FEMINIST AND QUEER THEORY

AN INTERSECTIONAL AND TRANSNATIONAL READER

EDITED BY

L. Ayu Saraswati
UNIVERSITY OF HAWAI'I AT MANOA

Barbara L. Shaw
ALLEGHENY COLLEGE

NEW YORK   OXFORD
OXFORD UNIVERSITY PRESS

Oxford University Press is a department of the University of Oxford.
It furthers the University's objective of excellence in research, scholarship,
and education by publishing worldwide. Oxford is a registered trade mark of
Oxford University Press in the UK and certain other countries.

Published in the United States of America by Oxford University Press
198 Madison Avenue, New York, NY 10016, United States of America.

Library of Congress Cataloging-in-Publication Data

Names: Saraswati, L. Ayu, author. | Shaw, Barbara L., author.
Title: Feminist and queer theory: an intersectional and transnational reader /
    L. Ayu Saraswati, University of Hawai'i at Manoa, Barbara L. Shaw, Allegheny College.
Description: First Edition. | New York : Oxford University Press, 2020. |
    Summary: "This is a feminist theory reader for college and graduate
    school level students"—Provided by publisher.
Identifiers: LCCN 2019044301 (print) | LCCN 2019044302 (ebook) |
    ISBN 9780190841799 (paperback) | ISBN 9780190057725 (ebook)
Subjects: LCSH: Feminist theory. | Queer theory. | Sex role—Study and teaching.
Classification: LCC HQ1190. S247 2020 (print) | LCC HQ1190 (ebook) |
    DDC 305.4201—dc23
LC record available at https://lccn.loc.gov/2019044301
LC ebook record available at https://lccn.loc.gov/2019044302

Printing number: 9 8 7 6 5 4 3 2 1
Printed by Sheridan Books, Inc., United States of America

CONTENTS

Theoretical Devices and Modes of Theory Production

Theorizing and Transforming: Situated Knowledge, Intersectionality, and Beyond

SECTION 2   THEORIZING AND TROUBLING THE BODY *195*

SECTION 3   CROSSING BORDERS AND TRANSNATIONAL MOVEMENTS *305*

Crossing Borders

Transnational Justice Movements

ABOUT THE EDITORS

L. Ayu Saraswati is associate professor and chair of the women's studies department at the University of Hawai'i, Manoa. She is the author of *Seeing Beauty, Sensing Race in Transnational Indonesia* and co-editor of *Introduction to Women's, Gender, and Sexuality Studies: Interdisciplinary and Intersectional Approaches*. Saraswati has also published numerous articles in *Feminist Studies, Meridians, Feminist Formations, Gender, Work, and Organization, Diogene, Women's Studies International Forum*, and *Sexualities*. More information about her work can be found on http://drsaraswati.com/.

Barbara L. Shaw, an associate professor of women's, gender & sexuality studies, holds the Brett '65 and Gwendolyn '64 Elliott Professorship for Interdisciplinary Studies, currently serves as the Director of Interdisciplinarity, and contributes to Black studies and global health studies at Allegheny College. She is the co-editor of *Introduction to Women's, Gender & Sexuality Studies: Interdisciplinary and Intersectional Approaches* and at work on a co-edited collection following a grant-driven curriculum transformation institute that she co-facilitated between 2016–2018. Shaw also is at work completing a single-authored manuscript tentatively titled, *Decolonizing Sexual Violence: Social Justice in Caribbean Women's Everyday Lives*.

PREFACE

The word "theory" sounds heavy. Indeed, a course on theory often has a reputation of being intense, intimidating, and full of abstract readings with verbose language that only experts in feminist and queer studies understand. This book, however, aims to challenge this perception as well as approaches to theory, theory-work, and theory-engagement. It invites students to think of and engage with theory differently: learning its scope; pushing on its boundaries; its interventions in political, social, and humanistic thought; and how it frames and makes sense of some of the most pressing issues of our time while recognizing their persistent histories.

Students are invited to think about theories as frameworks that craft, shape, and elucidate the sociocultural and political dynamics of our everyday lives. This suggests that theory exists all around us whether it is detected or not and provides language, indeed, a structural apparatus, for students to approach issues and understand social relations and systems of power. Theories are quite simply lenses for describing, explaining, and clarifying what we know and how we know it. Feminist and queer theory asks students to learn to see these frameworks more critically, offer new visions, and consider carefully how knowledge is produced, from what or whose point of view, and how power operates with its horizons on social change. Feminist and queer theories also carry with them political, social, cultural, and affective meanings that trace ideas that have long been circulating and built on, while also making clear that they are subject to refinement and change.

In *Feminist and Queer Theory: An Intersectional and Transnational Reader* (referred to as *FQT* in the following pages), as co-editors we have approached theory much like how we may think about how we build a story; it has the capacity to explain coherently and convincingly cultural dynamics and everyday phenomenon. As a process and an apparatus for how feminist and queer scholars go about producing knowledge, and more specifically developing lenses for naming how power is operationalized, theory is central to, indeed the basis for, imagining and enacting social change—in short, changing the story.

Before delving further into the world of "theories," in this Preface we would like to first clarify the key concepts that are at the heart of this book—feminist theory, queer theory, intersectionality, and transnationalism—and their relationships to one another. We do so without the intention to affix meanings to these concepts or draw reductive and linear relationships between them. In fact, some of the readings included in this volume may deploy more than one theory within a piece, and contradict one another across sections, as well as ask us to rethink the foundations in women's, gender, and sexuality studies so that students will think critically, build on, and creatively challenge how theory is imagined and what it does. Hence, these definitions are offered here as a point of departure, rather than a point of destination.

One additional note: *FQT* provides some advanced readings written by established and emerging scholars from around the world, some that have been previously published, as well as unpublished works, in order to explore more complex ideas that build on and challenge classic readings in women's, gender, and sexuality studies. This reader relies heavily on feminist *and* queer theories and makes a conscious effort to include works that speak from the spaces that rest in-between the two, as well as those that elucidate intersectionality and transnationalism. In broadest terms, this reader aims to shift how students think with and produce knowledge about feminist and queer theories, to unlearn the process of reading, learning, and producing frameworks to understand the broader world, and therefore to "unsettle" theory itself.

WHAT IS FEMINIST THEORY? WHAT IS QUEER THEORY?

What makes theory feminist? What makes it queer? These are the common questions asked in any feminist and/or queer theory reader and this book is no exception. From its earliest formations, feminist theory refused a single definition and embraced contradiction and contestation as a way of opening up pathways that name, critique, and put an end to racist capitalist heteropatriarchy. Some of its germinal scholar-practitioners named it as a body of work that described and explained women's oppression and inequality that created a second-class citizenry based on a gender binary. As a field of study that in the United States gained its academic currency in the 1970s, feminist theory critiques male-dominated canons that privilege whiteness and racial thought that does not include women; cisgendered assumptions that ignore trans and non-binary perspectives; and thought that begins with compulsory heterosexuality, able-bodied-ness, and national ethnocentrism in the humanities, social sciences, and increasingly in the physical sciences. For Elizabeth Grosz, "feminist theory is directed toward bringing about a future better than and different from the present; it is about revealing, elaborating, or unleashing the virtual forces that underlie (patriarchal, racist, militaristic, homophobic) actuality, those forces that enable the actual, the present, to become otherwise" (101). Certainly, what counts as a "better future" differs from theorist to theorist as students will read throughout this book. Some may focus on equality, others embrace equity through intersectional approaches in the United States, while some question if these critiques are adequate in addressing transnational systems of power embedded in capitalism.

Drawing on Clare Hemmings's insightful work in *Why Stories Matter: The Political Grammar of Feminist Theory* (2011), this volume takes as its starting point that feminist theories that have told particular stories grounded in the demands of political philosophies—often feminist responses to androcentric, "classic" texts—need an intervention "to allow a different vision of feminist past, present, and future" (20). The archive of feminist theory reaches beyond what we as co-editors bound together in this volume; thus, *FQT* is best understood as an introduction—the tip of the iceberg—for understanding Hemmings's new political grammar.

If feminist theory gained academic currency in the 1970s, queer theory flourished in the early 1990s (Binnie 1; Schippert 67). It was Teresa de Lauretis who first used the term "queer theory," as a title of an academic conference in California (Duong 371 fn.1). Since its inception, scholars have certainly provided varying and contested definitions of queer—some denying the umbrella term and preferring the acronym LGBTQPAI+ because queer no longer allows students to focus on lesbian, gay, bisexual, transgender, queer, pansexual, asexual, or intersex in their historical, political, and social specificity. In this text, we offer readings that explore both queer and LGBTQPAI+ situated lenses and have been mindful to select pieces that move beyond limiting identity politics. While the pieces respect and articulate the need to understand historically situated differences, the selections do not rest on identitarian claims for, of, or by a group, rights based on this discourse, or legal remedies for specific groups. Most readings share the understanding that "[q]ueer theory is a tough thing to pin down. Its deconstructive nature defies any simple definition or synopsis and from its inception, it has refused the definitional" (Cossman 2). As Hui-Ling Lin points out, "the concept of 'queer' does not concern definition, fixity or stasis, but focuses rather on de-centralization and transitivity" (36). That queer theory resists definition should not deter students from theorizing and incorporating it in our theory-work. Indeed, it is queer's "definitional indeterminacy, its elasticity, [which] is one of its constituent characteristics" that is embraced here (Jagose 1).

Beyond its definition, and similar to the work done by feminism and feminist theory, queer theory provides us with possibilities and ways to challenge power relations that we often refer to as "the norm." As David Halperin points out, queer is that which is "at odds with the normal, the legitimate, the dominant" (quoted in Cossman 3). Challenging the status quo and those institutions and people that benefit from it, "queer is an oppositional, resistant, transgressive movement, contrary and troubling to what surrounds and precedes in normalization" (Marchal 167). Not only defying the norm, queer can also be perceived as a "zone of possibilities" (Edelman 114). Thus, queer theory, much like feminist theorists who disrupt normative attachments to gender, race, class, sexuality, nationality, religion, ability, and age, forces us to theorize differently as it forgoes binary thinking; asks us to think beyond identity; and instead takes us into a third space, or what Gloria Anzaldúa named as the "borderlands"—a sociocultural, political, sometimes physical, and spiritual way of thinking beyond the field of deviant versus the (hetero)normative.

What makes theory feminist and queer is its investment in social justice and transformations with a keen interest in equity that reaches across all genders and liberation that stretches across race, socioeconomic status, sexuality, dis/ability, religion, nationality, age, and body size. Moreover, feminist and queer inquiry should not simply be perceived as modes for naming and refining identities. As bell hooks proposed, instead of saying "I am a feminist"—whereby feminist becomes an assumed, universal identity—she advises us to proclaim, "I advocate feminism" (hooks 31). In *FQT*, feminism is a constellation of ideologies rooted in gender equality and liberation that contests heteropatriarchy, transphobia, racism, xenophobia, ableism, ageism, and religious fundamentalism. hooks also helps us conceptualize how feminism and feminist theory is not limited to women simply because they are women nor prohibits men to advocate for feminist issues simply because they are men (31). LGBTQPAI+, nonbinary, genderqueer, and agender communities and transnational approaches are included within hooks's insights to expand our visions for racial, reproductive, and environmental justice alongside fair housing, employment, education, and judicial practices, for example. In other words, feminist and queer theory allows us to see the complex demands for political and social change in various contexts beyond one's personal identity and affiliation.

WHY INTERSECT FEMINIST AND QUEER THEORIES?

This reader is not simply a reader on feminist theory that *includes* queer theories. Rather, it theorizes at the *intersection* of feminist *and* queer theories as well as at the edges of feminist and queer theory, and by doing so, transforms and reshapes the boundaries of women's, gender, and sexuality studies. It pulls together feminist and queer theory in a way that shows how each field is constitutive of the other. It invites readers to think critically about the limitations of understanding feminist theory as separate but tangentially related to queer theory, and insists that feminist and queer theory take up intersectional and transnational approaches so that these analytical theoretical formations move beyond "additive" or US-centered perspectives. For example, social movements such as Black Lives Matter, Pride, reproductive justice, and students' demand to end sexual violence on campuses show us that the boundaries between feminism and LBGTQPAI+ liberation actually hold us back. The two (out of three) women who started Black Lives Matter, Alicia Garza and Patrisse Khan-Cullors, identify as queer; reproductive justice movements are reaching out to trans communities; and sexual violence on campus deeply affects women, men, trans/non-binary, and queer-identifying students. Mindful of the materiality of the circumstances that constitute our individual and collective lives, this reader includes theories articulated by writers who challenge boundaries among academic, creative, and community/activist work, and voices that have been excluded from theory texts. As such, *FQT* critically pushes on the edges of the fields *and* what it means to theorize.

Contextualizing theory and putting feminist and queer theory into conversation is also about possessing or having a stake and claim in theory and its genealogy. Although it may be counter-intuitive for some, theory-making is most useful and productive when it does *not* insist that the relationship between feminist and queer theories is a happy, coherent one; indeed, critique and dissonance opens up thoughtful spaces for creativity and new ideas to emerge if we collectively approach this process as a generative one in which feminist and queer communities build on each other's ideas and collaborate across our differences—even if it is contentious and painful in the process. The history between feminism and queer theories has not always been one that is harmonious. For instance, queer theory is often seen as a "break from feminism" in that it views gender as "colonizing"; and as Gayle Rubin demanded, in 1984, there needs to be "autonomous theory and politics specific to sexuality" (quoted in Cossman 3). The split between feminism and queer theory is also often attributed to how queer theory views feminism as about "sex wars"; and feminist theory views queer theory as "sexual libertarian and representation politics, overly male in orientation, devoid of ethicality, unconcerned with the material conditions of women and the role of sexuality in producing inequality" (Cossman 4). With both these approaches ignoring trans and genderqueer perspectives, as well as how people inhabit multiple social identities, geographic locations, and politics given the material relations of power that affect our daily lives, it is time to question the stark dichotomy. As students move through this text, they will encounter, study, and experience how and where contemporary feminist and queer theories converge, diverge, and ask them to think creatively about the possible horizons for coalitional and justice work.

This book is thus offered as a theory reader for the next generation of women's, gender, and sexuality studies students. Here "next generation" refers to students who came to feminism when it was already infused with queer theory, whether through digital cultures or in their households and communities. Furthermore, in many cases, they may have taken courses from a department/program that has expanded from women's studies, to women's and gender studies, to women's, gender, and sexuality studies. As a theory reader for the next generation, this book strives for balance between being contemporary (i.e., includes essays on current issues of science, digital, and technology and updates approaches to bodies, borders, migration, mobility, and antiviolence work) and offers some of the most cited and foundational essays in the field. This book thus aims to follow the flow of where the field is going, rather than further cementing the boundaries of discrete fields built on "classic" texts alone. It pushes students to think about what theory allows us to see and how it is the basis for our ideologies and actions rather than providing a roadmap for rehearsing what theory is. This book indeed encourages spaces where canonical texts (even the idea of "canon" itself) are challenged. The introductory essays that precede each section in this book are meant to incite and invite further inquiries into how key subject matter in women's, gender, and sexuality studies is framed, and the readings themselves provide examples for how theory informs writing and research projects. As students are encouraged to engage with the readings and *theorize* for themselves, this book offers a launching site that exemplifies how theory is a form of practice and work so students may have a hands-on experience with its rigors in framing humanistic interdisciplinary inquiry.

Intersecting queer and feminist theory, this book is inevitably interdisciplinary. It represents the breadth and depth of interdisciplinary thought in that it draws from scholarship in traditional disciplines as well as those that synthesize ideas across fields; provides multiple genres to emphasize that creative writing and interview essays (more exploratory and open-ended modes of imagining and reimagining relations of power) are also sites of theorizing; and consists of a mix of voices, perspectives, and approaches. These multiple entry points are meant to help students understand the broad scope of theory that moves us beyond the traditional, solo-authored academic theoretical articulations, the different stages of theory-production, and the various ways of engaging theories. Some essays may function more as theoretical memos or think pieces, whereas others are more expansive to demonstrate deep understandings of decades of bibliographies that inform their work. Interview essays are included to allow students to practice a different kind of engagement with theories. As AnaLouise Keating argues, interview/*entrevista* is "a process of looking (vista) between (entre) that enables a kind of 'immediacy rarely found in written work.' *La entra-vista* is a genre that stages rare moments of looking at the space between—interviewer and interviewee, speaking and writing, performer and audience, self and other" (Anthony and Rowe 353). In reading the interview essays, students are thus encouraged to learn what it means to theorize from the spaces between the interviewer and interviewee. Overall, it is our hope that this interdisciplinary approach encourages students to question why it is that theory has been traditionally practiced through dense, "insider" academic language that is often considered more credible than other forms of engagement. Theory is thus reimagined in this book as something that is more porous, more malleable, and more change and justice oriented, thus challenging not only what theory-work "should" look like but also what new feminist and queer political, sociocultural, and affective visions can emerge when creativity is allowed. The polyvocality in *FQT* is crucial in creating this space where no one theory is considered more privileged than others nor do they become or produce a coherent narrative of feminist and queer theory.

INTERSECTIONAL AND TRANSNATIONAL: CRITICAL PEDAGOGICAL APPROACHES

Creating this text as intersectional and transnational was a pedagogical choice. It was not a mere nod to acknowledge the importance of including works that engage how gender, race, sexuality, class, nationality, religion, age, body shape, and religion are constitutive of one another within material relations of power and elucidate the neocolonial ideologies of nation-building, global economies, and border crossings. Rather, intersectional and transnational approaches are modes of thinking and teaching that are essential—indeed integral—to understanding how and what knowledge gets produced, by whom, and with ramifications of what we learn and how we see the world.

In deploying intersectionality as a critical pedagogical approach, *FQT* provides students with a framework to think about women, gender, and sexuality as complex categories that consist of multiple and intersecting identities situated within axes of social, cultural, and economic power. It simultaneously questions the limitations of intersectionality in addressing the *fluidity* of these identities and the seemingly stasis construction of what gender, race, sexuality, class, nationality, body size, age, religion, and ethnicity mean in any given cultural context. While Kimberlé Crenshaw coined the term intersectionality in her groundbreaking scholarship that incorporates black feminist thought into critical legal studies (1989), and Patricia Hill Collins and Sirma Bilge build on her insights to craft their text, *Intersectionality* (2016), arguing for its applicability in transnational contexts, it is the visionary writing of the Combahee River Collective, Barbara Christian, Angela Davis, Paula Giddings, bell hooks, Audre Lorde, and Cherríe Moraga and Gloria Anzaldúa, to name a few scholar-activists that laid the groundwork for Crenshaw, Hill Collins, Bilge, and other feminist and queer theory scholars to name and reimagine why intersectionality is central in feminist and queer the-orizing. For example, a specific essay such as Angela Davis's "Transnational Solidarities" (included in section 4) shows students how Marxism, radical feminist thought, black femi-nism, and transnational feminism overlap and are required to show how race, class, gender, nation, and sexuality are co-constitutive of one another and needed for solidarity to be grounded and effective and for crafting change. In other words, in this book, intersectional-ity is not framed as a fixed and unproblematic concept.

In employing intersectional perspective critically, this book also integrates transnational feminist approaches that value how processes and practices of (neo)colonialism, globaliza-tion, and neoliberalism shape and re-shape systems of power vis-à-vis gender, race, sexual-ity, class, religion, (dis)ability, and age across and within national borders. Transnational feminism is understood here, according to M. Jacqui Alexander and Chandra Talpade Mohanty, as "a way of thinking" that allows us to understand women's conditions in dif-ferent locales who nonetheless share similar concerns; the different power relationships among people across and within nations; and the ways in which capitalism, racism, hetero/sexism, and other oppressive systems work in maintaining this unequal power structure across nations (24). Transnational feminism emerged "in response to the intensification of transnational flows associated with the contemporary epoch of globalization . . . [and] in response to a growing emphasis on the limits of territorially bound nation-states in a range of studies and theories that sought to make sense of the impact of globalization" (Fernandes 102). Engaging a transnational approach is *not* simply about studying condi-tions of people outside the United States or, worse, as a reiteration of nation-state, but rather as a site that allows us to "negotiate the circuits of travel between the local and the global, or to intuit the precise ways in which the local is constituted through the global" (Alexander and Mohanty 33). Moreover, this book also includes works that craft transna-tional analyses to focus on "the political significance of internal socioeconomic differentia-tion within non-Western contexts" (Fernandes 114). Ashwini Tambe's "Indian Americans in the Trump Era: A Transnational Feminist Analysis," included in section 4, for instance, exemplifies such an approach.

Transnationalism is indeed an important theoretical device, as Inderpal Grewal and Caren Kaplan note (and whose work is included in section 1), it is one that must be de-ployed in order to understand how and why "sexuality is globalized" (47). In a world where movement, dispersal, multiplicity, and flexibility describe the material realities of our every-day experiences, transnationalism emerges as a useful theoretical lens to understand how sexuality works in a postmodern world (Grewal and Kaplan 47). This is to say that sexual subjects should not simply be thought of as "purely oppositional or resistant to dominant institutions" and that "queer subjects are not always already avant-garde for all time and in all places" (51). At its core, transnationalism recognizes that "the nation does all sorts of ideological work, and when we take it for granted, that work becomes invisible" (Briggs et al. 643). Thus this book also asks students to grapple with settler-colonial relations of power naming its history as transnational and to imagine the political possibilities of indigenous theory and how its practice is part of the process of decolonization. This orientation allows us to do more than name ideological, political, economic, social, affective, and theoretical phenomena; it asks us as feminist and queer cultural critics to work in collaboration across national borders to better learn about the possibilities for creative movement building, social change, and decolonization.

It is also important to observe and make visible here that this book is conceived in the United States by two scholars currently residing and teaching in the United States trained to think through intersectional, transnational, and interdisciplinary lenses. Thus, efforts were made to include works from scholars residing in as well as theorizing about various locations across Asia, Africa, the Middle East, Australia, Europe, and the Americas to provide a more global perspective. The co-editors of this book hope that these works are not read as simply works that discuss issues "elsewhere," but rather that they are mindful of the politics of location and the theoretical and transnational connections formed and transformed across these locations.

In sum, transnational perspectives are offered in this book as a critical pedagogical approach to encourage students to be aware of how scholars in the United States may participate in epistemic violence when "imposing U.S. social categories on cultural transfigurations that were not U.S. based" and to therefore question such "epistemological assumptions" when producing and consuming theory, and to challenge how "hierarchies of place are normalized" (Alexander and Mohanty 36, 41). To theorize using a critical transnational queer and feminist approach means to recognize when scholars include works that focus on nonnormative, white, heterosexual abled bodies but then use them simply as a "normativizing gesture" that allows whiteness and Western philosophies to remain at the center and to do business as usual (Nagar and Swarr 15). It is also intended that being mindful of these dynamics generates conversations and serves as a threshold for students to contribute to transnational knowledge production and activism.

THE FOUR SECTIONS

This reader is divided into four sections. In organizing the essays, however, it is not based on a theme per se. Rather, they are structured in ways that allow them to challenge each other, and in turn, shape our readings of them. For example, it will be necessary to read and understand the foundations provided by readings in section 1 in order to grapple with the nuanced meanings of essays in other sections. In this way, theory builds on itself and becomes an iterative practice of knowing and thinking across social, cultural, national, and political similarities and differences moving from the abstract toward the applied. Reading critically is the cornerstone of an engaged praxis, and as María Lugones argues, "a politics of reading is a politics of knowledge-production" (22). Thus, if an essay is missing an explicit discussion on queer or feminist theory and/or a transnational or intersectional approach, rather than dismiss the usefulness of the essay, we encourage students to engage it in ways that question how our understanding of the field is enriched when the author's main argument is considered; how the argument would shift if the missing perspective is incorporated; and how it may be in conversation with other essays that address its gaps. Since a single essay cannot inscribe all that constitutes queer, feminist, transnational, and intersectional approaches, selections have been included that advance LGBTQPAI+ perspectives, feminist theory, anti-racism, disability studies, indigenous studies, and/or incorporate transnational inquiry in innovative and insightful ways. Studied together, they help us learn the complexity of an always-evolving and expanding field, and as such, we are practicing what Chela Sandoval theorized in *Methodologies of the Oppressed*: that while we rely heavily on iterations of theory, we simultaneously reoccupy and make new meanings of feminism and queer inquiry so that the process of decolonization (including of knowledge) and justice continues. Doing so evokes our collective theoretical imagination rather than simply presenting time-honored, canonized feminist and queer theories inviting students to think with one another about their ideas.

We also organize the sections in this book with how scholars do the work of theorizing based on some of the most pressing issues in the early twenty-first century—albeit not in a prescriptive mode. We ask students to consider what the relationship is between theory, social justice, and social transformation when we center global formations and local constructions of race, gender, sexuality, (dis)ability, class, nationality, religion, body size, and age as our starting points.

Section 1, "Theories, Stories, Histories," begins our conversation about theory as stories and the different forms that it takes. It aims to expand our ideas of what feminist and queer theories are and what they do, what it means to theorize from the intersection of feminist and queer theory and to theorize as a form of social justice work. It also introduces students to some of the framing devices that theorists use to produce theory and cultural critique and to understand how theory functions as an object of history, produced within time- and space-bound political and economic contexts, and formulated as part of a conversation within various communities committed to practices of social change. It urges us to destabilize and demystify processes of theorizing, and allows us to grasp what it means to theorize to transform and to do theory as a form of queer and feminist undertaking. We thus begin by posing these questions: What makes a story or theory feminist and/or queer? And why is intersectionality and transnationality required in its telling?

Section 2, "Theorizing and Troubling the Body," focuses on bodies as they have been a crucial aspect in feminist-queer theory production. It returns us to the materiality of the body and the feminist and queer modes of theorizing from and about the body. It helps us launch critical conversations about the body in its ambivalence, as it changes and ages, becomes diseased and ultimately deceased, and into a scholarly examination of the narratives and feelings surrounding these shifts. This section aims to answer, why does the body (and/or its parts, i.e., skin, hair, rectum, etc.) become a contested and important site and source for theorizing? How is the body theorized while simultaneously troubling its very biological and social constructions? What are the problems with theorizing about the body? How does (dis)embodiment work in the virtual world and in our theorizing about the body—particularly as it experiences and expresses pleasure and power? And, last, whose or which body matters sociopolitically and in our theorizing?

Section 3, "Crossing Borders and Transnational Movements," asks us to consider global and state power in crafting national borders, political economies of wealth and poverty, social and affective separations between people, and the production of in-between spaces where solidarities are built and feminist and queer communities speak back to systems of patriarchy and racism, entrenched class divides, precarious sexualities, and religious fundamentalisms. It opens with the frameworks and foundations that shed light on migration, mobility, diaspora, and what it means to belong in a world that increasingly exercises strictly policed nationalisms that erect both physical and cultural borders—particularly timely in an age where we see the re-emergence of white nationalism/supremacy and xenophobia purposefully weaponized in global politics. The subsection on transnational feminist and queer social movements ("Transnational Justice Movements") serves as a response to the current consolidation of power by looking specifically at intersectional and transnational movements for environmental, reproductive, religious, and indigenous justice that reach across borders. Migration and movement narratives are much more complicated, and the questions we pose for students as they make their way through this section are, what are the stories we tell about how people, ideas, and things (products tied to human capital) circulate? How do we make sense of lived experiences while also attending to public discourses that minoritize indigenous communities, people of color, and immigrants and refugees? How might national narratives change if they are told from migrants' point of view and we understand more about state violence and war, political economies, and sacrifices that people make to survive and support their families and communities? And what are some of the key social movements in the twenty-first century that seek to change the relations of power across national and cultural borders?

Section 4, "Resistance, Resilience, and Decolonizing Praxis," provides frameworks for students to think through the material, social, and affective realities of living in a violent world alongside imagining better futures through crafting feminist and queer theory horizons. Collectively, the readings in the first subsection ("Violence, Resistance, and Resilience") examine structural violence, political resistance, and individual and community resilience that women, women of color, and LGBTQPAI+ communities navigate and create globally. The pieces also suggest how violence must be paired with theoretical and social constructions of resistance, resilience, and praxis in order to move students beyond facile notions of equality and critique. The essays in the second subsection ("Feminist and Queer Theory Horizons") represent the depth and breadth of future directions of feminist and queer theory, looking to literature, science, spirituality, and political movements as pathways toward liberation. It includes works by scholar-activists who offer new ways of understanding coalitional politics, complex commonalities, queer horizons, and a world without as much pain and division. Questions that students will explore in Section 4 range from how can theory better help us understand systemic violence? What does decolonizing violence mean, especially within the Global North, and how might we better understand that there is more to the Global South than envisioning over three-quarters of the world's population as victims? And how does theory help us better understand the possibilities for the future even as they critique the present?

Ultimately, this book aims to explore the depth and breadth of theorizing itself, navigating its contradictions and collaborations, and it is done so to encourage us to create, enact, and practice its philosophies in our everyday lives. The book also hopes to demonstrate how theory provides the foundations that are necessary to build political, economic, and socio-cultural transformations.

REFERENCES

Alexander, M. Jacqui, and Chandra Talpade Mohanty. "Cartographies of Knowledge and Power: Transnational Feminism as Radical Praxis." *Critical Transnational Feminist Praxis*, edited by Amanda Lock Swarr and Richa Nagar. SUNY Press, 2010, pp. 23–45.

Anthony, Adelina, and Aimee Carillo Rowe. "Adelina Anthony Interview with Aimee Carillo Rowe." *Journal of Lesbian Studies*, vol. 21, no. 3, 2017, pp. 351–69.

Binnie Jon. *The Globalization of Sexuality*. Sage Publications, 2004.

Briggs, Laura, Gladys McCormick, and J. T. Way. "Transnationalism: A Category of Analysis." *American Quarterly*, vol. 60, no. 3, 2008, pp. 625–48.

Christian, Barbara. *Black Feminist Criticism: Perspectives on Black Women Writers*. Teachers College Press, 1985.

Collins, Patricia Hill, and Sirma Bilge. *Intersectionality*. Polity, 2016.

Combahee River Collective. *The Combahee River Collective Statement: Black Feminist Organizing in the Seventies and Eighties*. Kitchen Table: Women of Color Press, 1986.

Cossman, Brenda. "Continental Drift: Queer, Feminism, Postcolonial." *Jindal Global Law Review*, vol 4, no. 1, 2012, pp. 1–19. Law, Culture and Queer Politics in Neoliberal Times. Special Double Issue Part I: *Jindal Global Law Review*.

Crenshaw, Kimberlé. "Demarginalizing the Intersection of Race and Sex: A Black Feminist Critique of Antidiscrimination Doctrine, Feminist Theory and Antiracist Politics." *University of Chicago Legal Forum*, 1989, pp. 139–67.

Davis, Angela. *Women, Race & Class*. Vintage, 1983.

Duong, Kevin. "What Does Queer Theory Teach Us about Intersectionality?" *Politics & Gender*, vol. 8, no. 3, 2012, pp. 370–86.

Edelman, Lee. *Homographesis: Essays in Gay Literary and Cultural Theory*. Routledge, 1994.

Fernandes, Leela. *Transnational Feminism in the United States: Knowledge, Ethics, and Power*. New York University Press, 2013.

Giddings, Paula. *When and Where I Enter: The Impact of Black Women on Race and Sex in America*. Morrow, 1984.

Grewal, Inderpal, and Caren Kaplan. "Global Identities: Theorizing Transnational Studies of Sexuality." *GLQ: A Journal of Lesbian and Gay Studies*, vol. 7, no. 4, 2001, pp. 663–79.

Grosz, Elizabeth. "The Practice of Feminist Theory." *differences*, vol. 21, no. 1, 2010, pp. 94–108.

Hemmings, Clare. *Why Stories Matter: The Political Grammar of Feminist Theory*. Duke University Press, 2011.

hooks, bell. *Feminist Theory: From Margin to Center*. 1984. South End Press, 2000.

Jagose, Annamarie. *Queer Theory: An Introduction*. New York University Press, 1997.

Lin, Hui-Ling. "*Bodies in Motion: The Films of Transmigrant Queer Chinese Women Filmmakers in Canada*." PhD diss., University of British Columbia, 2011.

Lorde, Audre. *Sister Outsider: Essays and Speeches. Reprint*. Crossing Press, 2007.

Lugones, María. "Musing: Reading the Nondiasporic from the Diasporas." *Hypatia*, vol. 29, no. 1, 2014, pp. 18–22.

Marchal, Joseph. "Bio-Necro-Biblio-Politics? Restaging Feminist Intersections and Queer Exceptions." *Culture and Religion*, vol. 15, no. 2, 2014, pp. 166–76.

Moraga, Cherríe, and Gloria Anzaldúa. *This Bridge Called My Back: Writings by Radical Women of Color*. 4th Edition. SUNY Press, 2015.

Nagar, Richa, and Amanda Lock Swarr. "Introduction: Theorizing Transnational Feminist Praxis." *Critical Transnational Feminist Praxis*, edited by Amanda Lock Swarr and Richa Nagar. SUNY Press, 2010, pp. 1–20.

Sandoval, Chela. *Methodologies of the Oppressed*. University of Minnesota Press, 2000.

Schippert, Claudia. "Implications of Queer Theory for the Study of Religion and Gender: Entering the Third Decade." *Religion and Gender*, vol. 1, no. 1, 2011, pp. 66–84.

ACKNOWLEDGMENTS

The authors and OUP would like to thank the following reviewers who provided valuable and thoughtful feedback:

Kelly A. Dagan, Illinois College
Dawn Rae Davis, Monterey Peninsula College
Susan K. Freeman, Western Michigan University
Suzanne Gauch, Temple University
Elizabeth Groeneveld, Old Dominion University
Diane Grossman, Simmons College
Corie Hammers, Macalester College
Emily Klein, Saint Mary's College of California
Liam Oliver Lair, West Chester University
Vara Neverow, Southern Connecticut State University
Padini Nirmal, Clark University
Teresa M. Pershing, West Virginia University
Lisa Weasel, Portland State University
Denise Witzig, Saint Mary's College of California

THEORIES, STORIES, AND HISTORIES

The essays included in this section are carefully chosen to provide students with the necessary tools to address the following questions: How can we do theory differently? What would happen to our understanding of "theory" and to the "X" that it analyzes when we theorize in a way that goes beyond existing conventions of how or what to theorize? What do feminist and queer theories do? What does it mean to theorize from the intersection of feminist *and* queer theory, and to theorize as a form of social justice work? What makes a story/theory feminist and/or queer? And why are intersectionality and transnationality required in its telling?

By the end of this section, students will have learned the different ways of theorizing, various framing devices that theorists use to produce theory, and the multiple ways in which theory functions as an object of history, produced within a particular historical, political, and economical context. If theory is formulated as part of a conversation within and across diverse communities, then, hopefully, its practices can be seen as fundamental to producing transformation and moving us toward social justice.

This section is also designed with the intention to create fragile and fractured (rather than fixed) spaces that allow students to have robust discussions about theory production, while simultaneously challenging and going beyond the limitations of these theoretical framings. Collectively, and ultimately, the essays in this section urge students to destabilize and demystify existing processes of theorizing, and to grasp what it means to theorize, to transform, and to do theory as a form of queer and feminist undertaking.

TELLING STORIES, HISTORICIZING THEORIES

We would like to begin by asking a seemingly simple yet important question: Why do we theorize—and theorize in a specific way? The answer to this question will be as varied, of course, as the many theorists who do their theory-work. For bell hooks, writing in her 1991 essay, "Theory as Liberatory Practice" (included in this subsection), she came to theorizing because "I was hurting—the pain within me was so intense that I could not go on living. I came to theory desperate, wanting to comprehend—to grasp what was happening around and within me. . . . I saw in theory then a location for healing" (12). In this sense, theory is not something that exists outside the intimate space of our lives. But rather, theory *is* a necessary part of life because it has the capacity to heal and liberate us. Theorizing becomes a mode of survival—a way to save our lives.

This subsection thus begins with hooks's essay because it captures how this book approaches theory: as liberatory practice and integral to one's daily life. In framing theory as essential to one's life, hooks challenges the stereotype that positions theory as an academic abstraction that is divorced from everyday life. She also transgresses the binary thinking that juxtaposes theory to practice/activism. Indeed, as Robyn Warhol and Susan S. Lanser argue, feminist and queer theory itself can be considered as "a form of academic activism"; it challenges "assumptions which have served to keep gender inequalities and heteronormative epistemologies in place" (7). As a form of activism, (some) theories can indeed affect changes in the world. It is thus important to be mindful of what kind of theory we produce: does it support the status quo or challenge it?

The next reading in this book is an excerpt from Clare Hemmings's 2011 book, *Why Stories Matter: The Political Grammar of Feminist Theory*. Her work provides us with another foundational path to understand how we frame theory in this book: as a form of storytelling. That is, when we theorize, we inevitably tell stories. In women's, gender, and sexuality studies (WGSS) classrooms, we "tell many stories of gendered, racial, and sexual bodies" through the theories we produce, teach, and learn (Alexander and Mohanty 31). These stories/theories are never innocent in explaining what happened but are always embedded in power relations. They may obstruct and obfuscate what we once perceived as "real/the truth," or they may confirm it. Hemmings's work reminds us that it is important to understand the stories that feminism tells because they may be co-opted by and complicit with dominant narratives, such as global capitalism, hetero/sexism, racism, and so on. She thus urges us to tell our feminist stories *differently*, in ways that are more "ethically accountable" and "politically transformative" (20). Her piece is important as it pushes us to constantly think of the many other ways, beyond the suggestions in her book, that we can theorize—tell stories of—queerness and feminism in alternative and more progressive ways, with an eye toward social justice.

An example of how certain feminist stories have been useful in the past but may no longer have the same powerful impact in the present day (and therefore are not used as the organizing narratives in this book) are how the women's movement (mostly of white women) in the United States has been told through the "wave metaphor." The first wave of the women's movement has been traditionally marked by the suffragette movement beginning in 1848 with the Seneca Falls Convention and ending in 1920 with women's right to vote. The second wave represents the women's liberation movement of the 1960s and 1970s that fought for women's equality to men, such as in the workforce, reproductive rights, and sexual liberation. The third wave of the women's movement challenged the assumptions embedded in the white and middle-class women's movement of the second wave by pointing out the limitation of "woman" as a unified category and instead proposed the need to think through an intersectional framework.

The wave metaphor has been critiqued for oversimplifying the complexity of the women's movement that pre-dates Seneca Falls and has taken shape through small and notable actions across time and space, although some scholars have productively redefined it. For example, Nancy A. Hewitt finds "radio waves" as a more useful metaphor than the "oceanic wave" model (659). As she argues,

> Radio waves not only help us think about how competing versions of feminism coexist in the same time period, but they also continue to resonate even in moments of seeming quiescence. . . . Radio waves recognize explicit hierarchies of power (through wattage, volume, and geographical reach) that are crucial to understanding the dynamic interplay of feminists within a specific period and across time. (Hewitt 668)

Thus, here, Hewitt reworks the notion of the wave to provide new and more complex meanings of feminist movements as heterogenous, coexisting, and continuing.

Another way theories/stories of feminism have been organized in the past is through the different strands of liberal, radical, socialist, Marxist, psychoanalytic, postmodern/poststructural, and ecofeminist feminism. I summarize briefly here simply to provide students with a sense of what each taxonomy stands for: Liberal feminism refers to the demand that women and men level the playing field, such as asking for equal education for women, and equal pay for equal work. "Equality with men" is thus central in liberal feminists' fight for women's rights (Beasley 51). Radical feminism insists, however, that women need more than leveling the playing field. They see women's oppression as "the most fundamental form of oppression" and the basis of women's oppression is "their sex" (Beasley 54; Tong 71). As such, they often focus on issues of sexuality and reproduction, and seek systematic changes that happen at the root (*radix*) level (Beasley 57; Tong 72, 95). Both liberal and radical feminism may no longer fit in our present-day life when we are aiming to move away from the binary system of men versus women and toward a more gender inclusive understanding that may even challenge the very existence of gender itself (i.e., gender non-conforming, gender non-binary, etc.). Marxist and Socialist feminist theorists focus on the woman question and the ways in which political economy structures women's experiences. Marxist feminists see women's oppression as "a dimension of class power" and therefore focus on issues related to women's work, such as "wages for housework campaign" (Beasley 60; Tong 51, 54). The end to capitalism, they argue, is a pathway to end women's oppression (Beasley 61). Socialist feminism often draws from Marxist feminism, as well as radical feminism; however, socialist feminists focus on "dual-systems" that theorize the ways in which patriarchy (as ideology) work hand in hand with capitalism (as materiality) to oppress women in specific ways (Beasley 62; Tong 173, 175). The "unified-systems" theorists see patriarchy and capitalism as a unified system rather than a duality (Tong 175). Psychoanalytic feminism revisits Freudian analysis by focusing on the "pre-Oedipal stage" (rather than the Oedipus complex) of mother–infant relationship and the effect of psychology on subject (sexual) formation (Beasley 65; Tong 147). Postmodernist and poststructuralist feminism queries the taken-for-granted notion that there is "the truth" and challenges the category of women as a universal category (Beasley 81; Tong 217). Postmodernist feminists veer to deconstruction as its mode of knowing the world (Tong 219). Poststructural feminism, on the other hand, focuses on "the shifting, fragmented complexity of meaning (and relatedly of power), rather than a notion of its centralized order" (Beasley 91). Last, ecofeminism focuses on the connections between earth, women, and animal (other non-human beings), and how earth is often femi-nized (i.e., "mother earth," "virgin island," etc.) and is treated the same way as women are treated ("raped," "exploited," etc.). The end of women's oppression thus goes hand in hand with fighting for an end to ecological injustices.

These kinds of narratives, as Hemmings's text alludes us to, can no longer hold their center in our expanding field of women's, gender, and sexuality studies, and therefore, this book is not organized based on these taxonomies. We need stories that are more intersectional and transnational in their telling, which many theories told from these strands or metaphors are lacking, and that allow us to grasp the complexity that our growing field embodies.

The reading that comes after Hemmings's is Moon Charania's "Speaking in Tongues: Furtive Knowledge and/in the Pakistani GeoBody" (new). It is included here as it takes Hem-mings's argument a step further by arguing that storytelling itself can become "an oppo-sitional practice—a way to underscore the silences that surround the (fe)male body, the violence superimposed in their lives, and the ever-shifting matrix of oppression and resis-tance" (32). Working with her mother's story, particularly of the tongue—both as flesh and metaphor—Charania considers how stories can also be "a form of fugitive knowledge, always and already illegible to dominant modes of rational thought" (31). Being "illegible" to dom-inant narratives, her mother's story is thus "always and already queer; where queerness is informed by its historical specificity of sexual irregularities, . . . and where queerness im-plodes and exceeds disciplinary and theoretical conventions and opens up a way of writing that could track and understand the fragmented woman subject" (35). In short, Charania's writing questions the whole edifice of theory/storytelling while intersecting transnational feminist and queer theories in its telling.

The next reading included in this subsection is an excerpt from Leila J. Rupp's 2009 book, *Sapphistries: A Global History of Love between Women*. Her reading is purposefully placed in the beginning of the book to make visible how this book is committed to the non-heteronormative mode of theory production, to a transnational way of thinking, and to the notion of theory as history. Rupp's work thus challenges students to think about how to tell stories that put women who love women at the center; yet they escape the Western frame-work of sexuality—when the concept "lesbians" cannot be used in that specific geographical and historical context, for example. In doing theory-work at a global level, she reminds us, we need to look at stories that are similar across cultures as well as those that are specific to each of the different cultural settings. Moreover, Rupp's work also invites students to think of theory as a historical product. That is, theory always reflects historically and (inter) disciplinary-specific conversations within which it is produced and circulated; and theorists (not only theories) are also a product of their time. Hence, what can be theorized is deeply connected to how, why, and when thought emerges (we will explore more about this issue in the next subsection, "Theoretical Devices and Modes of Theory Production"). Suffice it to say, carefully reading theory within its historical contexts is important as it allows us to understand why a theorist would think the way that they do and why dominant ideologies operating at the time shapes the very contour and content of theories.

The reading that follows Rupp's is Inderpal Grewal and Caren Kaplan's "Global Identities: Theorizing Transnational Studies of Sexuality." This piece, published in 2001, is important in laying out the different ways in which the term "transnational" has been deployed in the US academy. It also charts what it means to employ a transnational frame in the study of sexuality. Whereas Grewal and Kaplan's piece highlights the transnational aspect of sexuality studies, E. Patrick Johnson's essay "Quare Studies, or (almost) Everything I know about Queer Studies I learned from My Grandmother," also published in 2001, is included here to highlight the importance of intersectionality. That is, queer theory, when not intersectional, hides queer of color's experiences. He thus proposes "quare" studies that expands US-based queer studies by focusing on the intersectional lives of "gays and lesbians of color" and honoring a practice of theorizing that recognizes it as a process that is discursive, historically specific, and "materially conditioned"—"theories in the flesh" (59).

Susan Stryker's 2004 essay, "Transgender Studies: Queer Theory's Evil Twin," which comes next, speaks specifically of the relationship between transgender studies and queer theories through the "shadow" metaphor. That is, embedded within systems of power and revealing of the power structure within which it is created, theories may inevitably have created their own "shadows." According to Stryker, "transgender studies has taken shape over the past decade in the shadow of queer theory" (71). Finding itself more invested in questions of embodiment that disability studies and intersex studies are centered around, transgender studies at times seek to break away from queer theory that she claims to be more invested in narratives of "sexual identity" that are more Western/Euro-American in its origin (70).

In sum, this first subsection, "Telling Stories, Historicizing Theories," proposes that by framing theory as story, history, and a liberatory practice, and by critically theorizing from the intersection of feminist *and* queer theories (and the disruptive spaces between the two), we may allow for different and more powerful stories/theories to be told. These feminist and queer stories/theories are different in that they challenge the normative conventions of storytelling by being disruptive or welcoming the "break" and by becoming a messy text— these theories "resist dichotomous thinking" (Burford and Orchard 210; Dean 387). Moreover, queer and feminist stories/theories also do the work of unsettling the current mode of theorizing by challenging the "blissful tidiness of the normal" and refusing to provide a "satisfying story" with "productive" endings (Chess 87; Manalansan "Queer" 567). Thus, as students read the essays in this book, they are encouraged to identify the various ways in which these feminist and queer stories/theories are disruptive, messy, and non-normative. Nonetheless, these messy ruptures may lead students to theorize differently.

THEORETICAL DEVICES AND MODES OF THEORY PRODUCTION

Theory is a product of ideological, political, and historical conditions of its time. It can support, challenge, complicate, and sometimes rewrite existing ideologies and power structure. It is thus important to make visible the devices that theorists use in their theory-work and the ways in which material conditions shape processes of theory production. The questions that students may ponder as they read the essays in this subsection of the book are, How does a person get to think and theorize that way? How does a subject get to be theorized in a specific way? What theoretical devices allow these theorists to theorize the way that they do?

What ideologies, discourses, historical, and material conditions shape their mode of theorizing, which in turn shape the theories they produce?

The first essay that launches this subsection is Chandra Talpade Mohanty's "Transnational Feminist Crossings: On Neoliberalism and Radical Critique," published in 2013, which focuses on neoliberalism both as a device to produce theory and a condition of possibility that shapes how theories travel and are reproduced and appropriated in a transnational context. Her piece is included here as an important meditation on feminist scholarship and the "traffic in feminist thought" in the age of neoliberal academic culture (76). She points out how within this neoliberal culture, radical theory is commodified, appropriated, assimilated, and domesticated into the "Eurocentric feminist globality," allowing feminist scholars to do "whiteness as usual" (77).

Akiko Takeyama's essay, "Possessive Individualism in the Age of Postfeminism and Neoliberalism: Self-Ownership, Consent, and Contractual Abuses in Japan's Adult Video Industry" (new), follows Mohanty's reading. Similar to Mohanty, Takeyama also uses neoliberalism as her theoretical device. However, Takeyama couples neoliberalism with postfeminism to interrogate both notions of consent and contract. Her work allows students to comprehend how existing legal framework of "consent" fails to address issues of sexual exploitation in a contractual condition, and thus exposes "consent" as a limited and problematic concept to understand women's sexuality.

Takeyama's work is followed by Amrita Banerjee's essay, "A Transnational Intervention into an Ethic of Care: Quandaries of Care Ethics for Transnational Feminisms" (new). These two texts (Takeyama's and Banerjee's), when read together, allow students to see how various theoretical devices provide theorists with diverse tools to produce different theories even as they wrestle with the same concept—in this case, the notion of "contract." Whereas Takeyama's work is an ethnographic examination of contract abuses in the adult video industry, Banerjee's essay is a philosophical investigation into the contract paradigm within the ethics of care. It is important to note here, however, although the two essays use different theoretical framing devices, they both employ a transnational feminist lens that interrogates how inequality underlies the legal and philosophical notions of "contract."

The next theoretical devices that students learn in this subsection are those employed in visual and virtual studies. To this end, we have included Megan Sibbett's essay, "Breaking Into Bad: The New Privileged Monsters, or, Straight, Middle-Class White Guys" (reading 11, new) that questions the emergence of a new white masculinity: the "anti-heroes" characters in American television. She focuses on Walter White, the "violent meth making, drug kingpin" from the television series *Breaking Bad* and argues that "such monstrosity wrapped around white, middle-class, heteronormativity vies with the monstrous queer other in showdowns that revitalize 'war on terror' ideologies for the preservation of heteronormative families" (98). Her essay invites us to be critical of our engagement with popular culture and to always ask, what is at stake when certain racialized, gendered, sexualized characters and narratives are produced in specific ways? What perceived threats do these pop culture representations aim to manage?

Another essay included in this subsection that addresses the contemporary virtual culture is Sarah E. S. Sinwell's "#MakeReyAsexual and #KeepJugheadAsexual: Asexuality, Queerness, and Representation on Twitter" (new). Sinwell's work explores Twitter campaigns to understand "how queer audiences and fans are promoting more positive and complex representations of asexual visibility in popular media" (104). Also interested in the importance of Twitter, but focusing on the high school/girl/youth culture, the last text in this subsection is Diza Edgina H.'s short fiction, "Praise and Prejudice" (new). Her creative writing critically examines the phenomena of heterosexual teenage girls who are fans of "Boys' Love" culture and who "ship" real life (rather than characters in television series) boys together. Indeed, heterosexual women have been the main audience of Boys' Love genre in the United States as well as in Japan (Wood; McLelland). Edgina's short story thus illustrates how this trend as well as other practices that seem to "praise" non-heteronormative sexuality may be a form of othering nonetheless.

In sum, readings in this subsection encourage students to be mindful of which theoretical framing devices and genres to employ, as well as which historical contexts and material conditions to incorporate, as they will inevitably shape the kind of theories that they produce.

THEORIZING AND TRANSFORMING: SITUATED KNOWLEDGE, INTERSECTIONALITY, AND BEYOND

Not all stories count as "theories," of course. What makes certain stories "theories" are their capacity to coherently and convincingly explain a particular phenomenon, and that they arrive at such stories/theories by way of systematic "researching" and being aware of one's location—social, historical, geographical, disciplinary—when producing these knowledges. This kind of responsible theory production is what Donna Haraway calls "situated knowledge." In her classic piece, "Situated Knowledges: The Science Question in Feminism and the Privilege of Partial Perspective," first published in *Feminist Studies* in 1988, and included in this subsection, Haraway introduces us to the importance of understanding feminist subjectivity. To produce situated knowledge, scientists (and theorists) should not assume an omniscient or god-like position. Rather, their knowledge should always be contextualized within *their* specific methodology and observation. As such, their findings can only be considered partial and therefore incomplete. Their theory/story is a form of *a truth* but not *the* truth. No one theory in women's, gender, and sexuality studies can provide us with a grand narrative of the absolute, unchanging/fixed, or universal truth.

Building on Haraway's essay and further questioning the position of science and therefore knowledge production as value-free, neutral, or innocent, and taking it to the twenty-first century, Neha Vora's essay, "A Transnational Feminist Critique of the March for Science" (new) reminds us that when people who march against the Trump administration's "anti-science" rhetoric adopt a stance that views science as neutral (non-situated) knowledge, they might have forgotten how science has been used as a technology that supports violence against women, people of color, and LGBTIQPA+ people—and in the military industrial complex. Science has also been responsible for projects that are imperialist or white supremacist. It is therefore important to always be critical of "science" and be aware of its problematic racist/sexist/heterosexist history.

Also working with Haraway's notion of situated knowledge and applying it to the digital world, Avery Dame-Griff, in his essay, "Algorithms Are a Feminist Issue" (new), exposes how an algorithm may not be innocent after all: it perpetuates whiteness as the unmarked category. For contents by people of color to be seen, they must be marked in a specific way. The search algorithm, he argues, "performs what Donna Haraway terms the 'god-trick'" (138). His work thus invites students to think of spaces where knowledge is produced in seemingly neutral and objective ways and to critically question these processes.

Alongside "situated knowledges," another concept that has become foundational in women's, gender, and sexuality studies is "intersectionality." Intersectionality was made known by works of Bonnie Thornton Dill, Maxine Baca Zinn, Kimberlé Crenshaw, and Combahee River Collective Statement of 1977 (Grzanka xiv). Kimberlé Crenshaw's 1989 essay, "Demarginalizing the Intersection of Race and Sex: A Black Feminist Critique of Antidiscrimination Doctrine, Feminist Theory and Antiracist Politics" (included in this subsection), provides us with a useful understanding of the working of intersectionality legally and politically as she makes clear, for example, how black women must impossibly choose either their race or gender to pursue discrimination cases under the law. It must be made clear, however, that while we include Crenshaw's important work that coined the term, we do not mean to suggest that she was *the* person to develop the theory. To do so would erase, according to The Santa Cruz Feminist of Color Collective, "the collaborative work feminist of color communities engaged in for decades to strategize resistance and defend their lives" (The Collective 32–33). Indeed, as Michael O'Rourke argues, "No one corpus of work . . . or no one particular project should be made to stand in for the whole movement" (103). Thus, we include Crenshaw's essay with the intention for it to be read alongside other essays in the subsection in order to understand the complexity of the contemporary meaning of intersectionality.

Why does "intersectionality" become an important concept in women's, gender, and sexuality studies? One of the reasons may be because it makes visible the ways in which women experience their gender differently—gender intersects with other categories of identities such as race, class, and sexuality to shape one's life experiences. Intersectionality also provides us with a lens through which we can see the interconnectedness of our lives and how power operates. That is, white women of a particular class can live the life that they do *because* women of color of a specific class live the life that they do (Barkley-Brown). For Kathy Davis, intersectionality has become a key concept in WGSS because it embodies the four characteristics of a successful social theory: (1) "it speaks to a primary audience concern" (70); (2) it provides "a novel twist to an old problem"—she speaks specifically on how feminist theory can answer the old problems of sexism, racism, and classism, and how it makes visible the material consequences of such categories (72–74); (3) it appeals "to a broad academic audience, bridging the gap between theory generalists and specialists" (74); and (4) it is "inherently ambiguous and obviously incomplete" (76). In reading the various intersectional essays in this book, students are thus encouraged to think for themselves why intersectionality has been an important concept in the field and useful for their learning process, and what are its limitations.

The next essay included in this subsection is Mel Michelle Lewis's "A Bridge Across Our Fears: Queer Feminist Intersectional Ethnic Studies as Interdisciplinary Praxis" (new).

Her essay takes intersectionality beyond providing a lens for understanding individual experiences and structural oppression and into the praxis of teaching. She shows us how her pedagogical approach is "itself an enactment of intersectional theory and praxis" (154). In demonstrating how intersectionality functions as theory and praxis, Lewis's essay also points to the ways in which intersectionality is not merely about *adding* a category of analysis to existing research topic. Rather, when incorporated mindfully, intersectionality could transform all fields involved—in her case: feminist, queer, and ethnic studies—simultaneously. Rosemarie Garland-Thomson has made a similar argument a couple of decades earlier when she started theorizing a then-new and now-burgeoning field of feminist disability studies. She argues, "thinking about disability *transforms* feminist theory. Integrating disability does not obscure our critical focus on the registers of race, sexuality, ethnicity, or gender, nor is it additive. . . . Integrating disability clarifies how this aggregate of systems operates together, yet distinctly, to support an imaginary norm and structure the relations that grant power, privilege, and status to that norm" (Garland-Thomson 4, emphasis ours).

A work that exemplifies and builds on Garland-Thomson's key intervention is Alison Kafer's 2013 book, *Feminist, Queer, Crip* (excerpted in this subsection). In her book, Kafer draws connections between feminist, queer, and disability studies to examine the "politics of crip futurity." She uses the framework of temporality and futurity in analyzing disability to problematize the assumption that people want the same future. She points out, "If disability is conceptualized as a terrible unending tragedy, then any future that includes disability can only be a future to avoid. A better future, in other words, is one that excludes disability and disabled bodies" (160). Her work is included in this subsection as it is important in providing us with evidence for how thinking with and through intersectionality allows students to understand *any* issue differently, in this case, to grasp how desire for the kind of future that they want may be produced under able-ist assumptions.

Finally, in ending section 1, we would like to return full circle to the issues that were brought up in the two essays that began this section: hooks's and Hemmings's texts. Both works invite us to ponder the questions of why we theorize and why we theorize/tell stories *differently*. In this book, we propose that we theorize not only for the sake of theorizing, finding truths, making sense of the world, or healing the pain—all of which are necessary and crucial. But also, we propose that we theorize to transform, which means that we must tell stories differently—ones that incorporate narratives of intersectionality and transnationality and that go beyond existing conventions of feminist and queer theorizing—and make spaces for changes to occur. As Marivel Danielson points out in her 2009 article included here, "Our Art Is Our Weapon: Women of Color Transforming Academia," we can make space through our citational practices. Unlike Hemmings, who recommends that we do institutional-based citations, Danielson suggests that we turn to people of color and marginalized people to trace our genealogy of knowledge. She asks, "why should a discussion of queer and colored bodies and their voices and work necessarily be translated or filtered through the theoretical scope and language of Foucault or Butler?" (181). Politics of citation that relies solely on mainstream academic sources and acknowledges one scholar (instead of a community) as the only person developing that theory indeed hides the fact that women of color have the capacity to theorize our own lives outside these works labeled as cannons.

Theorizing to transform, according to Danielson, also means that we reimagine the many forms a theory can take, including writings that are sensual and pleasurable. Beyond the "personal and political," she argues, lies the "poetic"—how eventually the *lives* within academia can also be transformed (193). Thus, to transform academia means that we "prioritiz[e] our holistic well-being and collective thinking" and "tak[e] turns working with our own and one another's words through simple writing exercises, longer papers, and conference presentations" (Color Collective 35). We do this despite the fact that academia values individual achievements and specific kinds of academic writings. This book is indeed produced in this spirit of collaboration—of collective thinking, of taking turns with each other's words, and of providing each other with emotional support that allows us to nurture our holistic well-being, even in the chaotic midst of writing and editing this book.

Theorizing to transform means that we continue to tell different stories of feminism and queer theories in ways that challenge the normative convention, and that we construct theory not as something that is found outside our lives or as the opposite of practice/activism. But rather, we construct theories by articulating them through and merging them with praxis, by being mindful of the power relations within which we produce theory, and by acknowledging theory, as hooks points out, as a liberatory practice that could move us toward social justice.

REFERENCES

Alexander, M. Jacqui, and Chandra Talpade Mohanty. "Cartographies of Knowledge and Power: Transnational Feminism as Radical Praxis." *Critical Transnational Feminist Praxis*, edited by Amanda Lock Swarr and Richa Nagar. SUNY, 2010, pp. 23–45.

Barkley-Brown, Elsa. "'What Has Happened Here': The Politics of Difference in Women's History and Feminist Politics." *Feminist Studies*, vol. 18, no. 2, 1992, pp. 295–312.

Beasley, Chris. *What Is Feminism?: An Introduction to Feminist Theory*. Sage, 1999.

Chess, Shira. "The Queer Case of Video Games: Orgasms, Heteronormativity, and Video Game Narrative." *Critical Studies in Media Communication*, vol. 33, no. 1, 2016, pp. 84–94.

Davis, Kathy. "Intersectionality as Buzzword: A Sociology of Science Perspective on What Makes a Feminist Theory Successful." *Feminist Theory*, vol. 9, no. 1, 2008, pp. 67–85.

Dean, Tim. "Sex and the Aesthetics of Existence." *Theories and Methodologies*, vol. 125, no. 2, 2010, pp. 387–92.

Garland-Thomson, Rosemarie. "Integrating Disability, Transforming Feminist Theory." *NWSA Journal*, vol. 14, no. 3, 2002, pp. 1–32.

Grzanka, Patrick. *Intersectionality: A Foundations and Frontiers Reader*, Westview Press, 2015.

Hewitt, Nancy A. "Feminist Frequencies: Regenerating the Wave Metaphor." *Feminist Studies*, vol. 38, no. 3, 2012, pp. 658–80.

hooks, bell. "Theory as Liberatory Practice." *Yale Journal of Law & Feminism*, vol. 4, no. 1, 1991–1992, pp. 1–12.

Manalansan IV, Martin F. "Queer Worldings: The Messy Art of Being Global in Manila and New York." *Antipode*, vol. 47, no. 3, 2015, pp. 566–79.

McLelland, Mark. "The World of Yaoi: The Internet, Censorship, and the Global 'Boys' Love' Fandom." *The Australian Feminist Law Journal*, vol. 23, no. 1, 2005, pp. 61–77.

O'Rourke, Michael. "The Afterlives of Queer Theory." *Continent*, vol. 1, no. 2, 2011, pp. 102–16.

The Santa Cruz Feminist of Color Collective. "Building on 'the Edge of Each Other's Battles': A Feminist of Color Multidimensional Lens." *Hypatia*, vol. 29, no. 1, 2014, pp. 23–40.

Tong, Rosemarie. *Feminist Thought: A More Comprehensive Introduction*. Westview Press, 1998. (Original work published 1989.)

Warhol, Robyn, and Susan S. Lanser. "Introduction." *Narrative Theory Unbound: Queer and Feminist Interventions*, edited by Robyn Warhol and Susan S. Lanser. Ohio State University Press, 2015, pp. 1–20.

Wood, Andrea. "'Straight' Women, Queer Texts: Boy-Love Manga and the Rise of a Global Counterpublic." *Women's Studies Quarterly*, vol. 34, no. 1/2, 2006, pp. 394–414.

1. THEORY AS LIBERATORY PRACTICE

Let me begin by saying that I came to theory because I was hurting—the pain within me was so intense that I could not go on living. I came to theory desperate, wanting to comprehend—to grasp what was happening around and within me. Most importantly, I wanted to make the hurt go away. I saw in theory then a location for healing.

I came to theory young, when I was still a child. In *The Significance of Theory* Terry Eagleton says:

> Children make the best theorists, since they have not yet been educated into accepting our routine social practices as "natural," and so insist on posing to those practices the most embarrassingly general and fundamental questions, regarding them with a wondering estrangement which we adults have long forgotten. Since they do not yet grasp our social practices as inevitable, they do not see why we might not do things differently.[1]

Whenever I tried in childhood to compel folks around me to do things differently, to look at the world differently, using theory as intervention, as a way to challenge the status quo, I was punished. I remember trying to explain at a very young age to Mama why I thought it was highly inappropriate for Daddy, this man who hardly spoke to me, to have the right to discipline me, to punish me physically with whippings: her response was to suggest I was losing my mind and in need of more frequent punishment.

Imagine if you will this young black couple struggling first and foremost to realize the patriarchal norm (that is of the woman staying home, taking care of household and children while the man worked) even though such an arrangement meant that economically, they would always be living with less. Try to imagine what it must have been like for them, each of them working hard all day, struggling to maintain a family of seven children, then having to cope with one bright-eyed child relentlessly questioning, daring to challenge male authority, rebelling against the very patriarchal norm they were trying so hard to institutionalize.

It must have seemed to them that some monster had appeared in their midst in the shape and body of a child—a demonic little figure who threatened to subvert and undermine all that they were seeking to build. No wonder then that their response was to repress, contain, punish. No wonder that Mama would say to me, now and then, exasperated, frustrated: "I don't know where I got you from, but I sure wish I could give you back."

Imagine then if you will, my childhood pain. I did not feel truly connected to these strange people, to these familial folks who could not only fail to grasp my world view but who just simply did not want to hear it. As a child, I didn't know where I had come from. And when I was not desperately seeking to belong to this family community that never seemed to really accept or want me, I was desperately trying to discover the place of my belonging. I was desperately trying to find my way home. How I envied Dorothy her journey in *The Wizard of Oz*, that she could travel to her worst fears and nightmares only to find at the end that "there is no place like home." Living in childhood without a sense of home, I found a place of sanctuary in "theorizing," in making sense out of what was happening. I found a place where I could imagine possible futures, a place where life could be lived differently. This "lived" experience of critical thinking, of reflection and analysis, became a place where I worked at explaining the hurt and making it go away. Fundamentally, I learned from this experience that theory could be a healing place.

"Theory as Liberatory Practice." *Yale Journal of Law & Feminism* 4, no. 1 (1991), 1–12. Reprinted with permission of bell hooks.

Psychoanalyst Alice Miller lets us know in her introduction to the book *Prisoners of Childhood*,[2] that it was her own personal struggle to recover from the wounds of childhood that led her to rethink and theorize anew prevailing social and critical thought about the meaning of childhood pain, of child abuse. In her adult life, through her practice, she experienced theory as a healing place. Significantly, she had to imagine herself in the space of childhood, to look again from that perspective, to remember "crucial information, answers to questions which had gone unanswered throughout [her] study of philosophy and psychoanalysis."[3] When our lived experience of theorizing is fundamentally linked to processes of self-recovery, of collective liberation, no gap exists between theory and practice. Indeed, what such experience makes more evident is the bond between the two—that ultimately reciprocal process wherein one enables the other.

Theory is not inherently healing, liberatory, or revolutionary. It fulfills this function only when we ask that it do so and direct our theorizing towards this end. When I was a child, I certainly did not describe the processes of thought and critique I engaged in as "theorizing." Yet, as I suggested in *Feminist Theory: From Margin to Center*,[4] the possession of a term does not bring a process or practice into being; concurrently one may practice theorizing without ever knowing/possessing the term just as we can live and act in feminist resistance without ever using the word "feminism."[5]

Often individuals who employ certain terms freely, terms like "theory" or "feminism" are not necessarily practitioners, whose habits of being and living most embody the action—the practice of theorizing or engaging in feminist struggle. Indeed, the privileged act of naming often affords those in power access to modes of communication that enable them to project an interpretation, a definition, a description of their work, actions, etc. that may not be accurate, that may obscure what is really taking place. Katie King's essay "Producing Sex, Theory, and Culture: Gay/Straight Remappings in Contemporary Feminism"[6] is a very useful discussion of the way in which academic production of feminist theory formulated in hierarchical settings often enables women, particularly white women, with high status and visibility to draw upon the works of feminist scholars who may have less or no

status, less or no visibility, without giving recognition to these sources. Discussing the way work is appropriated and/or the way readers will often attribute ideas to a well known scholar/feminist thinker even if that individual has cited in her work that she is building on ideas gleaned from less well known sources, and focussing particularly on the work of Chicana theorist, Chela Sandoval, King states: "Sandoval has been published only sporadically and eccentrically, yet her circulating unpublished manuscripts are much cited and often appropriated, even while the range of her influence is rarely understood."[7] Though King risks positioning herself in a caretaker role as she rhetorically assumes the posture of feminist authority, determining the range and scope of Sandoval's influence, the critical point she works to emphasize is that the production of feminist theory is complex, that it is less the individual practice than we often think and usually emerges from engagement with collective sources. Echoing feminist theorists, especially women of color who have worked consistently to resist the construction of restrictive critical boundaries within feminist thought, King encourages us to have an expansive perspective on the theorizing process.

Critical reflection on contemporary production of feminist theory makes it apparent that the shift from early conceptualizations of feminist theory which insisted that it was most vital when it encouraged and enabled feminist practice begins to occur or at least becomes most obvious with the segregation and institutionalization of the feminist theorizing process in the academy, with the privileging of written feminist thought/theory over oral narratives. Concurrently, the efforts of black women/women of color to challenge and deconstruct the category "woman," the insistence on recognition that gender is not the sole factor determining constructions of femaleness was a critical intervention which led to a profound revolution in feminist thought, one that truly interrogated and disrupted the hegemonic feminist theory produced primarily by academic women, most of whom were white.

In the wake of this disruption, this critical assault on white supremacy as it was made manifest in feminist critical practices alliances between white women academics and white male peers seemed to have been formed and nurtured around common efforts to formulate and impose standards of critical evaluation that would be used to define what is theoretical and what is not. These standards often led to appropriation and/or devaluation of work that did not "fit," that was suddenly deemed not theoretical, or not theoretical enough. In some circles, there seems to be a direct connection between white feminist scholars turning towards critical work and theory by white men, and the turning away of white feminist scholars from fully respecting and valuing the critical insights and theoretical offerings of black women/women of color.

Work by women of color and marginalized groups of white women (for example, lesbians, sex radicals), especially if written in a manner that renders it accessible to a broad reading public, even if that work enables and promotes feminist practice, is often de-legitimized in academic settings. Though such work is often appropriated by the very individuals setting restrictive critical standards, it is this work that they most often claim is not really theory or is not theoretical enough. Clearly, one of the uses these individuals make of theory is instrumental. They use it to set up unnecessary and competing hierarchies of thought which reinscribe the politics of domination by designating some work inferior, superior, more or less worthy of attention. In her essay, King emphasizes that "theory finds different uses in different locations."[8] It is evident that one of the many uses of theory in academic locations is in the production of an intellectual class hierarchy where the only work deemed truly theoretical is work that is highly abstract, jargonistic, difficult to read, and containing obscure references that may not be at all clear or explained. Literary critic Mary Childers declares that it is highly ironic that "a certain kind of theoretical performance which only a small cadre of people can possibly understand"[9] has come to be seen as representative of any production of critical thought that will be given recognition within many academic circles as "theory." It is especially ironic when this is the case with feminist theory. And, it is easy to imagine different locations, spaces outside academic exchange where such theory would not only be seen as useless, but would be seen as politically nonprogressive, as a kind of narcissistic self-indulgent practice that most seeks to create a gap between theory and practice so as to perpetuate class elitism. There are so many settings in this country where the written word has only slight visual meaning, where individuals who cannot read or write can find no use for a published theory however lucid or opaque. Hence, any theory that cannot be shared in everyday conversation cannot be used to educate the public.

Imagine what a change has come about within feminist movements when students, most of whom are female, come to women's studies classes and read what they are told is feminist theory only to feel that what they are reading has no meaning, cannot be understood, or when understood in no way connects to "lived" realities beyond the classroom. As feminist activists we might ask ourselves of what use is feminist theory that assaults the fragile psyches of women struggling to throw off patriarchy's oppressive yoke. We might ask ourselves, of what use is feminist theory that literally beats them down, leaves them stumbling bleary-eyed from classroom settings feeling humiliated, feeling as though they could easily be standing in a living room or bedroom somewhere naked with someone who has seduced them or is going to, who also subjects them to a process of interaction that humiliates, that strips them of their sense of value. Clearly, a feminist theory that can do this may function to legitimize women's studies and feminist scholarship in the eyes of the ruling patriarchy, but it undermines and subverts feminist movements. Perhaps, it is the existence of this most highly visible feminist theory that compels us to talk about the gap between theory and practice. For it is indeed the purpose of such theory to divide, separate, exclude, keep at a distance. And because this theory continues to be used to silence, censor, and devalue various feminist theoretical voices, we cannot simply ignore it. Concurrently, despite its uses as an instrument of domination, it may also contain important ideas, thoughts, visions, that could, if used differently, serve a healing, liberatory function. However, we cannot ignore the dangers it poses to feminist struggle which must be rooted in a theory that informs, shapes, and makes feminist practice possible.

Within feminist circles, many women have responded to hegemonic feminist theory that does not speak clearly to us by this hegemonic trashing theory, and as a consequence, further promoting the false dichotomy between theory and practice. Hence, they collude with those whom they would oppose. By internalizing the false assumption that theory is not a social practice, they promote the formation within feminist circles of a potentially oppressive hierarchy where all concrete action is viewed as more important than any theory written or spoken. Recently, I went to a gathering of women, predominantly black, where we discussed whether or not black male leaders, like Martin Luther King and Malcolm X, should be subjected to feminist critiques that pose hard questions about their stance on gender issues. The entire discussion was less than two hours. As it drew to a close, a black woman present who had been particularly silent, spoke to say that she was not interested in all this theory and rhetoric, all this talk, that she was more interested in action, in doing something, that she was just "tired" of all the talk.

Her response disturbed me: it is a familiar reaction. Perhaps she inhabits in her daily life a different world from mine. In the world I live in daily, the occasions where black women/women of color thinkers come together to rigorously debate issues of race, gender, class, and sexuality are rare. Therefore, I did not know where she was coming from when she suggested that talk, like the discussion we were having was common, so common as to be something we could dispense with or do without. I felt that we were engaged in a process of critical dialogue and theorizing that has long been taboo. Hence, from my perspective, we were charting new journeys, claiming for ourselves as black women an intellectual terrain where we could begin the collective construction of feminist theory.

In many black settings, I have witnessed the dismissal of intellectuals, the putting down of theory, and remained silent. I have come to see that silence as an act of complicity, one that helps perpetuate the idea that we can engage in revolutionary black liberation and/or feminist struggle without theory. Like many insurgent black intellectuals, whose intellectual work and teaching is often done in predominately white settings, I am often so pleased to be engaged with a collective group of black folks that I do not want to make waves, or make myself an outsider by disagreeing with the group. In such settings, when the work of

intellectuals is devalued, I have in the past rarely contested prevailing assumptions, or spoken affirmatively or ecstatically about intellectual process. Afraid that if I took a stance that would insist on the importance of intellectual work, particularly theorizing, or if I just simply stated that I thought it was important to read widely, I would risk being seen as uppity, or as lording it over. Thus I have often remained silent.

Risking these blows to sense of self now seem trite when considered in relation to the crisis we are facing as African Americans, to our desperate need to rekindle and sustain the flame of black liberation struggle. At the gathering I mentioned, I dared to speak, saying in response to the suggestion that we were just wasting our time talking, that I saw our words as an action, that our collective struggle to discuss issues of gender and blackness without censorship was as subversive a practice. Urging us to consider that many of the issues that we continue to confront as black people— low self-esteem, intensified nihilism and despair, repressed rage and violence that destroys our physical and psychological well-being—cannot be addressed by survival strategies that have worked in the past. Insisting to the group that we need new theories that can move us towards revolutionary struggle rooted in an attempt to understand both the nature of our contemporary predicament and the means by which we might collectively engage in resistance struggle that would transform our current reality, I was, however, not rigorous and relentless as I would have been in a different setting in my efforts to emphasize the importance of intellectual work, the production of theory as a social practice that can be liberatory. Though not afraid to speak, I did not want to be seen as the one who "spoiled" the good time, the collective sense of sweet solidarity in blackness. This fear reminded me of what it was like more than ten years ago to be in feminist settings, posing questions about theory and practice, particularly about issues of race and racism that were seen as potentially disruptive of sisterhood and solidarity.

It seemed ironic that at a gathering called to honor a black male leader who had often dared to speak and act in resistance to the status quo, black women were still negating our right to engage in oppositional political dialogue and debate, especially since this is not a common occurrence in black communities. Why did the black women there feel the need to police one another, to deny one another a space within blackness where we could unself-consciously talk theory? Why, when we could celebrate together the power of a black male critical thinker who dared to stand apart, was there this eagerness to repress any viewpoint that would suggest we might collectively learn from the ideas and visions of insurgent black female intellectuals/theorists who by the nature of the work they do are necessarily breaking with that stereotype that would have us believe that the "real" black woman is always the one who speaks from the gut, who righteously praises the concrete over the abstract, the material over the theoretical?

Again and again, black women find our efforts to speak, to break silences that would enable us to engage in radical progressive political debates on a number of fronts, opposed. There is a link between the silencing we experience, the censoring, the anti-intellectualism in predominantly black settings that are supposedly supportive (like all-black woman space), and that silencing that takes place in institutions wherein black women/women of color are told that we cannot be fully heard or listened to because our work is not theoretical enough. Cultural critic Kobena Mercer reminds us that "blackness is . . . complex and multifaceted" and that "black people can be interpolated into reactionary and anti-democratic politics."[10] Just as some elite academics who construct theories of "blackness" in ways that make it a critical terrain which only the chosen few can enter, using theoretical work on race to assert their authority over black experience, denying democratic access to the process of theory making, threaten collective black liberation struggle, so do those among us who react to this by promoting anti-intellectualism by declaring all theory as worthless. By reinforcing the idea that there is a split between theory and practice or by creating such a split, both groups deny the power of liberatory education for critical consciousness thereby perpetuating conditions that reinforce our collective exploitation and repression.

I was recently reminded of this dangerous anti-intellectualism when I agreed to appear on a radio show with a group of black women and men to discuss Sherazade Ali's *The Black Man's Guide to Understanding the Black Woman*,[11] where I listened to speaker after speaker express contempt for intellectual work, and speak against any call for the production of theory. One black woman was vehement in her insistence that "we don't need no theory." Ali's book, though written in plain language, in a style that makes use of engaging black vernacular, has a theoretical foundation. It is rooted in theories of patriarchy (for example, the sexist, essentialist belief that male domination of females is "natural"), that misogyny is the only possible response black men can have to any attempt by women to be fully self-actualized. Many black nationalists will eagerly embrace critical theory and thought as a necessary weapon in the struggle against white supremacy, but suddenly lose the insight that theory is important when it comes to questions of gender, of analyzing sexism and sexist oppression in the particular and specific ways it is manifest in black experience. The discussion of Ali's book is one of many possible examples illustrating the way contempt and disregard for theory undermines collective struggle to resist oppression and exploitation.

Within revolutionary feminist movements, within revolutionary black liberation struggles, we must continually claim theory as necessary practice within a holistic framework of liberatory activism. We must do more than call attention to ways theory is misused. We must do more than critique the conservative and at times reactionary uses some academic women make of feminist theory. We must actively work to call attention to the importance of creating a theory that can advance renewed feminist movements, particularly highlighting that theory which seeks to further feminist opposition to sexism, and sexist oppression. Doing this, we necessarily celebrate and value theory that can be and is shared in oral as well as written narrative.

Reflecting on my own work in feminist theory, I find writing—theoretical talk—to be most meaningful that which invites readers to engage in critical reflection and to engage in the practice of feminism. To me, this theory emerges from the concrete, from my efforts to make sense of everyday life experiences, from my efforts to critically intervene in my life and the lives of others. This to me is what makes feminist transformation possible. Personal testimony, personal experience, is such fertile ground for the production of liberatory feminist theory because usually it forms the base of our theory-making. While we work to resolve those issues (our need for literacy, for an end to violence against women and children, women's health and reproductive rights, our need for housing, for sexual freedom, etc. to name a few) that are most pressing in daily life, we engage in a critical process of theorizing that enables and empowers. I continue to be amazed that there is so much feminist writing produced and yet so little feminist theory that strives to speak to women, men and children about ways we might transform our lives via a conversion to feminist politics, to feminist practice. Where can we find a body of feminist theory that is directed toward helping individuals integrate feminist thinking and practice into daily life? For example, what feminist theory is directed toward assisting women who live in sexist households in their efforts to bring about feminist change?

We know that many individuals in the United States have used feminist thinking to educate themselves in ways that allow them to transform their lives. I am often critical of a lifestyle-based feminism, because I fear that any feminist transformational process that seeks to change society is easily co-opted if it is not rooted in a political commitment to mass based feminist movement. Within white supremacist capitalist patriarchy, we have already witnessed the commodification of feminist thinking (just as we experience the commodification of blackness), in ways that make it seem as though one can partake of the "good" that these movements produce without any commitment to transformative politics and practice. In this capitalist culture, feminism and feminist theory are fast becoming a commodity that only the privileged can afford. It is fast becoming a luxury item. This process of commodification is disrupted and subverted when feminist activists affirm our commitment to a politicized revolutionary feminist movement that has as its central agenda the transformation of society. From such a starting point, we automatically think of creating theory that speaks to the widest audience of people. I have written elsewhere and shared in numerous public talks and conversations that my decision about writing style, about not using conventional academic formats, are political decisions motivated by the desire to be inclusive, to reach as many readers as possible in as many different locations. This decision has had consequences both positive and negative. Students at various academic institutions often complain that they cannot include my work on required reading lists for degree-oriented qualifying exams because their professors do not see it as scholarly enough. Any of us who create feminist theory and feminist writing in academic settings in which we are continually evaluated know that work deemed "not scholarly" or "not theoretical" can result in one not receiving deserved recognition and reward.

Now, in my life these negative responses seem insignificant when compared to the overwhelmingly positive responses to my work both in and outside the academy. Recently, I have received a spate of letters from incarcerated black men who read my work and wanted to share that they are working to unlearn sexism. In one letter, the writer affectionately boasted that he had made my name a "household word around that prison." These men talk about solitary critical reflection, about using this feminist work to understand the implications of patriarchy as a force shaping their identities, their ideas of manhood. After receiving a powerful critical response by one of these black men to my . . . book *Yearning: Race, Gender and Cultural Politics*,[12] I closed my eyes and visualized that work being read, studied, talked about in prison settings. Since the location that has most spoken back to me critically about the study of my work is usually an academic one, I share this with you not to brag or be immodest, but to testify, to let you know from first-hand experience that all our feminist theory which is directed at transforming consciousness, that truly wants to speak with diverse audiences works: that this is not a naive fantasy.

In more recent talks, I have spoken about how "blessed" I feel to have my work affirmed in this way, to be among those feminist theorists creating work that acts as a catalyst for social change that crosses false boundaries. There were many times early on when my work was subjected to forms of dismissal and devaluation that created within me a profound despair. I think such despair has been felt by every black woman/woman of color thinker/theorist whose work is oppositional and moves against the grain. Certainly Michele Wallace has written poignantly in her introduction to the re-issue of *Black Macho and the Myth of the Superwoman*[13] that she was devastated and for a time silenced by the negative critical responses to her early work.

I am grateful that I can stand here and testify that if we hold fast to our beliefs that feminist thinking must be shared with everyone whether through talking or writing and create theory with this agenda in mind we can advance a feminist movement that folks will long, yes yearn, to be a part of. I share feminist thinking and practice wherever I am. When asked to talk in university settings, I search out other settings or respond to those who search me out so that I can give the riches of feminist thinking that I hold to anyone. Sometimes settings emerge spontaneously. Last month I was at a black-owned restaurant in the South and sat for hours with a diverse group of black women and men from various class backgrounds discussing issues of race, gender and class. Some of us were college-educated, others were not. We had a heated discussion of abortion, discussing whether black women should have the right to choose. Several of the Afrocentric black men present were arguing that the male should have as much choice as the female. One of the feminist black women present, a director of a health clinic for women, spoke eloquently and convincingly about a woman's right to choose.

During this heated discussion one of the black women present who had been silent for a long time, who hesitated before she entered the conversation because she was unsure about whether or not she could convey the complexity of her thought in black vernacular speech (in such a way that we, the listeners, would hear and understand and not make fun of her words), came to voice. As I was leaving, this sister came up to me and grasped both my hands tightly, firmly, and thanked me for the discussion. She prefaced her words of gratitude by sharing that the conversation had not only enabled her to give voice to feelings and ideas she had always "kept" to herself, but that by saying it she had created a space for her and her partner to change thought and action. She stared at me directly, intently, eye to eye, as we stood facing one another, holding hands and saying again and again, "there's been so much hurt in me." She gave thanks that our meeting, our theorizing of race, gender and sexuality that afternoon had eased her pain, testifying that she could

feel the hurt going away, that she could feel a healing taking place within. Holding my hands, standing body to body, eye to eye, she allowed me to empathically share the warmth of that healing. She wanted me to bear witness, to hear again both the naming of her pain and the power that emerged when she felt the hurt go away.

It is not easy to name our pain, to make it a location for theorizing. Patricia Williams in her essay, *On Being the Object of Property*,[14] names that even those of us who are "aware" are made to feel the pain that all forms of domination (homophobia, class exploitation, racism, sexism, imperialism) engender. Sharing from her experience, Patricia Williams says:

> There are moments in my life when I feel as though a part of me is missing. There are days when I feel so invisible that I can't remember what day of the week it is, when I feel so manipulated that I can't remember my own name, when I feel so lost and angry that I can't speak a civil word to the people who love me best. These are the times when I catch sight of my reflection in store windows and am surprised to see a whole person looking back. . . . I have to close my eyes at such times and remember myself, draw an internal pattern that is smooth and whole.[15]

It is not easy to name our pain, to theorize from that location.

I am grateful to the many women and men who dare to create theory from the location of pain and struggle, who courageously expose wounds to give us their experience to teach and guide, as a means to chart new theoretical journeys. Their work is liberatory. It not only enables us to remember and recover ourselves, it charges and challenges us to renew our commitment to an active, inclusive feminist struggle. We have still to collectively make feminist revolution. I am grateful that we are collectively searching as feminist thinkers/theorists for ways to make this movement happen. Our search leads us back to where it all began, to that moment when an individual woman or child, who may have thought she was all alone, began feminist uprising, began to name her practice, indeed began to formulate theory from lived experience. Let us imagine that this woman or child was suffering the pain of sexism and sexist oppression, that she wanted to make the hurt go away. I am grateful that I can be a witness, testifying that we can create a feminist theory, a feminist practice, a revolutionary feminist movement that can speak directly to the pain that is within folks, and offer them healing words, healing strategies, healing theory. There is no one among us who has not felt the pain of sexism and sexist oppression, the anguish that male domination can create in daily life, the profound and unrelenting misery and sorrow.

Mari Matsuda told us . . . that "we are fed a lie that there is no pain in war."[16] She told us that patriarchy makes this pain possible. Catharine MacKinnon reminded us that "we know things with our lives and we live that knowledge, beyond what any theory has yet theorized."[17] Making this theory is the challenge before us. For in its production lies the hope of our liberation, in its production lies the possibility of naming all our pain—of making all our hurt go away. If we create feminist theory, feminist movements that address this pain, we will have no difficulty building a mass-based feminist resistance struggle. There will be no gap between feminist theory and feminist practice.

NOTES

1. Terry Eagleton, The Significance of Theory 34 (1990).
2. Alice Miller, The Drama of the Gifted Child: The Search for the True Self xi–xv (1990) (earlier Published as Prisoners of Childhood) (1981).
3. Id. at xiv.
4. bell hooks, Feminist Theory: From Margin to Center (1984).
5. See generally id. at 17–31.
6. Katie King, *Producing Sex, Theory, and Culture: Gay/Straight Remappings in Contemporary Feminism*, in *Conflicts in Feminism* 82 (Marianne Hirsch & Evelyn Fox Keller eds., 1990).
7. Id. at 90.
8. Id. at 89.
9. Mary Childers & bell hooks, *A Conversation about Race and Class*, in Conflicts in Feminism, *supra* note 6, at 60, 77.
10. Kobena Mercer, *Travelling Theory: The Cultural Politics of Race and Representation* (interview quoted from personal knowledge of author).
11. Sherazade Ali, The Black Man's Guide to Understanding the Black Woman (1990).
12. bell hooks, Yearning: Race, Gender and Cultural Politics (1990).
13. Michele Wallace, Black Macho and the Myth of the Superwoman (1979).
14. Patricia Williams, *On Being the Object of Property*, in The Alchemy of Race and Rights: Diary of a Law Professor 216 (1991).
15. Id. at 228–29.
16. Mari Matsuda, speech given at the Conference (Feb. 9, 1991).
17. Catharine A. MacKinnon, *From Practice to Theory, or What Is a White Woman Anyway?*, 4 Yale J.L. & Feminism 13, 15 (1991).

2. *WHY STORIES MATTER: THE POLITICAL GRAMMAR OF FEMINIST THEORY*

INTRODUCTION

This . . . [Introduction] is on how feminists tell stories about Western feminist theory's recent past, why these stories matter, and what we can do to transform them. It explores their narrative form and charts their interaction with other stories about feminism and social change. It asks what might be at stake in feminist storytelling, and most importantly it seeks to intervene in these stories, to realign their political grammar to allow a different vision of a feminist past, present, and future.[1]

The work starts from the assumption that how feminists tell stories matters in part because of the ways in which they intersect with wider institutionalizations of gendered meanings. For example, stories that frame gender equality as a uniquely Western export, as a way to measure or enforce economic and democratic development, resonate disconcertingly well with feminist stories that place "feminism" as a radical knowledge project firmly in the Western past. When feminists celebrate the move beyond unity or identity, when they lament the demise of a feminist political agenda, or when they propose a return to a feminist vision from the past, they construct a political grammar that is highly mobile and does not belong only to feminists. It is not enough for feminists to lament what is most often perceived as the cooptation of feminism in global arenas. Feminist theorists need to pay attention to the *amenability* of our own stories, narrative constructs, and grammatical forms to discursive uses of gender and feminism we might otherwise wish to disentangle ourselves from if history is not simply to repeat itself.

This book is a claim for the continued radical potential of feminist theory and for the importance of telling stories differently. If Western feminists can be attentive to the political grammar of our storytelling, if we can highlight reasons why that attention might be important, then we can also intervene to change the way we tell stories. We can interrupt the amenability of the narratives that make up dominant Western feminist stories and tell stories differently.[2] Throughout this work I am pulled in two directions. One pull is the interest in highlighting overlaps among a range of stories about gender and feminism usually held apart. I want to examine commonalities across antagonistic Western feminist narratives, between these and postfeminist positions that reject such narratives, either in media and cultural contexts, or within the growing area of gender policy. Another is the belief that feminist theory is particularly well positioned to challenge these intersections because of its deep history of attention to differences, intersections, lies, and silences (Ware 2006). Feminist theory is certainly bound up in global power relations, particularly when we consider the various ways in which a presumed opposition between Western gender equality and non-Western patriarchal cultures is mobilized in temporal and spatial modes, but it also occupies a position of reflexive non-innocence that can break open those relations. Starting from invested attention to silences in the history of feminist theory, then, I suggest several ways of making the stories we tell both more ethically accountable and potentially more politically transformative.

This position is perhaps untenable—that feminism is both caught and freeing—but I hold it nevertheless and revisit this position throughout the work that follows. In this belief, I acknowledge the influence of other feminist theorists whose work, words, and lives have insisted, and continue to insist, on the potential of non-innocent theorizing for change. I read Rosi Braidotti's *Patterns of Dissonance* nearly twenty years ago, and was transported then by her certainty that passion was the point of theory, and that without that passion, feminist theory could have no real value (1991). I have always loved feminist theory for its utopianism, and I hope to contribute to the tradition of dogged optimism that allows its practitioners to understand and experience life differently. In this spirit, there are three overlapping strands to this work, all of which seek to allow for a different kind of feminist political thinking: the laying out of Western feminist storytelling in this intellectual space I call home; the exploration of the political grammar of feminist narratives that make up these stories and their consistency with other stories about feminism and gender; [and] the sketching out of interventions that start at the level of political grammar and propose ways of breaking open dominant narrative forms. Of these three strands, the last one is the most important, as it constitutes a starting point for a reflexive Western feminist accountability that shuttles back and forth between past and present in order to imagine a future that is not already known. My interventions focus specifically on citation tactics and on textual affect as starting points for unraveling the stuff of Western feminist storytelling to transformative effect.

STORYTELLING

So what are these stories I claim are told about Western feminist theory's recent past? The surprise that motivated much of the early research on this project was the uniformity of representations of Western feminist theoretical trajectories. Despite the complexity of the last few decades of feminist theory—its dizzying array of authors, objects, disciplines, and practices—the story of its past is consistently told as a series of interlocking narratives of progress, loss, and return that oversimplify this complex history and position

feminist subjects as needing to inhabit a theoretical and political cutting edge in the present. Let me give a flavour of these common threads here.

One: Progress. We used to think of "woman" or feminism as a unified category, but through the subsequent efforts of black and lesbian feminist theorists, among others, the field has diversified, and feminism itself has become the object of detailed critical and political scrutiny. Far from being a problem, difference within the category "woman," and within feminisms, should be a cause for celebration. Postmodern feminism has moved us still further towards a focus on political effect over identity politics and highlights the exclusions and inclusions social movements, including feminism, produce. In the process of intellectual and political advances, we have developed a variety of epistemological and methodological tools and critiqued the scope, reach, and ontological narrowness typical of Western feminism's earlier preoccupations and subjects. Since "woman" is no longer the ground of feminism, and the relationship between subject and object of feminist theory has been destabilized, an intellectual focus on gender or feminism alone may indicate an anachronistic attachment to false unity or essentialism.

Two: Loss. We used to think of "woman" or feminism as unified, but progressive fragmentation of categories and infighting have resulted in the increased depoliticization of feminist commitments. Conservative institutionalization of feminist thought and the generational popularity of "post-feminism" are empty parodies of a feminist social movement that has incontrovertibly passed. The demise of feminism can be understood as part of a more general political shift to the right that has also killed the viability of a left-wing alternative. Feminist academics and a new generation of women have both inherited and contributed to this loss, particularly through their lack of interest in recent feminist history and an acceptance of political individualism. Whatever the failings of previous feminist commitments, it was better to have a feminist movement than none at all. We need to risk academic and political marginalization by asserting uncomfortable truths about ongoing gender inequalities in the West and elsewhere.

Three: Return. We have lost our way but we can get it back, if we apply a little common sense to our current situation. We may have been convinced by the turn to language, a poststructuralist capacity to deconstruct power and value difference, but we know better now. We know now that critique does not alter power relations and indeed that these have endured and strengthened. We know now that postmodern feminism leads to relativism and political incapacity, while women everywhere remain disadvantaged. Perhaps earlier feminist theories might still have something to teach us about what we have in common as women, despite the valuable critiques of essentialism that have come since. On the bright side, we do not have to accept the opposition between fragmentation and unity; we can combine the lessons of postmodern feminism with the materiality of embodiment and structural inequalities to move on from the current theoretical and political impasse.

Despite each story's proclamations of difference from the other accounts, there are striking narrative similarities that link these stories and that facilitate discursive movement between them without apparent contradiction. . . . All three stories divide the recent past into clear decades to provide a narrative of progress or loss, proliferation or homogenization. Stories of return are equally invested in these distinctions to argue for what it is that we need to return to in order to rescue Western feminist theory. You may know without me telling you that "the past" most often refers to the 1970s, that reference to identity and difference denotes the 1980s, and that the 1990s stands as the decade of difference proper, as that which must be returned from in the noughts. The stories . . . [I am] concerned with tracing are thus "common stories."[3] Implicitly or explicitly too, each decade is understood to house particular schools of thought and particular theorists, irrespective of whether or not their work spans much longer periods. Thus Marxist or radical approaches give way to identity politics, which give way to deconstructivist critiques, which are replaced in turn by (new) materialism. And no doubt we have not seen the last shift. Whether positively or negatively inflected, the chronology remains the same, the decades overburdened yet curiously flattened despite each story's unique truth claims.

These stories describe and locate feminist *subjects* as well as events or schools of thought, of course, and this also makes them affectively saturated for both authors and readers. They are not neutral and do not ask us to remain neutral. They position their teller as a heroine of

the past, present, and future of Western feminist theory. To dispute where we have ended up in the present is to dispute not only a given account of feminist theory, but also its proper subject. So in a progress narrative as described above a radical or socialist feminist is not and cannot be its transcendent subject; she is left behind. Neither can a poststructuralist feminist be the ideal subject of a loss or return narrative; she needs to change her mind. In this respect claims for what has happened in feminist theory are also claims about individual status. One's own intellectual and political commitments are always at stake in these stories, as one sees oneself by turn marginalized by the passage of time, or at the cutting edge of contemporary thought and practice. These commitments also form the basis of generational claims of progress or loss, allowing for the deflection of personal hopes and regrets onto collectivities or general trends: previous generations made certain understandable mistakes; a generation of academics contributes to and pays the price for professional institutionalization; youth in general has no awareness of history, is apolitical, bored, or self-interested.

To return to one of the characteristics of the three stories of feminist theory, that of the decade by decade fixing of shifts in feminist theory, one key issue is who is identified as belonging to which decade. . . . [I]n progress narratives, black feminism frequently acts as catalyst for a more general, *later*, move to difference as proliferation. In the process, the former is consistently cited as taking place in the 1980s, while an essentialist radical feminism or myopic socialist feminism occupies the 1970s, and poststructuralism moves forward into the 1990s and sometimes beyond, free of both essentialism and identity restrictions. In a related vein, lesbian feminist theory is called to account by the pro-sex demands of the 1980s, with the 1990s belonging squarely to queer theorists. In loss narratives, the seventies are equally uniform, the 1980s an important decade of identity contestation but one ambivalently related to both 1970s radicalism and 1990s fragmentation. Whether politically brave or misguided, identity politics have given way completely to the professionalization of feminist knowledge in the 1990s, and we have yet to return from this lamentable state of affairs.

In all versions of this story, postmodern and poststructuralist feminism are understood to mark a break from feminism proper through their attack on the category "woman."[4] The separation of these theoretical traditions from their feminist genealogy has some important narrative and political effects. The first is that "other" critiques of unified womanhood (from identity politics perspectives, for example) become teleologically bound and their challenges transcended in turn. Thus black and lesbian feminist engagements become firmly identified with the past, become anachronistic, as do their presumed subjects. A second, related, effect is that the separation of postmodernism and poststructuralism from their complex feminist histories means that the former too emerge oddly subjectless and without reference to contests that characterize their own inclusions and exclusions. Such an imaginative separation is essential for return narratives to function, since postmodernism and poststructuralism need to be rendered as wholly abstract in order for the plea for a return to "the body" or "the social" to make sense. Indeed, these imperatives are recast in return narratives as the very reason we need to move away from postmodernism and poststructuralism: repeated cries of "Wither the body? Wither the material?" are not meant to be resolved but serve as rhetorical gestures that anchor Western feminist historiography.

. . .

CORRECTIVES

My damning presentation of Western feminist storytelling thus far might lead a reader to wonder what I am suggesting as an alternative. If Western feminist stories of progress, loss, and return share aspects of postfeminist political grammar that make untangling contemporary uses of "gender equality" difficult, what might a willing feminist theorist do? Tell different stories perhaps? Put together an alternative historiography that can tell a better story, one with fewer, or less harmful, exclusions? One that refuses to leave feminism behind, for example? I could, to paraphrase Hayden White (1992), marshal corrective efforts to set the story of Western feminist theory straight. I could point out the errors, as I have been doing, and suggest other pasts. I could, as many interlocutors at different stages of this project have suggested, prioritize difference over similarity and look for moments, and of course they

are myriad, when these stories are not reproduced, or not reproduced faithfully. I could intervene at the level of truth telling, then, and leave us with a fuller, richer version of the recent past of Western feminist theory than these dominant narratives allow.

Such projects are indeed important. Feminist historians have consistently sought to tell stories other than dominant ones, both in response to mainstream records, and as part of enriching feminist historiography.[5] I also have a great deal of respect for projects that seek to tell alternative stories that highlight what has been left out and endeavour to reinsert those omissions into the historical record. For example, Becky Thompson shows how retelling the history of Western feminism from a multiracial perspective would see the 1970s less as a heyday and more as a "low point of feminism—a time when many women who were committed to an antiracist analysis had to put their feminism on the back burner in order to work with women and men of color and against racism" (2002: 344).[6] Significantly, Thompson's work points to the importance of assuming not just that there will always be exceptions to the norm of any given historical account, but that these exceptions provide an epistemological challenge to accepted teleologies. Indeed, my own entry into this project arose partly from the experience of disjuncture between the linear stories told about the recent past of Western feminist theory and my encounters with multiple feminisms and feminist debates through this forty-to-fifty year period. I still remember my surprise when I first visited a feminist archive, perused newsletters and magazines from activist groups, and realized that discussions about sadomasochism in the lesbian community had been raging long before the "sex wars" and that black feminist and transnational critique had been a consistent component of feminist theory, rather than one initiated in the late 1970s or 1980s. For me, that moment of realization not only emphasized the importance of personal experience, luck if you like, in one's relationship to history, but also precipitated an ongoing discussion in my head about the best way to respond to absences from contemporary accounts.

Yet despite this genuine pull towards the corrective and the multiple, I do not finally think that attempting representation of this kind can be the answer to the particular problems of repetition and grammatical transferability identified . . . [here]. One reason for this resistance is that I have been persuaded by feminist historiographers' insistence that which story one tells about the past is always motivated by the position one occupies or wishes to occupy in the present. As Antoinette Burton (2001), Elizabeth Grosz (2002), Gayatri Spivak (1999a), Jennifer Terry (1991; 1999), and Eve Sedgwick (1991) all variously indicate, since fullness in representations of the past can never be reached, a corrective approach will always be likely to erase the conditions of its own construction, particularly if it purports to give us the final word. To correct the story which writers should we choose? How would this happen without reification? Who will tell this story? What methods might be proposed for fullness (Campt 2004)? In an early article outlining my concerns in this project, these questions are abruptly answered by a rather out-of-place footnote in which I provide a list of black feminist writers from the 1960s and 1970s as a way of making clear that the dominant stories I am critiquing are not only politically injurious but also inaccurate. . . . As one critic of this piece points out, the footnote both authenticates the desire to critique the existing ways of telling stories and reveals a more corrective approach than I otherwise claim to endorse (Torr 2007: 61). The stranded footnote remains uncontextualized and proposes an alternative history without fully delineating it, or being accountable for it. It hints at multiplicity but cannot find a way to represent it.

Similar problems arise when the Western feminist stories I have been sketching are set against geographical alternatives. In one strand of argument progress, loss, and return narratives are framed not as Western in general, but as Anglo-American in particular. Thus, the story that feminist theory has moved from radical or socialist feminism, through identity politics and into postmodernism and thence a "postcultural" turn, is sometimes critiqued by continental European feminists for positing Anglo-American trajectories as descriptive of the entirety of Western feminist theory. In this line of argument, the European alternative, often through the (re)claiming of sexual difference as current rather than surpassed, is offered as the corrective.[7] A fuller, more geographically representative theoretical reach is advocated and the story retold. Yet in the process, of course, only certain kinds of "European alternatives" can be incorporated: those standing in contrast to ones perceived as Anglo-American.[8] Not only does the "European alternative" thus posed risk simplifying the difference that it makes, but the Anglo-American centre remains static, too. In the volume *Italian Feminist Theory and Practice*, for example, the future may be Italian, but the Anglo-American feminist past continues to comprise a familiar move from sex to gender, from essentialism to deconstruction (Parati and West 2002). And in Chrysanthi Nigianni and Merl Storr's collection *Deleuze and Queer Theory* it is Anglo-American versions of the latter that are constraining, while continental inflections promise mobility (2009). In this respect, it is often the particular that is fleshed out, while the dominant that is corrected remains intact. Correction is bound to treasure what is found at the stereotyping expense of what is jettisoned.

What such geographical correctives miss are the ways in which dominant stories (Anglo-American or Western) traverse boundaries and operate in relation. They tend to substitute literal location for a politics of location (Rich 1986), and in doing so perpetuate stereotypes about who lives where and how stories travel.[9] Thus, the geopolitical power of located publishing and English as the global *lingua franca* means that feminist theory produced in an Anglo-American context is always likely to exceed its geography (King 1994). More importantly, conceptualizing of Anglo-American feminist theory's travels as direct *dissemination* fails to capture the transitions and translations that mark its movements back and forth and that highlight the nature of international engagement with its various forms (Bal 2002; Vasterling, Demény et al. 2006). For example, Sabine Hark's careful work on the discursive life of Judith Butler's *Gender Trouble* in Germany (2002) explores the ways in which dismissal of *Gender Trouble* by powerful feminist academics on the basis of its "seductive Americanness" masks and displaces central anxieties about queerness that the text also brings with it when it travels. Neither do what I continue to call *Western* feminist narratives of progress, loss, and return emerge only from Anglo-American sites, or even ones with English as a national language; they are produced and endorsed much more broadly than that. Journals such as *Nora: Nordic Journal of Women's Studies* and the *European Journal of*

Women's Studies generate the same stories about what has happened in Western feminist theory, even where this does not fit with the specific institutional context or political history at issue. To see these stories as geographically bounded, then, is to suggest that they do in fact accurately describe the history of feminist theory in Western (or indeed Anglo-American) contexts and that the failure is primarily one of inclusion rather than representation. Difference from dominant accounts is thus always elsewhere rather than within. In terms of the marginalization that those dominant narrations effect for particular subjects and histories, a belief in their geographically descriptive accuracy redoubles the racial and sexual exclusions that permeate those sites.

The realization of feminist theory's multiplicity, then, leads me to want to analyze not so much what other truer history we might write, but the politics that produce and sustain one version of history as more true than another, despite the fact that we know that history is more complicated than the stories we tell about it. Although I am always bound by my desire to see more multiplicity represented, this desire does not have to be approached from the perspective of plugging the gaps, as if this could ever be finally achieved, or as if which gaps one prioritizes were in need of no further explanation. Holding in mind multiple histories that remain un- or under-represented in the present should not determine the mode of one's response to that representation and does not automatically point to corrective redress as the most appropriate means to address the problem of omission. The moment, that snapshot of the discursive dissonance that makes up feminist history, might operate instead as a reminder that all histories are selective and motivated histories, even if they can make plain their "contested authorization" (Hemmings 2007a: 73). In line with my interest in what storytelling reveals about the politics of the present, my responses to Western feminist storytelling . . . start from, but do not conclude with, the multiple erasures and investments of the present. I seek to flesh out the substance of Western feminist stories and to intervene by experimenting with how we might tell stories differently rather than telling different stories.

. . .

INTERVENTIONS

Two particular storytelling tactics have emerged as central to my interest in the transformation of progress, loss, and return narratives throughout this project: attention to citation and to affect. I have mentioned both of these in passing thus far, but want to conclude this introduction by drawing out some of the threads of both approaches as they run through the text as a whole. Both citation and affect, I argue, are key techniques through which these narratives operate, through which they are secured and made believable. As I . . . demonstrate, . . . who is or is not cited as evidence in the case for Western feminist theory's recent past as a story of progress, loss, or return underwrites the decade by decade approach I have already begun to critique here. It is the primary technique through which people and approaches are assigned an era, positioned as pivotal to key shifts in theoretical direction, or written out of the past or present. Affect is similarly germane to the narratives I analyze and how they function. One of the ways in which the glosses I scrutinize appeal to the common sense of their reader without detailed discussion is through the mobilization of affect. Alternative ways of narrating the recent past of Western feminist theory are foreclosed in progress narratives, for example, through their celebratory tone that provides little space for dissent. Loss narratives, as laments, express and produce negative feelings that also allow a slide over what might be missing in a given account, and that paradoxically enough, might be said to underpin a positive affective state in the subject whose version of history is thus consolidated. As I outline further, . . . I am interested in affect as a core part of political grammar and, following Lauren Berlant (e.g., 1997; 2007; 2008), understand it as producing internal textual and external community cohesion that is difficult to resist. Both citation and affect seem like good places to start in thinking about my own storytelling tactics too, then, precisely because of their centrality to the dominant narratives I want to intervene in.

I have developed several ways of experimenting with citation in my analysis of Western feminist stories. . . . The first shines a spotlight on these stories as held in common irrespective of what else a given author may be arguing. Anyone who has ever published a piece of writing knows that which aspects of an article are assumed to need referencing, which ways of telling stories need further explanation or argumentation, are never individual decisions alone. As an editor or reviewer for more than one of the journals I examine, . . . my reading practices are shaped by the knowledge community within which I operate. When I review articles, my eye alights on certain things and not others; some parts of an article stick out, and there is a lot that passes my notice. Thus, my citation practice here combines with my choice to focus on journal articles rather than textbooks, single-authored books, or edited collections as a way of foregrounding knowledge practices as shared rather than individual. The primary tactic I employ is to cite the *source* of the extract I introduce—the journal and year—rather than the author, throughout. This tactic is intended to emphasize the role of journal communities—editors, boards, peer reviewers, and responses to publishing conventions and expectations—in the establishment of feminist (and broader academic) knowledge practices. It also provides a way of being able to focus on patterns across the journals, seeing them as a set, rather than being distracted by resonances across an individual oeuvre.

Citing place and time of publication in this way also underlines my commitment to non-corrective approaches to engaging Western feminist storytelling. It is intended to shift priority away from who said what, away from thinking about feminist theory in terms of "good" and "bad" authors, and away from the lures of prior agreement. In relation to the latter point, for example, a given author may well utilize aspects of a loss or return narrative despite the fact that they are more generally known (and liked or disliked) for endorsing progress narratives. Taking the authors out of the citation frame is thus a way of focusing attention on repetition instead of individuality, and on how collective repetition actively works to obscure the politics of its own production and reproduction. Other feminist authors have suggested similar moves. Christine Hughes, for example, suggests that we look at feminist texts not in terms of what is right or wrong about them, but in terms of their conditions of production, institutional resonance, and interpretative possibilities (2004), and Gayatri Spivak consistently warns us

against the individual author-blaming that mitigates against real recognition of historically and discursively constituted speaking locations (1999b). In this spirit, I also hope that the sustained approach to citation I take here works against the tendency to produce work that largely consists of extended critique of key authors: back and forth we go, arguing about who got it right. Instead, I see the narrative strands I analyze as creating stories that we all participate in and that constitute a process of collective knowledge production that locates us in particular ways. This citation tactic allows me to track the commonalities of utterance, the remarkably similar affects mobilized and produced, and to suggest that there is no "outside" of these processes, no single (or even multiple) alternative story one could tell that would finally "get it right," even while there remain ways of thinking stories differently.[10]

My second citation tactic . . . similarly intervenes at the representational level, though in a more assertive mode. . . . I examine citation practice in narratives of progress, loss, and return, focusing particularly on its role in temporally separating strands of feminist thought that could as easily be cited as co-extensive. Citation is important because it anchors an overall chronology, provides a semblance of detail, and has an appropriate status as evidence. This or that text will certainly have been published (or sometimes reissued) at the date cited, but this empiricism masks the selective nature of that evidence. The repeated choice in narrative glosses to cite black feminism as an eighties phenomenon, for example, tells us not just about that decade, but forms part of an overall chronology. Similarly it is an indisputable fact that Judith Butler's *Gender Trouble* was published in 1990, but its relentless citation as that which precipitates feminism into a new era of critique serves a much broader narrative function. In these and many other cases, citation works to position feminism as part of the past and contemporary work as apolitical or more political depending on textual affect. In my analysis of citation, . . . I focus both on the political productiveness of these practices—the kind of Western feminist present they instantiate—and on what is excluded through these practices. This examination of citation as key to the politics of the present forms the basis of the first major tactical intervention into Western feminist storytelling. . . . I develop an approach to narrative I call "recitation," which seeks to disrupt dominant narrative grammar and open up multiple re-readings of the present. Starting from what is precluded in dominant citational practice, I fold these hauntings back into the political grammar of Western feminist theory to produce a set of potential feminist realignments. I ask what happens when we recite stories in which feminism has been left behind by poststructuralism, by forcing absent presences back into the narrative, beginning from affective investments in what has been half-forgotten. One might describe this process as one that mobilizes my ambivalent corrective impulses as a starting point rather than endpoint of imagining otherwise. What kinds of historical and political possibilities does such a move allow us to imagine or temporarily inhabit? Recitation, then, combines with my other citation tactic of de-authorization to constitute a consistent intervention into the political grammar of Western feminist storytelling. . . .

My introduction of tactical recitation, above, states that I start from "what is precluded in dominant citational practice" and move forward, as if identifying absent presences were not itself a selective process. If citation is selective in ways I have suggested, then so too must be my own identification of what is lost. This is the danger of correctives I have been warning about throughout this introduction, of course. Consideration of this problem has lead me both to clarify that recitation is limited by its original frames of engagement (i.e., it is not an "anything goes" approach) and to explore more fully the importance of a motivated relation to Western feminist theory as the basis of a reflexive, accountable historiography. Feminist theory is filled with passion and with passionate attachments. Their expression forms the very stuff of feminist language, makes feminist theory alive, and produces passionate responses in audiences in turn. And one need only look at the hostile online responses to feminist writing in news media to see that these responses are just as motivated as their originals. Indeed, fury is one of the primary modes of antifeminist expression, despite its frequent claim to have moved beyond politics. Attempting to answer that question of motivation— in the stories I tell as well as those I analyze, and the relationship between these—has lead me to integrate questions of affect as central both to how narratives of progress, loss, and return function and as key to effective interventions at the level of a transformative political grammar.[11]

Affects of despair and hope, resentment and passion form the very currency of Western feminist narratives of progress, loss, and return. They presume a shared affective state, if not shared emotions.[12] Thus, loss narratives work through appealing to that sense of loss that narrator assumes is already present in the reader, providing a shared affective platform. Who is to blame for this loss, what needs to happen next and so on, is often less significant than this shared starting point, which overrides differences in historiographic interpretation. Progress narratives similarly presume a shared sense of pleasure at having overcome the worst excesses of a unified feminism, however we may have come to this present, more sophisticate, state of affairs. In this respect attention to the affective registers of Western feminist storytelling allows me to concentrate on the politics of the present in ways that are crucial for this project. Further, the use of emotional appeals in Western feminist narratives positions the teller of tales as heroic, triumphant, wounded, or marginalized in turn, bolsters this affective underside, and actively works to create agreement through identification. Indeed, lack of identification risks readerly positioning as the antiheroine: as self-interested, privileged, or narcissistic instead. Western feminist theorists make narrative judgements and foreclose other narrative possibilities, set subject up against object, theory against politics, now against then, and here against there, in part through mobilizing affect. Thus, although I am wary of being drawn into a critical process that privileges affect over politics in my reading of narrative, it is also clear to me that affect is part of the *texture* of narrative and political investments in feminist theory (Sedgwick 2003).

Following Gilles Deleuze and Silvan Tomkins respectively, Brian Massumi and Eve Sedgwick conceive of affects as having an ontological life that cannot be analyzed through epistemological frames or through their reduction to social structures (Massumi 2002; Sedgwick 2003). Yet perhaps they might also tell us something about the affective life of those same social structures, particularly when conceived of in terms of investments in past and future collectivities, as is the case in this project. Indeed, in following affect . . . what has struck me most is how this attention can reveal aspects of narrative meanings otherwise obscured, rather than revealing something outside of narrative altogether (Staunaes 2010). In this sense, alongside Lauren Berlant (1997; 2004) and the Jacques Derrida of *The Politics of Friendship* (1997), I understand analysis of affect as key to reading the relationship between the epistemological and the ontological. Elspeth Probyn's work on the tension between gendered epistemology and ontological experience as the basis for a reflexive feminist politics might indicate affect as a key object for a reflexive feminist criticism.[13] Further, attention to affect may take us along different paths because its presence often represents a substitution of one motivation for another (because direct reflection on affect is often too difficult) and thus needs to be analyzed through *association* rather than through opposition or exclusion.

If attention to affect is important in reading narratives of progress, loss, and return in all their complexity, it is also important intersubjectively in terms of how it positions me as well as other readers. As Sara Ahmed has indicated, the affective nature of intersubjective formation means that there is no "outside affect," no place to retreat to in order not to be moved (2004c; 2004d; 2004a). Indeed, it is partly through trying to trace my own relationship to Western feminist stories that I have become convinced of the importance of affect in the sustaining of critical attachment to one version of the past or another. Throughout this introduction and the mapping, . . . for example, I represent my own priorities as concerned with the pertinent racial and sexual absences that occur when feminist theory is understood to have left feminism behind and with the relation of these absences to larger social and political mobilizations of gender equality discourse. This is a rather admirable set of investments, I am sure you will agree, one definitionally likely to uncover less

worthy aims in the texts I read. Yet it proposes my critical position as outside of the narratives I examine, one invested in exposing their exclusions as if they were not also my own. Tracking my own affect is instructive, in that this "admirable neutrality" is of course impossible to sustain. . . . I am most unable to maintain this distance in my mapping of loss narratives, where I am directly implicated as a "co-opted professional feminist" in the accounts I read. My rage at being misrepresented is expressed as scorn, a set of emotional registers that enable me to preserve the prior convictions about poststructuralism as *not this* that I bring to the text. Intellectually and politically enlivened in the 1990s by queer, postcolonial, feminist poststructuralist theories, I see my past self, and the life and times of my pomo-comrades, dissolving in narratives that evoke "those days" as ones of critique alone. In loss narratives, we are not only subject to feminism's demise, we are also responsible for it; hence the spilling over of rage evidenced in textual tone. My smug interest in racial and sexual exclusions is thus tempered by a prior interest in their inclusion remaining part of the poststructuralism I need to remember myself by. . . .

Both interventions—recitation and affective mobilization—constitute experimental approaches to telling stories differently so that feminist theory might be less amenable to co-optation. Both experiments start from textual and political absences in the stories we already participate in, explicitly folding these back into narrative in order to reconfigure the political grammars of Western feminism. They offer ways of *approaching* feminist stories and politics over the temptation to produce a more correct account and thus prioritize the unknown over the known and refusal over acceptance. In this respect, both interventions develop new qualitative approaches that require attention to memory, desire, and uncertainty as central to feminist practice and radical politics, and that are intended for use, should you find them useful.

NOTES

1. I am grateful to one of the readers of the initial manuscript for the term "political grammar" and to both readers for their thoughtful and generous engagements.
2. I use the terms "story," "narrative," and "grammar" throughout [this Introduction]. By "stories" I mean, the overall tales feminists tell about what has happened in the last thirty to forty years

of Western feminist theory and indicate too their status as "myth" or "common opinion." By "narratives" I mean the textual refrains (content and pattern) used to tell these stories and their movement across time and space. By "grammar" I mean the techniques (oppositions, intertextual reference, and so on) that serve as narrative building blocks. I also use the term "political grammar" by which I mean to indicate the stitching together of all these levels as well as the broader political life of these stories. I have tried to be consistent in how these terms are used, but there are moments when of course technique and repetition are not distinct, or where I use other terms such as "history" to get me out of trouble.

3. You will notice that I have not provided references to particular authors in my overview here, relying on an initial sense of these stories as familiar. And it is indeed that familiarity that I am interested in, that motivates the range of "citation tactics" that I explore throughout, and that I explain later in this . . . [Introduction].

4. In Western feminist progress, loss, and return narratives postmodernism and poststructuralism are often represented as synonymous, or one or other is understood to stand in for both. I have tried not to reproduce the same slip, in part because I lean towards a poststructural approach myself. In representing my own understanding I tend to mark a (sometimes arbitrary, I admit) distinction by using "poststructuralism" to denote an attitude to text/subject/world over "postmodernism" as a critique of modernism or understanding of the social world as transformed by, for example, reflexive individualism.

5. It would seem odd to attempt to cite "feminist history" in a footnote, so let me gesture to one (London-based) project that seeks to enrich our knowledge of the past by focusing on complexities that are often overlooked: "History of Feminism Network: Celebrating, Exploring and Debating the History of Feminism"—***http://historyfeminism.wordpress.com/***.

6. See also Benita Roth's account of the emergence of a black feminist "vanguard" in the 1960s and 1970s, and Nancy MacLean's work, which links affirmative action to black and working class women's struggles in the same period (MacLean 1999; Roth 1999).

7. See Iris van der Tuin's article "'Jumping Generations,'" which links generation and geography very particularly, and my own response to this tendency in the same special issue of *Australian Feminist Studies* on "Feminist Timelines" (Hemmings 2009; van der Tuin 2009).

8. This may be one historiographical reason why the French Marxist tradition, including Christine Delphy, has been overlooked in preference for the sexual difference tradition more commonly associated with "écriture féminine" (See Braidotti 2000; Delphy 2000; Jackson 2001).

9. Caren Kaplan warns us that this happens when the careful contextualization of feminist positioning is replaced with localized universalisms or aestheticization (Kaplan 1994).

10. One clear danger of this approach is that it reduces an individual author's right of reply and makes it hard for readers to check the accuracy of my citation, too. I did try other approaches to citation of the journal glosses at one point, but author citation invariably drew me back into engaging with individual arguments, rather than the passing narratives an author might not even wish to claim. So, while acknowledging that this is a risky strategy in several ways, this aspect of citation practice remains central to this project.

11. My "turn to affect" in this project might strike readers familiar with my earlier critique of this term as rather ironic (Hemmings 2005a). In "Invoking Affect" I intervene in debates that herald the affective turn as a cutting-edge means to move beyond epistemological and political dead-ends. Suggesting that such calls produce a history of poststructuralism stripped of its feminist and postcolonial antecedents, I argue that invoking affect as new fails to provide a history to affect and makes us (as critics) inattentive to affect's intertwining with and production through

the social. The tone of this article is so critical that it might easily be read as a dismissal of the importance of affect altogether, although this was never my intention. My focus here then both starts from that interest in the social as lived in affective registers and results in the development of a warmer tone on my part.

12. Here I am making use of Silvan Tomkins' distinction between affects (as states) and emotions (as particular expressions of those states) (1963).

13. Elspeth Probyn understands the tension between the epistemological frames of gender and our ontological experiences of the same as the basis for feminist reflexivity (1993). A focus on affect as that which binds the epistemological and the ontological might also be thought of as part of a reflexive project.

3. SPEAKING IN TONGUES: FUGITIVE KNOWLEDGE AND/IN THE PAKISTANI GEOBODY

My mother tells me a story. She told me this story throughout my childhood and well into my adult life. For many years, I thought this story was strange and comical, even borderline ridiculous. But my mother narrated this story with such utter seriousness that it came to hold a mysterious accuracy. This story was about the tongue. Think about the human tongue, my mother would say—the tongue is soft and vulnerable, fleshy and pink, essential to both function (eating, speaking) and enjoyment (food and sex). But this tongue, for all its softness lives between thirty-two teeth—hard, strong, solid, and sharp. Any given moment, the teeth can damage, impair, tear the tongue, but the tongue has no choice, it has to learn to live among the teeth, in the midst of hardness, that could individually or collectively destroy it.

For my mother, this story of the tongue was the perfect allegory for woman. The very idea of the tongue living so intimately with that which can destroy it functions as a necro-metaphorization—a metaphor not just of death, but of "death worlds"—"forms of social existence in which vast populations are subjected to conditions of life conferring upon them the status of the living dead" (Agamben 40). I relay my mother's metaphoric story of women's survival, of the tongue's place in the mouth, among teeth, to crystalize patriarchal realities, imperial violences, nationalist struggles, and remind us that women, as Simone de Beauvoir stated, are often "imprisoned by the peculiarities of the body" (7).

This metaphorization of the human tongue I heard from her throughout my childhood bleeds over and into dominant feminist theorizations, closing the recent distance between women's stories and knowledge production, bloodying the pages of feminist theory with vocabularies of necro-politics, hetero-violence, women's survival, and the power of the tongue. In this story,

like so many others I heard from my mother throughout my childhood and in the last three years of more formal "interviews,"[1] both tongue/s and women are perversely marked by the queer interdependence of that which harms and that which heals, of endurance and survival, of silence and of story, of life and of death.

In this reading, I position feminist theory as constructive (experimental), destructive (subversive), and as the avant-garde (whose intent is to take on political function). I center feminist knowledge as home/less, un-contoured, undomesticated, wild and always crisscrossing over and through fugitive knowledges, the life of the racial, the landscapes of the geopolitical and the queerness undergirding it all. I argue that theory is not just words on a page. It is a life lived and unseen.

Feminist epistemologies, we know, have never been abodes of disinterested scholarship; rather, they have always been cleaved with contradictions, claiming unclaimed subjects, excavating the exiled, the buried, the queer. From this standpoint, in which theory is not the exclusive preserve of the academic elite, the feminist thinker takes the side of the excluded and the repressed. As a queer feminist theorist of color, I take this childhood story into serious consideration—I consider it a form of fugitive knowledge, always and already illegible to dominant modes of rational thought. I draw from Fred Moten, Frank Wilderson, and Saidiya Hartman, all of whom think about fugitive living as departing from dominant Anglo-Western notions that frame freedom as achievement and arrival, and instead offer fugitivity as the ways through which people of color *make way out of no way*. Indeed, the more I lean into the crevices of this strange story—the spaces between my mother's words—the more I see the skilled abilities of the marginalized to analyze the conditions of their own lives. In other words, I hear the quiet demand that room must be made for the subaltern.

STORY/S AS THEORY AND THEORY AS STORY/S

> "When you live in the ocean, you can't make enemies with the sharks." – my mother

"Buried knowledges of erudition"—as Michel Foucault (82) called them—requires conversation with those "low down on the hierarchy," whose unwritten subjects of history are beneath the required level of cognition, scientificity. To get at the precarious and fragile subject, Foucault continues, means listening "for something altogether different" (82). As a feminist, interested in writing about my mother, I am drawn to this Foucauldian notion as my interest centers around subjugated knowledges. When I speak of subjugated knowledges and feminist theory, I am specifically interested in the social and affective genealogies (read: historical stories) that have been repressed, disqualified, and marginalized by theoretical canons, sometimes even feminist canons.

What does it mean to use and situate this small story of the tongue offered by an im/migrant m/*other* of color into broader theoretical-political questions on racial capitalism, imperial patriarchies, and colonial conflict? How do we understand the *other* embedded in the figure of the m/*other*, especially the m/*other* of color? Answers to these questions demands cracking open feminist theory, disrupting the canonized subject of study, and asking, without apology, who have we forgotten?

I deliberately slash m/*other* as a linguistic variation to hint at and get at the politics of *otherness* embedded in the figure of the mother of color, and that for women of color, motherhood and the mechanisms of surviving as mothers are even further intensified, complicated, and fraught. By slashing m/other to highlight the *other*, I underscore the symbolic paradigm of the mother as always and already the other in feminist theory, as a metonymic figure left out of an entire repertoire of critical theory.

I attempt to grapple with these questions and these gaps by examining the role of my opening story as a vehicle of feminist theory, a way to theorize the complexities of m/others of color experience, and to take into account the social and political traces left behind in women of color's memories and resistance narratives. As the story on tongues demonstrates, the tongue is simultaneously the embodiment and the vehicle of resistance. It has to survive its own conditions in order to then tell the story of this survival. This strange little story—a play on words, a play on tongues—holds in it other forms of knowledges, what Chela Sandoval might call, a "methodology of the oppressed"—an alternative consciousness and oppositional expression that emerges through strange colloquialisms and odd tongues (2000). I am reminded, here, of Roland Barthes words: "Language is a skin: I rub my language against the other. It is as if I had words instead of fingers, or fingers at the tip of my words" (73). Barthes words appear to position language as feeling, as something that sticks. Thus, I came to recognize that my mother's speaking in tongues, about tongues, as similar to what Audre Lorde would call "beneath language," referring to the weight of whiteness in the English language, and how women of color created and constructed vocabularies unavailable to the dominant speaker (74). The task, then, of the politically engaged theorist is, as Aimé Césaire says, "My mouth shall be the mouth of those calamities that have no mouth" (30).

The social and geopolitical coordinates that made up my mother's life—an im/migrant, Muslim, Pakistani m/*other* living in the United States, raising her husband's (half) white children alongside her own very brown, very immigrant children within the constraints of hetero-patriarchal social formations that violated her (body), and made her violable to others' violence—implicated, interdicted, and immured her every day. Inciting, what Anne Czetkovich calls an "archive of feeling" and elucidating how systems of power are overlapping, continuous, proximate, embodied, and symbiotic, my m/other's tongue compels a different way of thinking about Pakistani women and the forms of living, suffering, enduring, and resisting that are ordinary, chronic, and cruddy (2003). Consequently, within her everyday, my mother would tell stories, allegories, and parables. She filled our childhood and her time with them. My mother, I learned, tells stories to make sense of her own historical present; and in so doing, her story on the tongue, for example, turns the intimate into the monumental. Storytelling, for her, became an oppositional practice—a way to underscore the silences that surround the fe/male body, the violence superimposed in their lives, and the ever-shifting matrix of oppression and resistance. In all of these stories, the conceptual and political accounting of power is evident: the parts always exceed the whole.

LIVING ARCHIVES

When I first started thinking about Pakistani women, I found myself drawn toward, and deeply critical of, what I identified as the increasing traffic and proliferation of the visual, the photographed and filmed "Pakistani woman." Wherever I went—from coffeehouses to classrooms to cocktail bars—I heard, with some variation, the insistent refrain, "but . . . isn't it worse for Pakistani women." The images and narratives produced—from Nicholas Kristoff's *Half The Sky* (2008) to mediascapes like *National Geographic* (2007) and *Newsweek* (2008) and even a range of Hollywood films, such as *Zero Dark Thirty* or television series, such as *Homeland*—belonged to an elite world of viewers. Each image and story was carefully made and pleasurable, even in their disturbances. This visual terrain of Pakistani women that circulated in transnational media and cultural circles returned to viewers their exact desires—the brown female *other* as abject, downtrodden, in need of a white savior.

Think, for example, of David Guggenheim's *He Named Me Malala*, a film based on the life and survival of Malala Yousafzai, the young teenager shot in the head by Taliban who is now lauded as a global activist for girls' education. While many critics saw the film as both structurally and cinematically "repetitive, heavy-handed, and superficial," they were deeply hesitant to critique it (Kramer). After all, the story "is so fascinating and important" that its underwhelming capture is almost beside the point. Or as CJ Johnson of *ABS News* states, "Guggenheim's film is not the kind that demands a big screen, but if you do see it at the cinema you might get what I got: that rare phenomenon of spontaneous audience applause at the film's conclusion. If that's because we were all thinking of Paris along with Malala, all the better." While the appeal to the visual and the visible is deployed as an answer to the histories of silence, this appeal is neither uncomplicated nor innocent. Visibility in and of itself

does not erase histories of silence nor does it challenge the structure of power and domination, symbolic and material, that determines who can and cannot be seen. Thus, the combined power of the visual still and the moving film lend itself to the discursive construction of "Pakistani women" whose trauma we must see and control.

With Orientalism so ready to hand a rubric for the relation of the *other*, it is difficult to resist seeing Pakistani women as simply the domestic oppressed. How, then, do we write stories of Pakistani women's being and becoming, subjectivity and trauma, displacement and dispossession, life and death, pleasure and pain outside these frames of spectatorship? By framing Pakistani women's stories as a social and political category, I recognize—against this orientalist impulse—that both the index of Pakistan and the signifier woman are subjects of a discourse at this particular political and cultural moment, each of which have complex and underwritten histories. However, I simultaneously remain alert to the ways in which my mother's stories, like so many others, can quickly become a bright object of, what José Muñoz calls "suburban spectatorship" (*Disidentifications* 4). I stand warned by indigenous scholars about how our work becomes trapped in ethnographic multiculturalism, a neoliberal representation domesticated by nation-state and capitalist imperatives. I engage in what Audra Simpson calls "ethnographic refusal," a refusal of containment, representation, and domestication of my mother's tongues. Conversely, then, I want to consider the ways my mother's story on the tongue, and her life stories more broadly, disrupt the orientalist and homogeneous understanding of Pakistani women, opening a space for feminist radicalism, within the specificities of class and sexualities.[2] Her story on the human tongue challenges the dominant narrative that feminism is what the West *gives* to the East. Instead, like Sara Ahmed, "feminism traveled to me, growing up in the West, from the East" (4) *and* "where we find feminism matters; from whom we find feminism matters" (4). Moreover, the category Pakistan[3] remains only one index of the many cultures, publics, and loyalties within which the story of the tongue operates. This story is not rooted in Pakistan nor can it be abstracted from Pakistan. Pakistan, and the category of the Pakistani woman, only partially captures the complexity of this narration and only marginally functions as a category by which to classify this story.

By tracking the story of the tongue—vulnerable, resilient, surviving—I elucidate how women of color positioned in complex geopolitical and geo-bodily spaces are, in Barbara Christian's (1987) words, "a race for theory"—always and already producing theory merely by living and surviving. Indeed, by conjoining the "geo" with the body, I underscore that women's stories are never luxuriously told outside the body. For example, my mother's departure from Pakistan was fraught with the politics of dis/possession of and over her body, her sexuality, her hetero and national belonging, experiences that led to the early formations of a language/a story of survival. But such stories need to be told very slowly, erasing the comforts of linearity, triumph, and optimisms. I think of dispossession from nation, from home, and from the viability of the body, as a queer feeling, a racialized relation, and disruption of hetero and national belonging, all of which come to be expressed in queer tongues and strange melancholia. José Muñoz taught us that "Melancholia for blacks, queers, or any queers of color, is not a pathology but an integral part of everyday lives . . . it is this melancholia that is part of our process dealing with all the catastrophes that occur in the lives of people of color, lesbians and gay men" (1999). Further, by offering my mother's story on the tongue as a site ripe for feminist theorizing, I offer up an insurgent vocabulary that can help me make sense of how notions of Pakistan, dispossession, violence, grief are experienced, and how particular forms of formal knowledge around these delimits the ways women of color can be talked about, their lives engaged, or their stories made public.

QUEER TONGUES

Let me close by noting the various ways I am thinking about "tongues," at the merger of my mother's story and feminist theorizing, with the important caveat that these are not the only ways to think about it. The phrase "mother tongue" often invokes nationalized and naturalized language, in co-occurrence with the notion of motherland—where land and language are implicated in subjectivity, power, and affect. The term

"tongues" also invokes varying Christian spiritual practices where the spiritual subject no longer has access to rational language, and comes to speak in ways that sonically surface like multiple languages working at once. This play on tongues holds important meanings tied to central theorems in this discussion—borderlands, unintelligibility, and chaos. This connotation of "speaking in tongues" emphasizes a private and privileged communication between a subject and her divine, inaccessible to others, outside the realm of public discourse and known language. But even this play on tongues incites nation and language, as the very idea of "speaking in tongues" reflects the subject's possession of a native tongue and is the ability to speak every language of every nation.

Fundamentally, if speaking in tongues is about transcendence—transcending your nativity, your body, your psyche, your positionality—then we have an interesting heteroglossia at play in this phrase. Mae Henderson argues that speaking in tongues, within the context of women of color, may be more usefully understood as the ability to speak in the multiple languages of public discourse. Revealing the concrete materialities of race, gender, and social power within which women of color come to speak in "tongues," Henderson underscores how this phrase stretches out and over the language of varied and complex social locations, embodiments, desires, and beliefs. Women of color, immigrants, and queers are often seen *not* just as disrupting discourse but language itself insofar as forms of marginalization produce their own vernacular, simultaneously drawing from and undercutting dominant language. Gloria Anzaldúa has provocatively stated that queer women of color "speak in tongues like the outcast and the insane" (165). Here, I am reminded of the figure of the *hijra* in the South Asian context (non-binary persons, transnationally understood as transgender), where they are often scorned as speaking gibberish because their Urdu vernacular is so affective and song-like (in *Urdu*, this is articulated as *bakwas*).

Let me also add here the oft-used turn of phrase "forked tongue"—a well-known Native American proverb indicating the act of saying one thing but meaning another, an insinuation of the hypocrisy of white men (Kramer Halaby). The tongue here comes to embody simultaneously white coloniality and white benevolence, in ways I find interesting and thoughtful insofar as it indicates how language has been central to oppression of colonized peoples. But even within this formation, we see the quintessential gendered and Judeo-Christian image of the serpent, a forked-tongue creature, duplicitous and dangerous, an association embedded within dominant readings of women of color's sexualities. I also think that the very idea of a forked tongue implies a sharpening of soft flesh, flesh as weaponized and disloyal—a characteristic often attributed to women's bodies and to queer desires.

Tongues—as carnal, as deceitful, as excessive—brings me to another important theorem in this discussion. Simply, my mother's story on the tongue is not outside the body or sexuality. A deeply intimate part of the body, the tongue, like women's bodies, has often been regarded as dirty and excessive, particularly in terms of sexuality. Queer sexuality, non-normative sex acts, often centralizes the mouth, and by doing so disturbs the futurity of penetrative sex. In this way, I am thinking about the tongue as flesh and metaphor, as an effective site of disrupting the futurity associated with heterosexuality and now, homo-exceptionalism.

Tongue/s as nation, as privatized vernacular, as illegible words, as dirty sex coagulates here, I argue, as fugitive, as *other*. Thus, I mobilize "tongues" as an analytic lever—a simultaneous incitement of the body and a means to track the affective associations that lack the structural coherence and stability necessary to the production of dominant knowledge. Indeed, I take my mother's stories—her speaking in tongues—as always and already unintelligible and illegible to dominant modes of rational thought and theoretical subject formation. Instead, senility, madness, passion, emotion, chaos, fragmentation are the burdens and benedictions of this kind of theorizing. In this way, my mother's story is always and already queer; where queerness is informed by its historical specificity of sexual irregularities, where queerness is bodily and that which challenges the limits of what can be understood as a body, where queerness assumes the presence of queer desire despite the silence, where queerness's varying expressions are often vilified as cowardly or dirty, and where queerness implodes and exceeds disciplinary and theoretical conventions and opens up a way of writing that could track and understand the fragmented woman subject.

NOTES

1. In my first book, *Will the Real Pakistani Woman Please Stand Up? Empire, Visual Culture and the Brown Female Body* (2015), my object of analysis was public and visual discourse, and as such, I pulled together an archive of mainstream Global North mediascapes around Muslim women that traced the increased traffic and proliferation of the visual, the photographed and filmed "Muslim woman" to excavate the US/Global North geopolitical and fetishistic fascination with *looking* at Muslim woman. Shortly after the publication of my first book, I began "interviewing" my mother. I recorded her stories, our conversations, and her conversations with her sisters and her brothers. Sometimes I asked questions, solicitous and probing; other times, most times, my mother (as she did throughout my life) would just begin telling an old story, or memory, and we would begin our descent into her past.

2. This reading is part of a larger book project, tentatively titled *Archive of Tongues: Memory, Trauma and Critical Theory* (Duke University Press). This project follows in the tradition of Audre Lorde, Gloria Anzaldúa, and Dionne Brand in the mode of creative non-fiction to get at the intersections of maternal knowledges and feminist theory, neo/colonialisms and diaspora, and the intimate geographies of brownness. Using what I call an archive of tongues—an intellectual practice that puts storytelling, history, affect and critical analysis in close dialogue—I collect an idiosyncratic archive of my mother's life-world. I see this archive, and the writing of this archive, as a thought experiment on the power of critical storytelling at the intersections of coloniality and memory.

3. Here, let me note that while divisions between the "West" and "Pakistan" or "formal" and "informal" knowledge are inherently problematic and will necessarily not be sustainable as a framework (a good thing, I think), my point of departure is that even as I deploy them, there are many points at which this distinction breaks down, as my thinking is that these "domains" are mutually constitutive, always assembling and re-assembling.

REFERENCES

Agamben, Giorgio. *State of Exception*. University of Chicago Press, 2005.

Ahmed, Sara. *Living a Feminist Life*. Duke University Press, 2017.

Anzaldúa, Gloria. *This Bridge Called My Back: Writings by Radical Women of Color*. 1980. SUNY Press, 2015.

Barthes, Roland. *A Lover's Discourse: Fragments*. Farrar, Strauss and Giroux, 1978.

Césare, Aimé. *Notebook of A Return To The Native Land*. Wesleyan Press, 2001.

Charania, Moon. *Will the Real Pakistani Woman Please Stand Up? Empire, Visual Culture and the Brown Female Body*. McFarland Press, 2015.

Christian, Barbara. "The Race for Theory." *Cultural Critique*, no.6, 1987, pp. 51–63.

Cvetkovich, Anne. *Archive of Feelings: Trauma, Sexuality and Lesbian Public Cultures*. Duke University Press, 2003.

Foucault, Michel. *The Hermeneutics of the Subject: Lectures at College de France, 1977–78*. Picador, 1997.

Henderson, Mae. "Speaking in Tongues: Dialogics and Dialectics and the Black Woman's Literary Tradition." *African American Literary Theory: A Reader, Ed*. Winston Napier. New York University Press, 2000.

Homeland. Developed by Howard Gordon and Alex Gansa. Showtime, 2011–2018.

Johnson, CJ. "Review of 'He Named Me Malala.'" *abcnews.net.au*, November 17, 2015, http://www.abc.net.au/nightlife/stories/4353932.htm. Accessed January 8, 2016.

Kramer, Gary. "Why 'He Named Me Malala' is a Missed Opportunity." *indiewire.com*, September 15, 2015, http://www.indiewire.com/article/telluride-review-why-he-named-me-malala-is-a-missed-opportunity-20150905. Accessed January 8, 2016.

Kristoff, Nicholas and Wudunn, Sheryl. 2009. *Half the Sky: Turning Oppression into Opportunity for Women Worldwide*. New York: Knopf Press.

Halaby, Raouf. "Beware Those Who Speak with Forked Tongues." *counterpunch.org*, July 7, 2015, http://www.counterpunch.org/2015/07/07/beware-those-who-speak-with-forked-tongues/. Accessed 30 May 2016.

Lorde, Audre. *Zami: A New Spelling of My Name*. The Crossing Press, 1982.

Muñoz, José Esteban. *Disidentifications: Queers of Color and the Performance of Politics*. University of Minnesota Press, 1999.

National Geographic. "Struggle for the Soul of Pakistan." September, 2007

Newsweek. "The Most Dangerous Place on Earth isn't Iraq. It's Pakistan." October, 2008

Sandoval, Chela. *Methodology of the Oppressed*. University of Minnesota Press, 2000.

Simpson, Audra. "On Ethnographic Refusal: Indigeneity, 'Voice' and Colonial Citizenship." *Junctures*, no. 9, 2007, pp. 77–80.

Zero Dark Thirty. Directed by Kathryn Bigelow, 2013.

4. *SAPPHISTRIES: A GLOBAL HISTORY OF LOVE BETWEEN WOMEN*: WHAT'S IN A NAME? (1890–1930)

In Deepa Mehta's controversial 1996 film *Fire*, Radha and Sita, sisters-in-law living in loveless marriages in a joint-family household, fall in love with each other. . . . After a first surprising kiss, they discover passion in each other's arms. When they make love for the first time, Sita, who is younger and the instigator, asks Radha, "Did we do anything wrong?" to which Radha replies, after a moment, "No." One day Ashok, Radha's celibate husband, discovers them in bed together. Sita is not sorry, but Radha wishes she had told him first. "What would you have said?" Sita asks. "'I love her, but not as a sister-in-law?' . . . Now listen, Radha, there's no word in our language that can describe what we are, what we feel for each other." Radha responds, "Perhaps you're right, seeing is less complicated."[1] Neither in this context nor in thinking about the naming of desire between women cross-culturally and historically is the statement that "there's no word in our language that can describe what we are, what we feel for each other" a simple one. It is important to remember this as we turn to a consideration of the naming of lesbianism by Western sexologists and the impact, and lack of impact, of that naming on various other parts of the world. For there have been many names for love, desire, and sex between women, and there has also been a great deal of unnamed love, desire, and sex between women. Both naming and leaving unnamed have their histories.

A once-familiar tale had it that until around the late nineteenth century, when sexologists categorized and named "the lesbian," there was no notion of a kind of woman who sought out sex with other women—in some times and places, any woman might fall prey to such a sin or crime; in other times and places, sex between women just did not happen. This idea was largely an echo of one about men's sexuality, since in the Western world (and elsewhere) there was a long tradition of elite men taking the right to penetrate anyone lower in the social scale, including not only women but boys, slaves, servants, and members of lower classes. Only an adult elite man enclosing another man, or desiring to do so, had consequences. This conception of male sexuality is what, according to the standard story, changed so dramatically in modern Western history, when as a result of the spread of new ideas, any man having sex with another man, no matter the part he played in the encounter, became a "homosexual."

Our understanding of this trajectory for men has become increasingly more complex, but what is most important here is that no similar change in the idea of sexuality applied to women. That is demonstrated by the fact that the crucial question about the wives of women living as men was whether they knew about the actual physical equipment of their husbands. If they did know, their willingness to enclose male women as well as men did not make them blameless.

Nor was the notion that some women desired and had sex with other women a novel idea in the nineteenth century. Consider what we have encountered already: in ancient Greece, tales of what Aeschylus described as "the warring Amazons, men-haters," who according to Diodorus of Sicily, were "greatly admired for their manly vigor"; Plato's fable of half-females searching desperately for their lost female half; the Aztec *patlācheh*, who "has sexual relations with women"; in ancient China, women engaged in *tui-shih* ("eating each other") and *mojingzi* ("rubbing mirrors"); "tribades"

Leila J. Rupp, *Sapphistries: A Global History of Love between Women* (New York: NYU Press, 2009): 142–151, 155–160. Reprinted with permission of NYU Press; permission conveyed through Copyright Clearance Center, Inc. Notes were renumbered.

in ancient Greece and Rome, in medieval Arabic texts, and in medieval, early modern, and modern Europe; *hetairistria* in ancient Greece, women who had sex with women; Sappho, to whom the association of same-sex desire has clung for centuries; *sahacat*, witches in sixteenth-century Fez, who "have sexual relations among themselves in a damnable fashion"; "God-insulting grannies," as the Orthodox Church in medieval eastern Europe called women who had sex with women; Indian *svairini*, Cocopa *warrhameh*, Mohave *hwame*, Maricopa *kwiraxame*, Montenegrin and Albanian sworn virgins, all of whom became social males and sometimes pursued sex with women; roaring girls and randy women; the "new Cabal" and "Anandryne Sect" in eighteenth-century England and France; Chinese sworn sisters and Urdu *Doganas* and *chapatbaz*. Sapphists.

Lots of names. Lots of conceptions, not only that women might make love to other women when no men were in sight but that some women might desire and seek out other women. . . .

BEFORE THE SEXOLOGISTS

Where there seems to have been little idea of a person with same-sex desires as a "kind of person" was outside Europe. In China, the Taoist tradition envisioned two forces, *yin* (associated with femininity and passivity) and *yang* (a masculine and active force), which need to exist in harmony. What mattered was not the biological sex of sexual partners but the preservation of *ch'i*, the life energy found in semen or vaginal secretions. Since women's *yin* is limitless, no sexual activities between women could sap *ch'i*.[2] Taoist ideas about sexuality had an impact on Japan, as well, where male-male love flourished alongside heterosexuality. In all these contexts, sexual relations between women as well as between men did not meet with condemnation, nor did they mark a woman engaged in sex with other women as a particular kind of being.

Some scholars have argued that what is essential for the emergence of the notion that people with same-sex desires are a kind of person is the concept of women and men as fundamentally different. In both the Chinese and European traditions, according to recent scholarship, the idea of women's and men's bodies as polar opposites is of relatively modern origin. Chinese physicians from the Song to the Ming dynasties (960–1644 [C.E.]) conceptualized the body as androgynous, viewing male bodies with too much *yang* and female bodies with too much *yin* as out of balance.[3] In a similar way, ancient Greek texts presented male and female bodies as quite similar, and that model had staying power in European history, although how dominant it was and how long it lasted is disputed. According to ancient Greek thinkers, bodily fluids were the same and reproductive organs comparable, with women's inside instead of out, making woman a lesser but not diametrically opposed man.[4] Anne Lister, the turn-of-the-eighteenth-century female rake, read about Aristotle's concept of the female body as inside-out male and took from it confirmation that her sexual desire for women was natural.[5]

In addition to changing ideas about gender difference, another scientific development that played a role in European conceptions of women's desire for women was the "rediscovery" of the clitoris in the sixteenth century.[6] With the practice of dissection, European anatomists began to notice this mighty organ, which the doctors, if not women themselves, had forgotten since ancient times. Now recognized as the source of women's sexual pleasure, the clitoris became the counterpart of the penis, a role formerly reserved for the uterus.[7] The doctors even agreed that the clitoris was essential to reproduction, for if women did not emit their seed during orgasm, they could not conceive. Knowledge of the clitoris gave rise to fears, as we have already seen, of what women with enlarged organs might do. Jane Sharp, a seventeenth-century midwife in England, described the possibilities: "sometimes it grows so long that it hangs forth at the slit like a Yard [the term for the penis], and will swell and stand stiff if it be provoked, and some lewd women have endeavoured to use it as men do theirs."[8] Sharp, like others before her, thought this mostly happened in Asia and Africa, but by the seventeenth century, as the cases of hermaphrodites and women passing as men make clear, the image of the tribade and her active clitoris was firmly entrenched in the Western world.

The question for us here is, was the tribade "a kind of person"? A seventeenth-century English medical text would suggest so, going on from a description of an enlarged clitoris to add, "And this part it is which those wicked women doe abuse called *Tribades*."[9] A travel text from the sixteenth century connects "feminine wantonness" in Turkish baths to the activities in "times past" of "the Tribades, of the number whereof was Sapho the Lesbian."[10] And we have already encountered the denunciations of English and French aristocratic women as tribades and sapphists. But what caused tribadism was unclear: perhaps women with unnaturally large clitorises pursued sex with other women, but perhaps it was use of the clitoris that made it grow. And, in any case, what were the limits of a normal clitoris?

There is no agreement, then, about when in the Western world we can begin to talk about women who desired other women as belonging in a discrete category.[11] But, whether or not the sixteenth-century tribade or the eighteenth-century sapphist represented a new conceptualization, what is clear is that these categories did not have the same global reach as the naming of the lesbian by the nineteenth-century sexologists.

A NAME THAT STUCK

By the late nineteenth century, European and U.S. doctors interested in what they defined as deviant sexuality began to talk across national borders about the problem of individuals who desired and had sex with others with biologically alike bodies. Medical and scientific attention to same-sex sexuality was part of the process of growing state involvement in civil society as a result of economic transformation across the industrialized world. The sexologists did not, of course, make up their ideas out of thin air. The emerging visible subcultures and communities of women and especially men with same-sex desires both piqued the doctors' interest and provided material for their theories. The doctors differed on the question of whether people were born with same-sex desires or acquired them for a variety of reasons, but all contributed to the notion that having such desires and engaging in same-sex sexual acts defined one as a particular kind of person.

Richard von Krafft-Ebing, the Viennese psychiatrist whose monumental and influential work *Psychopathia Sexualis* appeared in German in 1886, defined same-sex desire as a symptom, rather than the defining characteristic, of what he termed "inversion." What was inverted, or reversed, was gender: a woman would think, act, and feel as a man, and vice versa. Krafft-Ebing distinguished four kinds of female inverts with increasing degrees of deviance. One category consisted of women who "did not betray their anomaly by external appearance or by mental (masculine) sexual characteristics" but who were responsive to masculine women.[12] Here we finally meet the wives of female husbands. The second category was made up of women "with a strong preference for male garments." Next came women who assumed "a definitely masculine role." And finally, the "extreme grade of degenerative homosexuality" encompassed women who possess "of the feminine qualities only the genital organs; thought, sentiment, action, even external appearance are those of a man." Note that female masculinity, either as a characteristic of a woman or as her object of attraction, defined the female invert. Krafft-Ebing described one woman as "quite conscious of her pathological condition. . . . Masculine features, deep voice, manly gait, without beard, small breasts; cropped her hair short and gave the impression of a man in women's clothes."[13]

If Krafft-Ebing paid more attention to dress and manner than to sexual desire, sex came clearly into the picture with Havelock Ellis, a British sexologist whose early-twentieth-century writings both opposed sexual repression and labeled women's desire for women perverted. Ellis, married to a lesbian woman, differentiated between the congenital invert, who could not help her condition and should therefore be tolerated, and women in Krafft-Ebing's first category, who possessed a genetic predisposition for responsiveness to the advances of other women. These women, in an atmosphere such as a boarding school or women's club, had the potential to become homosexual, and Ellis feared that the advances in women's education and legal rights, along with the work of the women's movement, were creating a hotbed of potential homosexualization. The crushes so prevalent in girls' schools no longer seemed so innocent. As Ellis explained, "While there is an unquestionable sexual element in the 'flame' relationship, this cannot be regarded as an absolute expression of real congenital perversion of the sex-instinct."[14] But if crushes between school-girls did not point to a congenital condition, the atmosphere of the school or the women's movement might put women in danger of being seduced. Here is how Ellis, with no evidence whatsoever, described the women who would attract and be attracted to true inverts: "Their faces may be plain or ill-made but not seldom they possess good figures, a point which is apt to carry more weight with the inverted woman than beauty of face. . . . They are always womanly. One may perhaps say that they are the pick of the women whom the average man would pass by."[15]

Swiss neurologist August Forel, like Ellis and Krafft-Ebing, differentiated between women with a "hereditary disposition to inversion" and "sapphism acquired by seduction or habit."[16] The "pure female invert," he wrote, "feels like a man." He cited a case in which such an invert, "dressed as a young man, succeeded in winning the love of a normal girl." Even after the invert was discovered and sent to an asylum, the "normal girl" "continued to be amorous" when she visited her lover. Forel "took the young girl aside" to express astonishment at her feelings for the one who had deceived her. "Her reply," he wrote, "was characteristic of a woman: 'Ah! You see, doctor, I love him, and I cannot help it!'"

Forel's and Ellis's attention to sexual desire moved closer to the notion of homosexuality as defined by the sex of one's chosen sexual partner, although they still placed great emphasis on gender inversion in the case of those born "that way." In 1913, Ellis described inversion as referring to sexual impulses "turned toward individuals of the same sex, while all the other impulses and tastes may remain those of the sex to which the person by anatomical configuration belongs."[17] When Sigmund Freud introduced the distinction between sexual aim and sexual object—"aim" referring to a preference for genital, oral, or anal sex or for an enclosing or penetrating role, and "object" to the desired sexual partner—it marked a shift away from a focus on gender inversion. But this was truer in the case of men than women, for the sexologists continued the long tradition of associating female same-sex sexual desire with masculinity.

It is not surprising, given the history we have already encountered, that the sexologists at the end of the nineteenth century returned to a consideration of hermaphroditism, either physical or psychological. Perhaps, they thought, those masculine women were partly men; perhaps they had enlarged clitorises. Or perhaps they had a mind of one sex in a body of the other—making them a "third" or "intermediate" sex. Such was the concept embraced by a number of male sexologists who themselves desired other men, including Karl Ulrichs and Magnus Hirschfeld in Germany and Edward Carpenter in England. In the Netherlands, the director of the Dutch Institute for Research into Human Heredity and Race Biology in the 1930s sought to prove through analysis of identical twins that homosexuality was genetically determined. The female twins he found through the Dutch Scientific Humanitarian Committee, a spinoff of Hirschfeld's pioneering German organization, fit the traditional description of masculine women who preferred male activities, had deep voices, and felt no sexual attraction to men.[18] The biological argument of a "third sex" was an appealing concept for people with same-sex desires, for punishment made no sense if they could not help being who they were.

At the other end of the explanatory continuum, Sigmund Freud and his followers gave an enormous boost to the idea that social factors produced same-sex desire. Freud's attention to dynamics within families to explain homosexuality took same-sex desire out of the realm of the biological. Yet both kinds of explanations—the biological and the social—lived on (and continue to linger). One sexologist in 1919 claimed that people who had homosexual sex but in an appropriate sexual role—that is, "passive" lesbians and "aggressive" homosexual men—did so as a result of social factors, whereas "aggressive" lesbians and "passive" homosexual men could only be explained by "biological anomalies of development which are often coupled with unmistakable physical signs."[19] But whatever the cause of same-sex sexual desire, those who had it increasingly came to make up a category of person labeled "homosexual" or "lesbian."

The thinking of European scientists of sex reached beyond the United States to Japan and China, becoming a transnational conversation about sexuality. In Japan, the importation of Western science followed the end of Japanese resistance to contact with Western "barbarians" and the development of a more central-ized state.[20] The Japanese Forensic Medicine Association sponsored a Japanese translation of Krafft-Ebing's *Psychopathia Sexualis* that appeared in 1894, and ideas about legal rights for individuals becoming known as "homosexuals" also filtered into Japan. At the same time, German sexologists made use of knowledge about Japanese male same-sex sexual practices gleaned from Western travelers to Japan or Japanese visitors to Europe to describe a culture, like that of ancient Greece, accepting of male same-sex sexual acts.

Japanese thinking about same-sex sexuality focused almost entirely on male-male love: the concept of *homosexuality* as referring to both male-male and female-female interactions was, literally, quite foreign. When Japanese forensic pathologists first encountered Western texts, they coined a term in Japanese meaning "same-sex intercourse" to translate *homosexuality*, giving precedence to sexual acts, particularly anal intercourse. By 1887, Japanese texts mentioned "obscene acts" between women, using the German term "*Tribadie.*"[21] Yet Japanese authorities merged the concepts from the European sexologists with Japanese tradition, asserting that "intercourse between females" was most likely to occur when young women lived closely together without access to men, as in prison or wealthy households. Eventually the sexologists did place male and female same-sex sexuality in the same conceptual category, by the 1920s adopting as the standard term *dōseiai,* "same-sex love." As a result, Japanese experts began to pay more attention than they had previously to female same-sex love. Loanwords such as *lesbian* (*rezubian*) and *garcon* (*garuson,* from the French word for "boy"), meaning a masculine woman, became household words.[22] By the 1920s and 1930s, same-sex love had come to seem a peculiarly female phenomenon, as "modern institutions of entertainment" distracted schoolboys from homoeroticism.[23] This was one of the major ways that Western sexology affected Japanese thinking in this realm.

Japanese sexologists, like their European colleagues, disagreed about whether same-sex love was a biological or sociological phenomenon. Habuto Eiji, a well-known early-twentieth-century expert, distinguished between common feelings of love among preadolescent girls or directed at a teacher and a "hereditary element of mental disease" if such love lasted beyond puberty.[24] The concept of sexual inversion emerged in the assumption of gender difference between partners, that one would be masculine and the other feminine. Some Japanese sexologists rejected such a notion and emphasized that it was sex segregation in schools, textile mills, prisons, convents, nurses' quarters, and hospitals that treated prostitutes for venereal disease that caused girls and women to turn to one another. Whatever the cause, same-sex love might cause physical problems, including vaginal cramps and sterility, or insanity or lead to suicide or murder.[25] One sexologist even blamed same-sex love in girls' schools for "declining birth rates in civilized nations."[26]

In China, as in Japan, the introduction of European sexologists' concepts accompanied other forms of Western importation and fostered the new notion that male and female forms of same-sex love formed a conceptual unity, embodied in the term *tongxing ai* (same-sex love). As we have seen, female same-sex bonds had a place in Chinese culture, but "sisterhood" and "friendship" characterized such relationships, and sex acts between women did not signify a personal taste or an independent eroticism.[27] That changed in the course of the political, cultural, and intellectual flowering of the post–First World War May Fourth era. Western-oriented intellectuals embraced European sexology, sometimes imported through Japan, and spread a new term, *female same-sex love,* which encompassed older concepts of relationships between women such as those between co-wives. Terms such as *nüzi tongxing lian'ai* (female homosexuality), *qingyu zhi diandao* (sexual inversion), and *biantai* (perversion) came into the Chinese language.[28]

Havelock Ellis's influence can be seen in the emerging distinction between sexually inverted women, who displayed masculinity, and the pseudo-homosexuality of feminine schoolgirls who grew up to marry. Shan Zai (a pseudonym) published an article in a Shanghai women's journal in 1911 that quoted German and British sexologists and used German sexological terminology. He both asserted the similarity of male and female same-sex love—"when a woman falls in same-sex love with another woman, it is in fact the same as a man's being fond of having sex with beautiful boys"—and differentiated between inverts and women who "want to satisfy their erotic desire but have no opportunity to associate with men."[29] He also mentioned Sappho, tribades, and nuns.

Ellis was not the only sexologist translated into Chinese. Magnus Hirschfeld visited China in 1931 and lectured, in German with Chinese translation, to thirty-five audiences. In addition, the texts of Krafft-Ebing, Freud, and Edward Carpenter were translated and published in China. As in Japan, traditions of sex segregation came together with economic and social changes that were transforming gender and sexuality in a way that made distinctions between heterosexuality and homosexuality and ideas of sexual inversion make sense. As in the case of Japan, intellectuals took what was useful from Western thinking and translated it, in both a literal and figurative sense, into Chinese culture.

The writings of the sexologists, then, did three transformative things. They presented homosexuality, whether the result of biology or social context, as a condition that defined certain individuals. They combined what had often been viewed as quite disparate phenomena—male and female same-sex love—into the concept of homosexuality. And their ideas had resonance in diverse cultures where other Western influences and processes of economic development created receptive audiences. It is ironic that European thought about same-sex sexuality, which had long associated it with foreign cultures, beginning in the late nineteenth century created the conditions that underlie the contemporary notion in much of the world that homosexuality is a Western import.

. . .

WHAT WOMEN THOUGHT

We still need to ask, once the sexologists undertook the process of naming and defining the kind of people who loved others of the same sex, what did such definitions mean to women who loved other women? There is no simple answer to this question. Whereas language of perversion and morbidity offered little for them to embrace, the concept of a third sex could have its appeal. At the same time, even the positive pronouncements of the homosexual sexologists carried the potential to expose women living respectably in Boston marriages. For example, Magnus Hirschfeld's *The Homosexuality of Men and Women*, published in 1914, noted the frequency of same-sex couples creating "marriage-like associations characterized by the exclusivity and long duration of the relationships, the living together and the common household, the sharing of every interest, and often the existence of legitimate community property."[30] So for some women, the medicalization of same-sex love brought unwanted attention and shame. Some fell into the clutches of those who hoped to cure them of their desires. Others differentiated their romantic friendships from deviant lesbian love or ignored the new concepts altogether. Still others embraced the new definitions as providing an identity—even if a disparaged one—that made sense of their lives.

Ethel Smyth, a British composer, feminist, and masculine woman who formed passionate relationships with women and with one man, seemed to be referring to the medicalization and deviance of same-sex love when she wrote to her male lover in 1892, "I wonder why it is so much easier for me, and I believe for a great many English women, to love my own sex passionately rather than yours? . . . How do you account for it? I can't make it out for I think I am a very healthy-minded person and it is an everlasting puzzle."[31] Clearly reflecting the concepts of the doctors, in her memoirs she characterized her eroticized mother-daughter relationship with the wife of her music teacher as a "blend of fun and tenderness that saved it from anything approaching morbidity."[32] And late in life she considered whether an incestuous love for her mother was behind her passion for women.[33]

Jeannette Marks, a professor of English at Mount Holyoke College in Massachusetts, who lived in an intimate relationship for fifty-five years with Mary Woolley, the college's president, was one who worried that others might see her as a lesbian. In an essay she wrote in 1908, she denounced as "abnormal" "unwise college friendships" such as the one she had shared with Woolley and insisted that the only relationship that could "fulfill itself and be complete is that between a man and a woman."[34] British writers Eliza Lynn Linton and Vernon Lee reacted in different ways to medical theories of gender inversion. Linton was masculine and erotically attracted to women but considered gender inversion a sign of degeneracy and could only resolve her feelings by portraying herself as a man in her writing. Lee embraced the notion of a divided self, a masculine intellect with feminine feelings.[35]

Lu Yin, a May Fourth writer in Republican China, wrote about same-sex love and expressed unease about her desires. "Lishi's Diary," written in 1923, tells the story of a woman who does not wish to marry and whose feelings for her school friend Yuanqing change from "ordinary friendship" to "same-sex romantic love." They make plans to live together, and Lishi that night dreams that they are rowing a boat in the moonlight. Then Yuanqing's mother forces her to move away and plans to marry her off to her cousin. Yuanqing writes to Lishi, "Ah, Lishi! Why didn't you plan ahead! Why didn't you dress up in men's clothes, put on a man's hat, act like a man, and visit my parents to ask for my hand?"[36] In the end, Yuanqing repudiates their plan and Lishi dies of melancholia. Lu Yin herself married twice, but her writings suggest that she struggled with desire for women and worried that others might have "dreadful suspicions" about her.[37]

Others were less tortured but worked to distinguish themselves from the pathologized subjects described by the sexologists. In a 1930 autobiography, the pseudonymous American "Mary Casal" described her sexual relationship with another woman as "the very highest type of love" and "on a much higher plane than those of *the real inverts*."[38] In the same vein, U.S. prison reformer Miriam Van Waters, in an intimate relationship with her benefactor Geraldine Thompson from the 1920s to Thompson's death in 1967, struggled to differentiate her own "normality" from the gender inversion and pathology of lesbianism that she denounced in the women's reformatory that she supervised.[39] And yet other women forged ahead with their relationships, despite their familiarity with the writings of the sexologists. M. Carey Thomas, president of Bryn Mawr College in Pennsylvania, kept lists of books labeled "Lesbianism" and "Books on Sapphism" and admired and followed the trial of Oscar Wilde, yet she never expressed any unease over her overlapping relationships with the two loves of her life.[40] German feminists Anita Augspurg and Lida Gustava Heymann, who lived together as a couple for forty years and moved in transnational women's-movement circles familiar with the language

of the sexologists, reported unselfconsciously in their memoirs about marriage proposals they were offered by their farmer neighbor: "It took all of our effort to remain serious and make clear to the man the hopelessness of his desire. As he left, we shook with laughter."[41]

On the other hand, the concept of lesbianism as a defining characteristic allowed some women to embrace their own sexuality more fully. One of the women whose case histories appear in Havelock Ellis's *Sexual Inversion* credited sexology with being "a complete revelation" of her nature, and another credited Krafft-Ebing with cluing her into the fact that her "feelings" were "under the ban of society," although she rejected his notion that she was "unnatural and depraved."[42] British feminist Frances Wilder expressed her gratitude to homosexual sexologist Edward Carpenter, since his work made her realize, "I was more closely related to the intermediate sex than I had hitherto imagined."[43] Radclyffe Hall, who was "overjoyed and proud" that Havelock Ellis put his stamp of approval on *The Well of Loneliness*, had her famous character Stephen discover her true nature when she finds a copy of Krafft-Ebing's *Psychopathia Sexualis* with her father's notes in the margins.[44] Hall, a masculine woman herself, hoped that her novel would help young women come to terms with their desires as well as elicit sympathy from heterosexual readers.[45] . . . When the book went on trial for obscenity and Hall's lawyer sought to convince the court that "the relationship between women described in the book represented a normal friendship," Hall was furious.[46]

A particularly fascinating source on lesbian reaction to sexology can be found in the research of the Committee for the Study of Sex Variants, a group of experts who undertook a large-scale study of homosexuality in the 1930s in New York.[47] Women (and men), who were recruited largely from an urban bohemian context, provided family histories and underwent psychiatric and physical examinations. Following in a tradition we have encountered before, the gynecologist Robert Latou Dickinson set out to confirm his hypothesis that a woman's genitals would reveal innate sexual deviance as well as deviant sexual experience. In incredibly intrusive examinations, which involved measuring the clitoris with a ruler and the vagina with fingers, as well as tracing the vulva on a glass plate, the researchers sought to detect such signs as a large vulva, erectile clitoris, insensitive hymen, and small uterus. Not surprisingly, they found just what they were seeking, along with the expected signs of "inversion."

What they did not expect, however, was what they heard from some of the subjects, who insisted on the pleasures of their sex lives and bragged about their ability to satisfy their lovers. Ursula, described appreciatively by her lover, Frieda, as "a big, bold, mannish, fat woman who heaves into a room like a locomotive under full steam," confuses the doctor, telling him that she finds Frieda "tiny and very feminine, . . . very virile and aggressive." Refusing to confine sex to the genitals, she insists that "every part of the body becomes beautiful—caressing and kissing all parts of the body. . . . My sex life has never caused me any regrets."[48]

Perhaps playing with both traditional notions about lesbians and the experts' belief in the hypersexuality of Black women, a number of African American subjects boasted of their sexual technique: "I insert my clitoris in the vagina just like the penis of a man. . . . Women enjoy it so much they leave their husbands."[49] Or as another put it, "I think they are fond of me because of my large clitoris. I think that's the chief reason. They comment upon it. They whisper among themselves. They say, 'She has the largest clitoris.'"[50] And Marian J. insisted, "I became so expert in lingual caresses that I was noted in theatrical circles and in the fringe of polite society for my excellence. . . . Sometimes I put my tongue in the vagina to increase the sexual excitement." Although the subjects of this study sometimes adopted the negative spin of the sexologists, we can see that at least some of them played with those ideas and proudly asserted the superiority of their abilities and the rightness of their desires.

So, across the globe, in different locations, women who loved women ignored, rejected, feared, or welcomed the idea that they were a kind of person who could be named. But it is important to remember that not everyone, even in societies where the ideas of the sexologists circulated relatively freely, knew the names. One young British woman in the 1950s who was involved with another woman in college remembered telling a mutual friend about the relationship: "She said in surprise, 'But you're clearly the most obvious lesbian I've ever seen.' And my response was, 'The most

obvious what?' I'd never heard the word; I didn't know what she was talking about. She said, 'Well, women who fall in love with other women.' And for the first time in my life I had to sort of sit back and think, 'Oh, there's a word for something that I must be.'"[51]

The name *lesbian* was not the first to be applied to women with same-sex desires, but it was a powerful one. The women who formed romantic friendships or lived in marriages with other women or showed their masculinity or expressed desire for other women represented the source of the ideas of Krafft-Ebing and the others, and the stories of women such as Alice Mitchell and Maeda Otoki and Sandor Vay circled back from the courts and the doctors' offices to the newspapers, in the process fashioning the concept of the "female homosexual" or "lesbian."

It is hard to resist ending this chapter with Radclyffe Hall's *The Well of Loneliness*, which is all about the power of naming: Stephen Gordon's loving and sympathetic father finds Karl Heinrich Ulrichs's work and takes "to reading half the night, which had not hitherto been his custom."[52] He is coming to understand that his daughter Stephen is what Ulrichs called an *Urning*, or member of the third sex. He means to explain to his wife, Anna, who is cold toward Stephen, but he never can bring himself to utter the words. When a male suitor tells Stephen that he loves her and wants to marry her, and she reacts with terror and repulsion and outrage, she goes to her father to ask him if there is anything strange about her. He thinks, "Merciful God! How could a man answer? What could he say, and that man a father?"[53] So he lies, and then he dies before he can tell Anna or Stephen what she is. Stephen's teacher, Puddle, also finds herself unable to utter the truth. And then Stephen "fell quite simply and naturally in love, in accordance with the dictates of her nature," with a married woman neighbor.[54] Puddle sees, and she longs to help. She imagines going to Stephen and saying, "*I know.* I know all about it. . . . You're neither unnatural, nor abominable, nor mad; you're as much a part of what people call nature as anyone else; only you're unexplained as yet—you've not got your niche in creation. But some day that will come."[55] But she does not.

And then Stephen's married lover betrays her, and her mother turns against her. That is when she discovers the books locked away in her father's study. "For a long time she read; then went back to the bookcase and got out another of those volumes, and another . . . Then suddenly she had got to her feet and was talking aloud—she was talking to her father: 'You knew! All the time you knew this thing, but because of your pity you wouldn't tell me. Oh, Father—and there are so many of us.'"⁵⁶ Stephen recognizes herself as an invert and goes on her self-sacrificing way, ultimately giving up the love of her life, one of Ellis's "pick of the women whom the average man would pass by," forcing her into the arms of a male suitor.

A Chinese literary scholar, Zhao Jingshen, in 1929 wrote about the banning of *The Well of Loneliness*, finding humorous the fact that an ordinary love affair between two women so upset the authorities.⁵⁷ Yet he was perfectly aware of the language of abnormal sexual psychology and thought "same-sex love" "perverse." Such distinctions, like Hall's naming and Radha and Sita's inability to name their love, remind us of the complexities.

So the naming of the "lesbian" was both momentous and not. It was not momentous because, in some ways, the term simply replaced older names for women who made love to one another, combining masculinity (or attraction to masculinity) with the propensity to engage in same-sex sexual acts. It was not momentous because the new ways of viewing women who loved women did not reach everywhere, and not all women exposed to the work of the sexologists claimed or even reacted to the concepts.

On the other hand, it *was* momentous because the "lesbian," in all her cultural and linguistic variations, had a wider global reach as the ideas of the European sexologists spread to other parts of the world and merged with different cultural traditions. It was momentous because not only did it create a new conceptual unity between male and female same-sex sexuality in places such as Japan and China where they had previously been distinct, but it also gave the concept of lesbianism a Western origin. As we shall see, this change had its own momentous consequences, as the European notion of sex between women as a non-Western perversion gave way to the idea of lesbianism as a Western import. And it was also momentous because the concept of the lesbian underlay the development of different kinds of communities of women who desired women, beginning in the early twentieth century.

NOTES

1. On *Fire*, see Gopinath 2005.
2. See Carton 2006, 310.
3. Furth 1999; see Sang 2003.
4. Laqueur 1990. Sang 2003 makes the comparison between Chinese and European conceptions. See Traub 2002 and Park 1997 for critiques of Laqueur's thesis.
5. A. Clark 1996, 40.
6. Traub 2002; see also Park 1997.
7. See Gowing 2006; Traub 2002; Park 1997.
8. Quoted in Gowing 2006, 127.
9. Quoted in Traub 2002, 194.
10. Quoted in Traub 2002, 200.
11. Trumbach 1993 has the English sapphist being classified as a separate gender at the end of the eighteenth century, following the model of the earlier sodomite.
12. This and the following text from Krafft-Ebing quoted in Smith-Rosenberg 1989, 269. See also Terry 1999 for a full discussion of sexology.
13. Quoted in Smith-Rosenberg 1989, 270.
14. Quoted in Vicinus 1984, 619.
15. Quoted in Newton 1989, 270.
16. This and the following quotations from Forel quoted in Terry 1999, 63–64.

17. Quoted in Chauncey 1982–83, 122.
18. Everard 1986.
19. Quoted in Chauncey 1982–83, 138.
20. On Japan, see Pflugfelder 1999 and 2005.
21. Quoted in Pflugfelder 1999, 176.
22. See Robertson 1999.
23. Quoted in Pflugfelder 2005, 150.
24. Pflugfelder 2005, 143.
25. Pflugfelder 2005, 144.
26. Quoted in Pflugfelder 2005, 144.
27. Sang 2003.
28. Sang 2003, 24.
29. Quoted in Sang 2003, 107, 108.
30. Quoted in Marcus 2007, 49.
31. Quoted in Vicinus 2004, 83.
32. Quoted in Vicinus 2004, 127.
33. Vicinus 2004, 134.
34. Quoted in Faderman 1991, 53.
35. Vicinus 2004.
36. Quoted in Sang 2003, 139.
37. Quoted in Sang 2003, 144.
38. Quoted in Faderman 1991, 54.
39. See Freedman 1996a.
40. Horowitz 1994.
41. Quoted in Rupp 1997, 582.
42. Quoted in Doan 2001, 138, 137.
43. Quoted in Smith-Rosenberg 1989, 273.
44. Quoted in Doan 2001, 144.
45. See Vicinus 2004, 217.
46. Quoted in Newton 1989, 291; see also Doan 2001.
47. See Terry 1999.
48. Quoted in Terry 1999, 227.
49. Quoted in Terry 1999, 242.
50. Quoted in Terry 1999, 243.
51. Quoted in Jennings 2007b, 34.
52. Hall 1950, 26.
53. Hall 1950, 106.
54. Hall 1950, 146.
55. Hall 1950, 154.
56. Hall 1950, 204.
57. Sang 2003, 128.

INDERPAL GREWAL AND CAREN KAPLAN

5. GLOBAL IDENTITIES: THEORIZING TRANSNATIONAL STUDIES OF SEXUALITY

In modernity, identities inevitably become global. Indeed, few things remain local in the aftermath of the rise of capitalism. Just as goods and people come to circulate in new ways, so too identities emerge and come into specific relations of circulation and expansion. In this globalized framework of encounter and exchange, sexual identities are similar to other kinds of identities in that they are imbued with power relations. These power relations are connected to inequalities that result from earlier forms of globalization, but they have also generated new asymmetries. Our task is to examine both the specificities and the continuities within the globalization of sexual identities at the present juncture.

For the most part, throughout the twentieth century, what we might call politically "progressive" studies of sexuality emerged as a result of identity politics and social movements. Increasingly, with the rise of ethnic and postcolonial studies and the growing emphasis on diaspora in American studies, the scholarship on sexuality is globalized.[1] Yet thinking simply about global identities does not begin to get at the complex terrain of sexual politics that is at once national, regional, local, even "cross-cultural" and hybrid. In many works on globalization, the "global" is seen either as a homogenizing influence or as a neocolonial movement of ideas and capital from West to non-West.[2] Debates on the nature of global identities have suggested the inadequacy of understanding globalization simply through political economy or through theories of "Western" cultural imperialism and have pushed us to probe further the relationship between globalization and culture.[3] Yet how do we understand these emerging identities, given the divergent theories regarding the relationship between globalization and cultural formations? Can these identities be called "global identities," or is some other term more useful?

In light of the problems that some scholars have pointed out with the rhetoric of diversity and globality with respect to sexual identity, such that these discourses produce a "monumentalist gay identity" and elide "radical sexual difference," the term *transnational* seems to us more helpful in getting to the specifics of sexualities in postmodernity.[4] As we have argued elsewhere, the term *transnational* can address the asymmetries of the globalization process.[5] Yet it has become so ubiquitous in cultural, literary, and critical studies that much of its political valence seems to have become evacuated. Is this a function of globalization in its cultural aspects, of the ways in which it has become a truism that everyone and everything are always already displaced and hence "transnational"? Or is it a function of the modernist search for novelty and innovation leading to the adoption of a seemingly new term for a global world? Perhaps these two tendencies are intertwined, and this term works at this point because it has become "real" or "appropriate" in some way that it would do us good to examine. By thinking about the many ways in which the term is being rearticulated, we can understand the rhetorical imperative that underlies such uses. Since terms and critical practices are neither authentic nor pure, we do not wish to argue that one use is more correct than another. Rather, we need to examine the circulation of this term and its regulation through institutional sites, such as academic publishing, conference panels and papers, and academic personnel matters. By doing so, we can begin to understand how the study of sexuality remains bound by disciplinary constraints. A more interdisciplinary and transnational approach that addresses inequalities as well as new formations can begin more adequately to explore the nature of sexual identities in the current phase of globalization.

We can identify several primary ways in which the term *transnational* does a particular kind of work in the U.S. academy in general. First, it circulates widely as a more useful term to describe migration at the present time. This is the application that we find most often at work in anthropology, for example, in the work that theorizes migration as a transnational process.[6] In emphasizing labor migration, this approach leaves out other factors in the globalization of labor. We can also identify an application in the notion of "transnational flows," a concept that sometimes ignores inequities as well as those aspects of modernity that seem fixed or immobile.[7] Some Marxist commentators prefer the term *flexible* over the term *flow*, since it ties globalization to flexible accumulation in current capitalism.[8]

A second use of *transnational* is to signal the demise or irrelevance of the nation-state in the current phase of globalization.[9] A related "borderless world" argument suggests that cultures are more and more important or relevant than nations and that identities are linked to cultures more than to nations or to the institutions of the nation-state.[10] In this approach, the concept of transnational does not have to concern itself with the postcolonial state; that is, it erases political economy as well as new forms of governmentality. As Victoria Bernal has put it so powerfully, "Embracing globalization and transnationalism as forces that render the nation inconsequential may appeal to anthropologists and humanities scholars in part because it allows them to conveniently ignore the ambivalent and troubling postcolonial state in favor of more sympathetic social forms."[11] Thus, by eliminating the postcolonial nation-state, flows of people and shifts in culture appear to be almost inevitable and strangely ahistorical.

A third use of *transnational* that has become visible recently is as a synonym for *diasporic*. In this increasingly common usage, which follows on the current use of *transnational* as a term that describes cross-border migration, any reference to materials or evidence or texts from a region outside the United States is coded as "diasporic."[12] And everyone in the

United States is believed to be diasporic in some way. Often diasporics come to be figured as always in resistance to the nation-state in which they are located.[13] In this formulation, diasporic groups can be best understood through the politics of cultural identity or cultural citizenship. Thus subcultures of immigration and migration are always already diasporas. Here we are not arguing that people are better understood simply through the politics of the local. Rather, we are pointing to the mystification and romanticization of displacement that often accompany this formulation.[14]

A fourth use of *transnational* is to designate a form of neocolonialism. In this approach, *transnational* is a deeply problematic term, because it appears to be completely imbricated in the movements of transnational capital.[15] That is, the argument goes, globalization involves rapid movements of finance capital and thus facilitates a global economy in which transnational corporations have trampled on and destroyed local formations. In our view, this approach may inadvertently mystify what existed before the advent of late capitalism, whereas we would argue that earlier phases of globalization produced their own inequalities. Certainly, transnational capital is creating new forms of inequality and continuing older asymmetries. Consequently, a long historical viewpoint, indeed multiple views for many sites, is necessary.

A fifth use of *transnational* signals what has been called the NGOization of social movements.[16] In the wake of several decades of U.N. conferences on women, the emergence of global feminism as a policy and an activist arena, and the rise of human rights initiatives that enact new forms of governmentality, the term *transnational* has been adopted to stand for all of the above. Thus we find more and more references to "transnationalism from below" or to transnational women's movements (with *transnational* supplanting *global*).[17] Such a shift in usage is interesting and significant, since it signals an alternative to the problematic of the "global" and the "international" as it was articulated primarily by Western or Euro-American second-wave feminists as well as by multinational corporations, for which "becoming global" marks an expansion into new markets. Our response to this specific development is that we need to trace the histories of such movements through the modern period to understand how they have been tied to colonial processes and to imperialism. Thus such usage relied on a universal subject of feminism, while *transnational* could signal cultural and national difference. However, it is important to remain alert to these national and international histories, which are embedded in every so-called transnational social movement, regardless of the intention of committed individuals and organizations.

If we have pointed out some of the ways in which *transnational* is used so ubiquitously at the present moment, it is not to suggest that we should abandon the term on the grounds that it has been overused to the point of meaning nothing in particular. Since ignoring transnational formations has left studies of sexualities without the tools to address questions of globalization, race, political economy, immigration, migration, and geopolitics, it is important to bring questions of transnationalism into conversation with the feminist study of sexuality. The history of the way in which sexuality has been studied and described needs to be better understood. Many scholars working on sexuality have begun to identify how separate spheres of study have arisen as a result of the disciplinary divides in the U.S. academy. In this context, critical practices are at a bit of an impasse, relying heavily on conventional disciplinary approaches that are unable to address some key issues and problems.

What are these separate spheres? The first divide is the separation of sexuality from the study of race, class, nation, religion, and so on. If Western, Judeo-Christian culture has viewed sexuality as the other within each individual, the study of sexuality in the U.S. academy has been limited by the inability of the human sciences to address this feared aspect of human life. In general, in the social sciences sexuality has been discussed at length only as an attribute of "primitive" cultures—exerting a strong fascination and producing an enormous literature that continues to this day. As anthropologists begin to study their "own" cultures, we have begun to see some shifts in this dynamic. But the legacies of the rise of the human sciences remain. And the Western body stands as the normative body in scholarly discourse and in public policy.

We have to turn to the rise of biomedicine and the emergence of eugenics, gynecology, endocrinology, genetics, and psychology to understand fully the social and political stakes in viewing sexuality as distinct from race, class, nation, and other factors in modernity. Gender and sexual difference have become understood as attributes of bodies unmarked in any other way, despite copious evidence that all of these modern identities are interconnected. The binary gender model is so pervasive and universalized that it has become naturalized. In most queer studies in the United States, destabilization of gender binarism seems to remain in the zone of gender permutation or diversity rather than including considerations of histories of political economies and forms of governmentality.[18] For instance, if we can argue that historical analysis shows us that concepts of gender difference in medieval China were quite different from those in medieval Islamic cultures, we will begin to understand that the legacies of these traditions with attendant identities and practices produce new kinds of subjects in the present moment. Here we have to pause to note that we are not arguing that cultural specificity leads to complete difference. Rather, we want to add to this model of cultural difference a consideration of power, history, and analyses of contact and change.

In the study of sexuality in a transnational frame, we need a mapping of different medical traditions, conceptions of the body, scientific discourses, and, last but not least, political economies of the family. Such a mapping requires us to rethink the reliance on the family as a primary locus of difference and inequality. The family has been primarily treated as an entity that emerges in the context of a public-private split and as a result of divisions of labor. Internationalizing the public-private split and patriarchal divisions of labor has not changed the content of the scholarship much. Many of these approaches to the family produce representations of a heteronormative unit, a universal patriarchy, and, very often, a victimized and unified subject of feminism. If class comes to the fore in these analyses, sexuality remains in the realm of the exploitation and control of women via reproduction or trafficking. This emphasis on the family as a universal category of analysis also enables an allied mode of universalizing, that is, psychoanalytic criticism.

Psychoanalysis is a powerful mode of interpretation that has struggled with its universalizing tendencies.[19] That is, many psychoanalytic critiques admit to cultural limitations in the model but find it impossible to depart from it. If sexual desire is always already understood as produced in and through the family, then it would be difficult to detach it from a psychoanalytic approach. The family is an important figure in modernity, but it is not the only site of subject production. We want to argue that the study of sexuality in a transnational frame must be detached from psychoanalysis as a primary method in order to resist the universalization of the Western body as sexual difference. Psychoanalysis is a powerful interpretive tool, but it has become a form of biomedicine and cannot be utilized in ignorance of its own power structures.

Recently, new versions of psychoanalysis have sought to lift the cultural blinders from earlier work. These new works focus on the nation or the community as the family to provide new examples from diverse places. Although in recent years there has emerged an interest in expanding and rearticulating the notion of family and kinship, for the most part psychoanalytic cultural criticism may be of limited usefulness. Its Eurocentric biases can often be marshaled to reproduce nationalist formations.[20] Even Lacanian psychoanalysis cannot shake off its reliance on the modern European family as a central structuring metaphor. As we have said, this type of family may not make sense to people in other cultures and nation-states, nor can desire be understood solely in Western psychoanalytic terms. At the very least, the psychoanalytic framework may have to be different where relations between family and state are not the same as in the wealthier welfare states or where psychoanalysis is not medicalized or professionalized, as it is in Europe and North America.

The second instance of separated spheres that we wish to examine concerns the demarcation in the United States of international area studies from American studies. As Tani E. Barlow has argued, international area studies was implicated in the production of Cold War cultural and political knowledges about other cultures and nations.[21] American studies comes from a 1930s Marxist, popular-front effort to critique and oppose capitalism. During the conservative backlash of the Cold War, it was co-opted and became articulated as American exceptionalism. At that point, the whiteness of "American" studies became distinguishable from what was later called "ethnic studies." The emergence of ethnic studies has to be understood as a response to this conservative retrenching of an otherwise limited but more radical initial vision. So both international area studies and American studies as we know them today are Cold War productions generated to manage and negotiate the tensions that arose after the Second World War and during decolonization worldwide, that is, in distinction to the emergence of other nationalisms.

One consequence of these divisions has been that comparative work in international area studies and American studies remains bound by the nation-state. Although an analytic position of the comparison studies mode has given us some useful insights, it naturalizes and reproduces the nationalist basis of modern scholarship.[22] By questioning the distinctness of areas presupposed by the comparative framework and by respecting the specificities of historical and cultural conjectures, we might enable new insights into the workings of gender and patriarchy across various borders rather than simply within the parameters of the state or the nation. The changing nature of migrations, global flows of media, and capital demands a different notion of transdisciplinary scholarship.

How does the institutional divide between international area studies and American studies affect contemporary studies of sexuality? The academic study of sexuality that can be linked to the emergence of gay and lesbian politics of identity and new queer formations has focused on U.S. and European examples, with the primary emphasis on white, middle-class life.[23] Thus the disciplinary divides that emerge out of other political arenas are played out on campus and off, that is, in academic as well as in "community-based" or activist locations. As a result, much of the experience-based literature rearticulates the divide between a sexuality-based lesbian or gay or queer culture or identity and one that is based on race or class or ethnicity.[24] In recent years, both "articulation" theory and "intersectionality" approaches have attempted to resolve this problem by arguing for complex or hybrid subjects.[25] That is, the nationalist basis of these academic disciplinary formations has participated in producing sexual subjects as nationalist subjects or as cultural-nationalist subjects. A related issue that we are not going to dwell on here but that we have discussed elsewhere is the nature of the cosmopolitan subject as a mystified national subject in the guise of a "world" or global citizen.[26]

A third divide that we would like to bring up can be characterized as the tradition-modernity split. Following postcolonial studies, much has been said about this primary binary of Western culture. What is noteworthy, however, is the reemergence of this split in the international study of sexuality. As we noted above, nationalist biases and geopolitics contribute to this binary formulation, in which the United States and Europe are figured as modern and thus as the sites of progressive social movements, while other parts of the world are presumed to be traditional, especially in regard to sexuality. If any countries or nations depart from this model, it is because they are interpellated by "primitivism." In general, the United States and Europe come to be seen as unified sites of "freedom" and "democratic choice" over and against locations characterized by oppression.

In our work on female sexual surgeries and the global and cultural feminist discourse of "female genital mutilation" (FGM), we have argued that the tradition-modernity binary is foundational and even modern in that sexual subjects are produced as traditional in order to create feminist modern subjects.[27] Thus the global feminist is one who has free choice over her body and a complete and intact rather than a fragmented or surgically altered body, while the traditional female subject of patriarchy is forcibly altered, fragmented, alienated from her innate sexuality, and deprived of choices or agency. As we have discussed in relation to the film text by Alice Walker and Pratibha Parmar, *Warrior Marks*, freedom of choice in this nexus of modernity is marked by "coming out" as a lesbian. This is a complicated example, but suffice it to say at this juncture that a feminist and lesbian cosmopolitanism emerges over and against rural, African and Islamic "barbarism" in the name of saving "traditional women" from their own families. Although we see plenty of events and instances in the United States, for example, in which violence is enacted against gays and lesbians, against transgendered people, and against women, the displacement of the victims of sexualized violence to the Third World needs more discussion.

Another example of the tradition-modernity divide at work in the study of sexuality can be found in the literature on migration and refugee asylum. In such work, the process of migration to the United States, Europe, and other metropolitan locations is figured as the movement from repression to freedom.[28] That is, "backward," often rural subjects flee their homes and/or patriarchal families or violent, abusive situations to come to the modern metropolis, where they can express their true nature as sexual identity in a state of freedom. This narrative is a hallowed one in domestic "coming-out" discourses as well as in a burgeoning international human rights arena. Refugee asylum in the United States, for instance, produces gay and lesbian subjects through a political and legal articulation of such narratives. Some recent research suggests that it is virtually impossible to stay in the country without deploying such a narrative, thereby questioning its "natural" origins.[29] Further inquiry into this international context of immigration and asylum would need to focus on the ways in which the state becomes involved in producing sexual identities in an era of globalization. This is why we are arguing that a cultural or psychoanalytic understanding of so-called global lesbian and gay movements is inadequate. Nation-states, economic formations, consumer cultures, and forms of governmentality all work together to produce and uphold subjectivities and communities.

It is these kinds of examples and considerations that lead us to believe that we cannot think of sexual subjects as purely oppositional or resistant to dominant institutions that produce heteronormativity. In other words, as many have pointed out, queer subjects are not always already avant-garde for all time and in all places. For example, lesbian sexuality and practices in many sites have to struggle against patriarchal formations, while gay male sexualities may not. Our point is that, again, universalized models of resistance with idealized tropes or politics of identity obscure rather than elucidate the terrain of subjectivity in postmodernity.

A fourth link in this chain of examples of separate spheres is the global-local divide. In the context of globalization and some kinds of transnational studies, the local is seen as working against or in resistance to the global. That is, local and global constitute two separate spheres that never contaminate each other.

The global-local divide is a tempting device for many cultural critics, but, like all the other binaries we are discussing, this one obscures important aspects of postmodernity, not the least of which is that the local is often constituted through the global, and vice versa.[30] It is also a model that hails critics because of its liberatory and resistance qualities. In this formulation, the local serves as the space of oppositional consciousness and generates practices of resistance, and the global serves as an oppressive network of dominant power structures. In various critical engagements with this global-local binary, lesbian, gay, and queer theorists have argued that the site of the local destabilizes the homogenizing tendencies of global gay formations.[31] There is another formulation that advocates the globalizing of Euro-American identity politics of sexuality along the lines that we have discussed above, that is, to advance human rights and freedom of choice.

We think that there is another way to look at the tension between these heavily mediated practices that appear to signal "local" or "global." We would advocate a mode of study that adopts a more complicated model of transnational relations in which power structures, asymmetries, and inequalities become the conditions of possibility of new subjects. For example, we could look at the way social and political movements are cosmopolitan and class-based, generating new sites of power rather than simply forms of resistance.[32] We could also investigate the empowering practices of consumption and engagements with media and new technologies that create new subjects that trouble the model of rights and citizenship. Above all, there should be much more attention to the power relations of travel—contacts and transactions of all kinds—that are part of the knowledge production through which subjects are constituted. The social aspects of sexuality are always embedded in the material histories of these encounters and must be addressed in nuanced ways.

In many ways we are addressing the problem of writing history, a problem foregrounded by many theorists and critics working in gay and lesbian and queer studies.[33] That is, subjects are produced by the writing of history itself and thus may always be marked by a belated recognition or identification that is always already in the terms of the present. While we can see

this problem at work in the representation of the past, we are not always as aware of the limits of representation in the present. This problem of the present is especially egregious when we look at other cultures near or far. That is, identity politics have structured our view so profoundly that we literally cannot see the link between representation and subject formation in the ways that we are calling for vis-à-vis a transnational framework. Actually, what we are really grappling with here is not just representation; it is also the emergence of new forms of governmentality with an entire repertoire of strategies, regulatory practices, and instrumentalities linking the state to bodies. Thus representation is always linked to production, consumption, and regulation.[34]

Most of the identities we can recognize have emerged during the era of modernity encompassing the rise of capitalism and the nation-state in the context of imperialism. Our point is that sexual subjects are produced not just by the politics of identity or social movements but by the links between various institutions that accompany these social movements. Furthermore, we need to probe these connections and circuits to see how identities are upheld or made possible by institutions linked to the state. We find it problematic that in much work on sexual identities the state seldom has a hand in enabling these identities.[35] Most discussions of the state focus on queer or gay resistance to state-sanctioned heterosexism. While most states seem to oppose all forms of sexuality that are not related to reproduction or marriage, there have been cases where states (or institutions within states) have not been so uniformly in opposition. Although there is increasing discussion of the ways in which communities might be affected by institutions such as schools or the military, other state-linked or related institutions, such as universities and census boards, or institutions of the market, such as advertising, financial flows, and banks, are not often discussed in work on sexualities or sexual identities. Instead, communities seem to be simply produced by culture or by a culturalist notion of history, and by *culture* we mean in both the Arnoldian and the anthropological sense. This idea of culture signals a means of distinguishing between and ranking groups or seeing cultural formations as aesthetic categories.

What, then, is a transnational practice of the study of sexuality? There is a great deal of very exciting and useful work coming out of both interdisciplinary and disciplinary sites. Journals such as *GLQ* and *positions* have taken the lead in publishing new approaches, and there have been a plethora of conferences, workshops, and panels where these intersections have been increasingly evident.[36] Other institutional sites—such as centers for the study of sexuality or for gay, lesbian, and transgender studies; women's studies; gender studies; ethnic studies; and other interdisciplinary initiatives— are encouraging new scholarship and fostering various dialogues. Sexuality studies, like feminist and gender studies, is an increasingly important area of work in all kinds of disciplinary formations as well.

In our work on the film text of *Warrior Marks*, we began the project of creating a transnational framework for the study of sexual surgeries. We started by examining the ways in which colonial and postcolonial discourses of modernity and tradition have structured feminist and lesbian-feminist cultural production and identity politics as well as policy and activism in the Clinton era. Other parts of this long-term project include examinations of refugee asylum and other human rights practices and legal-juridical discourses that produce sexed subjects and identities. Another valence concerns the deployment of FGM discourse in social activism around infant sex assignment practices. Here the complicated issues involve the emergence of an intersex movement in the United States and the complexities of resisting recent biomedical practices by relying on notions of a natural body, conventions of sexual and gender difference, and colonial notions of tradition, barbarism, and mutilation. There is more that we can say about this project, but for now we would argue that the study of biomedicine must incorporate the kind of transnational frame that we are calling for in this essay.

Another area that engages not only our work but the work of many other scholars is travel and tourism.[37] As feminists in colonial and postcolonial discourse studies have argued, the emergence of travel in the modern period has been constitutive of many forms of orientalism and other ethnocentrisms.[38] Power differentials are always implicated in the activity of travel. Imperialism enabled forms of travel and exploration that produced circuits and flows of power and desire through which new forms of otherness and exoticism arose. From the "sotadic" zone in Richard Burton's travel narratives to Roland Barthes's "empire of signs" (not to forget Isabelle Eberhardt's peregrinations in male attire in North Africa), sexuality has been a primary subject of travel writing.[39] While over the last fifteen years both feminist and postcolonial critics have written extensively about travel in the era of imperialism, the field has been plagued by many of the critical limits that we have delineated here. In gay and lesbian and queer studies, the discussion of travel follows the parameters that we have critiqued thus far, for instance, the positioning of gay and lesbian travelers as transcending colonial power relations or functioning as agents of resistance.

Tourism is linked both to the colonial history of travel and to new forms of globalization in late capitalism. From global trafficking of women to sex tourism, the topic of tourism provides a window onto specific connections among nationalism, political economy, and cultural formations. The debate about global trafficking and sex tourism in certain locales, such as Thailand, Sri Lanka, and the Caribbean, for example, tends to portray sex workers as downtrodden victims of their patriarchies and "underdeveloped" economies. The figure of the "Third World prostitute," male or female, adult or child, is structured by the fantasy of rescue.[40] As Spivak's formulation argues, it is the old colonial project of saving the brown woman from her own kind—in these instances, we can expand this formulation to various subjects of capitalism and patriarchy, although there are important differences among these linked subjects.[41] There has been a lot of new work on these circuits of labor and desire, but much more needs to be done, especially in terms of media and visual culture.

We are also interested in new kinds of studies of migration and immigration that trouble the narratives of movement from oppression to freedom that we have already mentioned. Migration within nations as well as across different kinds of national boundaries has been studied in different disciplines; however, we need to pay attention to the different kinds of boundaries that are crossed or that cannot be crossed, and by whom. For instance, the family-based categories for immigration into the United States are profoundly antigay and -lesbian, but they also assume models of the family based on a hierarchy of nations and cultures. Other nation-states have enacted laws requiring HIV testing for entry as well as other invasive and homophobic practices. Here nationalism, gender, sexuality, and geopolitics must be considered, along with the political economy that underlies the regulation of immigration at the current moment.

One of the best examples of the issues we are raising here is the production of HIV/AIDS discourses over the last two decades. In this field we can discern a massive shift from the separate spheres to which we have been referring to the new forms of global and transnational policy discussions that have been created in response to this emergency. We see also the interconnections among state policies, nationalist agendas, pharmaceutical corporate practices, biomedical institutions, and the varied sexual subjects, cultures, and practices that become visible and targeted in new ways. The discourse of the modern nation-state's heteronormative family and of sexuality as the purview of males has been disrupted by the circulation of discourses of viruses, consumer actions, treatment strategies, theories of origins, and new sexual subjects. This example enables us to see the limits of the separate spheres approach as well as the interconnections that transnational subjects engender.

In conclusion, we would like to return to the five points with which we began our discussion of the circulation of the term *transnational*. We pointed out the limits of current uses of the term and linked these uses to articulations of knowledge formations. These limits include the production of various kinds of separate spheres or binaries, which prevent an approach to the study of sexuality that would usefully enable us to examine some of the areas of study that we have mentioned. Although other such topics can be considered, we have raised a few here as a contribution to a discussion that can build a bridge between the fields of global and transnational studies and those of sexuality, gender, women's, ethnic, and cultural studies in the U.S. academy. Such interdisciplinary work will enable us to understand global identities at the present time and to examine complicities as well as resistances in order to create the possibility of critique and change.

NOTES

1. See Jasbir Kaur Puar, "Global Circuits: Transnational Sexualities and Trinidad," *Signs* 26 (2001): 1039–65; Martin F. Manalansan IV, "Diasporic Deviants/Divas: How Filipino Gay Transmigrants 'Play with the World,'" in *Queer Diasporas*, ed. Cindy Patton and Benigno Sánchez-Eppler (Durham: Duke University Press, 2000), 183–203; Yukiko Hanawa, ed., "Circuits of Desire," special issue of *Positions* 2, no. 1 (1994); Elizabeth A. Povinelli and George Chauncey, eds., "Thinking Sexuality Transnationally," special issue of *GLQ* 5, no. 4 (1999); Phillip Brian Harper et al., eds., "Queer Transexions of Race, Nation, and Gender," special issue of *Social Text*, nos. 52–53 (1997); and Engin F. Isin and Patricia K. Wood, *Citizenship and Identity* (London: Sage, 1999).

2. For an influential account of this approach to globalization see Richard J. Barnet and John Cavanagh, *Global Dreams: Imperial Corporations and the New World Order* (New York: Touchstone, 1994); see also George Ritzer, *The McDonaldization of Society* (Thousand Oaks, Calif.: Pine Forge, 1993).

3. See Mike Featherstone, ed., *Global Culture* (London: Sage, 1990); Stuart Hall, "The Question of Cultural Identity," in *Modernity and Its Futures*, ed. Stuart Hall, David Held, and Tony McGrew (Cambridge: Polity, 1992), 274–316; Anthony D. King, ed., *Culture, Globalization, and the World System* (Minneapolis: University of Minnesota Press, 1997); and Fredric Jameson and Masao Miyoshi, eds., *The Cultures of Globalization* (Durham: Duke University Press, 1998).

4. See Lisa Rofel, "Qualities of Desire: Imagining Gay Identities in China," *GLQ* 5 (1999): 451–74.

5. See Inderpal Grewal and Caren Kaplan, "Introduction: Transnational Feminist Practices and Questions of Postmodernity," in *Scattered Hegemonies: Postmodernity and Transnational Feminist*

Practices, ed. Inderpal Grewal and Caren Kaplan (Minneapolis: University of Minnesota Press, 1994), 1–33.

6. See Linda Basch, Nina Glick Schiller, and Cristina Szanton Blanc, eds., *Nations Unbound: Transnational Projects, Postcolonial Predicaments, and Deterritorialized Nation-States* (Langhorne, Pa.: Gordon and Breach, 1994).

7. See Arjun Appadurai, *Modernity at Large: Cultural Dimensions of Globalization* (Minneapolis: University of Minnesota Press, 1999); Ulf Hannerz, *Transnational Connections* (London: Routledge, 1996); and Scott Lash and John Urry, *Economies of Signs and Space* (London: Sage, 1994).

8. See David Harvey, *The Condition of Postmodernity: An Enquiry into the Origins of Cultural Change* (Oxford: Blackwell, 1989).

9. See Appadurai, *Modernity at Large*.

10. See Hannerz, *Transnational Connections*.

11. Victoria Bernal, "The Nation and the World: Reflections on Nationalism in a Transnational Era," unpublished manuscript, 2001.

12. This usage is evident at conferences such as the American Studies Association meetings, as well as other meetings of humanities or social science academic organizations such as the American Anthropological Association. See also David L. Eng, *Racial Castration: Managing Masculinity in Asian America* (Durham: Duke University Press, 2001).

13. See Paul Gilroy, *The Black Atlantic: Modernity and Double Consciousness* (Cambridge, Mass.: Harvard University Press, 1993).

14. See Caren Kaplan, *Questions of Travel: Postmodern Discourses of Displacement* (Durham: Duke University Press, 1996).

15. See Lisa Lowe and David Lloyd, eds., *The Politics of Culture in the Shadow of Capital* (Durham: Duke University Press, 1997).

16. We take this phrase from Sabine Lang, "The NGOization of Feminism," in *Transitions, Translations, Environments: Feminisms in International Politics*, ed. Joan W. Scott, Cora Kaplan, and Debra Keates (New York: Routledge, 1997), 101–20.

17. See Teresa Carillo, "Cross-Border Talk: Transnational Perspectives on Labor, Race, and Sexuality," in *Talking Visions: Multicultural Feminism in a Transnational Age,* ed. Ella Shohat (New York: New Museum for Modern Art; Cambridge, Mass.: MIT Press, 1998), 391–412.

18. Although *The Lesbian and Gay Studies Reader*, ed. Henry Abelove, Michèle Aina Barale, and David M. Halperin (New York: Routledge, 1993), broke new ground in important ways, many of the essays in it focus on this approach to gender diversity. Since then, other publications have attempted to address this problem. See Gerald Hunt, ed., *Laboring for Rights: Unions and Sexual Diversity across Nations* (Philadelphia: Temple University Press, 1999); Amy Gluckman and Betsy Reed, eds., *Homo Economics: Capitalism, Community, and Lesbian and Gay Life* (New York: Routledge, 1997); Erica Rand, *Barbie's Queer Accessories* (Durham: Duke University Press, 1995); Donald Morton, ed., *The Material Queer: A LesBiGay Cultural Studies Reader* (Boulder, Colo.: Westview, 1996); and Roger N. Lancaster and Micaela di Leonardo, eds., *The Gender/Sexuality Reader: Culture, History, Political Economy* (New York: Routledge, 1997).

19. For a trenchant critique of such work see Gayatri Chakravorty Spivak, "French Feminism in an International Frame," in *In Other Worlds: Essays in Cultural Politics* (New York: Routledge, 1988), 134–53.

20. For instance, in the context of South Asian studies see the work of Ashis Nandy, *The Intimate Enemy: Loss and Recovery of Self under Colonialism* (Delhi: Oxford University Press, 1983).

21. Tani E. Barlow, "Colonialism's Career in Postwar China Studies," *positions* 1, no. 1 (1993): 224–67.

22. See Inderpal Grewal, *Home and Harem: Nation, Gender, Empire, and the Cultures of Travel* (Durham: Duke University Press, 1996); and Inderpal Grewal, Akhil Gupta, and Aihwa Ong, eds., introduction to "Asian Transnationalities," special issue of *positions* 7 (1999): 653–66.

23. Many writers have pointed out that analyses of race are often absent from works by gay and lesbian scholars. See Audre Lorde, *Sister/Outsider* (Trumansburg, N.Y.: Crossing, 1984); bell hooks, *Yearning: Race, Gender, and Cultural Politics* (Boston: South End, 1990); and Cherríe Moraga and Gloria Anzaldúa, *This Bridge Called My Back: Writings by Radical Women of Color* (Watertown, Mass.: Persephone, 1981). An example of work that does not address the relation between sexuality and race or ethnicity is Corey K. Creekmur and Alexander Doty, eds., *Out in Culture: Gay, Lesbian, and Queer Essays on Popular Culture* (Durham: Duke University Press, 1995). In the very influential *Lesbian and Gay Studies Reader*, most of the essays focus on Europe and North America, although some address the relationship among sexuality, sexual identities, and race. Lancaster and di Leonardo's anthology *The Gender/Sexuality Reader* provides a more cross-cultural perspective.

24. See Patton and Sánchez-Eppler, *Queer Diasporas*; Emilie L. Bergmann and Paul Julian Smith, eds., *¿Entiendes? Queer Readings, Hispanic Writings* (Durham: Duke University Press, 1995); Russell Leong, ed., *Asian American Sexualities: Dimensions of the Gay and Lesbian Experience* (New York: Routledge, 1996); and David Eng and Alice Hom, eds., *Q & A: Queer in Asian America* (Philadelphia: Temple University Press, 1998).

25. For articulation theory see Lawrence Grossberg, ed., "On Postmodernism and Articulation: An Interview with Stuart Hall," *Journal of Communication Inquiry* 10, no. 2 (1986): 45–60. For intersectional theory see Kimberlé Crenshaw, "Mapping the Margins: Intersectionality, Identity Politics, and Violence against Women of Color," in *After Identity: A Reader in Law and Culture*, ed. Dan Danielson and Karen Engle (New York: Routledge, 1995), 332–54.

26. See Kaplan, *Questions of Travel*; and Caren Kaplan, "Hillary Clinton's Orient: Cosmopolitan Travel and Global Feminist Subjects," *Meridians: Feminism, Race, Transnationalism* 2 (2001): 219–40.

27. See Inderpal Grewal and Caren Kaplan, "Warrior Marks: Global Womanism's NeoColonial Discourse in a Multicultural Context," *Camera Obscura* 39 (1996): 5–33.

28. See Olivia Espin, *Women Crossing Boundaries: A Psychology of Immigration and Transformations of Sexuality* (New York: Routledge, 1999).

29. See Inderpal Grewal, *Transnational America: Gender, Nation, and Diaspora* (Durham: Duke University Press, forthcoming).

30. See Rob Wilson and Wimal Dissanayake, eds., *Global/Local: Cultural Production and the Transnational Imaginary* (Durham: Duke University Press, 1996).

31. Katie King, "Local and Global: AIDS Activism and Feminist Theory," *Camera Obscura* 28 (1992): 79–100.

32. Lash and Urry, *Economies of Signs and Space*; Manuel Castells, *The Rise of the Network Society* (Cambridge, Mass.: Blackwell, 1996).

33. See Michel Foucault, *The History of Sexuality* (New York: Pantheon, 1978); David M. Halperin, "Is There a History of Sexuality?" *History and Theory* 28 (1989): 257–74; Halperin, "How to Do the History of Male Homosexuality," *GLQ* 6 (2000): 87–124; John D'Emilio, "Capitalism and Gay Identity," in *Powers of Desire: The Politics of Sexuality*, ed. Ann Snitow, Christine Stansell, and Sharon Thompson (New York: Monthly Review Press, 1983), 100–113; Carolyn Dinshaw, *Getting Medieval: Sexualities and Communities, Pre- and Postmodern* (Durham: Duke University Press, 1999); and Donna Penn, "Queer: Theorizing Politics and History," *Radical History Review*, no. 62 (1995): 28–30.

34. See Stuart Hall, introduction to *Representation: Cultural Representations and Signifying Practices*, ed. Stuart Hall (London: Sage, 1997), 1–11.

35. For work that does address the state in the context of transnationality see M. Jacqui Alexander, "Erotic Autonomy as a Politics of Decolonization: An Anatomy of Feminist and State Practice in the Bahamas Tourist Economy," in *Feminist Genealogies, Colonial Legacies, Democratic Futures*, ed. M. Jacqui Alexander and Chandra Talpade Mohanty (New York: Routledge, 1997), 63–100.

36. See Hanawa, "Circuits of Desire," in which some essays utilize approaches that engage with circulations of identity and sexuality. See also Povinelli and Chauncey, "Thinking Sexuality Transnationally"; and Harper et al., "Queer Transexions of Race, Nation, and Gender."

37. See Puar, "Global Circuits"; and Alexander, "Erotic Autonomy as a Politics of Decolonization."

38. See Mary Louise Pratt, *Imperial Eyes: Travel Writing and Transculturation* (New York: Routledge, 1992); Ella Shohat, "Gender and the Culture of Empire: Toward a Feminist Ethnography of the Cinema," *Quarterly Review of Film and Video*, no. 131 (1991): 45–84; Lisa Lowe, *Critical Terrains: French and British Orientalisms* (Ithaca: Cornell University Press, 1991); Reina Lewis, *Gendering Orientalism: Race, Femininity, and Representation* (London: Routledge, 1996); Grewal, *Home and Harem*; Anne McClintock, *Imperial Leather: Race, Gender, and Sexuality in the Colonial Context* (New York: Routledge, 1995); and Sara Mills, *Discourses of Difference: An Analysis of Travel Writing and Colonialism* (New York: Routledge, 1991).

39. See Richard Phillips, "Travelling Sexualities: Richard Burton's Sotadic Zone," in *Writes of Passage: Reading Travel Writing*, ed. James Duncan and Derek Gregory (London: Routledge, 1999), 70–91; and Phillips, "Imaginative Geographies and Sexuality Politics: The City, the Country, and the Age of Consent," in *De-centring Sexualities: Politics and Representations beyond the Metropolis*, ed. Richard Phillips, Diane Watt, and David Shuttleton (London: Routledge, 2000). Primary works include Richard F. Burton, *The Book of the Thousand Nights and a Night*, 6 vols. (New York: Limited Editions Club, 1934); Roland Barthes, *The Empire of Signs*, trans. Richard Howard (New York: Farrar, Straus and Giroux, 1982); and Isabelle Eberhardt, *The Passionate Nomad: The Diary of Isabelle Eberhardt* (Boston: Beacon, 1988).

40. See Kamala Kempadoo and Jo Doezema, eds., *Global Sex Workers: Rights, Resistance, and Redefinition* (New York: Routledge, 1998).

41. See Gayatri Chakravorty Spivak, "Can the Subaltern Speak?" in *Marxism and the Interpretation of Culture*, ed. Cary Nelson and Lawrence Grossberg (Urbana: University of Illinois Press, 1988), 271–313.

6. "QUARE" STUDIES, OR (ALMOST) EVERYTHING I KNOW ABOUT QUEER STUDIES I LEARNED FROM MY GRANDMOTHER

"QUARE" ETYMOLOGY (WITH APOLOGIES TO ALICE WALKER)

Quare (Kwâr), *n.* 1. meaning *queer*; also, opp. of *straight*; odd or slightly off kilter; from the African American vernacular for queer; sometimes homophobic in usage, but always denotes excess incapable of being contained within conventional categories of *being*; curiously equivalent to the Anglo-Irish (and sometimes "Black" Irish) variant of queer, as in Brendan Behan's famous play, *The Quare Fellow.*

—*adj.* 2. a lesbian, gay, bisexual, or transgendered person of color who loves other men or women, sexually or nonsexually, and appreciates black culture and community.

—*n.* 3. one who *thinks* and *feels* and *acts* (and, sometimes, "acts up"); committed to struggle against all forms of oppression—racial, sexual, gender, class, religious, etc.

—*n.* 4. one for whom sexual and gender identities always already intersect with racial subjectivity.

5. quare is to queer as "reading" is to "throwing shade."[1]

I AM going out on a limb. This is a precarious position, but the stakes are high enough to warrant risky business. The business to which I refer is reconceptualizing the still incubating discipline called queer studies. Now, what's in a name? This is an important question when, as James Baldwin proclaims in the titles of two of his works, I have "no name in the street" or, worse still, "nobody *knows* my name" (emphasis added). I used to answer to "queer," but when I was hailed by that naming, interpellated in that moment, I felt as if I was being called "out of my name." I needed something with more "soul," more "bang," something closer to "home." It is my name after all!

Then I remembered how "queer" is used in my family. My grandmother, for example, used it often when I was a child and still uses it today. When she says the word, she does so in a thick, black, southern dialect: "That sho'll is a quare chile." Her use of "queer" is almost always nuanced. Still, one might wonder, what, if anything, could a poor, black, eighty-something, southern, homophobic woman teach her educated, middle-class, thirty-something, gay grandson about queer studies? Everything. Or *almost* everything. On the one hand, my grandmother uses "quare" to denote something or someone who is odd, irregular, or slightly off kilter—definitions in keeping with traditional understandings and uses of "queer." On the other hand, she also deploys "quare" to connote something excessive—something that might philosophically translate into an excess of discursive and epistemological meanings grounded in African American cultural rituals and lived experience. Her knowing or not knowing vis-á-vis "quare" is predicated on her own "multiple and complex social, historical, and cultural positionality" (Henderson 147). It is this culture-specific positionality that I find absent from the dominant and more conventional usage of "queer," particularly in its most recent theoretical reappropriation in the academy.

E. Patrick Johnson and Mae G. Henderson, "'Quare' Studies, or (almost) Everything I know about Queer Studies I learned from My Grandmother," *Text and Performance Quarterly*, 21:1 (2001): 1–14, 18–25. Copyright © National Communication Association. Reprinted by permission of Taylor & Francis Ltd, www.tandfonline.com on behalf of The National Communication Association. Notes were renumbered.

I knew there was something to "quare," that its implications reached far beyond my grandmother's front porch. Little did I know, however, that its use extended across the Atlantic. Then, I found "quare" in Ireland.[2] In *Quare Joyce*, Joseph Valente writes,

> [. . .] I have elected to use the Anglo-Irish epithet *quare* in the title as a kind of transnational/transidiomatic pun. *Quare*, meaning odd or strange, as in Brendan Behan's famous play, *The Quare Fellow*, has lately been appropriated as a distinctively Irish variant of *queer*, as in the recent prose collection *Quare Fellas*, whose editor, Brian Finnegan, reinterprets Behan's own usage of the term as having "covertly alluded to his own sexuality." (4, emphasis in original)

Valente's appropriation of the Irish epithet "quare" to "queerly" read James Joyce establishes a connection between race and ethnicity in relation to queer identity. Indeed, Valente's "quare" reading of Joyce, when conjoined with my grandmother's "quare" reading of those who are slightly off kilter, provides a strategy for reading racial and ethnic sexuality. Where the two uses of "quare" diverge is in their deployment. Valente deploys quare to devise a queer literary exegesis of Joyce. Rather than drawing on "quare" as a *literary* mode of reading/theorizing, however, I draw upon the *vernacular* roots implicit in my grandmother's use of the word to devise a strategy for theorizing racialized sexuality.

Because much of queer theory critically interrogates notions of selfhood, agency, and experience, it is often unable to accommodate the issues faced by gays and lesbians of color who come from "raced" communities. Gloria Anzaldúa explicitly addresses this limitation when she warns that "queer is used as a false unifying umbrella which all 'queers' of all races, ethnicities and classes are shored under" (250). While acknowledging that "at times we need this umbrella to solidify our ranks against outsiders," Anzaldúa nevertheless urges that "even when we seek shelter under it ["queer"], we must not forget that it homogenizes, erases our differences" (250).

"Quare," on the other hand, not only speaks across identities, it *articulates* identities as well. "Quare" offers a way to critique stable notions of identity and, at the same time, to locate racialized and class knowledges. My project is one of recapitulation and recuperation. I want

to maintain the inclusivity and playful spirit of "queer" that animates much of queer theory, but I also want to jettison its homogenizing tendencies. As a disciplinary expansion, then, I wish to "quare" "queer" such that ways of knowing are viewed both as discursively mediated and as historically situated and materially conditioned. This reconceptualization foregrounds the ways in which lesbians, bisexuals, gays, and transgendered people of color come to sexual and racial knowledge. Moreover, quare studies acknowledges the different "standpoints" found among lesbian, bisexual, gay, and transgendered people of color—differences that are also conditioned by class and gender.[3]

Quare studies is a theory of and for gays and lesbians of color. Thus, I acknowledge that in my attempt to advance quare studies, I run the risk of advancing another version of identity politics. Despite this, I find it necessary to traverse this political mine field in order to illuminate the ways in which some strands of queer theory fail to incorporate racialized sexuality. The theory that I advance is a "theory in the flesh" (Moraga and Anzaldúa 23). Theories in the flesh emphasize the diversity within and among gays, bisexuals, lesbians, and transgendered people of color while simultaneously accounting for how racism and classism affect how we experience and theorize the world. Theories in the flesh also conjoin theory and practice through an embodied politics of resistance. This politics of resistance is manifest in vernacular traditions such as performance, folklore, literature, and verbal art.

. . .

"RACE TROUBLE": QUEER STUDIES OR THE STUDY OF WHITE QUEERS

At a moment when queer studies has gained momentum in the academy and forged a space as a legitimate disciplinary subject, much of the scholarship produced in its name elides issues of race and class. While . . . [authors] suggest that the label "queer" sometimes speaks across (homo)sexualities, they also suggest that the term is not necessarily embraced by gays, bisexuals, lesbians, and transgendered people of color. Indeed, the statements of Mack-Nataf, Blackman, and Cohen reflect a general suspicion that the label often displaces and rarely addresses their concerns.[4]

Some queer theorists have argued that their use of "queer" is more than just a reappropriation of an offensive term. Cherry Smith, for example, maintains that the term entails a "radical questioning of social and cultural norms, notions of gender, reproductive sexuality and the family" (280). Others underscore the playfulness and inclusivity of the term, arguing that it opens up rather than fixes identities. According to Eve Sedgwick, "What it takes–all it takes–to make the description 'queer' a true one is the impulse to use it in the first person" (9). Indeed, Sedgwick suggests, it may refer to

> pushy femmes, radical faeries, fantasists, drags, clones, leatherfolk, ladies in tuxedos, feminist women or feminist men, masturbators, bulldaggers, divas, Snap! queens, butch bottoms, storytellers, transsexuals, aunties, wannabes, lesbian-identified men or lesbians who sleep with men, or [. . .] people able to relish, learn from, or identify with such. (8)

For Sedgwick, then, it would appear that "queer" is a catchall term not bound to any particular identity, a notion that moves us away from binaries such as homosexual/heterosexual and gay/lesbian. Michael Warner offers an even more politicized and polemical view:

> The preference for "queer" represents, among other things, an aggressive impulse of generalization; it rejects a minoritizing logic of toleration or simple political interest-representation in favor of a more thorough resistance to regimes of the normal. For academics, being interested in Queer theory is a way to mess up the desexualized spaces of the academy, exude some rut, reimagine the public from and for which academic intellectuals write, dress, and perform. (xxvi)

The foregoing theorists identify "queer" as a site of indeterminate possibility, a site where sexual practice does not necessarily determine one's status as queer. Indeed, Lauren Berlant and Michael Warner argue that queer is "more a matter of aspiration than it is the expression of an identity or a history" (344). Accordingly, straight-identified critic Calvin Thomas appropriates Judith Butler's notion of "critical queerness" to suggest that "just as there is more than one way to be 'critical', there may be more than one (or two or three) to be 'queer'" (83).

Some critics have applied Butler's theory of gender to identity formation more generally. Butler calls into question the notion of the "self" as distinct from discursive cultural fields. That is, like gender, there is no independent or pure "self" or agent that stands outside socially and culturally mediated discursive systems. Any move toward identification, then, is, in her view, to be hoodwinked into believing that identities are discourse free and capable of existing outside the systems those identity formations seek to critique. Even when identity is contextualized and qualified, Butler still insists that theories of identity "invariably close with an embarrassed 'etc'." (*Gender* 143). Butler's emphasis on gender and sex as "performative" would seem to undergird a progressive, forward-facing theory of sexuality. In fact, some theorists have made the theoretical leap from the gender performative to the racial performative, thereby demonstrating the potential of her theory for understanding the ontology of race.[5]

But to riff off of the now popular phrase "gender trouble," *there is some race trouble here with queer theory.* More particularly, in its "race for theory" (Christian), queer theory has often failed to address the material realities of gays and lesbians of color. As black British activist Helen (Charles) asks, "What happens to the definition of 'queer' when you're washing up or having a wank? When you're aware of misplacement or displacement in your colour, gender, identity? Do they get subsumed [. . .] into a homogeneous category, where class and other things that make up a cultural identity are ignored?" (101–102). What, for example, are the ethical and material implications of queer theory if its project is to dismantle all notions of identity and agency? The deconstructive turn in queer theory highlights the ways in which ideology functions to oppress and to proscribe ways of knowing, but what is the utility of queer theory on the front lines, in the trenches, on the street, or anyplace where the racialized and sexualized body is beaten, starved, fired, cursed—indeed, where the body is the site of trauma?[6]

Beyond queer theory's failure to focus on materiality, it also has failed to acknowledge consistently and critically the intellectual, aesthetic, and political contributions of nonwhite and non-middle-class gays, bisexuals, lesbians, and transgendered people in the struggle against homophobia and oppression. Moreover, even when white queer theorists acknowledge these contributions, rarely do they self-consciously and overtly reflect on the ways in which their whiteness informs their critical queer position, and this is occurring at a time when naming one's positionality has become almost standard protocol in other areas of scholarship. Although there are exceptions, most often white queer theorists fail to acknowledge and address racial privilege.[7]

Because transgendered people, lesbians, gays, and bisexuals of color often ground their theorizing in a politics of identity, they frequently fall prey to accusations of "essentialism" or "anti-intellectualism." Galvanizing around identity, however, is not always an unintentional "essentialist" move. Many times, it is an intentional strategic choice.[8] Cathy Cohen, for example, suggests that "queer theorizing which calls for the elimination of fixed categories seems to ignore the ways in which some traditional social identities and communal ties can, in fact, be important to one's survival" ("Punks" 450). The "communal ties" to which Cohen refers are those which exist in communities of color across boundaries of sexuality. For example, my grandmother, who is homophobic, nonetheless must be included in the struggle against oppression in spite of her bigotry. While her homophobia must be critiqued, her feminist and race struggles over the course of her life have enabled me and others in my family to enact strategies of resistance against a number of oppressions, including homophobia. Some queer activists groups, however, have argued fervently for the disavowal of any alliance with heterosexuals, a disavowal that those of us who belong to communities of color cannot necessarily afford to make.[9] Therefore, while offering a progressive and sometimes transgressive politics of sexuality, the seams of queer theory become exposed when that theory is applied to identities around which sexuality may pivot, such as race and class.

As a counter to this myopia and in an attempt to close the gap between theory and practice, self and Other, Audre Lorde proclaims:

> Without community there is no liberation, only the most vulnerable and temporary armistice between an individual and her oppression. But community must

not mean a shedding of our differences, nor the pathetic pretense that these differences do not exist.

> [. . .] *I urge each one of us here to reach down into that deep place of knowledge inside herself and touch the terror and loathing of any difference that lives there. See whose face it wears. Then the personal as the political can begin to illuminate all our choices.* (112–13, emphasis in original)

For Lorde, a theory that dissolves the communal identity—in all of its difference—around which the marginalized can politically organize is not a progressive one. Nor is it one that gays, bisexuals, transgendered people, and lesbians of color can afford to adopt, for to do so would be to foreclose possibilities of change.

. . .

"QUARING" THE QUEER: TROPING THE TROPE

Queer studies has rightfully problematized identity politics by elaborating on the processes by which agents and subjects come into being; however, there is a critical gap in queer studies between theory and practice, performance and performativity. Quare studies can narrow that gap to the extent that it pursues an epistemology rooted in the body. As a "theory in the flesh" quare necessarily engenders a kind of identity politics, one that acknowledges difference within and between particular groups. Thus, identity politics does not necessarily mean the reduction of multiple identities into a monolithic identity or narrow cultural nationalism. Rather, quare studies moves beyond simply theorizing subjectivity and agency as discursively mediated to theorizing how that mediation may propel material bodies into action. As Shane Phelan reminds us, the maintenance of a progressive identity politics asks "not whether we share a given position but whether we share a commitment to improve it, and whether we can commit to the pain of embarrassment and confrontation as we disagree" (156).

Quare studies would reinstate the subject and the identity around which the subject circulates that queer theory so easily dismisses. By refocusing our attention on the racialized bodies, experiences, and knowledges of transgendered people, lesbians, gays, and bisexuals of color, quare studies grounds the discursive process of mediated identification and subjectivity in a political praxis that speaks to the material existence of "colored" bodies. While strategically galvanized around identity, quare studies should be committed to interrogating identity claims that exclude rather than include. I am thinking here of black nationalist claims of "black authenticity" that exclude, categorically, homosexual identities. Blind allegiance to "isms" of any kind is one of the fears of queer theorists who critique identity politics. Cognizant of that risk, quare studies must not deploy a totalizing and homogeneous formulation of identity. Rather, it must foster contingent, fragile coalitions as it struggles against common oppressive forms.

A number of queer theorists have proposed potential strategies (albeit limited ones) that may be deployed in the service of dismantling oppressive systems. Most significantly, Judith Butler's formulation of performativity has had an important impact not only on gender and sexuality studies, but on queer studies as well. While I am swayed by Butler's formulation of gender performativity, I am disturbed by her theory's failure to articulate a meatier politics of resistance. For example, what are the implications of dismantling subjectivity and social will to ground zero within oppressive regimes? Does an emphasis on the discursive constitution of subjects propel us beyond a state of quietism to address the very real injustices in the world? The body, I believe, has to be theorized in ways that not only describe the ways in which it is brought into being, but what it *does* once it *is* constituted and the relationship between it and the other bodies around it. In other words, I desire a rejoinder to performativity that allows a space for subjectivity, for agency (however momentary and discursively fraught), and, ultimately, for change.

Therefore, to complement notions of performativity, quare studies also deploys theories of performance. Performance theory not only highlights the discursive effects of acts, it also points to how these acts are historically situated. Butler herself acknowledges that the conflation of "performativity to performance would be a mistake" (*Bodies* 234). Indeed, the focus on performativity alone may problematically reduce

performativity and performance to one interpretative frame to theorize human experience. On the other hand, focusing on both may bring together two interpretative frames whose relationship is more dialogical and dialectical.

In her introduction to *Performance and Cultural Politics*, Elin Diamond proposes such a relationship between performance and performativity:

> When being is de-essentialized, when gender and even race are understood as fictional ontologies, modes of expression without true substance, the idea of performance comes to the fore. But performance both affirms and denies this evacuation of substance. In the sense that the "I" has no interior secure ego or core identity, "I" must always enunciate itself: there is only performance of a self, not an external representation of an interior truth. But in the sense that I do my performance in public, for spectators who are interpreting and/or performing with me, there are real effects, meanings solicited or imposed that produce relations in the real. Can performance make a difference? A performance, whether it inspires love or loathing, often consolidates cultural or subcultural affiliations, and these affiliations, might be as regressive as they are progressive. The point is, as soon as performativity comes to rest on *a* performance, questions of embodiment and political effects, all become discussible.
>
> Performance [. . .] is precisely the site in which concealed or dissimulated conventions might be investigated. When performativity materializes as performance in that risky and dangerous negotiation between doing (a reiteration of norms) and a thing done (discursive conventions that frame our interpretations), between somebody's body and the conventions of embodiment, we have access to cultural meanings and critique. Performativity [. . .] must be rooted in the materiality and historical density of performance. (5, emphasis in original)

I quote Diamond at length here because of the implications her construals of performance and performativity have for reinstating subjectivity and agency through the performance of identity. Although fleeting and ephemeral, these performances may activate a politics of subjectivity.

The performance of self is not only a performance/construction of identity for/toward an "out there" or merely an attachment or "taking up" (Butler, *Gender* 145) of a predetermined, discursively contingent identity. It is also a performance of self for the self in a moment of self-reflexivity that has the potential to transform one's view of self in relation to the world. People have a need to exercise control over the production of their images so that they feel empowered. For the disenfranchised, the recognition, construction and maintenance of self-image and cultural identity function to sustain, even when social systems fail to do so. Granted, formations/performances of identity may simply reify oppressive systems, but they may also contest and subvert dominant meaning systems. When gays, lesbians, bisexuals, and transgendered people of color "talk back," whether using the "tools of the master" (Lorde 110) or the vernacular on the street, their voices, singularly or collectively, do not exist in some vacuous wasteland of discursivity. As symbolic anthropologist Victor Turner suggests, their performances

are not simple reflectors or expressions of culture or even of changing culture but may themselves be active *agencies* of change, representing the eye by which culture sees itself and the drawing board on which creative actors sketch out what they believe to be more apt or interesting "designs for living." [. . .] Performative reflexivity is a condition in which a sociocultural group, or its most perceptive members, acting representatively, turn, bend, or reflect back upon themselves, upon the relations, actions, symbols, meanings, codes, roles, statuses, social structures, ethical and legal rules, and other sociocultural components which make up their public selves. (24, my emphasis)

Turner's theory of performative cultural reflexivity suggests a transgressive aspect of performative identity that neither dissolves identity into a fixed "I" nor presumes a monolithic "we." Rather, Turner's assertions suggest that social beings "look back" and "look forward" in a manner that wrestles with the ways in which that community exists in the world and theorizes that existence. As Cindy Patton warns, not everyone who claims an identity does so in the ways critics of essentialist identity claim they do (181).

Theories of performance, as opposed to theories of performativity, also take into account the context and historical moment of performance (Strine 7). We need to account for the temporal and spatial specificity of performance not only to frame its existence, but also to name the ways in which it signifies. Such an analysis would acknowledge the discursivity of subjects, but it would also "unfix" the discursively constituted subject as always already a pawn of power. Although many queer theorists appropriate Foucault to substantiate the imperialism of power, Foucault himself acknowledges that discourse has the potential to disrupt power:

Discourses are not once and for all subservient to power or raised up against it, any more than silences are. We must make allowances for the complex and unstable process whereby discourse can be both an instrument and an effect of power, but also a hindrance, a stumbling-block, a point of resistance and a starting point for an opposing strategy. Discourse transmits and produces power; it reinforces it, *but also undermines and exposes it, renders it fragile and makes it possible to thwart it.* (100–101, my emphasis)

Although people of color may not have theorized our lives in Foucault's terms, we have used discourse in subversive ways because it was necessary for our survival. Failure to ground discourse in materiality is to privilege the position of those whose subjectivity and agency, outside the realm of gender and sexuality, have never been subjugated. The tendency of many lesbians, bisexuals, gays, and transgendered people of color is to unite around a racial identity at a moment when their subjectivity is already under erasure.

Elaborating more extensively on the notion of performance as a site of agency for lesbian, gay, bisexual, and transgendered people of color, Latino performance theorist José Muñoz proposes a theory of "disidentification" whereby queers of color work within and against dominant ideology to effect change:

Disidentification is the third mode of dealing with dominant ideology, one that neither opts to assimilate within such a structure nor strictly opposes it; rather, disidentification is a strategy that works on and against dominant ideology. Instead of buckling under the pressures of dominant ideology (identification, assimilation) or attempting to break free of its inescapable sphere (counteridentification, utopianism), this "working on and against" is a strategy that tries to transform a cultural logic from within, always laboring to enact permanent structural change while at the same time valuing the importance of local and everyday struggles of resistance. (11–12)

Muñoz's concept of "disidentification" reflects the process through which people of color have always managed to survive in a white supremacist society: by "working on and against" oppressive institutional structures.

The performance strategies of African Americans who labored and struggled under human bondage exemplify this disidentificatory practice. For instance, vernacular traditions that emerged among enslaved Africans—including folktales, spirituals, and the blues—provided the foundation for social and political empowerment. These discursively mediated forms, spoken and filtered through black bodies, enabled survival. The point here is that the inheritance of hegemonic discourses does not preclude one from "disidentifying," from putting those discourses in the service of resistance. Although they had no institutional power, enslaved blacks refused to become helpless victims and instead enacted their agency by cultivating discursive weapons based on an identity as oppressed people. The result was the creation of folktales about the "bottom rail becoming the top riser" (i.e., a metaphor for the slave rising out of slavery) or spirituals that called folks to "Gather At the River" (i.e., to plan an escape).

These resistant vernacular performances did not disappear with slavery. Gays, lesbians, bisexuals, and transgendered people of color continued to enact performative agency to work on and against oppressive systems. Quare singers such as Bessie Smith and Ma Rainey, for instance, used the blues to challenge the notion of inferior black female subjectivity and covertly brought the image of the black lesbian into the American imaginary.[10] Later, through his flamboyant style and campy costumes, Little Richard not only fashioned himself as the "emancipator" and "originator" of rock-n-roll, he also offered a critique of hegemonic black and white masculinity in the music industry. Later still, the black transgendered singer Sylvester transformed disco with his high soaring falsetto voice and gospel riffs. Indeed, Sylvester's music transcended the boundary drawn between the church and the world, between the sacred and profane, creating a space for other quare singers, like Blackberri, who would come after him. Even RuPaul's drag of many flavors demonstrates the resourcefulness of quares of color to reinvent themselves in ways that transform their material conditions. Quare vernacular tools operate outside the realm of musical and theatrical performance as well. Performance practices such as vogueing, snapping, "throwing shade," and "reading" attest to the ways in which gays, lesbians, bisexuals, and transgendered people of color devise technologies of self-assertion and summon the agency to resist.[11]

Taken together, performance and quare theories alert us to the ways in which these disidentificatory performances serve material ends, and they do this work by accounting for the context in which these performances occur. The stage, for instance, is not confined solely to the theater, the dance club, or the concert hall. Streets, social services lines, picket lines, loan offices, and emergency rooms, among others, may also serve as useful staging grounds for disidentificatory performances. Theorizing the social context of performance sutures the gap between discourse and lived experience by examining how quares use performance as a strategy of survival in their day-to-day experiences. Such an analysis requires that we, like Robin Kelley, reconceptualize "play" (performance) as "work." Moreover, quare theory focuses attention on the social consequences of those performances. It is one thing to do drag on the club stage but quite another to embody a drag queen identity on the street. Bodies are sites of discursive effects, but they are sites of social ones as well.

I do not wish to suggest that quare vernacular performances do not, at times, collude with sexist, misogynist, racist, and even homophobic ideologies. Lesbian, bisexual, gay, and transgendered people of color must always realize that we cannot transgress for transgression's sake lest our work end up romanticizing and prolonging our state of struggle and that of others. In other words, while we may occasionally enjoy the pleasures of transgressive performance, we must transgress responsibly or run the risk of creating and sustaining representations of ourselves that are anti-gay, anti-woman, anti-transgender, anti-working class, and anti-black. Despite this risk, we must not retreat to the position that changes within the system are impossible. The social movements of the past century are testament that change is possible.

Ultimately, quare studies offers a more utilitarian theory of identity politics, focusing not just on performers and effects, but also on contexts and historical situatedness. It does not, as bell hooks warns, separate the "politics of difference from the politics of racism" (26). Quare studies grants space for marginalized individuals to enact "radical black subjectivity" (hooks 26) by adopting the both/and posture of "disidentification." Quare studies proposes a theory grounded in a critique of naïve essentialism and an enactment of political praxis. Such theorizing may *strategically* embrace identity politics while also acknowledging the contingency of identity, a double move that Angelia Wilson adroitly describes as "politically necessary and politically dangerous" (107).

. . .

BRINGIN' IT ON "HOME": QUARE STUDIES ON THE BACK PORCH

Thus far, I have canvassed the trajectory for quare studies inside the academy, focusing necessarily on the intellectual work that needs to be done to advance specific disciplinary goals. While there is intellectual work to be done inside the academy—what one might call "academic praxis"—there is also political praxis outside the academy.[12] If social change is to occur, gays, bisexuals, transgendered people, and lesbians of color cannot afford to be armchair theorists. Some of us need to be in the streets, in the trenches, enacting the quare theories that we construct in the "safety" of the academy. While keeping in mind that political theory and political action are not necessarily mutually exclusive, quare theorists must make theory work for its constituency. Although we share with our white queer peers sexual oppression, gays, lesbians, bisexuals, and transgendered people of color also share racial oppression with other members of our community. We cannot afford to abandon them simply because they are heterosexual. Cohen writes that "although engaged in heterosexual behavior," straight African Americans "have often found themselves outside the norms and values of dominant society. This position has most

often resulted in the suppression or negation or their legal, social, and physical relationships and rights" (["Punks"] 454). Quare studies must encourage strategic coalition building around laws and policies that have the potential to affect us across racial, sexual, and class divides. Quare studies must incorporate under its rubric a praxis related to the sites of public policy, family, church, and community. Therefore, in the tradition of radical black feminist critic Barbara Smith ("Toward"), I offer a manifesto that aligns black quare academic theory with political praxis.

We can do more in the realm of public policy. As Cohen so cogently argues in her groundbreaking book, *The Boundaries of Blackness*, we must intervene in the failure of the conservative black leadership to respond to the HIV/AIDS epidemic ravishing African American communities. Due to the growing number of African Americans infected with and contracting HIV, quare theorists must aid in the education and prevention of the spread of HIV as well as care for those who are suffering. This means more than engaging in volunteer work and participating in fund raising. It also means using our training as academics to deconstruct the way HIV/AIDS is discussed in the academy and in the medical profession. We must continue to do the important work of physically helping our brothers and sisters who are living with HIV and AIDS through outreach services and fundraising events, but we must also use our scholarly talents to combat racist and homophobic discourse that circulates in white as well as black communities. Ron Simmons, a black gay photographer and media critic who left academia to commit his life to those suffering with AIDS by forming the organization US Helping US, remains an important role model for how we can use both our academic credentials and our political praxis in the service of social change.

The goal of quare studies is to be specific and intentional in the dissemination and praxis of quare theory, committed to communicating and translating its political potentiality. Indeed, quare theory is "bi"-directional: it theorizes from bottom to top and top to bottom (pun intended!). This dialogical/dialectical relationship between theory and practice, the lettered and unlettered, ivory tower and front porch is crucial to a joint and sustained critique of hegemonic systems of oppression.

Given the relationship between the academy and the community, quare theorists must value and speak from what hooks refers to as "homeplace." According to hooks, homeplace "[is] the one site where one [can] freely confront the issue of humanization, where one [can] resist" (42). It is from homeplace that people of color live out the contradictions of our lives. Cutting across the lines of class and gender, homeplace provides a place from which to critique oppression. I do not wish to romanticize this site by dismissing the homophobia that circulates within homeplace or the contempt that some of us (of all sexual orientations) have for "home."[13] I am suggesting, rather, that in spite of these contradictions, homeplace is that site that first gave us the "equipment for living" (Burke 293) in a racist society, particularly since we, in all of our diversity, have always been a part of this homeplace: housekeepers, lawyers, seamstresses, hairdressers, activists, choir directors, professors, doctors, preachers, mill workers, mayors, nurses, truck drivers, delivery people, nosey neighbors, and (an embarrassed?) "etc." SNAP!.

Homeplace is also a site which quare praxis must critique. That is, we may seek refuge in homeplace as a marginally safe place to critique oppression outside its confines, but we must also deploy quare theory to address oppression within homeplace itself. One might begin, for instance, with the black church, which remains for some gays and lesbians, a sustaining site of spiritual affirmation, comfort, and artistic outlet. Quare studies cannot afford to dismiss, cavalierly, the role of the black church in quare lives. However, it must never fail to critique the black church's continual denial of gay and lesbian subjectivity. Our role within the black church is an important one. Those in the pulpit and those in the congregation should be challenged whenever they hide behind Romans and Leviticus to justify their homophobia. We must force the black church to name us and claim us if we are to obtain any liberation within our own communities.[14]

Regarding ideological and political conflicts in gay, lesbian, and transgendered communities of color, quare praxis must interrogate and negotiate the differences among our differences, including our political strategies for dealing with oppression and our politics of life choice and maintenance. Consequently, quare studies must also focus on interracial dating and the identity politics such couplings invoke. Writer Darieck Scott has courageously addressed this issue, but we need to continue to explore our own inner conflicts around our choices of sexual partners across racial lines. Additionally, quare studies should interrogate another contested area of identity politics: relations between "out" and "closeted" members of our community. Much of this work must be done not in the academy, but in our communities, in our churches, in our homes.

Unconvinced that queer studies is soon to change, I summon quare studies as an interventionist disciplinary project. Quare studies addresses the concerns and needs of gay, lesbian, bisexual, and transgendered people across issues of race, gender, class, and other subject positions. While attending to the discursive constitution of subjects, quare studies is also committed to theorizing the practice of everyday life. Because we exist in material bodies, we need a theory that speaks to that reality. Indeed, quare studies may breathe new life into our "dead" (or deadly) stratagems of survival.

. . .

NOTES

1. See Johnson, "SNAP! Culture" 125–128.
2. I have long known about the connection between African Americans and the Irish. As noted in the film *The Commitments*, "The Irish are the blacks of Europe." The connection is there—that is, at least until the Irish became "white." For a sustained discussion of how Irish emigrants obtained "white" racial privilege, see Ignatiev.
3. For more on "standpoint" theory, see Collins.

4. In *Bodies That Matter,* Judith Butler anticipates the contestability of "queer," noting that it excludes as much as it includes but that such a contested term may energize a new kind of political activism. She proposes that "[. . .] it may be that the critique of the term will initiate a resurgence of both feminist and anti-racist mobilization within lesbian and gay politics or open up new possibilities for coalitional alliances that do not presume that these constituencies are radically distinct from one another. The term will be revised, dispelled, rendered obsolete to the extent that it yields to the demands which resist the term precisely because of the exclusions by which it is mobilized" (228–29). To be sure, there are gay, bisexual, lesbian and transgendered people of color who embrace "queer." In my experience, however, those who embrace the term represent a small minority. At the "Black Queer Studies at the Millennium Conference" held at the University of North Carolina on April 7–9, 2000, for example, many of the conference attendees were disturbed by the organizers' choice of "queer" for the title of a conference on black sexuality. So ardent was their disapproval that it became a subject of debate during one of the panels.

5. See, for example, Hall and Gilroy, "'Race'."

6. I thank Michelé Barale for this insight.

7. While it is true that some white queer theorists are self-reflexive about their privilege and incorporate the works and experiences of gays, bisexuals, lesbians and transgendered people of color into their scholarship, this is not the norm. Paula Moya calls attention to how the theorizing of women of color is appropriated by postmodernist theorists: "[Judith] Butler extracts one sentence from [Cherríe] Moraga, buries it in a footnote, and then misreads it in order to justify her own inability to account for the complex interrelations that structure various forms of human identity" (133). David Bergman also offers a problematic reading of black gay fiction when he reads James Baldwin through the homophobic rhetoric of Eldridge Cleaver and theorizes that black communities are more homophobic than white ones (163–87). For other critiques of simplistic or dismissive readings of the works of gays, bisexuals, lesbians, and transgendered people of color see Ng, (Charles), and Namaste. One notable exception is Ruth Goldman's "Who is That *Queer* Queer," in which she, a white bisexual, calls other white queer theorists to task for their failure to theorize their whiteness: "[. . .] those of us who are white tend not to dwell on our race, perhaps because this would only serve to normalize us—reduce our queerness, if you will" (173).

8. For more on "strategic" essentialism, see: Case 1–12; de Lauretis; and Fuss 1–21.

9. For a sustained discussion of queer activists' disavowal of heterosexual political alliances, see Cohen, "Punks" 440–52.

10. For an analysis of Bessie Smith's explicitly lesbian blues songs, see Harrison 103–104.

11. See Riggs "Black Macho" and Johnson "SNAP!" and "Feeling."

12. I do not wish to suggest that the academy is not always already a politicized site. Rather, I only mean to suggest that the ways in which it is politicized are, in many instances, different from the ways in which nonacademic communities are politicized.

13. For a critique of the notion of "home" in the African American community vis-à-vis homophobia and sexism, see Clarke, Crenshaw, hooks, and Simmons.

14. For a sustained critique of homophobia in the black church, see Dyson 77–108.

REFERENCES

Anzaldúa, Gloria. "To(o) Queer the Writer: *Loca, escrita y chicana." Inversions: Writing by Dykes and Lesbians.* Ed. Betsy Warland. Vancouver: Press Gang, 1991. 249–259.

Baldwin, James. *Nobody Knows My Name: More Notes of a Native Son.* New York: Vintage, 1993.

Baldwin, James. *No Name in the Street*. New York: Dial, 1972.

Bergman, David. *Gaiety Transfigured: Gay Self-Representation in American Literature*. Madison: U of Wisconsin P, 1991.

Berlant, Lauren, and Michael Warner. "What Does Queer Theory Teach Us about X?" *PMLA* 110 (1995): 343–349.

Burke, Kenneth. *Philosophy of Literary Form*. Baton Rouge: Louisiana State UP, 1967.

Butler, Judith. *Bodies That Matter: On the Discursive Limits of "Sex."* New York: Routledge, 1993.

Butler, Judith. *Gender Trouble: Feminism and the Subversion of Identity*. New York: Routledge, 1990.

Case, Sue-Ellen. *The Domain Matrix: Performing Lesbian at the End of Print Culture*. Bloomington: Indiana UP, 1996.

(Charles), Helen. "'Queer Nigger': Theorizing 'White' Activism." *Activating Theory: Lesbian, Gay, Bisexual Politics*. Eds. Joseph Bistrow and Angelia R. Wilson. London: Lawrence and Wishart, 1993. 97–117.

Christian, Barbara. "The Race for Theory." *Cultural Critique* 6 (1985): 51–63.

Clarke, Cheryl. "The Failure to Transform: Homophobia in the Black Community." *Home Girls: A Black Feminist Anthology*. Ed. Barbara Smith. New York: Kitchen Table, 1983. 197–208.

Cohen, Cathy. *The Boundaries of Blackness: AIDS and the Breakdown of Black Politics*. Chicago: U of Chicago P, 1999.

Cohen, Cathy. "Punks, Bulldaggers, and Welfare Queens: The Radical Potential of Queer Politics?" *GLQ: A Journal of Lesbian & Gay Studies* 3 (1997): 437–465.

Collins, Patricia Hill. "The Social Construction of Black Feminist Thought." *Words of Fire: An Anthology of African-American Feminist Thought*. Ed. Beverly Guy-Sheftall. New York: New Press, 1995. 338–357.

The Commitments. Dir. Alan Parker. Lauren Films, 1991.

Crenshaw Kimberlé Williams. "Mapping the Margins: Intersectionality, Identity Politics, and Violence Against Women of Color." *Stanford Law Review* 43 (1991): 1241–99.

de Lauretis, Teresa. "The Essence of the Triangle, or Taking the Risk of Essentialism Seriously: Feminist Theory in Italy, the U.S. and Britain." *differences* 1.2 (1989): 3–37.

Diamond, Elin, ed. Introduction. *Performance & Cultural Politics*. New York: Routledge, 1996. 1–9.

Dyson, Michael Eric. "The Black Church and Sex." *Race Rules: Navigating the Color Line*. Reading, MA: Addison-Wesley, 1996. 77–108.

Foucault, Michel. *The History of Sexuality, Vol. 1*. Trans. Robert Hurley. New York: Random House, 1980.

Fuss, Diana. *Essentially Speaking: Feminism, Nature & Difference*. New York: Routledge, 1989.

Gilroy, Paul. "'Race', Class, and Agency." *There Ain't No Black in the Union Jack: The Cultural Politics of Race and Nation*. London: Hutchinson, 1987. 15–42.

Goldman, Ruth. "Who Is That *Queer* Queer?" *Queer Studies: A Lesbian, Gay, Bisexual and Transgender Anthology*. Eds. Brett Beemyn and Mickey Eliason. New York: NYU P, 1996. 169–182.

Hall, Stuart. "Subjects in History: Making Diasporic Identities." *The House That Race Built*. Ed. Wahneema Lubiano. New York: Pantheon, 1997. 289–299.

Harrison, Daphne Duval. *Black Pearls: Blues Queens of the 1920's*. New Brunswick: Rutgers UP, 1998.

Henderson, Mae. "*Speaking in Tongues*." *Feminist Theorize the Political*. Eds. Judith Butler and Joan W. Scott. New York: Routledge, 1992. 144–165.

hooks, bell. *Yearning*. Boston: South End, 1990.

Ignatiev, Noel. *How the Irish Became White*. New York: Routledge, 1995.

Johnson, E. Patrick. "Feeling the Spirit in the Dark: Expanding Notions of the Sacred in the African American Gay Community." 21 *Callaloo* (1998): 399–418.

Johnson, E. Patrick. "SNAP! Culture: A Different Kind of 'Reading'." *Text and Performance Quarterly* 3 (1995): 121–142.

Kelley, Robin D.G. "Looking to Get Paid: How Some Black Youth Put Culture to Work." *Yo Mama's Disfunktional!: Fighting the Culture Wars in Urban America*. Boston: Beacon, 1997. 43–77.

Lorde, Audre. *Sister Outsider*. Freedom, CA: Crossing, 1984.

Moraga, Cherríe, and Gloria Anzaldúa, eds. *This Bridge Called My Back: Writings by Radical Women of Color*. New York: Kitchen Table, 1983.

Moya, Paula M. L. "Postmodernism, 'Realism', and the Politics of Identity: Cherríe Moraga and Chicano Feminism." *Feminist Genealogies, Colonial Legacies, Democratic Futures*. Eds. M. Jacqui Alexander and Chandra Talpade Mohanty. New York: Routledge, 1997. 125–50.

Muñoz, José Esteban. *Disidentifications: Queers of Color and the Performance of Politics*. Minneapolis: U of Minnesota P, 1999.

Namaste, Ki. "'Tragic Misreadings': Queer Theory's Erasure of Transgender Identity." *Queer Studies: A Lesbian, Gay, Bisexual and Transgender Anthology*. Eds. Brett Beemyn and Mickey Eliason. New York: NYU P, 1996. 183–203.

Ng, Vivien. "Race Matters." *Lesbian and Gay Studies: A Critical Introduction*. Eds. Andy Medhurst and Sally R. Munt. London: Cassell. 215–231.

Patton, Cindy. "Performativity and Social Distinction: The End of AIDS Epidemiology." *Performativity and Performance*. Eds. Andrew Parker and Eve Kosofsky Sedgwick. New York: Routledge, 1995. 173–196.

Phelan, Shane. *Getting Specific*. Minneapolis: U of Minnesota P, 1994.

Riggs, Marlon. "Black Macho Revisited: Reflections of a SNAP! Queen." *Brother to Brother: New Writings by Black Gay Men*. Ed. Essex Hemphill. Boston: Alyson, 1991. 253–257.

Scott, Darieck. "Jungle Fever?: Black Gay Identity Politics, White Dick, and the Utopian Bedroom." *GLQ: A Journal of Lesbian & Gay Studies* 3 (1994): 299–32.

Sedgwick, Eve Kosofsky. "Queer and Now." *Tendencies*. Durham: Duke UP, 1993. 1–20.

Simmons, Ron. "Some Thoughts on the Issues Facing Black Gay Intellectuals." *Brother to Brother: New Writings by Black Gay Men*. Ed. Essex Hemphill. Boston: Alyson, 1991. 211–228.

Smith, Barbara. "Home." *Home Girls: A Black Feminist Anthology*. Ed. Barbara Smith. New York: Kitchen Table, 1983. 64–72.

Smith, Barbara. "Toward a Black Feminist Criticism." *All the Women Are White, All the Blacks Are Men, But Some of Us Are Brave*. Eds. Gloria T. Hull, Patricia Bell Scott, and Barbara Smith. Old Westbury, NY: Feminist Press, 1982. 157–175.

Smith, Cherry. "What Is This Thing Called Queer?" *Material Queer: A LesBiGay Cultural Studies Reader*. Ed. Donald Morton. Boulder: Westview, 1996. 277–285.

Strine, Mary. "Articulating Performance/Performativity: Disciplinary Tasks and the Contingencies of Practice." National Speech Communication Association Conference. San Diego, CA. November 1996.

Thomas, Calvin. "Straight with a Twist: Queer Theory and the Subject of Heterosexuality." *The Gay '90's: Disciplinary and Interdisciplinary Formations in Queer Studies*. Eds. Thomas Foster, Carol Siegel, and Ellen E. Berry. New York: NYU P, 1997. 83–115.

Turner, Victor. *The Anthropology of Performance*. New York: Performing Arts Journal [Publications], 1986.

Valente, Joseph. "Joyce's (Sexual) Choices: A Historical Overview." *Quare Joyce*. Ed. Joseph Valente. Ann Arbor: U of Michigan P, 1998. 1–18.

Walker, Alice. *In Search of Mothers' Gardens: Womanist Prose*. San Diego: Harcourt Brace Jovanovich, 1983.

Warner, Michael. Introduction. *Fear of a Queer Planet: Queer Politics and Social Theory*. Ed. Michael Warner. Minneapolis: U of Minnesota P, 1993. vii–xxxi.

Wilson, Angelia R. "Somewhere Over the Rainbow: Queer Translating." *Playing With Fire: Queer Politics, Queer Theories*. Ed. Shane Phelan. New York: Routledge, 1997. 99–111.

SUSAN STRYKER

7. TRANSGENDER STUDIES: QUEER THEORY'S EVIL TWIN

If queer theory was born of the union of sexuality studies and feminism, transgender studies can be considered queer theory's evil twin: it has the same parentage but willfully disrupts the privileged family narratives that favor sexual identity labels (like *gay, lesbian, bisexual,* and *heterosexual)* over the gender categories (like *man* and *woman)* that enable desire to take shape and find its aim.

In the first volume of *GLQ* I published my first academic article, "My Words to Victor Frankenstein above the Village of Chamounix: Performing Transgender Rage," an autobiographically inflected performance piece drawn from my experiences of coming out as a transsexual.[1] The article addressed four distinct theoretical moments. The first was Judith Butler's then recent, now paradigmatic linkage of gender with the notion of trouble. Gender's absence renders sexuality largely incoherent, yet gender refuses to be the stable foundation on which a system of sexuality can be theorized.[2] A critical reappraisal of transsexuality, I felt, promised a timely and significant contribution to the analysis of the intersection of gender and sexuality. The second moment was the appearance of Sandy Stone's "The 'Empire' Strikes Back: A Posttranssexual Manifesto," which pointedly criticized Janice G. Raymond's paranoiac *Transsexual Empire* and called on transsexual people to articulate new narratives of self that better expressed the authenticity of transgender experience.[3] I considered my article on transgender rage an explicit answer to that call. The third moment was Leslie Feinberg's little pamphlet, *Transgender Liberation.* Feinberg took a preexisting term, *transgender,* and invested it with new meaning, enabling it to become the name for Stone's theorized posttranssexualism.[4] Feinberg linked the drive to inhabit this newly envisioned space to a broader struggle for social justice. I saw myself as a fellow traveler. Finally, I perceived a tremendous utility, both political and theoretical, in the new concept of an antiessentialist, postidentitarian, strategically fluid "queerness." It was through participation in Queer Nation—particularly its San Francisco-based spin-off, Transgender Nation—that I sharpened my theoretical teeth on the practice of transsexuality.

When I came out as transsexual in 1992, I was acutely conscious, both experientially and intellectually, that transsexuals were considered abject creatures in most feminist and gay or lesbian contexts, yet I considered myself both feminist and lesbian. I saw *GLQ* as the leading vehicle for advancing the new queer theory, and I saw in queer theory a potential for attacking the antitranssexual moralism so unthinkingly embedded in most progressive analyses of gender and sexuality without resorting to a reactionary, homophobic, and misogynistic counteroffensive. I sought instead to dissolve and recast the ground that identity genders in the process of staking its tent. By denaturalizing and thus depriveleging nontransgender practices of embodiment and identification, and by simultaneously enacting a new narrative of the wedding of self and flesh, I intended to create new territories, both analytic and material, for a critically refigured transsexual practice. Embracing and identifying with the figure of Frankenstein's monster, claiming the transformative power of a return from abjection, felt like the right way to go.

Susan Stryker, "Transgender Studies: Queer Theory's Evil Twin under Thinking Sex/Thinking Gender," in *GLQ: A Journal of Lesbian and Gay Studies,* Volume 10, no. 2, pp. 212–215. Copyright, 2004, Duke University Press. All rights reserved. Republished by permission of the copyright holder, Duke University Press. www.dukeupress.edu.

Looking back a decade later, I see that in having chosen to speak as a famous literary monster, I not only found a potent voice through which to offer an early formulation of transgender theory but also situated myself (again, like Frankenstein's monster) in a drama of familial abandonment, a fantasy of revenge against those who had cast me out, and a yearning for personal redemption. I wanted to help define "queer" as a family to which transsexuals belonged. The queer vision that animated my life, and the lives of so many others in the brief historical moment of the early 1990s, held out the dazzling prospect of a compensatory, utopian reconfiguration of community. It seemed an anti-oedipal, ecstatic leap into a postmodern space of possibility in which the foundational containers of desire could be ruptured to release a raw erotic power that could be harnessed to a radical social agenda. That vision still takes my breath away.

A decade later, with another Bush in the White House and another war in the Persian Gulf, it is painfully apparent that the queer revolution of the early 1990s yielded, at best, only fragile and tenuous forms of liberal progress in certain sectors and did not radically transform society—and as in the broader world, so too in the academy. Queer theory has become an entrenched, though generally progressive, presence in higher education, but it has not realized the (admittedly utopian) potential I (perhaps naively) sensed there for a radical restructuring of our understanding of gender, particularly of minoritized and marginalized manifestations of gender, such as transsexuality. While queer studies remains the most hospitable place to undertake transgender work, all too often *queer* remains a code word for "gay" or "lesbian," and all too often transgender phenomena are misapprehended through a lens that privileges sexual orientation and sexual identity as the primary means of differing from heteronormativity.

Most disturbingly, "transgender" increasingly functions as the site in which to contain all gender trouble, thereby helping secure both homosexuality and heterosexuality as stable and normative categories of personhood. This has damaging, isolative political correlaries [*sic*]. It is the same developmental logic that transformed an antiassimilationist "queer" politics into a more palatable LGBT civil rights movement, with T reduced to merely another (easily detached) genre of sexual identity rather than perceived, like race

or class, as something that cuts across existing sexualities, revealing in often unexpected ways the means through which all identities achieve their specificities.

The field of transgender studies has taken shape over the past decade in the shadow of queer theory. Sometimes it has claimed its place in the queer family and offered an in-house critique, and sometimes it has angrily spurned its lineage and set out to make a home of its own. Either way, transgender studies is following its own trajectory and has the potential to address emerging problems in the critical study of gender and sexuality, identity, embodiment, and desire in ways that gay, lesbian, and queer studies have not always successfully managed. This seems particularly true of the ways that transgender studies resonate with disability studies and intersex studies, two other critical enterprises that investigate atypical forms of embodiment and subjectivity that do not readily reduce to heteronormativity, yet that largely fall outside the analytic framework of sexual identity that so dominates queer theory.

As globalization becomes an ever more inescapable context in which all our lives transpire, it is increasingly important to be sensitive to the ways that identities invested with the power of Euro-American privilege interact with non-Western identities. If the history and anthropology of gender and sexuality teach us anything, it is that human culture has created many ways of putting together bodies, subjectivities, social roles, and kinship structures—that vast apparatus for producing intelligible personhood that we call "gender." It is appallingly easy to reproduce the power structures of colonialism by subsuming non-Western configurations of personhood into Western constructs of sexuality and gender.

It would be misguided to propose transgender studies as queer theory for the global marketplace—that is, as an intellectual framework that is less inclined to export Western notions of sexual selves, less inclined to expropriate indigenous non-Western configurations of personhood. Transgender studies, too, is marked by its First World point of origin. But the critique it has offered to queer theory is becoming a point of departure for a lively conversation, involving many speakers from many locations, about the mutability and specificity of human lives and loves. There remains in that emerging dialogue a radical queer potential to realize.

NOTES

1. Susan Stryker, "My Words to Victor Frankenstein above the Village of Chamounix: Performing Transgender Rage," *GLQ* 1 (1994): 237–54.

2. Judith Butler, *Bodies That Matter: On the Discursive Limits of "Sex"* (New York: Rout-ledge, 1993).

3. Janice G. Raymond, *The Transsexual Empire: The Making of the She-Male* (Boston: Beacon, 1979); Sandy Stone, "The 'Empire' Strikes Back: A Posttranssexual Manifesto," in *Body Guards: The Cultural Politics of Gender Ambiguity,* ed. Julia Epstein and Kristina Straub (New York: Routledge, 1991), 280–304.

4. Leslie Feinberg, *Transgender Liberation: A Movement Whose Time Has Come* (New York: World View Forum, 1992).

CHANDRA TALPADE MOHANTY

8. TRANSNATIONAL FEMINIST CROSSINGS: ON NEOLIBERALISM AND RADICAL CRITIQUE

What happens to feminist scholarship and theory in our neoliberal academic culture? Have global and domestic shifts in social movement activism and feminist scholarly projects depoliticized antiracist, women-of-color, and transnational feminist intellectual projects? By considering how my own work has traveled, and what has been lost (and found) in translation into various contexts, I offer some thoughts about the effects of neoliberal, national-security-driven geopolitical landscapes and postmodern intellectual framings of transnational, intersectional feminist theorizing and solidarity work. Specifically, I suggest that the way my work has been adapted and developed within a few marginalized feminist scholarly and activist communities offers valuable lessons for all of us who are university-based feminists. It highlights the limitations of postmodernist feminist knowledge projects in the neoliberal academy.

. . .

Does postmodernism coupled with neoliberal knowledge economies in effect define a threshold of disappearance where one conceptual frame (systemic or intersectional) is quietly subsumed under and supplanted by another emerging frame, one that obscures crucial relations of power? In this essay, I explore a convergence between neoliberalism and postmodernism that depoliticizes radical theory (or insurgent knowledge as I prefer to call it). Coogan-Gehr's analysis of the tensions between a politics of territoriality (location and identity) and a politics of mobility (Foucault's notion of capillary politics) in US feminist scholarship on race is relevant to the discussion that follows.

NEOLIBERAL LANDSCAPES AND THE DEPOLITICIZATION OF ANTIRACIST FEMINIST THOUGHT

Neoliberalism has transformed material and ideological conditions in ways that have profound implications for radical critique and insurgent knowledges. Neoliberalism in the early twenty-first century is marked by market-based governance practices on the one hand (the privatization, commodification, and proliferation of difference) and authoritarian, national-security-driven penal state practices on the other. Thus, while neoliberal states facilitate mobility and cosmopolitanism (travel across borders) for some economically privileged communities, it is at the expense of the criminalization and incarceration (the holding in place) of impoverished communities.[1]

The past decade has witnessed dramatic cuts in public funding for education and increasing privatization of higher education around the world (see Hanhardt et al. 2010; Ayers and Ayers 2011). Julia Sudbury and Margo Okazawa-Rey (2009) argue that radical knowledges are domesticated by the neoliberal restructuring of higher education. As I suggest above, neoliberal intellectual culture may well constitute a threshold of disappearance for feminist, antiracist thought anchored in the radical social movements of the twentieth century. Radical theory can in fact become a commodity to be consumed; no longer seen as a product of activist scholarship or connected to emancipatory knowledge, it can circulate as a sign of prestige in an elitist, neoliberal landscape.

To trace this threshold of disappearance of antiracist feminist thought, what is needed is an analysis of

Chandra Mohanty, "Transnational Feminist Crossings: On Neoliberalism and Radical Critique," *Signs: Journal of Women in Culture and Society* 38:4 (2013): 967–991. © 2013 by The University of Chicago. All rights reserved.

neoliberalism and the knowledge economy that not only provides a critique of corporate rationality and labor practices in university settings and in the operation of state and transnational governing institutions but also addresses the impact of neoliberalism on social movements. Neoliberal governmentalities discursively construct a public domain denuded of power and histories of oppression, where market rationalities redefine democracy and collective responsibility is collapsed into individual characteristics (Giroux 2003). Such normative understandings of the public domain, where only the personal and the individual are recognizable and the political is no longer a contested domain, are indeed at the heart of "post" (feminist/race) discourses. For instance, what happens to the key feminist construct of "the personal is political" when the political (the collective public domain of politics) is reduced to the personal? Questions of oppression and exploitation as collective, systematic processes and institutions of rule that are gendered and raced have difficulty being heard when neoliberal narratives disallow the salience of collective experience or redefine this experience as a commodity to be consumed. If all experience is merely individual, and the social is always collapsed into the personal, feminist critique and radical theory appear irrelevant—unless they confront these discursive shifts.

Neoliberal discursive landscapes in the academy, and in state and transnational governance practices, are characterized by the privatization of the social justice commitments of post-1960s radical social movements and their attendant insurgent knowledges (originally institutionalized in women's and gender studies, race and ethnic studies, etc.). Privatizing commitments to race, class, and gender justice requires removing the social significance of racism, classism, or (hetero)sexism as institutionalized systems of power and inequality from the public domain, substituting individual prejudice and psychological dispositions or expressions of "hate" instead. This is a perfect example of a discursive shift, of a threshold of disappearance whereby critical feminist epistemological claims regarding experience, like "the personal is political," are transformed into privatized notions of individual experience. Here, political agency itself is redefined as an act of consumption, and I would argue that theory—feminist and/or antiracist—is trafficked as a

commodity disconnected from its activist moorings and social justice commitments (Giroux 2003).

The interwoven processes of privatization, consumption, and commodification of theory result in a politics of representation or a politics of presence disconnected from the power and political economy of rule. The epistemological and methodological claims of feminist and antiracist thought are transformed into a privatized politics of representation, disconnected from systematic critique and materialist histories of colonialism, capitalism, and heteropatriarchy (what Coogan-Gehr [2011] calls a politics of territoriality). This representational, discursive politics of gender, race, class, sexuality, and nation, disconnected from its materialist moorings, can thus be consumed more easily in institutional spaces. The complex political economy focus (highlighting power and hierarchy) of much feminist, antiracist theory, for instance, is either reduced to a politics of representation/presence/multiculturalism or seen as irrelevant in the context of a so-called postrace/postfeminist society. Thus, race and gender justice commitments, among others, are recoded as a politics of presence (or benign representation of various differences) in neoliberal universities.

. . .

FEMINISM ACROSS BORDERS: GEOPOLITICAL TRANSLATIONS

Undertaken to promote the objectives of gender, class, and racial justice, my scholarship and activism over the past three decades have been read and understood in multiple ways, varying with the material conditions and contexts of their reception.[2] The uses and translations of my work as it is embodied in particular sites, communities, and feminist projects illustrates both the productive adaptations of decolonizing antiracist feminist thought and the pitfalls of the convergence of postmodernist feminism and neoliberal logics in the academy.

Two essays of mine, in particular, have crossed multiple borders: "Under Western Eyes: Feminist Scholarship and Colonial Discourses" (Mohanty 1986) and "'Under Western Eyes' Revisited: Feminist Solidarity through Anticapitalist Struggles" (Mohanty 2003b). Reflecting on place-based reception and critical framing of this work illuminates the traffic in theory—the politics (and commodification) of theoretical travel across social/cultural and national borders.

The transition from "Under Western Eyes" to '"Under Western Eyes' Revisited" marks my explicit engagement with the rise of neoliberalism and the normalization of corporate practices in the academy. The circulation of these works in various geopolitical locales reveals feminist complicity in imperial and capitalist/neoliberal projects and points to the limitations of knowledge-making projects in academia. It also signals the continued relevance of systemic analyses of decolonization and resistance in transnational feminist praxis. "Under Western Eyes" was written from my location as a part-time teacher in the US academy, as an immigrant "third-world" woman at an elite institution. Written fifteen years later, '"Under Western Eyes' Revisited" marked a shift in my own location to a full professor of women's and gender studies in a less elite but still predominantly white liberal arts college. "Under Western Eyes" is an intervention explicitly addressing the colonizing gestures of feminist scholarship about women in the third world. It was written from within the context of a vibrant political and scholarly community of radical antiracist, transnational US women of color and a large and growing body of critical work by feminists from the global South. The essay was anchored in the experience of marginalization (and colonization) of the knowledges and intellectual agency of immigrant women of color in the United States. It was intended both as a critique of the universalizing and colonizing tendencies of feminist theorizing and as a methodological intervention arguing for historicizing and contextualizing feminist scholarship. "Under Western Eyes" had a clear political purpose and was written in collective solidarity with antiracist, cross-cultural feminist activist projects in the 1980s.

The publication journey of "Under Western Eyes" is instructive. It was first rejected by *Signs*. One external reader complained, "why did you waste my time on this essay? It says nothing of value!"[3] The essay was subsequently published in 1986 (in an issue dated 1984) by the Left literary/cultural studies journal *boundary 2*. It was immediately picked up and reprinted by the British feminist journal *Feminist Review* and simultaneously translated and published in German and Dutch feminist journals. "Under Western Eyes"

thus made its way into the US feminist academy via Europe. Since its publication in 1986, "Under Western Eyes" has been reprinted in numerous anthologies of feminist, postcolonial, area, development, and cultural studies, and translated into more than twenty Asian, Latin American, and Western and Eastern European languages. In the past twenty-five years, this essay has traveled widely across disciplinary, national, and linguistic borders. It is used as required reading in numerous disciplines from anthropology and international relations to literary and visual studies.

In contrast to "Under Western Eyes," '"Under Western Eyes' Revisited" marks not only a shift in my own location in the US academy but also a different intellectual/political moment of knowledge production as neoliberalism transformed material conditions in higher education in the United States and elsewhere in the world. While my status as a professor of women's and gender studies with access to some institutional power and an international audience was key to the way '"Under Western Eyes' Revisited" was received and the way it traveled across borders (this time *Signs* solicited the essay), the essay was also written as an intervention into cross-cultural feminist thought. It was written in part to respond to the ways that my previous work (including "Under Western Eyes"), had been absorbed within a hegemonic intellectual culture of postmodernism, primarily by rewriting the materialist basis of the discursive analysis of power and the call for attentiveness to specificity, historicity, and difference among women in marginalized communities into what was described, oddly enough, as support for a theoretical and methodological emphasis on "the local" and "the particular"—hence, against all forms of generalization. This particular misreading of my work ignored the materialist emphasis on a "common context of struggle" (Mohanty 2003b, 507) and undermined the possibility of solidarity across differences.[4]

As in earlier work, '"Under Western Eyes' Revisited" focuses on decolonizing feminism, a politics of difference and commonality, and specifying, historicizing, and connecting feminist struggles. The problematic reading of my earlier work meant that the material and historical continuities that were important to my argument in "Under Western Eyes" were lost in translation—as was the deep critique of Western feminist theory that called for a rethinking of how cross-cultural work is done in the context of racist and colonialist legacies. "'Under Western Eyes' Revisited" was written to address these losses and the depoliticization of my original project, as well as to model a form of feminist theorizing in the early twenty-first century—a feminist anticapitalist critique that constitutes a radical intervention in a neoliberal academic culture and corporate academy, advanced in conjunction with the rise of antiglobalization solidarity movements around the world.

While "Under Western Eyes" was written from a personal and institutional space of colonization and marginalization within Western feminism and the US academy, "'Under Western Eyes' Revisited" was written from the experience of struggling against neoliberal culture and postmodernist hegemony within the feminist theory establishment and women's and gender studies departments. I consider both essays to be oppositional gestures in feminist knowledge production in the United States. In 2003, "'Under Western Eyes' Revisited" was also an insurgent knowledge practice that claimed anticapitalist and anti-imperialist feminist space in the center of the corporate academy and contested the neoliberal appropriation of gender, race/ethnicity, and sexuality as "disciplined" objects of study. I was not claiming a voice for "third-world women" in the academy, since that project was already underway in the larger antiracist feminist/women-of-color communities, and it was already being domesticated by a neoliberal intellectual culture.

My intentions as an author, however, cannot control how my works are read. The final section of this essay traces the way my work has been taken up in different sites as it travels across borders. "Under Western Eyes" has resonated with readers who encounter the essay as immigrant, third-world women and women of color in academic and activist spaces where the narrow experiential politics of knowledge that "Under Western Eyes" critiques has significance. "'Under Western Eyes' Revisited" has been embraced by intellectuals, teachers, and activists in anticapitalist, antiglobalization, materialist feminist communities. Yet both essays have also been misread. In the context of the neoliberal, postmodern/poststructural capillary politics of mobility, both have been read too quickly as essentialist and reductive. In the end, however, these travels also expose the limits of the "posts" as knowledge-making projects.

MAPPING PLACE-BASED KNOWLEDGES AND THE TRAFFIC IN FEMINIST THOUGHT

Arturo Escobar (2008) suggests that theories of difference travel between place-based meanings and enactments of Eurocentric/colonial globality. Discussing the geopolitics of knowledge, Escobar rightly says that "the dynamic of an imperial globality and its regime of coloniality" is "one of the most salient features of the modern colonial world system in the early twenty-first century" (Escobar 2008,4). Brazilian feminist Claudia de Lima Costa (2006) frames the geopolitics of knowledge in terms of the uneven migration of analytical categories across borders, a process that causes some knowledge to be "lost in translation" as it travels to different hemispheres. Claiming that analytical categories have different rationalities depending on place, Costa looks at the traffic in theory by examining the ways that foundational feminist concepts like gender and women of color have traveled between US Latina and Latin American feminist spaces. Escobar and Costa both draw attention to North-South historical divides and to the colonial misappropriations and faulty translations of place-based theories of difference. Both suggest the need to reflect on the traffic in theory in a neoliberal landscape governed by global coloniality and Eurocentric globality. Writing about "traveling theories," Richa Nagar (2002) raises questions about accountability and political commitments in the theoretical languages and frames mobilized by transnational feminist scholars.[5]

Drawing on these ideas about the relation of place-based knowledge practices and cross-border traffic in theory, I explore below the way my ideas are read, understood, and utilized in Sweden, Mexico, and Palestine. In each space, the work is available in English and in translation (Swedish, Spanish, and Arabic). Although my work has traveled to other sites, I have chosen to focus on these locations because I can draw on multiple levels of engagement and collaboration with colleagues in these spaces. Thus, I can address questions of translation and travel of concepts as well as my own accountability to the ideas and communities I work with.[6] At each site, I begin with a brief discussion of the impact of neoliberalism and global coloniality on the knowledge economy and gender justice commitments and then explore the way my work is utilized by feminist colleagues engaged in struggles for gender, class, and racial justice in their own local/global contexts. The discussion of my work as it is taken up by activist and academic feminists in these sites indicates why systemic analyses of decolonization are so important for feminist communities—across borders.

Sweden is an interesting instance of neoliberal gender entanglements. Sweden is touted as one of the most progressive countries in terms of gender equity policy, and Swedish gender discourse is an example of close links between the state and grassroots and academic feminists (Lykke 2004; Liinason 2006, 2010, 2011). Since the 1990s, women's and gender studies projects and the equal opportunity policies of the Swedish state have been quite closely linked. Mia Liinason argues that the concept of gender is reproduced to underwrite a progressive success story (gender equality) of the nation. Similarly, Nina Lykke, Christine Michel, and Maria Puig de la Bellacasa (2001) have argued that since the 1990s, European Union policies have provided political and economic legitimation of gender equality at the national level, thus weaving the institutionalization of women's and gender studies together with national gender equality projects. The impact of neoliberalism on women's and gender studies programs in Europe has entailed a shift from radical feminist critique to an emphasis on policy-oriented work that produces "equal opportunity experts" (115).

In recent decades the development of antiracist and postcolonial feminist thought in Sweden (de los Reyes, Mulinari, and Molina 2002; Mulinari and Räthzel 2007) has led to pathbreaking scholarship on the racial and class parameters of Swedish "gender equality." Diana Mulinari and her colleagues (2007) draw on constructs of intersectionality and postcolonial feminism to anchor studies in the field of postcolonial Nordic feminism. These studies investigate notions of Nordic whiteness, exploring immigration policies and the centrality of race and ethnicity to the public landscape. The Swedish feminist debate on intersectionality and postcolonial feminism is both vibrant and multidimensional. For this reason, I found

it particularly interesting to look at how my work has been engaged and the struggles it seems to have made possible during a period when neoliberalism has gained purchase in the Swedish state, academia, and grassroots feminist movements.

Feminism without Borders was translated into Swedish in 2007. I can only track citations to the work in English (a major limitation, I admit), so I asked antiracist, postcolonial feminist scholar Diana Mulinari some direct questions about the impact of my work in Sweden.[7] Mulinari's assessment suggests that the constructs and theoretical/methodological aspects of my work, which have been utilized productively, include the critique of a Eurocentric and colonizing discourse of Western feminist theory, the significance of race and class intersectionality, the politics of location in the struggles of women in the global South and women of color in the United States (women-of-color epistemology), and the anticapitalist feminist analysis and notion of solidarity across borders. According to Mulinari, these themes have resonated in the academy, in art and cultural production, and in antiracist activism.[8]

Yet Mulinari also identified "misreadings" of my work that occur "through processes of appropriation . . . after acknowledging Mohanty in terms of a totemic symbol, (despite everything) 'the center,' (white) authors continue the doing of whiteness as usual, seldom analyzing the lack of women of color within the dynamics of knowledge production."[9] Mulinari's astute observation sheds light on the impact of neoliberalism on antiracist feminist projects, illuminating the appropriation of my work through a citational politics (use of Mohanty as "a totemic symbol"), a rhetorical gesture disconnected from the systemic and materialist analysis of power. Thus, even as my work has had a significant impact in Swedish intellectual, cultural, and activist circles, Mulinari charts an "appropriation." By "doing . . . whiteness as usual," hegemonic feminist knowledge production traffics antiracist feminist scholarship across borders, domesticating women-of-color epistemology in ways that either erase or assimilate it into a Eurocentric feminist globality. This is a powerful example of a representational politics characteristic of neoliberal landscapes that manages to erase the fundamental theoretical and methodological challenge of decolonization, which is central to my work.

Feminist scholarship in Latin America reveals different aspects of the limits and possibilities of traveling theories. Claudia de Lima Costa's work (2000, 2006) first introduced me to a discussion of what is "lost and found" in the translation of feminist theory across borders. Costa argues that the traffic in theory and the global export of feminist concepts across borders must be understood in terms of dominant and subordinate institutional configurations and historiographies across the North/South divide. Although Costa focuses specifically on US Latina and Latin American feminist translations, the theoretical points she makes about the potential untranslatability of certain concepts like women of color and the uneven migration of foundational concepts like gender are important considerations in understanding how my own work crosses geopolitical intellectual spaces. Costa's discussion of the way "gender" replaces "feminism" in the Brazilian academy is echoed in Liinason's (2010) analysis of how "gender" replaces "women" in the Swedish context. Both indicate the assimilation and domestication of feminism in neoliberal academic contexts. Focusing specifically on Ecuador and Brazil, Lynne Phillips and Sally Cole (2009) describe two disparate "translations" of feminism in the era of late neoliberalism, one from above and one from below (187). "UN-orbit" feminism is an approach toward gender equality embedded in systematic proposal-based global agendas (187). "Another-world" feminism is anchored in a decentralized, collaborative, diverse antiglobalization movement (187). Each of these accounts identifies contexts in which there are both faithful translations of insurgent knowledges and distorting appropriations.

In the Mexican context, scholars such as R. Aída Hernández Castillo (2002, 2010), Anna Sampaio (2004), and Michelle Téllez (2008) have deployed my work to foreground the agency of poor and indigenous women, drawing on notions of oppositional consciousness anchored in the lives of some of the most marginalized communities of women to suggest possibilities for feminist solidarity and alliance across borders.[10] In addition, they have used the notion of discursive colonialism to critique hegemonic Mexican feminism from the epistemological space of indigenous women in Mexico. As Hernández Castillo notes, my work has been particularly useful in developing critiques of hegemonic urban feminism:

> [Mohanty's] critique of the discursive colonialism of feminism has been applied to the strategies of hegemonic urban feminism towards indigenous women.... The concept of discursive colonialism has been used to refer to the power effect that the [representation] of indigenous and Afro-Latina women [as victims] can have in the lives and struggles of these groups. Also the concept of transcultural feminist work and the politics of solidarity has been used to reflect about the need to create links and alliances between different women in this difficult historical moment of militarization (in the name of the anti-drug war) and criminalization of social movements.
>
> Chandra Mohanty's theoretical-political work has contributed to the development of an indigenous women thought that is questioning ethnocentric visions of academic and political feminism in Mexico and its difficulty understanding evidence that subordination and gender inequality are not isolated, but intersect with ethnic exclusion, class, race and religion, etc. We could say that [her work] has decentered hegemonic conceptions of gender contributing to the reconceptualization of the concept of gender as a multidimensional category. Maya intellectuals from Guatemala in dialog with [Mohanty's] work are calling for recognition that there are multiple ways to articulate identities and gender projects within the constellation of actors and movements of a diverse and unequal Latin America.[11]

Hernández Castillo (rightly) suggests that an adequate critique of capitalism in the Latin American context must also engage a discussion of the globalization of the penal state. And she pinpoints particular contexts in which misreadings of my work occur: "Some urban Mexican feminists think that the first article generalizes 'white, urban feminism,' repeating the same mistakes that the article criticizes by homogenizing academic feminism."[12] This critique of the homogenization of academic feminism is anchored in a familiar postmodernist argument where "differences within" always trump critical analyses of dominant discourses, leading to a refusal to identify the existence of a hegemonic feminism that has systematic effects on marginalized communities. Thus, the very aspects of my work that are useful to indigenous and Maya feminist intellectuals in identifying discursive colonialism in Mexican academic and political feminism and in calling for the self-representation of indigenous women are dismissed by a critique that refuses to acknowledge its own hegemonic will to power in the neoliberal postmodern culture of Mexican feminism and the Latin American academy. Within privileged circles, my critique of the power of hegemonic feminism from the epistemological space of marginalized communities of women is misread as a representational politics focused primarily on differences within academic feminism. While those involved in the analysis of power and the systemic demystification of global capitalist and neocolonial processes from the epistemic location of poor and marginalized communities of women get me right, hegemonic versions of feminism, invested in privilege, tend to misread my work. These patterns are also evident in the Palestinian context, to which I turn now.

Neoliberalism is felt acutely in the context of the Palestinian women's movement. Given colonial occupation and the urgency of a national liberation struggle, many Palestinian feminist scholar-activists like Islah Jad (2007, 2009) and Eileen Kuttab (2008, 2010; see also Johnson and Kuttab 2001) call attention to the NGO-ization of the Palestinian women's movement post-Oslo. Since the first intifada, the impact of neoliberalism and colonial occupation have led to a dependency on donor-driven NGO funding, engendering a professionalization of social movements. Jad (2007) argues that this NGO-ization has led to the co-optation of grassroots social movements that posed a direct challenge to the occupation, opting instead for issue-based policy changes. Kuttab (2008, 2010) also explores the post-Oslo shaping of Palestinian feminism by neoliberal global frameworks, suggesting that since the 1990s, professionalized feminist NGOs have shifted the local focus from the intertwining of gender and national liberation to an international gender equity focus. According to Jad, it is in this context of depoliticization and professionalization of grassroots feminist struggles that my work entered the Palestinian intellectual/political feminist community:

> Your work came to Palestine in a moment where the discourse of "peace negotiation as the only option" was starting to prevail after the first Palestinian

popular uprising in 1987. Your work helped a great deal to deconstruct this hegemonic discourse that was working to marginalize what can be called "a home grown feminism" not driven by new liberal and universal discourse on women's rights. Your work was a cornerstone that helped us to defend our own notion of "militant feminism" that seeks to liberate the country and women in the same time.

> I think it deconstructed once and for all the notion of "sisterhood is global." [Instead] you founded "sisterhood" on the basis of solidarity and resistance to empire and to global capital, [reversing a tendency to see] contemporary feminism as "apolitical" and narrowly focused on "women" in isolation from their context.[13]

Unlike Mulinari and Hernández Castillo, Jad says categorically that my work "was not misread at all by us here; on the contrary it gave us a huge energy for reclaiming our 'militant feminism' and it helped a great deal to discredit the 'peace negotiation' camp that worked hard with donor funding to 'bring Israeli and Palestinian women' to build peace, assuming that feminism per se is capable to do wonders. Your work brought us back the spirit of resistance as the basis for solidarity."[14] Here again, Jad's assessment of the impact of my work suggests that the migration of concepts like discursive colonization; anticapitalist, anti-imperialist feminism; and solidarity based on mutuality and accountability is most significant in the Palestinian context. Indeed, Jad concurs with Mulinari and Hernández Castillo that the most important contribution of my work lies in the decolonization of knowledge, the politics of differences and commonality, and historicizing and specifying women's struggles and identities in the context of anticolonial, anticapitalist struggles within a neoliberal global culture.

Situating my work in the context of powerful divisions within transnational feminist praxis, Mulinari, Hernández Castillo, and Jad perceive my work as a critical intervention against hegemonic academic/political feminist formations. It creates a discursive space in which to decolonize feminist hegemonies by according epistemic privilege to the most marginalized communities of women. Thus, all three scholar-activists develop, in their own contexts, one of the central theoretical and methodological points of my work—the focus on a decolonization of feminist scholarship and theory and on women-of-color epistemology. Thus, this women-of-color epistemology inserts questions of racialization and the politics pertaining to racial/ethnic immigrant women into Nordic and Swedish feminist discourses, questions of indigenous women's struggles and agency into Latin American feminist engagements, and questions of Palestinian feminist militancy and agency into discourses of peace and reconciliation in the Israeli/Palestinian feminist context.[15] Each identifies systemic analyses of domination and resistance as key to radical feminist praxis—racism and anticapitalism/labor movements (Sweden), colonialism and racism/indigenous agency (Mexico), and colonialism/militant indigenous feminism (Palestine). It is significant that the communities that find my work useful in all three spaces—immigrant, indigenous, women of color—are mirrored in the United States as well, once again emphasizing the significance of systematic analysis of colonization and resistance while signaling the limits of the "post."[16]

Yet it is precisely the power of decolonizing feminist thought, grounded in women-of-color epistemology and engaging in systemic analysis, that global coloniality seeks to suppress. I began this essay with a discussion of neoliberal intellectual landscapes and the privatization and depoliticization of gender and racial justice commitments through the domestication of feminist thought in state and transnational governance practices, in academic/institutional cultures, and in the transformation of social movements into donor-driven social contracts. One of the primary aspects of this discussion was the privatization of social divisions and the individualization of experience—the collapse of notions of collectivity into the personal and the transformation of power and political agency into acts of consumption.[17]

As this brief examination of divergent receptions of my work in hegemonic and counterhegemonic sites makes clear, there is a threshold of disappearance of intersectional, systemic antiracist feminist projects within these neoliberal intellectual landscapes. Indiscriminately extending an overly general postmodernist skepticism to all social and political theory would serve the neoliberal agenda very well.[18] The neoliberal privatization and domestication of social justice commitments can go hand in hand with the postmodernist/poststructuralist dissolution of the systemic critiques of structures and institutions evident in intersectional, transnational materialist feminist engagements. This compromising of our politics reminds us that it is always important to turn the critique of privilege on ourselves. The dissolving of the systemic analyses of women of color and transnational feminist projects into purely discursive (representational) analyses of ruptures, fluidity, and discontinuities symptomatic of poststructural critique contributes to a threshold of disappearance of materialist antiracist feminist projects that target the state and other governing institutions. It is this danger of the appropriation of radical women of color and transnational feminist projects that should be of deep concern to us all.

The discussion of the travel and translation of my own work suggests the continuing importance of systemic analyses in radical antiracist feminist projects. It also points to the limits of knowledge projects in neoliberal academies. What would it mean to be attentive to the politics of activist feminist communities in different sites in the global South and North as they imagine and create cross-border feminist solidarities anchored in struggles on the ground? How would academic feminist projects be changed if we were accountable to activist/academic communities like the ones identified by Mulinari, Hernández Castillo, and Jad? I believe we need to return to the radical feminist politics of the contextual as both local and structural and to the collectivity that is being defined out of existence by privatization projects. I think we need to recommit to insurgent knowledges and the complex politics of antiracist, anti-imperialist feminisms.

NOTES

1. See Sampaio (2004), Davis and Mendieta (2005), Harvey (2005), and Sudbury (2005) for analyses of the links between neoliberalism, incarceration, criminalization, and new social movements.

2. For a sampling of critiques and responses to my work, see Marchand and Parpart (1995), Saliba (1995), Okin (1998), Clark (2002), Mendoza (2002), McLaughlin (2004), Ayotte and Husain (2005), Gupta (2006), Moallem (2006), Bradford (2007), and Mama (2009).

3. It is interesting to note that *Signs* reviewed "Under Western Eyes" during early to mid-1980s, a period described by Coogan-Gehr (2011) as representing an example of a "threshold of disappearance" (89) of the epistemological and methodological contributions of US Black feminists within feminist scholarship.

4. Scholars like Kevin Ayotte and Mary Husain (2005), Jyotsna Agnihotri Gupta (2006), and Chao-Ju Chen (2007), on the other hand, draw specifically on the connections between specificity and generalization, on the notions of solidarity across difference and the politics of accountability.

5. See also Alvarez (2000).

6. I draw on scholarly texts as well as personal communication with feminist scholars in all three sites, posing a series of questions to a key feminist colleague in each site. These are colleagues located within intellectual/activist communities I hold myself accountable to, communities that in fact are a part of the transnational, antiracist, decolonizing feminist project within which I situate myself. Clearly responses from single individuals do not constitute systematic research, but they do provide an embodied and horizontal dialogue across borders that is an important site of knowledge. These exchanges also answer a crucial question that can only be asked and answered directly, that is, the struggles my work furthers in these three sites.

7. I asked similar questions to feminist colleagues in Mexico (R. Aída Hernández Castillo) and Palestine (Islah Jad): "Can you describe briefly how you think my work is read in Sweden/Mexico/Palestine? What constructs/formulations/ideas/theories are most useful? What interventions (if any) into hegemonic discourses does my work make possible? What limitations can you identify in terms of how my work gets translated into a Swedish/Mexican/Palestinian context? How is/can it be misread?"

8. I believe it is worth quoting Mulinari at length since her voice represents a particular locus of struggle:

> "Under Western Eyes" . . . is not only acknowledged as a pathbreaking intervention, it has functioned as a basis for the analysis of how Eurocentric representations of "other women" are at play in topics going from social policy to the media in Sweden and in Scandinavia. Nearly all the works that take a critical approach towards the category of "race" frame their analysis in the arguments developed in Mohanty's article. Important to underline is that the article has had an impact that goes beyond feminist academic circles.. . .
>
> . . . Mohanty's work has in different ways made it nearly impossible to discuss gender without engaging in an intersectional analysis of the different axes of power inscribed in gendered identities with special emphasis on the category of "race." . . . *Third World Women and the Politics of Feminism* puts the Global South in general and women in particular at the center of the doing of (feminist) theory and has broken new ground regarding the location and the position of Southern feminisms.
>
> *Feminism without Borders* has had an impact not only among postcolonial, antiracist scholars but also on scholars exploring issues of social justice and solidarity. These new developments in her scholarship have strongly contributed to creating a bridge between postcolonial theory and labor studies and between critical development studies and ethnic/racial studies. Mohanty's focus and emphasis on labor makes her work unique among

postcolonial scholars, and this focus has been fruitful to introduce and to establish feminist postcolonial analysis in labor and organization studies. (E-mail exchange between Diana Mulinari and author, November 5, 2011.)

9. Ibid.
10. Hernandez Castillo writes regarding the impact of "Under Western Eyes" for indigenous women's resistance,

[Mohanty's] texts were translated and started to circulate broadly in a historical context in which indigenous autonomic demands for constitutional reforms opened a debate about how the recognition of collective rights and self-determination for indigenous peoples could endanger indigenous women's rights. In this context an important sector of the hegemonic feminist movement opposed the recognition of autonomous indigenous rights in the name of women's rights, using racist discourses against indigenous cultures and representing indigenous women only as victims of their patriarchal traditions. In this debate, indigenous women activists rejected the feminist representation of their cultures and denounced the colonial effect of these political and academic discourses. Some indigenous intellectuals started to use Chandra Mohanty's work to criticize the colonial effect that the victimization of indigenous women could have in their lives and struggles. At the same time the texts were used in several seminars organized by indigenous women in Guatemala, in which the subject of the decolonization of the Guatemalan academia was discussed. Important Maya intellectuals [such] as Aura Cumes, Emma Chirix, and Gladys Tzul have used Mohanty's texts to write about discursive colonialism and the need for new strategies of self-representation. (E-mail exchange between R. Aida Hernandez Castillo and author, November 18, 2011.)

11. Ibid.
12. Ibid.
13. E-mail exchange between Islah Jad and author, November 6, 2011.
14. Ibid.
15. This is in contrast to Moallem's (2006) critique of a modernist feminist internationalist agenda (under which my work is subsumed); there are no "others" to be rescued or centered in these articulations of my work.
16. See, especially, discussions of my work in Saliba (1995), Clark (2002), Ayotte and Husain (2005), Gupta (2006), and Mama (2009).
17. For useful discussions of postfeminism, neoliberalism, and the knowledge economy, see Larner (1995), Hall and Rodriguez (2003), Staunæs (2003), Braidotti (2005), Davies, Gottsche, and Bansel (2006), Genz (2006), Shope (2006), Choudry (2007), Feigenbaum (2007), McRobbie (2007), and McClennen (2008–9).
18. I have made similar critiques of postmodern skepticism elsewhere. See Alexander and Mohanty (1997, xvii–xviii; 2010) and Mohanty (2003b, 504–5; 2011).

REFERENCES

Alexander, M. Jacqui, and Chandra Talpade Mohanty. 1997. "Introduction: Genealogies, Legacies, Movements." In *Feminist Genealogies, Colonial Legacies, and Democratic Futures*, xiii–xlii. New York: Routledge.

Alexander, M. Jacqui, and Chandra Talpade Mohanty. 2010. "Cartographies of Knowledge and Power: Transnational Feminism as Radical Praxis." In *Critical Transnational Feminist Practice*, ed. Amanda Lock Swarr and Richa Nagar, 23–45. Albany, NY: SUNY Press.

Alvarez, Sonia E. 2000. "Translating the Global: Effects of Transnational Organizing on Local Feminist Discourses and Practices in Latin America." *Meridians* 1(1): 29–67.

Ayers, William, and Rick Ayers, eds. 2011. "Education under Fire: The U.S. Corporate Attack on Teachers, Students, and Schools." Special issue, *Monthly Review* 63, no. 3.

Ayotte, Kevin J., and Mary E. Husain. 2005. "Securing Afghan Women: Neocolonialism, Epistemic Violence, and the Rhetoric of the Veil." *NWSA Journal* 17(3):112–33.

Bradford, Clare. 2007. "Representing Islam: Female Subjects in Suzanne Fisher Staples's Novels." *Children's Literature Association Quarterly* 42(1):47–62.

Braidotti, Rosi. 2005. "A Critical Cartography of Feminist Post-postmodernism." *Australian Feminist Studies* 20(47):169–80.

Chen, Chao-Ju. 2007. "The Difference That Differences Make: Asian Feminism and the Politics of Difference." *Asian Journal of Women's Studies* 13(3):7–36.

Choudry, Aziz. 2007. "Transnational Activist Coalition Politics and the De/Colonization of Pedagogies of Mobilization: Learning from Anti-neoliberal Indigenous Movement Articulations." *International Education* 37(1):97–112, 133.

Clark, Roger. 2002. "Why All the Counting? Feminist Social Science Research on Children's Literature." *Children's Literature in Education* 33(4):285–95.

Coogan-Gehr, Kelly. 2011. "The Politics of Race in U.S. Feminist Scholarship: An Archeology." *Signs: Journal of Women in Culture and Society* 37(1):83–108.

Costa, Claudia de Lima. 2000. "Being Here and Writing There: Gender and the Politics of Translation in a Brazilian Landscape." *Signs* 25(3):727–60.

Costa, Claudia de Lima. 2006. "Lost (and Found?) in Translation: Feminisms in Hemispheric Dialogue." *Latino Studies*: 4(1–2):62–78.

Davies, Bronwyn, Michael Gottsche, and Peter Bansel. 2006. "The Rise and Fall of the Neo-liberal University." *European Journal of Education* 41(2):305–19.

Davis, Angela, and Eduardo Mendieta. 2005. *Abolition Democracy: Beyond Empire, Prisons, and Torture*. New York: Seven Stories.

De los Reyes, Paulina, Irene Molina, and Diana Mulinari. 2002. *Maktens olika förklädnader. Kön, Klass och etnicitet i det postkoloniala Sverige* [The various guises of power: Gender, class, and ethnicity in postcolonial Sweden]. Stockholm: Atlas.

Escobar, Arturo. 2008. *Territories of Difference: Place, Movements, Life*, Redes. Durham, NC: Duke University Press.

Feigenbaum, Anna. 2007. "The Teachable Moment: Feminist Pedagogy and the Neoliberal Classroom." *Review of Education, Pedagogy, and Cultural Studies* 29(4): 337–49.

Foucault, Michel. 1969. *The Archaeology of Knowledge*. New York: Routledge.

Genz, Stéphanie. 2006. "Third Way/ve: The Politics of Postfeminism." *Feminist Theory* 7(3):333–53.

Giroux, Henry. 2003. "Spectacles of Race and Pedagogies of Denial: Anti-Black Racist Pedagogy under the Reign of Neoliberalism." *Communication Education* 52(3/4):191–211.

Gupta, Jyotsna Agnihotri. 2006. "Towards Transnational Feminisms: Some Reflections and Concerns in Relation to the Globalization of Reproductive Technologies." *European Journal of Women's Studies* 13(1):23–38.

Hall, Elaine J., and Marnie Salupo Rodriguez. 2003. "The Myth of Postfeminism." *Gender and Society* 17(6):878–902.

Hanhardt, Christina, Laura Gutierrez, Miranda Joseph, Adela C. Licona, and Sandra K. Soto. 2010. "Nativism, Normatively, and Neoliberalism in Arizona: Challenges Inside and Outside the Classroom." *Transformations* 21(2):123–48.

Harvey, David. 2005. *A Brief History of Neoliberalism*. New York: Oxford University Press.

Hernández Castillo, R. Aída. 2002. "Indigenous Law and Identity Politics in Mexico: Indigenous Men's and Women's Struggles for a Multicultural Nation." *PoLAR* 25(1):90–109.

Hernández Castillo, R. Aída. 2010. "Indigeneity as a Field of Power: Multiculturalism and Indigenous Identities in Political Struggle." In *The Sage Handbook of Identities*, ed. Margaret Wetherell and Chandra Talpade Mohanty, 379–451. London: Sage.

Jad, Islah. 2007. "NGOs: Between Buzzwords and Social Movements." *Development in Practice* 17(4–5):622–29.

Jad, Islah. 2009. "The Politics of Group Weddings in Palestine: Political and Gender *Tensions*." *Journal of Middle East Women's Studies* 5(3):36–53.

Johnson, Penny, and Eileen Kuttab. 2001. "Where Have All the Women (and Men) Gone? Reflections on Gender and the Second Palestinian Intifada." *Feminist Review*, no. 69, 21–43.

Kuttab, Eileen. 2008. "Palestinian Women's Organizations: Global Cooption and Local Contradiction." *Cultural Dynamics* 20(2):99–117.

Kuttab, Eileen. 2010. "Empowerment as Resistance: Conceptualizing Palestinian Women's Empowerment." *Development* 53(2):247–53.

Larner, Wendy. 1995. "Theorizing Difference in Aoetearoa/New Zealand." *Gender, Place and Culture*, no. 2, 177–90.

Liinason, Mia. 2006. "Ph.D.'s, Women's/Gender Studies and Interdisciplinary." *NORA* 14(2):115–30.

Liinason, Mia. 2010. "Institutionalized Knowledge: Notes on the Processes of Inclusion and Exclusion in Gender Studies in Sweden." *NORA* 18(1):38–47.

Liinason, Mia. 2011. "Feminism and the Academy: Exploring the Politics of Institutionalization in Gender Studies in Sweden." PhD dissertation, Center for Gender Studies, Lund University.

Lykke, Nina. 2004. "Between Particularism, Universalism and Transversalism: Reflections on the Politics of Location of European Feminist Research and Education." *NORA* 12(2):72–82.

Lykke, Nina, Christine Michel, and Maria Puig de la Bellacasa. 2001. "Women's Studies: From Institutional Innovations to New Job Qualifications." *Report*, Advanced Thematic Network in Activities in Women's Studies in Europe, University of Southern Denmark. http://let.uu.nl/womens_studies/athena/whole_document.pdf.

Mama, Amina. 2009. "Rethinking African Universities: Gender and Transformation." *Scholar and Feminist Online* 7(2). http://sfonline.barnard.edu/africana/mama_01.htm.

Marchand, Marianne, and Jane L. Parpart, eds. 1995. *Feminism/Postmodernism/Development*. London: Routledge.

McClennen, Sophia A. 2008–9. "Neoliberalism and the Crisis of Intellectual Engagement." *Works and Days* 26 and 27(51/52 and 53/54):459–70.

McLaughlin, Lisa. 2004. "Feminism and the Political Economy of Transnational Public Space." *Sociological Review* 52(1):157–75.

McRobbie, Angela. 2007. "Top Girls? Young Women and the Post-feminist Sexual Contract." *Cultural Studies* 21(4–5):718–37.

Mendoza, Breny. 2002. "Transnational Feminisms in Question." *Feminist Theory* 3(3):295–314.

Moallem, Minoo. 2006. "Feminist Scholarship and the Internationalization of Women's Studies." *Feminist Studies* 32(2):332–51.

Mohanty, Chandra Talpade. 1986. "Under Western Eyes: Feminist Scholarship and Colonial Discourses." *boundary 2* 12(3):333–58.

Mohanty, Chandra Talpade. 2003a. *Feminism without Borders: Decolonizing Theory*, Practicing Solidarity. Durham, NC: Duke University Press.

Mohanty, Chandra Talpade. 2003b. "'Under Western Eyes' Revisited: Feminist Solidarity through Anticapitalist Struggles." *Signs* 28(2):499–535.

Mohanty, Chandra Talpade. 2011. "Imperial Democracies, Militarised Zones, Feminist Engagements." *Economic and Political Weekly of India* 46(13):76–84.

Mulinari, Diana, and Nora Räthzel. 2007. "Politicizing Biographies: The Forming of Transnational Subjectivities as Insiders Outside." *Feminist Review*, no. 86, 89–112.

Nagar, Richa. 2002. "Footloose Researchers, 'Traveling' Theories, and the Politics of Transnational Feminist Praxis." *Gender, Place and Culture* 9(2):179–86.

Okin, Susan Moller. 1998. "Feminism, Women's Human Rights, and Cultural Differences." *Hypatia* 13(2):32–52.

Phillips, Lynne, and Sally Cole. 2009. "Feminist Flows, Feminist Fault Lines: Women's Machineries and Women's Movements in Latin America." *Signs* 35(1):185–211.

Saliba, Therese. 1995. "On the Bodies of Third World Women: Cultural Impurity, Prostitution, and Other Nervous Conditions." *College Literature* 22(1):131–46.

Sampaio, Anna. 2004. "Transnational Feminisms in a New Global Matrix." *International Feminist Journal of Politics* 6(2):181–206.

Shope, Janet Hinson. 2006. "You Can't Cross a River without Getting Wet: A Feminist Standpoint on the Dilemmas of Cross-Cultural Research." *Qualitative Inquiry* 12(1):163–84.

Staunæs, Dorthe. 2003. "Where Have All the Subjects Gone? Bringing Together the Concepts of Intersectionality and Subjectification." *NORA* 11(2):101–10.

Sudbury, Julia. 2005, ed. *Global Lockdown: Race, Gender, and the Prison Industrial Complex*. New York: Routledge.

Sudbury, Julia, and Margo Okazawa-Rey. 2009. "Introduction: Activist Scholarship and the Neoliberal University." In *Activist Scholarship: Antiracsim, Feminism, and Social Change*, 1–16. Boulder, CO: Paradigm.

Téllez, Michelle. 2008. "Community of Struggle: Gender, Violence, and Resistance on the U.S./Mexico Border." *Gender and Society* 22(5):545–67.

AKIKO TAKEYAMA

9. POSSESSIVE INDIVIDUALISM IN THE AGE OF POSTFEMINISM AND NEOLIBERALISM: SELF-OWNERSHIP, CONSENT, AND CONTRACTUAL ABUSES IN JAPAN'S ADULT VIDEO INDUSTRY

Over the last three decades, feminist scholars and activists have debated the meaning of female sexual consent within patriarchal social and capitalist systems. The debate has shed light on the politics of female sexuality, a matter long kept behind closed doors, and significantly changed the public's attitude about what is considered consent and coercion. Fundamentally, however, the debate has failed to change either the legal frameworks or the liberal ideologies that underlie and sustain sexual and labor exploitation. This demands a fresh re-thinking of consent/coercion in late-capitalist societies.

The debate over female consent largely began in the late 1980s, when a heated discussion broke out about pornography in the United States and other countries. At the time, anti-pornography feminists claimed that pornography degraded female sexuality and was a form of violence against women (Barry; Dworkin and MacKinnon). In this view, the production of pornography is essentially coercive. Female actors who say they have consented to their performance and thereby embraced their sexual pleasure have succumbed to false consciousness. In contrast, sex-positive feminists contended that sex workers were not passive victims but rather free workers who offer sexual labor in exchange for wages. In other words, sex workers are autonomous agents who seek financial independence and alternative sexuality. This view has promoted sexual expression, with an emphasis on consent, as emancipatory (Rubin; Vance and Snitow). Despite different theorization of sexual consent, anti-pornography feminists and sex-positive feminists both essentialized consent and coercion as polar opposites. As a result, they have reinforced binary thinking and

essentialist views without questioning the very notions of consent and coercion, and the social consequences thereof, in the context of increasing demand for sexualized labor in postindustrial consumerism.

This reading thus critically examines the theoretical concept of consent. It argues that what I call "possessive individualism"—the core of liberal theory and social contract—has become intimately intertwined with socioeconomic values of freedom and empowerment in the era of postfeminism and neoliberalism. Specifically, I use the calculated ambivalence about sexual consent found in employment contracts in Japan's adult video (AV) industry to rethink liberal assumptions of self-ownership, consent, and equality. I ask, How do consumerism and commodification of anything salable—including femininity, sexuality, and sexual intercourse itself—shape meanings of freedom, consent, and empowerment? What is going on, for example, when women who have been recruited into performing in adult videos claim that they have been coerced into signing contracts and then legally forced to engage in sexual acts?

In what follows, I will first provide a brief overview of sex work in Japan's AV industry and the new possibilities and risks that have emerged. Then, based on my preliminary ethnographic research in 2015 and 2016 focusing on recruitment and contract-making in the industry, I will discuss how the notion of self-ownership and consent is a cultural construct based on possessive individualism. Drawing on Carol Pateman's (1988) classic work, *The Sexual Contract*, I take possessive individualism to be a perspective that values individuals as both owners of bodily properties (e.g., femininity, sexuality, and labor power) and decision makers who choose whether or not to contract these properties out as if they are material objects. In this conceptual framework, an employment contract treats employer and employee equally as autonomous subjects and undermines socioeconomic inequalities between them.

Building on Pateman's notion of sexual contract and feminist debates over sexual consent, my ultimate goal lies in problematizing the liberal notion of possessive individualism as a political fiction and revealing the ways that contract abuses are made sociolegally possible. I contend that possessive individualism makes it possible to understand how individuals self-objectify and capitalize on their own bodies without subjugating themselves to consuming others. What Rosalind Gill calls "postfeminist sensibility" welcomes sex work as part of individual freedom of choice and sexual expression, liberating women from conventional sexism and enhancing their sense of self-empowerment. In this celebratory air, young sexy women safely embrace femininity as a bodily property and commodify it (147). Postfeminist sensibility goes hand in hand with the neoliberal rhetoric of breaking away from bureaucratic conventions to promote private ownership in the name of advancing individual freedom, entrepreneurial creativity, and free exchange in market economies. Possessive individualism is thus not peculiar to Japan's adult video industry. Rather it reflects the ethos of postfeminism and neoliberalism, each of which valorize liberal notions of self-autonomy, consent, and equality.

JAPAN'S ADULT VIDEO INDUSTRY

The adult entertainment industry in industrialized countries generates billions of dollars each year (Weitzer 1). In Japan, the adult video market alone contributes an estimated 500 to 5,000 million US dollars a year to the global market, with some 35,000 video products created annually. More than 150 adult video talent agencies, mostly located in the Tokyo metropolitan area, aggressively scout young women on the street and recruit on average 2,000 to 3,000 women into the business every year. Increasing numbers of young Japanese women perform in these videos as so-called "AV actresses" (*ēbui joyū*). The industry demands youth and freshness. Two-thirds of female actresses are

replaced annually, and most of them are in their late teens and early twenties (Nakamura 16).

Successful AV stars embody the postfeminist sensibility. They achieve money, fame, and freedom through their work. Their success reinforces neoliberal values of individual freedom of choice, entrepreneurial creativity, and self-responsibility that Japan's politico-economic reforms have fostered since the 1980s (Takeyama). This success extends as well to Japan's neighbors (Coates; Wong and Yau). For example, Sora Aoi, for a time a moderately popular AV actress in Japan, became a superstar in China in the late 1990s as her videos began to circulate through informal networks of pirated DVDs and file-sharing. She is now a transnational celebrity, establishing her status as a "teacher" and "goddess" of sexual liberation and entrepreneurship for urban middle-class youth in Hong Kong, Taiwan, and South Korea.

Recently, however, Japan's AV industry has attracted public scrutiny as a result of the arrests and trials of former talent agency owners and their CEOs. In 2015, a Tokyo district court ruled against a talent agency that allegedly used a talent agreement to coerce a woman into acting in pornographic videos, exposing an industry rife with contractual abuses. It turned out that threats of breach of contract, which had resulted in outrageous violation fees and compensation money—24,600,000 yen (roughly 225,000 US dollars) in this case—bound the woman to her on-camera performances. The court decision has become a significant milestone, ruling employment contracts "null and void" when there is a "compelling reason" such as coercion against a worker's will. Since then, a number of AV actresses have sued their talent agencies for forcing them to perform on camera even when they did not want to. Three men, including a former president of a talent agency and two CEOs, were arrested in 2016 for allegedly coercing a woman to perform in adult videos.

In response, The Cabinet Office of Japan conducted a systematic investigation and produced a report in 2017 entitled "The Results of an Internet Survey to Grasp the Reality of Sexual Violence Against Young Men and Women." The report outlines rampant malpractice surrounding employment contracts and their enforceability. Only 42.6 percent of respondents who performed in pornographic films report that they read their employment contracts and fully understood them before they signed. Some of them confess that they did not want to bother reading the contract language, or did not expect that anything would go wrong during their employment. Others report that they were hustled into signing, or that they did not remember the moment of signing. And some others claim that neither a contract nor an agreement was presented to them. More than a quarter of the survey respondents report that they were asked during filming to perform sex acts on which they had not agreed, and one third of those performed anyway to avoid conflict (20–26).

As the court case in 2015 uncovered, some talent agencies and production companies threaten breach of contract or excessive penalty fees to force women to engage in non-contractual sexual acts. The case of Honoka, a well-known ex-AV actress in Japan, is a representative example of how a talent agency abuses power by imposing fines on actresses. In her 2010 autobiography, *Kago*, meaning the cage, Honoka describes the moment she could not escape becoming an adult video actress. The president of her agency threatened her when she refused to perform in a pornographic video for the first time: "You have verbally consented [to a performance in pornographic videos], haven't you? Once given, it becomes an official contract even though it is a verbally made one. If you cannot [fulfill it], there will be a penalty fee [for you to pay]. It will be six million yen in cash" (7). Honoka admits that she was susceptible to the president's persuasion because she dreamed of becoming a singer and needed the money. Nonetheless her first modeling job through the agency involved nudity and humiliated her. She refused a subsequent job to perform in an adult video. But like the woman in the 2015 court case, Honoka ended up becoming an AV actress to avoid paying exorbitant fines.

Some might wonder why these young women are so naïve. Why don't they simply walk away if they are abused? Why do these women, despite their protestations, continue to act in adult videos? These are the questions I will now turn to.

TRAJECTORY OF BUSINESS CONTRACTS

Unequal relationships start from the beginning and unfold through the process of recruitment to contract-making and to work conditions during filming.

A 26-year-old recruiter, who self-identifies as a social worker to help sex workers secure jobs, housing, and wellness in general, told me during an interview that he could easily identify "targets" whom he could turn into AV actresses. For example, those who carry a suitcase and aimlessly wander tend to be runaway youth or new arrivals from rural Japan; they are often in need of a place to stay and eager to find a job in Tokyo. Newcomers usually stop and listen to strangers, as they are not used to the speed of the city and customary practice of ignoring others on the street. He also targets women who seem reluctant to say "no" or who appear to be interested in show business so that he can ask them to stop and listen to him. Once he succeeds, he immediately invites them to his nearby talent agency. According to the recruiter, it is important to have a seamless flow from recruitment on the street to signing the talent agreement. Any delay or disturbance to the flow creates a moment for potential actresses to think twice and walk away.

At the talent agency office, a couple of agency staff, along with the recruiter, welcome women they have brought in. After a brief introduction, they typically explain their wide range of businesses, from commercial modeling to body parts modeling to acting in pornographic media. In the conversation, they emphasize modeling jobs and mention acting jobs in adult videos as an option only if there is interest. Making the job prospects sound good, they encourage the young woman to simply register her name and profile photos so that she can see what's available and then pick and choose. Registration is simple and easy: providing an identification document for photocopy and signing the contract. They know most women do what they are persuaded to do. The 2017 Internet Survey reinforces this point: 41.6% of respondents signed their contracts due to a lack of reasons to decline (The Cabinet Office of Japan 22). At this point, according to one NGO case worker I met, women who sign contracts without paying sufficient attention or receiving full disclosure of legal terms mostly assume that they have consented to registration of their names and profile photos for modeling jobs only, not acting jobs in adult videos.

Taking advantage of these young women's naiveté and misunderstanding, the talent agency effectively uses their expert knowledge in recruitment and contract-making to exploit them. Once the contract is signed, the document becomes an official record. The premise that a contract is a legal arrangement made between equally autonomous juridical subjects eliminates any trace of the existing gap between them—at least on paper and with regard to business know-how, negotiation skills, and socioeconomic power.

In an unequal employer–employee relationship, the weaker party, that is, the actress, is vulnerable to contract abuse and labor exploitation especially when there is very little regulation in the area of labor. The Japanese government does not regulate the adult video industry beyond existing legal clauses of obscenity and child protection from sexual commerce. Accordingly, it lacks a dedicated administrative office to oversee the industry. Meanwhile, the industry has rapidly grown over the last three decades, thus increasing demand for sexual labor. In the absence of public policy and oversight, talent agencies and video production companies have developed business models that profit greatly from AV actresses waiving their rights as workers and as copyright holders.

Employment contracts and labor practices in Japan's sex industry complicate simple distinctions between consent and coercion. Japanese contracts, including talent agreements, are typically very short and vague (Wagatsuma and Rosett). The contract usually does not specify employee compensation or agency commissions. It details the rights the production company holds, including copyrights and use of an actor's images and bio in promotional materials. By the same token, it binds an actress to duties and responsibilities such as health maintenance, STD prevention, management of physical appearance, confidentiality and film non-disclosure, and sometimes the contract itself. As such, a seemingly transparent and neutral contract is often intentionally vague and ill-defined so as to protect the business interests of a production company and not the rights and welfare of an actress. Sexual labor exploitation is then possible precisely because, as Pateman insightfully points out, "contracts about property in the person place right of command in the hands of one party to the contract"—in this case, the production side (8). Thus, consent itself possibly makes the weaker party legally vulnerable to contract abuse and labor exploitation.

SELF-OWNERSHIP, CONSENT, AND EQUALITY

Women's sexuality is, however, seen, theoretically, as a tool of female empowerment and as a leasable bodily property in a law-governed civil society at a time when postfeminist sensibility and neoliberal self-ownership value possessive individualism. This is because contract law has become pervasive, and the typical contract presumes a mutual agreement between equally autonomous individuals. Sociologist Pat O'Malley argues that the law of contract is inseparably linked to the "growth of liberalism and the formation of its subjects." Contract law does not only regulate economic lives; its apparent place at the heart of liberalism governs enterprising social activities in general (467).

Feminist scholars, however, have questioned liberal assumptions of free personhood, consent, and equality in contracts. Pateman argues that the free person is a gendered construct within a political fiction that equates men and women as juridically free subjects while eliding socioeconomic inequality (62). She contends that the free person—the core of liberal theory and the social contract—is a male subject who "owns his body and his capacities as pieces of property, just as he owns material property" (55).

The employment contract in Japan's AV industry also seems to be founded on possessive individualism: each individual owns his or her own bodily properties, such as femininity, sexuality, and acting capacity; another person can have access to these properties only with consent. This view of the Japanese contract relies on two problematic assumptions. The first is that the property in person is separable from its owner and leasable to another. This perspective entails boundaries between individuals and within an individual. A boundary that separates one individual from another creates each individual as a bounded entity as if one exists without any influence of others. Another boundary that separates an individual from his or her bodily property constitutes the individual as an autonomous subject as if one is a property owner and a decision maker of its use. This framework presupposes juridically autonomous and equal subjects and trumps the preexisting conditions of intersubjective relationships and socioeconomic inequalities (Pateman 56). The second assumption is that the property can be "contracted out without any injury to, determinant to, or diminishment of the individual self," who owns the property (Pateman 72). Based on this understanding, an employment contract allows the property owner to remain a free worker, not a slave, insofar as one agrees to contract out the property to another in exchange for a wage. The distinction between free worker and slave depends on whether one upholds the above two boundaries or abandons them.

These premises and boundaries reflect the possessive individualism embedded in postfeminist discourse: women freely separate their bodily property and creatively capitalize on it while breaking away from the conventional view of female sexuality, which is morally tied to the person as a whole. The assumptions and boundary-making also reflect notions of neoliberal self-ownership and entrepreneurial freedom: the contract permits not slavery but free work through which individuals commodify their bodily property in a market economy.

In reality, however, an employer, who owns the means of production and copyrights, and a worker, who owns only the property of their person, are not in an equal relationship. The employer in the adult video industry usually sets the terms of the employment contract to their advantage unless the actress is famous and has negotiation power. Upon consenting to a contract, it is she who is put under the director's command since her sexual performance is inseparable from her body *and* self in practice. Nonetheless, it is only her property, not the person as a whole, that a worker gives permission to be bought and sold. Like her sexual performance under the director's orders, commercial products of her obscene images are not so clearly separable from whom she *is*, either, in the eyes of general audience. As a result, the majority of AV actresses suffer the stigma attached to sex work in mainstream Japanese society. There is not much an actress can do, however, since her contract gives the production company the right to use and distribute her image. If an actress decides to quit her job prematurely, she then risks facing breach of contract threats that typically come with exorbitant violation fees and compensation money.

Employment contracts thus bind workers to disadvantageous conditions even though they are entirely legal. It is within this sociolegal reality that we should resituate sexual labor contracts and revisit Pateman's question posed more than a quarter century ago: "Why [is a] contract seen as the paradigm of free agreement?" (6). I contend with Pateman that the assumption of "free agreement" between two consenting parties expressed by contract is based on possessive individualism. Notions of self-ownership and property rights enable free agreement; individuals determine their use of property in the person freely as autonomous subjects.

Postfeminist sensibility and neoliberal rhetoric similarly hinge on these notions. In her 2007 article "Postfeminist Media Culture," social psychologist Rosalind Gill has laid out a wide array of interrelated themes that make up postfeminism: the notion of femininity as a bodily property; the shift from objectification to subjectification; and a focus on individualism, choice, and empowerment, among other paradigms (147). Postfeminism celebrates the process of individuals becoming subjects and enhancing self-empowerment even by way of objectifying themselves. By the same token, it downplays de facto gender hierarchies, labor subordination, and contract bondage. This perspective, in turn, feeds into the neoliberal market economy through the commercialization of female bodily properties.

As the case of Japan's adult video industry demonstrates, consent and coercion are closely intertwined and deeply embedded in sex industry contracts. Consent to something unpredictable and even predictably harmful can be made, as the Japanese AV actress, Honoka, exemplifies, to advance one's self-interests and realize one's dreams. Thinking of consent and coercion as binary opposites prevents a critical engagement of the assumptions underlying sexual and labor exploitation. Binary thinking discursively allows contract abuses to sound legal. Effective critical engagement means not fighting one another based on polarizing political agendas while at the same time turning a blind eye to abusive labor practices in the sex industries. What is needed is to eschew binary thinking and to critique the possessive individualism inherent in contemporary postfeminism and neoliberalism.

REFERENCES

Barry, Kathleen. *Female Sexual Slavery*. New York: New York University Press, 1984.

The Cabinet Office of Japan. *The Result of an Internet Survey That Grasps the Reality of Sexual Violence against Youth*. Tokyo: The Cabinet Office of Japan, 2017.

Coates, Jamie. "Rogue Diva Flows: Aoi Sola's Reception in the Chinese Media and Mobile Celebrity." *Journal of Japanese and Korean Cinema* 6, no. 1 (2014): 89–103.

Dworkin, Andrea, and Catharine A. MacKinnon. *Pornography and Civil Rights: A New Day for Women's Equality*. Minneapolis, MN: Organizing Against Pornography, 1988.

Gill, Rosalind. "Postfeminist Media Culture: Elements of a Sensibility." *European Journal of Cultural Studies* 10, no. 2 (2007): 147–66.

Honoka. *Kago (The Cage)*. Tokyo: Shufu no Tomo, 2010.

Nakamura, Atsuhiko. *Syokugyō Toshite No Av Joyū (Av [Adult Video] Actress as an Occupation)*. Tokyo: Gentōsya, 2012.

O'Malley, Pat. "Uncertain Subjects: Risks, Liberalism and Contract." *Economy & Society* 29, no. 4 (2000): 460–84.

Pateman, Carole. *The Sexual Contract*. Stanford, CA: Stanford University Press, 1988.

Rubin, Gayle. "Thinking Sex: Notes for a Radical Theory of the Politics of Sexuality." *Pleasure and Danger: Exploring Female Sexuality*. Ed. Carole S. Vance. New York: Routledge, 1984. 267–319.

Takeyama, Akiko. *Staged Seduction: Selling Dreams in a Tokyo Host Club*. Stanford, CA: Stanford University Press, 2016.

Vance, Carole S., and Ann B. Snitow. "Toward a Conversation About Sex in Feminism: A Modest Proposal." *Signs: Journal of Women in Culture and Society* 10, no. 1 (1984): 126–35.

Wagatsuma, Hiroshi, and Arthur Rosett. "Cultural Attitudes Towards Contract Law: Japan and the United States Compared." *Pacific Basin Law Journal* 2, no. 1–2 (1983): 76–97.

Weitzer, Ronald. "Sex Work: Paradigms and Policies." *Sex for Sale: Prostitution, Pornography, and the Sex Industry*. Ed. Ronald Weitzer. 2nd ed. New York: Routledge, 2010. 1–45.

Wong, Heung-Wah, and Hoi-yan Yau. *Japanese Adult Videos in Taiwan*. New York: Routledge, 2014.

AMRITA BANERJEE

10. A TRANSNATIONAL INTERVENTION INTO AN ETHIC OF CARE: QUANDARIES OF CARE ETHICS FOR TRANSNATIONAL FEMINISMS

An ethic of care is one of the key contributions by Western feminist philosophers to feminist theory and philosophical theory. Reflecting on practices of care, feminist philosophers have developed it as a subversive moral and political concept, and the basis for a sophisticated theoretical paradigm called care ethics. Care as a moral concept helps us to think about how we ought to relate to others. As a political concept, it helps us to think about a state's responsibility toward its citizens and to develop new ethical bases for public policies involving vulnerable groups. Recently, attempts have been made to apply care ethics to transnational feminist debates such as the global movement of women care workers from developing nations to more affluent ones to fill the care deficit there (Kittay, "Global Heart"); the use of military humanitarian intervention in situations of human rights violations, which often have heavily gendered connotations (Tronto, "Is Peacekeeping Care Work?"); and transnational commercial surrogacy where consumers from the Global North rent the wombs of women from the Third World (Parks). Care ethicists argue that anchor concepts from the care paradigm such as relationality and responsibility enables us to frame, interpret, and evaluate various issues in transnational feminisms.

In this essay, I argue that caution must be exercised in applying care ethics to transnational feminisms, and that we must first interrogate its decolonizing potential. In order to work through the question of decolonization, I call for a reversal of theoretical methodology, which involves an evaluation of central concepts from care ethics in relation to existing frameworks of transnational feminisms. It is, in other words, a transnational intervention into an ethic of care. Through this engagement, I want to drive home

the fact that we cannot simply take the transnational sphere as a passive domain for applications of an otherwise complete Western theory. Rather, transnational feminisms expose points of conceptual discomfort and incompleteness in the care paradigm, which it must address in order to productively collaborate with transnational feminisms.

First, I define relationality and responsibility as anchor concepts of the care paradigm, and key contributions of care ethics to transnational debates. These concepts are laid out after examining care ethics' dislodging of the liberal conception of reciprocity and the contract paradigm as primary modes of conceiving moral and political relations. Second, I argue that decentering reciprocity inaugurates several quandaries for transnational feminisms. A basic asymmetry appears to be built into the care paradigm, which in turn generates a colonizing conception of responsibility, threatens to deepen existing social and global inequalities, and may end up morally justifying the lack of reciprocity in feminist interactions across these inequalities. I conclude that is important to retain substantial moral weight for reciprocity, although it must learn to account for various asymmetries and vulnerabilities.

DECENTERING RECIPROCITY: MOVE TO RELATIONALITY AND RESPONSIBILITY

Care ethics arises as a critical reaction to certain dominantly masculinist philosophical theories on morals and justice such as the social contract theory. First articulated by classical liberal philosophers such as Thomas Hobbes, John Locke, and Jean-Jacques Rousseau, it gained new life in the writings of John Rawls in the twentieth century. The modern conception of reciprocity is intimately tied to the idea of a contract. A contract is, by definition, an agreement between independent and freely consenting individuals, who are the parties to it. This framework values independence and autonomy since a contract is impossible unless freely consented to by those that are governed by it. An everyday example of a contract would be an employment contract, which bind an employer and employee. The social contract tradition takes this idea of a contract in order to evolve a conceptual blueprint for conceiving of free and just social and political relations. The social contract is often taken to be governed by a more fundamental moral contract, which considers all human beings as equally worthy and as having some basic moral obligations toward each other. Care ethics offers a strong critique of the contract paradigm and the associated conception of reciprocity. I now turn to this critique, and explain how it generates anchor concepts of the care paradigm, namely, relationality and responsibility.

Perhaps the most sophisticated critique of the contract paradigm and one that is primarily directed to Rawls's conception of reciprocity is the dependency critique, which is articulated by Eva Kittay in *Love's Labor*. In Rawls's philosophy, the sociopolitical sphere is conceived as a sphere of cooperative activity in which individual self-interested citizens compete for certain basic goods. These goods are basic since they are desirable to all human beings, and include things such as rights, liberties, health, income, and the social bases of self-respect, among others. The main concern from the point of view of justice is to stipulate terms of fair cooperation so as to ensure that every individual (as a party to the social contract) shares equally in the benefits and burdens of the social contract. Equality and reciprocity, therefore, become critical in this framework. Equality, in turn, is defined through symmetry since each individual is placed equally in relation to other individuals, who are parties to the contract. When equality is defined as symmetry, then it entails reciprocity—each individual shares in the benefits and burdens of social cooperation according to a common benchmark of comparison, whereby nobody is morally entitled to more or less by virtue of their social position.

The dependency critique displaces equality-based reciprocity as the paradigmatic way of conceiving of social and political relations. Rather than viewing the sociopolitical sphere as one of competition among independent and self-interested agents, it conceives of it as a network of relations. Kittay observes, "A conception of society viewed as an association of equals masks inequitable dependencies, those of infancy and childhood, old age, illness and disability. While we are dependent, we are not well positioned to enter a competition for the goods of social cooperation on equal terms" (*Love's Labor* xi). Through her critique, Kittay emphasizes the sorts of relationships that are forms of dependencies and cannot be captured by the language of contract and reciprocity. Instead, her analysis focuses on non-reciprocal, and hence, non-contractual relationships such as those between a care-receiver and a care-giver as the primary site of moral meaning and on which to anchor claims of justice. There is a lack of reciprocity between the caregiver and care receiver in terms of agency, power, and vulnerability. In case of certain dependencies (e.g., infancy or severe disabilities), the care receiver might even be dependent on the caregiver for the satisfaction of basic needs. The caregiver, in turn, does not function as a self-interested agent and cannot compete for basic goods according to a common benchmark of comparison with other agents that are unencumbered by similar caring responsibilities. Since one individual's autonomy and interest is fundamentally affected by another, conceptual priority is accorded to security, well-being, and the nurturing of relations in the care paradigm rather than the independence and autonomy of the contract paradigm.

The shift of focus to non-reciprocal relations in care ethics means that the paradigmatic way of conceiving moral and political relations is to think of them primarily as a matter of attending to the needs of others (the care receiver) for whom one (the caregiver) takes responsibility. Responsibility, therefore, highlights the relatedness between the self and the other, the orientation of the self toward the other, an inequality of vulnerabilities on different sides of the caring relation, and finally an acceptance of some kind of burden on the part of the caregiver (Tronto, *Moral Boundaries* 103). These can be very important tools for theorizing transnational relations and multiple oppressions, along with identifying what we can do for one another on the basis of these relations. This is partly due to the fact that, as Joan Tronto rightly observes, "caring requires that one start from the standpoint of the one needing care or attention. It requires that we meet the other morally, adopt that person's, or group's, perspective and look at the world in those terms. . . . caring becomes a way to monitor, and perhaps to check the bad faith that might otherwise creep into the activities of feminist theorists" (*Moral Boundaries* 19). Lack of trust and bad faith between feminists is a real danger in transnational feminist collaborations and conversations since these happen across racial, cultural, linguistic, and religious differences as well as across international borders. Presence of differences means that diverse world views, diversity in feminist agendas, and even culturally varied meanings of feminism must be grappled with. In this scenario, a refusal to take another group's perspective or alternative feminist agendas seriously, dismissing another's viewpoint simply because it is different from one's own, and uncritically imposing one's own judgements on another are explicit examples of bad faith and may result in the breakdown of transnational relations. This is where care ethics serves as a valuable resource. By requiring us to morally start from the perspective of the other rather than the self, and trying to understand the world from their perspective, new bases of good faith and trustworthiness may be established. By putting such moral demands on us, argues Tronto, the care paradigm urges us to learn from each other's experiences (Tronto, *Moral Boundaries* 18).

I believe that a big challenge, and one that Tronto does not deal with, would be to define what it means to learn from each other's experiences and what such an exercise would involve within a heavily varied and fragmented transnational space. Difference and incommensurability in experiences and knowledges emanating from one's position amidst global inequalities is a regular feature of transnational relations. I will draw out some of these issues through my analysis of colonization next, which was also understood by colonizers as a project of care. The larger argument that I now turn to is that decentering reciprocity, or centering relationality and responsibility at the expense of reciprocity, poses unique problems from the perspective of transnational feminisms.

QUANDARIES OF AN ETHIC OF CARE FOR TRANSNATIONAL FEMINISMS

I share the care ethicists' concern with the liberal conception of reciprocity as the conscious relation between autonomous and equal individuals, since this definition may cover over actual vulnerabilities. Vulnerabilities in the social sphere arise due to the presence of various social hierarchies and structural inequalities, which creates special obstacles for members of marginalized groups compared to their more privileged counterparts along lines of gender, race, class, ability, nationality, and citizenship status, to name a few. It is here that care ethics with its recognition of relationality and vulnerability, and the moral requirement to begin from the perspective of the other rather than the self, becomes a significant resource for transnational feminisms. Despite this, I now argue against taking moral focus away from reciprocity in the context of transnational feminisms. My claim is that a basic asymmetry appears to be built into the care paradigm, which threatens to deepen existing material inequalities tied to one's position in social and global systems when it interacts with the latter. This generates a colonizing conception of responsibility and may end up morally justifying the lack of reciprocity in real-life feminist interactions across inequalities. This threat multiplies exponentially when the caregiver is a socially privileged individual compared to the care receiver in an act of caring.

In order to explain basic asymmetry, let's try to understand what the simplest elements of the care paradigm are, in keeping with the definition of care. The paradigm contains three formal elements: the giver (represented as X), the receiver (represented as Y), and the caring relation (represented as R). For the time being, let's not consider who is actually stepping into the shoes of X and Y in a particular instance of caring, and what their respective social positions are. We notice that in the definition of care, X is unequal to Y, since X and Y are unequally situated with respect to R. Asymmetry becomes a feature of R since R delineates basic inequalities in agency, power, and vulnerability between X and Y in their differential roles with respect to R. Although X is rendered somewhat vulnerable in the context of R since X may have to sacrifice some self-interest in order to care for Y, the vulnerability of Y in the context of R is significantly greater due to Y's dependence on X. Again, agency is unequally placed on the two sides of R since X will typically enjoy greater power compared to Y in the context of R, and this power may even be considered to be in Y's best interest (as is the case of a parent's care toward an infant). In so far as asymmetry is a feature of R, it becomes a formal feature of the care paradigm, and is induced by the paradigm.

Let us distinguish basic asymmetry from material asymmetries or inequalities in the context of a particular instance of caring by specific individuals. Such asymmetry is present when say Sally steps into the role of X/giver for Molly who becomes Y/receiver in the context of R/caring relation, and where Sally already occupies a socially and globally privileged position compared to Molly in respect to her race, class, and citizenship status. The asymmetry between Sally and Molly here delineates social and global inequalities, irrespective of whether Sally and Molly step into the roles of X and Y, respectively, in the context of R. We find this asymmetry, therefore, to be induced by social and global status. Status-induced asymmetry is different from basic asymmetry, as it is not a formal feature of the care paradigm. From the point of view of transnational feminisms, my worry is that asymmetries pertaining to status will deepen and actually find justification in light of the basic asymmetry of the care paradigm. Let us now consider some examples from transnational feminisms, which may be characterized as status-induced asymmetries, according to my definition.

Examples of status-induced asymmetries in the transnational sphere include "Third World Difference" (Mohanty 19) and "First World privilege" (Banerjee, "Race and a Transnational Reproductive Caste System" 122), which often structure and impact transnational feminist relations, especially those across the First World/Third World divide. I consider these to be status-induced since these are tied to social and global positions of individuals with respect to the First World/Third World divide. Chandra Mohanty in *Feminism Without Borders* outlines how cultural representations of Third World women in hegemonic Western feminisms are often mediated by Third World difference. Third World difference as a category, claims Mohanty,

can only be grasped in view of the domination of the world-system by the West. Amidst this domination, two mutually exclusive categories are created, namely, the West as the First World versus its other as the Third World. A unique feature of such categorization is that not only do we have two categories, but also one of them is privileged (becomes the norm) relative to the other, which only appears as a deviation from the norm.

When hegemonic Western feminisms perceive Third World women through Third World difference, the First World woman automatically becomes the norm and is defined in positive terms as possessing agency and being liberated. The Third World woman, on the contrary, can only be characterized in negative terms as objectified, oppressed, and lacking in all values characterizing her liberated counterpart. Third World difference as a conceptual category entails and works in tandem with "First World privilege" (Banerjee, "Race and a Transnational Reproductive Caste System" 122). First World privilege intersects with prevailing localized social hierarchies such as race, class, and caste, to give new life to various global inequalities across the First World/Third World divide. When transnational feminist interactions and acts of caring in the context of such interactions are mediated by status-induced asymmetries as those of Third World difference and First World privilege, the possibility of debate and dialogue across this divide on reciprocal terms (i.e., on free and equal terms) is severely obstructed to begin with. My worry is that this lack of reciprocity on the ground will gain new life from the basic asymmetry of the care paradigm since the latter morally justifies unequal agency on two sides of the caring relation. In this scenario, it may become virtually impossible for the Third World woman to speak back and demand reciprocation in the context of dialogue with her more privileged counterpart.

Ideological renderings of Third World women in the light of status-induced asymmetries such as Third World difference and First World privilege end up depriving them of agency and turning them into passive victims, whom First World women must enlighten and care for. The basic asymmetry of the care paradigm, in turn, threatens to deepen these existing status-induced inequalities. In order to explain this point, let us look at an example, namely, the historical project of colonization, which was heavily couched in the language of care according to Uma Narayan. Narayan claims that much turned on who defined these contested terms (133). In terms of the symbolic representation introduced above, we can represent the situation as follows: White women come to see colonization as a caring relation (R) in which they take the role of X/givers with respect to native peoples as Y/receivers, for whom X must take responsibility. The basic asymmetry in the care paradigm already skews the balance of agency and power in favor of X, while vulnerability of Y remains exponentially greater than X. The fact that the roles of X and Y are taken up by White women and native peoples, respectively, in the context of colonization (understood as a caring relation/R), and in a scenario where the social and global status of X is already unequal to Y, means that inequalities on the ground may deepen, interaction between X and Y on free and equal terms may become virtually impossible, and colonization gains moral justification by being couched in the language of responsibility to the other. We must not forget that in contemporary times, care is often evoked in a similar fashion to morally justify various transnational projects as the West's export of democracy to the world or rescue of Third World women from oppression. Such cases are typically characterized by strong assumptions about the epistemological and moral superiority of the West compared to its other, which then impacts key epistemological questions concerning the caring relation such as what needs must be met through care, and how these needs are to be translated cross-culturally and cross-nationally.

The irony of the colonial care discourse and others like it lies in the fact that while care ethics emphasizes the need to attend to the particular other, caring actually plays the opposite role of justifying the subjugation of entire peoples and of camouflaging global relations of domination as acts of care. Again, although the care paradigm asks us to attend to relations and vulnerabilities, the presence of status-induced asymmetries makes these relations prone to exploitation as care comes to be "defined in self-serving ways by the dominant and powerful" (Narayan 136). The unbalanced agency between the giver and receiver as an aspect of basic asymmetry further aggravates existing colonizing accounts of responsibility, and could even help justify the lack of reciprocity in transnational relations.

While recognizing the possibility of abuse in care, care ethicists claim that not all instances of care necessarily constitute an ethic of care (Held 11). Some care theorists also demand responsiveness and competence as aspects of care, whereby the caregiver is required to be attentive, develop trust, think from the standpoint of the receiver, and to carry out caring democratically (Tronto, "Is Peacekeeping Care Work?" 192). The point I am making, however, is that various status-induced asymmetries, which are operational in particular acts of caring and the differential experiences or meanings associated with the caring relation by parties on different sides of the relation (e.g., the colonizer vs. the colonized) creates tremendous problems for the epistemological projects of understanding, speaking, and hearing across this relation. Lack of attention to relationality and vulnerability is not the problem here. Rather, an acute awareness of the unequal nature of the relation propels further exploitations of these by already privileged parties and, therefore, complicates matters for the care paradigm on the decolonization front.

A transnational intervention into an ethic of care provides valuable insight on points of incompleteness within the care paradigm, which it must address as it seeks to collaborate with transnational feminisms. The most significant problem is that of basic asymmetry, which takes on an especially dangerous potential as it materializes amidst various status-induced asymmetries. The basic asymmetry threatens to deepen inequalities pertaining to social and global status, and creates obstacles for free and equal relations. Herein lies the colonizing potential of care, or at least its failure to decolonize. The concern of colonization discussed in this essay is different from one of simple paternalism of a caregiver toward the care receiver. While paternalism primarily focuses on individual attitudes and motives, my analysis retains focus on social positions and global inequalities. A transnational intervention reminds us that it is important to reserve substantial moral weight for reciprocity in order to overcome problems associated with the basic asymmetry of the care paradigm, although reciprocity must learn to account for asymmetries and vulnerabilities.

REFERENCES

Banerjee, Amrita. "Race and a Transnational Reproductive Caste System: Indian Transnational Surrogacy." *Hypatia*, vol. 29, no. 1, 2014, pp. 113–128.

Held, Virginia. *The Ethics of Care: Personal, Political, Global.* Oxford University Press, 2006.

Kittay, Eva Feder. *Love's Labor: Essays on Women, Equality and Dependency.* Routledge, 1999.

Kittay, Eva Feder. "The Global Heart Transplant and Caring across National Boundaries." *The Southern Journal of Philosophy*, vol. XLVI, 2008, pp. 138–165.

Mohanty, Chandra Talpade. *Feminism Without Borders: Decolonizing Theory, Practicing Solidarity.* 2003. Duke University Press, 2006.

Narayan, Uma. "Colonialism and Its Others: Considerations on Rights and Care Discourses." *Hypatia*, vol. 10, no. 2, 1995, pp. 133–140.

Parks, Jennifer A. "Care Ethics and the Global Practice of Commercial Surrogacy." *Bioethics*, vol. 24, no. 7, 2010, pp. 333–340.

Tronto, Joan C. *Moral Boundaries: A Political Argument for an Ethic of Care.* 1993. Routledge, 2009.

Tronto, Joan C. "Is Peacekeeping Care Work? A Feminist Reflection in the 'Responsibility to Protect.'" *Global Feminist Ethics: Feminist Ethics and Social Theory*, edited by Rebecca Whisnant & Peggy DesAutels. 2008. Rowman and Littlefield Publishers, Inc., 2010, pp. 179–200.

MEGAN SIBBETT

11. BREAKING INTO BAD: THE NEW PRIVILEGED MONSTERS, OR, STRAIGHT, MIDDLE-CLASS WHITE GUYS

Describing the first decade of the twenty-first century as television's newest "Golden Age," journalist Brett Martin applauds the booming innovation taken to write characters with "risky" morals. Such shows include *The Sopranos, The Wire, Dexter, Mad Men, Rescue Me, Breaking Bad*, and *The Walking Dead*. Walter White, the violent, meth-making drug kingpin of *Breaking Bad* (2008–2013), is one of the most celebrated anti-heroes of the era, setting a Guinness World Record in 2014 for the highest rated TV series. Emphasizing the risks of the Golden Age, Martin argues that the shows' patriarchs are characters "Americans would never allow into their living rooms: unhappy, morally compromised, complicated, deeply human people" (4). He views the characters as playing "a seductive game" with viewers "daring them to emotionally invest in, even root for, even love, a gamut of criminals" guilty of vampirism, adultery, polygamy, and serial murder (4). Other TV critics and creators also viewed the shows as taking never before seen risks with such characters. AMC executive Charlie Collier said that *Breaking Bad* was the network's "biggest risk" (Sepinwall 378). Yet Martin's assessment of viewers wanting to see complicated, morally ambiguous characters is misleading because criminal characters have long been a staple of film and television. So what is the actual risk?

First, the trope of the criminal has often been the marginalized "others"—characters who are not white, cisgender, straight, middle-class, or father figures. Second, the innovative risk rests on whether or not American viewers can be seduced, not by white, heteronormative criminals, but by men who become monstrous in order to make their criminality logical and necessary. While the risk might seem negligible, given all of their layers of privilege—race, class, gender,

sexuality—it is actually wagered on their privileged status as the "good guys" become the "bad guys" in order to continue to be the "good guys." Importantly, each belong to a pedigree of emerging white, normative monstrosity in television within the first decade of the "war on terror." Their award-winning arrival is not a coincidence. It is, indeed, a seductive game. But who is to be seduced and for what purposes? What *is* actually at stake when the white father figure becomes monstrous? Moreover, as theorizing whiteness and monstrosity emerges within critical media studies, and given the post-9/11 dirge of award-winning white, heteronormative monsters in popular television, what connections can be made between the surplus of narratives and the need to manage a patriotism and militarism in an ongoing "war on terror"? What violence do these new monsters manage?

I address these questions by situating Walter White (Bryan Cranston) from *Breaking Bad* within theorizations of monstrosity. I then discuss the technology of monstrosity within the post-9/11 rise of whiteness in monstrous figures followed by an explication of how such monstrosity wrapped around white, middle-class, heteronormativity vies with the monstrous queer other in showdowns that revitalize "war on terror" ideologies for the preservation of heteronormative families.

MONSTROUS AS OTHERNESS/QUEERNESS

Moving among theorizations of monstrosity within feminist, queer, and critical media studies, this reading critiques the celebrated white, heteronormative monstrosity that arrives to ease the messy discrepancies emerging with the "war on terror." Understanding the trope of the monster as other helps illuminate the significant emergence of the white, heteronormative monsters. As Jeffery Jerome Cohen points out, monsters created in popular culture often embody marginalized differences that are "cultural, political, racial, economic, and sexual" (7). In *Monsters in the Closet*, Harry Benshoff outlines the history of monsters in early horror films as they were consistently portrayed as the queer other who needed to be destroyed before fulfilling their singular purpose—the subversion of heteronormative society. Their demise, Benshoff explains, reinforced normality by eradicating any anti-heteronormativity (129).

The pervasive presence of the monstrous queer other saturates not just horror films but most other genres as well. Sean Griffin draws attention to Disney villains like Scar and Jafar, who, through their "refusal to support heteronormative patriarchy" and their queerness coded through their effeminate manners and their refusal to join a familial "circle of life," are cast as unforgivable (106). The tropic reiterations of defeating monsters across multiple genres do not just reflect dominant ideas of normality but they help form disciplinary systems. Monsters, then, are more than cultural signposts. Cohen positions the monster as a mechanism that polices the borders of what is permissible and possible by reinforcing notions of safety under the norms of the protective state (12). He cites colonial narratives where "one kind of difference becomes another as the normative categories of gender, sexuality, national identity, and ethnicity slide together," creating a polysemy that encodes monumental threats (11).

Writing about the Gothic novel, Halberstam explicates the anti-Semitic contexts of *Dracula*. But Halberstam argues that in theorizing monstrosity, we need to do more than merely bring attention to such critical interpretations. We must also ask how monsters "produce monstrosity as never unitary but always an aggregate of race, class, and gender" (88). The body of the monster represents an "economy [of] monstrous traits" so that a character like Dracula isn't simply a monster but "a technology of monstrosity" (88). Citing Foucault's analysis of the discursive creation of sexual identities, Halberstam shows how monstrous technology is tied to technologies of sex and other categories that situate historically and culturally contingent identities. Foucault enables an analysis between

monstrosity and the history of sexuality where systems of discipline regulate bodies and desire. Therefore, it isn't simply the monster but the text itself that produces and replicates "perverse identities" (Halberstam 89). As a technology, monstrosity not only provides but also produces meaning.

(WALTER) WHITE MONSTROSITY

If monstrosity is usually represented as anti-normativity that needs to be domesticated or eradicated, how is Walter monstrous? What is the monstrous technology of Walter White and the iteration of privileged monsters? As Halberstam argues, the technology of monstrosity does not simply construct and categorize identity. It is a discursive process of making meaning. Like Frankenstein cobbling together a monster, Walter's monstrosity is (re)produced through the perceived "risk" and "scandal" of the character laden with privilege and normality as he becomes evermore violent. It is further organized through the adversarial queer zombie horde surrounding him. Such maneuvers in monstrous technology contribute toward a heteronormative national monstrosity that withstands and reinforces the ongoing violence in the "war on terror," as I explain in the final sections.

In his character arc, Walter moves from being a mild high school teacher with terminal cancer to the menacing monster outside the door, as he boasts to his wife in his often quoted "I am the one who knocks" speech ("Cornered"). Through his escalating violence and rage, he becomes the monster to be feared. In the opening scene of the pilot episode, Walter appears as the one beset by monsters. Nearly naked, panicked, and seemingly lost, he runs through the New Mexico desert recording an emotional farewell to his pregnant wife and son ("Pilot"). Viewers do not yet know what pursues him, only that it is menacing enough to drive Walter to attempt suicide.

Initially, he manages his plan of family preservation with reluctant violence and criminality. "Pilot" foregrounds an approaching monstrosity as Walter is briefly portrayed as the marginalized other when a menacing diagnosis seemingly obliterates his privilege. As his naked vulnerability symbolizes, his privileged class, race, gender, citizenship, and sexuality seem worthless in the monstrous non-future of cancer. Furthermore, as the pilot unfolds, Walter is also running from other drug dealers whom he might not have successfully killed and through the ominous approaching sirens, possibly also the police. But, just after he fails to kill himself, a fire truck rather than a police car passes him, and no one pursues him. Like a zombie, Walter's privilege is re-animated after he does not die. He, in a sense, rises from the dead with a zombified whiteness where he battles and outsmarts the mostly non-white, non-heteronormative (non–family-rearing) drug makers, dealers, and traffickers. As the heteronormative patriarch, he occupies the monstrous space of the other in order to capitalize his income, his intellect, and patriarchal esteem while being beyond the legality of the state. His criminality and violence, entrenched within such privilege, is meant to be watched with admiration and a benevolent horror.

Throughout the series, the privileges that differentiate him from the monstrous others are on constant display. His name, along with his other white, male compatriots, Jesse Pinkman (Aaron Paul), Saul Goodman (Jimmy McGill), and Mike Ehrmantraut (Jonathan Banks), are perpetual reminders of their whiteness and masculinity. Within such a privileged monstrosity resides the risk imagined by the show's creators and producers. The risk taken by the Golden Age shows is not simply having an overabundance of shows consisting of white, male, anti-heroes making morally questionable self-interested decisions. What *is* risked is the maneuver from hero to anti-hero to monster, creating a new hegemony of monstrosity where the space of the monstrous, queer, criminal other is colonized with an aggressive white heteronormativity. What is at stake is the sense of moral supremacy within white, fatherly masculinity, or the "good" side of the erstwhile surplus of monster narratives.

In *Zombies, Migrants, and Queers: Race and Crisis Capitalism in Pop Culture*, Camilla Fojas argues that white characters in shows like *Breaking Bad*, *Weeds*, and *Arrested Development* "reconstitute their social subjectivities," adapting to economic crisis by "adopting survival strategies associated with a racialized underclass" (9). She adds that the protagonists "stand in for the marginal, occupying the same economic ruins and rubble as the racialized populations at the bottom of the socioeconomic strata" (11). The crises the white characters face become opportunities for "new forms of freedom" that utilize criminality within an entrepreneurial spirit (17). In fact, "racialized characters are ancillary but useful" as their histories and lives are mined for resources in the "reinvigoration of whiteness" (17). Walter, she states, represents a "threatened white masculinity" that is revised through his aggressive dominion into a "reconstructed version of post-crisis neoliberal masculinity" (32). Though Fojas does not situate such characters within the realm of monstrosity or specific post-9/11 crises, her assessment of the ways whiteness is capitalized relates to my own argument of the zombification of Walter's privilege as he moves into "breaking bad." In the context of bolstering heteronormative protection, Walter not only *stands in* for the marginalized other but also is at war with them.

Dialogue between Walter and Jesse, Walter's former student now under Walter's meth-making mentorship, highlights the move into monstrosity. Jesse skeptically asks Walter, "Some straight like you, giant stick up his ass [. . .] he's just gonna break bad?" ("Pilot"). Jesse's question emphasizes the technology of Walter's monstrosity—that rule-making heteropatriarchy will not break itself but it will break what it means to be "bad" in order to continue to thrive in the face of continued queer monstrosity. Importantly, the queer monstrous other does not disappear in the takeover. The whole series thus centers around the monster to monster dual where heteropatriarchy's formidable foe is depicted in the threats to Walter's newly thriving livelihood—the anti-futurity of cancer and Mexican, Latino, and Black characters involved in the Southwestern meth business, as I will discuss later as the zombie horde. First, however, the significant timing of the rise of Golden Era white monstrosity extends the analysis of meaning making within such monstrous technology.

POST-9/11 TRAJECTORIES OF MONSTROSITY

In *Monster Culture in the 21st Century*, Marina Levina and Diem-My T. Bui argue that monstrous narratives are more prevalent because they represent social anxiety over accelerated changes in the twenty-first century (1–2). Positioning monstrosity as a "necessary condition of our existence," they agree with political theorists Michael Hardt and Antonio Negri who write that "the new world of monsters is where humanity has to grasp its future" (as cited in Levina and Bui, 2). Thus, monstrosity manages "terror threats, global capitalism crises, new forms of warfare" as well as ambiguity in queer and sexual desires (2).

Jasbir Puar and Amit Rai explain that juridical powers are called forth through the figure of the monstrous queer other. They examine how the failed heterosexuality of the "monster-terrorist," became central to post-9/11 counterterrorism discourse and that monstrous figures emerging from Western civilizational discourse "haunt the prose of contemporary counterterrorism" (124). Counterterrorism discourse regularly centers a duality of monster and hero. The hero is propelled though the morals of a democratic heteropatriarchy that ensures the safety of Western families. As the monster is a "category of operational power," the image of the racialized "terrorist-monster" facilitates a normative "aggressive heterosexual patriotism" that sustains the "war on terror" (Puar and Rai, 119, 117). The monster is domesticated through concepts of democracy, freedom, and humanity that stand for "civilizational progress" (120).

Fox network's award-winning series *24* exemplifies the domesticating hero monster trope. Premiering two months after 9/11, the series featured a cisgender, white, straight father Jack Bauer (Kiefer Sutherland) working for a counterterrorism unit. The show championed Bauer's brazen torture tactics, and the character was solidly positioned as the heroic patriot. The show played out in real time as a digital clock counted down the time. But in the decade of *24*'s ticking clock, the tidy narrative of the "war on terror" had shifted. Narratives surrounding the war became controversial, complicated, or tiresome. The language framing the "war on terror" shifted to "invasion" and "occupation" of Afghanistan and Iraq as well as the "Iraq War" and the "War in Afghanistan." In 2004, the Torture Memos were leaked as well as photos of US soldiers illegally torturing Abu Ghraib detainees. WMDs that were the justification for the invasion of Iraq were not materializing; world opinion of the United States shifted as the legality of the wars was questioned; and drone bombings, which were increasing, missed targets. Without

a clear "victory" or convincing exit strategies, the urgency of the ticking clock no longer seemed applicable, and the Jack Bauer hero trope had worn itself out.

Television narratives shifted. Years into our post-9/11 era, monstrosity was no longer managed by the heroic patriot. The monstrous other also became diversified and complex, yet still existing in a place where normality and exceptionalism were managed. Evelyn Alsultany argues that through a celebratory US multiculturalism, television shows, like *The West Wing*, began portraying "limited and acceptable versions of diversity" (176). Cautioning against the perception that such diverse representations signal the end of racism, she emphasizes that these seemingly sympathetic representations are meant to be consumed along with dominant narratives of national security and post-race discourse that sustain notions of US exceptionalism. Therefore, instead of simply vilifying the other in order to justify war, the other is portrayed in a seemingly sympathetic complexity that protects US interests.

While the limited representations of diversity Alsultany highlights continue to be part of many television series, in *Breaking Bad* and other Golden Age shows, even shallow diversities are expunged by a white monstrosity that rises to regain its authority in question by positioning it against the increasingly monstrous queer other. The post-9/11 trajectory of monstrosity invests the white, heteronormative patriarch within monstrosity while retrenching the racialized other into a villainous monstrosity with deceptive representations of humanity. It ushers in a post-9/11 national posturing that we are monstrous only because we have to be. In *Breaking Bad*, the zombie horde of others and Walter's archenemy, Gustavo (Gus) Fring (Giancarlo Esposito) become the mechanism through which privileged monstrosity is fortified.

THE ZOMBIE HORDE

Walter's rising monstrosity is coupled with a horde of *Breaking Bad*'s others. His ongoing confrontation with increasingly sinister men sets a rapid pace for Walter's escalating violence and rash behavior. None of his numerous drug-world adversaries are white except for the gang of white supremacists he employs to kill

Fring's men and whom he later obliterates with an M60 machine gun. Most are not fathers or portrayed as fatherly in the ways that Walter is afforded. Furthermore, their monstrosities often descend into ruthless and irrational violence. They are unquestionably the villains that Walter must conquer in order to secure his meth empire. In most things, they represent an anti-heteronormativity carried over from 1930s horror films.

Underscoring their monstrosity, members of the horde are often portrayed through strange body movements resembling zombies. Exemplifying this, in their first scene, Marco and Leonel Salamanca (Luis and Daniel Moncada) walk slowly through a desert landscape in a trance, joining others who drag their bodies on knees and elbows toward the shrine of *Santa Muerte* ("*No Más*"). The brothers are repeatedly portrayed as zombies locked in kill mode. Later, after having his legs amputated, Leonel flings himself out of bed and drags his body toward the door, leaving a gory trail as he claws his way toward the fraternity of DEA agents gaping through the door's window ("I See You").

The zombie motif also overlays the death of Gustavo Fring. Not only does he wander through his own scenes with a distant persona, after he is supposedly killed by Walter's bomb, the camera puts the viewer outside the room as Gus surprisingly walks out, seemingly unscathed. Yet as he adjusts his tie, the camera pans from his profile to his front, one half of his face is his bloody skull with brains and gore hanging out ("Face Off"). In his final moments, Fring lingers as a zombie, suggesting he is not human.

Fring in particular exemplifies the queer monstrous other through his race, nationality, and non-heteronormative sexuality and gender. Fring has a darker skin tone than any of Walter's other enemies. His Chilean background connects him to the Pinochet dictatorship, echoing another 9/11 (1973) and US (CIA) backed military maneuver. His business partner is also portrayed as his closeted lover.

The closet trope further extends into his closeted monstrosity. He encompasses the undetectable threat sustaining the necessary monstrosity of Walter as his public appearance is a successful restaurateur and anti-drug philanthropist. The DEA, which employs Walter's oblivious brother-in-law, stands in for the official but incompetent state in the face of illusive targets. Because of Gus's undetectable monstrosity, Walter's presence is portrayed as all the more necessary. The duel between Walter and Gus is common to post-9/11 media. Mary K. Bloodsworth-Lugo and Carmen R. Lugo-Lugo argue that many post-9/11 films situate anxieties in "the wake of a 'changed America,'" and surmise how we "cope with an increasing number of post-9/11 'monsters'" (245). Protagonists slip into monstrosity, they note, when there is no reliable security outside of the self where deadly threats are difficult to discern; therefore, the only "solution" for the protagonist is to destroy the monstrous other—and in doing so, they recognize their own "monster within" (253). In *Breaking Bad*, those involved in the lucrative distribution of meth appear as border crossers whose physical presence is removed from the familial, heteronormative lives of everyone else. Gus, however, is well-regarded, and his notoriety enhances his unnoticed violence. The technology of Walter's monstrosity, which kills Gus by turning another drug kingpin into a suicide bomber, ushers in a new post-9/11 motto: If you see something, *do something*.

REPRODUCING SYSTEMS OF VIOLENCE

Monstrosity is often a mechanism for violence, or rather, violence is part of the technology of monstrosity. The earlier question of what is at stake now joins the question of what violence is produced and preserved? Morally complicated white monstrosity isn't only wagered but becomes the mechanism for securing white heteronormative patriotism as privilege and is re-animated into an endless war against the ever-lurking monstrous other. In her analysis of *District 9* and *Avatar*, Susana Loza argues that white characters become the alien in order to "manage white fears of invasion, contamination, segregation, miscegenation, and conquest" in a contemporary version of racial drag to "build and buttress the ever-shifting parameters of whiteness and Western identity" (53–54). Similarly, Walter, through monstrosity, refigures a national heteronormativity that had become unreliable as the "war on terror" progressed. Masculinity, via Walter, is reasserted in an insatiable drive for the preservation of the colonial patriarch. As Loza argues, the monstrosity of the white-becoming-alien surrounded by alien others reveals that we are "still re-enacting settler myths" (64). In the case of *Breaking Bad*, the transference of power, identity making, and what parades as necessary violence occurs through Walter, the justifiable, heteronormative monster. His violence is extraordinary and mundane, necessary and innocuous. *Breaking Bad* doesn't break down "bad," but breaks *into* bad, occupying it with an exceptionalism that bolsters ideas of necessary violence while further racializing and vilifying the former sole occupants of bad—the monstrous queer others.

REFERENCES

Alsultany, Evelyn. *Arabs and Muslims in the Media: Race and Representation After 9/11*. NYU P, 2012.

Benshoff, Harry M. *Monsters in the Closet: Homosexuality and the Horror Film*. Manchester UP, 1998.

Bloodsworth-Lugo, Mary K. and Carmen R. Lugo-Lugo. "The Monster Within: Post-9/11 Narratives of Threat and the U.S. Shifting Terrain of Terror." *Monster Theory: Reading Culture*, edited by Jeffrey Jerome Cohen. U of Minnesota P, 1996, pp. 243–255.

Cohen, Jeffrey Jerome. "Monster Culture: Seven Theses." *Monster Theory: Reading Culture*, edited by Jeffrey Jerome Cohen. U of Minnesota P, 1996, pp. 3–25.

"Cornered." *Breaking Bad*, season 4, episode 6, AMC, August 21, 2011.

"Face Off." *Breaking Bad*, season 4, episode 13, AMC, October 9, 2011.

Fojas, Camilla. *Zombies, Migrants, and Queers: Race and Crisis Capitalism in Pop Culture*. U of Illinois P, 2017.

Foucault, Michel, *The History of Sexuality*, vol. 1, trans. Robert Hurley. Vintage, 1980, pp. 105–106.

Griffin, Sean. "Pronoun Trouble: The 'Queerness' of Animation." *Spectator*, vol. 15, no. 1, 1994, pp. 94–109.

Halberstam, Judith. *Skin Shows: Gothic Horror and the Technology of Monsters*. Duke UP, 1995.

Hardt, Michael and Antonio Negri. *Multitude: War and Democracy in the Age of Empire*. Penguin, 2004.

"I See You." *Breaking Bad*, season 3, episode 8, AMC, May 9, 2010.

Levina, Marina and Diem-My T. Bui. "Introduction: Toward a Comprehensive Monster Theory in the 21st Century." *Monster Culture in the 21st Century: A Reader*, edited by Marina Levina and Diem-My T. Bui. Bloomsbury, 2014, pp. 1–13.

Loza, Susana. "Playing Alien in Post-Racial Times." *Monster Culture in the 21st Century: A Reader*, edited by Marina Levina and Diem-My T. Bui. Bloomsbury, 2014, pp. 53–72.

Martin, Brett. *Difficult Men: Behind the Scenes of a Creative Revolution: From the Sopranos and The Wire to Mad Men and Breaking Bad*. Penguin, 2014.

"No Más." *Breaking Bad*, season 3, episode 1, AMC, March 21, 2008.

"Pilot." *Breaking Bad*, season 1, episode 1, AMC, January 20, 2010.

Puar, Jasbir K. and Amit S. Rai. "Monster, Terrorist, Fag: The War on Terrorism and the Production of Docile Patriots." *Social Text*, vol. 20, no. 3, 2002, pp. 117–148.

Sepinwall, Alan. *The Revolution Was Televised: How The Sopranos, Mad Men, Breaking Bad, Lost, and Other Groundbreaking Dramas Changed TV Forever*. Touchstone, 2015.

SARAH E. S. SINWELL

12. #MAKEREYASEXUAL AND #KEEPJUGHEADASEXUAL: ASEXUALITY, QUEERNESS, AND REPRESENTATION ON TWITTER

Theorists of asexuality have often pointed to the invisibility of asexuality as a sexual orientation. It is only recently that asexuality has been represented within media culture. In films such as *Mysterious Skin* (Araki) and television series such as *Dexter* (Manos Jr.), asexuality is linked to the characters' criminal behavior and pathologies. In the popular sitcom *The Big Bang Theory* (Lorre and Prady), the asexual character of Sheldon (played by Jim Parsons) is associated with nerdiness and a possible personality disorder. In soap operas such as *Shortland Street* (Hollings, De Nave, and Daniel), teen television shows such as *Degrassi* (Moore and Schuyler) and *Losing It* (MTV), and crime series such as *House* (Shore), asexual characters are often represented as minor characters and rarely embody asexual identity outside of its problematic interrelationship with sexual pathology.

As a means of resisting these cultural (mis)understandings of asexuality, members of the asexual community have turned to Twitter and other social media outlets in order to voice their concerns about the contemporary state of asexual visibility in film and television. For instance, fans of the characters of Rey (played by Daisy Ridley) in *Star Wars: The Force Awakens* (Abrams) and Jughead (played by Cole Sprouse) in *Riverdale* (Aguirre-Sacasa) have turned to Twitter to call for even more visible and positive representation of asexuality onscreen. In this essay, I explore the campaigns to #MakeReyAsexual and #KeepJugheadAsexual on Twitter as a means of further examining how queer audiences and fans are promoting more positive and complex representations of asexual visibility in popular media.

Following in the footsteps of the It Gets Better Project of 2010, fans of both *Star Wars: The Force Awakens* and *Riverdale* are publicly calling for more mainstream visibility of asexuality in film and television. These Twitter campaigns enable members of the asexual community to resist the idea that asexuality is a pathology and pursue stories of aromantic and asexual relationships that push the boundaries of both heterosexual and queer identity. Questioning ideas of homosexuality and heteronormativity, these fans encourage the media to create asexual characters as a means of (re)defining sex, sexuality, and queerness. In this way, I argue that the creation of these Twitter campaigns worldwide is taking on the project of the LGBTIQPA+ (lesbian, gay, bisexual, trans, intersex, queer, pansexual, asexual, and other diverse identities) community by drawing attention to this need for asexuals to resist the erasure of their sexual identities, increase asexual visibility, and come out of the closet.

ASEXUALITY AND QUEER IDENTITY: HISTORIES AND DEFINITIONS

Asexuality has only recently been acknowledged as a sexual identity. Historically, asexuality was understood as a pathology, or a psychological or mental disorder. Rather than being seen as a sexual orientation, asexuality was associated with Hypoactive Sexual Desire Disorder (HSDD) and characterized in the *DSM-IV* as a mental disorder defined by lack of interest in sex (Bogaert 2004, 2006). By linking asexuality to abnormal psychology, asexuality was seen as both a mental and sexual dysfunction, much like the ways in which queerness and homosexuality were historically constructed in relation to sodomy and non-normative behavior (Bayer; Irvine).

Founded in 2001 by David Jay, The Asexual Visibility and Education Network (AVEN) was created as an online discussion forum for the asexual community worldwide. Working to counteract this construction of asexuality as a sexual pathology, AVEN defines asexuality as a sexual identity. An asexual is "a person who does not experience sexual attraction" (AVEN). Unlike celibacy, which is understood as a personal choice, asexuality is understood as a sexual orientation (AVEN). According to sex researcher Anthony Bogaert, between 1 and 6 percent of the American population describe themselves as asexual (2006, 241). Thus, the asexual community suggests incorporating an A (for asexual) within the LGBTIQPA+ community as a means of including asexuality within contemporary understandings of gender, sexuality, and queerness.

One cannot discuss the cultural significance of asexuality without also taking into account its relationship to queer theory. One of the most significant contributions of queer theory to the study of asexuality is Michel Foucault's description of sexuality as *the* open secret in *The History of Sexuality*. Foucault argues that in modern societies, sexuality is both obsessively talked about and condemned to prohibition, repression, and silence (1990). Thus, sexuality itself is seen as both private and public. Within the cultural imaginary, asexuality shares a particular relationship to the open secret and to silence. Since asexuality has been historically and culturally understood as taboo, pathologized, or even nonexistent, its entrenchment within the silence of the closet has often restricted discursive access to these ideas and identities (Bogaert, 2006). The Twitter campaigns to #MakeReyAsexual and #KeepJugheadA-sexual draw attention to this need for asexuals to increase their visibility by making Foucault's open secret more open and by coming out of the closet.

In *Epistemology of the Closet*, Eve Sedgwick continues to theorize this concept of the open secret in relation to sexuality. For Sedgwick, the closet is the defining structure of modern knowledge and of gay oppression. In the trope of the closet, she creates a model that incorporates not only sexuality but also other forms of language, knowledge, and existence. For many asexuals, sexuality is not only a secret but also an unknown sexual category. It is only following AVEN's creation in 2001 that asexuality has been understood as a sexual and cultural category (Bogaert, 2004, 2006; Scherrer; Cerankowski and Milks; Gressgard).

One of the most significant contributions that Sedgwick makes in relation to asexuality is her construction of other means of differentiating people in relation to sexuality besides sexual object choice. For instance, Sedgwick asks, why couldn't we be differentiated based on whether we prefer to have lots of sex or very little, whether sexuality makes up a large share of our self-perceived identity, whether auto-eroticism is a significant portion of our sex lives, and so forth. For asexuals, this understanding of a sexuality that includes how much we might have sex, or whether sexuality makes up a large share of our self-perceived identity or not, is a reminder that asexuals can also be included within queerness. Reading asexuality through a queer lens enables a rethinking of sexuality beyond its seemingly necessary relationship to sexual desire and enables us to create a place for asexuality within both queer theory and the LGBTIQPA+ community.

AVEN draws attention to the multiple ways in which asexuals experience their own sexualities, pointing out that "each asexual person experiences things like relationships, attraction, and arousal somewhat differently" (AVEN). For the asexual community, this includes those who experience romantic attraction (romantic asexuals) and those who do not (aromantic asexuals; Corrigan 1). At the same time, AVEN also acknowledges the fluidity of asexual identity by encouraging members of its community to choose to self-identify as asexual as long as they see fit. As Randi Gressgard notes in "Asexuality: From Pathology to Identity and Beyond," "Asexual identity has the potential to revitalize queer critique of naturalized gender and sexuality norms in so far as it destabilizes the sexual regime (of truth) that privilege sexual relationships" (69). These statements underscore the ability of asexuals both to self-identify as queer and/or LGBTIQPA+ and to create their own (romantic and aromantic) identities. By fostering an inclusive and fluid definition of asexuality that acknowledges the complexities of defining any (sexual) identity category, AVEN creates a space for queerly imagining asexuality via all of its complexities and variations.

ASEXUALITY IN THE MEDIA

Many of the cultural and social definitions of asexuality began with the formation of the asexual community online via AVEN. With over 19,000 users worldwide, AVEN hosts the world's largest asexual community and serves as a resource for the asexual community and its allies (Scherrer; Cerankowski and Milks). The site also hosts a large archive of resources on asexuality, including frequently asked questions, a survey about asexual demographics, a wiki, a bimonthly newsletter/magazine (*AVENues*), video links, and a number of forums on everything from asexuality itself, to meetups, personal ads, visibility and education projects, and an open-mic poetry area.

Representations of asexuality in film and television, on the other hand, have been fairly limited. In many cases, asexuality has been limited to its representation as a criminal behavior and a sexual pathology (*Mysterious Skin* and *Dexter*). In sitcoms such as *The Big Bang Theory*, the asexual character of Sheldon is often associated with nerdiness. Most often, asexual characters are represented as minor characters and rarely embody asexual identity outside of its problematic interrelationship with sexual pathology (*Degrassi, Losing It, House*). However, in the Netflix series *BoJack Horseman* (Bob-Waksberg) the character of Todd (voiced by Aaron Paul), has yet to be pathologized and has been able to explore his asexuality in a variety of ways (both romantically and aromantically). This paucity of asexual representation in contemporary media has led to a call not only for more positive representation of asexuals, but also for asexuals to identify themselves within the LGBTIQPA+ community.

The advent of campaigns such as #MakeReyAsexual and #KeepJugheadAsexual is not the first time that media fans have taken to Twitter in order to encourage and promote LGBTIQPA+ visibility and advocate for more representation in popular media. Hashtags like #WeNeedLGBTQStories have also been reminders of the popularity of such campaigns as #GiveElsaAGirlfriend (referring to the character of Elsa from *Frozen* (Buck), #GiveCaptainAmericaABoyfriend (following the release of *Captain America: Civil War*; Russo and Russo), and #MakePoeGay (again pointing to the significance of *Star Wars: The Force Awakens* within these fan communities). These campaigns point not only to the absence of LGBTIQPA+ characters within contemporary media more generally but also to alternative possibilities for queer media representation. As the GLAAD (formerly the Gay & Lesbian Alliance Against Defamation) 2015 Overview of Findings attests, "Of the 126 releases GLAAD counted from the major

studios in 2015, 22 (17.5%) contained characters identified as lesbian, gay, bisexual, or transgender." As seen here, GLAAD's Study does not even reference the inclusion of asexual characters within contemporary media. In this way, these Twitter campaigns serve as a reminder of the further limitations of LGBTIQPA+ media representation.

It is not by chance that the stories of the characters of Elsa, Captain America, and Poe were chosen by the LGBTIQPA+ community. These characters' lack of romantic/sexual/love interests have provided not only fodder for shipping (the fan act of creating fictional relationships between characters), but also an opportunity for fans to resist the status quo and create LGBTIQPA+ characters outside of more typical heteronormative narratives (Hills; Booth). As Emanuel Levy writes in *Cinema of Outsiders*, "The real issue is not so much gay content as gay sensibility, the 'gay look'—how gays and lesbians perceive and dissect Hollywood movies, how they read films against the grain, looking for meanings not just in the text but in the subtext" (480). By taking to Twitter to demand asexual representation, these fans are encouraging corporations such as Disney and Marvel to take on the queer project of resisting heteronormativity and promoting queer visibility.

#MAKEREYASEXUAL AND #KEEPJUGHEADASEXUAL: PRODUCING ASEXUAL VISIBILITY

The #MakeReyAsexual campaign began in May 2016 (just five months after the December 18, 2015, release of *Star Wars: The Force Awakens*). The asexual community focused on the character of Rey (played by Daisy Ridley) because of her character's refusal to be pigeonholed into the category of female love interest. As Rey is introduced as a character, she is masked and nongendered, until she uncovers her face for a drink of water in the desert. Though Finn (the storm trooper/rebel played by John Boyega) keeps trying to hold her hand, Rey proclaims, "Stop taking my hand." When he asks, "Do you have a boyfriend?" she answers, "None of your business." One can imagine a situation in which these interactions would lead to a more romantic or sexual encounter, but Rey refuses to be seen as only a love interest. Rather than making Rey heterosexual or "reducing her to a love interest," the asexual community campaigns to #MakeReyAsexual and advocates for more asexual representation in film.

In the summer of 2017, I examined over 400 tweets that had been posted with the #MakeReyAsexual and #KeepJugheadAsexual hashtags on Twitter. These Twitter postings range from May 2016 (when the #MakeReyAsexual campaign began) to January 2017 (when *Riverdale* premiered on the CW network). A number of themes emerged from the postings on the #MakeReyAsexual Twitter feed. For instance, many members of the asexual community advocate for Rey to be an asexual character as a means of normalizing asexuality.

> **Queen of Aces** @Michael_Paramo 24 May 2016
>
> **#MakeReyAsexual** because there is still a lot of ignorance surrounding asexuality. This could educate so many people about our community.

> ♡ @rrranpoes 24 May 2016
>
> **#MakeReyAsexual** because we get next to no rep in anything at all and it would be great to normalize asexuality as well as make it known:)

> ♡ @rrranpoes 24 May 2016
>
> **#MakeReyAsexual** to let it be known that for being asexual, you're not broken, would mean a lot to ace people everywhere

> **andrea // hoco sp** @daisyyquakes 24 May 2016
>
> **#MakeReyAsexual** because asexual people are invalidated by society all the time and they deserve a hero to represent them

Referring to the need to educate the community about asexuality, these postings indicate not only that there is a need for asexual representation but also a need for asexual representation outside the confines of sexual pathology. These Twitter postings point to the ways in which asexual people are often seen as invisible, invalidated, and pathologized by society. Therefore, they consider making Rey asexual a means of educating the public about asexuality in a way that both normalizes it and enables positive and heroic representation.

To this end, many of these posts explicitly acknowledge the paucity of representation of both the LGBTIQPA+ and asexual communities. Referencing characters such as serial killers and Sheldon from *The Big Bang Theory*, many of these posts allude to the need to resist these stereotypes and enable more "real,"

"valid," and "diverse" representations of the asexual community.

> **soph #kokobop** @dchyuns 24 May 2016
>
> **#MakeReyAsexual** we exist. We deserve much more representation. This would be massive for not just us but the LGBT community itself.

> **Estance Moriarty** @Constaniful 24 May 2016
>
> **#MakeReyAsexual**, because representation matters, Rey could speak to an entire generation, be a positive role model for all aces to look to.

> **f 🌈 at uni** @alecmagnvs 24 May 2016
>
> **#MakeReyAsexual** #MakeReyAromantic because aro and ace characters are practically non existent and #RepresentationMatters

> **Angie** @kekyoin 24 May 2016
>
> **#MakeReyAsexual** because the only representation we have are serial killers and sheldon from the big bang theory.

> **Rae Tharp** @the_bearprince 24 May 2016
>
> **#MakeReyAsexual** because aces have only had the pits of "representation" with Sheldon Cooper & other horrid references in mainstream

These posts not only acknowledge the need for more LGBTIQPA+ representation but also the need to represent asexuality outside the confines of sexual pathology and criminality. Remarking on the need to include asexuality within larger understandings of the LGBTIQPA+ community, these postings also see positive media representation as a means of promoting asexual visibility. This desire for positive representation of the asexual community is also evident in the Twitter campaign to #KeepJugheadAsexual.

Even before the new CW series *Riverdale* premiered in January 2017, fans of the *Archie* comic book series had supported keeping the character of Jughead Jones asexual. In an interview with Russ Burlingame at Comicbook.com in 2015, *Archie* comic book writer Chip Zdarsky discussed Jughead's asexuality, saying "There have been iterations of Jughead over the decades where he has been interested in girls, so there's room to play around if someone was inclined. For me though, I like an asexual Jughead. That's more interesting to me than writing him as just being behind everyone developmentally." Representing Jughead as asexual enables his character to be understood in more complex ways, both as a character and as a representation of the larger asexual community.

The actor who plays Jughead on *Riverdale*, Cole Sprouse, told *Hollywood Life* that he fought unsuccessfully to portray his character as asexual, saying "Asexuality is not one of those things in my research that is so understood at face value and I think maybe the development of that narrative could also be something very interesting and very unique and still resonate with people, and not step on anyone's toes" (Longeretta). Unlike the character of Rey (whose sexuality is undefined onscreen), the character of Jughead was historically represented in the *Archie* comic book canon as asexual. In this way, the campaign to #KeepJugheadAsexual is the asexual community's attempt to insist on more asexual representation on television.

In addition to advocating that *Riverdale* should stick to the canon by keeping Jughead asexual, many of these Twitter postings refer to the asexual community's desire not to have their identities erased.

> **AJ Madeline** @AJ_Madeline Jan 26
>
> #JugheadRepresents every single forgotten and erased aroace. We exist. Please don't erase us. **#keepjughead-asexual** @CW_Riverdale
>
> **AJ Madeline** @AJ_Madeline Jan 26
>
> #JugheadRepresents hope that I'm not alone. **#KeepJugheadAsexual**. Don't take away the little representation we have @CW_Riverdale
>
> **Maggie (Captain Ace)** @royai_alchemist Jan 26
>
> Jughead Jones is aromantic & asexual. @CW_Riverdale Don't erase my communities! #JugheadRepresents **#keepjugheadasexual** #aroacejugheadorbust
>
> **Bri** @Bri_Cheri Jan 15
>
> **#KeepJugheadAsexual** so fans can have some much needed visibility and an authentic, true to comics character. @CW_Riverdale

These Twitter campaigns are a reminder of the significance of media representation for the larger LGBTIQPA+ community. In the characters of Rey and Jughead, the asexual community is searching for their own representation online. Like those members of the queer community that were interviewed in *The Celluloid Closet* in 1996 (Rob Epstein and Jeffrey Freidman), the asexual community wishes to move beyond stereotypes of asexuals as psychopathic predators and desexualized nerds, and toward a representation of asexuals that encompasses a more fluid understanding of asexuality in relation to romance, sex, and queerness.

CONCLUSION

These Twitter campaigns create a space for asexuals to imagine themselves and their experiences and share them with the online community. As Kristin Scherrer writes in her study of AVEN users online, "it was only after encountering the language of asexuality and an asexual community that these participants took on the identity" (631). In these campaigns, asexuality is often constructed in relation to the larger LGBTIQPA+ community as a means of creating a social movement and a network of public visibility. At the same time, by defining asexuality within the larger cultural zeitgeist of such franchises as *Star Wars* and *Archie* comic books, these Twitter campaigns are a means of further promoting asexual visibility. As Alexander Doty attests, "some of the most exciting deployments of 'queer/queerness' are related to the word's ability to describe those complex circumstances in texts, spectators, and production that resist easy categorization, but that definitely escape or defy the heteronormative" (7). Reimagining asexualities together with all of their pluralities and intersections enables us to rethink the ways in which asexuality is constructed in relation to gender, sexuality, and queerness and creates a space for asexual "coming out."

REFERENCES

Abrams, J. J., dir. *Star Wars: The Force Awakens*. Walt Disney Studios, 2015.

Aguirre-Sacasa, Roberto, creator. *Riverdale*. Warner Brothers Television, 2017–present.

Araki, Gregg, dir. *Mysterious Skin*. Tartan Films, 2004.

Asexual Visibility and Education Network. 2008. http://www.asexuality.org. Accessed July 6, 2017.

Bayer, Ronald. *Homosexuality and American Psychiatry: The Politics of Diagnosis*. Princeton, NJ: Princeton University Press, 1987.

Bob-Waksberg, Raphael, creator. *BoJack Horseman*. Netflix, 2014–present.

Bogaert, Anthony. "Asexuality: Prevalence and Associated Factors in a National Probability Sample." *The Journal of Sex Research*, vol. 41, no. 3, 2004, pp. 279–287.

Bogaert, Anthony. "Toward a Conceptual Understanding of Asexuality." *Review of General Psychology*, vol. 10, no. 3, 2006, pp. 241–250.

Booth, Paul. *Digital Fandoms: New Media Studies*. New York: Peter Lang, 2010.

Buck, Chris and Jennifer Lee, dir. *Frozen*. Walt Disney Pictures, 2013.

Burlingame, Russ. "Chip Zdarsky Opens Up About Jughead." *Comicbook.com*. September 25, 2015. http://comicbook.com/2015/09/25/chip-zdarsky-opens-up-about-jughead. Accessed July 6, 2017.

Cerankowski, Karli June and Megan Milks. "New Orientations: Asexuality and Its Implications for Theory and Practice." *Feminist Studies*, vol. 36, no. 3, 2010, pp. 650–664.

Corrigan, Mark, Kristina Gupta, and Todd Morrison. "Introduction." In *Asexuality and Sexual Normativity: An Anthology*. New York: Routledge, 2014, pp. 1–9.

Doty, Alexander. *Flaming Classics: Queering the Film Canon*. New York and London: Routledge, 2000.

Epstein, Rob and Jeffrey Freidman, dir. *The Celluloid Closet*. Sony Pictures Classics, 1996.

Foucault, Michel. *The History of Sexuality, Volume I: An Introduction*. New York: Vintage Books, 1990.

GLAAD Overview of Findings. 2015. https://www.glaad.org/sri/2015/overview. Accessed July 6, 2017.

Gressgard, Randi. "Asexuality: From Pathology to Identity and Beyond." In *Asexuality and Sexual Normativity: An Anthology*. Edited by Mark Corrigan, Kristina Gupta, and Todd Morrison. New York: Routledge, 2014, pp. 68–81.

Hills, Matt. *Fan Cultures*. London: Routledge, 2002.

Hollings, Bettina, Catherine De Nave, and Jason Daniel, creators. *Shortland Street*. TVNZ2, 1992–present.

Irvine, Janice. *Disorders of Desire: Sexuality and Gender in Modern American Sexology*. Philadelphia: Temple University Press, 2005.

Jay, David. "The Computer in the Closet: A Look at Online Collective Identity Formation." 2003. http://web.archive.org/web/20040712040017/http://www.asexuality.org/AVENpaper.pdf. Accessed July 6, 2017.

Levy, Emanuel. *Cinema of Outsiders: The Rise of American Independent Film*. New York: New York University Press, 1999.

Longeretta, Emily, "Cole Sprouse Reveals He Fought for Jughead to be Asexual in 'Riverdale': I'll Keep Fighting," *Hollywood Life*, January 13, 2017. http://hollywoodlife.com/2017/01/13/riverdale-jughead-asexual-cole-sprouse-interview. Accessed July 6, 2017.

Lorre, Chuck and Bill Prady, creators. *The Big Bang Theory*. Warner Brothers Television, 2007–present.

Manos Jr., James, creator. *Dexter*. Showtime Networks, 2006–2013.

Moore, Yan and Linda Schuyler, creators. *Degrassi*. CTV, 2001–present.

MTV, creator. *Losing It*, 2014–2016.

Russo, Joe and Anthony Russo, dir. *Captain America: The Winter Soldier*. Marvel Studios, 2014.

Scherrer, Kristin. "Coming to an Asexual Identity: Negotiating Identity, Negotiating Desire." *Sexualities*, vol. 11, no. 5, 2008, pp. 621–641.

Sedgwick, Eve. *Epistemology of the Closet*. Berkeley: University of California Press, 1990.

Shore, David, creator. *House*. NBC Universal Television, 2004–2012.

13. PRAISE AND PREJUDICE

The thin, silky sheet quivers under its pin, cascading beneath the flowing ventilation units in the endless hallway of steely lockers. The poster is adorned with almost illegible scrawl, allowing only the faintest comprehension of enterprising 12th grader *Sara Machang*'s pursuit of "research correspondents." The qualifications are: a positive attitude, flexible schedule, and knowledge about the portrayal of queerness in Asian Media.

Sara should have been more demanding. She knows that, now, as she sits at an old, injured desk, swarmed by a pack of similarly aged girls who seem to have completely misinterpreted the positions.

With a weary start, Sara asks, "Why don't we all introduce ourselves? Let's all share our names, our grades, and our reason for interest in the project. I'm Sara Machang, and this is a senior project I'm planning to include with my Dean's Award recommendation letter."

A bright-eyed girl sitting opposite her decides that she's the bravest of the group. "Hi! I'm Ria, I'm a junior, and I'm an expert on gay characters in Asian culture because of my expertise on 'Boys' Love.'"

Sara's heart deflates a little at that, and continues to leak with each new introduction. The majority of her applicants are Boys' Love fans. Boys' Love, or BL, as any one of the fourteen individuals crowding the high school English classroom would call it, is a genre of romantic fiction. Though the genre of Boys' Love thrives as an extremely lucrative industry in Asian media—with BL dramas, movies, comics, or other—the term has been used by fans to apply to any instance, fictional or not, of sexual or romantic relationships between men.

The audience largely consists of straight female fans. Of course, there are exceptions of male, and/or non-heterosexual viewers; Sara herself is one such example of the latter, but it seems her group of counterparts are not.

The last girl's slight smile is brief and confident like the statement she delivers. "Cara. Senior. I used to be a straight couple shipper," translation: *supporter*, "But these days I'm *super* into BL stuff. Gay guys are just so adorable and hot." She gushes, the statement dripping down the ridges of Sara's ears.

Sara bites her cheeks the way she used to when she was tiptoeing around the closet. She inhales, letting herself cleanse—in from her nose and out through her mouth. "So, that's all for today, then. Thank you for your time everybody! Some of you will hear back from me."

As she's locking up the classroom, her younger brother, Sungi, texts her inquiries about any progress made. Sara simply replies: *It's not what I wanted, but I can use it.*

THE RESEARCH

The elimination rounds have shaved off a good 65% of her initial applicants. Sara's comfort is currently only shared with a manageable five interviewees as opposed to a small village of them. She centers her phone on the creaking wooden table and starts a voice memo. "Would you mind sharing your favorite aspects of BL, and why it attracts you more than straight-centric love stories, even though you all identify as straight?"

Cara is the first to nod. "Of course. I mean, I already told you that the guys in BL are seriously attractive, so that's a perk. The real winner, though, are the love stories! They're so romantic and scandalous. Boy/girl pairs are so average and *normal*. It's kind of a rush watching dramas or comedies showing something taboo."

"Right." Sara wraps her mind around that perspective, while attempting to fit her mouth around the label of *taboo*. "Are there any . . . tropes, characteristics, or typical plot lines in a BL story that you're partial to?"

Cara lets out an abrupt and appreciative squeal, but contains most of it in her throat. "Oh my God, I love when one of them used to be straight, but turns gay for the other one."

Sara stiffens. *There's a plethora of ways to describe someone who likes more than one gender, and you just used none of them.* "Okay, so what does that mean to you?"

"Well, for example," Cara fishes out her phone and shows Sara the promotional art for a Thai drama she's actually already familiar with. "This guy," She points to the taller of the two, "Was dating a girl at the beginning of the season, but he ends up accidentally sleeping with one of his male friends and they become a couple. There's just something so special about a guy *changing* for you, you know? Like, he didn't like guys, but he likes this one guy." She sighs. "It's romantic."

"And what about you?" Sara asks toward Talia. "Anything you like in BL?"

Talia shifts her weight in her chair, then flicks out a palm as if to mark where her conversation begins. "Well, the reason I like *Asian* BL, and not just any regular" (*White*?) "Gay couple in a show is because of the seniority in Asian culture. Unlike us in the Western world, they have age superiority dynamics of older and younger, like with *hyung/dongsaeng* in Korea, or *senpai/kohai* in Japan, or *P/nong* in Thailand. It's really hot that they call each other by those titles, like a constant reminder of who is the dominant caretaker figure."

Sara suddenly remembers she's the only one in the room personally familiar with Asian culture. These conventions of superiority of multiple countries in Asia are respectful. *I don't think twice about addressing my little brother or close friends with these names.* To hear someone say they find it attractive is interesting, to say the least.

Suddenly, Raelynn pipes up. "That totally has to do with *seme/uke* dynamics too!" She turns to Sara, who doesn't need the definition, but accepts it anyway. "Seme and uke are Japanese terms used when referring to BL couples. *Semeru* is the verb for attack, and *ukeru* means to receive, so they have to do with—"

"A top/bottom dynamic. Yeah, I get it."

Raelynn grins. "Personally, that's *my* favorite part of BL. Usually, age has to do with it. Typically, the top is the older, suave, womanizer type. The bottom is usually the cutesy, shy, more obviously gay one. But it's *especially* good when they make the older one the bottom, because then it's like he loves his boyfriend so much that he doesn't mind submitting to a junior. It's true love."

Sara physically relaxes into her chair, although her psychological state isn't remotely reflective of it. "I don't know if I would interpret it *that* way—"

Hailey suddenly jerks up, and Sara's heart leaps from her chest in surprise; the girl's been quietly fixated on her phone since the meeting began, stiff as a stone. "Wait, Sara *Machang*, right?" She asks with clear intent.

Sara takes a moment to swallow her shock. "Uh, yeah? It was on the poster."

"I just realized, *Machang* is Sung's last name—"

"*Sung*? My brother? Do you know him?"

"Not really," Hailey admits, "But he's well known." She exhales with relief. "*That's* why you seemed so familiar."

Sara scans the group. "I'm not following."

"I am." Talia adds. "It's @bonhwa-sungifanclub on Twitter."

Sara scrunches her nose up. *Bon-hwa? Who is—* "Oh, you mean *Benny*?" Sara asks back.

They know his Korean name? She sits, baffled. *Wait, why am I focused on them trying to make him more Asian? If that's even something you can do to actual Asian people.*

The nape of her neck tingles. "What did you just say about Twitter?"

"You haven't seen it?" Cara giggles. "Kinda ironic." Then she opens Twitter, searches up a user, and holds it in front of Sara's face.

The first post to fill up the screen is a picture of her very own little brother eating lunch by the science building with his best friend. Sungi is leaning on the table, resting his chin on his arms and watching Benny eat. A chuckle is dancing on his lips.

Sara can't help but smile; Sungi's been happy with Benny. Upon remembering the context of this reminiscing, her lips quickly sink into a frown. The Twitter page is brimming with similar pictures, all of Sungi and Benny, and all creepy, no matter how cute the scenes are of the two holding hands while leaving school or wearing matching hats. Even more disturbing are the replies speculating who is the seme and uke in *their* relationship. Sara can tell the girls kind of want to ask her, and she's thankful for the self-restraint from doing so.

"They look so good together." Cara notes, with a decisive click of the tongue.

Sara is unsure whether she should thank or dismiss them.

Talia nods furiously. "BonSung is *such* a cute bromance!"

Sure, if dating for the past year and a half makes you bros. Never before has Sarah so much wanted to betray her brother's privacy just to make a point.

Luckily, Hailey voices her same thoughts. "Bromance?"

Cara laughs, light, and melodic, and still chilling. "Come *on*, Sungi had girlfriends. He's not actually gay."

Raelynn feels a need to contribute. "But he could be gay for Bon-hwa." She knits her eyebrows together, forehead tugged into wrinkles of thought. "They're so much cuter than him and Lilian were."

Sara blinks, as if a splash of darkness will reset her surroundings. For a group of people that see queerness in everything, they don't have the most accurate gaydar.

"I mean, there's clearly intimacy between them," Hailey offers, "But I can't say what it is exactly."

A long sigh encircles them. The trail wisps from Cara's mouth. "I get what you mean. The fanservice these days is *so good*; we get couple moments with show bromances even when they're *not* in character! The actors are affectionate like a true gay couple, but deep down inside, I know they're not." She slouches in her chair, indulging in personal tragedy. "Shame."

Hailey agrees for different reasons. "It sucks. There are actually a handful of real BL celebrity couples in Asia that brave the public reaction to their love, and provide people with hope, but many actors in BL dramas get the benefits of acting like a gay couple and still have the privilege of being straight at the end of the day. It infuriates me that something with so much potential to make a positive impact, like *BL*, has created an industry where you can't even tell the difference between a fake relationship between two men and a real one. Fans feel entitled and acclimatized to the fanservice of straight idols. How are you supporting queer people if you don't want to interact with their real experiences?"

The other girls in the room have been stilled by the abrupt rant. If even a hair graces the floor, the scrape of fiber against carpet will be ear-splitting against the backdrop of silence.

Sara feels a welling optimism curl around her chest at the girl's words. With a light finger, she leans forward and presses the red recording button. After her phone chimes stop, she looks left and right over the disarray of emotions. "That's our first day, everyone." She claps her hands together, and smiles at the quieted, self-proclaimed gay supporters. Taking a line from Hailey's book, she asks rhetorically, "How are *you* supporting queer people?"

THE RECAP

Sara returns home as the sun does, finding three bundles of blankets hibernating on the couch. The piles are illuminated by the soft light of the television. "Hey guys." She greets with defeat, collapsing onto a cushion beside one of the fleece mountains.

A head pokes out of the blankets on the far end. "Hey," Sungi replies.

The purple throw blanket beside her buzzes, and suddenly her girlfriend, Mina, is erupting from within. "How was it?"

Sara buries her head into the layer wrapped around Mina's shoulder. "I don't know," is muffled into her side. "It's so taxing. I don't understand how people who worship gay characters can be so okay with silencing real queer people."

Benny emits an empathetic hum, and Sara is flung back to her discovery of the day.

"Hey, boys—" She coughs out. "Do you think anyone at school knows that you're dating?"

"Probably about as many as know about you and Mina." Sungi guesses.

"Well, after talking to the girls, it seems like a lot of people have picked up on it." Sara shares, forking over her phone to Sungi so he can see for himself. "This Twitter account is like a shipper's fan page for *you*."

Sungi cocks his head, then cradles the phone in his hands. The picture filling the screen was taken maybe three or four days ago, at a mall two blocks from school. It's a frozen moment between him and Benny sharing softened glances, cheek-splitting grins, and grazing each other's shoulders. Despite its simplicity, the snapshot is noticeably intimate. "Oh," he mutters, "I know about this."

"You know?" The only indicator that it's a question is the implied question mark tacked onto the back, because Sara's inquiry comes out flat like a statement.

"Uh, yeah. A bunch of people in my grade started joke-shipping me and Benny together back in 8th grade before we even went out, and then it actually took off around school. They take creepy pictures, and argue about who tops in a currently non-sexual relationship, and gush about how cute we are, but most of them still assume we're straight in reality because—"

"Because of your past girlfriends. Got it. People thinking that you're bi are probably the minority. Next biggest theory is likely that he turned you gay."

"Yeah." He turns to his boyfriend and cups his face. "Benny, you're incredibly attractive, and brilliant, and kind, but I don't know if you could make me stop liking girls."

Benny grins, "Couldn't I?"

Sungi thinks, for a moment, and shakes his head.

"You couldn't stop *me* from liking girls either," Sara adds.

Mina giggles, cocooning in the blanket again. "It runs in the family."

Sungi rolls his eyes and tosses Sara's phone back. He relaxes into the plush fabric swaddled around them, content with the present.

"So you're fine with this?" Sara asks.

He shrugs. "Not exactly, but it's uncontrollable. They want to fetishize our relationship, and they have the platform to, so they do. I think queer relationships are like a fantasy to them, just because it's not the norm. You rarely see instances of men and women idols in Asia forced to do fanservice with each other, but when it comes to same-gender showmances, or even real couples, people start to feel entitled to relationships between MLM—"

Benny scoffs. "*Clearly.*"

"Entitled as if these relationships aren't as genuine or valid as straight ones," Sungi finishes.

Sara almost scowls. "I would despise it. They've obsessed over your relationship and interactions— some people may have thought about you guys more than you have. What you *are* is theirs now."

Benny slings himself around Sungi and lets his eyes flutter shut. "Yeah, it's creepy, but at least we exist. There's not much of any queer female representation in these Queer Romance genres of Asia."

"Wait, really?" Sara pokes and prods.

"Really." Benny repeats.

THE ROUGH DRAFT

The room stirs with the white noise of sleeping monitors and wind dancing over wooden desks. The AC unit is knocking against itself, dying and being reborn every 20 minutes. The aged English room is warm and encompassing, closing its walls around the small group of girls. A tentative communion embeds itself into the circle, but not a word is shared.

Sara can only hear the hollow bubbles of water as someone gulps down their bottle, the harsh din of nails scratching erratically at skin, and the soft thuds of furious finger pads against phone screens. She interrupts the quiet symphony with a cough. "Thank you, everyone, for attending this follow-up meeting. It was an informative session."

The group nods back at her with appreciation, tucking their respective devices into their pockets or backpacks.

Sara has spent the last two hours viewing short snippets of each of her interviewees' favorite BL dramas, as well as clips of promotional fan-stage shows.

Her gaze was lazily locked to the screens before them, briefly absorbing the kinds of characters, tropes, and dialogue she was being thrown, but spent most of the time scrutinizing the reactions of her peers. She watched as their faces contorted into a multitude of expressions, ranging from joy, to disgust, to contempt.

Sara also watched in evolving comprehension as different documentations of fanservice were played on screen, whether it was kissing games likes passing playing cards from mouth-to-mouth, or playing up their relationship with excessive flirting. These tendencies are obviously part of the job for the actors, a majority of which are straight, which is exactly what deters Sara further.

Though the group's actions are dubiously supportive toward queer people, it's evident from the smiles stretching their lips that they truly hold these fictional relationships near and dear to their hearts.

It's also increasingly obvious to Sara, with each of their hidden scowls toward the Snivelling Girlfriend or Oblivious Admirer archetypes, that they despise the girls in these shows.

With a leap of faith, possibly inspired by a lack of oxygen circulation in the room, Sara decides to toe across that blurring line. "So, why don't you like the girls?"

Talia groans in annoyance. "Those b****es are always trying to split up the couple because they have a crush on one of them. God, it's annoying—"

Because they're one-note? Sara wonders.

"Because they're stopping the main boys from being together. I hate them." Talia mulls over the claim, rolling her tongue over the statement in her mouth. "But *some* dramas have a cool female friend who help the main characters out."

"Just one?"

"Maybe two." Talia adds thoughtfully. "They would usually set up the boys, that's the only time they're nice."

At the very least, they're not evil. Far from Sara's ideal criterion for positive female representation. Then, she thinks aloud: "What if the girls aren't interested in guys?"

Cara cocks an eyebrow. "Then what's the point of them?"

"Enrichment of characters? They can help the story? What's so different about two girls being in love?" Sara doesn't know, but it's clear the others do as they try and fail to conceal shudders. "More queer representation," Sara argues back, voice shaking with each suggestion.

"It's called *B-L*." Cara deadpans. "I mean, it's mostly about the guys."

"So you don't want girls in the storyline at *all*?"

"They're kind of unnecessary."

And, finally, Sara *gets* it. She understands, that this support of queer men is not always that. Instead, it can be the support of eliminating elements of women from romantic storylines. No girls to feel jealous of, just bottoms to empathize with. No need for realistic female characters, just the *evil b****es* who are born and bred for conflict. Not meaningful queer relationships, just the performance of something taboo.

Sara grits her teeth and grips her pen, as if the worn blade leaking ink is a sword dripping blood. "Why shouldn't *Boys' Love* and *Girls' Love* coexist?"

Cara tests her back. "Because I don't want to *see that*."

Sara's insides twist and melt and spill.

She adjourns the meeting in a fury, ushering out every girl, except the one that had stayed quiet. "You barely talked," Sara says, thankful and remorseful all at once.

Hailey sighs and discards her head into her hands. "It has more than one side." She shares, "Yes, there are horrible viewpoints, but you have to support progress and criticize stagnation. If we don't teach people how to portray people like us, who will encourage them to?"

And Sara freezes. *People like us.* She had just assumed. They had all assumed. It's an oversight; the lack of representation in the media is now pooling into the reflections of real life.

Sara drags her sword through the ripples of this pond.

THE FINAL VERSION

Mina peers over Sara's shoulder to get a better look at the Instagram post. "It's all done?"

"Yep." Sara smiles, tilting her phone toward Mina. "Done."

In the picture, their laughter is soaring; the brilliance of the scene is accentuated by the slight shake of the camera, indicating that the two photographers were enjoying themselves as well.

Mina chose the caption. "Girls and boys love Girls' Love and Boys' Love."

The Instagram account's name is @minasara_official, affectionately titling themselves as "A Project Celebrating Real Girls Love."

Sara studies the influx of comments that flood in. She dismantles every exclaim of shock or disgust, analyzes *who* feels this way and *why* they use harsh words and *how* she can change all this. She even sees Cara comment the underwhelmingly supportive, "*Kinda weird*," which feels soaked with chagrin and animosity.

It's brutal work, but one gem warms her up.

"Guess who's got competition? Love from me and @bennny" Commented by @sungimachang.

Mina laughs, and clicks on his account from Sara's phone.

Sungi had shared the same picture as them, but captioned it with the sensible, "Please get tired of us soon."

The comments below ranged from "Never!" and "You wish," to "Proud of you, much love."

The last comment Sara reads is heinous.

Cara's three words smack the wind out of her. They're short of sweet; rather, fatal.

"You're so cute." She comments.

So cute, Sara thinks, like a ragdoll on display, like a puppy in a glass box, like love that only inhabits the screen for your pleasure.

Discrimination, Sara thinks, still thrives when disguised as admiration.

DONNA HARAWAY

14. SITUATED KNOWLEDGES: THE SCIENCE QUESTION IN FEMINISM AND THE PRIVILEGE OF PARTIAL PERSPECTIVE

Academic and activist feminist inquiry has repeatedly tried to come to terms with the question of what *we* might mean by the curious and inescapable term "objectivity." We have used a lot of toxic ink and trees processed into paper decrying what *they* have meant and how it hurts *us*. The imagined "they" constitute a kind of invisible conspiracy of masculinist scientists and philosophers replete with grants and laboratories. The imagined "we" are the embodied others, who are not allowed *not* to have a body, a finite point of view, and so an inevitably disqualifying and polluting bias in any discussion of consequence outside our own little circles, where a "mass"-subscription journal might reach a few thousand readers composed mostly of science haters. At least, I confess to these paranoid fantasies and academic resentments lurking underneath some convoluted reflections in print under my name in the feminist literature in the history and philosophy of science. We, the feminists in the debates about science and technology, are the Reagan era's "special-interest groups" in the rarified realm of epistemology, where traditionally what can count as knowledge is policed by philosophers codifying cognitive canon law. Of course, a special-interest group is, by Reaganoid definition, any collective historical subject that dares to resist the stripped-down atomism of Star Wars, hypermarket, postmodern, media-simulated citizenship. Max Headroom doesn't have a body; therefore, he alone *sees* everything in the great communicator's empire of the Global Network. No wonder Max gets to have a naive sense of humor and a kind of happily regressive, preoedipal sexuality, a sexuality that we ambivalently—with dangerous incorrectness—had imagined to be reserved for lifelong inmates of female and colonized bodies and maybe also white male computer hackers in solitary electronic confinement.

It has seemed to me that feminists have both selectively and flexibly used and been trapped by two poles of a tempting dichotomy on the question of objectivity. Certainly I speak for myself here, and I offer the speculation that there is a collective discourse on these matters. Recent social studies of science and technology, for example, have made available a very strong social constructionist argument for *all* forms of knowledge claims, most certainly and especially scientific ones.[1] According to these tempting views, no insider's perspective is privileged, because all drawings of inside-outside boundaries in knowledge are theorized as power moves, not moves toward truth. So, from the strong social constructionist perspective, why should we be cowed by scientists' descriptions of their activity and accomplishments; they and their patrons have stakes in throwing sand in our eyes. They tell parables about objectivity and scientific method to students in the first years of their initiation, but no practitioner of the high scientific arts would be caught dead *acting on* the textbook versions. Social constructionists make clear that official ideologies about objectivity and scientific method are particularly bad guides to how scientific knowledge is actually *made*. Just as for the rest of us, what scientists believe or say they do and what they really do have a very loose fit.

Donna Haraway, "Situated Knowledges: The Science Question in Feminism and the Privilege of Partial Perspective," was originally published in *Feminist Studies*, Volume 14, Number 3 (Autumn 1988): 575–599. Reprinted by permission of the publisher, Feminist Studies, Inc., and Donna Haraway.

The only people who end up actually *believing* and, goddess forbid, acting on the ideological doctrines of disembodied scientific objectivity—enshrined in elementary textbooks and technoscience booster literature—are nonscientists, including a few very trusting philosophers. Of course, my designation of this last group is probably just a reflection of a residual disciplinary chauvinism acquired from identifying with historians of science and from spending too much time with a microscope in early adulthood in a kind of disciplinary preoedipal and modernist poetic moment when cells seemed to be cells and organisms, organisms. *Pace*, Gertrude Stein. But then came the law of the father and its resolution of the problem of objectivity, a problem solved by always already absent referents, deferred signifieds, split subjects, and the endless play of signifiers. Who wouldn't grow up warped? Gender, race, the world itself—all seem the effects of warp speeds in the play of signifiers in a cosmic force field.

In any case, social constructionists might maintain that the ideological doctrine of scientific method and all the philosophical verbiage about epistemology were cooked up to distract our attention from getting to know the world *effectively* by practicing the sciences. From this point of view, science—the real game in town—is rhetoric, a series of efforts to persuade relevant social actors that one's manufactured knowledge is a route to a desired form of very objective power. Such persuasions must take account of the structure of facts and artifacts, as well as of language-mediated actors in the knowledge game. Here, artifacts and facts are parts of the powerful art of rhetoric. Practice is persuasion, and the focus is very much on practice. All knowledge is a condensed node in an agonistic power field. The strong program in the sociology of knowledge joins with the lovely and nasty tools of semiology and deconstruction to insist on the rhetorical nature of truth, including scientific truth. History is a story Western culture buffs tell each other; science is a contestable text and a power field; the content is the form.[2] Period.

So much for those of us who would still like to talk about *reality* with more confidence than we allow to the Christian Right when they discuss the Second Coming and their being raptured out of the final destruction of the world. We would like to think our appeals to real worlds are more than a desperate lurch away from

cynicism and an act of faith like any other cult's, no matter how much space we generously give to all the rich and always historically specific mediations through which we and everybody else must know the world. But the further I get in describing the radical social constructionist program and a particular version of postmodernism, coupled with the acid tools of critical discourse in the human sciences, the more nervous I get. The imagery of force fields, of moves in a fully textualized and coded world, which is the working metaphor in many arguments about socially negotiated reality for the postmodern subject, is, just for starters, an imagery of high-tech military fields, of automated academic battlefields, where blips of light called players disintegrate (what a metaphor!) each other in order to stay in the knowledge and power game. Technoscience and science fiction collapse into the sun of their radiant (ir)reality—war.[3] It shouldn't take decades of feminist theory to sense the enemy here. Nancy Hartsock got all this crystal clear in her concept of abstract masculinity.[4]

I, and others, started out wanting a strong tool for deconstructing the truth claims of hostile science by showing the radical historical specificity, and so contestability, of *every* layer of the onion of scientific and technological constructions, and we end up with a kind of epistemological electroshock therapy, which far from ushering us into the high stakes tables of the game of contesting public truths, lays us out on the table with self-induced multiple personality disorder. We wanted a way to go beyond showing bias in science (that proved too easy anyhow) and beyond separating the good scientific sheep from the bad goats of bias and misuse. It seemed promising to do this by the strongest possible constructionist argument that left no cracks for reducing the issues to bias versus objectivity, use versus misuse, science versus pseudoscience. We unmasked the doctrines of objectivity because they threatened our budding sense of collective historical subjectivity and agency and our "embodied" accounts of the truth, and we ended up with one more excuse for not learning any post-Newtonian physics and one more reason to drop the old feminist self-help practices of repairing our own cars. They're just texts anyway, so let the boys have them back.

Some of us tried to stay sane in these disassembled and dissembling times by holding out for a feminist version of objectivity. Here, motivated by many of the same political desires, is the other seductive end of the objectivity problem. Humanistic Marxism was polluted at the source by its structuring theory about the domination of nature in the self-construction of man and by its closely related impotence in relation to historicizing anything women did that didn't qualify for a wage. But Marxism was still a promising resource as a kind of epistemological feminist mental hygiene that sought our own doctrines of objective vision. Marxist starting points offered a way to get to our own versions of standpoint theories, insistent embodiment, a rich tradition of critiquing hegemony without disempowering positivisms and relativisms and a way to get to nuanced theories of mediation. Some versions of psychoanalysis were of aid in this approach, especially anglophone object relations theory, which maybe did more for U.S. socialist feminism for a time than anything from the pen of Marx or Engels, much less Althusser or any of the late pretenders to sonship treating the subject of ideology and science.[5]

Another approach, "feminist empiricism," also converges with feminist uses of Marxian resources to get a theory of science which continues to insist on legitimate meanings of objectivity and which remains leery of a radical constructivism conjugated with semiology and narratology.[6] Feminists have to insist on a better account of the world; it is not enough to show radical historical contingency and modes of construction for everything. Here, we, as feminists, find ourselves perversely conjoined with the discourse of many practicing scientists, who, when all is said and done, mostly believe they are describing and discovering things *by means of* all their constructing and arguing. Evelyn Fox Keller has been particularly insistent on this fundamental matter, and Sandra Harding calls the goal of these approaches a "successor science." Feminists have stakes in a successor science project that offers a more adequate, richer, better account of a world, in order to live in it well and in critical, reflexive relation to our own as well as others' practices of domination and the unequal parts of privilege and oppression that make up all positions. In traditional philosophical categories, the issue is ethics and politics perhaps more than epistemology.

So, I think my problem, and "our" problem, is how to have *simultaneously* an account of radical historical contingency for all knowledge claims and knowing subjects, a critical practice for recognizing our own

"semiotic technologies" for making meanings, *and* a no-nonsense commitment to faithful accounts of a "real" world, one that can be partially shared and that is friendly to earthwide projects of finite freedom, adequate material abundance, modest meaning in suffering, and limited happiness. Harding calls this necessary multiple desire a need for a successor science project and a postmodern insistence on irreducible difference and radical multiplicity of local knowledges. *All* components of the desire are paradoxical and dangerous, and their combination is both contradictory and necessary. Feminists don't need a doctrine of objectivity that promises transcendence, a story that loses track of its mediations just where someone might be held responsible for something, and unlimited instrumental power. We don't want a theory of innocent powers to represent the world, where language and bodies both fall into the bliss of organic symbiosis. We also don't want to theorize the world, much less act within it, in terms of Global Systems, but we do need an earthwide network of connections, including the ability partially to translate knowledges among very different—and power-differentiated—communities. We need the power of modern critical theories of how meanings and bodies get made, not in order to deny meanings and bodies, but in order to build meanings and bodies that have a chance for life.

Natural, social, and human sciences have always been implicated in hopes like these. Science has been about a search for translation, convertibility, mobility of meanings, and universality—which I call reductionism only when one language (guess whose?) must be enforced as the standard for all the translations and conversions. What money does in the exchange orders of capitalism, reductionism does in the powerful mental orders of global sciences. There is, finally, only one equation. That is the deadly fantasy that feminists and others have identified in some versions of objectivity, those in the service of hierarchical and positivist orderings of what can count as knowledge. That is one of the reasons the debates about objectivity matter, metaphorically and otherwise. Immortality and omnipotence are not our goals. But we could use some enforceable, reliable accounts of things not reducible to power moves and agonistic, high-status games of rhetoric or to scientistic, positivist arrogance. This point applies whether we are talking about genes, social classes, elementary particles, genders, races, or texts; the point applies to the exact, natural, social, and human sciences, despite the slippery ambiguities of the words "objectivity" and "science" as we slide around the discursive terrain. In our efforts to climb the greased pole leading to a usable doctrine of objectivity, I and most other feminists in the objectivity debates have alternatively, or even simultaneously, held on to both ends of the dichotomy, a dichotomy which Harding describes in terms of successor science projects versus postmodernist accounts of difference and which I have sketched in this essay as radical constructivism versus feminist critical empiricism. It is, of course, hard to climb when you are holding on to both ends of a pole, simultaneously or alternatively. It is, therefore, time to switch metaphors.

THE PERSISTENCE OF VISION

I would like to proceed by placing metaphorical reliance on a much maligned sensory system in feminist discourse: vision.[7] Vision can be good for avoiding binary oppositions. I would like to insist on the embodied nature of all vision and so reclaim the sensory system that has been used to signify a leap out of the marked body and into a conquering gaze from nowhere. This is the gaze that mythically inscribes all the marked bodies, that makes the unmarked category claim the power to see and not be seen, to represent while escaping representation. This gaze signifies the unmarked positions of Man and White, one of the many nasty tones of the word "objectivity" to feminist ears in scientific and technological, late-industrial, militarized, racist, and male-dominant societies, that is, here, in the belly of the monster, in the United States in the late 1980s. I would like a doctrine of embodied objectivity that accommodates paradoxical and critical feminist science projects: Feminist objectivity means quite simply *situated knowledges*.

The eyes have been used to signify a perverse capacity—honed to perfection in the history of science tied to militarism, capitalism, colonialism, and male supremacy—to distance the knowing subject from everybody and everything in the interests of unfettered power. The instruments of visualization in multinationalist, postmodernist culture have compounded these meanings of disembodiment. The visualizing

technologies are without apparent limit. The eye of any ordinary primate like us can be endlessly enhanced by sonography systems, magnetic reasonance imaging, artificial intelligence-linked graphic manipulation systems, scanning electron microscopes, computed tomography scanners, color-enhancement techniques, satellite surveillance systems, home and office video display terminals, cameras for every purpose from filming the mucous membrane lining the gut cavity of a marine worm living in the vent gases on a fault between continental plates to mapping a planetary hemisphere elsewhere in the solar system. Vision in this technological feast becomes unregulated gluttony; all seems not just mythically about the god trick of seeing everything from nowhere, but to have put the myth into ordinary practice. And like the god trick, this eye fucks the world to make techno-monsters. Zoe Sofoulis calls this the cannibaleye of masculinist extraterrestrial projects for excremental second birthing.

A tribute to this ideology of direct, devouring, generative, and unrestricted vision, whose technological mediations are simultaneously celebrated and presented as utterly transparent, can be found in the volume celebrating the 100th anniversary of the National Geographic Society. The volume closes its survey of the magazine's quest literature, effected through its amazing photography, with two juxtaposed chapters. The first is on "Space," introduced by the epigraph, "The choice is the universe—or nothing."[8] This chapter recounts the exploits of the space race and displays the color-enhanced "snapshots" of the outer planets reassembled from digitalized signals transmitted across vast space to let the viewer "experience" the moment of discovery in immediate vision of the "object."[9] These fabulous objects come to us simultaneously as indubitable recordings of what is simply there and as heroic feats of technoscientific production. The next chapter, is the twin of outer space: "Inner Space," introduced by the epigraph, "The stuff of stars has come alive."[10] Here, the reader is brought into the realm of the infinitesimal, objectified by means of radiation outside the wave lengths that are "normally" perceived by hominid primates, that is, the beams of lasers and scanning electron microscopes, whose signals are processed into the wonderful full-color snapshots of defending T cells and invading viruses.

But, of course, that view of infinite vision is an illusion, a god trick. I would like to suggest how our insisting metaphorically on the particularity and embodiment of all vision (although not necessarily organic embodiment and including technological mediation), and not giving in to the tempting myths of vision as a route to disembodiment and second-birthing allows us to construct a usable, but not an innocent, doctrine of objectivity. I want a feminist writing of the body that metaphorically emphasizes vision again, because we need to reclaim that sense to find our way through all the visualizing tricks and powers of modern sciences and technologies that have transformed the objectivity debates. We need to learn in our bodies, endowed with primate color and stereoscopic vision, how to attach the objective to our theoretical and political scanners in order to name where we are and are not, in dimensions of mental and physical space we hardly know how to name. So, not so perversely, objectivity turns out to be about particular and specific embodiment and definitely not about the false vision promising transcendence of all limits and responsibility. The moral is simple: only partial perspective promises objective vision. All Western cultural narratives about objectivity are allegories of the ideologies governing the relations of what we call mind and body, distance and responsibility. Feminist objectivity is about limited location and situated knowledge, not about transcendence and splitting of subject and object. It allows us to become answerable for what we learn how to see.

These are lessons that I learned in part walking with my dogs and wondering how the world looks without a fovea and very few retinal cells for color vision but with a huge neural processing and sensory area for smells. It is a lesson available from photographs of how the world looks to the compound eyes of an insect or even from the camera eye of a spy satellite or the digitally transmitted signals of space probe-perceived differences "near" Jupiter that have been transformed into coffee table color photographs. The "eyes" made available in modern technological sciences shatter any idea of passive vision; these prosthetic devices show us that all eyes, including our own organic ones, are active perceptual systems, building on translations and specific *ways* of seeing, that is, ways of life. There is no unmediated photograph or passive camera obscura

in scientific accounts of bodies and machines; there are only highly specific visual possibilities, each with a wonderfully detailed, active, partial way of organizing worlds. All these pictures of the world should not be allegories of infinite mobility and interchangeability but of elaborate specificity and difference and the loving care people might take to learn how to see faithfully from another's point of view, even when the other is our own machine. That's not alienating distance; that's a *possible* allegory for feminist versions of objectivity. Understanding how these visual systems work, technically, socially, and psychically, ought to be a way of embodying feminist objectivity.

Many currents in feminism attempt to theorize grounds for trusting especially the vantage points of the subjugated; there is good reason to believe vision is better from below the brilliant space platforms of the powerful.[11] Building on that suspicion, this essay is an argument for situated and embodied knowledges and an argument against various forms of unlocatable, and so irresponsible, knowledge claims. Irresponsible means unable to be called into account. There is a premium on establishing the capacity to see from the peripheries and the depths. But here there also lies a serious danger of romanticizing and/or appropriating the vision of the less powerful while claiming to see from their positions. To see from below is neither easily learned nor unproblematic, even if "we" "naturally" inhabit the great underground terrain of subjugated knowledges. The positionings of the subjugated are not exempt from critical reexamination, decoding, deconstruction, and interpretation; that is, from both semiological and hermeneutic modes of critical inquiry. The standpoints of the subjugated are not "innocent" positions. On the contrary, they are preferred because in principle they are least likely to allow denial of the critical and interpretive core of all knowledge. They are knowledgeable of modes of denial through repression, forgetting, and disappearing acts—ways of being nowhere while claiming to see comprehensively. The subjugated have a decent chance to be on to the god trick and all its dazzling—and, therefore, blinding—illuminations. "Subjugated" standpoints are preferred because they seem to promise more adequate, sustained, objective, transforming accounts of the world. But *how* to see from below is a problem requiring at least as much skill with bodies and language, with the mediations of vision, as the "highest" technoscientific visualizations.

Such preferred positioning is as hostile to various forms of relativism as to the most explicitly totalizing versions of claims to scientific authority. But the alternative to relativism is not totalization and single vision, which is always finally the unmarked category whose power depends on systematic narrowing and obscuring. The alternative to relativism is partial, locatable, critical knowledges sustaining the possibility of webs of connections called solidarity in politics and shared conversations in epistemology. Relativism is a way of being nowhere while claiming to be everywhere equally. The "equality" of positioning is a denial of responsibility and critical inquiry. Relativism is the perfect mirror twin of totalization in the ideologies of objectivity; both deny the stakes in location, embodiment, and partial perspective; both make it impossible to see well. Relativism and totalization are both "god tricks" promising vision from everywhere and nowhere equally and fully, common myths in rhetorics surrounding Science. But it is precisely in the politics and epistemology of partial perspectives that the possibility of sustained, rational, objective inquiry rests.

So, with many other feminists, I want to argue for a doctrine and practice of objectivity that privileges contestation, deconstruction, passionate construction, webbed connections, and hope for transformation of systems of knowledge and ways of seeing. But not just any partial perspective will do; we must be hostile to easy relativisms and holisms built out of summing and subsuming parts. "Passionate detachment"[12] requires more than acknowledged and self-critical partiality. We are also bound to seek perspective from those points of view, which can never be known in advance, that promise something quite extraordinary, that is, knowledge potent for constructing worlds less organized by axes of domination. From such a viewpoint, the unmarked category would *really* disappear—quite a difference from simply repeating a disappearing act. The imaginary and the rational—the visionary and objective vision—hover close together. I think Harding's plea for a successor science and for postmodern sensibilities must be read as an argument for the idea that the fantastic element of hope for transformative knowledge and the severe check and stimulus of

sustained critical inquiry are jointly the ground of any believable claim to objectivity or rationality not riddled with breathtaking denials and repressions. It is even possible to read the record of scientific revolutions in terms of this feminist doctrine of rationality and objectivity. Science has been utopian and visionary from the start; that is one reason "we" need it.

A commitment to mobile positioning and to passionate detachment is dependent on the impossibility of entertaining innocent "identity" politics and epistemologies as strategies for seeing from the standpoints of the subjugated in order to see well. One cannot "be" either a cell or molecule—or a woman, colonized person, laborer, and so on—if one intends to see and see from these positions critically. "Being" is much more problematic and contingent. Also, one cannot relocate in any possible vantage point without being accountable for that movement. Vision is *always* a question of the power to see—and perhaps of the violence implicit in our visualizing practices. With whose blood were my eyes crafted? These points also apply to testimony from the position of "oneself." We are not immediately present to ourselves. Self-knowledge requires a semiotic-material technology to link meanings and bodies. Self-identity is a bad visual system. Fusion is a bad strategy of positioning. The boys in the human sciences have called this doubt about self-presence the "death of the subject" defined as a single ordering point of will and consciousness. That judgment seems bizarre to me. I prefer to call this doubt the opening of nonisomorphic subjects, agents, and territories of stories unimaginable from the vantage point of the cyclopean, self-satiated eye of the master subject. The Western eye has fundamentally been a wandering eye, a traveling lens. These peregrinations have often been violent and insistent on having mirrors for a conquering self—but not always. Western feminists also *inherit* some skill in learning to participate in revisualizing worlds turned upside down in earth-transforming challenges to the views of the masters. All is not to be done from scratch.

The split and contradictory self is the one who can interrogate positionings and be accountable, the one who can construct and join rational conversations and fantastic imaginings that change history.[13] Splitting, not being, is the privileged image for feminist epistemologies of scientific knowledge. "Splitting" in this context should be about heterogeneous multiplicities that are simultaneously salient and incapable of being squashed into isomorphic slots or cumulative lists. This geometry pertains within and among subjects. Subjectivity is multidimensional; so, therefore, is vision. The knowing self is partial in all its guises, never finished, whole, simply there and original; it is always constructed and stitched together imperfectly, and *therefore* able to join with another, to see together without claiming to be another. Here is the promise of objectivity: a scientific knower seeks the subject position, not of identity, but of objectivity, that is, partial connection. There is no way to "be" simultaneously in all, or wholly in any, of the privileged (i.e., subjugated) positions structured by gender, race, nation, and class. And that is a short list of critical positions. The search for such a "full" and total position is the search for the fetishized perfect subject of oppositional history, sometimes appearing in feminist theory as the essentialized Third World Woman.[14] Subjugation is not grounds for an ontology; it might be a visual clue. Vision requires instruments of vision; an optics is a politics of positioning. Instruments of vision mediate standpoints; there is no immediate vision from the standpoints of the subjugated. Identity, including self-identity, does not produce science; critical positioning does, that is, objectivity. Only those occupying the positions of the dominators are self-identical, unmarked, disembodied, unmediated, transcendent, born again. It is unfortunately possible for the subjugated to lust for and even scramble into that subject position—and then disappear from view. Knowledge from the point of view of the unmarked is truly fantastic, distorted, and irrational. The only position from which objectivity could not possibly be practiced and honored is the standpoint of the master, the Man, the One God, whose Eye produces, appropriates, and orders all difference. No one ever accused the God of monotheism of objectivity, only of indifference. The god trick is self-identical, and we have mistaken that for creativity and knowledge, omniscience even.

Positioning is, therefore, the key practice in grounding knowledge organized around the imagery of vision, and much Western scientific and philosophic discourse is organized in this way. Positioning implies responsibility for our enabling practices. It follows that politics and ethics ground struggles for and contests over what may count as rational knowledge. That is, admitted or not, politics and ethics ground struggles over knowledge projects in the exact, natural, social, and human sciences. Otherwise, rationality is simply impossible, an optical illusion projected from nowhere comprehensively. Histories of science may be powerfully told as histories of the technologies. These technologies are ways of life, social orders, practices of visualization. Technologies are skilled practices. How to see? Where to see from? What limits to vision? What to see for? Whom to see with? Who gets to have more than one point of view? Who gets blinded? Who wears blinders? Who interprets the visual field? What other sensory powers do we wish to cultivate besides vision? Moral and political discourse should be the paradigm for rational discourse about the imagery and technologies of vision. Sandra Harding's claim, or observation, that movements of social revolution have most contributed to improvements in science might be read as a claim about the knowledge consequences of new technologies of positioning. But I wish Harding had spent more time remembering that social and scientific revolutions have not always been liberatory, even if they have always been visionary. Perhaps this point could be captured in another phrase: the science question in the military. Struggles over what will count as rational accounts of the world are struggles over *how* to see. The terms of vision: the science question in colonialism, the science question in exterminism,[15] the science question in feminism.

The issue in politically engaged attacks on various empiricisms, reductionisms, or other versions of scientific authority should not be relativism—but location. A dichotomous chart expressing this point might look like this:

universal rationality	ethnophilosophies
common language	heteroglossia
new organon	deconstruction
unified field theory	oppositional positioning
world system	local knowledges
master theory	webbed accounts

But a dichotomous chart misrepresents in a critical way the positions of embodied objectivity that I am trying to sketch. The primary distortion is the illusion of symmetry in the chart's dichotomy, making any position appear, first, simply alternative and, second, mutually exclusive. A map of tensions and reasonances between the fixed ends of a charged dichotomy better represents the potent politics and epistemologies of embodied, therefore accountable, objectivity. For example, local knowledges have also to be in tension with the productive structurings that force unequal translations and exchanges—material and semiotic—within the webs of knowledge and power. Webs *can* have the property of being systematic, even of being centrally structured global systems with deep filaments and tenacious tendrils into time, space, and consciousness, which are the dimensions of world history. Feminist accountability requires a knowledge tuned to reasonance, not to dichotomy. Gender is a field of structured and structuring difference, in which the tones of extreme localization, of the intimately personal and individualized body, vibrate in the same field with global high-tension emissions. Feminist embodiment, then, is not about fixed location in a reified body, female or otherwise, but about nodes in fields, inflections in orientations, and responsibility for difference in material-semiotic fields of meaning. Embodiment is significant prosthesis; objectivity cannot be about fixed vision when what counts as an object is precisely what world history turns out to be about.

How should one be positioned in order to see, in this situation of tensions, reasonances, transformations, resistances, and complicities? Here, primate vision is not immediately a very powerful metaphor or technology for feminist political-epistemological clarification, because it seems to present to consciousness already processed and objectified fields; things seem already fixed and distanced. But the visual metaphor allows one to go beyond fixed appearances, which are only the end products. The metaphor invites us to investigate the varied apparatuses of visual production, including the prosthetic technologies interfaced with our biological eyes and brains. And here we find highly particular machineries for processing regions of the electromagnetic spectrum into our pictures of the world. It is in the intricacies of these visualization technologies in which we are embedded that we will find metaphors and means for understanding and intervening in the patterns of objectification in the world—that is, the patterns of reality for which we must be accountable. In these metaphors, we find means for appreciating simultaneously *both* the concrete, "real" aspect and the aspect of semiosis and production in what we call scientific knowledge.

I am arguing for politics and epistemologies of location, positioning, and situating, where partiality and not universality is the condition of being heard to make rational knowledge claims. These are claims on people's lives. I am arguing for the view from a body, always a complex, contradictory, structuring, and structured body, versus the view from above, from nowhere, from simplicity. Only the god trick is forbidden. Here is a criterion for deciding the science question in militarism, that dream science/technology of perfect language, perfect communication, final order.

Feminism loves another science: the sciences and politics of interpretation, translation, stuttering, and the partly understood. Feminism is about the sciences of the multiple subject with (at least) double vision. Feminism is about a critical vision consequent upon a critical positioning in unhomogeneous gendered social space.[16] Translation is always interpretive, critical, and partial. Here is a ground for conversation, rationality, and objectivity—which is power-sensitive, not pluralist, "conversation." It is not even the mythic cartoons of physics and mathematics—incorrectly caricatured in antiscience ideology as exact, hypersimple knowledges—that have come to represent the hostile other to feminist paradigmatic models of scientific knowledge, but the dreams of the perfectly known in high-technology, permanently militarized scientific productions and positionings, the god trick of a Star Wars paradigm of rational knowledge. So location is about vulnerability; location resists the politics of closure, finality, or to borrow from Althusser, feminist objectivity resists "simplification in the last instance." That is because feminist embodiment resists fixation and is insatiably curious about the webs of differential positioning. There is no single feminist standpoint because our maps require too many dimensions for that metaphor to ground our visions. But the feminist standpoint theorists' goal of an epistemology and politics of engaged, accountable positioning remains eminently potent. The goal is better accounts of the world, that is, "science."

Above all, rational knowledge does not pretend to disengagement: to be from everywhere and so nowhere, to be free from interpretation, from being represented, to . . . [be] fully self-contained or fully formalizable. Rational knowledge is a process of ongoing critical interpretation among "fields" of interpreters and decoders. Rational knowledge is power-sensitive conversation.[17] Decoding and transcoding plus translation and criticism; all are necessary. So science becomes the paradigmatic model, not of closure, but of that which is contestable and contested. Science becomes the myth, not of what escapes human agency and responsibility in a realm above the fray, but, rather, of accountability and responsibility for translations and solidarities linking the cacophonous visions and visionary voices that characterize the knowledges of the subjugated. A splitting of senses, a confusion of voice and sight, rather than clear and distinct ideas, becomes the metaphor for the ground of the rational. We seek not the knowledges ruled by phallogocentrism (nostalgia for the presence of the one true Word) and disembodied vision. We seek those ruled by partial sight and limited voice—not partiality for its own sake but, rather, for the sake of the connections and unexpected openings situated knowledges make possible. Situated knowledges are about communities, not about isolated individuals. The only way to find a larger vision is to be somewhere in particular. The science question in feminism is about objectivity as positioned rationality. Its images are not the products of escape and transcendence of limits (the view from above) but the joining of partial views and halting voices into a collective subject position that promises a vision of the means of ongoing finite embodiment, of living within limits and contradictions—of views from somewhere.

. . .

NOTES

1. For example, see Karin Knorr-Cetina and Michael Mulkay, eds., *Science Observed: Perspectives on the Social Study of Science* (London: Sage, 1983); Wiebe E. Bijker, Thomas P. Hughes, and Trevor Pinch, eds., *The Social Construction of Technological Systems* (Cambridge: MIT Press, 1987); and esp. Bruno Latour's *Les microbes, guerre et paix, suivi de irréductions* (Paris: Métailié, 1984) and *The Pasteurization of France, Followed by Irreductions: A Politico-Scientific Essay* (Cambridge: Harvard University Press, 1988). Borrowing from Michel Tournier's *Vendredi* (Paris: Gallimard, 1967), *Les microbes* (p. 171), Latour's brilliant and maddening aphoristic polemic against all forms of reductionism, makes the essential point for feminists: "*Méfiez-vous de la pureté; c'est le vitriol de l'ame*" (Beware of purity; it is the vitriol of the soul). Latour is not otherwise a notable feminist theorist, but he might be made into one by readings as perverse as those he makes of the laboratory, that great machine for making significant mistakes faster than anyone else can, and so gaining world-changing power. The laboratory for Latour is the railroad industry of epistemology, where facts can only be made to run on the tracks laid down from the laboratory out. Those who control the railroads control the surrounding territory. How could we have forgotten? But now it's not so much the bankrupt railroads we need as the satellite network. Facts run on light beams these days.

2. For an elegant and very helpful elucidation of a noncartoon version of this argument, see Hayden White, *The Content of the Form: Narrative Discourse and Historical Representation* (Baltimore: Johns Hopkins University Press, 1987). I still want more; and unfulfilled desire can be a powerful seed for changing the stories.

3. In "Through the Lumen: Frankenstein and the Optics of Re-Origination" (Ph.D. diss., University of California at Santa Cruz, 1988), Zoe Sofoulis has produced a dazzling (she will forgive me the metaphor) theoretical treatment of technoscience, the psychoanalysis of science fiction culture,

and the metaphorics of extraterrestrialism, including a wonderful focus on the ideologies and philosophies of light, illumination, and discovery in Western mythics of science and technology. My essay was revised in dialogue with Sofoulis's arguments and metaphors in her dissertation.

4. Nancy Hartsock, *Money, Sex, and Power: An Essay on Domination and Community* (Boston: Northeastern University Press, 1984).

5. Crucial to this discussion are Sandra Harding, *The Science Question in Feminism* (Ithaca: Cornell University Press, 1987); Evelyn Fox Keller, *Reflections on Gender and Science* (New Haven: Yale University Press, 1984); Nancy Hartsock, "The Feminist Standpoint: Developing the Ground for a Specifically Feminist Historical Materialism," in *Discovering Reality: Feminist Perspectives on Epistemology, Metaphysics, and Philosophy of Science,* eds. Sandra Harding and Merrill B. Hintikka (Dordrecht, The Netherlands: Reidel, 1983): 283–310; Jane Flax's "Political Philosophy and the Patriarchal Unconscious," in *Discovering Reality,* 245–81; and "Postmodernism and Gender Relations in Feminist Theory," *Signs* 12 (Summer 1987): 621–43; Evelyn Fox Keller and Christine Grontkowski, "The Mind's Eye," in *Discovering Reality,* 207–24; Hilary Rose, "Women's Work, Women's Knowledge," in *What Is Feminism? A Re-Examination,* eds. Juliet Mitchell and Ann Oakley (New York: Pantheon, 1986), 161–83; Donna Haraway, "A Manifesto for Cyborgs: Science, Technology, and Socialist Feminism in the 1980s," *Socialist Review,* no. 80 (March-April 1985): 65–107; and Rosalind Pollack Petchesky, "Fetal Images: The Power of Visual Culture in the Politics of Reproduction," *Feminist Studies* 13 (Summer 1987): 263–92.

Aspects of the debates about modernism and postmodernism affect feminist analyses of the problem of "objectivity." Mapping the fault line between modernism and postmodernism in ethnography and anthropology—in which the high stakes are the authorization or prohibition to craft *comparative* knowledge across "cultures"—Marilyn Strathern made the crucial observation that it is not the written ethnography that is parallel to the work of art as object-of-knowledge, but the *culture.* The Romantic and modernist natural-technical objects of knowledge, in science and in other cultural practice, stand on one side of this divide. The postmodernist formation stands on the other side, with its "anti-aesthetic" of permanently split, problematized, always receding and deferred "objects" of knowledge and practice, including signs, organisms, systems, selves, and cultures. "Objectivity" in a postmodern framework cannot be about unproblematic *objects*; it must be about specific prosthesis and always partial translations. At root, objectivity is about crafting *comparative* knowledge: How may a community name things to be stable and to be like each other? In postmodernism, this query translates into a question of the politics of redrawing of boundaries in order to have non-innocent conversations and connections. What is at stake in the debates about modernism and postmodernism is the pattern of relationships between and within bodies and language. This is a crucial matter for feminists. See Marilyn Strathern, "Out of Context: The Persuasive Fictions of Anthropology," *Current Anthropology* 28 (June 1987): 251–81; and "Partial Connections," Munro Lecture, University of Edinburgh, November 1987, unpublished manuscript.

6. Harding, 24–26, 161–62.

7. John Varley's science fiction short story, "The Persistence of Vision," in *The Persistence of Vision* (New York: Dell, 1978), 263–316, is part of the inspiration for this section. In the story, Varley constructs a utopian community designed and built by the deaf-blind. He then explores these people's technologies and other mediations of communication and their relations to sighted children and visitors. In the story, "Blue Champagne," in *Blue Champagne* (New York: Berkeley, 1986), 17–79, Varley transmutes the theme to interrogate the politics of intimacy and technology for a paraplegic young woman whose prosthetic device, the golden gypsy, allows her full

mobility. But because the infinitely costly device is owned by an intergalactic communications and entertainment empire, for which she works as a media star making "feelies," she may keep her technological, intimate, enabling, other self only in exchange for her complicity in the commodification of all experience. What are her limits to the reinvention of experience for sale? Is the personal political under the sign of simulation? One way to read Varley's repeated investigations of finally always limited embodiments, differently abled beings, prosthetic technologies, and cyborgian encounters with their finitude, despite their extraordinary transcendence of "organic" orders, is to find an allegory for the personal and political in the historical mythic time of the late twentieth century, the era of techno-biopolitics. Prosthesis becomes a fundamental category for understanding our most intimate selves. Prosthesis is semiosis, the making of meanings and bodies, not for transcendence, but for power-charged communication.

8. C.D.B. Bryan, *The National Geographic Society: 100 Years of Adventure and Discovery* (New York: Harry N. Abrams, 1987), 352.

9. I owe my understanding of the experience of these photographs to Jim Clifford, University of California at Santa Cruz, who identified their "land ho!" effect on the reader.

10. Bryan, 454.

11. See Hartsock, "The Feminist Standpoint: Developing the Ground for a Specifically Feminist Historical Materialism"; and Chela Sandoral, *Yours in Struggle: Women Respond to Racism* (Oakland: Center for Third World Organizing, n.d.); Harding; and Gloria Anzaldua, *Borderlands/La Frontera* (San Francisco: Spinsters/Aunt Lute, 1987).

12. Annette Kuhn, *Women's Pictures: Feminism and Cinema* (London: Routledge & Kegan Paul, 1982), 3–18.

13. Joan Scott reminded me that Teresa de Lauretis put it like this:

Differences among women may be better understood as differences within women. . . . But once understood in their constitutive power—once it is understood, that is, that these differences not only constitute each woman's consciousness and subjective limits but all together define the *female subject of feminism* in its very specificity, is inherent and at least for now irreconcilable contradiction—these differences, then, cannot be again collapsed into a fixed identity, a sameness of all women as Woman, or a representation of Feminism as a coherent and available image.

See Theresa de Lauretis, "Feminist Studies/Critical Studies: Issues, Terms, and Contexts," in her *Feminist Studies/Critical Studies* (Bloomington: Indiana University Press, 1986), 14–15.

14. Chandra Mohanty, "Under Western Eyes," *Boundary* 2 and 3 (1984): 333–58.

15. See Sofoulis, unpublished manuscript.

16. In *The Science Question in Feminism* (p. 18), Harding suggests that gender has three dimensions, each historically specific: gender symbolism, the social-sexual division of labor, and processes of constructing individual gendered identity. I would enlarge her point to note that there is no reason to expect the three dimensions to covary or codetermine each other, at least not directly. That is, extremely steep gradients between contrasting terms in gender symbolism may very well not correlate with sharp social-sexual divisions of labor or social power, but they may be closely related to sharp racial stratification or something else. Similarly, the processes of gendered subject formation may not be directly illuminated by knowledge of the sexual division of labor or the gender symbolism in the particular historical situation under examination. On the other hand, we should expect mediated relations among the dimensions. The mediations might move through quite different social axes of organization of both symbols, practice, and identity, such as race—and vice versa. I would suggest also that science, as well as gender or race, might

be usefully broken up into such a multipart scheme of symbolism, social practice, and subject position. More than three dimensions suggest themselves when the parallels are drawn. The different dimensions of, for example, gender, race and science might mediate relations among dimensions on a parallel chart. That is, racial divisions of labor might mediate the patterns of connection between symbolic connections and formation of individual subject positions on the science or gender chart. Or formations of gendered or racial subjectivity might mediate the relations between scientific social division of labor and scientific symbolic patterns.

The chart below begins an analysis by parallel dissections. In the chart (and in reality?), both gender and science are analytically asymmetrical; that is, each term contains and obscures a structuring hierarchicalized binary opposition, sex/gender and nature/science. Each binary opposition orders the silent term by a logic of appropriation, as resource to product, nature to culture, potential to actual. Both poles of the opposition are constructed and structure each other dialectically. Within each voiced or explicit term, further asymmetrical splittings can be excavated, as from gender, masculine to feminine, and from science, hard sciences to soft sciences. This is a point about remembering how a particular analytical tool works, willy-nilly, intended or not. The chart reflects common ideological aspects of discourse on science and gender and may help as an analytical tool to crack open mystified units like Science or Woman.

GENDER	SCIENCE
1) symbolic system	symbolic system
2) social division of labor (by sex, by race, etc.)	social division of labor (e.g., by craft or industrial logics)
3) individual identity/subject position (desiring/desired; autonomous relational)	individual identity/subject position (knower/known; scientist/other)
4) material culture (e.g., gender paraphernalia and daily gender technologies, the narrow tracks on which sexual difference runs)	material culture (e.g., laboratories, the narrow tracks on which facts run)
5) dialectic of construction and discovery	dialectic of construction and discovery

17. Katie King, "Canons without Innocence" (Ph.D. diss., University of California at Santa Cruz, 1987).

NEHA VORA

15. A TRANSNATIONAL FEMINIST CRITIQUE OF THE MARCH FOR SCIENCE

On April 22, 2017, members of the scientific community in the United States and globally, as well as others who were concerned about protecting and improving the role of science in society, marched on Washington, DC, and hundreds of other cities. The march took its inspiration from the highly successful Women's March following the inauguration of Donald Trump, and was in many ways a culmination of anger and concern at the Trump administration's seeming "anti-science" stance: beginning as early as Inauguration Day, web pages for environmental and other initiatives started to disappear from the White-House.gov website, followed by surveillance and firings at the National Parks Service, the Environmental Protection Agency, and other organizations that protect and study natural resources. In response to a climate of fear and intimidation within the Trump administration, as well as what many have described as a loose relationship with "facts," many government agencies even set up alternate Twitter sites from which they could report insider information and criticize the new leadership.

While some scientists felt it would be too political to conduct a March for Science, since science is meant to be an objective endeavor, a social media movement began to grow rather quickly around this cause.[1] The support for organizing a March for Science focused mainly on concerns around climate change, but many people took a broader stance that highlighted the increasing need to focus on objective empirical research in the face of the administration's "post-truth" approach to facts, whether academic or journalistic. By constantly referring to anything he did not agree with as "fake news" and by Tweeting fabricated information and insisting on "alternative facts," Trump and his administration have created a climate in which all truth claims are equally valid, regardless of whether they are based in any kind of evidence, and where those that have been validated through rigorous research by experts or through first-hand experience can be readily dismissed using rhetoric that plays to people's existing stereotypes or partisan emotions. In contrast to this "post-truth" approach, many found comfort in turning to science as a source of absolute truth claims.

Many of the signs and banners at the March directly highlighted this comparison, while also calling for better funding for scientific research to support the public good. Some examples included the following:

- More peer review; fewer alternate facts
- Defend not Defund (printed over an image of the earth)
- What do we want? Evidence-based Science! When do we want it? After Peer Review!
- I can't believe I'm marching for facts.

While there were occasional references to diversity in the signs that day, and a smattering of people of color in the crowds, the March for Science, like the Women's March that preceded it, was for the most part a white middle-class mobilization, one that actively silenced calls for better gender and race representation within the event by marginalized scientists while appropriating "diversity" as one of its taglines.[2] Criticisms of the event, which were not nearly as vocal or far-reaching as those of the Women's March, pointed to a need to think through these erasures, as well as those enacted when we choose to uncritically celebrate science as a site of public good, highlighting the ways that science, as a project of modernity and capital, has been from its inception entangled with relations of raced, gendered, and imperial inequality (Rusert).[3]

Modern science has also been the primary source of environmental destruction both historically and in the contemporary moment, with "conservation" or "climate" science making up a small proportion of the impacts of scientific knowledge production on the environment—for the most part, science's role in human history has been to destroy natural habitats and work against environmental justice, particularly for non-white and indigenous peoples. As academics and researchers, scientists, especially those who are asking the state for funding, have a responsibility to interrogate their own complicity in the imperial and anti-environmental projects (which often go hand in hand) that they are entangled in when they work for universities and accept funding from governmental agencies, not only from this administration, but as part of a legacy that can never claim that knowledge production occurs from a space that is not "political."

The most dangerous yet seemingly innocent claim made by the March for Science, however, is the doubling down on absolute truth and objectivity as the answer to a regime of sloppy "alternate facts" and outright lies. Feminists in particular have engaged all of these critiques of science and its history before; and the March for Science, if we turn to its discourses and platforms of activism as answers to the current political situation, threatens to undermine the very important ways that feminist scholars and activists,—specially those working from transnational, black, indigenous, and Global South perspectives—have radically contributed not only to rethinking the role of scientific knowledge in society but also the ways that we approach the production and dissemination of knowledge itself. This piece explores what it means to march for science in a "post-truth" era. I argue that to march for science means reinscribing science as a white liberal public sphere of exclusion rather than a true "public good" that serves those most impacted by both environmental injustice and the way that scientific objectivity silences certain histories and truths over others.

WHY CRITIQUE THE MARCH? WHY NOT JUST STRIVE FOR BETTER SCIENCE?

To arrive at the theoretical interventions I have developed for this piece, I utilized discourse analysis of social movement discussions and debates on social media, blog posts that utilized feminist and anti-colonial frameworks to highlight the legacies of science that the march was eliding, and woman of color commentary I had been following through the election cycle, which pointed out similar themes of exclusion and privilege. I also used my own Facebook page as forum through which I could invite academics and non-academics to generate theoretical interventions with me into what a more inclusive and decolonized science could look like. On the day of the March for Science, I posted a status on my Facebook page that led to a thread of over sixty comments, mostly by fellow academics and researchers. I criticized the march because "science" is also responsible for creating the very categories of race, gender, and sexuality that form the systems of oppression within which many people still struggle today ("AAA Statement on Race"; Gould; Hubbard; Yanagisako and Delaney). I also noted that "science" includes the military industrial complex, and that the US military is the largest polluter in the world (Ghosh 138; Terry). And I mentioned that the civilizational logics of capitalism and colonialism that have produced today's global inequalities continue in many ways within the scientific community (Haraway, *Primate Visions*; Lowe). So what are people marching for when they are marching for science, I asked?

I got several defensive responses and several supportive ones to my post, leading to an exchange that got quite heated at times. The defensive responses, which I define as "liberal" support of science, are the ones I want to focus on here because they are the ones that are naturalized in our academic and activist communities, and they appear on the surface to be innocent. They largely fall into the discourse of, "well yes, science has done some bad things in the past, but that was bad science." One person, a trained scientist himself, was very vehement in pointing out that the scientific method is essentially sound, but that when it is misapplied with racist assumptions, as it was with Nazi science, or with syphilis experiments on black men, this constituted "bad science." Another friend, a self-described feminist, pointed out all the good things science has given us, like antibiotics and birth control.

These responses, as several commentators, from sociologists to chemists to anthropologists to humanists also pointed out, rest on some common presumptions. The first is that science is inherently value-free:

the "bad" science is due to a few "bad apples," and those are now in the past because we live in a more progressive world. This is akin to the idea that the world is less racist, less sexist, and so forth, than it was before, a mythology that fits well with both white liberal fantasies of an America that is constantly improving and scientific modernity's ideas of perpetual progress. Whether the structures of heteropatriarchy, capitalism, and white supremacy are quantitatively different for those who suffer under them is debatable and arrogant for those in positions of power and privilege to presume they can measure.

In terms of science, "good" and "bad" are relative to those they impact, are sources of debate, and are highly complex and interconnected. One prime example is eugenics, a term that implies the worst of racist and Nazi science but is an ideology that continues today in many normalized practices, such as amniocentesis, sperm selection, and gene therapy in the planning of biological reproduction; the search for "gay" and other genes; and the Human Genome Project and its various applications. Birth control, one of the "good" outcomes of science cited by my feminist friend, is a controversial topic for women of color in particular because it has been forced on them in order to control their reproduction, tested on them for the benefit of white women, and held back from them in the Global South due to the influence of right-wing Christian evangelical ideologies on American foreign aid. These are but two examples of how "correcting" science's past mistakes does not produce a space of contemporary knowledge production free from the inequalities and power relations that exist outside the laboratory.

As science studies scholarship has shown very well, the presumption that knowledge can be produced objectively and apolitically is false because we as humans cannot escape language and culture and the historical and contemporary biases that come with them, as well as the material conditions under which we labor as academics and researchers (Haraway, "Situated Knowledges"; Fox-Keller). However, as one of my colleagues pointed out on the thread, most natural sciences and even social sciences continue to perpetuate the idea that scientific knowledge production occurs in a vacuum: "Have you seen some of the apologetics?

'But that was bad science. They weren't *real* scientists.'" And as someone else commented,

> The history of science, like the history of modernity, is a history of imperialism and slavery and othering. Fantastic scientists have tracked this history. I don't think it is a bad project to ask people to address this. I think sweeping it under the rug opens the door for the idea that facts can circulate "out there" without consequences. You should own the stakes of your research. Is this a horrible thing to ask of people?

Owning the stakes however, requires us to think about the entanglements between knowledge production and other realms of social activity, something that we have been taught not to do, especially in the academy, due to the separation of academic disciplines but especially due to the purification of science from culture and politics (Roberts and Turner).

This is a third premise in the liberal defense of science: that science stands in opposition to "political" disciplines, and, in the case of the March for Science, in opposition to an anti-science state. One of reasons for the march was to demand more funding—from the state in particular—for scientific research. The cuts in funding to social science, climate science, and those fields considered less important, or even politically charged, to the current administration does not mean that the state is anti-science. Asking the state to increase funding shows that scientists in this country rely heavily on state agencies as funding sources. Whether directly funded through grants from agencies like the National Science Foundation, or working for universities that receive federal and state funding (which includes private institutions), no academic researcher can claim that they are not entangled somehow with either the state or with corporations, who increasingly partner with universities on human and animal testing, fund research into new technologies and medicines, and jointly own patents (Chatterjee and Maira; Kerr).

The US state, under Trump, continues a legacy of imperial invasion in the Middle East, is intensifying surveillance and fortifying of the US/Mexico border, and is growing a police state that increasingly looks like a domestic occupying military. All of the weaponry and drones involved in these actions are built on scientific technology, invented and tested by scientists, using scientific methods, funded by state and corporate interests, usually in academic or joint research spaces. You are also marching for these things when you march under the banner of an apolitical innocent understanding of science. It is akin to George W. Bush's division of the world after 9/11 into "freedom-lovers" and "freedom-haters": of course one wants to be on the side of freedom, but this is an empty signifier—or even worse, it is one loaded with the heavy weight of colonial injustice. If we want better funding for better knowledge production, then we need better movements, and we need to hold the scientific community accountable for learning and teaching their histories, for intimately knowing their stakes. As a trained biologist recounted on my Facebook thread of her experience in graduate school,

> I never was asked formally or informally during my 13 years of training & being a scientist to ever more than cursorily think about any of this—and certainly never to consider how science centers & reifies white supremacy and all its attendant biases and oppressive actions. But I've seen scientists defend this position [that science is apolitical] vigorously.

It is here, by not clarifying history or stakes, that the March for Science reveals itself as an inherently contradictory and complicit mobilization. It claims science as an apolitical or neutral form of knowledge production that can be used for public good against a state that is deemed generally anti-science and "bad," but it is also asking that same state to paternalistically dole out funding for more scientific research. There is a liberal presumption built into this form of activism that both modern science and the modern state—two intertwined projects—are fundamentally self-correcting and in the service of the individual. However, within liberalism, the idea of the individual has only ever included the "unmarked subject," the white, cis-gendered, able-bodied, middle-class male, and not those "others" who have been produced through the very technologies of scientific knowledge and imperial governance that do not allow everyone to access state resources through such modes of political action and the embodied citizenship they affirm. The March on Science, then, needs to be considered for the public

sphere it produced, and who was left out of that public sphere. Those elisions link up to everyday academic practices of teaching sciences, and gesture to new ways of imagining a university in which responsibility for decolonial scientific practice and critical thinking is distributed differently, creating more inclusive citizenship and more inclusive knowledge production.

THE VALUE OF QUESTIONING TRUTH, EVEN IN A "POST-TRUTH" MOMENT

Every year, in my introductory anthropology class, I teach about scientific racism and how the biological idea that humans can be divided and ranked into distinct races was produced by modern science within the context of European imperialism. While these biological realities have long since been disproven, their ramifications linger in an array of medical, psychological, carceral, governmental, and representational technologies that continue to create hierarchies of humans in support of white supremacy, anti-blackness, and geopolitical disparity. Exploring the social construction of race alongside its entanglement with past and present biomedical understandings of human variation are crucial to the ethnographic project of understanding the everyday impacts of discrimination and injustice on marginalized communities. That is to say, an erasure of scientific race—it is not "real"—does not move us closer to understanding how very real race is as a structuring logic in today's world, both domestically in the United States, and globally, particularly in the civilizational logics used to justify US and Western military interventions in the Global South.

I similarly, in my introductory anthropology class, teach about the ways that Western Christian understandings of sex and sexuality and how they have informed secular science have led us to our current notions of gender duality and the various traits we attach to masculinity and femininity, as well as the investment in heteronormativity that has structured European definitions of "civilized" versus "uncivilized" cultures. We unpack the extent to which women's bodies themselves are shaped through societal expectations of strength and weakness; and how, when girls are given different opportunities to develop mentally and physically, they do not diverge significantly from boys. Cross-cultural examples also show us that what Westerners consider to be scientifically proven, like premenstrual syndrome, maternal instinct, or certain aspects of human sexuality, do not hold true universally, and are therefore not innate.

These are but a few of many ways that scholars use history, anthropology, gender studies, sociology, and other frameworks to place scientific "facts" within context, highlighting how knowledge is always produced under specific conditions, which include human cultural biases and certain genealogies of practice that are hard to move beyond. When we add in the pressure from funding agencies and insurance companies and lobbyists, other questions about the impacts of fuzzy ethical practices in scientific research and practice also come into relief, which many medical and environmental anthropologists have tracked on the ground, sometimes at great personal risk (Watters).

Why are the natural sciences not teaching these histories, their own histories? Why are they not asked by most institutions to offer courses on applied ethics? The study of science is often ghettoized into disciplines and interdisciplines that are underfunded and understaffed within universities, leaving "science" to claim the kind of position of neutrality from which an event like the March for Science can emerge. Were the sciences held more accountable for teaching their own complex historical and ongoing relationships with inequality and injustice, we might not have a "women in STEM" problem, or a lack of black engineers, for example—these are diversity anxieties that plague universities and they do not seem to be able to find answers to them regardless of how much they spin their wheels.

Perhaps the answer is to place difference and diversity inside of science more fully, instead of elevating the "scientific method" to a new religiosity that can stand outside and above politics and society.

While it may seem counter-intuitive, it is more important than ever to not turn to ideas like "truth" and "objectivity" as a response to a perceived threat of fascism—forms that have done much violence on women, people of color, and LGBTQ people in the past and continue to do so in the present. To do so enacts what Donna Haraway ("Situated Knowledges" 581) has called the "god trick," a view from nowhere, which is an impossible way of seeing. Why are we so keen to answer anti-science with lack of complexity? Shouldn't we be answering it with more intellectual curiosity and nuance? I don't think we need to look far to take on such projects, and it is not an indictment of scientific research at all to ask researchers to stop treating their work as if it is value-free. Valorizing neutral knowledge—a view from nowhere—risks complicity with modern projects of imperialism, white supremacy, and the military industrial complex. Claiming the political stakes and addressing the problematic histories of our disciplinary practices allows us to work more closely with the communities we want as our interlocutors and to truly move toward feminist decolonial knowledge projects. This would allow those most impacted by the legacies of modern science's destructive pathways—indigenous communities, the colonized, people of color, and women— to take the lead in imagining global environmental justice and allow scientific inquiry to benefit a truly "public" good.

ACKNOWLEDGMENTS

I want particularly to thank Daniela Bell, Sarah Gatson, and Saskia Van Bergen for their insightful comments on the fiery Facebook thread that inspired this article.

NOTES

1. See https://www.marchforscience.com/.
2. I assessed crowd diversity by looking at photographs from several national newspapers, and by asking colleagues and friends, white and non-white, from many parts of the country who attended their local marches to tell me what they saw. Most of the language from signs quoted was found at *politico*, http://www.politico.com/gallery/2017/04/22/ march-for-science-best-protest-signs-photos-002423?slide=0.

3. See, for example, "From the March for Science to an Abolitionist Science": https://www.fromthesquare.org/march-science-abolitionist-science/#.WX9eoIpGkxe; "The March for Science as a Microcosm of Liberal Racism": http://www.theroot.com/marginsci-the-march-for-science-as-a-microcosm-of-lib-1794463442; and "Race, History, and the #ScienceMarch": http://www.aaihs.org/race-history-and-the-sciencemarch/.

REFERENCES

"AAA Statement on Race." *American Anthropological Association*, http://www.americananthro.org/ConnectWithAAA/Content.aspx?ItemNumber=2583. Accessed September 17, 2017.

Chatterjee, P. and Maira, S., Eds. *The Imperial University*. University of Minnesota Press, 2014.

Fox-Keller, Evelyn. *Refiguring Life: Metaphors of Twentieth-Century Biology*. Columbia University Press, 1995.

Ghosh, Amitav. *The Great Derangement*. University of Chicago Press, 2016.

Gould, Stephen J. *The Mismeasure of Man*. W. Norton & Company, 1996.

Haraway, Donna. *Primate Visions: Gender, Race, and Nature in the World of Modern Science*. Routledge, 1990.

Haraway, Donna. "Situated Knowledges: The Science Question in Feminism and the Privilege of Partial Perspective." *Feminist Studies* vol. 14, no. 3, pp. 575–599, 1988.

Hubbard, Ruth. *The Politics of Women's Biology*. Rutgers University Press, 1990.

Kerr, C. *The Uses of the University*. Harper Torchbooks, 1966.

Lowe, Lisa. *The Intimacies of Four Continents*. Duke University Press, 2015.

Roberts, J. H. and J. Turner. *The Sacred and the Secular University*. Princeton University Press, 2000.

Rusert, Britt. "From the March for Science to an Abolitionist Science." *From the Square: NYU Press Blog*, April 20, 2017, https://www.fromthesquare.org/march-science-abolitionist-science/#.Wb-7FQ4prxon. Accessed September 17, 2017.

Terry, Jennifer. *Attachments to War: Biomedical Logics and Violence in Twenty-First Century America*. Duke University Press, 2017.

Watters, Ethan. "The Organ Detective: A Career Spent Uncovering a Global Market in Human Flesh." *Pacific Standard*, July 7, 2014, https://psmag.com/economics/nancy-scheper-hughes-black-market-trade-organ-detective-84351. Accessed September 17, 2017.

Yanagisako, Sylvia, and Carol Delaney. "Introduction." *Naturalizing Power*. Routledge, 1995.

AVERY DAME-GRIFF

16. ALGORITHMS ARE A FEMINIST ISSUE

Imagine you've just been assigned a research paper on a fairly narrow topic, like LGBT social movements in the 1970s or the work of author Sandra Cisneros. How would you learn more about this topic? Pre-internet, you would have visited the library to check out books or photocopy articles from periodicals or academic journals, all of which are filed using subject headings identifying their content. Determining if they're relevant to your specific project, however, likely would have required more in-depth reading. Nowadays, you can use your search engine of choice and put in several keywords. Your search results will include not just text web pages, but Wikipedia pages, video links, and even passages in published books. In most cases, you can safely assume these results are "relevant" to your assignment, no in-depth reading required. How does the search algorithm, which powers the engine you used, know these specific pages are the most relevant results, however?

In simple terms, the algorithm's human designers have taught it to objectively identify, in their view, relevancy in a variety of conditions. The algorithm, unlike human agents, treats information as value-neutral, which allows it to approach a query objectively. This emphasis on objectivity in a technology that remains largely opaque to its users is what makes, in my view, algorithms an important feminist issue. Algorithms, and search algorithms in particular, are central to many digital platforms, yet they're largely a "black box" to the average user, who can't access their inner workings and the cultural values that underlay their design.

However, I'm not interested in merely asserting that search engines can produce biased results, as other scholars have already described how search algorithms can emphasize commercial, popular, and/or American sites above others (Mowshowitz and Kawaguchi; Vaughan and Thelwall). Instead, I'm interested

in locating the algorithm's "objective" view of information within a larger history of supposedly value-neutral technological systems that reinforce existing norms. In each case, designers' implicit cultural assumptions are embodied through the technological object they design. Throughout, I'll draw on theory and methods from the field of feminist technoscience to unpack this process in the development of search algorithms. I'll then consider, using Donna Haraway's concept of situated knowledges, what a feminist objectivity might look like and how it could be embodied in design.

UNPACKING THE ALGORITHM

Before we get into search algorithms specifically, let's first briefly define an algorithm. In its broadest usage, an algorithm is a predefined sequence of actions that are successively performed depending on the output of each prior action. The algorithm ends once it's reached its final output. Often, they're visualized via flow charts, like the one in Figure 1.

Algorithms have long pre-existing modern computer technology in a variety of fields, but the term has gained greater cultural visibility with the rise of search technology built on algorithms. A search algorithm, like that maintained by Google, initially focuses on the placement of keywords in websites. For example, if you've just adopted a German Shepherd puppy, you might start researching training methods using the phrase "training German Shepherd." Whether or not the words "German Shepherd" and "training" (or other variants, like "train") appear on a given site is an initial determinant of relevance. However, terminology isn't foolproof: just relying only on keyword appearance could also identify as relevant a biographical piece about famous TV dog Rin Tin Tin, a news story on bomb-sniffing dogs, or the home page for a German Shepherd breeder. Instead, most search algorithms

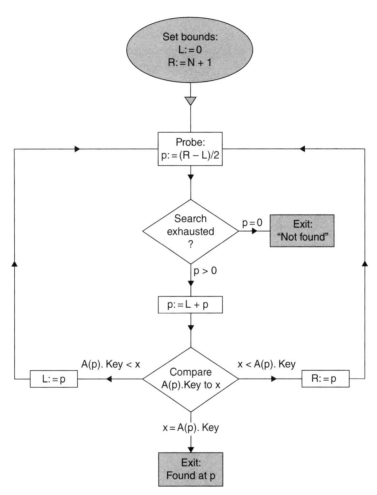

Binary Search
Given: array *A* with attribute *key*,
elements 1 to N ordered on the values of *key*
so that *A(1). Key* ≤ *A(2). Key* ≤ ... ≤ *A(N). Key*
Find index *p* such that *A(p).Key* = *x*.

FIGURE 1. Flowchart depicting an algorithm to search a sorted list for the location of a specific item, such as finding a word in a dictionary. Credit: Public domain image created by WikiMedia User Nicky McLean. Source: https://commons.wikimedia.org/wiki/File:BinarySearch.Flowchart.png.

include other measures to identify quality information, such as number of links to that page, visitors' expressed interest in them, or site age (Hillis et al.). A similar assumption also underlies the "Suggestions" sidebar on websites or video streaming platforms like YouTube: people who watched that video also watched these videos on the same topic, so you would likely also want to watch these videos.

However, these measures of relevance don't always produce relevant results for all users. In my research on how contemporary trans individuals use the internet, multiple participants of color reported they had difficulty finding content by people of color in their search results. The "generic" terms they might use to identify themselves in online spaces ("ftm," "mtf," etc.) produced search results dominated by white individuals. To find videos or social media content relevant to their specific experiences, they had to use specific keywords signifying racial or ethnic identity. These participants' experiences reflect a wider cultural reality: while they were able to find content by other trans-identified people of color, the algorithm's understanding of broad cultural concepts like "transgender," "ftm," and "mtf"—as trained by its human creators and users—emerges from a baseline assumption of whiteness.

The algorithm, then, materializes the existing representational imbalance into a set of search results. This focus on how technology materializes cultural concepts is at the core of feminist technoscience. Ideas like masculinity and femininity "acquire their meaning and character" by being embedded within technology (Wajcman, "Feminist Theories of Technology" 149). These ideas can shape both an object's form, such as its color scheme or the materials used in its construction, and its function, or its utility. For example, tools marketed as "for women" may not only be decorated with light pastel colors but also be smaller and lighter—limiting what tasks can be completed with them. This "mutual shaping approach" highlights how the gendering of objects persists beyond their design to affect their application in day-to-day use (Wajcman, "Feminist Theories of Technology" 149). Feminist technoscience scholars have highlighted the materialization of gender in a variety of fields, from domestic technology (Wajcman, *Feminism Confronts Technology*), reproductive technology (Hartouni), and biotech (Balsamo) to robotics and artificial intelligence (Suchman, *Human-Machine Reconfigurations*). In this essay, I take a more expansive focus, looking beyond gender to consider how a variety of interlocking sociocultural aspects of self (gender, race, ethnicity, ability, etc.) are materialized through technology.

Feminist technoscience also interrogates how designers' perspective and assumptions profoundly influence the objects they produce. The history of film chemistry provides an illustrative example. Because white individuals were assumed as the target market by companies like Kodak, consumer-grade film was designed with white skin tones as the ideal standard, and darker skin tones often failed to develop clearly. This state remained largely unchanged until companies advertising products that came in multiple shades of brown, such as chocolate and wood furniture, complained to Kodak that their film failed to illustrate nuances in between their products (Roth, "Looking at Shirley"). Moreover, the embedding of norms goes beyond material technology. In her analysis of the development of the UNIX operating system (OS), whose design serves as the basis for all modern OSs, Tara McPherson traces the correlations between the political climate surrounding UNIX's designers during the 1970s and their final design decisions. At that time, there was an increasing "social and political embrace of modularity and encapsulation," a marked shift away from the cross-group alliances common in labor and anti-racist organizing during the 1930s and 1940s. UNIX's design mirrors this approach, emphasizing not the interrelationships of data but data as "discrete modules or nodes" in a manner that "[managed] and [controlled] complexity" (McPherson 25, 30). In other words, instead of navigating data stored on a hard drive via their connections to each other, UNIX and all OSs that followed are organized via a hierarchical filing system that partitions data into clearly identified folders and subfolders.

Beyond just interrogating how norms become embedded in design, feminist technoscience also challenges disciplinary norms, such as objectivity and neutrality in particular, that exclude other ways of knowing. Though objectivity's exact definition and use has always been disputed, its one consistent aspect among all definitions is the idea of value-neutrality, used at different moments as objectivity's "myth, mask, shield and sword" (Proctor 262). Yet neutrality is itself also an unstable concept: a viewpoint is only as neutral as the social and cultural milieu from which it emerged. What seems like a value-neutral, objective viewpoint to a room of individuals with a shared background may be anything but for those outside the room. Thus, science and other technical fields have long prioritized the viewpoints of those "in the room," who often represent dominant social groups.

In the realm of search algorithms, objectivity and relevance are core values that underlay their design and development (van Couvering, "Is Relevance Relevant?"). Commercial search engines' algorithms are heavily shaped by the work of research scientists, who use value-neutral numerical metrics to more efficiently identify causal links within their datasets. From this work emerges the technology users interact with, enabling them to "act on the world effectively and efficiently" (van Couvering, "Is Relevance Relevant?"). Ideally, the most effective results are those most relevant to the user's needs. Yet as van Couvering finds in her interviews with search professionals, relevance can often only be determined on a subjective, case-by-case basis.

In order to achieve "objective" relevance, search professionals turn these subjective cases into objective problems through mathematical modelling, creating a quantifiable, improvable model fine-tuned through "relevance judgments," or sets of test data, as one search employee put it (van Couvering, "Is Relevance Relevant?"). And in some cases, an algorithm will also draw on one's past search history and other data to create "customized" results that are, presumably, even more relevant. Companies reinforce their algorithm's objectivity through marketing that emphasizes the algorithm's mathematical nature, objectivity, and "inhuman agency" (Sandvig, "Art & Infrastructures"). Unlike humans, search algorithms are understood as "magical agents" whose unbiased results consistently enable and empower users, with a wider disregard for algorithms' possible downsides (Hillis et al. 58).

PERFORMING THE GOD TRICK

As I mentioned earlier, participants of color in my research didn't often see content by other people of color in their search results. When they're searching for information using trans-specific terms like "transgender," "ftm," or "mtf," in one sense we could see how their search results are by the algorithm's standards objectively relevant. The results they get contain these terms, so they pass the initial test. Assuming they've also been judged relevant by the appropriate "relevance judgment" model, these pages, videos, blog

posts, and so forth likely contain information that would answer the average user's query. Yet just presenting relevant results doesn't solve the core problem: objectively relevant content still retains its culturally situated, decidedly non-objective context. Because the algorithm has focused on the average user, they've produced the cultural "average" of transgender identity, whiteness. In this way, white-as-norm is materialized and embedded in the algorithm. Further searches validate the existing "relevance judgment," and the dominance of whiteness continues for the algorithm's life trajectory. Moreover, since most search algorithms are proprietary, users can't access their code, which would shed light on how algorithms determine relevance.

In these cases, users have some agency. As Jenna Burrell notes of spam filtering algorithms in these moments, "machine thinking" sometimes has to be resolved by "human interpretation" (9). For the user of color, they interpret the results as not relevant and instead have to add a race- or ethnicity-related term to get relevant results. However, the necessity of human interpretation assumes the human user already knows enough to successfully interpret their results. For those questioning their identity, they may use search engines to answer a deeply personal question: am I transgender? In this case, the results they receive may not only help them answer this question, they may also shape how questioning individuals understand their self-identity. A user of color who sees only white faces associated with "transgender" may feel disassociated from the concept. Furthermore, if they're unfamiliar with community-specific language related to gender identity and presentation (boi, stud, etc.), they don't yet have the interpretative skills necessary to identify information that might be more relevant to their situation.

I'd argue that in their design and development, search algorithms and the engines built around them occupy a "gaze from nowhere," which allows the "unmarked category [to] claim the power to see and not be seen, to represent while escaping representation" (Haraway 188). As we can see in the previous example, the whiteness of search results goes unmarked by the algorithm, while content by people of color must be specifically labeled as such in order to be "seen," so to speak—a process that can sometimes reduce one's complex embodied self down to semantic labels. Even these labels can be limiting. As Sandy Stone notes in her widely cited essay, "The Empire Strikes Back: A Posttransexual Manifesto," the trans body doesn't only replicate cultural notions of gender but also offers opportunities to reconfigure and disrupt them. A single term or set of terms—a process of slicing one's sense of self into ever smaller, disembodied partitions—may not be able to fully account for an individual's complex gender identity and presentation.

In this way, the search algorithm performs what Donna Haraway terms the "god trick" of disembodied "infinitely mobile vision . . . seeing everything from nowhere" (189). But the "god trick" is an illusion, an attempt to disconnect vision from the embodied individuals who view and are viewed—or in this case, who search and are searched. For Haraway, however, achieving a usable, if imperfect, understanding of objectivity isn't entirely impossible. Instead of universality, objectivity must be grounded in partial perspective and particular embodiment, in actors' "situated knowledges." All actors, both human and otherwise, occupy specific positions, their "view from somewhere." These viewpoints, when put in conversation, can join together to form a "collective subject position" from which to interpret the world (Haraway 196).

What would it mean to rethink objectivity in such terms? In our example, we can identify a variety of partial subject positions: the research scientist who fine-tunes the algorithm, the designer focused on designing the best solution for a human user, the marketer who has to explain and promote their product to the public, and the user who inputs their query. Moreover, these positions are not limited to human actors. Particularly with the rise of machine learning, the search algorithm has its own viewpoint, from which it interprets the world as a body of knowledge to be processed and indexed. Each of these actors have agency to shape what knowledge is produced, from how the research scientist develops measurement metrics to the user who modifies their query when the results don't reflect their viewpoint on the world.

FEMINIST POSSIBILITIES

Ultimately, design need not be destiny. By interrogating the embedded norms within technology, feminist technoscience reminds us "that 'things could be

otherwise'"—in other words, that current technologies didn't result from an inevitable arc of progress but arose from deliberate decisions and choices made by their creators (Wajcman, "Feminist Theories of Technology" 150). By asking what this "otherwise" might look like, we can imagine new possibilities. An operating system structured around the category of queer, as Kara Keeling proposes in her article "Queer OS," could challenge and complicate existing hegemonic norms. For Keeling, a Queer OS enables new and unanticipated relationships between both individuals and their environments, particularly when it might otherwise seem they have little in common (154). How might designers, then, go about building systems that support such relationships?

Participatory design, a design approach that involves non-designers at every step of the process, is a key part of any such effort. Lucy Suchman, drawing on Haraway's situated knowledges, argues designers must put themselves within a position of "located accountability," focusing their attention on how people use an object or system in their specific environment ("Located Accountabilities" 96). Effective design, instead of "design from nowhere," requires crossing the boundaries between designer and user to facilitate meaningful encounters between their "different partial knowledges" (Suchman, "Located Accountabilities" 94–95). Suchman describes her own efforts during the late 1990s to redesign a large law firm's document management process. In that project, each party had different investments and understandings. The designers were invested in producing a meaningful design object to help streamline document encoding for cases, but each of the possible users had different understandings of the actual task: Lawyers viewed encoding as "mindless labor" that could be automated or outsourced to cut costs, while the document analysts, who made up the firm's litigation support staff, saw their job as "knowledge work" requiring an in-depth understanding of a case's specific parameters. Suchman and her colleagues, then, had to bridge all of these knowledges to produce a process that simultaneously helped the document analysts and reduced costs for the firm ("Located Accountabilities" 98–99). In algorithm design, it might be important to consider from the outset when to bring in other perspectives, like prospective users, to see the project from a different angle.

Technological objects must also, Suchman argues, be developed for the environments where they'll be used, not in an "ideal" enclosed environment maintained by a design firm ("Located Accountabilities" 99). In example, the infrared sensors used in motion detection technology such as faucets, soap dispensers, and security cameras are triggered by the reflection of light off human skin. However, the amount of light reflected back will vary based on skin tone, a difference that has led to multiple examples of sensors not detecting Black users. If an object using infrared technology is only tested in the "enclosed" environment of a design firm filled with white and lighter-skinned users, then it's more likely the resulting product won't work properly for the full spectrum of possible users. In these cases, testing an object in its everyday environment could correct this issue. By exposing the sensor to a variety of human skin tones through product tests in high traffic environments, designers can determine the gain necessary for the sensor to consistently detect users with all shades of skin color. In the same way, more situation-specific evaluation of relevance—shifting focus from the ideal user of the mathematical model to multiple users' everyday interactions—might offer new and unexpected results.

Shaowen Bardzell's work in Feminist Human-Computer Interaction (HCI) offers a similar plan for bringing feminist concerns to bear on technological design. As Bardzell rightly suggests, "feminism has far more to offer than pointing out instances of sexism after the fact" (Bardzell 1308). The integration of feminist principles into design practice can generate, she argues, new approaches to both the design process and studies of user practices. Bardzell encourages designers to focus not on the "ideal user" but the user as a self-disclosing subject, who has some agency to define how they are represented (Bardzell 1307). She uses the example of the Amazon recommendation algorithm, which allows users to "fix" recommendations by offering more specific detail on their purchase—or even excluding the item from the recommendation algorithm entirely (1308). Last, disciplines must be placed in conversation across their traditional boundaries in order to generate new conversations. In their article "Feminist Technoscience Rearranging in the Black Box of Information Technology," the authors recount their experiences attempting to bring feminist concerns into their work in technical fields like computer science or systems design, all of which often appear as impenetrable "black boxes" to outsiders (Björkman et al.). By translating feminist concerns for a non-feminist audience, they made interventions in a variety of ways, from transgressing traditional boundaries between roles and disciplines, drawing attention to implicit disciplinary assumptions in their teaching, to emphasizing the non-linearity of technological design. As the authors found, doing such "translation work" can facilitate new collaborations with unexpected partners (Björkman et al. 92).

These methods—located accountability, technology in its everyday environment, supporting user agency, and translation work—can guide designers working on both algorithms and a variety of other technological objects. Successful implementation, however, requires not just a change in practice but a change in perspective: admitting that no one can see it all and entering into a conversation about how to see better together.

REFERENCES

Balsamo, Anne Marie. *Technologies of the Gendered Body: Reading Cyborg Women*. Durham: Duke University Press, 1996.

Bardzell, Shaowen. "Feminist HCI: Taking Stock and Outlining an Agenda for Design." *Proceedings of the SIGCHI Conference on Human Factors in Computing Systems* (2010): 1301–1310.

Björkman, Christina, Pirjo Elovaara, and Lena Trojer. "Feminist Technoscience Rearranging in the Black Box of Information Technology." *Gender Designs IT: Construction and Deconstruction of Information Society Technology*, Ed. Isabel Zorn et al. Wiesbaden: VS Verlag für Sozialwissenschaften, 2007. 79–94.

Burrell, Jenna. "How the Machine 'Thinks': Understanding Opacity in Machine Learning Algorithms." *Big Data & Society* 3, no. 1 (2016): https://doi.org/10.1177/2053951715622512.

Haraway, Donna Jeanne. *Simians, Cyborgs, and Women: The Reinvention of Nature*. New York: Routledge, 1991.

Hartouni, Valerie. *Cultural Conceptions: On Reproductive Technologies and the Remaking of Life*. Minneapolis: University of Minnesota Press, 1997.

Hillis, Ken, Michael Petit, and Kylie Jarrett. *Google and the Culture of Search*. New York: Routledge Taylor & Francis Group, 2013.

Keeling, Kara. "Queer OS." *Cinema Journal* 53, no. 2 (2014): 152–157.

McPherson, Tara. "U.S. Operating Systems at Mid-Century: The Intertwining of Race and UNIX." *Race after the Internet*. Ed. Lisa Nakamura and Peter A. Chow-White. New York: Routledge, 2012. 21–37.

Mowshowitz, Abbe, and Akira Kawaguchi. "Measuring Search Engine Bias." *Information Processing & Management* 41, no. 5 (2005): 1193–1205.

Proctor, Robert. *Value-Free Science?: Purity and Power in Modern Knowledge*. Cambridge, MA: Harvard University Press, 1991.

Roth, Lorna. "Looking at Shirley, the Ultimate Norm: Colour Balance, Image Technologies, and Cognitive Equity." *Canadian Journal of Communication* 34, no. 1 (2009): 111–136.

Sandvig, Christian. "Seeing the Sort: The Aesthetic and Industrial Defense of 'The Algorithm'." *Media-N: Journal of the New Media Caucus* 10, no. 03 (2014): http://median.newmediacaucus.org/art-infrastructures-information/seeing-the-sort-the-aesthetic-and-industrial-defense-of-the-algorithm/.

Stone, Sandy. "The Empire Strikes Back: A Posttranssexual Manifesto." *The Transgender Studies Reader*. Ed. Susan Stryker and Stephen Whittle. London: Routledge, 2006. 221–235.

Suchman, Lucille Alice. *Human-Machine Reconfigurations: Plans and Situated Actions*. 2nd ed. Cambridge: Cambridge University Press, 2007.

Suchman, Lucy. "Located Accountabilities in Technology Production." *Scandinavian Journal of Information Systems* 14, no. 2 (2002): 91–105.

Van Couvering, Elizabeth. "Is Relevance Relevant? Market, Science, and War: Discourses of Search Engine Quality." *Journal of Computer-Mediated Communication* 12, no. 3 (2007): 866–887. https://academic.oup.com/jcmc/article/12/3/866/4582998.

Vaughan, Liwen, and Mike Thelwall. "Search Engine Coverage Bias: Evidence and Possible Causes." *Information Processing & Management* 40, no. 4 (2004): 693–707.

Wajcman, Judy. *Feminism Confronts Technology*. University Park: Pennsylvania State University Press, 1991.

Wajcman, Judy. "Feminist Theories of Technology." *Cambridge Journal of Economics* 34, no. 1 (2010): 143–152. https://academic.oup.com/cje/article-abstract/34/1/143/1689542.

KIMBERLÉ CRENSHAW

17. DEMARGINALIZING THE INTERSECTION OF RACE AND SEX: A BLACK FEMINIST CRITIQUE OF ANTIDISCRIMINATION DOCTRINE, FEMINIST THEORY AND ANTIRACIST POLITICS

One of the very few Black women's studies books is entitled *All the Women Are White, All the Blacks Are Men, But Some of Us are Brave.*[1] I have chosen this title as a point of departure in my efforts to develop a Black feminist criticism[2] because it sets forth a problematic consequence of the tendency to treat race and gender as mutually exclusive categories of experience and analysis.[3] In this . . . [reading], I want to examine how this tendency is perpetuated by a single-axis framework that is dominant in antidiscrimination law and that is also reflected in feminist theory and antiracist politics.

I will center Black women in this analysis in order to contrast the multidimensionality of Black women's experience with the single-axis analysis that distorts these experiences. Not only will this juxtaposition reveal how Black women are theoretically erased, it will also illustrate how this framework imports its own theoretical limitations that undermine efforts to broaden feminist and antiracist analyses. With Black women as the starting point, it becomes more apparent how dominant conceptions of discrimination condition us to think about subordination as disadvantage occurring along a single categorical axis. I want to suggest further that this single-axis framework erases Black women in the conceptualization, identification and remediation of race and sex discrimination by limiting inquiry to the experiences of otherwise-privileged members of the group. In other words, in race discrimination cases, discrimination tends to be viewed in terms of sex- or class-privileged Blacks; in sex discrimination cases, the focus is on race- and class-privileged women.

This focus on the most privileged group members marginalizes those who are multiply burdened and obscures claims that cannot be understood as resulting from discrete sources of discrimination. I suggest further that this focus on otherwise-privileged group members creates a distorted analysis of racism and sexism because the operative conceptions of race and sex become grounded in experiences that actually represent only a subset of a much more complex phenomenon.

After examining the doctrinal manifestations of this single-axis framework, I will discuss how it contributes to the marginalization of Black women in feminist theory and in antiracist politics. I argue that Black women are sometimes excluded from feminist theory and antiracist policy discourse because both are predicated on a discrete set of experiences that often does not accurately reflect the interaction of race and gender. These problems of exclusion cannot be solved simply by including Black women within an already established analytical structure. Because the intersectional experience is greater than the sum of racism and sexism, any analysis that does not take intersectionality into account cannot sufficiently address the particular manner in which Black women are subordinated. Thus, for feminist theory and antiracist policy discourse to embrace the experiences and concerns of Black women, the entire framework that has been used

Kimberlé Crenshaw, "Demarginalizing the Intersection of Race and Sex: A Black Feminist Critique of Antidiscrimination Doctrine, Feminist Theory and Antiracist Politics." *University of Chicago Legal Forum*, 140 (1989): 139–167. Reprinted with permission.

as a basis for translating "women's experience" or "the Black experience" into concrete policy demands must be rethought and recast.

. . .

I. THE ANTIDISCRIMINATION FRAMEWORK

A. THE EXPERIENCE OF INTERSECTIONALITY AND THE DOCTRINAL RESPONSE

One way to approach the problem of intersectionality is to examine how courts frame and interpret the stories of Black women plaintiffs. While I cannot claim to know the circumstances underlying the cases that I will discuss, I nevertheless believe that the way courts interpret claims made by Black women is itself part of Black women's experience and, consequently, a cursory review of cases involving Black female plaintiffs is quite revealing. To illustrate the difficulties inherent in judicial treatment of intersectionality, I will consider three Title VII[4] cases: *DeGraffenreid v General Motors,*[5] *Moore v Hughes Helicopter,*[6] and *Payne v Travenol.*[7]

1. *DeGraffenreid v General Motors.*

In *DeGraffenreid,* five Black women brought suit against General Motors, alleging that the employer's seniority system perpetuated the effects of past discrimination against Black women. Evidence adduced at trial revealed that General Motors simply did not hire Black women prior to 1964 and that all of the Black women hired after 1970 lost their jobs in a seniority-based layoff during a subsequent recession. The district court granted summary judgment for the defendant, rejecting the plaintiffs' attempt to bring a suit not on behalf of Blacks or women, but specifically on behalf of Black women. The court stated:

> [P]laintiffs have failed to cite any decisions which have stated that Black women are a special class to be protected from discrimination. The Court's own research has failed to disclose such a decision. The plaintiffs are clearly entitled to a remedy if they have been discriminated against. However, they should not be allowed to combine statutory remedies to create a new 'super-remedy' which would give them relief beyond what the drafters of the relevant statutes intended. Thus, this lawsuit must be examined to see if it states a cause of action for race discrimination,

sex discrimination, or alternatively either, but not a combination of both.[8]

Although General Motors did not hire Black women prior to 1964, the court noted that "General Motors has hired . . . female employees for a number of years prior to the enactment of the Civil Rights Act of 1964."[9] Because General Motors did hire women—albeit *white women*—during the period that no Black women were hired, there was, in the court's view, no sex discrimination that the seniority system could conceivably have perpetuated.

After refusing to consider the plaintiffs' sex discrimination claim, the court dismissed the race discrimination complaint and recommended its consolidation with another case alleging race discrimination against the same employer.[10] The plaintiffs responded that such consolidation would defeat the purpose of their suit since theirs was not purely a race claim, but an action brought specifically on behalf of Black women alleging race *and* sex discrimination. The court, however, reasoned:

> The legislative history surrounding Title VII does not indicate that the goal of the statute was to create a new classification of "black women" who would have greater standing than, for example, a black male. The prospect of the creation of new classes of protected minorities, governed only by the mathematical principles of permutation and combination, clearly raises the prospect of opening the hackneyed Pandora's box.[11]

Thus, the court apparently concluded that Congress either did not contemplate that Black women could be discriminated against as "Black women" or did not intend to protect them when such discrimination occurred.[12] The court's refusal in *DeGraffenreid* to acknowledge that Black women encounter combined race and sex discrimination implies that the boundaries of sex and race discrimination doctrine are defined respectively by white women's and Black men's experiences. Under this view, Black women are protected only to the extent that their experiences coincide with those of either of the two groups.[13] Where their experiences are distinct, Black women can expect little protection as long as approaches, such as that in *DeGraffenreid,* which completely obscure problems of intersectionality prevail.

2. *Moore v Hughes Helicopter, Inc.*

Moore v Hughes Helicopters, Inc. [14] presents a different way in which courts fail to understand or recognize Black women's claims. *Moore* is typical of a number of cases in which courts refused to certify Black females as class representatives in race *and* sex discrimination actions.[15] In *Moore*, the plaintiff alleged that the employer, Hughes Helicopter, practiced race and sex discrimination in promotions to upper-level craft positions and to supervisory jobs. Moore introduced statistical evidence establishing a significant disparity between men and women, and somewhat less of a disparity between Black and white men in supervisory jobs.[16]

Affirming the district court's refusal to certify Moore as the class representative in the sex discrimination complaint on behalf of all women at Hughes, the Ninth Circuit noted approvingly:

> . . . Moore had never claimed before the EEOC that she was discriminated against as a female, *but only* as a Black female. . . . [T]his raised serious doubts as to Moore's ability to adequately represent white female employees.[17]

The curious logic in *Moore* reveals not only the narrow scope of antidiscrimination doctrine and its failure to embrace intersectionality, but also the centrality of white female experiences in the conceptualization of gender discrimination. One inference that could be drawn from the court's statement that Moore's complaint did not entail a claim of discrimination "against females" is that discrimination against Black females is something less than discrimination against females. More than likely, however, the court meant to imply that Moore did not claim that *all* females were discriminated against *but only* Black females. But even thus recast, the court's rationale is problematic for Black women. The court rejected Moore's bid to represent all females apparently because her attempt to specify her race was seen as being at odds with the standard allegation that the employer simply discriminated "against females."

The court failed to see that the absence of a racial referent does not necessarily mean that the claim being made is a more inclusive one. A white woman claiming discrimination against females may be in no

better position to represent all women than a Black woman who claims discrimination as a Black female and wants to represent all females. The court's preferred articulation of "against females" is not necessarily more inclusive—it just appears to be so because the racial contours of the claim are not specified.

The court's preference for "against females" rather than "against Black females" reveals the implicit grounding of white female experiences in the doctrinal conceptualization of sex discrimination. For white women, claiming sex discrimination is simply a statement that but for gender, they would not have been disadvantaged. For them there is no need to specify discrimination as *white* females because their race does not contribute to the disadvantage for which they seek redress. The view of discrimination that is derived from this grounding takes race privilege as a given.

Discrimination against a white female is thus the standard sex discrimination claim; claims that diverge from this standard appear to present some sort of hybrid claim. More significantly, because Black females' claims are seen as hybrid, they sometimes cannot represent those who may have "pure" claims of sex discrimination. The effect of this approach is that even though a challenged policy or practice may clearly discriminate against all females, the fact that it has particularly harsh consequences for Black females places Black female plaintiffs at odds with white females.

Moore illustrates one of the limitations of antidiscrimination law's remedial scope and normative vision. The refusal to allow a multiply disadvantaged class to represent others who may be singularly disadvantaged defeats efforts to restructure the distribution of opportunity and limits remedial relief to minor adjustments within an established hierarchy. Consequently, "bottom-up" approaches, those which combine all discriminatees in order to challenge an entire employment system, are foreclosed by the limited view of the wrong and the narrow scope of the available remedy. If such "bottom-up" intersectional representation were routinely permitted, employees might accept the possibility that there is more to gain by collectively challenging the hierarchy rather than by each discriminatee individually seeking to protect her source of privilege within the hierarchy. But as long as antidiscrimination doctrine proceeds from the premise that employment systems need only minor adjustments, opportunities for advancement by disadvantaged employees will be limited. Relatively privileged employees probably are better off guarding their advantage while jockeying against others to gain more. As a result, Black women—the class of employees which, because of its intersectionality, is best able to challenge all forms of discrimination—are essentially isolated and often required to fend for themselves.

In *Moore*, the court's denial of the plaintiffs bid to represent all Blacks and females left Moore with the task of supporting her race and sex discrimination claims with statistical evidence of discrimination against Black females alone.[18] Because she was unable to represent white women or Black men, she could not use overall statistics on sex disparity at Hughes, nor could she use statistics on race. Proving her claim using statistics on Black women alone was no small task, due to the fact that she was bringing the suit under a disparate impact theory of discrimination.[19]

The court further limited the relevant statistical pool to include only Black women who it determined were qualified to fill the openings in upper-level labor jobs and in supervisory positions.[20] According to the court, Moore had not demonstrated that there were any qualified Black women within her bargaining unit or the general labor pool for either category of jobs.[21] Finally, the court stated that even if it accepted Moore's contention that the percentage of Black females in supervisory positions should equal the percentage of Black females in the employee pool, it still would not find discriminatory impact.[22] Because the promotion of only two Black women into supervisory positions would have achieved the expected mean distribution of Black women within that job category, the court was "unwilling to agree that a prima facie case of disparate impact ha[d] been proven."[23]

The court's rulings on Moore's sex and race claim left her with such a small statistical sample that even if she had proved that there were qualified Black women, she could not have shown discrimination under a disparate impact theory. *Moore* illustrates yet another way that antidiscrimination doctrine essentially erases Black women's distinct experiences and, as a result, deems their discrimination complaints groundless.

3. *Payne v Travenol.*

Black female plaintiffs have also encountered difficulty in their efforts to win certification as class representatives in some race discrimination actions. This problem typically arises in cases where statistics suggest significant disparities between Black and white workers and further disparities between Black men and Black women. Courts in some cases[24] have denied certification based on logic that mirrors the rationale in *Moore*: The sex disparities between Black men and Black women created such conflicting interests that Black women could not possibly represent Black men adequately. In one such case, *Payne v Travenol*,[25] two Black female plaintiffs alleging race discrimination brought a class action suit on behalf of all Black employees at a pharmaceutical plant.[26] The court refused, however, to allow the plaintiffs to represent Black males and granted the defendant's request to narrow the class to Black women only. Ultimately, the district court found that there had been extensive racial discrimination at the plant and awarded back pay and constructive seniority to the class of Black female employees. But, despite its finding of general race discrimination, the court refused to extend the remedy to Black men for fear that their conflicting interests would not be adequately addressed;[27] the Fifth Circuit affirmed.[28]

Notably, the plaintiffs in *Travenol* fared better than the similarly situated plaintiff in *Moore*: They were not denied use of meaningful statistics showing an overall pattern of race discrimination simply because there were no men in their class. The plaintiffs' bid to represent all Black employees, however, like Moore's attempt to represent all women employees, failed as a consequence of the court's narrow view of class interest.

Even though *Travenol* was a partial victory for Black women, the case specifically illustrates how antidiscrimination doctrine generally creates a dilemma for Black women. It forces them to choose between specifically articulating the intersectional aspects of their subordination, thereby risking their ability to represent Black men, or ignoring intersectionality in order to state a claim that would not lead to the exclusion of Black men. When one considers the political consequences of this dilemma, there is little wonder that many people within the Black community view the specific articulation of Black women's interests as dangerously divisive.

In sum, several courts have proved unable to deal with intersectionality, although for contrasting reasons. In *DeGraffenreid,* the court refused to recognize the possibility of compound discrimination against Black women and analyzed their claim using the employment of white women as the historical base. As a consequence, the employment experiences of white women obscured the distinct discrimination that Black women experienced.

Conversely, in *Moore,* the court held that a Black woman could not use statistics reflecting the overall sex disparity in supervisory and upper-level labor jobs because she had not claimed discrimination as a woman, but "only" as a Black woman. The court would not entertain the notion that discrimination experienced by Black women is indeed sex discrimination—provable through disparate impact statistics on women.

Finally, courts, such as the one in *Travenol,* have held that Black women cannot represent an entire class of Blacks due to presumed class conflicts in cases where sex additionally disadvantaged Black women. As a result, in the few cases where Black women are allowed to use overall statistics indicating racially disparate treatment Black men may not be able to share in the remedy.

Perhaps it appears to some that I have offered inconsistent criticisms of how Black women are treated in antidiscrimination law: I seem to be saying that in one case, Black women's claims were rejected and their experiences obscured because the court refused to acknowledge that the employment experience of Black women can be distinct from that of white women, while in other cases, the interests of Black women were harmed because Black women's claims were viewed as so distinct from the claims of either white women or Black men that the court denied to Black females representation of the larger class. It seems that I have to say that Black women are the same and harmed by being treated differently, or that they are different and harmed by being treated the same. But I cannot say both.

This apparent contradiction is but another manifestation of the conceptual limitations of the single-issue analyses that intersectionality challenges. The point is that Black women can experience discrimination in

any number of ways and that the contradiction arises from our assumptions that their claims of exclusion must be unidirectional. Consider an analogy to traffic in an intersection, coming and going in all four directions. Discrimination, like traffic through an intersection, may flow in one direction, and it may flow in another. If an accident happens in an intersection, it can be caused by cars traveling from any number of directions and, sometimes, from all of them. Similarly, if a Black woman is harmed because she is in the intersection, her injury could result from sex discrimination or race discrimination.

Judicial decisions which premise intersectional relief on a showing that Black women are specifically recognized as a class are analogous to a doctor's decision at the scene of an accident to treat an accident victim only if the injury is recognized by medical insurance. Similarly, providing legal relief only when Black women show that their claims are based on race or on sex is analogous to calling an ambulance for the victim only after the driver responsible for the injuries is identified. But it is not always easy to reconstruct an accident: Sometimes the skid marks and the injuries simply indicate that they occurred simultaneously, frustrating efforts to determine which driver caused the harm. In these cases the tendency seems to be that no driver is held responsible, no treatment is administered, and the involved parties simply get back in their cars and zoom away.

To bring this back to a non-metaphorical level, I am suggesting that Black women can experience discrimination in ways that are both similar to and different from those experienced by white women and Black men. Black women sometimes experience discrimination in ways similar to white women's experiences; sometimes they share very similar experiences with Black men. Yet often they experience double-discrimination—the combined effects of practices which discriminate on the basis of race, and on the basis of sex. And sometimes, they experience discrimination as Black women—not the sum of race and sex discrimination, but as Black women.

Black women's experiences are much broader than the general categories that discrimination discourse provides. Yet the continued insistence that Black women's demands and needs be filtered through categorical analyses that completely obscure their experiences guarantees that their needs will seldom be addressed.

B. THE SIGNIFICANCE OF DOCTRINAL TREATMENT OF INTERSECTIONALITY

DeGraffenreid, Moore and *Travenol* are doctrinal manifestations of a common political and theoretical approach to discrimination which operates to marginalize Black women. Unable to grasp the importance of Black women's intersectional experiences, not only courts, but feminist and civil rights thinkers as well have treated Black women in ways that deny both the unique compoundedness of their situation and the centrality of their experiences to the larger classes of women and Blacks. Black women are regarded either as too much like women or Blacks and the compounded nature of their experience is absorbed into the collective experiences of either group or as too different, in which case Black women's Blackness or femaleness sometimes has placed their needs and perspectives at the margin of the feminist and Black liberationist agendas.

While it could be argued that this failure represents an absence of political will to include Black women, I believe that it reflects an uncritical and disturbing acceptance of dominant ways of thinking about discrimination. Consider first the definition of discrimination that seems to be operative in antidiscrimination law: Discrimination which is wrongful proceeds from the identification of a specific class or category; either a discriminator intentionally identifies this category, or a process is adopted which somehow disadvantages all members of this category.[29] According to the dominant view, a discriminator treats all people within a race or sex category similarly. Any significant experiential or statistical variation within this group suggests either that the group is not being discriminated against or that conflicting interests exist which defeat any attempts to bring a common claim.[30] Consequently, one generally cannot combine these categories. Race and sex, moreover, become significant only when they operate to explicitly *disadvantage* the victims; because the *privileging* of whiteness or maleness is implicit, it is generally not perceived at all.

Underlying this conception of discrimination is a view that the wrong which antidiscrimination law addresses is the use of race or gender factors to interfere with decisions that would otherwise be fair or neutral. This process-based definition is not grounded in a bottom-up commitment to improve the substantive conditions for those who are victimized by the interplay of numerous factors. Instead, the dominant message of antidiscrimination law is that it will regulate only the limited extent to which race or sex interferes with the process of determining outcomes. This narrow objective is facilitated by the top-down strategy of using a singular "but for" analysis to ascertain the effects of race or sex. Because the scope of antidiscrimination law is so limited, sex and race discrimination have come to be defined in terms of the experiences of those who are privileged *but for* their racial or sexual characteristics. Put differently, the paradigm of sex discrimination tends to be based on the experiences of white women; the model of race discrimination tends to be based on the experiences of the most privileged Blacks. Notions of what constitutes race and sex discrimination are, as a result, narrowly tailored to embrace only a small set of circumstances, none of which include discrimination against Black women.

To the extent that this general description is accurate, the following analogy can be useful in describing how Black women are marginalized in the interface between antidiscrimination law and race and gender hierarchies: Imagine a basement which contains all people who are disadvantaged on the basis of race, sex, class, sexual preference, age and/or physical ability. These people are stacked—feet standing on shoulders—with those on the bottom being disadvantaged by the full array of factors, up to the very top, where the heads of all those disadvantaged by a singular factor brush up against the ceiling. Their ceiling is actually the floor above which only those who are *not* disadvantaged in any way reside. In efforts to correct some aspects of domination, those above the ceiling admit from the basement only those who can say that "but for" the ceiling, they too would be in the upper room. A hatch is developed through which those placed immediately below can crawl. Yet this hatch is generally available only to those who—due to the singularity of their burden and their otherwise privileged position relative to those below—are in the position to crawl through. Those who are multiply burdened are generally left below unless they can somehow pull themselves into the groups that are permitted to squeeze through the hatch.

As this analogy translates for Black women, the problem is that they can receive protection only to the extent that their experiences are recognizably similar to those whose experiences tend to be reflected in antidiscrimination doctrine. If Black women cannot conclusively say that "but for" their race or "but for" their gender they would be treated differently, they are not invited to climb through the hatch but told to wait in the unprotected margin until they can be absorbed into the broader, protected categories of race and sex.

Despite the narrow scope of this dominant conception of discrimination and its tendency to marginalize those whose experiences cannot be described within its tightly drawn parameters, this approach has been regarded as the appropriate framework for addressing a range of problems. In much of feminist theory and, to some extent, in antiracist politics, this framework is reflected in the belief that sexism or racism can be meaningfully discussed without paying attention to the lives of those other than the race-, gender- or class-privileged. As a result, both feminist theory and antiracist politics have been organized, in part, around the equation of racism with what happens to the Black middle-class or to Black men, and the equation of sexism with what happens to white women.

Looking at historical and contemporary issues in both the feminist and the civil rights communities, one can find ample evidence of how both communities' acceptance of the dominant framework of discrimination has hindered the development of an adequate theory and praxis to address problems of intersectionality. This adoption of a single-issue framework for discrimination not only marginalizes Black women within the very movements that claim them as part of their constituency but it also makes the illusive goal of ending racism and patriarchy even more difficult to attain.

II. FEMINISM AND BLACK WOMEN: "AIN'T WE WOMEN?"

Oddly, despite the relative inability of feminist politics and theory to address Black women substantively, feminist theory and tradition borrow considerably from Black women's history. For example, "Ain't I a Woman" has come to represent a standard refrain in feminist discourse.[31] Yet the lesson of this powerful oratory is not fully appreciated because the context of the delivery is seldom examined. I would like to tell part of the story because it establishes some themes that have characterized feminist treatment of race and illustrates the importance of including Black women's experiences as a rich source for the critique of patriarchy.

In 1851, Sojourner Truth declared "Ain't I a Woman?" and challenged the sexist imagery used by male critics to justify the disenfranchisement of women.[32] The scene was a Women's Rights Conference in Akron, Ohio; white male hecklers, invoking stereotypical images of "womanhood," argued that women were too frail and delicate to take on the responsibilities of political activity. When Sojourner Truth rose to speak, many white women urged that she be silenced, fearing that she would divert attention from women's suffrage to emancipation. Truth, once permitted to speak, recounted the horrors of slavery, and its particular impact on Black women:

> Look at my arm! I have ploughed and planted and gathered into barns, and no man could head me—and ain't I a woman? I could work as much and eat as much as a man—when I could get it—and bear the lash as well! And ain't I a woman? I have born thirteen children, and seen most of 'em sold into slavery, and when I cried out with my mother's grief, none but Jesus heard me—and ain't I a woman?[33]

By using her own life to reveal the contradiction between the ideological myths of womanhood and the reality of Black women's experience, Truth's oratory provided a powerful rebuttal to the claim that women were categorically weaker than men. Yet Truth's personal challenge to the coherence of the cult of true womanhood was useful only to the extent that white women were willing to reject the racist attempts to rationalize the contradiction—that because Black women were something less than real women, their experiences had no bearing on true womanhood. Thus, this 19th-century Black feminist challenged not only patriarchy, but she also challenged white feminists wishing to embrace Black women's history to relinquish their vestedness in whiteness.

Contemporary white feminists inherit not the legacy of Truth's challenge to patriarchy but, instead, Truth's challenge to their forbearers. Even today, the difficulty that white women have traditionally experienced in sacrificing racial privilege to strengthen feminism renders them susceptible to Truth's critical question. When feminist theory and politics that claim to reflect *women's* experience and *women's* aspirations do not include or speak to Black women, Black women must ask: "Ain't *We* Women?" If this is so, how can the claims that "women are," "women believe" and "women need" be made when such claims are inapplicable or unresponsive to the needs, interests and experiences of Black women?

The value of feminist theory to Black women is diminished because it evolves from a white racial context that is seldom acknowledged. Not only are women of color in fact overlooked, but their exclusion is reinforced when *white* women speak for and as *women*. The authoritative universal voice—usually white male subjectivity masquerading as non-racial, non-gendered objectivity[34]—is merely transferred to those who, but for gender, share many of the same cultural, economic and social characteristics. When feminist theory attempts to describe women's experiences through analyzing patriarchy, sexuality, or separate spheres ideology, it often overlooks the role of race. Feminists thus ignore how their own race functions to mitigate some aspects of sexism and, moreover, how it often privileges them over and contributes to the domination of other women.[35] Consequently, feminist theory remains *white,* and its potential to broaden and deepen its analysis by addressing non-privileged women remains unrealized.

An example of how some feminist theories are narrowly constructed around white women's experiences is found in the separate spheres literature. The critique of how separate spheres ideology shapes and limits women's roles in the home and in public life is a central theme in feminist legal thought.[36] Feminists have attempted to expose and dismantle separate spheres ideology by identifying and criticizing the stereotypes that traditionally have justified the disparate societal roles assigned to men and women.[37] Yet this attempt

to debunk ideological justifications for *women's* subordination offers little insight into the domination of *Black* women. Because the experiential base upon which many feminist insights are grounded is white, theoretical statements drawn from them are over generalized at best, and often wrong.[38] Statements such as "men and women are taught to see men as independent, capable, powerful; men and women are taught to see women as dependent, limited in abilities, and passive,"[39] are common within this literature. But this "observation" overlooks the anomalies created by crosscurrents of racism and sexism. Black men and women live in a society that creates sex-based norms and expectations which racism operates simultaneously to deny; Black men are not viewed as powerful, nor are Black women seen as passive. An effort to develop an ideological explanation of gender domination in the Black community should proceed from an understanding of how crosscutting forces establish gender norms and how the conditions of Black subordination wholly frustrate access to these norms. Given this understanding, perhaps we can begin to see why Black women have been dogged by the stereotype of the pathological matriarch[40] or why there have been those in the Black liberation movement who aspire to create institutions and to build traditions that are intentionally patriarchal.[41]

Because ideological and descriptive definitions of patriarchy are usually premised upon white female experiences, feminists and others informed by feminist literature may make the mistake of assuming that since the role of Black women in the family and in other Black institutions does not always resemble the familiar manifestations of patriarchy in the white community, Black women are somehow exempt from patriarchal norms. For example, Black women have traditionally worked outside the home in numbers far exceeding the labor participation rate of white women.[42] An analysis of patriarchy that highlights the history of white women's exclusion from the workplace might permit the inference that Black women have not been burdened by this particular gender-based expectation. Yet the very fact that Black women must work conflicts with norms that women should not, often creating personal, emotional and relationship problems in Black women's lives. Thus, Black women are burdened not only because they often have to take on responsibilities that are not traditionally feminine but, moreover, their assumption of these roles is sometimes interpreted within the Black community as either Black women's failure to live up to such norms or as another manifestation of racism's scourge upon the Black community.[43] This is one of the many aspects of intersectionality that cannot be understood through an analysis of patriarchy rooted in white experience.

. . .

NOTES

1. Gloria T. Hull et al., eds. *But Some of Us Are Brave* (The Feminist Press, 1982).

2. For other work setting forth a Black feminist perspective on law, see Judy Scales-Trent, *Black Women and the Constitution: Finding Our Place, Asserting Our Rights* (*Voices of Experience: New Responses to Gender Discourse*), 24 Harv CR-CL L Rev 9 (1989); . . . Angela Harris, *Race and Essentialism in Feminist Legal Theory* (unpublished manuscript on file with author); and Paulette M. Caldwell, *A Hair Piece* (unpublished manuscript on file with author).

3. The most common linguistic manifestation of this analytical dilemma is represented in the conventional usage of the term "Blacks and women." Although it may be true that some people mean to include Black women in either "Blacks" or "women," the context in which the term is used actually suggests that often Black women are not considered. See, for example, Elizabeth Spelman, *The Inessential Woman* 114–15 (Beacon Press, 1988) (discussing an article on Blacks and women in the military where "the racial identity of those identified as 'women' does not become explicit until reference is made to Black women, at which point it also becomes clear that the category of women excludes Black women"). It seems that if Black women were explicitly included, the preferred term would be either "Blacks and white women" or "Black men and all women."

4. Civil Rights Act of 1964, 42 USC § 2000e, et seq as amended (1982).

5. 413 F Supp 142 (E D Mo 1976).

6. 708 F2d 475 (9th Cir 1983).

7. 673 F2d 798 (5th Cir 1982).

8. *DeGraffenreid*, 413 F Supp at 143.

9. Id at 144.

10. Id at 145. In *Mosley v General Motors*, 497 F Supp 583 (E D Mo 1980), plaintiffs, alleging broad-based racial discrimination at General Motors' St. Louis facility, prevailed in a portion of their Title VII claim. The seniority system challenged in *DeGraffenreid*, however, was not considered in *Mosley*.

11. Id at 145.

12. Interestingly, no case has been discovered in which a court denied a white male's attempt to bring a reverse discrimination claim on similar grounds—that is, that sex and race claims cannot be combined because Congress did not intend to protect compound classes. White males in a typical reverse discrimination case are in no better position than the frustrated plaintiffs in *DeGraffenreid*: If they are required to made their claims separately, white males cannot prove race discrimination because white women are not discriminated against, and they cannot prove sex discrimination because Black males are not discriminated against. Yet it seems that courts do not acknowledge the compound nature of most reverse discrimination cases. That Black women's claims automatically raise the question of compound discrimination and white males' "reverse discrimination" cases do not suggest that the notion of compoundedness is somehow contingent upon an implicit norm that is not neutral but is white male. Thus, Black women are perceived as a compound class because they are two steps removed from a white male norm,

while white males are apparently not perceived to be a compound class because they somehow represent the norm.

13. I do not mean to imply that all courts that have grappled with this problem have adopted the *De-Graffenreid* approach. Indeed, other courts have concluded that Black women are protected by Title VII. See, for example, *Jefferies v Harris Community Action Ass'n.*, 615 F2d 1025 (5th Cir 1980). I do mean to suggest that the very fact that the Black women's claims are seen as aberrant suggests that sex discrimination doctrine is centered in the experiences of white women. Even those courts that have held that Black women are protected seem to accept that Black women's claims raise issues that the "standard" sex discrimination claims do not. See Elaine W. Shoben, *Compound Discrimination: The Interaction of Race and Sex in Employment Discrimination*, 55 NYU L Rev 793, 803–04 (1980) (criticizing the *Jefferies* use of a sex-plus analysis to create a subclass of Black women).

14. 708 F2d 475.

15. See also *Moore v National Association of Securities Dealers*, 27 EPD (CCH) ¶ 32,238 (D DC 1981); but see *Edmondson v Simon*, 86 FRD 375 (N D 111 1980) (where the court was unwilling to hold as a matter of law that no Black female could represent without conflict the interests of both Blacks and females).

16. 708 F2d at 479. Between January 1976 and June 1979, the three years in which Moore claimed that she was passed over for promotion, the percentage of white males occupying first-level supervisory positions ranged from 70.3 to 76.8%; Black males from 8.9 to 10.9%; white women from 1.8 to 3.3%; and Black females from 0 to 2.2%. The overall male/female ratio in the top five labor grades ranged from 100/0% in 1976 to 98/1.8% in 1979. The white/Black ratio was 85/3.3% in 1976 and 79.6/8% in 1979. The overall ratio of men to women in supervisory positions was 98.2 to 1.8% in 1976 to 93.4 to 6.6% in 1979; the Black to white ratio during the same time period was 78.6 to 8.9% and 73.6 to 13.1%.

For promotions to the top five labor grades, the percentages were worse. Between 1976 and 1979, the percentage of white males in these positions ranged from 85.3 to 77.9%; Black males 3.3 to 8%; white females from 0 to 1.4%, and Black females from 0 to 0%. Overall, in 1979, 98.2% of the highest level employees were male; 1.8% were female.

17. 708 F2d at 480 (emphasis added).

18. Id at 484–86.

19. Under the disparate impact theory that prevailed at the time, the plaintiff had to introduce statistics suggesting that a policy or procedure disparately affects the members of a protected group. The employer could rebut that evidence by showing that there was a business necessity supporting the rule. The plaintiff then countered the rebuttal by showing that there was a less discriminatory alternative. See, for example, *Griggs v Duke Power*, 401 US 424 (1971); *Connecticut v Teal*, 457 US 440 (1982).

A central issue in a disparate impact case is whether the impact proved is statistically significant. A related issue is how the protected group is defined. In many cases a Black female plaintiff would prefer to use statistics which include white women and/or Black men to indicate that the policy in question does in fact disparately affect the protected class. If, as in Moore, the plaintiff may use only statistics involving Black women, there may not be enough Black women employees to create a statistically significant sample.

20. Id at 484.

21. The court buttressed its finding with respect to the upper-level labor jobs with statistics for the Los Angeles Metropolitan Area which indicated the there were only 0.2% Black women within comparable job categories. Id at 485 n 9.

22. Id at 486.

23. Id.

24. See *Strong v Arkansas Blue Cross & Blue Shield, Inc.*, 87 FRD 496 (E D Ark 1980); *Hammons v Folger Coffee Co.*, 87 FRD 600 (W D Mo 1980); *Edmondson v Simon*, 86 FRD 375 (N D 111 1980); *Vuyanich v Republic National Bank of Dallas,* 82 FRD 420 (N D Tex 1979); *Colston v Maryland Cup Corp.*, 26 Fed Rules Serv 940 (D Md 1978).

25. 416 F Supp 248 (N D Miss 1976).

26. The suit commenced on March 2, 1972, with the filing of a complaint by three employees seeking to represent a class of persons allegedly subjected to racial discrimination at the hands of the defendants. Subsequently, the plaintiffs amended the complaint to add an allegation of sex discrimination. Of the original named plaintiffs, one was a Black male and two were Black females. In the course of the three-year period between the filing of the complaint and the trial, the only named male plaintiff received permission of the court to withdraw for religious reasons. Id at 250.

27. As the dissent in *Travenol* pointed out, there was no reason to exclude Black males from the scope of the remedy *after* counsel had presented sufficient evidence to support a finding of discrimination against Black men. If the rationale for excluding Black males was the potential conflict between Black males and Black females, then "[i]n this case, to paraphrase an old adage, the proof of plaintiffs' ability to represent the interests of Black males was in the representation thereof." 673 F2d at 837–38.

28. 673 F2d 798 (5th Cir 1982).

29. In much of antidiscrimination doctrine, the presence of intent to discriminate distinguishes unlawful from lawful discrimination. See *Washington v Davis*, 426 US 229, 239–45 (1976) (proof of discriminatory purpose required to substantiate Equal Protection violation). Under Title VII, however, the Court has held that statistical data showing a disproportionate impact can suffice to support a finding of discrimination. See *Griggs*, 401 US at 432. Whether the distinction between the two analyses will survive is an open question. See *Wards Cove Packing Co., Inc. v Atonio*, 109 S Ct 2115, 2122–23 (1989) (plaintiffs must show more than mere disparity to support a prima facie case of disparate impact). For a discussion of the competing normative visions that underlie the intent and effects analyses, see Alan David Freeman, *Legitimizing Racial Discrimination Through Antidiscrimination Law: A Critical Review of Supreme Court Doctrine*, 62 Minn L Rev 1049 (1978).

30. See, for example, *Moore*, 708 F2d at 479.

31. See Phyliss Palmer, The Racial Feminization of Poverty: Women of Color as Portents of the Future for All Women, *Women's Studies Quarterly* 11:3–4 (Fall 1983) (posing the question of why "white women in the women's movement had not created more effective and continuous alliances with Black women" when "simultaneously . . . Black women [have] become heroines for the women's movement, a position symbolized by the consistent use of Sojourner Truth and her famous words, "Ain't I a Woman?").

32. See Paula Giddings, *When and Where I Enter: The Impact of Black Women on Race and Sex in America* 54 (William Morrow and Co, Inc, 1st ed. 1984).

33. Eleanor Flexner, *Century of Struggle: The Women's Rights Movement in the United States* 91 (Belknap Press of Harvard University Press, 1975). See also bell hooks, *Ain't I a Woman* 159–60 (South End Press, 1981).

34. "'Objectivity' is itself an example of the reification of white male thought." Hull et al., eds, *But Some of Us Are Brave* at XXV (cited in note 1).

35. For example, many white females were able to gain entry into previously all white male enclaves not through bringing about a fundamental reordering of male versus female work, but in large part by shifting their "female" responsibilities to poor and minority women.

36. Feminists often discuss how gender-based stereotypes and norms reinforce the subordination of women by justifying their exclusion from public life and glorifying their roles within the private sphere. Law has historically played a role in maintaining this subordination by enforcing the exclusion of women from public life and by limiting its reach into the private sphere. See, for example, Deborah L. Rhode, *Association and Assimilation*, 81 Nw U L Rev 106 (1986); Frances Olsen, *From False Paternalism to False Equality: Judicial Assaults on Feminist Community, Illinois 1869–95*, 84 Mich L Rev 1518 (1986); Martha Minow, *Foreword: Justice Engendered*, 101 Harv L Rev 10 (1987); Nadine Taub and Elizabeth M. Schneider, *Perspectives on Women's Subordination and the Role of Law*, in David Kairys, ed, *The Politics of Law* 117–39 (Pantheon Books, 1982).

37. See works cited in note 36.

38. This criticism is a discrete illustration of a more general claim that feminism has been premised on white middle-class women's experience. For example, early feminist texts such as Betty Friedan's *The Feminine Mystique* (W. W. Norton, 1963), placed white middle-class problems at the center of feminism and thus contributed to its rejection within the Black community. See Hooks, *Ain't I a Woman* at 185–96 (cited in note 33) (noting that feminism was eschewed by Black women because its white middle-class agenda ignored Black women's concerns).

39. Richard A. Wasserstrom, *Racism, Sexism and Preferential Treatment: An Approach to the Topics*, 24 UCLA L Rev 581, 588 (1977). I chose this phrase not because it is typical of most feminist statements of separate spheres; indeed, most discussions are not as simplistic as the bold statement presented here. See, for example, Taub and Schneider, *Perspectives on Women's Subordination and the Role of Law* at 117–39 (cited in note 36).

40. For example, Black families have sometimes been cast as pathological largely because Black women's divergence from the white middle-class female norm. The most infamous rendition of this view is found in the Moynihan report which blamed many of the Black community's ills on a supposed pathological family structure.. . .

41. See Hooks, *Ain't I a Woman* at 94–99 (cited in note 33) (discussing the elevation of sexist imagery in the Black liberation movement during the 1960s).

42. See generally Jacqueline Jones, *Labor of Love, Labor of Sorrow; Black Women, Work, and the Family from Slavery to the Present* (Basic Books, 1985); Angela Davis, *Women, Race and Class* (Random House, 1981).

43. As Elizabeth Higginbotham noted, "women, who often fail to conform to 'appropriate' sex roles, have been pictured as, and made to feel, inadequate—even though as women, they possess traits recognized as positive when held by men in the wider society. Such women are stigmatized because their lack of adherence to expected gender roles is seen as a threat to the value system." Elizabeth Higginbotham, *Two Representative Issues in Contemporary Sociological Work on Black Women*, in Hull et al., eds, *But Some of Us Are Brave* at 95 (cited in note 1).

MEL MICHELLE LEWIS

18. A BRIDGE ACROSS OUR FEARS: QUEER FEMINIST INTERSECTIONAL ETHNIC STUDIES AS INTERDISCIPLINARY PRAXIS

Poetry is not only a dream and vision; it is the skeleton architecture of our lives. It lays the foundations for a future of change, a bridge across our fears of what has never been before.

—Audre Lorde, "Poetry is not a Luxury," *Sister Outsider*

I describe myself as a feminist Black queer studies interdisciplinary scholar working at the nexus of intersectional queer critical race studies and pedagogies of social justice praxis. I am proud to have an MS, MA, and PhD, all in women's studies. Audre Lorde's work, including the poem "Poetry is not a Luxury" excerpted above, is central to my intersectional education, and my musings on intersectionality and pedagogy. I claim women's studies as my "dream and vision," in the language of her poem. Indeed, intersectionality is the "architecture of my life" and is central to theorizing queer feminist ethnic studies.

Over the last several years, I have taught in and directed women's studies and Africana studies. I am now embarking on a journey as the director of a new intersectional ethnic studies major program. I posed a question to Lorde: "How will I bridge women's studies, queer studies, and ethnic studies in the context of this new major? How will I lay a foundation for the future of change we so desperately need?" And the Lorde said, let us build "a bridge across our fears of what has never been before" (37–38). In this essay, I will do the following: (a) offer you as women's studies students the opportunity to think deeply about intersectionality, not just as a theory but as a praxis that can be enacted through teaching and learning; (b) share how women's studies shapes the theoretical framework for my interdisciplinary project of developing queer feminist intersectional ethnic studies; and (c) provide ways

for you to think about the inner workings of interdisciplinary pedagogy and how we come to learn what we learn in courses that employ intersectionality.

I often seek direction from the brilliance of queer writers of color of the twentieth century, my intellectual and spiritual elders and ancestors. This essay reflects on "conversations" I've had with these writers and their texts as I embark on developing an ethnic studies major that integrates Black queer feminist studies as an intentional area of emphasis. My inquiry—"What can queer feminist intersectional ethnic studies lens tell us about interdisciplinarity and its future formations?"—is meant to highlight the voices of scholars, artists, and activists who work at the intersections. I theorize a queer feminist intersectional ethnic studies pedagogy and praxis that allows students to explore how we might "dream and vision" an intersectional location. This means that I frame the work of Lorde, Bayard Rustin, James Baldwin, Gloria Anzaldúa, and Cherríe Moraga; organizations such as Kitchen Table Press and Combahee River Collective; and uprisings such as the Stonewall Riots as having already built a bridge that we need only explicitly traverse. You may have encountered some of these theorists, artists, and activists. I invite you to "dream and vision," using an intersectional praxis, in your own classes when you encounter these dynamic materials. Finally, this essay will conclude with an appreciation of Black Lives Matter and AFRO-PUNK, contemporary movements whose praxis can be linked to the foundations of intersectional work. I argue that a queer feminist ethnic studies lens can reveal the ways in which these movements both draw on the past and present new possibilities for what "has never been done before."

With my own interdisciplinary positionality, orientation toward Black queer feminist studies, and the parameters for this essay in mind, I have chosen to focus on bridge builders who are foundational to my own work to serve as examples. I acknowledge there are many other foundational individuals and works that might serve to illuminate the lineage of queer feminist intersectional ethnic studies. I will explore how selected luminaries are foundational to queer feminist intersectional ethnic studies as I seek to develop it. Then I will examine the ways in which this foundation has been taken up in contemporary movements who have centered and operationalized intersectionality.

INTERSECTIONALITY: BUILDING A BRIDGE AT THE CROSSROADS

The conceptual framework for intersectionality, a term coined by legal scholar Kimberlé Crenshaw in her influential article "Mapping the Margins: Intersectionality, Identity Politics, and Violence Against Women of Color," and taken up by scholars, activists, and social justice practitioners, is often used to illuminate structural oppression as well as resistance and resilience of those on the margins. Conveying the function of an intersectional framework, Patricia Hill Collins and Sirma Bilge write, "People's lives and the organization of power in a given society are better understood as being shaped not by a single axis of social division . . . but by many axes that work together and influence each other" (2). Intersectionality, then, is a crucial element in illuminating a queer feminist intersectional ethnic studies lens; indeed, this work stands on the shoulders of many thinkers whose bodies, identities, and experiences led them to articulate what we now call intersectionality, long before the term was used to understand social and political complexities from a queer feminist person of color perspective. The anthology *This Bridge Called My Back*, edited by Gloria Anzaldúa, and Cherríe Moraga, exemplifies the articulation of this complexity.

Cherríe Moraga writes, "*This Bridge Called My Back* was collectively pinned with the hope for 'revolutionary solidarity,'" a concept at the center of the project. She continues: "For the first time in the United States, women of color, who had been historically denied a shared political voice, endeavored to create bridges of consciousness through the exploration, in print, of their diverse classes, cultures and sexualities" (xvi). Anzaldúa and Moraga's text not only addresses the intersections of race, ethnicity, class, gender, sexuality, nation, and many other dimensions of identity and experience; it also is a prototype for queer feminist intersectional ethnic studies praxis. By drawing together the voices of the contributors of the anthology and making visible the connected experiences, struggles, and transformative power of the writers, Anzaldúa and Moraga enacted intersectional theory with their publication. Reflecting on the foundational nature of *Bridge*, Moraga notes that although *Bridge* documented "the living experience of what academics now refer to as 'intersectionality,' where multiple identities converge at the crossroads of a woman of color life," we must acknowledge "'holes in the walls' of our thinking remain wide and many and there is an abundant amount of 'bridging' left to be done" (xxii). These remaining "holes" necessitate that we first, name *Bridge* as foundational in its content and its framing, and second, theorize a pedagogy and praxis that continues to build bridges between feminist theory, queer theory, and critical race theory. *Bridge* was conceived to highlight the woman of color life as always already inclusive of a queer feminist exploration of ethnicity. I have made texts like *Bridge* central in my ethnic studies introductory course in order to illuminate the foundations that already undergird intersectional thinking, and to facilitate further theorizing at the nexus of race, class, gender, sexuality, and other dimensions of identity and experience. This pedagogical approach is itself an enactment of intersectional theory and praxis.

REVOLUTIONARY SOLIDARITY: CREATION STORIES

Thinking deeply about *Bridge* as a template for queer feminist intersectional ethnic studies pedagogy and praxis led me to questions about how to more intentionally examine the creation story of the text's publication. This creation story provides an example of how subjugated knowledges can theorize in chorus, providing multiple perspectives on the personal as political, and offering models for interrogating structural oppressions. Reflecting on Lorde's involvement in the founding of Kitchen Table Press, Beverly Guy-Sheftall writes, "Kitchen Table: Women of Color Press was founded in 1980 by Audre Lorde and Barbara Smith for the purpose of publishing mainly feminist women of color; its mission was also to provide a political support network for feminists and lesbians of color as well" (18). Moraga writes, "[*Bridge*] was collectively pinned with the hope for 'revolutionary solidarity' at the center of the project" (xvi). Illuminating the creation stories of solidarity projects, in this instance, the first edition of the publication of *Bridge* by Kitchen Table Press is also central to developing a queer feminist intersectional ethnic studies pedagogy and praxis.

Central to theorizing queer feminist intersectional ethnic studies pedagogy and praxis is providing ways to access hidden knowledges. I teach students to assess their sources by learning more about author's perspectives; I also ask students to think of each text as a "political project" that goes beyond the content. I encourage students to examine how the text came to be; the press or placement of the material; relationships between contributors, editors, and co-authors; and the situatedness of those involved. My students discover all manner of complexities, including love relationships, political alliances, institutional barriers, contention, and alliances. In this way, models for revolutionary solidarity are revealed alongside the content. Theorizing solidarity, intersectionality, feminist visioning, and liberatory praxis are a part of "reading" the essays of each text, as well as "reading" all of the knowledges made available by examining the political project of a text. Kitchen Table Press as a model for political solidarity, and interpersonal complexity does not disappoint.

Asserting the centrality of Black queer women's knowledges, Guy-Sheftall names Kitchen Table Press in a litany of organizations, publishers, and publications whose ideology and praxis were, in Lorde's words, "foundations for a future of change." Guy-Sheftall writes, "Indeed, Black queer women have been central to the development of Black feminist and Black queer ideology and praxis," and that "Black lesbians have been denied their rightful place in African American cultural, intellectual, and political history" (231). By revealing this history to students as a part of their

engagement with the material, I seek to assert a more holistic queer feminist intersectional ethnic studies pedagogy that examines the exigency for establishing these bodies named above. This "reading" of the text explores the personal and political commitments that they supported and engages the challenges inherent in sharing knowledges produced by feminist women of color, alongside the analysis of the textual content.

Another formative work in queer feminist intersectional ethnic studies, the Combahee River Collective's (CRC) *A Black Feminist Statement*, further highlights revolutionary solidarity as central to the development of any holistic solidarity project. Guy-Sheftall notes that from its creation, the CRC practiced solidarity and coalition building, working with "other women of color, white feminists, and progressive men" (18). Perhaps their most significant contribution was "breaking the silence about homophobia within the black community and providing lesbians and heterosexual women with opportunities to work together" (16). The CRC enacted what today we might call a "queering" of social justice projects at the intersection of race or gender. Acknowledging and learning from the creation story of CRC's solidarity work during the 1970s and early 1980s is also central to the development of a queer feminist intersectional ethnic studies.

SIMULTANEITY: CROSS THAT BRIDGE WHEN WE GET [QUEER]

Unlike the CRC, movements for justice and liberation from the 1960s through the 1970s did not have solidarity and simultaneity as a central tenant and have been critiqued for their singular approach to issues. The phrase, "cross that bridge when we get to it," comes to mind. We often study civil rights movements, feminism, antiwar movements, and gay liberation through this same univariate model in the curriculum. Recovering the vibrant intersectional praxis of the past is also a part of the queer feminist intersectional ethnic studies pedagogical project.

By centering an understanding of simultaneity that is always already queer, queer feminist intersectional ethnic studies makes visible the history of many individuals and communities who have been deeply engaged in intersectional work. What would it mean to center the Stonewall Riots, for example, as a principal moment of resistance in ethnic studies? The field centers social movements, resistance, and progressions toward justice, born of moments like Stonewall. Cheryl Clarke asserts that the majority of those participating in the 1968 riot were Black and Latino patrons. She notes, "These riots caused gays and lesbians around the country to come out of their closets and fight heterosexist oppression" (225). A queer feminist intersectional ethnic studies inquiry into Stonewall provides the opportunity to examine what Lorde calls "the skeleton architecture of our lives" from many perspectives. We are only beginning to reframe Stonewall as an uprising with transwomen and gender non-conforming femmes of color at the center.

Centering Stonewall offers not only the opportunity to examine the intersections of race, ethnicity, gender identity and expression, and sexual orientation, but also the simultaneity of police profiling and state violence and carceral issues, the criminalization of sex work, poverty, among many other dimensions of oppression and resistance. Queering ethnic studies may also reclaim voices silenced in the margins, and add complexity and nuance to political stances and debates. Reclaiming and reframing the knowledge production, activism, and creativity of James Baldwin and Bayard Rustin offer such an opportunity to queer the field.

An examination of Baldwin and Rustin's lives and works offer us ways to examine race, masculinity, sexuality, activism, and dissonance within movements. "Today, among my generation of black writers and readers, James Baldwin is almost universally adored," writes Thomas Chatterton Williams. Baldwin's writings are among the cannon in Black literary studies, and may be found among the "special topics" in women and gender studies or English courses, among others. Baldwin's *Giovanni's Room* may also be found on a queer studies syllabus. Queer feminist intersectional ethnic studies as a reclamation project is particularly attentive to instances of erasure or silencing at the intersections. Williams writes, "[I]t is easy to forget the degree to which [Baldwin] was disparaged and even savaged by both black and white critics, to both his right and his left, while still alive." Williams specifically notes Eldridge Cleaver's "venomous

homophobic assault in *Soul on Ice.*" Queer feminist intersectional ethnic studies provides a lens through which to theorize this complex point of contention. This lens not only reveals the depth and breadth inherent in Baldwin's political and creative work, and the transformative power of Cleaver's leadership and writings, but also asserts the problematics of Black masculinity and taboo sexuality within the struggle for Black liberation, which is critical to an intersectional ethnic studies inquiry. This inquiry is also interdisciplinary and multimodal. Another multimodal example critical to reclamation is the work of the gifted of pacifist, organizer, cultural worker, and musical talent Bayard Rustin. Rustin was the chief organizer of the 1963 March on Washington for Jobs and Freedom during which Martin Luther King Jr. gave his well known speech, emphasizing the phrase, "I Have a Dream."

Reflecting on the life and times of Rustin, John D'Emilio writes, "The boundary between public and private proved very porous in Rustin's life. As I dug through the evidence and interviewed those who knew him, it became abundantly clear that his sexuality—or, more accurately, the stigma that American society attached to his sexual desires—made him forever vulnerable" (5). Queer feminist intersectional ethnic studies theorizes this intra-community vulnerability at the nexus of Black sexuality, Black masculinity, and the pursuit of Black liberation. Indeed, asserting Rustin as a central leader in the civil rights movement is in itself a reclamation project. D'Emilio notes that Rustin's influence was marginalized because of homophobia. Rustin had to navigate in ways "that unpredictable eruptions of homophobia might not harm these causes," D'Emilio laments, "It is little wonder that so few Americans today know who he is" (5). Queer feminist intersectional ethnic studies seeks to know who Rustin is and reclaim the voices of those marginalized at the intersections. It can reclaim Rustin's work, articulate his centrality, and value his complexities with a multimodal approach. It is also as important to listen to Rustin sing freedom songs and Negro spirituals, and to explore the "queerness" of his musical studies and performances, and connect them to his commitment to a nonviolent pacifist politic, as it is to learn about his organizing and transnational approach to liberation.

In presenting examples of Lorde, Anzaldúa and Moraga, Kitchen Table Press, the Combahee River Collective, Baldwin, and Rustin, I have theorized a historical foundation for queer feminist intersectional ethnic studies pedagogy and praxis. I have shown how a framing of the work happening in the margins during the 1960s and 1970s is foundational to inquiries about intersectionality, and provides an opportunity to think deeply about intersectionality as both a theory and praxis of the teaching and learning process. The foundational work lives on in forms that mirror the formative intersectional examples above. It can be seen in the activism and cultural production of Black Lives Matter, AFROPUNK, and other contemporary movements for justice and liberation, which I will turn to next.

BRIDGE CROSSING: A FUTURE OF CHANGE

The final element in formulating a queer feminist intersectional ethnic studies as introduced in this essay is the practice of emphasizing the continuum of intersectional work that laid the foundation for contemporary intersectional movements. Black Lives Matter and AFROPUNK have emerged as critical political and cultural movements for Black liberation. Exploring their guiding principles, structures, and commitments, and linking them to foundational intersectional work is critical for cultivating a future of change. Examining the core values of each complex movement provides an opportunity to engage "what has never been done before," in Lorde's words, and explore how bridge work continues to be done, again and again, in new, innovative, and increasingly complex and inclusive ways.

Black Lives Matter's guiding principles echo the "revolutionary solidarity" discussed by Moraga earlier in this essay. This solidarity was demonstrated by the creative process for the text *Bridge*. Kitchen Table Press and the CRC also created opportunities to break the silence about homophobia within the black community and racism within the feminist movement, while providing a framework for solidarity work at multiple intersections. Black Lives Matter principles that exemplify a contemporary revolutionary solidarity include an unapologetically Black positioning that is attentive to sexism, misogyny, and male-centeredness; sexual identity, gender identity, gender expression, economic

status, ability, disability, religious beliefs or disbeliefs, immigration status or location, heteronormativity, ageism, ableism, and economic justice. This inclusive intersectional platform builds on the foundational work of Lorde, Anzaldúa and Moraga, Kitchen Table Press, the Combahee River Collective, Baldwin, and Rustin by simultaneously engaging personal and political dimensions of identity and experiences with a clear power analysis, intersectional liberation model, and commitment to social justice praxis.

AFROPUNK also draws on the foundations of revolutionary solidarity by bridging with a clear and concise statement about the politics of the movement. Banners that flank the stage proclaim, "No sexism. No racism. No ableism. No ageism. No homophobia. No fatphobia. No transphobia. No hatefulness" (AFROPUNK FEST Brooklyn). The AFROPUNK Global Initiative also seeks to "disrupt and dismantle persistent bias in media by building positive identities of self and community. . . . With the many unique voices behind the AFROPUNK movement, the global initiative leverages our collective cultural power to drive progressive social change"(AFROPUNK Global Initiative). Thus, Black Lives Matter and AFROPUNK engage an intersectional legacy while explicitly naming an increasingly more inclusive political praxis. Including these movements, and examining them as a continuation of solidarity work from the 1960s and 1970s, is also at the heart of queer feminist intersectional ethnic studies. The bridge across foundational radical solidarity becomes clearer and can be highlighted through intersectional studies in ways that give blossoming scholar activists and cultural workers a legacy and history in which to root their work as they engage contemporary movements.

I return to Lorde's words, my inspiration for a "dream and vision," as I embark on this journey of creating a queer feminist intersectional ethnic studies major. I have theorized queer feminist intersectional ethnic studies by asserting an intersectionality as an approach with a rich queer feminist of color history, reclaiming the complexities of luminaries who built a "bridge across our fears" before we called it intersectionality, and illustrating how contemporary movements are rooted in and expand on this history, is at the heart of this project. The texts and assignments for the introductory course will reflect this bridge, and I hope to fully develop a dynamic and innovative curriculum for the new major that will excite and inspire students while offering them analytical tools and creative inspiration that will support their own social justice pursuits. I read this intention back to Lorde as my own "dream and vision"; indeed, it is the poetry of my pedagogy.

REFERENCES

"AFROPUNK FEST Brooklyn." Accessed July 18, 2017. https://afropunk.com/festival/brooklyn/.

"AFROPUNK Global Initiative." Accessed July 18, 2017. https://afropunk.com/tag/afropunk-global-initiative/.

Baldwin, James. *Giovanni's Room*. Random House, 2000.

Black Lives Matter. "Guiding Principles." *Black Lives Matter*, http://scalar.usc.edu/works/utsa-blacklivesmatter-digital-archive/black-lives-matter-guiding-principles.

Clarke, Cheryl. "Living the Texts Out: Lesbians and the Uses of Black Women's Traditions." In *Theorizing Black Feminisms: The Visionary Pragmatism of Black Women*. Stanlie James, Ed. Psychology Press, 1993, pp. 214–227.

Cleaver, Eldridge. *Soul on Ice*. Delta, 1999.

Collins, Patricia Hill, and Sirma Bilge. *Intersectionality*. Polity, 2016.

Combahee River Collective. *A Black Feminist Statement*. 1977.

Crenshaw, Kimberle. "Mapping the margins: Intersectionality, identity politics, and violence against women of color." *Stan. L. Rev.* 43 (1990): 1241–1299.

D'Emilio, John. *Lost Prophet: The Life and Times of Bayard Rustin*. Simon and Schuster, 2003.

Guy-Sheftall, Beverly. *Words of Fire: An Anthology of African-American Feminist Thought*. New Press, 1995.

Lorde, Audre. *Sister Outsider: Essays and Speeches*. Crossing Press, 1984.

Moraga, Cherríe. "Catching Fire: Preface to the Fourth Edition." In *This Bridge Called My Back, Writings by Radical Women of Color*. Gloria Anzaldúa and Cherríe Moraga, Eds. 4th ed. State University of New York Press, 2015, pp. xv–xxv.

Rustin, Bayard. *Time on Two Crosses: The Collected Writings of Bayard Rustin*. Cleis Press Start, 2003.

Williams, Thomas Chatterton. "Breaking Into James Baldwin's House." *The New Yorker*, October 28, 2015. http://www.newyorker.com/news/news-desk/breaking-into-james-baldwins-house.

ALISON KAFER

19. *FEMINIST, QUEER, CRIP*: INTRODUCTION: IMAGINED FUTURES

I dream of more inclusive spaces.

—Kavitha Koshy, "Feels Like Carving Bone"

I have never consulted a seer or psychic; I have never asked a fortune-teller for her crystal ball. No one has searched my tea leaves for answers or my stars for omens, and my palms remain unread. But people have been telling my future for years. Of fortune cookies and tarot cards they have no need: my wheelchair, burn scars, and gnarled hands apparently tell them all they need to know. My future is written on my body.

In 1995, six months after the fire, my doctor suggested that my thoughts of graduate school were premature, if not misguided. He felt that I would need to spend the next three or four years living at home, under my parents' care, and only then would it be appropriate to think about starting school. His tone made it clear, however, that he thought graduate school would remain out of reach; it was simply not in my future. What my future did hold, according to my rehabilitation psychologist and my recreation therapist, was long-term psychological therapy. My friends were likely to abandon me, alcoholism and drug addiction loomed on my horizon, and I needed to prepare myself for the futures of pain and isolation brought on by disability. Fellow rehab patients, most of whom were elderly people recovering from strokes or broken hips, saw equally bleak horizons before me. One stopped me in the hallway to recommend suicide, explaining that life in a wheelchair was not a life worth living (his son, he noted offhandedly, knew to "let him go" if he was eventually unable to walk).

My future prospects did not improve much after leaving the rehabilitation facility, at least not according

to strangers I encountered, and continue to encounter, out in the world. A common response is for people to assume they know my needs better than I do, going so far as to question my judgment when I refuse their offers of help. They can apparently see into my immediate future, forecasting an inability to perform specific tasks and predicting the accidents and additional injuries that will result. Or, taking a longer view, they imagine a future that is both banal and pathetic: rather than involving dramatic falls from my wheelchair, their visions assume a future of relentless pain, isolation, and bitterness, a representation that leads them to bless me, pity me, or refuse to see me altogether. Although I may believe I am leading an engaging and satisfying life, they can see clearly the grim future that awaits me: with no hope of a cure in sight, my future cannot be anything but bleak. Not even the ivory tower of academia protected me from these dismal projections of my future: once I made it to graduate school, I had a professor reject a paper proposal about cultural approaches to disability; she cast the topic as inappropriate because insufficiently academic. As I prepared to leave her office, she patted me on the arm and urged me to "heal," suggesting that my desire to study disability resulted not from intellectual curiosity but from a displaced need for therapy and recovery. My future, she felt, should be spent not researching disability but overcoming it.

These grim imagined futures, these suggestions that a better life would of necessity require the absence of impairment, have not gone unchallenged. My friends, family, and colleagues have consistently conjured other futures for me, refusing to accept ableist suggestions that disability is a fate worse than death

Alison Kafer, *Feminist, Queer, Crip* (Bloomington: Indiana University Press, 2013): 1–19. Reprinted with permission of Indiana University Press.

or that disability prohibits a full life. Those who have been most vocal in imagining my future as ripe with opportunities have been other disabled people, who are themselves resisting negative interpretations of their futures. They tell stories of lives lived fully, and my future, according to them, involves not isolation and pathos but community and possibility: I could write books, teach, travel, love and be loved; I might raise children or become a community organizer or make art; I could engage in activist struggles for the rights of disabled people or get involved in other movements for social justice.

At first glance, these contradictory imagined futures have nothing in common; the first casts disability as pitiable misfortune, a tragedy that effectively prevents one from leading a good life, while the second refuses such inevitability, positioning ableism—not disability—as the obstacle to a good life. What these two representations of the future share, however, is a strong link to the present. How one understands disability in the present determines how one imagines disability in the future; one's assumptions about the experience of disability create one's conception of a better future.

If disability is conceptualized as a terrible unending tragedy, then any future that includes disability can only be a future to avoid. A better future, in other words, is one that excludes disability and disabled bodies; indeed, it is the very *absence* of disability that signals this better future. The *presence* of disability, then, signals something else: a future that bears too many traces of the ills of the present to be desirable. In this framework, a future with disability is a future no one wants, and the figure of the disabled person, especially the disabled fetus or child, becomes the symbol of this undesired future. As James Watson—a geneticist involved in the discovery of DNA and the development of the Human Genome Project—puts it, "We already accept that most couples don't want a Down child. You would have to be crazy to say you wanted one, because that child has no future."[1] Although Watson is infamous for making claims about who should and shouldn't inhabit the world, he's not alone in expressing this kind of sentiment.[2] Watson's version simply makes clear some of the assumptions underlying this discourse, and they are assumptions that cut to the heart of this project. The first is that disability is seen as the sign of no future, or at least of no good future. The second, and related, assumption is that we all agree; not only do we accept that couples don't want a child with Down syndrome, we know that anyone who feels otherwise is "crazy."[3] To want a disabled child, to desire or even to accept disability in this way, is to be disordered, unbalanced, sick. "We" all know this, and there is no room for "you" to think differently.

It is this presumption of agreement, this belief that we all desire the same futures, that I take up in this book. I am particularly interested in uncovering the ways the disabled body is put to use in these future visions, attending to both metaphorical and "corporeal presence and absence."[4] I argue that disability is disavowed in these futures in two ways: first, the value of a future that includes disabled people goes unrecognized, while the value of a disability-free future is seen as self-evident; and second, the political nature of disability, namely, its position as a category to be contested and debated, goes unacknowledged. The second failure of recognition makes possible the first; casting disability as monolithic fact of the body, as beyond the realm of the political and therefore beyond the realm of debate or dissent, makes it impossible to imagine disability and disability futures differently. Challenging the rhetoric of naturalness and inevitability that underlies these discussions, I argue that decisions about the future of disability and disabled people are political decisions and should be recognized and treated as such. Rather than assume that a "good" future naturally and obviously depends upon the eradication of disability, we must recognize this perspective as colored by histories of ableism and disability oppression. Thus, in tracing these two failures of recognition—the disavowal of disability from "our" futures—I imagine futures otherwise, arguing for a cripped politics of access and engagement based on the work of disability activists and theorists.

What *Feminist, Queer, Crip* offers is a politics of crip futurity, an insistence on thinking these imagined futures—and hence, these lived presents—differently. Throughout the course of the . . . [Introduction], I hold on to an idea of politics as a framework for thinking through how to get "elsewhere," to other ways of being that might be more just and sustainable. In imagining more accessible futures, I am yearning for an elsewhere—and, perhaps, an "elsewhen"—in which disability is understood otherwise: as political, as valuable, as integral.

Before going any further, I admit to treading tricky ground here. "A future with disability is a future no one wants": while I find it absolutely essential to dismantle the purported self-evidence of that claim, I can't deny that there is truth to it. Not only is there abstract truth to it, there's personal, embodied truth: it is a sentiment I myself hold. As much joy as I find in communities of disabled people, and as much as I value my experiences as a disabled person, I am not interested in becoming more disabled than I already am. I realize that position is itself marked by an ableist failure of imagination, but I can't deny holding it. Nor am I opposed to prenatal care and public health initiatives aimed at preventing illness and impairment, and futures in which the majority of people continue to lack access to such basic needs are not futures I want.[5] But there is a difference between denying necessary health care, condoning dangerous working conditions, or ignoring public health concerns (thereby causing illness and impairment) and recognizing illness and disability as part of what makes us human.[6] While definitively mapping that difference is beyond the scope of this book—and, I would argue, neither fully possible nor desirable—sketching out some of the potential differences is exactly the work we need to be doing.

DEFINING DISABILITY: A POLITICAL/RELATIONAL MODEL

The meaning of disability, like the meaning of illness, is presumed to be self-evident; we all know it when we see it. But the meanings of illness and disability are not nearly so fixed or monolithic; multiple understandings of disability exist. Like other disability studies scholars, I am critical of the medical model of disability, but I am equally wary of a complete rejection of medical intervention. In [what] . . . follow[s], I offer a hybrid political/relational model of disability, one that builds on social and minority model frameworks but reads them through feminist and queer critiques of identity. My concern with imagining disability

futures differently frames my overview of each model; thinking about the kinds of futures imagined or implicit in each definition provides a useful lens for examining the assumptions and implications of these frameworks.

Despite the rise of disability studies in the United States, and decades of disability rights activism, disability continues to be seen primarily as a personal problem afflicting individual people, a problem best solved through strength of character and resolve. This individual model of disability is embodied in the disability simulation exercises that are a favored activity during "disability awareness" and diversity events on college campuses (including, in years past, my own). For these kinds of events, students are asked to spend a few hours using a wheelchair or wearing a blindfold so that they can "understand" what it means to be blind or mobility-impaired.[7] Not only do these kinds of exercises focus on the alleged failures and hardships of disabled bodies (an inability to see, an inability to walk), they also present disability as a knowable fact of the body. There is no accounting for how a disabled person's response to impairment shifts over time or by context, or how the nature of one's impairment changes, or, especially, how one's experience of disability is affected by one's culture and environment. Wearing a blindfold to "experience blindness" is going to do little to teach someone about ableism, for example, and suggests that the only thing there is to learn about blindness is what it feels like to move around in the dark. The meaning of blindness, in other words, is completely encapsulated in the experience of wearing a blindfold; there is simply nothing else to discuss. Although these kinds of exercises are intended to reduce fears and misperceptions about disabled people, the voices and experiences of disabled people are absent. Absent also are discussions about disability rights and social justice; disability is depoliticized, presented more as nature than culture. As Tobin Siebers notes, these are exercises in "personal imagination" rather than "cultural imagination," and a limited imagination at that.[8]

This individual model of disability is very closely aligned with what is commonly termed the medical model of disability; both form the framework for dominant understandings of disability and disabled people. The medical model of disability frames atypical bodies and minds as deviant, pathological, and defective, best understood and addressed in medical terms. In this framework, the proper approach to disability is to "'treat' the condition and the person with the condition rather than 'treating' the social processes and policies that constrict disabled people's lives."[9] Although this framing of disability is called the "medical" model, it's important to note that its use isn't limited to doctors and other service providers; what characterizes the medical model isn't the position of the person (or institution) using it, but the positioning of disability as an exclusively medical problem and, especially, the conceptualization of such positioning as both objective fact and common sense.[10]

Indeed, some of the most passionate defenses of the medical model of disability occur outside the hospital or clinic. Literary critic Denis Dutton exemplifies this pattern of thought, condemning a writing manual for its attempt to describe disability in social rather than medical terms. Dutton refutes the need for such attention to disability language, countering that *it is the medical condition that is the problem, not the words that describe it.*"[11] Because disability is a purely medical problem, Dutton finds no need to engage with disability as a category of analysis; concepts such as able-bodiedness, healthiness, and the normal body, or conditions such as "blindness, wheelchairs, polio, and cretinism" do not require or merit critical attention for they are merely facts of life.[12] For Dutton, disability is a self-evident, unchanging, and purely medical phenomenon, and the meanings, histories, and implications of "cretinism," for example, are not available for debate or dissent.

Thus, in both the individual and medical models, disability is cast as a problematic characteristic inherent in particular bodies and minds. Solving the problem of disability, then, means correcting, normalizing, or eliminating the pathological individual, rendering a medical approach to disability the only appropriate approach. The future of disability is understood more in terms of medical research, individual treatments, and familial assistance than increased social supports or widespread social change.

Disability studies scholars and disability activists, however, refute the premises of the medical/individual framework. Rather than casting disability as a natural, self-evident sign of pathology, we recast disability in social terms. The category of "disabled" can only be understood in relation to "able-bodied" or "able-minded," a binary in which each term forms the borders of the other. As Rosemarie Garland-Thomson explains, this hierarchical division of bodies and minds is then used to "legitimat[e] an unequal distribution of resources, status, and power within a biased social and architectural environment."[13] In this construction, disability is seen less as an objective fact of the body or mind and more as a product of social relations.

Thus, the definitional shift away from the medical/individual model makes room for new understandings of how best to solve the "problem" of disability. In the alternative perspective, which I call the political/relational model, the problem of disability no longer resides in the minds or bodies of individuals but in built environments and social patterns that exclude or stigmatize particular kinds of bodies, minds, and ways of being. For example, under the medical/individual model, wheelchair users suffer from impairments that restrict their mobility. These impairments are best addressed through medical interventions and cures; failing that, individuals must make the best of a bad situation, relying on friends and family members to negotiate inaccessible spaces for them. Under a political/relational model of disability, however, the problem of disability is located in inaccessible buildings, discriminatory attitudes, and ideological systems that attribute normalcy and deviance to particular minds and bodies. The problem of disability is solved not through medical intervention or surgical normalization but through social change and political transformation.

This is not to say that medical intervention has no place in my political/relational model. By my reckoning, the political/relational model neither opposes nor valorizes medical intervention; rather than simply take such intervention for granted, it recognizes instead that medical representations, diagnoses, and treatments of bodily variation are imbued with ideological biases about what constitutes normalcy and deviance. In so doing, it recognizes the possibility of simultaneously desiring to be cured of chronic pain and to be identified and allied with disabled people.[14] I want to make room for people to acknowledge—even mourn—a change in form or function while also acknowledging that such changes cannot be understood apart from the context in which they occur.

In juxtaposing a medical model with a political one, I am not suggesting that the medical model is not itself political. On the contrary, I am arguing for increased recognition of the political nature of a medical framing of disability. As Jim Swan argues, recognizing that a medical model is political allows for important questions about health care and social justice: "How good is the care? Who has access to it? For how long? Do they have choices? Who pays for it?"[15] Swan's questions remind us that medical framings of disability are embedded in economic realities and relations, and the current furor over health care reform underscores the political nature of these questions. Moreover, as scholars of feminist science studies, reproductive justice, and public health continue to make clear, medical beliefs and practices are not immune to or separate from cultural practices and ideologies. Thus, in offering a political/relational model of disability, I am arguing not so much for a rejection of medical approaches to disability as for a renewed interrogation of them. Insisting upon the political dimension of disability includes thinking through the assumptions of medical/individual models, seeing the whole terrain of "disability" as up for debate.[16]

My framing of disability as political/relational is intended as a friendly departure from the more common social model of disability. Like Margrit Shildrick and Janet Price, my intent is to "demand an unsettling of its certainties, of the fixed identities of which it is bound up" and to pluralize the ways we understand bodily instability.[17] Although both the social and political/relational models share a critique of the medical model, the social model often relies on a distinction between impairment and disability that I don't find useful. In that framework, impairment refers to any physical or mental limitation, while disability signals the social exclusions based on, and social meanings attributed to, that impairment.[18] People with impairments are disabled by their environments; or, to put it differently, impairments aren't disabling, social and architectural barriers are. Although I agree that we need to attend to the social, asserting a sharp divide

between impairment and disability fails to recognize that *both* impairment and disability are social; simply trying to determine what constitutes impairment makes clear that impairment doesn't exist apart from social meanings and understandings. Susan Wendell illustrates this problem when she queries how far one must be able to walk to be considered able-bodied; the answer to that question, she explains, has much to do with the economic and geographic context in which it is addressed.[19] What we understand as impairing conditions—socially, physically, mentally, or otherwise—shifts across time and place, and presenting impairment as purely physical obscures the effects of such shifts. As feminist theorists have long noted, there is no mention of "the" body that is not a further articulation of a very particular body.[20]

At the same time, the social model with its impairment/disability distinction erases the lived realities of impairment; in its well-intentioned focus on the disabling effects of society, it overlooks the often-disabling effects of our bodies. People with chronic illness, pain, and fatigue have been among the most critical of this aspect of the social model, rightly noting that social and structural changes will do little to make one's joints stop aching or to alleviate back pain. Nor will changes in architecture and attitude heal diabetes or cancer or fatigue. Focusing exclusively on disabling harriers, as a strict social model seems to do, renders pain and fatigue irrelevant to the project of disability politics.[21]

As a result, the social model can marginalize those disabled people who are interested in medical interventions or cures. In a complete reversal of the individual/medical model, which imagines individual cure as the desired future for disability, a strict social model completely casts cure out of our imagined futures; cure becomes the future no self-respecting disability activist or scholar wants. In other words, because we are so often confronted with the medical framing of disability as unending burden, or as a permanent drag on one's quality of life, disability rights activists and scholars tend to deny our own feelings of pain or depression; admitting to struggling with our impairments or to wanting a cure for them is seen as accepting the very framings we are fighting against, giving fodder to the enemy, so to speak. But by positioning ourselves only in opposition to the futures imagined through the medical model, and shutting down communication and critique around vital issues, we limit the discourses at our disposal. As Liz Crow warns, in refusing to acknowledge pain, fatigue, or depression, "our collective ability to conceive of, and achieve, a world which does not disable is diminished."[22]

Finally, drawing a hard line between impairment and disability, and having this distinction serve as the foundation for theorizing disability, makes it difficult to explore the ways in which notions of disability and able-bodiedness affect everyone, not just people with impairments.[23] Anxiety about aging, for example, can be seen as a symptom of compulsory able-bodiedness/able-mindedness, as can attempts to "treat" children who are slightly shorter than average with growth hormones; in neither case are the people involved necessarily disabled, but they are certainly affected by cultural ideals of normalcy and ideal form and function. Or, to take this idea in a different direction, friends and family members of disabled people are often affected by ableist attitudes and barriers, even if they are not themselves disabled. Their social lives may shrink, for example, because others are uncomfortable or embarrassed by their stories of illness and adaptation, or friends may feel guilty inviting them to inaccessible houses; difficulty accessing reliable and affordable attendant care or finding appropriate housing certainly affects entire families, not only the disabled person herself or himself. Moreover, not only does disability exist in relation to able-bodiedness/ able-mindedness, such that disabled and abled form a constitutive binary, but also, to move to a different register of analysis, disability is experienced in and through relationships; it does not occur in isolation. My choice of a *relational* model of disability is intended to speak to this reality.

Similarly, my articulation of a *political* framing of disability is a direct refusal of the widespread depoliticization of disability. Dutton's medicalized description of disability assumes that "cretinism" is a natural category, derived purely from objective medical study and irrelevant to discussions of politics or prejudice; proclaiming the naturalness of disability, he goes on to ridicule attempts to discuss disability in terms of language or identification.[24] By asserting that we cannot

(or should not) resignify disability identities and categories, refusing to recognize the impact disability rhetoric and terminology might have on understandings of disability (and thus on the lives of disabled people), and insisting that medical approaches to disability are completely objective and devoid of prejudice or cultural bias, Dutton completely removes disability from the realm of the political. In doing so, he forecloses on the possibility of understanding disability differently; divorcing disability and disabled people from understandings of the political prohibits incorporating disability into programs of social change and transformation or, in other words, into visions of a better future. Once disability has been placed solely in the medical framework, and both disability and the medical world are portrayed as apolitical, then disability has no place in radical politics or social movements—except as a problem to be eradicated.

A political/relational model of disability, on the other hand, makes room for more activist responses, seeing "disability" as a potential site for collective reimagining. Under this kind of framework, "disability awareness" simulations can be reframed to focus less on the individual experience of disability—or imagined experience of disability—and more on the political experience of disablement. For example, rather than placing nondisabled students in wheelchairs, the Santa Barbara-based organization People in Search of Safe and Accessible Restrooms (PISSAR) places them in bathrooms, armed with measuring tapes and clipboards, to track the failures and omissions of the built environment. As my fellow restroom revolutionaries explain in our manifesto, "This switch in focus from the inability of the body to the inaccessibility of the space makes room for activism and change in ways that 'awareness exercises' may not."[25] In creating and disseminating a "restroom checklist," PISSAR imagines a future of disability activism, one with disability rights activists demanding accessible spaces: contrast that approach with the simulation exercises, in which "awareness" is the future goal, rather than structural or systemic change.

In reading disability futures and imagined disability through a political/relational model, I situate disability squarely within the realm of the political. My goal is to contextualize, historically and politically, the meanings typically attributed to disability, thereby positioning "disability" as a set of practices and associations that can be critiqued, contested, and transformed. Integral to this project is an awareness that ableist discourses circulate widely, and not only in sites marked explicitly as about disability; thus, thinking about disability as political necessitates exploring everything from reproductive practices to environmental philosophy, from bathroom activism to cyberculture. I am influenced here by Chantal Mouffe, who argues that "the political cannot be restricted to a certain type of institution, or envisaged as constituting a specific sphere or level of society. It must be conceived as a dimension that is inherent to every human society and that determines our very ontological condition."[26] To say that something is "political" in this sense means that it is implicated in relations of power and that those relations, their assumptions, and their effects are contested and contestable, open to dissent and debate.

In other words, I'm concerned here with what Jodi Dean calls "the *how* of politics, the ways concepts and issues come to be political common sense and the processes through which locations and populations are rendered as in need of intervention, regulation, or quarantine."[27] This focus on the *how* of politics parallels the first set of questions that motivate my project: Is disability political? How is it political? How is the category of disability used to justify the classification, supervision, segregation, and oppression of certain people, bodies, and practices? Addressing these questions requires a recognition of the central role that ideas about disability and ability play in contemporary culture, particularly in imagined and projected futures.

After stressing the importance of the "how" of politics, Dean insists on the need "to take *depoliticization* seriously, to address the means through which spaces, issues, identities, and events are taken out of political circulation or are blocked from the agenda—or are presumed to have already been solved."[28] Attending to the ways in which disability is political leads to my second set of motivating questions: How has disability been depoliticized, removed from the realm of the political? Which definitions of and assumptions about disability facilitate this removal? What are the effects of such depoliticization? I'm not so much arguing for or positing a chronology here—"disability used to be

political and now it's not"—as highlighting the need for disability studies to attend to the specific ways in which ableist understandings of disability are taken as common sense.[29] Such attention is vital in a context in which, as Susan Schweik notes, disability-based discrimination and prejudice are often condemned not as markers of structural inequality but of cruelty or insensitivity; this kind of rhetoric "sidesteps the reality of social injustice, reducing it to a question of compassion and charitable feelings."[30]

These questions—of politicization and of depoliticization—lie at the root of my interest in political frameworks of the future: Do the futures I examine . . . assume and perpetuate the depoliticization of disability, and if so, how? What is it about disability that makes it a defining element of our imagined futures, such that a "good" future is one without disability, while a "bad" future is overrun by it? Why is disability in the present constantly deferred, such that disability often enters critical discourse only as the marker of what must be eliminated in our futures or what was unquestioningly eliminated in our pasts? And, most importantly, why are these characterizations taken for granted, recognized as neither partial nor political?

IDENTIFYING DISABILITY: BODIES, IDENTITIES, POLITICS

Seeing disability as political, and therefore contested and contestable, entails departing from the social model's assumption that "disabled" and "nondisabled" are discrete, self-evident categories, choosing instead to explore the creation of such categories and the moments in which they fail to hold. Recognizing such moments of excess or failure is key to imagining disability, and disability futures, differently. Thus I understand the very meanings of "disability," "impairment," and "disabled" as contested terrain.[31] Disability can then be understood, in Jasbir Puar's framework, as an *assemblage*, where "[c]ategories—race, gender, sexuality [and, I would add, disability]— are considered as events, actions, and encounters between bodies, rather than as simply entities and attributes of subjects."[32]

Thus, a political/relational framework recognizes the difficulty in determining who is included in the term "disabled," refusing any assumption that it refers to a discrete group of particular people with certain similar essential qualities. On the contrary, the political/relational model of disability sees disability as a site of questions rather than firm definitions: Can it encompass all kinds of impairments—cognitive, psychiatric, sensory, and physical? Do people with chronic illnesses fit under the rubric of disability? Is someone who had cancer years ago but is now in remission disabled? What about people with some forms of multiple sclerosis (MS) who experience different temporary impairments—from vision loss to mobility difficulties—during each recurrence of the disease, but are without functional limitations once the MS moves back into remission? What about people with large birthmarks or other visible differences that have no bearing on their physical capabilities, but that often prompt discriminatory treatment?

Government and nongovernmental organizations alike frequently issue guidelines for determining who is disabled and thus eligible for certain programs and protections. Such groups, ranging from the World Health Organization to the US Social Security Administration, would not have to be so precise in defining "disability" if such definitions were without controversy; the very fact that so much energy is funneled into defining disability and impairment suggests the fundamental instability of the terms. Moreover, the desire for fixed definitions cannot be divorced from the economic effects of such fixing. The Social Security Administration uses its definitions of disability to determine who qualifies for benefits and at what level; the US Supreme Court has continued to revisit the Americans with Disabilities Act in order to determine who merits protection under its provisions and who does not. Both entities rule as if there were bright lines between disabled and non-, even though the need for such rulings suggests otherwise. But there is clearly a notion that there are people whose claims do not rise to the level of disability, and who therefore are undeserving of such protections.

In contrast, the disability theory and politics that I develop in these pages do not rely on a fixed definition of "disability" and "disabled person" but recognize the parameters of both terms as always open to debate. I am concerned here with disability not as a category

inherent in certain minds and bodies but as what historian Joan W. Scott calls a "collective affinity." Drawing on the cyborg theory of Donna Haraway, Scott describes collective affinities as "play[ing] on identifications that have been attributed to individuals by their societies, and that have served to exclude them or subordinate them."[33] Collective affinities in terms of disability could encompass everyone from people with learning disabilities to those with chronic illness, from people with mobility impairments to those with HIV/AIDS, from people with sensory impairments to those with mental illness. People within each of these categories can all be discussed in terms of disability politics, not because of any essential similarities among them, but because all have been labeled as disabled or sick and have faced discrimination as a result. Simi Linton illustrates this fundamental diversity of the disability community when she writes,

> We are everywhere these days, wheeling and loping down the street, tapping our canes, sucking on our breathing tubes, following our guide dogs, puffing and sipping on the mouth sticks that propel our motorized chairs. We may drool, hear voices, speak in staccato syllables, wear catheters to collect our urine, or live with a compromised immune system. We are all bound together, not by this list of our collective symptoms but by the *social and political circumstances that have forged us as a group.*[34]

Linton's formulation strikes me as a fitting place to begin this exploration of accessible futures, primarily because it reads more as promise than fact. Both disability studies and disability movements have been slow to recognize potential linkages among people who hear voices, people with compromised immune systems, and people using wheelchairs. Although there have been notable exceptions, disability studies, especially in the humanities, has focused little attention on cognitive disabilities, focusing more often on visible physical impairments and sensory impairments.[35] Chronic illness has become more common in these discussions, but only in particular forms; discussion of chronic fatigue syndrome and mental disability has increased thanks to the work of scholars such as Susan Wendell, Ellen Samuels, and Margaret Price, but diabetes, asthma, and lupus remain largely unexplored by disability studies scholars.[36] (This oversight is all the more troubling given the fact that diabetes occurs disproportionately among "members of racial and ethnic minority groups in the United States," and asthma is a common side-effect of living in heavily polluted neighborhoods, which, unsurprisingly, are more likely to be populated by poor people.)[37] I repeat Linton's formulation then in an effort to call it into being, to invoke it as a possibility for thinking disability differently. I want to hold on to the possibility of a disability studies and a disability movement that does take all of these locations seriously, that feels accountable to these bodies and identities and locations.

One of the arguments I will make, . . . however, is that part of the work of imagining this kind of expansive disability movement is to simultaneously engage in a critical reading of these very identities, locations, and bodies. We must trace the ways in which we have been forged as a group, to use Linton's terminology, but also trace the ways in which those forgings have been incomplete, or contested, or refused. We need to recognize that these forgings have always already been inflected by histories of race, gender, sexuality, class, and nation; falling to attend to such relations will ensure that disability studies remains, as Chris Bell puts it, "white disability studies."[38] We must, in other words, think through the assumptions and erasures of "disabled" and "disability," reckoning with the ways in which such words have been used and to what effect.

Doing so might mean imagining a "we" that includes folks who identify as or with disabled people but don't themselves "have" a disability. Scholars of chronic illness have started this work, arguing for the necessity of including within disability communities those who lack a "proper" (read: medically acceptable, doctor-provided, and insurer-approved) diagnosis for their symptoms. Doing so not only provides such people with the social supports they need (everything from access to social services to recognition from friends and family), it also presents disability less as diagnostic category and more as collective affinity; moving away from a medical/individual model of disability means that disability identification can't be solely linked to diagnosis.

Less familiar, and potentially more complicated, would be people identifying with disability and lacking not only a diagnosis but any "symptoms" of impairment. How might we understand the forging of a group that includes, in Carrie Sandahl's and Robert McRuer's framings, a "nondisabled claim to be crip?[39] Hearing Children of Deaf Adults, or CODAs, would be a clear example of this kind of identification, as CODAs consider themselves part of Deaf communities, and some even claim Deaf identity, but are not themselves deaf or hard-of-hearing.[40] But does claiming crip require this kind of blood or kinship tie? What might it mean for lovers or friends to claim crip, or to understand themselves as "culturally disabled"? Or for theorists and activists committed to rethinking disability and able-bodiedness/able-mindedness to make such claims? Can claiming crip be a method of imagining multiple futures, positioning "crip" as a desired and desirable location regardless of one's own embodiment or mental/psychological processes? As McRuer notes, these practices run the risk of appropriation, but they also offer a vital refusal of simplistic binaries like disabled/nondisabled and sick/healthy.[41] Claiming crip, then, can be a way of acknowledging that we all have bodies and minds with shifting abilities, and wrestling with the political meanings and histories of such shifts. Thus, to circle back to the notion of "we" as more promise than fact: thinking through what nondisabled claims to crip might entail will require exploring whether such claims might be more available, or more imaginable, to some people than others (and on what basis).

Attention to these kinds of questions—the histories and effects of disability claims, the different availability and viability of disability identification—distinguishes this kind of "nondisabled claim to crip" from the well-intentioned but deeply ableist declaration that "we are *all* disabled." The latter obscures the specificities I call for here, conflating all experiences of physical, mental, or sensory limitation without regard to structural inequality or patterns of exclusion and discrimination. It is for this reason that Linton cautions against "erasing the line between disabled and nondisabled people," explaining that "naming the category" of disabled remains necessary because it effectively "call[s] attention to" disability-based discrimination. But I suggest that exploring the possibilities of nondisabled claims, as well as attending to the promises and dangers of the category's flexibility, can facilitate exactly this kind of critical attentiveness.[42] To claim crip critically is to recognize the ethical, epistemic, and political responsibilities behind such claims; deconstructing the binary between disabled and able-bodied/able-minded requires *more* attention to how different bodies/minds are treated differently, not less.

Attending to the epistemological challenges raised by disability claims introduces yet another set of questions about claiming crip. Thinking through this collective "we," this forging of crip communities, means accounting for those who do "have" illnesses or impairments, and who might be recognized by others as part of this "disabled we," but who do not recognize themselves as such. This group would include the largest proportion of disabled people: those folks with hearing impairments, or low vision, or "bum knees," or asthma, or diabetes who, for a whole host of reasons, would claim neither crip identity nor disability. Even though most people with impairments might fall into this camp, it is actually the hardest group for me to address; . . . indeed, I think it is the hardest group for disability studies and disability rights activism to address.[43] Given my (our) focus on disability rights and justice, on radical queercrip activism, on finding disability desirable, how am I (how are we) to deal with those who want no part of such names?

One answer to these questions is that it doesn't matter whether such people claim crip or not: rethinking our cultural assumptions about disability, imagining our disability futures differently, will benefit all of us, regardless of our identities. As Ladelle McWhorter notes, "The practices and institutions that divide, for example, the 'able-bodied,' 'sane,' and 'whole' from the 'impaired,' 'mentally ill,' and 'deficient' create the conditions under which all of us live; they structure the situation within which each one of us comes to terms with ourselves and creates a way of life.[44] As someone writing and teaching disability studies, as someone imagining readers and students with a whole range of bodies and minds, I find hope in McWhorter's prediction, in her articulation of a better future. Much as feminist activism benefits people who want no part of feminism, disability studies and activism ideally benefit people who are not interested or invested in either.[45] At the same time, I'm certain this is not the only, or

not the full, answer. As I embark on this journey into accessible futures, I want to highlight the question of crip affiliation, what it means, what it entails, what it excludes.

FEMINIST, CRIP, QUEER: A NOTE ON TERMS, METHODS, AND AFFILIATIONS

I became disabled before I began reading feminist theory, yet it was feminist theory that led me to disability studies. It was through reading feminist theoretical approaches to the body that I came intellectually to understand disability as a political category rather than as an individual pathology or personal tragedy. Feminist theory gave me the tools to think through disability and the ways in which assumptions about disability and disabled bodies lead to resource inequalities and social discrimination. Just as feminist theorists had questioned the naturalness of femininity, challenging essentialist assumptions about "the" female body, I could question the naturalness of disability, challenging essentialist assumptions about "the" disabled body. My understanding of the political/relational model of disability has been made possible by my engagement with the work of feminist theorists, an engagement that I hope will become clear in the following pages. Simply put, feminism has given me the theoretical tools to think critically about disability, the stigmatization of bodily variation, and various modes and strategies of resistance, dissent, and collective action.

I locate this project, then, within the larger field of feminist theory and politics. Although I examine a range of radical political visions, some explicitly feminist and others less so, I understand my investment in radical politics as a feminist investment. As many historians of feminism and women's studies have noted, feminism has long been interested in bridging theory with practice. Activists and scholars alike continue to explore the ways in which theory can inform political practice; conversely, feminists often theorize from practice, developing concepts and frameworks based on the strategies, conversations, conflicts, and achievements of feminist activists. My interest in radical politics derives in part from my theoretical and activist commitment to blending theory with practice, a commitment that I associate with feminism. I think it only appropriate to make this indebtedness explicit as I begin my exploration of possible futures, given recent disability studies texts that have downplayed or dismissed any connections to feminism; my readings and my imaginings are resolutely feminist.[46]

They also are undeniably crip, a term that has much currency in disability activism and culture but still might seem harsh to those outside those communities. Indeed, that harshness is a large part of its appeal, as suggested by essayist Nancy Mairs: "People– crippled or not—wince at the word 'crippled' as they do not at 'handicapped' or 'disabled.' Perhaps I want them to wince."[47] This desire to make people wince suggests an urge to shake things up, to jolt people out of their everyday understandings of bodies and minds, of normalcy and deviance. It recognizes the common response of nondisabled people to disabled people, of the normative to the deviant—furtive yet relentless staring, aggressive questioning, and/or a turning away from difference, a refusal to see.[48] This wincing is familiar to many disabled people, but here Mairs turns it back on itself, almost wincing back. Like "queer," "crip" and "cripple" are, in Eli Clare's formulation, "words to help forge a politics."[49]

Two related examples of such forging, of crafting an inducement to wince, would be Carrie Sandahl's preference for "crip studies" and "crip theory" over "disability studies" and Robert McRuer's decision to name his theoretical project *Crip Theory.* According to both Sandahl and McRuer, disability studies and crip theory differ in orientation and aim: crip theory is more contestatory than disability studies, more willing to explore the potential risks and exclusions of identity politics while simultaneously and "perhaps paradoxically" recognizing "the generative role identity has played in the disability rights movement."[50] I see *Feminist, Queer, Crip* as engaging in exactly this kind of contradictory crip theory, and I use both "crip" and "crip theory" as a way to stake my claim alongside the activists and cultural workers engaged in these multiple sites of radical politics.[51]

One of the most productive and provocative elements of crip theory, and of crip in general, is the potential expansiveness of the term. As Sandahl notes, "cripple, like queer, is fluid and ever-changing, claimed

by those whom it did not originally define. . . . The term crip has expanded to include not only those with physical impairments but those with sensory or mental impairments as well."[52] I agree with Sandahl, and this potential flexibility is precisely what excites me about crip theory, but, as with Linton's "we are everywhere," this inclusiveness is often more hope than reality. Many expressions of crip pride or crip politics often explicitly address only physical impairments, thereby ignoring or marginalizing the experiences of those with sensory or mental impairments. Others position crip as a way of naming opposition to cure, potentially making it difficult for "crip theory" to encompass the perspectives and practices of those who both claim disability identity and desire an end to their own impairments. Thus, I move back and forth between naming this project one of "feminist and queer disability studies" and one of "crip theory," raising the possibility that the two can be, and often are, intertwined in practice; indeed, given the rich analyses of identity that circulate within feminist and queer studies, a "feminist and queer disability studies" may very well engage in the "paradoxical" approach to identity practiced in crip theory while making room for those who do not or cannot recognize themselves in crip.[53]

Similarly, throughout *Feminist, Queer, Crip,* I combine references to bodies with references to minds and pair "compulsory able-bodiedness" with "compulsory able-mindedness."[54] If disability studies is going to take seriously the criticism that we have focused on physical disabilities to the exclusion of all else, then we need to start experimenting with different ways of talking about and conceptualizing our projects.[55] At the same time, I'm well aware that my use of such terms is partial in both senses of the word: I am invested in shifting the terrain of disability studies even as my own performances of it bear the marks of its current terrain, and I have only just begun to scratch the surface of what able-mindedness might mean in relation to able-bodiedness. Thus, as with Linton's "we" and Sandahl's "crip," I use "mind" alongside "body" in the hope that writing and reading "bodies and minds" or "compulsory able-bodiedness/able-mindedness" makes me think disability differently. Rather than assuming that the mere use of such language is sufficient in and of itself, I'm calling for an engagement with the hard work of actually making such coalitions happen. As I suggest, . . . such expansiveness—mind and body, a crip of us all—can never be fully or finally achieved, but serves as a kind of hopeful horizon, "fluid and ever-changing," as Sandahl notes, and used in ways unimagined in advance.

Queer (theory) readers will likely recognize this talk of fluidity, ever-changing horizons, and paradoxical treatments of identity as kin to queer projects, and, like Sandahl and McRuer, I position crip theory in general, and this project in particular, as such. "Queer" also remains contested terrain, with theorists and activists continuing to debate what (and whom) the term encompasses or excludes; it is this kind of contestation I welcome for disability. Indeed, Butler argues for queer as a "site of collective contestation" to be "always and only redeployed, twisted, queered."[56] The circularity of that definition—queerness is something always to be queered—serves only to support this desire for dissent and debate. In naming my project "queer," then, I am wanting both to twist "queer" into encompassing "crip" (and "crip," "queer") and to highlight the risks of such twisted inclusion. Critical examinations of compulsory able-bodiedness and compulsory able-mindedness are queer and crip projects, and they can potentially be enacted without necessarily flattening out or stabilizing "crip" and "queer."[57] What is needed, then, are critical attempts to trace the ways in which compulsory able-bodiedness/able-mindedness and compulsory heterosexuality intertwine in the service of normativity; to examine how terms such as "defective," "deviant," and "sick" have been used to justify discrimination against people whose bodies, minds, desires, and practices differ from the unmarked norm, to speculate how norms of gendered behavior—proper masculinity and femininity—are based on nondisabled bodies; and to map potential points of connection among, and departure between, queer (and) disability activists. As we shall see, one productive site for such explorations is the imagined future invoked in popular culture, academic theory, and political movements; *Feminist, Queer, Crip* begins to trace some of these queer/crip connections.

I want, then, to position this book as a fundamentally coalitional text. The "feminist, queer, crip" named in the title signals methodology as much as content. This work quite obviously, and necessarily, involves bringing disability identities and experiences to bear on existing feminist and queer theoretical frameworks. It is not simply, or not only, an additive intervention, however. While I am indeed arguing that disability needs to be recognized as a category of analysis alongside gender, race, class, and sexuality, my larger goal is to address how disability is figured in and through these other categories of difference.[58] What work does able-bodiedness do, for example, in feminist appropriations of the cyborg, or queer uses of reproductive technologies, or ecofeminist imaginings of a better life? How does reckoning with histories and experiences of disability, in other words, critique or transform feminist environmental philosophy or queer approaches to assisted reproductive technologies? I want to explore the theoretical terrain opened up by reading disability into those queer narratives and feminist analyses that never use the word "disability." How might such readings shift our understandings of terms like "disabled," or "queer," or "feminist"? Or how might they expand our understanding of what it means to do cross-movement work, both in terms of theoretical development and activist practice? *Feminist, Queer, Crip* argues that a coalitional politics requires thinking disability, and disabled bodies, differently—recognizing the work done by disability and able-bodiedness/able-mindedness in different political visions, for example, or acknowledging the exclusions enacted in the desire for a unified disability community.

I know that in carefully delineating my affiliations here—feminist, queer, crip—I run the risk of further reifying these categories, thereby presenting them as discrete, separable identities. This kind of personal and theoretical positioning has long been a mainstay of feminist intersectional scholarship, and, as Puar warns, too easily requires the "stabilizing of identity across space and time."[59] But taking such risks feels necessary because we are operating in a theoretical and activist context in which this combination of analytics and practices too rarely appears. It feels important at this particular moment to identify explicitly as feminist, queer, crip—even as I want to trouble such identifications—and to explicitly practice feminist, queer, crip work. I'm calling attention to these shifting positions not to fix them in place, but to get them moving on the questions that face those of us committed to and invested in such positions.

I'm writing out of a concern, for example, about the silence of disability studies scholars and disability activists in response to how our movements have often (been) publicly aligned with the right. Where were the public feminist/queer/crip responses to Sarah Palin? How might we have intervened in the representation of her as a disability rights advocate, questioning the blurring of antichoice ideologies and disability critiques of prenatal testing? Or how might a feminist/queer/crip-informed analysis expand or complicate queer theoretical texts that rely on a trope of mobility for their analyses or that tend to allegorize rather than analyze disability and disabled bodies? Or, when only a small handful of papers and presentations at the annual Society for Disability Studies conference make explicit use of feminist and queer theories in their analyses, does it not become essential to name and inhabit these very intersections?[60] And, importantly, how can we do this kind of naming, demand these kinds of analytic and political practices, without stabilizing feminist/queer/crip or gender/sexuality/disability, without treating these very categories, nodes, and positions as themselves self-evident? I'm wanting this particular imagining of accessible futures—my imagining of accessible futures—to carve out a place on the theoretical/political map where feminist/queer/crip can feed and inform each other, even as they are always already bound up in each other. More, I'm wanting this imagining to generate more such imaginings, such that the nodes on the map and the map itself multiply, proliferate, regenerate. We need multiple iterations of crip theory, ones that its practitioners might not always recognize, ones that contest and exceed its very parameters, and ones that take this particular iteration to task.

In the hopes of such proliferations, questions take center stage throughout *Feminist, Queer, Crip*. Part of this focus is stylistic, aesthetic; I like the cadence of a question. But it is also, and primarily, methodological. If one of my goals with this project is to get us to think disability differently, to begin to see both the category and the experience of disability as contested and contestable, then what better way to do that then to ask questions? (I've started already.) Rhetorical

questions are common in conclusions as authors hint at their next projects, or discover new problems, or point toward the need for more research. I'm including such questions in the introduction as a reminder that I should imagine readers talking back, taking these ideas in new directions, turning my own questions back on me in different contexts or to different effects. The format of the question insists on seeing these complex subjects—the future of the child with Down syndrome or the desirability of disability—as debatable, contestable: as *in question*. It also opens up the possibilities of new answers, shifting answers, unforeseen answers. . . . I am interested in a crip politics of access and engagement that is resolutely a work in progress, open-ended, aiming for but never reaching the horizon. Questions keep me focused on the inconclusiveness of my conclusion, of the desire to think otherwise.

This . . . [project] contains not only unanswered questions but also contradictions and logical inconsistencies. . . . I am much more critical about deselecting disability (i.e., terminating a pregnancy because tests reveal potential "genetic anomalies") than I am about selecting for disability (i.e., using a sperm donor who carries a desired genetic trait), even though both practices involve parents wanting to have a child like themselves. Such contradictions are inevitable in a project like this one, reflecting our convoluted approaches to disability; I am writing in a culture in which inconsistency about disability is commonplace. Might it be logically inconsistent, for example, that we claim to value the lives of disabled people even as we create (and mandate) more and more prenatal tests to screen out "undesirable" fetuses? Glossing over these inconsistencies, or pretending that they can be easily and definitively resolved, simplifies the complexities inherent in questions of social justice. The desire for clear answers, free of contradiction and inconsistency, is understandable, but I want to suggest that accessible futures require such ambiguities. Following Puar, I believe that "contradictions and discrepancies . . . are not to be reconciled or synthesized but held together in tension. They are less a sign of wavering intellectual commitment than symptoms of the political impossibility to *be on one side or the other*."[61] Indeed, part of the problem I'm tracing in these pages is the assumption that there is only one side to the question of disability and that we're all already on it.

In this spirit, my use of "we" and "they," "them," and "us," shifts throughout. . . . To always use the third person in discussing disabled people would be to impose a distancing between myself and my subject that rings false. It also would run counter to this notion of "claiming crip," denying the possibility of a deep and abiding connection to the identities, bodies, minds, and practices discussed here. At the same time, to always use the first person would be to answer in advance the question of a unified community of disabled people, to presume not only that we all share the same positions but also that one person—and in this case, I—can accurately represent the whole. In other words, when it comes to the vexed issue of personal pronouns, I will occasionally use "we/us" even when I am not an obvious member of the group being discussed, and, by the same token, will occasionally use "they/them" even when I am obviously included in the category. I do this to trouble the very notion of "obvious" identifications as well as the disabled/able-bodied and disabled/nondisabled binaries.[62] Even though I am a disabled person, I do not exist apart from the ableist discourses circulating through US society; to act as if my impairments render me immune to, or incapable of, ableist rhetoric and ideology would be to deny the insidiousness of compulsory able-bodiedness and able-mindedness.[63] "I," Sedgwick reminds us, can be a powerful heuristic, and so can "we," "they," "you," and "them."[64]

NOTES

1. Michael Gerson, "The Eugenics Temptation," *Washington Post*, October 24, 2007, A19.

2. I have borrowed my phrasing here from Ruth Hubbard. See her "Abortion and Disability: Who Should and Who Should Not Inhabit the World?" in *The Disability Studies Reader*, ed. Lennard J. Davis (New York: Routledge, 2006), 93–103. For an overview of Watson's career by one of his former assistants, see Charlotte Hunt-Grubbe, "The Elementary DNA of Dr. Watson," *Sunday Times* (UK), October 14, 2007. In that article, Watson laments that "all our social policies are based on the fact that [Africans'] intelligence is the same as ours—whereas all the testing says not really." He has been quoted elsewhere as supporting the abortion of fetuses that contain "the gay gene," if such tests eventually become possible, although he later claimed he was simply defending women's right to choose under any circumstances. V. MacDonald, "Abort Babies with Gay Genes, Says Nobel Winner," *Telegraph* (UK), February 16, 1997; Steve Boggan and Glenda Cooper, "Nobel Winner May Sue over Gay Baby Abortion Claim," *Independent* (UK), February 17, 1997; and Richard Dawkins, "Letter: Women to Decide on Gay Abortion," *Independent* (UK), February 19, 1997.

   Watson is often described as a provocateur, willing to put things in the most shocking way to make a point, and, as a result, it is tempting to dismiss his comments as extreme and isolated. But his personal penchant for the outrageous doesn't change the fact that many of his assumptions, particularly about disability, are quite pervasive. The filing of wrongful birth suits would be another manifestation of this notion that no one wants disabled children; in these suits, parents sue their doctors for failing to catch disabling conditions in utero and thereby preventing them from aborting the fetus.. . .

3. In his deployment of "crazy," Watson employs the same kind of "common sense" logic he uses regarding Down syndrome: in this framework, "obviously" both conditions are undesirable and irredeemable. Part of my project . . ., then, is to work to counteract this assumption about both mental illness and cognitive disabilities. That work occasionally involves occupying and reimagining epithets like "crazy."

4. Monica J. Casper and Lisa Jean Moore, *Missing Bodies: The Politics of Visibility* (New York: New York University Press, 2009), 4.

5. Although disability theorist Tom Shakespeare and journalist Norah Vincent hold opposing views about the worth and need for disability studies (with Shakespeare "for" and Vincent "against"), they share the belief that casting disability as desirable leads, logically, to the belief that we can intentionally disable other people. Vincent suggests, for example, that adhering to such a position must mean that one is opposed to giving pregnant women access to folic acid because it decreases the incidence of certain impairments. Shakespeare argues that "if impairment were just another difference"—not negative but neutral—"there would be nothing wrong with painlessly altering a baby so they could no longer see, or could no longer hear, or had to use a wheelchair." Contrast their position with that of Nirmala Erevelles, who argues that a critical disability response to the question of desiring disability is not to deny such a possibility but rather to explore the social and material conditions under which such desire is possible. Nirmala Erevelles, *Disability and Difference in Global Contexts: Enabling a Transformative Body Politic* (New York: Palgrave Macmillan, 2011), 29. Tom Shakespeare, *Disability Rights and Wrongs* (London: Routledge, 2006), 64; Norah Vincent, "Enabling Disabled Scholarship," *Salon*, August 18, 1999.

6. For an account of disability as human biodiversity, see Rosemarie Garland-Thomson, "Welcoming the Unbidden: The Case for Preserving Human Biodiversity," in *What Democracy Looks Like: A New Critical Realism for a Post-Seattle World*, ed. Amy Schrager Lang and Cecelia Tichi (New Brunswick, NJ: Rutgers University Press, 2006), 77–87. See also Kenny Fries, *The History of My Shoes and the Evolution of Darwin's Theory* (New York: Carroll & Graf, 2007).

7. Although most simulation exercises focus on mobility-impairment/wheelchairs and blindness/blindfolds, I have heard of exercises employing deafness/noise-canceling headsets and, astonishingly, speech impairment/marbles (i.e., asking students to try to speak with marbles in their mouths). Other disabilities, however, seem beyond the reach of these exercises. There are not simulations, for example, of chronic illness, pain, or fatigue, perhaps because people assume they already know what those sensations feel like. I suspect simulations are limited to those conditions that sound fun to experience because they come with props or accoutrements, e.g., canes and wheelchairs. Mental disability and multiple chemical sensitivities are less visible and perhaps therefore more frightening; it would be harder to know when the simulation was beginning and ending, thereby interrupting the distancing dynamic on which these exercises ultimately rely. Some impairments are harder to take on and off.

8. Tobin Siebers, *Disability Theory* (Ann Arbor: University of Michigan Press, 2008), 29. For another critique of disability simulation exercises, see Art Blaser, "Awareness Days: Some Alternatives to Simulation Exercises," *Ragged Edge Online*, September/October 2003. . .

9. Simi Linton, *Claiming Disability: Knowledge and Identity* (New York: New York University Press, 1998), 11.

10. Nor do all medical professionals employ an individual/medical model of disability; service providers are also often allies and activists, and there certainly are medical professionals who themselves have disabilities. Thus, as Leslie J. Reagan notes, "[t]he disabilities critique of the medical model . . . perhaps may be best understood as a critique of the entire society, rather than of the medical profession alone, for prioritizing medicine and medical solutions over social reconstruction." Leslie J. Reagan, *Dangerous Pregnancies: Mothers, Disabilities, and Abortion in Modern America* (Berkeley: University of California Press, 2010), 65.

11. Denis Dutton, "What Are Editors For," *Philosophy and Literature* 20 (1996): 551–66, accessed September 24, 2009, http://www.denisdutton.com/what_are_editors_for.htm; emphasis in original.

12. To clarify this point, Dutton provides a list of the symptoms of cretinism: "The bodily symptoms (including limb stunting, enlarged lips, open, drooling mouth, broad, flat face, sallow skin,

etc.), and intellectual subnormality to the level of imbecile or moron, are actual medical conditions." Dutton, "What Are Editors For."

13. Rosemarie Garland-Thomson, "Integrating Disability, Transforming Feminist Theory," in *Gendering Disability*, ed. Bonnie Smith and Beth Hutchison (New Brunswick, NJ: Rutgers University Press, 2004), 77.

14. For one of the most well-known examples of this phenomenon, see Susan Wendell, *The Rejected Body: Feminist Philosophical Reflections on Disability* (New York: Routledge, 1996).

15. Jim Swan, "Disabilities, Bodies, Voices," in *Disability Studies: Enabling the Humanities*, ed. Sharon L. Snyder, Brenda Jo Brueggemann, and Rosemarie Garland-Thomson (New York: Modern Languages Association, 2002), 293.

16. Shakespeare suggests that the focus on the medical model as the main site for disability critique is misguided; "when closely analyzed, it is nothing but a straw person" because no one actively and explicitly argues for such an approach to disability. Although I agree that a notion of "the" medical model is unnecessarily simplistic and reductionist—medical approaches to disability are not monolithic, and many service providers support social change on top of any medical treatments—medical constructions and definitions of disability, impairment, and disabled bodies/minds remain the most culturally pervasive frameworks. Shakespeare, *Disability Rights and Wrongs*, 18.

17. Janet Price and Margrit Shildrick, "Uncertain Thoughts on the Dis/abled Body," *Vital Signs: Feminist Reconfigurations of the Bio/logical Body*, ed. Margrit Shildrick and Janet Price (Edinburgh: Edinburgh University Press, 1998), 243, 246.

18. B. J. Gleeson, "Disability Studies: A Historical Materialist View," *Disability and Society* 12, no. 2 (1997): 193. See also Shakespeare, *Disability Rights and Wrongs*.

19. Wendell, *Rejected Body*, 14. See also Shelley Tremain, "On the Subject of Impairment," in *Disability/Postmodernity: Embodying Political Theory*, ed. Mairian Corker and Tom Shakespeare (New York: Continuum, 2002), 32–47.

20. See, for example, Adrienne Rich, "Notes Toward a Politics of Location," *Blood, Bread, Poetry: Selected Prose, 1979–1985* (New York: W. W. Norton, 1994): 210–31.

21. Nor, suggests Michael Bérubé, can the social model adequately address cognitive or intellectual impairments; although social and structural changes are both necessary and long overdue, "it's possible that [a] cognitively impaired person . . . would be impaired by any built environment." Michael Bérubé, "Term Paper," *Profession* (2010): 112. For other recent critiques of the social model, particularly its foreclosure of certain questions from debate, see Julie Livingston, "Insights from an African History of Disability," *Radical History Review* 94 (Winter 2006): 111–26; Anna Mollow, "'When *Black* Women Start Going on Prozac': Race, Gender, and Mental Illness in Meri Nana-Ama Danquah's *Willow Weep for Me*," *MELUS* 31, no. 3 (2006): 67–99; Anna Mollow and Robert McRuer, introduction to *Sex and Disability*, ed. Robert McRuer and Anna Mollow (Durham, NC: Duke University Press, 2012), 1–34; and Shakespeare, *Disability Rights and Wrongs*.

22. Liz Crow, "Including All of Our Lives: Renewing the Social Model of Disability," in *Encounters with Strangers: Feminism and Disability*, ed. Jenny Morris (London: The Women's Press, 1996), 210. For sharp analyses and moving insights on the importance of trauma and depression to radical projects—what Heather Love calls "feeling backward"—see Ann Cvetkovich, *An Archive of Feelings: Trauma, Sexuality, and Lesbian Public Cultures* (Durham, NC: Duke University Press, 2003); and Heather Love, *Feeling Backward: Loss and the Politics of Queer History* (Cambridge, MA: Harvard University Press 2007).

23. Tom Shakespeare, "The Social Model of Disability," in *The Disability Studies Reader*, 2nd ed., ed. Lennard J. Davis (New York: Routledge, 2006), 199.

24. Dutton uses race as his primary example, arguing that there can be no disability equivalent to the "Black is Beautiful" movement of the 1960s.

25. Simone Chess, Alison Kafer, Jessi Quizar, and Mattie Udora Richardson, "Calling All Restroom Revolutionaries!" in *That's Revolting! Queer Strategies for Resisting Assimilation*, ed. Matt Bernstein Sycamore (New York: Soft Skull, 2004), 189–206.. . .

26. Chantal Mouffe, *The Return of the Political* (London: Verso, 1993), 3.

27. Jodi Dean, "Introduction: The Interface of Political Theory and Cultural Studies," in *Cultural Studies and Political Theory*, ed. Jodi Dean (Ithaca, NY: Cornell University Press, 2000), 6.

28. Dean, "Introduction: The Interface of Political Theory," 4; emphasis mine.

29. For an examination of ableism, see Fiona Kumari Campbell, *Contours of Ableism: The Production of Disability and Abledness* (New York: Palgrave Macmillan, 2009). On compulsory able-bodiedness, see Robert McRuer, "Compulsory Able-Bodiedness and Queer/Disabled Existence," in *Disability Studies: Enabling the Humanities*, ed. Sharon L. Snyder, Brenda Jo Brueggemann, and Rosemarie Garland-Thomson (New York: Modern Language Association, 2002): 88–99; and Alison Kafer, "Compulsory Bodies: Reflections on Heterosexuality and Able-bodiedness," *Journal of Women's History* 15, no. 3 (2003): 77–89.

30. Susan M. Schweik, *The Ugly Laws: Disability in Public* (New York: New York University Press, 2009), 280.

31. For other critical accounts of disability identity, see Gloria Anzaldúa, "Disability and Identity," in *The Gloria Anzaldúa Reader*, ed. AnaLouise Keating (Durham, NC: Duke University Press, 2009), 298–302; Robert McRuer, *Crip Theory: Cultural Signs of Queerness and Disability* (New York: New York University Press, 2006); Anna Mollow, "Identity Politics and Disability Studies: A Critique of Recent Theory," *Michigan Quarterly Review* 43, no. 2 (2004): 269–96; and McRuer and Mollow, introduction to *Sex and Disability*.

32. Ben Pitcher and Henriette Gunkel, "Q&A with Jasbir Puar," *darkmatter Journal*, accessed December 3, 2009, http://www.darkmatter101.org/site/2008/05/02/qa-with-jasbir-puar/.

33. Joan W. Scott, "Cyborgian Socialists?" in *Coming to Terms: Feminism, Theory, Politics*, ed. Elizabeth Weed (New York: Routledge, 1989), 216.

34. Linton, *Claiming Disability*, 4, emphasis mine.

35. The field of philosophy has a fair number of texts dealing with cognitive impairments, partly because of the importance of, and discourses around, rationality in the field. Disability studies approaches to these topics within the field, however, remain quite rare. For exceptions, see, for example, Licia Carlson, "Cognitive Ableism and Disability Studies: Feminist Reflections on the History of Mental Retardation," *Hypatia* 16, no. 4 (2001): 128–33; Licia Carlson, *The Faces of Intellectual Disability* (Bloomington: Indiana University Press, 2010); and Sophia Isako Wong, "At Home with Down Syndrome and Gender," *Hypatia* 17, no. 3 (2002): 89–117. There is also a critical set of historical texts addressing cognitive impairments through a disability studies lens. See, for example, Martin S. Pernick, *The Black Stork: Eugenics and the Death of "Defective" Babies in American Medicine and Motion Pictures since 1915* (New York: Oxford University Press, 1996); and James W. Trent, Jr., *Inventing the Feeble Mind: A History of Mental Retardation in the United States* (Berkeley: University of California Press, 1995).

36. Margaret Price, *Mad at School: Rhetorics of Mental Disability and Academic Life* (Ann Arbor: University of Michigan Press, 2011); Ellen Samuels, "My Body, My Closet: Invisible Disability and the Limits of Coming-Out Discourse," *GLQ: A Journal of Lesbian and Gay Studies* 9, nos. 1–2 (2003):

233–55; and Susan Wendell, "Unhealthy Disabled: Treating Chronic Illnesses as Disabilities," *Hypatia: A Journal of Feminist Philosophy* 16, no. 4 (2001): 17–33.

37. Signorello et al. explain that "[r]easons for racial disparities in diabetes prevalence are not clear, but behavioral, environmental, socioeconomic, physiological, and genetic contributors have all been postulated." Their findings suggest that these differences cannot be attributed to "race" per se, but to other established risk factors including socioeconomic status. L. B. Signorello et al., "Comparing Diabetes Prevalence between African Americans and Whites of Similar Socioeconomic Status," *American Journal of Public Health* 97, no. 12 (2007): 2260. For a critique of race-based medicine, see Dorothy Roberts, *Fatal Invention: How Science, Politics, and Big Business Re-create Race in the Twenty-first Century* (New York: The New Press, 2011).

38. Chris Bell, "Introducing White Disability Studies: A Modest Proposal," in *The Disability Studies Reader,* 2nd ed. (New York: Routledge, 2006): 275–82. Nirmala Erevelles and Andrea Minear offer a productive reading of theories of intersectionality through the lens of disability studies; they work in both directions, interrogating the whiteness of disability studies and the inattention to disability in critical race studies. Nirmala Erevelles and Andrea Minear, "Unspeakable Offenses: Untangling Race and Disability in Discourses of Intersectionality," *Journal of Literary and Cultural Disability Studies* 4, no. 2 (2010): 127–45. See also Corbett Joan O'Toole, "The Sexist Inheritance of the Disability Movement," in *Gendering Disability,* ed. Bonnie G. Smith and Beth Hutchison (New Brunswick, NJ: Rutgers University Press, 2004), 294–95.

39. Carrie Sandahl, "Queering the Crip or Cripping the Queer: Intersections of Queer and Crip Identities in Solo Autobiographical Performance," *GLQ* 9, nos. 1–2 (2003): 27; Robert McRuer, *Crip Theory: Cultural Signs of Queerness and Disability* (New York: New York University Press, 2006), 36.

40. Robert Hoffmeister, "Border Crossings by Hearing Children of Deaf Parents: The Lost History of Codas," in *Open Your Eyes: Deaf Studies Talking,* ed. H-Dirksen L. Bauman (Minneapolis: University of Minnesota Press, 2008), 189–215; see also Lennard J. Davis, *My Sense of Silence: Memoirs of a Childhood with Deafness* (Champaign: University of Illinois Press, 2000). Brenda Jo Brueggemann offers a productive examination of deaf identity and the space between identities. Brenda Jo Brueggemann, *Deaf Subjects: Between Identities and Places* (New York: New York University Press, 2009).

41. McRuer, *Crip Theory,* 36–37.

42. Linton, *Claiming Disability,* 13. See also Carlson, *Faces of Intellectual Disability,* 192–94.

43. Drawing on her work on disability in Botswana, Julie Livingston suggests the term "debility" as an alternative to disability because it encompasses chronic illness, aging, and a wide range of impairments, not just "disability per se." Livingston, "Insights," 113.

44. Ladelle McWhorter, foreword to *Foucault and the Government of Disability,* ed. Shelley Tremain (Ann Arbor: University of Michigan Press, 2005), xv.

45. For a discussion of the inclusion of women who do not identify as feminists in feminist political activism and coalition work, see Sohera Syeda and Becky Thompson, "Coalition Politics in Organizing for Mumia Abu-Jamal," in *Feminism and Antiracism: International Struggles for Justice,* ed. France Winddance Twine and Kathleen M. Blee (New York: New York University Press, 2001), 193–219.

46. In some of his recent work on disability and identity politics, Lennard J. Davis provides a progress narrative of theories of identity in which he consigns the work of feminist and queer theorists to earlier, problematic stages, with disability—a disability apparently separate from feminist and queer theory—offering a solution to the problems of identity politics. See *Bending*

Over Backwards: Disability, Dismodernism, and other Difficult Positions (New York: New York University Press, 2002), 9–32. For a brief critique of Davis's representation of feminist and queer theory and activism, see McRuer, *Crip Theory*, 202.

My desire to make these links explicit echoes the work of Gayatri Gopinath, who, in her study of queer diasporas, "challenges the notion that these fields of inquiry [queer and feminist scholarship] are necessarily distinct, separate, and incommensurate." Gayatri Gopinath, *Impossible Desires: Queer Diasporas and South Asian Public Cultures* (Durham, NC: Duke University Press, 2005), 16.

47. Nancy Mairs, *Plaintext: Essays* (Tucson: University of Arizona Press, 1992), 9.

48. On the dynamic of staring, see Rosemarie Garland-Thomson, *Staring: How We Look* (New York: Oxford University Press, 2009).

49. Eli Clare, *Exile and Pride: On Disability, Queerness, and Liberation* (Boston: South End Press, 1999), 70.

50. Sandahl, "Queering the Crip," 53n1; McRuer, *Crip Theory*, 35.

51. "Critical disability studies" is another term describing this orientation toward disability and disability studies; as Margrit Shildrick describes it, critical disability studies is the frame favored "by those . . . for whom the original challenge of the social model of disability no longer provides an effectively dynamic model." Margrit Shildrick, *Dangerous Discourses of Disability, Subjectivity, and Sexuality* (New York: Palgrave Macmillan, 2009), 15.

52. Sandahl, "Queering the Crip," 27.

53. Part of my reluctance to articulate a strict boundary between feminist disability studies (or queer disability studies) and crip theory stems from an awareness that contradictory strategies and epistemologies often circulate under the same name. Merri Lisa Johnson explains, for example, that some work marked "feminist disability studies" refuses all medical terminology while other feminist disability studies approaches do not; similarly, some "disability studies" texts deconstruct the disabled/nondisabled binary while others reify it. Moreover, I worry about the possibility of "crip theory" being positioned as a successor narrative to disability studies, as if all the problems with the field could be solved with this one shift in approach. (After all, crip theory could also be critiqued, in Bell's terms, as *white* crip theory.) I hasten to add that neither McRuer nor Sandahl have positioned crip theory this way, and both continue to practice and claim "disability studies"; I believe their distinction invites a contestatory approach to both disability and disability studies while remaining invested in the promises of the field as a whole. For an example of a theorist who is interested in mapping the differences between feminist disability studies and crip feminism, see Merri Lisa Johnson, "Crip Drag Swan Queen: Two Readings of Darren Aronofsky's *Black Swan*," National Women's Studies Association Conference, Atlanta, GA, November, 2011.

54. "Compulsory able-mindedness" is a way of capturing the normalizing practices, assumptions, and exclusions that cannot easily be described as directed (exclusively) to *physical* functioning or appearance. Kristen Harmon suggests, for example, that "able-bodiedness" cannot sufficiently address what she calls "compulsory hearing." Kristen Harmon, "Deaf Matters: Compulsory Hearing and Ability Trouble," in *Deaf and Disability Studies: Interdisciplinary Perspectives*, ed. Susan Burch and Alison Kafer (Washington, DC: Gallaudet University Press, 2010), 42. For extensive analyses of compulsory able-mindedness in terms of mental disability, see Andrea Nicki, "The Abused Mind: Feminist Theory, Psychiatric Disability, and Trauma," *Hypatia* 16, no. 4 (2001): 80–104; and Margaret Price, *Mad at School: Rhetorics of Mental Disability and Academic Life* (Ann Arbor: University of Michigan Press, 2010).

55. Anna Mollow makes a similar argument in her discussion of depression and mental illness; to engage fully with questions of mental illness, disability studies will need to shift its guiding frameworks and terminologies. Mollow, "'When *Black* Women Start Going on Prozac.'" See also Elizabeth J. Donaldson, "Revisiting the Corpus of the Madwoman: Further Notes toward a Feminist Disability Studies Theory of Mental Illness," in *Feminist Disability Studies*, ed. Kim Q. Hall (Bloomington: Indiana University Press, 2011), 91–113.

56. Judith Butler, *Bodies That Matter: On the Discursive Limits of "Sex"* (New York: Routledge, 1993), 223.

57. Carrie Sandahl expresses the same hope, and concern, noting that queer theory (and, I would add, disability studies) has a "tendency to absorb and flatten internal differences, in particular to neutralize its constituents' material and cultural differences and to elevate the concerns of gay white men [or middle-class white male wheelchair users] above all others." Sandahl, "Queering the Crip," 27.

58. Mattilda suggests that it is in the "messiness" of intersectional work that "the possibility for a rigorous analysis emerges." Jason Ruiz, "The Violence of Assimilation: An Interview with Mattilda aka Matt Bernstein Sycamore," *Radical History Review* 100 (Winter 2008): 239.

59. Jasbir K. Puar, *Terrorist Assemblages: Homonationalism in Queer Times* (Durham, NC: Duke University Press, 2007), 212.

60. Of course, this lack is even more pronounced in the other direction; papers on disability studies topics or drawing on disability theory remain few and far between at many cultural studies and critical theory conferences.

61. Puar, *Terrorist Assemblages,* 209; emphasis in original.

62. Janet Price and Margrit Shildrick play with this desire for and practice of disability identification in some of their collaborative work, as do Robert McRuer and Anna Mollow. See Price and Shildrick, "Uncertain Thoughts"; and Mollow and McRuer, introduction to *Sex and Disability*.

63. John B. Kelly's analysis of quad rugby offers a potent reminder that ableism or, in his framing, the ideology of ability, affects relationships *between* disabled people. John B. Kelly, "'It Could Have Been Worse': Quadriplegic Athletes and the Ideology of Ability," Society for Disability Studies Annual Meeting, Chicago, June 2000.

64. Eve Kosofsky Sedgwick, *Tendencies* (Durham, NC: Duke University Press, 1994), xiv. See also Margaret Price, "'Her Pronouns Wax and Wane': Psychosocial Disability, Autobiography, and Counter-Diagnosis," *Journal of Literary and Cultural Disability Studies* 3, no. 1 (2009): 11–33.

MARIVEL DANIELSON

20. OUR ART IS OUR WEAPON: WOMEN OF COLOR TRANSFORMING ACADEMIA

I look at my fingers, see plumes growing there. From the fingers, my feathers, black and red ink drips across the page. *Escribo con la tinta de mi sangre.*

—Gloria Anzaldúa, *Borderlands: The New Mestizo*

Ela Troyano's 1994 short film *Carmelita Tropicana: Your Kunst Is Your Waffen* stars Troyano's sister Alina as her performative alter-ego, Carmelita Tropicana, a radical Cuban-born, New York City, Lower East Side–dwelling, lesbian performance artist with a penchant for colorful sequined costumes, platform sneakers, and fruit as a fashion accessory. In the film's opening scene, Carmelita prides herself on being "good with the tongue." The film's title, *Your Kunst Is Your Waffen* (*Your Art Is Your Weapon*), is a mixture of German and English that illustrates her linguistic talents and artistic ideology while simultaneously (and certainly not inadvertently) sounding a little sexy and scandalous to non–German speaking viewers who might only guess at the meanings of "kunst" and "waffen."

Another of Troyano's performances, *Memorias de la revolución/Memories of the Revolution*, tells of Carmelita Tropicana's origins and also develops the critical metaphor of art as a weapon. The drama begins in 1955 Havana as Carmelita and her friends and family attempt to overthrow the evil dictator Maldito. When the assassination plot fails, Carmelita is forced to flee her home in a small rowboat, which quickly becomes lost at sea. As she is tossed about the choppy waters, the Virgin Mary appears to Carmelita and informs her she has been selected to be "the next hottest Latin Superstar" (A. Troyano 37). The Virgin–played by the cast's only male actor—also instructs: "Oh, the revolution. Let it be your art. Your art is your weapon. To give dignity to Latin and Third World women: this is your struggle" (38).

Before this drag queen Virgin exits, she warns Carmelita that along with its rewards (of superstardom and eternal youth), her artistic mission will have a price. The Virgin cautions, "listen Carmelita, there is more. You must never, ever, ever . . . let a man touch you. You must remain pure, like me," to which Carmelita quickly retorts, "Believe me, to Carmelita Tropicana Guzmán Jiménez Marquesa de Aguas Claras, that is never to be a problem" (38). So we come to understand Carmelita's revolution as an artistic one, specifically grounded in the interests of Latina and Third World Women, and necessarily queer in nature (since Carmelita reinterprets the Virgin's allusion to celibacy as a call for radical lesbianism). In this way, *Memorias de la revolución* and *Your Kunst Is Your Waffen* provide readers and audiences with specifically queer and Latina frameworks for cultural revolution.

This metaphor of art as weapon suggests a framework with which to understand the creative, political, and—certainly not least of all—theoretical possibilities offered to readers and viewers of artistic expression in general, and of queer U.S. Latina creativity specifically. Tropicana's translation of art into weapon is most powerfully understood not as destructive but rather deconstructive in as much as politically and socially conscious art is able to break down cultural stereotypes and institutions of oppression. In Tropicana's performance, as well as the context of this project as a whole, a weapon is also a tool that not only takes apart but also rebuilds. The artistic production of Latina lesbians is equally reconstructive through its practices of building and rebuilding spaces for the launching of theory, history, and identity from the perspectives, the mouths, and the bodies of queer Latinas in the United States.

Queer Latina art as a weapon can be understood as destructive in as much as it is able to break down cultural stereotypes and institutions of oppression. Works such as Carmelita Tropicana's "excess-as-norm" performance of Latinidad in *Your Kunst Is Your Waffen* and *Memorias de la revolución* reinscribe outrageous cultural stereotypes as purported by dominant discourse and have the potential to dislodge stereotypical images from their fossilized foundations. So we see the power of queer Latina art to dismantle and deconstruct existing structures of oppression, but how can this same art be recontextualized as equally reconstructive?

. . .

The critical work I explore . . . spans several decades and traverses a wide range of genres and stylistic approaches to theoretical production. My analysis traces the way creativity—defined here as the personal, emotional, and poetic investment of an author into her critical work—is used by queer women of color as a tool to both penetrate the mainstream space of hegemonic academia and to create new spaces within academia for the production of and respect for alternative modes of scholarship. In this way, as both an invasion of mainstream space and the creation of strategic home spaces within, a movement toward a revolution of academia led by queer women of color can be seen to encompass the frameworks of space-making and homecoming as examined/observed throughout this project.

LIVING LANGUAGE AND SCHOLARSHIP

In a similar metanarrative to that offered by Emma Pérez's *Gulf Dreams*, Juana María Rodríguez cautions readers in the preface to her 2003 publication *Queer Latinidad: Identity Practices, Discursive Spaces*: "Do not believe everything I say. I am learning to feel at ease with ambiguity. Most of [this] text is not imaginative fiction, but it is a product of my critical imagination" (2). Rodríguez's suggestion of a "critical imagination" signifies a move toward creativity as a scholarly tool. Stepping outside scientific paradigms of fact and unbiased invisibility of the researcher, Rodríguez imagines

a criticism that not only holds itself accountable for ideological influences but also defines itself through such distinctions and specificities. For Rodríguez, then, theory is more story than science, more dream than diagnosis.

In fact, Rodríguez reiterates her role not as a critic, but a narrator, emphasizing a facilitation process whereby her authorial role and ideological interest in the text are openly acknowledged. This self-proclaimed title enables her to align her text more closely with art and literature than anthropology or medical science. Creativity, in this context, impacts both scholar and subject, since telling a story is wholly distinct from defining a subject, as Rodríguez explains: "This text is not about representing communities or a set of subjects. I am more concerned with ways of looking than constructing credible objects of analysis" (3). Rodríguez's investment in "ways of looking" echoes Moraga's earlier poetic petition for "other ways of seeing" (3). Such a shift in scholarly focus, from the literal and figurative "nailing down" of subjects of inquiry to the process and practices through which we as scholars attempt to "see" such subjects and the work they create, offers hope for a more inclusive, viable, and consequently sustainable notion of academia.

As a professor, author, and activist, bell hooks is careful to differentiate between intellectual life and academic careerism. In doing so, she locates a space from which to think critically, engage with theory, and produce scholarly texts from outside the historically hallowed halls and ivory towers of mainstream academia. She underlines the lack of support for nontraditional theory-making within traditional academia, particularly for practices that utilize creativity as critical weaponry: "It is precisely because common structures of evaluation and advancement in various academic jobs require homogeneous thought and action, judged usually from a conservative standpoint, that academia is often less a site for open-minded creative study and engagement with ideas and more a space of repression that dissenting voices are so easily censored and/or silenced" (*Remembered Rapture* 140).

Further, hooks indicates that a revolution of scholarship working toward the survival of the voices and ideas of marginalized communities not only embraces creativity and artistry as theoretical practices, but also seeks out alternative sites for the production and exploration of meaning. She deems "dangerous" the limitation of revolution to solely "academic" institutions. Like Tropicana's art as weapon, hooks sees creativity as offering a vital framework for contextualizing subversive movements and discourse. Increasingly, anyone willing to look is able to locate these spaces of creative theoretical production in the novels, poetry, film, political and social organizing, performance and visual art of individuals who have felt alienated by the goals and structure of traditional academia. These hegemonic institutions provide little inspiration or support for artistic endeavors that engage with theoretical and critical issues yet fail to conform to established (white Anglo male) standards of critical production.

What happens when the presumed boundaries separating literature and scholarship become blurred? What does it mean to read creative and literary texts as theoretical works? To ask such a question reveals an already fossilized ideology regarding the imagined divisions between these two "categories."

theory	→	creativity
true	→	fictional
unbiased	→	biased
impersonal	→	emotional
critical	→	political
analytical	→	poetic

The preceding paradigm privileges theory as an exclusive category. It is also constructed upon inherently racist, sexist, and homophobic ideologies, since the positionalities of the subjects responsible for creating the ideal models are rarely seen to contribute to the value systems embedded within these ideals. Inherent discrimination can also be attributed to the fact that hegemonic theory necessitates an unbiased discourse that eludes all subjects outside the default universal white male heterosexual whose work benefits from a suspended mode of gender, racial, and sexual invisibility. As soon as a scholar emerges from this fantastic realm of invisibility, as woman, queer, person of color, or all three, her discourse stands a much greater risk of being dismissed as emotional, personal, biased, and political in as much as it engages with the impact of race, gender, and sexuality. Though these issues impact the universal subject (white, male, heterosexual) as

much as they do the marginalized subject, the latter has constructed an academic institution that allows his work to slip from the marked positionalities it actually occupies and that are used to limit the impact, dissemination, and reception of works by individuals of marginalized communities.

This study of alternative theory-making begins with the notion of the body. Issues of corporeality are certainly relevant to the study of creative work by women of color, specifically within discussions of texts, authors and artists grappling with racial and ethnic identity, queer brown desire, and the literal staging of queer Latina bodies in performative and cinematic works. Yet as I approach a theoretical discussion of the body as it pertains to queer women of color, I am prompted to confront the question of whether it is appropriate to discuss this aforementioned body without the critical work of Michele Foucault. Can I offer analyses of the politics of gender for women of color without Judith Butler's interpretation of drag and performance?[1] Can I have these critical conversations and complete these projects without grounding my arguments in the ideas and language of white European precursors whose purportedly universal and groundbreaking work on gender and the body has absorbed the majority of academic attention over the past century[?] Yet why should a discussion of queer and colored bodies and their voices and work necessarily be translated or filtered through the theoretical scope and language of Foucault or Butler? Simply because these voices were (published) first, should it follow that they should occupy a more privileged space on university shelves[?] The fact is, for most academics, it does and they do. What I propose for my own work—as a direct corollary to my previous work with queer Latina creative texts as critical weaponry—is a reading of and thinking about textual production of women and lesbians of color from within the rich legacy of critical thought by women and lesbians of color themselves. I do not dispute that mainstream theoretical voices can dialogue in productive ways with texts by women of color and other marginalized authors and artists. To the contrary, I cite both Foucault and Butler briefly here, and I have engaged the work of Anglo lesbian and male postcolonial theorists throughout this work. I simply posit that the aforementioned texts may be read in equally insightful ways via other critical traditions and methodologies, and that hegemonic resistance to such scholarly inclusions stems not from any lack of relevance or applicability, but rather from an investment in the exclusive and elitist nature of this hegemony known as academia.

It will probably be thought naive or even ignorant to approach discussions of queer subjectivity, body politics, and female desire without first grounding myself in foundational foremothers and fathers of European descent who have previously overwhelmed discourse on these topics of the academic mainstream. However, I am willing to risk such accusations and criticisms of my work in order to offer the perhaps gravely offensive possibility that we as women and lesbians of color may in fact be capable of explaining, understanding, and theorizing ourselves, our bodies, our experiences, and our voices entirely outside previously hailed discourse on women, gays and lesbians, sexuality, subjectivity, and power emerging from mainstream academic sources.

As Audre Lorde so powerfully stated over two decades ago, "The master's tools will not dismantle the master's house," and, similarly, while a mastery of increasingly dense and technical theory may earn me tenure at a well-respected research institution, my wielding of those hegemonic tools will not dismantle the increasingly elitist house of academia (Lorde 112). As long as theory requires a translation for users and use outside university walls, it will continue to produce limited revolutions for a privileged few. Appropriation, as Lorde views it, can be insufficient. If we cannot forge a new and more expansive definition of theory and the language that surrounds it, we as scholars will be perpetuating a colonialist system that relegates certain texts (most frequently those of women, queers, and people of color) to the patronizing realm of descriptive production rather than the revolutionary discourse these texts often represent. Scholarly exclusivity has a price, and entirely too often it is the silencing of the voices and contributions of queer women of color. Trinh T. Minh-ha notes this, the flaw of appropriated discourse: "Stolen language will always remain that other's language . . . Words thoroughly invested with realities that turn out to be not-quite-yet-mines are radically deceptive" (20). The hollowness

of dominant diction—a critical language forged apart from the minority critic who may invoke it—yields a discursive incompletion closely aligned with Albert Memmi's characterization of assimilation as an impossible prospect for colonized subjects.

In this state of failed appropriation, Cindy Cruz posits the performance of hegemonic theory by women of color as "bodiless entity" when such discourse requires that minority scholars shed all designations of difference (gender, sexuality, racial, class, etc.) in order to assume the unmarked status of universality (read: white Anglo male heterosexual). Cruz explains that this denial of brown, female, and often queer bodies produces a theory divorced from material issues of community and self. Yet she also affirms the subversive possibilities afforded to a scholar when appropriation of dominant discourse is discarded in favor of writing and producing theory from within the aforementioned categories of difference (Cruz 659).

The scholar in possession of a brown and lesbian body, or in this case the body inscribed as messy text, is not only disruptive to the canon, but is also excessive in its disorderly movements and conduct. Nothing provokes the custodians of normality and objectivity more than the excessiveness of a body (Cruz 659). Given the potential threat posed to traditional academia by the excesses of queer Latina difference, Emma Pérez's envisioning of *un sitio y una lengua* underlines the need for and works toward a space and a language expressly for this unwelcomed messy text.

To defend the primacy or inherent superiority of a primarily white European foundation of philosophy and women's studies is to concomitantly defend the oppressive systems of power that enabled those voices to develop, emerge first, and define that foundation. To declare that a scholar must establish an understanding and fluency in these foundational theories before engaging subsequent discussions of more specialized work on women and lesbians of color is to declare allegiance to the very systems that relegate those voices to the position of the margins. As minority groups of all sorts fully understand, this paradigm of intellectual development does not exist in reverse. Knowledge of the voices and theories of women and lesbians of color is almost always considered to be in excess, extra, rarely essential to the discourse of a well-trained scholarly mind.

In her first book, a collection of poetry and short fiction, *Chicana Falsa*, Michele Serros notes a double standard regarding the learning of Spanish as an Anglo or a Chicana:

> My skin is brown
> just like theirs,
> but now I'm unworthy of the color
> 'cause I don't speak Spanish the way I should
>
> . . .
>
> A white person gets encouragement,
> praise,
> for weak attempts at a second language.
> "Maybe he wants to be brown
> like us."
> and that is good.
> My earnest attempts
> make me look bad,
> dumb. (Serros 31)

The dynamic this poetic *testimonio* illustrates is one of essential knowledge. The speaker's authenticity and authority as a Chicana is perceived as damaged by her inability to wield the language inextricably tied to this identity by the Latinos who criticize her. In her efforts to "be Chicana," the poetic voice discovers that this label comes with a prescribed set of characteristics and required knowledge—her essentialized Chicano space demands Spanish fluency upon admission, the antithesis of Pérez's *sitio y lengua*.

In academia, hegemonic theory of primarily white Europeans is the currency with which scholarly authority is earned/purchased. And while Serros's bilingualism is overlooked because of her partial fluency in Spanish, an Anglo man is praised for his efforts to speak even a few words. Serros must know both languages fluently, while the Anglo is hailed for the minimalist of attempts at a second language. In the same way Serros's bilingualism is a requisite, we as women of color in academia are expected to be fluent in the languages of both traditional theory and those that emerge from and speak to our own communities and specifically focus on our bodies, voices, and experiences as racial, ethnic, and sexual minorities.

A foundation comprised of the latter voices alone is insufficient to claim intellectual entitlement in most traditional academic settings, not enough to warrant tenure or publication. Yet survival in a university setting is scarcely possible without such voices. Hence, for many women of color scholars, existence in academia necessitates a theoretical bilingualism not often recognized or rewarded.

As scholars and women of color, we are informed that we must first establish our critical voices in this accepted language before moving on to include alternative voices and modes of theoretical discourse. Barbara Christian maps out this unequal paradigm, noting, "I was supposed to know them, while they were not at all interested in knowing me" (72). Yet a theory/theorist is criticized very little for not adequately addressing issues of queers, women, and people of color, aside from the critiques produced by these excluded communities themselves. This double standard results from an academy constructed upon racist and exclusionary principles, where the values of scholarship reflect the colonialist aims of its creators. Hegemonic critical theory is no more essential, no more primary, no more universal than that of women and queers of color. This universality—like most notions of universality—is equal parts delusion and colonial instrument. For those of us who are indeed advocating a world free from delineation and distribution of privilege along lines of race, class, gender, and sexuality, it would behoove us to begin to dismantle those divisions within the discourse of this very academy first.

As a young scholar, over just the past few years I have heard and read the stories of countless women of color with established university careers openly and adamantly distancing themselves from the academy. "Academic" is becoming an increasingly negative label, especially—and perhaps most critically—among communities of color who are already largely disenfranchised from systems of education in the United States. I have also noticed as of late several calls for papers that engage with the challenge of translating theory into practice so as to bridge the gaps between academic and activist. And, indeed, the *Oxford English Dictionary* defines theory as abstract knowledge that is "distinguished from or opposed to practice." Yet a tangled web of dichotomies reveals this interpretation of theory to be incomplete. In her book *The Color of Privilege*, Aída Hurtado traces the shifting frameworks underlying both mainstream and Third World feminist movements. Hurtado discusses how mainstream (largely white and Anglo) feminist endeavors employed the model that private is political, implying that issues of personal relevance (distribution of household labor, child development, gendered beauty ideals, etc.) impacted the political lives of women as much as issues outside of home, family, and intimate relationships. In contrast, Hurtado explains the shift in paradigm for feminists of color who invoke the equation that public is personal in order to extend the focus of a women's and human rights movement to public institutions of oppression (racism, affirmative action, disenfranchisement) with personally relevant impact on the lives of women of color (18). This paradigmatic shift is important in providing a model of the opening up of critical spaces for the unique and diverse perspectives of women of color scholars and activists. When slightly adjusted to address the practice of theoretical or scholarly production versus the practice of activism or artistry, Hurtado opens up the space for the reformulated equation that theory is practice, rather than theory preceding practice. Certainly theory-making is every bit as personal and emotionally invested as are the practices of creativity or political action.

Numerous critics have pointed out that for communities of color, theory and practice have been unnaturally fractured into separate fields since, as they observe, in the most revolutionary sense theory is practice. And since practice for women of color and other communities includes literature, art, activism, performance, organization, and—most important—survival, theory is necessarily all of these things. Privileging theory over practice and ignoring their inherent connectedness will condemn academia to inevitable obsolescence. Beginning from such an understanding of scholarly production allows many more options for the production of theory, the practices of activist scholars, and academic sanity/survival.

This study has taken as its methodology the declaration that all forms of critical production—regardless of their format—may be considered for their theoretical implications for communities of color and beyond. In the pages that follow, I will map out a framework for theoretical discourse that respects the fluidity of discursive production for women—and specifically lesbians—of color. It is my hope that projects such as this one will lend themselves to an expansion of our definitions of theory, its shapes, functions, purposes, and possibilities so that ultimately the academy might abandon its elitist tendencies and facilitate a sort of discursive multilingualism for all participants that is simultaneously theory and practice such that the translation between the two becomes obsolete.

. . . It seems to me so often that a discussion of theory—defined in the form of the critical essay—begins all work around an issue. This traditional model sets up a research project by first establishing an overview of theoretical discourse in a field, while literary and testimonial texts follow. I suggest, however, that works by women of color can be viewed productively not as a division of primary (creative) and secondary (critical or theoretical) works, but rather as an active dialogue between these two discursive modes, which can—in fact—be seen to blur into each other within the very works examined in this project. In this way, through the conscious and celebratory incorporation of personal and emotional expression within their theoretical production, women and specifically lesbians of color begin to disrupt traditional academic practices.

I find a discussion of ongoing radical transformations of hegemonic academia here useful and appropriate for several reasons. I believe that women of color and specifically queer women of color, as multiply marginalized subjects, tend to experience and understand most intimately the inadequacies of contemporary structures of higher education. Historically, these hallowed halls and ivory towers were not created for us as women, people of color, queers, and working-class, though perhaps the structures themselves may have been constructed by us, our hands, shoulders, and backs.

Those who designed this space of critical scholarship known as academia did so according to their own unique needs, desires, and interests—to form their own *sitio y lengua*, one might argue (not so much for survival but advancement). As subsequent communities begin to gain limited and rigidly policed access to university spaces, these subjects are most often the first to recognize the insufficiencies of the existing system. To use Audre Lorde's image of the master's house, many scholars of color, specifically women and queers among them, find the house of academia unacceptable, a roof that hangs too low, walls too close, a door frame much too narrow to afford entrance to the diverse specificities represented across intersecting communities. Lorde notes, then, "the master's tools will not dismantle the master's house," so for those of us who find the current structure both cramped and uninhabitable, her paradigm suggests several viable options.

First, one might undertake a massive remodeling project in which this master's tools are appropriated and transformed through the imposition of new positionalities and ideologies. As a restructuring of the original, this option offers limited change but represents perhaps the most realistic possibility for mutual understanding, since it necessitates literal and figurative cohabitation within difference. Contrastingly, some scholars find that these tools cannot ever be adequately stripped of their previous ideological content and that entirely new tools must be fashioned. Both approaches are evident in my earlier discussion of identity labels and the politics of representation, since some accepted or reappropriated existing terms while others created entirely new linguistic manifestations. Although a reappropriation of the master's instruments may succeed at taking apart the offending structures, some will argue that our time, breath, sweat, and energy might be better spent building entirely new structures of our own original design.

Given that these institutions of higher education were founded and developed with particular ideologies and intentions, minority academics—ones perhaps not envisioned in the founders' original vision because of their racial, cultural, sexual, and/or gender identities—have learned to survive as well as build entire careers from their critical and creative responses to this system's vast insufficiencies. For marginalized scholars who succeed at penetrating this dominant center of power, academia becomes an exercise in professional, financial, social, and psychological survival. Certainly, though, many respected and established underrepresented scholars have found support, success, and a home in hegemonic academia, in its language

and traditions. I do not intend the preceding narrative as dismissive or disrespectful toward any theorist or theory. My methodological approach here is wholly productive, rather than destructive. I seek not to tear down but to build additional alternatives, to trace the possible paths, and understand the revolutions waged daily by groundbreaking scholars emerging from all directions of intellectual production—from within the university and beyond.

NOTES ON INVISIBILITY

> I am a man of substance, of flesh and bone, fiber and liquids—and I might even be said to possess a mind. I am invisible, understand, simply because people refuse to see me.
>
> —Ralph Ellison, *Invisible Man*

> As the semester went on, my self began to slowly vanish. I would soon become invisible. Although I knew I was physically there, attentively listening, taking in as much as I possibly could, I also knew that I was the only one aware of my presence. Completely ignored in a silence, I was growing numb.
>
> —Caridad Souza, *Telling to Live*

In his 1947 novel *Invisible Man*, Ralph Ellison offers an eloquent and insightful theoretical reflection on the dynamics of invisibility through the voice of an anonymous young male African American narrator. Despite vast political, social, and psychological implications, Ellison's narrator concedes that this condition is "sometimes advantageous" and admits, "after existing some twenty years, [I] did not become alive until I discovered my invisibility" (7). How might his described state of invisibility enable this African American man, or for that matter a Latina, or a queer woman of color to become alive rather than remaining silenced, erased, and obliterated? Just as Emma Pérez's *Gulf Dreams* exposed the potential repercussions of speaking out against violation, Ellison's narrator points out that rejecting one's invisibility prompts violent resistance: "You ache with the need to convince yourself that you do exist in the real world, that you're a part of all the sound and anguish, and you strike out with your fists, you curse and you swear to make them recognize you. And, alas, it's seldom successful" (4). Again we bear witness to Memmi's theory of impossible revolution for the colonized subject and Minh-ha's state of "almost-not-quite" linguistic incompletion. It is in the reactive nature of this struggle that one finds insight into the futility of a revolutionary movement grounded in the disproving of dominant ideology as ideological construction or fantasy. Homi Bhabha argues against such an approach to colonialist stereotypes where qualifications of good/bad or true/false overshadow the epistemological dismantling of the discursive tools of oppression. "To judge the stereotype image on the basis of a prior political normativity is to dismiss it, not to displace it, which is only possible by engaging with its effectivity" (Bhabha 67). According to Bhabha's theory, Ellison's protagonist fails in his resistance when he aims to prove his existence as truth in opposition to dominant perception of his invisibility. This attempt could be likened to the treatment of stereotype as positive/negative and right/wrong. Bhabha's theory suggests such evaluations yield little in the way of social change, while a grappling with the functionality of stereotype—how it works and why it is effective or ineffective within a system of meaning—offers greater transformative impact.

Mitsuye Yamada's contribution to *This Bridge Called My Back* parallels that of Ellison's protagonist: "I had become invisible to white Americans, and it clung to me like a bad habit. Like most bad habits, this one crept up on me because I took it in minute doses like Mithradates' poison and my mind and body adapted so well to it I hardly noticed it was there" (Yamada 37). For Yamada, the stereotypical subservience and silence surrounding popular Asian and Asian American representations left her struggling to convince herself and others of her active role in the political and social movements with which she was associated. Yet Yamada's invisibility extended beyond the boundaries of mainstream white America and into her own family, where her political convictions and activist involvement were deemed inconsequential, not because of her race but because of her gender.

Silence and invisibility have been ingrained into the purported essence of an Asian American female subject, a trait authorized as truth unless proven otherwise. However Yamada's text works toward an unraveling of such chains of knowledge, identifying the weakest points where these generalizations fail to correspond to any heterogeneous lived reality of Asian American identity. In fact, the author insists, "Invisibility is not a natural state for anyone," and thus not a valid characteristic of any individual's essential self (40). Yamada's interpretation of invisibility is characterized by both its positive and negative repercussions, as she views it as concomitantly oppressive and utilitarian in nature.

Notions of invisibility and its dichotomous partner of hypervisibility frame many of the contributions to the 2001 publication *Telling to Live: Latina Feminist Testimonios*. Discussions of the inhospitable environment of academia for women of color are common but covert, and *Telling to Live* offers numerous testimonios from a wide range of Latina feminist authors, academics, and artists. In a collectively written introduction to the section "Alchemies of Erasure," the Latina Feminist Group's members recognize the complexity of their perceived presence: "*Somos tan invisibles que somos visibles. Parece contradicción pero no lo es*" (del Alba Acevedo et al., 167). In fact, the collective notes, there is a distinct power associated with invisibility, in that one's perceived absence allows for increased observation, exploration, and interrogation, "the better to see, to hear, to notice, to learn" (167).

Yet of the four thematic sections that make up the collection—empowerment, the body, desire, and erasure in academia—this last section contains by far the greatest percentage of anonymous entries. Surely the presence of this literary and professional "witness protection program" evidences the continued hostility toward those ungrateful subjects who dare speak out against the current content and character of traditional academia. A quick glance at other selections' titles maps a disquieting journey through higher education for U.S. Latinas: "Snapshots from My Daze at School," "Between Perfection and Invisibility," "Diary of a Llorona with a Ph.D.," "Welcome to the Ivory Tower," "Lessons Learned from an Assistant Professor," "Don't You Like Being in the University," "Temporary Latina," "La Tra(d)ición," and "I Still Don't Know Why." Half of the above have anonymous authors. The collective assures readers, "When a woman has to be made invisible, it is because she is powerful, and her presence reverberates, touching everything in its path" (167). Unfortunately, to speak of such invisibilities is threatening, an assertion of self-worth as well as a critical attack on the institutions of power that perpetuate such silences. The above titles and their nameless authors illustrate that to speak as an invisible woman, to finally declare one's voice and insist upon being heard, one must continue to be veiled under the cloak of anonymity, a top-secret *sitio*. She who is unseen often may only speak from within the position of the unnamed.

In order to trace some of the ways in which women of color use creativity to push at the boundaries of critical and theoretical production, it is useful to map out some of the reasons why authors feel inclined to break silences and write as well as some of the goals and intentions of their writing according to the writers themselves. Many scholars, across racial, ethnic, class, sexual, and gender lines, have dedicated their time to learning the game that is traditional academia so as to either deconstruct it from within or knowingly or unknowingly reinforce it. To be sure, this . . . [essay], as well as this project as a whole, does not concern itself with such approaches—though I do not deny the merits of these practices. Instead, I take as a common thread an authorial resistance to both the rules and implications of the game of hegemonic academia. In the works resulting from this sense of resistance I find inspiration and hope for the promise of an academic revolution grounded in the words, work, and voices of women of color, queer women of color, and others who work toward a respect of difference and a dismantling of oppressive and colonialist rule.

In "Speaking in Tongues: A Letter to 3rd World Women Writers," Gloria Anzaldúa's contribution to her and Cherríe Moraga's foundational collection, *This Bridge Called My Back*, Anzaldúa addresses issues of intention and audience in her theoretical production. She maps this process by tracing her selection of literary genre and the evolution of her contribution: "It began as a poem, a long poem. I tried to turn it into an essay but the result was wooden, cold. I have not yet unlearned the esoteric bullshit and pseudo-intellectualizing that school brainwashed into my writing. . . . How to begin again. How to approximate the intimacy and immediacy I want. What form? A letter, of course" (Anzaldúa, "Speaking in Tongues" 165).

In this simple but invaluable choice lies the radical conceptualization of theory as both intimately personal and inherently dialogic. Anzaldúa's epistolary format positions her as both theorist and subject situated within the very community to whom she speaks. Anzaldúa's theoretical production speaks to specific subjects, for specific purposes, and from specified positionalities in such a way that overtly rejects the default universality and authorial invisibility purported by hegemonic theorists. In doing so, Anzaldúa is able to provide theories of writing that are not only about Third World women but expressly to and in collaboration with Third World women. This intellectual process is an inherently collective pursuit with a theorist who involves and embraces her intended audience as readers, participants, and active contributors. Anzaldúa's willingness to directly proclaim a specific positionality and ideology consequently places under suspicion all those works and writers who fail to acknowledge the equally specific ideological agendas behind their theories.

In her letter, Anzaldúa provides support and encouragement for her audience, Third World women writers, as she outlines some of the vital reasons why writing can be an invaluable tool for the diverse communities represented under this category. First, she suggests that the writing of Third World women affords individuals the opportunity to imagine alternate worlds that counteract the brutal realities of daily life for marginalized subjects.[2] This practice of queer world-making has underlined previous . . . analyses, as authors and artists like Terri de la Peña, Marga Gomez, and Carmelita Tropicana/Alina Troyano use their creative voices to construct alternate worlds by transforming the dynamics of existing spaces (i.e., México, Hollywood, prison) and ideological constructs (gender, identity, home). Anzaldúa asserts that writing offers important challenges to existing structures of oppression: "Because the world I create in the writing compensates for what the real world does not give me" (169). In this sense, writing becomes the means through which alternatives to the master's house are constructed according to the specific and multiply diverse positionalities of women and queer women of color writers. Finally, Anzaldúa reveals, "I write because I'm scared of writing but I'm more scared of not writing" (169). Writing is necessary because the threat of being criticized is far less dangerous than the threat of being silenced and erased altogether. There is no pretense of authorial omnipotence, only an insistence on the irrefutable presence of Anzaldúa's voice, and that of the communities to which she speaks, and of the dialectic contained within.

Anzaldúa notes that writing may also be used as a tool for community and coalition building for and between letter writers and letter readers. She illustrates the unique power of writing to touch the lives of readers as she assures us of our collective condition. "As I grope for words and a voice to speak of writing, I stare at my brown hand clenching the pen and think of you thousands of miles away clutching your pen. You are not alone" (169). The new house being created here is the notion of writing as a practice specifically by and for women of color. We are not alone because, although our marginalization from traditional centers of academic practice continues to be palpable, this theory and this theorist speak to us. By fashioning a mode of theorizing from within a personal letter that directly and specifically speaks to communities of women of color, Anzaldúa establishes her audience as a vital factor in her intellectual production. We are able to observe how the shape or format of theory can impact both how and by whom intellectual work is received.

Another important element determining the scope and reception of theory is the language in which it is written. In an article that shall set the tone for this . . . [essay], Barbara Christian calls on her readers to consider the question "For whom are we doing what we are doing when we do literary criticism?" (77). Barbara Christian also expresses her concern for the increasingly exclusionary nature of scholarly language by offering a sound reproach of traditional philosophical writing: "I am appalled by the sheer ugliness of the language, its lack of clarity, its unnecessarily complicated sentence constructions, its lack of pleasurableness, its alienating quality. It is the kind of writing for which composition teachers would give a first-year student a resounding F" (72). The article in which Christian makes this assertion, "The Race for Theory," criticizes the type of impenetrable language upon which justifications of a necessarily elitist and exclusionary academia are built. Her title

offers a twofold meaning for readers. First, Christian uses the phrase to describe the competitive process through which traditional academics launch theories into their fields of study with the increasingly abstract and monolithic approaches to scholarship exemplified by their dense language and entangled syntax, as described earlier. Christian also invokes the phrase to reiterate the ways in which theorizing has always been a part of the creative and intellectual practices of communities of color, although often in ways rarely recognized by mainstream academics and institutions. Christian assures both this traditional academia and other readers: "My folk, have always been a race for theory—though more in the forms of the hieroglyph, a written figure that is both sensual and abstract, both beautiful and communicative" (68). In this article, Christian expresses distaste for the lack of pleasure in traditional scholarly language and notes the valuable potential of an approach to writing that is both abstract and sensual. Her insistence on the sensuality of writing and intellectual expression marks one of the many alternative paths being forged in academia by women and queer women of color scholars and artists.

Audre Lorde also discusses the power of developing such sensuality in women's writing in her 1978 paper "The Uses of the Erotic: The Erotic as Power." In her discussion Lorde develops a conceptualization of the erotic as an empowering creative energy and a celebration of the life force of women. The erotic as a force is simultaneously joyful and collective in nature. Contrasted from the non-emotional practice of sexuality devoid of feeling (as in pornography), Lorde's model envisions the erotic as a revolutionary tool for the empowerment of women through writing and other practices where sensuality and potential pleasure define the work being produced. Under this framework, Lorde explains, "The aim of each thing which we do is to make our lives and the lives of our children richer and more possible. Within the celebration of the erotic in all our endeavors, my work becomes a conscious decision—a longed-for bed that I enter gratefully and from which I rise up empowered" (340). Embracing the power of the erotic within one's writing, then, allows this work to transform a chore or burden into a nourishing and pleasurable practice. Given the hostile environment present in so many universities for women of color, the shifting of scholarship from a tedious game into a spiritually and emotionally fulfilling act of joy and celebration enables many minority scholars to not only survive but also thrive (psychically if not always professionally or financially) in traditional academic settings.

So what does Lorde's elucidation of the erotic look like and how does it translate into the theoretical practices of other women and queer women of color? In the work of all the artists and authors examined in this study—not only those within this . . . [essay]—the deployment of creativity in order to theorize, produce meaning, and create alternative worlds represents one primary way in which the power of the erotic is utilized by queer women of color. Creative energy and personal positionality charge theoretical language with new dialectics and incendiary passions. Even small shifts in wording of a text impact both how and by whom that work will be received, as Aurora Levins Morales declares: "The language people use reveals important information about who they identify with, what their intentions are, for whom they are writing or speaking . . . Unnecessarily specialized language is used to humiliate those who are not supposed to feel entitled. It sells the illusion that only those who can wield it can think" (70).

If we can think of academia, in its traditional sense, as one example of a master's house, then according to Levins Morales's theory of language and audience overly dense and complicated language could be thought of as the awkwardly shaped doorway through which only those individuals of a particular shape and size may pass. This traditionally accepted language is useless to some scholars, both because of its inherently exclusive nature and its distance from community-based activist and human rights movements. Given these responses to traditional theoretical language as defined and rewarded by hegemonic academia, to what degree can we interpret this language as and example of the master's tools from Lorde's previously discussed model? To what extent can these linguistic tools be utilized in the act of dismantling preexisting systems of oppression within the university system and beyond? And, finally, if there is to be a mode of linguistic expression that we deem both oppressive and consequently ineffective at promoting change—at

least for women of color—what alternatives exist and are being incorporated into the critical work of women of color and queer women of color scholars? Trinh T. Minh-ha utilizes her poetic theory coupled with photographic images in order to incite women of color to action as she dares us to transform language into the tools of our own fashioning: "So where do you go from here? where do I go? and where does a committed woman writer go? Finding a voice, searching for words and sentences: say some thing, one thing, or no thing: tie/untie, read/unread, discard their forms; scrutinize the grammatical habits of your writing and decide for yourself whether they free or repress. Again, order(s). Shake syntax, smash the myths, and if you lose, slide on, unearth some new linguistic paths. Do you surprise? Do you shock? Do you have a choice?" (Minh-ha 20). Here Minh-ha's position on language aligns itself with Homi Bhabha's treatment of stereotype. Both scholars avoid simplistic classifications of good or bad, instead opting to engage with the mechanics of use and effectiveness. In spite of Minh-ha's previous accounting of the insufficiencies of dominant language for minority authors, ultimately she drops the decision at the feet of the writer herself, whom she instructs to "decide for yourself." In this act, her recognition of individual agency, Minh-ha interrupts the existing discourses of power that laud one language (white, Anglo, male, heterosexual) while condemning another (brown, immigrant, female, queer).

COLORING WOMEN'S STUDIES

It is easy and/or expected to say that heterosexual women (not to be understood as "white women" simply because I have not specified a particular race) possess more institutional privilege than lesbians (again of all and no particular race, class, or gendered population).[3] Heterosexual privilege, as examined by Aída Hurtado rewards conformist (heteronormative) women with access to more central positions in dominant structures of power primarily ruled by their white male partners. Yet for women of color—and to a further degree queer women of color—the racial privilege enjoyed (whether openly or ignorantly/obliviously) by white women (feminists and lesbians included) simultaneously perpetuates the oppression of communities of color, and specifically other women of color (21–22). It is, of course, no surprise that willingness of many white women to accept their contributing role as oppressors in any paradigm of power is limited if not absent in far too many academic departments, feminist organizations, support groups, and social interactions. Hurtado's analysis of privilege extends to include lesbian subjects for whom access to the centers of power and the "rewards of seduction" are denied. Lesbians, Hurtado notes, "in having distance from white patriarchy, are more likely to have the psychological, social and physical space to invent themselves outside the confines of gender seduction" (23). Additionally she posits lesbianism as an inherently subversive tool, in that it "undermines the unconquerable biological divide of patriarchal inheritance laws through biological ties" (22). This rewriting and reappropriation of family via queer and nonbiological connections provides a framework for . . . [previous] texts. For some, then, sexual alterity provides the ultimate vehicle from which to challenge the politics of exclusion and marginalization based on all forms of difference.

Female undergraduate and graduate students of color, despite their relative newness within institutions of higher education, walk the same threatening halls and confront similar issues of silence, invisibility, and hostility as full-time faculty. As grade-earning students, scholars-in-training, and future job-seekers, they experience many of the same professional pressures to conform as do faculty pursuing tenure in the university system. What they write, how and for whom they write it, where they publish, whose help they seek, are all questions that serve to direct their futures as respected academics or resented outsiders. Yet despite the supposed lures of conformity, many young scholars choose not to be forced into a singular model of intellectual and academic activity. Often this requires dissatisfied students to insist upon the inherent interconnectedness of politics and scholarship and how each scholar's sexuality, race, class, and gender positionality inform her or his work.

One group of students engaged in such a critical, political, and creative revolution of hegemonic academia emerged from the Women's Studies Department at Portland State University under the self-proclaimed title "Raging Exotics: Women of Color Caucus." In the fall of 2000 at the University of Arizona, founding members of Raging Exotics alongside Women's Studies students from the Tucson campus offered a workshop at this conference proudly entitled "The Future of Women's Studies Conference." The panel detailed the student organization's history, goals, and personal experiences and traumas lived by women of color students within Women's Studies academic departments as well as the field in general. Although the group offered copies of their work in print, the most vibrant form of theorizing occurred as the panel and audience performed the lived experience of collaboration and confrontation in this "live" venue.

As a graduate student deeply invested in the experiences and voices of women authors and artists, I always viewed Women's Studies as an integral part of my research. I was excited to attend the University of Arizona conference, despite my own semitraumatic experiences with race and politics in Women's Studies departments and classrooms at both my graduate and undergraduate institutions. I had hope—as I have had in the past—that in this conference on the "future of Women's Studies" I might finally locate a space from which to speak and to situate my own research that I still believe is unquestionably relevant to this field that purports to study women's lives, voices, and work.

That morning my companion and I arrived early, but no sooner had we reached the registration table when anticipation turned to cool alienation and frustration when the women in charge could not locate my folder. Though my friend and I registered together, only her name and folder could be found. The individual helping me wondered aloud, Had I paid? Had I sent in my registration materials? Had I completed the forms properly? In the end, there was nothing she could do, and she was quick to reiterate this several times in the face of my disbelief. Seeing how upset I was at being quite literally cast out of this particular Women's Studies world, my friend quickly offered me her registration materials so I might participate in her place. Looking back, I am willing to concede, due to lack of proof, not conviction, that this confusion about the registration was not related to my brown and my friend's white skin. However, the politics of race and ensuing social and academic tensions failed to dissolve away, remaining an overt reminder of just how unsteady this future was. Just around the corner at the workshop sign-up table, I was quickly informed that there was no room left in the panel entitled "Raging Exotics: Women of Color Transforming Silence into Action."

Knowing this panel would deal with the stories and struggles of female students of color within the field of Women's Studies, I knew I would probably never again find a session that so perfectly fit my needs, desires, and interests as a woman of color, scholar, and student working, though never seemingly welcomed, in this field. It was particularly upsetting that such a unique and important session would be restricted to only a limited audience of preregistered members. Conference planners clearly did not anticipate the sizable crowd this workshop would draw, perhaps due to an underestimation of the relevance of queer women of color discourse to the future of Women's Studies. Conference organizers might cite safety precautions, but I would also point to the underlying or even blatant fear of communities of color coming together, organizing, and constructing political, social, academic, and cultural revolutions. Perhaps incendiary ideas rather than fire codes were the underlying concern. A return to Cindy Cruz's assurance that "nothing provokes the custodians of normality and objectivity more than the excessiveness of a body" reminds us that difference and mobilization among marginalized groups can, indeed, spark the fear and hostility of any ruling party (659). In my mind, the threat of such possibilities loomed large in the situating of this "Raging Exotics" workshop in a small remote classroom rather than in one of the area's other larger venues, an auditorium or conference room, which were used for other events and speakers that were no doubt deemed both more popular and less dangerous.

Over the course of their panel, "Raging Exotics" members Monica Steen, Lamya Chidiac, and Emi Koyama, joined by two local University of Arizona Women's Studies students, would present their own experiences, each reading a prepared statement about the unique forms of racism and ignorance with which she grapples on a daily basis as a student in the Portland State University's Women's Studies Department. In addition to their panel presentations, the students offered copies of their independently published zine.

In this publication, the "Raging Exotics" established their goals as well as demands of audiences and readers alike: "The issues we are talking about are still very traumatic for us, so we may get emotional in the course of the presentation. Do not freak out or use our emotions as an excuse to devalue our words. And if you are white, take responsibility for your discomfort upon hearing our very difficult stories. We are not talking about skinheads or KKK; we are talking about perfectly well-intentioned feminists who end up hurting us due to their ignorance and prejudice" (Raging Exotics Zine).

However, before they could begin their presentation, the validity of their experiences and theories would be performed as a profoundly troublesome introduction. That afternoon I entered the tiny, almost empty classroom with an Anglo female friend who insisted on sitting silently in the back row. When I suggested we move closer to the front of the room, she shook her head and pointed to a sign written in large letters on a blackboard at the side of the room: "This is a space for Women of Color to speak and express ourselves. If you are not a Woman of Color please keep your comments brief. If you do not respect this request we will tell you to stop. This workshop is not about you."

I sat and watched as women entered, filling the room, reading the sign, and reacting with varying degrees of melodrama, outrage, indignation, fear, righteousness, humor, and fierce accord. One older woman appeared disturbed and seemed to scoff at the sign's request. She strolled calmly into the classroom, claiming a seat in the front row directly across from the panelists, as if initiating a duel. Before the speakers began, the woman rose from her seat and walked to the center of the table where they had placed a stack of their self-created zines. She first read a sign indicating that the publication was free to women of color and five dollars for allies. In a loftily sarcastic voice, the women challenged, "What if you're 1/16 Cherokee. Does that count?" Clearly upset, one of the panelists managed to state firmly, "I find your statement offensive. I think you should leave." The woman offered that she was just joking and, if given the benefit of the doubt, could have been lightly directing an anti-essentialist nudge at the workshop organizers' establishing statement.

When she was met with only stunned silence, she turned to face the now nearly full and shocked audience and implored, "Do you think I should leave?" No doubt expecting a warm and supportive match to her own indignation at the situation, she received, instead, only our own awkward silence and stares. Another panelist quietly argued that perhaps she should be allowed to stay, but the stand-off would not so easily be diffused. Finally, incredulous, the woman turned, gathered her things, and exited the room as the rest of us watched speechless. Perhaps none of us had ever observed a scene where an older Anglo professor, with clear institutional knowledge and authority, had been shut down by a young woman of color student. Perhaps we had never seen or experienced a space in which insensitive quips, derogatory joking, and carelessly tossed racist statements were neither tolerated, nor reciprocated. Perhaps we had only dreamed of such spaces where women of color took precedence even in the company of other dominant groups. And we sat speechless now, not realizing these spaces could actually exist, that we would ever be fortunate enough to locate them, to situate ourselves, our bodies, voices, and experiences within such a site.

In this pivotal moment, graduate students, young and largely queer women of color, assembled a space of their own along the lines of similarity as well as shared difference from larger dominant spheres. They defined this sitio with specific boundaries to indicate whose participation was relevant and permissible. The attention to voice, *la lengua*, was also imperative, as they were clear in their desire to allow the words and experiences of women of color to not only emerge but also to dominate or at least saturate the discursive focus of the workshop. In addition to invoking such voices, the members of "Raging Exotics" attempted to remove any dominant voices deemed distractionary, demeaning, or dismissive. Even seemingly supportive gestures were deconstructed into their most basic dominant parts, as when one white French woman began to cry as she expressed how upset she was that someone would think her oppressive when all she intended to do was help. After continuing to speak between tearful gasps for roughly a five-minute uninterrupted stretch, one panelist responded dryly that this workshop "was not about her [the French woman]." Whether intentional

or not, the woman's emotions shifted the panel's intended focus from the unique experiences and needs of women of color in academia to the guilt and indignation of Caucasian female scholars. Rather than rush to the side of this woman, the students simply recognized the attempt to shift attention and refocused on their own critical agenda. The attempt, of course, was to cease what Gloria Anzaldúa calls reactive communication, where a struggle takes the form of action/reaction where all critical thought is focused on combating the ideas of others, rather than offering up new and original ideas of one's own. For the "Raging Exotics," the goal was to act and speak, rather than respond to the issues and inquiries of another. Yet Pérez deems such a sitio strategic, since even the original thoughts and speech presented in the room that afternoon were responses to actions and words of the now silenced Anglo women. Painful exclusions, bitter dismissals, and tokenized treatment marked most of the experiences shared that day. Though the imposed Anglo silence rule removed these women's discourse from the hour or so of discussion—following the conflict and indignant ejection of one woman—the sitio was provisional, not permanent or lasting in its ability to silence or remove the structures of power present among feminist scholars.

Subsequent to the temporary refuge of such *sitios*, Anzaldúa urges further interaction across differences to locate allies and productive coalitions in spite of continued inequalities: "it is not enough to stand on the opposite river bank, shouting questions, challenging patriarchal, white conventions . . . it's a step towards liberation from cultural domination. But it's not a way of life. At some point, on our way to a new consciousness, we will have to leave the opposite bank, the split between the two mortal combatants somehow healed so that we are on both shores at once and, at once, see through serpent and eagle eyes" (*Borderlands* 100–101). As we all stepped into the classroom for this particular workshop, we were fortunate to bear witness to the realm of the "Raging Exotics" sitio, where theories—like those of the scholars and artists discussed throughout this book—made space for us to speak, think, and believe in the possibility of a home in academia. Women of color scholars have forged new paths for performing critical analysis and shaping scholarly work in and out of academia. As evidenced above, nowhere, not even in a space that is consciously designed to meet the decolonizing principles of Emma Pérez's *sitio y lengua*, is entirely free from the impact of hierarchies of power and privilege.

The scene also illustrates the painful ramifications of creating such home spaces where universal inclusivity is rejected. It must be noted that all parties in the conflictive exchange that took place in the Raging Exotics workshop pay distinct prices for their words and/or silences in academia. The Raging Exotics incident brings to life Aída Hurtado's theorization of Chicana and Latina feminism as a blasphemic challenge to nationalist and patriarchal structures. In a conference space of intended unification of allies via the collective experiences of gender oppression, feminists of different races, ethnicities, spiritualities, classes, and national affiliations found unity elusive at best. While the students of color seized their opportunity to make

home in the university, and to limit the participation and consequent *lenguas* of Anglo women attendees, many other women of color in academia are unable to locate or inhabit such home spaces. The lures of tenure, job security, departmental harmony, and financial stability all factor into the shape of any scholar's public voice. The stereotype of the angry person of color—an archetype Chicano performance troupe Culture Clash deems "confused and full of rage"—permeates across gender lines, merging with another stereotype, that of the angry feminist, yielding a landscape of professional landmines and potential hazards to career advancement. When scholarly work is both personal and political, and, in the case of all the critical work examined here, poetic as well, academic fields of study and the lives made possible within are transformed.

. . .

NOTES

1. If you answered no to this question, see Michel Foucault, *The History of Sexuality, Volume I: An Introduction,* trans. Robert Hurley (New York: Vintage Books, 1990).

2. Nearly two decades later, José Esteban Muñoz, in his book *Disidentifications: Queers of Color and the Performance of Politics* (Minneapolis: University of Minnesota, 1999), suggests a similar practice in the work of queer performers of color, which he terms "Queer World-Making."

3. For a foundational text on the complications of invisible or unmarked status of Anglo and male identity categorizations, see *All the Women Are White, All the Blacks Are Men, But Some of Us Are Brave: Black Feminist Studies,* ed. Gloria T. Hull, Patricia Bell Scott, [and] Barbara Smith (New York: Feminist Press at City University of New York, 2003).

THEORIZING AND TROUBLING THE BODY

In the field of women's, gender, and sexuality studies, the body has taken on a particular significance because our understandings of its key terms—such as trans/cis, wo/men, gender, and sexuality—are often "performed" through the body. As Margrit Shildrick and Janet Price point out in their anthology, *Feminist Theory and the Body*, "feminism has from the start been deeply concerned with the body—either as something to be rejected in the pursuit of intellectual equality according to a masculinist standard, or as something to be reclaimed as the very essence of the female" (2–3). Beyond feminist theorizing, the body has indeed been important "to all forms of theory" (Shildrick and Price 2).

In this section, we pose questions that allow students to further theorize and trouble the body: why does the body (and/or its parts, i.e., skin, hair, rectum, etc.) become a contested and important site and source for theorizing? How do we theorize the body while simultaneously problematizing its very biological and social constructions? What are the problems with theorizing about the body? How does dis/embodiment work in the virtual world and in our theorizing about the body—particularly as it experiences and expresses pleasure and power? And, lastly, whose or which body matters sociopolitically and in our theorizing?

This section addresses these questions by focusing on feminist and queer modes of theorizing from and about the body. Selected essays are chosen to launch us into critical conversations about the body as it changes and ages, becomes diseased and deceased, and into a scholarly examination of the narratives and feelings surrounding these shifts. By the end of the section, students will have learned the myriad ways in which scholars in the field have theorized and troubled the body, and hold it as a critical and crucial site of knowledge production.

RETURNING TO THE BODY: WHICH/WHOSE/WHAT BODIES?

This subsection begins with Trinh T. Minh-Ha's essay, "Write Your Body," originally published in 2009 and reprinted here, because it delivers a theoretical pathway that leads us toward a critical understanding of how theorizing (and) the body is approached in this book: that theorizing itself is an embodied practice. We need to write, feel, think, and theorize, in her words, "(with) our entire bodies rather than only (with) our minds or hearts" (203). Knowledge itself can even be considered, according to Elizabeth Grosz, as "a product of a bodily drive to live and conquer" (*Space* 37). The body therefore has a crucial relationship with knowledge production. In Minh-Ha's essay, "our" body refers specifically to the female body—often falsely constructed as it may be, as "intrinsically unpredictable, leaky and disruptive" (Shildrick and Price 2). Minh-Ha's insistence that women should write with their entire body can thus be read as an attempt to value the female body and reposition the body as something that is not outside of and separate from us—as something we "*have*"— but rather, as something that we "*are*" (203). Moreover, and just as importantly, her essay begins this subsection as it forces us, or rather, becomes a force in our theory-work, to frame the body not only as discursive but also as material bodies.

What does the *materiality* of the body refer to? How is it different from an understanding of the body as *discursive*? A Discursive body means that its performativity and legibility depends on specific ways of thinking—such as through medical, religious, and racial discourses, and so forth—that shape its meanings. Racial discourses, for example, provide socially constructed meanings for the color of our skin or the texture of our hair—meanings that are then translated into how others will think of and treat us in different and often hierarchical ways because of our skin color. To think of the materiality of the body, then, is to pay attention to the "corporeality" of the body—the body as a living, breathing, or even dying entity, without essentializing or reducing it simply to its biology (Kuhlmann and Babitsch 434; Grosz, *Volatile*). For Jay Prosser, "the body's materiality" can be understood as "its fleshiness, its nonplasticity, and its nonperformativity" (62).

Certainly, by making a gesture to focus on the materiality of the body, this book does not succumb to the idea that the body is only meaningful as a material body. We consider this stance as a way to bring back the corporeality of the body that has often been overlooked in "Western philosophical thought and contemporary feminist theory" (Grosz, *Volatile* 3) and only perceived as a "route to analyzing power, technology, discourse, language" (Prosser 13), rather than an important subject/object of analysis in itself.

Analyzing the body only as a discursive body misses how different material practices shape the body, quite literally (Bakare-Yusuf 313). The food we eat, the exercises we do, and the beauty practices that we perform are all examples of how the discursive body *and* the materiality of the body are articulated through each other. For instance, while eating reminds us of the materiality of the body that *needs* to be fed to continue to exist, what kind of food—organic, low calorie, vegan, gluten-free diet, how many times and when we eat, why and how we eat—and what kind of body we want to have are practices whose meanings are often shaped through particular discourses about the body.

Some key scholars in the field have indeed paved the way for a perspective on the body that emphasizes and highlights the materiality of the body while acknowledging its intricate relationship with the discursive body. Anne Balsamo, for example, considers that the body is "a site of the mutually constitutive interaction between discourses *about* the body and the materiality *of* specific bodies" (*Technologies* 163). For Donna Haraway, "the material female body is actually constructed by and within discourse" (quoted in Balsamo, *Technologies* 12).

Sitting at the liminal point between nature and nurture, the body, according to Grosz, is an "open materiality" (*Volatile* 191). Grosz even offers a new term called "corporeal feminism" that considers how "(1) the body is a central symbolic resource for cultural work; (2) the discursive, symbolic body and the material body are mutually determining; and, (3) gender is often a submerged discourse within many studies of the body and culture" (quoted in Balsamo, *Technologies* 11).

The interview-style essay that follows Minh-Ha's texts takes us further into this complex relationship between the material and the discursive body. James Burford and Sam Orchard's 2014 piece, "Chubby Boys with Strap-ons: Queering Fat Transmasculine Embodiment" is a conversation between James Burford and Sam Orchard, a New-Zealand based creator of a weekly web-comic *Rooster Tail* about his experiences on transitioning and embodying what he calls a fat transgender body. This essay weaves together narratives of the materiality of the body (i.e., his experience of going to an endocrinologist and being told to lose nine kilograms before he can be prescribed testosterone) and the discursive body (i.e., the experience of trying to love his "fat" trans body in a fat- and trans-phobic world that tells him otherwise). Burford and Orchard's interview piece that simultaneously highlights both material/medical as well as subjectivity/representation/discourse is important here because works that focus on the materiality of the trans body, as Prosser astutely observes, often "isolate medical discourses to the exclusion of subjective accounts. . . . The transsexual appears as medicine's passive effect, a kind of unwitting technological product: transsexual subject only because subject to medical technology" (7). Burford and Orchard's essay, on the other hand, challenges this dichotomy and critically examines subjectivities, medical discourses, and materiality of the body in ways that highlight how each is articulated through the others.

Christina Lux's poem, "Wildlife Refuge" (new), which comes after Burford and Orchard's essay, continues to address the medical/discursive body but shifts its focus to cis women's health—in particular, how a woman would feel during a breast cancer screening. Her poem invites us to ponder: can the lump be figured as a seed, a sign of new, perhaps hopeful, life? How may we think of the body differently through the metaphor of the seed? At its core, Lux's poem invites us to think about technology, science, and their relationship to women's bodies, an issue that Chikako Takeshita also addresses in her 2011 piece on the IUD, "'Keep Life Simple': Body/Technology Relationships in Racialized Global Contexts" (included here). In her work, Takeshita focuses on Mirena's marketing strategy and its use among women in the Global North to show "the transnational and racial political economies of women's bodies, health, and reproductive interests" (220). She shows us how certain technological and bodily practices further perpetuate inequality and how IUD discourse constructs subjects that are racialized and class based. While some women's bodies are consumers of medical devices, others are framed as "overproducing fertility machines" (231). As such, her text speaks directly to conversations about reproductive justice in a global context, especially ones that aim to "challenge global capitalist priorities—the structures that keep resources scarce for the many and plentiful for the few" (Briggs et al. 122).

The next essay takes students into a journey beyond human bodies. This book makes an effort to challenge the field's dominant focus on human bodies by insisting that animal bodies and their sexual behavior also matter when producing critical feminist and queer theories. Stacy Alaimo's 2010 piece, "Eluding Capture: The Science, Culture, and Pleasure of 'Queer' Animals" invites students to "look to queer animals, not as a moral model or embodiment of some static universal law, but in order to find, in this astounding biological exuberance, a sense of vast diversity, deviance . . . and a proliferation of astonishing differences that make nonsense of biological reductionism" (236). Alaimo's essay is also important in challenging the flawed discourse that frames homosexual behavior as unnatural and only belonging to the human world. In bringing non-human subjects into the conversation about bodies, this first subsection hopes to make visible and denaturalize both heteronormativity and hierarchy that exist among different species. We need to be mindful, for example, when we compare a person to an animal or a non-human subject by way of words such as someone is in "a vegetative state," that it is often used as a way to lessen their subjectivity or as a racist or ableist offense (Kim 297). The advertisement during the late nineteenth century United States that likened Chinese people to rats (or referring to their hair as "tail"), for example, relies on the racist logic that stereotypes Chinese people as rats who could "stir up fears of infection," and who were considered less than the assumed-superior White human race (Chen 110).

From *living* human and non-human bodies, this subsection then moves to *dead* bodies. Joanne Clarke Dillman's essay, "'Dominated, Opened and Entered': Theorizing the Dead Woman in Contemporary Media Representation" (new), the last essay in this section, takes up the issue of dead women's bodies in media, specifically in two television series: *The Bridge* and *The Killing*. It shows us how "women often have brutal, slow deaths, and their bodies are often posed in a graphic, sexualized fashion"; whereas "the deaths and corpses of male characters tend to be treated differently" (248). By way of understanding how we treat the body of dead women in media, we would understand whose bodies, whose lives matter. As Sharon Patricia Holland argues, if we want to know a nation, we can examine how it "treats its dead" (Holland 18). Although it may seem that the line separating living and dead bodies is clear, in reality, it may be neither simple nor straightforward. As Jasbir Puar asks, "Where does a body—and its aliveness—begin and where does it end? If we view information itself as a form of life (or life itself as a compendium of information) we might be led to ask: What is a life? When does it begin and end? And, who owns it? What defines living? In turn, what counts as a death—as dying?" (164). Indeed, technology may support certain racialized/gendered/sexualized bodies to live longer, but not other bodies. In other words, the merging of the materiality of the body with the discursive body can be understood by way of examining which bodies are considered worthy of living. Which and how bodies should die or be treated after their death is ultimately about the body as both a materiality and a discourse, which is the main thread that is carried throughout this first subsection.

TROUBLING BODIES, TROUBLED BODIES

The essays included in this second subsection focus on bodies that are perceived as troubled as well as those that create trouble. Here, trouble is not necessarily considered a "bad" thing. Judith Butler's 1990 work, "Gender Trouble, Feminist Theory and Psychoanalytic Discourse" launches this subsection to help students understand how "trouble" could be employed as a productive trope or a constructive launch pad to unpack the very assumption about gender and its relationship to bodies. This text—no longer representative of Butler's most current theoretical work because she has revised her thinking of gender performativity in *Undoing Gender* (2004)—remains canonical and important as it marked a historical shift, indeed a new direction in the field, by challenging definitions of sex and gender. In it, she argues that sex, like gender, is also socially constructed, that gender is performative, and we perform gender through the repetitive acts that we do through and with our bodies. Prior to the publication of Butler's books in the early 1990s, sex (equated with biology, or "nature") is often put in juxtaposition with gender (understood as socially constructed, or "nurture"). In the case of bodies in drag, for instance, she makes clear that "in imitating gender, drag implicitly reveals the imitative structure of gender itself" (263).

Further questioning the meanings of bodies and sexualities as they travel in a transnational context, Hendri Yulius Wijaya's essay, "The Queer Child in Transnational Indonesia: Fear, Futurity, and Rectum Politics" (new) shows us how because "LGBT movements are gaining momentum across the globe [that] they provoke fear and anti-LGBT sentiments in Indonesia" (269). In other words, rather than providing a catalyst for progressive changes for LGBTQPAI+ communities in Indonesia, global LGBTQPAI+ movements provoke fear in Indonesia. It is this fear that drove AILA (An Islamic pro-family group also known as Family Love Alliance) to demand that same-sex practices between consented adults be criminalized—only homosexual practices that involve persons under the age of eighteen are considered illegal.

Queer bodies have also been perceived to create troubles in the context of "family togetherness." Drawing on affect theories in a transnational context, Vanita Reddy, in her essay, "Family Togetherness, Affect Aliens, and the Ugly Feelings of Being Included" (new) shows us how family gathering often exposes the aggressive heteronormative love that structures how particular bodies are grouped together in ways that produce "ugly feelings" for "affect aliens"—"subjects who feel out of line with an affective community when [they] do not experience 'pleasure from proximity to objects that are already attributed as being good'" (272). For instance, "certain subjects are grouped together for photographs and/or are photographed more often—parents with their children, or married or dating or engaged couples" (271). In the process, this structure of body arrangements (that regulates which bodies become "legible in the hetero-repro-generational terms" or are considered problematic) affectively alienates people whose lives "are lived out of sync and out of pace with this economy of love—the uncoupled cousin, the queer (spinster) aunt, the divorced uncle, the widowed mother who chooses to remain single, the bachelor, the femme boy-child" (272).

This subsection ends with a poem, Kimberly Dark's "It Was a Lovely Dinner" (new) to bring us full circle to Butler's notion of gender performativity that begins this subsection. Specifically, Dark addresses how women perform their gender through their body hair—an issue that has become "the last taboo," seen as both trivial and monstrous at the same time (Lesnik-Oberstein 2). Her poem exposes the complexity of how women are always questioned no matter what they do with their hair. To leave them as they are, to lead a "mammal life," as she calls it, is to be seen as "unkempt." To shave them, however, is to be perceived to infantilize one's self. Women's bodies and their hair are thus seen as already and always problematic.

Questioning and interrogating when, which, whose, where, and how certain bodies are deemed troubling and creating trouble through a myriad of thought-provoking examples in this subsection thus allows students to see how power works through the body, and how (micro-)managing these bodies and their performativity of gender and sexuality has been crucial to the maintenance of the power hierarchy. Consequently, feminist and queer theorists have grappled and made central "the body" in their analyses.

BODIES, SEX, AND DESIRE: EMBODYING POWER

The third subsection is intended to continue the conversation in the second subsection on how power operates through the body. However, it shifts its focus from bodies considered as troubled/troubling and oppressed (in the second subsection) to bodies as a site of embodying, articulating, and challenging power (in this subsection). More specifically, this subsection interrogates the articulation of power and/in/through the body by way of issues of desire and the erotic. Hence, Audre Lorde's essay, "The Uses of the Erotic: The Erotic as Power" (first published in 1978) is included here to open and ground this subsection. Lorde's essay is powerful in redefining erotic as "an internal sense of satisfaction to which, once we have experienced it, we know we can aspire"; and arguing that when women embody their erotic power, they are "less willing to accept powerlessness, or those other supplied states of being which are not native to [them], such as resignation, despair, self-effacement, depression, self-denial" (279). Because accessing power of the erotic empowers women, and empowered women are considered "dangerous," women are then "taught to separate the erotic demand from most vital areas of [their] lives other than sex" (240). It is therefore important, she argues, that women reclaim their erotic power.

Annamarie Jagose's 2014 book chapter, "Counterfeit Pleasures: Fake Orgasm and Queer Agency" follows the conversation on women's body through her analysis of fake orgasm. In this text, Jagose points out that if fake orgasm were to be read through a Foucauldian lens, such a heterosexual act may be seen as "evidence of a feminine docility consistent with the disciplinary regimes of normalization" (287). Reading it from a different perspective that highlights female agency, she argues, fake orgasm can be understood as "a sexual practice in its own right" and "as a positive cultural practice, an erotic invention that emerges from a set of culturally specific circumstances as a widespread sexual observance, a new disposition or way of managing one's self in sexual relations. Fake orgasm, therefore, is not simply the simulation of orgasm but a dense complex of effects enfolding an indexically female, twentieth-century heterosexual practice" (291). Her work thus shifts our understanding of fake orgasm from a signifier of powerlessness to an empowering mode of sexual articulation and performativity for women.

Also demonstrating how women use their body as a means of articulating power specifically in the digital age, Karina Eileraas Karakuş's essay, "An (Im)modest Revolution?: Nudity, Modest Fashion, and Cultural Appropriation on the Global Runway" (new), analyzes the "modest fashion revolution . . . alongside the nude protest of Aliaa Elmahdy in

Egypt during the 'Arab Spring' to understand how women's bodies and their relationship to dress bear particularly revolutionary meanings that assume heightened symbolic power in the digital age" (296). She contends that "nude protest and the modest fashion movement raise crucial questions about the meanings of sexual and national fantasy, desire, fear, identity, and citizenship, especially relative to historical debates and legislation that seek to regulate how, under what circumstances, and for whose pleasure and benefit women's bodies are authorized to appear or perceived to 'belong' in the public sphere" (296). In bringing the digital world into the conversation about bodies, Karakuş's essay forces us to think about the (im)possibilities of body in the virtual world. Although the virtual world has been imagined to free us from the limitation of the body, "a body-free universe," it has unfortunately reinforced rather than challenged the physical world's racist/hetero/sexist stereotypes (Balsamo, "Forms of" 284). At the same time, however, the digital world has provided more marginalized people with various spaces and platforms to be present and articulate their voices, and thus challenges and creates some ruptures to contemporary power structure.

In sum, all of the essays included in this section would help students comprehend how the body is shaped through both its discursivity and materiality—its biological and social constructions, why certain human/non-human/living/dead bodies and their parts (i.e., hair, rectum, etc.) matter more or are considered more troubling than others, and how power works through the body and thence how the body functions as a site of power articulation, as well as a productive site of feminist and queer theorizing.

REFERENCES

Bakare-Yusuf, Bibi. "The Economy of Violence: Black Bodies and the Unspeakable Terror." *Feminist Theory and the Body: A Reader*, edited by Janet Price and Margrit Shildrick. Routledge, 1999, pp. 311–23.

Balsamo, Anne. "Forms of Technological Embodiment: Reading the Body in Contemporary Culture." *Feminist Theory and the Body: A Reader*, edited by Janet Price and Margrit Shildrick. Routledge, 1999, pp. 278–89.

Balsamo, Anne. *Technologies of the Gendered Body: Reading Cyborg Women*. Duke University Press, 1999.

Briggs, Laura et al. "Roundtable: Reproductive Technologies and Reproductive Justice." *Frontiers: A Journal of Women Studies*, vol. 34, no. 3, 2013, pp. 102–25.

Chen, Mel Y. *Animacies: Biopolitics, Racial Mattering, and Queer Affect*. Duke University Press, 2012.

Grosz, Elizabeth. *Space, Time, and Perversion: Essays on The Politics of Bodies*. Routledge, 1995.

Grosz, Elizabeth. *Volatile Bodies: Toward a Theory of Corporeal Feminism*. Indiana University Press, 1994.

Holland, Sharon. *Raising the Dead: Readings of Death and (Black) Subjectivity*. Duke University Press, 2000.

Kim, Eunjung. "Unbecoming Human: An Ethics of Objects." *GLQ: A Journal of Lesbian and Gay Studies*, vol. 21, no. 2–3, 2015, pp. 295–320.

Kuhlmann, Ellen and Birgit Babitsch. "Bodies, Health, Gender: Bridging Feminist Theories and Women's Health." *Women's Studies International Forum*, vol. 25, no. 4, 2002, pp. 433–42.

Lesnik-Oberstein, Karin. "The Last Taboo: Women, Body Hair and Feminism." *The Last Taboo: Women and Body Hair*, edited by Karin Lesnik-Oberstein. Manchester University Press, 2006, pp. 1–17.

Prosser, Jay. *Second Skins: The Body Narratives of Transsexuality*. Columbia University Press, 1998.

Puar, Jasbir. "Prognosis Time: Towards a Geopolitics of Affect, Debility and Capacity." *Women & Performance: A Journal of Feminist Theory*, vol. 19, no. 2, 2009, pp. 161–72.

Shildrick, Margrit and Janet Price. "Openings on the Body: A Critical Introduction." *Feminist Theory and the Body: A Reader*, edited by Janet Price and Margrit Shildrick. Routledge, 1999, pp. 1–16.

21. WRITE YOUR BODY

It wrote itself through me. "Women must write through their bodies." Must not let themselves be driven away from their bodies. Must thoroughly rethink the body to re-appropriate femininity. Must not however exalt the body, not favor any of its parts formerly forbidden. Must perceive it in its integrity. Must and must-nots, their absolution and power. When armors and defense mechanisms are removed, when new awareness of life is brought into previously deadened areas of the body, women begin to experience writing/the world differently. This is exciting and also very scary. For it takes time to be able to tolerate greater aliveness. Hence the recurrence of musts and must-nots. As soon as a barrier is destroyed, another is immediately erected. Call it reform or expansion. Or else, well-defined liberation revolution. Closure and openness, again, are one ongoing process: we do not *have* bodies, we *are* our bodies, and we are ourselves while being the world. Who can endure constant open-endedness? Who can keep on living completely exposed? We write—think and feel—(with) our entire bodies rather than only (with) our minds or hearts. It is a perversion to consider thought the product of one specialized organ, the brain, and feeling, that of the heart. The past convention was that we desire because we are incomplete, that we are always searching for that other missing half. More recently, we no longer desire-because, we simply desire, and we desire as we are. "I am a being of desire, therefore a being of words," said Nicole Brossard, "a being who looks for her body and looks for the body of the other: for me, this is the whole history of writing."[1] Gathering the fragments of a divided, repressed body and reaching out to the other does not necessarily imply a lack or a deficiency. In writing themselves, women have attempted to render noisy and audible all that had been silenced in phallocentric discourse. "Your body must be heard," Hélène Cixous insists, "[Women] must invent the impregnable language that will wreck partitions, classes and rhetorics, regulations and codes."[2] Touch me and let me touch you, for the private is political. Language wavers with desire. It is "the language of my entrails," a skin with which I caress and feel the other, a body capable of receiving as well as giving: nurturing and procreating. Let it enter and let it go; writing myself into existence also means emptying myself of all that I can empty out—all that constitutes Old Spontaneous/Premeditated Me—without ceasing from being. "Every woman is the woman of all women" (Clarice Lispector). Taking in any voice that goes through me, I/i will answer every time someone says: I. One woman within another, eternally. "Writing as a woman. I am becoming more and more aware of this," notes Anaïs Nin, "All that happens in the real womb, not in the womb fabricated by man as a substitute . . . . woman's creation far from being like man's must be exactly like her creation of children, that is it must come out of her own blood, englobed by her womb, nourished by her own milk. It must be a human creation, of flesh, it must be different from man's abstractions."[3] Man is not content with referring to his creation as to his child, he is also keen on appropriating the life-giving act of childbearing. Images of men "in labor" and "giving birth" to poems, essays, and books abound in literature. Such an encroachment on women's domain has been considered natural, for the writer is said to be either genderless or bisexual. He is able to chat with both man's and woman's voices. This is how the womb is fabricated. Women began to be spoken of as if they were wombs on two feet when the fetus was described as a citizen, the womb was declared state property, legislation was passed to control it, and midwifery

Trinh T. Minh-Ha, "Write Your Body," *Woman, Native, Other: Writing Postcoloniality and Feminism* (Bloomington, IN: Indiana University Press, 2009): 36–44.

was kept under continual medical supervision—in other words, when women were denied the right to create. Or not to create. With their bodies. "All that happens in the real womb": writing as an "intrinsic" child/birth process takes on different qualities in women's contexts. No man claims to speak from the womb, women do. Their site of fertilization, they often insist, is the womb, not the mind. Their inner gestation is in the womb, not in the mind. The mind is therefore no longer opposed to the heart; it is, rather, perceived as part of the womb, being "englobed by it." Men name "womb" to separate a part of woman from woman (to separate it from the rest that forms her: body and mind), making it possible to lay legal claim to it. By doing so, they create their own contradictions and come round to identifying her with their fabrication: a specialized, infant-producing organ. Women use "womb" to re-appropriate it and re-unite (or re-differ) themselves, their bodies, their places of production. This may simply mean beating the master at his own game. But it may also mean asserting difference on differences. In the first case, the question is chiefly that of erecting inverted images and defying prohibitions. Annie Leclerc wrote:

> Let me first tell you where I get what I'm saying from, I get it from me, woman, and from my woman's belly. . . . Who would have told me, will I ever be able to tell, from what words shall I weave the bewildering happiness of pregnancy, the very rending, overwhelming happiness of giving birth. . . .
>
> So much the worst for him, I will have to speak of the joys of my sex, no, no, not the joys of my mind, virtue or feminine sensitivity, the joys of my woman's belly, my woman's vagina, my woman's breasts, sumptuous joys of which you have no idea at all.
>
> I will have to speak of them since it is only from them that a new, woman speech will be born.
>
> We will have to divulge what you have so relentlessly put in solitary confinement, for that is what all our other repressions build themselves upon.[4]

Woman's writing becomes "organic writing," "nurturing-writing" (*nour-ricriture*), resisting separation. It becomes a "connoting material," a "kneading dough," a "linguistic flesh." And it draws its corporeal fluidity from images of water—a water from the source, a deep, subterranean water that trickles in the womb, a meandering river, a flow of life, of words running over or slowly dripping down the pages. This keeping-alive and life-giving water exists simultaneously as the writer's ink, the mother's milk, the woman's blood and menstruation.[5] Logical backlash? An eye for an eye, a tooth for a tooth. Not quite, it seems. A woman's ink of blood for a man's ink of semen (an image found, for example, in Jacques Derrida's hymeneal fable: a sexual union in which the pen writes its in/dis/semination in the always folded/never single space of the hymen). In the second case—that of asserting difference on differences—the question of writing (as a) woman is brought a step further. Liquid/ocean associated with woman/mother is not just a facile play on words inherited from nineteenth-century Romantics (*mer-mère* in French). Motherhood as lived by woman often has little to do with motherhood as experienced by men. The mother cannot be reduced to the mother-hen, the wet-nurse, the year-round cook, the family maid, or the clutching, fear-inspiring matron. Mother of God, of all wo/mankind, she is role-free, non-Name, a force that refuses to be fragmented but suffocates codes (Cixous). In her maternal love, she is neither possessed nor possessive, neither binding nor detached nor neutral. For a life to maintain another life, the touch has to be infinitely delicate: precise, attentive, and swift, so as not to pull, track, rush, crush, or smother.[6] Bruised, half-alive, or dead is often the fate of what comes within the masculine grip. Woman, as Cixous defines her, is a whole—"whole composed of parts that are wholes"—through which language is born over and over again. (The One is the All and the All is the One; and yet the One remains the One and the All the All. Not two, not One either. This is what Zen has been repeating for centuries.) To the classic conception of bisexuality, the self-effacing, merger-type of bisexuality, Cixous opposes "The *other bisexuality* . . . that is, each one's location in self (*repérage en soi*) of the presence—variously manifest and insistent according to each person, male or female—or both sexes, nonexclusion either of the difference or of one sex, and, from this 'self-permission,' multiplication of the effects of the inscription of desire, over all parts of my body and the other body."[7] The notion of "bisexual, hence neuter" writing together with the fantasy of a "total" being are concepts that many men have actively promoted to do away with differentiation. Androgyny is another name for such a co-optation. Saying that a great mind is androgynous (and *God knows* how many times we have heard this line—supposedly from Coleridge—and in how many disguises it appears) is equivalent to saying that "the mind has no sex" (also read "no gender"). In the salvation theme of androgyny, the male is still seen as the active power of generation and the female as the passive one (a defective male, due to the absence of androgen). Thus Janice Raymond suggests as a substitute the word "integrity"; she expands it and redefines it as "an unfolding process of becoming. It contains within itself an insatiable generativeness, that is, a compulsion to reproduce itself in every diverse fashion."[8] In every diverse fashion . . . Laying claim to the specificity of women's sexuality and the rights pertaining to it is a step we have to go through in order to make ourselves heard; in order to beat the master at his own game. But reducing everything to the order of sex does not, obviously, allow us to depart from a discourse directed within the apparatuses of sexuality. Writing does not translate bisexuality. It (does not express language but) fares across it.

THE BODY IN THEORY

It must be different from man's abstractions. Different from man's androgenization. Man's fragmentization. Ego is an identification with the mind. When ego develops, the head takes over and exerts a tyrannical control over the rest of the body. (The world created must be defended against foreign infiltration.) But thought is as much a product of the eye, the finger, or the foot as it is of the brain. If it is a question of fragmenting so as to decentralize instead of dividing so as to conquer, then what is needed is perhaps not a clean erasure but rather a constant displacement of the two-by-two system of division to which analytical thinking is often subjected. In many cases emphasis is necessarily placed upon a reversal of the hierarchy implied in the opposition between mind and body, spiritual and material, thinking and feeling, abstract and concrete, theory and practice. However, to prevent this counter-stance from freezing into a dogma (in which the dominance-submission patterns remain unchanged), the strategy of mere reversal needs to be displaced

further, that is to say, neither simply renounced nor accepted as an end in itself. In spite of the distant association, one example that comes to mind are the procedures which in Asia postulate not one, not two, but three centers in the human being: the intellectual (the *path*), the emotional (the *oth*), and the vital (the *kath*). The martial arts concentrate on developing awareness of the latter, which they call the *tantien* or the *hara*. This center, located below the navel (the oth being connected with the heart, and the path with reason), radiates life. It directs vital movement and allows one to relate to the world with instinctual immediacy. But instinct(ual immediacy) here is not opposed to reason, for it lies outside the classical realm of duality assigned to the sensible and the intelligible. So does certain women's womb writing, which neither separates the body from the mind nor sets the latter against the heart (an attitude which would lead us back to the writing-as-birth-delivering-labor concept and to the biologico-metaphorization of women's bodies previously discussed) but allows each part of the body to become infused with consciousness. Again, bring a new awareness of life into previously forgotten, silenced, or deadened areas of the body. Consciousness here is not the result of an accumulation of knowledge and experience but the term of an ongoing unsettling process. The formula "Know thyself" has become obsolete. We don't want to observe our organism from a safe distance. We do not just write about our body, whether in a demonstrative (objectivist) or a submissive (subjectivist) discourse. Knowledge leads no more to openings than to closures. The idealized quest for knowledge and power makes it often difficult to admit that enlightenment (as exemplified by the West) often brings about endarkenment. More light, less darkness. More darkness, less light. It is a question of degrees, and these are two degrees of one phenomenon. By attempting to *exclude* one (darkness) for the sake of the other (light), the modernist project of building universal knowledge has indulged itself in such self-gratifying oppositions as civilization/primitivism, progress/backwardness, evolution/stagnation. With the decline of the colonial idea of advancement in rationality and liberty, what becomes more obvious is the necessity to reactivate that very part of the modernist project at its *nascent* stage: the radical calling into question, in every undertaking, of everything that one tends to take for granted—which is a (pre- and postmodernist) stage that should remain constant. No Authority no Order can be safe from criticism. Between knowledge and power, there is room for knowledge-without-power. Or knowledge at rest—"the end of myths, the erosion of utopia, the rigor of taut patience,"[9] as Maurice Blanchot puts it. The terrain remains fresh for it cannot be occupied, not even by its specific creator. The questions that arise continue to provoke answers, but none will dominate as long as the ground-clearing activity is at work. Can knowledge circulate without a position of mastery? Can it be conveyed without the exercise of power? No, because there is no end to understanding power relations which are rooted deep in the social nexus—not merely added to society nor easily locatable so that we can just radically do away with them. Yes, however, because in-between grounds always exist, and cracks and interstices are like gaps of fresh air that keep on being suppressed because they tend to render more visible the failures operating in every system. Perhaps mastery need not coincide with power. Then we would have to rethink mastery in terms of non-master, and we would have to rewrite women's relation to theory. "Writing the body" may be immediately heard by a number of male or genderless writers as "imitating" or "duplicating the body." It may be further read as "female self-aggrandizement" or "female neurosis." (It falls on deaf ears, most likely. . . .) *There is no such thing as a direct relation to the body*, they assert. For them writing the body means writing *closer* to the body, which is understood as being able to express itself directly without any social mediation. The biological remains here conveniently separate from the sociohistorical, and the question "where does the social stop in the biological?" and vice versa, is not dealt with. They read "writing the body" as "the (biological) body writing itself." They either can't hear the difference or believe there is only *one way* of hearing it: the way they define it. Putting an end to further explorations they often react with anger: *that's not deep enough! What is it supposed to mean?* If we take the case of Roland Barthes, who also passionately writes the (impetus of the) body, the question of depth and meaning no longer exerts its tyranny: he might be fetishist, some of them admit, but We love his fetishism;

it's *intelligently* written! and theoretically sound! Through the works of a number of male writers, "writing the body" may be accepted as a concept because attempts at theorizing it have been carried out, and it has its own place as theoretical object. But when this concept-practice is materialized, the chance of its being understood or even recognized as such never goes without struggle. On the one hand it is a commonplace to say that "theoretical" usually refers to inaccessible texts that are addressed to a privileged, predominantly male social group. Hence, to many men's ears it is synonymous with "profound," "serious," "substantial," "scientific," "consequential," "thoughtful," or "thought-engaging"; and to many women's ears, equivalent to "masculine," "hermetic," "elitist," and "specialized," therefore "neutral," "impersonal," "purely mental," "unfeeling," "disengaging," and—last but not least—"abstract." On the other hand, it is equally common to observe that theory threatens, for it can upset rooted ideologies by exposing the mechanics of their workings. It shakes established canons and questions every norm validated as "natural" or "human." And it undermines a powerful tradition of "aesthetics" and "scholarship" in the liberal arts, in the humanities as well as in the social sciences. To say this is also to say that theory is suspicious, as long as it remains an occupied territory. Indeed, theory no longer is theoretical when it loses sight of its own conditional nature, takes no risk in speculation, and circulates as a form of administrative inquisition. Theory oppresses, when it wills or perpetuates existing power relations, when it presents itself as a means to exert authority—the Voice of Knowledge. In the passage from the heard, seen, smelled, tasted, and touched to the told and the written, language has taken place. Yet in the articulation of language, what is referred to, phenomenally and philosophically, is no more important than what is at work, linguistically, in the referring activity. To declare, for example, that so-and-so is an authority on such-and-such matter (implying thereby that s/he has written with authority on the subject concerned and that this authority is recognized by his/her peers) is to lose sight of the radicalness of writing and theorizing. It is to confuse the materiality of the thing named—or the object of discussion—with the materiality of the name—the modalities of production and reception of meaning—and to give up all attempt at understanding the very social and historical reality of the tools one uses to unmask ideological mystifications—including the mystification of theory. What is at stake is not so much the referential function of language as the authority of language as a model for natural cognition and a transparent medium for criticizing and theorizing. The battle continues, as it should, on several fronts. If it is quite current today to state that language functions according to principles that are not necessarily (like) those of the phenomenal world, it is still unusual to encounter instances where theory involved the voiding, rather than the affirming or even reiterating, of theoretical categories. Instances where poeticalness is not primarily an aesthetic response, nor literariness merely a question of pure verbalism. And instances where the borderline between theoretical and non-theoretical writings is blurred and questioned, so that theory and poetry necessarily mesh, both determined by an awareness of the sign and the destabilization of the meaning and writing subject. To be lost, to encounter impasse, to fall, and to desire both fall and impasse—isn't this what happens to the body in theory? For, in theorizing, can women afford to forget, as Marguerite Duras puts it, that "men are the ones who started to speak, to speak alone and for everyone else, on behalf of everyone else. . . . They activated the old language, enlisted the aid of the old way of theorizing, in order to relate, to recount, to explain this new situation"?[10] Indeed, women rarely count among those whom Catherine Clément describes as being "greedy of the slightest theoretical breaking of wind that is formulated, eager not to miss any coach of a passing train in which they hop in flocks behind their chief, whoever he may be, provided that they are not alone and that it is a question of things of the mind."[11] Difference needs not be suppressed in the name of Theory. And theory as a tool of survival needs to be rethought in relation to gender in discursive practice. Generally speaking, it is not difficult to agree with Duras that "men don't translate. They begin from a theoretical platform that is already in place, already elaborated. [Whereas] the writing of women is really translated from the unknown, like a new way of communicating rather than an already formed language. But to achieve that, we have to turn away from

plagiarism." More specifically speaking, however, it is difficult to be content with statements she puts forth such as: "Reverse everything. Make women the point of departure in judging, make darkness the point of departure in judging what men call light, make obscurity the point of departure in judging what men call clarity. . . ."[12] Unless "point of departure" is constantly re-emphasized so that, again, reversal strategies do not become end points in themselves. Language defying language has to find its own place, in which claiming the right to language and disqualifying this same right work together without leading to the mystical, much-indulged-in angst that pervades many men's works. By its necessary tautness, writing the body in theory sometimes chokes to the breaking point. But the break, like the fall and impasse mentioned earlier, is desired. I do not write simply to destroy, conserve, or transmit. To re-appropriate a few sentences of Blanchot's, I write in the thrall of the impossible (feminine ethnic) real, that share of the detour of inscription which is always a de-scription.[13] From jagged transitions between the analytical and the poetical to the disruptive, always shifting fluidity of a headless and bottomless storytelling, what is exposed in this text is the inscription and de-scription of a non-unitary female subject of color through her engagement, therefore also disengagement, with master discourses. Mastery ensures the transmission of knowledge; the dominant discourse for transmitting is one "that annihilates sexual difference—where there is no question of it." "Her discourse, even when 'theoretical' or political, is never simple or linear or 'objectivized,' universalized; she involves her story in history" (Cixous).[14] Like Monique Wittig's and Sande Zeig's bearers of fables, women "are constantly moving, they recount, among other things, the metamorphosis of words from one place to another. *They* themselves *change* versions of these metamorphoses, *not in order to further confuse the matter but because they record the changes.* The result of these changes is an avoidance of fixed meanings. . . . They agree upon the words that they do not want to forgo. Then they decide, according to their groups, communities, islands, continents, on the possible tribute to be paid for the words. When that is decided, they pay it (or they do not pay it). Those who do so call this pleasantly 'to write one's life with one's blood,' this, they say, is the least they can do."[15] "Writing the body" is that abstract-concrete, personal-political realm of excess not fully contained by writing's unifying structural forces. Its physicality (vocality, tactility, touch, resonance), or edging and margin, exceeds the rationalized "clarity" of communicative structures and cannot be fully explained by any analysis. It is a way of making theory in gender, of making of theory a politics of everyday life, thereby re-writing the ethnic female subject as site of differences. It is on such a site and in such a context that resistance to theory yields more than one reading. It may be a mere form of anti-intellectualism—a dis-ease that dwells on the totalizing concept of theory and practice and partakes in the Master's norms of clarity and accessibility while perpetuating the myth of the elite versus the mass, of those who think versus those who do not think. It may also be a distrust of the use of language about language and could be viewed in terms of both resistance and attraction to language itself. For to say that language is caught within a culturally and sexually dominent ideology is not to deny the heterogeneous history of its formation or, in other words, to refuse to "see race, class *and* gender determinations in the formation of language" (Gayatri C. Spivak).[16] Woman as subject can only redefine while being defined by language. Whatever the position taken ("no position" is also a position, for "I am not political" is a way of accepting "my politics is someone else's"), the love-hate,

inside-outside, subject-of-subject-to relation between woman and language is inevitably always at work. That holds true in every case—whether she assumes language is a given, hence the task of the writer is merely to build vocabularies and choose among the existing possibilities; whether she decides to "steal" demonstrative and discursive discourse from men (Clément), since language cannot free itself from the male-is-norm ideology and its subsuming masculine terms; whether she asserts that language is primarily a tool for transmitting knowledge, therefore there is no attributable difference between masculine and feminine writing and no shift needs to be made (in language and) in metalanguage, whose repressive operations "see to it that the moment women open their mouths—women more often than men—they are immediately asked in whose name and from what theoretical standpoint they are speaking, who is their master and where they are coming from: they have, in short, to salute . . . and show their identity papers";[17] whether she affirms that language is heterogeneous, claims her right to it, and feels no qualms in reproducing existing power relations because she has discoursed on this issue; or whether she insists that the production of woman-texts is not possible without a writing that inscribes "femininity," just as writing woman cannot address the question of difference and change (it cannot be a political reflection) without reflecting and working on language.

NOTES

1. Quoted by Karen Gould in "Setting Words Free: Feminist Writing in Quebec," *Signs* 6, no. 4 (Summer 1981), p. 629.
2. Hélène Cixous, "The Laugh of the Medusa," trans. K. Cohen and P. Cohen, *Signs* 1, no. 4 (Summer 1976), pp. 880, 886.
3. Anaïs Nin, "Diary," *By A Woman Writt*, pp. 294, 299.
4. Annie Leclerc, *Paroles de femme* (Paris: Grasset, 1974), pp. 11–12 (my translation).
5. For a detailed analysis of these images, see Irma Garcia, *Promenade femmilière*, vol. 2 (Paris: Des Femmes, 1981).
6. I have discussed the relationship between body, mother, cry (voice), hand, and life in Trinh T. Minh-ha, "L'innécriture: Féminisme et littérature," *French Forum* 8, no. 1 (January 1983), pp. 45–63.
7. Cixous, "The Laugh of the Medusa," p. 884.
8. Janice Raymond, "The Illusion of Androgyny," *Quest* 2, no. 1 (Summer 1975), p. 66.

9. Maurice Blanchot, *The Writing of the Disaster,* trans. A. Smock (Lincoln: Univ. of Nebraska Press, 1986), p. 38.

10. Marguerite Duras, "Smothered Creativity," *New French Feminism,* ed. E. Marks & I. de Courtivon (Amherst: Univ. of Massachusetts Press, 1980), p. 111.

11. Catherine Clément. *Les Fils de Freud sont fatigués* (Paris: Grasset, 1978), p. 137 (my translation).

12. Duras, in *New French Feminism,* pp. 174–75.

13. Blanchot, *The Writing of the Disaster,* p. 38.

14. Hélène Cixous & Catherine Clément, *The Newly Born Woman,* trans. Betsy Wing (Minneapolis: Univ. of Minnesota Press, 1986), pp. 146, 92.

15. Monique Wittig & Sande Zeig, *Lesbian Peoples. Material for a Dictionary* (New York: Avon, 1979), p. 166.

16. Gayatri Chakravorty Spivak, Interview, *Art Network* 16 (Winter 1985), p. 26.

17. Cixous, "Castration or Decapitation?" *Signs* 7, no. 1 (Autumn 1981), p. 51.

JAMES BURFORD AND SAM ORCHARD

22. CHUBBY BOYS WITH STRAP-ONS: QUEERING FAT TRANSMASCULINE EMBODIMENT

INTRODUCTION

Rooster Tails is a weekly web-comic that has followed Sam Orchard's transition from "shy girl" to "awkward semi-butch chubby nerd" since 2010. Orchard's comic has contributed to an emerging archive of cultural work around fat transgender embodiment, including among others, Wyatt Riot's writing and video work and the writing and tumblring of Mey DJneres (e.g., 2013). Our present text is nourished by an emerging community of scholarship that connects transgender embodiment, food and body size (see Bergman 2009, Cooper 2012, Watson-Russel 2012). In activist conversations, and increasingly in academic ones (e.g., Vade and Solovay 2009), the connections between transgender and fat rights struggles have been articulated. A clear pathway into analysis has been to examine the ways in which both fat and trans* people, and fat trans* people, are expected to reproduce societal value systems—that is: fat people *should want* to become thin, and trans* people *should* want to be model examples of the binary gender system. Often, these values emerge through the figures of the "trans* person trapped in the wrong body" and/ or "thin person trapped in a fat body." Orchard's comics trouble both of these accounts, and therefore have the potential to prompt and invigorate future conversations in the intersecting fields of trans* and fat studies. While not intended as such, we also suggest our work might serve as a response to some fat studies research, and conversations in fat activisms, that make encompassing claims about representing trans* fat embodiment by invoking acronyms like LGBT. Too often we have found that such promises of inclusion fail to deliver. Indeed, sometimes the "t" appears to be mere relish adorning

and "inclusifying" the main meal of lesbian and gay studies. This is an issue we address, in a small way, by publishing a conversation between two people who (at the time of writing) shelter under the broad trans* umbrella, and focus on accounts of fat embodiment in trans* cultural work.

Our text is a co-constructed conversation between the two authors. It is a product of an extended series of email exchanges during the early months of 2013, which were then worked into a dialogic text. In taking up this methodology of representation, we intended to create a "messy text" (Marcus 1998)—a break with the representational technologies of traditional writing forms. We are attracted to the potential of such texts to resist dichotomous thinking by proliferating different and indeed divergent accounts. Working in this way frees us as authors to disagree with each other, and ourselves. In response, we invite you (the reader) to read this text differently. . . . As for the conversation itself, we suggest you might wish to read it aloud. Perhaps you will notice which senses are activated, what thoughts come to mind, and which feelings are evoked. Consider which of our words you may wish to spit out, and those you wish to savour. We'd ask you, too, to observe the moments where you might wish to speak back—what is it that you want to say, and how do you want to say it?

> Sam, it's a real pleasure to have a chance to speak to you about your comics. I'd like to begin by acknowledging that yours is an autobiographical project about your transition, so your body and the changes it goes through are always in your comics, and will be at the centre of our talk. It is then—in a spirit of co-authorial fairness—that I'd also like to "come out"

about my embodiment. Rather than tell (my? a?) story its traditional way from "the beginning," I'd like to start with right now. From the perspective of an outsider looking at me as I type, I imagine (fantasise) they would see me as a camp, cis-male person who is plump. If they were to address me, they would almost certainly use male pronouns. If they looked harder still they might notice my queer deportment, my large rings, my too-sweet fragrance, and colourful clothing. My size would likely go unremarked, except perhaps as tall, or "solid." When I chat with my doctor; they sometimes admonish me to lose some weight, but are generally surprised to find out that, according to abstract measures such as the BMI, my body falls within the "obese" category (maybe I've been training?). Unfortunately, this "coming out" doesn't really satisfy me. It doesn't tell much about my own attachments, the way my body has travelled through time, or my subjective feelings about it—and perhaps such a story is for another chapter. I would like the reader to be in possession of a couple of extra clues however: While today I may be read as both relatively "male" and "average" sized, my body bears the marks of weight loss, and gain. I am also a person who has lived experience of non-normative gender identity and expression, and the social costs and many pleasures associated with this.

Sam, in looking through *Rooster Tails* from 2010 to the present it's clear that over the years there have been some changes in the way you draw yourself. You seem to have become bigger in the comic, and increasingly represent yourself with a squishy tummy. Does this represent changes to your own body over this time, or is it more about your increasing comfort around including the fullness of your body in your work?

I think the changes are a combination of my drawing ability/style, actual changes in my body size, and my increasing comfort with my own fatness. When I first started *Rooster Tails*, I drew all characters with big heads and skinny necks/bodies. This was probably a result of my drawing ability and finding my own style, as well as my level of comfort with fatness in general.

I think that my consciousness of fat-phobia and fat-pride has been developing over the last four years, and that gets reflected through the increasingly diverse body shapes I draw in my comics. My critical consciousness around fat issues is in constant development, and has also been very much connected to my transition (by transition I don't mean medical interventions of testosterone—although that has played a part in changing my body shape—I mean thinking about and embodying ways of living as a transmasculine person).

As a young girl I was very conscious of weight. I was a chubby teen, and felt very uncomfortable about my tummy. I spent a good number of years with my arms wrapped around my waist, in an attempt to hide my stomach. For teenage women weight is seen as an indicator of attractiveness, and certainly my weight contributed to my feeling that I was "failing" at being a girl. When I came out as someone who was attracted to women, and entered into dyke communities, I was surprised and heartened by the level of acceptance around body diversity, and how my chubbiness contributed to making me a "successful" butch. Then, as I began transitioning towards the masculine/boy end of the gender spectrum, and engaging with gay male and transmale communities, I began experiencing body-policing again. This was obviously different to that which I experienced as a girl, but involved similar messages around "fat is bad/unattractive." Within small gay male communities, I felt as though I had to be super skinny, or super ripped to be attractive to other men. Within transmasculine communities, I felt as though weight was seen as feminine, or, rather, as feminising, as in: "urgh, look at my curves." Then, as I moved to larger queer communities, with more bear scenes, the discourses around "sexiness" and body weight changed again.

These transitions and differing community expectations caused me to think about weight and body issues. As well as the fact that I have a partner who finds chubby people attractive. It has caused me to examine my relationship with my body, as well as my relationship to different communities' values around body weight and attractiveness. I think over time I've made a point of talking about chubby bodies, particularly chubby trans* bodies, in a positive way, so as to disrupt some of those negative discourses. And, as I am a chubby transguy myself, who writes an autobiographical comic, depicting my own embodiment has been a part of that.

As a reader, I appreciate the intimacy of your work, in particular your willingness to allow us to witness paradoxical thoughts. I'm thinking here of a series of comics in 2011 which explored your feelings about your own body size. You indicated that you were planning to lose weight in order to feel more comfortable binding in the heat and humidity of Auckland, but also because your endocrinologist told you to. . . . These accounts sit alongside others in your collection which are more assertive, calling out fat phobia, and proliferating positive images of chubby trans* guys. In bringing this up, it's not my intention to point out "bad (fat) politics," instead I am interested in how these kinds of inconsistencies are actually quite consistent with my own experience, and possibly the experiences of others who are not thin. Even though, as a queer and feminist knowledge worker, I critique discourses around body normativities, I do at times, actually quite often, desire to be thinner. I also, with varying degrees of commitment, engage in exercise. Increasingly, this is exercise that I frame as a project around feeling good about moving in my body, but other times, if I am honest, it is undertaken by a disciplining self who wants to trim and tighten. Being able to see these moments of ambivalence in your work is important for me as a reader. It is an invitation to reflect on the messiness of practicing a progressive fat politics, and experiencing our own desires about our bodies in a world structured by fat-shaming and obesity hysteria. How do you feel about these paradoxes in your work?

Like you said, these inconsistencies have been consistent with how I experience, and value, my body. Just as we live in a heterosexist/cissexist world and we have to constantly deal with our own internalised homo/trans phobias, so too do we have to deal with our internalised fat phobias in a fat phobic world.

For me, I have found it really hard to work out how to love myself, and love my body, in the face of a world that quite consistently points out its unattractiveness. Whether I'm unattractive because I'm a perceived-female-bodied butch person, a perceived-male-bodied femme person (or just a generally non-normatively gendered person), or I'm unattractive because I'm queer-looking, or I'm unattractive 'cause I have curves,

it all impacts my self-esteem. It also makes it hard to fight against, in a world where mass media bombards me with messages that whatever I'm doing with my body, I'm "not doing it right." So, yeah, I think my analysis is fraught, 'cause *I* feel fraught about it. *I* find it hard to keep positive, and to continue loving myself when the world is telling me I shouldn't.

I don't see people like me on television or in films, I've never seen someone who looks like me being portrayed as attractive. I feel really sad about that. I feel sad because I can't change mainstream media. I feel sad that I buy into it. I feel sad that even when my boyfriend tells me that he finds me/my body attractive, I think he's only saying that to be "nice" to me. On a political level, I know that fat phobia exists, and it's awful, and I can be critical of it—but I also feel the impacts of it, and know it influences how I feel about myself, and that's incredibly disheartening. I want to be able to be empowered and stand up and say "fuck you all, my body is fearless, and amazing, and curvy and delicious!" and sometimes I can, and I do that. So, I think that the inconsistencies in my comics are a reflection of where I'm at.

Yes, I think this is an important issue to talk about in a number of activist communities, where there seems to be an expectation that our politics will neatly fit with our experience, [t]hat we won't or at least shouldn't feel ashamed, guilty or depressed about our bodies, and if we do this should be quickly tidied up and repackaged. Reflecting back on my community development practice, I am aware that I have done this myself. I recall facilitating a support group and trying to steer conversations about fatness away from painful, complex or ambivalent feelings and toward "good" ones, like pride. But I feel we can lose something when we do this, potentially something quite critical. This phenomenon of paradoxes seems to connect with some important articles I have read in the field of fat studies, like Robyn Longhurst's (2011) autoethnography about her experience of simultaneously critiquing and desiring slimness, and Karen Throsby and Debra Gimilin's (2010) work in the same vein. It also reminds me of Samantha Murray's (2005) work on the guilt of potentially "selling out" on her fat politics by engaging in a dieting practice.

Yep, I agree—I think that for me it's about finding a way to work from a strengths perspective, while still owning that part of our strength comes from the resilience we develop from dealing with the hard stuff that internalised and externalised phobias bring with them. I think there's a way to own both the awesome stuff and the hard stuff in a way that values our whole selves, without going down the "only positivity is accepted" route, or the "we are all victims" route.

> The other thing I noticed about the 2011 comic was the line about your endocrinologist, what happened there?

Yes, the endocrinologist experience . . . sigh. It has required a lot of processing to find a "strengths" perspective from the whole ordeal. In 2011, I decided, after many years, of living as Sam and being a dude, that I was in a place where taking testosterone was important for me. I don't want to use the term "physical transition" here, 'cause I feel like I had already been doing that for years, but this was the first time that I had sought medical interventions, and it was in the form of starting hormones.

I was referred to a doctor at the sexual health clinic in Auckland, who is not actually an endocrinologist, but at the time had become the go-to doctor to refer trans* patients . . . to. In New Zealand there isn't a standard pathway for care when it comes to medical transitions, so trans* people often have really different experiences of accessing/attempting to access hormones. This has been outlined in the New Zealand Human Rights Commission's report *To be who I am/ Kia noho au ki toku ano ao*, which has found that the provision of public health services to be "patchy and inconsistent [with] major gaps in availability, accessibility, acceptability and quality of medical services required by a trans* person seeking to transition" (2008: 50). In this instance, the doctor in question had set criteria that he used to assess whether he would write prescriptions for hormones. One criterion that he used was weight. He used the BMI to assess me, and said he would only prescribe me testosterone if I lost 9kgs.

I felt like I'd been kicked in the guts. The whole process left me feeling heartbroken and humiliated. I had been living as a guy for three years at that point, had been thinking about gender my whole life, and had finally decided that I felt "ready" to begin taking testosterone. Instead of an informed consent model, where a doctor points out the risks and benefits of medical intervention (which I had already researched myself when it came to testosterone), I felt like I was being told by a father figure "no, you're not allowed that, you haven't been good enough, show me that you really want it and then maybe I'll let you."

This was a first for me. No doctor had ever told me to lose weight, or refused to prescribe me medication because of my weight. I went home and researched the BMI, and found out about how problematic it is around gender (as well as culture/race). I had no idea whether my doctor was using the scale for me as a "female" or "male," he never explained to me why the BMI was important in terms of transitioning, he just told me that I should lose the weight or it would be too "dangerous" to prescribe me testosterone, and that I should probably join Weight Watchers or Jenny Craig (I was a student at the time, with no disposable income, which meant this was a financial impossibility from the outset).

I talked to my partner, and to close friends (I was too humiliated at the time to talk with others about it), and got reassurance that he was a dick . . . but I still took the doctor's words on board. Doctors were supposed to know best, they were supposed to be kind, they were supposed to know how to keep us healthy— was I being precocious thinking that I knew better than him? Was I making excuses about my body? I felt like a failure. And I felt angry at myself for feeling like a failure. As I look back on it now, this comic reminds me of that feeling of holding that inconsistent subjectivity— simultaneously feeling outraged as well as awful and insecure. I wanted to punch the doctor, but I also felt that I really had to lose the weight because otherwise I would continue to be a "bad fat person" who didn't "deserve" to go on T.[1] It was really rough. In my comics I often use Joe (the character of my boyfriend) as a sounding board to explore alternative perspectives on an issue. This was true for one of my comics around this issue; I felt like I was oscillating between Joe's outrage and my own shame.

> I recall that time myself, both reading your comic and talking with you. I remember feeling angry about the way you had been treated, and a kind of aching

despair that trans* friends, and some of the university students I was doing advocacy with, seemed compelled to follow often mindless medical dictates, not only with regard to fatness, but around gender identity too. But in this case you kind of outmanoeuvred the doctor, right? Joe organised a fundraiser among friends so you could pay to go to another endo' who gave you the prescription.

Yes, in the end I knew that I would end up in a much worse position (physically and emotionally) if I tried to lose the weight. It would impact my self-esteem, my relationship with my body (which was already quite fraught), my relationship to food (which is a huge part of my self-care), and my relationship with Joe. It also felt like I was colluding with the doctor, and I really didn't feel like I could do that. So, yeah, I was lucky enough to have a partner who fundraised for me to go to a private endocrinologist, and bypass the public system altogether. It meant that I didn't battle to change the structural oppression, but it did enable me to get the interventions I needed. It's important to acknowledge here that not everyone has the resources, whether financial or cultural, to beat the system in this way.

> For the next couple of questions, I'd like to broaden out our conversation to examine the social context in which your work is produced. It is clear that discussions about fat are not only common with health workers. As you touched on earlier, discussions about fatness seem to take particular routes in transmasculine communities and media. How have you seen these play out?

There's some real diversity in the way that weight is discussed in various communities, a majority of the time there is a "fat = bad" message, but that can come from a variety of places. Part of identity is about finding yourself in the reflection of others. I had never seen a transmasculine person (that I knew of) on television or in real life before I was 24. The only one I can think of was Hilary Swank's Brandon Teena in *Boy's Don't Cry*, and I had always seen that character written about as a lesbian who dressed like a boy, so I didn't make the "trans" connection. I had no idea that we existed. So, when I met my first transguy and things clicked into place ("aha! that is me too!"), I began looking for

more and more reflections. I was living in Dunedin, a small city in the South Island, so there was a tiny pool of transguys to pester.

I took to the Internet, as I had when coming out as someone who liked women, to see what I could find. My experiences of Internet-based transmasculinity, through tumblrs, Facebook groups, etc., were often white-centric and skinny. These groups told me that curves were bad—because "girls" had curves, and so being less feminine meant being skinny, or being muscly, but definitely not being curvy. This seemed particularly true for noho (no masculinising hormones) boys (like me at the time)—without testosterone redistributing fat away from your hips and butt, you should do everything in your power to make them as small as possible, because that would mean you would be more likely to "pass." Passing is a fraught term, and is not the ideal for everyone, but that is a whole other discussion.

> I have noticed a couple of alternative discourses that constitute fat transmasculine embodiment in seemingly contradictory ways. My primary exposure is to a discourse which emphasises the benefits of losing fat, or more specifically engaging in diet and exercise in order to try and lose certain curves that might normatively be read as cis-feminine, in favour of "angularity." An example of this can be seen in a post by blogger Elliot DeLine on the website originalplumming.com. He observed that his ideal transmasculine embodiment would be "the cute, skinny, hipster boy" or the "intellectual, emo twink" (DeLine 2012). We can also see this in the work of Kyle Lukoff who speaks about his experience with anorexia, and his attempts to "starv[e] away" breasts and hips (Lukoff 2010: 123). But DeLine's skinny, hipster boy seems quite a different kind of trans masculine embodiment to that described by S. Bear Bergman in her chapter "Part-time Fatso" (2009. In this work Bergman positions "bulk" as something that can be helpful for giving male cues.

I think there are some interesting differences between the "socially acceptable weight" in different community contexts. There's something about bulk that can be read as a masculine indicator. This is true for when I'm being read in the context of bear communities; not being a twink is regarded [as] hot. Similarly, in heterosexual cis-male spaces, size can be read as relating to power, and being able to take up space. It's interesting that fatness, thinness and muscle bulk can be seen as positives for male/masculine people, whereas women/feminine people are supposed to be neither muscular nor fat. I feel as though there's a bit more room to move within male spaces.

I feel that when I'm being read as a woman, or within transmasculine communities, my weight is more likely to be seen as a sign of weakness. It is more likely to be read within discourses around failure—too curvy to be seen as male, or too fat to be attractive. The weakness is expressed through the related ideas that fatness is a result of "not having enough self-control/ discipline," or being "too lazy."

> Bergman has also reflected on the significant differences ze has encountered in public space whether ze is read as a fat woman or transmasculine butch person, as ze puts it ze is "Fat one minute (as a woman) and just a big boy in the next," with resulting differences in whether ze is assumed to want a diet coke or a side of fries. Mey DJneres (2013) has also examined this from her perspective as a fat trans woman, noting that when she began presenting as a woman her size became "fair play" for both public negativity as well as fetishisation. Have you noticed changes in the way your body is received as you have transitioned?

I was more likely to be policed around my body when I presented as a girl. It seems more socially acceptable to offer suggestions, or just plain make assumptions about food choices (like that you should be drinking diet coke if you're a woman, or that you shouldn't be ordering the extra-large with a side of whatever). I have definitely noticed a shift in the portion sizes that I'm given in dining halls, or even at friend's places—I'll be offered more, and seconds, without hesitation these days. Whereas before, people seemed to be embarrassed (I was definitely also embarrassed) to offer me seconds, thirds, or fourths— because it is seen as "breaking the rules" or shameful for girls to eat a lot. When I was younger, my brothers and I would have eating competitions at home. But, as I became a teenager, it became "gross," "unladylike"

and embarrassing for everyone if I tried to partake in those sorts of competitions.

> Now I'd like to talk about your 2011 collection "Chubby boys with strap-ons." As we have spoken about previously, fatness, or as you have put it "curviness" is often constituted as feminine, or pretransition. In particular, the curves of the chest, butt and thighs, which are often read as indexing cis-feminine embodiment. Was "Chubby boys with strap-ons" a direct response to this?

Yes! I wanted to create art that would disrupt the audience(s).

I wanted to have a direct conversation with the transmasculine Internet communities that I had engaged with to disrupt the value that was being placed on skinny (white) transmasculine bodies. I wanted to show that boys with curves are hot, boys of all colours are hot. It was intended to be a "fuck you, I'm sexy" response to the common discourses that I felt de-valued me.

The other direct conversation I wanted to have was with a cis-centric audience. I had drawn an illustration of Wolverine a few years ago for my university magazine's queer issue. The picture was of Wolverine wearing just boots and a harness with a bright yellow dildo. It was really wonderful how many cis-centric people just didn't understand it—"why is he wearing a strap-on if he's a guy?" I wanted to recreate this image with more "real" transboys (because as much as I'd like Wolverine to be trans*, I am not sure that any of the X-Men creators really envisioned that for him). The idea of having erotic boys wearing strap-ons with dildos, in empowered poses, felt like it was an important disruption of what sexiness could look like, and what sexy men could look like.

I think that one of the things that happens when we live in a phallo-centric society is that the penis becomes one of the most central thoughts for people. This seems especially true for both sexuality and gender identity; with cis gay men it seems society gets fascinated about which partner's dick goes into what orifice, with cis lesbians there seems to be a focus on questioning about whether you can "really" have sex if there's no dick present, with trans women the conversations revolve around whether she still has got "that part" or if she's "had the surgery," and the opposite is true for transguys. So I wanted to really disrupt that conversation—to show a silicone phallus—to highlight the construction of gender (they literally put on their dicks, or dildos, depending on how they identify)—to show that a silicone dick/dildo is just as sexy as one made from skin and nerves—to disrupt the idea that trans bodies are somehow "lacking" or "embarrassing."

> "All my curves are sexy" and "All man" *[images]* seem like important pieces of work. In the first of these you have created a transmasculine figure with a large and unbound chest, and in the second a figure with large hips and butt. But it is not only the images that do work. Throughout this collection the text also seems to assert different modes of discourse about the transmasculine body. What I find most striking is the way that it creates an erotic politics for fat trans guys. Your boys are naked and erect. They look directly at us and smile, or dance. It seems they are not only celebrated—but you have gone further and positioned curvy-transmasculine embodiment as both desired and desirable. Your boys are sexy, and they know it.

Yes they are! I think a lot of the time I have felt that I (and people with my body type/shape/gender identity) should feel ashamed, ugly and undesirable. So this was a reaction to that. These boys love the way they look. I especially love the "All my curves are sexy"

boy, because he is being cheeky, and proudly showing off his curvy chest. I think that's so important, especially since a really dominant narrative around trans* people is that we hate our bodies, and transguys especially hate the parts that are seen to be "feminine" like our hips and our breasts/chests/pecs.

> Your project seems fabulously queer. Not only does your work queer transmasculine embodiment and identity, by proliferating alternative and (to some) incoherent images and accounts of masculinities, it seems to me that your comic makes an important contribution to queering fat transmasculine embodiment by your representation of yourself, and your boys, as masculine and chubby, desirable and desired. Can we expect more work of this kind?

I hope that my work will continue to challenge norms of desire, and celebrate difference. Part of the reason I started creating comics was because there was a lack of media that represented and celebrated me and the people that I love. I spent a long time feeling sad about that, and critiquing it, and then felt empowered enough to say "fuck it, if 'they're' not going to create it, then I am." I have so many questions and I love complications in our embodiments and our identities—I find that interesting and compelling, so I think that I'll just keep exploring that stuff, asking questions, trying things, and see what happens.

NOTE

1. Testosterone.

REFERENCES

Bergman, S. B. 2009. Part-time fatso, in *The Fat Studies Reader*, edited by S. Solovay and E. Rothblum. New York: New York University Press, 139–142.

Cooper, C. 2012. A queer and trans fat activist timeline: Queering fat activist nationality and cultural imperialism. *Fat Studies: An Interdisciplinary Journal of Body Weight and Society*, 1(1), 61–74.

DeLine, E. 2012. Timid boy, eating. *Original Plumming*. [Online, 9 February] Available at: http://www.originalplumbing.com/2012/02/09/timid-boy-eating/ [accessed 3 May 2013].

DJneres, M. 2013. Fat, trans and (working on being) fine with it. *Autostraddle*. [Online, 28 March] Available at: http://www.autostraddle.com/fat-trans-and-working-on-being-fine-with-it-168108/ [accessed 3 May 2013].

New Zealand Human Rights Commission. 2008. To be who I am/kia noho au ki toku ano ao, the report of the Transgender Inquiry. Human Rights Commission.

Longhurst, R. 2011. Becoming smaller: Autobiographical spaces of weight loss. *Antipode*, 44(3), 1–21.

Lukoff, K. 2010. Taking up space, in *Gender Outlaws. The Next Generation*, edited by K. Bornstein and S. B. Bergman. Berkeley: Seal Press, 122–127.

Marcus, G. 1998. *Ethnography through Thick and Thin*. Princeton: Princeton University Press.

Murray, S. 2005. Doing politics or selling out? Living the fat body. *Women's Studies: An Interdisciplinary Journal*, 34(3–4), 265–277.

Throsby, K. and Gimilin, D. 2010. Critiquing thinness and wanting to be thin, in *Secrecy and Silence in the Research Process: Feminist Reflections*, edited by R. Ryan-Flood and R. Gill. Oxon Routledge, 105–116.

Vade, D. and Solovay, S. 2009. No apology: Shared struggles in fat and transgender law, in *The Fat Studies Reader*, edited by E. Rothblum and S. Solovay. New York: New York University Press, 167–175.

Watson-Russel, D. (2012). Growing Boys: Trans* Male Narratives on Food and the Construction of Bodies, unpublished dissertation, La Trobe University.

23. WILDLIFE REFUGE

reeds perfectly painted,
sway, not quite bow;
boy, yellow-hooded coat,
blue binoculars bouncing,
running, camera in hand,
so not to miss
a scurrying squirrel,
an egret taking off.
i hoped to snap a photo
of him myself, my son,
meandering
down the curve of the path,
not anticipating
he would come running, my boy,
eager to discover
the magic of creation.
as yesterday,

holding a slice of orange
up to the window's light:
see mom? this is how you tell
it has a seed!
it was near translucent,
the veins showing,
the seed a small nodule.
not unlike my right breast,
which the nurse practitioner
kneaded, kept kneading, kneading,
asked me to knead:
do you feel that?
to me it felt
like that nodule and the veins
in the translucent orange,
or perhaps . . . a few seeds.

Context: Wildlife refuge visit after breast cancer screening at Planned Parenthood, December 2016.

24. "KEEP LIFE SIMPLE": BODY/TECHNOLOGY RELATIONSHIPS IN RACIALIZED GLOBAL CONTEXTS

After the birth of my second child in 2005, I had my second IUD inserted. This time it was a Mirena, which releases a synthetic progestin, levonorgestrel, from an intrauterine capsule and prevents pregnancy for five years without replacement. The device is one of the most effective contraceptive methods, comparable to surgical sterilization. In clinical trials, the pregnancy rate was less than 1 percent, and fertility returned to normal levels after users discontinued the device. The ParaGard, the other IUD product available in the United States, is a copper-bearing IUD that lasts ten years. Although the two types of devices have similar contraceptive efficacy and reversibility, users of the two different devices typically experience significantly different side effects. Whereas the copper T tends to increase menstrual bleeding and cramping, the levonorgestrel-releasing IUD (LNG-IUD) reduces them. Clinical trials found that menstrual bleeding completely stops in 20 percent of Mirena users, a condition known as amenorrhea.

Several months after the Mirena insertion, I developed amenorrhea, which I embraced. As someone not particularly attached to menstruation as something that defines my femininity, I greatly appreciated not having to endure the inconveniences and physical discomfort that accompanied the monthly period. As an environmentalist, I was pleased not to have to produce any more tampon and sanitary napkin trash. This was a wonderfully liberating corporeal experience.[1] Mirena users who post their experience on the Internet often echo my sentiment. One thirty-five-year-old woman, for instance, wrote, "I LOVE my Mirena. . . . Mirena has made me feel free, not moody, no pain, no period."[2] Internet postings also reveal, however, that a significant

number of women are experiencing undesirable side effects such as weight gain, mood swings, and loss of libido. These symptoms were not frequently observed in clinical trials but nevertheless are real and bothersome for these women.[3] Still other postings indicate that many women who are on Mirena after having tried other contraceptive methods are satisfied with the device. Sometimes Internet blogs mention the women's gynecologists, who are equally enthusiastic about this highly effective contraceptive. These doctors believe the device is safe and free of adverse side effects, and they view the altered menstrual pattern in a favorable light.

Mirena is marketed successfully within a pharmaceutical-marketing rubric of "lifestyle drugs." In other words, when a woman has a positive Mirena experience, the device is functioning as a pharmaceutical product that "promise[s] a refashioning of the material body with transformative life-enhancing results."[4] In recent years, pharmacological therapies claiming to treat baldness, sleep difficulties, excessive weight gain, mild depression, general aging, and sexual performance have become increasingly popular. These medications are not treatments for serious diseases. Rather, they treat or prevent various mild conditions that are often labeled a "problem." Taking a drug not only resolves the problem, but may also enhance the individual's life experience and productivity. For instance, low libido is now considered to be a health issue that can be fixed by medication for erectile dysfunction, which could simultaneously contribute to a man's overall well-being by increasing his sexual appetite, restoring what he perceives to be his manliness, and improving his outlook on life.[5] Similarly, decreased productivity at work might be treated

---

Takeshita, Chikako. *The Global Biopolitics of the IUD: How Science Constructs Contraceptive Users and Women's Bodies* (Cambridge, MA: MIT Press, 2011). Copyright © 2011 MIT Press. All rights reserved. Notes were renumbered.

with antidepressants, which are presumed to lift one's mood and help get through tasks more easily.[6]

Menstrual regulation and suppression medications that have become popular are yet another type of lifestyle drug. Feminist scholars Laura Mamo and Jennifer Fosket show that menstruation is cast as inconvenient, undesirable, and even unnatural in the marketing campaigns of Seasonale, the first oral contraceptive to reduce the number of menstrual periods from twelve to four a year. Various similar products are now being offered as a seemingly natural solution to what is sometimes viewed as a nagging female problem. By changing the material body, lifestyle drugs transform life from the inside out. Direct marketing to consumers of pharmaceutical products communicate this idea by presenting images of people whose lives are positively transformed by the medication.

When Mirena appeared on the TV screen around 2007, the commercial only briefly mentioned shorter, lighter periods as a common occurrence in users. Yet because the cultural narrative that renders menstrual suppression a positive lifestyle choice had already been solidified with period-reducing oral contraceptives, viewers were prepared to accept and appreciate the device's major side effect as a bodily enhancement. The advertisement, which shows a mother of three young boys appreciating her freedom from having to worry about birth control, conveys two additional ways the device improves women's lives through transforming the body. First, the ad suggests that the easy-to-use long-acting contraceptive enables a woman to "keep life simple." Second, it sends the message that retaining the option to have more children is another lifestyle choice that Mirena, a reversible method, allows a woman to make. To this end, the clip announces that the mother has "changed her mind" and concludes with a picture of her holding an adorable new baby girl standing with the rest of her happy upper-middle-class suburban white family.

To an average TV watcher, Mirena appears to be a new contraceptive product with unique features that promise to make a user's life better. The representation of the lifestyle IUD, however, obscures the history of the device and the broad spectrum of biopolitical interests that its development has engaged along the

way. This chapter examines the making of Mirena, while revealing the behind-the-scenes aspects of this now increasingly popular contraceptive method and reconstructs the historical paths that produced this device. This activity, which I call *diffraction* after Donna Haraway's optical metaphor, shows how contemporary IUDs came to be, while simultaneously grasping the multiple meanings the device now embodies. The historical trajectories that made Mirena and the copper-bearing IUD ParaGard what they are today involved creating and reinforcing inequities among women of different races, classes, nationalities, ages, and levels of modernity. By tracking the backstories of how Mirena is represented, marketed, and embodied in the global North, this chapter brings into relief the transnational and racial political economies of women's bodies, health, and reproductive interests.

FROM A POPULATION CONTROL TOOL TO A COMMERCIAL PRODUCT

The period-free IUD that some of us love was created over the course of three decades. The first study to look at the effect of intrauterine administration of hormones was supported by the Ford Foundation and published in the journal *Fertility and Sterility* in 1970.[7] The Chicago researchers who inserted progesterone-releasing capsules into the womb observed changes in the uterine lining similar to those induced by oral contraceptives. They concluded that locally administering a hormonal substance in the uterus could be a way to increase the contraceptive effectiveness of IUDs.

Using discriminatory language common at the time to describe ideal IUD users, the authors related their study to the need for population control. According to them, women "in the less advanced countries" who lack "sophistication and motivation" were good candidates for this method because it achieves prolonged contraception "without special patient cooperation."[8] Early IUD studies presumed that women of the global South were not self-motivated to contracept, which justified the need for this new birth control method that could be imposed on women who, according to the population control advocates, were otherwise unwilling to limit their fertility or incapable of doing so. Studies of hormone-releasing IUDs initially drew their justification from a perceived need to increase reproductive control over former colonial subjects.

The primary goal of adding progesterone to an IUD was to decrease pregnancy rates of the existing plastic devices, which ranged from 2.3 to 10.8 per 100 women in one year. The researchers were pleased to find that no one wearing the progesterone-releasing device got pregnant during the study. The hormonal compound available at the time, however, lasted for only about twelve weeks, making the life span of the device "too short . . . to be meaningfully used in population control."[9] Nevertheless, the authors decided that what they had observed showed enough promise to suggest further development of this method.

THE NEXT-GENERATION IUD

Research on hormone-releasing IUDs started at a time when developers were becoming frustrated with the performance of plastic IUDs. The effort to improve the inert devices by tinkering with their physical configurations seemed to take them nowhere. In the late 1960s, developers began investigating bioactive substances that could be added to IUDs to simultaneously increase contraceptive efficacy, reduce expulsion rates, and decrease bleeding and pain. The Population Council started developing copper-bearing devices with this intention in 1969. Other bioactive compounds such as estrogen and antiprogestin substances were also experimentally added to intrauterine devices, but these did not yield promising results.

This was also a time when the safety of the oral contraceptives was starting to be publicly questioned. It was becoming apparent that hormones from the oral contraceptive entering the bloodstream could cause severe headache, breast tenderness, and mood change, as well as rare but serious adverse consequences such as a fatal blood clot. This realization boosted the idea of administering hormones locally in the uterus, which theoretically would avoid systemic hormonal side effects. Within a few years, the authors of the 1970 study managed to develop a device that lasted six months. After testing it for twelve months,

they concluded that its contraceptive effect was very good, although it needed to last longer for population management.[10] By the mid-1970s, a California-based company independently developed and started marketing a one-year progesterone-releasing IUD they called Progestasert, which stayed on the market on a small scale for the next couple of decades.[11]

The development of a multiyear hormone-releasing IUD, however, had to wait for the discovery of a synthetic progestin with high potency per unit weight that can be released slowly over many years. Such a compound emerged several years later from the Population Council's work to develop a hormone-releasing subdermal contraceptive implant. Sheldon Segal recounts his excitement when the idea of the "under-the-skin pill" came to him, and he experimentally implanted capsules filled with various hormones into rats in the council's laboratory.[12] Soon after, in 1970, the Population Council established the International Committee for Contraception Research (ICCR) to facilitate collaboration among a team of international scientists. The committee embarked on the development of the subdermal contraceptive with Elsimar Coutinho of Brazil as the head of the project.[13] After testing no fewer than ten compounds and a number of different capsules and rods, the research team selected levonorgestrel as the most promising progestin and ultimately produced the contraceptive method known as the Norplant.[14]

Another ICCR scientist, Tapani Luukkainen of Finland, led the development of the levonorgestrel-releasing IUD, and after more than a decade of testing to determine the appropriate dosage through a series of clinical trials, he introduced it in Finland in 1990 with the brand name Levonova.[15] Rebranded as Mirena in some other countries, the device was inserted in approximately 1 million women around the globe before it received approval from the U.S. Food and Drug Administration (FDA) in 2000 and started being sold to American women in 2001.

THE NORPLANT SAGA

Ironically, the Norplant, to which Mirena owed its hormonal compound, had been virtually withdrawn from the American market by 2001. The social reception of the Norplant after its introduction in the United States in 1990 was "mired in controversy, suspicion, and even ethnic conflicts" due to socially problematic applications of the device.[16] The idea of the under-the-skin pill was conceived when the Population Council was seeking a superior long-acting reversible contraceptive after it had come to realize that the IUD would not fulfill its expectation to become the one-size-fits-all solution for the problem of excess fertility in the global South. Norplant was in essence the next-generation imposable method and carried with it all of the problematic assumptions about controlling what the council saw as "excessively fertile" women's bodies. The biopolitical quality embedded in the implant technology was immediately expressed in the applications of Norplant in the United States. Within a few years, lawmakers proposed more than forty bills that either mandated Norplant use for women who received government assistance or targeted women who are poor, convicted, or addicted to drug[s] and alcohol in order to prevent them from having children.[17] Norplant was also offered to poor inner-city adolescents at no cost in school-based clinics in Baltimore. The contraceptive implant was also distributed to the Native American population.[18] All of these applications were met with suspicion due to the "deep worries about discrimination in the United States on the basis of class, race, and gender."[19]

. . .

THE PROBLEM OF MENSTRUAL BLEEDING

To discuss the issue of bleeding in IUD users, it is necessary to start back once again in the late 1960s when researchers admitted that they had failed to develop an ideal plastic device. They conceded that design innovation efforts focused too much on increasing the contraceptive efficacy and uterine retention and not enough on reducing side effects. Pain and bleeding resulted in so many discontinuations of the contraceptive method that the U.S. Agency for International Development (USAID) eventually decided to prioritize funding for research on a "bloodless, comfortable IUD."[20] Incidentally, the 1970 study had found that intrauterine hormone capsules decreased uterine contractions and vaginal bleeding. IUD researchers hence characterized progesterone as a "uterine tranquilizer" and hoped

that future hormone-releasing IUDs would improve the overall efficacy of the contraceptive method by reducing cramping, pain, and bleeding.[21]

Although researchers knew these side effects were an obstacle to broader acceptance of IUDs, data to understand the problem in detail were scarce. Complaints of pain and discomfort were often characterized as psychological, and physicians dismissed them as a normal part of using the device for which certain women had low tolerance thresholds. The Cooperative Statistical Program (CSP), the multilocation large-scale statistical program that took place between 1963 and 1968 and validated the contraceptive efficacy of the IUD, reflects a lack of emphasis on women's subjective experiences. The study simply bundled "bleeding and/or pain" as a single category of reason for IUD removal.[22] It did not provide information on whether the patient requested removal because she could not tolerate menstrual cramping, had debilitating abdominal or back pain, experienced too much bleeding, found her period unacceptably prolonged, had too much midcycle spotting, or experienced some combination of symptoms. This made it impossible to analyze the relationship between side effects and removal in detail.

Because pain is difficult to measure objectively, systematic research on pain with IUD use is almost nonexistent. Blood loss, however, is quantifiable and is a source of health concern; hence, some researchers turned to measuring it in their studies. Studies found that, on average, women lose about 35 milliliters of blood during a menstrual period. Common plastic IUDs, which were larger in size and therefore more irritating to the uterus than smaller copper-bearing IUDs, increased the blood loss by 20 to 50 milliliters. The smaller copper-bearing IUDs increased blood loss by only 10 to 30 milliliters, although they prolonged the period by two days. The particular progesterone-releasing devices being tested decreased blood loss by 40 percent.[23] Although no research had confirmed that IUDs could cause anemia, developers suggested that increased menstrual bleeding might cause the health of poor women of the global South to decline since approximately half of them already had anemia or were borderline anemic. These data raised some hope in the minds of researchers that hormone-releasing IUDs might be distributed to women of the global South as protection against anemia.[24]

THE CULTURAL SIGNIFICANCE OF MENSTRUATION

In the meantime, IUD developers also began to notice that dropout rates of subjects from their studies who complained of bleeding and pain varied dramatically from place to place. A 1970 study of 14,000 users in thirty countries found that removal due to bleeding and pain was relatively rare in Europe. Yet they found significant variance in the global South. Parts of India, for example, had a much higher incidence of dropouts from studies compared to other parts of the country, whereas incidents in the Philippines were much lower.[25]

These findings prompted the Population Council to sponsor another study, this one investigating the effect of culture on IUD acceptance. Elizabeth Whelan reported that Orthodox Jewish women were five times more likely than non-Orthodox Jewish women to discontinue the IUD on account of prolonged or irregular bleeding because their religious practice mandated that women refrain from various religious, daily, and sexual activities during their period. She also identified religious texts that could have similar effects on women of other faiths.[26] Subsequently the 1979 *Population Reports*, which summarized the status of IUD research for family planning programmers and other health professionals, stated: "In countries where menstruating women are not permitted to prepare certain foods, carry on their usual household tasks, perform religious rites, or engage in sexual intercourse, any prolongation of bleeding or midcycle spotting disrupts personal and household routines. As a result, not only the IUD user but also her husband and mother-in-law may insist on removal of the device."[27] This shows that users' cultural beliefs began to be seen as part of the problem that led to the discontinuation of IUDs.

As an organization overseeing reproductive health around the globe, the World Health Organization (WHO) also recognized that menstrual disturbances, such as no bleeding, excessive bleeding, or irregular bleeding, were responsible for one-fourth to one-half of all first-year dropouts of contraceptive methods such as the IUD, progestin-only oral contraceptive, progestin-estrogen combination pill, and progesterone injection. Between 1973 and 1979, the WHO conducted an investigation of attitudes toward menstruation among 5,000 women from fourteen cultures.[28] Interviews with women affirmed that an increase in the number of bleeding days might be unacceptable in certain cultures because it interferes with day-to-day household or religious activities. Three-quarters of the Hindu women interviewed, for instance, said they avoided cooking for their families during menstruation; almost all respondents in Egypt, Indonesia, and Pakistan and three-quarters of Yugoslavian Muslim women believed that a woman should not visit temples when she is bleeding. The study also found that while many women felt that increased blood loss would make them physically weaker, some also believed that decreased blood loss would cause discomfort due to retention of blood within the body. Importantly, the study concluded that most women did not want any changes in their menstrual patterns.

As the WHO report was coming out, the Population Council discovered that its latest levonorgestrel-releasing device was experiencing a 20 percent discontinuation rate due to amenorrhea or other hormonal side effects.[29] At this early phase in the testing of the device, researchers had not understood that levonorgestrel stopped menstrual bleeding altogether in 20 percent of users. The initial high dropout rate therefore was later attributed to uninformed physicians who removed the device out of concern that was actually unwarranted. But this explanation provided only a small consolation since the WHO study had also found that the majority of women interviewed stated that they were "not prepared to accept" a contraceptive if it led to amenorrhea.[30] The rates of women rejecting amenorrhea varied from 53 percent of British women to 91 percent of Punjab women in Pakistan, while their reasons ranged from fear of impairing their health by disallowing what they viewed as "bad blood" to purge and reluctance to tamper with nature to the negative indications of menopause and infertility associated with having no periods.

Defying the original expectation that reduced blood loss and less cramping with progesterone-releasing devices would increase IUD acceptance in the global South, the 1982 *Population Reports* concluded that removal rates in several trials were similar to or worse for the hormone-releasing devices as compared to the copper-bearing ones.[31] Although levonorgestrel had achieved the "bloodless, comfortable IUD" sought by USAID, the cultural significance of menstruation appeared to be working against the acceptance of an otherwise effective device. As this perception unfolded, the conceptual division between users of the global North and South widened.

CONFIGURING THE MODERN WOMAN/CONSUMER

The WHO study also offered subtle yet significant insight into who may be more inclined to accept modern contraceptive methods that alter menstrual patterns. For instance, the report noted that beliefs associated with menstruation, such as that one should not bathe or visit the temple while bleeding, were more commonly held by "older, less educated, rural women." In contrast, a woman who was "prepared to accept" amenorrhea was reportedly "younger, better educated, [and] urban."[32] Family planning in the global South has been closely linked to the idea of modernity representing enlightenment values of secularism, rationality, scientism, and optimism for the future. As Nilanjana Chatterjee and Nancy Riley point out, the modern subject has been construed as a rational, autonomous individual who can control her environment and shape her own future by embracing scientific knowledge and technological innovations.[33] As researchers took notice of the cultural significance of menstrual disturbance, however, they began to see that some women who lacked education and led a preindustrial lifestyle were not modern enough to accept scientific methods of fertility control that change bleeding patterns.

The presumed unpreparedness of women of the global South to accept the new contraceptive was compounded by the way clinical studies in the region were interpreted and represented. An Indian study comparing the copper-bearing to the levonorgestrel-releasing device found that the continuation rate of the latter was significantly lower due to amenorrhea and irregular bleeding.[34] The seven-year study initiated by the Population Council, which took place mostly in clinics located in the global South, including Brazil, Egypt, Chile, the Dominican Republic, . . . and Singapore, also showed a better continuation rate for the copper-bearing device.[35] The double-blind test protocols that prevented physicians from providing adequate counseling about amenorrhea may have increased the number of removals in these trials. But this background was obscured when the 1995 *Population Reports* simply noted that LNG-IUD removal rates were higher than copper-bearing IUDs in the global South due to amenorrhea.[36] The report left the impression that LNG-IUD was not well suited for women in underdeveloped areas who embody premodern ideas about menstruation.

The *Population Reports* then presented a contrasting conclusion from a European study, which had resulted in less common discontinuation for bleeding and pain with the LNG-IUD than with the copper IUD.[37] The comparable success of the LNG-IUDs in the European study conducted in Denmark, Finland, Hungary, Norway, and Sweden was attributed to having provided detailed information regarding the contraceptive method to the women who received it. Health care personnel in the European trial explained to their patients how the effect of the hormone reduces the buildup of the uterine lining that sheds during menstruation. They also informed them that amenorrhea is not a sign of pregnancy or menopause, that the ovarian function is continuing even in the absence of menstruation, and that amenorrhea does not reduce the ability to conceive after removing the device. In addition, Scandinavian women were told that the LNG-IUD had a high level of effectiveness, which motivated them to continue using the method. Some were also advised of the device's benefits, such as increased hemoglobin, better iron stores, general well-being, and relief from dysmenorrhea and prolonged bleeding. Information regarding what women should expect to experience with this device as well as its health benefits were also disseminated through mass media. Tapani Luukkainen, whose name is often associated with the invention of LNG-IUDs, explains that offering open and accurate information has contributed to the acceptance of this method of contraception.[38]

Based on the positive responses in Europe, Luukkainen announced: "When adequately advised beforehand, most women who develop amenorrhea learn to like the new freedom."[39] This seemingly non-problematic statement fails to recognize that a medicalized explanation of the female reproductive system may have resonated with the women in the European study due to their cultural upbringing. Medical anthropologist Emily Martin has found that middle-class American women more readily identified with the scientific model of menstruation as compared to working-class women, who resisted medical explanations of their embodied experiences.[40] Martin's findings suggest that certain groups of women are more amenable to seeing their bodies in physiological terms, making them good candidates for accepting the information of the hormonal effects on their reproductive systems. Luukkainen does not address how "adequate advising" may work for women whose understanding of their bodies departs significantly from the medicalized version. His suggestion to educate women may certainly be effective for the middle class of the global North but does not necessarily take all women into consideration. In fact, as Stacy Pigg points out, knowledge of bodies is always cultural and there exists no neutral biological language that is equivalent across cultures. Insisting on Western scientific understandings of reproduction thus could constitute "epistemological colonization" or violence.[41]

WRITING OFF LESS MODERN WOMEN

After the comparative clinical trials in the global South showed a lower retention rate for hormonal devices, there has been little attempt to see if acceptance by these women could be improved if they were "adequately advised." In fact, interest in women who were not ready to accept amenorrhea faded as researchers turned their attention to women who might "learn to like" the period-less lifestyle. If there are indeed health benefits of this device, such advantages are being denied to women of the global South, who are implicitly written off as being not modern enough to appreciate the new technology.

Perhaps IUD developers have simply lost interest in women who they deem as less modern. But there is also little incentive for family planning supporters to strongly promote the distribution of this device overseas, now that the copper-bearing devices are widely accepted. This is particularly so since they are just as effective in preventing pregnancy and are much more economical. When asked whether USAID would provide Mirena to overseas family planning programs, Dr. James D. Shelton, senior medical scientist of the agency's Office of Population, gave this answer on his Q&A Web site, *Jim Shelton's Pearls:* "Cost is likely to be an insurmountable hurdle. . . . Bear in mind, the Copper-T-380A is an excellent and inexpensive IUD. So after factoring in the costs of introducing a new method, the advantages of Mirena would only justify USAID large-scale procurement in the face of a very attractive price."[42] This statement construes Mirena as being too expensive for aid agencies to supply to women in the global South because the copper T is an adequate cheaper alternative.

In order to close some of the economic gap, the Population Council and Mirena manufacturer Schering Oy established the International Contraceptive Access Foundation (ICA) in 2004. ICA offers a combination of donation and subsidized sale (for a maximum of $40 per device) to the public sector for a limited number of units. The ICA also conducts projects in twelve countries supporting Mirena use in family planning programs.[43] Nevertheless, the $40 price tag is still vastly more expensive than the $ 1.64 that USAID supplies the copper T for. Copper IUDs can actually be obtained as cheaply as $0.25 a unit.[44] The economic factor clearly widens the gulf between the reproductive choices of women in the global North and South.

The economic divide is present in the United States as well. Mirena costs around $500 at a doctor's office, compared to about $250 for ParaGard, in addition to the office visit charges and fees for screening tests.[45] State Medicaid programs may cover Mirena at various levels of reimbursement, and an uninsured patient whose income is below the poverty level can apply for a free device with her provider through a program funded by Bayer Healthcare Pharmaceuticals.[46] More often than not, however, women must cover all or part of the expense. Paradoxically, despite the high initial cost, IUDs, including the Mirena, are the most cost-effective form of reversible contraception.[47]

As ideas formulated regarding who would accept a device that dramatically changes menstrual patterns, who could be educated to appreciate decreased menstrual bleeding, and who could afford the high initial expenses, the original intention to promote the hormone-releasing IUD in the global South to boost contraceptive acceptance evaporated. Developers instead found new interest in applying the device's unique side effect to gynecological treatments, as we shall see next. Looking at these ironic transitions teaches us a few things: biopolitical investments in women's bodies diverge over space and time; developers transfer their interests from one type of device application to another without explicit reflections on how they perpetuate inequality; and technological practices are imagined with implicit assumptions about differences between women of the global South and North. Significantly, shifting interests kept the momentum for the exploration of hormone-releasing devices.

. . .

THE BIOPOLITICAL SCRIPT OF MENSTRUAL SUPPRESSION TECHNOLOGIES

Surpassing the device's promise for the diseased patients is the appeal that device-induced menstrual pattern changes has for general consumers. Contraceptives that are approved as menstrual management methods have paved the way for Mirena to be perceived as having a similar benefit. Less apparent is the fact that the histories of these medications are intimately linked to the development of the LNG-IUD with overlapping researchers.

IS MENSTRUATION OBSOLETE?

Contraceptive developers were paying attention to altered menstrual patterns before they became an issue for IUD users. During the 1950s, Gregory Pincus, the inventor of the first oral contraceptive, noticed that his trial subjects became distressed when they experienced amenorrhea, which led him to believe that women wanted to feel that they were menstruating naturally. Then the director of biological research of G. D. Searle, the first company to market oral contraceptives, told Pincus that he "did not want to take part in the development of any compound that might interfere with

the menstrual cycle."[48] In response, Pincus devised a way of mimicking nature by creating the seven-day bleeding period every twenty-one days, which is actually caused by taking sugar pills for a week instead of hormones.[49] The inventors of the oral contraceptive thus effectively configured a woman whose "normal" periods consist of a twenty-eight-day menstrual cycle twelve times a year.

Forty years later, contraceptive researchers started to reconfigure the menstruating subject. After decades of experience with contraceptive methods that inadvertently affected menstrual patterns, Elsimar Coutinho and Sheldon Segal, who were involved in the development of both the Norplant and the LNG-IUD, published *Is Menstruation Obsolete?* Their 1999 book contends that menstruation is "an unnecessary, avoidable byproduct of the human reproductive process."[50] The authors state that regular and recurrent menstruation throughout most of a woman's fertile years is a fairly recent phenomenon of the industrialized world: women used to have very few periods when they nursed babies for an extended period of time and gave birth multiple times throughout their reproductive lives. The authors argue that the common perception that menstruation is a natural event that is somehow beneficial to women has no scientific basis.

Since there were no products indicated for menstrual suppression on the market yet, Coutinho and Segal proposed that women should start using available methods to stop menstruation "with the cooperation and supervision of their physicians."[51] This could be done, for instance, by skipping the sugar pills in standard oral contraceptives. The authors predicted that suppressing menstruation "would forge a major advance in women's health, led by women" and that "today's proposal would become tomorrow's new paradigm."[52] Subscribing to the idea that biological differences hold women down and proposing to liberate them from their innate imperative, the authors quoted the most prominent birth control activist of all times, ending the book by stating, "The pioneer feminist Margaret Sanger wrote 'No woman is completely free unless she has control over her own reproductive system.' Let this new freedom begin."[53] Their prediction about the new paradigm has for the most part come true. Although pharmaceutical companies, instead of women, led the way with their new products, the idea that a woman could suppress her menstruation to free herself from an unnecessary burden has taken hold among consumers in North America and Europe.

MARKETING MENSTRUAL SUPPRESSION PRODUCTS

Laura Mamo and Jennifer Fosket illustrate how Seasonale, an oral contraceptive that produces menses-like bleeding cycles four times a year, rewrote the norms of menstruation and menstruating subjects through its product campaign. In the absence of either pathology or an at-risk state that requires medication, the Seasonale campaign constructed menstruation as an inconvenience and an obstacle that the drug could eliminate. It told women, "There is no medical reason to have [a period] when you are on the pill," suggesting that since the periods that pill users experience are in effect created by the medication, reducing the frequency of unnatural periods is perfectly reasonable.[54] Its marketing discourse also "produced associations between cleanliness and femininity, between freedom of movement and women's bodies, and between limited menstrual flow and natural embodiment," thereby reconfiguring the nonmenstruating woman as desirable and feminine.[55]

Since the launch of Seasonale by Duramed Pharmaceuticals in 2003, a number of similar products have been introduced. Seasonique from Duramed also induces menstrual-like bleeding every three months. The TV commercial for this product shows a physician, who announces, "There is no medical need to have a monthly period on the pill. Lots of women are having four periods a year." Based on what she learned from the doctor, a young woman in the ad decides to use the drug, conveying to the viewers that such a decision is a logical one. A rival product, Loestrin 24 Fe from Warner Chilcott, reduces monthly bleeding to three days or less. This product is marketed with a catchphrase, "Say so long to a period that's too long." Its advertisement features Cammie, a young, active, and attractive woman living in an artsy neighborhood in New York City. Suggestive scenes of a bouquet of red roses and of a man's arm around her waist send the message that the drug produces an appealing heterosexual female body that is available for sex for more days each month. Finally, the most recent product, Lybrel from Wyeth Pharmaceuticals (now Pfizer), eliminates bleeding entirely within about six months by continuously taking progestin-estrogen combination birth control pills. As with other lifestyle drugs, modifying the material body with menstrual suppression products produces culturally and socially meaningful positive changes in the identities and lives of their users.

MIRENA'S ADDITIONAL BENEFIT AND GOVERNMENTALITY

Mirena is not explicitly marketed as a menstrual regulation product. Yet some of its informational material, such as the pamphlet provided to prescribing physicians, highlights the side effect as an "additional benefit."[56] The 2006 educational DVD for patients also promotes this aspect with an illustrative episode of an apparently athletic career-oriented woman, who recommends Mirena to her sister because she likes not having her period. The 2008 TV commercial, which introduced the product widely to prospective consumers, merely mentions a "shorter lighter period" as a common side effect. Yet since many women are already familiar with menstrual-suppression contraceptives, they are likely to interpret reduced bleeding as a bonus feature.

Women who blog about how much they love Mirena regularly attribute their satisfaction to their nonmenstruating bodies as much as they do to not having to worry about forgetting to take the pill.[57] The precedence of menstrual-suppression medications prepared Mirena users to view their experience with the device as an enhancement of lifestyle. These commercial products have reconfigured menstruation and the menstruating subjects, successfully transforming the meaning of monthly periods from a necessary part of womanly embodiment to an event that can be manipulated to suit one's lifestyle.

A biopolitical script based on market logic and capitalist lifestyle has been co-configured into menstrual-suppressing contraceptives. As Patrick Joyce points out, the emergence of liberalism in Europe "depended on cultivating a certain sort of self, one that was reflexive and self-watching."[58] The enlightened women who make conscious decisions about how they are going to manage their reproductive lives and maximize their bodily functions to live life smartly and productively are *ruled through freedom*. The marketing of this lifestyle drug relies on self-governing subjects whose desires are cultivated through the advertising, who exercise their right to manage their own fertility, and who choose to maintain their reproductive health. In the context of the American market, the biopolitical subjects of the long-acting menstrual-free IUD are largely invested in as a site of consumption rather than as an overtly fertile population. They are the subjects of liberal governmentality. A closer investigation of how IUD users are represented in product promotional materials, however, offers additional insight into how governance over women's bodies is delicately differentiated at intersections of race and class.

THE RACIAL ECONOMY OF IUD PROMOTION IN THE UNITED STATES

Marketing endorsements of IUDs today argue that the contraceptive method has advantages over the pill and barrier methods because it has long-term effectiveness that offers convenience and a lower rate of user failure. They also promote it as being favorable compared to surgical sterilization: the device's contraceptive effect is reversible, and it preserves future fertility. Not all women's reproductive choices, however, are represented equally in the advertisements. The device's benefits tend to be advertised through representations of women who are subtly differentiated in accordance with cultural expectations about how certain groups of women should regulate their reproductive capacities. While the construction of the North/South divide in IUD applications reflected ideas about modernity based on regionalized racialization and economics, promotional materials for the devices within the United States reveal that biopolitical interests are segmented based on race and class, mirroring American social relations.

Terri Kapsalis makes a similar observation in a three-page Norplant advertisement printed in a nurse practitioner's journal in 1992, arguing that they implicitly reinforce race-based reproductive politics.[59]

Both of the two white women featured in the ad have children and appear modern, wealthy, and family oriented. The first woman chose Norplant because she is mostly certain that she completed her family but would like to leave open the option of having more children, while the second one is using the implant to time the birth of the next child she plans to have. Both are photographed with their children. The African American woman in the advertisement, in contrast, has no children. Rather, she is using Norplant so that she can finish nursing school before she has a family. Kapsalis points out that the representation of the childless African American woman reflects the idea that a black woman should establish herself economically before she has children and signals that Norplant will aid this process. She argues that these advertisement images and narratives "play into current dominant constructions of proper African American women's reproductive identity."[60] I would add that a strong expectation toward family orientedness in white women is also embedded in these advertisements.

Subtle but racially distinct similar messages are present in the marketing of IUDs. Of the two products available in the United States, the ParaGard Web site shows far more diversity than the Mirena site.[61] Women represented on the Mirena site are mostly upper-middle-class white women with their male partners and children; only one light-skinned African American woman can be found posing with her even lighter-skinned baby girl, but without a male partner, in a tastefully decorated nursery.[62] One can deduce that the primary target niche market for this product is well-to-do mothers.

In comparison, ParaGard reaches out to a broader consumer base, including women who have not had children. The product home page features five racially diverse women. With a scroll of the mouse, the viewer can read the reason each woman chose ParaGard. The Asian woman, who is "single and planning for the future," is "in a serious relationship, but not ready for a family." She represents a woman of color who is expected to establish her livelihood before she has children. The race of the woman in a business suit standing confidently in the center can be read as either a dark-haired white person or a very light-skinned

Latina. She represents a career-oriented woman who wants to put off having a family. One of the African American women appeals to prospective users who are "concerned about hormonal health risks" and want "highly effective birth control" without hormones and their side effects. The other African American woman is "living the change of life" and represents older consumers. Her testimony reads: "Done with family. Done with pills, patches, and rings. Wants simple birth control to last until menopause." Whereas the Asian and Latina/white women clearly express the desire to have children in the future, the two African American women do not. The second woman explicitly states her childbearing is complete, and the first woman makes no mention of wanting a child.

African American women's desire to restrain their fertility is a culturally appropriate script that is also played out in the representation of Mirena users. The Mirena patient education DVD features women of color in only one of the four episodes: two African American women discuss Mirena as a good option for them because their chaotic lives with children make it challenging to remember to take the pill. One of them (whose feature can also be read as a non–African American woman of color) is pregnant with her second child and asks her gynecologist if Mirena is right for her; the white female doctor assures her that it is not too early to plan on getting it during her postnatal checkups. An ideal user for Mirena as represented in this episode reiterates the notion that the IUD is a suitable contraceptive for women who are unreliable pill users (who are often marked by their race, class, and young age) and for restraining the fertility of women of color.

The three educational DVD episodes involving white women include the one I have already mentioned, which features an athletic businesswoman who appreciates not having her period. The second skit shows a new mom with her husband. She wishes she did not have to fiddle with the diaphragm whenever the couple finally has a moment to themselves. Sure enough, her doctor recommends Mirena. This scenario highlights the sexual spontaneity and convenience that Mirena users in a stable relationship enjoy. The last episode presents a blond white woman with three children. She says she considered tubal ligation,

but decided to get a Mirena instead because she is not completely sure if she is done having children.

There is a striking similarity between this woman and the fifth woman shown on the ParaGard Web site. She is also a blond white woman, who "loves being a mom." With a scroll of the mouse, we learn that she "adores her kids. Wonders what it would be like to have more. Wants hassle-free birth control that won't limit her options." The Mirena TV commercial also emphasizes reversibility as an advantage of this contraceptive method, concluding the clip with a picture-perfect American family with their fourth newborn child. But with a closer and critical look, this so-called option is presented as appropriate only for middle- to upper-middle-class white family-oriented mothers. There is an enduring pattern that shows a cultural preference toward fecund women to be portrayed as white and well-to-do and toward women of color to express the need to suppress reproduction.

In an essay titled "Will the 'Real' Mother Please Stand Up?: The Logic of Eugenics and American National Family Planning," Patricia Hill Collins argues that in the United States, "where social class, race, ethnicity, gender, sexuality, and nationality comprise intersecting dimensions of oppression, not all mothers are created equal."[63] The idealized mother best suited for the tasks of reproducing both the American nation and seemingly American values is embodied by an affluent white woman bearing American citizenship who reproduces her biological children and physically participates in every facet of their lives. These kinds of mothers, whom Collins calls "real" mothers, encounter social policies, institutional arrangements, and ideological messages that encourage and support them to continue to reproduce. For instance, the availability of medical services to combat infertility simultaneously supports and obligates upper-middle-class white women to reproduce their biological offspring. Images of large, happy families with distinctly white upper-middle-class features such as the ones shown on IUD commercials are examples of the encouragement that "real" mothers receive. In contrast, mothers who are considered less fit and even unfit are discouraged from having children and do not receive similar support for parenting. The reproductive options that are prescribed to working-class black women, in particular, often derive from the racist notion of poor African American women who have too many children and become "welfare queens." Collins argues that both positive and negative eugenics, which are based on the race and class of the mothers, are still present in contemporary American society. We indeed see them manifest in contraceptive advertisements.

On the surface, ParaGard and Mirena IUDs have joined the myriad birth control options available to American consumers. Yet various aspects of the contraceptive method are matched up with culturally sanctioned body/technology relationships. Although sometimes bodies cross over the dichotomous categories, reversibility is generally stressed for what are viewed as real American mothers, and other aspects, such as the ease of use and long-term effectiveness, are promoted through the bodies of women of color. The initial emphases IUD researchers placed on controlling the birthrates of undesirable populations and disciplining women's bodies to suppress socially problematic pregnancies are still embodied by this seemingly progressive lifestyle product.

BODY/TECHNOLOGY RELATIONSHIPS IN RACIALIZED GLOBAL CONTEXTS

During its fifty years of development, the IUD discourse has generated diverse body/technology relationships while representing scientific findings in biopolitically and geopolitically meaningful ways. From being the population control tool it once was foreseen to become, the hormone-releasing device diversified into a gynecological treatment, a menstrual-suppression technique, and an alternative to tubal ligation. The diversification, however, applies for the most part only to the global North. The International Contraceptive Access Foundation, an organization that donates free LNG-IUDs to family programs overseas, states, "ICA aims to serve the needs of women and families in the developing world to achieve their desired family size and birth spacing."[64] As this statement suggests, the biopolitics of contraceptive technologies in the global South continue to focus on fertility, although the rhetoric has moved away from justifying mass insertions. The pairing of excessively fertile bodies and an effective long-acting contraceptive technology remains the dominant paradigm there.

Contested meanings of menstruation have contributed to reinforcing the divide between bodies in the global South and North by creating an additional dichotomy between "backward" and "modern" contraceptive users. Women who were deemed not ready to appreciate amenorrhea due to their cultural beliefs about menstruation were left behind in the popularization of the hormone-releasing device. Meanwhile, those regarded as accepting of the scientific explanation of why women should embrace less menstrual bleeding were thrust into a new paradigm of bodily enhancement and lifestyle medications. The cost of Mirena, too, has contributed to the separation between underprivileged women, for whom effective contraceptives are rendered adequate, and economically privileged women, for whom a favorable contraceptive should offer extra benefits.

As Mirena's common side effect acquired new meanings, body/technology relationships in the global North expanded. IUD developers interested in treating menstrual disorders and uterine ailments reconceptualized the device as a therapeutic technology and gynecological patients as treatable bodies. Much less concerned with reproduction, this body/technology coupling represents the biopolitics of health maintenance. The mensesfree body/device also entered a market already sold on the idea of artificial menstrual suppression as lifestyle choice. Liberal governmentality or self-management for achieving better health, higher productivity, and a happier life connects the desiring consumer to this new contraceptive with an additional benefit.

The latest body/technology relationships in IUD promotional materials also represent contemporary eugenics ideologies promoted within the framework of individualism. The 1995 Hastings Center Report on the ethics of long-acting contraceptives signify a shift in the approach to suppressing undesirable pregnancies from targeting specific groups to holding individuals responsible. Authors of the report take great caution not to approve of broad use that may suggest racial and class discrimination. Yet at the same time they explore acceptable ways to discourage what they see as irresponsible reproduction. The overall report leaves an opening for an argument to be made for promoting long-acting contraceptive methods in limited cases that are evaluated on an individual basis.

The individualist approach easily blends with a consumerist framework and naturalizes the coupling of racialized bodies, understood as potentially "unfit mothers," with long-acting and user-failure-free contraceptives. Meanwhile, white mothers' bodies are unproblematically paired with the reversible feature of the IUD, implicitly promoting positive eugenics through consumption.

By following the development of Mirena, this . . . essay traced how diverse biopolitical subjects were constructed within the IUD discourse in accordance with cultural expectations about race and class, as well as the global political economy of women's bodies that render some as overproducing fertility machines and others as sites of consumption of medical services and devices. It also revealed how various body/technology pairings were configured, forming a network of relationships that reflect the racialized global context within which technoscientific interventions in women's bodies are imagined.

NOTES

1. For more detailed perspective on my academic and personal journey with an IUD, see Takeshita (2010).
2. Posting on an online medication discussion resource, medications.com: http://www.medications .com/effect/view/34880 (accessed November 2010).
3. See for example, http://lifeaftermirena.blogspot.com.
4. See Mamo and Fosket (2009).
5. See Loe (2004) and Mamo and Fishman (2004).
6. Blum and Stracuzzi (2004).
7. Scommegna et al. (1970).
8. Ibid. (201, 202).
9. Ibid. (209).
10. See Scommegna et al. (1974). This research was also funded by the Ford Foundation. This time, they tested a T-shaped progesterone-releasing device in 249 women for twelve months. No pregnancies resulted.
11. See Huber et al. (1975) and Piotrow, Rinehart, and Schmidt (1979).
12. See Segal (2003).
13. Population Council (1970).
14. Norplant consists of six levonorgestrel-containing matchstick-size rods that are implanted beneath the skin of a woman's forearm to prevent pregnancy for five years.
15. Prager and Darney (2007).
16. Moskowitz, Jennings, and Callahan (1995, S1).
17. See Watkins (2010a, 2010b).
18. Smith (2005b).
19. Moskowitz, Jennings, and Callahan (1995, S2).
20. Huber et al. (1975, B-38).
21. "Uterine tranquilizer" appears in ibid.
22. See Tietze and Lewitt (1968).
23. See Liskin (1982).
24. See Treiman and Liskin (1988).
25. See Bernard (1970).
26. Whelan (1975).
27. Piotrow, Rinehart, and Schmidt (1979, B-66).

28. The WHO (1981) study was conducted between 1973 and 1979 and involved 5,322 parous women from fourteen cultural groups in Egypt, India (Hindu high caste, Hindu low caste), Indonesia (Javanese, Sudanese), Jamaica, Korea, Mexico, Pakistan (Punjab, Sind), the Philippines, United Kingdom, and Yugoslavia (Muslim, non-Muslim).

29. See Liskin (1982).

30. WHO (1981, 12).

31. See Liskin (1982).

32. WHO (1981, 13).

33. Chatterjee and Riley (2001).

34. The continuation rates for the levonorgestrel IUD were 74.5, 58.7, and 38.8 percent at one, two, and three years, respectively. The continuation of copper devices ranged from 82.4 to 84.4 percent at year 1, 66.6 to 69.9 percent at year 2, and 45.4 to 50.4 percent at year 3. This was a double-blind trial, which disallowed physicians to provide consultation to women who received the LNG-IUD about possible amenorrhea. Thus the high discontinuation rate may have partly been corrected with counseling. See Indian Council of Medical Research (1989).

35. See Sivin et al. (1991).

36. Treiman et al. (1995).

37. Ibid. For the original report of the European study, see Andersson, Odlind, Goran Ryobo (1994).

38. Luukkainen (1994).

39. Ibid. (39).

40. Martin (2001).

41. See Pigg (2001). See also Adams and Pigg (2005).

42. Jim Shelton, "IUD Mirena," Dr. Jim Shelton's Pearls. January 15, 2001. http://info.k4health.org/pearls/2001/01-15.shtml (accessed November 2010) Shelton explains: "In the private sector at least, the price is likely to be in the hundreds of dollars. Over the years AID staff have had discussions with Schering (and with its predecessor Leiras) about an acceptable public sector price. Although we have never been able to reach accord, we will keep trying." USAID was not supplying Mirena at the time of writing this.

43. Under their agreement, product donations to international development agencies and public health organizations can be made up to 1 percent of non-U.S. market unit sales (about 53,000 IUDs by 2007). In addition, the company will sell up to 3 percent of non-U.S. market unit sales for under $40 to qualified public sector organizations. ICA has projects in Brazil, Curasao, Dominican Republic, Ecuador, El Salvador, Ghana, Kenya, Indonesia, Nigeria, Paraguay, Saint Lucia, and South Africa. http://www.ica-foundation.org/ (accessed November 2010).

44. Rademacher et al. (2009). Available at http://www.k4health.org/toolkits/iud/essential-knowledge-about-lng-ius (accessed November 2010).

45. These cost figures are based on my own experience between 2002 and 2005. Prices vary depending on the provider, and distributors' business decisions may affect future prices.

46. ARCH Foundation, https://www.thearchfoundation.org/ (accessed November 2010).

47. Rademacher et al. (2009). See also Trussell, Lalla, and Doan (2008).

48. Oudshoorn (1994, 121).

49. Ibid.

50. Coutinho and Segal (1999, 163).

51. Ibid.

52. Ibid. (164).
53. Ibid.
54. Mamo and Fosket (2009, 933).
55. Ibid. (931).
56. Mirena promotional material from October 2006 for prescribing physicians.
57. See note 2.
58. Joyce (2003, 4).
59. Kapsalis (1997).
60. Ibid. (53).
61. ParaGard product Web site: https://www.paragard.com/ (accessed November 2010).
62. Mirena product Web site: http://www.mirena-us.com/index.jsp (accessed November 2010).
63. Collins (1999, 266).
64. www.ica-foundation.org (accessed November 2010).

STACY ALAIMO

25. ELUDING CAPTURE: THE SCIENCE, CULTURE, AND PLEASURE OF "QUEER" ANIMALS

We're Deer. We're Queer. Get Used to It. A new exhibit in Norway outs the animal kingdom.

—Alisa Opar

Biological Exuberance is, above all, an affirmation of life's vitality and infinite possibilities: a worldview that is at once primordial and futuristic, in which gender is kaleidoscopic, sexualities are multiple, and the categories of male and female are fluid and transmutable. A world, in short, exactly like the one we inhabit.

—Bruce Bagemihl

[W]e are acting with the best intentions in the world, we want to add reality to scientific objects, but, inevitably, through a sort of tragic bias, we seem always to be subtracting some bit from it. Like a clumsy waiter setting plates on a slanted table, every nice dish slides down and crashes on the ground. Why can we never discover the same stubbornness, the same solid realism by bringing out the obviously webby, "thingy" qualities of matters of concern?

—Bruno Latour

"Nature" and the "natural" have long been waged against homosexuals, as well as women, people of color, and indigenous peoples. Just as the pernicious histories of Social Darwinism, colonialism, primitivism, and other forms of scientifically infused racism have incited indispensable critiques of the intermingling of "race" and nature,[1] much queer theory has bracketed, expelled, or distanced the volatile categories of nature and the natural, situating queer desire within an entirely social, and very human, habitat. This now compulsory sort of segregation of queer from nature is hardly appealing to those who seek queer green places, or, in other words, an environmentalism allied with gay affirmation, and a gay politics that is also environmentalist. Moreover, the question of whether nonhuman nature can be queer provokes larger questions within interdisciplinary theory regarding the relations between discourse and materiality, human and more-than-human worlds, as well as between cultural theory and science. In short, we need more robust, complex ways of productively engaging with materiality—ways that account for the diversity and "exuberance" of a multitude of naturecultures, ways that can engage with science as well as science studies. Queer animals—"matters of concern" for queer, green, human cultures—may foster such formulations.

. . . Popular science books, such as Bruce Bagemihl's monumental *Biological Exuberance: Animal Homosexuality and Natural Diversity* (1999) and Joan Roughgarden's *Evolution's Rainbow: Diversity, Gender, and Sexuality in Nature and People* (2004), as well as the work of Myra J. Hird, present possibilities for radically rethinking nature as queer, by documenting the vast range of same-sex acts, same-sex childrearing pairs, intersex animals, multiple "genders," "transvestism," and transsexuality existing throughout the more-than-human world. Bagemihl's 750-page volume, two-thirds of which is "A Wondrous Bestiary" of "Portraits of Homosexual, Bisexual, and Transgendered Wildlife," astounds with its vast compilation of species "in which same sex activities have been scientifically documented" (1999, 265). Bagemihl restricts himself to

Stacy Alaimo, "Eluding Capture: The Science, Culture, and Pleasure of 'Queer' Animals," *Queer Ecologies: Sex, Nature, Politics, Desire*, ed. Mortimer-Sandilands, Catriona, Bruce Erickson (Bloomington: Indiana University Press, 2010): 52–72. Reprinted with permission of Indiana University Press; permission conveyed through Copyright Clearance Center, Inc.

mammals and birds, but even so, he discusses nearly three hundred species and "more than two centuries of scientific research" (1999, 1–2). Rich not only with scientific data, but also with photos, illustrations, and charts, Bagemihl's exhaustively researched volume renders any sense of normative heterosexuality within nature an absurd impossibility. Joan Roughgarden's book, *Evolution's Rainbow: Diversity, Gender, and Sexuality in Nature and People* (2004), which consists of three sections, "Animal Rainbows," "Human Rainbows," and "Cultural Rainbows," paints an expanse of sexual diversity across both animal and human worlds. In October 2006, the Naturhistorisk Museum in Oslo, Norway, opened "the first-ever museum exhibition dedicated to gay animals." "Against Nature?" sought to "reject the all too well known argument that homosexual behavior is a crime against nature" by displaying species known to engage in homosexual acts. The exhibit "outs" these animals by telling a "fascinating story of the animals' secret life . . . by means of models, photos, texts, and specimens" (Against Nature 2007). Ironically, the patriarchal diorama of the early twentieth century that served, as Donna Haraway argues, as a "prophylactic" against "decadence" (1990, 26), is followed by an exhibition that unveils sexual diversity in the world of animals. Queer animals have also gained notoriety with the controversy over a German zoo's plan "to test the sexual orientation of six male penguins which have displayed homosexual traits" and set them up with female penguins because they want "the rare Humboldt penguins to breed" (Gay Outrage 2005). After the public outcry, zoo director Heike Kueke reassured people that they would not forcibly break up the homosexual penguin couples, saying, "Everyone can live here as they please" (*Ananova* 2005). *Dr. Tatiana's Sex Advice to All Creation: The Definitive Guide to the Evolutionary Biology of Sex,* includes a letter from a manatee worried that their son "keeps kissing other males," signed "Don't Want No Homo in the Florida Keys." Dr. Tatiana replies: "It's not your son who needs straightening out. It's you. Some Homosexual activity is common for animals of all kinds" (Judson 2003, 143). More surprising, perhaps, the television sex show host Dr. Susan Block, with her explicit website replete with porn videos and sex toys, promotes a peaceful philosophy of

"ethical hedonism," based on "the Bonobo Way." "The Bonobo Way," which includes a great deal of "lesbian" sex, "supports the repression of violence and the free, exuberant, erotic, raunchy, loving, peaceful, adventurous, consensual expression of pleasure" (Block 2007).[2]

According to the website for the "Against Nature?" exhibit (2007), "Homosexuality has been observed in most vertebrate groups, and also from insects, spiders, crustaceans, octopi and parasitic worms. The phenomenon has been reported from more than 1,500 animal species, and is well documented for 500 of them, but the real extent is probably much higher" (Against Nature 2007). Notwithstanding the sheer delight of dwelling within a queer bestiary that supplants the dusty, heteronormative Book of Nature, the recognition of the sexual diversity of animals has several significant benefits. Most obviously, scientific accounts of queer animals insist that heteronormativity has damaged and diminished scientific knowledge in biology, anthropology, and other fields. Roughgarden charges that "the scientific silence on homosexuality in animals amounts to a cover-up, deliberate or not," thus scientists "are professionally responsible for refuting claims that homosexuality is unnatural" (2004, 128). Bruce Bagemihl (1999) and Myra J. Hird (2004b) document how the majority of scientists have ignored, refused to acknowledge, closeted, or explained away their observations of same-sex behavior in animals, for fear of risking their reputations, scholarly credibility, academic positions, or heterosexual identity. Most notably, Bagemihl includes a candid reflection of biologist Valerius Geist, who "still cringe[s] at the memory of seeing old D-ram mount S-ram repeatedly": "I called these actions of the rams *aggrosexual* behavior, for to state that the males had evolved a homosexual society was emotionally beyond me. To conceive of those magnificent beasts as 'queers'—Oh God!" (Bagemihl 1999, 107). A queer-science-studies stance parallel to that of feminist empiricism would insist that the critique and eradication of heteronormative bias will result in a better, more accurate account of the world—simply getting the facts (not-so) straight. Although Margaret Cuonzo warns of the possibility for homosexist, anthropocentric, "or even egocentric" bias in accounts of queer animals (2003, 231), these possibilities seem highly unlikely given the pervasive heteronormativity not only in science, but in the wider culture.[3] Moreover, as Catriona Mortimer-Sandilands argues, citing the case in which ecologists assumed that the lesbian behavior of seagulls "must be evidence of some major environmental catastrophe" (and it wasn't), "the assumption that heterosexuality is the only natural sexual form is clearly not an appropriate benchmark for ecological research" (2005). In short, environmental sciences require better accounts of the sexual diversity of natural creatures; otherwise heteronormative bias may render it even more difficult to understand the effects of various toxicants.

. . .

From a cultural studies perspective that focuses on discursive contestation, it is easy to see queer animals as countering the pernicious and persistent articulation of homosexuality with what is unnatural. The multitude of examples given by Bagemihl (1999) and Roughgarden (2004), not to mention the explicit photos and illustrations, strongly articulate "queer" with "animal," making sexual diversity part of a larger biodiversity. This cultural studies model of political-discursive contestation, however, may, by definition, bracket all that which is not purely discursive—ironically, of course, the animals themselves—and thus limit the possibilities for imagining a queer ethics and politics that is also environmentalist. (This difficulty is part of a larger problem within cultural theory of finding ways of allowing matter to matter.) But even within the paradigm of discursive contestation, trouble arises, since the normative meanings of nature and the natural have long coexisted with their inverse: nature as blank, dumb, or even debased materiality. In other words, if conservatives are hell-bent on damning homosexuals, they will, no doubt, simply see all this queer animal sex as shocking depravity and consign those of us who are already outside of the Family of Man to the howling wilderness of bestial perversions. No doubt the rather sweet-looking illustrations of say, female hedgehog "courtship" and cunnilingus included in Bagemihl's book, which would delight many a gay-affirmative viewer, would disgust others (Bagemihl 1999, 471).

Rather than simply toss queer animals into the ring of public opinion to battle the still pervasive sense that homosexuality is unnatural, we need to embrace the possibilities for the sexual diversity of animal behavior to help us continue to transform our most basic sense of what nature and culture mean. For many cultural critics, who fear that any engagement with nature, science, or materiality is too perilous to pursue, queer animals are segregated into a universe of irrelevance. But it is possible, I think, to look to queer animals, not as a moral model or embodiment of some static universal law, but in order to find, in this astounding biological exuberance, a sense of vast diversity, deviance (in the way that Ladelle McWhorter [1999] recasts the term),[4] and a proliferation of astonishing differences that make nonsense of biological reductionism. Moreover, it is crucial that we see animals not as genetically driven machines but as creatures embedded within and creating other "worlds" or naturecultures, as Haraway (2003) puts it.

EPISTEMOLOGY OF THE ZOOLOGICAL CLOSET

Eve Sedgwick's paradigm of the "open secret" captures the way in which nonhuman animals have been fixed within a zoological closet: many people have witnessed some sort of same-sex activity between animals and yet still imagine the natural world as unrelentingly straight. Such determined ignorance emerges from a heteronormative epistemology. As Sedgwick explains, ignorance—as well as knowledge—has power: "These ignorances, far from being pieces of the originary dark, are produced by and correspond to particular knowledges and circulate as part of particular regimes of truth" (1990, 8). Decades ago, when my brother was young, my mother bought him a pair of hamsters. Fearing we would be overrun by a proliferation of tiny mammals, she chose two females. My brother was baffled and my mother stunned to discover the spectacle of their seemingly nonstop oral sex. Despite this family memory, I must admit that I was rather astonished by Hird's, Roughgarden's, and Bagemihl's accounts of the enormous variety of sexual diversity throughout the nonhuman world. Who knew? This sense of astonishment, as I will discuss, below, can rouse a queer-green, ethical/epistemological/aesthetic response, even as it may be implicated in regimes of closeted knowledges.

The sexual diversity of animals, I contend, matters. Predominant modes of social theory, however, which still assume a radical separation of nature and culture, tend to minimize the significance of queer animals. Just as most feminist theory has engaged in a "flight from nature" (see Alaimo 2000), most cultural critics have cast out queer animals from the field of cultural relevance. Jonathan Marks, for example, in *What it Means to Be 98% Chimpanzee: Apes, People, and Their Genes* (2002) takes his place in a long line of people who have attempted to clearly demarcate human from animal by seizing upon some key difference: "One of the outstanding hallmarks of human evolution is the extent to which our species has divorced sexuality from reproduction. Most sexuality in other primates is directly associated with reproduction" (2002, 110). Just as language, tool use, and other supposed keys to the Human Kingdom have been usurped by evidence of similar accomplishments across a range of species, the deluge of evidence of same-sex sex among animals collapses this claim. Marks, however, contends that the female "same-sex genital stimulation" of the bonobo is exceptional, arguing that "virtually all primates are sexually active principally as a reproductive activity" (111). Paul Vasey's extensive studies of Japanese macaques, discussed below, as well as the accounts of hundreds of other species that engage in same-sex pleasures, counter Marks's assertion. More generally, however, Marks criticizes the way in which we, as humans, look to other primates, especially chimps, as the key to understanding our "true" selves: "They are us, minus something. They are supposed to be our pure biology, unfettered by the trappings of civilization and its discontents. They are humans without humanity. They are nature without culture" (165). On this point, Marks offers a demystifying critique, especially of the way in which the cultural framework of the scientists may be mistaken as "a contribution of the chimps, rather than for our own input" (ibid.). Even as it is useful to expose the popular pursuit of seeking the primal truth of the human within the animal, and even as it is likewise important to wrestle with the thorny epistemological problems that animal ethology poses, I would argue that it is also crucial to critique the narrow evolutionary narrative of progress inherent in the notion that "they" are "nature without

culture." Nonhuman animals are also cultural creatures, with their own sometimes complex systems of (often nonreproductive) sex. The overall effect of Marks's debunking—when unaccompanied by any attempt to formulate productive ways of engaging with scientific accounts of animals—is to banish animals to a wilderness of irrelevance, where they serve as the backdrop for the erection of human achievement.

Jennifer Terry offers an incisive discursive critique of "the scientific fascination with queer animals," in which "animals provide models for scientists seeking to determine a biological substrate of sexual orientation" (2000, 152). She exposes how "reproductive sexuality provides the master narrative in studies of animal sexuality and tethers queer animal behavior to the aim of defining reproduction as the ultimate goal of sexual encounters" (154). Drawing on Haraway's work, Terry begins her essay by stating that "animals help us tell stories about ourselves, especially when it comes to matters of sexuality" (151). She concludes by arguing that the "creatures that populate the narrative space called 'nature' are key characters in scientific tales about the past, present, and future. Various tellings of these tales are possible, but they are always shaped by historical, disciplinary, and larger cultural contexts" (185). Terry illuminates such contexts in a useful way throughout the essay. This mode of critique, however, framed as it is by the emphasis on "narrative space," cages animal sexual practices within human stories. Although Terry draws heavily on Haraway, Haraway herself, especially in her . . . [more] recent work, seems wary of modes of cultural critique that bracket the materiality and the significance of the nonhuman: "Dogs, in their historical complexity, matter here. Dogs are not an alibi for other themes; dogs are fleshly material-semiotic presences in the body of technoscience. Dogs are not surrogates for theory; they are not here just to think with. They are here to live with" (2003, 5). Even as Haraway executed one of the most dazzlingly complex and multidimensional scientific/cultural critiques in her 1990 masterpiece *Primate Visions*, she insisted that the "primates themselves—monkeys, apes, and people—all have some kind of 'authorship'" (1990, 8). Her work on primates and dogs, especially, demonstrates this sort of commitment to them—to the world—even as she admits "how science 'gets at' the world remains far from resolved" (1990, 8). I do not have the space here to explore the debates in science studies regarding these broader epistemological questions. I contend, however, that we need models capacious enough to include both cultural critique and a commitment to uncovering material realities and agencies.[5]

Cynthia Chris, in *Watching Wildlife*, exposes the heteronormativity of wildlife films, explaining that most "wildlife films posit heterosexual mate selection as not only typical but inevitable and without exception" (Chris 2006, 156). Even the show *Wild and Weird—Wild Sex*, "downplays—even avoids—same-sex behaviors in the cavalcade of animal sexualities it frames as varied" (157). Despite her analysis of the heteronormativity of the wildlife genre, however, Chris ultimately warns against celebrating queer animals:

> Evidence of same-sex behaviors among animals and genetic influences on homosexuality among humans is used as ammunition in battles waged over gay rights for which advocates might be better off relying on other discourses through which civil rights are claimed. Such evidence remains inconclusive, uneasily generalizable across species, subject to wildly divergent interpretations, and likely to fail the endeavor of understanding animal behavior on its own terms. (165)

Chris's conflation here of animal sexual behavior with "genetic influences on homosexuality among humans" is disturbing, in that it assumes that if animals do something, they do it because of genetic programming. The extent to which any sexual orientation could possibly be influenced by genetic factors is a question that is entirely separate from the sexual diversity of animals. Rather than assuming that the "genetic human" is the thing that is equivalent to animality, it would be much more accurate to think of animal sex as both cultural and material, and genetics as much more of a dynamic process, inextricably interwoven with organism and environment.[6] While Chris would rather have us "rely on other discourses," in part because the evidence for queer animals is "uneasily generalizable across species and subject to wildly divergent interpretations," I will argue below that this very sense of being not generalizable is what makes accounts of animal

sexual diversity so potent. They highlight a staggering expanse of sexual diversity in nonhuman creatures that is the very stuff of a vaster biodiversity. Environmentalists and queers can engage with accounts of the sexual diversity of animals, allowing them to complicate, challenge, enrich, and transform our conceptions of nature, culture, sex, gender, and other fundamental categories.

Roger N. Lancaster in *The Trouble with Nature: Sex in Science and Popular Culture* wades through "a toxic waste dump of ideas" hoping to "discover sophisticated new biological perspectives on sex and sexuality" but encountering instead "the same old reductivism warmed over" (2003, xi). He argues that the "attempts at supposedly 'queering' science . . . consolidate an astonishingly *heteronormative* conception of human nature" (29). While he presents incisive critiques of heteronormativity and scientific reductivism, many of his arguments endorse a strict nature/culture opposition. Such an opposition, of course, underwrites the very reductivism that he supposedly opposes.[7] For example, he argues that "society, bonding, hierarchy, slavery, rape, and harem" are "concepts, relations, and activities characteristic of humans" and implies that "facts of nature" and "facts of culture" should remain utterly separate (61). While "slavery, rape, and harem" leap out as all-too-human in terminology, there is certainly solid evidence for "society, bonding, [and] hierarchy" within many animal species.[8] Lancaster advocates that we "reject the naturalized regime of heteronormativity in its totality" in order to be "finished with the idea of normal bodies once and for all" (31). Ironically, even as Lancaster's book casts scientific accounts of nature as nothing but "trouble," the surprising range of sexual diversity within nonhuman animals could actually foster Lancaster's utopian dream. Even Lancaster himself becomes momentarily seduced by Bagemihl's book, which he warns is "anthropomorphic" and "fetishistic," a collection of "charms and talismans of a coming science that would at least be progressive once again" (114).

When nature and culture are segregated within different disciplinary universes, detrimental oppositions result, in which animal sex is reduced to a purely reproductive function and in which human sexuality—in its opulent range of manifestations—becomes, implicitly, at least, another transcendent human achievement that places us above the brute mating behaviors of nonhuman creatures. Rather than continuing to pose nature/culture dualisms that closet queer animals as well as animal cultures, and rather than attempting to locate the truth of human sexuality within the already written book of nature, we can think of queer desire as part of an emergent universe of a multitude of naturecultures.

PURSUING PLEASURES, CREATING CULTURES

Human-animal dualisms, which reduce animal sex to a mechanical act of instinct or genetic determinism, should be supplanted with models of naturecultures (Haraway 2003), in which sexual activity is always indivisibly material and social.[9] Interestingly, unlike much of the scholarship in the humanities, many scientific accounts of animal sex do not reduce it to mechanistic forces or genetically determined instinct. Sex, in nonhumans as well as humans, is partly a learned, social behavior, embedded within and contributing to particular material-social environments. Kristin Field and Thomas Waite, for example, begin their study of male guppies with the following premise: "On a longer timescale, social environment and 'learned sexuality' can have dramatic effects on the expression of species-typical sexual behavior" (Field and Waite 2004, 1381; Woodson [2002], cited in Field and Waite [2004]). In terms of environmental ethics and politics, it is crucial to acknowledge animals as cultural beings, enmeshed in social organizations, acting, interacting, and communicating. An understanding of animal cultures critiques the ideology of nature as resource, blank slate for cultural inscription, or brute, mechanistic force. Lest we imagine that the view of animal-as-machine without feelings, sentience, or value vanished with Descartes, Werner Herzog's comments in *Grizzly Man* (2005) that tag a particular bear as Treadwell's "murderer" at the same time they announce that the "blank stare" of the bear betrays the bear's dreadful vacuity remind us that the demonization and mechanization of animals persists. Even as sexual activity has been assumed to be a biological drive, the recognition of the sheer astonishing diversity of animal "sex-gender systems" (Rubin 1975), provokes us to understand animals as "cultural" beings. Bagemihl himself argues that it is "meaningful to speak of the 'culture' of homosexuality in animals, since the extent and range of variation that is found (between individuals or populations or species) exceeds that provided by genetic programming and begins to enter the realm of individual habits, learned behaviors, and even community-wide 'traditions'" (1999, 45). Myra J. Hird concurs, arguing that "it is no longer feasible to maintain that only humans have culture: there are as many cultures as there are species with cultural behavior because each species is neurophysiologically unique" (2004b, 93).

The pursuit of pleasure may itself be a dynamic force within some animal cultures. Two of the most prominent markers of culture, in fact—tool use and language—have arisen, for some animals, as modes of sexual pleasuring. Drawing on the research of Susan Savage-Rumbaugh, which began in the 1970s, Bagemihl describes the "'lexicon' of about a dozen hand and arm gestures—each with a specific meaning" that bonobos use to "initiate sexual activity and negotiate various body positions with a partner (of the same or opposite sex)" (1999, 66). He includes a chart illustrating these hand movements and translating them into commands such as "Approach" or "Move Your Genitals Around" (67). Bagemihl argues that among primates, humans included, "as sexual interactions become more variable, sexual communication systems become more sophisticated." He concludes, that "it is possible, therefore, that sexuality—particularly the fluidity associated with nonreproductive sexual practices—played a significant role in the origin and development of human language" (69). Bagemihl's claim for the influence of sexuality on the development of tools is equally bold. Citing examples of how many primates not only use, but manufacture, objects to aid with masturbation, Bagemihl claims that "the pursuit of sexual pleasure may have contributed, in some measure, to our own heritage as creatures whose tool-using practices are among the most polymorphous of any primate" (71). Bagemihl's arguments are compelling, and certainly subvert the grand narratives of the Origins of Man, which lay claim to tool making and language as exclusively human. His claim, however, may still be problematic, in that there is a sense in which nonhuman sexual practices become significant because of their role within linear narratives that culminate in the development of the human. But only a slight shift here is needed to read these examples of tool use and language development as part of particular animal naturecultures in which the pursuit of sexual pleasure is one of the most quintessentially "cultural" sorts of activities. Indeed, it is difficult not to be impressed with the creativity, skill, tenacity, and resourcefulness of a female bonnet macaque who "invented some relatively sophisticated techniques of tool manufacture, regularly employing five specific methods to create or modify natural objects for insertion into her vagina":

> For example, she stripped dry eucalyptus leaves of their foliage with her fingers or teeth and then broke the midrib into a piece less than half an inch long. She also slit dry acacia leaves in half lengthwise (using only a single half) and fashioned short sticks by breaking longer ones into several pieces or detaching portions of a branch. Implements were also vigorously rubbed with her fingers or between her palms prior to being inserted into her vagina, and twigs, leaves, or grass blades were occasionally used unmodified. (70–71)

An artist at work. It is tempting to read this account through Roger N. Lancaster's notion of desire: "This desire is on the side of poetry, in the original and literal sense of the word: *poiesis*, 'production,' as in the making of things and the world. Not an object at all, desire is what makes objects possible" (2003, 266). Even as Lancaster places desire "squarely within a social purview" (266), elaborating an ultrahuman sort of sexuality that is all culture and no nature, the tool-making, language-creating, culturally embedded, pleasurable practices of nonhuman animals invade this ostensibly human terrain, muddying the terms.

Whereas many cultural critics cast animal sex into the separate sphere of nature, many scientific accounts of queer animal sex have rendered them too cultural, so as to render them not sexual. Indeed, Block's philosophy of the ethical hedonism of the bonobo is indicative of a general understanding, in the wider culture, that the "reason" bonobos have so much sex, including same-sex sex, is to reduce social conflicts. Such explanations may well make all that

mounting seem like just another chore. Whereas Block celebrates the eroticism of the bonobos, many scientific accounts of same-sex genital activities emphasize their social functions in such a way as to define them as anything other than sex. As Vasey and his colleagues explain, much same-sex sexual behavior has been interpreted as "sociosexual," meaning "sexual in terms of their external form, but . . . enacted to mediate some sort of adaptive social goal or breeding strategy" (Vasey 2004b, 399). Take, for example, the 1998 textbook *Primate Sexuality*, by Alan F. Dixon. The chapter "Sociosexual Behavior and Homosexuality" begins by making it clear that what might look like same-sex sex among nonhuman primates is merely "motor patterns": "The form and functions of sociosexual patterns vary between species, but the important point is that motor patterns normally associated with sex are sometimes incorporated into the nonsexual sphere of social communications" (147). In order to claim that these "motor patterns" are not sex, he places "sex" in a sphere entirely separate from "social communications," a strange segregation for either hetero or homo sexual relations.[10] Obviously, as Vasey explains, "sexual motivation and social function are not mutually exclusive" (Vasey 2004a, 351). Social function, then, often closets same-sex animal sex by black-boxing pleasure and elevating the social into an abstract and disembodied calculus. The gleeful-erotic illustrations appearing in Dixon's textbook, however, counter the reduction of these activities to mechanistic motor patterns by depicting several entirely different same-sex primate mounts, that—to a less mechanistically constrained eye—suggest such things as desire, effort, playfulness, pleasure—and sex.

Within this landscape of Byzantine heteronormativity, scientists who do suggest that same-sex genital activity may be something like sex often do so tentatively. M. K. Shearer and L. S. Katz state that female goats "may mount other females to obtain sexual stimulation. To the observer, there appears to be a hedonistic component associated with the body pressure and motions involved while mounting" (2006, 36). Vasey must put forth a strong case to even begin to claim that the sexual behavior between female Japanese macaques is, in fact, sexual:

Despite over 40 years of intensive research in populations in which females engage in same-sex mounting and courtship . . . there is not a single study in existence demonstrating any sort of sociosexual function for these behaviors. Rather, all the available evidence indicates that female-female mounting and courtship are not sociosexual behaviors. Female Japanese macaques do not use same-sex mounting and courtship to attract male sexual partners, impede reproduction by same-sex competitors (Gouzoules and Goy, 1983; Vasey, 1995), form alliances, foster social relationships outside consortships (Vasey, 1996), communicate about dominance relationships (Vasey, Faroud, Duckworth, and Kovacovsky; 1998), obtain alloparental care (Vasey, 1998), reduce social tension associated with incipient aggression (Vasey et al., 1998), practice for heterosexual activity (i.e. female-male mounting), or reconcile conflicts. (Vasey 2004b, 399)

Clearly, same-sex activity between animals is considered not-sex until proven otherwise. All possibilities for its existence—other than pleasure—must be ruled out before it can be understood as sex.[11] The predominant scientific framework, oddly, parallels the mainstream environmentalist conception of nature that Sandilands critiques as "both actively de-eroticized and monolithically heterosexual" (Sandilands 2001, 176).[12] As Sandilands explains, drawing upon the work of Greta Gaard, "[e]rotophobia is clearly linked to the regulation of sexual diversity; normative heterosexuality, especially in its links to science and nature, has the effect of regulating and instrumentalizing sexuality, linking it to truth and evolutionary health rather than to pleasure and fulfillment (2001, 180). Queer animals may play a part, then, in helping us question "eco-sexual normativity" through asserting "polymorphous sexualities and multiple natures" (Sandilands 1999, 92–93). Queer animals may also foster an ontology in which pleasure and eroticism are neither the result of genetically determined biological drives nor tools in cultural machinations, but are creative forces simultaneously emergent within and affecting a multitude of naturecultures. Pleasure, in this sense, may be understood within Karen Barad's notion of performativity as "materialist, naturalist, and posthumanist," "that allows matter its due as an active participant

in the world's becoming, its ongoing 'intra-activity'" (2003, 803).

ELUDING CAPTURE

A universe of differing naturecultures, propelled by the pursuit of pleasure as well as other forces, can hardly serve as a foundation for biological reductionism, gender essentialism, heteronormativity, or models of human exceptionalism. The multitude of utterly different models of courtship, sexual activity, childrearing arrangements, gender, transsexualism, and transvestism that Bagemihl and Roughgarden document portray animal lifeworlds that cannot be understood in reductionist ways. Myra J. Hird argues that biology "provides a wealth of evidence to confound static notions of sexual difference" (2004a, 85). Her exuberant essay encourages us to imagine *The Joy of Sex* for plants, fungi, and bacteria. Schizophyllum, for instance, has more than 28,000 sexes. And sex among these promiscuous mushrooms is literally a 'touch-and-go' event, leading Laidman to conclude that for fungi there are 'so many genders, so little time'" (86). Hird presents a convincing case for embracing queer natures as the quintessential boundary transgressors, rather than assuming that "living and non-living matter" is "the stubborn, inert 'outside' to transgressive potential" (85). She concludes her piece by noting that since "gay parenting, lesbianism, homosexuality, sex-changing, and other behaviors in animals are prevalent in living matter, [i]t is at least curious that queer theory does not devote more space to the abundant queer behavior of most of the living matter on this planet" (88).

Indeed, animal sex may de-sediment intransigent cultural categories, beginning with heteronormativity, though not ending there. For example, Vasey and his colleagues, in an investigation of female-female mounting behavior, conclude that "[f]emale mounting in Japanese macaques is not a defective counterpart to male mounting. There is no evidence that females were attempting to execute male mounts, but failing to do so" (Vasey et al. 2006, 127). Rather, the female mounting is "female-typical," exhibiting a strikingly different repertoire of movements (126). The macaques may remind us of Judith Butler's argument that homosexuality is not an imitation of heterosexuality, and Jeanne Hamming's argument that the dildo is not "a representation of a penis," but instead, a "postgender, nonphallic signifier" (Hamming 2001, 330). Vasey himself argues that his study "raises the much broader issue of what constitutes male or female behavior," since it makes little sense to characterize mounting as "male" when "females, in certain populations, engage in this behavior so frequently, and do so in a female-typical manner" (Vasey et al. 2006, 127). Most feminist theory distinguishes between sex and gender, positing "gender" as a cultural, and thus solely human construct. Roughgarden, on the other hand, sees gender in nonhuman animals, defining it as "the appearance, behavior, and lived history of a sexed body" (2004, 27). She notes that "many species have three or more genders" (28), such as the white-throated sparrow, which has "four genders, two male, and two female." These genders are distinguished by either a white stripe or a tan stripe, which correspond to aggressive and territorial versus accommodating behaviors. As far as sex goes, 90 percent of the breeding involves a tan-striped bird (of either sex) with a white-striped bird (of either sex) (9). Haraway's call to see animals as other worlds, replete with "significant otherness" (2003, 25) resounds when trying to make sense of the multitude of animal cultures that just don't fit within human—even feminist, even queer—models. Just as animal sex (and gender) may complicate the foundations of feminist theory, animal practices may also denaturalize familiar categories and assumptions in queer theory and gay cultures. For one thing, nearly all the animal species, as well as individual animals, that have been documented as engaging in same-sex relations also engage in heterosexual sex, meaning that "universalizing" models of sexuality work better for most nonhuman animals than "minoritizing" models. The queer animals I've been referring to, as a convenient shorthand, are queer in a multitude of ways, but rarely do any of them correspond to early-twenty-first-century categories of gay or lesbian. Roughgarden explains that most male bighorn sheep live in "homosexual societies," courting and copulating with other males, via anal penetration. It is the nonhomosexual males who are considered "aberrant": "The few males who do not participate in homosexual activity have been labeled 'effeminate'

males. . . . They differ from 'normal males' by living with the ewes rather than joining all-male groups. These males do not dominate females, are less aggressive overall, and adopt a couched, female urination posture. These males refuse mounting by other males" (2004, 138). As Roughgarden contends, these sheep challenge gay/straight categories: "The 'normal' macho bighorn sheep has full-fledged anal sex with other males. The 'aberrant' ram is the one who is straight—the lack of interest in homosexuality is considered pathological" (138). Inevitably, in an attempt to understand the remarkable differences in animal cultures, most accounts draw upon human categories and terms. Even as she critiques the "biased vocabulary" of scientists, Roughgarden uses many terms lifted too unproblematically from twentieth-century American culture, such as "domestic violence" and "divorce," which flattens and distorts the significant otherness of animal cultures.

Interestingly, both Roughgarden and Bagemihl argue that many non-Western cultures have a greater knowledge of and appreciation for the sexual diversity of the nonhuman world. Roughgarden, for example, notes that in the South Sea Islands of Vanuatu, pigs have "been bred for their intersex expressions": "Among the people of Sakao, seven distinct genders are named, ranging from those with the most egg-related external genitalia to those with the most sperm-related external genitalia" (2004, 37). Similarly, Bagemihl contends that contemporary theoretical accounts of sexual diversity pale next to both the scientific accounts of animal sexuality and the knowledge systems of particular indigenous groups who recognize animal sexual diversity:

> The animal world—right now, here on earth—is brimming with countless gender variations and shimmering sexual possibilities: entire lizard species that consist only of females who reproduce by virgin birth and also have sex with each other; or some multigendered society of the Ruff, with four distinct categories of male birds, some of whom court and mate with one another; or female Spotted Hyenas and Bears who copulate and give birth through their "penile" clitorides, and male Greater Rheas who possess "vaginal" phalluses (like the females of their species) and raise young in two-father families; or the vibrant transsexualities of coral reef fish, and the dazzling intersexualities of gyandromorphs and

chimeras. In their quest for "postmodern" patterns of gender and sexuality, human beings are simply catching up with the species that have preceded us in evolving sexual and gender diversity—and aboriginal cultures have long recognized this. (1999, 260–61)

Despite the scientific aim to make sense of the world, to categorize, to map, to find causal relations, many who write about sexual diversity in nonhuman animals are struck with the sense that the remarkable variance regarding sex, gender, reproduction, and childrearing among animals defies our modes of categorization, even explodes our sense of being able to make sense of it all. These epiphanic moments of wonder ignite an epistemological-ethical sense in which, suddenly, the world is not only more queer than one could have imagined,[13] but more surprisingly itself, meaning that it confounds our categories and systems of understanding. In other words, queer animals elude perfect modes of capture. In Andrew Pickering's model, science is "an evolving field of human and material agencies reciprocally engaged in a play of resistance and accommodation in which the former seeks to capture the latter" (1995, 23). Paradoxically, this model allows us to value scientific accounts of sexual diversity in nonhuman animals, in the sense that these accounts are accounting for something—something more than a (human) social construction—and yet, it also encourages an epistemological-ethical stance that recognizes the inadequacy of human knowledge systems to ever fully account for the natural world.

By eluding perfect modes of capture, queer animals dramatize emergent worlds of desire, action, agency, and interactivity that can never be reduced to a background or resource against which the human defines himself. Haraway, defining her term "companion species," explains: "There are no pre-constituted subjects and objects, and no single sources, unitary actors, or final ends. . . . A bestiary of agencies, kinds of relatings, and scores of time trump the imaginings of even the most baroque cosmologists" (2003, 6). Such responses emanate from a queer, green, place, in which pleasure, desire, and the proliferation of differing lifeworlds and interactions provoke intense, ethical, reactions. As Brian Massumi argues, "intensity is the unassimilable" because, "structure is the place where nothing

ever happens, that explanatory heaven in which all eventual permutations are prefigured in a self consistent set of invariant generative rules" (2002, 27). Many responses to sexual diversity in nonhuman creatures emanate this sort of intensity of the unassimilable. Volker Sommer, for example, concludes his epilogue to *Homosexual Behavior in Animals: An Evolutionary Perspective*, by asking: "Is the diversity of sexual behavior that we can observe in nature anything other than mindbogglingly beautiful?" (2006, 370). In a review of Bagemihl's book, Duane Jeffery comments that "nature's inventiveness far outruns our meager ability to categorize her productions," adding that "the sheer inventiveness—exuberance—of nature overwhelms" (2005, 72). Roughgarden, herself a transgender woman and ecologist, notes that in writing her book she "found more diversity than [she] had ever dreamed existed," calling her book the "gee-whiz of vertebrate diversity" (2004, 2), an expression that captures the reader's response as much as the book's content. Bagemihl carefully wraps up his "labor of love" with layers of wonderment. We first encounter the poem "Snow" by Louis MacNeice (which includes the line "World is crazier and more of it than we think"), then two lines from e. e. cummings—"hugest whole creation may be less/incalculable than a single kiss"—both of which stand as epigraphs to the entire volume, then an epigraph by Einstein for the introduction: "The most beautiful thing we can experience is the mysterious. It is the source of all true art and science. He to whom this emotion is a stranger, who can no longer pause to wonder and stand rapt in awe, is as good as dead: his eyes are closed" (Bagemihl 1999, 1). A grand, two-page map of "The World of Animal Homosexuality," on the second and third pages of the introduction, invites us to see the earth as an entirely different place, one populated with a multitude of queer sexualities. Unlike Latour's clumsy waiter whose "nice dishes" crash to the ground, Bagemihl wishes to deliver "'the facts' about animal behavior'" as well "captur[ing] some of their 'poetry'": "In addition to being interesting from a purely scientific standpoint, these phenomena are also capable of inspiring our deepest feelings of wonder, and our most profound sense of awe" (1999, 6). Such wonder and awe, may, I hope, help foster queer-green ethics, politics, practices, and places.

NOTES

1. For more on race and nature see Moore, Kosek, and Pandian (2003). . . . Dana Seitler documents the emergence of sexual "perversity" as interconnected with other categories: "the construction of perversity appears as part of a story in which race, gender, physical deformation, sexuality, and many other bodily forms and practices emerge in ontologically and epistemologically interdependent ways" (2004, 74).

2. Susan Block is not the only one inspired by bonobo sex. Barbara Ehrenreich, in a piece entitled, "Let Me Be a Bonobo," predicts a "surge in trans-species people, who will eagerly go over to the side of the chimps." She explains that another "reason to make the human-to-ape transition is the sex": "Bonobos, genetically as close to humans as larger chimpanzees, use sex much as we use handshakes—as a form of greeting between individuals in any gender combination" (Ehrenreich 2007, x). Kelpie Wilson's science fiction novel *Primal Tears* features a half-bonobo, half-human protagonist named "Sage" (2005). Interestingly, the same sort of alliance between sexual freedom and environmentalism that Susan Block promotes becomes a problem in the novel when some of Sage's fans transform her "Rainbow Clubs"—which are intended to promote the protection of endangered bonobos—into sex clubs.

3. Cuonzo also refers to the "'other minds' problem," questioning whether, say, the illustrations in Bagemihl's book, "pictures of animals in what looks like sexual activity," are, in fact, sex: "But how do we know that these behaviors are what they seem to be?" (2003, 230). While it is epistemologically and ethically useful to underscore the limits of human knowledge, it is just as problematic—if not perverse—to then conclude that because we cannot, absolutely, know these behaviors "are" sex, then they are not. Certainly, heterosex between animals is not held up to such a high standard of "proof." Cuonzo's skepticism seems a perfect example of how cultural critics are much better (in Latour's terms) at "subtracting reality."

4. McWhorter's brilliant recasting of deviance articulates sexual deviance with evolutionary deviation, resulting in a formulation that generates a queer green ethics: "It was deviation in development that produced this grove, this landscape, this living planet. What is good is that the world remain ever open to deviation" (1999, 164).

5. See the essays within *Material Feminisms* (Alaimo and Hekman 2008) for a range of approaches that combine postmodernism, poststructuralism, and social construction with a commitment to productively engaging with the materiality of human bodies and more-than-human natures and environments. Hekman and I argue that a paradigm shift is underway in which the linguistic turn that has dominated humanities scholarship is being transformed by theories that engage with material forces. Hekman's essay "Constructing the Ballast: An Ontology for Feminism" (2008) provides an excellent map of four different "settlements" in contemporary theory in which this new paradigm is emerging.

6. See, for example, Evelyn Fox-Keller's critique of genetic determinism in *The Century of the Gene* (2002). Another striking counterpoint to genetic determinism would be Ronnie Zoe Hawkins's contention that "the message of the genome is the opposite of biological determinism: our primate biology provides us with a tremendous amount of behavioral flexibility, while our social and cultural environments are often in the role of maintaining practices that have become maladaptive" (2002, 60–61).

7. See Lynda Birke's discussion of how most critiques of biological determinism apply only to humans, which means that they not only ignore the behavior of other animals but also rely upon a strict human/animal dichotomy (1994, 110–30).

8. My facile division of this terminology raises larger epistemological and ethical questions regarding the discourses for animal sex. Terms that seem too anthropomorphic disrespect the differences of various nonhuman creatures. Terms that seem too anti-anthropomorphic shore up the human/animal divide, casting animals as mechanistic creatures of instinct or genetic determinism. Clearly there is no way out of this dilemma; our terms are strands within these webs of meaning, relation, and effect.

9. One aspect of the new materialism in science studies, or of "material feminisms" (see Alaimo and Hekman 2008), is an openness to the transgressive, progressive potential for theoretical engagements with materiality. Myra J. Hird puts it succinctly in "Naturally Queer": "We may no longer be certain that it is nature that remains static and culture that evinces limitless malleability" (2004a, 88). Roughgarden states: "Biology need not be a purveyor of essentialism, of rigid universals. Biology need not limit our potential" (2004, 180). In *Undomesticated Ground*, I discuss a range of women writers, from the late nineteenth century to the present, who challenge the conception of nature as a ground of fixed essences, rigid sexual difference, and already apparent norms, values, and prohibitions (Alaimo 2000, 17).

10. Frans de Waal writes that some "authors and scientists are so ill at ease [with the bonobo's sexuality] that they talk in riddles. . . . It's like listening to a gathering of bakers who have decided to drop the word 'bread' from their vocabulary, making for incredibly circumlocutory exchanges. The sexiness of bonobos is often downplayed by counting only copulations between adults of the opposite sex. But this really leaves out most of what is going on in their daily lives. It is a curious omission, given that the 'sex' label normally refers to any deliberate contact involving the genitals, including petting and oral stimulation" (2005, 93).

11. Similarly, Cynthia Chris argues that within television wildlife shows homosexuality is "not a natural act to be understood on its own terms, but a phase of foreplay prior to the real reproductive deal, an assertion of power, or an experience though which one risks subordination. Pleasure for these creatures, is strictly on the rocks" (2006, 165).

12. Queer animals may disrupt the prevalent marketing of nature as the quintessentially wholesome (straight) family recreational site. Just as I always wonder, every time I teach Whitman's "Song of Myself," what decades of school children (and their teachers) thought about that blatant homosexual moment within the poem, I wonder how dolphin-tour operators respond to the question, "What are they doing?!" when, say, a group of male dolphins, penises very much in plain sight, rub against each other in a frenzy of pleasure, right next to the tour boat. Oh, to have access to an archive of these conversations!

13. The reference alludes to the J. B. S. Haldane quote "The Universe is not only queerer than we suppose, it is queerer than we can suppose," which Bagemihl, Hird, and Lancaster all use as an epigraph.

REFERENCES

Against Nature? An Exhibition on Animal Homosexuality. 2007. Naturhistorisk museum, Oslo Norway. http://www.nhm.uio.no/besokende/skiftende-utstillinger/againstnature/index-eng.html.

Alaimo, Stacy. 2000. *Undomesticated Ground: Recasting Nature as Feminist Space.* Ithaca, N.Y.: Cornell University Press.

Alaimo, Stacy, and Susan J. Hekman, eds. 2008. *Material Feminisms.* Bloomington: Indiana University Press.

Ananova. 2005. Penguins Can Stay Gay. http://www.ananova.com/news/story/sm_1284769.html.

Bagemihl, Bruce. 1999. *Biological Exuberance: Animal Homosexuality and Natural Diversity*. New York: St. Martin's Press.

Barad, Karen. 2003. Posthumanist Performativity: Toward an Understanding of How Matter *Comes to Matter. Signs: Journal of Women in Culture and Society* 28.3: 801–31.

Birke, Lynda. 1994. *Feminism, Animals, and Science: The Naming of the Shrew*. Buckingham, U.K.: Open University Press.

Block, Susan. 2007. The Bonobo Way. http://www.blockbonobofoundation.org/.

Chris, Cynthia. 2006. *Watching Wildlife*. Minneapolis: University of Minnesota Press.

Cuonzo, Margaret. 2003. Queer Nature, Circular Science. In *Science and Other Cultures: Issues in Philosophy of Science and Technology*, ed. Robert Figueroa and Sandra Harding, 221–33. New York: Routledge.

De Waal, Frans. 2005. *Our Inner Ape: A Leading Primatologist Explains Why We Are Who We Are*. New York: Riverhead Books.

Dixon, Alan F. 1998. *Primate Sexuality: Comparative Studies of the Prosimians, Monkeys, Apes, and Human Beings*. Oxford, U.K.: Oxford University Press.

Ehrenreich, Barbara. 2007. Let Me Be a Bonobo. *Guardian*, Thursday, May 10, 32.

Field, Kristin L., and Thomas A. Waite. 2004. Absence of Female Conspecifics Induces Homosexual Behavior in Male Guppies. *Animal Behavior* 68: 1381–89.

Fox-Keller, Evelyn. 2002. *The Century of the Gene*. Cambridge, Mass.: Harvard University Press.

Gay Outrage over Penguin Sex Test. 2005. *BBC News*. http://news.bbc.co.uk/2/hi/europe/4264913.stm, February 14.

Gouzoules, H. and Robert W. Goy. 1983. Physiological and social influences on mounting behavior of troop-living female monkeys *(Macaca fuscata)*. *American Journal of Primatology* 5.1: 39–49.

Hamming, Jeanne. 2001. Dildonics, Dykes and the Detachable Masculine. *European Journal of Women's Studies* 8.3: 329–41.

Haraway, Donna J. 1990. *Primate Visions: Gender, Race, and Nature in the World of Modern Science*. New York: Routledge.

Haraway, Donna J. 2003. *The Companion Species Manifesto: Dogs, People, and Significant Otherness*. Chicago: Prickly Paradigm Press.

Hawkins, Ronnie Zoe. 2002. Seeing Ourselves as Primates. *Ethics and the Environment* 7.2: 60–103.

Hekman, Susan. 2008. Constructing the Ballast: An Ontology for Feminism. In Material Feminisms, ed. Stacy Alaimo and Susan Hekman, 85–119. Bloomington: Indiana University Press.

Herzog, Werner, dir. 2005. Motion picture. *Grizzly Man*. Lions Gate Entertainment.

Hird, Myra J. 2004a. Naturally Queer. *Feminist Theory* 5.1: 85–89.

Hird, Myra J. 2004b. *Sex, Gender and Science*. New York: Palgrave.

Jeffrey, Duane. 2005. Review of Joan Roughgarden's *Evolution's Rainbow. Politics and the Life Sciences* 23.2 (10 November): 71–77.

Judson, Olivia. 2003. *Dr. Tatiana's Sex Advice to All Creation: The Definitive Guide to the Evolutionary Biology of Sex*. New York: Vintage Books.

Lancaster, Roger N. 2003. *The Trouble with Nature: Sex in Science and Popular Culture*. Berkeley and Los Angeles: University of California Press.

Latour, Bruno. 2004. Why Has Critique Run Out of Steam? From Matters of Fact to Matters of Concern. *Critical Inquiry* 30: 225–48.

Marks, Jonathan. 2002. *What it Means to Be 98% Chimpanzee: Apes, People, and Their Genes*. Berkeley and Los Angeles: University of California Press.

Massumi, Brian. 2002. *Parables for the Virtual: Movement, Affect, Sensation*. Durham, N.C.: Duke University Press.

McWhorter, Ladelle. 1999. *Bodies and Pleasures: Foucault and the Politics of Sexual Normalization*. Bloomington: Indiana University Press.

Moore, Donald S., Jake Kosek, and Anand Pandian, eds. 2003. *Race, Nature, and the Politics of Difference*. Durham, N.C.: Duke University Press.

Mortimer-Sandilands, Catriona. 2005. Unnatural Passions? Notes Toward a Queer Ecology. *Invisible Culture* 9. http://www.rochester.edu/in_visible_culture/Issue_9/title9.html.

Opar, Alisa. 2006. We're Deer. We're Queer. Get Used to It: A New Exhibit in Norway Outs the Animal Kingdom. *Plenty Magazine: Environmental News and Commentary,* October 25.

Pickering, Andrew. 1995. *The Mangle of Practice: Time, Agency, and Science*. Chicago: University of Chicago Press.

Roughgarden, Joan. 2004. *Evolution's Rainbow: Diversity, Gender, and Sexuality in Nature and People*. Berkeley and Los Angeles: University of California Press.

Rubin, Gayle. 1975. The Traffic of Women: Notes on the "Political Economy" of Sex. In *Toward an Anthropology of Woman*, ed. Rayna Reiter, 157–85, 198–200. New York: Monthly Review Press.

Sandilands, Catriona. 1999. Sex at the Limits. In *Discourses of the Environment*, ed. Eric Darier, 79–94. Oxford, U.K.: Blackwell.

Sandilands, Catriona. 2001. Desiring Nature, Queering Ethics: Adventures in Erotogenic Environments. *Environmental Ethics* 23.2: 169–88.

Sedgwick, Eve Kosofsky. 1990. *Epistemology of the Closet*. Berkeley and Los Angeles: University of California Press.

Seitler, Dana. 2004. Queer Physiognomies; Or, How Many Ways Can We Do the History of Sexuality? *Criticism* 46: 71–102.

Shearer, Meagan K., and Larry S. Katz. 2006. Female-Female Mounting among Goats Stimulates Sexual Performance in Males. *Hormones and Behavior* 50: 33–37.

Sommer, Volker. 2006. Against Nature?! An Epilogue about Animal Sex and the Moral Dimension. *In Homosexual Behaviour in Animals: An Evolutionary Perspective*, ed. Paul Vasey and Volker Sommer, 365–71. Cambridge: Cambridge University Press.

Terry, Jennifer. 2000. "Unnatural Acts" in Nature: The Scientific Fascination with Queer Animals. *GLQ* 6.2: 151–93.

Vasey, Paul L. 2004a. Pre- and Postconflict Interactions between Female Japanese Macaques during Homosexual Consortships. *International Journal of Comparative Psychology* 17: 351–59.

Vasey, Paul L. 2004b. Sex Differences in Sexual Partner Acquisition, Retention, and Harassment during Female Homosexual Consortships in Japanese Macaques. *American Journal of Primatology* 64: 397–409.

Vasey, Paul L., Afra Foroud, Nadine Duckworth, and Stefani D. Kovacovsky. 2006. Male-Female and Female-Female Mounting in Japanese Macaques: A Comparative Study of Posture and Movement. *Archives of Sexual Behavior* 35.2: 117–29.

Wilson, Kelpie. 2005. *Primal Tears*. Berkeley, Calif.: Frog Limited.

Woodson, J. C. 2002. Including "Learned Sexuality" in the Organization of Sexual Behavior. *Neuroscience and Biobehavioral Reviews* (Jan. 26): 69–80.

JOANNE CLARKE DILLMAN

26. "DOMINATED, OPENED AND ENTERED": THEORIZING THE DEAD WOMAN IN CONTEMPORARY MEDIA REPRESENTATION

INTRODUCTION

Graphic images of the imagined dead woman are ubiquitous today in film, television, and other media. A notorious recent example is the animal rights campaign by PETA that equates women's dead bodies to beef. In one set of images, (seemingly) dead women splattered with "blood" are wrapped in cellophane on plastic trays ("PETA Strikes Again"). In other displays, image and word are linked as in an advertisement (@peta. "Meat Is Murder"). Rather than its relation to language, though, what we remember is the image itself. Images have a "surplus value" (Mitchell); they can exceed the significations to which they have been employed. The PETA images also show, as W.J.T. Mitchell observes, that images "cannot say no to what they signify" (Dikovitskaya 238). Although the preferred meaning is the need to boycott meat, the images provoke outrage because they also reflect a callous sexism. Thus, images differ from language-based signification. The filmmaker Pier Paolo Pasolini understood this when he wrote, "Images are always concrete, never abstract" (171). In this essay, I critically examine meanings of the dead woman's body in media through case studies of *The Bridge* and *The Killing* television series.

Images, television shows, and films—centered on dead bodies or not—are linked to the context of their production. My work relates dead women in visual representations to the contexts of globalization, antifeminism, and post 9/11 anxieties (Clarke Dillman). I also draw a connection between women who have been murdered in real life and the patterns of murder now so conventionalized in films and television shows. I argue that a show's narrative storyline involving a detective and a killer is in a different register than that

of its visual violence and corpse images. This means that although the killer is caught by a show's end, indicating that the case is closed, nothing changes the fact that gruesome images of a woman tortured, raped, or beaten to death have been used to manipulate the viewer. In a culture ordered by "male preoccupations" (Bal 17–18), women *mean*; that is, they signify beyond themselves for the culture that produces them. And as Sarah Webster Goodwin and Elisabeth Bronfen note, in representation "death is gendered" (13). Women often have brutal, slow deaths, and their bodies are often posed in a graphic, sexualized fashion. The deaths and corpses of male characters tend to be treated differently.

For these reasons, I disagree with Amy Sullivan's characterization of the BBC show *The Fall* (2013–), which features women's corpses and graphic depictions of violence against women, as "the most feminist show on television" because, among other things, its detective's gender is a "non-issue." The gender of the dead bodies on which the show depends *is* an issue. Moreover, I argue that the increasing courage and brilliance of the woman detective is offset by the increasing viciousness of the serial killer and the increasingly graphic violence he visits on women victims.

The cultural studies perspective understands the representational arena as a site of struggle over contentious issues. After 9/11 and especially during the era of globalization, dead women in representation signify a cultural anxiety related to women's changing status in social life. How can women become equal to men without men losing power and privilege? As Angela McRobbie notes, despite the claim that equality of the sexes has "achieved the status of common sense"

(6) and differentiates the West from less developed cultures (1), women's equality remains contested. If this contestation cannot be spoken, it is repressed and returns in other sites, such as movies and television shows. Michel Foucault describes a similar phenomenon in his discussion of sexuality and the repressive hypothesis (10). The repetition of graphic violence and its outcomes—death and the corpse image—in many "entertainment" sites across the visual field suggests a powerful, unconscious resentment over women's real-world gains.

Imagery of dead women has reached a point of saturation in contemporary representation. In one example, AMC's *The Bridge* (2013–2014) takes up a story-line related to the murders of women along the border in Ciudad Juárez. In the representational arena as in the real world, this proliferation of dead female bodies is rooted in a number of interrelated factors: shifts in gender politics brought about by the affirmation of women's rights and what Manuel Castells calls "men's defense of their privileges" (194); escalation of patri-archal, fundamentalist views of "family values" that stand in direct opposition to women's bodily auton-omy; and the destabilization of Mexican social norms in the wake of "free trade." In *The Killing*, also on AMC, the dead woman's body becomes a floating signifier, in that brutal graphic images indicating sexual or gen-dered violence are shown repeatedly throughout the first two seasons to explore social stereotypes and male behavior. This narrative pathway allows the show to lure the viewer with signs that indicate gendered vio-lence, only to erode the truth value of those very signs, as I have also discussed in the context of *CSI* (Clarke Dillman 97).

And yet signs of gendered violence generally sig-nify intelligibly that the violence is being enacted against women for a reason. For men of all classes and nationalities, the power and prerogatives aligned with male identity—in the home, on the job, and in reli-gious institutions—appear to be under threat. Since the 1960s and 1970s, women have shattered educa-tional barriers all over the world, taken up positions in the world's elite professions, integrated into the armed forces, and played sports from grade school to the professional level. That women and many men have embraced these changes is apparent for all to see.

What has persisted in response is a legacy of violence directed at women as scapegoat. For Vivian Fox, "at-titudes towards women" that place them as "inferior" and traditional beliefs about women's inferiority ". . . have imprinted a psychic cultural memory that lingers and continues to motivate belief and behavior despite historic change" (16). One arena that Fox does not consider is the media and its power to shape a culture's beliefs, an area that I will turn to now.

HISTORICAL REPRESENTATIONS OF DEAD WOMEN IN MEDIA

Violent reactions to women's gains that are imprinted on their (dead) bodies visibly play out in the media arena. For example, Brian Jarvis notes that of the one thousand films about serial killers in the Internet Movie Database (IMDb), the majority have been cre-ated since the early 1990s (327). Widespread fascina-tion with the female corpse onscreen can be dated back to this moment, a time that Susan Faludi marks as the onset of a backlash against the second wave feminist movement. Certainly, a number of novels and films with a serial killer narrative and images of graphic violence against women stem from 1980s and 1990s, including Thomas Harris's novels *Silence of the Lambs* (1988, film 1991) and *Red Dragon* (1981), which is the basis of the films *Manhunter* (1986) and *Red Dragon* (2002), and Bret Easton Ellis's novel *Ameri-can Psycho* (1991) and the film version with Christian Bale (2000). The British TV series *Prime Suspect* also first appeared in 1991. As Deborah Jermyn (2003) notes, Detective Chief Inspector Jane Tennison pitted her wits not only against a serial killer, but also against a hostile work environment. *Prime Suspect* was also hugely successful in the United States. *CSI: Crime Scene Investigation* (2000–2015) and its various spin-offs also cultivated the fascination with graphic images of women's dead bodies, and deployed those bodies for "killer ratings" (March).

According to Jarvis, "The serial killer is driven by the desire to achieve mastery, virility, and control: his objective is to dominate and possess the body and the mind of his victims. . . . [T]he killer/victim dyad produces a polarization of gender norms: the killer embodies an uber masculinity while the victim, who

is *dominated*, *opened* and *entered* [my italics] personi-
fies a hyper-femininity" (333). The violated corpse or
corpse image reduces the woman to her embodiment.
Through the performative acts of this violence, the
woman is forced, unwillingly, to take up a culturally
determined feminine position. Is this not what Judith
Butler would consider to be violence as "regulatory
norm" (2)? It seeks to limit the movement of women
as social actors through violation and warning. The
violated body is the mark and ground of woman's
difference; she is reduced to body again and again in
representation precisely because in the contemporary
global context women are no longer so limited. This is
an instance of how "[violence] is engendered as 'symbolic action'" (Domínguez-Ruvalcada and Corona 4).

In studies of dead women, scholars have noted the
variety of arenas in which the dead woman as signifier
has been put to cultural use. In her study of the Book
of Judges, Mieke Bal develops a feminist method of
interpretation to locate the dead woman in relation to
"the reality that brought [her story] forth and to which
it responded" (3). This method offers a way to theorize the proliferation of female corpses in the media
in the contemporary moment. Scholars have also examined dead women in art and literature (Bronfen),
crime thrillers like *Prime Suspect* and *The Fall* (Jermyn),
and *CSI* (Tait). Brian Norman's study of literature and
my examination of film, television, and news interpret
works that place a woman under erasure of death as
the condition for her emergence in the story space (as
in *The Lovely Bones*). All of these scholars share an interest in the "spectacle of the ruined body" (Pinedo 6). In
her study of Jack the Ripper, Judith Walkowitz marks
industrialization as the historical locus in which he
emerged and notes how boys, husbands, men on the
street, and police officers used the threat of the Ripper
to discipline and scare girls and women (561–563).
Today's corpse images perform a similar function.

CONTEMPORARY EXAMPLES: *THE BRIDGE* AND *THE KILLING*

Series such as *The Bridge*, based on the Scandinavian
series *Bron/Broen* (2011–present), and *The Killing*,
adapted from the Danish series *Forbrydelsen* ("The
Crime," 2007–2012; unavailable in the United States),

show how dead women signify for their cultures in
the early twenty-first century. Indeed, in *Bron/Broen*,
the detective Saga remarks, after a female corpse is discovered on the middle of a bridge in the first episode,
"This is meant to send a message." Despite this opening, however, *Bron/Broen* is not specifically interested
in gendered murder, while AMC's *The Bridge* never
loses sight of the killings of women in Ciudad Juárez,
Mexico. *The Bridge* also follows the storyline of Sonya,
an El Paso detective who loses her sister to a violent
serial killer.

The Bridge suggests that serial killers are an American phenomenon when the Mexican drug lord Fausto,
upon reading the newspaper, asks, "What is a serial
killer?" For Fausto, killing is "just business." And as
his henchman notes, Fausto could not be mistaken
for a serial killer because serial killing involves "sexu-
ales," and, he "does not enjoy it." But the signification
that human life is cheap in the Mexican context still
comes through the bodies of young women; women
are symbolic currency. *The Bridge* implies that the
Mexican police are themselves the killers of the missing women of Juárez. In their discussion of real-life
murder victims on the U.S.-Mexico border, Héctor
Domínguez-Ruvalcada and Ignacio Corona write, ". . .
these women are not killed in random acts of fury,
but because they constitute or 'symbolize' a particular group of women . . . from an economic perspective women have come to personify social change and
ultimately liberation from the traditional webs of institutional and social control" (5). By gaining employment, women accrue financial clout and freedom from
dependence on the male breadwinner in the family,
destabilizing that social institution.

Nothing in *The Bridge* can be read in isolation.
While the bridge is a material structure straddling the
boundary between Mexico and the United States, the
credit sequence depicts the border as porous, with a
constant flow of traffic between El Paso and Ciudad
Juárez belying rigid border distinctions. In the opening
episode, "the bridge" between cultures is constituted
by the female body left in the center of the road on the
span between the two locales. Implicating institutions
in both countries, the body is grotesquely comprised
of the torso and head of a middle-aged (female) American judge and the lower half of a disappeared young

Mexican woman. Does this suggest that the "ruling elite" is above the border and the "labor-producing body" is below, that the Mexican body is mule to the American arbiter of justice, that both are victimized/feminized? The dead women are symbolic of resentment over female intrusion into the realms of justice and work. This body is made to stand in for a whole region destroyed by "free trade," trafficking, and drug violence.

On *The Bridge*, it is men who generally enact spectacular violence. On the U.S. side, a cuddly, patriarchal sheriff never tires of the autistic ticks of Sonya, the El Paso detective. He avenges the death of Sonya's sister, though this does not play out as he expects. A deranged border terrorist turns out to be a middle-aged white American male FBI agent. On both sides of the border, law enforcement is compromised. The FBI, the CIA, and the Mexican police are violent and riddled through with corruption.

With such a high level of violence, all of the central characters are marked by loss. To avenge the deaths of his wife and son, rogue FBI agent David Tate kills the son of Mexican detective Marco. Tate is also responsible for the two women who comprise the broken body left on the bridge in the opening episode. Another storyline revolves around Eva, a Mexican maquiladora worker trapped in the system of abuse who Mexican policemen drug, rape, and leave for dead. She is saved from death by the creepy, born-again social worker Steven and by the efforts of Sonya, Marco, and the sheriff. The second season unleashes an unhinged Mennonite accountant, Eleanor Nacht, whose vengeance is also grounded in loss; Social Services took her child because it was conceived through sexual abuse by her patriarchal father. Eleanor quotes Bible verses while serving as accountant and killer for Fausto.

A transnational theme resonates in *The Bridge*, just as it did in the original Scandinavian television series set at the border between Denmark and Sweden: women are the signs men use to communicate anger. While much of *The Bridge's* storyline is faithful to the Scandinavian original, it is in relation to the women characters and their social context that one finds many of the departures from *Bron/Broen*. For example, in the original series, the detective, Saga, has a sister who dies from suicide, not gendered violence. The

Ciudad Juárez murders are particular to the Mexican locale and the globalization era. *The Bridge* suggests that these murdered women are responsible for their own deaths, but they are actually the disposable bodies stemming from an endemic state corruption. Because the police act with impunity, the only recourse of family members is to check the fields in the desert for the murdered bodies of their missing loved ones. At the end of the second season, a government attorney is determined to expose the Police Department's widespread corruption, but he is gunned down, and his evidence is destroyed.

Two multiseason narrative arcs involving gendered violence comprise the central storylines of the four seasons of AMC's *The Killing*, set in Seattle, Washington. In the first season, detectives Sarah Linden and Stephen Holder work to uncover the murderer of the teenager Rosie Larsen. In all four seasons, *The Killing's* depiction of graphic violence conforms to the pattern set by shows like *CSI*. Photos of victims at crime scenes and from autopsies show us what happened, and, as the series progresses, remind us of the bodily trauma of the victims. In season one, for example, images of Rosie Larsen's bruised and battered wrists, scored with rope marks, are visually linked to the wrists of the crucified Christ in the church where her funeral is held, suggesting early on that the killer may be a church member.

Over the course of four seasons, a generalized atmosphere of hostility to women is palpable through callous sexism at the precinct and throughout the workday. During the initial two-season arc, male colleagues tease Sarah by giving her a blow-up doll at her going-away party. A teenage male suspect seethes with privilege and anger, calling Sarah a bitch. Middle schoolers the same age as Sarah's son also deride her as a "bitch." A janitor with teen porn magazines spies on amorous students in the high school's basement "cage," where because of all the blood, it is thought that Rosie Larsen was murdered. But when the janitor is ruled out as a suspect, the show appears to forget about the blood and the cage. What happened there? The show moves on. In addition, the violent propensity of masculinity is critiqued through Stan's history as a hitman and Belko's gleeful participation in the beating of a teacher. These instances of flawed masculinity are countered by the two Muslim males who become the object of an FBI surveillance operation because of their efforts to help a young Muslim girl escape female genital mutilation. For this they are surveilled as Muslim terrorists.

In this narrative arc, *The Killing* repeatedly defers confirmation of the identity of the true killer while offering one plausible male suspect after another, including those with political and financial clout. After two seasons, the shocker ending is that, although Rosie Larsen had been beaten and hunted like prey by a male political consultant, her killer is her aunt Terri.

The third and fourth season storyline escalates the search for one girl's killer to the search for a rapacious serial killer whose victims are young teens. The grisly violence is also escalated; we are shown photos of victims with nearly severed heads and hands with missing fingers. Out of a shallow lake deep in the forest come seventeen victims in bright red biohazard body bags. When detectives interrogate an intended victim who escaped the serial killer, the visible stitching on her neck and nose demand that viewers contemplate the violence of her ordeal. As earlier in the series, suspicion falls on one man after another. Is the killer the pedophile pornographer, the veterinarian who stitched up the escaped girl, the homeless shelter minister, Holder's partner Reddick, or the head of the Special Investigations Unit, Lieutenant Skinner? Despite *The Killing*'s effort—like *The Bridge*'s—to implicate women in violent actions that end in death, what both series underscore is the generalized threat of violence men pose to women and girls.

The identity of the serial killer is finally revealed to be Lieutenant Skinner, although Seattle's institutional power brokers hush this up. *The Killing* then abruptly jumps to several years later. Stephen Holder, now the father of a young girl and divorced, meets up with Sarah Linden, who has been gone for some time. Holder playfully asks Linden, "Did you find the bad guy?" After a thoughtful pause, she responds, "No. There is no bad guy; just life." This attempt to disavow that there are "bad guys," after the show has wallowed in toxic masculinity, depravity, and graphic imagery of gendered violence, rings hollow, as does the effort to unite Linden and Holder. Like the effort to implicate women in violence, these plot moves are manipulative fantasies, designed for audiences so desensitized to graphic violence that the show is left only with unthinkable or implausible choices. *The Killing* has revealed a Seattle awash in women's bodies and lawless behavior; fifteen minutes of strained happiness at the end cannot undo that.

These examples show how media texts that tell stories centered around dead women's bodies increasingly demand higher and higher levels of graphic violence, rendering these women increasingly more disposable and anonymous. A feminist analysis that only looks at the brave female detective or the vanquishing of the killer overlooks what these shows depend on, which is a violent encounter with a woman's disposability.

REFERENCES

Bal, Mieke. *Death and Dissymmetry: The Politics of Coherence in the Book of Judges*. Chicago: University of Chicago Press, 1988.

Bronfen, Elisabeth. *Over Her Dead Body: Death, Femininity, and the Aesthetic*. New York: Routledge, 1992.

Butler, Judith. *Bodies That Matter: On the Discursive Limits of "Sex."* New York: Routledge, 1993.

Castells, Manuel. *The Power of Identity*. 2nd ed. Malden, MA: Blackwell Pub., 2004.

Clarke Dillman, Joanne. *Women and Death in Film, Television, and News; Dead but Not Gone*. New York: Palgrave, 2014.

Demme, Jonathan, et al. *The Silence of the Lambs*. Orion Pictures, 1991.

Dikovitskaya, Margaret. "An Interview with W.J.T. Mitchell." *Visual Culture: The Study of the Visual after the Cultural Turn*. Cambridge, MA: MIT Press, (2005): 238–257.

Domínguez-Ruvalcada, Héctor, and Ignacio Corona. *Gender Violence at the U.S.-Mexico Border: Media Representation and Public Response*. Tucson: University of Arizona Press, 2010.

Ellis, Bret Easton. *American Psycho: A Novel*. New York: Vintage Books, 1991.

Faludi, Susan. *Backlash: The Undeclared War Against American Women*. New York: Anchor Books, 1991.

Foucault, Michel. *The History of Sexuality, Volume I: An Introduction*. Translated by Robert Hurley. New York: Vintage Books, 1990.

Fox, Vivian. "Historical Perspectives on Violence against Women." *Journal of International Women's Studies* 4.1 (November 2002): 15–34.

Harris, Thomas. *The Silence of the Lambs*. New York: St. Martin's Press, 1988.

Harris, Thomas. *Red Dragon*. New York: Putnam, 1981.

Harron, Mary, et al. *American Psycho*. Lionsgate, 2000.

Goodwin, Sarah Webster and Elisabeth Bronfen. "Introduction." *Death and Representation*, edited by Sarah Webster Goodwin and Elisabeth Bronfen. Baltimore, MD: The Johns Hopkins University Press, 1993. 3–25.

Jarvis, Brian. "Monster's Inc.: Serial Killers and Consumer Culture." *Crime, Media, Culture* 3 (2007): 326–344.

Jermyn, Deborah. "Silk Blouses and Fedoras: The Female Detective, Contemporary TV Crime Drama and the Predicaments of Postfeminism." *Crime, Media, Culture* 13.3 (2016): 259–276. doi:10.1177/1741659015626578.

Jermyn, Deborah. "Women with a Mission: Lynda LaPlante, DCI Jane Tennison and the Reconfiguration of Television Crime Drama." *Cultural Studies* 6.1 (2003): 46–63.

Mann, Michael, et al. *Manhunter*. Karl-Lorimar Video, 1986.

March, Anna. "Dead Girls, Killer Ratings: 'Game of Thrones,' 'True Detective' and TV's Epidemic of Violence against Women." *Salon*, April 14, 2015, http://www.salon.com/2015/04/14/dead_women_killer_ratings_game_of_thrones_true_detective_and_tvs_epidemic_of_violence_against_women_partner/.

McRobbie, Angela. *The Aftermath of Feminism: Gender, Culture, and Social Change*. Los Angeles: Sage Publications, 2009.

Menaul, Christopher, *et al. Prime Suspect*, Series 1. ITV Studios Limited., 1991.

Mitchell, W.J.T. "The Surplus Value of Images." *Mosaic* 35.3 (September 2002).

Norman, Brian. *Dead Women Talking: Figures of Injustice in American Literature*. Baltimore, MD: The Johns Hopkins University Press, 2013.

Pasolini, Pier Paolo. "The 'Cinema of Poetry.'" *Heretical Empiricism*. Translated by Louise K. Barnett, edited by Ben Lawton and Louise K. Barnett. Bloomington: Indiana University Press, 1988.

@peta. "Meat is Murder." *Twitter*, May 25, 2014, https://twitter.com/peta/status/470628117879324672.

"PETA Strikes Again in San Francisco: Women Stand in as Literal Pieces of Meat." *About-Face*, March 22, 2012, https://www.about-face.org/peta-strikes-again-today-in-san-francisco-women-stand-in-as-literal-pieces-of-meat/.

Pinedo, Isabel. *Recreational Terror: Women and the Pleasure of Horror Film Viewing*. Albany: State University of New York Press, 1997.

Ratner, Brett, et al. *Red Dragon*. Universal Pictures, 2002.

Sullivan, Amy. "The Fall: The Most Feminist Show on Television." *The Atlantic*, January 23, 2015, https://www.theatlantic.com/entertainment/archive/2015/01/the-fall-the-most-feminist-show-on-television/384751/.

Tait, Sue. "Autoptic Vision and the Necrophilic Imaginary in CSI." *International Journal of Cultural Studies* 9.1 (2006): 45–62.

Walkowitz, Judith R. "Jack the Ripper and the Myth of Male Violence." *Feminist Studies*, 8.3 (1982): 543–574.

27. GENDER TROUBLE, FEMINIST THEORY AND PSYCHOANALYTIC DISCOURSE

Within the terms of feminist theory, it has been quite important to refer to the category of "women" and to know what it is we mean. We tend to agree that women have been written out of the histories of culture and literature that men have written, that women have been silenced or distorted in the texts of philosophy, biology, and physics, and that there is a group of embodied beings socially positioned as "women" who now, under the name of feminism, have something quite different to say. Yet, this question of being a woman is more difficult than it perhaps originally appeared, for we refer not only to women as a social category but also as a felt sense of self, a culturally conditioned or constructed subjective identity. The descriptions of women's oppression, their historical situation or cultural perspective has seemed, to some, to require that women themselves will not only recognize the rightness of feminist claims made in their behalf, but that, together, they will discover a common identity, whether in their relational attitudes, in their embodied resistance to abstract and objectifying modes of thought and experience, their felt sense of their bodies, their capacity for maternal identification or maternal thinking, the nonlinear directionality of their pleasures or the elliptical and plurivocal possibilities of their writing.

But does feminist theory need to rely on a notion of what it is fundamentally or distinctively to be a "woman"? The question becomes a crucial one when we try to answer what it is that characterizes the world of women that is marginalized, distorted, or negated within various masculinist practices. Is there a specific femininity or a specific set of values that have been written out of various histories and descriptions that can be associated with women as a group? Does the category of woman maintain a meaning separate from the conditions of oppression against which it has been formulated?

For the most part, feminist theory has taken the category of women to be foundational to any further political claims without realizing that the category effects a political closure on the kinds of experiences articulable as part of a feminist discourse. When the category is understood as representing a set of values or dispositions, it becomes normative in character and, hence, exclusionary in principle. This move has created a problem both theoretical and political, namely, that a variety of women from various cultural positions have refused to recognize themselves as "women" in the terms articulated by feminist theory with the result that these women fall outside the category and are left to conclude that (1) either they are not women as they have perhaps previously assumed or (2) the category reflects the restricted location of its theoreticians and, hence, fails to recognize the intersection of gender with race, class, ethnicity, age, sexuality, and other currents which contribute to the formation of cultural (non)identity. In response to the radical exclusion of the category of women from hegemonic cultural formations on the one hand and the internal critique of the exclusionary effects of the category from within feminist discourse on the other, feminist theorists are now confronted with the problem of either redefining and expanding the category of women itself to become more inclusive (which requires also the political matter of settling who gets to make the designation and in the name of whom) or to challenge the place of the category as a part of a feminist normative

Judith Butler, "Gender Trouble, Feminist Theory and Psychoanalytic Discourse," in *Feminism/Postmodernism*, ed. Linda J. Nicholson (New York, NY: Routledge, 1990): 324–340. Reprinted with permission of Judith Butler.

discourse. Gayatri Spivak has argued that feminists need to rely on an operational essentialism, a false ontology of women as a universal in order to advance a feminist political program.[1] She concedes that the category of women is not fully expressive, that the multiplicity and discontinuity of the signified rebels against the univocity of the sign, but she suggests that we need to use it for strategic purposes. Julia Kristeva suggests something similar, I think, when she recommends that feminists use the category of women as a political tool without attributing ontological integrity to the term, and she adds that, strictly speaking, women cannot be said to exist.[2]

But is it the presumption of ontological integrity that needs to be dispelled, or does the practical redeployment of the category without any ontological commitments also effect a political consolidation of its semantic integrity with serious exclusionary implications? Is there another normative point of departure for feminist theory that does not require the reconstruction or rendering visible of a female subject who fails to represent, much less emancipate, the array of embodied beings culturally positioned as women?

Psychoanalytic theory has occupied an ambiguous position in the feminist quandary over whether the category of women has a rightful place within feminist political discourse. On the one hand, psychoanalysis has sought to identify the developmental moments in which gendered identity is acquired. Yet, those feminist positions which take their departure from the work of Jacques Lacan have sought to underscore the unconscious as the tenuous ground of any and all claims to identity. A work that makes both arguments, Juliet Mitchell's *Psycho-analysis and Feminism* (1974), sought not only to show that gender is constructed rather than biologically necessitated but to identify the precise developmental moments of that construction in the history of gendered subjects. Mitchell further argues on structuralist grounds that the narrative of infantile development enjoyed relative universality and that psychoanalytic theory seemed, therefore, to offer feminists a way to describe a psychological and cultural ground of shared gender identification.[3] In a similar position, Jacqueline Rose asserts: "The force of psychoanalysis is therefore precisely that it gives an account of patriarchal culture as a trans-historical and cross-cultural force. It therefore conforms to the feminist demand for a theory which can explain women's subordination across specific cultures and different historical moments."[4] As much as psychoanalytic theory provided feminist theory with a way to identify and fix gender difference through a metanarrative of shared infantile development, it also helped feminists show how the very notion of the subject is a masculine prerogative within the terms of culture. The paternal law which Lacanian psychoanalysis takes to be the ground of all kinship and all cultural relations not only sanctions male subjects but institutes their very possibility through the denial of the feminine. Hence, far from being subjects, women are, variously, the Other, a mysterious and unknowable lack, a sign of the forbidden and irrecoverable maternal body, or some unsavory mixture of the above.

Elaborating on Lacanian theory, but making significant departures from its presumptions of universal patriarchy, Luce Irigaray maintains that the very construct of an autonomous subject is a masculine cultural prerogative from which women have been excluded. She further claims that the subject is always already masculine, that it bespeaks a refusal of dependency required of male acculturation, understood originally as dependency on the mother, and that its "autonomy" is founded on a repression of its early and true helplessness, need, sexual desire for the mother, even identification with the maternal body. The subject thus becomes a fantasy of autogenesis, the refusal of maternal foundations and, in generalized form, a repudiation of the feminine. For Irigaray, then, it would make no sense to refer to a female subject or to women as subjects, for it is precisely the construct of the subject that necessitates relations of hierarchy, exclusion, and domination. In a word, there can be no subject without an Other.[5]

Psychoanalytic criticism of the epistemological point of departure, beginning with Freud's criticism of Enlightenment views of "man" as a rational being and later echoed in Lacan's critique of Cartesianism, has offered feminist theorists a way of criticizing the disembodied pretensions of the masculine knower and exposing the strategy of domination implicit in that disingenuous epistemological gesture. The destabilization of the subject within feminist criticism becomes a tactic in the exposure of masculine power and, in some French feminist contexts, the death of the subject spells the release or emancipation of the suppressed feminine sphere, the specific libidinal economy of women, the condition of *écriture feminine*.

But clearly, this set of moves raises a political problem: If it is not a female subject who provides the normative model for a feminist emancipatory politics, then what does? If we fail to recuperate the subject in feminist terms, are we not depriving feminist theory of a notion of agency that casts doubt on the viability of feminism as a normative model? Without a unified concept of woman or, minimally, a family resemblance among gender-related terms, it appears that feminist politics has lost the categorial basis of its own normative claims. What constitutes the "who," the subject, for whom feminism seeks emancipation? If there is no subject, who is left to emancipate?

The feminist resistance to the critique of the subject shares some concerns with other critical and emancipatory discourses: If oppression is to be defined in terms of a loss of autonomy by the oppressed, as well as a fragmentation or alienation within the psyche of the oppressed, then a theory which insists upon the inevitable fragmentation of the subject appears to reproduce and valorize the very oppression that must be overcome. We need perhaps to think about a typology of fragmentations or, at least, answer the question of whether oppression ought to be defined in terms of the fragmentation of identity and whether fragmentation *per se* is oppressive. Clearly, the category of women is internally fragmented by class, color, age, and ethnic lines, to name but a few; in this sense, honoring the diversity of the category and insisting upon its definitional nonclosure appears to be a necessary safeguard against substituting a reification of women's experience for the diversity that exists.[6] But how do we know what exists prior to its discursive articulation? Further, the critique of the subject means more than the rehabilitation of a multiple subject whose various "parts" are interrelated within an overriding unity, a coalitional subject, or an internal polity of pluralistically related points of view. Indeed, the political critique of the subject questions whether making a conception of identity into the ground of politics, however internally complicated, prematurely forecloses the possible

cultural articulations of the subject-position that a new politics might well generate.

This kind of political position is clearly not in line with the humanist presuppositions of either feminism or related theories on the Left. At least since Marx's *Early Manuscripts*, the normative model of an integrated and unified self has served emancipatory discourses. Socialist feminism has clearly reformulated the doctrine of the integrated subject in opposition to the split between public and private spheres which has concealed domestic exploitation and generally failed to acknowledge the value of women's work, as well as the specific moral and cultural values which originate or are sustained within the private sphere. In a further challenge to the public/private distinction in moral life, Carol Gilligan and others have called for a reintegration of conventional feminine virtues, such as care and other relational attitudes, into conventional moral postures of distance and abstraction, a kind of reintegration of the human personality, conceived as a lost unity in need of restoration. Feminist psychoanalytic theory based in object-relations has similarly called for a restructuring of child-rearing practices which would narrow the schism between gender differences produced by the predominating presence of the mother in the nurturing role. Again, the integration of nurturance and dependency into the masculine sphere and the concomitant assimilation of autonomy into the feminine sphere suggests a normative model of a unified self which tends toward the androgynous solution. Others insist on the deep-seated specificity of the feminine rooted in a primary maternal identification which grounds an alternative feminine subject, who defines herself relationally and contextually and who fails to exhibit the inculcated masculine fear of dependency at the core of the repudiation of the maternal and, subsequently, of the feminine. In this case, the unified self reappears not in the figure of the androgyne but as a specifically feminine subject organized by a founding maternal identification.

The differences between Lacanian and post-Lacanian feminist psychoanalytic theories on the one hand and those steeped in the tradition of object-relations and ego psychology on the other center on the conception of the subject or the ego and its ostensible integrity. Lacanian feminists such as Jacqueline

Rose argue that object-relations theorists fail to account for the unconscious and for the radical discontinuities which characterize the psyche prior to the formation of the ego and a distinct and separate sense of self. By claiming certain kinds of identifications are primary, object-relations theorists make the relational life of the infant primary to psychic development itself, conflating the psyche with the ego and relegating the unconscious to a less significant role. Lacanian theorists insist upon the unconscious as a source of discontinuous and chaotic drives or significations, and they claim that the ego is a perpetually unstable phenomenon, resting upon a primary repression of unconscious drives which return perpetually to haunt and undermine the ostensible unity of the ego.[7]

Although these theories tend to destabilize the subject as a construct of coherence, they nevertheless institute gender coherence through the stabilizing metanarrative of infantile development. According to Rose and to Juliet Mitchell, the unconscious is an open libidinal/linguistic field of discontinuities which contest the rigid and hierarchizing codes of sexual difference encoded in language, regulating cultural life. Although the unconscious thus becomes a locus of subversion, it remains unclear what changes the unconscious can provide considering the rigid synchronicity of the structuralist frame. The rules constituting and regulating sexual difference within Lacanian terms evince an immutability which seriously challenges their usefulness for any theory of social and cultural transformation. The failure to historicize the account of the rules governing sexual difference inevitably institutes that difference as the reified foundation of all intelligible culture, with the result that the paternal law becomes the invariant condition of intelligibility, and the variety of contestations not only can never undo that law but, in fact, require the abiding efficacy of that law in order to maintain any meaning at all.

In both sets of psychoanalytic analyses, a narrative of infantile development is constructed which assumes the existence of a primary identification (object-relations) or a primary repression (the *Ürverdrangung* which founds the Lacanian male subject and marks off the feminine through exclusion) which instantiates gender specificity and subsequently informs, organizes, and unifies identity. We hear time and again

about *the* boy and *the* girl, a tactical distancing from spatial and temporal locations which elevates the narrative to the mythic tense of a reified history. Although object-relations poses an alternative version of the subject based in relational attitudes characteristically feminine and Lacanian (or anti-Lacanian), theories maintain the instability of the subject based in the disruptive potential of the unconscious manifest at the tentative boundaries of the ego; they each offer story lines about gender acquisition which effect a narrative closure on gender experience and a false stabilization of the category of woman. Whether as a linguistic and cultural law which makes itself known as the inevitable organizing principle of sexual difference or as the identity forged through a primary identification that the Oedipal complex requires, gender meanings are circumscribed within a narrative frame which both unifies certain legitimate sexual subjects and excludes from intelligibility sexual identities and discontinuities which challenge the narrative beginnings and closures offered by these competing psychoanalytic explanations.

Whether one begins with Freud's postulation of primary bisexuality (Juliet Mitchell and Jacqueline Rose) or with the primacy of object-relations (Chodorow, Benjamin), one tells a story that constructs a discrete gender identity and discursive location which remains relatively fixed. Such theories do not need to be explicitly essentialist in their arguments in order to be effectively essentialist in their narrative strategies. Indeed, most psychoanalytic feminist theories maintain that gender is constructed, and they view themselves (and Freud) as debunking the claims of essential femininity or essential masculinity. Indeed, this seems to be the case when we consider Freud's claim, for instance, in *The Three Essays on the Theory of Sexuality* that heterosexuality is not a given of biological life but a developmental accomplishment,[8] his theory of primary bisexuality,[9] and his further claim in *New Introductory Lectures on Psychoanalysis* that to become a woman is a laborious construction which takes the repression of primary bisexuality as its premise.[10]

At its most general level of narrative development, the object-relations and Lacanian versions of gender development offer (1) a utopian postulation of an originally predifferentiated state of the sexes which

(2) also preexists the postulation of hierarchy, and (3) gets ruined either by the sudden and swift action of the paternal law (Lacanian) or the anthropologically less ambitious Oedipal injunction to repudiate and devalue the mother (object-relations). In both cases, an originally undifferentiated state of the sexes suffers the process of differentiation and hierarchization through the advent of a repressive law. "In the beginning" is sexuality without power, then power arrives to create both culturally relevant sexual distinction (gender) and, along with that, gender hierarchy and dominance.

The Lacanian position proves problematic when we consider that the state prior to the law is, by definition, prior to language and yet, within the confines of language, we are said somehow to have access to it. The circularity of the reasoning becomes all the more dizzying when we realize that prior to language we had a diffuse and full pleasure which, unfortunately, we cannot remember, but which disrupts our speech and haunts our dreams. The object-relations postulation of an original identification and subsequent repudiation constructs the terms of a coherent narrative of infantile development which works to exclude all kinds of developmental histories in which the nurturing presence of the nuclear family cannot be presupposed.

By grounding the metanarratives in a myth of the origin, the psychoanalytic description of gender identity confers a false sense of legitimacy and universality to a culturally specific and, in some contexts, culturally oppressive version of gender identity. By claiming that some identifications are more primary than others, the complexity of the latter set of identifications is effectively assimilated into the primary one, and the "unity" of the identifications is preserved. Hence, because within object-relations the girl-mother identification is "founding," the girl-brother and girl-father identifications are easily assimilated under the already firmly established gender identification with women. Without the assumption of an orderly temporal development of identifications in which the first identifications serve to unify the latter ones, we would not be able to explain which identifications get assimilated into which others; in other words, we would lose the unifying thread of the narrative. Indeed, it is important to note that primary identifications establish gender in

a substantive mode, and secondary identifications thus serve as attributes. Hence, we witness the discursive emergence of "feminine men" or "masculine women," or the meaningful redundancy of a "masculine man." Without the temporal prioritization of primary identifications, it would be unclear which characterizations were to serve as substance and which as attributes, and in the case in which that temporal ordering were fully contested, we would have, I suppose, the gender equivalent of an interplay of attributes without an abiding or unifying substance. I will suggest what I take to be the subversive possibilities of such a gender arrangement toward the end of my remarks.

Even within the psychoanalytic frame, however, we might press the question of identification and desire to a further limit. The primary identification in which gender becomes "fixed" forms a history of identifications in which the secondary ones revise and reform the primary one but in no way contest its structural primacy. Gender identities emerge and sexual desires shift and vary so that different "identifications" come into play depending upon the availability of legitimating cultural norms and opportunities. It is not always possible to relate those shifts back to a primary identification which is suddenly manifest. Within the terms of psychoanalytic theory, then, it is quite possible to understand gendered subjectivity as a history of identifications, parts of which can be brought into play in given contexts and which, precisely because they encode the contingencies of personal history, do not always point back to an internal coherence of any kind.

Of course, it is important to distinguish between two very different ways in which psychoanalysis and narrative theory work together. Within psychoanalytic literary criticism, and within feminist psychoanalytic criticism in particular, the operation of the unconscious makes all narrative coherence suspect; indeed, the defenders of that critical enterprise tend to argue that the narrative capacity is seriously undermined by that which is necessarily excluded or repressed in the manifest text and that a serious effort to admit the unconscious, whether conceived in terms of a repressed set of drives (Kristeva) or as an excluded field of metonymic associations (Rose), into the text disrupts and inverts the linear assumptions of coherent narrativity. In this sense, the text always exceeds the narrative; as the field of excluded meanings, it returns, invariably, to contest and subvert the explicitly attempted narrative coherence of the text.

The multiplication of narrative standpoints within the literary text corresponds to an internally fragmented psyche which can achieve no final, integrated understanding or "mastery" of its component parts. Hence, the literary work offers a textual means of dramatizing Freud's topographical model of mind in motion. The nonliterary use of psychoanalysis, however, as a psychological explanatory model for the acquisition and consolidation of gender identification and, hence, identity generally fails to take account of itself as a narrative. Subject to the feminist aim to delimit and define a shared femininity, these narratives attempt to construct a coherent female subject. As a result, psychoanalysis as feminist metatheory reproduces that false coherence in the form of a story line about infantile development where it ought to investigate genealogically the exclusionary practices which condition that particular narrative of identity formation. Although Rose, Mitchell, and other Lacanian feminists insist that identity is always a tenuous and unstable affair, they nevertheless fix the terms of that instability with respect to a paternal law which is culturally invariant. The result is a narrativized myth of origins in which primary bisexuality is arduously rendered into a melancholic heterosexuality through the inexorable force of the law.

Juliet Mitchell claims that it is only possible to be in one position or the other in a sexual relation and never in both at once. But the binary disjunction implicit to this gendered law of noncontradiction suggests that desire functions through a gender difference instituted at the level of the symbolic that necessarily represses whatever unconscious multiplications of positions might be at work. Kristeva argues similarly that the requirements of intelligible culture imply that female homosexuality is a contradiction in terms, with the consequence that this particular cultural manifestation is, even within culture, outside it, in the mode of psychosis. The only intelligible female homosexuality within Kristeva's frame is in the prohibited incestuous love between daughter and mother, one that can only be resolved through a maternal identification and the quite literal process of becoming a mother.[11]

Within these appropriations of psychoanalytic theory, gender identity and sexual orientation are accomplished at once. Although the story of sexual development is complicated and quite different for *the* girl than *the* boy, it appeals in both contexts to an operative disjunction that remains stable throughout: one identifies with one sex and, in so doing, desires the other, that desire being the elaboration of that identity, the mode by which it creates its opposite and defines itself in that opposition. But what about primary bisexuality, the source of disruption and discontinuity that Rose locates as the subversive potential of the unconscious? A close examination of what precisely Freud means by bisexuality, however, turns out to be a kind of bi-sexedness of libidinal dispositions. In other words, there are male and female libidinal dispositions in every psyche which are directed heterosexually toward opposite sexes. When bisexuality is relieved of its basis in the drive theory, it reduces, finally, to the coincidence of two heterosexual desires, each proceeding from oppositional identifications or dispositions, depending on the theory, so that desire, strictly speaking, can issue only from a male-identification to a female object or from a female-identification to a male object. Granted, it may well be a woman, male-identified, who desires another woman, or a man, female-identified, who desires another man, and it may also be a woman, male-identified who desires a man, female-identified, or similarly, a man, female-identified, who desires a woman, male-identified. One either identifies with a sex or desires it, but only those two relations are possible.

But is identification always restricted within the binary disjunction in which it has been framed so far? Clearly, within psychoanalytic theory, another set of possibilities emerges whereby identifications work not to consolidate identity but to condition the interplay and the subversive recombination of gender meanings. Consider that in the previous sketch, identifications exist in a mutually exclusive binary matrix conditioned by the cultural necessity of occupying one position to the exclusion of the other. But in fantasy, a variety of positions can be entertained even though they may not constitute culturally intelligible possibilities. Hence, for Kristeva, for instance, the semiotic designates precisely those sets of unconscious fantasies and wishes that exceed the legitimating bounds of paternally organized culture; the semiotic domain, the body's subversive eruption into language, becomes the transcription of the unconscious from the topographical model into a structuralist discourse. The tenuousness of all identity is exposed through the proliferation of fantasies that exceed and contest the "identity" that forms the conscious sense of self. But are identity and fantasy as mutually exclusive as the previous explanation suggests? Consider the claim, integral to much psychoanalytic theory, that identifications and, hence, identity, are in fact *constituted* by fantasy.

Roy Schafer argues in *A New Language for Psychoanalysis* that when identifications are understood as internalizations, they imply a trope of inner psychic space that is ontologically insupportable. He further suggests that internalization is understood better not as a process but as a fantasy.[12] As a result, it is not possible to attribute some kind of ontological meaning to the spatial internality of internalizations, for they are only fantasied as internal. I would further argue that this very fantasy internal psychic space is essentially conditioned and mediated by a language that regularly figures interior psychic locations of various kinds, a language, in other words, that not only produces that fantasy but then redescribes that figuration within an uncritically accepted topographical discourse. Fantasies themselves are often imagined as mental contents somehow projected onto an interior screen, a conception conditioned by a cinematic metaphorics of the psyche. However, identifications are not merely fantasies of internally located objects or features, but they stand in a transfigurative relation to the very objects they purport to internalize. In other words, within psychoanalytic theory, to identify with a figure from the past is to figure that figure within the configuration of interior psychic space. Identification is never simply mimetic but involves a strategy of wish fulfillment; one identifies not with an empirical person but with a fantasy, the mother one wishes one had, the father one thought one had but didn't, with the posture of the parent or sibling which seems to ward off a perceived threat from some other, or with the posture of some imagined relation whom one also imagines to be the recipient of love. We take up identifications not only to receive love but also to deflect from it and its dangers;

we also take up identifications in order to facilitate or prohibit our own desires. In each case of identification, there is an interpretation at work, a wish and/or a fear as well, the effect of a prohibition, and a strategy of resolution.

What is commonly called an introject is, thus, a fantasied figure within a fantasied locale, a double imagining that produces the effect of the empirical other fixed in an interior topos. As figurative productions, these identifications constitute impossible desires that figure the body, active principles of incorporation, modes of structuring and signifying the enactment of the lived body in social space. Hence, the gender fantasies constitutive of identifications are not part of the set of properties that a subject might be said to have, but they constitute the genealogy of that embodied/ psychic identity, the mechanism of its construction. One does not have the fantasies, and neither is there a one who lives them, but the fantasies condition and construct the specificity of the gendered subject with the enormously important qualification that these fantasies are themselves disciplinary productions of grounding cultural sanctions and taboos—a theme to which I will momentarily turn. If gender is constituted by identification and identification is invariably a fantasy within a fantasy, a double figuration, then gender is precisely the fantasy enacted by and through the corporeal styles that constitute bodily significations.

In a separate context, Michel Foucault challenges the language of internalization as it operates in the service of the repressive hypothesis. In *Discipline and Punish*, Foucault rewrites the doctrine of internalization found in Nietzsche's *On the Genealogy of Morals* through the language of *inscription*. In the context of prisoners, Foucault writes, the strategy has not been to enforce a repression of their desires but to compel their bodies to signify the prohibitive law as their ownmost essence, style, necessity. That law is not internalized, but it is incorporated, with the consequence that bodies are produced which signify that law as the essence of their selves, the meaning of their soul, their conscience, the law of their desire. In effect, the law is at once fully manifest and fully latent, for it never appears as external to the bodies it subjects and subjectivates. "It would be wrong," Foucault writes, "to say that the soul is an illusion, or an ideological effect.

On the contrary, it exists, it has a reality, it is produced permanently around, on, within, the body by the functioning of a power that is exercised on those that are punished. . . ."[13] The figure of the interior soul understood as "within" the body is signified through its inscription *on* the body, even though its primary mode of signification is through its very absence, its potent invisibility, for it is through that invisibility that the effect of a structuring inner space is produced. The soul is precisely what the body lacks; hence, that lack produces the body as its other and as its means of expression. In this sense, then, the soul is a surface signification that contests and displaces the inner/outer distinction itself, a figure of interior psychic space inscribed on the body as a social signification that perpetually renounces itself as such. In Foucault's terms, the soul is not imprisoned by the body, as some Christian imagery would suggest, but "the body becomes a prisoner of the soul."[14]

The redescription of intrapsychic processes in terms of the surface politics of the body implies a corollary redescription of gender as the disciplinary production of the figures of gender fantasy through the play of presence and absence in the body's surface, the construction of the gendered body through a series of exclusions and denials, signifying absences.

But what determines the manifest and latent text of the body politic? What is the prohibitive law that generates the corporeal stylization of gender, the fantasied and fantastic figuration of the gendered body? Clearly, Freud points to the incest taboo and the prior taboo against homosexuality as the generative moments of gender identity, the moments in which gender becomes fixed (meaning both immobilized and, in some sense, repaired). The acquisition of gender identity is thus simultaneous with the accomplishment of coherent heterosexuality. The taboo against incest, which presupposes and includes the taboo against homosexuality, works to sanction and produce identity at the same time that it is said to repress the very identity it produces. This disciplinary production of gender effects a false stabilization of gender in the interests of the heterosexual construction and regulation of sexuality. That the model seeks to produce and sustain coherent identities and that it requires a heterosexual construction of sexuality in

no way implies that practicing heterosexuals embody or exemplify this model with any kind of regularity. Indeed, I would argue that in principle no one can embody this regulatory ideal at the same time that the compulsion to embody the fiction, to figure the body in accord with its requirements, is everywhere. This is a fiction that operates within discourse, and which, discursively and institutionally sustained, wields enormous power.

I noted earlier the kinds of coherences instituted through some feminist appropriations of psychoanalysis but would now suggest further that the localization of identity in an interior psychic space characteristic of these theories implies an expressive model of gender whereby identity is first fixed internally and only subsequently manifest in some exterior way. When gender identity is understood as causally or mimetically related to sex, then the order of appearance that governs gendered subjectivity is understood as one in which sex conditions gender, and gender determines sexuality and desire; although both psychoanalytic and feminist theory tend to disjoin sex from gender, the restriction of gender within a binary relation suggests a relation of residual mimeticism between sex, conceived as binary[15] and gender. Indeed, the view of sex, gender, and desire that presupposes a metaphysics of substance suggests that gender and desire are understood as attributes that refer back to the substance of sex and make sense only as its reflection.

I am not arguing that psychoanalytic theory is a form of such substantive theorizing, but I would suggest that the lines that establish coherence between sex, gender, and desire, where they exist, tend to reenforce [sic] that conceptualization and to constitute its contemporary legacy. The construction of coherence conceals the gender discontinuities that run rampant within heterosexual, bisexual, and gay and lesbian contexts in which gender does not necessarily follow from sex, and desire, or sexuality generally, does not seem to follow from gender; indeed, where none of these dimensions of significant corporeality "express" or reflect one another. When the disorganization and disaggregation of the field of bodies disrupts the regulatory fiction of heterosexual coherence, it seems that the expressive model loses its descriptive force, and that regulatory ideal is exposed as a norm and a fiction that disguises itself as a developmental law that regulates the sexual field that it purports to describe.

According to the understanding of identification as fantasy, however, it is clear that coherence is desired, wished for, idealized, and that this idealization is an effect of a corporeal signification. In other words, acts, gestures, and desire produce the effect of an internal core or substance, but produce this on the surface of the body, through the play of signifying absences that suggest, but never reveal, the organizing principle of identity as a cause. Such acts, gestures, enactments, generally construed, are performative in the sense that the essence of identity that they otherwise purport to express becomes a *fabrication* manufactured and sustained through corporeal signs and other discursive means. That the gendered body is performative suggests that it has no ontological status apart from the various acts which constitute its reality, and if that reality is fabricated as an interior essence, that very interiority is a function of a decidedly public and social discourse, the public regulation of fantasy through the surface politics of the body. In other words, acts and gestures articulate and enacted desires create the illusion of an interior and organizing gender core, an illusion discursively maintained for the purposes of the regulation of sexuality within the obligatory frame of reproductive heterosexuality. If the "cause" of desire, gesture, and act can be localized within the "self" of the actor, then the political regulations and disciplinary practices which produce that ostensibly coherent gender are effectively displaced from view. The displacement of a political and discursive origin of gender identity onto a psychological "core" precludes an analysis of the political constitution of the gendered subject and its fabricated notions about the ineffable interiority of its sex or of its true identity.

If the inner truth of gender is a fabrication and if a true gender is a fantasy instituted and inscribed on the surface of bodies, then it seems that genders can be neither true nor false but are only produced as the truth effects of a discourse of primary and stable identity.

In *Mother Camp: Female Impersonators in America*, anthropologist Esther Newton suggests that the structure of impersonation reveals one of the key fabricating mechanisms through which the social construction of gender takes place. I would suggest as well that drag fully subverts the distinction between inner and outer psychic space and effectively mocks both the expressive model of gender and of the notion of a true gender identity. "At its most complex," Newton writes, "[drag] is a double inversion that says, 'appearance is an illusion.' Drag says [Newton's curious personification], my 'outside' appearance is feminine, but my essence 'inside' {the body} is masculine." At the same time it symbolizes the opposite inversion: "my appearance 'outside' {my body, my gender} is masculine but my essence 'inside' myself is feminine."[16] Both claims to truth contradict one another and so displace the entire enactment of gender significations from the discourse of truth and falsity.

The notion of an original or primary gender identity is often parodied within the cultural practices of drag, cross-dressing, and the sexual stylization of butch/femme identities. Within feminist theory, such parodic identities have been understood to be either degrading to women, in the case of drag and cross-dressing, or an uncritical appropriation of sex-role stereotyping from within the practice of heterosexuality, especially in the case of butch/femme lesbian identities. But the relation between the "imitation" and the "original" is, I think, more complicated than that critique generally allows. Moreover, it gives us a clue to the way in which the relationship between primary identification, that is, the original meanings accorded to gender, and subsequent gender experience might be reframed.

The performance of drag plays upon the distinction between the anatomy of the performer and the gender that is being performed. But we are actually in the presence of three separate dimensions of significant corporeality: anatomical sex, gender identity and gender performance. If the anatomy of the performer is already distinct from the gender of the performer, and both of those distinct from the gender of the performance, then the performance suggests a dissonance not only between sex and performance but between sex and gender, and gender and performance. As much as drag creates a unified picture of "woman" (what its critics often oppose), it also reveals the distinctness of those aspects of gendered experience which are falsely naturalized as a unity through the regulatory fiction of heterosexual coherence. In imitating gender, drag implicitly reveals the imitative structure of gender itself—as well as its contingency. Indeed, part of the pleasure, the giddiness of the performance is in the recognition of a radical contingency in the relation between sex and gender in the face of cultural configurations of causal unities that are regularly assumed to be natural and necessary. In the place of the law of heterosexual coherence, we see sex and gender denaturalized by means of a performance which avows their distinctness and dramatizes the cultural mechanism of their fabricated unity.

The notion of gender parody defended here does not assume that there is an original which such parodic identities imitate. Indeed, the parody is *of* the very notion of an original; just as the psychoanalytic notion of gender identification is constituted by a fantasy of a fantasy, the transfiguration of an other who is always already a "figure" in that double sense, so gender parody reveals that the original identity after which gender fashions itself is itself an imitation without an origin. To be more precise, it is a production which, in effect, that is, in its effect, postures as an imitation. This perpetual displacement constitutes a fluidity of identities that suggests an openness to resignification and recontextualization, and it deprives hegemonic culture and its critics of the claim to essentialist accounts of gender identity. Although the gender meanings which are taken up in these parodic styles are clearly part of hegemonic, misogynist culture, they are nevertheless denaturalized and mobilized through their parodic recontextualization. As imitations which effectively displace the meaning of the original, they imitate the myth of originality itself. In the place of an original identification which serves as a determining cause, gender identity might be reconceived as a personal/cultural history of received meanings subject to a set of imitative practices which refer laterally to other imitations, and which, jointly, construct the illusion of a primary and interior gendered self or which parody the mechanism of that construction.

Inasmuch as the construct of women presupposes a specificity and coherence that differentiates it from that of men, the categories of gender appear as an unproblematic point of departure for feminist politics. But if we take the critique of Monique Wittig seriously, namely, that "sex" itself is a category produced in the interests of the heterosexual contract,[17] or if we consider Foucault's suggestion that "sex" designates an artificial unity that works to maintain and amplify the regulation of sexuality within the reproductive domain, then it seems that gender coherence operates in much the same way, not as a ground of politics but as its effect. The political task that emerges in the wake of this critique requires that we understand not only the "interests" that a given cultural identity has, but, more importantly, the interests and the power relations that establish that identity in its reified mode to begin with. The proliferation of gender style and identity, if that word still makes sense, implicitly contests the always already political binary distinction between genders that is often taken for granted. The loss of that reification of gender relations ought not to be lamented as the failure of a feminist political theory, but, rather, affirmed as the promise of the possibility of complex and generative subject-positions as well as coalitional strategies that neither presuppose nor fix their constitutive subjects in their place.

The fixity of gender identification, its presumed cultural invariance, its status as an interior and hidden cause may well serve the goals of the feminist project to establish a transhistorical commonality between us, but the "us" who gets joined through such a narration is a construction built upon the denial of a decidedly more complex cultural identity—or nonidentity, as the case may be. The psychological language which purports to describe the interior fixity of our identities as men or women works to enforce a certain coherence and to foreclose convergences of gender identity and all manner of gender dissonance—or, where that exists, to relegate it to the early stages of a developmental and, hence, normative history. It may be that standards of narrative coherence must be radically revised and that narrative strategies for locating and articulating gender identity ought to admit to a greater complexity or it may be that performance may preempt narrative as the scene of gender production. In either case, it seems crucial to resist the myth of interior origins, understood either as naturalized or culturally fixed. Only then, gender coherence might be understood as the regulatory fiction it is—rather than the common point of our liberation.

NOTES

1. Remarks, Center for the Humanities, Wesleyan University, Spring 1985.

2. Julia Kristeva, "Woman Can Never Be Defined," *New French Feminisms*, ed. Elaine Marks and Isabelle de Courtivron (New York: Schocken, 1984).

3. Juliet Mitchell, *Psycho-analysis and Feminism* (New York: Vintage, 1975), p. 377.

4. Jacqueline Rose, "Femininity and its Discontents," *Sexuality in the Field of Vision* (London: Verso, 1987), p. 90.

5. Luce Irigaray, "Any Theory of the Subject Has Already Been Appropriated by the Masculine," *Speculum of the Other Woman*, trans. Gillian Gill (Ithaca, NY: Cornell University Press, 1985), p. 140. See also "Is the Subject of Science Sexed?," *Cultural Critique*, Vol. I, Fall 1985, p. 11.

6. For an interesting discussion of the political desirability of keeping the feminist subject incoherent, see Sandra Harding, "The Instability of the Analytical Categories of Feminist Theory," *Sex and Scientific Inquiry*, ed. Sandra Harding and Jean F. O'Barr (Chicago: University of Chicago Press, 1987).

7. See Jacqueline Rose's argument in "Femininity and its Discontents," *Sexuality in the Field of Vision*, pp. 90–94.

8. Sigmund Freud, *Three Essays on the Theory of Sexuality*, trans. James Strachey (New York: Basic Books, 1975), p. 1.

9. Freud, *Three Essays*, p. 7; see also "The Ego and the Superego," *The Ego and the Id*, trans. Joan Riviere (New York: Norton, 1960), pp. 22–23.

10. See Freud, Chapter 33, "Femininity," *New Introductory Lectures*, trans. James Strachey (New York: Norton, 1965), p. 116.

11. For a fuller exposition of Kristeva's positions, see my article "The Body Politics of Julia Kristeva" in the French Feminism issue of *Hypatia: A Journal of Feminist Philosophy*, Vol. 3, no. 3, pp. 104–108.

12. Roy Schafer, *A New Language for Psychoanalysis* (New Haven, CT: Yale University Press, 1976), p. 177.

13. Michel Foucault, *Discipline and Punish* (New York, Panthenon, 1977), p. 29.

14. *Foucault, Discipline and Punish*, p. 30.

15. The assumption of binary sex is in no sense stable. For an interesting article on the complicated "sexes" of some female athletes and the medicolegal disputes about how and whether to render their sex decidable, see Jerold M. Loewenstein, "The Conundrum of Gender Identification, Two Sexes Are Not Enough," *Pacific Discovery*, Vol. 40, No. 2, 1987, pp. 38–39. See also Michel Foucault's *The History of Sexuality, Volume I: An Introduction*, trans. Robert Hurley (New York: Vintage, 1980), pp. 154–155; and *Herculine Barbin, Being the Recently Discovered Memoirs of a Nineteenth-Century French Hermaphrodite*, trans. Richard McDougall (New York: Pantheon, 1986), pp. vii–xvii. For a feminist analysis of recent research into "the sex gene," a DNA sequence which is alleged to "decide" the sex of otherwise ambiguous bodies, see Anne Fausto-Sterling, "Recent Trends in Developmental Biology: A Feminist Perspective" (Departments of Biology and Medicine, Brown University).

16. Esther Newton, *Mother Camp: Female Impersonators in America* (Chicago: University of Chicago, 1972), p. 103.

17. Monique Wittig, "The Category of Sex," *Feminist Issues*, Vol. 2, p. 2.

HENDRI YULIUS WIJAYA

28. THE QUEER CHILD IN TRANSNATIONAL INDONESIA: FEAR, FUTURITY, AND RECTUM POLITICS

INTRODUCTION

The internationalization of lesbian, gay, bisexual, and transgender (henceforth LGBT) human rights and US marriage equality have triggered a national crackdown over LGBT people in Indonesia. In 2016, politicians, government officials, religious leaders, and a number of civil society organizations made derogatory public statements in which homosexuality was conflated with immorality, foreign intervention, mental illness, and direct threats to youth's morality and the nation. Although in the past few decades attacks against LGBT Indonesians were sporadic and carried out by religious vigilante groups, since 2016, the recent anti-LGBT sentiments have been translated into systematic legal steps to criminalize both homosexual practices and identities. An Islamic pro-family group, Family Love Alliance (*Aliansi Cinta Keluarga/AILA*), has demanded the Constitutional Court through judicial review processes to revise the Criminal Code by including and classifying consented sexual practices of same-sex adults into a criminal act. They argue that there has been systematic public campaign of LGBT in Indonesia, including the push for same-sex marriage (Constitutional Court 13–15). The current penal code only outlaws homosexual practices that involve persons under the age of eighteen.

Driven by fear of transnational forces of LGBT rights and marriage equality, AILA deployed multiple discourses during the Courtroom hearings to assert their claims that homosexuality is dangerous. One of these discourses is articulated by way of posing trivial causality between gay sex and AIDS epidemic. Moreover, during the proliferation of these sexuality discourses, the figure of queer child was also inadvertently emerged and constituted. The group, through

connecting the cause of homosexuality with anal sex pleasure, came to justify the peril of tolerating anal sex that, according to them, has led children to become gay. Aside from the underpinning dubious logics and evidence, this argument was emotionally appealing because it was articulated through the figure of a child with a child's perceived vulnerabilities.

Through a discourse analysis of the Court's judicial review minutes (*risalah sidang*) and anal sex represented by AILA, I examine not only the discursive production of anus as a site of homosexuality but also the emergence of the figure of the queer child to uncover how fear and the futurity of nation-state is imagined through the child's body and their sexuality. Positioning such emergence in the intensified war against homosexuality in Indonesia, I ask: what are the underlying cultural and sexual logics behind this rectum-ization of homosexuality? Why is the cause of homosexuality tethered imaginatively and discursively to anus? What effects are produced and sustained through this discursive formulation? As I argue in this essay, this enactment of such a queer child in Indonesia uncovers how such a transnational "spectral figure" (imaginary figure produced through particular narratives) interacts with specific local cultural and historical contexts.

DISCIPLINING HOMOSEXUALITY IN TRANSNATIONAL INDONESIA

Although homosexuality is not illegal, negative attitudes toward it have persisted since the emergence of homosexual identities in Indonesia. While homosexual practices have existed for a long time, Tom Boellstorff (81) argues that people with same-sex desires and attractions began to identify themselves as *gay* and

Permission to reprint this article has been secured from New Mandala, where a portion of this work has been published before under the title "The Criminalisation of LGBT People in Indonesia."

lesbi in the early 1980s when homosexual identities became widespread through the Indonesian media. At this historical juncture, it was common for Indonesian *gay* and *lesbi* people to see their sexuality as "illness," despite the simultaneous creation of a homosexual selfhood. As a consequence, Indonesian homosexuals recognized their identity as a passage before adulthood, signified by heterosexual marriage, and thus did not seek to defend their rights as a self-identified minority (Howard 13). They placed their sexuality after family, nation, or God and saw heterosexual marriage as a primary marker of an ideal adulthood and citizenship of a "normal" Indonesian (Offord 145). This reflects the traditional heteronormative family norms set by the authoritarian New Order (1966–1998) that promoted heterosexual nuclear family as an indicator of successful citizenship.

Such notions of heteronormativity nevertheless continue to the post-reform era (1998 to present), after the collapse of Soeharto's regime. Besides illness and abnormality, other common discourses used to prohibit homosexuality coalesce around religious and nationalist rhetoric. The former associates homosexuality with sins, whereas the latter conceives gay and lesbian identity as an unprecedented outcome of Western influence and intervention, which is irreconcilable with local social-cultural norms. Such claim also coincides with the globalization of LGBT identities and rights since the early 2000s, in which international humanitarian organizations and transnational LGBT organization networks increasingly channel technical and/or financial supports to Indonesia's LGBT organizations, leading to the mushrooming and greater visibilities of the LGBT activism, as well as the increased use of human rights discourse on sexuality and gender issues. Although Indonesian LGBT people and activism do not strive for marriage equality, the US legalization of same-sex marriage in 2015 has brought unexpected effects on the national gender and sexuality landscapes. Government representatives, civil society organizations, and politicians reduce and conflate any LGBT-related activism with efforts to import marriage equality.

The assumption that internationalization and visibilities of LGBT rights would result in greater acceptance and tolerance toward sexual minorities in Indonesia is problematic. What has to be considered in the production of global and even universalized LGBT subjects through transnational human rights rubrics is its inseparability from shared liberal values in Western societies (Altman & Symons *Queer Wars*). As the term LGBT is increasingly used in Indonesia and sexuality is treated as a basis of citizenship-rights claiming, efforts to transplant it to non-Western countries where sex is still deemed taboo would potentially result in further conservative backlash and damage to local communities. The increased visibilities inadvertently lead to increased vulnerabilities as well, particularly when LGBT individuals become specifically singled out and identified.

The above understanding, however, has not often been interrogated in many scholarships of transnationality, which are still more focused on cultural conformity, homogenous identities, weakening nation-state control, fluid geospatial boundaries, and new forms of Western imperialism as the direct outcomes of globalization (Grewal and Kaplan 663–666). Drawing from Aihwa Ong (243), I assert that current transnational studies tend to overlook the emergent maneuvers that produce new practices of surveillance, control, and border policing as a response to the Westernized or transnational forces of sexual identity and sexual rights discourse. Since it has become a public matter, sexuality appears to be a fertile ground for such new contestations and configurations to unfold and manifest. As we shall see, such emergent disciplinary tactics do not merely involve concrete actions through discursive practices and policies but also through the deployment of emotional registers, particularly fear.

Motivated by the fear of globalized LGBT rights discourse, recent discursive practices to outlaw LGBT subjects have produced a more complex view of homosexuality. The "concretization" of LGBT subjects/identities in which individuals are pinpointed, labeled, and made into sexual subjects, inevitably invites conservative counteraction to "identify" and "pin down" homosexual subjects and causes. Coming from an Islamic group AILA, a cutting-edge discourse that emerges at this historical juncture and becomes the central theme of my analysis here is that the cause and peril of homosexuality tends to coalesce around anus (Constitutional Court 10). AILA's main argument is that anal sex pleasures and its repeated actions will turn a boy into a gay man. Such "sexual conversion" is then presented as a threat to nation-state, through subsequently conflating gay sex with the widespread of HIV, sexually transmitted diseases, and Kaposi Sarcoma among gay people (Constitutional Court 10–16). While the latter is claimed based on the empirical data from the United States after the legalization of same sex marriage, the former postulation is more complex, which I argue is related to the production of a queer child figure.

The figure of queer and sexualized child, as an outcome of a disciplinary regime and incitement to sexuality discourse, is not too foreign in the West. In *The History of Sexuality* (1978), Michel Foucault contends that the efforts to discipline children's sexuality have multiplied the forms of sexuality discourse that subsequently constructed knowledge and regulation that were beyond children's grasp. Situating it in the Victorian period, he argued that the obsession about children's sexuality was "evident in the war against onanism, which in the West lasted nearly two centuries" ("The History of Sexuality" 104). The proliferation of such discourse relied on the nature of perilous sexual potentials of children that needed parental controls. The figure produced here, as later appeared in Freudian analysis, was the sexually malleable child who gradually learned to be a modern civilized subject through regimes of discipline and control. Built on this conception, children have always been perceived as innocent yet sexually uninhibited and insatiable humans that require tight controls and surveillance. In other words, bodies and sexualities become productive sites to manage population. Children as a population category are directed to become re-productive subjects, as their bodies must be "subjugated to power" to "foster life or disallow it to the point of death" ("Right of Death and Power over Life" 261). In the United States, the figure of the queer child appeared in the 1970s during the wars against homosexuality. This spectral figure was constructed and deployed by conservative groups in response to the emerging LGBT rights discourses and movements (Rosky 639–640). They argued that if homosexuality was allowed to flourish in public, homosexuals would socially indoctrinate and become role models for these queer children. The

figure of the Indonesian queer child, however, is constructed through its biological body—that is, his anus.

RECTUM-IZATION OF HOMOSEXUALITY, FEAR, AND FUTURITY

Anus, alongside its sexual potentialities and meanings, is a productive discursive site. There are diverse cultural constructions of anal sex that deserve critical attention. Introducing the term "phallic sexuality," Simon Hardy argues that because modern Western sexual culture revolves around the centrality of a penis or "phallus," anus has become interchangeable with vagina, underlining its "passive" role. Nonetheless, this assumption limits different possibilities and meanings intimately produced and reproduced through anal sex, including "a contraceptive method," "a routine variation of sexual repertoire," "an ultimate intimacy between couple," and "a heterosexual substitute for heterosexual men in absence of women" (Hardy 114–120). Positioning it in the AIDS crisis in the late 1980s, Leo Bersani (222) points out that anal sex is often represented as pathological, dirty, and self-annihilating. This analysis lends a critical lens to interrogate anal sex as it unpacks various meaning-makings attached to a specific body part. Moreover, it also allows us to examine the underpinning logics that make such meanings palpable.

AILA argues that a boy who is raped and anally penetrated [*sodomi*] will experience pleasure, due to the existence of the prostate inside his anal canal (Constitutional Court 10). The pleasure signified by the ejaculation of the insertee will thus drive him to repeat the action and consequently become "gay." As the prevalence of gays and/or LGBTs living with HIV is higher than heterosexuals in Indonesia, AILA thus declares that the state's indifference to the danger of LGBT sexuality that will only lead to an HIV epidemic, which will consequently imperil the State's budget and reduce citizens' productivity (Constitutional Court 14–15).

In Indonesia, the term "anal sex," or what is dubbed "*tempong*" [to attack] in Indonesian gay slang, is indeed a new addition to the local homosexuality discourse and vernacular, as the gay identity emerged in Indonesia (Boellstorff 101). Since the 1990s, anal sex has become a major attention in HIV prevention efforts for gay or transgender men, and men having sex with men (MSM). Condom promotions and classification of sexual practices on the basis of their HIV risks have constructed anal sex as a high-risk sexual practice and as increasingly associated with gay sexuality. Furthermore, since heteronormativity places superior values on traditional gender norms and reproductive heterosexuality, anal sex is also perceived as an unnatural act and an ultimate threat to masculinity.

While it is associated with unnatural acts and high-risk sex, anal sex also acquires another common pejorative name "sodomi" (sodomy), as used by AILA in their argument (Constitutional Court 10). This term, imbued with religious reference, is commonly used in Indonesia to refer to sexual violence against children that involves forced anal penetration. Such negative evocation has been developed through high-profile cases of sexual violence against children since the late 1990s. Indonesian people were alarmed and startled with the arrests, murders, and rape against children by, among others, a thirty-five-year-old "homosexual" man popularly known as *Robot Gedek*." In the 2000s, the sodomy cases also continued to proliferate in public through the media. In 2010, forty-nine-year-old Baekuni sodomized and murdered four street children; in 2014, teachers from Jakarta International School (JIS) were accused of sodomizing their students; and a twenty-four-year-old man sodomized 28 children and harassed sixteen more children (Yulius, "The Criminalization of LGBT People in Indonesia"). Those are only a few examples of "extreme" cases that received strong reactions from the public.

Because "sodomy" was the term that was used by the mass media when covering these cases, its "dangerous impacts" have intensively been conflated with homosexuality. According to Indonesian scholar Moh Yasir Alimi, mass media representations and reports of such crime established direct links between homosexuality and criminal acts, delineating not only the "abnormality" of homosexuality, but also its potential threats to "other people" and subsequently the "nation" (106–108). Specifically, the figure of the queer child has been used as evidence to show how homosexuals are threats to others. Popular discourses often represent how sodomy destroys the children's

future and causes emotional damage. It is worth it to note here that violation and rape will undoubtedly traumatize the children. However, the issue I would like to raise is that the current discourse promoted by AILA frames and highlights that their future will be imperiled because they will "become gay," instead of because of these traumatic events are violations of their bodily integrity.

Besides making such a dubious conflation between sexual practices (anal sex) and sexual identity/orientation (gay/homosexual), AILA also argues that the victim will always seek to repeat the action, become gay after such encounters, and then fall into uncontrollable and unsafe sexual acts. The assumption that these children would continue their lives and grow up to be gay men exposes the condition that I call the "rectum-ization" of homosexuality in Indonesia. This refers to the problematic assumption that homosexuality resides as an inherent trait located in the rectum—a boy is anally penetrated once, feels the pleasure of anal sex, longs for similar encounters, and then is turned into a gay man. The figure of the child is therefore imagined as a queer child, for he has latent and insatiable homosexual desires even prior to the encounter. He thus only needs an encounter, a contact, and a trigger to manifest his homosexual desire.

More than simply representing homosexuality, the figure of the queer child also sustains the connections between sexualities, futurity, and nation-state. That is, AILA argues that those queer bodies will threaten the nation-state for their vulnerabilities to HIV and STDs if they become gay. These will reduce citizens' productivity and imperil State's budgets (Constitutional Court 14–16). They argue that the State has to pay IDR 1,000,000 (USD 90) per month per person to cover individuals living with sexual diseases, which will subsequently destroy both national resilience [*ketahanan nasional*] and the quality of Indonesian people (Constitutional Court 18). To address this, AILA calls for an immediate action, as they claim that "our future [is] in those children's hands" [*masa depan kita ada di tangan mereka*] (Constitutional Court 18). As such, the figure of the child is thus framed as needing surveillance, control, and guidance from adults, who claim to have adequate expertise and life experience to ensure the child's upward movement. Indeed, queer theory scholar Kathryn Bond Stockton demonstrates that child growth has always been figured as "vertical movement upward toward full stature, marriage, work, reproduction, and the loss of childishness" (4). In Indonesia, heterosexual marriage is still deemed as a dominant marker of adulthood and a primary unit in society. It is no exaggeration that children's bodies are always directed to this stage, to ensure their reproductive adulthood in the future. Thus, the "ideal future" and the "figure of child" are seamlessly stitched together, as both are always envisioned through their upward vertical movement to reproductive-heterosexuality.

Moreover, the figure of the child as part of the population is perceived as a growing-up figure that will sustain the nation-state through their capacity to reproduce population through heteronormative ideology. Individuality (or a "people") is flattened out and melts into a collective (or population), for whom the state controls its specific variables, from birth, marriage, family organization, and its use of sex ("The History of Sexuality" 24–27). These peculiar variables, particularly sex, are then regulated and managed for "the greater good of all" and "the maximum potentials" in which population is viewed as wealth, productive manpower, and labor capacity ("The History of Sexuality" 24–25).

The articulation of the queer child figure therefore signals the "futural" failures to conform to these ideals and thus shows the temporal dimension of fear. While clearly noting the close relation between fear and the uncertainty of the future, Sara Ahmed demonstrates that "fear presses us into that future as an intense bodily experience in the present" (65). As a consequence, the object of such feeling affects us in the present, as if the "imagined" consequences are always "certain" and already "here" in the present. Through the spectral figure of the queer child, AILA projects these "futural" failures into the tangible present, albeit

their dubious evidence: the sexually insatiable queer child, reproductive failure, and even unproductive bodies affected by HIV and other STDs that endanger the nation-state productivity and survival.

The reductionist emplacement of gay identity onto anus also further strengthens and contributes to the shaping of children's bodies that requires more intimate control. Homosexuality is glued and placed on a bodily part that in turn sexualizes the children's bodies. Through this strategy, fear of homosexuality does not only attach to children's bodies, but also allows those bodies to be sexually distinguished from the adult bodies. Given all this, fear and control of (homo)sexuality becomes mobile and ubiquitous, following children's bodies wherever they move to. This then invites surveillance that polices and disciplines those bodies to prevent them from falling into "homosexuality" and its subsequent un-(re)-productivity.

CONCLUSION

This essay argues that a new form of control over sexuality in Indonesia is partly affected by transnational forces and the globalization of LGBT rights. That is, as LGBT movements are gaining momentum across the globe, they provoke fear and anti-LGBT sentiments in Indonesia. In the process of pushing against these globalized LGBT rights and demanding that same-sex practices be criminalized, AILA has inadvertently constructed the figure of the queer child who needs state's protection and investment because the future of the nation is in their hands. This argument thus extends existing scholarship on anti-LGBT sentiments in Indonesia in that it highlights how fear of transnational LGBT movements fuels tighter regulatory practices of sexuality. Although at the time of writing, AILA's proposal has not been adopted into policy, anti-LGBT sentiments in Indonesia are still very much present.

REFERENCES

Ahmed, Sara. *The Cultural Politics of Emotion*. Edinburgh: Edinburgh University Press, 2004.

Alimi, Yasir Moh. *Dekonstruksi Seksualitas Pascakolonial*. Yogyakarta: LKIS, 2004.

Altman, Dennis, and Jonathan Symons. *Queer Wars*. Cambridge, UK: Polity, 2016.

Bersani, Leo. "Is the Rectum a Grave?" *AIDS: Cultural Analysis/Cultural Activism*, vol. 43, October, Winter 1987, pp. 197–222.

Boellstorff, Tom. *The Gay Archipelago*. Princeton: Princeton University Press, 2005.

Constitutional Court *(Makhamah Konstitusi Republik Indonesia)*. *Risalah Sidang Perkara Nomor 46/PUU-XIV/2016*, Monday, August 1, 2016.

Foucault, Michel. *The History of Sexuality: An Introduction*. Penguin Books, 1978.

Foucault, Michel. "Right of Death and Power Over Life." *The Foucault Reader*, edited by Paul Rabinow. New York: Vintage Books, 2010, pp. 258–272.

Grewal, Inderpal, and Caren Kaplan. "Global Identities: Theorizing Transnational Studies of Sexuality." *GLQ: A Journal of Lesbian and Gay Studies*, vol. 7, no. 4, 2001, pp. 663–679.

Hardy, Simon. "Anal Sex: Phallic and Other Meaning." *Introducing the New Sexuality Studies*, edited by Steven Seidman, Nancy Fischer, and Chet Meeks. New York: Routledge, 2006, pp. 114–120.

Howard, Richard S. "Falling into the Gay World: Manhood, Marriage, and Family in Indonesia." ProQuest Dissertations Publishing, 1996.

Offord, Baden. "Singapore, Indonesia and Malaysia: Arrested Development!" *The Lesbian and Gay Movement and the Nation-state*, edited by Manon Tremblay, David Paternotte, and Carol Johnson. Farnham, UK: Ashgate, 2011, pp. 135–152.

Ong, Aihwa. *Flexible Citizenship: The Cultural Logics of Transnationality*. Durham: Duke University Press, 1999.

Rosky, Clifford J. "Fear of the Queer Child." *Buffalo Law Review*, vol. 61, no. 3, 2013, pp. 607–697.

Stockton, Kathryn Bond. *The Queer Child, or Growing Sideways in the Twentieth Century*. Durham: Duke University Press, 2009.

Yulius, Hendri. "The criminalisation of LGBT people in Indonesia." *New Mandala*. N.p., Dec. 20, 2016. Accessed July 5, 2017. http://www.newmandala.org/criminalisation-lgbt-people-indonesia.

VANITA REDDY

29. FAMILY TOGETHERNESS, AFFECT ALIENS, AND THE UGLY FEELINGS OF BEING INCLUDED

Every holiday season or every occasion in which getting-together-as-blood-based-kin is part of social convention, such as birthdays, anniversaries, and weddings, I am overwhelmed by how much love surrounds me. I find myself thinking: "How did I get this lucky to have such amazing people around me? How did I get lucky enough to be born into this group of beautiful, intelligent, kind, and genuinely thoughtful people?" I know many of us think this about our families, but really, mine is pretty great. Really, really great.

And then—or, more accurately, as I'm having that feeling—I experience a pang of dis-ease, a feeling of being out of place and out of sync with what's happening around me. And that feeling is tied to the irresolute and aggressive heteronormativity of this love.

What I will go on to explain as the "bad" or "ugly feelings" of being included in family togetherness applies to those of us who fall outside normative economies of love and attachment. My use of the phrase "ugly feelings," of course, draws from literary scholar Sianne Ngai's book by the same name. Ngai defines ugly feelings as negative emotions that register social powerlessness. Ngai implores us to turn toward rather than away from these ugly feelings—namely, envy, irritation, anxiety, "stuplimity," and paranoia—as a way of reckoning with the "ambivalent feelings of suspended agency" (1) that are part of how we experience social powerlessness. Rather than read this ambivalence as a kind of individual defeat, she shows how these moments of forced passivity and arrested agency critique therapeutic attempts to overcome social norms; instead, they force us to address the social power of these norms (3).

By "us," I refer not only to self-identified queers, where "queer" is assimilated into a political identity. I refer also to those heterosexual-identified folks who fall outside multiple heteronormativities. Following black feminist Cathy Cohen's cautionary critique of the limiting radical potential of political identities that emerged out of a critical genealogy of queer theory in the US academy, I am here attentive to the danger of presupposing any natural antagonism between "queer" and "heterosexual." Cohen elaborates on how this antagonism dissolves a more productive and transformative sexual politics, one that would challenge "the normalizing tendencies of hegemonic sexualities rooted in ideas of static, stable sexual identities and behaviors" (438). This is a radical queer politics that would allow us to see how, for example, the figure of the black welfare queen, because of the way she is read as hyperreproductive, uncoupled, matriarchal, and reliant on economic aid from the state rather than as economically self-reliant, is positioned as always already outside the boundaries of sexual respectability in ways that are proximate to more recognizably queer figures such as the black bulldyke. Like Cohen, then, I am concerned with the way that sexual respectability is routed through monogamy, marriage, childbearing, "couplehood," domesticity, and the capitalist relations that structure them. Just as the gender binary disciplines even those who adhere to its socially mandated roles of femininity and masculinity, these forms and institutions of sexual respectability discipline and manage everyone who participates in occasions of family togetherness.

But this disciplining is especially pronounced for those of us who maintain tense, strained, or even hostile relationships to these occasions. Many of us feel the ugly feelings of family togetherness when certain subjects are grouped together for photographs and/or are photographed more often: parents with their children, or married or dating or engaged couples; what gifts are given: gender-specific and ableist toys and clothes; how sleeping arrangements are made: bigger rooms or those with private bathrooms that go to couples and couples with children; what news is shared: who is married, engaged, pregnant, bought a house; what "counts" as news: same list; and how future plans are made: at what *couple*'s *home* the festivities will take place next year.

It's worth making clear that "family togetherness" is not the problem. It's the structures of that togetherness that so often fail to guarantee a more equitable distribution of tenderness, affection, recognition, attention, and value for the lives that are lived out of sync and out of pace with this economy of love—the uncoupled cousin, the queer (spinster) aunt, the divorced uncle, the widowed mother who chooses to remain single, the bachelor, the femme boy-child. In the absence of an alternative economy of love that would allow for a more equitable distribution of our affective (and economic) resources, the normative injunction in these moments is for these subjects to assimilate—to invest in being the aunt, the cousin, the child, and the mother—rather than pay any real or sustained attention to the adjectives that modify those familial nouns. This then ensures that we become legible in the hetero-repro-generational terms that are set for us, the terms that are already structuring the conversations and compliments and looks and actions that are taking place as soon as we step into a room full of family.

For some of us—maybe even many of us—the generation of good feeling among kin can make us feel like what feminist Sara Ahmed calls "affect aliens," subjects who feel out of line with an affective community when we do not experience "pleasure from proximity to objects that are already attributed as being good" ("Happy Objects" 37)—in this case, biological kin. To put it differently, affect aliens are understood as outside of a well-established and collectively agreed on orientation toward happy objects. For Ahmed, orientation "involves different ways of registering the proximity of objects and others" and a way of directing our "attention and energy" (*Queer Phenomenology* 3). In some ways, the family form is already one that is assumed to be a happy object, even prior to its encounter—it is why it is held as so aspirational, even (or especially) for gay subjects; this is why so many of us are oriented toward it. Feeling like an affect alien within the family-as-happy object can be read as a lack of willingness to experience joy or as an act of willfulness to be contrary or difficult. Affect aliens can be willful, yes. But the willfulness is not about the choice not to be joyful (though this is and can be an important choice since there is

nothing necessarily innocent about joy). Willfulness informs the other choices we make—to be uncoupled, unmarried, non-reproductive, non-monogamous, and so forth, even and especially when those choices feel like the most mundane thing in the world or when they don't feel like choices at all.

To say that family togetherness creates bad feeling is to risk being labeled the requisite feminist killjoy, the family outlier whose feminism means she must kill the joy that others experience and want to experience under the sign of "family togetherness." I am not going to challenge the label of the killjoy because I think she is much too culturally and politically valuable. Instead, we should think of the feminist killjoy as a critically productive figure—someone who exposes the way that heteronormative forms of love and attachment hold out "the promise of happiness," or happiness as a social good. Happiness as a social good through the belief that proximity to certain norms and ideals creates happiness, which make certain forms of personhood—such as being part of a romantic couple rather than being single—more valuable than others. Drawing on black, feminist, and queer critiques of happiness, Ahmed argues that happiness is "used to describe social norms as social goods" (*The Promise of Happiness* 2), so that the promise of happiness is rarely if ever constructed as a social ill. Happiness-as-a-social good means that happiness "itself becomes a duty" (*The Promise of Happiness* 7)—a duty to be happy when together in the family. This means that to not feel *individual* joy and to reveal, explicitly or implicitly, one's joylessness through non-engagement, withdrawal, and opting out of certain familial practices, or by calling out how these practices produce alienation is often to risk guaranteeing the family's *collective* unhappiness.

In being called the killjoy is the assumption that we and other affect aliens are somehow ungrateful for the invitation to be included in the experience of family togetherness: "No one is saying you cannot participate or that we don't want you here. You are of course part of the family and always will be. Please come join us!" Or, the assumption is that somehow, if we just tried a little harder or that if we could put our feminist, non-binary, non-ableist frames aside for just this once, we could experience that joy without caution or misgiving: "You are, after all, a sister, aunt, cousin, mother, etc., too! You are getting in your own way of experiencing shared joy in these roles!"[1] These assumptions are so violating because they mistake feelings of affect alienation for feelings of exclusion. To be alienated can certainly be a symptom of exclusion, such as when one is not invited or welcomed into a group or community. But it can also be a symptom of being included. Alienation of this latter kind (and the kind that I am writing about), happens when one is made to feel like an outsider to *the terms upon which belonging is defined.* That we affect aliens are already invited in, in other words, becomes the condition of possibility *for* our alienation once we accept that invitation.

These feelings of affect alienation are especially pronounced within the dynamics of the immigrant and diasporic family. The immigrant family is one in which nostalgia—defined by a loss of and desire for homeland—operates as a dominant structure of feeling. We might understand success in the family structure through sexual respectability as a way of coping with such feelings of loss. Asian American literary scholar erin K. Ninh has written about the ways in which the structure of the Asian immigrant family has largely been ignored in studies of the Asian American racialization. Ninh is concerned with the intergenerational structures of power that obtain between immigrant parents and daughters in particular. She claims that the immigrant family is "ordered by a capitalist logic and ethos" and "arranged around the disciplined and profitable docile body" of the immigrant daughter (6) whose professional and personal successes or failures become an index of the family's successes or failures. In thinking about the kinds of alienation-in-belonging that I am discussing here, we might extend Ninh's claims to the way that the good capitalist (daughterly) subject also becomes an index of the *success of the family form* itself. Success in one's family (marriage, children, and a high-paying job) works not only to aid in "forgetting" diasporic nostalgia, but also to mitigate the experience of cultural alienation within the US nation. To demonstrate to ourselves that we can successfully create belonging by reproducing the "happy family" in the diaspora becomes a way of not having to fully confront the structural violences of national alienation and migrant melancholia.

The representation of familial success (economic) and successful family forms (hetero-reproductive) are so pervasive in immigrant and diasporic contexts, I would argue, because of the historical construction of Asian Americans as "perpetual aliens" in the US nation. Despite their nominal inclusion within the nation on the basis of professional success and economic achievement since the passage of Immigration and Nationality Act of 1965 that lifted immigration restrictions based on national origin quotas and established a new immigration policy based on family reunification and skilled labor, Asian Americans have faced more than 100 years of immigration exclusion and restriction laws. Aiding and abetting such state practices of exclusion, Asian Americans have often invested—materially and psychically—in their own construction as the "good minority," cultivating hard work, family values, and capitalist success and achievement, especially over and against criminalized Latinos and blacks. Despite the critical impulse of many Asian American studies scholars to debunk the model minority myth as a narrative of cultural essentialism that obscures the powerful history of twentieth- and twenty-first century Asian American political activism and cross-racial collaborations and the material realities of working-class, working-poor Asian immigrant families, Ninh and others have argued that the narrative of Asian achievement can be rethought as not merely a myth but as a powerfully aspirational narrative that reveals the immigrant family as an "intermediary and agent" (11) of the nation.[2] For it is not only the production of the good capitalist (daughterly) subject but also the *production of good feeling* as a form of social (if not only economic) capital that ameliorates the diasporic family's feelings of national alienation.[3] If family togetherness is a form of social capital, then the presence of affect aliens amidst family togetherness reminds us about the ways that both familial and state forms of belonging rely on assimilation.[4]

To imbue the lives of affect aliens with value would require a different relation to time, even a different organization of time, one outside of what queer studies scholar Elizabeth Freeman has called chrononormativity. Chrononormativity names the way that people are "bound to one another, engrouped, made to feel coherently collective through particular orchestrations of time" (3). A non-chrononormative version of togetherness would look like valuing alternative organizations of time that are not linear, progressive, developmental, and bound up in capitalist logics of productivity. Instead of the normative joys of marriages, pregnancies, births, and home ownership, it would mean imbuing with collective value and meaning those events and relationships that fall off the chrononormative timeline—a month-long meditation retreat, taking care of someone else's child, friendship, a solo trip around the world. It would also involve imbuing with value and meaning those events and relationships that are normatively shameful or marked by hardship and pain: surviving a break-up, surviving dating, gender transitioning, recovering from or enduring chronic illness, being the sole provider for a child or parent, investing in professional over romantic attachments, interspecies intimacies, etc. I actually believe that being "made to feel collectively coherent"

in these and other ways would benefit everyone, not just affect aliens.

So, to be clear: I never feel excluded from my family's togetherness since I almost always opt in and since I want to feel connected to the people I love. Rather, I have felt and feel alienated from the terms on which that togetherness is often structured, from what are held as shared values, what gets recognized as meaningful, beautiful, and worthy of celebration. That's why this isn't a grievance about exclusion and a petulant cry for inclusion. It's not really a grievance at all. It's an observation about the aggressively and oppressively ingenious ways that heteronormativity structures how we express—even how we can think to express—our affective attachments. Maybe it's also expression of a deep and abiding quiet grief that many of us affect aliens live with when we choose to remain deeply attached to our biological kin.

NOTES

1. I realize that in expressing the ugly feelings of familial inclusion I risk minimizing the privilege of being included since so many whose gender and sexuality does not conform to the heteronormative codes of respectability and economic productivity can never feel the guarantee of inclusion to begin with. For these folks, familial disenfranchisement and disownment are the social costs for violating those codes. Yet to hold the position that inclusion is merely or primarily a privileged position when compared to outright exclusion is to miss the very real ways that being included cannot guarantee visibility on our own terms. It is also to miss the way that inclusion can and does reproduce invisibility in ways that insist on respectability as the *sine qua none* of individual gender and sexuality. Here I am thinking of the ways that, for example, the homonormative gay couple (especially with children) is far more likely to attain desired forms of visibility within the liberal family form than the queer figures and relations that I just mentioned.

2. Here I follow the work of Ninh and Shalini Shankar who argue that even or especially when Asian Americans fall outside of model minority racialization, model minority narratives nonetheless remain powerful as aspirational narratives of racial success and achievement. This is why anti-Black and anti-Latino racisms are perpetuated among many working-class Asian American communities, even in the face of class proximities to these other racial groups.

3. In my book *Fashioning Diaspora*, I discuss the Asian African poet Shailja Patel's prose-poem *Migritude* in which she elaborates on the concept of "shilling love" as exposing the way that familial love both expresses and is conditioned by economic and political realities. Shilling love is a form of love and attachment that is expressed and secured through the quiet pursuit of upward mobility and capitalist accumulation as responses to anti-Asian racial violence and political upheaval among Asian Indians in the black majority nation of postcolonial Kenya. Each stanza of "Shilling Love" begins with the juxtaposition of the Kenyan shilling's loss in value to the British pound as Patel recalls that her "parents never say they love us" but instead "they save and count/

count and save" (27). The counting of money is, in effect, an accounting of the distribution of love within the migrant family since the family's economic situation determines "who gets to leave/and who has to stay/who breaks free/and what they pay" (26). As a political economy of love, shilling love denaturalizes love as a sentimental mode of kin relations; instead, love is mediated through the historical exigencies of political and economic upheaval.

4. I want to thank Anantha Sudhakar for succinctly capturing this relationship between the state and the family form in Ninh's work.

REFERENCES

Ahmed, Sara. "Happy Objects." *The Affect Theory Reader*. Eds. Melissa Gregg and Gregory Seigworth. Durham: Duke UP, 2007.

Ahmed, Sara. *The Promise of Happiness*. Durham: Duke UP, 2010.

Ahmed, Sara. *Queer Phenomenology: Orientations, Objects, Others*. Durham: Duke UP, 2006.

Cohen, Cathy. "Punks, Bulldaggers, and Welfare Queens: The Radical Potential of Queer Politics?" *GLQ* 3.4 (May 1997): 437–465.

Freeman, Elizabeth. *Time Binds: Queer Temporalities, Queer Histories*. Durham: Duke UP, 2010.

Ngai, Sianne. *Ugly Feelings*. Cambridge, MA: Harvard UP, 2007.

Ninh, Erin. *Ingratitude: The Debt-Bound Daughter in Asian American Literature*. New York: NYU Press, 2011.

Patel, Shailja. *Migritude*. Los Angeles: Kaya Press, 2010.

Reddy, Vanita. *Fashioning Diaspora: Beauty, Femininity, and South Asian American Culture*. Philadelphia: Temple UP, 2016.

Shankar, Shalini. *Desiland: Teen Culture, Class, and Success in Silicon Valley*. Durham: Duke UP, 2008.

30. IT WAS A LOVELY DINNER

Now I guess I'll have to buy a razor,
tidy things up a bit. Not a clean shave
neither will I call in for waxing.
A little tidying is enough, besides,
one can get into trouble with older
feminists. I've been questioned before.
"Do you mean to look like a child?"
"Why do you think I'd want a little girl?"
"Don't you feel right in your adult body?"

These are the right questions, of course,
wrong timing, as wax shops hang banners
on every city block and
hairlessness equates hygiene.
One can get into trouble either way.
Who wants to be seen as unkempt?
As having "let oneself go?"

The life of the body, beneath clothes,
unprepared for external gaze

is just mammal life. Well, mine is.
I think I'll shave this, let that grow,
pluck here. Decades have past
since my gleeful conscious patterning,
removal and arrangement of body hair.
I'm simply no longer entertained and
only consider it from the perspective
of an invited guest.

We have another dinner date,
just two days since the last
I'm "tough to leave alone,"
she writes in email and when
I note my body's pleasure upon
reading her invitation and flirty quip,
wrapped in sheets, I roll over in
morning twilight with a delighted squeal.
When I hear and see my joy,
the next thought is:
Well, I guess I'll have to buy a razor.

31. USES OF THE EROTIC: THE EROTIC AS POWER

There are many kinds of power, used and unused, acknowledged or otherwise. The erotic is a resource within each of us that lies in a deeply female and spiritual plane, firmly rooted in the power of our unexpressed or unrecognized feeling. In order to perpetuate itself, every oppression must corrupt or distort those various sources of power within the culture of the oppressed that can provide energy for change. For women, this has meant a suppression of the erotic as a considered source of power and information within our lives.

We have been taught to suspect this resource, vilified, abused, and devalued within western society. On one hand the superficially erotic has been encouraged as a sign of female inferiority—on the other hand women have been made to suffer and to feel both contemptible and suspect by virtue of its existence.

It is a short step from there to the false belief that only by the suppression of the erotic within our lives and consciousness can women be truly strong. But that strength is illusory, for it is fashioned within the context of male models of power.

As women, we have come to distrust that power which rises from our deepest and non-rational knowledge. We have been warned against it all our lives by the male world, which values this depth of feeling enough to keep women around in order to exercise it in the service of men, but which fears this same depth too much to examine the possibilities of it within themselves. So women are maintained at a distant/inferior position to be psychically milked, much the same way ants maintain colonies of aphids to provide a life-giving substance for their masters.

But the erotic offers a well of replenishing and provocative force to the woman who does not fear its revelation, nor succumb to the belief that sensation is enough.

The erotic has often been misnamed by men and used against women. It has been made into the confused, the trivial, the psychotic, the plasticized sensation. For this reason, we have often turned away from the exploration and consideration of the erotic as a source of power and information, confusing it with its opposite, the pornographic. But pornography is a direct denial of the power of the erotic, for it represents the suppression of true feeling. Pornography emphasizes sensation without feeling.

The erotic is a measure between the beginnings of our sense of self, and the chaos of our strongest feelings. It is an internal sense of satisfaction to which, once we have experienced it, we know we can aspire. For once having experienced the fullness of this depth of feeling and recognizing its power, in honor and self-respect we can require no less of ourselves.

It is never easy to demand the most from ourselves, and from our lives, and from our work. To go beyond the encouraged mediocrity of our society is to encourage excellence. But giving in to the fear of feeling and working to capacity is a luxury only the unintentional can afford, and the unintentional are those who do not wish to guide their own destinies.

This internal requirement toward excellence which we learn from the erotic must not be misconstrued as demanding the impossible from ourselves nor from others. Such a demand incapacitates everyone in the process, for the erotic is not a question only of what we do. It is a question of how acutely and fully we can feel in the doing. For once we know the extent to which we are capable of feeling that sense of satisfaction and fullness and completion, we can then observe which of our various life endeavours bring us closest to that fullness.

The aim of each thing which we do is to make our lives and the lives of our children more possible and more rich. Within the celebration of the erotic in all our endeavours, my work becomes a conscious decision—a longed-for bed which I enter gratefully and from which I rise up empowered.

Of course, women so empowered are dangerous. So we are taught to separate the erotic demand from most vital areas of our lives other than sex. And the lack of concern for the erotic root and satisfactions of our work is felt in our disaffection from so much of what we do. For instance, how often do we truly love our work?

The principal horror of any system which defines the good in terms of profit rather than in terms of human need, or which defines human need to the exclusion of the psychic and emotional components of that need—the principal horror of such a system is that it robs our work of its erotic value, its erotic power and life appeal and fulfillment. Such a system reduces work to a travesty of necessities, a duty by which we earn bread or oblivion for ourselves and those we love. But this is tantamount to blinding a painter and then telling her to improve her work, and to enjoy the act of painting. It is not only next to impossible, it is also profoundly cruel.

As women, we need to examine the ways in which our world can be truly different. I am speaking here of the necessity for reassessing the very quality of all the aspects of our lives and of our work.

The very word "erotic" comes from the Greek word *eros,* the personification of love in all its aspects—born of Chaos, and personifying creative power and harmony. When I speak of the erotic, then, I speak of it as an assertion of the life-force of women; of that creative energy empowered, the knowledge and use of which we are now reclaiming in our language, our history, our dancing, our loving, our work, our lives.

There are frequent attempts to equate pornography and eroticism, two diametrically opposed uses of the sexual. Because of these attempts, it has become fashionable to separate the spiritual (psychic and emotional) away from the political, to see them as contradictory or antithetical. "What do you mean, a poetic revolutionary, a meditating gunrunner?" In the same way, we have attempted to separate the spiritual and the erotic, reducing the spiritual thereby to a world of flattened affect—a world of the ascetic who aspires to feel nothing. But nothing is farther from the truth. For the ascetic position is one of the highest fear, the

gravest immobility. The severe abstinence of the ascetic becomes the ruling obsession. And it is one, not of self-discipline, but of self-abnegation.

The dichotomy between the spiritual and the political is also false, resulting from an incomplete attention to our erotic knowledge. For the bridge which connects them is formed by the erotic—the sensual—those physical, emotional, and psychic expressions of what is deepest and strongest and richest within each of us, being shared: the passions of love, in its deepest meanings.

The considered phrase, "It feels right to me," acknowledges the strength of the erotic into a true knowledge, for what that means and feels is the first and most powerful guiding light towards any understanding. And understanding is a handmaiden which can only wait upon, or clarify, that knowledge, deeply born. The erotic is the nurturer or nursemaid of all our deepest knowledge.

The erotic functions for me in several ways, and the first is in the power which comes from sharing deeply any pursuit with another person. The sharing of joy, whether physical, emotional, psychic or intellectual, forms a bridge between the sharers which can be the basis for understanding much of what is not shared between them, and lessens the threat of their difference.

Another important way in which the erotic connection functions is the open and fearless underlining of my capacity for joy. In the way by body stretches to music and opens into response, hearkening to its deepest rhythms, so every level upon which I sense also opens to the erotically satisfying experience, whether it is dancing, building a bookcase, writing a poem, examining an idea.

That self-connection shared is a measure of the joy which I know myself to be capable of feeling, a reminder of my capacity for feeling. And that deep and irreplaceable knowledge of my capacity for joy comes to demand from all of my life that it be lived within the knowledge that such satisfaction is possible, and does not have to be called marriage, nor god, nor an afterlife.

This is one reason why the erotic is so feared, and so often relegated to the bedroom alone, when it is recognized at all. For once we begin to feel deeply all the aspects of our lives, we begin to demand from ourselves and from our lives, pursuits that they feel in accordance with that joy which we know ourselves to be capable of. Our erotic knowledge empowers us, becomes a lens through which we scrutinize all aspects of our existence, forcing ourselves to evaluate those aspects honestly in terms of their relative meaning within our lives. And this is a grave responsibility, projected from within each of us, not to settle for the convenient, the shoddy, the conventionally expected, nor the merely safe.

During World War II, we bought sealed plastic packets of white, uncolored margarine, with a tiny, intense pellet of yellow coloring perched like a topaz just inside the clear skin of the bag. We would leave the margarine out for a while to soften, and then we would pinch the little pellet to break it inside the bag, releasing the rich yellowness into the soft pale mass of margarine. Then taking it carefully between our fingers, we would knead it gently back and forth, over and over, until the color had spread throughout the whole pound bag of margarine, leaving it thoroughly colored.

I find the erotic such a kernel within myself. When released from its intense and constrained pellet, it flows through and colors my life with a kind of energy that heightens and sensitizes and strengthens all my experience.

We have been raised to fear the yes within ourselves, our deepest cravings. For the demands of our released expectations lead us inevitably into actions which will help bring our lives into accordance with our needs, our knowledge, our desires. And the fear of our deepest cravings keeps them suspect, keeps us docile and loyal and obedient, and leads us to settle for or accept many facets of our oppression as women.

When we live outside ourselves, and by that I mean on external directives only, rather than from our internal knowledge and needs, when we live away from those erotic guides from within our selves, then our lives are limited by external and alien forms, and we conform to the needs of a structure that is not based on human need, let alone an individual's. But when we begin to live from within outward, in touch with the power of the erotic within ourselves, and allowing that power to inform and illuminate our actions upon the world around us, then we begin to be responsible to ourselves in the deepest sense. For as we begin to recognize our deepest feelings, we begin to give up, of necessity, being satisfied with suffering, and self-negation, and with the numbness which so often seems like their only alternative in our society.

Our acts against oppression become integral with self, motivated and empowered from within.

In touch with the erotic, I become less willing to accept powerlessness, or those other supplied states of being which are not native to me, such as resignation, despair, self-effacement, depression, self-denial.

And yes, there is a hierarchy. There is a difference between painting a back fence and writing a poem, but only one of quantity. And there is, for me, no difference between writing a good poem and moving into sunlight against the body of a woman I love.

This brings me to the last consideration of the erotic. To share the power of each other's feelings is different from using another's feelings as we would use a Kleenex. And when we look the other way from our experience, erotic or otherwise, we use rather than share the feelings of those others who participate in the experience with us. And use without consent of the used is abuse.

In order to be utilized, our erotic feelings must be recognized. The need for sharing deep feeling is a human need. But within the European-American tradition, this need is satisfied by certain proscribed erotic comings together, and these occasions are almost always characterized by a simultaneous looking away, a pretense of calling them something else, whether a religion, a fit, mob violence, or even playing doctor. And this misnaming of the need and the deed give rise to that distortion which results in pornography and obscenity—the abuse of feeling.

When we look away from the importance of the erotic in the development and sustenance of our power, or when we look away from ourselves as we satisfy our erotic needs in concert with others, we use each other as objects of satisfaction rather than share our joy in the satisfying, rather than make connection with our similarities and our differences. To refuse to be conscious of what we are feeling at any time, however comfortable that might seem, is to deny a large part of the experience, and to allow ourselves to be reduced to the pornographic, the abused, and the absurd.

The erotic cannot be felt secondhand. As a Black Lesbian Feminist, I have a particular feeling, knowledge, and understanding for those sisters with whom I have danced hard, played, or even fought. This deep participation has often been the forerunner for joint concerted actions not possible before.

But this erotic charge is not easily shared by women who continue to operate under an exclusively European-American, male tradition. I know it was not available to me when I was trying to adapt my consciousness to this mode of living and sensation.

Only now, I find more and more woman-identified women brave enough to risk sharing the erotic's electrical charge without having to look away, and without distorting the enormously powerful and creative nature of that exchange. Recognizing the power of the erotic within our lives can give us the energy to pursue genuine change within our world, rather than merely settling for a shift of characters in the same weary drama.

For not only do we touch our most profoundly creative source, but we do that which is female and self-affirming in the face of a racist, patriarchal, and anti-erotic society.

ANNAMARIE JAGOSE

32. COUNTERFEIT PLEASURES: FAKE ORGASM AND QUEER AGENCY

Pleasure does not represent anything; there are no counterfeit pleasures.

—Arnold Davidson, "Foucault,
Psychoanalysis, and Pleasure"

Physical practices of the fist-fucking sort . . . are in effect extraordinary counterfeit pleasures *[extraordinaires falsifications de plaisir]*.

—Michel Foucault, "Le gai savoir"
(from Halperin, *Saint Foucault*)

In *On Love*, his philosophical primer disguised as a novel, Alain de Botton uses the trajectory of the romance narrative to investigate various metaphysical considerations underlying the experience of falling in love; desiring another, in both unrequited and requited registers; having sex; forming a couple; coming unstuck over an infidelity; contemplating suicide; and—eventually—falling in love again. The modern cast to this love story is evident in de Botton's inclusion of a fake-orgasm episode in which the beloved Chloe attempts to extend her orgasmic performance by smuggling in, among her four genuine contractions, four imitations. "It was at first hard for me to imagine," reports Chloe's lover,

> an untruth lasting 3.2 seconds fitted into a sequence of eight 0.8-second contractions, the first and the last two [3.2s] of which were genuine. It was easier to imagine a complete truth, or a complete lie, but the idea of a truth-lie-truth pattern seemed perverse and unnecessary. Either the whole sequence should have been false or the whole genuine. Perhaps I should have disregarded intentionality in favor of a physiological explanation. Yet whatever the cause and whatever the level of explanation, I had begun to notice that Chloe had begun to

simulate all or part of her orgasms. 0.8+ / 0.8+ / 0.8– / 0.8– / 0.8– / 0.8– / 0.8+ / 0.8+ = total length 6.4.[1]

If this feat raises the suspicions of her lover, then the narrative work performed here by fake orgasm ought to arouse ours. It is not only that the narrator is able to detect the difference between authentic and inauthentic contractions with a superhuman accuracy, incorporating into his everyday routines of sexual responsiveness a disciplinary surveillance of female orgasm that supplements the limits of human perception by drawing on the observational powers associated, post-Kinsey, with such representational technologies as the electroencephalograph, the electrocardiograph, and magnetic resonance imaging, but that he also immediately understands the significance of Chloe's clonic performance, intuiting from the simulated portions of her orgasm that she has begun to dissociate herself emotionally from the relationship.[2] Subscribing to a widespread cultural narrative that aligns orgasm with truth and fake orgasm with falsehood, *On Love's* narrator sorrowfully registers the imitative neuro-muscular clutches that Chloe attempts to pass off as the real thing. Despite his empiricist attempts not to give intentionality any interpretive weight and his claim not to understand "the cause" or "the level of explanation," he takes Chloe's performance as certain evidence that she is slipping the bonds of love that have previously bound them to each other. Some weeks later, when Chloe breaks off the relationship, she formalizes this with a letter whose phrasings, however difficult they are for her abandoned lover to absorb, he has already anticipated in their generic form via those four false contractions: "I cannot continue to deny you the love you deserve. . . . You'll always be beautiful to me . . . I hope we can stay friends."

This . . . essay is about fake orgasm. Or rather it is, despite earlier fixations and intentions, a[n] . . . essay that has turned out to be about fake orgasm. There is something pleasing about the happenstance of this critical swerve since, in its everyday instantiations, fake orgasm itself is, however habituated, however frequently arrived at, seldom intended from the start. Given near-axiomatic understandings of what constitutes, politically speaking, good sex and bad, fake orgasm crystallizes as a critical object under the compacting pressure of the kinds of stories queer and, more generally, progressive, left-of-center theory wants sex to tell. Given the centrality of sex for the legibility and intelligibility of modern subjectivities, it is not surprising that sex has often been the ambivalent focus of quotidian and utopian projects of sociopolitical transformation. The longing to maintain some relation between sexual practice and social change, between erotic and political yearnings, persists in queer and feminist theory despite, and in many ways alongside, Foucault's influential debunking of the repressive hypothesis and his concomitant skepticism about the ease with which "the sexual cause . . . becomes legitimately associated with the honor of a political cause."[3] Foucault's work on sexual discipline and later sexual ethics has determined the kinds of sex queer theory thinks with and, as a consequence, continues to shape queer theoretical understandings of what sexual styles, demographics, and scenarios are recognizable as political.[4]

Insofar as fake orgasm is customarily characterized as unpolitical—considered unfeminist, for instance, and regarded in most analyses as a practice abjected by feminism—it affords a welcome because [of an] improbable opportunity for rethinking the relation between sex and politics.[5] If it is a rhetorical commonplace in feminist critical projects to take fake orgasm as a figure for feminine capitulation to masculinist values—in short, as a figure for feminism's failure—then, in pursuing beyond the bounds of common sense the question of how fake orgasm might be politically consequential, this . . . essay frees up space for the articulation of some questions that approach the issue of sex and politics aslant, that reframe what is political about sex.[6] As a critical figure, fake orgasm brings to visibility the presumptions that underpin claims to the transformative capacities or potentials of

some sex acts, some amatory transactional relations or erotic spaces but not others. It therefore acts as a useful reminder that the critical value accorded to certain sex acts is often in the service of systems of discrimination more ideological than erotic. Because what we want from sex is never, it seems, fake orgasm, and because fake orgasm has many practitioners but few champions, it has the potential to estrange us productively from our more familiar knowledges about the relations between erotic practice and the desire for social transformation.

. . .

BODIES AND PLEASURES

Foucault's invocation of "bodies and pleasures" occurs in the last pages of *The History of Sexuality*, Volume 1 and marks a shift from the book's dominant register of critique to the specification of a future-directed strategy, however tantalizingly underdescribed. "The rallying point for the counterattack against the deployment of sexuality," writes Foucault in a much-quoted passage, "ought not to be sex-desire, but bodies and pleasures."[7] Unsurprisingly, a great deal of critical work has subsequently focused on Foucault's speculatively abstract reference to bodies and pleasures, specifying what it might mean exactly and whether it represents an efficacious tactical move with regard to the deployment of sexuality. In a series of interviews with the gay press during the late 1970s and into the 1980s, that period described by Gilles Deleuze as "the fairly long silence following *The History of Sexuality*," Foucault elaborated on what might be entailed by "a different economy of bodies and pleasures."[8] The relation of Foucault's interviews to his critical works has been the subject of scholarly discussion. Particular interest has been paid to those interviews that fall in the gap between the publication in 1978 of *The History of Sexuality, Volume 1* and the publication in 1985 of *The Use of Pleasure: The History of Sexuality, Volume 2*, a gap that marks a significant turn—for some critics, an about-turn—in Foucault's work, from an interest in processes of subjectification under modern disciplinary power to a concern with ancient ethical practices of self-cultivation.[9] Despite Amanda Anderson's argument that the homogenizing of Foucault's work as a single project subscribes to a "charismatic fallacy" in which Foucault's argumentative incoherencies and radical shifts in conceptual paradigms are dissolved under the glamorizing influence of the proper name of the celebrity theorist, Foucault's queer critical reception has been productively shaped by a tendency to read the interviews as providing a conceptual bridge, via their recourse to contemporary gay subcultural practices, between the two works.[10] For queer critics, this shift in focus in Foucault's second volume is largely seen as intellectually continuous with his enigmatic call to bodies and pleasures insofar as his interest in ancient Greek and Roman sexual ethics is connected in part to his desire to think about contemporary gay subcultures as affording opportunities for aesthetic stylization that transform the self.[11] Thus, when discussing the resonances between ancient ethics and queerness, Halperin argues that Foucault's interest in aesthetics as a way of life is shaped "by his reading of the ancient ethical texts at least as much as by his personal contacts with the rapidly developing gay and lesbian communities."[12] Arnold Davidson similarly notes that it "would have given Foucault genuine pleasure to think that the threat to everyday life posed by ancient philosophy had a contemporary analogue in the fears and disturbances that derive from the self-formation and style of life of being gay."[13] In queer critical commentary, Foucault's work on ancient ethics provides him with a conceptual vocabulary for thinking about how bodies and pleasures might rearticulate gayness as a way of life, via "a homosexual *askesis* that would make [homosexuals] work on [themselves] and invent . . . a manner of being that is still improbable."[14]

Hinting at it in *The History of Sexuality, Volume 1* and sketching it out in more detail in subsequent interviews, Foucault argues that the counterdisciplinary, or, as he says, "nondisciplinary," reorganization of the body through the production of new pleasures is required to counter the disciplinary system of sexuality, whose most effective strategy remains, of course, its annexation of the body as its expression. "We must invent," says Foucault, "with the body, with its elements, surfaces, volumes, and thicknesses, a nondisciplinary eroticism—that of a body in a volatile and diffused state, with its chance encounters and unplanned pleasures."[15] Not some authentic substrate that houses the subject and affords unmediated access

to pleasure, the body here is a site whose comprehensive disciplinary inscription makes it strategically available for political ends, opening it up as a resource for "fabricating other forms of pleasure."[16] In advocating the invention of "a general economy of pleasure not based on sexual norms," Foucault distinguishes pleasure from the normalizing operations of desire.[17] In his work, pleasure, as specifically opposed to desire, is crucially implicated in the forging of a particular relation to the self, a relation of experimentation and invention that has the potential to reorganize experiences of embodiment and hence sexual subjectivity. Where desire is concerned with psychologization, and the deep attachment of an interiorized sexual subjectivity to the classificatory categories of sexology, pleasure is concerned with intensification and the temporary dissolution of the subject.[18] As Foucault puts it, "Pleasure has no passport, no identification papers."[19] For Foucault, intense sexual pleasure, particularly that which reorganizes the body's erogeneity, is productively impersonal insofar as it has the capacity to reorder momentarily the subject's sense of self, to detach the individual from the stable, coherent identity through which modern sexuality is administered and regulated.

With a few exceptions, the queer critical take-up of Foucault's point about the invention of pleasures has tended largely to read over the ancient Greco-Roman contexts specified in the second and third volumes of *The History of Sexuality*, preferring to focus, as previously noted, on the modern, predominantly male, public sex cultures that Foucault himself discusses in various interviews, taking as key examples the same sexual practices, fist-fucking and anonymous sex, for example, and the same sexual architectures, such as bathhouses and sex-on-site venues. In insisting on not only the existence but also the vibrant resourcefulness of marginalized twentieth-century sex cultures, in demonstrating that, far from being immoral or merely self-indulgent, such practices might constitute an ethical and political intervention in stock liberal understandings of freedom, privacy, and selfhood, these discussions are invaluable for understanding the normalizing, disciplinary force of sexuality. There is, however, also a sense in which critical discussions of subaltern sexual practices risk reifying them as necessarily radical and transformative in ways that are quite at odds with the Foucauldian project, as if, like a faulty battery that keeps draining energy from a car's electrical systems, the newly revamped model Foucault offers cannot hold its conceptual charge. Too often, the assumed obviousness or self-evidence of the transformative political potential of subcultural sexual practices relies on the persistent belief that dissident sex pits itself against power in the name of liberation, and bodies and pleasures, rehabilitated against the ambition of Foucault's intellectual project, are folded back into personalizing models of selfhood or are reified as the deeply impersonal practices of specific queer sex cultures, which amounts to something similar.

Given the apparent ease with which some sex cultures or practices are associated with the advancement of political aims, and given, too, that others are written off as erotic dead ends, it is worth remembering that, despite frequent questioning, Foucault himself refuses to specify any particular program of resistance. "I do not think," he writes, "that there is anything that is functionally—by its very nature—absolutely liberating. Liberty is a practice."[20] In valorizing gay subcultural sexual practices as "the creation of pleasure," Foucault is not therefore recommending particular sexual acts or scenarios but articulating the ways certain historically specific forms of sexual innovation strategically refuse the regulatory system of sexuality.[21] Far from credentialing certain forms of sex as necessarily transformational, Foucault's insistence that sex is "an imaginary point determined by the deployment of sexuality"—which is to say that sex is less something we have than something that has us—calls for a transformation in our understanding of sex itself.[22] "It is," writes Foucault, "precisely this idea of sex in itself that we cannot accept without examination."[23] Queer theory after Foucault might yet be more strenuously shaped by this claim, might relax its own certainty about what sex is and what its political effects are, and might open up the range of what it thinks of as its proper objects.

A QUASI-HISTORY OF FAKE ORGASM

If fist-fucking is, as we post-Foucauldians have come to learn, "the sexual invention of the twentieth century," then it is not the only sexual practice to emerge newly as a widespread sexual observance in the twentieth century.[24] Less celebrated but no less ingenious,

fake orgasm is also a twentieth-century sexual invention. The degree to which fake orgasm has been constructed as a problem, rather than an innovation, is the impetus for venturing a quasi-history here, necessarily brief and partial. Mostly transacted in private, sex—even so-called public sex—leaves little archival trace, privately authored ephemera such as letters, diaries, and memoirs supplementing what can be indirectly deduced from official civil and legal records such as registers of marriages and births or court proceedings. Although often represented as a corrective to the fuzziness of sexual knowledge, sexual self-reporting is also problematic, because informants are prone, for a range of social reasons, to exaggeration, omission, and fabrication. It is therefore notoriously difficult to ascertain from publicly available data actual human sexual behavior, let alone the historical career of a particular sexual practice. Fake orgasm presents a further difficulty because in practice it is ideally neither acknowledged nor recognized. Seldom detected by other parties in the interpersonal contexts in which it is practiced, fake orgasm can barely be said to meet the minimum requirements of a sexual event.

Leaving only the faintest historical spoor, fake orgasm's archive is idiosyncratic and incomplete: a bunch of expert and folk talk, recommendations and denunciations both, buoyed along on the public privacies of women's intimate culture and their osmotic permeation of popular mass-mediated knowledges that gives rise to speculations about the status of orgasm as a communicative event within modern regimes of intimacy.[25] To the extent that it can be considered to have one, the official story of fake orgasm is a narrative of extinction. According to this story, women's erotic capacities and requirements were once so little valued or understood that women routinely simulated orgasm in heterosexual intercourse; now that female sexual agency is widely acknowledged and even celebrated, the necessity for such artifice is radically diminished, fake orgasm being the vestigial evidence of an older sexual order passing from visibility.[26] Prominent subscribers to this account, William Masters and Virginia Johnson imagine that their work on human sexual response eliminates fake orgasm. Unlike their predecessor Alfred Kinsey, Masters and Johnson are disinclined to consider fake orgasm an unobjectionable part of the contemporary sexual landscape.[27] Consistent with the interventionist nature of their behavioral modification programs, Masters and Johnson are intent on eradicating fake orgasm as a practice, suggesting, on two very different grounds, that their own research ensures its cultural extinction. On the one hand, they argue, now that women know how to secure adequate sexual stimulation in sexual encounters with men, fake orgasm is no longer necessary: "The female's age-old foible of orgasmic pretense has been predicated upon the established concept that obvious female response increases the male's subjective pleasure during coital opportunity. With need for pretense removed, a sexually responding woman can stimulate effectively the interaction upon which both the man's and the woman's psychosocial requirements are culturally so dependent for orgasmic facility."[28] On the other, they suggest that, given recent advances in the scientific registration of female sexual response, fake orgasm is no longer plausible: "With the specific anatomy of orgasmic-phase physiology reasonably established, the age-old practice of the human female of dissimulating has been made pointless. The obvious, rapid detumescence and corrugation of the areolae of the breasts and the definable contractions of the orgasmic platform in the outer third of the vagina remove any doubt as to whether the woman is pretending or experiencing orgasm."[29] If the continued cultural life of fake orgasm into the twenty-first century suggests Masters and Johnson oversimplified the historical contexts that enable it as a specific practice, there is also reason to be skeptical about their presumption that fake orgasm is an "age-old" occurrence.[30] Although discourses of fake orgasm are easily able to hitch a ride on the long-standing figuration of femininity in terms of dissimulation and undecidability, the historical opportunity for fake orgasm to be consolidated as a widespread and acknowledged practice appears only when two incongruous ideological formations emergent in the late nineteenth century around a heterosexuality newly defined in terms of heteroeroticism stall out against each other by the middle of the twentieth century, each functioning as the other's enabling ground and constraining limit.[31] Let's call them the sexual incompatibility of the heterosexual pair and the erotic, ethical relations of parity and reciprocity publicly rehearsed around that couple.

By now, the sexual incompatibility of the heterosexual couple is an open secret, promulgated by "a whole public environment of therapeutic genres" that Lauren Berlant and Michael Warner describe as "dedicated to witnessing the constant failure of heterosexual ideologies and institutions."[32] The cultural repository for this "secret" is vast, yet, as the subtle logic of the open secret testifies, the ubiquity of some knowledge formations is precisely what sustains and energizes their cultural circulation as if they were occult truths. From marital advice manuals published early in the twentieth century to contemporary sexual self-help titles, from sexological discussions of the male drive to mastery and the female drive to modesty, in the Mars and Venus erotics of much contemporary expert and popular sex advice, from second-wave feminist critiques of received understandings of what sex is to the dream of simultaneous orgasm kept alive outside mainstream cinematic and pornographic imaginings by the various techniques and training protocols of renegade sex therapists, the disclosure that heterosexuality is in trouble never fails to arrive freshly as the diagnosis of a particularly contemporary crisis, its signature sex act failing to deliver the reciprocal sexual satisfactions it nevertheless emblematizes.

Sex survey after sex survey, never mind the unofficial informational circuitry of gossip and anecdote, suggest that, without additional clitoral stimulation, women do not reliably have orgasms in coitus. Acknowledging the problems inherent in drawing conclusions from thirty-two quantitative sex surveys that employ different methodologies, Elisabeth A. Lloyd nevertheless notes that the studies, conducted between 1921 and 1995, consistently indicate that among women who masturbate, approximately 95 percent regularly achieve orgasm by this method, while only some 25 percent of women who have penetrative sex always orgasm in that context.[33] It might be the case that the statistical parceling of this "news," which is so conventional to the genre, speaks less to the clout of the quantitative for such social-science research than the ongoing difficulty of presenting this information in a culturally memorable format. The difficulty of retaining this information, of recognizing it and according it the status of cultural fact, is no doubt linked to its intrinsic feminization, as is its strategic circulation as masculinized "hard data" rather than as the feminized forms of complaint or testimony.[34] However cannily got up as a sound bite, the fate of such information is to be repeated again and again without ever loosening the cultural imagination's allegiance to heterosexual intercourse and its figuration of the sexual reciprocity that is the ethical model for modern heterosexuality.[35]

Although it has frequently been misrecognized as just such a strategy, drawing attention to the public failures of heterosexuality is not in itself an unsettling or destabilizing gesture, as is readily evidenced by the failure of those failures to register significantly against heterosexuality's social value. Far from being the end of the road, or even a malfunction, failure is a part of modern heterosexuality's support system, buoyed by aspiration, consolation, and optimism: the everyday bricolage of emotional making do. Widely known, but known inside circuits of transmission that do not allow for its solidification as a transparent fact, the sexual incompatibility of the heterosexual couple can consequently keep arriving on the cultural scene as news, in large part because such diagnoses are almost always in the service of some more optimistically framed project, the failure of heterosexual sexual reciprocity a resource for the hopeful possibility that it might nevertheless yet be realized. Drip-fed by failure, this order of optimism is not the Pollyannaish kind, fattened on buoyancy and confidence. It has a closer affinity with the hope that Eve Kosofsky Sedgwick describes as "a fracturing, even traumatic thing to experience."[36] For now let's just say that whatever the futures of the intimate public cultures currently articulated in the name of heterosexuality, one thing is certain: the demonstration of the capricious relation between coital sex and female orgasm does not prevent heterosexual intercourse continuing to figure, however ambivalently, the optimistic expression of a sexual ideology whose privileged ethical terms are equality and mutuality.[37] It is under these specific historical circumstances that the much discussed, although little theorized, feminine heterosexual practice of fake orgasm emerges.

Characterizing fake orgasm as a traditionally feminine social practice is not to disavow the fact that men also have the capacity and, at times, the proclivity to fake orgasm.[38] Similarly, the evidence of fake orgasm's occurrence across a range of sexual exchanges does not invalidate the analysis of it as paradigmatically heterosexual. Indeed, the insistent reminder that fake orgasm also occurs in nonfemale subjects and non-heterosexual encounters is in large part an attempt to dissociate it in its typicality from the heterosexual regimen. The finding that 17 percent of men had faked an orgasm in the last twelve months, for instance, circulated more prominently in media reports of the Durex Sex Survey of 2004 than the finding that 39 percent of women had. Rather than presume some equal-opportunity mode of theorizing, whose evenhanded commitment to a socially neutral set of descriptors necessarily deadens it to the conditions it sets out to describe, thinking about fake orgasm in its case-study declension as feminine and heterosexual enables a consideration of the ways it is a response to historically specific sexual expectations and knowledges that forcefully emerged during the twentieth century.[39] In particular, fake orgasm is legible as a registration of the embodied tensions implicit in an asymmetrically gendered access to sexual pleasure that persists internal to the democratization of gender within modern heterosexual intimacies that are significantly structured by notions of mutuality and reciprocity.

Although Foucault can hardly be taken as my license, his insistence that "it is the agency of sex that we must break away from" tempts me to consider fake orgasm as an inventive bodily technique that differently addresses itself to the regulatory apparatus of sexuality.[40] In doing so, I am not turning away from—far less disparaging—the rich archive of gay sexual subcultures, with their erotic innovation and the new forms of sociality those practices open on to, so much as widening the critical frame for thinking about different historically determined inhabitations of bodies and pleasures. Taking the contemporary scenarios and figures preferred by Foucault as a privileged example, rather than the material form, of counterdisciplinary transformation suggests other possibilities, possibilities perhaps gendered otherwise, that might take very different forms, unforeseen and almost certainly unrecognizable in terms of a gay subcultural template. When Foucault extols, for very different reasons, the same erotic practices long associated with transgression and freedom in the critical model he contests, it is useful to ask what other contexts or lifeworlds yield up different, perhaps unlikely, practices whose relation to pleasure might be newly recognizable as political to the extent that they are legible as open-ended exercises in self-transformation.

FAKE ORGASM AS COUNTERDISCIPLINARY PRACTICE

Given that fake orgasm is commonly derided or lamented as a debased sexual masquerade that emerges as a feminine strategy in the context of heterosexual relations organized around a specifically male sexual gratification, the masculinist measure of which can be seen in its indifference to securing female pleasure while nevertheless requiring its registration, it seems reasonable to ask: In what imagined world might the fake orgasm be recognizable as a political practice? When standard feminist discourse on fake orgasm is translated into Foucauldian terms, for instance, fake orgasm is most commonly taken for evidence of a feminine docility consistent with the disciplinary regimes of normalization. It is, however, the implausibility of contemplating fake orgasm as signifying anything other than sexual subjection, the massive and unmitigated unlikeliness of reading fake orgasm as a counterdisciplinary tactic, that most recommends its consideration. The unintelligibility of fake orgasm in terms of the queer theorizing of subaltern pleasures exerts critical pressure on our axiomatic understandings of the social forms the political properly takes.

Without doubt, fake orgasm is part of a network of effects and behaviors that naturalizes dominant cultural norms such as the masculinization of sexual desire, the promotion of intercourse as the signature act of heterosexuality, and the representation of orgasm as the true expression of an interiorized sexual self. This indisputable fact, however, has tended to obscure the possibility that fake orgasm might also be, and be for that very reason, an innovative sexual practice that makes available a mode of feminine self-production in a constrained field of possibility. Pushing against the commonsense plausibility that credits certain transgressive acts and identities with resistant potential, I am suggesting instead that the more valuable insight afforded by Foucault's call to bodies and pleasures is the recognition that one's relation to the disciplinary system of sexuality is necessarily articulated with

regard to historically specific and bounded sites of contestation.[41] Without discounting the significance of women's sexual self-determination, it remains possible to suggest that the example of fake orgasm enables a point of critical purchase on the normalizing discipline of sexuality.

Insofar as the fake orgasm fakes orgasm, it has tended to be read as a poor semblance of the real thing. Suspending our belief in the tight cultural fit between sex and authenticity, however, as indeed the circulation of fake orgasm as an intelligible concept requires us to do, we can refigure the fake orgasm as less an imitation of orgasm than a critique of its disciplinary imperatives. We can think, for example, about fake orgasm in relation to Foucault's strategic cultivation of impersonality and pleasure. According to dominant understandings of sex and sexuality, fake orgasm can only seem impersonal; it is not a true expression of one's personhood. By the same logic, fake orgasm can have nothing to do with pleasure; in miming pleasure, it removes itself from the scene of pleasure. It is because fake orgasm must be impersonal and cannot be pleasurable that it is always also a problem. I want to suggest instead that the impersonality of fake orgasm is bound inextricably with its pleasures and, furthermore, that Foucault's call to bodies and pleasures, his call for the revaluation of impersonality and pleasure in relation to sexual practice, enables us to refigure the implausibly Foucauldian—and perhaps even more implausibly feminist—fake orgasm not as a problem but as a counterdisciplinary practice.

Fake orgasm is impersonal in a number of interrelated ways where impersonality might be calculated as something nonspecific to the individual, as something shared among strangers, or as something of the self that exceeds the self. First, in the body's performative recollection of past pleasures or its fabrication of pleasures only ever experienced in the mode of simulation, fake orgasm draws on the conventions or protocols of orgasm, citing a representational code, the impersonality of which is evidenced not simply by its being distributed across a number of popular cultural discourses such as pornography, sexology, and mainstream cinema but also by its being indistinguishable, at least as far as anyone else is concerned, from your previous orgasms and the orgasms of others, strangers perhaps to you, except in your impersonal capacity to impersonate their orgasmic pleasures. Second, the communicative mode of fake orgasm is not interpersonal but impersonal, because it substitutes for the personalizing intimacies of the couple a dissimulated scene that, if it taps into any communal feeling, draws that sense from an impersonal sexual public, that dispersed, imaginary, and uneroticized community of other heterosexual women who also fake orgasm, habitually or from time to time. Third, in its practiced but never quite complacent counterfeiting of orgasm, fake orgasm produces at once a hyperconsciousness of what one is doing and an estrangement from those same acts. The dissembling production of the self as other than what one is gives rise to an alterity internal to oneself that, though it might be experienced as less the heady rush of self-transcendence customarily associated with utopian sexual practices than a leveling alienation or even a traumatized falling away from self, functions as a breach in the usual fiction of self-continuity whose strategic possibilities remain an open question.

If it seems that fake orgasm cannot be talked about in terms of pleasure as customarily perceived, then it is salutary to remember that Foucault's mobilization of the term is equally estranged from everyday understandings of pleasure. In trying to get a fix on the ways the alienations and traumas of fake orgasm, no less than its competencies and experimentations, resonated for me in terms of Foucault's admittedly very differently nuanced work on pleasure, I kept returning to an interview conducted in 1982, in which Foucault says: "I think that pleasure is a very difficult behavior. It's not as simple as that to enjoy one's self."[42] Here Foucault problematizes the thing he is frequently enough taken to be promoting, the self-evidential and self-licensing character of pleasure. To say that pleasure is "a very difficult behavior" is not to advocate some kind of feel-good hedonism in which pleasure would be the unmediated measure of the political efficacy or worth of this or that practice. Focusing on the tactical merits of the disaggregating force of extreme pleasures, Foucault's readers tend to skip over this reminder that pleasure and enjoying oneself are not easy matters, despite the fact that Foucault's key contemporary examples, fistfucking and s&m, insofar as they negotiate relations to pleasure through pain, resistance, and discomfort, refuse customary definitions of pleasure. In focusing

on Foucault's claim that "pleasure is a very difficult behavior," I do not mean to suggest so much that the attainment of pleasure is sometimes difficult, the logic often enough of feminist and therapeutic interventions with regard to fake orgasm, but rather that pleasure itself might be difficult, might be demanding, intricate, perhaps even disagreeable or objectionable. In framing fake orgasm in terms of pleasure, I'm insisting on the subtext of Foucault's "ethics of pleasure," the counterintuitive possibility that pleasure does not necessarily feel good.[43]

If, with the invocation of subtexts and counterintuition, I have wandered, under cover of his name, some distance from Foucault, that distance remains critically productive. The appeal of fake orgasm as a figure through which to revisit the political dimension of certain sexual practices depends less on its assimilability to received understandings of what makes sex political than its bad fit with those naturalized narratives. In failing to be legible in these ways, fake orgasm intervenes in the presumption that to register as political, sexual practices must be keyed to productive action, must move things along and make stuff happen. Not easily absorbed by the templates of political recognizability common to much queer theorizing, fake orgasm troubles notions of the political defined in terms—however collective, however impersonal—of agency, action, and intentionality.[44] The degree to which fake orgasm falls short of the potential Foucault and subsequent queer theorists attribute to various minoritarian sexual practices is precisely the degree to which it supports a different understanding of political action or subjectivity.

Consider, for instance, that seam of argument that runs through Foucault's interviews most articulately— and, as a consequence of the genre of the interview, most partially and fragmentedly—in which the advocacy of impersonal, even radically antisocial, "bodies and pleasures" gets fastened to an optimism that gay male public-sex cultures will thereby secure new ways of life, what Foucault refers to as "other forms of pleasure, of relationships, coexistences, attachments, loves, intensities."[45] Halperin remarks on this productivity when he notes "the specifically political significance Foucault attached to the invention of the new pleasures produced by fist-fucking or recreational drugs as well as to the invention of new sexual environments, such as saunas, bathhouses, and sex clubs, in which novel varieties of sexual pleasure could be experienced."[46] "In fact," Halperin goes on to speculate, "what may have intrigued Foucault most about fist-fucking was the way a specific nonnormative sexual practice could come to provide the origin and basis for such seemingly remote and unrelated events as bake sales, community fundraisers, and block parties."[47] In this formulation, what seems most promising, then, about the protocols and scenarios of gay male public sex as a technology for unseating oneself with tender violence from the constraints of normative sexual subjectivity—for connecting with the raw promise inherent in the phrase getting fucked up—is the more widely transacted and more familiar optimism that such scenes will afford improved forms of sociability, enhanced ways of being in and of the world, that they will, that is to say, open on to the same but still alluring horizon of nearly every other political project or impulse: something different, something better.

As noted earlier, Bersani critiques this pastoralizing transubstantiation of the erotic into a social good, scoffing at those "gays [who] suddenly rediscover their lost bathhouses as laboratories of ethical liberalism, places where a culture's ill-practiced ideals of community and diversity are authentically put into practice."[48] Dismissing as part of a wider redemptive recuperation of sex Foucault's call for a reinvention of the body as the site of new pleasures, he laments instead "the degeneration of the sexual into a relationship," which he sees as a regrettable declension in what otherwise might be the "more radical disintegration and humiliation of the self."[49] Refusing to reframe sex as a form of political action committed to pluralism and equality, a form in which "getting buggered is just one moment in the practice of those laudable humanistic virtues," Bersani instead touts gay sex as an opportunity for shattering the masculine self, emphasizing, in particular, anal sex between men as "a particular sex act" capable of inhabiting differently the phobic conflation of homosexuality and death by living it repetitively as a survivable suicide.[50] Across Halperin's and Bersani's opposed critical readings of Foucault's call to "bodies and pleasures," it is remarkable to note the strikingly similar evaluation of scenarios of gay male public sex

that continue to figure as politically resistant because they are indexed either to the invention of new affiliative forms of the social or, contrariwise, to newly embraceable possibilities of dissolution and shattering for the subject.[51] No matter whether they are read with or against Foucault's invocation of "bodies and pleasures," for both critics the erotic practices associated with male-male sexual subcultures continue to offer the most recognizable models for political engagement through sexual practice.

Compared to the endlessly generative promise of the anonymous, promiscuous, and cruisy scenes of male-male public sex, fake orgasm does not promise much in the way of such transformed lifescapes. The impersonal pleasures of fake orgasm, even as I have imagined them, barely open out on to anything, secure nothing definite, play themselves out on the high rotation of the broken promise. Fake orgasm is therefore disqualified from the scene of the political, regarded at best as a making do, a biding of time, falling well short of the promise of queer sex cultures and their muscular bringing into being of new social constellations. The political progressivism of the one and the political recidivism of the other hardly bear specifying, so ubiquitously does each circulate as common knowledge in left critical theorizing. Against the brunt of this knowledge commonly held, however, fake orgasm continues to hold open an alternate way of thinking about the political, offering not a future-directed strategy for political transformation but an eloquent figure for political engagement with the conditions of the present.

SEXUAL FEELING

Stymied yet resourceful, persistent almost to the point of anachronism, fake orgasm can be thought political to the degree that it indexes a future lived strenuously as a disappointing repetition in the present. As a figure, and perhaps also as a practice, fake orgasm condenses something of what it feels like to experience, repetitively, the constraints of the present as the source of a highly labile optimism capable of replenishing itself from the very scenes of its own disappointment, if not quite its extinction. Such an optimism is highly ambivalent, perhaps even cruel. Lauren Berlant has revivified the pat phraseology of "cruel optimism," using the term to describe "a relation of attachment to compromised conditions of possibility." "Where cruel optimism operates," she writes, "the very vitalizing or animating potency of an object/scene of desire contributes to the attrition of the very thriving that is supposed to be made possible in the work of attachment in the first place."[52] Berlant associates cruel optimism with what she calls "the politically depressed position," noting, in an earlier version of this work, "the centrality of optimistic fantasy to reproducing and surviving in zones of compromised ordinariness."[53] Berlant's work on the negativity of political feeling has been productive for my thinking about fake orgasm, yet if I hesitate to follow her in distinguishing taxonomically between different orders of optimism—the cruel as opposed to the benign or, at least, the less cruel—it is because I suspect that, in the everyday theater of the political, her "thriving" and "surviving," as their rhyming resemblance suggests, might be hard to tell apart. In the present tense that marks the real time of the political, who can say with certainty whether she is "thriving" or "surviving," both situations only confirmable after the fact, when all that can be known is the striving? In addition to all the other things it might or might not mean, fake orgasm speaks to these radically mixed feelings of political engagement, figuring the wedged-open possibility of return to some scene of deadening familiarity that might yet be repeated differently even if, more probably, done just the same.

My thinking here therefore also resonates with Heather Love's meditations on what she calls "backward feelings," such as depression, abjection, and shame, which, via their queer attachment to various scenes of negativity, suggest that the political is not always recognizable in terms of its upbeat and forward-looking mien. Accordingly Love speaks up for the importance for queer politics of an optimism that is not hygienically quarantined from the despondency it is more usually understood to counter and correct, "a form of hope inseparable from despair, a structure of feeling that might serve as a model for political life in the present."[54] Her hunch that backward feelings "teach us that we do not know what is good for politics" fits with my argument that, by being an abjected erotic practice associated with failure, self-recrimination, and embarrassment, fake orgasm is

closely calibrated to, rather than disqualified from, the political.[55] Love's argument, like that of other queer theorists who argue for the potential of the unintelligible, the unproductive, and the wasteful, invites us to rethink the political less in terms of efficacious actions or exercises of intentionalist agency than as a mode of experiencing without necessarily changing the world, as an affective engagement indiscernible within models that take real-world traction as politics' true measure. More readily than the apparently heroic, self-authoring subjects that stand for resistance, world-making, or ethical reinvention in different strands of much queer theorizing about sexual subcultures, fake orgasm affords the valuable recognition that action might be ineffectually repetitive, that agency might be, as Kathleen Stewart writes, "strange, twisted, caught up in things, passive, or exhausted. Not the way we like to think about it. Not usually a simple projection toward a future . . . agency is frustrated and unstable and attracted to the potential in things."[56] More easily framed as a bad habit, a passive accession to a scene of oppression, or a recidivist slide to a superseded style of femininity, the difficulty with which fake orgasm is recognizable as political attests to the importance of alternative political imaginaries for queer conceptualizations of erotic practice and identity.

In making this claim, I'm not calling for fake orgasm in the sense of recommending it as a liberatory, transformative, or even oppositional sexual practice. (What would it mean anyway to call for fake orgasm? Despite the almost universal opprobrium it attracts, fake orgasm has no trouble maintaining itself as a sexual practice with a recognizable cultural profile.) Rather, the mode for my thinking about fake orgasm is not therapeutic or remedial but critical theoretical, or, even better, critical hypothetical. "Hypothesizing is easier than proving," writes Sedgwick and, like Sedgwick, when it comes to revising the political valence of fake orgasm, "I cannot imagine the protocol by which such hypotheses might be tested."[57] Stopping short of ascribing a political intentionality to the sexual agent who fakes her orgasm, my reading of fake orgasm does not discount, but rather draws its counterintuitive energies from, the probable fact that most women who fake would rather have an orgasm. Far from ascribing a political objective to the woman who fakes orgasm or even a political utility to fake orgasm, my license here is instead the persistence of fake orgasm as an observance and a social concept and the pressure this applies to traditional understandings of the political efficacy of sexual practice. Given this persistence, fake orgasm needs to be conceptualized outside the narrow logics in which it is customarily thought, outside, that is, the logics of deceit (the exemplary male perspective) or dissatisfaction (the exemplary female one). My motivation for this is the possibility of thinking differently about a discredited and traditionally feminine sexual practice—one customarily associated with conservative rather than radical ends, suburban rather than subcultural scenarios—retrieving it for a recognition of the ways fake orgasm, when taken seriously, suggests different possibilities for thinking sex and politics together.

What does it mean to take fake orgasm seriously? I don't mean to say here the thing that is most readily heard in relation to fake orgasm. Taking fake orgasm seriously usually means recognizing it as a problem, the seriousness of which motivates calls for its eradication. Whether it is seen as a sociocultural problem of women's access to full sexual expression, as an ethical problem organized around notions of deceitfulness, as a problem of false consciousness in which women imitate sexual pleasure rather than secure it through challenging the dominant model of heterosexual sex, or as a psychosomatic problem in which the reiterative performance of fake orgasm trains the body against orgasm proper, fake orgasm is regarded first and foremost as a problem. If, however, we resist classifying fake orgasm as a problem—resist, too, reading it as the symptom of a broader problem with heteroeroticism—it is possible to recognize fake orgasm as a sexual practice in its own right. The very least thing secured by such a taxonomic shift is no small thing: a recognition of fake orgasm as a positive cultural practice, an erotic invention that emerges from a set of culturally specific circumstances as a widespread sexual observance, a new disposition or way of managing one's self in sexual relations. Fake orgasm, therefore, is not simply the simulation of orgasm but a dense complex of effects enfolding an indexically female, twentieth-century heterosexual practice that, by putting into prominent circulation the problem of the legibility of sexual pleasure, troubles the presumed truth or authenticity of sex itself, recognizes that norms are self-reflexively inhabited by a wider range of social actors than is commonly presumed, and asks us to rethink the conditions of legibility for political agency.

NOTES

1. De Botton, *On Love,* 165. The bracketed text is part of the original work.
2. The specification of orgasmic contractions at intervals of precisely 0.8 seconds is, of course, a finding of Masters and Johnson, who note that in women "the orgasmic platform may respond initially with a spastic contraction lasting 2 to 4 seconds before the muscle spasm gives way to the regularly recurrent 0.8-second contractions" *(Human Sexual Response,* 78).
3. Foucault, *The History of Sexuality,* 6.
4. How or where to draw the contours of political recognizability is itself a political question. As Judith Butler argues, "To become political, to act and speak in ways that are recognizably political, is to rely on a foreclosure of the very political field that is not subject to political scrutiny" ("Is Kinship Always Already Heterosexual?" 19). What desires or practices, claims or stakes get to count as political depends very much on how the field of the political is imagined and thus the constitution of that field is itself politically consequent.
5. See, for example, the last sentences of Rachel Maines's *The Technology of Orgasm* (122–23), in which fake orgasm is singled out as the female erotic practice that must be renounced in order for androcentric sexual norms to become a thing of the past. For a vernacular example of the appropriately feminist aversion to fake orgasm, consider one of Shere Hite's anonymous respondents who answers the question "Do you ever fake orgasms?" with "I used to, but not since

I learned the submissive implications of it and the fact that I had a real right to genuine plea-sure" *(The Hite Report,* 207).

6. The tendency for fake orgasm to be read ultimately as the failure of feminism is clearly evident in Gayatri Chakravorty Spivak's discussion of it in relation to the persistent critical and theoreti-cal troping of femininity in terms of deception and being other than what it seems. Initially, Spivak takes up the model of fake orgasm to critique the deconstructive figuration of feminin-ity. Commenting on Jacques Derrida's positive reframing of the misogynistic representation of women's impersonation of sexual pleasure as representing the citational character of writing and, more generally, the indeterminacy of sexual difference, Spivak seems momentarily to cel-ebrate the capacity of fake orgasm to destabilize phallocentric logics of sexual possession: "If men think they have or possess women in sexual mastery, they should be reminded that, by this logic, women can destroy the proper roles of master and slave. Men cannot know when they are properly in possession of them as masters (knowing them carnally in their pleasure) and when in their possession as slaves (duped by their self-citation in a fake orgasm)" ("Love Me, Love My Ombre Elle," 22). In a further essay, however, Spivak notes as a problem the double displace-ment this effects for the woman who stands in for a universal condition she can only embody at one remove: "The woman who is the 'model' for deconstructive discourse remains a woman generalized and defined in terms of the faked orgasm and other varieties of denial" ("Displace-ment and the Discourse of Woman," 45). If, in the first instance, what is being denied is male certainty with regard to sexual hierarchy, in the second the denial is registered at the expense of the feminine, that historical figure who can ill afford to have fake orgasm metaphorize relations between the sexes, still less the human condition.

7. Foucault, *The History of Sexuality,* 157.

8. Deleuze, "Foldings, or the Inside of Thought," 315; Foucault, The History of Sexuality, 159.

9. The French originals, *La Volonté de savoir: Histoire de la sexualité, 1* and *L'usage des plaisirs: Histoire de la sexualité, 2,* were published in 1976 and 1984, respectively.

10. A. Anderson, *The Way We Argue Now,* 149. Deleuze insists that Foucault's historical scholarship was always motivated by contemporary coordinates and that, for this reason, moreover, his popular interviews are key to his work: "There's one key thing that runs right through Foucault's work: he was always dealing with historical formations (either short-term or, toward the end, long-term ones), but always in relation to us today. He didn't have to make this explicit in his books, it was quite obvious, and left the business of making it still clearer to interviews in news-papers. That's why Foucault's interviews are an integral part of his work" (*Negotiations,* 105–6).

11. An important exception to this queer critical tendency is Judith Butler's reading of Foucault's last works as a repudiation of the speculatively utopian conclusion to *The History of Sexuality, Volume 1.* She interprets his turn away from the program of work he anticipated with that publication and his focus instead in the second and third volumes on ancient ethics as evidence of "the distance that Foucault ultimately takes from this most thrilling of his political rallying calls" ("Revisiting Bodies and Pleasures," 13).

12. Halperin, *Saint Foucault,* 72.

13. Davidson, "Ethics as Ascetics," 134.

14. Foucault, "Friendship as a Way of Life," 206.

15. Foucault, "Sade," 227.

16. Foucault, "The End of the Monarchy of Sex," 144.

17. Foucault, "The History of Sexuality," 191.

18. For more sustained discussions of the distinction Foucault makes between desire and pleasure, see Davidson, "Foucault, Psychoanalysis, and Pleasure," 45–49, and Halperin, *Saint Foucault,* 92–97.

19. Quoted in Macey, *The Lives of Michel Foucault*, 364.

20. Foucault, "An Ethics of Pleasure," 264.

21. Foucault, "Sex, Power, and the Politics of Identity," 169.

22. Foucault, *The History of Sexuality*, 155.

23. Foucault, *The History of Sexuality*, 152.

24. Žižek, "The Ongoing 'Soft' Revolution," 293.

25. Popular discussions of fake orgasm—mostly directed at female readers— cover a range of positions. See, for example, Tavris, "The Big Bedroom Bluff"; Jeffery, "Where Is the Real Orgasm?"; Reynolds, "Do You Still Fake Orgasm?"; Kaplan, "Are You Lying in Bed?"; Dormen, "Faking It?"; Lerner, "The Big O"; Feltz, "So What If You Fake It!"; Swift, "Yes, You Should Fake It"; Haze, "Faking It"; M. Brown, "Can He Tell If You're Faking an Orgasm?"; and Koli, "Is Your Guy Faking It in Bed?"

26. Even phenomena such as "faking cyberorgasms" suggest the necessity for a more complex account. See Ben-Ze'ev, *Love Online*, 6.

27. Defending his data by drawing attention to the very high coefficients of correlation between what husbands and wives say, Kinsey is satisfied that he can demonstrate the veracity of independently collected data in every category of inquiry but two, one of which concerns the frequency of female orgasm. In this instance, Kinsey notes, "the male believes that his female partner experiences orgasm more often than she herself reports; but it is to be noted that the wife sometimes deceives her husband deliberately on that point." Less concerned with human sexual behavior at this point than the robustness of his research data, Kinsey offers no analysis of the circumstances under which wives mislead their husbands about the occurrence of their own orgasms, his lack of interest in this direction reinforcing a sense that, however regrettable for statistical accuracy, fake orgasm is a wifely commonplace and commonly undetected on the part of husbands (Kinsey et al., *Sexual Behavior in the Human Female*, 127–28).

28. Masters and Johnson, *Human Sexual Response*, 138.

29. Masters and Johnson, *Human Sexual Response*, 134. Whereas Masters and Johnson seem here to attribute to men observational powers more usually associated with the laboratory, more recent neuroscientific research uses simulated orgasm as a laboratory control to demonstrate, via positron emission tomography, patterns of cerebral blood flow consistent with female orgasm. Although comparing orgasm to simulated orgasm allows the research team to conclude that orgasm is marked by "decreased rCBF [regional cerebral blood flow] in the prefrontal cortex and left temporal lobe," fake orgasm continues to haunt the study. Despite building in a protocol that solicits the experimental subject's self-report as to whether an orgasm has been achieved, the team decided to reject two reported orgasms on the grounds that they returned rectal pressure data closely resembling simulated orgasm in the same subjects. "Therefore," concludes the team, having just admitted that the differences between the simulated orgasm and the real orgasm it is intended to authorize are difficult to fix, "the orgasms included in the present study are likely to be 'real'" (Georgiadis et al., "Regional Cerebral Blood Flow," 3315, 3314).

30. Nearly ten years later and despite the massive popularization of their findings, Masters and Johnson were still inveighing against fake orgasm, although this time on moral rather than pragmatic grounds: "'Pretending' or 'faking' are euphemisms for 'lying' and lying divides people. This is especially true in bed" (*The Pleasure Bond*, 247). See also Darling and Davidson, "Enhancing Relationships."

31. For an account that, under cover of historically overarching discourses of female insincerity, conflates fake orgasm in the twentieth century with early modern simulations of virginity, see Marjorie Garber's "I'll Have What She's Having," in Garber, *Symptoms of Culture*, 217–35.

32. Berlant and Warner, "Sex in Public," 320.

33. Lloyd, *The Case of the Female Orgasm*, 25 and 36. For a full discussion of the surveys, see Lloyd's second chapter, "The Basics of Female Orgasm," 21–43.

34. Lauren Berlant notes this tendency of female testimony never to arrive on the public scene: "When any woman testifies publicly 'as woman' she is unknown: her knowledge is marked as that which public norms have never absorbed, even when there's nothing new about the particular news she brings" ("Trauma and Ineloquence," 47).

35. The widespread, if unassimilated, knowledge that penetrative intercourse unreliably secures female sexual pleasure therefore constitutes one of the tightly impacted contradictions that structure the heart of modern heterosexuality. Another is the idea that women want men to talk to them more while men want women to have sex with them more. For a brilliant reading of this gendered complaint, see Vogler, "Sex and Talk." Vogler argues that sex and talk can be thought of as similar strategies for accessing a depersonalized relation to the self, an intimacy that is valued in terms of its capacity to unloose the self from itself rather than its ability to restore the self to itself or manufacture a better self. Although Vogler's essay takes up the gendered malaise that characterizes case-study heterosexuality via an interrogation of Immanuel Kant's prioritization of rationality and will for ethical conduct, her promotion of a sexual subjectivity imagined in a mode of impersonality over a fully self-knowing subject forged in the crucible of interpersonal communication has been useful for my thinking in the next section . . . about the implications of Foucault's ethics of self-fashioning for fake orgasm.

36. Sedgwick, "Paranoid Reading and Reparative Reading," 24.

37. There have been feminist attempts, of course, to code heterosexual intercourse otherwise, as a figure for gendered relations of dominance and inequity. See, for example, Dworkin, *Intercourse*. While these perspectives have remained culturally marginal, they receive a kind of backhanded vernacular recognition in the everyday variations on "fuck you" that circulate as expressions of contemptuous dismissal.

38. For a recent scholarly account of male fake orgasm that finds that "the modal sexual activity during which participants had pretended was PVI [penile-vaginal intercourse]" and that such pretense occurs most frequently in the context of an established relationship, see Muehlenhard and Shippee, "Men's and Women's Reports of Pretending Orgasm," 558.

39. For an account that takes fake orgasm as an exemplary articulation of the contradictory forces that structure specifically heterosexual relations, see C. Roberts et al., "Faking It."

40. Foucault, *The History of Sexuality*, 157.

41. Foucault argues as much in relation to the historic situatedness of homosexuality when he writes: "Homosexuality is an historic occasion to re-open affective and relational virtualities, not so much through the intrinsic qualities of the homosexual, but due to the biases against the position he occupies" ("Friendship as a Way of Life," 207).

42. Foucault, "An Interview by Stephen Riggins," 129.

43. Foucault, "An Interview by Stephen Riggins," 131.

44. So established is this queer theoretical template that Gregory Tomso can write uncritically of "the politically resistant, identity-and subjectivity-alerting effects of certain forms of male-male sex celebrated by queer theorey" ("Viral Sex," 273).

45. Foucault, "The End of the Monarchy of Sex," 144.

46. Halperin, *Saint Foucault*, 93.

47. Halperin, *Saint Foucault*, 99.

48. Bersani, "Is the Rectum a Grave?" 222.

49. Bersani, "Is the Rectum a Grave?" 218, 217. The relation of Bersani's essay to Foucault's project is complicated. Bersani argues that the feminist and gay and lesbian politics of sexual liberation he opposes "received its most prestigious intellectual justification from Foucault's call—especially in the first volume of his *History of Sexuality*— for a reinventing of the body as a surface of multiple sources of pleasure." Not only does Bersani read *History of Sexuality, Volume 1* as a further instantiation of the liberatory discourses that work influentially critiques, but he also pushes, in the final phrasing of his essay, as if it were an oppositional strategy to the one offered by Foucault, what reads more easily as its paraphrase, "jouissance as a mode of ascesis" (Bersani, "Is the Rectum a Grave?" 219, 222). Halperin also notes the latter in *Saint Foucault*, 218n192.

50. Bersani, "Is the Rectum a Grave?" 219, 220. Although Bersani suggests toward the close of his essay that the normative masculine subjectivity sacrificed in anal sex is "an ideal shared—differently—by men and women," he more consistently disregards the possibility that women of any erotic persuasion have access to the ego transformations exclusively indexed in his argument to male homosexual erotic practice. Here again is the tendency to accord political and critical significance to erotic practices associated with particular identity groups. More readily perhaps than any masculine ideal of the subject, receptive anal sex can be practiced as easily by women as men, a possibility Bersani overlooks when he privileges anal sex between men by comparing it with vaginal sex between men and women. Significantly, for Bersani, it is not that anal sex between men, like vaginal sex between men and women, is an opportunity for ego-shattering. Rather, anal sex between men is imbued with critical force to the degree to which it is "associated with women but performed by men" ("Is the Rectum a Grave?" 222, 220).

51. If in my account the proper names of Halperin and Bersani seem neatly aligned with the two sides of this interpretative standoff, it should be noted that each scholar in his broader project encompasses the critical perspective more prominently associated with the other. Thus Halperin argues, "If [Foucault] does seem to suggest that getting fisted is, in some sense, good for you, he does so only because he believes that getting fisted is, in another sense, extremely bad for you. Only something so very bad for the integrated person that the normalized modern individual has become can perform the crucial work of rupture, of social and psychological disintegration, that may be necessary in order to permit new forms of life to come into being" (*Saint Foucault*, 107). Similarly, Bersani comes to argue, in ways that soften his earlier position, for what he calls "homo-ness," an attribute associated with relationality, however impersonal, rather than disintegrated selves: "An anticommunal mode of connectedness we might all share, or a new way of coming together: that, and not assimilation into already constituted communities, should be the goal of any adventure in bringing out, and celebrating, 'the homo' is all of us" (*Homos*, 10).

52. Berlant, *Cruel Optimism*, 24–25.

53. Berlant, *Cruel Optimism*, 27, and Berlant, "Cruel Optimism," 35.

54. Love, *Feeling Backward*, 26.

55. Love, *Feeling Backward*, 27.

56. Stewart, *Ordinary Affects*, 86. See also Lauren Berlant's suggestion in *Cruel Optimism* that "lateral agency," by which she means "an activity of maintenance, not making; fantasy, without grandiosity; sentience, without full intentionality; inconsistency, without shattering; embodying, alongside embodiment" (100) might be a more useful concept than sovereignty for thinking about the constrained spaces in which many subjects under late capitalism get by.

57. Sedgwick, *Epistemology of the Closet*, 12.

33. AN (IM)MODEST REVOLUTION?: NUDITY, MODEST FASHION, AND CULTURAL APPROPRIATION ON THE GLOBAL RUNWAY

My message is gender equality and my body is no sin.

—Aliaa Elmahdy

If we don't invent a language, if we don't find our body's language, it will have too few gestures to accompany our story.

—Luce Irigaray

Modest fashion is going viral. The first modest fashion show in the United States was staged during New York Fashion Week in September 2016, with another show in London in February 2017. Both events followed on the heels of Istanbul's First International Modest Fashion Week in May 2016. International media, fashion, film, and technology moguls were conspicuously present at these runway shows. Given such mainstream visibility and high profile turnout, it is safe to say not only that modest fashion is trending, but that it has definitively "arrived" on the global fashion runway with unique style, force, and implications.

This essay will make sense of the modest fashion revolution relative to today's geopolitical climate marked by heightened Islamophobia, neo-Orientalism, sexual and racial violence, and xenophobia, perhaps most evident in a tidal wave of bans on women's right to wear the burkini, hijab, and niqab in public and, increasingly, private spaces throughout the EU—as in the March 2017 ruling by the European Court of Justice that allows private companies to ban female employees from wearing the hijab at work (Bilefsky). I will analyze this revolution alongside the nude protest of Aliaa Elmahdy in Egypt during the "Arab Spring" to understand how women's bodies and their relationship to dress bear particularly revolutionary meanings that assume heightened symbolic power in the digital age. While nude protest and modest fashion deploy modes of dress from opposite ends of the spectrum, both stage the female body in public space in ways that seek to intercept the sexualized gaze and, by so doing, redress women's bodies as well as the body politic in times of upheaval.

Nude protest and the modest fashion movement raise crucial questions about the meanings of sexual and national fantasy, desire, fear, identity, and citizenship, especially relative to historical debates and legislation that seek to regulate how, under what circumstances, and for whose pleasure and benefit women's bodies are authorized to appear or perceived to "belong" in the public sphere. I will ask how Aliaa's nude protest in Egypt and Sweden as well as the modest fashion revolution speak to contemporary geopolitical anxieties in Turkey, the United States, the EU, and beyond with respect to national, cultural, and religious identities and their relationship to difference, assimilation, and sexual violence. What happens when modest fashion and nude protest hit the global digital runway? What are the effects of both forms of revolution for varied local and transnational audiences?

I will also ask whether there are circumstances under which nudity and modest fashion may lose their revolutionary potentials. To this end, I will consider contexts in which nudity may be perceived to reinforce hypersexualized or exploitative readings of female embodiment. I will also examine the modest fashion movement as it intersects with forms of cultural, ethnic, and religious appropriation. How do the meanings of nudity and modest fashion obfuscate and even empty out as they are staged across diverse national, religious, and cultural borders and affiliations? I will consider the "global beauty" aesthetic and its implications for the politics of cultural and religious assimilation and appropriation.

REVOLUTIONARY (UN)DRESSING?: NUDE PROTEST AND HYPERSEXUALIZATION

On November 17, 2011, a group of Egyptian law students filed suit against Egyptian blogger Aliaa Magda Elmahdy for "violating morals, inciting indecency and insulting Islam" (Mezzofiore). A few weeks earlier, on October 23, the 19-year-old Elmahdy had posted nude selfies and images of naked men to her blog, "A Rebel's Diary" (Elmahdy). This was a radical act that resulted in calls to punish and kill her. Elmahdy's activism emerged at a historical moment of despair regarding the direction of the Egyptian revolution. The military had consolidated power in the previous months, despite mass mobilizations that forced President Hosni Mubarak to step down in February.

In a November 2011 interview, Elmahdy framed her act as part of an ongoing struggle for sex equality in the new Egypt: "(Sexism) against women in Egypt is unreal, but I will battle it until the end" (Fahmy). Elmahdy's nude protest followed revelations by Samira Ibrahim that the military had conducted "virginity" tests on her and other Egyptian women activists who police had violently removed from Tahrir Square on March 9, 2011. As the military state bolstered itself against deeper transformations, harassment and violence against fully dressed girls and women in public space had intensified rather than improved, especially in Cairo. In sum, the context in which Elmahdy took her radical action was particularly hostile to women's presence in public space and their political activism. Elmahdy's activism re-stages the naked female body as a tool of political dissent, and by so doing highlights the "tensions around national identity that animate the contemporary Arab public sphere" (Mourad 62).

In December 2012, Elmahdy founded a branch of the Ukrainian feminist organization Femen in Egypt. Death threats prompted her to flee to Sweden in early 2013, where she was granted political asylum. She continued her body activism through street theater with Femen in Sweden and postings on her blog. She broke with Femen in October 2013, and continues her body activism through self-authored visual and narrative blog posts that often focus on resisting sexual violence and control.

I argue that Elmahdy is a revolutionary subject who provocatively fuses aesthetics and dis-identification politics in a self-branding, digital age. Her nude protests perform imagined violence and rage at the sexual status quo. Elmahdy sex(t)s revolution by calling attention to its embodied sexual-gendered elisions and exclusions. She challenges revolutionary and iconographic registers that subordinate matters related to gender, femininity, sex, and the body. Elmahdy's digital activism foregrounded sex and the female body in a way that underscored their political primacy. In effect, she used fantasy to stage a revolt against the sexual status quo. Elmahdy's activism illustrates the "paradoxical" nature of all spaces, which offer opportunities for counterhegemonic rupture even when they are sexist, racist, or homophobic (Rose 20). When she performatively inserted her body where it is least expected, she reshaped the landscape of feminist protest and female nudity despite the perils of cyberspace, the complicated charge attached to female nudity, and the ideological disagreements that immediately emerged among feminists in Egypt and the Arab world about Elmahdy's strategy.

Human bodies exert unique force, even in the digital age. Bodies represent humanity in its most primal form. Our bodies are expressive and fragile, prone to bruises, breaks, cuts, fractures, and scars (Eileraas). Bodily forms of protest communicate "a radically superior commitment to one's cause, because putting one's body in harm's way reflects far higher stakes"(Kraidy 73). When protestors obstruct the paths of tanks and soldiers, light themselves afire, or hunger strike, they pose a metaphysical question: "What is my body—my life—worth to you?" Bodily protest asks how different lives are valued and whose experiences are officially erased or sanctified in collective memory.

Women's bodies compose particularly fraught symbolic terrain, especially when they are out of place, as they disrupt sacrosanct gendered dichotomies of public/private. Women's oppositional nakedness demands a pause not only because all public nudity signifies as inappropriate, but because militant or unashamed female nudity challenges the conventional visual economy of male entitlement and female passivity within public space. By launching her nude body into cyberspace to viral effect (Michael), Elmahdy criticizes not only the regulation of female visibility, but also state policing and violation of women's bodies and masculinist ambivalence about the presence of women in public space.

Many Arab activists, in Egypt as well as the Egyptian diaspora, rallied to support Elmahdy. Egyptian-American actress Amanda Banoub commended Elmahdy for "displaying genuine purity and modesty without a single layer of clothing"(Mezzofiore). Lebanese journalist Joy Majdalani Habib writes:

> Not only did Aliaa el Mahdy break the taboo of nudity, she also countered the tyranny of the male gaze that strives to enclose the female body in one of two categories: either a desirable object to lust upon or a shameful object to hide under heavy sheets. (Habib)

Mikdashi further notes that Elmahdy

> is not "waiting" for the "right moment" to bring up bodily rights and sexual rights in post-Mubarak Egypt. Her nudity aims to reinvigorate a conversation about the politics of sex and the uneven ways it is articulated across the fields of gender, capital, and control. She is staring back at us. (Mikdashi)

By forcing attention to the naked female body, Elmahdy questions persistent paradigms that frame women's nudity, sexuality, political activism, and presence in public space as either irrelevant distractions or sources of shame. Elmahdy's actions demonstrate how "the gendered human body is at once a medium of expression and a discursive battlefield" (Kraidy 73). She challenges a figurative landscape where women's bodies too often serve as symbolic war zones between Western and Eastern actors and ideologues. On one side are those who invoke women's status and bodies as in need of liberation/modernization. And on the other are those who constitute them as repositories of national, cultural, or religious tradition. Elmahdy refuses such binary frames when she rages against sexual inequality, gendered double standards, and political marginalization that reduce women to silent victims or erotic spectacles. If, as Ernest Renan suggests, nationalism depends on forgetting, Elmahdy uses embodied digital protest to remember sexuality and gender-based violence as sources of trauma and shame historically integral to projects of revolution and state formation (Renan).

Elmahdy rewrites the female nude from object of the male gaze and heteronormative fantasy to autonomous feminist subject. In the Orientalist painterly tradition of the *odalisque*, naked women wait passively for men to enter and command the scene. In this sense, as John Berger argues, the surveyed female nude is dominated by the male spectator (Berger). Elmahdy rewrites this dynamic of passive femininity and male domination. She provocatively re-stages the genre of the female nude through self-authored, sex-positive oppositional nakedness. She deploys her body as "erotic capital" where the desired return is not the voyeuristic male gaze, but rather social and political empowerment for women (Hakim).

Elmahdy insists that women's bodies are central to revolutionizing art, politics, and history. She re-tools the female nude, investing it with explicitly confrontational sexual and political agency. When she opens her legs and exposes her genitals in her self-portrait, Elmahdy openly defies conventional expectations of female modesty within the national, cultural, and religious contexts of Egypt and Islam. Through content and composition, her nude self-portrait conveys an innocent and insouciant sexiness that has been described as seductive, alluring, erotic, and unintentional. But it is also insolent (Shoair). Her portrait is arresting in its simplicity and iconic in its determination to put sexuality into a conversation with revolution. Through her careful blend of nudity and simple fashion accessories, she fuses the intimate, hidden chamber of the *boudoir* with a conversation about power in public space, cyberspace, and representational space more broadly. Rather than occupying the least amount of space, as girls and women are conditioned to do (Kilbourne; Bartky), Elmahdy dominates the space in her self-presentation. She transforms the photographic field into a space of expansive possibility by writing herself into history as a political and sexual agent.

(COUNTER-) REVOLUTIONARY DRESSING?: MODEST FASHION AND CULTURAL APPROPRIATION

While less eye-catching than nudity, "modest fashion" is increasingly gaining visibility on runways from Istanbul to New York. Fueled by young, style-savvy Muslim women who have often felt invisible to mainstream designers, modest fashion centers on the desire to look chic while abiding by Islamic codes of modesty. The rise in modest fashion over the past decade coincides with the emergence of "Generation M"—a new generation of Muslims who embrace faith alongside popular culture, and who use fashion to convey religious identity and modern aesthetics by pairing traditional values with Western designer labels. Nearly two-thirds of Generation M is younger than 30, and most women within this demographic are digitally connected, marrying later, and in possession of a disposable income (Paton).

Haute couture designers and fast-fashion chains are suddenly awakening to the sartorial needs of this demographic, as Muslim consumers comprise a growing percentage of the global fashion market. A 2011 report estimates that Muslims will make up over 26% of the world's population by 2030, and a more recent study predicts their spending on clothing and shoes will reach $488 billion by 2019, or 15% of global spending (Petrilla; Fernandez; Pew Research Center). Muslim women, in particular, are heralded as the "next big untapped fashion market" (Petrilla). Fashion designers concentrate their efforts on the holy month of Ramadan, which is increasingly recognized as a shopping holiday when many Muslims buy new clothes and dress up. In 2014, US fashion house DKNY became one of the first Western brands to launch a Ramadan collection aimed at a wealthy Arab clientele. Modest and Muslim fashion are no longer on the periphery of the industry, nor can the industry afford to ignore them (Paton). Hijabi women fashion bloggers, in particular, comprise a veritable digital *umma* of sorts. To tap into this influential online community, Dolce & Gabbana launched a luxury collection of abayas and headscarves in 2016 in the Middle East, Paris, and London. Conservative British designer Marks & Spencer released a burkini in summer 2016 following public debate over the burkini ban on beaches in France. Earlier this year, Nike launched a "pro hijab," a headscarf designed of high-tech fabrics aimed at female Muslim athletes.

Because timing is everything in fashion as in politics, it is vital to contextualize this moment of modest fashion's mainstream "arrival" to the global catwalk. Since September 11, 2001, and especially for the past few years of incendiary events throughout the EU and the United States, including Charlie Hebdo in Paris and Donald Trump's election as President of the United States, anti-immigrant, anti-Islam populism and Islamophobic hate crimes have been on the rise. President Trump regularly shares Islamophobic worldviews that capitalize on discourses of fear and "othering" to build "a better America"—one that seeks to ban Muslim immigrants, among others, from its shores. Against this volatile backdrop, Shepard Fairey's "We the People" illustration of Munira Ahmed has gained increasing sociopolitical currency as an iconic image of resistance in the Trump era.

At the same time, especially in the wake of the 2011–2013 "Arab Spring" or revolutions throughout the Middle East, North Africa, and Turkey, a digital *umma* is taking shape online—one that consists primarily of young Muslim bloggers and netizens eager to engage in creative and critical practices of digital citizenship and solidarity. Within this online community organized around affirmations and contestations of Muslim identity, new styles, tastes, and trends are continually fashioned, negotiated, and recycled. Such spaces of belonging are vital for those who lack a legitimately recognized homeland; who feel their religious identity is under attack; who face increasing controls on freedom of speech within conventional media channels; or who are able to enjoy significant mobility and anonymity online relative to the modes of scrutiny and regulation their bodies would attract in public space (Ali). Hijab tutorials and blogs devoted to "modest chic" attract millions of followers on Instagram and YouTube.

Given the historical context and geopolitical landscape in which modest fashion is taking root, I argue that its ascendance within the public eye constitutes a revolution of aesthetic and political dimensions. As Pardis Mahdavi notes of sexual and stylistic subcultures in Tehran, fashion rebellion often serves not only as a means of creative self-expression, but also as a subaltern space in which to negotiate identities marked by the dominant regime or culture as "deviant," marginal, pathological, or transgressive; and as a mode of political intervention that seeks to reconfigure the public sphere. In this sense, the contemporary rise of modest fashion on the global runway can be regarded as revolutionary against the backdrop of Islamophobic policies and practices in the United States and the EU. It doubles as revolutionary within an industry widely held to promote damaging body and beauty ideals, low self-esteem and eating disorders, and heavily invested in fulfilling the desires of an objectifying, heteronormative male gaze that works, as Fatima Mernissi notes, to produce an "invisible harem" or state of internal colonization for those negatively impacted by its ideals (Mernissi).

Modest dress provokes anxiety and panic in France, where the banning of hijabs, niqabs, and burkinis in response to racial tensions, security fears, debates about national identity, and xenophobic immigration policies has simultaneously ignited and stymied public discourse for the past two decades. Debate over modest fashion in France centers on core French republican values of *laicite*, or secularism; *fraternite*, or national identity and solidarity; and *egalite*, or equality. This dialogue pits distinctly "French," secular visions of "freedom" and identity against religious—especially sartorial, and disproportionately Islamic—practices. Such practices are figured as antithetical to the republic inasmuch as they are perceived to thwart women's "liberation" in a nation theoretically prefaced on equality (Friedman; Rubin "From Bikinis to Burkinis"). In a shocking application of this logic, a school in northeastern France sent a 15-year-old student home twice in two weeks in April 2015 for wearing a long skirt that the principal judged was "an ostentatious sign of the girl's Muslim faith" (Rubin "French School Deems Teenager's Skirt"). Similarly, Laurence Rossignol, former French minister for women and families, sparked controversy when she expressed this perspective in an interview in March 2016. Rossignol compared women who choose to wear the hijab or burqa to "American negroes who were in favor of slavery." Furthermore, she described major brands that promote Islamic or modest dress as "socially irresponsible," and suggested that such fashion "promotes the confinement of women's bodies" (Wilsher). That same month, Pierre Berge, a former partner of Yves Saint Laurent, accused big fashion houses that cater to the Muslim market as participating in the "enslavement of women" ("French Fashion Mogul Pierre Berge Hits Out at 'Islamic' Clothing"). Feminist scholarship on the politics of beauty importantly recalls the ways in which Berge's notion of "enslavement" could be applied to traditional Western fashion and beauty standards as well (Mernissi; Wolf; Rhode). For many feminist critics, the comments of Rossignol and Berge evoke a disturbing legacy of white, Western, colonial or "rescue feminism" that speaks for or on behalf of Third World, especially Muslim, women in accordance with Western definitions of "liberation" (Abu-Lughod).

Eager to reject these stereotypes, many postcolonial and Muslim feminist critics view modesty as a welcome counterpoint to the culture of mandatory self-exposure and sexual objectification that prevails in Western societies. Such advocates frame modest fashion as "revolutionary," understanding it as a means to combine fashionable self-presentation with feminist empowerment, or a deliberate attempt to limit women's exposure and sexual objectification. Some feminists view modest dress, especially the hijab, as a tool to subvert the voyeuristic male gaze by removing the female body from the field of vision or rendering it "invisible" to prurient onlookers. In this sense, modest fashion challenges a sense of male entitlement to (see and access) women's bodies that pervades Western culture. Others regard modest chic as a strategy with which to "turn the female body inside out" and map out alternate circuits of visibility and desire for female bodies as they traverse public space (Gokariksel and Secor).

The modest fashion movement commercializes Islam, raising valid questions about cultural appropriation. Can non-Muslim designers genuinely create fashion for Muslim audiences without exploiting religious principles as yet another means to turn a profit? Muslim critics of modest chic emphasize its oxymoronic coupling of Islam with conspicuous consumption to attract a sexualized gaze. They maintain that the aim of fashion—to attract attention, fascination, allure, and envy through the gaze—directly contradicts Muslim religious imperatives of modesty and humility.

From this perspective, it might be argued that a more "revolutionary" fashion statement could be found in Turkey's gradual easing and reversal of the hijab ban in public schools and workplaces, which began with a landmark decision by the Higher Education Board in 2010 (Toksabay and Villelabeitia). Designed in part by the Erdogan administration as an affirmation of Islam that would challenge Western influence, including the secularization of public space under Ataturk, this legal move paved the way for the contemporary flourishing of modest fashion. More significantly, it attempts to invite into public space genuine freedom of expression, whether embodied in religious or secular terms. On the sidewalks of Istanbul today, the relatively peaceful co-existence of hijabis and those adopting distinctly secular, Westernized styles gestures toward new aesthetic and political horizons and coalitions.

In Turkey, where modest fashion originated and Muslim identity is openly expressed in public space, critiques of haute couture "modest fashion" often center on religious and cultural appropriation. From this perspective, Western, Judeo-Christian brands control and benefit from the exploitation of the Muslim principle of modesty in ways that tend to overlook the differing needs of different communities; disrespect cultural and religious tradition; and deepen existing political and socioeconomic patterns of exploitation between East and West (Pham; Fung). A recent article in Turkish newspaper *Daily Sabah* describes Dolce & Gabbana's foray into modest chic as "outdated" and "mediocre" compared to the designs of traditional Islamic fashion houses. On a positive note, the article suggests that "in a world where it is always the *hijabis* who, due to their visibility, suffer the consequences of terrorist acts that are so wrongfully associated with Islam," the momentous occasion of top Western brands catering to the Muslim market may instill *Muslimah* pride. On the other hand, the author reads haute couture modest fashion as "far from revolutionary" and advises Western fashion labels interested in modest chic to "take a much-needed trip to the Middle East to see what they are up against"—local designers "who know *hijabis* best and who have been serving us when there was nobody around to pay attention to our needs" ("D&G's Islamic Fashion Collection Far from Revolutionary," *Daily Sabah*).

Yet the rise of Islamic fashion is also revolutionary in that it seeks to reconfigure colonial power dynamics between East and West in an era marked by heightened Islamophobia and widespread cultural panic about the appropriation of "difference" within the body politic. European and Scandinavian nations are increasingly grappling with Islamophobia, xenophobia, and the ascendance of right-wing nationalist political parties in response to growing immigrant and refugee populations. While France leans further toward Le Pen and relies on burqa and burkini bans to define the contours of what it means to be a "French" citizen, similar sentiment is gaining ground in Germany, Belgium,

and the Netherlands. Fearful of stigmatizing migrants as potential rapists, most European politicians have avoided the question of whether men arriving from more conservative societies might engage in violence against women once they move to societies where liberal dress codes prevail. But Norway recently instituted an educational curriculum that seeks to inculcate new immigrants in "Norwegian" values, especially gender equality and sexual norms (Higgins).

The geographic flow of "modest fashion" from East to West has prompted a flurry of debates over cultural and religious appropriation, neo-Orientalism, and Islamophobia. When *Vogue* launched *Vogue Arabia* from its Dubai office last year, Gigi Hadid appeared on the inaugural front cover sporting a jeweled hijab. Muslim and non-Muslim audiences alike have debated the meaning and effect of this image. Some Western viewers celebrate the photo in the name of "cultural diversity." For these viewers, Hadid's veiled portrait is "a powerful image which is at once glamorously high-fashion, whilst also nodding to the modest dress codes which many of the magazine's readers will abide by" (Holt). Conversely, many Muslim feminist commentators understand the cover as a gesture of neo-Orientalism or colonial feminism. Such critics understand the image to engage in cultural and religious appropriation of Islamic veiling practices—one that empties out or erases their underlying meaning and intent. Furthermore, "modest fashion" is presented to *Vogue Arabia* readers in the form of Gigi Hadid, a fashion model that neither identifies as Muslim nor adheres to modest codes of dress in personal or professional life. Surprisingly, these contradictions coalesce on the cover of a publication whose target audience is a woman who "celebrates her tradition," and whose editorial mission aims to "eradicate misconceptions around the Arab and Muslim diaspora" (Paton). As such conflicting interpretations reveal, "tensions around the right to bare skin (or not) and what freedom really looks like still simmer across the world" (Paton).

CONCLUSION

Despite their contrary aims, modest fashion and nude protest illuminate—in endlessly fascinating ways—a paradoxical transnational feminist body politic fractured by difference, yet actively contesting the meanings of female embodiment for times and spaces still to come. Both naked and modestly dressed bodies insert a pause for reflection that invites us to consider anew possibilities for genuinely inclusive revolutionary symbolic spaces, digital republics, public squares, and feminist futures. On the streets of Istanbul and Stockholm, the catwalks of London, and the internet, the meanings of "freedom," "resistance," and female embodiment are being powerfully and radically contested, negotiated, and redefined. This explosive mix of street theatre and ideological struggle plays out in moving, disturbing, and sometimes exhilarating ways, and opens up new horizons for imagining women's bodies relative to visual culture and feminist political strategies of "liberation."

REFERENCES

Abu-Lughod, Lila. "Do Muslim Women Really Need Saving?: Anthropological Reflections on Cultural Relativism and Its Others." *American Anthropologist* vol. 104, no. 3, September 2002, 783–390.

Ali, Amro, and Dina El-Sharnouby, "Youth and Citizenship in the Digital Era: Critique of an Emerging Phenomenon," *Jadaliyya*, July 6, 2012. www.jadaliyya.com/pages/index/6304/youth-and-citizenship-in-the-digital-era_critique.

Bartky, Sandra Lee. "Foucault, Femininity and the Modernization of Patriarchal Power." In *Writing on the Body: Female Embodiment and Feminist Theory*, ed. Katie Conboy, Nadia Medina, and Sarah Stanbury. New York: Columbia University Press, 1997, 129–154.

Berger, John. *Ways of Seeing*. New York: Penguin, 1972.

Bilefsky, Dan. "Ban on Head Scarves at Work is Legal, E.U. Court Rules." *New York Times*, March 14, 2017. www.nytimes.com/2017/03/14/world/europe/headscarves-ban-european-court.html.

"D&G's Islamic Fashion Collection Far from Revolutionary." *Daily Sabah* (March 2017). www.dailysabah.com/feature/2016/01/07/dgs-islamic-fashion-collection-far-from-revolutionary.

Eileraas, Karina. "Sex(t)ing Revolution, Femen-izing the Public Square: Aliaa Magda Elmahdy, Nude Protest, and Transnational Feminist Body Politics." *Signs* vol. 40, no. 1, Autumn 2014, 40–52.

Elmahdy, Aliaa Magda. *Statement, Femen protest*, Stockholm, July 1, 2013.

Fahmy, Mohamed. "Egyptian Blogger Aliaa Elmahdy: 'Why I Posed Naked.'" *CNN*, November 19, 2011. www.cnn.com/2011/11/19/world/meast/nude-blogger-aliaa-magda-elmahdy/.

Fernandez, Chantal. "How Should Designers Approach Creating Fashion for Muslim Women?." *Fashionista* (1 April 2016).

"French Fashion Mogul Pierre Berge Hits Out at 'Islamic' Clothing." *The Guardian* (March 30, 2016). www.theguardian.com/fashion/2016/mar/30/fashion-mogul-pierre-berge-hits-out-at-islamic-clothing.

Friedman, Vanessa. "What Freedom Looks Like." *New York Times*, April 13, 2016. www.nytimes.com/2016/04/14/fashion/islamic-fashion-france.html.

Fung, Richard. "Working Through Appropriation." *Fuse* V.XVI, no. 5+6, Summer 1993, 16–24.

Gokariksel, Banu, and Anna Secor. "The Veil, Desire, and the Gaze: Turning the Inside Out." *Geography Faculty Publications*, (Fall 2014), Paper 3.

Habib, Joy Majdalani. "Who's Afraid of Alia El-Mahdy?" *Middle Eastern Women's Rights Knowledge Base: Red Lips High Heels*, March 11, 2013. See http://www.redlipshighheels.com/whos-afraid-of-aliaa-el-mahdy/.

Hakim, Catherine. "Erotic Capital." *European Sociological Review* vol. 26, no. 5, 2010, 499–518.

Higgins, Andrew. "Norway Offers Migrants a Lesson in How to Treat Women." *New York Times*, December 19, 2015. www.nytimes.com/2015/12/20/world/europe/norway-offers-migrants-a-lesson-in-how-to-treat-women.html.

Holt, Bethan. "Is It Controversial That Gigi Hadid Wore a Veil on the Cover of *Vogue Arabia?*" *The Telegraph* (March 3, 2017).

Irigaray, Luce. *This Sex Which Is Not One*, trans. Catherine Porter. Ithaca: Cornell University Press, 1985.

Kilbourne, Jean. *"The More You Subtract, the More You Add": Cutting Girls Down to Size*. New York: Simon & Schuster, 1999.

Kraidy, Marwan M. "The Revolutionary Body Politic: Preliminary Thoughts on a Neglected Medium in the Arab Uprisings." *Middle East Journal of Culture and Communication* vol. 5, no. 1, 2012, 73.

Mernissi, Fatima. "Size 6: The Western Woman's Harem." In *Scheherazade Goes West: Different Cultures, Different Harems*. New York: Washington Square Press, 2001, 208–220.

Mezzofiore, Gianluca. "Aliaa Magda Elmahdy, the Egyptian Nude Blogger, Sued for 'Insulting Islam.'" *International Business Times*, November 18, 2011, www.ibtimes.co.uk/aliaa-magda-elmahdy-egyptian-nude-blogger-sued-252058.

Michael, Maggie. "Woman Activist Nude Blog Sparks Free Expression Uproar in Egypt." *Daily News Egypt*, November 17, 2011: http://www.dailynewsegypt.com/2011/11/17/activist-posts-herself-nude-sparks-outrage/.

Mikdashi, Maya. "Waiting for Alia." *Jadaliyya*, November 20, 2011. www.jadaliyya.com/pages/index/3208/waiting-for-alia.

Mourad, Sara. "The Naked Body of Alia: Gender, Citizenship, and the Egyptian Body Politic." *Journal of Communication Inquiry* vol. 38, no. 1, 2014, 62.

Paton, Elizabeth. "Asserting a Muslim Fashion Identity." *New York Times*, November 1, 2016.

Petrilla, Molly. "The Next Big Untapped Fashion Market: Muslim Women." *Fortune*, July 15, 2015. fortune.com/2015/07/15/muslim-women-fashion/.

Pew Research Center. "The Future of the Global Muslim Population." January 27, 2011.

Pham, Minh-ha T. "Fashion's Cultural Appropriation Debate: Pointless." *The Atlantic*, May 15, 2014. www.theatlantic.com/entertainment/archive/2014/05/cultural-appropriation-in-fashion-stop-talking-about-it/370826/.

Renan, Ernest. "What Is a Nation?" In Ernest Renan, *Qu'est-ce qu'une nation?* Paris: Presses-Pocket, 1992.

Rhode, Deborah. *The Beauty Bias: The Injustice of Appearance in Life and Law*. Oxford: Oxford University Press, 2010.

Rose, Gillian. *Feminism and Geography: The Limits of Geographical Knowledge*. London: Polity, 1993.

Rubin, Alissa. "French School Deems Teenager's Skirt an Illegal Display of Religion." *New York Times*, April 29, 2015. www.nytimes.com/2015/04/30/world/europe/french-school-teenagers-skirt-illegal-display-religion.html.

Rubin, Alissa. "From Bikinis to Burkinis, Regulating What Women Wear." *New York Times*, August 27, 2016. www.nytimes.com/2016/08/28/world/europe/france-burkini-bikini-ban.html.

Shoair, Mohammed. "Elmahdy: Egypt's Nude Rebel." *Al Akhbar*, November 15, 2011.

Toksabay, Ece, and Ibon Villelabeitia. "In Quiet Revolution, Turkey Eases Headscarf Ban." *Reuters*, October 17, 2010. www.reuters.com/article/us-turkey-headscarf/in-quiet-revolution-turkey-eases-headscarf-ban-idUSTRE69G0DX20101017.

Wilsher, Kim. "French Women's Rights Minister Accused of Racism Over Term 'Negro.'" *The Guardian*, March 30, 2016. www.theguardian.com/world/2016/mar/30/french-womens-rights-minister-laurence-rossignol-accused-racism-negro.

Wolf, Naomi. *The Beauty Myth: How Images of Beauty Are Used Against Women*. New York: Harper Collins, 1991.

CROSSING BORDERS
AND TRANSNATIONAL MOVEMENTS

Theorizing migration, diasporas, belongings, and borders through intersectional and transnational feminist and queer lenses has never been more urgent given today's political climate. Borders, walls, indigenous land encroachment, and the movement of people are weaponized to secure defined-yet-mythical homelands, to deport people who work under exploitive conditions, and to craft layers of violence that deny women, people of color, and LGBTQPAI+ communities human rights. Whether literally etched in the geopolitical landscape or figuratively cutting across sociocultural groups and individuals, borders establish relations of power by separating and dividing people based on nationality, gender, race, sexuality, abilities, socioeconomic status, and religion and spiritual practices.

This section of readings examines relations of power that link local experiences to global socioeconomic and political dynamics so that we begin to see how we are radically interconnected through our differences (Keating). With the public resurgence of white nationalism in the Global North and South—from the United States to Brazil to Turkey and beyond—alongside the deep divisions between people cultivated through heteropatriarchy, religious, neocolonial, and neoliberal social structures, this section asks us to re-examine the political grammar of the nation-state and nationality, citizenship and belonging, and easy dichotomies of "us" and "them" as central projects in feminist and queer theory. In Western societies, migration is embedded in Eurocentric ideologies that ask us to believe that people who have been marginalized systemically want to assimilate in search of freedom. Migration narratives are much more complicated, and some of the questions posed in this section are the following: What are the stories we tell about how people, ideas, and things (products tied to human capital) circulate? How do these narratives become solidified while so often leaving feminist and queer subjectivities, lived experiences, and their attending public discourses—what Inderpal Grewal names as "gendered knowledge formations"—about indigenous communities, people of color, and immigrants and refugees on the margins (Grewal 1)? How might national perspectives change if they are told from a migrant's point of view and we understand more about state violence and war, political economies, and sacrifices that people make to survive and support their families and communities? And what are some of the key social movements in the twenty-first century that seek to change the relations of power across national and cultural borders?

Feminist and queer theory asks us to think about the colonial histories that remapped land; continuously reproduce the porousness of borders; and where and how women, people of color, and/or LGBTQPAI+ communities live in-between a place that was left behind and a place of arrival. According to Avtar Brah in *Cartographies of Diaspora*, diasporic space is where movement happens and reveals what can be hidden by the certifying processes of migration and citizenship. Rather than looking to the rhetoric of nation-states in the Global North, what if we turn our attention to the continuous connection people have to one another, the economies that shape migration, and the violence that people may experience? Brah contends that diaspora connects exclusionary politics of belonging in the Global North to their colonial histories in the Global South. While her theorizing emerges from research within specific South Asian-British communities, contemporary feminist and queer scholars continue to draw on its insights to think through the roots of gendered discrimination and racism embedded in nationalistic approaches to immigration. It is important to note that diaspora space is not a celebration of a new "home" or an available "homeland" to migrants—indeed, borders are not free from racial, gender, and class injustices. Rather, mapping movement enables us to see how imperial relations of power are reinscribed along national borders.

This section also directs students to explore how and why feminist and queer scholar-activists organize transnational social movements as we seek new geographic and cultural reconfigurations that embrace free movement, collectivity, sharing, liberation, people over profit, and religious and spiritual freedom. In turning our attention toward movements for change, Eithne Luibhéid provides a framework for thinking through the spatiality and temporality of transformation: naming it as something that "cannot be understood within progressive, unilinear, and Eurocentric models" (Luibhéid 170). Asking us to think about "queer" as more than a theoretical naming of identitarian politics, she suggests that feminist and queer scholars "deploy the term queer to acknowledge that all identity categories are burdened by legacies that must be interrogated, do not map neatly across time and space, and become transformed through circulation within specific, unequally situated local, regional, national, and transnational circuits" (Luibhéid 170). This section explores how queer *and* feminist theory are necessary frameworks for understanding migration, mobility, and the politics of location and belonging globally. Theories help make sense of how we are all connected to one another through relations of power, and this knowledge can build sustainable solidarity in the name of change across borders.

CROSSING BORDERS

Whether in the name of indigenous sovereignty or Iraqi refugee rights and freedoms, feminist and queer theorists interrogate the nation as a social construct beyond that of certifying documents, legal citizenship, and shared identity by centering people systemically minoritized and tracing their everyday experiences through transnational exchanges in capital, policy, economies, and violence. Nira Yuval-Davis in "Gender and Nation" named the nation as a site that produces a dualistic system for women; accordingly, women exist both inside and outside its bounds, and the nation creates subjects who are asked to understand their futures as interdependent (an argument for both ethnic and religious inclusion and exclusion). As such, women are granted political rights (e.g., the right to vote if they are eligible citizens) though they "have still not been given full civil and social rights" (625). In her "Women, Citizenship and Difference," Yuval-Davis refines her argument to elucidate how citizenship is also deeply tied to a politics of belonging that must be seen through a prism of gender, race, ethnicity, and class. In the first reading included in this subsection, written in 2013, Heidi Safia Mirza ("'A Second Skin'") expands on Yuval-Davis's ideas and provides a framework for understanding belonging as a process of negotiation. By examining how Muslim women in Britain negotiate oppression as immigrants and within their own communities, Mirza names the centrality of "embodied intersectionality" and "explores how the intersection of race, gender and religion is written on and experienced within the body" (314) and how women's everyday existence—indeed "Muslim women's agency which, as the women's narratives reveal, continually challenges and transforms hegemonic discourses of race, gender and religion" (315). Neither victim nor granted power, Muslim women negotiate their immigrant status and play an active role in reshaping what it means to be Muslim and women in the UK.

Communities of women and LGBTQPAI+ people learn to negotiate crossing borders because of the ways that masculinity and political economies fortify and militarize them in the name of sovereignty (Enloe 2000, 2007). This directly impacts the everyday worlds of women, and in the next reading written specifically for this reader, "Permanent Transients," Isis Nusair examines how so with specificity and through ethnographic research with Iraqi women who have been classified by the Jordanian government as refuges. In troubling the term "refugees," she argues that women's stories challenge and have the potential to transform Orientalist ideology and nation-states themselves where refugees come to call "home." Here Orientalism refers to what Edward Said (and many following him) theorizes as the dangers of Western imagination constructing the Orient or the East in opposition to the Occident or the West. In naming Orientalism as a Western construction, his critical work demystifies how Asia, the Middle East, and North Africa "is . . . the place of Europe's greatest and richest and oldest colonies . . . and one of its deepest and most recurring images of the other" (1). Borrowing from this framework, Nusair contends that this understanding must be gendered and elucidates how representations of women as refugees matter and get played out on women's bodies. Her work provides an avenue to "talk back" to Western mediated narratives by centering Iraqi refugee women's narratives as theory. Crossing borders and hearing about Iraqi women's experiences is "not only about power but also about lived experiences and how power is reproduced and maintained" in refugee communities (332). Nusair provides theoretical and historical context for understanding this humanitarian crisis and how it directly affects women, and most importantly, values Iraqi women's refugee voices as theorists, as the subject with vision that can lead feminist research and activism.

White, male, able-bodied, and gender conforming citizens in the Global North have unprecedented access to the world without harassment at or within its the borders if they have the economic means and proper documents to secure passports and visas. Lisa Lowe argues in *Immigrant Acts* that these "juridical, legislated, territorially situated, and culturally embodied" markers of citizenship "powerfully shape who the citizenry is, where they dwell, what they remember, and what they forget" (Lowe 2). In the next new reading, M. Soledad Caballero navigates how this razor-sharp terrain exists in both Santiago, Chile, during days of the coup and in the imagination and memory of an "immigrant" in the United States in her poem "The Spell." Similar to Nusair's insistence that Iraqi women refugees become the theorists, Caballero's poetry is a form of theory-making. It explores the everyday experience of "diaspora living" through memory and mixes the images of home (sopaipillas, knitted blankets, clothes hanging to dry in the sunlight) with militarism (tanks and soldiers) and a now life led in English in the Midwest. "Diaspora living is heavy" because it "claimed . . . memories" and rewrites childhood years (336). The stories are not of belonging but exile and silences.

And while diaspora may be inscribed through whispered memories of the homeland, in Gayatri Gopinath's (2005) "Impossible Desires," she theorizes how "the queer racialized body becomes a historical archive for both individuals and communities" to understand the boundaries of nation and belonging (337). In drawing our attention to the absence of queer, female South Asian representations, she "use[s] the notion of "impossibility as a way of signaling the unthinkability of a queer female subject position within various mappings of nation and the diaspora." This moves her work beyond naming something that has been rendered invisible and silent to interrogating the "deep investments" in keeping her subject position "unimaginable," especially within cultural forms and practices such as film and literature (344).

In the next reading, published in 2003, Martin F. Manalansan wonders out loud in "Migrancy, Modernity, Mobility" why the experiences of immigrant gay men are absent from public discourses, national archives, and representations within mainstream popular culture. Drawing on his ethnographic research with Filipino gay men living in New York City between 1990 and 1995, he theorizes "the interscalar connections between the lived locality and the larger seemingly more expansive sites of the city, the nation, and the global" (352). While some critical queer theory may elucidate the global circuits themselves—as Gopinath does in her work—Manalansan anchors these large sociopolitical structures to the daily lives of migrant gay men. In doing so he argues that we can see intersectionality more clearly— that Filipino gay men experience the interlocking oppressions of race, gender, class, sexuality, and nationality—and this troubles "the conventional time-space binary" of diaspora and mobility "by expressing the ways in which memory is spatialized and space is entangled with intimate habits, routines, personal histories, and deviant chronologies" (353). In short, a linear, postcolonial narrative of crafting a clear "them" against a clear "us" vis-à-vis imperial discourse and political economies does not and cannot capture what it is like to become *and* live as a queer, racialized person in a specific place.

Digital feminist and queer activist spaces engage us politically and challenge us to think through how gender compliance is reinforced in crossing national and cultural borders. They serve as public outlets to ask that the state be obligated to issue certifying documents that reflect how citizens self-identify, thereby allowing trans, nonbinary, and genderqueer people easier passage and inclusion into the body politic. Aren Z. Aizura asks a different kind of question in his 2012 piece titled "Transnational Transgender Rights and Immigration Law": "What would happen if we thought about trans and gender-variant freedom outside and against the framework of the nation state?" (361). Said differently, to agree to the state's mandate to be visible in a particular way according to "the nation state's idea about what . . . [transgender and gender variance] means," Aizura argues two things: (1) that the community becomes a part of the law-rights machinery and (2) to exist outside of this and advocate for trans and gender variant people's unfettered mobility will require turning "'trans' in an anti-identitarian direction" (361). By beginning the piece with a story of Naz, "a trans woman from Iran who was featured in a number of documentaries about transsexuality in Iran" and migrated to Turkey and sought asylum in Canada and who ultimately committed suicide, "taking on the lessons of particular feminist and queer antiracist work on intersectionality, and also challenging some of the limits of intersectional analysis" (361) brings new urgency for thinking about the rigidity of citizenship and borders, what it means to belong in any given cultural space, as well as the borders between transgender, queer, and feminist studies.

In the next reading, "La Conciencia de la Mestiza: Towards a New Consciousness" (1987), Gloria Anzaldúa lays bare the danger of borders for those who are not white or Mexican, do not identify as heterosexual, and rebel against the patriarchy. The writing itself exists in the linguistic borderlands of Spanish, indigenous languages, and English to make clear that a new consciousness that loves and accepts herself and that must learn to live in-between cultural spaces—in the borderlands (both on the contemporary border between Texas and Mexico as well as straddling the pre- and post-conquest of indio-mestizo land)—and to embrace ambiguity. Anzaldúa situates Chicana lesbian individuals and their spiritual-psychological well-being within harsh and unwelcoming familial, social, and national dynamics. What continues to resonate for students since the publication of *Borderlands/La Frontera* (the source of her reading in this book) is the way in which she recognizes that it is not enough to respond to racism, sexism, classism, and xenophobia by "stand[ing] on the opposite river bank, shouting questions, challenging patriarchal, white conventions" (375). Ultimately, hers is a call to see those who have been systemically minoritized, including within their own communities, to see themselves anew. "I seek our woman's face, our true features, the positive and the negative seen clearly, free of the tainted biases of male dominance. I seek new images of identity, new beliefs about ourselves, our humanity and worth no longer in question" (380). And importantly, that *la mestiza* will lead the way toward this liberation through decolonization of mind, body, and spirit.

TRANSNATIONAL JUSTICE MOVEMENTS

Social movements are born out of necessity and the cohesion of several moments where people become, as civil rights activist and politician Fannie Lou Hamer declared, "sick and tired of being sick and tired." Understanding theories of migration, mobility, and cultural belonging are important because knowledge forms the foundations for enacting social change to begin to address and heal the deep divisions along the lines of gender, race, class, sexuality, able-bodiedness, religion, and nationality that have been built and nurtured by the state and individuals who benefit from our separation and pain. In *The Promise of Happiness* and her blog, Sara Ahmed embarks on a project of feminist world-making by naming feminist theorists-activists-educators-students—across our differences—as feminist killjoys. She theorizes killjoys as willful subjects with agency, productive anger, and the ability to see that being happy within a system of violence may not be happiness and that change-making requires scholar-activists to speak and act polyphonically. In short, she gives feminist and queer identifying people permission to raise our voices, critique, work for change together, and that in doing so, we do not have to comply with social norms of being happy. There's a lot to be angry about and feminist killjoys are needed. And when we revisit the Combahee River Collective alongside Audre Lorde's *Sister Outsider*, and Bernice Johnson Reagon's inscription of coalitional politics, it becomes clear that collective actions—movements that recognize interlocking oppressions across national and cultural borders—are and have been feminist and queer avenues toward sociopolitical change. In this subsection, scholar-activists look closely at the ways in which intersectional and transnational movements have taken shape in our contemporary world with over half the readings written for this collection and within present, twenty-first century frameworks.

This subsection begins with Christina Holmes's new piece "Feminist Approaches to Environmentalism" to reignite discussions about how space and place are intimately woven into gendered racial justice work. She traces the genealogies of feminist interventions in sustaining the environment and begins by provocatively asking, "Who does 'ecofeminism' belong to and why should we care?" (383). By way of conclusion, she notes that feminists cannot afford to stand on the sidelines while discussions of climate change, clean air/water regulations, and erosions of our national parks and indigenous territories deeply affect women and queer people of color. As we look at the ongoing man-made disasters in Flint, Michigan, and Puerto Rico, our national analyses must be infused with what Holmes theorizes as eco-womanism and borderlands environmentalism so that we can see the roots of who is being affected by policies that embolden heteropatriarchy, racism, and capitalism.

But what if organizations such as the Human Rights Campaign begin with the assumption that their approach to LGBTQPAI+ protections and rights is *the* approach to transnational queer activism? In the next reading written by Karma Chávez in 2017, "Queer Migration Politics as Transnational Activism," she rhetorically asks this question before thinking through how a more radical, transnational approach is needed. While a wide-ranging array of monographs exist that critique mainstream international gay and lesbian activism because of its neocolonial, anti-black, and neoliberal foundations (see Johnson and Henderson), Chávez theorizes how "transnational queer activism from and in the global South and North works closely with communities on the ground and challenges logics and systems that often shape mainstream engagement with, and promotion of, transnational queer or LGBTI activism" (390). The key, it seems, to a queer migration politics is to learn the local histories of LGBTQPAI+ activism with specific communities—whether it is Kenya or in Kentucky—and work directly and in coalition with people experiencing discrimination and systemic violence. What becomes clear is that queer, global movement building does not hinge on identitarian politics but if activists are on the ground, in local communities—indeed at home—and willing to be self-reflexive and put in the time to build trust and lasting relationships, queer movements could be sustainable across national and cultural borders.

As Elora Halim Chowdhury notes in the next reading published in 2009, "'Transnationalism Reversed,'" much of the postcolonial and transnational feminist/queer theory that is produced within Global North contexts is for academic audiences who are actively building an archive of critique—who are engaging in "vigorous debates over location, privilege and colonial baggage" (400). And while epistemological interventions into Orientalist, Islamophobic, and anti-blackness construction of the "Other" are important, Chowdhury also argues these concerns may be "derailing the practical and exigent issues on the ground . . . furthering women's oppression" (400). She begins her work by naming herself as an academic in the Global North and someone who is deeply interested in what happens *within* feminist movements themselves. The work that needs to be done is less about naming "third world" or women in the Global South as oppressed but supporting and shining a light on what, for example, Bangladeshi women must overcome (vis-à-vis local and regional politics and religious expectations and restrictions) in order to enter employment, be free from domestic violence, and experience bodily integrity. Chowdhury's work may in fact point us to the future directions of intersectional and transnational feminist and queer theory whereby women making changes in their communities in India, Vietnam, South Africa, Iraq, Jamaica, and so on are the theorists because engaging with their practices provides pathways for sustainable social change.

When feminist and queer transnationalism is reversed and repressive regimes create hostile living conditions, key concepts in Western theory-making such as representation and visibility may not be the clearest or safest pathways to movement building. Context matters, and in S. M. Rodriguez's new piece ("Invisibility Matters") that draws on their ethnographic work in Uganda, they argue that "'coming out of the closet' relies on the assumption that visibility is a one-way street" toward progress. Moreover, a "full understanding of queer visibility includes the when's, how's, and why's of staying hidden especially after the initial rupture of public existence" (415). This makes all the more sense when Anti-Homosexuality Acts impose punishments for existing as lesbian, gay, bisexual, trans, and queer. And while those in the Global North may offer asylum and refugee status to LGBTQPAI+ individuals in Uganda and elsewhere, Rodriquez theorizes that "these campaigns have both fueled the cultural imperialism claims and frustrated the efforts of many kuchu activists" (417). Such actions assume that the "West knows best" how to "save" people when in fact these actions disrupt Ugandan activists from doing their work in ways that keep people invisible and undetected yet connected to one another within resilient communities in their homespaces.

Movement building stretches beyond enacting ideas and practices of social justice. In the next new article written specifically for this anthology, Brandy Nālani McDougall theorizes in "Sovereign Bodies, Sovereign Chic" that fashion and beauty within indigenous women's activism is meaningful and powerful. While Western feminism has eschewed beauty as a heteropatriarchal construction that objectifies and disempowers women, McDougall argues that "the layered-ness of Indigenous women's activist fashion is complex and should be seen as both a phenomena of cultural strength and continuity as well as a response to a forced discontinuity and part of the violence of colonial biological and cultural genocide campaigns" (421).

This theoretical twist suggests that scholar-activists consider how beauty and fashion are defined as powerful within indigenous feminist communities, and thus invites us to redefine how we engage in aesthetics. A fashion movement "encourages participation through social media activism, with people creating, posting, and sharing . . . memes" and images of politicized clothing, jewelry, and tattoos (421) and may be interpreted as indigenous women not only having "sovereignty over their bodies" but also "reclaiming Indigenous women's power in the face of institutions that have encouraged and excused gender and environmental violence" (421). The power of visual and digital culture is its potential to empower communities of women when they may otherwise be silenced by dominant culture and both become tools in movement building.

Section 3 closes with a conversation between feminist and queer scholars located in Canada, Lebanon, and Hawai'i who offer their questions and reflections of the Women's March(es) in 2017 following the 45th U.S. presidential election. What it reveals through very clear language and experiences is a snapshot at how movements are simultaneously local and global. The need for women's marches to protest racism and sexism may have seemed and felt universal for those who participated within the United States. Yet, when women mobilized in their corners of the world, the inflections of harassment and sexual misconduct alongside questions about whose voices and experiences were included/excluded and where/how the march was organized mattered. Of particular importance in naming the challenges inherent in organizing masses of people to protest, the authors (Jennifer Nish, Kimberly A. Williams, and L. Ayu Saraswati, "Marching and Crossing Borders") note of how noninclusive organizing practices and mediated narratives circulated to undermine and divide the efforts by feminist and LGBTQPAI+ communities. Ultimately, the fact that people showed up marks the need for the women's marches.

While the arc of justice is indeed long, it bends as we create collectivities that work in coalition toward more open borders and equitable futures that value intersectional and transnational approaches to social change. In this section, students will learn that feminist and queer inquiry is interested in theorizing—or telling the stories—of mobility, movement, and connection with one another. Through critique and understanding how national narratives delimit people's experiences based on gender, race, class, sexuality, nationality, religion, and ability alongside how movements reorient normative frameworks of nationalism, citizenship, and belonging, the story is a hopeful one that change is possible and taking shape in the midst of sociopolitical urgencies.

REFERENCES

Ahmed, Sara. *The Promise of Happiness*. Duke University Press, 2010.

Brah, Avtar. *Cartographies of Diaspora: Contesting Identities*. Routledge, 1996.

The Combahee River Collective. *The Combahee River Collective Statement: Black Feminist Organizing in the Seventies and Eighties*. Kitchen Table: Women of Color Press, 1986.

Enloe, Cynthia. *Globalization and Militarism: Feminists Make the Link*. Rowman & Littlefield Publishers, 2007.

Enloe, Cynthia. *Maneuvers: The International Politics of Militarizing Women's Lives*. University of California Press, 2000.

Grewal, Inderpal. *Transnational America: Feminisms, Diasporas, Neoliberalisms*. Duke University Press, 2005.

Johnson, E. Patrick, and Mae G. Henderson, eds. *Black Queer Studies: A Critical Anthology*. Duke University Press, 2005.

Keating, AnaLouise. *Transformation Now!: Toward a Post-Oppositional Politics of Change*. University of Illinois Press, 2013.

Lorde, Audre. *Sister Outsider: Essays and Speeches*. Reprint. Crossing Press, 2007.

Lowe, Lisa. *Immigrant Acts: On Asian American Cultural Politics*. Duke University Press, 1996.

Luibhéid, Eithne. *Queer Migrations: Sexuality, Citizenship and Border Crossings*. University of Minnesota Press, 2005.

Reagon, Bernice Johnson. "Coalition Politics: Turning the Century." *Home Girls: A Black Feminist Anthology,* edited by Barbara Smith. Kitchen Table: Women of Color Press, 1983.

Said, Edward. *Orientalism*. Routledge, 1978.

Yuval-Davis. Nira. "Gender and Nation." *Ethnic and Racial Studies* 16:4 (1993): 621–632.

Yuval-Davis, Nira. "Women, Citizenship and Difference." *Feminist Review* 57 (Autumn 1997): 4–27.

HEIDI SAFIA MIRZA

34. "A SECOND SKIN": EMBODIED INTERSECTIONALITY, TRANSNATIONALISM, AND NARRATIVES OF IDENTITY AND BELONGING AMONG MUSLIM WOMEN IN BRITAIN

INTRODUCTION: MUSLIM WOMEN, MIGRATION AND ISLAMOPHOBIA

In this article I explore how the intersection of race, gender and religion is written on and experienced within the body. Drawing on the black feminist framework of "embodied intersectionality" the paper examines the narratives of three professional transnational Muslim women of Turkish, Pakistani and Indian heritage living and working in Britain. As an Indo-Caribbean woman of Muslim heritage also living and working in Britain, I am particularly interested in how the internal subjective world of transnational professional Muslim women is produced by and performed through the external affective Islamophobic discourses that circulate in the West. I explore how Muslim women who are externally seen as embodying a "dangerous" or "oppressed" religious gendered identity subjectively "live out" what it means to be a "Muslim woman" when working and living in a transnational context. I draw on three professional Muslim women's narratives of "self" and survival to reveal multiple layers of power, both seen and unseen in the making of the female Muslim "self." In particular I focus on her religious, racial and ethnic identity as manifested through her subjective expressions of faith, home and belonging. The women, who were of Pakistani, Indian and Turkish heritage, are part of the transnational educated mobile classes whose families

have moved from South Asia and the Middle East to study and work in Europe—and as in these women's cases, in transglobal industries such as universities and international NGOs.

Stuart Hall talks of the importance of analysing the economic, political and cultural modalities of historically specific forms and sites when attempting to understand post war global migrancy. He argues that the transformations, displacements and condensations of a particular historic moment define new emergent "diasporic" spaces (Hall, 2012). The journeys of the Muslim women to Britain come at a time of growing national concern over the Muslim presence in the "West" in general, and in Britain in particular. There are now 3 generations of British born Muslim-British who make up 4.2% of the British population (BRIN, 2010). With a population growth rate among Muslims purported to be ten times faster than the rest of the British society, there has been a hysterical reaction in the press about Muslims over-running Britain signalled by the most popular name of newborns in Britain being "Mohammed" (Doyle, 2010).

This raises the question, "how does anti-Islamic hostility play out on the Muslim female body in post colonial Britain?" Since the 2001 bombing of the Twin Towers on 9/11 in New York and more recently the 2005 7/7 bombings by young British Muslim men in London there has been an overwhelming

Heidi Mirza, "'A Second Skin': Embodied Intersectionality, Transnationalism, and Narratives of Identity and Belonging among Muslim Women in Britain," *Women's Studies International Forum* 36 (2013): 5–15. Reprinted with permission of Elsevier; permission conveyed through Copyright Clearance Center, Inc.

preoccupation with the embodied Muslim women in British public spaces (Meetoo & Mirza, 2007). In particular the Muslim woman wearing the veil has preoccupied the media and they face openly hostile reactions in a climate of State sanctioned gendered Islamophobic discrimination. The scholarly interventions of transnational postcolonial critical race feminists show how the Muslim female body has become a battlefield in the symbolic war against Islam and the perceived Muslim enemy "within" (Jiwani, 2006; Razack, 2008; Razack, Smith, & Thobani, 2010). Sara Ahmed (2003: 377) argues that discourses of fear and anxiety which have circulated since September 11th work by securing what is the "truth" about "the other." She states, "Fear operates as an affective economy of truth. Fear slides between signs and sticks to some bodies and not others. For example the judgement that someone 'could be' a terrorist draws on past and affective associations that stick various signs (such as Muslim, fundamentalist, terrorist) together. At the same time, fear is reproduced precisely by the threat that such bodies 'may pass (us) by.' Such bodies become constructed as fearsome and as a threat to the very truths that are reified as "life itself."

In this article I ask what the consequences are for transnational professional Muslim women who are caught up in the Islamophobic space occupied by the postcolonial Muslim diaspora in Britain. Muslim women who migrate to the "West" are at the confluence of many competing claims and counter claims in the ensuing discourse of terror and securitization produced by the global threat from Islamic extremism. In the West's ideological "war against terror" the "Muslim woman" has come to symbolise the "barbaric Muslim other" in our midst. This is articulated through Muslim women being pathologised as voiceless victims of their "backward" communities who are in need of "saving" by the enlightened "West" (Abu-Lughod, 2002; Zahedi, 2011). The visibility of patriarchal community and group cultural practices such as forced marriage and honour crimes conveniently contribute to the Western "Orientalist" construction of the racialised "other's" barbaric customs and cultures (Said, 1985). Muslim women's dress has become interchangeable with essentialist notions of ethnicity, traditionalism and religion. In these constructions the veil is given a symbolic meaning far greater than its religious and social status. The

Muslim women's private reasons for wearing the headscarf (hijab) or niqab (full face veil) have become public property, a "weapon" used by many different competing interests, from male politicians in France to white feminists in Belgium to argue their cases for and against assimilation, multiculturalism, secularism and human rights (Coene & Longman, 2008; Killian, 2003; Scott, 2007). However as the Islamic feminist Haleh Afshar (2008) poignantly points out, a woman's right to wear the veil should be a matter of choice whether it be a personal, religious, or political one.

As this study reveals the three transnational professional Muslim women were bound, not by territory or nationality, but by embodied practices of contingent and reconfigured "Muslimness" such as the wearing or not of the hijab, going to the Mosque, eating halal food, and other acts of gendered resistance and accommodation. The notion of "embodied intersectionality" which I now turn to enables an understanding of how power comes to be written through and within the raced and sexed body. Moreover it provides a theoretical framework illuminating Muslim women's agency which, as the women's narratives reveal, continually challenges and transforms hegemonic discourses of race, gender and religion.

"EMBODIED INTERSECTIONALITY": A CONCEPTUAL FRAMEWORK FOR UNPACKING RACE, GENDER AND RELIGION

It could be argued that transnational Muslim women coming to Britain from particular postcolonial histories, ethnicities, cultures, and nation-states, are each positioned within the dominant and intersecting modalities of race, class and gender in very different ways. Thus in order to investigate how the intersectional dynamics of race, gender and religion shape their ethnic identity and sense of self it is important to develop a conceptual framework for analysis which looks at the situated ways racialised and gendered boundaries are produced and experientially "lived through" a faith based Muslim female subjectivity. As an analytic framework intersectionality provides a complex ontology of "really useful knowledge" which has been used to systemically reveal the everyday lives of black and postcolonial ethnicised women who are simultaneously positioned in multiple structures of dominance and power as gendered, raced, classed, colonized, and sexualized others (Mirza, 2009a). Intersectionality, a term developed by Kimberlé Crenshaw (1989, 1991) rearticulated the scholarship of black feminists such as the Combahee River Collective, Angela Davis, Audre Lorde and Patricia Hill Collins who were concerned with understanding the matrix of domination in which cultural patterns of oppression are not only interrelated, but are bound together and influenced by the intersectional systems of society (Collins, 1990: 222). It offered a way into understanding how particular identities (i.e. black and female) are tied to particular inequalities (i.e. violence against women) in different historical times and geographic places (McKittirick, 2006). Moreover intersectionality enables us to see that different dimensions of social life cannot be separated out into discrete and pure strands. As Brah and Phoenix write, "We regard the concept of intersectionality as signifying the complex, irreducible, varied, and variable effects which ensue when multiple axis of differentiation—economic, political, cultural, psychic, subjective and experiential—intersect in historically specific contexts" (Brah & Phoenix, 2004: 76). In this sense intersectionality draws our attention to the ways in which identities, as subject positions, are not reducible to just one or two or three or even more dimensions layered onto each other in an additive or hierarchical way. Rather intersectionality refers to the converging and conterminous ways in which the differentiated and variable organizing logics of race, class and gender and other social divisions such as sexuality, age, disability, ethnicity, culture, religion and belief structure the material conditions which produce economic, social and political inequality in women's real lived lives.

It is argued, not without controversy, that intersectionality—as a black feminist standpoint epistemology—is contextual and contingent privileging the situated knowledge of marginalised social agents as they are interpellated into hegemonic social, economic and political discourses (Anthias, 2011; McCall, 2005; Nash, 2008; Puar, 2007; Yuval-Davis, 2006). However to focus on women's "lived lives" is not to privilege the unstable notion of experience (Applebaum, 2008) or sublimate the indeterminacy of the body (Puar, 2007) when constructing a theoretical and methodological framework. It is precisely because intersectionality

is able to knit together the macro-economic political social discourses which structure inequities with a complex array of individuated subjectivities which by imposition, choice or desire are written on and lived within the body, that makes its ontological instability a powerful tool for analysis. The notion of embodied intersectionality as a postcolonial black feminist critical theory of gendered racialisation uses the malleability of the concept of intersectionality and takes it a stage further. By providing a way to methodologically operationalise intersectionality we are able to map the effect of gendered and raced Islamophobic discourses as lived in and through Muslim women's embodied subjectivities.

Embodied intersectionality not only seeks to theorise the complexities of race, gender, class, and other "positional" social divisions as lived realities (i.e. how the women experience the world holistically as a "Muslim, middleclass, heterosexual woman") but also interrogates how this experience is affectively mediated by the body and lived through Muslim female subjectivity (Mirza, 2009b). That is, it looks at how the external materiality of their situatedness (the political, economic and social structures that produce inequality) is constituted, reconfigured and lived through their corporeal representation (i.e. as racialised "dangerous" or "oppressed" others). It seeks to demonstrate how intersectional "othering" which arises at unique historical moments (i.e. when the category "Muslim woman" is invested with a particular affective and linguistic meaning), is organized into systematic social relations and practices. At the intersection of the material external world and the embodied interior world the identity of the Muslim female marginal subject comes into being (Alexander & Knowles, 2005). As Butler (1993) argues it is through the repetition of norms on the surface of bodies that the boundaries and fixity of social worlds materialise.

The embodiment of power and disempowerment written through and within the sexed, raced and classed body is particularly important if we are to understand how religious identity is performed, experienced and articulated through the women's sense of self in the context of the all consuming hegemonic racist and sexist discourses such as Western Islamophobia and patriarchal Islamic dominance. Thus for the Muslim women in this study, their dress, religious disposition (piety), cultural attachments—such as food, ethnic pride, speech and style, show not only their ethnic identity (as performed) but how such embodied practices need to be understood as meaningful signs and expressions of a reflexive female Muslim agency. The Muslim female voices in the autobiographically articulated narrative interviews reveal the ways in which regulatory discursive power and privilege are "performed" or exercised in the everyday material world of the socially constructed "Muslim woman" in the "West." By drawing on personalised embodied accounts of the Muslim women in the study we can reveal the processes of "being and becoming" a gendered, raced and classed subject of discourse. The notion of "embodied intersectionality" thus enables us to see how, through the articulation of their identities, Muslim women continually resist and rename the regulatory effects of hegemonic gendered, raced and classed discourses of inequity and subjugation in their daily lives. Such resistance is played out in the subjecthood of racialised Muslim women, whose agency ultimately challenges and transcends such dominance.

METHODOLOGY: MAPPING THE INTERSECTIONAL NARRATIVES OF MUSLIM WOMEN

The aim of this paper is to explore the embodied intersection of race, gender and religion and how the internal subjective world of transnational professional Muslim women is performed by and produced through the external affective Islamophobic discourses that circulate in the West. The interviews with the three Muslim professional women whose narratives inform this analysis were undertaken in 2009 as part of the larger study for the cognitive testing for the ethnicity boost of the UK Longitudinal Household Survey, *Understanding Society*[1] (Nandi & Platt, 2009). For this larger study in-depth semi structured interviews were conducted with 13 respondents to help inform the design of the main survey questions for the ethnicity strand of the survey. The 13 interviewees were both male and female, from various ethnic heritages, such as African Caribbean, Middle-Eastern, South Asian, and European and included the three Muslim women discussed here. The interviewees were in their 30s,

educated to at least Master's level and were in professional occupations or studying for a higher degree.

The interviews were carried out by a team of four ethnically diverse female interviewers including myself.[2] They were conducted in English and adhered to the University of Essex ethical codes of consent and confidentiality. The respondents were selected through the researchers' networks and work place contacts in several universities located in cities in the south east of England. In a 60–90 minute face-to-face interview with a researcher, each interviewee was asked the same structured questions about their ethnic identity across several different dimensions traditionally associated with ethnic affiliation. This included country of birth, parental country of birth, region of upbringing, language, religion and skin colour (Phinney, 1992). However to probe the salience of these domains we also asked semi-structured questions interrogating deeper expressions of ethnicity focusing on "group belonging" and "sense of self." This included questions such as pride in one's heritage, importance of ancestors, future wishes for their children, importance of food and language, as well as core values and principles with regard to faith and belief. The interviews were recorded and the transcripts were circulated among the team members for interpretation and reflection. They were then thematically cross-coded interrogating the texts for detailed subjective expressions of "group belonging" and "sense of self." The analysis of each interview was undertaken by 2 different researchers to ensure consistency and validity in mapping the various cross-cutting dimensions of ethnic identity.

The narratives of the three Muslim women of Turkish, Pakistani and Indian heritage were selected for this study as they raised interesting issues about the complexity of race, gender, religion and transnational identity pertinent to a black feminist analysis of embodied intersectionality. The in-depth interviews interrogating "group belonging" and "sense of self" brought to the fore issues of religious identity, subjectivity and the body for Muslim women. As a transnational postcolonial woman of colour I recognised the auto-biographical stories they told of border-crossing, journeys of the "self" and their relationship to the wider Muslim female diaspora. I felt compelled to look deeper and unravel the "identity affects" emerging within the women's narratives. The women's narratives emerged from the interviews rather than the interviews consciously being set up as narrative interviews. Ludhra and Chappell (2011: 107) tell a similar story about reflexively reviewing their methodology when they found that the dialogic space of the traditional interview provided an emancipatory opportunity for South Asian girls to share their "inner thoughts and consider their lives in a way never asked before." While a narrative focus may capture marginalised voices, the reading of a narrative is not about finding the "truth" about their condition, but about creating a text which provides an insight into the discourses through which the subject makes sense of "self" and their experience (Cole, 2009).

THE WOMEN: SHARING NARRATIVES OF TRANSNATIONALISM AND BELONGING

In this introduction to the women in the study, their names are anonymised, as are the places of work and any other identifiable details, such as local place names. All three women were highly educated professionals with strong cross-national affiliations and had either dual citizenship or permission to work in the UK. Yet they all expressed a strong sense of being rooted in their ethnic cultures and religious identity through attachments to place, which was expressed through language, dialect, food, memories and family.

Mehrunissa is in her 30s and a lawyer from Bombay in India. She came to Britain in 2006, and works in a charitable organisation within a university in a major city in the south east of England. She is applying for British citizenship and lives with her husband who is also from India. She describes herself as ". . . a foreign lawyer from India." But she loves living in the city because it is like Bombay ". . . loads of people, fast. . . . I love buildings, tall buildings, sky scrapers and people all around, I like the crowd and noise around." She sees herself as a "Bombayite" which she says is ". . . Like you're from Essex but you're in the UK." For her, place and nation are very important to her sense of self which is simultaneously articulated, as she explains,

". . . Bombay it's very important because I was born and brought up and if I go somewhere then people would know—Oh you're from Bombay—not from India . . . that's very important, your language, your

dialect . . . but in my mind I will always be Indian. There's a saying that you can take away Indians from India but you can't take away Indianness from an Indian!"

Fatima is a lecturer in a university in a major city in the south east of England. She is a Dutch citizen with the right to work in [the] UK. She is in her mid 30s and sees herself as "very international" a "new European." She is the daughter of a migrant worker who came to live in the Netherlands thirty years ago, but never returned to Turkey. She was born in Turkey in a rural mountain region, but from 7 she grew up in a town in the north east of the Netherlands. She went to school and attended a university in Istanbul from age 13. She came back to Finish her degree and then worked In the Netherlands. Her husband is also Turkish, but moved to be with her in the Netherlands. He stays in the Netherlands because as a third country national he has many problems travelling to and from UK and entering the Netherlands— so reluctantly they are separated.

She explains she feels most at home in the small town in the Netherlands where she grew up and where friends and family still live—"it is a very important city for me. We bought our house there where I was growing up and it was—that neighbourhood was between two rails, one train rail going to (my home town) and the other going to Utrecht so if you come from the airport entering the city you will see our house. So when I enter (this town) and see my ex-house I see myself walking there and going to school, playing, having arguments with my parents—was very interesting. It gives you a nice feeling and sad feeling because you see that life is going on—this is a sad feeling, it could be nice—it depends which mood you are. Many of my memories are there, but I shouldn't forget to mention that the city or the village or the mountain (in Turkey) where I was born is also very important for me."

Amina is in her mid 30s, and a researcher at a rights based NGO in a large metropolis in south east England. She is single and has dual citizenship—Canadian and British. Though born in Britain she left [the] UK at age 4 because her parents found it "too racist." Now her home is in Toronto, Canada where her family lives. She is emphatic that she is not British ("they speak funny over there and have a queen!"). However she describes herself to others as a Canadian, or British Canadian if she is in other places like Nigeria. Being born in the UK Is Important to her sense of self only when in Canada. Amina has a strong sense of a South Asian identity which comes from her parents. Her mother is Indian but lived in Bangladesh and her father is from Pakistan. She has no real close experiences of those places except through her parents and grandparents. She rationalises herself as being more generally "South Asian" as she says her history is "kind of made up" because of partition. Thus being South Asian is for her, ". . . more about a cultural thing than a place thing." She explains,

> "I'd probably have more in common with a white Canadian than I would with a South Asian Indian. I mean I think you know, basically, I'm Canadian, I'm not Indian. That's how I think, how I value it, how I kind of move round in the world. We used to joke that about if you show up in India, like within about three seconds they'll figure out you're not from there just by the way you stand, the way you put the same clothes on that they're wearing, they can just spot it— it's the same kind of thing."

Turning to the analysis of the Muslim women's narratives in the following section, three emerging themes frame the discussion. First is our consideration of the women's embodied reality as raced and gendered Muslim women in Britain and their emergent racialised consciousness post 9/11. Second is the theme of embodied modesty articulated through the women's religious agency and the gendered discourse of the hijab. Third is their "nomadic disposition" as a transnational subject which is embodied and articulated through [their] . . . sense of belongingness to diasporic and other Muslim communities.

POSTCOLONIAL DISJUNCTIONS: RACISM AS A "KIND OF GAUZE"

Bodies that are visually recognised as religiously raced and gendered clearly carry unequal value depending on their position in space and place (Skeggs, 1997). The embodied experience of being a transnational woman "out of place" is articulated by the postcolonial feminist writer Lata Mani. She writes, "The disjunctions between how I saw myself and the kind of

knowledge about me that I kept bumping into in the West opened up new questions for social and political inquiry" (Mani, 1989: 11). The women in the study were conscious of the "disjunction" between how they saw themselves as Muslim women and how they were racially constructed as a "female Muslim other" in Britain. As Mehrunissa explains:

> "A white person may call us black but I would never call myself . . . you can see your skin and visible characteristics, for instance the dressing, the physical appearance. That would not be of so much importance to you as it would be for others—like, for me, ok I'm Indian but the person sitting opposite me—what impact will it have after he looks at me. . . . So when I go for an interview they will look at me as a nation. I will be going for an interview but they will say— 'This girl is a nation'—so that character, physical appearance, my skin will affect others. Discrimination always comes from the other" (Mehrunissa).

Mehrunissa talks about being seen as a "girl who is a nation." As a "raced" transnational Indian migrant she is knowingly no longer just an "I"—an individual, Mehrunissa—but a homogenous, collective "Us"— that is a representation of a "brown" alien invader nation. She describes the way in which her "character, physical appearance, my skin will affect others." The Muslim female body, like the black body in the Frantz Fanon classic analysis of raclalisation is "sealed in to the crushing object hood of the skin." As Fanon writes,

> Not only must the black man be black, he must be black in relation to the white man. The Black man does not know at what moment his inferiority comes into being through the other. In the white world the man of colour encounters difficulties in the development of his bodily schema—a slow composition of me as a body in the middle of a spatial and temporal world—such seems to be the schema. It does not impose itself on me; it is rather a definitive structuring of the self and the world—definitive because it creates a real dialectic between my body and the world (Fanon, 1986: 11).

Mehrunissa examines her relationship with her body when understanding the world as an embodied "other." As an Indian middle class Muslim woman, her identifiable dress and national markers (colour and accent) become an extension of her skin. Her embodied intersectional identity is both chosen (in the context of her habitus as a Muslim female Indian) and imposed (she is known and racialised as a Muslim female Indian). Her multi-layered habitus is thus "given and given off" through her skin colour, speech, dress, and body disposition. Bourdieu suggests that one's habitus—that is ways of standing, speaking walking, feeling, and thinking—shows how the body is in the social world but also how the social world is in the body (Bourdieu, 1990). Habitus, as a personalised embodied experience is not only classed but also deeply racialised. Simmonds, the black feminist writer explains,

> "As a black woman, I know myself inside and outside myself. My relation to this knowledge is conditioned by the social reality of my habitus. But my socialised subjectivity is that of a black woman and it is at odds with the social world of which I am a product, for this social world is a white world . . . in this white world I am a fresh water fish that swims in sea water. I feel the weight of the water on my body" (Simmonds, 1997: 226–7).

Like Mehrunissa, Amina was also conscious of her body being encountered as a racialised object. Amina also talks of the weight of the heavy "gauze" of racism which she has to "work through" in Britain but feels the lightness of "nothing" in her home town of Toronto where she feels accepted.

> . . . I feel more "raced" here than I felt in Canada . . . Yeah, and it's like a kind of gauze you're trying to work through when you meet people—it's just heavy—it's just not there in Toronto I can just walk around, it's just nothing. And here there are different layers of it too. I've been told that I need to, like specifically say certain things in an interview because my accent is going to put them off. So if I'm speaking on race and gender I need to make a point of the fact that I'm "of colour" so that on radio they'll know otherwise they're going to think I'm American and they'll think I'm white and therefore not an authority on my topic (Amina).

In her narrative Amina describes being seen and not seen through "different layers" in different places. In Britain she has to actively make adjustments to accommodate others. This work Amina must do to legitimate her authority over her topic (minority women's rights). She is asked to prove her "authentic" credentials to speak on behalf of her own when she can't be visibly seen on the radio. Sara Ahmed talks eloquently on the way black subjects are expected to "happily" perform essentialised otherness in white organisations so those places can claim to be diverse through embodying the "diversity" of others. She writes, "What does diversity mean for those of us who look different, and who come, in the very terms of our appearance, to embody diversity? . . . through diversity, the organisation is represented "happily" as "getting along," as committed to equality, as anti-racist. . . . But you must smile—you must express gratitude for having been received. If your arrival is a sign of diversity, then you are a success story" (Ahmed, 2009: 46).

Like Amina, Fatima was also a "success story." "Success," as Bradford and Hey (2007: 600) explain, is a neoliberal discourse of our time in which a person's psychological capital, "is constituted in practices of self-esteem, confidence and self-belief . . . producing desires and emotions including rage, shame, resentment and pain as well as power and pleasure." As a sociologist and lecturer in a high status university Fatima understood that her success was predicated upon her psychological capital to negotiate the markers of her difference in her professional life, such as skin colour, language, and her headscarf. She talks here about the visual and social "disjunctions" that her presence creates in racialised places.

> I see myself different because I have a different religion than the majority religion and I have a different culture. I use different languages. They could see me as different but I do not see myself as different. I never think of this, like I would think well they didn't offer me the job because of discrimination because I'm wearing a headscarf, because this is different. I won't know what I would think if I were not wearing a headscarf. I was surprised actually, as a sociologist I was studying race and colour and bla, bla, bla and when I came to the UK I faced this—skin colour is very important here. Very interesting actually, in the Netherlands it's not that—well, we have Sudanese for instance very much discussed is headscarves and moustaches of Turkish man for instance (laughter) (Fatima).

Both Amina and Fatima manage their racialised experiences in Britain by expressing nostalgia for "home." In the countries where they grew up, Canada and Netherlands, they see racism as less rife than in Britain. Theories of identity describe the self-in-process of becoming, which is always by its nature incomplete, unstable, and potentially transformative (Hall, 1992). The women's reflections of a "better place back home" encapsulate the transnational migratory process where cross border mobility disrupts definitions of cultural identity and unsettles associations between people and place (Song, 2005). This, as Butcher (2009) argues can lead to a re-evaluation of identity in which people seek to re-find points of comfort in order to manage difference. In this sense the women's "knowing nostalgia" for a non-racist utopia back home (they admit "home" is also racist) is about recreating spaces of comfort and safety through re-memory (Reynolds, 2005) in order to survive working and living in new hostile racist spaces.

DIASPORA SPACES: ISLAM AS "A SECOND SKIN"

For the women in the study being a Muslim was a crucial aspect of their sense of self and ethnic belonging. In contrast to the more outwardly collective masculine expressions Muslimness, in which Islam has been mobilised as a political and nationalistic power resource in civil society (Balzani, 2010: Werbner, 2007), the women expressed their faith as a private transcendental spiritual space from which they derived an inner strength. As Fatima explains, being a Muslim is very important to her sense of who she is. She describes her belief as a "second skin" which extends to her dress. She cannot imagine not having a headscarf, which is as much about her inner spiritual life as well as a naturalised external way of being.

> Being religious or a Muslim is very important for me, it shapes and gives the power for me and when I feel weak, normally I do not feel weak, well I'm not a weak person but many times I could feel weak, then religion is very important for me. I pray and I take time for myself. I have this feeling that a power bigger than me protects me. Having this religious feeling and this religious belief gives you the look to see the life. I mean the very thin line through the life, you connect things with each other and you make sense of everything and that's why religion is so important for me (Fatima).

Saba Mahmood (2005) seeks to explain this form of embodied gendered religious agency through the understanding of acts of piety or taqwa. She argues on Muslim women's religious disposition, such as obedience to God brings spiritual rewards in and of itself to the women. The Egyptian women she studied in the mosque movement produced "virtuous selves" through conscious acts of "shyness" in which the female body is used as an instrument to attain [a] state of embodied piety. Mahmood suggests that in order to understand the Islamic female forms of moral subjectivity and embodied spiritual interiority, we must move beyond Western Imperialist notions of libratory emancipation and the deterministic binaries of resistance/subordination by which Muslim female subjectivity and agency are so often judged. Thus rather than seeing Fatima's practices and beliefs through the Western normative assumptions about Muslim female docility, complicity, and resistance to patriarchal conservative cultural values, we must understand her agency and acts of faith within the broader political and social environment. As Manal Hamzeh (2012) points out the *hijab* is a socially constructed gendering discourse that has hegemonised women's ways of thinking and acting for centuries. As she explains, the "hijab is a multidimensional embodiment of interwoven subtle values and practices—the visual, spatial, and ethical" (Hamzeh, 2012: 2). Fatima's ethically derived transcendental identity was not unlike the spatially situated young Bangladeshi women in Halima Begum (2008). Begum describes the ways in which the second generation British born Bangladeshi women preferred to express their visually apparent "Muslimness" as an embodied inner private belief when situated within and excluded from the physically unsafe male dominated nationalistic Bangladeshi streets of the East End of London.

While it has been shown that some Muslim women choose to veil in order to reassert their Muslimness as a political statement in the wake of 9/11 (Buitelaar, 2006; Housee, 2004; Killian, 2003), Amina and Mehrunissa still articulated a strong sense of

"Muslimness" though they themselves did not wear a headscarf. In her study of Pakistani Muslim women in Glasgow, Siraj (2011) shows how Muslim conservative ideology pervasively produced an idealised view of Muslim femininity even among those who chose not to wear the hijab. This commitment to modesty and the "idea" of the hijab need to be understood in relation to the identity choices that are available for Muslim women in Islamophobic contexts. Buitelaar (2006: 260) argues that having to respond to essentialist images of "the Muslim" has a strong impact on how intersectionality is experienced by those who among other many identifications see themselves as Muslims. She writes, "They (Muslim women in the Netherlands) are left with few generally accepted narratives to communicate the ways in which their various identifications are simultaneously (in)formed by prevailing conceptions about gender, ethnicity, religion, class, nationality etc." Thus Amina, who also saw herself as primarily a South Asian Canadian, still expressed a strong affinity with other Muslims, like going to festivals and celebrations in the Mosque, which she talked about as being an "unconscious and innate" experience. When asked if she feels a sense of belonging with other Muslims, she replies,

> Yeah, it is important to who I am but what I assert will be different at different times so I'm Muslim that's the easiest for most people but I'm a particular sub-set of a minority and so it depends on how specific you want to get on what that means. A lot of people think they know something about me by knowing that I'm Muslim and so I'll employ that if it's needed in the context but they, in my eyes, they don't particularly know anything additional about me just because I've said Muslim other than I've chosen to ally myself with that identity for a particular reason (Amina).

Mehrunissa explains that it is not just the "appearance" of the headscarf but also her name and her Asian culture, and in particular eating halal food that are identifiers of her Muslimness. For her being a Muslim is,

> . . . Very, very important, not only important to me, also it should be, appearance-wise. When you look at a Muslim girl, all covered, you can immediately identify them because Islam says that you should have the identity of your religion. But I'm not covering my

head so maybe people will not think of me in the first place that she's Muslim—they can see Asian—but later on if I introduce myself they would know by my name that I am (Mehrunissa).

For all the women, Islam was a conscious site of memory and belonging—a "second skin" through which their ethnic and religious identity was embodied and lived out through their subjectivity and sense of self. Like the Muslim American women activists in Zahedi (2011) the women were constantly redefining themselves in relation to hegemonic Islamophobic and patriarchal discourses. In this context Islam and being a Muslim meant different things to each woman. Amina used the physical space of the Mosque as her site of contestation. For Mehrunissa it was through her culture and food, for Fatima it was her headscarf and Islamic practices. Brah (1996) talks about the ways in which transnational migration creates "diaspora spaces" in new places of settlement. Here culture, class and communities become contested "sites" which are reshaped when "individual and collective memories and practices collide, reassemble and reconfigure" (Brah, 1996: 193). The women could be seen to be dialogically constructing "diaspora spaces" by both listening to and negotiating dominant external discourses about Islam and Muslims and then using them to re-construct their own shifting and contingent narratives of what it is to be a "Muslim woman."

Such narratives, however, are deeply disrupted by the heightened political sentiment against Muslim women. Naima Bouteldja (2011) shows how the Islamophobic political discourse in France legitimated a public free-for-all "witch hunt" against women wearing the veil. The persecution of women extended to internally colonized Muslim and Arab communities living in France who accused their own women wearing the burqa (full dress including the face) of "shaming" the entire community, and "dirtying the religion" (Open Society Foundations, 2011). Killian (2003) shows the power of dominant cultural repertoires and political and policy structures in shaping Muslim women's views of themselves. In her study of North African Muslim women's response to the French "headscarf affair" she found that older poorly educated women in France drew on traditional Islamic discourses from the Maghreb, while younger well educated Muslim women drew on French secularism to defend the headscarf as a matter of personal liberty and cultural expression.

As well educated and professional women, Amina, Mehrunissa and Fatima all distanced themselves from "the imagined other Muslims" who were "not like them." Fatima explains, "there are many Muslims which I do not want to belong to. But I am a religious person which is a very important part of my life." Mehrunissa talks about Muslims having different ideologies which for her would bring about "conflicts of interest." While religion was important to Amina's sense of self she does not want to be, "paralysed or suffer guilt" about being a Muslim, she explains,

> I know quite a few Muslims who are, I mean, partly just because of the current context, but quite defensive, lack confidence as far as the ease that they feel about the world. I know a lot of people who are just bunkered down in their "Muslimness" and have a very narrow understanding of what it is to be Muslim and that kind of thing (Amina).

Amina's statement that "I know a lot of (other) people who are just bunkered down in their 'Muslimness'" is articulated against an essentialist notion of authenticity—i.e. what it is to be a "real" Muslim. Buitelaar (2006) argues that to understand the accounts of Muslim women's intersecting identifications we need to employ the theory of the "dialogical self." She suggests that the Moroccan Muslim woman living in the Netherlands whose life-story she tells, orchestrates multiple voices within herself that speak from different *I-positions*. Fatima's statement that "there are many Muslims which I do not want to belong to" points to her social positioning and religious and ethnic identification. Buitelaar explains, "Identity is the temporary outcome of our responses to the various ways in which we are addressed on the basis of our positions in power relations in and between the different social and cultural fields in which we participate["] (Buitelaar, 2006: 261). Thus for Amina, Mehrunissa and Fatima, their ambivalent relationship to "other Muslims" speaks to the racially inscribed religious and political voices that intersect and inform their *I-positions* in their narratives.

NEGOTIATING MODERNITY: TRANSNATIONAL "CHAMELEONS"

Transnational mobility across national sites engenders a process of identity re-evaluation as the familiar cultural frames of reference that underpin identities are disrupted in new and different places (Butcher, 2009; Song, 2005: Zine, 2007). Indeed these transnational women dislocated from their real and "imagined" homelands and positioned as a Muslim minority in Britain occupy transnational spaces in which the modalities of race, class and gender intersect with hostile anti-immigrant British nationalism and globalized anti-Islamic discourses. In these diasporic spaces they negotiate this disruption through a range of raced, classed and gendered identity strategies which they embody through language and culture.

Amina who is of Canadian, Pakistani, Indian, British, and Bangladeshi heritage sees herself as "worldly" and "nomadic." She is like a chameleon, a "shape-shifter," with many layers of national and cultural identity that she employs simultaneously as the need arises. She explains,

> A lot of my social identity is basically bound up in an idea of being worldly and nomadic and that's what I take from being me. So what it means to be Canadian, what it means to be South Asian, whatever, they're quite different and they're interesting in their own ways. If I could I'd get passports for, you know—have all five passports—go around travelling everywhere (Amina).

However it is within the negating discourse of multiculturalism and virulent discourses of Islamophobia that Amina's search for multiple and shifting identities must be located (Mirza, 2012). Anita Fábos (2012) argues the British discourse regarding the limits of multiculturalism has been framed in terms of home, family, and belonging, which has striking implications for migrant and refugee women who are seen as embodying an "unhomely" threat to Britishness. In her study of Muslim Arab Sudanese women in Britain, Fábos talks about the impact these negative connotations have on the women. She explains, "The reactions to these ascribed identities include a distancing from the assumptions that Sudanese form part of the 'black' community, development of strategies of belonging that rely on transnational networks, and a commitment to Islamic 'authenticity'" (2010: 224). Resisting being "named" by employing multiple identities that link outward toward a global transnational identity constitutes an embodied reaction to endemic racism and exclusion faced in Britain. As Amina Mama writes, "Black women do not simply accept these images of themselves but over time use collective histories within oppressive social orders to counteract racism and sexism" (Mama, 1995).

One such embodied act of resistance is to use powerful hegemonic symbols such as language to negotiate modernity. Fatima who speaks 3 languages fluently—Turkish, Dutch and English expresses her determination to "become" universal through speaking English. She explains,

> English is the language where I express my universal identity. I mean, with English I can express my identity and share my thoughts, my ideas with this language and that gives me a refreshed feeling that I know English (Fatima).

While Fatima is aware of colonial subjugation through language from her schooling "back home," in her statement there is an implicit acceptance of the hegemony and power of English as a way to express herself and be understood. Frantz Fanon (1990: 27) calls for the "decolonising of the native intellectual" as a means to "change the order of the world" in the wake of the violent colonial suppression and destruction of indigenous knowledges and culture in the Western Imperial project (Smith, 2008; Young, 1990). Spivak (1990) describes the necessary process of decolonisation for "third world" Asian/Indian postcolonial intellectuals working in universities in the West, which includes strategically positioning themselves in the academy. As Mehrunissa explains, this involves speaking the colonizers' language.

> English speaking is more important than your own language, than your national language. Why?—Because in India, the communication, the mode of study is in English; when you go out anywhere you will not be speaking your language—here people don't know any other language other than English whereas in our country people know various, many

Asian languages, so those people get used to so many languages (Mehrunissa).

Though they all spoke English fluently the women were still strongly rooted to their ethnic and cultural "belonging" through a strong sense of place. They consciously created meaningful diasporic communities, across a number of nation-states which they recalled through gendered memories of childhood and family. These were strongly recalled through culturally specific smells, hearing, touch and particularly the taste of food. Fatima who feels most at home with friends and family in her home town in the Netherlands still holds on to emotional memories of growing up in Turkey.

> I was born in a village and this village is a mountain village where the houses are situated very far from each other, so if you have a gun and shoot from a gun, the next house won't hear the sound—so very far from each other. And my mother used to live in this mountain with me, my sister two years older than me and my brother 12 years older than me. When the time comes, it's May here, spring time and they cut the grass and it dries and gives a smell, so if I first smell this smell I have to immediately think of those villages where I grew up because that is the smell of those villages. My mother can't read or write, she's illiterate because they didn't have schools there but she's very tough. She lived there without my father for eight years and she saved money by selling cheese, meat and that kind of things. She bought very nice gold for us. Gold is very important in Turkey; people save gold, not money. So yeah, I think I have some features from that region too (Fatima).

Fatima's feelings of longing and belonging are embodied personal geographies that are shaped by people, place and time. Louise Ryan (2008: 300) in her study of working class Irish women nurses who came to Britain describes the "emotional terrain of transnational journeys." She suggests that through global care chains migrant women manage their families and expectations of support and obligation. She argues that migrant women's emotional reactions are rooted in bodily processes, such as feelings of homesickness and the stoical need to conform to the ideal of the successful migrant. This insight into the "psychic landscape" (Reay, 2005) of postcolonial transnational Muslim women reveals the ways in which the shared identification of race, class and gender is embodied and lived out through a collective consciousness and memory.

CONCLUSION: MUSLIM WOMEN AT THE CROSS ROADS OF RACE, GENDER AND RELIGION

In this article I explored the intersectional dynamics of race, gender and religion by looking at the relationship between the gendered Islamophobic discourses that circulate in the "West" and the embodied identity of transnational professional young Muslim women living in Britain. The three Muslim professional women's subjectivity and narratives of "self" were expressed firstly through "the gauze" of their racialised consciousness borne of living in Britain, secondly through the "second skin" of their faith and embodied modesty, and thirdly, as "transnational chameleons" with tangible embodied memories of "home." In their dialogic conversations of gendered religious racialisation the women's voices revealed how the intersectionality of race, gender, and religion was lived out on and within the Muslim female body.

I began by asking what the consequences are for transnational professional Muslim women of being caught up in the Islamophobic space occupied by the postcolonial Muslim diaspora in Britain. Framing the analysis was the macro discourse of anti-Islamic hostility in Britain and its production of the raced and gendered Muslim female body. In her essay on the construction of the racially objectified "Muslim woman," the postcolonial Muslim feminist anthropologist Lila Abu-Lughod argues that we must be vigilant of West's reifying tendency "to plaster neat cultural icons like 'the Muslim woman' over messy historical and political dynamics" (Abu-Lughod, 2002: 784). The transnational professional Muslim women in the study were indeed caught up in the messy historical and political dynamics of the post-9/11 Islamophobic media discourse and its overwhelming preoccupation with the "embodied" Muslim women in British public spaces. While Muslim women and Islamic feminists (Abu-Lughod, 2002; Badran, 2009; Mernissi, 1996) have taken issue with the simplistic cultural constructions of Muslim women in the media, it nevertheless remains a macro regulatory discourse that framed the Muslim women's daily lived reality. In what Haw (2009) describes as the "mythical feedback loop," the media's emphasis on signifying stories of "backward" Muslim practices, such as veiling, impacts on the identity of the wider British Muslim community, which in turn affects Muslim women's internal felt world and sense of self.

In the study Fatima's veiled Muslim body was visually recognised and marked as religiously raced and gendered in Britain. As a Turkish, (now) middle class Muslim woman, her identifiable dress (hijab) and racialised national markers (skin colour and accent) determined how she was seen and thus "known" as an "other." As Sara Ahmed (2004) explains the figure of the veiled Muslim woman challenges the values that are crucial to the multicultural nation, such as freedom and culture, making her a symbol of what the nation must give up to be itself. Thus being visibly "non-assimilated" in a multicultural society invites a certain type of benign surveillance as "standing out" invokes deep feelings of need, rejection and anxiety within the majority "white other" culture. The Muslim woman's demand to be "different" (i.e. wear the veil) is seen as a rejection of the welcoming embrace or "gift" of the multicultural "host" society. The "disjuncture" that this racialisation engendered within Fatima produced her as a "knowing subject." Fatima was conscious of how her Muslim body was encountered as racialised object (Lorde, 1984). However it was through her religious disposition that she expressed her embodied gendered religious agency. Her headscarf was experienced as a "second skin," and personal embodied acts of piety such as wearing the hijab became an "identity affect" which enabled her to move beyond the simplistic cultural constructions of Muslim women in the media that negates Muslim female agency.

As transnational subjects the professional Muslim women were able to draw on meaningful diasporic communities of belonging across a number of nation-states based on a continuing shared identification and sense of consciousness of kind (Bilge & Denis, 2010: 3). Such transcendental diasporic situatedness challenges classic notions of the mobile transnational migrant as rational strategic agents (Butcher, 2009; Ley, 2005). The alternative geographies of the women's new emergent "diasporic" spaces were bounded not by territory or nationality but by embodied practices of contingent and reconfigured gendered "Muslimness," as manifested in the wearing or not of the hijab, going to the Mosque, eating halal food, and other acts of postcolonial resistance and accommodation such as speaking English. For them "home" was powerfully recalled through "other knowledges" (hooks, 1991; Smith, 2008). These "other knowledges" invoked decolonised spaces which the women "felt" through their embodied sensory memories of childhood, shaped by people and places, and spatially articulated through a rooted sense of belonging to the "land of their ancestors." However dialogically, the women's embodied lived reality as raced and gendered Muslim women was also marked by the affective racist immigration and Islamophobic discourses of hate and fear in which they were now embedded as transnational female migrants.

The notion of "embodied intersectionality," as I have developed here, enables us to move beyond the limitations of modernist "capacity endowed" categories of race, class, gender, sexuality and disability which have "gridlocked" feminist theorising on difference (Anthias, 2011; Puar, 2011).The framework of embodied intersectionality enables us to see not only how the women were constructed as recognisable visible Muslim others in discourse, but how that affective representation is signified and mediated by the body and experienced as a lived reality. The embodiment of power and disempowerment written through and within the sexed and raced body is particularly important if we are to understand how religious identity is performed, experienced and articulated through the women's subjectivity and sense of self. The all consuming hegemonic racist and sexist discourses inherent within Western Islamophobia and fundamentalist, nationalist Islamic patriarchy frames her social reality. The Muslim female voices in the autobiographically articulated narrative interviews revealed the ways in which regulatory discourses of gendered and raced inequity and subjugation are "performed" or exercised in the everyday material world of the socially constructed "Muslim woman" in the "West." By drawing on the embodied accounts of Fatima, Amina and Mehrunissa, the process of "being and becoming" an intersectionally situated gendered and raced subject of discourse reveals not only the discursive effects of hegemonic power and privilege which "name" the Muslim woman, but also highlights her embodied agency to consciously rename her identity as lived at the intersecting cross-roads of her transnational journey.

NOTES

1. *Understanding Society* is a world leading study of the socio-economic circumstances and attitudes of 100,000 individuals in 40,000 British households. It is funded by the Economic and Social Research Council (ESRC) at the Institute for Social and Economic Research (ISER), University of Essex. See http://www.understandingsociety.org.uk/.
2. The team members on this project were Lucinda Platt, Heidi Safia Mirza, Alita Nandy, and Punita Chowbey. I thank my colleagues for their kind permission to use the data and take full responsibility for the analysis developed here.

REFERENCES

Abu-Lughod, Lila (2002). Do Muslim women really need saving? Anthropological reflections on cultural relativism and its others. *American Anthropologist, 104*(3), 783–790.

Afshar, Haleh (2008). Can I see your hair? Choice, agency and attitudes: The dilemma of faith and feminism for Muslim women who cover. *Ethnic and Racial Studies, 31*(2), 411–427.

Ahmed, Sara (2003). The politics of fear in the making of worlds. *International Journal of Qualitative Studies in Education, 16*(3), 377–398.

Ahmed, Sara (2004). *The cultural politics of emotions*. Edinburgh: Edinburgh University Press.

Ahmed, Sara (2009). Embodying diversity: Problems and paradoxes for black feminists. *Race Ethnicity and Education, 12*(1), 41–52.

Alexander, Claire, & Knowles, Caroline (2005). *Making race matter: Bodies, space and identity*. Basingstoke: Palgrave MacMillan.

Anthias, Floya (2011). Intersections and translocations: New paradigms for thinking about cultural diversity and social identities. *European Educational Research Journal, 10*(2), 204–217.

Applebaum, Barbara (2008). "Doesn't my experience count?" White students, the authority of experience and social justice pedagogy. *Race Ethnicity and Education, 11*(4), 405–414.

Badran, Margot (2009). Feminism in Islam secular and religious convergences. *Oxford: Oneworld*.

Balzani, Marzia (2010). Masculinities and violence against women in South Asian communities: Transnational perspectives. In Ravi K. Thiara, & Aisha K. Gill (Eds.), *Violence against women in South Asian communities: Issues for policy and practice*. London: JKP.

Begum, Halima (2008). Geographies of inclusion/exclusion: British Muslim women in the East End of London. *Sociological Research, 13*(5) (Online http://www.socresonline.org.uk)

Bilge, Sirma, & Denis, Ann (2010). Introduction: Women, intersectionality and diasporas. *Journal of Intercultural Studies, 31*(1), 1–8.

Bourdieu, Pierre (1990). *In other words: Essays toward a reflexive sociology*. Cambridge: Polity Press.

Bouteldja, Naima (2011). *France's false battle of the veil*. The guardian (Monday 18 April http://www.guardian.co.uk/commentisfree/2011/apr/18/france-false-battle-of-the-veil (28.9.2012))

Bradford, Simon, & Hey, Valerie (2007). Successful subjectivities? The successification of class, ethnic and gender positions. *Journal of Education Policy, 22*(6), 595–614.

Brah, Avtar (1996). *Cartographies of diasponnra: Contesting identities*. London: Routledge.

Brah, Avtar, & Phoenix, Ann (2004). Ain't I a woman? Revisiting intersectionality. *Journal of International Women's Studies, 5*(3), 75–86.

BRIN (2010). *How many Muslims?* British religion in numbers: The PEW forum report.: Manchester University (https://www.brin.ac.uk/news/?p=598 (accessed 28.9.12))

Buitelaar, Marjo (2006). I am the ultimate challenge: Accounts of intersectionality in the life-story of a well-known daughter of a Moroccan migrant worker in the Netherlands. *European Journal of Women's Studies, 13*(3), 259–276.

Butcher, Melissa (2009). Ties that bind: The strategic use of transnational relationships in demarcating identity and managing difference. *Journal of Ethnic and Migration Studies, 35*(8), 1353–1371.

Butler, Judith (1993). *Bodies that matter: On the discursive limits of "sex."* New York: Routledge.

Coene, Gily, & Longman, Chia (2008). Gendering the diversification of diversity: The Belgium hijab (in) question. *Ethnicities, 8*(3), 302–321.

Cole, Barbara (2009). Gender, narratives and intersectionality: Can personal experience approaches to research contribute to "undoing gender"? *International Review of Education, 55*, 561–578.

Collins, Patricia Hill (1990). *Black feminist thought: Knowledge consciousness and the politics of empowerment*. London: Routledge.

Crenshaw, Kimberlé W. (1989). Demarginalising the intersection of race and sex: A black feminist critique of anti-discrimination doctrine, feminist theory and antiracist politics. *The University of Chicago Legal Forum, feminism in the law: Theory, practice and criticism* (pp. 138–167).

Crenshaw, Kimberlé W. (1991). Mapping the margins: Intersectionality, identity politics, and violence against women of color. *Stanford Law Review, 43*(6), 1241–1299.

Doyle, Jack (2010). *Mohammed is now the most popular name for baby boys ahead of Jack and Harry. Daily mail 28th* October http://www.dailymail.co.uk/news/ (accessed 28.9.12)

Fábos, Anita (2012). Resisting blackness, embracing rightness: How Muslim Arab Sudanese women negotiate their identity in the diaspora. *Ethnic and Racial Studies, 35*(2), 218–237.

Fanon, Frantz (1986). *Black skin white masks* (3rd edn). London: Pluto Books.

Fanon, Frantz (1990). *The wretched of the earth* (5th edn). London: Penguin Books.

Hall, Stuart (1992). New ethnicities. In J. Donald, & A. Rattansi (Eds.), *"Race," culture and difference* (pp. 252–259). London: Sage/OU Press.

Hall, Stuart (2012). Avtar Brah's cartographies: moment, method, meaning. *Feminist Review, 100,* 27–38.

Hamzeh, Manal (2011). Deveiling body stories: Muslim girls negotiate visual, spatial, and ethical hijabs. *Race Ethnicity and Education, 14*(4), 481–506.

Hamzeh, Manal (2012). *Pedagogies of deveiling: Muslim girls and the hijab discourse.* Charlotte, North Carolina: Information Age Publishing (IAP).

Haw, Kaye (2009). From hijab to jilbab and the "myth" of British identity: Being Muslim in contemporary Britain a half-generation on. *Race Ethnicity and Education, 12*(3), 363–378.

hooks, B. (1991). *Yearning: Race gender and cultural politics.* London: Turnaround Press.

Housee, Shirin (2004). Unveiling South Asian female identities post September 11: Asian female students' sense of identity and experiences of higher education. In Ian Law, Deborah Phillips, & Laura Turney (Eds.), *Institutional racism in higher education.* Stoke on Trent: Trentham Books.

Jiwani, Yasmin (2006). *Discourses of denial: Mediations of race, gender and violence.* Vancouver: UBC Press.

Killian, Caitlin (2003). The other side of the veil: North African women in France respond to the headscarf affair. *Gender and Society, 17*(4), 567–590.

Ley, David (2005). Shaky borders? Transnational migrants as strategic actors. In Henk van Houtum, Oliver Kramsch, & Wolfgang Zierhofer (Eds.), *B/ordering space.* Aldershot: Ashgate Publishing.

Lorde, Audre (1984). *Sister outsider: Essays and speeches.* Berkeley California: The Crossing Press Feminist Series.

Ludhra, Geeta, & Chappell, Anne (2011). "You were quiet—I did all the marching": Research processes involved in hearing the voices of South Asian girls. *International Journal of Adolescence and Youth, 16,* 101–118.

Mahmood, Saba (2005). The politics of piety: The Islamic revival and the feminist subject. *Princeton: University Press.*

Mama, Amina (1995). *Beyond the masks: Race, gender and subjectivity.* London: Routledge.

Mani, Lata (1989). Multiple mediations: Feminist scholarship in the age of multiple mediations. *Inscriptions, 5,* 1–23.

McCall, Leslie (2005). The complexity of intersectionality. *SIGNS Journal of Women Culture and Society, 30*(31), 1771–1802.

McKittirick, Katherine (2006). *Demonic grounds: Black women and the cartography of struggle.* Minneapolis: University of Minnesota Press.

Meetoo, Veena, & Mirza, Heidi Safia (2007). "There is nothing honourable about honour killings": Gender, violence and the limits of multiculturalism. *Women's Studies International Forum, 30*(3), 187–200.

Mernissi, Fatima (1996). *Women's rebellion and Islamic memory.* London: Zed Books.

Mirza, Heidi Safia (2009a). Plotting a history: Black and postcolonial feminisms in "new times." *Race Ethnicity and Education, 12*(1), 1–10.

Mirza, Heidi Safia (2009b). *Race, gender and educational desire: Why black women succeed and fail.* London: Routledge.

Mirza, Heidi Safia (2012). Multiculturalism and the gender gap: The visibility and invisibility of Muslim women in Britain. In Waqar I. U. Ahmad, & Ziauddin Sardar (Eds.), *Britain's Muslims, Muslim Britain: Making social and political space for Muslims* (London).

Nandi, Alita, & Platt, Lucinda (2009). Developing ethnic identity questions for understanding society: The UK household longitudinal study. *Understanding society working paper series no. 03.:* ISER, University of Essex.

Nash, Jennifer, C. (2008). Re-thinking intersectionality. *Feminist Review, 89*(1–15).

Open Society Foundations (2011). *Unveiling the truth.* Why 32 women wear the full-face veil in France (http://www.soros.org/initiatives/home/articles_publications/publications/unveiling-the-truth-20110411 (accessed 28.9.12))

Phinney, Jean S. (1992). The multigroup ethnic measure: A new scale for use with diverse groups. *Journal of Adolescent Research, 7,*156–176.

Puar, J. K. (2007). *Terrorist assemblages: Homonationalism in queer times.* (Durham).

Puar, Jasbir K. (2011). *I would rather be a cyborg than a goddess: Intersectionality, assemblage, and affective politics.:* European Institute for Progressive Cultural Policies EIPCP (http://eipcp.net/transversal/0811/puar/en (28.9. 2012))

Razack, Sherene (2008). *Casting out: The eviction of Muslims from Western laws & politics.* Toronto: University of Toronto Press.

Razack, Sherene, Smith, Malinda, & Thobani, Sunera (Eds.). (2010). *States of race: Critical race feminism for the 21st century.* Toronto: Between the Lines Press.

Reay, Diane (2005). Beyond consciousness? The psychic landscape of social class. *Sociology, 39*(5), 911–928.

Reynolds, Tracey (2005). *Caribbean mothers: Identity and experiences in the UK.* London: Tufnell Press.

Ryan, Louise (2008). Navigating the emotional terrain of families "here" and "there": Women, migration and the management of emotions. *Journal of Intercultural Studies, 29*(3), 299–313.

Said, Edward (1985). *Orientalism: Western concepts of the orient.* Harmondsworth: Penguin.

Scott, Jallach Wallach (2007). *The politics of the veil.* New Jersey: Princeton University Press.

Simmonds, Felly (1997). My body myself: How does a black woman do sociology? In Heidi S. Mirza (Ed.), *Black British feminism.* London: Routledge.

Siraj, Asifa (2011). Meanings of modesty and the hijab amongst Muslim women in Glasgow, Scotland. *Gender, Place and Culture, 18*(6), 716–731.

Skeggs, Beverley (1997). *Formations of class and gender: Becoming respectable.* London: Sage.

Smith, Linda Tuhiwai (2008). *Decolonising methodologies: Research and indigenous peoples.* London and New York: Zed Books.

Song, Miri (2005). Global and local articulations of Asian identity. In C. Alexander, & C. Knowles (Eds.), *Making race matter: Bodies, space and identity.* Basingstoke: Palgrave MacMillan.

Spivak, Gayatri, Chakravorty (1990). Questions of multiculturalism. In Sarah Harasym (Ed.), *The post-colonial critic: Interviews, strategies and dialogues* (pp. 59–60). New York: Routledge.

Werbner, Pnina (2007). Veiled interventions in pure space: Honour shame and embodied struggles among Muslims in Britain and France. *Theory Culture and Society, 24*(2), 161–186.

Young, Robert (1990). *White mythologies: Writing history and the West.* London: Routledge.

Yuval-Davis, Nira (2006). Intersectionality and feminist politics. *European Journal of Women's Studies, 13*(3), 193–209.

Zahedi, Asraf (2011). Muslim American women in the post-11 September era. *International Feminist Journal of Politics, 13*(2), 183–203.

Zine, Jasmin (2007). Safe havens or religious "ghettos"? Narratives of Islamic schooling in Canada. *Race Ethnicity and Education, 10*(1), 71–92.

ISIS NUSAIR

35. PERMANENT TRANSIENTS: GENDERING THE NARRATIVES OF IRAQI WOMEN REFUGEES IN JORDAN

INTRODUCTION

This article is based on ethnographic research conducted between 2007 and 2011 with Iraqi women refugees in Jordan and with representatives of the United Nations and national and international aid organizations. I analyze the gendered nature of the women's experiences leaving Iraq and seeking refuge in Jordan. The women interviewed, whose names have been changed to protect their identity, arrived in Jordan after the 2003 United States-led invasion of Iraq, with most arriving between 2005 and 2006. The women's age ranged from 18 to 72, and I deliberately chose to interview women who came from different parts of Iraq and had different economic, educational, political, ethnic, and religious backgrounds. My research is informed by feminist participatory research methodology, relational/reflective approaches, and the historicization of the women's context. I privilege an ethnographic approach in which the voices of the women frame my conceptual understanding and analysis of their situation rather than apply theoretical frameworks to their narratives and in this way constrain the meaning I might derive. Instead, I reflect on the multiple layers of meaning in what the women reveal in their shifting, lived experiences.

FIXED TEMPORALITY

The invisibility of the consequences of the US-led invasion of Iraq in 2003, particularly its impact on population displacement, raises questions about accountability and the impact of the war on the day-to-day lives of Iraqis in general and refugees in particular. Contrary to United Nations predictions, Iraqis did not leave their country immediately after the 2003 US-led invasion; they left in massive numbers after the 2006 bombing of the mosque in Samarra. With the increased assassinations, kidnapping for ransom,

violence, instability, and threats on people's lives, over two million Iraqis left for neighboring countries, and two million were internally displaced. One million of those are estimated to have arrived in Syria and half a million in Jordan. Both Jordan and Syria are not signatories to the 1951 Refugee Convention. Jordan signed in 1998 a Memorandum of Understanding with UNHCR (United Nations High Commissioner for Refugees) that allowed asylum seekers to stay in the country pending refugee status determination (UNHCR, 2012–2013, 2007). Without a legal status, refugees had to constantly pay fees to renew their visas. They were not allowed to work unless they deposited large sums of money in the bank, and many had to rely on aid agencies for provision of basic services of food, shelter, and schooling for their children. The majority of Iraqis in Jordan are urban refugees (not placed in refugee camps) and live in the capital Amman.

I refrain from using the term "guests" to describe Iraqi refugees in Jordan. "Guests" is the official term used to connote hospitality and the temporary nature of the Iraqi refugees' presence in the country. Many refugees referred directly to this contradiction and explained the lack of rights associated with the term "guests" and the fact that many of them have been "guests" in Jordan for a number of years (see Chatelard). Hana, a widow in her fifties, described the transient nature of her presence in Jordan as contingent: "we do not know our destiny. The Jordanian government might ask us to leave at any moment. . . . There is no rest for a guest. It is heavy, if we were to work, the situation could have been better. . . . I am responsible for the house and the kids. The responsibility of a daughter and disabled child is on me." Suad, a woman in her early sixties whose house was broken into and who was kidnapped in Iraq in 2006, added, "There is no stability. Our living in Amman is temporary as they might ask us to leave at any moment. If it were not for my kids, I would not be here." She concluded by saying that restoring stability to her country will take a long time to resolve and that her extended family is dispersed in the Arab Gulf states and in Europe.

Since all the women interviewed left Iraq to protect their children from violence, they reiterated a sense of no return back to their homeland. Sameera, born in 1958, has been in Jordan since 2007. She came to Jordan with her children following the assassination of her husband in 2007. Sameera is not registered with the United Nations. She described how she does not have any ambition to go back to Iraq, and that not much is left of this life. She concluded by saying, "We have seen a lot." Nadia, an Iraqi painter in her early seventies, described how people were afraid to say a word under the Ba'th regime, and how she does not interact much with the Jordanian society. "Nothing is left. . . . Our group [family] is dispersed. This is our situation, some are in Qatar, New Zealand, and Sweden. . . . When they [the Americans] occupied us, they did not bring a democratic life and the situation became worse. Now we miss the Saddam [Hussein] days. . . . Many families do not have money to go back and visit their homes. This is a long-term stay for us for where could we go?" Zeina, a medical doctor who was kidnapped and severely harassed for five days in 2004, said that she came to Jordan to overcome the shock that she went through. "I need security to go back. We are thankful to Jordan but the prospect of return worsens by the day. . . . There was a loss of security, and everything collapsed." Although the majority of the women interviewed did not provide details of the violence they were exposed to while in Iraq, they emphasized the witnessing act of the horrors of war.

CONTESTING TERMINOLOGY

Peter Nyers argues in *Rethinking Refugees* that the politics of being a refugee has as much to do with the cultural expectation of certain qualities and behaviors that are demonstrative of "authentic" "refugeeness" (e.g., silence, passivity, victimhood) as it does with legal definitions of regulations (Nyers xv). He adds, "the refugees' relationship to the political can be described as a kind of 'inclusive exclusion.' Refugees are included in the discourse of 'normality' and 'order' only by virtue of their exclusion from the normal identities and ordered spaces

of the sovereign state" (xiii). Sama, an Iraqi performance artist in her early fifties, started the interview by saying, "I do not like the word refuge. I prefer shelter. . . . There is no security and if it was not for my son, I would not have left." She described how in the last five years, she has been unable to perform theatrically or on television despite the proposals she receives. "I feel that I cannot reflect what the country [Iraq] is going through."

This sense of paralysis was echoed by many women refugees who were traumatized by what they went through before their arrival in Jordan (see Dahl). They expressed the limits on their space and the contradictions they live through, especially that they came to Jordan seeking security and found instability instead. This instability is a product of the temporality of their presence in the country, as they have to constantly pay fees to renew their visas and avoid deportation. Sana, a woman in her late twenties, said, "We sacrificed everything for security. . . . The main thing is to feel stable and be respected as human beings. If there is work, no one is incapable." Rabiha, a journalist in her late fifties, described the contradiction between visibility and invisibility when talking about her job. She publishes daily and weekly articles in a major Jordanian newspaper, and her articles are translated regularly into different languages. Although she is a well-known journalist in the region, she was granted residency in Jordan through her son's work permit.

References to trauma as well as paralyses were particularly present in the narratives of younger women as they were still navigating a personal and professional path for themselves. Nadine, a woman in her early twenties who studied computer science in Iraq said, "My life passes me by, stops, like a machine that has not been used for a long time. I need to get out of this paralysis that I am in. . . . Sometimes I see my future as black, that my life will end here with no chance to advance, and that the situation will become worse . . . [we are] like refugees with no past, present or future." Nadine described how she was followed by a car with militia men while in Iraq and how she had to flee with her mother to Amman as her father and brother remained behind. She emphasized throughout the interview that if her country were to return to the way it was, she would immediately go back. For her, the Iraq she knew and grew up in is no longer there.

This was echoed by Hanan and Zeina, two sisters who fled to Jordan with their dad and other sister as their mother and brothers remained behind. They fled because of threats made against the older sister, Hanan, who worked as a translator with the Americans. Zeina, a school teacher by training, described how depressed she feels and how she gained weight as she stays mostly at home cooking and watching TV. She described her two-year experience of working in a factory in Amman as exploitative with no opportunity for advancement. "They would not pay for work permits or health insurance. There is no stability. . . . I feel like an intruder, I am not for this place and nothing in it connects me to it. . . . We as Iraqis hope that they will give us asylum and a place to settle. There is no security, neither here nor there. Everything is hanging." Hanan describes the limitations on her space and her inability to politically organize for Iraqi refugee rights in Jordan. She described how the Mukhabarat (Jordanian Intelligence Agency) called her for questioning about her activities.

Suha, a divorced woman in her late thirties with three children (one of them is disabled), described how she felt alienated. "There are lots of people without families. They do not have self-confidence and they have no confidence in others. . . . Iraqis are tormented . . . I am alone and my burden is heavy. . . . I need a home where I could settle down. . . . The hope is to leave. That is how we could get our rights and feel secure. We are supposed to be refugees but not here. Here is temporary. . . . Despite the Saddam regime, Iraq was our country . . . the situation today is barbaric. . . . We got used to exile and difficulties" She concluded the interview by saying, "maybe it will be better in a foreign country. . . . Things will not improve in Iraq even after ten years. . . . It is hard to see the country fall apart in front of your eyes. This is what hurts. I live in constant worry yet I am optimistic and won't despair. . . . My hope is to gain independence and immigrate."

The Ba'th regime controlled Iraq from 1968 until 2003. The majority of Iraqi women interviewed described the militarization of their lives and the continuities between the past and present; their current status in Jordan and their living through the Iran-Iraq war (1980–1988); the Gulf War (1991); and life under the sanctions regime (1990–2003; see Ismael and Ismael). Sama vividly recalled living under the Ba'th regime. She said, "terror was implanted even among the members of the same family. . . . When I remember it now, I feel the bitterness more than when we lived it. We live in exile, we flee from the unknown." She spoke about the impact of the Iran-Iraq war; "it was then that things started to deteriorate. We lived as if suffocated and pretended to be living. . . . I used to walk by the wall [to protect herself from the Ba'th regime] and if my death would have made a difference I would have sacrificed myself." Suha recalled how under the sanctions regime, they were unable to achieve anything. "You were unable to develop; only sleep and eat." These were the same words that many women refugees used to describe their situation in Jordan. She added, "the war [with Iran] started when we were children. We grew up with war and bombing, and something died inside. We lived from one war to another; we were barely living."

BODY POLITICS AND THE CONTINUUM OF VIOLENCE

Both Cockburn and Kelly analyze the continuum of violence before, during, and in the aftermath of conflict as well as the link between sexual violence and other forms of violence. Violence in this context is not only about power but also about lived experiences and how power is reproduced and maintained (Nordstrom and Robben 8-9). As bodies are vested with gendered and sexualized meanings, women's experiences of their bodies are produced through multiple social and political relationships defined by religion, class, race, sexuality, and ethnicity (see Žarkov). The body of the Iraqi woman became a site of contestation of power structures and a struggle over the meanings and constructions of masculinity and femininity, especially during the Iran-Iraq war, under the sanctions regime, and in the aftermath of the 2003 US-led invasion. The Ba'th regime's attempt to increase birth rates during the war with Iran limited access to contraceptives and highlighted the masculine image of the Iraqi male war hero (see Al-Ali). Al-Jawaheri (2008) and Al-Ali (2007) describe the effects of the sanctions regime on Iraqi women and their increased insecurity and vulnerability in light of economic destitution, a changing social climate, and decline in educational and employment opportunities.

Under the sanctions, and especially in the aftermath of the 2003 US-led invasion, women's bodies became a site for marking the religious and political/social conservatism of the new Iraq (see Al-Ali and Pratt).

This vulnerability and insecurity was illustrated by many of the women interviewed. Jamila, a university professor in her early sixties said, "under the sanctions, there was hunger and some women sold their honor to leave Iraq in all ways possible. When the woman leaves with nothing, all she has is her body." Hanan emphasized throughout the interview how the instability of the situation and of being a refugee falls on the woman. "It is hard financially on the man, he feels lost and this has negative consequences on the family. . . . It is not only that I am not legal, I also do not like to be threatened with that and with the fact that they could deport me at any second. . . . I am tired and my brain is frozen. . . . People hide their Iraqi identity and when you speak with an Iraqi accent, you get higher prices and they ask you political questions." Nasra, an accountant in her early forties said, "when asked, I say that I am Sunni and not Shi'a, and I am able to imitate the Jordanian accent. To be a woman and on your own is hard."

Nasra repeated a saying I heard from many women refugees on how as strangers they should be polite (*ya ghareeb koun adeeb*). Here the connection is clear between being polite and being invisible as a refugee. Nadine's mother, Arwa, emphasized how she does not trust anyone, and shared how she changes her accent and wears sunglasses in public in order to pass as non-Iraqi. Arwa is well aware of the limits of her agency, especially that she does not have health insurance and is barely surviving in Jordan with the remittance that her husband and son send from Iraq. Suha echoed this emphasis on the need to keep silent and negotiate the different terrains of what it means to be a woman refugee in Jordan. She added, "I worked as a secretary for two years. The owner was good in the beginning but then his son would say, 'Watch out from my father' [that he might ask for sexual advances]. . . . As a consequence, I left work and started to wear a headscarf. I should have rights where I live." Suha described how she changed her place of residence to be close to the Iraqi community in Amman, and how she changes her accent when leaving that community in order to pass as non-Iraqi.

The refugee as an "other" is never only ethnic but also always gendered and sexualized, albeit in ambiguous and conflictual ways (see Žarkov). Within this context, refugee women constitute an extreme form of the "other" that is both vulnerable and an object of domination, and where the physicality of the body could hardly be separated from the symbolic meanings vested in it (11). Within this context, the violation of women's bodies acts as a symbol of the violation of the country. Violence against women is regarded as a "natural" circumstance of war and conflict, and women frequently face social stigma or are accused of promiscuity if they live alone. This was the case with many single, divorced, and widowed women I interviewed. Suha made clear throughout the interview that she does not reveal to her neighbors that she is divorced. Khawla, a woman in her mid-thirties, said that her husband, who was a member of the Ba'th regime, was assassinated in 2004. She was scared for her children and came to Jordan the following year. "We came to Jordan seeking aid and I had to become independent. I used to work as a hairdresser before I got married. I came back to work to support my children. . . . The kids are confined. I am managing and my neighbors are good. They are always watching though because I am on my own." Khawla added, "The owner of the house rang my doorbell once at four in the morning asking for water. I told him to come in and showed him my three kids who were sleeping on the floor. He left immediately." She added, "Our kids are tired from what they went through. . . . I won't go back to Iraq, Iraq is lost." Although there is demand for hairdressers, Khawla gets paid a fixed salary of 110 JD (about $150). She sells part of the ration that she receives through the United Nations to help with the house expenses. "I had a big house in Baghdad, but Baghdad is in the past. If it wasn't for good and generous people, I would not have made it." Khawla, as did many other women refugees, emphasized the limits on her space and the gendered and sexualized nature of these limitations.

THE LIMITS OF THE RESEARCH PROCESS

In a context where many refugee women are in dire need of aid, it was imperative for me to emphasize that the research I was carrying out will help expose the issues but not necessarily resolve the problems. This challenge exposes the limits of the research process itself in affecting meaningful change in the life of the refugees (see Bloch et al.). The women were well aware of this limitation. Suha said, "Iraqis are tired and need solutions and not surveys and application forms. We need tangible things." Many women emphasized that despite these limitations they needed to make their stories heard. Hajdukowski-Ahmed et al. argue in *Not Born a Refugee Woman* that through voice and voicing, agency and power are reclaimed by marginalized groups. Yet Olujc reminds us that we may give voice to the survivors of violence but we can never restore their lives (as quoted in Hajdukowski-Ahmed et al. 19). Many of the aid workers I interviewed emphasized how difficult it was to provide psychological aid to Iraqi refugees who have other stressing material needs. Although many of the women interviewed suffered from trauma, they still had to carry the responsibility of caring for their families and keeping their needs as secondary.

The open-ended nature of the interviews where the focus was on the causes that prompted the women to leave Iraq and the transition and challenges they currently face as Iraqi women refugees in Jordan opened a space for the women to reflect on their experiences and construct a narrative that analyzed their situation and visions for the future. Nyers warns against emptying all notions of political agency from refugee subjectivity (14), especially that the prevailing attitude in conventional analyses of refugee movements is one that provides no place for refugees to articulate their experiences and struggles or to assert their (often collectively conceived) political agency (xiv).

Relating to the refugee experience as a politicized process of contestation and becoming emphasizes the connection and continuum between their life before and after their arrival in Jordan. I was constantly reminded as I conducted the interviews of the need to be attentive to the complexity embedded in the women's narratives and their coping mechanisms. The majority of the women did not elaborate or provide graphic details of what they went through before leaving Iraq. They positioned their experiences as part of a larger collective and made clear connections between the hardships they had to endure while living under the Ba'th regime and sanctions, and in the aftermath of the US-led invasion in 2003.

CONCLUSION

I conducted the research with a firm political engagement to analyze the gendered nature of Iraqi refugee experience in Jordan. This engagement raised questions about where research ends and intervention begins. My activist background and academic training in feminist analysis push me to link theory with practice and think of research as a space for social change.

My analysis focuses on how Iraqi women refugees constructed meanings and practices to deal with the challenges they face on a daily basis as women refugees in Jordan, and the consequences of the transient nature of displacement and the impact it has on their physical and mental health. The longer refugees remain in exile, the more difficult and complicated it may be to return (see Bloch et al.). Most of the Iraqi women I spoke with were interested in repatriation into a third country. Since viable options were almost entirely outside the realm of control of refugee women, they were still resilient and constantly searching for ways to improve their situation. Yet, can they sustain this situation for the short and long term, and could they continue to live for years to come in this third space that grants them a limited opportunity to seek asylum, return to Iraq, or settle in Jordan?

REFERENCES

Al-Ali, Nadje. *Iraqi Women: Untold Stories from 1948 to the Present.* Zed Books, 2007.

Al-Ali Nadje and Nicola Pratt. *What Kind of Liberation? Women and the Occupation of Iraq.* University of California Press, 2009.

Al-Jawaheri, Yasmin Husein. *Women in Iraq: The Gender Impact of International Sanctions.* I.B. Tauris, 2008.

Bloch, Berry et al. "Refugee Women in Europe: Some Aspects of the Legal and Policy Dimensions." *International Migration,* 38(2) (2000): 20–40.

Chatelard, Géraldine. "The Politics of Population Movements in Contemporary Iraq: A Research Agenda." In *Writing the History of Iraq: Historiographical and Political Challenges*. R. Bocco, J. Tejet, and P. Sluglett (eds.). World Scientific Publishers/Imperial College Press, 2011.

Cockburn, Cynthia. "The Continuum of Violence: A Gender Perspective on War and Peace." In *Sites of Violence: Gender and Conflict* Zones. Wenona Giles and Jennifer Hyndman (eds.). University of California Press, 2004.

Dahl, Solveig et al. "Traumatic Effects and Predictive Factors for Posttraumatic Symptoms in Displaced Bosnian Women in a War Zone." *Journal of Traumatic Stress*, 11(1) (2005): 137–145.

Hajdukowski-Ahmed, Maroussia et al. *Not Born a Refugee Woman: Contesting Identities, Rethinking Practices*. Berghahn Books, 2008.

Ismael, Jacqueline, and Shereen Ismael. "Gender and State in Iraq." In *Gender and Citizenship in the Middle East*. Joseph Suad (ed.). Syracuse University Press, 2000.

Kelly, Liz. "Wars Against Women: Sexual Violence, Sexual Politics and the Militarized States." In *States of Conflict: Gender, Violence and Resistance*. Susie Jacobs et al. (eds.). Zed Books, 2000.

Nordstrom, Carolyn, and Antonius C. G. M. Robben (eds.). *Fieldwork Under Fire: Contemporary Studies of Violence and Culture*. University of California Press, 1996.

Nyers, Peter. *Rethinking Refugees: Beyond States of Emergency*. Routledge, 2006.

UNHCR Global Appeal 2012–2013, Jordan. http://www.unhcr.org/4ec231020.pdf. Accessed February 13, 2018.

UNHCR Statistics on Displaced Iraqis Around the World. April 2007. http://www.unhcr.org/461f7cb92.pdf. Accessed February 13, 2018.

Žarkov, Dubravka. *The Body of War: Media, Ethnicity, and Gender in the Break-up of Yugoslavia*. Duke University Press, 2007.

36. THE SPELL

Diaspora living is heavy. There are moments
I think about the smell of bread and sopaipillas,
the morning fog coating the sky. The buildings
gleaning beneath the Andes. It is early, the color
of the night clings to cement streets, the air is
cold, bitter. The dawn enters through windows,
underneath doors, translucent, the gossamer
of water drops and spider webs. In this light,
I am still a child, still hidden beneath knitted
blankets, still living in Spanish, surrounded
in the thickness of family. It is a time of stories.

Still, the shadow is there. It lingers, a snake
waking slowly. It knows its prey lives in every
corner. Before migration, before life in other
languages, before memories got lost in the five
thousand miles between Santiago and the Midwest,
the story of the coup claimed my memories. It
marked all stories, it marked all light. It fed
the snow in the mountains, the screams in
the stadium. It fed all life with the secrets of
the missing. It lingered. It was a fierce companion.
It kept its promise. I live under its spell.

Thirty years later, I am still its daughter. Spend
my immigrant days in its wake, stuck in the diaspora,
writing about a past that does not belong to me,
but only belongs to me when the callampas looked
like silk, the color of a silver blue ocean, when I
walked past shanty towns on my way to school,
and draping clothes lines strung across makeshift
dirt roads. Even then, I knew there was hunger
inside. The thin, metal houses sprung up like
mushrooms after a rainfall. The week before, there
had been nothing. This was the coup. These were
the years of silence, my childhood years.

Tanks, soldiers snaked around the city, a machine
of violence and sadness. There was no Chicago boys'
miracle. The blood in the river was blood. The hunger
creeping through the city was hunger. The disappeared
who were taken in black vans were taken. Their bodies
not just a story. This is the living I did not live, but
this is the past I remember, the living I dream at night.
The whispers, low voices, the fear of dusk closing in,
men, women hiding in building archways, running from
guns and boots, fighting curfews with rocks, glass bottles,
with pain, running home to families restless, waiting.

Running, fighting, bleeding, dying, we all did some
in those years of hunger. Did I? I was barely a girl.
This is the divide in the diaspora of memory. I am
hostage only to the stories. The people who bled or
screamed or ran, they are at the bottom of the Pacific,
ground up in blank, muddy graves, bones imbedded,
hidden in coliseum walls, forgotten. Exiled fathers,
sisters, lovers. I have not found them but as a song,
a wailing tune, a funeral march, charred bone and
shadows. Pulpy eulogy, this spell of history, this story
of the diaspora, dingy, broken memory.

GAYATRI GOPINATH

37. IMPOSSIBLE DESIRES

In a particularly memorable scene in *My Beautiful Laundrette* (dir. Stephen Frears, 1985), British Pakistani screenwriter Hanif Kureishi's groundbreaking film about queer interracial desire in Thatcherite Britain, the white, working-class gay boy Johnny moves to unbutton the shirt of his lover, the upwardly mobile, Pakistan-born Omar. Omar initially acquiesces to Johnny's caresses, but then abruptly puts a halt to the seduction. He turns his back to his lover and recalls a boyhood scene of standing with his immigrant father and seeing Johnny march in a fascist parade through their South London neighborhood: "It was bricks and bottles, immigrants out, kill us. People we knew . . . And it was you. We *saw* you," Omar says bitterly. Johnny initially recoils in shame as Omar brings into the present this damning image from the past of his younger self as a hate-filled skinhead. But then, as Omar continues speaking; he slowly reaches out to draw Omar to him and embraces Omar from behind. The final shot frames Omar's face as he lets his head fall back onto Johnny's chest and he closes his eyes.

The scene eloquently speaks to how the queer racialized body becomes a historical archive for both individuals and communities; one that is excavated through the very act of desiring the racial Other. For Omar, desiring Johnny is irrevocably intertwined with the legacies of British colonialism in South Asia and the more immediate history of Powellian racism in 1960s Britain.[1] In his memory of having seen Johnny march ("we *saw* you"), Qmar in a sense reverses the historical availability of brown bodies to a white imperial gaze by turning the gaze back onto Johnny's own racist past. The scene's ambiguous ending—where Omar closes his eyes and succumbs to Johnny's caresses—may suggest that Omar gives in to the historical amnesia that wipes out the legacies of Britain's racist past. Yet the

meaning and function of queer desire in the scene are far more complicated than such a reading would allow. If for Johnny sex with Omar is a way of both tacitly acknowledging and erasing that racist past, for Omar, queer desire is precisely what allows him to remember. Indeed, the barely submerged histories of colonialism and racism erupt into the present at the very moment when queer sexuality is being articulated. Queer desire does not transcend or remain peripheral to these histories but instead it becomes central to their telling and remembering: there is no queer desire without these histories, nor can these histories be told or remembered without simultaneously revealing an erotics of power.

Upon its release in 1985, *My Beautiful Laundrette* engendered heated controversy within South Asian communities in the UK, some of whose members took exception to Kureishi's matter-of-fact depiction of queer interracial desire between white and brown men, and more generally to his refusal to produce "positive images" of British Asian lives.[2] The controversy surrounding its release prefigured the at times violent debates around queer sexuality and dominant notions of communal identity that took place both in South Asia and in the diaspora over the following decade.[3] In New York City, for instance, the South Asian Lesbian and Gay Association waged an ongoing battle throughout the 1990s over the right to march in the annual India Day Parade, a controversy I will return to later. . . . And in several Indian cities in December 1998, . . . Indian-Canadian director Deepa Mehta's film *Fire* was vociferously attacked by right-wing Hindu nationalists outraged by its depiction of "lesbian" sexuality. These various battles in disparate national locations speak to the ways in which queer desires, bodies, and subjectivities become dense sites of meaning in the production and reproduction of notions of "culture," "tradition," and communal belonging both in South Asia and in the diaspora. They also signal the conflation of "perverse" sexualities and diasporic affiliations within a nationalist imaginary, and it is this mapping of queerness onto diaspora that is the subject of this book.

Twenty years later, Kureishi's film remains a remarkably powerful rendering of queer racialized desire and its relation to memory and history, and acts as a touchstone and precursor to much of the queer South Asian diasporic cultural production that I discuss in *Impossible Desires*.[4] . . . *In Kureishi's film*, . . . queer desire reorients the traditionally backward-looking glance of diaspora. Stuart Hall has elegantly articulated the peculiar relation to the past that characterizes a conservative diasporic imaginary. This relation is one where the experience of displacement "gives rise to a certain imaginary plenitude, recreating the endless desire to return to 'lost origins,' to be one again with the mother, to go back to the beginning."[5] If conventional diasporic discourse is marked by this backward glance, this "overwhelming nostalgia for lost origins, for 'times past,'"[6] a queer diaspora mobilizes questions of the past, memory, and nostalgia for radically different purposes. Rather than evoking an imaginary homeland frozen in an idyllic moment outside history, what is remembered through queer diasporic desire and the queer diasporic body is a past time and place riven with contradictions and the violences of multiple uprootings, displacements, and exiles. Joseph Roach, in his study of Atlantic-rim performance cultures, uses the suggestive phrase "forgotten but not gone" to name that which produces the conditions for the present but is actively forgotten within dominant historiography.[7] Queer diasporic cultural forms and practices point to submerged histories of racist and colonialist violence that continue to resonate in the present and that make themselves felt through bodily desire. It is through the queer diasporic body that these histories are brought into the present; it is also through the queer diasporic body that their legacies are imaginatively contested and transformed. Queer diasporic cultural forms thus enact what Roach terms "clandestine countermemories" that bring into the present those pasts that are deliberately forgotten within conventional nationalist or diasporic scripts.[8] If, as Roach notes, "the relentless search for the purity of origins is a voyage not of discovery but of erasure,"[9] queer diasporic cultural forms work against the violent effacements that produce the fictions of purity that lie at the heart of dominant nationalist and diasporic ideologies.

Significantly, however, Kureishi's excavation of the legacies of colonialism and racism as they are mapped onto queer (male) bodies crucially depends on a particular fixing of female diasporic subjectivity. The film's female diasporic character Tania, in fact, functions in a classic homosocial triangle as the conduit and foil to the desire between Johnny and Omar, and she quite literally disappears at the film's end. We last see her standing on a train platform, suitcase in hand, having left behind the space of the immigrant home in order to seek a presumably freer elsewhere. Our gaze is aligned with that of her father as he glimpses her through an open window; the train rushes by, she vanishes. It is unclear where she has gone, whether she has disappeared under the train tracks or is safely within the train compartment en route to a different life. She thus marks the horizon of Kureishi's filmic universe and gestures to another narrative of female diasporic subjectivity that functions quite literally as the film's vanishing point. Kureishi's framing of the female diasporic figure makes clear the ways in which even ostensibly progressive, gay male articulations of diaspora run the risk of stabilizing sexual and gender hierarchies.

My Beautiful Laundrette presents a useful point of departure in addressing many of the questions that concern me. . . . As the film makes apparent, all too often diasporas are narrativized through the bonds of relationality between men. Indeed, the oedipal relation between fathers and sons serves as a central and recurring feature within diasporic narratives and becomes a metaphor for the contradictions of sameness and difference that, as Stuart Hall has shown, characterize competing definitions of diasporic subjectivity.[10] For Freud, the oedipal drama explains the consolidation of proper gender identification and heterosexual object choice in little boys, as masculine identification with the father is made while feminine identification with the mother is refused. In his 1952 work *Black Skin, White Masks*, Frantz Fanon resituates the oedipal scenario in the colonial context and shows how, for racialized male subjects, the process whereby the little boy learns to identify with the father and desire the mother is disrupted and disturbed by the (black) father's lack of access to social power.[11] Fanon's analysis, . . . makes evident the inadequacy of the Oedipus complex in explaining the construction of gendered subjectivity within colonial and postcolonial regimes of power. While I am interested in identifying how queer diasporic texts follow Fanon in reworking the notion of oedipality in relation to racialized masculinities, I also ask what alternative narratives emerge when this story of oedipality is jettisoned altogether. For even when the male-male or father-son narrative is mined for its queer valences (as in *Laundrette* or in other gay male diasporic texts I consider here), the centrality of this narrative as the primary trope in imagining diaspora invariably displaces and elides female diasporic subjects. The patriarchal and heteronormative underpinnings of the term "diaspora" are evident in Stefan Helmreich's exploration of its etymological roots:

> The original meaning of diaspora summons up the image of scattered seeds and . . . in Judeo-Christian . . . cosmology, seeds are metaphorical for the male "substance" that is traced in genealogical histories. The word "sperm" is metaphorically linked to diaspora. It comes from the same stem [in Greek meaning to sow or scatter] and is defined by the OED as "the generative substance or seed of male animals." Diaspora, in its traditional sense, thus refers us to a system of kinship reckoned through men and suggests the questions of legitimacy in paternity that patriarchy generates.[12]

These etymological traces of the term are apparent in Kureishi's vision of queer diasporic subjectivity that centralizes male-male relations and sidelines female subjectivity. . . . *Impossible Desires* examines a range of South Asian diasporic literature, film, and music in order to ask if we can imagine diaspora differently, apart from the biological, reproductive, oedipal logic that invariably forms the core of conventional formulations of diaspora. It does so by paying special attention to *queer female subjectivity in the diaspora*, as it is this particular positionality that forms a constitutive absence in both dominant nationalist and diasporic discourses. More surprisingly perhaps, and therefore worth interrogating closely, is the elision of queer female subjectivity within seemingly radical cultural and political diasporic projects that center a gay male

or heterosexual feminist diasporic subject. *Impossible Desires* refuses to accede to the splitting of queerness from feminism that marks such projects. By making female subjectivity central to a queer diasporic project, it begins instead to conceptualize diaspora in ways that do not invariably replicate heteronormative and patriarchal structures of kinship and community. In what follows I lay out more precisely the various terms I use to frame the texts I consider—*queer diasporas, impossibility,* and *South Asian public cultures—as* they are hardly self-evident and require greater elaboration and contextualization.

QUEER DIASPORAS

In an overview of recent trends in diaspora studies, Jana Evans Braziel and Anita Mannur suggest that the value of diaspora—a term which at its most literal describes the dispersal and movement of populations from one particular national or geographic location to other disparate sites—lies in its critique of the nation form on the one hand, and its contestation of the hegemonic forces of globalization on the other.[13] Nationalism and globalization do indeed constitute the two broad rubrics within which we must view diasporas and diasporic cultural production. However, the concept of diaspora may not be as resistant or contestatory to the forces of nationalism or globalization as it may first appear. Clearly, as Braziel and Mannur indicate, diaspora has proved a remarkably fruitful analytic for scholars of nationalism, cultural identity, race; and migration over the past decade. Theories of diaspora that emerged out of Black British cultural studies in the 1980s and 1990s, particularly those of Paul Gilroy and Stuart Hall, powerfully move the concept of diaspora away from its traditional orientation toward homeland, exile, and return and instead use the term to reference what Hall calls "a conception of 'identity' which lives with and through, not despite, difference; by hybridity."[14] This tradition of cultural studies, to which my project is deeply indebted, embraces diaspora as a concept for its potential to foreground notions of impurity and inauthenticity that resoundingly reject the ethnic and religious absolutism at the center of nationalist projects. Viewing the (home) nation through the analytical frame of diaspora allows for a reconsideration of the traditionally hierarchical relation between nation and diaspora, where the former is seen as merely an impoverished imitation of an originary national culture.[15] Yet the antiessentialist notion of cultural identity that is at the core of this revised framing of diaspora functions simultaneously alongside what Hall terms a "backward-looking conception of diaspora,"[16] one that adheres to precisely those same myths of purity and origin that seamlessly lend themselves to nationalist projects. Indeed while the diaspora within nationalist discourse is often positioned as the abjected and disavowed Other to the nation, the nation also simultaneously recruits the diaspora into its absolutist logic. The policies of the Hindu nationalist government in India in the mid– to late 1990s to court overseas "NRI" (non-resident Indian) capital[17] is but one example of how diaspora and nation can function together in the interests of corporate capital and globalization.[18] Hindu nationalist organizations in India are able to effectively mobilize and harness diasporic longing for authenticity and "tradition" and convert this longing into material linkages between the diaspora and (home) nation.[19] Thus diasporas can undercut and reify various forms of ethnic, religious, and state nationalisms simultaneously. Various scholars have pointed out the complicity not only between diasporic formations and different nationalisms but also between diaspora and processes of transnational capitalism and globalization.[20] The intimate connection between diaspora, nationalism, and globalization is particularly clear in the South Asian context, as the example of NRI capital underwriting Hindu nationalist projects in India makes all too apparent.

Vijay Mishra importantly distinguishes between two historical moments of South Asian diasporic formation: the first produced by colonial capitalism and the migration of Indian indentured labor to British colonies such as Fiji, Trinidad, and Guyana in the late nineteenth and early twentieth centuries; and the second a result of the workings of "late modern capital" in the mid– to late twentieth century. Significantly, in addition to producing labor diasporas, colonial capitalism also produced what Kamala Visweswaran terms a "middleman minority" that served the interests of the colonial power and acted as a conduit between British colonial administrators and the indigenous populations in East Africa and other locations in the British Empire.[21] The legacies of this initial phase of South Asian diasporic formation in the nineteenth century are apparent in the second phase of migration engendered by globalization in the mid– to late twentieth century. Mishra defines this diaspora of "late modern capital" as "largely a post-1960s phenomenon distinguished by the movement of economic migrants (but also refugees) into the metropolitan centers of the former empire as well as the 'New World' and Australia."[22] While South Asian migrants in the 1960s were allowed entry into the UK primarily as low-wage labor, the class demographic and racialization of South Asians in the United States was strikingly different. Vijay Prashad has pointed out how the 1965 Immigration and Nationality Act, which shifted the criteria for U.S. citizenship from a quota system to "family reunification," encouraged the immigration of large numbers of Indian professionals, primarily doctors and scientists; this demographic was particularly appealing to the U.S. government in that it was seen as a way to bolster U.S. cold war technological supremacy.[23] Visweswaran argues that this professional technocratic elite in the United States functions in effect as a latter-day middleman minority, working in collusion with dominant national interests in both the United States and in India. Mishra, Prashad, and Visweswaran thus point to the ways in which South Asian diasporic formations engendered by colonial capitalism (in the form of labor diasporas) and those engendered by globalization and transnational capitalism (in the form of a bourgeois professional class) function in tandem with different national agendas.

Clearly, then, the cultural texts that emerge from these different historical moments in South Asian diasporic formation must be seen as inextricable not only from the ongoing legacies of colonialism and multiple nationalisms but also from the workings of globalization. Indeed theories of diasporic cultural production that do not address the imbrication of diaspora with transnational capitalism shore up the dominance of the latter by making its mechanisms invisible. In an astute critique of Paul Gilroy's influential formulation of black diasporic culture in *The Black Atlantic*, Jenny Sharpe argues that globalization provides the unacknowledged terrain upon which the diasporic cultural productions that Gilroy celebrates take shape. Sharpe notes that the transnational cultural practices that Gilroy draws on are rooted in urban spaces in the First World: "to consider London and New York as global city centers is to recognize the degree to which Gilroy's mapping of the black Atlantic follows a cartography of globalization."[24] Sharpe's analysis is a particularly useful caution against a celebratory embrace of diasporic cultural forms that may obscure the ways in which they are produced on the terrain of corporate globalization. Thus just as diaspora may function in collusion with nationalist interests, so too must we be attentive to the ways in which diasporic cultural forms are produced in and through transnational capitalist processes.

The imbrication of diaspora and diasporic cultural forms with dominant nationalism on the one hand, and corporate globalization on the other, takes place through discourses that are simultaneously gendered and sexualized. Feminist scholars of nationalism in South Asia have long pointed to the particular rendering of "woman" within nationalist discourse as the grounds upon which male nationalist ideologies take shape.[25] Such scholarship has been instructive in demonstrating how female sexuality under nationalism is a crucial site of surveillance, as it is through women's bodies that the borders and boundaries of communal identities are formed. . . . Feminist scholarship on South Asia has also, for the most part, remained curiously silent about how alternative sexualities may constitute a powerful challenge to patriarchal nationalism.[26] Nor has there been much sustained attention paid to the ways in which nationalist framings of women's sexuality are translated into the diaspora, and how these renderings of diasporic women's sexuality are in turn central to the production of nationalism in the home nation.[27] In an article on Indian indentured migration to Trinidad, Tejaswini Niranjana begins this necessary work by observing that anticolonial nationalists in India in the early twentieth century used the figure of the amoral, sexually impure Indian woman abroad as a way of producing the chaste, virtuous Indian woman at "home" as emblematic of a new "nationalist morality."[28] The consolidation of a gendered bourgeois nationalist subject in India through a configuration of its disavowed Other in the diaspora underscores the necessity of conceptualizing the diaspora and the nation as mutually constituted formations.

However, . . . Niranjana's article still presumes the heterosexuality of the female diasporic and female nationalist subject rather than recognizing institutionalized heterosexuality as a primary structure of both British colonialism and incipient Indian nationalism. The failure of feminist scholars of South Asia and the South Asian diaspora to fully interrogate heterosexuality as a structuring mechanism of both state and diasporic nationalisms makes clear the indispensability of a queer critique. A queer diasporic framework insists on the imbrication of nation and diaspora through the production of hetero- and homosexuality, particularly as they are mapped onto the bodies of women.

Just as discourses of female sexuality are central to the mutual constitution of diaspora and nation, so too is the relation between diasporic culture and globalization one that is mediated through dominant gender and sexual ideologies. Feminist theorists have astutely observed that globalization profoundly shapes, transforms, and exploits the gendered arrangements of seemingly "private" zones in the diaspora such as the "immigrant home."[29] But while much scholarship focuses on how global processes function through the differentiation of the labor market along gendered, racial, and national lines, how discourses of sexuality in the diaspora intersect with, and are in turn shaped by, globalization is only beginning to be explored.[30] Furthermore, the impact of globalization on particular diasporic locations produces various forms of oppositional diasporic cultural practices that may both reinscribe and disrupt the gender and sexual ideologies on which globalization depends.

The critical framework of a specifically *queer* diaspora, then, may begin to unsettle the ways in which the diaspora shores up the gender and sexual ideologies of dominant nationalism on the one hand, and processes of globalization on the other. Such a framework enables the concept of diaspora to fulfill the double-pronged critique of the nation and of globalization that Braziel and Mannur suggest is its most useful intervention. This framework "queers" the concept of diaspora by unmasking and undercutting its dependence on a genealogical, implicitly heteronormative reproductive logic. Indeed, while the Bharatiya Janata Party-led Hindu nationalist government in India acknowledged the diaspora solely in the form of the prosperous, Hindu, heterosexual NRI businessman, there exists a different embodiment of diaspora that remains unthinkable within this Hindu nationalist imaginary. The category of "queer" in my project works to name this alternative rendering of diaspora and to dislodge diaspora from its adherence and loyalty to nationalist ideologies that are fully aligned with the interests of transnational capitalism. Suturing "queer" to "diaspora" thus recuperates those desires, practices, and subjectivities that are rendered impossible and unimaginable within conventional diasporic and nationalist imaginaries. A consideration of queerness, in other words, becomes a way to challenge nationalist ideologies by restoring the impure, inauthentic, nonreproductive potential of the notion of diaspora. Indeed, the urgent need to trouble and denaturalize the close relationship between nationalism and heterosexuality is precisely what makes the notion of a queer diaspora so compelling.[31] A queer diasporic framework productively exploits the analogous relation between nation and diaspora on the one hand, and between heterosexuality and queerness on the other: in other words, queerness is to heterosexuality as the diaspora is to the nation. If within heteronormative logic the queer is seen as the debased and inadequate copy of the heterosexual, so too is diaspora within nationalist logic positioned as the queer Other of the nation, its inauthentic imitation. The concept of a queer diaspora enables a simultaneous critique of heterosexuality and the nation form while exploding the binary oppositions between nation and diaspora, heterosexuality and homosexuality, original and copy.

If "diaspora" needs "queerness" in order to rescue it from its genealogical implications, "queerness" also needs "diaspora" in order to make it more supple in relation to questions of race, colonialism, migration, and globalization. An emerging body of queer of color scholarship has taken to task the "homonormativity" of certain strands of Euro-American queer studies that center white gay male subjectivity, while simultaneously fixing the queer, nonwhite racialized, and/or immigrant subject as insufficiently politicized and "modern."[32] My articulation of a queer diasporic framework is part of this collective project of decentering whiteness and dominant Euro-American paradigms in theorizing sexuality both locally and transnationally.

On the most simple level, I use "queer" to refer to a range of dissident and non-heteronormative practices and desires that may very well be incommensurate with the identity categories of "gay" and "lesbian." A queer diasporic formation works in contradistinction to the globalization of "gay" identity that replicates a colonial narrative of development and progress that judges all "other" sexual cultures, communities, and practices against a model of Euro-American sexual identity.[33] Many of the diasporic cultural forms I discuss . . . do indeed map a "cartography of globalization," in Sharpe's terms, in that they emerge out of queer communities in First World global cities such as London, New York, and Toronto. Yet we must also remember, as Lisa Lowe and David Lloyd point out, that "transnational or *neo-colonial* capitalism, like colonialist capitalism before it, continues to produce sites of contradiction that are effects of its always uneven expansion but that cannot be subsumed by the logic of commodification itself."[34] In other words, while queer diasporic cultural forms are produced in and through the workings of transnational capitalism, they also provide the means by which to critique the logic of global capital itself. The cartography of a queer diaspora tells a different story of how global capitalism impacts local sites by articulating other forms of subjectivity, culture, affect, kinship, and community that may not be visible or audible within standard mappings of nation, diaspora, or globalization. What emerges within this alternative cartography are subjects, communities, and practices that bear little resemblance to the universalized "gay" identity imagined within a Eurocentric gay imaginary.

Reading various cultural forms and practices as both constituting and constituted by a queer South Asian diaspora resituates the conventions by which homosexuality has traditionally been encoded in a Euro-American context. Queer sexualities as articulated by the texts I consider here reference familiar tropes and signifiers of Euro-American homosexuality—such as the coming-out narrative and its attendant markers of secrecy and disclosure, as well as gender inversion and cross-dressing—while investing them with radically different and distinct significations. It is through a particular engagement with South Asian public culture, and popular culture in particular, that this defamiliarization of conventional markers of homosexuality takes place, and that alternative strategies through which to signify non-heteronormative desire are subsequently produced. These alternative strategies suggest a mode of reading and "seeing" same-sex eroticism that challenges modern epistemologies of visibility, revelation, and sexual subjectivity. As such, the notion of a queer South Asian diaspora can be understood as a conceptual apparatus that poses a critique of modernity and its various narratives of progress and development.[35] A queer South Asian diasporic geography of desire and pleasure stages this critique by rewriting colonial constructions of "Third World" sexualities as anterior, pre-modern, and in need of Western political development—constructions that are recirculated by contemporary gay and lesbian transnational politics. It simultaneously interrogates different South Asian nationalist narratives that imagine and consolidate the nation in terms of organic heterosexuality.

The concept of a queer South Asian diaspora, then, functions on multiple levels. . . . First, it situates the formation of sexual subjectivity within transnational flows of culture, capital, bodies, desire, and labor. Second, queer diaspora contests the logic that situates the terms "queer" and "diaspora" as dependent on the originality of "heterosexuality" and "nation." Finally, it disorganizes the dominant categories within the United States for sexual variance, namely "gay and lesbian," and it marks a different economy of desire that escapes legibility within both normative South Asian contexts and homonormative Euro-American contexts.

The radical disruption of the hierarchies between nation and diaspora, heterosexuality and homosexuality, original and copy, that queer diasporic texts enact hinges on the question of translation. . . . In restoring the prior text as central to the discussion of the contemporary text, and in tracing the ways in which representations of queerness shift from "original" to "remake," I ask what is both lost and gained in this process of translation. Reading diasporic texts as translations may seem to run the risk of reifying the binary between copy and original; it risks stabilizing the "nation" as the original locus that diaspora merely attempts to replicate. Just as the nation and the diaspora are mutually constitutive categories, by extension so too do the "original" national text and its diasporic

translation gain meaning only in relation to one another. Tejaswini Niranjana, in her study of translation as a strategy of colonial subjectification, observes that translation functions within an idiom of fidelity, betrayal, and authenticity and appears "as a transparent representation of something that already exists, although the 'original' is actually brought into being through translation."[36] In the juxtaposition of texts that I engage in, the queerness of either text can only be made intelligible when read against the other.[37] Furthermore, reading contemporary queer representations (such as Mehta's *Fire)* through their "originals" . . . militates against a developmental, progress narrative of "gay" identity formation that posits the diaspora as a space of sexual freedom over and against the (home) nation as a space of sexual oppression. Rather, I am interested in how the erotic economies of the prior text are mapped differently within a diasporic context. Translation here cannot be seen as a mimetic reflection of a prior text but rather as a productive activity that instantiates new regimes of sexual subjectivity even as it effaces earlier erotic arrangements.

Finally, in its most important intervention into dominant nationalist and diasporic formations, the framework of a queer diaspora radically resituates questions of home, dwelling, and the domestic space that have long concerned feminist, queer, and postcolonial scholarship. Historians of colonialism and anticolonial nationalism in India have examined in detail the ways in which home and housing were crucial to the production of both a British colonial and Indian anticolonial nationalist gendered subjectivity in the nineteenth century.[38] Partha Chatterjee argues that in late-colonial India, "the battle for the new idea of womanhood in the era of nationalism was waged in the home . . . it was the home that became the principal site of the struggle through which the hegemonic construct of the new nationalist patriarchy had to be normalized."[39] Contemporary nationalist and diasporic discourses clearly bear the marks of these colonial and anticolonial nationalist legacies of "home" as a primary arena within which to imagine "otherness" in racial, religious, national, and gendered terms. The "home" within both discourses is a sacrosanct space of purity, tradition, and authenticity, embodied by the figure of the "woman" who is enshrined at its center, and marked by patriarchal gender and sexual arrangements. It is hardly surprising, then, that the home emerges as a particularly fraught site of contestation within the queer diasporic texts I discuss. . . .

Just as the home has been a major site of inquiry within feminist postcolonial scholarship, queer studies has also been particularly attuned to the home as a primary site of gender and sexual oppression for queer and female subjects.[40] Yet while many lesbian and gay texts imagine "home" as a place to be left behind, to be escaped in order to emerge into another, more liberatory space, the queer South Asian diasporic texts I consider here are more concerned with remaking the space of home from within. For queer racialized migrant subjects, "staying put" becomes a way of remaining within the oppressive structures of the home—as domestic space, racialized community space, and national space—while imaginatively working to dislodge its heteronormative logic.[41] From the two sisters-in-law who are also lovers in Deepa Mehta's film *Fire,* to a British Asian gay son's grappling with his immigrant father in Ian Rashid's short film *Surviving Sabu,* to the queer and transgendered protagonists of Shani Mootoo's and Shyam Selvadurai's novels, home is a vexed location where queer subjects whose very desires and subjectivities are formed by its logic simultaneously labor to transform it.

Historian Antoinette Burton writes of how, in the memoirs of elite women writers in late-colonial India, the "home" itself becomes an archive, "a dwelling-place of a critical history rather than the falsely safe space of the past."[42] Similarly, the queer diasporic texts I discuss . . . provide a minute detailing and excavation of the various forms of violence and, conversely, possibility and promise that are enshrined within "home" space. These queer diasporic texts evoke "home" spaces that are permanently and already ruptured, rent by colliding discourses around class, sexuality, and ethnic identity. They lay claim to both the space of "home" and the nation by making both the site of desire and pleasure in a nostalgic diasporic imaginary. The heteronormative home, in these texts, unwittingly generates homoeroticism. This resignification of "home" within a queer diasporic imaginary makes three crucial interventions: first, it forcefully repudiates the elision of queer subjects from national and diasporic memory;

second, it denies their function as threat to family/community/nation; and third, it refuses to position queer subjects as alien, inauthentic, and perennially outside the confines of these entities.

IMPOSSIBILITY

Because the figure of "woman" as a pure and unsullied sexual being is so central to dominant articulations of nation and diaspora, the radical disruption of "home" that queer diasporic texts enact is particularly apparent in their representation of queer female subjectivity. I use the notion of "impossibility" as a way of signaling the unthinkability of a queer female subject position within various mappings of nation and diaspora. My foregrounding of queer female diasporic subjectivity . . . is not simply an attempt to merely bring into visibility or recognition a heretofore invisible subject. Indeed, as I have suggested, many of the texts I consider run counter to standard "lesbian" and "gay" narratives of the closet and coming out that are organized exclusively around a logic of recognition and visibility. Instead, I scrutinize the deep investment of dominant diasporic and nationalist ideologies in producing this particular subject position as impossible and unimaginable. Given the illegibility and unrepresentability of a non-heteronormative female subject within patriarchal and heterosexual configurations of both nation and diaspora, the project of locating a "queer South Asian diasporic subject"—and a queer female subject in particular—may begin to challenge the dominance of such configurations. Revealing the mechanisms by which a queer female diasporic positionality is rendered impossible strikes at the very foundation of these ideological structures. Thus, while this project is very much situated within the emergent body of queer of color work that I referenced earlier, it also parts ways with much of this scholarship by making a queer female subject the crucial point of departure in theorizing a queer diaspora. In so doing, *Impossible Desires* is located squarely at the intersection of queer and feminist scholarship and therefore challenges the notion that these fields of inquiry are necessarily distinct, separate, and incommensurate.[43] Instead, the book brings together the insights of postcolonial feminist scholarship on the gendering of colonialism, nationalism, and globalization, with a queer critique of the heteronormativity of cultural and state nationalist formations.[44]

The impossibility of imagining a queer female diasporic subject within dominant diasporic and nationalist logics was made all too apparent in the battle in New York City between the South Asian Lesbian and Gay Association (SALGA) and a group of Indian immigrant businessmen known as the National Federation of Indian Associations (NFIA), over SALGA's inclusion in the NFIA-sponsored annual India Day Parade. The India Day Parade—which runs down the length of Madison Avenue and is an ostensible celebration of India's independence from the British in 1947—is an elaborate performance of Indian diasporic identity, and a primary site of contestation over the borders and boundaries of what constitutes "Indianness" in the diaspora. In 1992 the newly formed SALGA applied for the right to march in the parade only to be brusquely turned down by the NFIA. Later that same year, right-wing Hindu extremists demolished the Babri Masjid, a Muslim shrine in Ayodhya, India, setting off a frenzy of anti–Muslim violence. These two events—the destruction of the Babri Masjid in Ayodhya, and the resistance on the part of the NFIA to SALGA's inclusion in the parade in New York City—are not as unrelated as they may initially appear. Paola Bacchetta has argued that one of the central tenets of Hindu nationalist ideology is the assignation of deviant sexualities and genders to all those who do not inhabit the boundaries of the Hindu nation, particularly Indian Muslims.[45] Thus, while these two events are certainly not comparable in terms of scale or the level of violence, together they mark the ways in which terrifyingly exclusivist definitions of communal belonging are relayed and translated between nation and diaspora within the realm of public culture, through intersecting discourses of gender, sexuality, nationality, and religion. The literal erasure of Muslims from the space of the (Hindu) nation coincides with the symbolic effacement of queer subjects from a "home" space nostalgically reimagined from the vantage point of the diaspora. Indeed the battle between SALGA and the NFIA that continued throughout the 1990s makes explicit how an Indian immigrant male bourgeoisie (embodied by the NFIA) reconstitutes Hindu nationalist discourses of communal belonging in India by interpellating

"India" as Hindu, patriarchal, middle class, and free of homosexuals.[46] This Hindu nationalist vision of home and homeland was powerfully contested by SALGA at the 1995 parade, where once again the group was literally positioned at the sidelines of the official spectacle of national reconstruction. One SALGA activist, Faraz Ahmed (aka Nina Chiffon), stood at the edge of the parade in stunning, Bollywood-inspired drag, holding up a banner that proclaimed, "Long Live Queer India!" The banner, alongside Ahmed's performance of the hyperbolic femininity of Bollywood film divas, interpellated not a utopic future space of national belonging but rather an already existing queer diasporic space of insurgent sexualities and gender identities.

That same year, the NFIA attempted to specify its criteria for exclusion by denying both SALGA and Sakhi for South Asian Women (an anti-domestic violence women's group) the right to march on the grounds that both groups were, in essence, "antinational." The official grounds for denying Sakhi and SALGA the right to march was ostensibly that both groups called themselves not "Indian" but "South Asian." The possibility of Pakistanis, Bangladeshis, or Sri Lankans marching in an "Indian" parade was seen by NFIA members as an unacceptable redefinition of what constituted the so-called Indian community in New York City. In 1996, however, the NFIA allowed Sakhi to participate while continuing to deny SALGA the right to march. The NFIA, as self-styled arbiter of communal and national belonging, thus deemed it appropriate for women to march as "Indian women," even perhaps as "feminist Indian women," but could not envision women marching as "Indian queers" or "Indian lesbians"; clearly the probability that there may indeed exist "lesbians" within Sakhi was not allowed for by the NFIA.

The controversy surrounding the India Day Parade highlights how hegemonic nationalist discourses, produced and reproduced in the diaspora, position "woman" and "lesbian" as mutually exclusive categories to be disciplined in different ways. Ananya Bhattacharjee's work on domestic violence within Indian immigrant communities in the United States, for instance, demonstrates how immigrant women are positioned by an immigrant male bourgeoisie as repositories of an essential "Indianness." Thus any form of transgression on the part of women may result in their literal and symbolic exclusion from the multiple "homes" which they as immigrant women inhabit: the patriarchal, heterosexual household, the extended "family" made up of an immigrant community, and the national spaces of both India and the United States.[47] Sunaina Maira's ethnography of South Asian youth culture in New York City further documents the ways in which notions of chastity and sexual purity in relation to second-generation daughters are "emblematic not just of the family's reputation but also, in the context of the diaspora, of the purity of tradition and ethnic identity, a defense against the promiscuity of 'American influences.'"[48] Both Bhattacharjee and Maira valuably point to the complex ways in which the gendered constructions of South Asian nationalism are reproduced in the diaspora through the figure of the "woman" as the boundary marker of ethnic/racial community in the "host" nation. The "woman" also bears the brunt of being the embodied signifier of the "past" of the diaspora, that is, the homeland that is left behind and continuously evoked. But what remains to be fully articulated in much feminist scholarship on the South Asian diaspora are the particularly disastrous consequences that the symbolic freight attached to diasporic women's bodies has for non-heteronormative female subjects. Within the patriarchal logic of an Indian immigrant bourgeoisie, a "nonheterosexual Indian woman" occupies a space of impossibility, in that she is not only excluded from the various "home" spaces that the "woman" is enjoined to inhabit and symbolize but, quite literally, simply cannot be imagined. Within patriarchal diasporic and nationalist logic, the "lesbian" can only exist outside the "home" as household, community, and nation of origin, whereas the "woman" can only exist within it. Indeed the "lesbian" is seen as "foreign," as a product of being too long in the West, and therefore is annexed to the "host" nation where she may be further elided—particularly if undocumented—as a nonwhite immigrant within both a mainstream (white) lesbian and gay movement and the larger body of the nation-state.

The parade controversy makes clear how the unthinkability of a queer female diasporic subject is inextricable from the nationalist overvaluation of the heterosexual female body; but it also functions in tandem with the simultaneous subordination of gay male subjectivity. Thus, . . . I pay close attention to the highly specific but intimately related modes of domination by which various racialized, gendered, classed, and sexualized bodies are disciplined and contained by normative notions of communal identity. The rendering of queer female diasporic subjectivity as "impossible" is a very particular ideological structure: it is quite distinct from, but deeply connected to, the fetishization of heterosexual female bodies and the subordination of gay male bodies within dominant diasporic and nationalist discourses.[49] *Impossible Desires* attempts to track the mutual dependency and intersections between these different modes of domination, as well as the particular forms of accommodation and resistance to which they give rise. . . . Thus, in their elision of queer female diasporic subjectivity, gay male and liberal feminist frameworks may be complicit with dominant nationalist and diasporic discourses.

While the phrase "impossible desires" refers specifically to the elision of queer female diasporic sexuality and subjectivity, I also use it to more generally evoke what José Rabasa, in his analysis of the Zapatista rebellion in Chiapas, Mexico, calls "a utopian horizon of alternative rationalities to those dominant in the West."[50] Noting that one of the rallying cries of the movement is "Exigíd lo imposible!" (Demand the impossible!), Rabasa understands the Zapatistas' evocation of pre-Columbian myths combined with a pointed critique of the North American Free Trade Agreement and former president Raúl Salinas's economic reforms as articulating a particular vision of time, history, and national collectivity that runs counter to that of dominant Mexican nationalism. The "impossibility" of the Zapatistas' subaltern narrative, argues Rabasa, lies in its incompatibility with the "modern" narratives of dominant nationalism that relegate indigenous people to the realm of the pre-political and the premodern. The power of the Zapatistas thus "resides in the new world they call forth—a sense of justice, democracy, and liberty that the government *cannot* understand because it calls for its demise."[51] It may initially appear incongruous to begin a study of gender, sexuality, and migration in the South Asian diaspora with an evocation of an indigenous peasant struggle in southern Mexico. However I find the notion of "the impossible," as articulated by Rabasa's reading of Zapatismo, to have a remarkable resonance with the project [I have] engaged in. . . . The phrase "Exigíd lo imposible!," in relation to a queer South Asian diaspora, suggests the range of oppositional practices; subjectivities, and alternative visions of collectivity that fall outside the developmental narratives of colonialism, bourgeois nationalism, mainstream liberal feminism, and mainstream gay and lesbian politics and theory. "Demanding the impossible" points to the failure of the nation to live up to its promises of democratic egalitarianism, and dares to envision other possibilities of existence exterior to dominant systems of logic.

SOUTH ASIAN PUBLIC CULTURES

I attempt to read the traces of "impossible subjects" as they travel within and away from "home" as domestic, communal, and national space. In so doing, I ask how we can identify the multitude of "small acts," as Paul Gilroy phrases it, that fall beneath the threshold of hegemonic nationalist and diasporic discourses.[52] This project of mapping the spaces of impossibility within multiple discourses necessitates an engagement with particular cultural forms and practices that are at the margins of what are considered legitimate sites of resistance or the "proper objects" of scholarly inquiry. The term "South Asian public cultures," in my project, functions to name the myriad cultural forms and practices through which queer subjects articulate new modes of collectivity and kinship that reject the ethnic and religious absolutism of multiple nationalisms, while simultaneously resisting Euro-American, homonormative models of sexual alterity. My understanding of the term builds on Arjun Appadurai and Carole Breckenridge's definition of "public culture" as a *"zone* of cultural debate" where "tensions and contradictions between national sites and transnational cultural processes" play out.[53] It is within the realm of diasporic public culture that competing notions of community, belonging, and authenticity are brought into stark relief. Such an understanding of public culture reveals the intimate connections between seemingly unrelated events such as the India Day Parade controversy and the destruction of the Babri Masjid that I just described. The queer diasporic public culture . . . takes the form of easily "recognizable"

cultural texts such as musical genres, films, videos, and novels that have a specifically transnational address even as they are deeply rooted in the politics of the local. But because queer diasporic lives and communities often leave traces that resist textualization, they allow us to rethink what constitutes a viable archive of South Asian diasporic cultural production in the first place.[54] Thus the archive of queer public culture that I track here also encompasses cultural interventions that are much harder to document, such as queer spectatorial practices, and the mercurial performances and more informal forms of sociality (both on stage and on the dance floor) that occur at queer night clubs, festivals, and other community events. This queer diasporic archive is one that runs against the grain of conventional diasporic or nationalist archives, in that it documents how diasporic and nationalist subjectivities are produced through the deliberate forgetting and violent expulsion, subordination, and criminalization of particular bodies, practices, and identities. This archive is the storing house for those "clandestine countermemories," to once again use Joseph Roach's phrase, through which sexually and racially marginalized communities reimagine their relation to the past and the present. By narrating a different history of South Asian diasporic formation, a queer diasporic archive allows us to memorialize the violences of the past while also imagining "other ways of being in the world,"[55] as Dipesh Chakravarty phrases it, that extend beyond the horizon of dominant nationalisms.

This different mode of conceptualizing the archive necessitates different reading strategies by which to render queer diasporic subjects intelligible and to mark the presence of what M. Jacqui Alexander terms an "insurgent sexuality" that works within and against hegemonic nationalist and diasporic logic.[56] Indeed, the representations of non-heteronormative desire within the texts I consider . . . call for an alternative set of reading practices, a queer diasporic reading that juxtaposes what appear to be disparate texts and that traces the cross-pollination between the various sites of non-normative desires that emerge within them. On the one hand, such a reading renders intelligible the particularities of same-sex desiring relations within spaces of homosociality and presumed heterosexuality; on the other hand, it deliberately wrenches particular scenes and moments out of context and extends them further than they would want to go. It exploits the tension in the texts between the staging of female homoerotic desire as simply a supplement to a totalizing heterosexuality and the potential they raise for a different logic and organization of female desire. Because it is consistently under erasure from dominant historical narratives, the archive of a queer diaspora is one that is necessarily fractured and fragmented. I therefore employ a kind of scavenger methodology that finds evidence of queer diasporic lives and cultures, and the oppositional strategies they enact, in the most unlikely of places—the "home" being one such key location. As we see in relation to "home," often what looks like a capitulation to dominant ideologies of nation and diaspora may in fact have effects that dislodge these ideologies; conversely what may initially appear as a radically oppositional stance may simply reinscribe existing power relations.

NOTES

1. For an analysis of the racist ideology espoused by the British politician Enoch Powell in the 1960s, see Anna Marie Smith, *New Right Discourse on Race and Sexuality*.
2. See Ian Iqbal Rashid, "Passage to England," for a discussion of *My Beautiful Laundrette's* reception by the "cultural left" in the UK in the 1980s.
3. In its most general sense, the term "communal" is used here and throughout the book to reference notions of community and collectivity; more specifically, my use of "communal" is meant to evoke the term "communalism," which in the South Asian context names a politics of religious nationalism and the persecution of religious minorities, particularly on the part of the Hindu right.
4. The category of "South Asian" encompasses populations that originated *from* Bangladesh, Bhutan, India, Nepal, Pakistan, and Sri Lanka. Ananya Bhattacharjee provides a useful gloss on the term, which gained increasing currency in the 1980s and 1990s within progressive communities in the United States in order to signal a broad politics of coalition that rejected the narrow nationalisms of mainstream South Asian diasporic organizations. Bhattacharjee notes that despite its progressive valence, "South Asian" as an identity marker remains a deeply problematic term, given its origins in area studies and cold war rhetoric, as well as its capacity to evade questions of Indian regional hegemony. See "The Public/Private Mirage," 309–10. Despite these limitations, I find the category "South Asian" invaluable in tracing the lines of commonality and difference between various experiences of racialization of diasporic communities within different national locations. Clearly the history of racialization of immigrants from the Indian subcontinent is vastly different depending on religion, class, and nation of origin in each of these national sites. Nevertheless the term continues to be useful as it produces strategic transnational identifications that allow for a critique of dominant notions of community in both South Asia and the diaspora.
5. Stuart Hall, "Cultural Identity and Diaspora," 245.
6. Ibid.
7. Joseph Roach, *Cities of the Dead*, 2.
8. Ibid., 20.
9. Ibid., 6.
10. Hall, "Cultural Identity and Diaspora," 245.
11. Frantz Fanon, *Black Skin, White Masks*, 151–53.
12. Stefan Helmreich, "Kinship, Nation and Paul Gilroy's Concept of Diaspora," 245.
13. Braziel and Mannur, "Nation, Migration, Globalization," 7.
14. Hall, "Cultural Identity and Diaspora," 244.

15. For an elaboration of how diasporic cultural forms reverse the diaspora-nation hierarchy, see Gayatri Gopinath, "Bombay, U.K., Yuba City."

16. Hall, "Cultural Identity and Diaspora," 244.

17. For instance, as Anupam Chander documents, the right-wing Hindu nationalist government of the Bharatiya Janata Party (BJP) issued "Resurgent India Bonds" following the international sanctions imposed on India after its nuclear tests in 1998. The BJP promoted the bonds by appealing to the diasporic nationalism of NRIS in an attempt to encourage them to invest in the "homeland." See Chander, "Diaspora Bonds." See also Vijay Prashad, *The Karma of Brown Folk,* 21, for a discussion of the Indian government's production of the category of "NRI" as an attempt to garner foreign exchange.

18. Another stark illustration of the double-sided character of diaspora was apparent during the savage state-sponsored violence against Muslims in Gujarat, India, in February 2002. The Hindu nationalist state government in Gujarat received the support of NRIS even while other anticommunalist NRI organizations in New York and San Francisco mobilized against the violence and the government's complicity in the killing and displacement of thousands of Indian Muslims.

19. Sunaina Maira, for instance, documents the ways in which second-generation Indian American youth in the United States are drawn to Hindu religious nationalist ideology as a way of fulfilling a desire to be "truly Indian." Maira, *Desis in the House,* 137.

20. I understand "globalization" and "transnationalism" as a range of processes that, following Arjun Appadurai's formulation, includes the global movements of labor, technology, capital, media, and ideologies. See Appadurai, "Disjuncture and Difference in the Global Cultural Economy." While transnationalism is the result of the exigencies of late capitalism, I also concur with Lisa Lowe and David Lloyd's assessment that understanding transnationalism as the homogenization of global culture "radically reduces possibilities for the creation of alternatives"; "Introduction," in *The Politics of Culture in the Shadow of Capital,* I. . . . [I am] therefore concerned with the particular cultural forms and practices that arise out of, and in contestation to, transnational capitalism.

21. Visweswaran, "Diaspora By Design," 5–29.

22. Vijay Mishra, *Bollywood Cinema,* 235.

23. Prashad, *The Karma of Brown Folk,* 74.

24. Jenny Sharpe, "Cartographies of Globalisation, Technologies of Gendered Subjectivities." I thank the author for permission to discuss her unpublished manuscript.

25. Some of the most influential works in the broad field of gender and nationalism in South Asia include the following: Kumkum Sangari and Sudesh Vaid, eds., *Recasting Women*; Zoya Hassan, ed., *Forging Identities*; Lata Mani, *Contentious Traditions*; Ritu Menon and Kamala Bhasin, eds., *Borders and Boundaries.*

26. Key exceptions include Ruth Vanita, ed. *Queering India*; Giti Thadani, *Sakhiyani*; Shohini Ghosh, "*Hum Aapke Hain Koun …!*"; Paola Baccheta, "When the (Hindu) Nation Exiles its Queers."

27. See Purnima Mankekar, "Brides Who Travel," for an examination of representations of diasporic women's sexuality in Hindi cinema.

28. Tejaswini Niranjana, "Left to the Imagination." See also Madhavi Kale, *Fragments of Empire,* for a discussion of Indian women's sexuality in the British Caribbean and discourses of both Indian and British nationalism.

29. See, for instance, Lisa Lowe's analysis of Asian immigrant women's labor in "Work, Immigration, Gender."

30. For collections that begin to map out this terrain, see Arnaldo Cruz Malavé and Martin Manalansan, eds., *Queer Globalizations*; Elizabeth Povinelli and George Chauncey, eds., *Thinking Sexuality Transnationally.*

31. Following from George Mosse's groundbreaking analysis of sexuality in Nazi Germany in *Nationalism and Sexuality*, an important body of work has emerged over the past decade that has unraveled the complex interrelation between discourses of sexuality and those of the nation. For a few key examples of this increasingly large and complex field, see Andrew Parker, ed., *Nationalisms and Sexualities*; M. Jacqui Alexander, "Erotic Autonomy as a Politics of Decolonization"; Anne McClintock, *Imperial Leather*; and more recently Licia Fiol Matta, *A Queer Mother for the Nation*.

32. Some exemplary instances of this growing body of literature in U.S. ethnic studies include the following: Martin Manalansan, *Global Divas*; José Muñoz, *Disidentifications*; Juana María Rodríguez, *Queer Latinidad*; Robert Reid Pharr, *Black Gay Man*; Philip Brian Harper, *Are We Not Men?*; David L. Eng, *Racial Castration*; Roderick Ferguson, *Aberrations in Black*; Nayan Shah, *Contagious Divides*.

33. See Martin Manalansan, "In the Shadow of Stonewall," for an important interrogation of contemporary gay transnational politics.

34. Lowe and Lloyd, *The Politics of Culture in the Shadow of Capital*, I.

35. The imbrication of narratives of "progress," "modernity," and "visibility" is made obvious in what Alexander terms "prevalent metropolitan impulses that explain the absence of visible lesbian and gay movements [in non-Western locations] as a defect in political conciousness and maturity, using evidence of publicly organized lesbian and gay movements in the U.S. . . . as evidence of their orginary status (in the West) and superior political maturity." Alexander, "Erotic Autonomy as a Politics of Decolonization," 69.

36. Tejaswini Niranjana, *Siting Translation*, 3.

37. I thank Alys Weinbaum for her thoughtful feedback on the question of translation.

38. Antoinette Burton, *Dwelling in the Archive*.

39. Partha Chatterjee, *The Nation and Its Fragments*, 133.

40. Biddy Martin and Chandra Talpade Mohanty, "Feminist Politics."

41. For an elaboration of the notion of "staying" for queer subjects, see Anne Marie Fortier, "Coming Home."

42. Burton, *Dwelling in the Archive*, 29.

43. As such, I trace the genealogy of this project back to the rich body of radical women of color scholarship of the late 1970s and 1980s that insistently situated lesbian sexuality within a feminist, antiracist, and anticolonial framework. Such work includes Audre Lorde's *Zami*; Cherrie Moraga, *Loving in the War Years*; Cherrie Moraga and Gloria Anzaldúa, eds., *This Bridge Called My Back*; Gloria Anzaldúa, *Borderlands/La Frontera*; Barbara Smith, ed., *Home Girls*.

44. Queer Euro-American scholarship has done the crucial work of revealing the heteronormativity of dominant U.S. nationalism. Such work includes Gayle Rubin's groundbreaking essay "Thinking Sex"; Michael Warner, *The Trouble with Normal*; Lisa Duggan, *Sapphic Slashers* and *The Twilight of Equality?*

45. Paola Baccheta, "When the (Hindu) Nation Exiles its Queers."

46. For a discussion of how the "Indian immigrant bourgeoisie" constructs itself as unnamed and universal, see Ananya Bhattacharjee, "The Habit of Ex-Nomination."

47. Bhattacharjee, "The Public/Private Mirage."

48. Maira, *Desis in the House*, 49.

49. I thank Chandan Reddy for asking me to elaborate on the specificity of different modes of domination.

50. José Rabasa, "Of Zapatismo."

51. Ibid., 421.

52. Paul Gilroy, *Small Acts.*

53. See Appadurai and Breckenridge, "Public Modernity in India," for an explication of the term "public culture" in relation to South Asia. The authors use "public culture" in contradistinction to Habermas's notion of the "public sphere" as a depoliticized zone dominated by the mass media. Instead, the term "public culture" captures the sense of resistance, co-optation, critique, and agency with which subaltern groups interact with popular culture.

54. José Muñoz theorizes the ephemeral nature of queer cultural production in "Gesture, Ephemera, Queer Feeling," 433. For an extended discussion of queer archives and public cultures, see Ann Cvetkovich, 1–14.

55. Dipesh Chakravarty, *Provincializing Europe,* 66.

56. M. Jacqui Alexander, "Erotic Autonomy as a Politics of Decolonization," 86.

MARTIN F. MANALANSAN

38. MIGRANCY, MODERNITY, MOBILITY: QUOTIDIAN STRUGGLES AND QUEER DIASPORIC INTIMACY

I was sitting in a cramped apartment in Queens, New York, in the spring of 1992 after talking for more than an hour with Roberto, one of my informants, when he suddenly blurted, "Look around you, this is not the glamorous life that people back in Manila think I have. They all believe I live in a brownstone or a spacious house on Fifth Avenue—like the ones in the movies and TV. They don't know the daily drama I have to go through here just to make it. Although if you ask me whether I would exchange the struggle here with a cushy life over back in the Philippines, never darling, never!"[1]

The complicated twists and turns of Roberto's declaration reveal a particular dimension of gay life that is often missed if not ignored in queer scholarship—the daily life struggles and experiences of queer immigrant men of color. This essay focuses on my ethnographic fieldwork research with Filipino gay immigrant men living in the New York City area. I use the term "gay" as a provisional term and intersperse it with "queer" as a rubric and to signal the cultural dissonance queer immigrants experience with identity categories and cultural practices.

I conducted research from 1990 to 1995 focusing on the various strategies of identity articulation and self-formation of Filipino gay immigrants. My fieldwork involved over a hundred informal interviews and countless observations in various sites such as bars, households, and streets, but the whole project is built around fifty life history interviews of Filipino gay immigrants who have a median age of thirty-one and have lived in the United States from two years to thirty years.[2]

I am interested in the ways the seemingly mundane activities of daily life construct a vital arena in which to investigate various underexplored issues, specifically the connections between everyday life, intimacy, and diasporic queer identity formation. While there has been an emerging body of scholarship in recent years around the travails and travels of gay identity and peoples within a globalizing world, most of these works have concentrated on social movements that provide panoramic snapshots of people and communities on the verge of universal queer comradeship. While the works of Barry, Dyvendak, and Krouwel and Altman[3] have ably analyzed global efforts of queer social movements that are demanding rights and creating viable communities in various parts of the world, they have overemphasized collective and organized acts with little or no regard to how queer subjects apprehend and negotiate the cultural products of these transnational movements of ideas, technology, and people.

Following Appadurai's reworking of locality,[4] I am interested in the interscalar connections between the lived locality and the larger seemingly more expansive sites of the city, the nation, and the global. More important, this essay is a response to the overvalorization of circuits and flows in the study of queer globalization and transnationalism; it highlights how queer subjects mediate these processes.[5]

While heavily influenced by the body of lesbian and gay community research, my work departs from it by centering on the seemingly private and banal aspects of queer people's lives. While most ideas about queer community and identity formations are based on organized public enactments of gayness and lesbianness, the focus on the everyday reveals not only the inadequacy of conventional narratives where self and community progressively unfold, it also points to the complexities of various intersections and borderlands of race, gender, class, and sexuality in diasporic and immigrant groups. The every-day also troubles, if not resists, the conventional time-space binary by expressing the ways in which memory is spatialized and space is entangled with intimate habits, routines, personal histories, and deviant chronologies.[6] Moreover, influenced by the works of the social theorist Michel de Certeau and the feminist sociologist Dorothy Smith,[7] I take the everyday as a crucial "problematic" and as a site of tactical maneuvers for creating selves and forging relationships for marginalized groups, particularly diasporic queers everywhere. In other words, the focus on the quotidian life unveils the veneer of the ordinary and the commonplace to lay bare the intricate and difficult hybrid negotiations and struggles between hegemonic social forces and voices from below.

This essay documents a specific instance, a case or moment if you will, that grounds the cultural, political, and historical specificities of Filipino diasporic gay men's experiences within the uneven yet hegemonic power of global capitalist expansion. These men's experiences are anchored to the Philippines' long enduring political, cultural, historical, and economic connections to the United States and being part of the intensification of movement of labor and capital in the late twentieth century.[8] Yet this contextual anchoring is a backdrop to the creative tensions between these men's individual predicaments and larger social forces.

Everyday life is a site for critically viewing and "reading" modernity.[9] Unlike traditional historiography, which depends on grand narratives of "famous men" and great events, the narrative of everyday life reveals the rich intricacies of the commonplace. Everyday life intersects and engages with the intimate, the private, and the search for home in modern life. While these three sites are not necessarily equivalent to each other, I would argue that they meet at critical junctures, especially in the displaced lives of queer immigrants.

Intimacy, according to Lauren Berlant, is a crucial yet ambivalent practice in modern life because of its connections to domesticated and normative forms of relationships and spaces such as home, family, and privacy.[10] If home, privacy, and domesticity are vexed locations for queer subjects, particularly those in the diaspora,[11] then it follows that queers struggles toward finding, building, remembering, and settling into a home, as well as the displacements brought about by

migration, create a sphere of what has been called diasporic intimacy.[12] Diasporic intimacy constitutes these struggles that showcase the different ways in which the state, public life, and the "world" outside intrude on and permeate these seemingly bounded, private, and domestic spaces of home and how diasporic subjects confront them. The process of creating diasporic intimacy can be achieved either through counterpublic cultural productions[13] or through more mundane routes that translate and transform "the habitual estrangements of everyday life abroad."[14] Therefore, I suggest that everyday life is the space for examining the creation and rearticulation of queer selves in the diaspora.

My analysis of the everyday is shaped by my understanding of biyuti and drama, which are two emic concepts or idioms typically used in Filipino gay slang or what is called "swardspeak." Swardspeak, as I describe in earlier essays,[15] is an argot that showcases the hybrid cultural engagements of Filipino gay men; the syntax and lexicon of this speech style include Tagalog, Spanish, and English words in a virtual linguistic amalgam. More important, language as exemplified by swardspeak is one of the more crucial spaces for diasporic queers to inhabit particular positions and selves. The deployment of these linguistic concepts of biyuti and drama in the analysis aims to create the lenses through which Filipino gay men's voices, images, and ideas are filtered.

While biyuti and drama betray their provenance from the English language, their deployment in everyday discourse reveals their complex and intricate articulation with various issues of race, gender, class, sexuality, and nationality. "Biyuti,"[16] which may in fact refer to aesthetic experiences and features, also points to a particular notion of the self as highly mercurial and plastic. "Biyuti" is deployed in such situations as a daily greeting: "Kumusta na ang biyuti mo ngayon?" or "How is your biyuti today?" The closely related notion of drama refers to a theatricalized notion of the self and everyday life. Depending on the context, drama can refer to occupation, sexual orientation, health, or daily travails: "Ano ang drama mo ngayon?" or "What is your drama today?"; or conspiratorially when two Filipino gay men are speaking about another person's business, "Ano ba ang drama niya?" or "Now what is this guy's drama?"

The idioms of biyuti and drama are not mere instances of linguistic mimicry between the queer colonized and the gay metropole. Biyuti is not a literal appropriation of American gay camp aesthetics. Rather, Filipino gay men's worldview resonates with cultural practices of what is called Island Southeast Asia, which includes the Philippines and Indonesia. The play of surface, the logic of managing "turbulent hearts,"[17] and the presentation of the self in daily life are not products of the modern or postmodern West but are actually embedded in premodern rituals and ideas in Southeast Asia.[18]

This essay analyzes how these notions are deployed in everyday life situations and how they may illuminate the predicament of Filipino gay immigrant men as diasporic subjects. Through my ethnographic forays into queer everyday life, I seek to arrive at what Gayatri Gopinath termed "a more nuanced understanding of the traffic and travel of competing systems of desire in a transnational frame."[19] I present pivotal vignettes of two Filipino gay immigrants that provide the fulcrum for the mobilization of other narratives. These narratives are glimpses into the ways in which space, time, and selfhood are engaged with and confronted by Filipino gay men in the diaspora.

THE STORY OF AN APARTMENT

The first vignette is about Alden, a middle-aged Filipino gay man, and focuses on his apartment in Greenwich Village. Unlike most cinematic and televisual unreal renderings of the spacious and sophisticated New York City apartment, the small studio apartment will strike many New York City natives as typical, with nothing to really distinguish or mark it as different from other apartments of this type in the city. The living, sleeping, and eating/cooking quarters are situated within a space of twenty by thirty feet.

The furniture exuded a slightly worn quality that Alden acknowledged to be emblematic of a kind of bohemian lifestyle of the "old" Village that is slowly being eroded by the influx of straight white yuppies into the expensive condos and townhouses. Having lived in the same apartment since the early seventies, Alden is one of the lucky few in the city to be in a rent-stabilized apartment, paying a mere four hundred dollars a month to live there.

This apartment, Alden contends, is not just a place but also a story—the story of his life in America. Alden came to America in 1971, and he first lived with a female cousin in New Jersey. His parents thought that it would be important to have somebody to look after him and to serve as a surrogate parent. However, when he arrived at his cousin's house, the cousin declared that she was not about to be responsible for Alden. She admonished Alden to become more self-reliant, since that is what was needed to be able to succeed in America. He was expected to carry his own weight and pay part of the rent. Alden was dismayed at first, but after a while he admitted that it was "a different drama" that he had to learn.

He moved out after six months and stayed with a couple of Filipino men whom he knew from the private school he attended in Manila. After a few petty quarrels about rent, Alden moved out. He found this apartment after a few weeks of searching. He said that finding something on his own was a turning point. For him, it marked a distancing from his way of life in the Philippines where he lived in a big house with his parents, grandparents, unmarried sibling, and several maids. He shared a room with his brothers until he was seventeen. Getting his own room allowed him to create a world for himself. Remembering that moment, he looked around his present studio and said, "When I got my room [at seventeen], I did a full interior decoration. I went crazy and I made it really fabulous. . . . [My mother came into my room and then] she told me to throw out the loud curtains and throw pillows. . . . She said it looked like a [cheesy] dance hall. Here [in my Greenwich Village apartment] I can put in whatever I want. Look at that Herb Ritts poster [of a naked man]. I would not even think of putting that up back home; my mother would upbraid me."

Alden's apartment studio was a study in contrasts. Right across from the wall with the poster of a naked man is a corner he dubbed alternately the "guilt corner" or his "Filipino corner." This corner was in fact a wall filled with photographs, mainly of family members in the Philippines. Occupying the central part of this wall, right next to the television set and VCR, was an altar. He proudly showed me several religious images and statues his mother made him bring to America, mostly antiques that were owned by his great-grandmother. The religious figures included a crucifix, the Virgin Mary, and the Infant Jesus of Prague. When I asked him why he called this his "guilt corner," he said that sometimes life in America can get so frenetic and stressful that he sometimes forgets to call his family back home. After an extremely busy week at work, he would sit on his sofa and stare at the pictures and statues and suddenly feel guilty, then make his weekly overseas call to the Philippines. After a series of sexual encounters, the power of the corner would also befall him, and he would suddenly feel the impulse to pray and would try to become, as he said facetiously, "virtuous" again.

His apartment consists of two parts or sides, the American side with the poster and sofa and the Filipino side with the altar and family pictures. He said that by crossing the room, he traverses two boundaries of his two selves. "This part of the apartment is like the Philippines. So I only need to sashay to the other side, and I am back in America. This is how I feel, always going back and forth even if I have not actually gone home."

Alden still lives in his studio apartment to this day. He does not plan to move because of the rather prohibitive prices of new apartments in the city. When I last visited him in December 1995, a full year after our interview, he had replaced the Herb Ritts poster of the naked man with prints of French impressionists. He reasoned that he was getting old and Herb Ritts was quite passé. The altar was still there on the opposite wall. It still held the same arrangement of religious figures, except for a small bud vase with a yellow rose. Alden reminded me that his aunt was ailing back in the Philippines and he was praying for her.

EVERYDAY ROUTES TO GAY MODERNITY

Let us move both literally and figuratively from Alden's apartment to another vignette and another dimension of the everyday. Our move is from the meanings of mundane spaces to the meanings of banal activities—chores or routines. Roldan, a forty-year-old informant, arrived in the United States during the early eighties. I followed his daily activities for two straight weeks and off and on for several months. I kept a diary and recorded his daily, weekly, and monthly activities. The following are highlights of the two-week detailed record I made of his daily life. I knew him for five years before I asked him to allow me a voyeuristic view of his activities.

Every day Roldan got up early. He spent most of his weekdays at work and his weekends doing chores around his apartment in Queens. On Wednesday of the first week, after breakfast and putting on his office garb, he looked at the mirror and said, "Nobody would guess who is under this suit and tie. They might think I am a Wall Street executive or a successful career girl [he giggles]—oh, I really need more coffee—I must still be dreaming. People will take one look at me and say—immigrant—fresh off the boat." He then twirled around the mirror: "You know, people in the office treat me a little differently." When I asked him what he meant by a different treatment, he said, "it is difficult to say—you know my biyuti is Asian (Asiatika), so you never really know whether they think right away that I am effeminate or if they think I am gay because I am a thin frail-looking Asian . . . who knows?"

When I pressed further about this issue, he said, "When I used go to bars in the Village or Chelsea, I felt left out—you know I don't look good in a tight T-shirt. But then, when another Filipino gay friend told me about these cross-dressing bars—all of a sudden I found a different world where these gorgeous white men found me attractive." Roldan then revealed how he started to regularly go to cross-dressing bars in Manhattan every weekend. He said, "I used to think that I came to America to be gay, but then I realized that I came to America to be a real bakla." In this statement, "bakla" is a broad Tagalog rubric that encompasses cross-dressing, hermaphroditism, homosexuality, and effeminacy. He was referring to the fact that he always perceived gayness and gay culture as rooted both in the United States and ultramasculine images and practices. He was reflecting on the fact that he has become more of the bakla than the gay man he thought he was going to be in America because of his weekend leisure activities.

At the same time he was talking about this, Roldan talked about the dangers of being a cross-dresser in public. He was afraid of getting caught and thrown in jail. He was not worried about the embarrassment such a situation may potentially cause but about how such an incident might jeopardize his stay in America. I have known for a long time that Roldan was an undocumented immigrant. He confessed to me about his status in this way: "You know my biyuti is TNT." "TNT" is an acronym used in Filipino queer language or swardspeak and literally means "always in hiding"

He was proud of the fact that no one in the office knew about his immigration status. In fact, he once worked in a personnel department, and one of his duties was to check on the paperwork regarding job candidates' eligibility to work in the United States. Despite this irony, Roldan talked about the difficulty of being in such a legal limbo. He once considered a green card marriage but backed out. When I asked him why he backed out, he answered, "Do you think my biyuti can pass INS scrutiny? I don't think so, sister! One look at me and they will say—oh a big fag, a big bakla!" I countered that maybe the authorities may just see him as another slim Asian man. He said, "Oh, there is too much risk to do that drama, too much . . . I am too afraid." Then he paused for a second and said, "Well, you may be right. I know through the bakla grapevine that there is this . . . [he mentions a famous female impersonator in the Philippines] who was in a green card marriage. Darling, he is now a U.S. citizen. Oh well, he is used to the stage—I am not . . . or maybe I am not always on stage." Then he laughed, this time a little sadly.

He mentioned how he really cannot risk being caught in this situation. He has a family in the Philippines who are dependent on his monthly financial remittances. One weeknight, during the two-week period, Roldan received an urgent phone call from his mother. The phone call was unusual since they always talked on weekends. After talking to her for thirty minutes, Roldan hung up the phone with an irritated facial expression and breathed a long sigh. I asked him if anything was wrong. He said that his mother had just informed him that his youngest sister, whom he was sending to one of the most exclusive private schools in Manila, wanted to get married. She was seventeen years old. Roldan's mother wanted him to talk to the sister to convince her to continue her studies. Roldan was fuming mad, not only at his sister, but also at his mother who expected him to play surrogate father via an overseas phone call. Besides, he said, his father was still alive, but because of his vital role of being provider, he was by default given authority over specific family issues.

He made it clear to me that his family was not poor but middle-class. The money and goods he regularly sends back enable his family to be more comfortable economically, especially during the troubled times in the Philippines. He said that he was looking forward to the day when his responsibility would end. After saying this, he shook his head and admitted that

his previous statement was in fact wishful thinking. Then in a voice of surrender he said, "ganyan talaga ang drama—that is how the drama goes."

His weekends, apart from his jaunts to the cross-dressing bars, also included attendance at Sunday mass. He once took me to a church in Greenwich Village with a large Filipino congregation. As part of the service, slips of paper that people dropped in a box near the altar were taken out and read. These slips of paper contained petitions for God's intervention in mundane situations. There were petitions for better health and safe trips back to the Philippines, but there was a significant number of petitions about receiving the green card or passing the nursing licensure examinations. Roldan said, "You can't really mistake this drama for anything but Filipino."

STAGING QUEER DIASPORIC LIVES

These two vignettes provide an affirmation of the view that immigrants, particularly those from the Third World, "always perceive themselves onstage, their lives resembling a mediocre fiction with occasional romantic outbursts and gray dailiness."[20] Moreover, as Shohat and Stam have argued, these immigrants—or as they call them, "hybrid diasporic subject[s]"—are "confronted with the 'theatrical' challenge of moving, as it were, among diverse performative modes of sharply contrasting and ideological worlds."[21] In other words, citizenship for queers of color and diasporic queers—like Filipinos and those Latino immigrants and exiles that Roque Ramirez and Peña examine …—is not a birthright nor is it about the romance of dissidence; instead, it is about survival and making it.

Diasporic queers in particular refuse the assimilative framework; they not so much carry with them the baggage of tradition but rather are in constant negotiation, or—to use the idioms of biyuti and drama—selfhood and belonging are framed in the process of cultural translation and transformation. The concept of biyuti and drama partakes of this negotiated space between tradition and modernity as queer immigrants move or "sashay" between local, national, and global spaces. Their deployment by Filipino immigrant men living in New York City points to the kind of negotiations that create an "imperfect aesthetics of survival"[22] as well as a counternarrative to the prevailing view of the immigrant route as a movement away from tradition in the homeland and settling into an assimilated modern life in the land of settlement. Moreover, these idioms constitute what can be considered an alternative form of modernity.[23] The bakla or the Filipino gay man is neither a ludic nor an anachronous figure, but a subject in constant mediation whose modernity is not always dependent on Western mainstream queer culture.

The space of the everyday, as in Alden's apartment, portrays an ironic kind of movement inherent in "settling in." His narrative also portrays the possibility of performance in the global/local stage. That is, the story of his apartment narrates in spatial terms the constant engagements with experiences of emplacement and displacement. While physical distance from his family and the Philippines has allowed Alden to create his intimate, seemingly private local space, the routine intrusions and almost habitual hauntings of familial images, voices, and sentiments of both family and organized religion unravel the locality of his Village studio and showcase its transnational connections.

The Philippine corner and the American wall not only reconstruct national landscapes, but also are spatialized translations of desire and propriety. The grammars of desire and propriety are expressed in the kinds of situational and diachronic movement between guilt and pleasure, and between land of settlement and the homeland. It is perhaps no wonder that Alden, who has not been home, realizes a kind of homecoming when certain sentiments arise after sexual encounters or after missing his usual weekly overseas phone call to his family. The ambivalent and troubled relationship between "being at home" and "homecoming" beset queer immigrants like Alden. As such, they are in perpetual motion, shuttling between settling in and feeling displaced.

Diasporic people today are more than ever faced with creating multistranded relationships with the homeland and their new land of settlement.[24] No longer is assimilation the only fate for the present-day immigrant. Immigrants are compelled and propelled by new developments in technology and by increasing mobility of capital to devise a flexible performative repertoire that increases their survival and success in an increasingly unequal yet global world. Familial ties for both Alden and Roldan—as well as for many of my informants—mark the continuity and discontinuity of the immigrant experience. Phone calls, monetary remittances, and regular trips back to the homeland rescue the queer immigrant from this assimilative fate.

Roldan's mental and physical reflections in front of his mirror on a workday reveal how the routine regimes of race and gender permeate if not infect daily assessment of situations involving confrontations, disputes, and obedience.[25] Roldan's astute observation of the forms of racialization in America and their articulation with gender points to the power of his daily experiences and their impact on identity.[26] Because of this situation, bakla as an identity becomes a possibility in the metropole. While bakla is seen as rooted to the homeland, it becomes a tool to negotiate Roldan's cultural discomfort with mainstream gay public life. Immigration narratives are conventionally and popularly constructed as a linear movement from tradition to modernity, but Roldan's observation of being bakla in America rejects this particular teleology. At the same time, his condition is not a retreat from modernity; rather, it unwittingly destabilizes a monolithic gay identity. Roldan's recuperation of bakla, of alienation to both transgender and gay identity politics, is a result of the kinds of daily barrage of images, ideas, and bodies.

The intimate spaces and routines of the everyday may be seen by many as a kind of retreat from worldliness by an individual or a kind of bounded warm refuge of authenticity from the harsh realities of the public sphere, but, as many of my informants have unwittingly performed, for immigrants and exiles the everyday is an incomplete if not imperfect colonization of the wildness and trauma of displacement.[27] The everyday is an important arena open to manipulation and intrusion by the state. Roldan's fear of being caught by the INS or other authorities extends to his practice of cross-dressing and his cultural discomfort with gay mainstream practices. His routines are tracked by his own fear of being found out as an illegal alien, while at the same time he consciously accepts his place in the queer cultural world in New York City. He realizes that the script or, more appropriately, the drama of dissimulation is a crucial tactic for his legal, cultural, and physical survival. His marginal status in relation to what are considered authentic forms of citizenship and belonging compels him to refigure his routines and recreate his biyuti in America.

A CAUTIONARY HOPEFULNESS

The narratives of Filipino gay men may suggest a dystopic and rather bleak fate. However, I am dissatisfied with current fashionable skepticism over liberation and its overemphasis on failed dreams and dim futures. I am neither resurrecting a grand narrative of redemption nor positing the notion of the global as modernity's triumph over the local. Rather, the ethnographic examples above recast seemingly static locales, such as apartments and routines, into spaces of fervently mobile fictions, tactics, and strategies. And as such, I am convinced that a cautionary hopefulness is very appropriate at this juncture, since Filipino gay men are creating alternative routes for selfhood and belonging despite the unrelenting forces of globalization and the weight of Western institutions and practices. In other words, we need to look beyond the dizzying and often loud noise of overarching global circuits and flows, such as cyberspace images and other technological marvels, and appreciate these voices from below.

In this regard, I want to highlight the opportunities in the ambivalent and often contradictory nature of the quotidian. As I have demonstrated, the narratives of daily life in Filipino gay men's terms are constituted through the drama of survival and the biyuti of pleasure and belonging. These idioms illustrate the ambivalent yet transformative potential of quotidian engagement. Henri Lefebvre warns against the pitfalls of skepticism over the burden and dreariness of *la vie quotidienne*.[28] Instead, Lefebvre urges readers to look beyond the paralyzing effects of the banal and the routine and to appreciate its changeability and dynamism. Following Lefebvre, I finally submit that the everyday struggles of queer subjects within a globalizing world form a strategic path leading not to a teleologically determined home but rather to other more exciting possibilities.

NOTES

1. Most interviews were conducted in Taglish or code-switching from Tagalog and English. Names of informants have been changed to protect their anonymity.

2. According to the 2000 U.S. census, Filipinos in the United States number around 1.8 million, second only to the Chinese, who are the biggest group of Asian Americans with 2.3 million.

3. Adam Barry, Jan Willem Dyvendak and Andre Krouwel, eds., *The Global Emergence of Gay and Lesbian Politics: National Imprints of a Worldwide Movement* (Philadelphia: Temple University Press, 1994); and Dennis Altman, "Rupture and Continuity? The Internationalization of Gay Identities," *Social Text* 48 (1996): 77–94.

4. Arjun Appadurai, *Modernity at Large: Cultural Dimensions of Globalization* (Minneapolis: University of Minnesota Press, 1996).

5. Elizabeth Povinelli and George Chauncey, "Thinking Sexuality Transnationally: An Introduction," *GLQ* 5, no. 4 (1999): 445.

6. For an excellent ethnography of immigrant spaces and ethnicity among Filipino Americans in California, see Rick Bonus, *Locating Filipino Americans: Ethnicity and the Cultural Politics of Space* (Philadelphia: Temple University Press, 2000).

7. Michel de Certeau, *The Practice of Everyday Life* (New York: Cambridge University Press, 1984); and Dorothy Smith, *The Everyday World as Problematic: A Feminist Sociology* (Boston: Northeastern University Press, 1987). See also Keya Ganguly, *States of Exception: Everyday Life and Postcolonial Identity* (Minneapolis: University of Minnesota Press, 2001).

8. See the following for critical historiographies of Philippine-U.S. relations: Oscar V. Campomanes, "Afterword: The New Empire's Forgetful and Forgotten Citizens; Unrepresentability and Unassimilability in Filipino American Postcolonialities," *Critical Mass: A Journal of Asian American Cultural Criticism* 2, no. 2 (1995):145–200; Epifanio San Juan, "Configuring the Filipino Diaspora in the United States," *Diaspora* 3, no. 2 (Fall 1994): 117–34.

9. Svetlana Boym, *Common Places: Mythologies of Everyday Life in Russia* (Cambridge: Harvard University Press, 1994), 20. See also David Frisby and Mike Featherstone, eds., *Simmel on Culture: Selected Writings* (London: Sage, 1997), for key studies on the everyday and modernity.

10. Lauren Berlant, "Intimacy: A Special Issue," *Critical Inquiry* 24, no. 2 (1998): 287.

11. David Eng, "Out Here and Over There: Queerness and Diaspora in Asian American Studies," *Social Text*, no. 52–53 (1997): 31–52; and Gayatri Gopinath, "Homo Economics: Queer Sexualities in a Transnational Frame," in *Burning Down the House*, ed. Rosemary M. George (Boulder, CO: Westview Press, 1998).

12. Paul Gilroy, *The Black Atlantic: Modernity and Double Consciousness* (Cambridge: Harvard University Press, 1993), 16.

13. *American Sexualities: Dimensions of the Gay and Lesbian Experience*, ed. Russell Leong (New York: Routledge, 1996). Both Gopinath's and Gilroy's notions of diasporic intimacy focus on the creation of public cultural forms, such as bhangra music or hip-hop, respectively.

14. Boym, *Common Places*, 51.

15. "Performing Filipino Gay Experiences in America: Linguistic Strategies in a Transnational Context," in *Beyond the Lavender Lexicon: Authenticity, Imagination, and Appropriation in Lesbian and Gay Language*, ed. William Leap (New York: Gordon and Breach, 1996); and "Speaking of AIDS: Language and the Filipino Gay Experience in America," in *Discrepant Histories: Translocal Essays in Philippine Cultures*, ed. Vicente Rafael (Philadelphia: Temple University Press, 1996).

16. My spelling of "biyuti" instead of "beauty" is to signal the former's departure from the constrictions of the English word and also to acknowledge the unique pronunciation styles and usage by Filipino gay men. In some cases, the word is shortened to "biyu" or "B.Y." to signal attractiveness.

17. This is from the title of the book by Unni Wikan, *Managing Turbulent Hearts: A Balinese Formula for Living* (Chicago: University of Chicago Press, 1990), which showcases the idiom of self-transformation as crucial in the construction of persons and selves in Southeast Asia.

18. See the following for a theorization of the notion of beauty in the Philippines: Fennell Cannell, *Power and Intimacy in the Christian Philippines* (Cambridge: Cambridge University Press, 1999); and Mark Johnson, *Beauty and Power: Transgendering and Cultural Transformation in the Southern Philippines* (Oxford: Berg, 1997).

19. Gopinath, "Homo Economics," 116.

20. Svetlana Boym, "On Diasporic Intimacy: Ilya Kabakov's Installations and Immigrant Homes," *Critical Inquiry* 24, no. 2 (1998): 502.

21. Ella Shohat and Robert Stam, *Unthinking Eurocentrism: Multiculturalism and the Media* (London: Routledge, 1994), 42.

22. Boym, "On Diasporic Intimacy."

23. In my book, *Global Divas: Filipino Gay Men in the Diaspora* (Durham, NC: Duke University Press, 2003), I develop this idea of an alternative modernity among Filipino gay men in the diaspora.

24. See Linda Basch, Nina Glick Schiller, and Cristina Blanc-Szanton, *Nations Unbound: Transnational Project, Postcolonial Predicaments, and Deterritorialized Nation-States* (New York: Gordon and Breach, 1994).

25. This includes the hegemonic "whiteness" prevalent in gay mainstream cultural images and products.

26. See Lisa Lowe, *Immigrant Acts: On Asian American Cultural Politics* (Durham, NC: Duke University Press, 1996), for an excellent discussion of gender and Asian American citizenship.

27. Boym, "On Diasporic Intimacy," 500.

28. Henri Lefebvre, *Critique of Everyday Life* (London: Verso, 1991).

AREN Z. AIZURA

39. TRANSNATIONAL TRANSGENDER RIGHTS AND IMMIGRATION LAW

IMAGINING RIGHTS

On a panel called Queer Necropolitics at the American Anthropological Association meeting in 2009, Sima Shakhsari related the story of Naz, a trans woman from Iran who was featured in a number of documentaries about transsexuality in Iran. In the global North, recent media attention to the situation of trans people in Iran has anxiously deliberated on the visibility of their "suffering." The symptoms of this suffering may include social and familial repudiation, difficulty finding work, and the seemingly odd juxtaposition of a sympathetic medical establishment and government that, simultaneously, imprison gays and lesbians. Such media portrayals explicitly beg a further anxious query of whether trans people in Iran are not simply gays and lesbians undergoing enforced surgical mutilation to live with their partners.[1] As Shakhsari pointed out, the rash of documentaries on Iranian trans people generally portray transsexual subjects as stuck in Iran as a repressive "elsewhere," juxtaposed with the ostensible freedom of queer life in the global North. Naz, however, did not remain in Iran. After the documentaries were filmed, she went to Turkey and from there applied successfully for asylum in Canada. A year after arriving in Canada, Naz committed suicide, alone in state-subsidized housing from which she would soon have been evicted.

What happened to Naz is neither uncommon nor unexpected. Immigrants to the "developed" regions of North America, Australia, and Europe are subject to a host of laws regulating their lives and racializing and criminalizing the undocumented. The reality of Naz's suicide acts as a counter-narrative to a familiar story in which an oppressed queer or trans person living in a developing country, a dictatorship, or a fundamentalist Islamic state immigrates to the "West" to encounter freedom, hope, and a better life. This narrative is a staple of feature films and documentaries about gender-variant and queer people immigrating.[2] This immigration narrative folds into the (often-mistaken) assumption that models for transgender rights are generally initiated in "Western" nation-states—the United States, Canada, Australia, the European Union—and will later spread to other, less-progressive "corners" of the globe.

Of course, models for transgender rights and citizenship *do* move, spread, and emerge, and often in locations that might seem unlikely. For example, the first International Congress on Gender Identity and Human Rights was held in Barcelona in 2010; but the agenda was not shaped by European or North American activists as much as by the presence of activists from India, Chile, Argentina, Thailand, the Philippines, Venezuela, South Africa, and a host of other locations. As gender-variant life has become more socially visible in particular locations around the world, concurrently more struggles are occurring to produce legislation, regulations, and administrative apparatuses that accord gender-variant subjects the privileges of citizenship (i.e., rights specific to gender-variant people).[3] What Paisley Currah calls a "transgender rights imaginary" are the arguments and counter-arguments, rights claims, and forms of law being deployed in these struggles.[4] Transgender-rights discourses are already contested: Many have critiqued the tendency to incorporate medicalized understandings of surgical transsexuality in the law or to enshrine a white, heterosexual, middle-class subject of rights as the "ideal" gender-variant subject. Yet the difficulty of survival for gender-variant people in the "developed" nations we champion as modem and progressive challenges this transgender-rights imaginary and begs a *different* question: What would happen if we thought about trans and gender-variant freedom outside and against the framework of the nation-state?

In this . . . [essay], I intervene in emerging imaginaries of transgender rights and their usefulness in understanding and combating the global regulation of immigration and its effects on the lives of gender-variant people. In the realm of immigration, a transgender-rights imaginary can be seen emerging in several sites. One is a publication called *Immigration Law and the Transgender Client* (hereon referred to as *Immigration Law*), co-authored by the New York-based advocacy group Immigration Equality and the San Francisco-based Transgender Law Center. The only handbook available globally that addresses transgender immigration issues in detail, *Immigration Law* is intended as a practice manual for attorneys who represent gender-variant clients. Informally, this handbook also acts as a primer for gender-variant immigrants (or potential immigrants) to the United States on how to navigate different visa categories. Although it deals specifically with U.S. law, as a policy document it presages similar documents that may emerge in nation-states with a similarly high level of immigration and an exceptionalist image as the liberatory location in which people may live as trans without harm. Through a close reading of *Immigration Law,* I interrogate the limits of neoliberal-rights frameworks that produce gender-variant people as subjects who must perfectly perform regulatory procedures to gain access to rights. In this framework, political transformation is displaced onto individuals, who are asked to be visible as "transgender subjects" (hence also to conform to the nation-state's idea about what that means) for their cases to become part of the precedential law-making machine. In doing so, *Immigration Law* exemplifies the limits and inconsistencies of a political practice oriented exclusively toward "rights."

Following this reading, I broaden the discussion to ask what work intersections between transgender studies, queer studies, and feminism can accomplish toward generating new strategies to prevent death. I argue that what we need is a trans theory that not only acknowledges its debts to feminist theory and incorporates a feminist critique of heteronormativity but also that turns "trans" in an anti-identitarian direction. Although it is important to acknowledge that transgender is an identity category whose subjects' access to freedom will be divided along the cuts of affluence, racialization, gender, and citizenship, we also need to look at where and how bodies escape or act clandestinely outside those categories—and at moments in which the categories of immigrant, transgender person, man, and woman become incoherent and inconsistent. This means taking on the lessons of particular feminist and queer antiracist work on intersectionality, and also challenging some of the limits of intersectional analysis.

It is neither new nor insurrectionary to write about borders in trans theory. With few exceptions until very recently, trans theory has examined those figural "borders" regulating traffic between genders rather than watching what happens to gender-variant people at real borders, appropriating the metaphor of the immigrant "without land or nation" to understand transgender experience without considering that many trans people are, in fact, immigrants.[5] For example, the slogan on the Web page of TransX, an Austrian transgender-activist organization, reads, *"Wir öffnen Geschlechterngrenzen* [We open gendered borders]." Even as TransX fights against the deportation of its asylum-seeker members from the European Union, the "opening-borders" metaphor risks annexing talk of the border to gender alone. Existing scholarly accounts of transgender immigration law often perform a similar error. Rather than analyzing discrimination against transgender immigrants as part of the broader immigration industrial complex that recognizes or misrecognizes different immigrant bodies using different tactics, case notes and reviews on transgender immigration generally begin with a critique of the legal mechanics of fixing the "truth" of gendered bodies (i.e., medico-legal interpretations of corporeal requirements to be recognized as transgender). With few exceptions, this critique is framed as though that were an end in itself, culminating in the argument that lawmaking should incorporate improved models of recognition.[6]

This . . . essay bypasses the task of "finding a better model." Rather, I probe how different regimes of gender definition regularly collide in a site where such collisions remain by-products of a much-more administratively violent biopolitics aimed at regulating national and racialized borders and directing labor flows. The differentiated recognition of gender-variant bodies has become just another part of the machinery of institutions that control geographic mobility, a new technique of control to modulate enclosure or opportunity.[7] Under these conditions, we need to look at the bigger picture. For such theorists as Dean Spade, this means resisting the move to frame law reform—particularly antidiscrimination and hate-crimes legislation—as the primary political goal of trans politics and remaining alert to how trans-political projects are mobilized toward neoliberal goals of inclusion, optimization, and incorporation.[8] Rather than framing queer or transgender as categories that are excluded or invisible within the *polis*, Spade investigates how the emerging inclusion and visibility of transgender and gender identity as legal and administrative categories are fraught, often producing "targeted insecurities and death" for those who are unclassifiable or misclassified.[9] Spade's focus on populations most at risk of death or lifelong precariousness—such as immigrants, the incarcerated, those who engage in informal economies, and people of color—is instructive here: These populations are also targeted for increased surveillance and regulation in the context of sustained, ongoing wars—on drugs, on terror, on immigration.

This . . . essay contributes to that project by situating the forms of power that produce and govern gender-variant bodies within a framework that looks beyond the nation-state (and especially beyond the United States). Gender-variant movement needs to be understood as part of global movement, and trans communities need to be understood as composed not of "citizens" but of people who are also undocumented, stateless, or constantly on the move. This commitment is both personal and theoretical. As an Australian citizen living in the United States, I encounter immigration systems regularly. However, my status as a white academic whose skills are in demand have thus far meant successful, if nerve-wracking, visa-application procedures (so long as I avoid presenting my female-assigned birth certificate alongside the passport that designates me as male, and possibly even then). As a scholar of transnationality, it is impossible for me to ignore how the majority of writing on queer and transgender studies and transnationality restricts critical attention to one nation-state or one diasporic community. This is not to say that we should make universalizing assumptions of generality at the expense of focusing on the local, acknowledging the specificity of juridical governmentalities, or acknowledging the specificity of differently racialized or ethnicized communities. What I sketch out here is a tactical commitment to approaching localized struggles as linked transnationally and politically, enabling us to grasp the contact points that bind gender-variant people into global migratory regulatory regimes regardless of which geographical regions they were born in, are traveling to, or are traveling from.

FOR A BIOPOLITICS OF TRANS MIGRATION

Despite the recent overuse of biopolitics as a conceptual tool, Michel Foucault's insight that modern politics deploys the optimization and extension of life to control its subjects does necessary work here.[10] To push against the assumption that the nation-state marks the perimeter of politics means tracing the trajectories of immigrants *before* they reach "destination" nation-states while recognizing that vectors of global-migration flow are modulated by many national borders acting as filters.[11] Not only national governments but international and localized nongovernmental organizations and institutions contribute to global/local "regimes of mobility control."[12] These regimes deploy a variety of contradictory mechanisms to optimize labor flows, to filter particular kinds of subjects into and out of territories, to secure those populations, and to manage popular political discourse around protecting nation-states from, or opening nation-states to, immigration.

Far from offering a perspective on immigration that privileges institutional calls for better "human rights," theorizing mobility control this way permits us to approach "humanitarian" and "nonhumanitarian" immigration laws as part of the same flexible set of assemblages, aimed at modulating the enclosures just in time, case by case. These assemblages include stratified visa categories (such as temporary-work visa categories, skilled-worker visa categories, partnership or family visa categories, or asylum-seeker visa categories); the detention and deportation of undocumented migrants or those who overstay their visas, often aimed at particular racialized populations; and transnational outsourcing of detention camps to nation-states located on migration routes to "developed" countries.

From this perspective, borders are not simply about exclusion. Rather, as Angela Mitropoulos puts it, "the regulation and transformation of the movements of bodies (become calculable, exchangeable) through space, the habituating of space as market and movement as commerce."[13] The words "calculable" and "exchangeable" here alert us to how encountering the border forces us not only to become legible subjects in stratified categories (asylum seeker, permanent resident, temporary worker, skilled worker, student, visiting researcher, "illegal alien," citizen) but also to reinvent ourselves as entrepreneurial subjects under contract with the nation-state. In exchange for permission to enter a territory legally, we agree to comply with visa requirements—to work or to not work, to pay the agreed-upon fees, to leave on time, to present ourselves as hard-working, responsible, or, in the case of queer or transgender asylum seekers, as the traumatized victims of "barbaric" third-world trans- or homophobia. The symbolic and material debt incurred in such an exchange ensures the pliability and self-surveillance of the immigrant herself.

In exchange for *not* entering legally, undocumented migrants clandestinely fill a growing need for domestic or unskilled labor in "modernized" nation-states. Yet the undocumented are also characterized as having broken a contract with the state and are thus subject to an illegalized existence at higher risk of detention or deportation and the inability to harvest the other contractual benefits potentially accorded to "good immigrant" behavior, such as health benefits, sick leave, or collective bargaining. Like the Schmittian exception that enables the sovereign to suspend democracy (thus, for Schmitt, defining sovereignty itself), the suspension of the contract is built into contractualism: "the failure of will to prevail over 'custom,' the non-identity of the contracting parties, the inability of certain people to 'control themselves.'"[14] At this juncture, racializing logics dictate that "those people" were never appropriate multicultural subjects to begin with and may be ejected forthwith. Calls for immigration reform often follow the same divisive logic, pitting "good" against "bad" immigrants. For example the now-demolished DREAM Act would have been the most progressive immigration-reform bill on the agenda in the United States, in that it would have entitled undocumented minors to permanent residence on the condition that they complete college or serve in the military. Populist support for the DREAM Act framed the U.S. government as benevolently excusing "innocent" children for the crimes of their undocumented parents.[15] Simultaneously, however, it must be acknowledged that those parents' low-waged labor is central to the survival of millions of American corporations and government bodies, so much so that, at least in Indiana, Democrats and Republicans alike condemned the undocumented criminalizing SB590 law as counterproductive for Indiana's (crisis-beset) economy.

Within this framework, the legibility or illegibility of subjects is paramount. Thus it should not surprise us that, for gender-variant people, negotiating borders is filled with risk and anxiety: the risk that one's documents will not match up with the gender read by strangers or immigration officials on the basis of appearance or the risk of being apprehended as being "in disguise" and therefore a potential threat. Recall the famous memo sent by the U.S. Department of Homeland Security in 2005 warning TSA guards to be on the alert for "cross-dressed" terrorists.[16] The new generation of airport X-ray body scanners picks up "inconsistencies" not by matching appearance with documents but by looking at the body's surface. Such biometric surveillance techniques complement skirmishes taking place at an administrative and legislative level, toward which I now turn.

CALCULABLE UNDER WHAT NAME?

> I can't find any information or guidance whatsoever, for transgendered people wishing to immigrate to the UK to be with their partner. There is no mention anywhere that I have found of how a trans person should properly apply, or under what visa category.[17]

This plea for assistance, written by a participant on the United Kingdom Lesbian and Gay Immigration Group (UKLGIG) online forum, appeared at the beginning of a thread entitled "Transgender visa application no help available." "It's as if Trans people do not exist," the post continued. A male citizen of the United Kingdom, the forum participant lived in the Philippines with his partner, a Filipina trans woman. They intended to return to the United Kingdom to live. Under the United Kingdom's relatively progressive partnership immigration laws, foreign nationals can obtain residency in the United Kingdom if they are married heterosexual partners, same-sex civil partners, or unmarried domestic partners of U.K. citizens. Unmarried partners must show they have cohabited for two years prior to immigrating, while civil partnerships or marriages do not have to provide evidence of prior cohabitation. The participant and his partner preferred to apply as a heterosexual couple—the author of the post considered himself to be a heterosexual male, and his partner identified as a woman. However, she was unable to obtain documents listing her gender as female in the Philippines. Because her documents designated her as male, it seemed that they must apply to the U.K. immigration authorities as same-sex civil partners. Once in the United Kingdom, she intended to gain legal recognition as a woman under the U.K.'s Gender Recognition Act (GRA), a process that would take two years of documented living as a woman. Neither party wanted to enter into a same-sex civil partnership as men—which would, at any rate, be dissolved once she was legally recognized as a woman under the GRA. If they applied as unmarried partners, the couple could not meet the requirements, because during their five-year long-distance relationship, they had not cohabited for two years. The forum participant could not decide how to proceed and found no helpful information in bureaucratic channels. Hence, he had turned to UKLGIG for assistance. "If anyone has a view on this, and can point me at the contact for immigration services in U.K. immigration, both myself and my as yet unmarried trans Fiancee would be very grateful," he wrote.

The dilemma in which this forum participant and his partner found themselves has all the hallmarks of a classical immigration story: faceless bureaucratic institutions, labyrinthine application procedures, a disconnect between the left and right hands of the body politic. It is a characteristic example of what transgender immigrants must contend with in nation-states that legally recognize either transgender persons' change of legal gender designation or same-sex

partnerships but do not consider how one may contradict the other. Because the Gender Recognition Act and same-sex civil-partnership laws were passed by the U.K. Parliament in the same year, this example seems particularly farcical. The two forms of legal recognition seem plagued by discontinuity at precisely the point where an overlap would assist those who may be most in need of legal protection. At any rate, volunteer advisers in the UKLGIG message board offered advice regarding whether the length of time the couple had cohabited might "count" toward legitimating their unmarried partnership status but had no wisdom regarding the specificity of transgender immigration procedures. One moderator suggested the forum participant write to his member of Parliament, and there the exchange ended. UKLGIG's Web site still does not offer any advice for transgender immigration or asylum applicants. This episode illustrates how contradictory and complex immigration law may be for gender-variant people to negotiate. It also illustrates the need for comprehensive information about trans issues and the paucity of that information in purportedly T-inclusive LGBT immigration-advocacy work in the United Kingdom.

By contrast, the United States has quite comprehensive information available for transgender immigrants and their legal advocates in the form of a handbook, *Immigration Law and the Transgender Client*. Produced by Immigration Equality and the Transgender Law Center, the handbook articulates its target as two major problems that contribute to the increased marginalization, detention, and deportation of gender-variant immigrants to the United States, the misapplication of the law in cases involving gender-variant applicants, and the high prevalence of immigration attorneys offering transgender immigrants inaccurate legal advice.[18] It offers indispensable advice not only for immigrants seeking permanent residency but also for advocates acting for undocumented or criminalized immigrants in immigration detention.

However, a close reading of key chapters illustrates that *Immigration Law* requires its transgender "clients" to engage in precisely the form of neoliberal contractualism I critique above. Most of the advice offered deals with petitions for U.S. permanent residency through spousal and fiancée petition or asylum, because these are the categories of permanent-residency petition for which transgender status is perceived to have definite bearing on the outcome. To win permanent residency, the handbook insists, one must perform the correct legal maneuvers to gain strategic success within a system blatantly structured to filter entry exclusively to those who already have such skills.

Although Immigration Equality has worked extensively on lobbying for the Uniting American Families Bill to pass, which would open up permanent-residency petitions to binational same-sex partners, here the aim is more limited: to prevent the misapplication of the law and to quietly encourage law reform through precedent. Both policy initiatives address themselves to people who are already living in the United States, whether documented or undocumented. Advice is explicitly not provided for refugees—the refugee category under U.S. law designates those who apply under a humanitarian convention from outside the country, as opposed to asylum, which designates those who apply under a humanitarian category from inside the United States. These tactics may be the most immediately practical contribution either Immigration Equality or the Transgender Law Center can make with the resources at its disposal. Both organizations retain staff attorneys who represent trans and LGBT clients *pro bono*; the handbook's comprehensive "practice tips" demonstrate an ongoing familiarity with the logistics of negotiating lengthy application procedures. However, by focusing on how transgender immigrants can strategically negotiate immigration regulations with their attorneys through formalized case law, *Immigration Law* renders the struggle for freedom from harassment, discrimination, criminalization, and incarceration as an individual task. Although it is commendable that someone is doing this work at all, *Immigration Law*'s format relinquishes the opportunity to create connections between immigrants in a more networked or collective struggle to transform public policy on immigration or to assist those who prefer not to be outed as transgender or have the "correct" documents at all.

The key question here is whether changing one's administrative gender is more important than moving through an invasive permanent-residency application process with as little difficulty as possible. *Immigration Law* addresses itself to an attorney who is not familiar

with transgender issues and offers a number of preliminary tips so the attorney can treat their client with respect.

These include suggestions that the attorney do the following: "narrow the issues" by steering away from discussing the client's gender identity if it will not affect the client's immigration status; permit the client to direct the attorney how to address and perceive them; refrain from making assumptions about the client's gender identity based on their appearance; and use the correct name, pronoun, and mode of address in all correspondence with the client. This should happen, the authors write, even if the client self-presents in correspondence or appointments using their legal name:

> Often, clients will tell their attorneys their legal name (i.e., their birth name) rather than the name they feel comfortable using. If your client's legal name clearly does not match his or her corrected gender, you should ask whether there is another name that is preferred.[19]

The authors also counsel that an attorney should see that the client makes all possible attempts to change their legal name and gender classification on documents. Ideally this should take place before an individual starts an immigration record. Thus, the authors advise attorneys that

> it is easier for your client to begin his or her immigration record with the name that corresponds to the gender identity. Therefore, especially for immigration clients, it is important to do all that you can to get your client's paperwork in order to file the application in the correct name. If your client has not legally changed his or her name, however, you will generally not be able to file in the name your client chooses. Nonetheless, it is best to explain in the cover letter to USCIS [U.S. Citizenship and Immigration Services] that your client is transgender and generally goes by a different name.[20]

It is clearly admirable to advise non-trans-"friendly" lawyers on how to be trans-friendly in their interactions with clients and to pursue whatever will make life easier for the client in terms of name and gender-classification changes. However, I want to trouble the final advice that an attorney should inform USCIS of the client's transgender status, *even when filing applications under the birth name.* The assumption here is that social, bodily, and administrative gender should be consistent. The corollary assumption is that a client will desire eventually to be administratively legible as the gender she socially identifies as and that name changes should be made before embarking on an immigration process that may take years. But must a gender-variant person always change their administrative gender? Depending on the state, it is not always possible or practical. In the United States, where a person might not need to change their gender classification on legal documents to access hormone therapy or surgeries, changing a legal name or gender classification may be unnecessary. This is not to say that the option to change legal identifiers should not be available—it should. Rather, I question the necessity of being visibly marked as transgender in a process that renders immigrants vulnerable to surveillance, discrimination, and violence. Being administratively marked as transgender may make a gender-variant individual vulnerable to harassment from immigration officials. This is particularly important, because (as the handbook reminds readers in the same chapter) gender-variant immigrants may think of themselves in ways that are not consistent with Euro-American understandings of transgender as exclusively about gender identity rather than sexual orientation.

The implicit project animating *Immigration Law's* emphasis on transgender visibility becomes more clear in the chapter on spousal and fiancée permanent-residency petitions. To make clear the stakes of this reading, a brief summary of bureaucratic approaches to transgender permanent-residency applications is necessary here. In the United States, marriage-based petitions for permanent residency involving a transgender person are not officially "legal." But they can and have been approved by a mazelike process that exploits policy inconsistencies between different arms of government. Officially, USCIS's policy is to not recognize marriages between parties where one or both individuals claim to be transsexual, "regardless of whether either individual has undergone sex reassignment surgery, or is in the process of doing so."[21] (It is unclear whether this is because of common garden-variety transphobia or because officially allowing transsexual marriages might stray too near a perceived infraction

of the Defense of Marriage Act, or both.[22]) After an application is first denied by USCIS, however, applicants are free to appeal. The Board of Immigration Appeals (BIA), administered by the Department of Justice, will often reverse the original decision and approve the petition. This approval dates from a 2005 case, *In re Lovo Lara*, what *Immigration Law* calls a "shockingly favorable precedential decision," which inaugurated a complex test to ensure the legality of a marriage.[23] The *Lovo Lara* requirements include the following: that it be proven not to contravene the Defense of Marriage Act, which stipulates that a marriage be between a man and a woman; that the marriage be legal in the jurisdiction in which it occurred; that the transgender individual (or individuals) obtain "complete" surgical gender reassignment prior to making the petition; and that the applicant's gender is recognized administratively through a corrected birth certificate.

In *Immigration Law's* chapter on binational marriage petitions, the conflict between performing a legibly proper transgender identity and flying under the radar becomes even more explicit. Because around 25 percent of successful petitions for U.S. permanent residency each year are marriage-based petitions, *Immigration Law's* chapter on marriage is deservedly extensive. (Advice on how transgender employees might negotiate employer-initiated sponsorship for permanent residency warrants two paragraphs, the assumption being that workers skilled enough to attract employer sponsorship do not require human-rights advocates). So-called "green-card" marriage is notorious for the resources the Immigration and Nationalization Service (INS) devotes to surveillance and interrogation of binational couples in attempt to ensure that these marriages are based on romantic love rather than convenience.[24] The authors offer advice on how to negotiate marriage-based petitions for permanent residency through all the permutations of transgender embodiment and foreign or national status, offering hypothetical situations to illustrate how the law works. For example, they advise that if a couple is married in a state that does not recognize such marriages, they should apply to have the marriage declared void and remarry in a state that *does* recognize the marriage. For couples who marry in a state that recognizes same-sex marriage, the authors stipulate that they should ensure they are marrying as a man and a woman, not as a same-sex couple (because, of course, same-sex marriages are not recognized federally).

A short section near the end of the chapter mentions cases involving a "Homosexual-Identified Couple but No Surgery." To quote the section in full:

> A lesbian-identified couple is comprised of Bette who was born anatomically female and Tina who was born anatomically male but identifies as female. Tina has had no surgery and has taken no steps to change her gender marker on identity documents. For immigration purposes, this couple should be able to marry as an opposite sex couple and succeed with a marriage-based petition. . . .[25]

In theory, this strategy might make the petitioning easier, because there may be no need to out one's self as transgendered or transsexual to U.S. immigration officials. For a gender-variant person who does not desire to change the gender recorded on their documents and is marrying a person recognized to be the "opposite" gender, this seems like the most common-sense way to negotiate the system. Why be visible as transgender at all if it is possible to fly under the radar? After all, the point of a successful marriage-based petition in this case is not to be outed as transgender but to obtain permanent residency for an individual who may not even be transgendered at all. In the following paragraph, the authors subtly undercut this logic. Many transgender-rights organizations, they point out, will not accept cases like this to represent—in particular, Immigration Equality and the Transgender Law Center, *Immigration Law*'s coauthors. "We feel uncomfortable," the authors explain, "advocating with DHS [Department of Homeland Security] for the position that a transgender individual who self-identifies as (in this example) female should be legally considered male simply because she has had no surgery."[26] The booklet offers some advice to private legal practitioners who choose to take on cases of this kind, however: the decision of whether to "pass" as a normal heterosexual couple or whether to disclose that one partner is transgender "but has had no surgery."

I could make a number of demurrals in response to this curious section. To begin with, the question of surgical status seems an incidental, not to mention

euphemistic, way of putting it. What is being proposed is that a person pass as their birth-assigned gender to enter into a marriage that everyone but the state would regard as queer. Because "passing" takes many forms and is rather less concerned with embodied "reality" than appearance, the person's surgical status should not matter. Secondly, what "transgender" means is very particular here. To the authors, it evidently means an uncomplicated transition from male to female or female to male, in which (as I note above) social, administrative, and embodied gender all ought to be consistent. Finally, the comment that transgender-rights organizations would "feel uncomfortable" advocating that a person is non-trans when they are "really" transgender gestures subtly to a subtext of political expediency: *If we say you are non-trans, the authors seem to be saying, then the Department of Homeland Security will not recognize you when you say that you are trans. You cannot have it both ways.*

Of course, there may be additional political costs for legal advocates who admit they represent clients who pursue this strategy on paper. If it became public, it would be easy for INS and the Department of Homeland Security to claim transgender-immigration lobbyists were secretly pushing same-sex marriages through the back door, as it were. Given that queer and transgender foreigners embody a threat to heterosexuality and to the cohesion of the nation and that anxiety about defending marriage from homosexuality hovers spectrally about every transgender marriage case, it is unsurprising that lobbyists should desire their own cases to present watertight instances of heterosexual transgender people. It could also be argued that providing representation to couples who can access heterosexual privilege, however precarious, is not the concern of an organization dedicated to GLBT rights. (The perennial *ressentiment* of some gay and lesbian community members who perceive trans people to be "lying" about their correct genders to claim advantages must surely raise its ugly head here.[27]) However, given Immigration Equality's other policy focus on bringing about legislative recognition of binational same-sex relationships, a refusal of association with even the whiff of same-sex partnership seems odd.

Is this simply another case of Immigration Equality's investment in a "normative discourse on belonging," as Karma Chávez puts it in an incisive critique of the Immigration Equality publication *Family, Unvalued: Discrimination, Denial and the Fate of Binational Same-Sex Couples under U.S. Law?*[28] *Family, Unvalued* reports on nine hundred interviews with binational same-sex couples affected by the U.S. government's refusal to recognize same-sex partnerships under immigration law. Chávez argues that *Family, Unvalued* plays to a perceived middle ground on immigration issues by framing same-sex couples as homonationalist good citizens, with the same desires to unite in romantic fusion and reproduce the nation as heterosexual couples. Meanwhile, U.S. citizens' claims for rights to reunite their queer families via legal means deflect attention from undocumented immigrants—whose numbers are far higher, and whose criminalization and public demonization is far more serious, than legalized immigrants. Normative belonging signals a shift where the proper performance of citizenship offers a justification for legal reform rather than the ideal of universal rights.[29]

Reading *Immigration Law and the Transgender Client* as another, transgender-focused facet of the discourse on normative belonging seems apt. Yet I want to stress another aspect of the "normative" here. *Immigration Law* rewards those who have the capacity to be entrepreneurial and to decide in advance on the best legal strategy. One can safely assume that although the targeted readers are immigration attorneys, the "smart" gender-variant prospective immigrant to the United States will discover the existence of the handbook, pore over it, and arrive in a lawyer's office already familiar with the necessary procedures. In this sense, it calls into being a neoliberal entrepreneurial subject who is always and forever calculating her exchangeability.[30]

INTERSECTIONAL TACTICS

What political tactics might refuse the logics of neoliberal calculability? Does a theorization of calculability run the risk of evacuating an analysis of racialization and sexual normativities? For these techniques do, in fact, still perform important filtering procedures for who counts as a body to be embraced by the nation or expunged from it.

Queer, feminist, and pro-immigrant work that deploys intersectionality as a critical tool may be instructive here. To illustrate what I mean by this, I want to detour into a discussion of theoretical and activist critical work on links between queer and immigrant politics. Eithne Luibhéid's work on the interlinking of sexuality and migration in the U.S. nation-state historically frames immigration as the locus of control of sexuality and vice versa. In a reading of *Family, Unvalued,* Luibhéid refuses the homonationalist desire to gain queer rights through designating queer couples as "family." Rather than complying with the seemingly static categories of "legal" and "illegal," Luibhéid reframes these seemingly universal categories as processes of legalization and illegalization that are contingent and shift according to need. The inclusion of queer couples as a category recognized in permanent residency application, she argues, would mean that same-sex couples would be subject to the same surveillance as heterosexual couples. Luibhéid questions the biopolitics of intimacy that deploy couple relationships as strategies to reproduce good citizens through economic and social incentives. She concludes by arguing that we should address how "other crosscutting social hierarchies also shape the production of il/legal status."[31] "Could the campaign be reframed to address the multiple, intersecting bases on which legal and illegal statuses are produced?" she asks.

A number of groups working on immigrant and queer issues have released statements arguing for an appreciation of the intersections between queer and immigrant politics. The New York-based group Queers for Economic Justice (QEJ) released a statement called *Queers and Immigration: A Vision Statement* in 2008; joint statements addressing measures against queer rights and immigration rights were made by the Arizona-based Coalición de Derechos Humanos (CDH) and Wingspan in the lead-up to and after the 2006 Arizona state election that included four anti-immigrant propositions and an antigay amendment to the state constitution. QEJ's *Vision Statement* makes a number of calls on issues that affect not only queer immigrants but also immigrants (in general) and queers: for example, repealing the ban on HIV travelers to the United States, refuting the proposed building of a U.S.-Mexico border wall, calling for an end to the criminalization of harboring undocumented immigrants, and so on. The statement ends with a resounding call for queer and immigrant-rights organizers to "address the intersection where we live and love and struggle."[32]

Chávez calls the political work these statements do a form of "differential belonging," in contrast to the normative belonging discourse of *Family, Unvalued.* For Chávez, these critiques reject normative inclusion by focusing on the connections between queers and immigrants (and other kinds of bodies) as threats to the nation and the focus of blame within national-ist discourse, drawing attention to the simultaneous homophobia, racism, and xenophobia of govern-ment: "At a fundamental level, migrants and queers are scapegoats that are easily blamed for a multitude of societal problems."[33] Thus, rather than focusing on the family as the mode of immigrant inclusion (which simultaneously excludes those who do not participate in recognizable family structures—i.e., queers), CDH, Wingspan, and QEJ "rhetorically craft a justification for belonging across lines of difference."[34]

What would an intersectional approach look like in relation to a transgender-rights imaginary? Such an approach might resist a rights framework that privi-leges those who already have access to the most eco-nomic resources and forms of social capital and who fit best into the dominant medico-legal understanding of male and female. Instead, it might address the di-lemmas and needs of transgender people who are most vulnerable to violence, death, and discrimination. This might involve an analysis of how laws stigmatizing apparently unrelated populations, such as prisoners, sex workers, and undocumented immigrants, impact gender-variant people (who are statistically overrepre-sented in each of these categories). Many groups orga-nizing on such principles already exist in the United States: For example, the Sylvia Rivera Law Project (SLRP) works to increase the political participation and visibility of low-income people and people of color who are gender variant. Its mission statement states that SLRP begins from the premise that "gender self-determination is inextricably intertwined with racial, social and economic justice."[35] It is clear that groups such as QEJ, SLRP, CDH, Wingspan, and others do very important work—work that is being done by no one else in the broader lobbying-focused political arena.

However, I want to challenge the assumption that an intersectional analysis is sufficient to harness a po-litical project that desires to improve the lives of people who do not count as subjects at all under a national

framework and paradoxically are also integral to that nation's economic stability. An analysis of intersecting oppressions and the corollary that different groups must work coalitionally across lines of difference as-sumes the coherence and stability of identity catego-ries. As Jasbir Puar puts it, intersectional models of subjectivity may still limit us if they presume the auto-matic primacy and singularity of the disciplinary sub-ject and its identitarian interpellation."[36] Puar ascribes this insight to the affective turn within critical theory, citing Brian Massumi's resistance to positionality as gridlock as well as feminist and queer work on affect as the feelings or sensations that precede identity cat-egories.[37] But we also need to challenge intersectional theories of politics that posit those who are excluded (strangers) as the groups who must form coalitions. If we accept an analysis of capitalist neoliberalism as relentlessly *inclusive* of bodies as long as they can pres-ent themselves as calculable (and even when they are not), we must also acknowledge that the imaginaries of liberal aspiration exhort us all to *become* calculable as the first step to self-improvement.

An analysis of gender-variant immigration that relies too heavily on intersectional politics risks rein-stating terms such as transgender, queer, gay, person of color, immigrant, low-income, and family as uncon-tested or universal. When a person migrates through a number of different nation-states in which currency-exchange rates and what constitutes "poverty" fluctuate wildly, how does she come to know herself as "low-income"? When a feminine-appearing person who was assigned male at birth uses female pronouns but characterizes herself as *bakla, sao prophet sorng, waria, fa'fafine, travesti,* or *hijra (or gay)*—all non-English terms that denote different gender-variant embodiments and identities—from which U.S. support organization will she seek assistance if she needs it? If we assume that "the border" always means the U.S.-Mexico border, what transnational networks that see borders as in-terconnected and coterminous are lost? Or, to give an example closer to my personal experience, perspectives on what counts as "white" in Australia and the United States differ entirely: in Australia, close Greek and Ital-ian friends are racialized as nonwhite according to the white Australia policy's shifting historical definitions, while in the United States, Greek- or Italian-American friends are now considered to be white. Their capacity to intervene in particular antiracist political debates thus changes according to geographical location (and contradictory racialized interpretations of the right to speak collide in transnational e-mail list and Weblog skirmishes). Intersectional political projects risk failure without an assessment of how transnational flows of people interrupt, transform, and resist these shifting lines of demarcation.

My final note on intersectional politics regards the symbolic burden placed on trans women of color, many times immigrants, to represent themselves consistently as victims of the most heinous crimes of transphobic violence. The Transgender Day of Remembrance (TDOR), which tallies a global list of transgender people murdered each year and commemorates their deaths with vigils and memorial services annually on November 21, offers a salutary example. Implicitly or explicitly, the statistics quoted on each nation-state imprint a shocking transnational sensibility on proceedings (nothing exemplifies this more ironically than watching mostly white Midwestern college students at a 2009 TDOR vigil in Indiana struggle to pronounce the "foreign" names of those on the list). Yet TDOR vigils often end in calls for nation-bound legislative recompense, such as national hate-crime laws, which would not help most of the people on the list of dead—not to mention that many seem to be vulnerable as sex workers or undocumented immigrants who are also subject to criminalizing anti-sex-work laws or the violence of numerous security agencies.[38]

A similar effect can be seen in writing on the global feminization of labor: As Neferti Tadiar puts it, writing on feminist critiques of globalization, "immigrant female domestic and/or sex workers . . . come to embody the material consequences of the gendered, racialized, and sexualized aspects of the normative logics of the capitalist economy."[39] Under this regime of representation, the subject "serves as the axiomatic form of human equivalence" who becomes the only player in moral-political narratives of dramatic suffering.[40] As with the story of Naz, whom I discuss at the beginning of this chapter, narratives about dead trans women of color too often mobilize suffering to support the exceptionalist lie that life is better in the center—except on those occasions when it is proved, after all, not to be better. The abstraction of these bodies into subjects of suffering also prevents the formation of a political model that might begin by understanding precisely how the privileges and freedoms of those who are documented, or not sex workers, or not transgender, are cosubstantial with and intimately connected to those spoken for, in ways we cannot anticipate in advance. These ways may not be about law reform, rights, representation, or belonging at all.

EXITING, IMPERCEPTIBLY

Throughout this chapter, I offer examples of salutary moments in which legislative recognition or nongovernmental attempts at negotiating recognition of gender-variant people fail. The example of the poster on the UKLGIG message board illustrates how "gender recognition" and "same-sex partnership recognition" neither remove the necessity of demonstrating one's legitimate gender at all points nor remove the boundaries between same-sex and heterosexual partnerships. When it is impossible to verify gender transitions, an unsurpassable gulf is created between subjectivation as a "same-sex partner" and a heterosexual "fiancée." My discussion of *Immigration Law* similarly demonstrates how even minimal, partial recognition of transgender immigrants within U.S. spousal permanent-residency petitions depends on the willingness of the gender-variant person to be administratively visible as transgender *and* to commit to a male or female legal identity. That discussion also illustrates how nongovernmental organizations can be compliant with and supportive of these conditions. Finally, I critique the assumptions of intersectional politics as reliant on the stability of categories of identity that clearly are not stable geographically.

If we are to take these failures seriously, we also need to acknowledge that the bodies we are dealing with in speaking of gender-variant immigration often do not desire visibility at all. It is a truism of transgender and transsexual community advice that the best way to obtain identity documents with the correct gender classification is to walk into any given bureaucratic institution and claim indignantly that the gender designation on the license or certificate is mistaken. One then relies on the embarrassment of the "customer service representative" one approaches to effect a quick, clandestine keystroke transforming one from M to F or vice versa. The same kinds of advice columns often recommend passing as the gender listed on one's documents while moving through airport security, even if one never does at any other time. That is to say, at times it is easier not to be visible (and vulnerable) as transgender—and there is no contradiction in working around the law to ensure one's safety. Undocumented immigrants, too, have a vested interest in passing under the radar. As theorists of migration and gender variance, it is our business to remain fidelitous to that need. In that case, it might be salient to reconceive of "the political" as designating exclusively representational and specular tactics. As post-autonomist theorist Yann Moulier-Boutang writes in an interview on the politics of flight, "It is the interpretation of the silences that interests me: to seize the silences, the refusals, and the flight as something active."[41]

In this final section, I challenge us to rethink gender-variant immigration as a form of flight, or exodus: a performance of politics without necessarily privileging visibility. This also means acknowledging that the mobility and flexibility of immigrants, and the "spread" of a transgender rights imaginary, may be convenient to capitalism. Emerging forms of transgender rights also bring into being new disciplinary mechanisms that operate transnationally. They depend on the capacity of bodies to be mobile in order to enclose them. This is not to downplay the efforts made by gender-variant activists and lobby groups to fight for transgender rights in an enormous number of jurisdictions across the globe. But it is to mark those struggles also as a way to bring gender-variant subjects into new networks of circulation that demarcate the political spaces in which "freedom" or "tyranny" are said to inhere.

. . . I [have] researched the movements of gender-variant people: migrating to access health care if it does not exist in one's home; moving to access different forms of juridical recognition or laws about reassigning gender classification, marriage, work, and so forth; moving to earn more valuable currencies in the European Union or North America; and moving to take advantage of unfamiliar places as laboratories for tweaking with the intricate social interconnections that create, sustain, or shut down passing or identifying as any kind of gender. My research subjects lived in a number of locations across the globe and responded to my questions about their mobility in wildly differing ways. They all negotiated risk, danger, a desire for autonomy or mobility, and the incapacity to move. The desire of my informants to be mobile seemed be coterminous with a pragmatic and expert knowledge about how to negotiate visa restrictions, currency-exchange value, and transnational differences in expression of gender variance. Rather than consigning these tactics to the realm of the contingent, I regard them as politicized strategies of exodus.

Exodus gives one name to a political strategy that refuses to invest in the constitution of a state or in the affective and juridical forms of relation to statehood, such as inclusion or recognition. Exodus is an "engaged withdrawal," a refusal to participate, a means of flight.[42] Exodus is not necessarily passive, either: When Moulier-Boutang exhorts readers to view silences, refusals, and flight as something active, he asks us to reorient our conceptions of the political not only as recognition. Another name for similar strategies is imperceptible politics: the politics of the everyday.[43] Imperceptible politics approaches immigration as a "constituent force of the current social transformation"—millions of people moving, sustained by networks of solidarity, cooperation, sharing resources, and knowledge of how to navigate without identifying one's self or how to best negotiate the filtering systems of multiple borders. This is a politics that is not quietist but quiet, not visible but disidentifying and invisible in the specular economies of representation and calculability inhabited by both non-governmental organizations and the state. Such silences and invisibilities are not necessarily apolitical but trace the refusal of an easy dialectic between recognition and misrecognition, visibility and invisibility, or discipline and escape. Read collectively as tactics moving toward a form of exodus, the practices of gender-variant mobility might be understood as a desertion of the calculus of contractualism, marginalizing categories, classificatory systems, refusals of adequate health care, discriminatory institutions, and misrecognitions gender-variant people must contend with almost everywhere. Rather than contributing to a transgender-rights imaginary, contributing to this imperceptible politics demands the emergence of an *unimaginary*: not imagined and future-oriented but present-minded, oriented to real, everyday, and important tactics; not based on identity politics, but on seeing the cosubstantiality and intimacy of all bodies, all the time.

NOTES

1. For a critique of this tendency, see Afsaneh Najmabadi, "Transing and Transpassing across Sex-Gender Walls in Iran," *WSQ: Women's Studies Quarterly* 36, nos. 3–4 (2008): 23–42.

2. Also see the Israeli film *Paper Dolls (Bubot Niyar)*, dir. Tomer Heymann, 2006.

3. In this . . . essay, I use the term "gender variant" to designate persons who do not conform to the logic that one must remain the gender assigned at birth for the duration of one's life or that gender can be only male or female. This avoids deploying identity categories, such as transgender or transsexual, with which many gender-variant people disidentify and that tend to be used in a universalizing manner.

4. Paisley Currah, "The Transgender Rights Imaginary," in *Feminist and Queer Legal Theory: Intimate Encounters, Uncomfortable Conversations*, ed. Martha Fineman, Jack E. Jackson, and Adam P. Romero (London, UK: Ashgate, 2009), 245–258.

5. On the appropriation of the border metaphor, see Aren Aizura, "Of Borders and Homes: The Imaginary Community of (Trans) Sexual Citizenship," *Inter-Asia Cultural Studies* 7, no. 2 (2006): 289–309; Nael Bhanji, "Diasporic Trans/scriptions: Home, Transsexual Citizenship, and Racialized Bodies," in *Transgender Migrations: The Bodies, Borders and (Geo) Politics of Transition*, ed. Trystan Cotton, 157–175 (New York: Routledge, 2011).

6. See, for example, Nan Seuffert, "Reflections on Transgender Immigration," *Griffith Law Review* 18, no. 3 (2009): 428–452; John A. Fisher, "Sex Determination for Federal Purposes: Is Transsexual Immigration Via Marriage Permissible under the Defense of Marriage Act," *Michigan Journal of Gender and Law* 10 (2003–2004): 237–268. An exception is Pooja Gehi, "Struggles from the Margins: Anti-immigrant Legislation and the Impact on Low-Income Transgender People of Color," *Women's Rights Law Report* 30 (2008): 315–346.

7. On modulation as a technique of societies of control, see Gilles Deleuze, "Postscript on the Societies of Control," *October* 59 (1992): 3–7.

8. Dean Spade, "Trans Law and Politics on a Neoliberal Landscape," *Temple Political and Civil Rights Law Review* 18, no. 2 (2009): 354.

9. Ibid., 368.

10. On biopolitics, see Michel Foucault, "From the Power of Sovereignty to Power over Life," in *Society Must Be Defended: Lectures at the College de France 1975–1976*, ed. Mauro Bertani and Alessandro Fontana (New York: Picador, 2003), 239–264. On the overuse of biopolitics, see Melinda Cooper, Anna Munster, and Andrew Goffey, "Biopolitics, for Now," *Culture Machine* 7 (2005), www.culturemachine.net/index.php/cm/article/ view/24/31 (accessed June 20, 2009).

11. For example, although the U.S.-Mexico border is the locus of the xenophobic specular imaginary of U.S. nationalism, the border between Guatemala and Mexico is heavily policed by numerous formal and informal law-enforcement agencies. The European Union's Schengen Treaty designates all the E.U. countries as one supranational territory that outsources detention camps for undocumented migrants to nations on the borders of Europe placed in high-flow locations, such as Morocco, Tunisia, Turkey, Croatia, and so forth.

12. These institutions include the United Nations High Commission for Refugees and the International Organization for Migration. On regimes of mobility control, I cite Dimitris Papadopoulos, Niamh Stephenson, and Vassilis Tsianos, *Escape Routes: Control and Subversion in the 21st Century* (London, UK: Pluto Press, 2008), 162; but also see the work of Angela Mitropoulos.

13. Angela Mitropoulos, "Halt, Who Goes There?" in *City-State: A Critical Reader on Surveillance and Social Control,* ed. Louise Boon-Kuo and Gavin Sullivan (Sydney, Australia: UTS Community Law and Legal Research Centre, 2002), 73.

14. Angela Mitropoulos, "The Materialization of Race in Multiculture," *darkmatter* 2 (February 23, 2008), www.darkmatterl01.org/site/2008/02/23/the-materialisation-of-race-in-multiculture (accessed January 3, 2011). On the Schmittian exception, see Carl Schmitt, *Political Theology: Four Chapters on the Concept of Sovereignty,* trans. George Schwab (Chicago, IL: University of Chicago Press, 1985).

15. See "Letter to the DREAM Movement: My Painful Withdrawal of Support for the DREAM Act," http://anti-fronteras.com/2010/09/18 (accessed October 5, 2010).

16. "Maintaining Awareness Regarding Al-Qaeda's Potential Threats," Department of Homeland Security, September 4, 2003, www.dps.state.vt.us/homeland/library_aware.htm.

17. United Kingdom Lesbian and Gay Immigration Group online forum, www.uklgig.org.uk/phpBB/viewtopic.php?f=4&t=2228&hilit=transgender (accessed April 13, 2011).

18. Immigration Equality and the Transgender Law Center, *Immigration Law and the Transgender Client,* section 1.2.4.1, www.immigrationequality.org/template3.php?pageid=1135 (accessed November 3, 2011).

19. Ibid., section 1.2.4.

20. Ibid., section 1.2.4.1.

21. Yates Memo Regarding Transgender Immigration Applicants, http://immigrationequality.org/uploadedfiles/MicrosoftWord-App(2).pdf (accessed February 21, 2011).

22. The U.S. Defense of Marriage Act (1996) stipulates that marriage is between a man and a woman.

23. *Immigration Law and the Transgender Client,* section 1.2.4.1.

24. The preoccupation with romantic heterosexual coupledom as the only legitimate idea of family worthy of immigration sponsorship has been critiqued by many, including Eithne Luibhéid, who points out how U.S. immigration control has historically served as a mechanism for "constructing, enforcing and normalizing dominant forms of heteronormativity" and simultaneously casting a variety of non-heteronormative bodies as threats. See Eithne Luibhéid "Sexuality, Migration, and the Shifting Line between Legal and Illegal Status," *GLQ: A Journal of Lesbian and Gay Studies* 14, nos. 2–3 (2008): 296.

25. *Immigration Law and the Transgender Client,* section 4.6.6.

26. Ibid.

27. A critical dissection of the stereotype of trans people as "deceivers" can be found in Talia Mae Bettcher, "Evil Deceivers and Make-Believers: On Transphobic Violence and the Politics of Illusion," *Hypatia* 22, no. 3 (Summer 2007): 44–65.

28. Karma Chávez, "Border (In)Securities: Normative and Differential Belonging in LGBTQ and Immigrant Rights Discourse," *Communication and Critical/Cultural Studies* 7, no. 2 (2010): 141.

29. Ibid., 142.

30. For the term "entrepreneurial subject," I am indebted to Wendy Brown's essay "Neo-liberalism and the End of Liberal Democracy," *Theory and Event* 7, no. 1 (2003), in Wendy Brown, *Edgework: Critical Essays on Knowledge and Politics* (Princeton, NJ: Princeton University Press, 2005), 37–59.

31. Luibhéid, "Sexuality, Migration, and the Shifting Line between Legal and Illegal Status," 307.

32. Queers for Economic Justice, "Queers and Immigration: A Vision Statement," *Scholar and Feminist Online* 6, no. 3 (2008), www.barnard.edu/sfonline/immigration/qej_01.htm (accessed May 13, 2011)

33. Chávez, "Border (In) Securities," 147.

34. Ibid., 148.

35. Sylvia Rivera Law Project, http:/slrp.org/about (accessed January 1, 2011).

36. Jasbir Puar, *Terrorist Assemblages: Homonationalism in Queer Times* (Durham, NC: Duke University Press, 2007), 206.

37. See Brian Massumi, *Parables for the Virtual: Movement, Affect, Sensation* (Durham, NC: Duke University Press, 2002), 2–3.

38. A more insightful critique of Transgender Day of Remembrance than I have room for here is Sarah Lamble's "Retelling Racialized Violence, Remaking White Innocence: The Politics of Interlocking Oppressions in Transgender Day of Remembrance," *Sexuality Research and Social Policy: Journal of NSRC* 5, no. 1 (March 2008): 24–42.

39. Neferti Tadiar, "Towards a Vision of Sexual and Economic Justice," *Scholar and Feminist Online* 7, no. 3 (2009), www.barnard.edu/sfonline/sexecon/print_tadiar.htm (accessed March 4, 2011).

40. Ibid., 3.

41. Yann Moulier-Boutang and Stany Grelet, "The Art of Flight: An Interview with Yann Moulier-Boutang," *Rethinking Marxism* 13, no. 3–4 (2001): 227.

42. Paolo Virno, "Virtuosity and Revolution: The Political Theory of Exodus," in *Radical Thought in Italy: A Potential Politics,* ed. Michael Hardt and Paolo Virno (Minneapolis: University of Minnesota Press, 1996), 189.

43. Papadopoulos, Tsianos, and Stephenson, *Escape Routes,* 220.

GLORIA ANZALDÚA

40. LA CONCIENCIA DE LA MESTIZA: TOWARDS A NEW CONSCIOUSNESS

Por la mujer de mi raza
hablará el espíritu.[1]

José Vasconcelos, Mexican philosopher, envisaged *una raza mestiza, una mezcla de razas afines, una raza de color—la primera raza síntesis del globo.* He called it a cosmic race, *la raza cósmica,* a fifth race embracing the four major races of the world.[2] Opposite to the theory of the pure Aryan, and to the policy of racial purity that white America practices, his theory is one of inclusivity. At the confluence of two or more genetic streams, with chromosomes constantly "crossing over," this mixture of races, rather than resulting in an inferior being, provides hybrid progeny, a mutable, more malleable species with a rich gene pool. From this racial, ideological, cultural and biological cross-pollinization, an "alien" consciousness is presently in the making—a new *mestiza* consciousness, *una conciencia de mujer.* It is a consciousness of the Borderlands.

UNA LUCHA DE FRONTERAS/A STRUGGLE OF BORDERS

Because I, a *mestiza,*
continually walk out of one culture
and into another,
because I am in all cultures at the same time,
alma entre dos mundos, tres, cuatro,
me zumba la cabeza con lo contradictorio.
Estoy norteada por todas las voces que me hablan
simultáneamente.

The ambivalence from the clash of voices results in mental and emotional states of perplexity. Internal strife results in insecurity and indecisiveness. The *mestiza*'s dual or multiple personality is plagued by psychic restlessness.

In a constant state of mental nepantilism, an Aztec word meaning torn between ways, *la mestiza* is a product of the transfer of the cultural and spiritual values of one group to another. Being tricultural, monolingual, bilingual, or multilingual, speaking a patois, and in a state of perpetual transition, the *mestiza* faces the dilemma of the mixed breed: which collectivity does the daughter of a darkskinned mother listen to?

El choque de un alma atrapado entre el mundo del espíritu y el mundo de la técnica a veces la deja entullada. Cradled in one culture, sandwiched between two cultures, straddling all three cultures and their value systems, *la mestiza* undergoes a struggle of flesh, a struggle of borders, an inner war. Like all people, we perceive the version of reality that our culture communicates. Like others having or living in more than one culture, we get multiple, often opposing messages. The coming together of two self-consistent but habitually incompatible frames of reference[3] causes *un choque,* a cultural collision.

Within us and within *la cultura chicana,* commonly held beliefs of the white culture attack commonly held beliefs of the Mexican culture, and both attack commonly held beliefs of the indigenous culture. Subconsciously, we see an attack on ourselves and our beliefs as a threat and we attempt to block with a counterstance.

But it is not enough to stand on the opposite river bank, shouting questions, challenging patriarchal, white conventions. A counterstance locks one into a duel of oppressor and oppressed; locked in mortal combat, like the cop and the criminal, both are reduced to a common denominator of violence. The counterstance refutes the dominant culture's views and beliefs, and, for this, it is proudly defiant. All reaction is limited by, and dependent on, what it is reacting against. Because the counterstance stems from a problem with authority—outer as well as inner—it's a step towards liberation from cultural domination. But it is not a way of life. At some point, on our way to a new consciousness, we will have to leave the opposite bank, the split between the two mortal combatants somehow healed so that we are on both shores at once and, at once, see through serpent and eagle eyes. Or perhaps we will decide to disengage from the dominant culture, write it off altogether as a lost cause, and cross the border into a wholly new and separate territory. Or we might go another route. The possibilities are numerous once we decide to act and not react.

A TOLERANCE FOR AMBIGUITY

These numerous possibilities leave *la mestiza* floundering in uncharted seas. In perceiving conflicting information and points of view, she is subjected to a swamping of her psychological borders. She has discovered that she can't hold concepts or ideas in rigid boundaries. The borders and walls that are supposed to keep the undesirable ideas out are entrenched habits and patterns of behavior; these habits and patterns are the enemy within. Rigidity means death. Only by remaining flexible is she able to stretch the psyche horizontally and vertically. *La mestiza* constantly has to shift out of habitual formations; from convergent thinking, analytical reasoning that tends to use rationality to move toward a single goal (a Western mode), to divergent thinking,[4] characterized by movement away from set patterns and goals and toward a more whole perspective, one that includes rather than excludes.

The new *mestiza* copes by developing a tolerance for contradictions, a tolerance for ambiguity. She learns to be an Indian in Mexican culture, to be Mexican from an Anglo point of view. She learns to juggle cultures. She has a plural personality, she operates in a pluralistic mode—nothing is thrust out, the good the bad and the ugly, nothing rejected, nothing abandoned. Not only does she sustain contradictions, she turns the ambivalence into something else.

She can be jarred out of ambivalence by an intense, and often painful, emotional event which inverts or resolves the ambivalence. I'm not sure exactly how. The work takes place underground—subconsciously. It is work that the soul performs. That focal point or fulcrum, that juncture where the *mestiza* stands, is where phenomena tend to collide. It is where the possibility of uniting all that is separate occurs. This assembly is not one where severed or separated pieces merely come together. Nor is it a balancing of opposing powers. In attempting to work out a synthesis, the self has added a third element which is greater than the sum of its severed parts. That third element is a new consciousness—a *mestiza* consciousness—and though it is a source of intense pain, its energy comes from continual creative motion that keeps breaking down the unitary aspect of each new paradigm.

En unas pocas centurias, the future will belong to the *mestiza*. Because the future depends on the breaking down of paradigms, it depends on the straddling of two or more cultures. By creating a new mythos—that is, a change in the way we perceive reality, the way we see ourselves, and the ways we behave—*la mestiza* creates a new consciousness.

The work of *mestiza* consciousness is to break down the subject-object duality that keeps her a prisoner and to show in the flesh and through the images in her work how duality is transcended. The answer to the problem between the white race and the colored, between males and females, lies in healing the split that originates in the very foundation of our lives, our culture, our languages, our thoughts. A massive uprooting of dualistic thinking in the individual and collective consciousness is the beginning of a long struggle, but one that could, in our best hopes, bring us to the end of rape, of violence, of war.

LA ENCRUCIJADA / THE CROSSROADS

A chicken is being sacrificed
at a crossroads, a simple mound of earth
a mud shrine for *Eshu*,
Yoruba god of indeterminacy,
who blesses her choice of path.
She begins her journey.

Su cuerpo es una bocacalle. La mestiza has gone from being the sacrificial goat to becoming the officiating priestess at the crossroads.

As a *mestiza* I have no country, my homeland cast me out; yet all countries are mine because I am every woman's sister or potential lover. (As a lesbian I have no race, my own people disclaim me; but I am all races because there is the queer of me in all races.) I am cultureless because, as a feminist, I challenge the collective cultural/religious male-derived beliefs of Indo-Hispanics and Anglos; yet I am cultured because I am participating in the creation of yet another culture, a new story to explain the world and our participation in it, a new value system with images and symbols that connect us to each other and to the planet. *Soy un amasamiento*, I am an act of kneading, of uniting and joining that not only has produced both a creature of darkness and a creature of light, but also a creature that questions the definitions of light and dark and gives them new meanings.

We are the people who leap in the dark, we are the people on the knees of the gods. In our very flesh, (r)evolution works out the clash of cultures. It makes us crazy constantly, but if the center holds, we've made some kind of evolutionary step forward. *Nuestra alma el trabajo*, the opus, the great alchemical work; spiritual *mestizaje*, a "morphogenesis,"[5] an inevitable unfolding. We have become the quickening serpent movement.

Indigenous like corn, like corn, the *mestiza* is a product of crossbreeding, designed for preservation under a variety of conditions. Like an ear of corn—a female seed-bearing organ—the *mestiza* is tenacious, tightly wrapped in the husks of her culture. Like kernels she clings to the cob; with thick stalks and strong brace roots, she holds tight to the earth—she will survive the crossroads.

Lavando y remojando el maíz en agua de cal, despojando el pellejo. Moliendo, mixteando, amasando, haciendo tortillas de masa.[6] She steeps the corn in lime, it swells, softens. With stone roller on *metate*, she grinds the corn, then grinds again. She kneads and moulds the dough, pats the round balls into *tortillas*.

We are the porous rock in the stone *metate*
squatting on the ground.
We are the rolling pin, el maíz y agua,
la masa harina. Somos el amasijo.
Somos lo molido en el metate.
We are the *comal* sizzling hot,
the hot *tortilla*, the hungry mouth.

We are the coarse rock.
We are the grinding motion,
the mixed potion, somos el molcajete.
We are the pestle, the *comino, ajo, pimienta*,
We are the *chile colorado*,
the green shoot that cracks the rock.
We will abide.

EL CAMINO DE LA MESTIZA / THE MESTIZA WAY

Caught between the sudden contraction, the breath sucked in and the endless space, the brown woman stands still, looks at the sky. She decides to go down, digging her way along the roots of trees. Sifting through the bones, she shakes them to see if there is any marrow in them. Then, touching the dirt to her forehead, to her tongue, she takes a few bones, leaves the rest in their burial place.

She goes through her backpack, keeps her journal and address book, throws away the muni-bart metromaps. The coins are heavy and they go next, then the greenbacks flutter through the air. She keeps her knife, can opener and eyebrow pencil. She puts bones, pieces of bark, *hierbas*, eagle feather, snakeskin, tape recorder, the rattle and drum in her pack and she sets out to become the complete *tolteca*.

Her first step is to take inventory. *Despojando, desgranando, quitando paja*. Just what did she inherit from her ancestors? This weight on her back—which is the baggage from the Indian mother, which the baggage from the Spanish father, which the baggage from the Anglo?

Pero es difícil differentiating between *lo heredado, lo adquirido, lo impuesto*. She puts history through a sieve, winnows out the lies, looks at the forces that we as a race, as women, have been a part of. *Luego bota lo que no vale, los desmientos, los desencuentos, el embrutecimiento. Aguarda el juicio, hondo y enraizado, de la gente antigua.* This step is a conscious rupture with all oppressive traditions of all cultures and religions. She communicates that rupture, documents the struggle. She reinterprets history and, using new symbols, she shapes new myths. She adopts new perspectives toward the darkskinned, women and queers. She strengthens her tolerance (and intolerance) for ambiguity. She is willing to share, to make herself vulnerable to foreign ways of seeing and thinking. She surrenders all notions of safety, of the familiar. Deconstruct, construct. She becomes a *nahual*, able to transform herself into a tree, a coyote, into another person. She learns to transform the small "I" into the total Self. *Se hace moldeadora de su alma. Según la concepción que tiene de sí misma, así será.*

QUE NO SE NOS OLVIDEN LOS HOMBRES

> *"Tú no sirves pa'nada—*
> you're good for nothing.
> *Eres pura vieja."*

"You're nothing but a woman" means you are defective. Its opposite is to be *un macho*. The modern meaning of the word "machismo," as well as the concept, is actually an Anglo invention. For men like my father, being "macho" meant being strong enough to protect and support my mother and us, yet being able to show love. Today's macho has doubts about his ability to feed and protect his family. His "machismo" is an adaptation to oppression and poverty and low self-esteem. It is the result of hierarchical male dominance. The Anglo, feeling inadequate and inferior and powerless, displaces or transfers these feelings to the Chicano by shaming him. In the Gringo world, the Chicano suffers from excessive humility and self-effacement, shame of self and self-deprecation. Around Latinos he suffers from a sense of language inadequacy and its accompanying discomfort; with Native Americans he suffers from a racial amnesia which ignores our common blood, and from guilt because the Spanish part of him took their land and oppressed them. He has an excessive compensatory hubris when around Mexicans from the other side. It overlays a deep sense of racial shame.

The loss of a sense of dignity and respect in the macho breeds a false machismo which leads him to put down women and even to brutalize them. Coexisting with his sexist behavior is a love for the mother which takes precedence over that of all others. Devoted son, macho pig. To wash down the shame of his acts, of his very being, and to handle the brute in the mirror, he takes to the bottle, the snort, the needle, and the fist.

Though we "understand" the root causes of male hatred and fear, and the subsequent wounding of women, we do not excuse, we do not condone, and we will no longer put up with it. From the men of our race, we demand the admission/acknowledgment/disclosure/testimony that they wound us, violate us, are afraid of us and of our power. We need them to say they will begin to eliminate their hurtful put-down ways. But more than the words, we demand acts. We say to them: We will develop equal power with you and those who have shamed us.

It is imperative that *mestizas* support each other in changing the sexist elements in the Mexican-Indian culture. As long as woman is put down, the Indian and the Black in all of us is put down. The struggle of the *mestiza* is above all a feminist one. As long as *los hombres* think they have to *chingar mujeres* and each other to be men, as long as men are taught that they are superior and therefore culturally favored over *la mujer*, as long as to be a *vieja* is a thing of derision, there can be no real healing of our psyches. We're halfway there— we have such love of the Mother, the good mother. The first step is to unlearn the *puta/virgen* dichotomy and to see *Coatlalopeuh-Coatlicue* in the Mother, *Guadalupe*.

Tenderness, a sign of vulnerability, is so feared that it is showered on women with verbal abuse and blows. Men, even more than women, are fettered to gender roles. Women at least have had the guts to break out of bondage. Only gay men have had the courage to expose themselves to the woman inside them and to challenge the current masculinity. I've encountered a few scattered and isolated gentle straight men, the beginnings of a new breed, but they are confused, and entangled with sexist behaviors that they have not been able to eradicate. We need a new masculinity and the new man needs a movement.

Lumping the males who deviate from the general norm with man, the oppressor, is a gross injustice. *Asombra pensar que nos hemos quedado en ese pozo oscuro donde el mundo encierra a las lesbianas. Asombra pensar que hemos, como feministas y lesbianas, cerrado nuestros corazónes a los hombres, a nuestros hermanos los jotos, desheredados y marginales como nosotros.* Being the supreme crossers of cultures, homosexuals have strong bonds with the queer white, Black, Asian, Native American, Latino, and with the queer in Italy, Australia and the rest of the planet. We come from all colors, all classes, all races, all time periods. Our role is to link people with each other—the Blacks with Jews with

Indians with Asians with whites with extraterrestrials. It is to transfer ideas and information from one culture to another. Colored homosexuals have more knowledge of other cultures; have always been at the forefront (although sometimes in the closet) of all liberation struggles in this country; have suffered more injustices and have survived them despite all odds. Chicanos need to acknowledge the political and artistic contributions of their queer. People, listen to what your *jotería* is saying.

The *mestizo* and the queer exist at this time and point on the evolutionary continuum for a purpose. We are a blending that proves that all blood is intricately woven together, and that we are spawned out of similar souls.

SOMOS UNA GENTE

Hay tantísimas fronteras
que dividen a la gente,
pero por cada frontera
existe también un puente.

—Gina Valdés[7]

Divided Loyalties. Many women and men of color do not want to have any dealings with white people. It takes too much time and energy to explain to the downwardly mobile, white middle-class women that it's okay for us to want to own "possessions," never having had any nice furniture on our dirt floors or "luxuries" like washing machines. Many feel that whites should help their own people rid themselves of race hatred and fear first. I, for one, choose to use some of my energy to serve as mediator. I think we need to allow whites to be our allies. Through our literature, art, *corridos,* and folktales we must share our history with them so when they set up committees to help Big Mountain Navajos or the Chicano farm workers or *los Nicaragüenses* they won't turn people away because of their racial fears and ignorances. They will come to see that they are not helping us but following our lead.

Individually, but also as a racial entity, we need to voice our needs. We need to say to white society: We need you to accept the fact that Chicanos are different, to acknowledge your rejection and negation of us. We need you to own the fact that you looked upon us as less than human, that you stole our lands, our personhood, our self-respect. We need you to make public restitution: to say that, to compensate for your own sense of defectiveness, you strive for power over us, you erase our history and our experience because it makes you feel guilty—you'd rather forget your brutish acts. To say you've split yourself from minority groups, that you disown us, that your dual consciousness splits off parts of yourself, transferring the "negative" parts onto us. (Where there is persecution of minorities, there is shadow projection. Where there is violence and war, there is repression of shadow.) To say that you are afraid of us, that to put distance between us, you wear the mask of contempt. Admit that Mexico is your double, that she exists in the shadow of this country, that we are irrevocably tied to her. Gringo, accept the doppelganger in your psyche. By taking back your collective shadow the intracultural split will heal. And finally, tell us what you need from us.

BY YOUR TRUE FACES WE WILL KNOW YOU

I am visible—see this Indian face—yet I am invisible. I both blind them with my beak nose and am their blind spot. But I exist, we exist. They'd like to think I have melted in the pot. But I haven't, we haven't.

The dominant white culture is killing us slowly with its ignorance. By taking away our self-determination, it has made us weak and empty. As a people we have resisted and we have taken expedient positions, but we have never been allowed to develop unencumbered—we have never been allowed to be fully ourselves. The whites in power want us people of color to barricade ourselves behind our separate tribal walls so they can pick us off one at a time with their hidden weapons; so they can whitewash and distort history. Ignorance splits people, creates prejudices. A misinformed people is a subjugated people.

Before the Chicano and the undocumented worker and the Mexican from the other side can come together, before the Chicano can have unity with Native Americans and other groups, we need to know the history of their struggle and they need to know ours. Our mothers, our sisters and brothers, the guys who hang out on street corners, the children in the playgrounds, each of us must know our Indian lineage, our *afro-mestizaje,* our history of resistance.

To the immigrant *mexicano* and the recent arrivals we must teach our history. The 80 million *mexicanos* and the Latinos from Central and South America must know of our struggles. Each one of us must know basic facts about Nicaragua, Chile and the rest of Latin America. The Latinoist movement (Chicanos, Puerto Ricans, Cubans and other Spanish-speaking people working together to combat racial discrimination in the marketplace) is good but it is not enough. Other than a common culture we will have nothing to hold us together. We need to meet on a broader communal ground.

The struggle is inner: Chicano, *indio*, American Indian, *mojado*, *mexicano*, immigrant Latino, Anglo in power, working class Anglo, Black, Asian—our psyches resemble the bordertowns and are populated by the same people. The struggle has always been inner, and is played out in the outer terrains. Awareness of our situation must come before inner changes, which in turn come before changes in society. Nothing happens in the "real" world unless it first happens in the images in our heads.

EL DIA DE LA CHICANA

I will not be shamed again
Nor will I shame myself.

I am possessed by a vision: that we Chicanas and Chicanos have taken back or uncovered our true faces, our dignity and self-respect. It's a validation vision.

Seeing the Chicana anew in light of her history. I seek an exoneration, a seeing through the fictions of white supremacy, a seeing of ourselves in our true guises and not as the false racial personality that has been given to us and that we have given to ourselves. I seek our woman's face, our true features, the positive and the negative seen clearly, free of the tainted biases of male dominance. I seek new images of identity, new beliefs about ourselves, our humanity and worth no longer in question.

Estamos viviendo en la noche de la Raza, un tiempo cuando el trabajo se hace a lo quieto, en lo oscuro. El día cuando aceptamos tal y como somos y para donde vamos y porque—ese día será el día de la Raza. Yo tengo el compromiso de expresar mi visión, mi sensibilidad, mi percepción de la revalidación de la gente mexicana, su mérito, estimación, honra, aprecio, y validez.

On December 2nd when my sun goes into my first house, I celebrate *el día de la Chicana y el Chicano*. On that day I clean my altars, light my *Coatlalopeuh* candle, burn sage and copal, take *el baño para espantar basura*, sweep my house. On that day I bare my soul, make myself vulnerable to friends and family by expressing my feelings. On that day I affirm who we are.

On that day I look inside our conflicts and our basic introverted racial temperament. I identify our needs, voice them. I acknowledge that the self and the race have been wounded. I recognize the need to take care of our personhood, of our racial self. On that day I gather the splintered and disowned parts of *la gente mexicana* and hold them in my arms. *Todas las partes de nosotros valen.*

On that day I say, "Yes, all you people wound us when you reject us. Rejection strips us of self-worth; our vulnerability exposes us to shame. It is our innate identity you find wanting. We are ashamed that we need your good opinion, that we need your acceptance. We can no longer camouflage our needs, can no longer let defenses and fences sprout around us. We can no longer withdraw. To rage and look upon you with contempt is to rage and be contemptuous of ourselves. We can no longer blame you, nor disown the white parts, the male parts, the pathological parts, the queer parts, the vulnerable parts. Here we are weaponless with open arms, with only our magic. Let's try it our way, the *mestiza* way, the Chicana way, the woman way."

On that day, I search for our essential dignity as a people, a people with a sense of purpose—to belong and contribute to something greater than our *pueblo*. On that day I seek to recover and reshape my spiritual identity. *¡Anímate! Raza, a celebrar el día de la Chicana.*

EL RETORNO

All movements are accomplished in six stages,
and the seventh brings return.

—I Ching[8]

Tanto tiempo sin verte casa mía,
mi cuna, mi hondo nido de la huerta.

—"Soledad"[9]

I stand at the river, watch the curving, twisting serpent, a serpent nailed to the fence where the mouth of the Rio Grande empties into the Gulf.

I have come back. *Tanto dolor me costó el alejamiento.* I shade my eyes and look up. The bone beak of a hawk slowly circling over me, checking me out as potential carrion. In its wake a little bird flickering its wings, swimming sporadically like a fish. In the distance the expressway and the slough of traffic like an irritated sow. The sudden pull in my gut, *la tierra, los aguaceros.* My land, *el viento soplando la arena, el lagartijo debajo de un nopalito. Me acuerdo como era antes. Una región desértica de vasta llanuras, costeras de baja altura, de escasa lluvia, de chaparrales formados por mesquites y buizaches.* If I look real hard I can almost see the Spanish fathers who were called "the cavalry of Christ" enter this valley riding their *burros,* see the clash of cultures commence.

Tierra natal. This is home, the small towns in the Valley, *los Pueblitos* with chicken pens and goats picketed to mesquite shrubs. *En las colonias* on the other side of the tracks, junk cars line the front yards of hot pink and lavender-trimmed houses—Chicano architecture we call it, self-consciously. I have missed the TV shows where hosts speak in half and half, and where awards are given in the category of Tex-Mex music. I have missed the Mexican cemeteries blooming with artificial flowers, the fields of aloe vera and red pepper, rows of sugar cane, of corn hanging on the stalks, the cloud of *polvareda* in the dirt roads behind a speeding pickup truck, *el sabor de tamales de rez y venado.* I have missed *la yegua colorada* gnawing the wooden gate of her stall, the smell of horse flesh from Carito's corrals. *Hecho menos las noches calientes sin aire, noches de linternas y lechuzas* making holes in the night.

I still feel the old despair when I look at the unpainted, dilapidated, scrap lumber houses consisting mostly of corrugated aluminum. Some of the poorest people in the U.S. live in the Lower Rio Grande Valley, an arid and semi-arid land of irrigated farming, intense sunlight and heat, citrus groves next to chaparral and cactus. I walk through the elementary school I attended so long ago, that remained segregated until recently. I remember how the white teachers used to punish us for being Mexican.

How I love this tragic valley of South Texas, as Ricardo Sánchez calls it; this borderland between the Nueces and the Rio Grande. This land has survived possession and ill-use by five countries: Spain, Mexico, the Republic of Texas, the U.S., the Confederacy, and the U.S. again. It has survived Anglo-Mexican blood feuds, lynchings, burnings, rapes, pillage.

Today I see the Valley still struggling to survive. Whether it does or not, it will never be as I remember it. The borderlands depression that was set off by the 1982 peso devaluation in Mexico resulted in the closure of hundreds of Valley businesses. Many people lost their homes, cars, land. Prior to 1982, U.S. store owners thrived on retail sales to Mexicans who came across the border for groceries and clothes and appliances. While goods on the U.S. side have become 10, 100, 1000 times more expensive for Mexican buyers, goods on the Mexican side have become 10, 100, 1000 times cheaper for Americans. Because the Valley is heavily dependent on agriculture and Mexican retail trade, it has the highest unemployment rates along the entire border region; it is the Valley that has been hardest hit.[10]

"It's been a bad year for corn," my brother, Nune, says. As he talks, I remember my father scanning the sky for a rain that would end the drought, looking up into the sky, day after day, while the corn withered on its stalk. My father has been dead for 29 years, having worked himself to death. The life span of a Mexican farm laborer is 56—he lived to be 38. It shocks me that I am older than he. I, too, search the sky for rain. Like the ancients, I worship the rain god and the maize goddess, but unlike my father I have recovered their names. Now for rain (irrigation) one offers not a sacrifice of blood, but of money.

"Farming is in a bad way," my brother says. "Two to three thousand small and big farmers went bankrupt in this country last year. Six years ago the price of corn was $8.00 per hundred pounds," he goes on. "This year it is $3.90 per hundred pounds." And, I think to myself, after taking inflation into account, not planting anything puts you ahead.

I walk out to the back yard, stare at *los rosales de mamá.* She wants me to help her prune the rose bushes, dig out the carpet grass that is choking them. *Mamagrande Ramona también tenía rosales.* Here every Mexican grows flowers. If they don't have a piece of dirt, they use car tires, jars, cans, shoe boxes. Roses are the Mexican's favorite flower. I think, how symbolic—thorns and all.

Yes, the Chicano and Chicana have always taken care of growing things and the land. Again I see the four of us kids getting off the school bus, changing into our work clothes, walking into the field with Papi and Mami, all six of us bending to the ground. Below our feet, under the earth lie the watermelon seeds. We cover them with paper plates, putting *terremotes* on top of the plates to keep them from being blown away by the wind. The paper plates keep the freeze away. Next day or the next, we remove the plates, bare the tiny green shoots to the elements. They survive and grow, give fruit hundreds of times the size of the seed. We water them and hoe them. We harvest them. The vines dry, rot, are plowed under. Growth, death, decay, birth. The soil prepared again and again, impregnated, worked on. A constant changing of forms, *renacimientos de la tierra madre.*

This land was Mexican once
was Indian always
and is.
And will be again.

NOTES

1. This is my own "take off" on José Vasconcelos' idea. José Vasconcelos, *La Raza Cósmica; Misión de la Raza Ibero-Americana* (México: Aguilar S.A. de Ediciones, 1961).
2. Vasconcelos.
3. Arthur Koestler termed this "bisociation." Albert Rothenberg, *The Creative Process in Art. Science, and Other Fields* (Chicago, IL: University of Chicago Press, 1979), 12.
4. In part, I derive my definitions for "convergent" and "divergent" thinking from Rothenberg, 12–13.
5. To borrow chemist Ilya Prigogine's theory of "dissipative structures." Prigogine discovered that substances interact not in predictable ways as it was taught in science, but in different and fluctuating ways to produce new and more complex structures, a kind of birth he called "morphogenesis," which created unpredictable innovations. Harold Gilliam, "Searching for a New World View," *This World* (January, 1981), 23.
6. *Tortillas de masa harina:* corn tortillas are of two types, the smooth uniform ones made in a tortilla press and usually bought at a tortilla factory or supermarket, and *gorditas,* made by mixing *masa* with lard or shortening or butter (my mother sometimes puts in bits of bacon or *chicharrones).*
7. Gina Valdés, *Puentes y Fronteras: Coplas Chicanos* (Los Angeles, CA: Castle Lithograph, 1982), 2.
8. Richard Wilhelm, *The I Chine or Book of Changes*, trans. Cary F. Baynes (Princeton, NJ: Princeton University Press, 1950), 98.
9. "*Soledad*" is sung by the group *Haciendo Punto en Otro Son.*
10. Out of the twenty-two border counties in the four border states, Hidalgo County (named for Father Hidalgo who was shot in 1810 after instigating Mexico's revolt against Spanish rule under the banner of *la Virgen de Guadalupe)* is the most poverty-stricken county in the nation as well as the largest home base (along with Imperial in California) for migrant farmworkers. It was here that I was born and raised. I am amazed that both it and I have survived.

CHRISTINA HOLMES

41. FEMINIST APPROACHES TO ENVIRONMENTALISM: ECOFEMINISM, ECOWOMANISM, AND BORDERLANDS ENVIRONMENTALISM

Who does "ecofeminism" belong to and why should we care? As a field that consciously holds "eco" and "feminism" in tension, it joins two of most influential social movements in recent history. The term was introduced in the late 1970s and early eighties by Americans Mary Daly and Ynestra King and by French writer Françoise d'Eaubonne, each of whom speculated about how women's oppression relates to the domination of nature (Gaard, *Ecofeminism Now!*). By the 1987 "Ecofeminist Perspectives" conference, "the word ecofeminism began to be widely used to describe a politics which attempted to combine feminism, environmentalism, antiracism, animal rights, anti-imperialism, antimilitarism, and non-traditional spiritualities" (Sturgeon, "The Nature of Race" 263). The unwieldy breadth of issues brought together makes ecofeminist theory hard to pin down, but we now have a number of genealogies that track its emergence, initial insights, and subsequent theoretical developments. Genealogies explore how a discourse takes hold at a particular moment in time, who it imagines as its relevant subjects (e.g., white feminist academics, grassroots activists), and how it gets taken up, refused, or transformed as it circulates (Foucault 76-77). Genealogies are important because how we tell stories is important—we do not tell them in a non-innocent way that is free of investments (Hemmings). Stories help us think, feel, and act in new ways or they can close us off to possibilities. I provide an overview of how ecofeminism has evolved with and against the environmental justice movement before considering how ecowomanist and borderlands environmentalisms sit at the intersection of ecofeminism and environmental justice. Telling ecofeminist history through a narrow lens of Western feminist theoretical schools, as has been the case in much of the literature, explains

some things about how women's environmental activism gains meaning, but it also affirms the idea that environmentalism and feminism are the terrains of white and middle-class women. There are multiple feminist environmentalisms with different origins, interests, actors, and understandings of oppression; our theory (and thus, our action) grows stronger when we recognize this. A multiplicitous feminist environmentalism invites new actors to identify ecological elements in their social justice agenda and contribute to theory and coalition building in their own way.

ECOFEMINISM

Karen Warren broadly defines ecofeminism through the statement that "there are important connections between how one treats women, people of color, and the underclass on one hand and how one treats the nonhuman natural environment on the other" (*Ecofeminism* xi). She elaborates that these human-nature connections may be empirical, linguistic, literary, religious, or historical, to name just a few. Because of the interdisciplinary nature of ecofeminism and the numerous topics it enfolds, the field has been seen as porous, maybe too much so as one critic complained that "when [ecofeminism] contains all peoples and all injustices, the fine tuning and differentiation lose out" (qtd. in Gaard, "Ecofeminism Revisited" 33). A common way genealogists differentiated ecofeminism's contributions to feminist analysis was to locate its roots in Western feminist philosophy, theorizing it through liberal, radical cultural, and socialist feminisms. Liberal feminism identifies women's oppression in legal, political, and economic barriers to opportunities afforded to (some) men (Tong 2). They might argue that women, especially low-income and women of color who live in neighborhoods with a high toxic burden, should have access to safe neighborhoods and laws that extend equal protections; further, "Given equal educational opportunities to become scientists, natural resource managers, regulators, lawyers, and legislators, women, like men, can contribute to the improvement of the environment" (Merchant, *Radical Ecology* 200-201). As liberal philosophy is grounded in an equal rights approach that valorizes the freedom of rational agents participating in a social contract, many believe it does not offer a deep enough critique about how such approaches rely on a hierarchy of humans over animals and the environment (Gruen 75). It also fails to note that those who have benefitted from the legal, political, and economic systems in place have historically done so from the extracted value of exploited *others* (i.e., "natural resources" such as trees, oil, and the labor of minoritized humans).

Genealogies then track radical and socialist responses. For radical feminists, patriarchy oppresses women, and it is "characterized by power, dominance, hierarchy, and competition" across institutions in the public and private spheres (Tong, 2). While liberal feminisms minimize gender differences, radical cultural feminists reassert differences between men and women. They claim that women can better understand the natural world because of socialized relationships that bring them closer to nature or because of their traits of care, empathy, and the potential for reproduction. For example, Daly's *Gyn/Ecology* "is primarily concerned with the mind/spirit/body pollution inflicted through patriarchal myth and language on all levels" (9). We should rid ourselves of the polluting internalized messages of male domination and find gynocentric ways of being: invent new myths, celebrate female goddesses, and summon ways of writing in a woman's voice. Citing Rachel Carson's bravery in raising the alarm about ecological disaster in *Silent Spring*, Daly urges that, "by breaking the imposed silence we help to spring other prisoners of patriarchy whose biophilic tendencies have not been completely blighted or blocked" (22). Though Daly and other radical feminists are critiqued for making universal, essentialist claims about women, they remind us to locate the body in feminist theory and politics, value interconnectedness between humans and the more-than-human world, and attend to the important role

spirituality plays in justice work (Griffin; Spretnak). Yet an analysis of patriarchy that does not consider how racism, heterosexism, and other forces intersect with or play a larger role than sexism in people's lives shows the shortcomings of some radical writing.

Socialist ecofeminists argue that capitalism *and* patriarchy oppress women, the poor, and people of color; capitalist patriarchies also exploit the environment. Socialist feminists believe that, "insofar as there is a gender and class (/caste/race)-based division of labor and distribution of property and power, gender and class (/caste/race) structure people's interactions with nature and so structure the effects of environmental change on people and their responses to it" (Agarwal 126). In other words, we need to look more closely at the materialist sources of oppression as Carolyn Merchant does in *The Death of Nature*. She shows how the domination of women and nature occurred simultaneously through the mechanization of farming and the domestication of animals. The development of this European masculine ethos of control via technological advances led to a particular kind of political economy. Critics respond that, although socialist ecofeminists problematize the unitary category "woman" and theorize a multiple systems approach to oppression, "nature" is essentialized. It shows up in theory as a natural resource or degraded habitat only insofar as it relates to women's activities (Sandilands 68-74; Casselot). It has no life or agency of its own.

In addition to sorting ecofeminism into categories of Western feminist thought, genealogists emphasize how hierarchical dualisms undergird oppressive thinking, valuing male over female, culture over nature, whiteness over racialized otherness, human over animal. Warren theorizes a "logic of domination" in Western thought that bolsters dualisms, connecting sexism, racism, speciesism and other "isms" conceptually (Warren, *Ecofeminist Philosophy* 47). Similarly, in "Toward a Queer Ecofeminism," Greta Gaard considers those dualisms alongside ascetic/erotic and heterosexual/homosexual binaries. She points out one set of equivalences among the first terms and another across the second so that maleness is associated with rationality, culture, independence, and normative heterosexuality; in contrast, "queers are feminized, animalized, eroticized, and naturalized in a culture that devalues women, nature, and sexuality. We can also examine how persons of color are feminized, animalized, eroticized, and naturalized" (119). We find traces of this in language such as "the rape of mother earth" or "virgin forest," naming homosexuality and disability as "unnatural," "sins against nature," and designating female slaves as "breeders" with contemporary echoes in discourse surrounding welfare in the United States.

While Warren, Gaard, and others trained in humanistic inquiry theorize symbolic woman-nature connections, scholars in the social and natural sciences use empirical research to study links between women and their environments. From them we learn that women make up the majority of the world's farmers; they are typically tasked with feeding and caring for family and community members, and therefore are responsible for the health of their families and environments. Vandana Shiva, a physicist known for critiquing western-style agribusiness's impacts on poor farmers, explains women's relationship to seeds and why it matters: "For an Indian woman farmer, rice is not only food, but also a resource of cattle fodder and straw for thatch. . . . Women have been seed custodians since time immemorial, and their knowledge and skills should be the basis of all crop-improvement strategies" (168). Genetically modified rice crops may grow fast and provide a high economic yield for a short time, but they also degrade the soil, require expensive fertilizers, trap a farmer in debt, and undermine the value of biodiversity. This empirical study matters because it shows the importance of knowledge systems outside of the masculinist, colonialist episteme. Women seed custodians may have resources for alternate ways of organizing social, political, environmental, and economic life.

Taxonomies based on how women in specific environments are connected symbolically or empirically to nature avoid essentialism and the problem of how to make sense of activism in non-Western contexts. Why should we expect Western feminist theories to explain the work of the seed custodians described above? Theories of anti-colonialism and a native understanding of the spiritual value of seeds have explanatory power without ethnocentrism implied by interpreting the behavior of *others* through the lens of the West. Tracing ecofeminism back to specific Western feminist theory traditions or even a history originating in the peace and

antinuclear movements limits what counts as ecofeminist theories, histories, and actors. Recently published genealogies now remind us of ecofeminism's ties to twentieth-century gay and lesbian communities that reclaimed rural and urban landscapes (Mortimer-Sandilands and Erickson). Animal-focused ecofeminists recall an earlier history, drawing on conceptual connections and non-violence activism in the contemporaneous examples of British and American suffragettes, antivivisection activists, workers rights advocates, and Gandhian resistance against British rule (Adams and Gruen 8-9). My aim is to build on this work and open ecofeminist genealogies up to include those parallel movements and theories that share some of the same aims, actors, and histories as ecofeminism, but arrive at them from different starting places.

We can start with the environmental justice movement, which, like ecofeminism, intervened in the largely male and white-dominated environmentalism that focused on natural resource conservation and preservation. Environmental justice developed from grassroots activists protesting environmental racism related to issues such as locally unwanted land uses (e.g., placement of incinerators), food deserts, gentrification, and lead poisoning. Many environmental justice organizations developed from civil rights organizations and strategies (Bullard and Wright); however, they have been criticized for minimizing the role of gender, sexuality, and consideration for non-human others (Peña 145-146; Stein; Hourdequin). Dorceta Taylor responds to these criticisms, explaining that "[t]he absence of large numbers of environmental justice campaigns based solely or primarily on gender equality is no denial of the importance of the issue; it is the result of a strategy to mobilize a broad and effective coalition to help people and communities survive" (64). Nonetheless, while a whole community may be impacted by lead in tap water, pregnant ciswomen and transmen face unique risks to their developing fetuses. Environmental justice scholars that recognize material bodily differences, as well as ideologies that contribute to the disposability of those specific populations, are in a position to better understand how power operates and to build coalitions among trans and disability rights groups, child advocacy groups, and feminist and anti-racist movements.

Ecowomanism and borderlands environmentalism partially developed from but do not fit entirely within ecofeminism or environmental justice; and as such, they attend to some of the blind spots in those movements. Using the theoretical moves introduced earlier, we'll look briefly at ecowomanist and borderlands environmentalisms to count what is significant about their genealogies, including movement histories, actors, and theoretical contributions. These approaches offer a broader understanding of intersectionality and transnationality in their analysis of human-nature relationships, and understanding them better opens us up to stronger solidarities.

ECOWOMANISM AND BORDERLANDS ENVIRONMENTALISM

The Commission for Racial Justice's "Toxic Wastes and Race in the United States" broke ground in exposing the disproportionate impact of environmental toxins borne by African American communities, and many writers show how racializing discourses primitivized black bodies to justify colonization and slavery (Crenshaw 411; hooks 62; Ahuja 557). Ecowomanism builds on these analyses, ecofeminism's logic of domination, and the theory of womanism introduced by Alice Walker (Harris). Womanism focuses on the histories and experiences of African American women and it takes women's Afrocentric spiritual practices and writing for the community as vital to healing against injustice.

An ecowomanist exploration of speciesism helps us better understand interlocking systems of oppression and the importance of freeing *all* "others." Making a case for veganism, A. Breeze Harper explains why a plant-based diet should be part of antiracist, antipoverty praxis. This is especially so in a country that targets African Americans with fast food ads for salt and fat laden beef, resulting in high rates of obesity, heart disease, and diabetes (29). She advocates compassionate consumption to heal the bodies of those made ill by their food, the bodies of animals harmed by factory farming, and the bodies of those who live and work in degraded environments near ranches and factory farms. Harper acknowledges that the image of veganism is popularly embodied by white and middle-class young women, but she interrupts that story and

offers an analysis that not only welcomes women of color into veganism, but theorizes how speciesist labor practices intersect with and rely on racial, gender, and class hierarchies. Importantly, she uses examples from black lives to make her case.

Delores Williams also tackles gendered racism and speciesism while reminding us that conceptions of "human" and "nature" are so interconnected within some African American spiritual traditions that it doesn't make sense to separate social and environmental justice. Williams "uncovers parallels between acts of violence against the earth and systemic patterns of violent experience in the historical lives of women of African descent . . . by identifying the destructive methods of strip-mining used to extract coal from the earth, and comparing these to the exploitative ways black women were used for breeding during American slavery" (qtd. in Harris 35). Williams refuses hierarchical thinking that elevates humans above all else; and in naming the dual exploitation of women and the land a "sin," she marks both the earth and black women as sacred, rewriting the discursive violence that figures them as objects. While radical ecofeminist spiritualities were criticized for focusing on self-care rather than social transformation, ecowomanism draws from environmental justice movement activists that found organizing models, rhetorical skills, and leaders in churches serving African Americans. It also draws on Alice Walker's sense of spirituality that celebrates women's creative and community-building powers (e.g., seeing genius in gardens, quilts, and song). Bridging ecofeminism, environmental justice, and womanism, ecowomanism creates a space to recognize the interconnections among spiritual, social, and environmental well-being as understood from the social locations occupied by black women. It provides a lens to recognize environmental histories, actors, and approaches outside of genealogies of mainstream environmentalism and ecofeminism.

Chicana feminist environmentalism has its own historical trajectory that is not wholly contained within ecofeminism or environmental justice. In *Mexican-Americans and the Environment*, Devon Peña expands the history of the environmental justice movement beyond its focus on African American activists by folding Mexican American-led movements into discussions of environmental racism. He names farm workers against chemical exposure, urban residents against gentrification, land grant heirs seeking restoration of land, and rural colonia residents fighting for sanitation as environmental justice actors (153–155). Yet as is the case with other environmental justice literatures, the intersections of gender and sexuality are under-theorized. Even among accounts of the United Farm Workers politicizing issues of labor and land, Cesar Chavez takes center stage over co-founder Delores Huerta. And like ecowomanism that puts black women at the center of its analysis, Chicana feminist environmental approaches start from the lives of Mexican American women (Davis).

"Borderlands environmentalism" refers to the ecologically specific regions of the US Southwest and to Gloria Anzaldúa's *Borderlands/La Frontera* (Holmes). Many read Anzaldúa, but not in the context of a Chicanx land ethic and environmental consciousness. Those unfamiliar with Mexican American history may miss intertextuality with the Chicano movement's *El Plan Espiritual de Aztlán* that lays out an agenda for a society free from white supremacist Anglo rule. "Aztlán" names the Southwest homeland of the Aztecs, and the manifesto proclaims "Aztlán belongs to those who plant the seeds, water the fields, and gather the crops and not to the foreign Europeans" (*El Plan*). If the movement's male leaders imagined a Chicano nation with heterosexual women submitting to the roles of dutiful wife, mother, and Catholic daughter, Chicana feminists imagined a more inclusive homeland. Anzaldúa resignified the Southwest into a "borderlands" home for the "the squint-eyed, the perverse, the queer, the troublesome, the mongrel, the mulatto, the half-breed, the half-dead; in short: those who cross over, pass over, or go through the confines of the 'normal'" (25). Here Anzaldúa self-consciously takes up the colonialist discourses that animalized people of color to claim denigrated identities such as "mongrel" and "half-breed" for their subversive potential. She refuses human/animal dualism, just as she does American/Mexican. Related, as she makes sense of sexism in the Chicano movement, racism in the feminist movement, and ubiquitous homophobia and ableism that leave her feeling without a home or people, she calls on pre-Aztec mythology and spiritual traditions to find a new set of values. In the chapter "Entering the Serpent," she searches out the dark, creative, feminine, and underground aspects of self and culture; she tries to reintegrate and heal from dualisms that split body from soul, human from nature, male from female. On their surface, the ecological connections Anzaldúa makes do not differ much from Daly's. However, the sources and goals of her ecological consciousness do. Anzaldúa writes, "Like the ancient Olmecs, I know earth is a coiled Serpent. Forty years it's taken me to enter into the Serpent, to acknowledge that I have a body, that I am a body and to assimilate the animal body, the animal soul" (48). Building on ecofeminist and environmental justice literatures, but also on the historical knowledge and spiritual traditions of precolonial indigenous peoples, experiences of the body, nature, and spirituality become key sites of theory-building for Anzaldúa and other Chicana feminists who work in the tradition of borderlands environmentalism.

CONCLUSION

In the face of escalating climate disasters, pushback against clean air and water regulations, and encroachments on national parks and native territories, ecofeminists challenge feminist theory to take eco-social justice seriously. They practice self-reflexivity as they analyze how the field represents itself. They sort various writers into one feminist philosophical school or another and look at how ecofeminists characterize "woman" and theorize oppression through a single versus multiple systems approach. Most genealogists also protest the oversimplification of ecofeminism as essentialist, which led to its dismissal by academic feminists (many undergraduates majoring in women's and gender studies never learn about ecofeminism!). From this we see how *context* regarding how and why histories and taxonomies are told is just as important as the theories they generate—and, indeed, that it shapes how we understand those theories. To attend as carefully to context as is possible in this brief essay, I look primarily at the United States, though others provide good transnational accounts of eco-social justice (Sturgeon, *Ecofeminist Natures*; Braidotti et al.). I also take care not to extend the label "ecofeminism" to examples of ecowomanism or borderlands environmentalism. To paraphrase Dorceta Taylor, if there was a clear fit between women of color activists and ecofeminism, women of color would have joined the movement and embraced the name; since there wasn't, they made their own movements and joined alliances where possible (70). After all, "Intersectionality invites us to take up a *radical coalitional orientation* grounded in solidarity, rather than sameness as a basis for working collectively to eradicate inequalities" (May 18). We can and should understand the taxonomies that shaped ecofeminism since the 1970s even as we recover other histories that have always been present, including those offered by queer ecologies, animal studies, ecowomanism, and borderlands environmentalism. Rather than understanding feminist approaches to environmentalism through an atomistic lens, these new genealogies expose different facets of interconnected phenomena and situated standpoints offer points of contact where coalitions can be forged.

REFERENCES

Adams, Carol, and Lori Gruen, eds. *Ecofeminism: Feminist Intersections with Other Animals & the Earth.* Bloomsbury, 2014.

Agarwal, Bina. "The Gender and Environment Debate: Lessons from India." *Feminist Studies*, vol. 18, no. 1, 1992, pp. 119–158.

Ahuja, Neel. "Postcolonial Critique in a Multispecies World." *PMLA*, vol. 124, no. 2, 2009, pp. 556–563.

Anzaldúa, Gloria. *Borderlands/La Frontera.* 2nd edition, Aunt Lute Books, 1999.

Braidotti, Rosi, et. al. *Women, the Environment and Sustainable Development: Towards a Theoretical Synthesis.* Zed, 1994.

Bullard, Robert, and Beverly Wright. "The Quest for Environmental Equity: Mobilizing the African-American Community for Social Change." *American Environmentalism*, edited by Riley Dunlap and Angela Mertig, Taylor and Francis, 1992, pp. 39–49.

Casselot, Marie-Anne. "Ecofeminist Echoes in New Materialism?" *PhænEx*, vol. 11, no. 1, 2016, pp. 73–96.

Commission for Racial Justice, United Church of Christ. "Toxic Wastes and Race in the United States." *Public Access Data, Inc.*, 1987.

Crenshaw, Kimberlé. "Whose Story Is It Anyway? Feminist and Antiracist Appropriations of Anita Hill." *Race-ing Justice, Engendering Power*, edited by Toni Morrison, Pantheon, 1992, pp. 402–440.

Daly, Mary. *Gyn/Ecology: The Metaethics of Radical Feminism.* Beacon, 1978.

Davis, Malia. "Philosophy Meets Practice: A Critique of Ecofeminism through the Voices of Three Chicana Activists." *Chicano Culture, Ecology*, edited by Devon Peña, Arizona UP, 1998.

El Plan Espiritual de Aztlán. (1969). *MECHA*, University of Michigan, http://www.umich.edu/~ mechaum/Aztlan.html. Accessed August 2, 2017.

Foucault, Michel. "Nietzsche, Genealogy, History." *The Foucault Reader*, edited by Paul Rabinow, Pantheon, 1984.

Gaard, Greta, director. *Ecofeminism Now!* Video. Medusa Productions, 1996.

Gaard, Greta. "Ecofeminism Revisited: Rejecting Essentialism and Re-Placing Species in a Material Feminist Environmentalism." *Feminist Formations*, vol. 23, no. 2, 2011, pp. 26–53.

Gaard, Greta. "Toward a Queer Ecofeminism." *Hypatia*, vol. 12, no. 1, 1997, pp. 114–137.

Griffin, Susan. *Woman and Nature: The Roaring Inside Her.* Harper & Row, 1978.

Gruen, Lori. "Dismantling Oppression: An Analysis of the Connection between Women and Animals." *Ecofeminism*, edited by Greta Gaard, Temple UP, 1993, pp. 60–90.

Harper, A. Breeze. "Social Justice Beliefs and Addiction to Uncompassionate Consumption." *Sistah Vegan*, edited by A. Breeze Harper, Lantern, 2010, pp. 20–41.

Harris, Melanie L. "Ecowomanism: Black Women, Religion, and the Environment." *The Black Scholar*, vol. 46, no. 3, 2016, pp. 27–39.

Hemmings, Clare. "Telling Feminist Stories." *Feminist Theory*, vol. 6, no. 2, 2005, pp. 115–139.

Holmes, Christina. *Ecological Borderlands: Body, Nature, and Spirit in Chicana Feminism*. Illinois UP, 2016.

hooks, bell. *Black Looks: Race and Representation*. South End, 1992.

Hourdequin, Marion. *Environmental Ethics*. Bloomsbury Academic, 2015.

May, Vivian M. *Pursuing Intersectionality, Unsettling Dominant Imaginaries*. Routledge, 2015.

Merchant, Carolyn. *The Death of Nature: Women, Ecology, and the Scientific Revolution*. Harper & Row, 1989.

Merchant, Carolyn. *Radical Ecology*. 2nd edition, Routledge, 2005.

Mortimer-Sandilands, Catriona, and Bruce Erickson, eds. *Queer Ecologies*. Indiana UP, 2010.

Peña, Devon. *Mexican-Americans and the Environment*. Arizona UP, 2005.

Sandilands, Catriona. *The Good-Natured Feminist*. Minnesota UP, 1999.

Shiva, Vandana. "Women's Indigenous Knowledge and Biodiversity Conservation." *Ecofeminism*, edited by Maria Mies and Vandana Shiva, Zed, 1993, pp. 164–173.

Spretnak, Charlene. "Ecofeminism: Our Roots and Our Flowering." *Reweaving the World*, edited by Irene Diamond and Gloria Orenstein, Sierra Club Books, 1990, pp. 3–14.

Stein, Rachel, ed. *New Perspectives on Environmental Justice: Gender, Sexuality and Activism*. Rutgers UP, 2004.

Sturgeon, Noël. *Ecofeminist Natures: Race, Gender, Feminist Theory and Political Action*. Routledge, 1997.

Sturgeon, Noël. "The Nature of Race: Discourses of Racial Difference in Ecofeminism." *Ecofeminism*, edited by Karen Warren, Indiana UP, 1997, pp. 260–278.

Taylor, Dorceta E. "Women of Color, Environmental Justice, and Ecofeminism." *Ecofeminism*, edited by Karen Warren, Indiana UP, 1997, pp. 38–81.

Tong, Rosemarie. *Feminist Thought: A More Comprehensive Introduction*. Westview, 1998.

Warren, Karen. *Ecofeminist Philosophy: A Western Perspective on What It Is and Why It Matters*. Rowman and Littlefield, 2000.

Warren, Karen, ed. *Ecofeminism: Women, Culture, Nature*. Indiana UP, 1997.

KARMA R. CHÁVEZ

42. QUEER MIGRATION POLITICS AS TRANSNATIONAL ACTIVISM

Organizations like the US-based Human Rights Campaign have set their sights on international pursuits after the achievement of marriage equality in the United States, and President Obama, in a landmark visit to Kenya and Ethiopia in summer 2015, chastised East African countries for their records on LGBTI rights. As this occurs, many are rightfully concerned about the next phase of LGBTI activism.[1] Both are examples of a specific viewpoint that communicates and participates in the idea that the problems of LGBTI rights now exist outside US borders, not within them. Maintaining borders between "us" and "them," such rhetoric also suggests that US solutions are universal ones.

If those examples do not reflect how we should think the queer or LGBTI in relation to the transnational, and I firmly maintain they *don't,* how should we think queer activism transnationally? In its most mainstream forms, transnational gay and lesbian activism has centered on global gay human rights, international "equality" agendas and other campaigns, tourism and mobility, global homophobia, and visibility politics. It has also often trafficked in Islamophobia, anti-blackness, neocolonialism, and, very obviously, neo-liberal capitalism.[2] In its most radical forms, transnational queer activism from and in the global South and North works closely with communities on the ground and challenges logics and systems that often shape mainstream engagement with, and promotion of, transnational queer or LGBTI activism. These confronted logics and systems include newer formations like homonationalism, homotransnationalism and pinkwashing, alongside enduring ones such as colonialism, liberalism, capitalism and imperialism.[3]

Significant powerful writing addresses the mainstream global gay rights industry and the radical queer projects that challenge it and broader systems of oppression.[4] My focus is, instead, on local/national instantiations of what I call queer migration politics—political work in the many intersections and interstices among queer (though not necessarily LGBTI) and migration politics.[5] Queer migration politics are often locally or nationally focused, but the ways they can challenge borders and bordering logics offer fresh insight into the old adage, "think globally, act locally." These are useful for thinking queer activism transnationally out of the approaches mentioned above. Queer migration politics challenge static borders of nation-states and us vs. them logics.

Transnationalism is often associated with heightened mobility, but often, queer migration politics are incredibly confined to singular locales—nation-states, states or provinces, cities or even neighborhoods.[6] This geographical confinement is due to people's precarious legal status and the risk for arrest, incarceration, and deportation.[7] When queer migration activists are not geographically constrained, queer migration politics frequently target the laws or practices of particular locales because it is those local, state or national policies that most directly restrict and constrain their daily lives.[8] Even when seemingly focused only on or from a locale, or toward a local or national concern, queer migration politics also simultaneously point at, and outside, the boundaries of nation-states.

Queer migration politics regularly question or confront the legitimacy of borders and restrictive policies that enforce their existence and thereby expunge

Karma Chávez, "Queer Migration Politics as Transnational Activism," *The Scholar & Feminist Online* 14.2 (2017). Reprinted with permission of Karma Chávez.

particular people. As Wendy Brown explains, nation-states "exhibit a passion for wall-building," both literally and metaphorically, when it comes to the movement of people.[9] Jenna M. Loyd, Matt Mitchelson and Andrew Burridge explain that walls and cages are erected in the name of national sovereignty, which then renders certain people "illegal" and "criminal."[10] When confronting bordering logics for the movement of people, queer migration politics challenge national sovereignty. The move of queer migration politics differs from much mainstream immigration politics that often, through a logic of inclusion, reinforce the legitimacy of national borders. The challenges of queer migration politics to sovereignty operate as part of the waning of nation-state sovereignty logics, but in emphasizing people (not capital), work against the logics of neoliberal globalization.[11]

In this essay, I discuss two instantiations of queer migration politics that iterate different challenges to national sovereignty, borders and bordering through critiquing the laws of a singular nation-state: in both cases, the United States. These examples show that seemingly-contained challenges to a nation-state's laws or imaginaries are actually challenges to bordering logics and perhaps to national sovereignty. I selected these two seemingly disparate cases because they illustrate the importance of location and borders for queer migration politics throughout different periods of neoliberal globalization. Although these cases are "cherry-picked" in one sense, I drew them from extensive research into different iterations of queer migration politics throughout the late 20th and early 21st centuries and put forth these two as ideal types. As instances of queer resistance, they both stand in opposition to the tendencies of mainstream immigration politics and the global gay rights industry that help to call attention to the situatedness of borders, relationships among the global and local, and the functions of normativities.

First, I consider activist responses to US President Barack Obama's November 2014 executive orders on immigration, which in part allegedly shifted his administration's focus away from deporting "families" and toward deporting "felons." Queer migration activists, many of whom are the most marginalized by state-level policies, responded to this framing by queering literal and metaphorical bordering logics in important ways. Second, I turn to activist responses to the 1990 and 1992 International AIDS Conferences, which were scheduled to be held in the United States, despite the US ban on HIV-positive migrants and visitors. Here, activists built and drew upon transnational networks of AIDS workers in order to challenge the legitimacy of US national law and its self-proclaimed status as leader of the global economic-political order.

QUEER MIGRATION POLITICS FROM NATIONAL TO TRANSNATIONAL

On November 20, 2014, the Obama administration announced the end of a controversial program known as Secure Communities, or S-Comm. S-Comm was a massive program that functioned more or less as an extension of a provision in the Immigration and Nationality Act called 287(g). 287(g) allows local law enforcement agencies to enter an agreement with Immigration and Customs Enforcement (ICE) that essentially deputizes these local agencies as ICE agencies; S-Comm made it so that any person who was arrested and booked into a local jail would have their information run through an FBI criminal database and also through Department of Homeland Security (DHS) immigration databases to see if they were deportable. If so, ICE could issue a "detainer," which asked the local jail to let them know when a non-US citizen would be released. ICE could then decide whether to bring the person into federal custody. S-Comm was controversial because it terrorized entire communities by opening them up to possible deportation for only minor police interaction, criminalized anyone suspected of being undocumented, and led to hundreds of thousands of deportations. Immigrants and advocates championed the end of S-Comm, but what did Obama propose in its place?

An Informational announcement from US Citizenship and Immigration Services put it this way: "On November 20, 2014, President Obama announced a series of executive actions to crack down on illegal immigration at the border, prioritize deporting felons not families, and require certain undocumented immigrants to pass a criminal background check and pay taxes in order to temporarily stay in the U.S. without fear of deportation."[12] Most mainstream media and many immigrant rights organizations emphasized only this latter point: the extension of the President's deferred action program beyond youth to the parents of US citizens or legal permanent residents. Few focused on the other pieces centered on a program DHS Secretary Jeh Johnson introduced as "PEP," the Priority Enforcement Program. Under PEP, as the name suggests, immigration officials would focus only on "priority" targets, specifically the following:

1. Those who threaten national security, public safety or border security: including "terrorists" or those suspected of espionage, members of street gangs, aggravated felons and those apprehended at borders;
2. Those convicted of three (non-traffic or separate immigration related) misdemeanors, one significant misdemeanor, visa abusers, or those who cannot prove they have been here since January 1, 2014; and
3. Those with "other immigration violations."[13]

Another November 20 memo from Johnson, "Policies for the Apprehension, Detention and Removal of Undocumented Immigrants," added some clarification to the application of PEP, noting, "Nothing in this memorandum should be construed to prohibit or discourage the apprehension, detention, or removal of aliens unlawfully in the United States who are not identified as priorities herein."[14] In other words, the three priority groups should be used as guidelines, but anyone could still be removed even if not considered part of one of the priority groups. Both S-Comm and PEP were instruments of national sovereignty designed to strengthen the US state's ability to both enforce its international borders and reinforce walls between who is worthy of belonging and who must be excluded.

When it comes to the administration's framing of PEP, bordering logics were front and center in the catch phrase "felons, not families." The "deporting felons, not families" rhetoric must be read as a direct response to outrage with the Obama administration's policies that split hundreds of thousands of families by deporting some 2.5 million people from 2009-2016. Pleas to stop dividing families have long been central to immigrant rights and justice advocacy, but the singularity of this rhetoric has arguably been even more prominent since Obama took office. This rhetoric of the immigrant rights movement is often paired with contentions that immigrants are not criminals. Both strategies by the

movement enact bordering logics that imply some are worthy of inclusion and others are not. One could easily contend that Obama took this catch line directly from the mainstream immigrant rights movement.

Queer migration activists, before and after Obama's announcement, have confronted both of these rhetorical devices, and have especially critiqued how reliance on "family" arguments create exclusionary distinctions. In my book, *Queer Migration Politics*, I wrote about a number of challenges to such arguments, including several pieces from scholar-activist-writer Yasmin Nair and the now-defunct Queers for Economic Justice (QEJ)'s "Queers and Immigration: A Vision Statement" (2007). The QEJ statement highlights the problem with accepted definitions of family within law and in the rhetoric of advocates; as the authors noted, "the broad universe of non-heteronormative family units created by LGBTQ immigrants is automatically excluded from receiving immigration benefits. Both the LGBTQ and immigrant rights communities need to 'work towards expanding their narrow definitions of 'family' in order to better serve all immigrants, including LGBTQ immigrants."[15] The statement also argues that criminalization of people associated with unauthorized immigrants in the form of harboring provisions functions to divide people's kin networks. The task is to simultaneously confront both the boundaries around family and the divisions created to keep people separate. Both confrontations not only resist divisive logics, but they also intervene in the legitimacy of the nation-state's ability to make such determinations about family and criminality.

After Obama's November 2014 announcements, most advocates celebrated the extension of the deferred action program that provided select undocumented youth with a work permit,[16] but some also brought a queer critique to bear upon who would be left out, and, in fact, targeted as deportable priorities. Based on interviews with several activists, Julianne Hing reported that the following groups were among those left out of the deferred action order: parents of undocumented youth who benefited from the 2012 Deferred Action for Childhood Arrivals (DACA), seasonal workers without connections to US citizen children, LGBT immigrants—especially youth and trans people—who are more likely to have been homeless and therefore to have committed low-level criminal offenses, domestic violence survivors who can't get visas under the Violence Against Women Act, and black immigrants who are more likely to be racially profiled by police and therefore either have a felony record or have family members who do.[17] These groups were left out or targeted because the Obama administration did not recognize their family relationships as legitimate or worthy of inclusion, and/or because the administration failed to acknowledge how even "legitimate" families might be harmful and thus create conditions that put someone in a deportable position.

Several partners in the Not One More Deportation Campaign, which claimed a significant role in Obama's decision to issue executive orders, also commented on the contradiction in Obama's framing with specific emphasis on LGBT people. Yesenia Valdez, a national organizer for Familia: Trans and Queer Liberation Movement noted,

> As a community, we know that we do not fit the normal definition of families that continue to dominate public discourse. Many LGBTQ undocumented immigrants do not have families that are US citizens or permanent residents that could allow them to qualify for the program. Additionally, we know that our community, especially trans women of color, is unfairly targeted by law enforcement through racial discrimination or for engaging in survival sex work. These daily realities mean that many members of our LGBTQ community will be left out of the president's plan.[18]

Like the QEJ statement, Familia refused to accept the legitimacy of any program that reinforced troubling divisions. Opal Tometi, the executive director for the Black Alliance for Just Immigration and co-founder of Black Lives Matter, recognized that black people are most likely to be impacted by enforcement measures, adding: "We won't stand for a system that criminalizes us, and then pits family against people who may have a criminal record."[19] Tometi also reiterated concerns both about limiting definitions of family and the negative impacts on families that such divisions between alleged "felons" vs. "families" create. Although these instances of queer migration politics are on one level from within the nation-state toward that nation-state, the challenge to border logics between those who are worthy and unworthy of belonging then questions the right of the nation-state to enforce such divisions.

These instances of queer migration politics demonstrate that queer transnational resistance is not just the work of mobile cosmopolites, but can also be the labor of those most marginalized by state policy. Here, activists brought a queer critique to bear upon powerful national fictions about family and belonging and how such fictions reinforce literal and metaphorical borders. I now turn attention to an earlier instance of queer migration politics that also centers the local/national and directly challenges borders. Here, activists enacted a kind of queer resistance by relying on transnational networks and creating transnational publicity to challenge unjust national laws.

QUEER MIGRATION POLITICS FROM TRANSNATIONAL TO NATIONAL

Controversy regarding the 1990 and 1992 international AIDS Conferences (IAC) provides another opportunity to examine how queer migration politics offer a way to imagine the relationship between the localized and the global through a critique *and* use of borders. These protests surrounded the ban preventing HIV-positive people migrating to, or regularizing their status in, the United States. The first IAC was held in 1985; the International AIDS Society was founded in 1988 and tasked with facilitating the organization of future conferences. IACs are the largest meeting of AIDS workers, and, over time, grew beyond only scientists to also include sociologists, behaviorists and people living with HIV. As with most large conferences, sites for future events are selected well in advance, so the choice of San Francisco for the 1990 IAC preceded the 1987 federal ban on HIV-positive migrants from coming to the United States. Because HIV-positive, non-US citizens would no longer be allowed to travel to the United States to attend the conference, this severely limited who would be able to participate in the important conversations scheduled on US soil.

The question of the ban apparently did not come up quickly enough, or perhaps organizers believed that the ban would, in fact, be lifted beforehand. As a result, organizers did not move the 1990 conference on the grounds that there was too little time to do so.[20]

Interested organizations from around the world began to call for a boycott of the conference in November 1989 on several grounds, including that this would prevent some people from attending, lead to the harassment or violation of privacy for those who did, and tacitly condone the actions of the US federal government.[21] Despite organizers' attempts to persuade the Bush administration to change the policy, and its leaders' ability to obtain temporary waivers for participants, 130 groups and organizations boycotted the conference in the end.[22] Some observers claimed that as many as 2,000–3,000 people did not register who otherwise would have.[23]

The IAC was already a contested site in the minds of AIDS activists. As Deborah Gould notes of this time period, the federal government was ignoring the issue and refusing to put funding toward it while all levels of government considered policies like quarantine and mandatory testing.[24] Although scientists often wanted to be allies, they regularly missed the importance of political perspective and dismissed the queer, in-your-face approach of political activists. Local activists from ACT UP and immigrant rights groups organized massive protests of the conference's events. Protestors staged media spectacles, marched, and chanted outside the San Francisco conference building.

The boycott and protests, built through existing transnational networks, used border restrictions to generate "transnational publicity," or "the rhetorical crafting and circulation of discourse by a broad range of advocacy groups, individuals, and organizations that intervene in particular rhetorical situations, constraining and enabling the options that publics have in responding to the issues and subjects they take up."[25] Protestors' actions opened space for scientists to express political views they might not have otherwise expressed, at times blurring boundaries between activist and scientist. To indicate solidarity with those who boycotted and express opposition to discriminatory laws, many conference attendees wore red armbands, as recommended by the Bay Area Physicians for Human Rights. Some delegates read protest statements before or during their scientific presentations, including Lars Olaf Kallings, then-president of the International AIDS Society.[26]

Reportedly, some official delegates gave their passes to protestors who were then able to bypass security to attend and disrupt the closing session, namely Health and Human Services Secretary Louis Sullivan, who gave the conference's last speech. This was one of the most widely covered actions staged by activists. The introduction given by Paul Volberding, IAC Chair, used the word "honorable" to describe Sullivan. Whether the official cue, activists immediately began groaning, and the sound steadily increased. Volberding waited. The audience never quieted. Sullivan then started his speech. Protestors charged the stage, played sirens, whistles and horns, held signs, and started chanting. Activist interruptions stalled the proceedings for several minutes. Eventually the chants erupted into screams of, "Shame! Shame!" as activists shook their fists in rhythm. They threw crumpled paper and paper airplanes at the stage. Sullivan maintained his calm and only once addressed the protest. His words remained inaudible as he continued his speech praising the Bush administration's advancements and financial resources in the fight against AIDS. In this instance, protestors clearly had an effect and brought scientists into political space. Afterwards, some scientists were quoted as agreeing that Sullivan deserved such treatment because of the discriminatory policies he advocated and represented.[27] Boycotters and protestors thus intervened in one specific event in order to draw attention to one country's laws that had global impacts.

While the 1991 conference was scheduled for Florence, Italy, the 1992 conference was again set to be held in the United States, this time in Boston. As it became clearer that the ban would not be lifted before the conference, rumblings of boycott began to emerge. After much discussion, conference organizers decided to move the conference abroad to Amsterdam. This did not deter activists from using the occasion to generate more transnational publicity aimed at US border restrictions. As the conference approached, the Immigration Working Group (IWG) of ACT UP Golden Gate and ACT UP San Francisco led the international charge, using attention focused on the Amsterdam conference as an opportunity to further pressure the US government.[28]

The IWG called July 19, 1992 as a "Day Against Travel and Immigration Restrictions" in order to draw attention to the US policy.[29] Urging organizations to stage appropriate "high visibility actions" that the media would capture and circulate, the IWG suggested sites like Immigration and Naturalization Services (INS) offices, but also "symbolic and real borders." In addition, members spent that spring writing letters to celebrities, world leaders, and global ACT UP chapters to gain more support and attention. These letters were addressed to leaders including French President Mitterrand, European member of Parliament Bandrés Molet, and celebrities such as Magic Johnson and Elizabeth Taylor. Letter writers sought transnational publicity by targeting key opinion leaders and stakeholders to put wanted pressure on the United States.[30]

Activists also sent letters to conference organizers, demanding time at the podium to focus specific attention on US policy in the ways activists desired. Most specifically, they requested that Tomás Fábregas, an HIV-positive legal permanent resident from Spain who lived in the United States, be the person with AIDS selected to speak at the opening ceremony. This was a request the conference organizers repeatedly did not approve, reportedly to avoid an "unwieldy opening ceremony."[31] For years, Fábregas played a crucial part in activism drawing attention to the US policy, building links between queer direct action groups like ACT UP, predominantly gay non-profits like the San Francisco AIDS Foundation, and immigration advocacy groups such as the Coalition for Immigrant and Refugee Rights and Services. Although he risked being banned from returning to the United States, Fábregas decided to travel to Amsterdam to represent others in more vulnerable positions that would not be able to do so. He was not allowed to address the IAC, but in choosing to take the trip, he relied on existing transnational publicity to both challenge US sovereignty and simultaneously protect him from the US applying its sovereignty by deporting him.

The centerpiece of the protest strategy in Amsterdam involved ACT UP's transnational publicity and a press conference by ACT UP to denounce US policy, connecting that policy with similar laws in countries with which the US may not want to be compared. These media events throughout the conference opened up possibilities for audiences to make connections among and between countries, policies and treatment of HIV-positive people. Before, during and after the July conference, Fábregas publicly dared US immigration authorities to detain and deport him as he sought

to re-enter US territory after attending the conference in Amsterdam.

Fábregas' remarks at the press conference he coordinated along with Elizabeth Taylor's organization AmFAR (American Foundation for AIDS Research) on July 23, 1992 and upon his return to the United States on July 25 show how focusing on the localized or national context has significant transnational implications as this becomes the site for fostering transnational publicity and subsequent networks and connections. In his statements, Fábregas used the US national border both as a literal site and a metaphor for all borders, as a theatre in which to call for transnational coalition. In his Amsterdam statement, Fábregas begins by suggesting he is merely there to offer his personal experience as "a person trapped by the dangerous and discriminatory HIV and immigration travel restrictions." He personally speaks of those in the United States and how stressful the policy has been for him and his partner, but he does not look to make the occasion about him. He goes on,

> We are joined by over four and one half million people of every nationality who have been forced by the U.S. government to submit to HIV testing when applying for residency in the United States of America. And we are joined by the seventeen million foreign born currently living through the U.S. who need to be reached, and can be reached, but are not being reached with the education and support of services we know are effective in preventing the transmission of HIV. I am one of them, and I can assure you that those seventeen million will not seek an HIV test if the result means possible deportation.

Here, Fábregas notes the connection between all those who suffer under such policies, calling out the irony that these policies actually enable rather than prevent the spread of HIV for people who can and should be reached, and are not being reached due to the policy. But Fábregas recognizes his relative privilege and does not intend to make his experience a representative for all others. He continues: "I am here today. But I left many friends at home who cannot risk making their story known." Fábregas begins by telling the story of another member of the ACT UP immigration working group, a Brazilian national who cannot get his permanent residency approved because he contracted HIV (in the United States). Fábregas describes the negative health impacts his friend experiences under the stress, but he again stops, wishing not to make the experience of people in the United States a stand-in for all others. He also builds connections between the US policy with African students required to take HIV tests to study in Belgium, and Burmese sex workers in Thailand who work until they contract HIV and then are deported and often killed when they return home. Fábregas' use of this last example shows how so-called first world countries like the US and Belgium are implicated in the extreme example of Burma and Thailand as they are each presented as manifestations of similar policies and logics. In blurring the experiences and subjectivities among and between European immigrant gays in the US, African students in Belgium, and Burmese sex workers in Thailand, Fábregas calls on those who hear his speech to understand the complex interrelatedness and impacts of HIV/AIDS for a transnational community. Here, queer resistance challenges bordering logics between supposed developed and underdeveloped countries and among different kinds of people living with HIV/AIDS.

Fábregas ends his statement at the press conference in Amsterdam by telling George Bush when and where his flight arrives back to the United States. Upon his arrival and wearing a "No Borders" t-shirt, Fábregas denounced US policy, even as he reentered the country without major incident. His arrival speech focuses entirely on the US policy, even as he repeats many of the same points from his speech two days prior. The Bush administration didn't bother detaining Fábregas. This lack of response reveals the porousness of the US border and the farce of border restrictions, even as borders and bordering logics constantly threaten and thus participate in the deaths of so many.[32] While his actions and the government's inaction may not pose a direct challenge to national sovereignty as Fábregas certainly hoped would happen, Fábregas again reveals the US border and the restrictions that constitute it as sites where transnational coalition is possible.

CONCLUDING THOUGHTS

At a time when large Western organizations and the governments of large Western countries advocate for a particular brand of international gay politics, this paper offers some thoughts on alternative ways to think about transnational queer activism. Specifically, by discussing two instances of queer migration politics that primarily target the laws of particular nation-states, I show that seemingly contained challenges to a nation-state's laws or imaginaries are actually challenges to bordering logics and perhaps even to national sovereignty. Moreover, such challenges can also serve as mechanisms for activating and fortifying transnational publicity, networks and connections. Queer migration politics may manifest in ways that don't address borders and bordering, but given the centrality of both within queer migration politics, this current runs strong. What I hope this paper shows is that even when thinking about transnational queer activism, the biggest and most important struggles at home and elsewhere might very well be where we currently are.

NOTES

1. J. Lester Feder, "Human Rights Campaign's Move into International Work Puts Global LGBT Advocates on Edge," *BuzzFeed News* November 5, 2013, http://www.buzzfeed.com/lesterfeder/human-rights-campaigns-move-into-international-work-puts-glo#.qczkRL1ZB; Kristen Holmes and Eugene Scott, "Obama Lectures Kenyan President on Gay Rights," *CNN* July 25, 2015, http://www.cnn.com/2015/07/25/politics/obama-kenya-kenyatta/.

2. Jin Haritaworn, Adi Kuntsman, and Silvia Posocco, eds., *Queer Necropolitics* (New York: Routledge, 2014); "Murderous Inclusions," *International Feminist Journal of Politics* 15, no. 4 (2013); Scott Long, "'Gay Killings,' Emos, and Iraq: What's Going On," A Paper Bird: Sex, Rights, and the World, March 8, 2012, http://paper-bird.net/2012/03/08/gay-killings-emos-and-iraq-whats-going-on/, January 3, 2013; "HRC and the Vulture Fund: Making Third World Poverty Pay for

LGBT Rights," Paper Bird, November 4, 2013, http://paper-bird.net/2013/11/04/hrc-and-the-vulture-fund-making-third-world-poverty-pay-for-lgbt-rights/.

3. Homonationalism, a term coined by Jasbir Puar, explains the way certain gay identities are taken up in the service of the nation against brown, usually Muslim, others. Homotransnationalism is an extension of this concept by Jin Haritaworn and Paola Bacchetta that describes "the production and specifically transnational circulation of neocolonial, orientalist, sexist, and queerphobic discourses, such as about persecuted Muslim women or queers" (134). Palestinian feminist Ghadir Shafie describes pinkwashing as "a deliberate strategy used by Israel's government, agencies, and the Israeli LGBT community to exploit Israel's relatively progressive stance on gay rights, and deflect international attention from its gross violations of human rights and international law" (83). Pinkwashing can also be used by and concerning other entities, but most directly connects to Israel in popular understanding. See: Paola Bacchetta and Jin Haritaworn, "There Are Many Transatlantics: Homonationalism, Homotransnationalism and Feminist-Queer-Trans of Color Theories and Practices," in *Transatlantic Conversations: Feminism as Traveling Theory*, ed. Kathy Davis and Mary Evans (Farnham, UK: Ashgate, 2011); Jasbir K. Puar, *Terrorist Assemblages: Homonationalism in Queer Times* (Durham, NC: Duke University Press, 2007); Ghadir Shafie, "Pinkwashing: Israel's International Strategy and Internal Agenda," *Kohl: A Journal for Body and Gender Research* 1, no. 1 (2015).

4. For some good work that challenges oppressive logics, see: Jin Haritaworn, *Queer Lovers and Hateful Others: Regenerating Violent Times and Places* (London: Pluto Press, 2015); Selections from: Haritaworn, Kuntsman, and Posocco, eds., *Queer Necropolitics*, Jin Haritaworn, Tamsila Tauqir, and Esra Erdem, "Gay Imperialism: Gender and Sexuality Discourse in the 'War on Terror,'" in *Out of Place: Interrogating Silences in Queerness/Raciality*, ed. Adi Kuntsman and Esperanza Miyake (York, UK: Raw Nerve Books, 2008); Joseph A. Massad, *Desiring Arabs* (Chicago: University of Chicago Press, 2007). See especially Massad's chapter on the Gay International. Some recent work that addresses more of the "global gay rights industry": Phillip Ayoub and David Paternotte, eds., *LGBT Activism and the Making of Europe: A Rainbow Europe?* (New York: Palgrave Macmillan, 2014); Jordi Díez, *The Politics of Gay Marriage in Latin America: Argentina, Chile, and Mexico* (Cambridge: Cambridge University Press, 2015); Ryan R. Thoreson, ed. *Transnational LGBT Activism: Working for Sexual Rights Worldwide* (Minneapolis: University of Minnesota Press, 2014).

5. Karma R. Chávez, *Queer Migration Politics: Activist Rhetoric and Coalitional Possibilities* (Urbana: University of Illinois Press, 2013). A quick note on the distinction I make between LGBTI and queer: LGBTI is primarily an identity or set of identity markers which people use as the basis for political actions. See Nicholas De Genova, "The Queer Politics of Migration: Reflections on 'Illegality' and Incorrigibility," *Studies in Social Justice* 4, no. 2 (2010); Eithne Luibhéid, "Introduction: Queer Migration and Citizenship," in *Queer Migrations: Sexuality, U.S. Citizenship, and Border Crossings*, ed. Eithne Luibhéid and Lionel Cantú Jr. (Minneapolis: University of Minnesota Press, 2005). As for queer, certainly this has a variety of meanings that are in no way agreed upon by theorists or activists. My use of queer in relation to im/migration politics has multiple meanings—it may, at times, refer to politics by people who identify as LGBTI or queer as a marker of sexual or gender identity and use that identity as a way to orient their politics; it may also refer to bring[ing] a queer approach to immigration politics, which can mean radical/in-your face politics (see De Genova), or politics based on a queer critique of the normativity of borders and relationality (see Luibhéid, "Introduction").

6. On transnationalism, see: Laura Briggs, Gladys McCormick, and J. T. Way, "Transnationalism: A Category of Analysis," *American Quarterly* 60, no. 3 (2008); Inderpal Grewal, *Transnational America: Feminisms, Diasporas, Neoliberaiisms* (Durham, NC: Duke University Press, 2005).

7. Eithne Luibhéid, "Sexuality, Migration, and the Shifting Line between Legal and Illegal Status," *GLQ* 14, no. 2–3 (2008).

8. See my *Queer Migration Politics*. See also, for example: Hinda Seif, "'Unapologetic and Unafraid': Immigrant Youth Come out from the Shadows," *New Directions for Child and Adolescent Development* 134 (2011); Lynn Stephen, Jan Lanier, Ramón Ramírez, and Marcy Westeriing, "Building Alliances: An Ethnography of Collaboration between Rural Organizing Project (ROP) and CAUSA in Oregon" (New York: New York University and Leadership for a Changing World, 2005); Melissa Autumn White, "Documenting the Undocumented: Toward a Queer Politics of No Borders," *Sexualities* 17, no. 8 (2014).

9. Wendy Brown, *Walled States, Waning Sovereignty* (Brooklyn, NY: Zone Books, 2010).

10. Jenna M. Loyd, Matt Mitchelson, and Andrew Burridge, "Introduction: Borders, Prisons, and Abolitionist Visions," in *Beyond Walls and Cages: Prisons, Borders, and Global Crisis*, ed. Jenna M. Loyd, Matt Mitchelson, and Andrew Burridge (Athens: University of Georgia Press, 2012).

11. It is beyond the scope of this short essay, but it is important to note that the waning of nation-state sovereignty in globalization that Brown identifies does not necessarily mean progressive change leading toward global social justice; sovereignty may simply shift elsewhere to other global sites.

12. "Executive Actions on Immigration," *US Citizenship and Immigration Services* November 20, 2014, http://www.uscis.gov/immigrationaction. Accessed July 19, 2017.

13. Jeh Charles Johnson, "Secure Communities," Department of Homeland Security Memorandum, November 20, 2014, https://www.dhs.gov/sites/default/files/publications/14_1120_memo_secure_communities.pdf. Accessed July 19, 2017.

14. Jeh Charles Johnson, "Policies for the Apprehension, Detention and Removal of Undocumented Immigrants," Department of Homeland Security Memorandum, November 20, 2014, https://www.dhs.gov/sites/default/files/publications/14_1120_memo_prosecutorial_discretion.pdf. Accessed July 19, 2017. Of course, starting under the Trump administration in January 2017, all Obama-era immigration orders ended with the exception of Deferred Action for Childhood Arrivals. Trump began his administrative term by issuing four of his own draconian executive orders regarding immigration.

15. Queers for Economic Justice. "Queers and Immigration: A Vision Statement." Scholar and Feminist Online, 6.3 (2008), http://sfonline.barnard.edu/immigration/qej_01.htm.

16. Carlos, "'We should be deporting felons, and not families'—an immigrant student speaks out." *PBS Extras: Student Voices* December 10, 2014, http://www.pbs.org/newshour/extra/student_volces/we-should-be-deporting-felons-and-not-famiIles-an-immigrant-student-speaks-out/.

17. Julianne Hing, "Who Will Lose Under Obama's Executive Action," *Colorlines* November 21, 2014, http://www.colorlines.com/articles/who-will-lose-under-obamas-executlve-action, accessed July 19, 2017.

18. "#Not1More: Our Victories and Our Fights Will Continue." Not One More Deportation, Press Release, November 20, 2014, http://www.notonemoredeportation.com/2014/11/20/not1more-our-victories-and-our-fights-will-continue/, accessed July 19, 2017.

19. Opal Tometi, "Statement from Opal Tometi, the Executive Director of the Black Alliance for Just Immigration regarding President Obama's executive action on immigration and deportation," BAJI Blog November 22, 2014, http://www.blackalliance.org/edresponse/, accessed July 19, 2017.

20. Tomás Fábregas, Memo to ACT UP Golden Gate, "US Policy on HIV infected Foreigners," August 6, 1991. GLBT Historical Society, Jorge Cortiñas Papers, Collection Number 1998-42, Box 2, Folder 8. Retrieved March 27–29, 2013.

21. Kelly Toughill, "US Eases Visa Rules for AIDS Conference," *Toronto Star*, April 17, 1990. It is difficult to say who first called for the boycott as stories conflict. Some sources say the UK Consortium was the first; others say it was the Geneva-based League of Red Cross and Red Crescent Societies. See: Peter McIntyre, "Aids Meeting Faces Boycott over Rules on Entry to US," *Independent*, November 20 1989, 3.

22. Eric Sawyer, "Absolutely Fabregas," *Poz* (June 1997), last accessed March 23, 2013.

23. n.a., "Restrictions Set Off AIDS Session Boycott," Sf. *Louis Post-Dispatch*, June 15, 1990.

24. Deborah B. Gould, *Moving Politics: Emotion and Act Up's Fight Against AIDS* (Chicago: University of Chicago Press, 2009), 11.

25. Sara L. McKinnon, *Gendered Asylum: Race and Violence in US Law and Politics* (Urbana: University of Illinois Press, 2016), 22.

26. Andrew Orkin, "Policy Protests, Scientific Spats Take Centre Stage at Sixth International AIDS Conference," *Canadian Medical Association Journal* 143, no. 4 (1990).

27. Paul Taylor, "Protest Disrupts Close of AIDS Conference; Activists, Scientists Decry US Policy," *Globe and Mail*, June 25, 1990.

28. There are many indications of this throughout the Tomás Fábregas Papers, Collection 1996-44 and the Jorge Cortiñas Papers, Collection 1998-42 at the GLBT Historical Society. I cite specific instances throughout.

29. ACT UP Immigration Working Group Letter to ACT UP Members. 1992. GLBT Historical Society. Tomás Fábregas Papers, Collection 1996-44, Box 1. Folder 2. Retrieved March 28, 2013.

30. See for example, several letters to Elizabeth Taylor, dated March 20, 1992; March 18, 1992; June 2, 1992; and June 29, 1992; GLBT Historical Society, Tomás Fábregas Papers, Collection Number 1996-44, Box 1, Folders 5 and 6. Retrieved March 27–29, 2013. See letter to Magic Johnson on February 27, 1992, Box 1, Folder 2. See letter to Bandres Molet on June 15, 1992, Box 1, Folder 5. See letter to President Mitterand on June 10, 1992, Box 1, Folder 5.

31. See "Letter to Jonathan Mann," March 20, 1992. GLBT Historical Society, Tomás Fábregas Papers, Collection Number 1996-44, Box 1, Folder 2. Retrieved March 27–29, 2013. Already in March, this letter indicates that the request has been denied at least one time on the grounds that It would make the opening ceremony "unwieldy." "Letter from Richard Rochon to Jonathan Mann," June 22, 1992, Box 1, Folder 8. GLBT Historical Society, Tomás Fábregas Papers, Collection Number 1996-44, Box 2, Folder 5. Retrieved March 27–29, 2013.

32. "Statement of Tomás Fábregas." July 25, 1992. GLBT Historical Society, Tomás Fábregas Papers, Collection Number 1996-44, Box 2, Folder 5. Retrieved March 27–29, 2013.

ELORA HALIM CHOWDHURY

43. "TRANSNATIONALISM REVERSED": ENGAGING RELIGION, DEVELOPMENT AND WOMEN'S ORGANIZING IN BANGLADESH

INTRODUCTION

As a feminist activist and scholar interested in women's transnational organizing in Bangladesh, I have followed with curiosity a sudden soar in the Western media over the last several years of reports depicting the nation as alternatively "the site of the next Islamist revolution" and a model developing nation. The first of these images of Bangladesh was tied to a series of attacks on NGOs, women clients of NGOs, progressive intellectuals, and leaders of a secular leaning political party by Islamist groups, many of whom claim transnational allegiances with growing networks of extremist organizations in the region. The second image is associated with the globally acclaimed Grameen Bank and its founder Professor Muhammad Yunus winning the 2006 Nobel Peace Prize. Development initiatives empowering poor brown[1] Muslim women through micro loans, and Dr. Yunus as the moderate brown Muslim male voice have both gained prominence in the context of a global climate of stark contrasts between Western "civilization" and Islamic reticence to join it. Several questions come to mind in response to these categorical representations of the third largest Muslim majority nation:

1. Why the shift from a developing nation status to that of a moderate/violent Islamic country?
2. In what ways are women perceived to be the measure of development or lack thereof?
3. In the age of transnational feminism, what kinds of mobilizations and alliances are possible as women activists in Bangladesh face the multiple challenges of neoliberal development, patriarchy, and rising religious extremism regionally as well as resurgent Orientalism globally?

My positions and perspectives are shaped by the multiple roles I occupy as an academic from a third world country located in the North American academy writing and teaching about women in "Other" contexts, and as an activist in Bangladesh who has worked with both local and international NGOs in mobilizing campaigns against gender violence. In the post September 11th climate, discussions about women's emancipation in the Muslim world have taken on a new kind of intensity. However, the concerns of transnational feminists located primarily in the North can be perceived as overly "academic" (focusing on important and vigorous debates over location, privilege and colonial baggage) and derailing the practical and exigent issues on the ground (such as mobilizing global awareness and resources for constituencies in immediate need of assistance). Some would consider these debates even "dangerous" or unnecessary while giving voice to faith based constituencies, which are at times uncritically perceived by certain progressive circles as furthering women's oppression.

As a feminist scholar occupying multiple and often contradictory locations, I fully understand the importance of scholarly concerns problematizing Orientalist framings of gender violence in non-Western locations. Yet I am equally cognizant of the difficult conditions in which local activists organize; conditions which involve time and resource constraints, working with recalcitrant state services and international aid agencies, and making use of transnational networks which can perpetuate unidimensional images of women's oppression under indigenous patriarchy. These conditions may render irrelevant or suspend the pertinence of scholarly concerns that in theory should inform activist agendas. Here, I do not mean to reify the activist/academic binary nor do I intend to suggest that activists are not aware of complex global power configurations shaping local contexts. Instead I suggest that a) these debates may very well be more pressing for academics located in the North and b) in the process of instigating urgent action and forging complex negotiations they may lose pragmatic relevance. My purpose is to open up a more honest and nuanced discussion around transnational feminist praxis that addresses the troubling yet real disconnect between criticism and urgent action. How do we address feminist complicity in and mount dissent against the scattered hegemonies of neoimperialism, fundamentalism, and patriarchies?

The available literature on Islamization in Bangladesh has focused little on its relationship to the national women's movement, which historically has been aligned with the nationalist movement for liberation. This movement has remained secular[2] in orientation as a means to create a distinct identity from the colonizing West Pakistani state ideology of "authentic" Islam. Post-independence, the women's movement has been equally influenced by "modernizing" forces of international development initiatives. The secular-nationalist stance of the women's movement understands Islamists as a force external to the nation and bolstered by the unpunished war-collaborators from 1971 who have gained prominence in the political life of the nation over the years. In fact, the very visible urban based progressive movements in Bangladesh have collectively taken a strong stance against Islamization, perhaps at the expense of attention to the complex ways in which the contemporary social and political landscapes have shifted since 1971 leading to a strengthening in national and local based Islamist politics. Although the Liberation War, and women's important role in it, is undoubtedly an inspiring legacy for women's activism in Bangladesh, the framing of all contemporary feminist struggles in that light—as the women's rights leaders often do—leads to the marginalization of *other* struggles incommensurate with the politics of Bengali nationalism and development. The

challenges that the women's movement in Bangladesh currently confronts require a more nuanced analysis that goes beyond the Islamist/secular-nationalist binary and engages a more self-reflexive lens to acknowledge the linkages that connect disparate power structures, including feminist ones, that have differential implications for differently located women.

The landscape of contemporary Bangladeshi politics is such that divisions like nationalist, secularist, and Islamist are no longer clear, if they ever were at all. Historians Sugata Bose and Ayesha Jalal (1998) encourage understanding "regional dissidence" in the subcontinent, as it is manifested in secular democratic as opposed to authoritarian and Islamic government in terms of the "historical dynamics of the transition from colonialism" (Bose and Jalal, 1998, 203). They point out that historically these modalities of governance: democracy, authoritarianism, secularism, and religion-based, "have coexisted if not been thoroughly imbricated" within the nation (Bose and Jalal, 1998, 203). Too often the women's movement (and feminist politics generally) in Bangladesh is uncritically coupled with the secularist one of the civil society or the NGO sector. These groups in turn are deemed as the progressive voice in the backdrop of a weak state with dubious allegiances to Islamist parties. Both the state and the civil society, however, are implicated in donor-driven modernization and "nation-building" initiatives with contradictory consequences not always entirely "emancipatory" for women. In such an intricate web of relationships it is difficult to tease out autonomous agendas for any of these constituencies. Nor is it easy to understand the specific constraints that the women's movement must negotiate, constraints that might involve confronting instead of aligning with so-called secular/modernizing forces of NGOization. Indeed, the interface of globalization, national development, and rising militant Islamic politics is where the women's movement's attention needs to be shifted. Therefore, in this paper I argue for a more nuanced analysis of the perceived dichotomy of Islamist/secularist politics in Bangladesh and the class based women's movement's responses to it such that the women's movement/feminist agenda is not uncritically conflated with a secularist/democratic one. Moving beyond this dualistic framework that serves a narrow and elitist agenda, we must call for more serious attention to the links between Islamist and secular agendas, and imagine feminist dissent that is more accountable to those constituencies that are seemingly "benefiting" yet abjectly affected by the promise of secular development.

WOMEN'S NGOS: COMPLICIT OR/YET DISSIDENT?

As Najma Chowdhury's (2001) account of implementing women's rights in Bangladesh shows, the impetus behind women's organizing post-1971 reflects the merging interests of state and economic development strategies from international organizations such as the United Nations, donor agencies or "development partners," and global corporations that bring capital into the country in the form of direct foreign investment. She asserts that women specific NGOs as well as those with a major focus on women, are an important part of the national women's movement in Bangladesh (Chowdhury, 2001, 212). The leadership of women-focused NGOs is provided by women while most of those that are not women-focused are led by men with women serving at mid and lower levels. Chowdhury points out that some women's organizations distinguish themselves from NGOs because their service is not salaried but voluntary. Nevertheless, they too solicit donor funds for projects and often partner with NGOs who provide them with the infrastructure to access subjects of development, namely poor women. One of the major predicaments then for the women's movement is to carve out an autonomous space from colonialist discourses of donor-driven development agendas, the state's conflicting ideologies subscribing to these agendas, and the Islamist visions of a moral society.

In Bangladesh the headquarters for women's NGOs are primarily concentrated in urban areas and are largely led by Western-educated urban elites who advocate women's rights within a secular modernist framework. This class-based women's movement is highly visible and active in the public arena. On any given day if one were to look through the national newspapers there would be a plethora of seminars and workshops on topics related to women, gender, and development and featuring familiar speakers: professors, lawyers, researchers, NGO advocates and professionals who circulate with high frequency in national and international conferences. The large rural population in Bangladesh is mostly poor, illiterate, unemployed/underemployed, and alienated from the nation building project. This nation building project, however, does not exclude women entirely. Leaders of the two major political parties are women and the position of prime ministership has been held alternately by these two women from 1991 until 2006. Bangladesh has a Ministry of Women's Affairs, Women In Development (WID) focal points, a National Policy for the Advancement of Women, reserved Parliamentary seats and non-professional and clerical and custodial posts for women, and a national umbrella women's organization entrusted with improving conditions faced by women. These opportunities benefit mostly certain sectors of the population, namely educated and urban based women rather than women in rural areas (Karim, 2004, 301).

Women's rights organizations are using the UN mandate for gender mainstreaming and international human rights treaties to put pressure on the government. Moral shaming of the government in the global community by pressuring it to comply with the international treaties has been an effective mobilizing tool for women activists in the global South even as it means integrating gender mainstreaming as an "external" discourse rather than an organic "internal" one to define movement agendas. As Liz Kelly (2005) has suggested, mainstreaming a gender perspective into development and human rights discourse and practice has been more of an exercise in mainstreaming activists than ensuring gender mainstreaming's methodological incorporation at all levels. It implies a "rhetorical absorption of a gender perspective" rather than meaningful infusing of gender discourse and transformation of gender relations (Kelly, 2005, 472). Women's NGOs in Bangladesh have been able to exploit the globalizing force of human rights and women's rights ideology by taking on the mandates and implementation of the Convention on the Elimination of All Forms of Discrimination Against Women (CEDAW).[3] While Bangladesh is a signatory to international treaties, and therefore obligated to protect the human rights of all its citizens, the various successive governments continue to remain ambiguous regarding policy on gender and ineffective in operationalizing gender mainstreaming. One example is the way that the government has manipulated the "religion card" while simultaneously projecting modernist and Islamist identities for their own political agendas.

Najma Chowdhury (2001) captures the tremendous enthusiasm with which women leaders in Bangladesh participated in the formulation of national plans of action, monitoring tools, and measurable targets for gender mainstreaming even though the implementations of these have been met with tepid response. The Bangladesh National Preparatory Committee Towards Beijing, a coalition of over two hundred individuals and organizations encompassing civil society, women activists, researchers, professionals, workers, development organizations, grassroots workers, cultural organizations, and human rights groups, engaged in awareness raising and mobilizing for nearly eighteen months previous to the World Conference on Women in Beijing in 1995. The main agenda items of this Committee included lobbying the government to withdraw reservations pertaining to CEDAW and spotlighting violence against women. Post-Beijing, national workshops and taskforces were formed which broadened access to government level policy making to civil society advocacy groups. The tangible outcomes of these alliances have included strategies to strengthen the capacity of law-enforcement authorities and agencies to deal with crimes of violence against women with minimal intervention in the social arena that inhibits the majority of the population's access to such legal machinery (Chowdhury, 2001, 217). Critiquing the festival-like organizing stimulated by transnational forums such as the Beijing Conference, Suzanne Bergeron (2006) citing Gayatri Spivak, likened the U.N.-sponsored World Conferences on Women held in Beijing in 1995 as representing a kind of "global theater" that puts on a show of global unity in spite of the absence of subaltern women and continuing to engage in colonialist power relations. Bergeron notes that according to Spivak these conferences further the image of global unity while obfuscating the premise of the conferences, which is the "unspoken assumption of the U.N. that the South is not capable of governing itself" (Bergeron, 2006, 161). Women's groups at the conference rallied around issues identified by the global platform instead of allowing for issues to be defined by local groups based on their specific situations.

Transnational organizing thus often follow the mandates of global feminist advocacy as well as government priorities instead of diverse local concerns. This point emerges more clearly when we take into consideration Chowdhury's (2001) point that as the time for submission of the Bangladesh report to the CEDAW drew closer in 1995, the government surreptitiously withdrew some of the reservations to Article 2 having to do with equal enjoyment of family benefits and guardianship and custody of children. By not publicizing the withdrawal of reservations and keeping it out of a public debate, the government chose to maintain a "politics of silence" presumably to protect itself from appearing inconsistent in revising yet supporting gender discriminatory policy (Chowdhury, 2001, 226). The NGOization of women's organization in this sense depoliticized a nascent women's movement in the post-independence era.

In an interview, Bangladeshi feminist scholar and activist Meghna Guhathakurta suggests that Islamization has tended to influence restrictions on women's rights in the legal arena to a greater extent than the mainstream political and economic spheres, which are most heavily determined by the flows of the political economy than by Islamist ideology (Eclipse, 1994). Official policies have espoused the Beijing Platform of Action and passed the National Women's Advancement Policy crafted with progressive feminist and human rights groups. In contrast to this track record however, in 2004 the Bangladesh National Party (BNP) government secretly introduced changes to the National Women's Advancement Policy (NWAP) without discussing it in Parliament or with women's groups (Siddiqi, 2006). Moving away from the principle of equality found in an earlier 1997 document formulated under the Awami League (AL) government, the revised policy restricts women's rights to inheritance and control over resources, employment, political and economic autonomy. Dina Siddiqi suggests that, "In terms of employment, the new policy calls for efforts to employ women in 'appropriate' professions. What constitutes appropriate is left open to interpretation" (Siddiqi, 2006). Furthermore, women are barred from holding the highest positions in the judiciary, the diplomatic corps, and key administrative bodies. The government has neither formally endorsed nor rejected the revised documents but the common understanding is that these changes were brought on by the Islamist parties with which the government was in alliance. Curiously, adds Siddiqi, the donor endorsed

Poverty Reduction Strategy Paper still reflects the principles of the 1997 document. She also notes that a group of 35 women's and other social justice based organizations have formed a coalition, the Shamajik Protirodh Committee, to protest the underhanded revisions to the NWAP. This coalition protests the BNP government's secretive alliances with Islamists, however is not equally critical of the limited ways that gender mainstreaming has translated in economic and social arenas for diverse groups of women.

In a recent conversation with a women's movement activist in Bangladesh, I learned that the emphasis on Poverty Reduction Strategy Paper (PRSP) by the government reflects its class-based top down approach. The PRSP, which is developed by member countries along with the World Bank and the IMF is an imposed agenda, one that is not grounded in country-specific needs and realities. Together with the implementation plans of Millennium Development Goals (MDGs), donor-driven gender mainstreaming overlooks differential realities of women by class, ethnicity and religion. While the national government historically laid out program goals for development in five-year cycles, that strategy had been replaced by gender mainstreaming through MDGs and the PRSP mandates. Further, the push for gender mainstreaming puts the Ministry of Women and Children Affairs at the lead for ensuring the integration of gender in other government sectors. This, according to sociologist Dr. Sadeka Halim, is not an effective strategy given the marginalization of the Ministry of Women and Children Affairs in relation to other Ministries. The "burden" of gender integration remains with the Women's Ministry, with its members approaching other sectors for assessment of gender component in their work. Dr. Halim maintains the onus should actually be on the other ministries to approach the Women's Ministry, which they rarely do because gender is not a priority for them. Replacing national five-year plans with the imposed agenda of the PRSP is "unconstitutional" according to Dr. Halim and perpetuates the elitist vision of donor and urban based women's development (Halim, 2008a, b).

Furthermore, MDG assessments often do not pay close attention to local complexities of gender relations on the ground. Naila Kabeer (2005) argues that the third Millennium Development Goal, gender equality and women's empowerment, is clearly an important goal yet disappointingly narrow in its vision of implementation. It ignores the crucial reality that unequal social relationships result in differential access to resources that are understood to ameliorate women's participation in education, employment and politics—the three indicators of gender equality and empowerment. For example, in a report on "Gender Needs Assessment of MDG-3" commissioned by United Nations Development Program (UNDP), Dr. Halim notes, "Bangladesh has made considerable progress in terms of reducing the discrimination between men and women" (Halim, 2008a, b, 2), and that gender parity has been achieved in primary school enrollment. However, the report goes on to reveal that not all regional divisions (there are six in total) have reached the aforementioned parity, and surprisingly the division with the highest literacy rate has not reached gender parity in primary education. In addition, in the last five years, five divisions have shown a negative annual growth rate of primary school enrollment. Although no conclusive data is yet available, Dr. Halim notes areas with high populations of minorities (defined by ethnic, religious, socio-economic status) have less parity and enrollment.

Gender parity in secondary school enrollment has also been reached in Bangladesh. In the last fifteen years, enrollment of girls have surpassed that of boys and between 1991 and 1995 enrollment of boys witnessed a substantial decrease. Dr. Halim, author of the UNDP report notes that the impressive enrollment of girls in secondary school can be attributed to the government assisted Female Secondary School Assistance Program (FSSAP) launched in the late 1980's. The program offers cash incentive or stipend to secondary school girls to cover a large portion of direct school expenses and provides tuition assistance to the schools. As at the primary level, secondary school level growth rates also differ according to division with three divisions noting a decrease in enrollment. Between the years of 2000 and 2005, growth rates in rural areas were negative and urban areas witnessed a decline.

At the tertiary level, however, by 2005 women's enrollment targets stood at 24%. Between 1997 and 2005 female enrollment declined from 31 to 24% while male enrollment increased from 61 to 76%. Dr. Halim notes in the report that stipend-related interventions must be available at the tertiary level to address gender parity. In the area of non-agricultural employment, by 2005 the male to female ratio reached roughly 85:15. The annual growth rate has decreased for females in recent years. In the area of political participation, the numbers are most disheartening with women holding 12.6% of the seats in National Parliament (which allocates 30 reserved seats to women out of 330), reflecting a decrease from the two previous parliamentary democracy governments (Halim, 2008a, b, 3).[4]

Kabeer explains that education increases women's ability to deal with matters in the public sphere more effectively as well as exercise more control within the family and community. However, in the context of societal gender inequality the effects of education may take on different meanings. For instance, where women's roles in society are defined by their reproductive function, education is seen as a means to acquire suitable husbands and take on subordinate roles within family and wage work spheres. Social inequalities are also present in the delivery of education where gender discrimination leads to lower expectations and achievements among women. Moreover, a hidden content of education curriculum usually is the devaluation of work that is generally taken up by the poor and women. Kabeer observes that policy makers recognize that educating women leads to the improvement of the welfare of the family, but they neglect to emphasize education that is geared towards better equipping women as equals in society. Based on these observations, we can see how the attainment of MDG goals can be illusory because the effects are not uniformly experienced by all women.

In other goal areas Kabeer shows that women's participation in wage work increases self-esteem and confidence among women. Wage work is a way for women to achieve greater respect within the family and community as well as acquire skills to negotiate with various actors in wider society and participating in political activities. Women workers in the garment industry expressed that they are able to negotiate marriage relations and oppressive family and community structures by moving away from home and developing alternative communities of support in their new work and living spaces. However, paid work often involves harsh and exploitative working conditions with little recourse for organizing against or protesting them. In the area of political participation, notes Kabeer, greater

attention needs to be paid to strengthening women's voices in local rather than national government. The later tends to draw its members from more elite factions of society who may not respond to the needs of poor women. Kabeer concludes that while the formulation of the MDG might reflect the success of global movements for social justice, the translation of them "into a series of technical goals, to be implemented mainly by the very actors and institutions that have blocked their realization in the past" minimize their potential for greater change (Kabeer, 2005, 22). Policy changes have to allow women to participate more effectively, she suggests, so attainment of goals can be tested beyond the numerical parity of capacity to challenge and question unjust practices. Kabeer asks the key question, ". . . to what extent the international community is prepared to provide support to women at the grassroots—support which will ensure that they have the collective capabilities necessary. ..." (Kabeer, 2005, 24). Exercising collective capability is connected to having transformative agency, not hollow "empowerment" indicators.

Lamia Karim (2004) and Elora Shehabuddin (1999) have criticized the urban based women's movement for either exploiting unequal social relations with their clients or having little understanding of women's realities in rural Bangladesh. These scholars bring to our attention that women who staff and run NGOs lead vastly different lives from the women who are their clients. While not intending to lessen the very important work that women's rights organizations do, it is nevertheless critical to acknowledge that privilege based on religion, ethnicity, and class result in perpetuating the clientelist social structure of Bangladesh and hinder feminist alliances.

The consequences of unacknowledged privilege is brought up by Meghna Guhathakurta (2004) in a discussion of the contested ways violence and victimization have been understood by the mainstream women's movement and the state and indigenous community struggles for citizenship, particularly women in the Chittagong Hill Tracts (CHT) of Bangladesh. While the state conceptualizes violence against women primarily in its physical manifestation, the women's movement has also located its causes in patriarchal and class based structural inequalities.

Critical reading of the writings of Kalpana Chakma, the organizing secretary of the Hill Women's Federation (HWF)—an organization that mounted a powerful response to the state brutalization of the Jumma people[5]—reveals the multiple challenges facing indigenous women against "politicomilitary" interventions of the Bengali state, patriarchal oppression in the Hill Tracts, poverty, and struggles to retain cultural identity. Guhathakurta surmises, ". . . Kalpana's feminism also differs sharply from that of her middle-class Bengali sisters because unlike them her life struggles force her to confront and engage military and ethnic/racial domination in a way that is not easily comprehensible to the privileged Bengali" (Guhathakurta, 2004, 201). Her writings also frame struggles for gender and ethnic justice within the broader struggle for Bengali democracy, nationalism, and freedom: ". . . we are part of the student's movement who had created '52, '69, '71. And '90!" (Guhathakurta, 2004, 202). Although Jumma struggles are labeled as a threat to the sovereignty of the Bengali nation, this statement casts them as a democratic movement for self-determination within the nation of Bangladesh.

Despite the flourishing civil society sector in Bangladesh, very few organizations have expressed interest in the CHT issue. Following the abduction and alleged murder of Kalpana Chakma in 1996 and the subsequent organizing among the Jumma people as well as various human rights reports in the mainstream media, the women's movement has joined together with the indigenous women's group, albeit not along the conceptualization of the larger struggles so eloquently defined by Kalpana Chakma. Guhathakurta notes that although the HWF participated in the International Women's Day Rally in 1994 and went to the NGO Forum of the Women's Conference in Beijing in 1995 (although Kalpana Chakma could not go because of lack of funds) with their slogan "Autonomy for Peace," barely two lines appeared about their struggles in the summary of the official NGO report. Middle class Bengali organizations are so driven by the development discourse and its narrow conceptualization of gender mainstreaming, that there are serious limitations to engaging more critically in questions of ethnicity and nationality as they intersect with gender. While showing support to the hill women around

generalized notions of human rights violations by the state, the same women's organizations fail to interrogate notions of citizenship, nation, self-determination and ethnicity—the very ideals upon which the Bengali nationalist movement was mobilized.

Women activists in Bangladesh work within the development focused NGO paradigm, thus we have to analyze the limits of it on feminist praxis. NGOs, with their dependent links to the government, multinationals, donors, and other NGOs hinder forceful criticisms and acknowledgements to the limits of a developmentalist paradigm. These institutional structures may provide feminists opportunities to mobilize resources and forge alliances particularly in the transnational arena and in the realm of policy advocacy, but they may also inhibit forging more radically transformative alliances across class, ethnicity, grassroots agendas.

In a 2004 study commissioned by CARE Bangladesh that explores current initiatives for women's empowerment undertaken by the NGO communities, Santi Rozario convened 25 organizations involved in promoting women's rights. An important observation made in her report is the extent to which the agenda of the groups are donor driven, manifesting in project-based work that is time-bound and product-oriented. This kind of programming did not foster collaboration among women's groups around common themes. Instead, the donor driven agenda engenders a climate of competition among these groups. The most significant common issue among the groups is violence against women, not surprisingly since the global women's movement has been most successful in leveraging this as a common platform. However, the framing of gender violence within this platform has limitations in enabling a fundamental critique of women's role in society because of the way physical violence (understood as a consequence of patriarchy) is considered detached from structural violence (requiring an analysis of global capitalism and racism). This issue based strategy tackling violence against women facilitates generating publicity and criminalization of spectacular acts of violence, but it has not effectively confronted social conditions that enable gendered violence nor has it dealt with women's lack of access to due process and the ability to lead secure lives. For instance, Rozario reports delivering legal aid in and of itself would not make much difference to the practice of dowry as re-flected in the statement of a young man: "I can tell you this, if there is one case against dowry from this village, no man will come forward to marry any girls from this village" (Rozario, 2004, 18). Challenging patriarchal norms that measure women's worth by her marriageability are as important as providing legal services. Rozario's report makes the important point that despite laws against the giving and taking of dowries, most dowry-related violence cases are only reported when a woman has been assaulted because of unmet dowry demands, not when a dowry transaction has been made. This brings home the earlier point made about the success of global feminism and gender main-streaming in criminalizing violence against women yet the inability in confronting structural violence.

Another striking gap in women's NGO organizing is the lack of solidarity across and even within class lines. Programs that foster competition instead of col-laboration perpetuate the patron-client relationship between urban elite feminists who can participate in and are conversant in the language of global feminist platforms, and their counterparts, women often based in rural contexts or even urban contexts but lacking the professional skills required to be participants in global development apparatus. The competitive model is rep-licated even in development programs for women who have to become members of NGOs in order to avail services. Rozario reports that while in theory NGOs are supposed to provide health/legal/educational services to all members of any given community, in reality they do so only to their members while charging non-members higher fees.

Organizations are further polarized along party lines, seriously influencing the kinds of responses they mount towards important campaigns such as Uniform Family Code and female students' movements against sexual harassment. There is a tendency for women's organizations, following the general trend among civil society, to line up alongside the Awami League (AL) or the Bangladesh National Party (BNP), the two major political parties who have ruled the nation for much of its thirty seven years of independence. Although poli-cies regarding gender do not differ in any great detail from one political platform to another, they do capit-ulate to alliances with the Islamist parties to varying degrees, thereby consolidating the "Islamic"/"Secular" bifurcation. The AL was the political party that led the secular nationalist independence struggle and, while both parties have embraced secular modernist development initiatives for nation building, the BNP has made more overt alliances with Islamists over the years. The AL's more recent support of Islamist plat-forms has been met with harsh criticisms from pro-gressive constituencies including women's groups. These vacillations clarify the intricate co-dependencies between various state and nonstate actors and the need for analysis that recognizes the cross-fertilizations in discourses of religiosity, secular development, and global feminism shaping women's organizing strate-gies in Bangladesh.

BRAHMANBARIA RALLY—VYING FOR SOCIAL CONTROL

The complex positionality of NGOs and their contra-dictory relationship to their constituencies are crystal-lized in the competing representations of a women's rally led by the NGO Proshika in Brahmanbaria, Bangladesh in December 1998 in the work of Ali Riaz and Lamia Karim respectively. Riaz (2004) describes the events of that day as an attack by Islamists on women who took part in an NGO-led rally to celebrate the liberation of Brahmanbaria from Pakistani Army in 1971 while the local police failed to intervene. Lamia Karim's (2004) account of the same event however, exposes how democratizing impulses of NGOs are in conflict with the clientelist relationship they have with their women constituencies whom they profess to em-power. Here, the secular progressive underpinnings of NGOs which are heralded as democratic and modern-izing forces in Bangladesh come to be seen as making poor women particularly vulnerable and accessible to physical and structural violence.

The late 1990s witnessed a spate of violence against NGOs, their staff, women clients as well as poor women. According to most media reports and women activists, these were symbolic of the threat moderniza-tion projects posed to more orthodox factions of so-ciety, namely Islamists. Anthropologist Dina Siddiqi's analysis of Eclipse, a film made by women activists in Bangladesh in response to fatwa related violence against women in the 1990s, demonstrates how similar ideas are reflected within progressive organizing as well. She argues, in Eclipse, Islam is seen as an "external threat" to the nation and its women and "Islamist violence" is carried out by those groups who opposed the nationalist struggle of Bangladesh. Analyzing the attack on the Proshika-led women's rally in December 1998 sheds light on this particular debate pitting Islam against nation, and framing women activists' agendas as secular nationalist.

In December 1998, Proshika, one of the biggest NGOs in Bangladesh organized a *Mela* (village fair) for its women members in Brahmanbaria. The location is significant because it is where a historic victory was won by the Bengali Liberation forces against the Pakistani army in 1971. Moreover, it is known as a conservative and influential hub of Islamist groups and Qwami Madrassas. *Melas* and folk theater, historically associated with Bengali Hindu culture and often used as tools of grassroots organizing and consciousness raising by NGOs, were considered blasphemous by the Islamist groups in the area who issued a fatwa against them. Subsequently, Proshika, not to be outdone by the Islamists, changed the *Mela* into a public rally to commemorate the 1971 liberation war. The *Mela* symbolically strengthened Proshika's secular progressive positioning, invoking the memory of 1971, not an uncommon strategy in Bangladesh among the progressive communities.

The rally was attended by approximately 10,000 impoverished women and men where madrassah students and clergy launched an attack. It sent the NGO staff scattering to take shelter in the nearby homes of villagers. Women attendees in particular were beaten, their clothes were torn off and insults were hurled at them for daring to gather in public in spite of the fatwa. For at least two days following the rally, NGO offices, schools, and staff homes were looted, burned, and torn down. The presence of state law enforcement was notably absent despite existing laws against issuing fatwas. Riaz sees the event as a clash between Islamists and secular progressives. According to him, "Their [NGO workers] only crime was that they didn't heed the warnings of the Islamists to join a gathering deemed 'un-Islamic.' . . . The NGO activists in particular were forced to flee the city. Thus, twenty-seven

years after independence, Brahmanbaria returned to the media spotlight, once again as a battleground, this time between the secularists and the Islamists. And this time, the secularists had to take cover, at least for that day" (Riaz, 2004, 90). In contrast, Karim notes not without irony that the leaders of the NGO having fled to the capital "in their imported SUVs" began holding seminars to raise awareness and support to mobilize against Islamism (Karim, 2004, 306). She further notes that feminist leaders in Dhaka also responded by blaming the gradual Islamization of society as the source of violence against women leaving the opportunistic NGO politics in this case unscathed.

Lamia Karim notes that her interviews with men and women borrowers of the NGO revealed that they had little choice in the matter of attending the rally in the first place as their loan approval depended on it. What is more, the attendees were unaware of the fatwa issued by the Islamist group against potential attendees and they did not know that the *Mela* had been changed to a rally by the NGO in an attempt to challenge the Islamists' move. Karim further shows that the Islamists' reaction towards women—particularly poor rural women—was class based since a women's rally attended by middle class women activists from Dhaka a few days earlier had gone unchallenged. In a climate of increasing socioeconomic disempowerment of both men and women, and the loss of employment and underemployment of men, "modernizing" forces of NGOs represent a layered threat. The NGOization of society within the context of globalization is perceived to go hand in hand with Westernization and even Christianization (Karim, 2004).

As Dina Siddiqi (1998) has argued, NGOs have become a powerful symbol of change in the domain of gender relations and the social order. The hierarchical gender practices that Islamist parties seek to protect overtly clash with the seeming modernist ideologies of NGOs (Siddiqi, 1998, 216–217). Women NGO staff in particular have been attacked by religious extremist groups as have NGO schools and offices. Ironically, despite the anti-Christian rhetoric no missionary schools have been attacked nor the more radical NGOs with overt feminist agendas. It is the large NGOs of Bangladesh (such as BRAC and Proshika) which have been at the brunt of much of Islamist attacks. Siddiqi connects BRAC's iconic position and visibility to these attacks. She astutely states, "This kind of movement (Islamist) must ultimately be located within the specific predicaments of modernity, in particular the tensions of the postcolonial nation-state and the contingencies of global capitalism." In the context of Bangladesh, she concludes, politicization of Islam has been state-sponsored rather than a "fundamentalist" people's movement (Siddiqi, 1998, 212–213). In other words, the allegiances forged between ruling political parties and Islamist parties at the national level have emboldened Islamists' power at the local levels.

Like NGOs and state sponsored development initiatives, Islamist groups themselves are also invested in mobilizing poor women for bolstering their group support. Riaz suggests that these Islamist groups accuse NGO education programs of spreading atheism and Western development aid organizations of continuing colonial era structures by transforming existing gender relations to the detriment of the family (Riaz, 2004, 123). Digging deeper, Riaz also reveals that rural power structure in Bangladesh—patron clientelist in nature—is grating against shifting gender dynamics. The state has been complicit in maintaining the rural power structure as a means to maintain its link to the rural population. Developmentalist agendas of the NGOs on the other hand, have relied on "active" participation of women in credit and educational programs which have directly confronted the rural power structures' assignation of proper female behavior. As Dina Siddiqi has recently argued, the advent of NGOs has reconstituted local power structures. Patronage of religious leaders and other formations of local elites like rural moneylenders and large landowners are being replaced by NGOs providing low interest loans. Simultaneously, these different elite formations are strengthening their alliances in opposition to the shifting social and economic tides in rural society. At the same time, madrassas are losing students to NGO education programs. Siddiqi posits, "The intensification of corrupt patronage systems sustained by foreign assistance and the increasing presence of, and opposition to, NGOs provide a fertile ground for Islamist rhetoric" (Siddiqi, 1998, 217).

The state and NGOs have both failed to protect poor women citizens and left them vulnerable to physical violence that is the manifestation of power struggles among various interest groups whose existence is at times legitimized by invoking the rights of poor women. Although Proshika depicted women's participation in the *Mela* as democratization and the religious groups saw it as unIslamic, the women involved saw it as meeting the conditions of their NGO contracts. In this instance, integrating gender into development required their visibility in the form of participation in a public rally without ensuring social and economic empowerment to make this participation a real choice. Furthermore, it hinted that the vehicles of women's empowerment—NGOs in particular—are just as interested in self-promotion in a fashion that is ostensibly recognizable by international development structures (galvanizing bodies of poor brown Muslim women in the public space) as in attaining goals of gender mainstreaming. As Liz Kelly (2005) points out, the turn to gender mainstreaming has resulted in increased donor support for NGOs, although not always for feminist ones who have thought through these issues. Intergovernmental organizations have become major players in choosing large NGOs over smaller long standing feminist ones to be their service providers thus entrenching new hierarchies.

Feminist scholar Chandra Mohanty (2003) has argued that much of the literature on globalization has marked the centrality of race, class, and gender in critiquing global capitalist development but racialized gender still remains a largely unmarked terrain. In other words, poor women constituencies of state, NGO and Islamist group-led social mobilization are subject to racialized patriarchal marginalization in the context of globalization. Furthermore, the political economy of capitalist development brings into sharp focus the intersections of colonialism, capitalism, race, class, and gender as they discipline the labor and public and private lives of the poor in the third world and other women of color disproportionately. The abject victimization of the impoverished women and men at the Brahmanbaria rally is an instance where we see the intersecting forces of global capitalist development through NGOs who are integrating poor women into the market through micro-credit initiatives. Rising religious extremism itself is a complex phenomenon inseparable from the particular dynamics of modernization and global capitalism, and global feminism's resolute allegiance to the so-called belief of progressive development.

CONCLUSION

In 2000, I was in the audience of a forum in Dhaka where women activists were presenting an appraisal of the Beijing Platform for Action (1995) five years after its declaration. Speakers and audience included representatives from prominent national and women's NGOs. Also in the audience were staff and clients of NGOs, many of whom had traveled long distances to be part of a ceremony, which clearly had a celebratory ring. Following a presentation by a representative of BRAC—known globally as a model development organization whose education and health programs have been replicated worldwide—a member of the audience who identified himself as an ordinary citizen of Bangladesh who worked hard to provide for his family and who had traveled from Kishoreganj to hear the "national development plan" for Bangladeshis said, "I did not come hear [*sic*] to listen to a progress report from BRAC. I want to know what plans the NGOs have to improve the lives of the poor (*gorib manusher jonno apnara ki korchen?*)" This man did not get an answer that day and the stir he momentarily created in the room was quickly suppressed as the facilitator stepped on to the platform and moved on with the program.

As an inside-outsider, I have often wondered about the relative absence of critique on the ground of development and social mobilization in Bangladesh. I have seen first-hand the difficult terrain of transnational organizing treaded by devoted feminists in Bangladesh, even as they depend on framing issues in essentialist terms to mobilize disparate communities to take urgent action. NGOs occupy such a powerful social space in Bangladesh that they seemed to have appropriated the space of dissent even among progressive intellectuals and activists. In fact, much of the organizing, production and dissemination of knowledge, and social mobilization occur through NGOs and not against them. NGOs contract professionals as consultants and researchers, organize national, regional and local forums, employ increasing numbers of graduates interested in grassroots development work, and mobilize constituencies for social and political action. How

do we have conversations in this context engaging the particular ways in which NGOs have become the vehicle of neoliberal governance, control and disciplining of post-colonial subjects even as they produce new identities and meanings, in smaller scale, that disrupt the global order?

I would like to return to the question of what kinds of mobilizations are possible as women activists in Bangladesh confront the scattered hegemonies of rising religious extremism in the region, neoimperialism and Islamophobia globally, and neocolonial development initiatives that make use of poor Bangladeshi women's participation to bolster their own sustainability. Although I agree with much of Karim's (2004) astute analysis of unequal power relations between NGO-based urban feminists and poor rural women clients of NGOs, I am not comfortable in relegating urban women's activism as wholly uninformed and clientelist. As this paper has shown, the urban based women's movement in Bangladesh has flourished as a result of transnational networking and availing global feminist instruments. At the same time, such alliances hinder a more nuanced engagement with diverse women's realities on the ground. This contradictory consequence of global women's organizing efforts whereby new kinds of hierarchies emerge and only certain kinds of organizing are visible has been noted by Elizabeth Friedman (1999) as an example of "transnationalism reversed." Anthropologist Sally Merry's ethnographic work on the making and implementing of human rights policy on gender in the UN reveals how participants seem to perpetuate an image of a national culture with regard to women's status in order to maximize the impact of their situation. Instead of explaining how culture is used in struggles over class, kinship, ethnic or religious identity, activists often invoke an essential culture as detrimental to women's emancipation. Sally Merry writes, ". . . in the context of an international setting and universal principles, acknowledging such complexity would diminish the political impact of her [the woman activist's] statement" (Merry, 2006,18). International documents and country reports on Bangladesh are rife with such "progress narratives" where women are perceived to be victims of culture and indigenous patriarchy deflecting attention from other kinds of analysis. Even if feminists use essentializing discourses of gender and culture consciously and strategically, we must persistently ask about the implications for transnational solidarity and praxis. Saba Mahmood's work (2005) is especially insightful in this discussion as she astutely observes that feminism is both an analytic and political project, and while the two certainly inform one another they ought not to be collapsed in to one. There is value in keeping the possibilities of the analytic project open in the interest of thinking beyond immediate or urgent political action. The expediency of mobilizing campaigns under difficult circumstances may lead to silencing critical voices, as we saw happening in Beijing related organizing as well as the constructing of a nationalist identity to counter Islamist "threat." Nevertheless, ongoing reflection and dialogue are essential if NGOs are to effectively serve and integrate their constituencies in to development initiatives.

Minoo Moallem (1999) views both feminism and fundamentalism within modernity instead of as competing discourses. Just as Islamic fundamentalism in the West is linked to the racialization of Muslims as a peoples without history and the demonization of Islamic masculinity as barbaric and Islamic femininity as victimized and subordinate, Western egalitarian feminism is tied to the notion of feminist progress narrative of women's emancipation from backwards tradition to enlightened modernity. Moallem sees cross-fertilization between feminism and fundamentalism and co-complicity in, ". . . perpetuating power relations, either by sustaining the boundaries of a totalistic ideology (in the case of fundamentalist feminists), or by creating restricted boundaries through a replacement of patriarchy with matriarchy, or by limiting women's issues to only one set of relations, and thus putting an end to any constructive sociological discussion" (Moallem, 1999, 325). Sometimes these forces can function as rivals, but they can also act together in their rigidified positions and categories. Subject positions emerging from such formations remain cut off from historical and geopolitical contexts. Moallem proposes ". . . embracing a transnationalism rooted in the recognition of the various intersecting social relations or nation, 'race,' ethnicity, class, gender, and sexuality and the positionality of the self" (Moallem, 1999, 342). Further, feminism must disrupt its own complicity with

perpetuating rigidified analysis of women's oppression within transnational spheres of mobilization. Following this line of thinking NGO based organizing, important as it is as a venue for social change, must interrogate this rigid dichotomy between secular development and religious oppression and find more nuanced causes of conflicts such as the one that unfolded in Brahmanbaria.

Raka Ray's (1999) work conceptualizing women's organizing in India within Pierre Bourdieu's notion of political fields is instructive here. She suggests that organizations are embedded in and respond to a set of unequal socially constructed structures and relations. They act not as free agents but rather within the context of asymmetrical power relations within a given field, which ought to be understood "both as configurations of forces and as sites of struggle" that perpetuate yet disrupt existing dynamics (Ray, 1999, 7). Instigating action within the structure of global UN-based feminism is imbricated within the culture of such a field that inhibits multi-axial analysis of diverse women's positionalities and realities. Ray explains, "The political field includes such actors as the state, political parties, and social movement organizations (in which I would add international organizations who push the agenda of gender mainstreaming in local contexts), who are connected to each other in both friendly and antagonistic ways, some of whose elements are more powerful than others, and all of whom are tied together by a particular culture" (Ray, 1999, 7). Based on this understanding of women's movements location within a political field, one can surmise that the notion of autonomy is illusive. Rather, Ray presents the term "protest fields" to imply subgroups and networks that oppose the logic of power relations in the larger political field even as they are constrained by them. Ray's analysis of women's movements juxtaposed with Moallem's assertion of Western egalitarian feminism's (one that appears to dominate global feminist scripts of fashioning "other" women's needs and desires in the image of the liberated western subject) complicity in furthering imperialist discourses of modernity and development opens up an important dialogue. Binary analysis of women's organizing as secular/Islamist or modern/underdeveloped freezes up conversations that recognize the heterogeneous ways in which women activists negotiate their environments. My work here seeks to illuminate intra-movement tensions in the context of Bangladesh in an attempt to theorize and imagine feminist alliances that are more equitable and just across borders of nation, class and community.

As feminist activists, scholars, and practitioners we need to be more attentive to the protest field conversations that rupture the asymmetrical plane of political fields and open up more productive dialogue for effective transnational praxis.

NOTES

1. A term widely used to describe South Asians as a racialized community in the West.
2. In the context of Bangladesh, secular at the nation's founding and as defined by "father of the nation" Mujib implied co-existence and tolerance of plural religious beliefs and practices as opposed to a strict separation of religion from state. Subsequent regimes however as a result of complex global and regional social, economic and political forces dropped secularism from the Constitution and declared Islam as the state religion. Increasingly however and particularly in relation to current global politics it is important to keep in mind for any discussion on Islam vs secularism the ways in which the latter has been deployed in the service of imperialism by idealizing a linear narrative of progress and development in opposition to the term religious/Islamic. Gil Anidjar (2006) quotes Talal Asad, "the 'religious' and the 'secular' are not essentially fixed categories" but gain in prominence and hegemony by the culture—more specifically, "Western Christendom" (Gil Anidjar, "On Secularism" pp. 57-8). Furthermore, Ashis Nandy (2002) has argued that the birth of secularism as an ideology in modernity makes it deeply intolerant because modernity undermines faith in favor of secular values of rationality and development which is achieved by abandoning or devaluing "traditional" belief systems. A belief in secular development, constructed as the opposite of traditional belief systems, overlooks the accommodating ways faith systems co-existed historically.
3. The state of Bangladesh has ratified CEDAW with reservations to Article 2, which has to do with the implementation of shari'a law in personal/family matters.
4. It should be noted, the report was published before the outcome of the . . . election in 2008.
5. The ethnic nationalities of the CHT are collectively known as Jumma people.

REFERENCES

Anidjar, Gil (2006). Secularism. *Critical inquiry, 33*(1), 52–77.

Bergeron, Suzanne (2006). *Fragments of development: Nation, Gender, and the Space of Modernity.* Ann Arbor: The University of Michigan Press.

Bose, Sugata, & Jalal, Ayesha (1998). *Modern South Asia: History, culture, political economy.* London: Routledge.

Chowdhury, Najma (2001). The politics of implementing women's rights in Bangladesh. In Jane H. Bayes & Nayereh Tohidi (Eds.), *Globalization, gender, and religion: The politics of women's rights in Catholic and Muslim contexts* (pp. 203–230). New York: Palgrave.

Eclipse (1994). Ain O Salish Kendro Bangladesh: Dhaka.

Friedman, Elisabeth (1999). The effects of "transnationalism reversed" in Venezuela: assessing the impact of UN global conferences on the women's movement. *International Feminist Journal of Politics, 1*(3), 357–381.

Guhathakurta, Meghna (2004). Women negotiating change: the structure and transformation of gendered violence in Bangladesh. *Cultural Dynamics, 16*(2/3), 193–211.

Halim, Sadeka (2008). *Gender Needs Assessment MDG-3 Situational Analysis Report.* Submitted to the General Economic Division and UNDP, Dhaka, Bangladesh. June 22.

Halim, Sadeka (2008, October 6). Personal interview.

Kabeer, Naila (2005). Gender equality and women's empowerment: A critical analysis of the third Millennium Development Goal. *Gender and Development, 13*(1), 13–24.

Karim, Lamia (2004). Democratizing Bangladesh: State, NGOs, and militant Islam. *Cultural Dynamics, 16*(2/3), 291–318.

Kelly, Liz (2005). Inside Outsiders: Mainstreaming Violence Against Women into Human Rights Discourse and Practice. *International Feminist Journal of Politics, 7*(4), 471–495.

Mahmood, Saba (2005). Feminist theory, agency and the liberatory subject. In F. Nouraie-Simone (Ed.), *On Shifting Ground* (pp. 111–152). New York: Feminist Press.

Merry, Sally E. (2006). *Human rights and gender violence: Translating international law into local justice.* Chicago: University of Chicago Press.

Moallem, Minoo (1999). Transnationalism, Feminism and Fundamentalism. In Caren Kaplan, Norma Alarcon, & Minoo Moallem (Eds.), *Between woman and nation: nationalisms, transnational feminisms, and the state* (pp. 320–348). Durham: Duke University Press.

Mohanty, Chandra (2003). *Feminism Without borders: decolonizing theory, practicing solidarity.* Durham: Duke University Press.

Nandy, Ashis (2002). *Time Warps: Silent and Evasive Pasts in Indian Politics and Religions.* New Brunswick: Rutgers University Press.

Ray, Raka (1999). *Fields of Protest: Women's Movements in India.* Minneapolis: University of Minnesota Press.

Riaz, Ali (2004). *God Willing: The Politics of Islamism in Bangladesh.* Lanham: Rowman & Littlefield Publishers, Inc.

Rozario, Santi (2004). Building Solidarity Against Patriarchy. *Report for CARE Bangladesh.*

Shehabuddin, Elora (1999). Contesting the illicit: gender and the politics of Fatwas in Bangladesh. *Signs: Journal of Women in Culture and Society, 24*(4), 1011–1044.

Siddiqi, Dina (1998). Taslima Nasreen and others: The contest over gender in Bangladesh. In Herbert L. Bodman, & Nayereh Tohidi (Eds.), *Women in Muslim Societies: diversity Within Unity* (pp. 205–227). Boulder: Lynne Rienner Publishers.

Siddiqi, Dina (2006). In the Name of Islam? Gender, Politics and Women's Rights in Bangladesh: *Harvard Asia Quarterly.* Retrieved August 9, 2008 from http://ww.asiaquarterly.com/index2.

S. M. RODRIGUEZ

44. INVISIBILITY MATTERS: QUEER AFRICAN ORGANIZING AND VISIBILITY MANAGEMENT IN A TRANSNATIONAL AGE

"Kensington Gardens and Golf," I say to Samuel, who has become my trusted *boda-boda* (motorbike taxi) driver.

"Ma'am?" he responds. I repeat it, to no avail. He knows the neighborhood well, but has never heard of the venue. Samuel looks at me, puzzled, and I'm worried that he's having a hard time understanding my accent again.

After an hour of riding around, lost, and of conversation about my accent, lack of religion, and how I'm not yet engaged, Samuel points into the distance, *"Maybe it's that!"* We see a beautiful sign grounded in vast gardens that covered the hill. I ask him if he had ever seen the area before to which he responds, *"No ma'am, it is beautiful but I've never noticed it. Perhaps it is for the Europeans?"* I understand immediately what he means; it strikes me that not one Ugandan person from whom we had asked directions had ever been to this place. I wonder, even today, if Cherish chose the venue based on proximity to her home or desire to experience the grounds.

I call Cherish when I'm at the entrance. We first met just a year before in New York, where she attended an event hosted by the community organization that I serve. She tells me that she has already arrived. I join her at the bar in the front, where she sits with the overpriced beer she had ordered to justify being in this commercial space. It's clear that she didn't intend on paying for it; a vibe that the server undoubtedly picked up on. The waitress looks relieved when I show up. I let Cherish know that I actually didn't have enough shillings on me to buy her more than two drinks since I had to pay more than I anticipated for the boda ride.

We begin talking about various topics. Mostly, we focus on the history and future of her organization and what my intentions are for my writing. Also, in light of a conversation that I had with others about my desire to meet with her, we broach the subject of alliance building. After a pause in the largely casual, honest, and relaxed conversation, I look at the picturesque sign on the hill; observe the wedding bustle; and eventually I catch the eyes of the server, who was raptly watching us, more confused than hostile.

We, together, are visibly strange. We are exposed but likely illegible in this environment. Cherish, a transwoman, is clearly trying to manage the visibility of her queerness—she's dressed "as a man" (her words), but she can't be read as manly. Her vibrancy, her sass, her sway, her effeminate gestures are giving her away. She's somewhere in between and outside of genders, in this moment. In this overwhelmingly cis-space and we both sit here, in a completely unreadable relationship.

I imagine the server's confusion. Why am I with her? Why is she acting this way? Why does she expect me to pay for her drink? Why has she brought a laptop and me a notebook? We don't look like an average pair of professionals: I look young and I'm underdressed in my blue jeans and simple t-shirt. She maybe smiles too much; is too sweet "for a man." There is an economic power dynamic that is obvious and inverted, as I am read as a woman (a reading that I do not identify with, but acknowledge).

It's all queer and I'm hyperaware of our strangeness, as everyone stares. We're uncovered, unprotected, but our interactions are genuine and comfortable and it is clear that we share a likeness or familiarity. It occurs to me that this is the type of organizing experience that I value, the very beginning of a collaborative relationship. However, importantly, this is also a formation that is growing increasingly subjected to scrutiny by government and ordinary citizens like the server.

In this moment, the Anti-Homosexuality Bill (AHB) has passed into an Act that has not yet been nullified. The "era" of the AHB lasted between 2009 and 2014 and is one marked by heightened nationalist anxiety in which LGBT people (*kuchus*) and the Non-Governmental Organizations (NGOs) that service and/or employ them are subjected to an unmistakably hostile gaze. The AHB, originally proposed to penalize "aggravated homosexuality" with the death penalty, passed into an Act when that penalty reduced to a maximum of a life sentence. The concept of aggravated homosexuality included repeat offenses, same sex pedophilia, same sex parent-child incest, sex while living with HIV, administering a drug to enable sex, or sexually engaging with someone who has a disability. The Bill also, for the first time in any country, defined "homosexuality" as a criminal term, departing from the colonial language of "sodomy" or buggery (Rodriguez 405). This circumstance exemplifies what M. Jacqui Alexander, a transnational, decolonial feminist theorist, calls a "repressive and regressive gaze" on queerness, on behalf of the postcolonial state (Alexander 5). Postcolonial state powers enact an aggressive, law-based heterosexualization in order to assert national cohesion and a respectable image (Alexander).

Perhaps it is an obvious next step, then, in this climate of anti-gay policing, to question the role of visibility, invisibility, and alliance-building as survival and empowerment strategies of kuchu activists. This essay examines these concepts and asks *when do queer bodies choose to remain invisible?* Also, *how and why do allies violate that autonomy?* I use "bodies" to refer to both organizational structures—bodies of queer people and to one's individual, physical body.

The methodological approach that I embrace in order to explore this question has been called *engaged ethnography* or *feminist activist ethnography* (Craven and Davis). The term methodology, as used here, encompasses both the logic behind the questions I ask and the way that I go about answering the questions. An *ethnography* is an approach that involves entrenching oneself in a setting and writing thick description of what one observes and experiences. The *engagement* exists in various forms such as systematically recording my interactions, thoughts, questions, and surroundings and actively participating in a range of LGBT protests, parties, and parades. I especially engage in an emotional way, by caring deeply about the topic

and the people involved in such activism. These forms of engagement challenge traditional academic approaches that value "objectivity" but are understood as important methodological interventions (Craven and Davis; Juris 164). In doing so, this engaged methodology ensures that I critically evaluate and theorize from a point of connection because my main motivation is to contribute to the autonomy and dignity of the parties involved.

Importantly, this essay is written with accessibility in mind. Theory-work need not be inaccessible or detached from experience; it also does not necessitate academic formatting or difficult language. I use ethnographic storytelling to illuminate how theorizing from situated observations enables us to understand social problems more fully. I have personally experienced invisibility practices and challenges with allies, and therefore I intimately understand how they develop.

Last, I note that each name used here for kuchus (such as "Cherish") is a pseudonym, and each location within Kampala has been renamed in order to protect and respect the privacy and spatial autonomy of the participants. These activists often speak publicly and share pieces of themselves and their struggles; and yet, by honoring anonymity, I leave it up to them to opt into and out of these conversations upon their choosing.

WHEN DO QUEER BODIES CHOOSE TO REMAIN INVISIBLE?

The narrative of "coming out of the closet" relies on the assumption that visibility is a one-way street: a queer body exits the closet and enters into a realm of full transparency. Once one is out of the closet, one does not return willingly (if ever). This transparency leads to representation, and representation leads to progress. However, this clean trajectory is a fallacious imagining. A full understanding of queer visibility includes the when's, how's, and why's of staying hidden, especially after the initial rupture of public existence. For example, Ashley Currier, a sociologist who studies Southern African LGBT activism, states that visibility decisions include both the management of visibility and invisibility as organizing tools for queer empowerment. A group may use "simultaneous strategies of visibility and invisibility when it wants to work with certain organizations in coalitions, for instance, but not be publicly visible to everyone" (Currier, 2007, 25). African queer groups choose select visibility in order to opt into alliances, yet they also need to choose public invisibility in openly hostile contexts.

Invisibility offers a modicum of safety. It allows for a strategic determination of how to confront systemic power structures—which power structures to bother confronting and when to do so. To live as African (or of African descent) *and* poor *and* queer is to live as activists, whether or not one is visibly protesting, organizing, or speaking publicly. We are constantly interacting with power structures that are here to end us. Navigating (in)visibility is a strategy that queers become fluent in, often in our youth. This written articulation of the importance of strategic invisibility matters especially for kuchu Ugandans, as they battle involuntary exposure as well as the state or interpersonal violence that often occurs in response to their presence in public.

When I use the term *strategic invisibility*, I refer to a range of actions. On a personal level, actions such as wearing gender-conforming clothing or speaking in the tonality assumed of the gender that people think you are can encompass strategic invisibility. This looks like me wearing a long, modest skirt in Kampala, an article of clothing I never wore before. It also looks like Cherish wearing "men's" clothing in public. This is not to imply successfully passing (being regarded as the target identity): at times, queerness is suspected and there is nothing that dressing cis* can do to protect someone. However, this would all count as *personal invisibility*.

Interpersonal invisibility may look like lying, evading the truth, or having a cover story. Although many regard "lying" as unethical, it can be strategic and done for safety. In a potentially life-threatening situation, when a parent or police officer asks about queer engagement, assuming an alternate identity is an important and useful tool.

Organizational invisibility encompasses clandestine practices engaged in often in the histories of many countries and in present-day Uganda. This includes hosting a meeting in private homes, using passcodes for entry or for sharing information, or occupying an unmarked building for organizational purposes.

Last, *national invisibility* occurs when groupings of LGBT people do not make large, public appearances.

It can happen intermittently or indefinitely. For example, 2007 was the first time that a kuchu organization made a public appearance large enough to make national headlines, despite having existed for four years (Rodriguez). Some organizations choose to go underground for a period in order to collectivize, plan, and reemerge stronger. For example, if an organization seeks to plan and execute a campaign, they may opt into invisibility during their efforts, and into visibility following a press conference. This strategy makes the safety of the community feasible and calls attention to success.

The Anti-Homosexuality Bill had a strong influence on these visibility decisions, stifling the activists' ability to work publicly in Kampala. A clause called "The Promotion of Homosexuality," while never passed into law, continued to develop as a legal concept equally detrimental to kuchu visibility. Criminalizing the Promotion of Homosexuality is the Parliament of Uganda's attempt to ensure that no organization or individual teaches safe same-sex sexual engagement, financially supports a kuchu group, or enables open kuchus to reside or work on private property.

While lawmakers formally withdrew the Promotion of Homosexuality clause, the Non-Governmental Organisations (NGO) Act developed and became law shortly after, in 2016. The NGO Act (2016) increases the government's ability to monitor and "dissolve" any organizing deemed contrary to the nation's goals. The Act establishes committees with which each NGO in the country would register. The committees thereby would "guide and monitor organizations in carrying out their activities" (4, II, d), among other responsibilities. In this context, *organizational invisibility* becomes an absolute requirement for each grouping of activists, as this legislation extends past the criminalization of same-sex sexual acts and into kuchu organizing in its very essence.

The NGO Act is an attempt to manage the NGOization of gay rights movements and the spread of the message that homosexuality is natural, okay, or healthy. Although the Promotion of Homosexuality is no longer an operational legal concept, organizers (kuchu and otherwise) understood the NGO Act as an extremely invasive and limiting national effort. It consolidates what "Uganda" stands for and against by coordinating civil society in such a way that its focus must necessarily complement the agenda of the government. This effort, or what I call *homophobic nationalism,* developed as the government framed European and American financial support of LGBT activism as a form of cultural imperialism, or erasure of Ugandan cultural values through economic domination (Rodriguez 411).

Kuchu organizers know that the required registration of all organizations would push them further into obscurity. According to the NGO Act, each organization must divulge information about the whereabouts of meetings and activities and its operations and purpose. If an unregistered group is discovered in meeting, it is vulnerable to government scrutiny. If an organization meets or acts without a valid permit, it is liable, on conviction, to a fine. There is also the possibility that, if this law is broken, the organization's director or officer serves a sentence not exceeding eight years in prison (VIII, 31(11), b). The legislation thus criminalizes co-ordinated kuchu activity; therefore, the Promotion of Homosexuality manifested in a more insidious way.

HOW AND WHY DO ALLIES VIOLATE THE "INVISIBILITY" AUTONOMY?

Despite the international silence surrounding the NGO Act, the AHB propelled Uganda to the forefront of global media. In the wake of the proposed legislation, even before its passage, transnational alliances formed both within Africa and between Uganda and Western nations. The campaigns of Western allies, in particular, have rested on two assumptions: (1) the known activists in Uganda need to be made more visible in order to garner material and political support from powerful elites; and (2) the unknown LGBT people of Uganda, who are suffering without profile or attention, need assistance. For the latter, this support has largely been in the form of fundraising and coordinating efforts to get them out of the hostile, anti-gay climate. However, many of these campaigns have both fueled the cultural imperialism claims and frustrated the efforts of many kuchu activists.

One such project was named "The New Underground Railroad," which began with the organizing efforts of American Quakers who call themselves the "Religious Society of Friends." They had reportedly "coordinated passage" out of Uganda for 107 kuchus as of 2014 (Schlanger). The project received backlash

both locally and on as widely known of an outlet as Buzzfeed, which featured an extensive and balanced critique. The critique rested largely on the operability of the campaign. Neil Grungras, of the Organization for Refuge, Asylum, and Migration (ORAM), which works on LGBT refugee issues, told Buzzfeed, "In order to run a program like that successfully . . . you have to invest tremendous resources to understand the situation on the ground." Grungras also critiques this type of campaign for its difficulty in responsibly allocating donor funds. However, even ORAM admitted to shutting down its own LGBT refuge project (Schlanger).

Activist and entrepreneur, Isaac, tells me, as an indirect response to this phenomenon, *"You cannot evacuate a community that keeps being born.* These [projects that focus on getting gays out of Uganda] guzzle money and do not help." His critique, although appreciative of international allies, is that it diverts funds from more sustainable, kuchu-led ideas. My critique is of how such evacuation attempts incite nationalist backlash. They reproduce an image that gay Ugandans do not want to be Ugandan or identify with the country. For these reasons, kuchu groups try to minimize the number of campaigns dedicated to this effort, as well as the amount of visibility that each effort receives.

Regardless, many "Save Gay Ugandans" fundraisers popped up after the Anti-Homosexuality Act (AHA) to "help LGBT people escape Africa." The "Rescue Fund to Help LGBT People Escape Africa" raised $14,025 in one month and was one of three similar fundraisers. A very well respected kuchu organizer, Oliver, tells me about the lack of accountability that these fundraisers have. He is in a leadership position of one of the oldest LGBT rights organizations in Uganda and is dedicated to creating sustainable progress for kuchus. His organization has attempted to follow the numbers for how much the founder makes from these and cannot see where the money actually goes. The organization also questions whether or not kuchu Ugandans receive it, and if so, who they are. He is used to having access to such details, as the organization positions itself to know most kuchus in the city and events that would lead one to seek refuge.

The person who initiates these fundraisers, on the other hand, publicly defends that she has contacts that are not affiliated with Oliver's organization and are in desperate need. Her circumvention of the major kuchu organizations is, in her words, a way to make sure that they do not monopolize the resources. The obvious controversy remains. Neither she—who lives in the United States and is not Ugandan—nor those who have spearheaded the New Underground Railroad have heeded the advice of kuchu organizers. They raise tremendous amounts of money to "rescue" kuchus and relocate them, rather than invest in the movements to create a sustainable living situation for LGBT people in Uganda. These campaigns do not rely on clandestine fundraising or collectivizing methods, as they would if they received support from local organizations. Therefore, they actually rely on strategies of *visibility* that may ultimately harm those who wish to remain in the country.

There's a tough divide here. On one hand, the threat of violence becomes unbearably high, especially for those affiliated with the movement. Due to international alliances, kuchus are more publicly recognized. Locally, they're associated with the breakdown of national morality and pride, and are made vulnerable by this negative association. On the other hand, everyone that I've spoken with in the movement says that asylum in and of itself is not what the movement should be about; that the amount of funds dedicated to "evacuating" kuchus surmounts the amount of support that self-sustaining projects receive. I argue that this is because nationalist violence is more visible, more recognizable to Westerners than the globalized economic violence of colonialism's aftermath.

The common anti-gay sentiment shared around the continent that "homosexuality is unAfrican" relies on the belief that inherent in the kuchu identity is a *desire* to leave Uganda (or Africa) and live in proximity to white or European others. It is a nationalist argument that reverses the logic of refuge, centering desire as opposed to an imminent *need* to leave. It also doesn't take into account the shared national oppression in the world system: that the majority of kuchu Ugandans experience limited access to Western countries.

Liberal American campaigns that raise money for Ugandans to move to other countries forget that long before the newest *de jure* travel ban, there was a *de facto* ban on issuing visas to travelers from most African countries. Additionally, even if received in the United States or a European nation, the chance of obtaining legal,

protected status in the country is slim. Many kuchus have been sent back to Uganda in high profile (hypervisible) deportations after spending years attempting asylum in the UK, Sweden, and Norway—countries considered "more liberal" and easier to access than the United States. These deportations typically follow courts that could not prove the queer sexuality or gender of the applicant along the white, Western, and homonormative understanding of queerness (Llewellyn 695). Importantly, the courts also demonstrate a narrow imagining of the harm that LGBT people experience while criminalized and hyper-policed.

CONCLUSION

In the era of the Anti-Homosexuality Bill and Act, global attention to Uganda and local attention to kuchus both spiked. The nationalist vigilance of kuchu organizing leads to conflicting processes: kuchus desire invisibility in order to fortify communal strength and yet international communities create hypervisible campaigns in order to amass global support for LGBT Ugandans. This conflict has no resolution, yet it holds important revelations about assumptions of LGBT progress that disregard the importance of invisibility and autonomy. The theories of visibility, developed by Currier's research on South African and Namibian queer organizing, have been advanced here by a perspective that enables an exploration of various levels of strategic invisibility. Additionally, it helps us to reframe the idea of what a goal is in transnational, feminist organizing. We can witness that allies often define their own goals, based in cultural assumptions that do not acknowledge the needs or realities of those in the local contexts. Grounding an analysis of transnational campaign work in questions of strategic visibility helps us to examine the complications of allying through a shared identity (e.g. queer, "progressive") across different racial or economic contexts. The only way forward is through a decolonial praxis, in which an activist or academic acts through self-reflection, sustained dialogue, and critical, contextualized thought.

Note: All names used in reference to interview participants are pseudonyms. Identifying information has been changed for the safety of the activists.

REFERENCES

Alexander, M. Jacqui. "Not Just (Any) Body Can Be a Citizen: The Politics of Law, Sexuality and Post-coloniality in Trinidad and Tobago and the Bahamas." *Feminist Review*, no. 48, 1994, pp. 5–23.

Craven, Christa, and Dána-Ain Davis, eds. *Feminist Activist Ethnography: Counterpoints to Neoliberalism in North America*. Lexington Books, 2013.

Currier, Ashley. "The Visibility of Sexual Minority Movement Organizations in Namibia and South Africa." PhD diss., U of Pittsburgh, 2007.

Currier, Ashley. *Out in Africa: LGBT organizing in Namibia and South Africa*. University of Minnesota Press, 2012.

Juris, Jeffrey S. "Practicing Militant Ethnography with the Movement for Global Resistance in Barcelona." In *Constituent Imagination: Militant Investigations, Collective Theorization*, edited by E. Biddle, D. Graeber, and S. Shukaitis. AK Press, 2007, pp. 164–176.

Llewellyn, Cheryl. "Homonationalism and Sexual Orientation-Based Asylum Cases in the United States." *Sexualities* 20, no.5–6, 2017: 682–698.

Non-Governmental Organisations Act, 2016, *The Uganda Gazette* No. 14, Volume CIX, March 3, 2016.

"Rescue Fund to Help LGBT People Escape Africa." *Indiegogo.* https://www.indiegogo.com/projects/rescue-fund-to-help-lgbt-people-escape-africa#/updates/all. Imaged featured on web page by Ben Curtis, AP. Accessed April 2014.

Rodriguez, S.M. "Homophobic Nationalism: The Development of Sodomy Legislation in Uganda." *Comparative Sociology* 16, no.3, 2017: 393–421.

Schlanger, Zoe. "American Quakers are Running New Underground Railroad to Help LGBT Ugandans Flee." *Newsweek*, July 11, 2014.

BRANDY NĀLANI McDOUGALL

45. SOVEREIGN BODIES, SOVEREIGN CHIC: INDIGENOUS WOMEN'S ACTIVIST FASHION AND THE FASHIONING OF LAND PROTECTION MOVEMENTS

When European men first began settling North America, they feminized the lands describing them as "virgin" territories, empty of inhabitants and ready to be claimed by (masculinized) European powers. While North America was clearly inhabited by hundreds of distinct nations before their successive arrivals, these settlers in attributing virginity to the land also sought to establish their right to sovereignty over territory and natural resources by emphasizing emptiness. Extending this gendered metaphor, colonial representations often associated the land with Native women's bodies, seeing both as "open, 'rapeable,' [and] inviting male penetration and exploration" (Ramirez 107); yet, beyond the metaphor, settlement occurred through various forms of violence, including sexual violence against Indigenous women and girls, and has continued. The Indian Law Resource Center ("Ending Violence Against Native Women") reports that Native women are 2.5 times more likely than other women to face sexual violence or physical assault, with 1 in 3 Native women being raped and 3 in 5 being assaulted at some point in their lifetimes. They note that "due to under-reporting, the actual numbers are almost certainly higher."

Notably, scholars theorizing Indigenous feminisms assert that the high rates of sexual, domestic, and other forms of violence against Indigenous women are directly linked to settler colonialism, a form of colonialism that is structured to eliminate and replace Indigenous peoples so as to claim and occupy their land (see Lefevre for an overview of major sources). Patrick Wolfe describes settler colonialism as an ongoing structure that follows a "logic of elimination" of Indigenous peoples to provide "access to territory," as "territoriality is settler colonialism's specific, irreducible element" (388). He asserts that elimination may take the form of genocide or forced removal amounting to "the summary liquidation of Indigenous people," as well as biological and cultural assimilation wherein "the native repressed continues to structure settler-colonial society" (390). Gender violence exists within the structure of settler colonialism and occurs as a form of native repression that, along with other strategies, has enabled settlers to acquire and maintain control of land and natural resources and to establish their own cultural and political systems.

In collecting and examining a history of institutionalized sexual violence against Indigenous women, Andrea Smith concludes that because "Native people continue to live on the lands rich in energy resources that government or corporate interests want, the sexual colonization of Native people will continue. Native bodies will continue to be depicted as expendable and inherently violable as long as they continue to stand in the way of the theft of Native lands" (82). Statistics gathered in a recent report by the Women's Earth Alliance and Native Youth Sexual Health Network reinforce the connection between environmental violence and violence against Indigenous bodies, demonstrating that disproportionately, Indigenous communities "are sites of chemical manufacturing and waste dumping, while others [live with] large encampments of men ('man camps') who work for the gas and oil industry. The devastating impacts of environmental violence, therefore, ranges from sexual and domestic violence, drugs and alcohol, murders and disappearances, reproductive illnesses and toxic exposure, threats to culture and Indigenous lifeways, crime, and other social stressors" (2).

Emphasizing the correlation between environmental violence (including extractive industries, pollution, and toxic dumping), and violence against Indigenous women, scholars and activists such as Sarah Deer, Joanne Barker, Renya Ramirez, Andrea Smith, Mishuana Goeman, Jennifer Nez Denetdale, Lisa Kahale'ole

Hall, Maile Arvin, and Dian Million have urged that Indigenous sovereignties must account for this legacy of settler colonial violence and its impact on our lands, bodies, and communities. Building on this important work and focusing on the fashion of Indigenous women's activism in land and water protection movements, I examine this theory in action, the ways that Indigenous women in North America and in the Pacific consciously recognize ongoing gender and environmental violence while also recasting their lands and themselves as sites of power, healing, beauty, teaching, and inspiration. Specifically, I analyze examples of women's activist fashion within Idle No More, Murdered and Missing Indigenous Women (MMIW), and We Are Mauna Kea, emphasizing the inherent power of Indigenous women as well as that of the bodies of lands and waters they protect and honor.

INDIGENOUS WOMEN'S ACTIVIST FASHION REDEFINING BEAUTY, REFASHIONING ACTIVISM

I apply the term "Indigenous women's activist fashion" to refer to only Indigenous cultural productions that include traditional and contemporary forms of regalia; the use of ancestral materials (often specific to and from Indigenous homelands) to create forms of fashion; contemporary or introduced forms that incorporate ancestral aesthetic designs and symbols; and forms that emphasize specific political views to protect and/or celebrate Indigenous lands, peoples, and social justice movements. This entails everything that may adorn the body, including clothing, jewelry, and tattoos, and the cultural and aesthetic revitalization movements (modes of political activism in and of themselves) that often give rise to, support, and accompany these forms of activist fashion. Indeed, the layeredness of Indigenous women's activist fashion is complex and should be seen as both a phenomena of cultural strength and continuity as well as a response to a forced discontinuity and part of the violence of colonial biological and cultural genocide campaigns.

This study takes up an overlooked focus of analysis—Indigenous women's beauty and fashion as defined by Indigenous women's activism—and examines the rhetorics (the art of discourse through which a person strives to inform or persuade an audience) and aesthetics (how one defines beauty and pleasure) of movements that refashion women's activism as beautiful and powerful. Such fashion, I argue, redefines and furthers notions of beauty on Indigenous women's terms—equating beauty with activist engagement—while also fostering Indigenous women as educators and leaders informed by cultural memory and genealogies intimately connected to land and water. Moreover, because the movements that produce Indigenous activist fashion are publicized through visual images posted on social media platforms, this medium of educational dissent creates and fosters meaningful spaces for expressions of settler, male, and other-gendered solidarity. While several studies have examined the use of social media in protest movements globally, how social media has been leveraged within Indigenous movements remains underrepresented. In examining how fashion is used rhetorically and aesthetically through shared images on social media to grow these women-led movements, I am interested in how Indigenous women activists open up various modes of activist participation and assert a sovereignty of beauty and strength over their bodies by wearing their political activism and culture and assuming their roles as leaders and teachers in their communities.

SOVEREIGN CHIC: AESTHETIC AND RHETORICAL EXAMPLES OF INDIGENOUS WOMEN'S ACTIVIST FASHION

The popular grassroots movement Idle No More (#idlenomore) is led by Indigenous women and has very quickly become one of the largest Indigenous movements in history. Mobilizing both social media and fashion to share its message to "call all people to join in a peaceful revolution to honor Indigenous sovereignty and to protect the land and water" since its inception in Canada in 2012, Idle No More (INM) educates the general public about treaty rights and other Indigenous sovereignty issues tied to land and water, "criticiz[ing] settler colonialism and resource extraction" yet not "agitating against settlers but rather against continued colonialism and unleashed capitalism. The movement turns towards settlers because everybody depends on clean water and, as Idle No More stresses, only through combined efforts is change possible" (John 46). The open forum of social media, as both a mechanism and approach, enables the wider participation of supporters, Indigenous and settler alike; and INM's message encourages such solidarity through what social media theorist Zeynep Tufekci calls an "oppositional information/action cascade" (Tufekci).

Because of their popularity, speed, reach, ease of use, and relative accessibility, Twitter, Facebook, YouTube, and Instagram continue to be leveraged as sites for INM to share their message as well as to rally support for their cause via teach-ins, rallies, and other forms of protest and public education. Images of Indigenous activist women wearing INM t-shirts and/or Indigenous regalia at these events are publicized through memes (or more precisely image macros) that also featured inspirational quotations from these women. For example, a meme featuring 14-year-old Ta'Kaiya Blaney (Tla'amin Nation) depicts her speaking at a rally protesting pipelines and reads, "The question is not only what land we will leave for our children, but what children we will leave for our land." Another features Mi'kmak activist Shelley A. Young holding a protest sign at a rally, her fist raised in the air, and quotes her saying, "We do not plan on stopping. No money in the world is worth destroying our land and our water" (Idle No More). Both women are proudly adorned in the regalia of their nations at public rallies, which audiences can assume are part of the land movements they seek to protect. Their youth (though other memes feature women elders), the strength of their message, along with the leadership they embody and possess as women rhetorically and aesthetically inspire collective dissident action. These memes along with many others are shared by INM on Facebook and Instagram, through hashtags on Twitter, and on the INM website, which features two buttons under each meme—one to "Add your reaction" and one to "Share." The memes are then shared by countless more supporters on social media and garner hundreds of likes and comments. This sharing, in turn, encourages supporters to create and share their own memes by example so feminist knowledge may be actively accessed and crafted by many people around the world, often with other social movements expressing solidarity in struggle.

The fashion accompanying INM further serves as a means of publicizing and funding the movement and enables others wanting to openly demonstrate their support. This fashion is most recognizable through t-shirts with logos designed by First Nations artists Aaron Paquette (Metis) and Andy Everson (Comox), who both use variations of an upturned fist holding up a single feather in resistance. Other forms of fashion—from hoodies and scarves to baby onesies—with INM logos can also now be purchased online. INM fashion works rhetorically and aesthetically to inspire dissident action and aligns its wearer and the wearer's body with the messages of Indigenous resistance, sovereignty, water, and land, placing its wearer in a distinct political and pedagogical position.

Another instance of Indigenous activist fashion rests in the Murdered and Missing Indigenous Women and Girls (#MMIW and #MMIWG) movement, which is dedicated to raising greater public awareness about the violence facing Aboriginal women. Representing just 3% of the Canadian population, violence against Aboriginal women and girls is disproportionately high, as they are 3.5 times more likely than other women to experience violence. The Native Women's Association of Canada's (NWAC) research indicates that, between 2000 and 2008, Aboriginal women and girls represented as many as 10% of all female homicides in Canada. Of the 582 documented cases in the NWAC database (the NWAC concludes the number must be much higher, but is limited in its ability to investigate cases from the 1990s and earlier), 55% of the cases involve women and girls under age 31, with 17% under the age of 18, and with the majority of cases (70%) occurring in urban areas. Disturbingly, only 53% of murder cases involving Aboriginal women or girls have led to charges of homicide (NWAC). Though rooted in Canada, the MMIWG movement contributes to a global feminist production of knowledge for the public that urges action be taken to bring justice to end gender violence. The awareness campaigns of MMIWG has inspired similar research in the United States, where a database of murdered and missing Indigenous women is still in the process of being built by grassroots initiatives.

Two examples of Indigenous activist fashion of the MMIWG draw their powerful impact from not being worn. The Anishnabek nation created a "blanket of hope" in 2015 by collecting 1,181 single earrings donated from different women to represent the 1,181 Indigenous women and girls who have been reported missing or have been murdered since 1980. Earrings were pinned to a pink Pendleton blanket. The collective effect was a beautiful, shining tapestry from afar; yet, upon closer examination, viewers could see the diversity and overwhelming number of the earrings, and perhaps even ascertain the unique personalities of both the women they once adorned and the many they are meant to memorialize. One of the organizers, Jody Cotter, shared the single earrings were intended to represent a sense of loss, the blanket, a sense of comfort (Porter). Similar displays of donated single earrings have since been part of other community projects throughout Canada and the United States. Planned in solidarity with Canada, Sing Our Rivers Red (SORR) of the United States, for example, plans a traveling earring exhibit (to which women and girls may donate earrings to honor the missing and murdered), sewing circles, and other events with interested communities and schools (Sing Our Rivers Red). These earrings displays are central to initiating difficult conversations in communities about the personal trauma of victims, institutionalized patriarchal violence and its connections to environmental violence, and the ways that Indigenous women's and girls' lives continue to be devalued.

Another example may be seen in Jaime Black, a Metis artist based in Winnepeg, who created The REDress Project, an artistic installation using fashion as "an aesthetic response to the more than 1,000 missing and murdered Aboriginal women in Canada" (Black, REDress Project). The project collects red dresses through community donations and hangs them from hangers in public spaces throughout Canada to highlight the gendered and racialized nature of violent crimes against Aboriginal women. In using the title, REDress, Black emphasizes its double meaning—both the red dress marking the women and girls who are no longer with us, but also the redress still needed for the historical and contemporary violence inflicted on Indigenous communities in Canada as part of the project of settler colonialism. The title, thus, establishes connections between this critical issue and historical and current policies that fostered violence against Indigenous women and girls. Rhetorically and aesthetically, the hung dresses effectively mark the absence of

the missing and murdered in everyday spaces, such as a university courtyard or a park. Black's choice of red for the dresses, notwithstanding the double meaning of the project's title, presents a memorable image for the viewer but also evokes the symbolism of red as the color of life and blood for many First Nations communities as well as the violence these Indigenous women have faced (Edwards). Because of her dedication to opening up dialogues about the issue and offering spaces to honor and memorialize for those who have lost loved ones, Black encourages public participation in the project, asking people to hang red dresses outside of their homes and businesses. This participation fosters a sense of communal healing and responsibility to remember the missing and murdered and to protect Indigenous women and girls from further violence; it also welcomes a public discourse molded by feminist knowledge production.

The final example I offer is the fashion associated with the We are Mauna Kea (WAMK) movement. Mauna Kea is the highest mountain in the world, measuring from the seafloor to the summit at 32,000 feet. Though home to the primary aquifer for Hawai'i island, endangered and severely endangered species, and several Hawaiian cultural sites and burial grounds, Mauna Kea is now also home to 13 telescopes that have caused irreversible ecological damage. The University of Hawai'i plans to further develop the summit by building an 18-story high Thirty-Meter Telescope (TMT) complex with a footprint of over five acres and excavations reaching 20 feet into the ground, further violating legal protections for Hawaiian traditional and customary rights and desecrating the environment.

Protests against the construction of telescopes on Mauna Kea have ensued for decades (see Goodyear-Ka'ōpua for further discussion), but the use of social media by WAMK has made protests against the TMT much more visible and accessible. Following the success of other Indigenous movements effectively using social media, #WeareMaunaKea is led by two women, Pua Case (Kanaka Maoli) and her daughter Hawane Rios (Kanaka Maoli/Chamorro), and has gained international attention. Over the past four years, WAMK activists emphasizing they are "protectors" and not protestors have formed peaceful human blockades to stop construction, sharing videos and live feeds of their efforts. In 2015, the protectors succeeded in having all earth-moving machines removed from the site; but in 2017, the courts recommended a state permit be issued and the TMT be allowed to proceed. At the time of writing this essay, WAMK is regrouping both legally and on the ground, anticipating the return of construction.

WAMK posts videos, memes, and news stories to keep fellow protectors and supporters informed and participating in the movement regardless of their location. Among the images of Mauna Kea that have circulated are photos of Hawane Rios dressed in regalia standing in front of a bulldozer and a large drill. Verging on the theatrical, as her yellow pā ʻū (skirt) and hair blow in the wind, the photos suggest her alignment with and invocation of mana wahine and the female deities dwelling on the mountain. Mana wahine encompasses the spiritual and political power and dimensions of femaleness. Kuʻualoha Hoʻomanawanui describes mana wahine as being "rooted in traditional concepts such as moʻokūʻauhau [genealogy], aloha ʻāina [a love and patriotism stemming from genealogical connections to the land], and kuleana (responsibility)" (28). As such, the images of Rios performing mana wahine underscore the sacredness of Mauna Kea as well as her commitment as a Kanaka Maoli woman with genealogical ties to the land to protect and stand with Mauna Kea against the massive complex. In turn, the images also emphasize the continuance of an ancient feminine protective power embodied by the mountain itself.

The movement encourages participation through social media activism, with people creating, posting, and sharing WAMK memes, as well as their own photos and selfies expressing solidarity. Memes include people using a hand signal created for Mauna Kea (two hands forming a triangle), holding signs, and wearing clothing and/or jewelry purchased from #WeWearMaunaKea, an online marketplace featuring various grassroots vendors of political t-shirts, hats, and jewelry who donate proceeds to the protectors, funding bail money and supplies. Among the most popular with women is the Poliʻahu shawl designed by Pomai Bertelman. Each of the 13 shawl colors represents a different deity associated with Mauna Kea (most of whom are female), rhetorically and aesthetically emphasizing the sacredness of the mountain and its importance within Hawaiian religion and ecology, while also recognizing mana wahine and genealogical ties Kānaka have with the mountain.

While these examples demonstrate a conscientious use of clothing and jewelry to suit and support Indigenous women's activism, they also illustrate an active fashioning of Indigenous women's activism as beautiful and powerful. That social media has increased the reach of this activism—mobilizing the quick visual impact and wide international reach made possible through memes, videos, tweets, live streams, and news posts—underscores the power of these women-led movements' rhetorical and aesthetic appeals for social justice and sovereignty. These appeals through fashion teach the public about perspectives that counter colonial institutions and ideologies and represent reclamations, or more precisely, reaffirmations of Indigenous women's power. As women wear the fashion, they place themselves in the role of leader and educator in their communities, answering questions about the movements they represent and inspiring others to support these grassroots movements.

Aside from the pedagogical, Indigenous activist fashion may be read as a means of women exercising sovereignty over their bodies. Though faced with many stylish possibilities, these women choose to wear symbolic Indigenous designs and bold political statements that counter mainstream colonial beliefs and leave them vulnerable to public scrutiny and confrontation. This is no small feat, given the disproportional violence Indigenous women's bodies continue to face. Rather, the choice to wear Indigenous activist fashion puts Indigenous feminist theory into action by reclaiming Indigenous women's power in the face of institutions that have encouraged and excused gender and environmental violence.

While these aesthetic and rhetorical appeals through fashion are powerful, they are also intended to be beautiful. They are image-conscious and performative, even theatrical, in their expressions and promotions of Indigenous women's beauty, but they do so for far more than just beauty's sake. Indigenous women's beauty is redefined in these appeals by Indigenous women themselves as a grounding in one's land and culture as well as a dedication to social and environmental justice. This redefinition of beauty is a powerful form of women's sovereignty, one that depicts Indigenous culture as fashionable and Indigenous women as enduring leaders and protectors.

REFERENCES

Black, Jaime. *Redress Project*, http://www.theredressproject.org. Accessed October 15, 2017.

Edwards, Samantha. "Q&A: Jaime Black, the Artist Hanging Red Dresses Around U of T Campus." *Toronto Life*. March 24, 2017. Accessed August 22, 2017.

"Ending Violence Against Native Women." Indian Law Resource Center, indianlaw.org/issue/Ending-Violence-Against-Native-Women. Accessed October 15, 2017.

Goodyear-Kaʻōpua, Noelani. "Protectors of the Future, Not Protestors of the Past: Indigenous Pacific Activism and Mauna a Wakea." *South Atlantic Quarterly* 116.1 (2017): 184–194.

Hoʻomanawanui, Kuʻualoha. "Mana Wahine: Feminism and Nationalism in Hawaiian Literature." *Anglistica* 14.2 (2010): 27–43.

Idle No More. Idle No More, www.idlenomore.ca. Accessed October 15, 2017.

John, Sonja. "Idle No More-Indigenous Activism and Feminism." *Theory in Action* 8.4 (2015): 38–54.

Lefevre, Tate A. *Settler Colonialism*. Oxford University Press, 2015.

NWAC. NWAC, www.nwac.ca. Accessed October 15, 2017.

Porter, Jody. "'Blanket of Hope' Honours Missing, Murdered Indigenous Women." CBC News. January 16, 2015. Accessed August 22, 2017.

Ramirez, Renya. "Healing, Violence, and Native American Women." *Social Justice* 31.4 (2004): 103–116.

Sing Our Rivers Red, singourriversred.wordpress.com. Accessed August 22, 2017.

Smith, Andrea. "Not an Indian tradition: The Sexual Colonization of Native Peoples." *Hypatia* 18.2 (2003): 70–85.

Tufekci, Zeynep. "New Media and the People-Powered Uprisings." MIT Technology Review, www.technologyreview.com/s/425280/new-media-and-the-people-powered-uprisings. August 30, 2011. Accessed October 15, 2017.

Wolfe, Patrick. "Settler Colonialism and the Elimination of the Native." *Journal of Genocide Research* 8.4 (2006): 387–409.

Women's Earth Alliance and Native Youth Sexual Health Network. *Violence on Our Land, Violence on our Bodies: Building an Indigenous Response to Environmental Violence*. Land Body Defense, http://landbodydefense.org/uploads/files/VLVBReportToolkit2016.pdf. Accessed October 15, 2017.

JENNIFER NISH, KIMBERLY A. WILLIAMS, AND L. AYU SARASWATI

46. MARCHING AND CROSSING BORDERS: A TRANSNATIONAL CONVERSATION

On January 21, 2017, one day after the inauguration of the 45th President of the United States, millions of women across the globe participated in the historic Women's March. Two American feminist scholar-activists working in Lebanon and Canada, Jennifer Nish and Kimberly A. Williams, took part in their local events. This essay is a constructed conversation about their experiences of that day, critically reflecting on their positions as transnational scholars, facilitated by this anthology's co-editor, L. Ayu Saraswati.

AYU: *Tell us a little bit about yourself.*

JENNIFER: I received my PhD from the University of Kansas and I'm an assistant professor of Rhetoric and Composition at the American University of Beirut, Lebanon. I identify as a feminist, and am invested in anti-oppression theorizing, acting, and organizing in my professional and personal life.

KIMBERLY: My PhD is in Women's Studies from the University of Maryland. I direct the Women's & Gender Studies Program at Mount Royal University in Calgary, Canada. I'm a white settler feminist trying to live and work unsettled in the land of the Blackfoot, Nakoda, and Tsuut'ina peoples.

AYU: *How did the Women's March emerge in your city?*

KIMBERLY: Calgary's march was a response to the 2016 US election and the Women's March being planned for the day after the inauguration. Preparation was initiated offline among a small group of friends, who created a Facebook event page that went live on January 12, 2017.

JENNIFER: As in Calgary, the Beirut event responded to discussions about the Women's March in the United States. Planning was initiated on Facebook and included people of multiple nationalities. Organizers used some Women's March Global (WMG) ideas and tools, including listing the event on the WMG website and discussing the WMG's

values statement and HERS (Health, Economic Security, Representation, and Safety) framework. These were never simply adopted as-is but rather presented as something to discuss in relation to the participants' goals, values, and experiences, and with our context in Beirut in mind. Organizers wanted the event to be an inclusive and safe space. The event was held at the Dammeh Cooperative, a Beirut women's cooperative that supports feminist and socioeconomic justice work.

KIMBERLY: "Inclusivity" is so tricky, isn't it? For me, and I would guess for you, too, Jennifer, the theory and practice of inclusivity emerge from intersectional feminist theory, which is rooted in Black feminist thought such as Crenshaw's argument that "different things make different women vulnerable" (in Miller, par. 9). But I worry when "inclusivity" turns into placating anti-feminists, moderates, and others who are more comfortable with a broad human rights approach. This happened in Calgary: organizers repeatedly expressed on Facebook and in the media that the event was "inclusive" and open "to all people who support human rights." But some local activists, drawing implicitly on the feminist theorists who have for decades critiqued the human rights framework for its lack of a gender-based lens (see, e.g., Binion; Grewal 2005; and Qureshi), argued that focusing on "human rights" would dilute the effectiveness of the event for targeting gender-based oppression, especially in Alberta, which has a terrible track record (Hussey and Jackson; McInturff 48–51). I worry, too, that this type of "inclusive" feminism ends up supporting the appeasement politics of diversity and inclusion initiatives rather than what Crenshaw originally had in mind, which is equity and justice (Stewart).

JENNIFER: Absolutely! Although inclusivity and safety weren't explicitly defined, organizers' use of the terms overlaps with their use in many US activist and university spaces to mean that participants welcome and respect one another, especially with the goal of supporting those who are marginalized due to structural oppressions. I've certainly witnessed (and sometimes participated in) conversations here about the complexity of inclusivity in feminist spaces, where inclusivity seems to conflict with the need for, say, literal or conversational space dedicated specifically to gender-based concerns.

I'm glad you mentioned "human rights," because WMG uses this phrase. At face value, human rights seems to be such a simple way to draw social justice causes together. However, human rights frameworks have often been mobilized unevenly and with political interests in mind. For example, the typical human rights violation occurs when a powerful country or organization (say, the United States or the UN) critiques or intervenes in a country that is presumably less democratic or less developed. Violence or oppression in the West is not usually seen as a violation of human rights because people are assumed to already have human rights and states are assumed to be able to uphold them (Grewal, *Transnational America* 129). Many feminist organizations and conversations have assumed that Western women have more rights than women in other places and allowed Western women to define "global" feminist agendas and shape feminist work in other places (Grewal, *Transnational America* 142–145).

AYU: *From your observation, what was specific about your local March?*

KIMBERLY: The question that loomed above all others in Calgary was, Why had the organizers chosen the controversial Famous Five Monument as the march's starting point? Canada's Famous Five were five white, middle- and upper-class Albertan women who, in the early twentieth century, successfully got the Supreme Court of Canada to acknowledge that women are persons under the law. While many glorify them as trailblazers for Canadian women, others have critiqued some of the women for advocating eugenics, their exclusionary attitude toward non-white immigrants, and their patronizing attitude toward sex workers (Acorn).

Truthfully, these attitudes and approaches did not differentiate the Famous Five from many other American and British feminists of their generation, cultural background, and social class (Dionne). However, it appears that the Calgary organizers were either unaware of the Famous Five's troubling legacy and/or unprepared for the criticism levied at them for having chosen the monument as the march's starting point (done, ironically, out of a concern for accessibility, since the statue is within a block of several public transit hubs). Still, the simmering debate taking place on the Facebook event page reached a boiling point just before the march.

On January 18, one user asked if it might be possible to (1) acknowledge and make transparent the Famous Five's problematic politics and/or (2) change the starting point location. Organizers felt it would be too confusing to make any changes to the location at that late date. As for the first request, it does not seem to have ever been acknowledged. By January 21, though, Women's March Calgary's initial lack of intersectional feminist praxis and/or inexperience at feminist activism had been resolved; organizers put together a dynamic event emceed by local Nigerian-Canadian feminist comedian, Adora Nwofor, and featuring a number of speakers from Calgary's robust and dynamic social justice community. Topics included not only the Famous Five's problematic legacy but also trans visibility, sex worker rights, immigration, poverty, gender-based violence, and settler colonialism.

JENNIFER: The event in Beirut was actually a "Day of Action," which wasn't easy to articulate within the WMG framework. The WMG invited people to join protest *marches* (i.e., events in which people gather and move together along a planned, visible, public route), and people expected sister events to take this form even though a number of events named or described themselves differently. The dominant narrative of worldwide participation in news stories and blog posts represents events in a fairly singular way, neglecting their variety in favor of a unitary story listing the number of marches, cities, and continents in which people participated. Participants held events that were shaped by local contexts and concerns—for example, the goals of participants, viable locations, and local laws. For example, the event in Yangon, Myanmar, was a "solidarity picnic"; the event description specified that political activity is forbidden for foreigners and either high-risk or prohibited for citizens (Anonymous Annie). This variation shows that elements of culture (in this case, a particular form of political engagement) change as they flow across borders and boundaries, depending on "where, by whom, and for what reason" they are used (Grewal and Kaplan 12–14).

The Beirut event was much smaller than many of the events in the United States and Europe. Many participants, though certainly not all, were US citizens or had spent time living or working in the United States. The event was focused on developing relationships among people concerned about the issues highlighted by the Women's March but also drew participants' attention to relevant local initiatives. Organizers shared a list of local groups and networks focused on progressive causes (e.g., sexual health, sexual violence, LGBT rights, racism and migrant workers' rights) and asked participants to discuss and add to the list during the event. Participants also discussed ways to support feminist ideas in their professional and personal lives in Beirut (e.g., a group of teachers discussed ways to learn more about feminist

principles so they could apply this knowledge to their classrooms). Participants used the Women's March as a catalyst to connect with one another and consider how to collaborate and act.

AYU: *Were there any particular challenges that the movement in your city had to address?*

JENNIFER: Organizers were wary of responding to journalists, artists, and others who asked for photos or interviews with participants in Beirut. They agreed that no one was discouraged from participating personally by sending in photos or speaking to the press, but no one would participate on behalf of the group. Some conservative critics of the US events suggested that if marchers were really concerned about women, they should protest at the Saudi embassy or focus on the "real" oppression of women in the Middle East. Women's March Global (@WM_Global) responded to one such critique on Twitter by referencing the Beirut event, as well as an event in Riyadh (Saudi Arabia) and an event in Erbil (Iraq). I sent several tweets about the Beirut event, and one Twitter user replied by asking if there were any "indigenous" events; he also assumed participants in a photo that I shared were students and the event was tied to a university (perhaps due to my Twitter bio, which states that I work at an American university, and/or a photo of participants in a space that looks like a classroom). The implication, I think, is that participants weren't Lebanese women, and therefore our event wasn't authentic.

These examples highlight the importance of critical attention to narratives that circulate about feminist activity. The Beirut event was attended by many US-Americans, which is logical for an event framed in relation to US politics. There are many feminist and LGBTQIA activists, groups, and initiatives in Beirut, both new and old. In the months following the Beirut Day of Action, many of these groups collaborated to plan, attend, and/or support marches and other events for International Women's Day, migrant domestic workers' rights, and Beirut Pride Week, drawing much more participation and local attention than the Day of Action. One can imagine feminists in

Beirut choosing not to attend the Day of Action for any number of reasons: opposition to US imperialism, wariness of Western feminists' history of treating non-Western women as homogenous and oppressed (Mohanty) and in need of "saving" (AbuLughod), or simply because they see other work as more useful and relevant.

KIMBERLY: In addition to questions and critiques about starting the march from the Famous Five monument, organizers also contended with some anti-feminist trolling, notably by Stephanie Smith, a local self-identified transwoman whose main critique of the Women's March was that it was anti-male because it did not expressly advocate for an end to male circumcision. Smith also charged feminists with hypocrisy because the Women's March in Washington, DC, explicitly prevented anti-choice groups from participating.

Despite her critique, and much to the dismay of some local activists, the Calgary organizers never explicitly banned anti-choice groups—or *any* groups, for that matter—from joining the march. They even repeatedly asked Smith and another anti-feminist troller, Liz Morehouse, to join the organizing committee if they wanted their perspectives considered, but neither took them up on that invitation.

AYU: *Using a transnational feminist lens, how would you analyze the event and its relationship to US politics?*

JENNIFER: The Women's March emerged from US-oriented conversations, which shapes who participates and how, even outside the United States. Many of the "global" events were organized and attended by US citizens living in other countries (though not exclusively). After January 21, participation looks different: a list of "local chapters" continuing their work through the WMG website include groups in Australia, Canada, Germany, Mexico, the Netherlands, New Zealand, Sweden, and Switzerland. Conversations about the events would have been enriched by considering which people were taking part in WMG and how their location shapes their engagement, rather than simply listing a series of locations where events took place.

The rhetoric used to frame the events also points to some shortcomings of the Women's March, both within the United States and globally. For example, the unifying principles for the Women's March are very focused on domestic concerns and neglect the ways that US foreign policy causes oppression globally through economic and military policy and action. The first principle, "ending violence," should encompass this concern; yet the language of police brutality, racial profiling, and the "criminal justice system" don't point to the violence produced or supported by the US state that is a major concern for many women and people outside of the United States (and especially in the Global South).

KIMBERLY: Nationalist myths celebrate Canada as the global "good guy" to the US's "bad guy." This superiority myth is particularly virulent in at least three ways. First, Canadians congratulate themselves for having a national, free health care system, which they do not; Canada's public health care systems vary significantly by province, and they are paid for by income taxes and/or monthly premiums. Second, a good number of Canadians believe that their country long ago eradicated all forms of discrimination. Canadians forget, however, the existence of slavery in the Eastern provinces as well as the last 500 years of settler colonialist occupation, the capitalist exploitation of Indigenous lands, and systemic attempts to eradicate Indigenous cultures. Third, there is what legal scholar Paulette Regan describes as the "peacekeeper myth" that, because it "reinforces the popular belief that the settling of Canada was relatively peaceful," allegedly accomplished through treaty-making with Indigenous peoples rather than genocide (14), enables settler Canadians to ignore our own complicity in past and present colonial projects.

Canada's relationship to and with the United States is thus a complicated one. Economically and militarily entwined with the United States in ways far too complex to unpack here, Canadians simultaneously admire, fear, and detest the country with which they share the world's longest unfortified border. Was Women's March Canada able to mobilize support because the United States is a long-time easy target of Canadian nationalist rhetoric?; and/or because there was genuine acknowledgment of the myriad ways in which myriad forms of oppression and discrimination are, as they are in all settler nations, thoroughly embedded into the very fabric of Canadian systems and institutions?

AYU: *Very complicated indeed. Did the Women's March accomplish its goals?*

JENNIFER: The Beirut event accomplished most of its aims, which were modest: to participate in the energy and organizing catalyzed by the Women's March, to connect people interested in feminist and anti-oppression organizing, and to provide opportunities to take concrete action during the event. The work continued with a group of people who formed a Beirut chapter of a group called Progressive Action, Global Exchange (PAGE), an organization focused on activism for US Americans abroad.

KIMBERLY: The Calgary march did accomplish its aims, which, as in Beirut, were modest. The goal was to perform, in concert with progressive activists across Canada and around the world, a mass act of resistance against the divisive and discriminatory rhetoric used during the 2016 US Presidential election campaign, and in advocacy of inclusivity and human rights. The event took the form of a short march, ending with a rally on the steps of City Hall. An estimated 3,500 people attended the event, which was the largest political gathering in provincial history.

AYU: *Finally, what does it mean for you, as a transnational scholar, to participate in this transnational event?*

JENNIFER: For me, advocating feminism is an ongoing process that requires reflection and learning as well as action. I apply this to my teaching, research, and activism. I try to be mindful of my privileges (e.g., citizenship, race, class, sexual orientation) and their effects, and to educate myself about local and regional politics, history, and culture (generally and with respect to gender and sexuality). This is important for my daily life, so that I can productively contribute to feminist

acts in Beirut. I also want to be able to usefully engage both the genuine questions and problematic comments I receive from colleagues, friends, relatives, and even strangers about my experiences here. Learning from my experiences here is especially important because it intersects with major systems of oppression (e.g., the US "War on Terror" and Islamophobia).

The Beirut Day of Action was complicated for me because I want to resist the power relations through which privileged voices and perspectives are often circulated and engaged with more than those of people who are marginalized. As a US citizen, I want to engage with US politics and participate in US feminist work; but since so many US narratives marginalize non-Western culture and politics, I was hesitant to participate in a feminist event so centered on US politics in this particular place. But after reading posts about the event and attending the first meeting, I observed that other participants were making an effort to be mindful of our location and position within it. For example, at one of the first meetings I attended, a fellow US citizen who had initiated the meetings expressed her hesitation to engage with journalists. She didn't explicitly say "I don't want to speak for feminists in Beirut," but I interpreted her reluctance this way. Knowing that others in the group were mindful of these power dynamics helped me feel more comfortable participating.

KIMBERLY: I am a US citizen and longtime feminist activist. I am the daughter of elderly parents who rely on the US Medicare and Social Security systems. I am the cisgender co-conspirator of a genderqueer partner who deserves to pee in peace. I have friends who might be killed tomorrow because they're Black, Muslim, or Indigenous. I am also a legal resident of a nation-state to which I am an immigrant—but not the sort of "immigrant" currently being targeted by Canadian white nationalists. I am simultaneously *not home* and not *at* home. Unable to be physically present to march in the streets with friends and family at "home" in Washington, DC, while also legally ineligible to participate in Canada's formal political processes, I often feel quite powerless to help fix the myriad problems in either country.

But like Jennifer has in Beirut, I have made it my feminist business to learn about local and regional politics, history, and culture, as well as the scholarship on gender and sexuality that undergirds feminist and social justice praxis here in Canada. I recognize the privilege of being a feminist scholar-activist. It is literally my job to make a difference in how the future unfolds. So I wake up every morning with one goal: to do my best (while making as few mistakes as possible) to deploy my many privileges to end oppression and advocate for social justice. I've also got Congress on speed dial.

REFERENCES

AbuLughod, Lila. *Do Muslim Women Need Saving?* Harvard UP, 2013.

Acorn, Annalise. "Snapshots Then and Now: Feminism and the Law in Alberta." *Alberta Law Review*, vol. 35, no. 1, 1996, p. 140.

Anonymous Annie. "Yangon Solidarity Picnic." The Action Network, Women's March / Sister March Network, 2017, actionnetwork.org/events/yangon-solidarity-picnic. Accessed September 18, 2017.

Binion, G. "Human Rights: A Feminist Perspective." *Human Rights Quarterly*, vol. 17, no. 3, 1995, pp. 509–526. *Project MUSE*, doi:10.1353/hrq.1995.0022

Dionne, Evette. "Women's Suffrage Leaders Left Out Black Women," *Teen Vogue*, August 18, 2017, http://www.teenvogue.com/story/womens-suffrage-leaders-left-out-black-women. Accessed 19 Aug. 2017.

Grewal, Inderpal. "'Women's Rights as Human Rights': Feminist Practices, Global Feminism, and Human Rights Regimes in Transnationality." *Citizenship Studies*, vol. 3, no. 3, 1999, pp. 337–354.

Grewal, Inderpal. *Transnational America: Feminisms, Diasporas, Neoliberalisms*. Duke UP, 2005.

Grewal, Inderpal, and Caren Kaplan. *Scattered Hegemonies: Postmodernity and Transnational Feminist Practices*. U of Minnesota P, 1994.

Hussey, Ian, and Emma Jackson. "Gendering the Downturn: Is the NDP Doing Enough for Alberta Women?" *Parkland Institute*, May 4, 2017, http://www.parklandinstitute.ca/gendering_the_downturn. Accessed August 14, 2017.

McInturff, Kate. "The Best and Worst Places to be a Woman in Canada 2016: The Gender Gap in Canada's 25 Biggest Cities." *Canadian Centre for Policy Alternatives*, October 13, 2016, https://www.policyalternatives.ca/publications/reports/best-and-worst-places-be-woman-canada-2016. Accessed August 14, 2017.

Miller, Hayley. "Kimberlé Crenshaw Explains The Power of Intersectional Feminism in 1 Minute." *Huffington Post Canada*, August 11, 2017, http://www.huffingtonpost.ca/entry/kimberle-crenshaw-intersectional-feminism_us_598de38de4b090964296a34d. Accessed August 14, 2017.

Mohanty, Chandra Talpade. *Feminism without Borders: Decolonizing Theory, Practicing Solidarity*. Duke UP, 2003.

Qureshi, Shazia. "Feminist Analysis of Human Rights Law." *Journal of Political Studies*, vol. 19, no. 2, 2012, pp. 41–55.

Regan, Paulette. *Unsettling the Settler Within: Indian Residential Schools, Truth Telling, and Reconciliation in Canada*. U of British Columbia P, 2010.

Stewart, Dafina-Lazarus. "Language of Appeasement." *Inside Higher Ed*, March 30, 2017, https://www.insidehighered.com/views/2017/03/30/colleges-need-language-shift-not-one-you-think-essay. Accessed August 19, 2017.

RESISTANCE, RESILIENCE, AND DECOLONIZING PRAXIS

Scroll through social media, turn on the news, watch a box office film, discuss contemporary politics, and it is easy to see that violence circumscribes our lives. In this section, scholars theorize the structures of systemic violence. They ask students to think through how relations of power are embedded in gender, race, class, sexuality, nationality, religion, and ability and form the foundations of violence. These epistemologies are woven into the fabric of our institutions, social systems, understandings of cultural identities, and relationships. Digital activism (whether it is #IBelieveSurvivors, #SayHerName, or #AbolitionNow), street protests, writing, visual arts, music, feminist jurisprudence, some nonprofits, and sometimes our daily individual practices create resistant cultural spaces. The fight against violence and oppression is constant so much so that feminist and queer scholar-teacher-activists in this section theorize resilience alongside resistance to injustices, injuries, and harm. In this section, students will learn the importance of naming the roots of violence; understanding feminist and queer decolonizing practices; and in the final subsection, how contemporary feminist and queer theories crafts horizons that reimagine and provide possibilities for social transformation, justice, and freedom.

While this section draws upon intersectional and transnational approaches to theorizing systemic violence by naming power and social control as its roots, this by no means suggests that individual acts of violence are not worthy of attention. They are and are also embedded in relations of power. Collectively, the readings analyze what binds all forms of violence. Mainstream stories that dominate 24/7 "air time" are shaped by the materiality of our lives and discursively shape what we know and how we know it. They tell us about Supreme Court Justices accused of rape, the murder of black young trans and nonbinary individuals, women, and men alongside the overwhelming statistics that tell us about privatized, intimate abuse. Feminist and queer theory ask us to think about how gender and race operate such that Anita Hill and Christine Blasey Ford's voices are silenced while men can present themselves on the international stage as angry and injured in order to retain some of the most powerful positions in the nation; how gender, race, class, and sexuality

are co-constitutive of one another so that the state (police) can target, surveil, and disproportionately imprison communities of color while violence against of trans and nonbinary
individuals remain unsolved; and how intersectional and transnational approaches matter
in understanding how intimate and sexual violence are sustained.

Individual acts are horrific, traumatizing, and as Elaine Scarry persuasively argues in *The
Body in Pain: The Making and Unmaking of the World*, the pain of human suffering exists
beyond language. What we emphasize here is that while there are white, Christian men that
exert power, individual police officers that abuse his/her/their power, and single bombers
that target mosques and synagogues, their actions are intimately linked to systems of heteropatriarchy, white nationalism and colonialism, and a network of groups and sometimes
the state that structure unthinkable violence.

Violence has historical weight, it has been built, and many women, people of color,
queer and trans, disabled, and/or religious communities across the globe know how pernicious and ubiquitous it is. Whether it is physical and mental violence between two people;
the symbolic violence embedded in heteropatriarchy such that men/women/trans people
are complicit with its construction of power; or the structural violence that is embedded in
institutions such that people remain silent in fear of retaliation, further silencing, or possibly
bodily harm, violence can silence resistance and those who endeavor to create change. The
pieces in the first subsection of section 4, "Violence, Resistance, and Resilience," when read
together, suggest how we might reconsider individual acts as manifestations of a deeply connected system of power and control to frame a range of violence that affects women, people
of color, and/or LGBTQPAI+ communities; how it enters our lives in small ways and not just
in dramatic form as the media may suggest; and who or what benefits from the control and
power that violence produces.

Feminist and queer theory has from their inception critiqued how oppression and privilege are yoked and that to name these relations of power begins the process of dismantling
the violence of hetero/sexism, racism, classism, white nationalism, able-ism, homophobia,
and transphobia. This naming provides the foundations for the raising of our collective
consciousness, and this unlearning is the first step of decolonization. Emerging from indigenous, ethnic studies, and feminist, queer, and critical race and Latin American theory, decolonial thinking reframes universal modes of thinking or the settler-colonial logics that craft
the meanings of, for example "gender," "race," and "progress." (see Lugones; Mignolo; Pérez;
Sandoval). Decolonization requires not just a reframing but a conscious un-thinking of
western European paradigms that establish a modern, colonial, gender system so that people
are divided into discreet categories—or what María Lugones names as "terms of atomic, homogeneous, separable categories" ("Toward" 742). In "Toward a Decolonial Feminism," she
writes, "[i]f woman and black are terms for homogeneous, atomic, separable categories, then
their intersection shows us the absence of black women rather than their presence" (742).
To unlock this mode of thinking means that scholars-activists-practitioners-students could
look to local and indigenous knowledges that "resist modern, capitalist modernity that are
in tension with its logic" (742). An example of this could be when communities draw on
restorative justice models to address wrongdoing instead of punitive systems that support
the prison industrial complex.

As the readings make clear in the final subsection of this book, "Feminist and Queer Horizons," knowing must be integrated with reimagined practices to produce meaningful change. While no theorist can offer a blueprint for how to go about doing this work, they collectively ask key questions such as what is possible if we decolonize knowledge that is embedded in social institutions (e.g., how we craft families and the rhetoric used in media); what social worlds might we imagine if queer and feminist theory move beyond critique and toward reimagining and transformation; and how do individual and collective stories inform a radical praxis of resistance, pleasure, and solidarity in order to re-envision our communities and reframe social change?

VIOLENCE, RESISTANCE, AND RESILIENCE

This subsection begins with Qwo-Li Driskill's "Stolen from Our Bodies: First Nations Two-Spirits/Queers and the Journey to a Sovereign Erotic," originally published in 2004, in part because it starts with an indigenous song-story—a method of decolonial praxis that offers theoretical insight as it elucidates violence, resistance, and resilience in indigenous communities. Driskill centers indigenous knowledge and experiences before weaving how the pain and trauma from sexual assault are "entangled with a history of colonization" with how First Nation survivors have their lives stolen *and* are living warriors (443). Given the robust literature on how these layers of violence are a form of genocide (see Dunbar-Ortiz; Gutiérrez; Smith; Stannard), Driskill pivots on this point drawing on the main points in Audre Lorde's "The Uses of the Erotic: The Erotic as Power" (included in Section 2) to theorize what it means to embody "erotic wholeness and/or heal from the historical trauma that First Nations people continue to survive" (443–44).

The "Sovereign Erotic" in Driskill's work redefines the erotic to include our sense/feelings as a part of how we know the world around us *and* reclaims a history of two-spirit people lost to violently imposed colonial definitions of sexuality. Likewise, sovereignty has layered meanings: that native communities have governing authority over themselves *and* the right of all indigenous peoples to have control over their own bodies. Poignantly, Driskill also names the English language—including the sociopolitical taxonomies of "queer," "transgender," and "gay" deployed in feminist and queer theory—as forms of violence if we try to include two-spirit within them. "While homophobia, transphobia, and sexism are problems in Native communities, in many of our tribal realities these forms of oppression are the result of colonization and genocide that cannot accept women as leaders, or people with extra-ordinary genders and sexualities" (444). This piece theorizes the simultaneous layers of how violence affects our bodies/sense of being and that it is best understood within systems of power that have been written, executed, and re-rooted across time and space.

The next reading builds on the theme of colonial violence and turns its attention to feminism, rhetoric embedded in reproductive rights, and the politics of transnational adoption. In her new piece, "Transnational Adoption and the Paradox of Reproductive Rights," Jenny Heijun Wills argues that it is "Western liberal feminism [that] reiterates racial power imbalances and oppressions through the intended generous act of transnational adoption as white adoptive families see themselves as saving brown and black children from brown and black families and spaces" (451). Drawing on the work of David Eng in *The Feeling of Kinship*, Wills also names queer normative family structures—those that reproduce heteronormative nuclear families—as part of the apparatus that re-roots *and* re-routes racial oppression and gender inequality within diaspora communities.

Intersectional reproductive justice movements have a long history of mobilizing against state policies and laws that constrain the bodily freedom of women and girls of color and is perhaps most precisely defined on SisterSong's web page as "the human right to maintain personal bodily autonomy, have children, not have children, and parent the children we have in safe and sustainable communities." Those committed to reproductive justice work in solidarity with anti-racist, feminist, and disability rights groups to name sterilization abuse, forced birth control, and coercive disinformation as forms of violence and violations of human rights. However, as Wills argues in her piece, a transnational approach also asks us to question what it means for those in the West to adopt children from, for example, South Korea. While both liberal and progressive reproductive groups argue for bodily autonomy (albeit differently), the "Adoption Industrial Complex" has the potential to erase the rights of non-Western women and children (see McKee).

In the next reading, "What's Wrong with Rights?," published in 2011, Dean Spade theorizes that rights are not just a paradox, but when they are *not* reimagined by the redistribution of power, they become arms of an administratively violent set of laws. Focusing specifically on violence against trans communities, he argues that while "the logic of visibility and inclusion surrounding anti-discrimination and hate crime laws campaigns is very popular," this liberal reform framework hinges on communities, the police, and courts not treating trans individuals as second- (or third-)class citizens (458). While laws are established to protect people, harm, injury, violence, and death sometimes comes from law and order itself—from police or perhaps in jail while awaiting trial. The logic of reform may be popular, he contends, but the system itself is deeply flawed and not being addressed. Therefore, as Spade argues, "hate crime laws do not have a deterrent effect [because] they focus on punishment and cannot be argued to actually prevent bias-motivated violence . . . and anti-discrimination laws are not adequately enforced" (458). If legal strategies are developed based on the experiences of trans people—if the stories of violence, resistance, and resilience are listened to within "capitalism's murderous structures"—then justice systems will be better equipped to address, prevent, and end brutality (463).

Following the presidential election of 2016, communities that are systemically marginalized braced for and have experienced more violence in their lives. According to an article titled "Hate Groups Reach Record High" posted to the Southern Poverty Law Center's website, 2019 has seen "the fourth straight year of hate group growth" with a "30 percent increase that has coincided with Trump's campaign and presidency." From the hurling of insults to the xenophobia that drives Muslim bans and the closing of borders to the entrenched heteropatriarchy that threatens access to abortion, birth control, and health care—all provide fuel to a white nationalism grounded in heteropatriarchy. In the next new reading written for this collection, "Indian Americans in the Trump Era: A Transnational Feminist Analysis," Ashwini Tambe makes clear the scale of harm, divisiveness, injury, and pain by looking at the South Asian Indian diaspora. In it, she envisions a more expansive conceptualization of transnational feminism—one that moves beyond being "concerned with the cross-border circulation of people, capital, or ideas" to analyzing clear connections between the local-national-global circuitries. Tambe looks closely "how Indian Americans have responded to rising levels of xenophobia . . . [and] how progressive organizing has given rise to flexible transnational solidarities," and how the Trump era has also heralded "a contradiction in mainstream Indian political leanings" that critique the administration's rhetoric and policies all the while supporting the rise of a more politically conservative India (468).

Attempts at intervening in the consolidation of power under Trump has meant that everyday people—not just feminist and queer activists—have gravitated toward one another to fight public racism, hetero/sexism, and increased poverty; and groups that might not normally find common ground are working strategically and in solidarity to combat the tide of hate and violence. As Tambe argues, by way of Grewal and Kaplan, these moments "are a reminder of the value of forging connections and alliances across different identities around common issues, planks, and priorities" (473). Reaching across borders, whether within our own communities or across oceans, remains urgent and a call for all of us to practice what we collectively theorize in the midst of unthinkable violence, regression, and repression.

Writing is powerful and can bring individuals and communities together to think and sometimes act. What might we collectively learn and what may take shape if we begin to think of literature—of African women's literature—as feminist theory? As Barbara Boswell explores in the next new article, "African Women's Literature as Feminist Theory," the stories of resistance and resilience that African women tell matter and are at the center for change not just on the African continent but across oceans. She, like so many in this collection, is concerned with "the very fabric of what counts as knowledge," especially since "the circuits of dissemination and the politics of citation of theory produced in western locations often sees theory constructed in the global south . . . unexamined and not cited in the ongoing production of global feminist knowledge," (475). Indeed, if we think carefully about the conspicuous absence of writing from Africa, Latin America, the Caribbean, and Asia in transnational feminist and queer thought, it may be easier to see how Western epistemologies are forms of ongoing colonial violence. Drawing in part on the body of postcolonial work (such as Spivak) alongside African feminist theorists (such as Amina Mama), Boswell's framing challenges US-based constructions of transnational feminist theory and pivots those in the Global North to think through how fiction produced by African women *is* theory and "provide an entry point into the politics of decolonial gender, sexuality and knowledge construction" (476). Art moves us beyond naming what decolonization might look like within feminism and gives it texture—words that create new imagined and sociocultural spaces.

If feminist and queer theory hinges on what and how narratives are told about discursive and material relations of power, Cherríe Moraga pushes on the edges of this framework by questioning and considering what sociocultural narratives stick—what stories compel us to become a more tightly knit community with one another in the piece "La Güera" (originally written in 1976). Not withstanding her mother's own story of illiteracy and a lifetime of working factory and piecework alongside her own deep understanding that she "had it made" to be fair-skinned like her Anglo father, Moraga powerfully writes that it was her coming out as a lesbian that most deeply connected her to her mother—and by extension, all oppressed women. "It wasn't until

I acknowledged and confronted my own lesbianism in the flesh, that my heartfelt identification with and empathy for my mother's oppression . . . was realized. My lesbianism is the avenue through which I have learned the most about silence and oppression, and it continues to be the most tactile reminder to me that we are not free human beings" (482).

Moraga integrates the personal and political by weaving together silences and a spectra of violence that take shape in our homes, in our larger social worlds, *and* within feminist and queer communities. Indeed, the ideas in her piece ask us not just to understand but *feel* how and why progressive thought, indeed theory in and of itself, does not automatically translate into transformed feminist and queer cultural spaces. Moraga writes, "I think this phenomenon is indicative of our failure to seriously address ourselves to some very frightening questions: How have I internalized my own oppression? How have I oppressed" (483). Published decades ago, her words remain salient in naming what is at the heart of perpetuating systems of violence that keep women, people of color, and/or the LGBTQPAI+ community separated from one another; and thus, this piece remains central to the processes of decolonization and social change.

FEMINIST AND QUEER THEORY HORIZONS

Some of the field's founding ideas continue to represent the horizons of feminist and queer theory. Sara Ahmed has done this reclamation work in *Living a Feminist Life* (2017) and the chapter reprinted here, "Lesbian Feminism," begins with a reminder that "in order to survive what we come up against, in order to build worlds from the shattered pieces, we need a revival of lesbian feminism" (486). To be sure, reigniting lesbian feminism is not at the expense of rethinking (trans)gender, though it is to say that lesbian feminism remains one of the central tenets of feminist and queer theory, and we need to continue taking seriously what it means for two women *to be*—in public, in private, and as theory-makers and change-makers. Rather than claiming it as a sociopolitical space that will transform systemic structures, Ahmed's work on naming lesbian feminism is about the ordinary, daily battle "for recognition [that] comes out of rage against the injustice of how some dwell by the dispossession of others" (491).

The inspiration for the title of this subsection comes from José Muñoz's *Cruising Utopia* (2009), and the inclusion of "Queerness as Horizon" honors him as a theorist who saw beyond critique and toward possibility. Although he passed away too young, his insistence that queer theory imagine "[t]he not-quite-conscious [as] . . . potentiality that must be called on, and insisted on, if we ever to look beyond the pragmatic sphere of the here and now, the hollow nature of the present" (501), facilitates our transformation in perspective and recalibrates our compass toward the future. For example, naming the sociopolitical nightmare of a Trump administration that is poised to chip away at and eventually eliminating rights is important but it is not the settled place where theory can live. In his own words, "gay pragmatic organizing is in direct opposition to the idealist thought that I associate as endemic to a forward-dawning queerness that calls on a no-longer-conscious in the service of imagining a futurity" (501). In reading Muñoz, it is important to consider what it means when he claims that "we are not quite queer yet, that queerness, what we will really know as queerness, does not yet exist" (501). Such thought may allow us to embrace creativity, see beyond borders and boundaries, and live beyond the taxonomies that build walls within and between queer communities and feminists.

Looking to the horizons requires that we not only look beyond compulsory heterosexuality (see Rich 1986) and heteronormative family structures in feminist and queer theory (see Duggan; Muñoz) but to *rethink* monogamy itself. And what if we begin to rethink it from the starting point of where queer-feminist theory intersects with science? In Angela Willey's robust manifesto "Biopossiblity," which was written in 2016, she challenges students to think beyond how feminist and queer theory has theorized science through critique and instead to imagine its findings as a partner in explaining how monogamy is neither natural or affixed to being human. More generally, she claims that "it is with desire for 'social justice' . . . that I turn to the molecular . . . [to craft] a manifesto [that] is a speculative exploration of the uses of a materialism grounded in the epistemological interventions of feminist and postcolonial science studies and queer historicizations of sexuality" (509–10). "Biopossiblity" fuses together methodologies, scientific knowledge, and feminist and queer theory to ask, "how do we engage the molecular with queer feminist desires for new biocultural stories and forms?" (510). The horizons in feminist and queer theory require deep cross-fertilization, and as Audre Lorde theorized that there are no "hierarchy of oppressions," Willey charges us to think and work across entrenched disciplinary boundaries if we want to queer knowledge production itself.

In the next reading, written for this reader, "Decolonizing Religion, Transforming Spirit," AnaLouise Keating and Kakali Bhattacharya also argue women's, gender, and sexuality studies scholars' general unwillingness to engage in religion limits what we know and how we know it. When we "conflate religion with spirituality and then downplay or avoid them . . . [they shut] out those for whom religion and/or spirituality are more complex than this knee-jerk rejection presumes" (523). To rely on the false binary of religion/spirituality and secular thinking, they argue, constrains how we think through intersectional and transnational feminisms as well as how we might imagine and move beyond oppositional thinking that re-roots the hierarchies embedded in dyads such as "mind/body, subject/object, spirit/matter, male/female, and reason/intuition" (523). Drawing on the work of Gloria Anzaldúa and their own experience—what they name as autohistoria-teorías—the authors argue that living within material and spiritual worlds and looking inward is a "de/colonial praxis" that moves us beyond theory-making and toward "social critique, metaphysical exploration, and personal/collective transformation" (524). Their work begs the question, if we all had more spiritually driven understandings of our gendered and racialized selves, what are the possibilities for change? Taken together with Willey's work and interestingly juxtaposed with it, Keating and Bhattacharya return us to the question of what is possible if we decolonize knowledge itself.

Feminist and queer theory has long embraced personal narrative as a form of writing theory—indeed as a starting point to reframe seemingly fixed knowledges. Stories not only alter what we think but how we think, and Eli Clare's *Brilliant Imperfection* (2017) transforms our understanding of disability. There is a lengthy and relatively recent history of feminist and queer scholars who argue that disability studies is feminist and queer theory and therefore both need to take seriously the relations of power that dis/abled bodies experience (see, e.g., Garland-Thomson 2002; 2005; Hall; McRuer). In Moving through Cure (included in this subsection), Clare names curing disability and medically managing transgender bodies as the root of the problem. As a young person, he knew that his mother was not happy having a disabled child and was on the receiving end of how much time and money the family spent seeking a cure. Medicine seeks to eliminate disease and make people well; and when disability is without question understood as a disease and gender is understood as a binary, it redirects our attention to the person who needs to be fixed so that she/he/they can lead a "normal" life. In short, when the layers of disability, gender, and sexuality are seen through this lens, it erases people's subjectivity. Clare asks us to think deeply about why we imagine paralysis, cerebral palsy, bipolar, and/or the "diagnosis" of gender dysphoria as needing a cure? What is wrong with people living within their bodies and seeking meaning in their lives, indeed pleasure, in their disabilities?

In the final two readings in this book, we turn our attention to where decolonizing praxis is taking place: in art and in transnational movements to free political prisoners. In the first instance, Jayna Brown's "A World on Fire: Radical Black Feminism in a Dystopian Age" (2018) reignites a black revolutionary feminism that is, in her words, "already queer, as they critique normativity and normativizing processes and challenge a 'politics of respectability,' the long-engrained anxieties about hypersexualization that have kept more moderate black feminist discourse from exploring sexualities" (539). Moving away from neoliberal language and political impulses in the media that claim easy empowerment, she turns her attention to film, and specifically *Born in Flames* (1983), to theorize revolution. Brown gravitates to this text because it shows us through image and language that it is in the everyday where theorizing of political tactics for a revolution take place. Thus, revolution is not interested in leadership or market visibility; those committed to it and especially those minoritized within violent systems know that change "demands that we deconstruct, and reconstruct, all the laws that suppress, and oppress, all of us" and is not grand; instead it is a daily practice (540). While Spade argues for new legal strategies in "What's Wrong with Rights" (also in Section 4), Brown draws our attention to how change happens culturally and in the texture of our daily lives. As she argues, revolution and transformation will not become manifest through social institutions; rather, it will be built slowly between people, in neighborhoods, communities, grassroots organizations, and require feminist and queer coalitions that meet the needs of the poor, women and people of color, LGBTQPAI+ communities, those dis/abled, and im/migrants. In our dystopian era, Brown's work and the film crystalizes for us how politics, white house administrations, courts, and neoliberal-based media are the battlegrounds—not the vehicles for change.

We conclude this book with a selection from Angela Davis's *Freedom is a Constant Struggle* (2016), "Transnational Solidarities," in which she draws together her many talks around the world and names political imprisonment, indeed the prison industrial complex itself, as genocide. Transnational solidarity returns us to the centrality of theory as storytelling. It requires that we understand our "histories never unfold in isolation [and that] we cannot truly tell what we consider to be our own histories without knowing the other stories. And often we discover that those other stories are actually our own stories" (551). We hope what is evident throughout this text is that storytelling is done in layers. It is not just that the most contemporary theories are the most compelling; it is that they build on one another so that we may deeply understand what intersectionality and transnationalism means. To do so, according to Davis, allows us to see the connections between police violence in Ferguson with the militarization and politicization in Gaza.

Thus storytelling does not just offer us one version of feminist and queer theories but layers that can be excavated across time and space so that we can know more "about the conjunctures of race and class and ethnicity and nationality and sexuality and ability" (551). Davis's poignant words make clear that the United States does not hold the key in crafting theories and knowledge about how to see these intersections, and that we will have a greater chance at transformation, justice, and change if we listen and learn from one another across and through our differences as well as across and through our struggles. In short, Davis claims that "feminism provides methodological guidance for all of us who are engaged in serious research and organized activist work [because it] urges us to develop understandings of social relations, whose connections are often initially only intuited" (554). Unless we move through a deliberate process of decolonization that feminist and queer theory offers—that is, an unlearning of the workings of the state, capitalism, racism, and heteropatriarchy—we may continue to "do the work of the state in and through our interior lives" (554). She concludes her piece asking us to do "something quite extraordinary . . . [and] be willing to stand up and say no with our combined spirits, our collective intellects, and our many bodies"—to be agents of change in whatever ways are possible in our lives (555).

This section has examined systemic violence, collective resistance, the resilience of individuals and communities, and has explored the following questions: How can theory better help us understand systemic violence? What does decolonizing violence mean, especially within the Global North, and how might we better understand that there is more to the Global South than envisioning over three-quarters of the worlds population as victims? And how does theory help us better understand the possibilities for the future even as they critique the present? Together, the readings offer insights toward transformations that embrace humanity/people over profit, systemic change over reform, and decolonizing practices that facilitate community-building and collective action. This volume has explored the depth and breadth of theorizing itself—ranging from its ideas and arguments to the form it takes—and how theory itself has the capacity to frame and explain everyday dynamics and cultural phenomena through relations of power that shape our diverse and shared lives. If intersectional and transnational feminist and queer theories provide the foundations for imagining, navigating, and building new approaches to collectivity, social change, and liberation, then the stories that we tell through theory-making (be it poetry, indigenous song-story, or evidence-based abstract thought) matter in crafting what we know and how we know it.

REFERENCES

Ahmed, Sara. *Living a Feminist Life*. Duke, 2017.
Clare, Eli. *Brilliant Imperfection: Grappling with Cure*. Duke, 2017.
Duggan, Lisa. *Twilight of Equality: Neoliberalism, Cultural Politics, and the Attack on Democracy*. Beacon, 2004.
Dunbar-Ortiz, Roxanne. *An Indigenous People's History of the United States*. Beacon, 2015.

Eng, David. *The Feeling of Kinship: Queer Liberalism and the Racialization of Intimacy*. Duke, 2010.

Garland-Thomson, Rosemarie. "Integrating disability, Transforming Feminist Theory." *NWSA Journal*, vol. 14, no. 3, Fall 2002, pp. 1–32.

Garland-Thomson, Rosemarie. "Feminist Disability Studies." *Signs*, vol. 30, no. 2, Winter 2005, pp. 1557–1587.

Grewal, Inderpal and Caren Kaplan. *Scattered Hegemonies*. University of Minnesota Press, 1994.

Gutiérrez, Ramón. *When Jesus Came, the Corn Mothers Went Away: Marriage, Sexuality, and Power in New Mexico, 1500–1846*. Stanford University Press, 1998.

Hall, Kim Q., ed. *Feminist Disability Studies*. Indiana University Press, 2011.

Keating, AnaLouise. *Transformation Now!: Toward a Post-Oppositional Politics of Change*. University of Illinois Press, 2013.

Lorde, Audre. "There is No Hierarchy of Oppression." *Homophobia and Education*. New York: Council on Interracial Books for Children, 1983.

Lugones, Maria. "Heterosexualism and the Colonial Modern Gender System." *Hypatia*, vol. 22, no. 1, Winter 2007, pp. 186–209.

Lugones, Maria. "Toward a Decolonial Feminism." *Hypatia*, vol. 25, no. 4, Fall, 2010, pp. 742–59.

Mama, Amina. *Beyond the Masks: Race, Gender and Subjectivity*. Routledge, 1995.

McKee, Kimberly. "The Transnational Adoption Industrial Complex: An Analysis of Nation, Citizenship, and the Korean Diaspora." PhD diss., Ohio State University, 2013.

McRuer, Robert. *Crip Theory: Cultural Signs of Queerness and Disability*. University Press, 2006.

Mignolo, Walter. *The Darker Side of Western Modernity: Global Futures, Decolonial Options*. Duke University Press, 2011.

Muñoz, José Esteban. *Cruising Utopia*. NYU Press, 2009.

Muñoz, José Esteban. *Disidentifications: Queers of Color and the Performance of Politics*. University of Minnesota Press, 1999.

Pérez, Emma. *The Decolonial Imaginary: Writing Chicanas into History*. Indiana University Press, 1999.

Rich, Adrienne. "Compulsory Heterosexuality and the Lesbian Existence." *Signs*, vol.5, no. 4 Summer 1980, pp. 631–660.

Sandoval, Chela. *Methodology of the Oppressed*. University of Minnesota Press, 2000.

Scarry, Elaine. *The Body in Pain: The Making and Unmaking of the World*. Oxford University Press, 1987.

Sister Song. "Reproductive Justice." www.sistersong.net/reproductive-justice/. Accessed December 28, 2018.

Smith, Andrea. *Conquest: Sexual Violence and American Indian Genocide*. Duke University Press (reprint), 2015.

Southern Poverty Law Center. "Hate Groups Reach Record High." https://www.splcenter.org/news/2019/02/19/hate-groups-reach-record-high. Accessed May 5, 2019.

Spivak, Gayatri. "Can the Subaltern Speak?" *Marxism and the Interpretation of Cultures*, edited by Cary Nelson and Lawrence Grossberg. University of Illinois Press, 1988.

Stannard, David. *American Holocaust: The Conquest of the New World*. Oxford University Press, 1993.

47. STOLEN FROM OUR BODIES: FIRST NATIONS TWO-SPIRITS/QUEERS AND THE JOURNEY TO A SOVEREIGN EROTIC

This is a Warrior Song
From one poor Skin to another
And I don't know what I'm lookin' for
But I know I've found you
These words will shuffle across concrete
Will float across the Rockies
To the Smokey Mountains
We were stolen from
We were stolen from
We were stolen from our bodies
We were stolen from our homes
And we are fighters in this long war
To bring us all back home
And this is a Warrior Song
From one poor Skin to another
And I don't know what I'm lookin' for
But I know I've found you
U-ne-la-nv-hi U-we-tsi
I-ga-gu-yv-he-yi
Hna-quo-tso-sv Wi-yu-lo-se
But I know I've found you
And this is a Warrior Song
From one poor Skin to another
And I don't know what I'm lookin' for
But I know I've found you[1]

This song came to me one night a few years ago as I began to understand that healing our sexualities as First Nations people is braided with the legacy of historical trauma and the ongoing process of decolonization. Two-Spirits are integral to this struggle: my own resistance to colonization as a Cherokee Two-Spirit is intimately connected to my continuing efforts to heal from sexual assault and the manifestations of an oppressive overculture on my erotic life. Like other Two-Spirit people, I am making a journey to a Sovereign Erotic that mends our lives and communities.[2]

I mention my experiences with trauma in this essay because sexual assault, sexism, homophobia, and transphobia are entangled with the history of colonization. Sexual assault is an explicit act of colonization that has enormous impacts on both personal and national identities and because of its connections to a settler mentality, can be understood as a colonial form of violence and oppression. My own journey back to my body, and the journeys of other First Nations people back to their bodies, necessarily engage historical trauma. In her book *Shaking the Rattle: Healing the Trauma of Colonization*, Barbara-Helen Hill (Six Nations, Grand River Territory) writes:

> All of the abuse and addiction that we are seeing in communities are symptoms of the underlying cause, the oppression and the stress of living in isolation on reservations or in Native communities within the larger non-Native communities. . . . Healing the spirit of the individual will eventually spread to healing the spirit of family and this in turn will spread out into the communities. . . .(36)

When I speak of a Sovereign Erotic, I'm speaking of an erotic wholeness healed and/or healing from the historical trauma that First Nations people continue to

Qwo-Li Driskill, "Stolen from our Bodies: First Nations Two-Spirits/Queers and the Journey to a Sovereign Erotic," *Studies in American Indian Literatures*, Series 2, Vol. 16, No. 2 (SUMMER 2004): 50–64. Reprinted with permission of University of Nebraska Press; permission conveyed through Copyright Clearance Center, Inc.

survive, rooted within the histories, traditions, and resistance struggles of our nations. I am in agreement with Audre Lorde when she writes, "Our erotic knowledge empowers us, becomes a lens through which we scrutinize all aspects of our existence, forcing us to evaluate those aspects honestly in terms of their relative meaning in our lives" (57). I do not see the erotic as a realm of personal consequence only. Our relationships with the erotic impact our larger communities, just as our communities impact our senses of the erotic. A Sovereign Erotic relates our bodies to our nations, traditions, and histories.

The term "Two-Spirit" is a word that resists colonial definitions of who we are. It is an expression of our sexual and gender identities as sovereign from those of white GLBT movements. The coinage of the word was never meant to create a monolithic understanding of the array of Native traditions regarding what dominant European and Euro[-]American traditions call "alternative" genders and sexualities. The term came into use in 1990 at a gathering of Native Queer/Two-Spirit people in Winnipeg as a means to resist the use of the word "berdache," and also as a way to talk about our sexualities and genders from within tribal contexts in English (Jacobs et al. 2). I find myself using both the words "Queer" and "Trans" to try to translate my gendered and sexual realities for those not familiar with Native traditions, but at heart, if there is a term that could possibly describe me in English, I simply consider myself a Two-Spirit person. The process of translating Two-Spiritness with terms in white communities becomes very complex. I'm not necessarily "Queer" in Cherokee contexts, because differences are not seen in the same light as they are in Euro[-]American contexts. I'm not necessarily "Transgender" in Cherokee contexts, because I'm simply the gender I am. I'm not necessarily "Gay," because that word rests on the concept of men-loving-men, and ignores the complexity of my gender identity. It is only within the rigid gender regimes of white America that I become Trans or Queer. While homophobia, transphobia, and sexism are problems in Native communities, in many of our tribal realities these forms of oppression are the result of colonization and genocide that cannot accept women as leaders, or people with extra-ordinary genders and sexualities.[3] As Native people, our erotic lives and identities have been colonized along with our homelands.

My family is diasporic, descendants of so many removals of so many kinds it becomes difficult to count them all. Survivors of so many genocides that one simply bleeds into the next. As a Red-Black person, the Trail of Tears and other forced relocations are not the first removals of my peoples.[4] I find myself obsessed with the notion of "home" on many levels. I have not only been removed from my homelands, I have also been removed from my erotic self and continue a journey back to my first homeland: the body. "We were stolen from our bodies / We were stolen from our homes."

Sexual assault was not something that was tolerated in most of our cultures before invasion. In Lakota custom, for example, the "Rare Knife" was given to Lakota women to use only to cut off the heads of men who abused her or her children.[5] Consequently, abuse was rare in Lakota lifeways before white supremacist patriarchy enforced violence against women and children. Wilma Mankiller reminds us,

> Europeans brought with them the view that men were the absolute head of households, and women were to be submissive to them. It was then that the role of women in Cherokee society began to decline. One of the new values Europeans brought to the Cherokees was a lack of balance and harmony between men and women. It was what we today call sexism. This was not a Cherokee concept. Sexism was borrowed from Europeans. (20)

Sexual violence is rampant in all communities in the United States. Recent events within the Catholic Church show how often sexual abuse of children is silently condoned. Sexual abuse must be seen with an understanding of the history of colonization, which uses sexuality as a tool to gain power over others and to control women's bodies. In this country the *white wing* attempts to make abortion illegal at the same time women of color and poor women continue to survive forced sterilization. It is no accident that white masculinity is constructed the way it is in the United States, as European invasion of the Americas required a masculinity that murders, rapes, and enslaves Native and African peoples. It is a masculinity that requires men to be soldiers and conquerors in every aspect of their lives. A masculinity rooted in genocide breeds a culture of sexual abuse. It is vital to remember that most of our traditions did not allow such behavior. Healing from assault is intimately joined with decolonization and the reclamation of indigenous understandings of the world.

> We were stolen from our bodies
> We were stolen from our homes
> And we are fighters in this long war
> To bring us all back home

A colonized sexuality is one in which we have internalized the sexual values of dominant culture. The invaders continue to enforce the idea that sexuality and non-dichotomous genders are a sin, recreating sexuality as illicit, shocking, shameful, and removed from any positive spiritual context. Queer sexualities and genders are degraded, ignored, condemned, and destroyed. As people often raised under dominant culture's values through our homes, televisions, or teachers, Two-Spirit erotic lives continue to be colonized. Native people survive a legacy of spiritual and sexual abuse at the hands of soldiers, missionaries, clergy, and teachers who have damaged our senses of Self and wounded our sacred connection to our bodies. The boarding school systems in the United States and Canada are one example of the ways our sexualities, genders, and spirits have been colonized by the invaders. Boarding schools continue to have severe repercussions on our communities, including colonized concepts of gender and sexuality. To decolonize our sexualities and move towards a Sovereign Erotic, we must unmask the specters of conquistadors, priests, and politicians that have invaded our spirits and psyches, insist they vacate, and begin tending the open wounds colonization leaves in our flesh.

I have seen no study that tells how many Two-Spirit people commit suicide or turn to drugs and alcohol to cope with the shame colonization brings to our sexualities and genders.[6] How many Two-Spirit people are forced to leave their families and thus their primary connection to their traditions because of homophobia and transphobia? How many of us grapple with deep shame because of our sexualities and/or genders? Our sexualities harbor bruises left by a white supremacist culture. We find ourselves despising our bodies and sexualities, unable to speak of our own erotic lives and desires even with our lovers. We see dominant culture's concepts of the erotic and know they have nothing to do with our Two-Spirit bodies, often causing us to dissociate from our erotic selves or assimilate dominant culture's concepts into our lives. Marilou Awiakta (Cherokee/Appalachian) writes, "Thinking of sex as an it and women as sex objects is one of the grooves most deeply carved into the Western mind. This groove in the national mind of America will not accept the concept of sex as part of the sacred and generative power of the universe—and of woman as a bearer of the life force" (252). It is not only First Nations people who have internalized dominant culture's concepts of sexuality and gender. The legacy of colonization seeps into every aspect of life in this country, even if only Native folks and other people of color recognize it.

Beth Brant (Bay of Quinte Mohawk) writes about the importance of Two-Spirit engagement in a process of healing from historical trauma:

> Much of the self-hatred we carry around inside us is centuries old. This self-hatred is so coiled within itself, we often cannot distinguish the racism from the homophobia from the sexism. We carry the stories of our grandmothers, our ancestors. And some of these stories are ugly and terrorizing. And some are beautiful testaments to endurance and dignity. We must learn to emulate this kind of testimony. Speaking ourselves out loud—for our people, for ourselves. To deny our sexuality is to deny our part in creation. (63)

To understand our place in creation, I look at the stories within my tradition that celebrate difference. To my knowledge as a non-fluent Cherokee speaker, there is currently no term in Cherokee to describe Two-Spirit people. We simply *are*. However, within our stories are roadmaps for contemporary Cherokee Two-Spirits. Many of our stories address difference, the embodiment of dichotomies, and journeys between worlds. Craig Womack (Oklahoma Creek-Cherokee) reminds us, "Rather than disrupting society, anomalies actually reify the existing social order. . . . That which is anomalous is also an important source of power. The Southeastern belief system is not an oppositional world of good and evil" (*Red on Red* 244). Our stories as First Nations people keep us alive in a world that routinely destroys and discards us. Though our stories were present as survival cartographies before the invasion of Turtle Island by Columbus and the crowned power of Spain, our stories are perhaps even more vital to our survival now, during the European occupation of our homelands.[7]

It is in our stories, including our written literatures, that I search for meaning and reflection of my Two-Spirit body in order to survive a world in which people like me are routinely killed. How do I make sense of the murder of F. C. Martinez Jr., a Diné/Cheyenne Nádleeh youth killed in June 2001 in Cortez, Colorado? How do I make sense of the February 2002 murder of Amy/Raymond Soos, a Two-Spirit of the Pima Nation whose naked body was found in Phoenix, Arizona? How do I make sense of the strangled and beaten body of Alejandro Lucero, Hopi Nation, whose body was found on March 4, 2002, also in Phoenix? How do I make sense of the slaughter of "Brandon Teena," always spoken of as white, who was actually of mixed "Sioux" and white ancestry, his life erased by transphobic murderers and his Nativeness erased by white Queer and Trans folks?[8] How do we as Two-Spirits remain whole and confident in our bodies and in our traditions when loss attempts to smother us? I return to our stories.

Many Cherokee stories deal with characters considered outsiders, who live in liminal spaces, help bring about necessary change, and aid in the process of creation. In one story, a water spider brings fire to the other animals after many larger and stronger animals attempt to retrieve it and fail. She creates a bowl and straps it to her back with spider silk in order to carry fire across the water. In another version of the story, a dragonfly assists her by pushing the bowl from behind (Mooney 431). This story is significant to Cherokee Two-Spirits because so much of it deals with the embodiment of opposites. Spider is specifically a water-spider, and in Mooney's recording of the story, a species of spider that is black with red stripes, opposite sacred colors in Cherokee cosmology (Mooney 241). Dragonfly also dwells between worlds of water, air, and earth. In Cherokee cosmology, fire is associated with the female principal and water is associated with the male principal. Dragonfly and spider become beings that help join these realities.

A Sovereign Erotic is a return to and/or continuance of the complex realities of gender and sexuality that are ever-present in both the human and more-than-human world, but erased and hidden by colonial cultures. Oppression is used by the "settlers" to "tame" our "wild" and "savage" understandings of our Selves, to injure our traditional understandings of the world, to pit us against each other along divisions of gender, sexuality, skin tone, geography, "blood-quantum," (dis)ability, and class so that the powers that be have less work to do in maintaining control over our homelands, our bodies, and our spirits.[9]

In discussing the colonization of Queer African and First Nations bodies and sexualities, elias farajajé-jones writes:

> My . . . African ancestors stood on auctioning blocks in this country where their bodies were offered for sale. They were subjected to the white "gaze" quite literally; their genitalia were touched and inspected in a very public way. The bodies of my First Nations (Tsalagi/Cherokee) ancestors were forcibly removed, infected, massacred, locked up. They were so effectively removed and locked up that they do not even enter into the erotic fictions of the dominating culture. (Kay et al. 328)

Knowing this, Two-Spirit writers, artists, and scholars should turn to and create our own Sovereign Erotic literatures.

IN OUR OLDEST LANGUAGE

Tsuj'/Boy, you are ga-lv-lo'/sky
continually above me
I am eloh'/earth your hands reach
inside to aching molten rock
Your fingers gilded wings
that rise and thrust against
dark muscle rhythms
rock me until I am coiled
around you blooming
Your lightning tongue
summons me to skim
the sweltering expanse of your back
tempts me to nv-yo-i/the rocky place
between your thighs where
you are hard as a cedar flute
a-s-da-ya/taut
as a drum
Water swells at your bank

threatens to break loose
But I am slow
so slow
and steady as a panther
Nibble and suck
strawberries
Flick my tongue across their dark tips
u-wa-n-sv ale tsu-wo-du/ripe and beautiful
Lure their flavor to the surface of your skin
My mouth hungry for your pulse
even and soft on my lips
My hands blanketed by your hair
Your chest silvered and wet
against mine
V:v/Yes
Our moans a low fierce rumble
a coming storm[10]

Two-Spirit people are creating literatures that reflect Sovereign Erotics, and in doing so participate in the process of radical, holistic decolonization. The erotic within First Nations literatures is rarely examined, and Two-Spirit erotics are often ignored. Womack observes, "I would speculate that a queer Indian presence . . . *fundamentally* challenges the American mythos about Indians in a manner the public will not accept. Deeply embedded in the romanticism about Indians are ideas regarding gender. . . . The queer Indian fits none of these popular imaginings" *(Red on Red* 280).

In Her I Am by Chrystos (Menominee) has received praise from other Two-Spirit, Lesbian, and Queer identified women, but has been largely ignored by critics. Not only is this due to the fact that unapologetic Lesbian erotica threatens heteropatriarchal culture, but also because the Sovereign Erotic set forth in her book deals with histories of abuse and colonization that deeply complicate the text. *In Her I Am* demonstrates radical Two-Spirit woman-centered erotics as tools for healing from colonization. The poem "Against" grapples with genocide, abuse, and homophobia and their effects on sexual relationships:

We're survivors of childhood violence with black eyes
in common from mothers who hated our difference

[. . . . .]

Your people as well as mine slaughtered in millions
Queer we're still open season My fingermarks on your
ass are loving you
[. . . . .]
Desire red & raw as wounds we disguise we're open
season. (Chrystos 4–25)

It is poems such as this, which examine the complexities of sexuality within an abusive culture, that are needed in order for Two-Spirit people to engage with healing and (re)creating Sovereign Erotic spaces in our lives and work. Chrystos writes,

Because sex has been split off from us as women in a colonizer culture, we ourselves police our pleasure. . . . We need to engage in a radical discussion & redefinition of our sexuality, a discussion which has been co-opted to issues of biology (abortion & conception), rather than sexual freedom, remembering that freedom needs the bones of responsibility to flourish. (83)

Chrystos undertakes this redefinition through the creation of erotic poems for other Native Two-Spirit women that encompass First Nations traditions and histories. In "Woman" the gathering of wild rice is eroticized:

will you come with me moving
through rivers to soft lakebeds
[. . . . .]
Will you go with me down the long waters smoothly
shaking life into our journey. (Chrystos 1–6)

Likewise, "Tenderly Your" situates the erotic within historical memory:

We're in the grass of prairies our grandmothers rode
Sweet smell of distant cookpots edges the blue
Your kisses are a hundred years old & newly born.
(Chrystos 3–5)

The poem continues by discussing the erotic as a tool for healing from trauma:

Flaming ride us past our rapes our pain
past years when we stumbled lost [. . . . .]
This
is why we were made by creation. (9–14)

Sovereign Erotics are also reflected in Craig Womack's *Drowning in Fire*. Through the narrative of Josh Henneha, lines between historical memory and contemporary lives spiral into one another. The erotic relationship that develops between Josh and Jimmy weaves itself into a history of Creek resistance to allotment and Oklahoma statehood. Snake motifs throughout the text represent both the supernatural tie-snake, an embodiment of opposites, and the Snake faction in Creek resistance history. During a sexual encounter between Josh and Jimmy, snakes appear:

> There were snakes everywhere, shimmering rainbows of color and motion, circles and circles. . . . A copperhead was dancing around one of Jimmy's Air Jordans lying on the floor. A giant rattlesnake sat coiled around the copperhead and the tennis shoes, shaking his tail like an accompaniment to the swaying dance inside the circles they had made, the snakes within snakes. . . . The whip snake came down from the lamp, crawled over our way, placed his head on the edge of the sparse white sheet, and flicked his tongue at us. (Womack, *Drowning in Fire* 200)

Womack also connects the erotic to the sacred through the relationship between Josh and Jimmy. After the couple makes love in a creek, Josh dreams:

> I dreamed that I came back a year later with him and the pond was no longer there, only a large, shimmering

mud flat. . . . In the dried-up creekbed, at the exact spot where Jimmy had come in the creek, had grown a red cedar. My Aunt Lucy stepped out from behind it, and she laughed at the way she'd startled us. "See, boys," she said, nodding at the cedar, "now you know where those trees come from." (*Drowning in Fire* 279)

The Sovereign Erotics created by Two-Spirits are part of the healing of the wounded bodies of ourselves, our lands, and our planet. Collections of First Nations erotic writing that include the work of Two-Spirit writers such as *Without Reservation: Indigenous Erotica* edited by Kateri Akiwenzie-Damm (Anishanaabe) and Red Ink Magazine's Love & Erotic Issue (Volume 11:1) are quickly emerging in North America. We were stolen from our bodies, but now we are taking ourselves back. First Nations Two-Spirits are blooming like dandelions in the landscape of a racist, homophobic, and transphobic culture's ordered garden. Through over 500 years of colonization's efforts to kill our startling beauty, our roots have proven too deep and complicated to pull out of the soil of our origin, the soil where we are nurtured by the sacrifices that were made by our ancestors' commitment to love us.

And we are fighters in this long war
to bring us all back home

NOTES

1. The Cherokee used in the poem is a translation of "Amazing Grace."

2. My use of the term "sovereign" is in no way an attempt to challenge or replace the legal definitions of sovereignty. As Native nations, sovereignty specifically refers to the legal relationships our nations have with other governments and nations, including the United States. By using the terms "sovereign" and "sovereignty" in relationship to tribally specific and traditional understandings of our bodies, sexualities, genders, erotic senses of self, terms employed in the formation of identities, or other non-legal contexts, I'm using the words as metaphors for relationships between Native people and nations and the non-Native nations, people, values, and understandings that occupy and exist within our traditional lands.

3. While I am choosing to focus on erotics as a site of decolonization and sovereignty, it should be made clear that I do not think of the term "Two-Spirit" as a pan-Native term synonymous with "Gay," or "Lesbian." The various traditions being called "Two-Spirit" are often much more about gender identity and gender expression than about sexual orientation. I also realize the problematic nature of using one term for our various and vastly differing tribal traditions, understandings, and identities. I am choosing to use the term "Two-Spirit" throughout this essay because it does not make me splinter off sexuality from race, gender from culture. It was created specifically to hold, not diminish or erase, complexities. It is a sovereign term in the invaders' tongue.

4. It should also be remembered that Cherokees and other First Nations people were sold into slavery. For a thorough discussion of the enslavement of First Nations peoples, see Cherokee/Assateague-Gingaskin scholar Ron Welburn's essay "The Other Middle Passage: The Bermuda-Barbados Trade in Native American Slaves" in *Roanoke and Wampum: Topics in Native American Heritage and Literatures* (2001).

5. Dagmar Thorpe's (Sauk and Fox/Potawatomi/Kickapoo) interview with Charlotte Black Elk (Lakota) (157).

6. As of the writing of this essay, there is a study being conducted, however, through the University of Washington's School of Social Work called the Two-Spirit Honor Project.

7. An invasion, it should be remembered, rooted in the murder and expulsion of Sefardí Jews and Muslim North Africans during the Inquisition.

8. While he used the names Billy and Brandon, "Brandon Teena" is a name created by activists by switching the first and last names given to Brandon at birth. I learned of Brandon's mixed blood ancestry through an unlikely text, *All She Wanted* by Aphrodite Jones. The book is widely criticized in Trans communities for its transphobia and sensationalistic "true-crime" style. In a particularly racist passage that at once romanticizes Brandon's Native features and celebrates his light skin and eyes, Jones writes, "Their grandfather on their fathers side was a full-blooded Sioux Indian, so Teena . . . was an exotic-looking infant. To JoAnn (Brandon's mother), she almost looked black, even though it was only her hair that was dark. Teena was beautiful, blessed with the bluest Irish eyes" (Jones 29). Besides "Sioux," Brandon's tribal affiliation is not mentioned. *All She Wanted* is the only book about Brandon's life and murder, and in some ways remains more factual than the highly popular film *Boys Don't Cry*.

9. (Dis)ability, as an alternative to "disability," was coined in 1999 by radical activist and writer Colin Kennedy Donovan and appears in the 'zine *Fuck Pity: Issue Number One: Not Yr Goddamn Poster Child*. I have chosen to use this term because it draws attention to "disability" as a social and political construct rather than an inherent "condition" blamed on our bodies and minds.

10. By the author, originally published in *Red Ink Magazine*.

REFERENCES

Akiwenzie-Damm, Kateri, ed. *Without Reservation: Indigenous Erotica*. Cape Croker Reserve ON: Kegedonce Press, 2003.

Awiakta, Marilou. *Selu: Seeking the Corn-Mother's Wisdom*. Golden CO: Fulcrum, 1993.

Brant, Beth. *Writing as Witness: Essay and Talk*. Toronto: Women's Press, 1994.

Chrystos. *In Her I Am*. Vancouver BC: Press Gang, 1993.

Donovan, Colin Kennedy. *Fuck Pity: Issue Number One: Not Yr Goddamn Poster Child*. Seattle: Independently Published, 2000.

Driskill, Qwo-Li. "In Our Oldest Language." *Red Ink Magazine. Love & Erotics*. Volume 11.1. Tucson: University of Arizona, Fall 2003.

Hill, Barbara-Helen. *Shaking the Rattle: Healing the Trauma of Colonization*. Penticton BC: Theytus Books, 1995.

Jacobs, Sue-Ellen, Wesley Thomas, and Sabine Lang, eds. *Two-Spirit People: Native American Gender Identity, Sexuality and Spirituality*. Urbana: U of Illinois P, 1997.

Jones, Aphrodite. *All She Wanted*. New York: Pocket Books, 1996.

Kay, Kerwin, Jill Nagle, and Baruch Gould, eds. *Male Lust: Pleasure, Power, and Transformation*. Binghamton NY: Harrington Park, 2000.

Lorde, Audre. *Sister Outsider*. Freedom CA: Crossing Press, 1984.

Mankiller, Wilma. *Mankiller: A Chief and Her People*. New York: St. Martin's, 1993.

Mooney, James. *History, Myths, and Sacred Formulas of the Cherokees*. Ashville NC: Bright Mountain Books, 1992.

Thorpe, Dagmar. *People of the Seventh Fire: Returning Lifeways of Native America*. Ithaca NY: Akwe:kon Press, 1996.

Welburn, Ron. *Roanoke and Wampum: Topics in Native American Heritage and Literatures*. New York: Peter Lang, 2001.

Womack, Craig S. *Drowning in Fire*. Tucson: U of Arizona P, 2001.

Womack, Craig S. *Red on Red: Native American Literary Separatism*. Minneapolis: U of Minnesota P, 1999.

JENNY HEIJUN WILLS

48. TRANSNATIONAL ADOPTION AND THE PARADOX OF REPRODUCTIVE RIGHTS

Commencing in the years following World War II and formalized during the Korean War, transnational adoption has grown into a multimillion-dollar industry that is as morally complex as it is lucrative. On one side of the conversation, proponents describe the shortage of accessible kinship for young people, particularly in lands where options for domestic adoption and first mothers' rights are limited. On the other side, opponents note the ways that transnational adoption reiterates global power inequalities as the majority of cases center white, middle-class families in "the West" adopting young people of color from supposedly poorer conditions. Combining the nefarious practices of child trafficking and the non-guarantee of citizenship for adoptees in their new countries (e.g., The Adoptee Rights Campaign estimated thirty-thousand transnational adoptees raised in the United States are without citizenship), the link between (neo)colonialism and transnational adoption, and the racial alienation experienced by adoptees, especially when they are raised in homogenous white families and communities, it is no wonder that some adult transnational adoptees and their allies are calling for what scholar and blogger Daniel Ibn Zayd calls "the new abolition." Nonetheless, countries like South Korea continue to send young people overseas for adoption, thereby growing a program that has lasted nearly seventy years. Other prolific countries of origin include (but are not limited to) China, India, Guatemala, Ethiopia, Haiti, and Vietnam. The result is large populations of diasporic subjects raised in places like Canada, the United States, and Australia, in addition to nations in Western Europe, who exemplify the precarious ways that race, ethnicity, kinship, class, and nationality are constructed but also complicated designations. These experiences are inextricably linked to issues of gender and sexuality—in terms of all members of the transnational adoption constellation: first families, adoptive families, and adoptees, as well as siblings, extended family members, and even adoption workers and policymakers. Most notable among these issues is the so-called right to parent—a right that extends mainly to Western adoptive families, including queer families that some scholars argue use transnational adoption as a tool of entering heteronormativity at the sacrifice of first families from everywhere else.

In this essay, I chart the ways Western liberal feminism reiterates racial power imbalances and oppressions through the intended generous act of transnational adoption as white adoptive families see themselves as saving brown and black children from brown and black families and spaces. This dynamic was especially prevalent during the rise of adoption from China, when Western adoptive families were particularly motivated to adopt so-called unwanted female babies whom they felt they were saving from both the literal and moral poverty of the "Orient": that is, economic destitution and a misogynistic culture that privileges male children. Next, I summarize some different feminist perspectives on this debate, highlighting the ways that intersectional, global feminism seems to come up against more white-centered, Western liberal feminisms in relation to this topic. Last, I engage with David Eng's argument in *The Feeling of Kinship* when he suggests that transnational adoption is being used by same-sex couples to participate in heteronormative nuclear family-building in ways that render invisible brown and black (birthing) labor. In doing so, my essay questions the manners in which white feminist and queer kinship is constructed in relation to the transnational adoption industry and the ironic ways these liberal forms of family-building reiterate global raced and gendered inequalities. Notions of "rights-based" actions are complex and problematized; and in this case, these rights-based actions are linked to reproductive justice—specifically, the right to be a parent. In all, I illustrate the ways that feminist perspectives are used by both proponents and opponents of transnational adoption, with the concluding observation that supporters tend to affirm Western-liberal feminist approaches while transnational adoption abolitionists lean more toward radical, intersectional, global feminist perspectives. I will begin this discussion with a brief historical survey of transnational adoption, focusing on Asian adoption as it is both the catalyst for what would become what Kimberly McKee calls the "Adoption Industrial Complex," and it is the most prolific "resource" for adoptable young people.

LIBERALISM, RELIEF, AND ASIAN ADOPTION

Considered the necessary solution for the increasing number of biracial "war babies" or "GI babies" born in South Korea who were not claimed by their Korean mothers or their American military personnel fathers, transnational adoption was originally imagined as a relief program in the 1950s (Wills, "Transnational" 102). Korean adoptees were adopted by civilian families, unlike earlier transnational adoptees (from Austria, Germany, Greece, and Japan) who were raised by military families in other countries. Central to the discourse motivating and perpetuating Korean adoption in these early years was a critique of South Korea's racism and sexism that targeted biracial people and unwed mothers. And while it is inarguable that "the protective and homogenous Korean society had no place for these racially different children," Western liberals capitalized on the "rhetorical narrative . . . that imagined multiracial 'war babies' as unwanted, destitute, and fated to grow up in a racist society that would forever reject them" (Wills, "The Gift" 161). Transnational Asian adoption was immediately framed as a rescue mission; young people were seen as needing relief from racist and sexist societies, unfit first families, and economically unsure lands. Leading the call for Western families, and especially American families, to adopt young people from South Korea were white liberal feminists like Pulitzer and Nobel prize winning author Pearl Buck, whose discourse included exceptionalist rallies that Americans could take the moral high ground and care for the young people marginalized and oppressed in their own lands. With this in mind, we can see how transnational adoption shores up the definitiveness of the nation-state; kinship, opportunity, and success are isolated away from individual experience and are pronounced through the geographic and cultural confines of nationalism.

Transnational adoption advocates framed adopting from Asia as a relief program in the final moments of the war in Vietnam, when the now notorious "Operation Babylift" evacuated thousands of *presumed* orphaned Vietnamese young people for the express purpose of being adopted by Western families. The program was hasty despite its humanitarian intentions, and as scholar Jodi Kim pronounces, cannot be separated from "America's protracted episodes of empire-building and war-making" (223). Moreover, as scholar Catherine Ceniza Choy outlines, Orientalist ideologies fed into Asian adoption industries as Western media "perpetuated stereotypical representations of a homogenous Asia and its peoples' inability to care for abandoned children in general" (41). Exceptionalist rhetoric implied that "American rescue might be the only option for the well-being of [Vietnamese] children" and that adoption was the most effective tool (41). As a result, many young people were separated from their first families, including their first mothers, and transported to foreign lands under the auspices of often-inaccurate orphan visas—an irony given the weight placed on these documents by nation states. Peter Selman estimates the number of young people evacuated in the months leading up to the fall of Saigon at two thousand and notes, "[e]ver since, adoption from Vietnam has been surrounded by controversy and accusations of corruption" (62). As young people were hastily shuffled away into orphanages and then sent overseas for adoption, few attempts to contact family members were made.

Discourse shifted in ways perhaps most relevant to this collection with the rise of Asian adoption from China which, in its earliest moments of popularity, was inextricably tied to the Family Planning Policy that came into effect in 1979. Forced contraception and sterilization was just one nefarious aspect of what became colloquially known as China's "One-Child Policy" that was meant to quell overpopulation and some of its social and environmental ramifications. Westerners "no longer [felt the need to] step in and adopt unwanted multiracial children, but saw themselves as the saviours of abandoned infants who had been rejected by their patriarchal and sexist Chinese families and societies" (Wills, "The Gift" 165). Indeed, when scholar Helena Grice states, "The *story* of Chinese adoption to U.S. parents is also a tale of gender woe, as almost all Chinese children adopted by overseas parents are abandoned little girls," her gesture to the significance of narrative, characterization, and story here is notable (125, emphasis mine). This is not said to deny the fact that thousands of female babies were relinquished to orphanages. The point here is that the discourses that motivated the replacement of South Korea as the leading country of origin by China hinged on a narrative of indignation over the abandonment of Chinese female babies as a recent example of "codified gender violence and discrimination against Chinese women" (Grice 127). The fact is that these so-called abandonments were a by-product of a more insidious situation and that transnational adoption arguably became a band-aid solution to gender inequality and violence that enabled the core injustice to continue. The good intentions of Western liberalism, particularly the desire to save black and brown children through the auspices of individualism and care, cannot attend to these larger, systemic problems.

Peak year 2005 saw approximately fourteen thousand young people adopted from China to countries around the world (Selman 67), but as scholar Sara Dorow points out, these adoption "practices—as well as the children themselves—have taken on forms of public and symbolic significance that exceed what the numbers suggest" (10). From the lauding of celebrity adoptions of China-born young people to the ubiquity of adopted Asian girls in popular film and television, Asian adoptees (and particularly young people from China) have become naturalized symbols of twenty-first century transracial kinship. The result is that adoption from China has become a synecdoche for transnational Asian adoption in much of our contemporary imaginary. In addition to the large waves of transnational Asian adoption from Korea, Vietnam, and China are adoptions from other countries of origin, including Japan, the Philippines, and

India (Selman 57). Relevant in all of these instances is the way that Orientalism shapes assumptions that young people must be removed from their original environments and that the Western intervention of transnational adoption can stave off the damage of colonial oppression if those antecedents are even acknowledged. To extrapolate from Gayatri Chakravorty Spivak's memorable statement in "Can the Subaltern Speak," when she summarizes the relationship between colonizer and colonized as "[w]hite men are saving brown women from brown men," we might consider transnational and transracial adoption as a colonial technology whereby white families are saving brown children from brown families (93).

FEMINIST THOUGHTS ON TRANSNATIONAL AND TRANSRACIAL ADOPTION

It is not surprising that transnational adoption has captivated feminist imaginations for years. Feminist proponents of transnational adoption argue for (Westerners') rights to parent without biological reproduction or the use of invasive and patriarchal reproductive technologies. And indeed, transnational adoption is an important method of family-building for many people, including those for whom biological reproductive kinship is inaccessible (including people who have tried and cannot conceive, older people, single people, people with disabilities, and queer people). Alternatively, feminist opponents of transnational adoption emphasize the social injustices incurred by black and brown women who may be oppressed by their social and economic environments and the ways that certain Western feminists use transnational adoption to benefit from their struggles. Scholars Patricia Fronek, Denise Cuthbert, and Indigo Willing summarize the feminist paradox of transnational adoption succinctly: "Discourses surrounding the rights of the child define [transnational adoption], yet in reality its practice characteristically pits the rights of the poor against those of the privileged. That is, it pits women affected by their social and economic conditions against relatively affluent women hoping to parent a child" (351). From their perspective, there are implicit power imbalances that frame the ways adoption is discussed on the one side as a feminist alternative to reproductive technology and on the other as a feminist issue of people's right to kinship—and more specifically, their right to parent. When it comes to thinking about other people's right to parent their own children or young people's rights to be raised in a culturally compatible environment, these conversations tend to distribute privilege in global hegemonic ways.

In her short essay, "The Fantasy of the Global Cabbage Patch," Karen Dubinsky distances herself from the ethical binary of "rescue and kidnap [that] dominate contemporary discussions of transnational adoption," but concludes that "[a]doption politics are complicated politics, and feminists have made their way into both realms of this debate" (339, 340). On one side, arguments are made that adoption upends the "normative nuclear family," challenging the patriarchal ways that blood and essentialist approaches of reproduction shape women's lives. On the other side, some contend that transnational adoption not only removes first mothers' agency in deciding to raise their own children, but that in some instances becomes connected to social systems that "punish sexually active women," offering individual recourse from rigid and misogynistic societies but accommodating those ideologies in the long run (Dubinsky 340). Discussing Human Rights in China, Helena Grice offers graphic accounts of state-sanctioned late-term abortions and infanticides, presenting transnational adoption as the most positive (albeit still problematic) solution to the policing of Chinese women's bodies. According to Grice, "the phenomenon of Chinese American adoption is specifically gendered," and her article provides a handful of examples of white, Western liberal adoptive parents attempting to navigate complex, intersectional issues (128).

But while Grace is forgiving of transnational adoption because it is a better alternative to more violent responses to reproductive rights in China, Dorothy Roberts, in "Feminism, Race, and Adoption Policy," addresses white, Western feminist approaches to imagining adoption a solution to social injustice which is, she argues, "a particularly selfish way to approach child welfare that perpetuates rather than challenges America's racial hierarchy" (246). Speaking specifically about the disproportionate number of black children in American foster care, Roberts states:

Feminists should reject the emphasis on adoption to cure the ills of foster care and insist on fundamental change in our approach to child welfare. . . . Feminists should see the racial disparities in adoption as a powerful reason to radically transform the child welfare system into one that generously and noncoercively supports families. (246)

Roberts' argument speaks directly to and summarizes nicely the feminist paradox around transracial adoption, and especially transracial adoption of black children in the United States. But I think her insights can also be applied to other contexts of transracial adoption, including transnational adoptions. In other words, one might call on feminists to stop lauding the surface benefits of transnational adoption if those actions enable (or at least pass over) ongoing racial and gender inequality. It is worth noting as well that in many countries of origin, scholarship and activism about transnational adoption is led by feminist scholars, whether they are challenging state-sanctioned reproduction policies or calling for greater sexual agency and rights for unwed mothers. There is also a sizeable contingent of returned adoptees, many of whom are utilizing feminist methods and critiques, and are actively fighting for rights, including one's right to their personal history and agency files. Thus, in sum, as Dubinsky rightfully notes, transnational adoption is indeed a feminist issue regardless of which side of the debate one finds themselves, and perhaps it is another telling example of how radical, intersectional, transnational feminism comes up against more Western-liberal iterations.

QUEER KINSHIP AND TRANSNATIONAL ADOPTION

In recent years, queer families of various subject positions have rightfully fought for kinship rights, including the right to parent young people. The dilemma of rights-based claims to adopt versus rights-based claims to be raised in one's first family and first culture or rights-based claims to raise one's own children is perhaps most complex in the contexts of queer kinship, as both proponents and opponents of transnational adoption here have been marginalized and oppressed by the hegemonic powers of heteronormativity, patriarchy, and white supremacy. Scholars Fronek, Cuthbert, and Willing argue that, "in the domain of inter country adoption, access to children for adoptive family formation is cast as the right to parent or the right to form a family" and that "increasingly, this 'right' is being claimed by those— single people, older adults, and gay and lesbian couples—formerly excluded from heterosexual norms of parenthood" (351). This reality is meaningful and highlights the reasons why transnational adoption is such a prescient topic when it comes to queer rights as well as other people's rights to kinship.

In order to analyze different modes of queer kinship, literary critic David Eng explores the historical emergence of queer liberalism in *The Feeling of Kinship* by using transnational adoption as a multifaceted example of queer liberalism. Eng gives the example of a US insurance company commercial that features a white lesbian couple that has recently adopted a female infant from Asia. He suggests that the "emergence of queer family and queer kinship depends on the faithful reproduction of the heteronormative conjugal family" (99) and that the Asian adoptee is the catalyst for this recreation. Expanding on the work of anthropologist Ann Anagnost, Eng remarks, "The desire for parenthood as economic entitlement and legal right . . . not only by heterosexuals but also, and increasingly, by homosexuals seems to stem in large part from an unexamined belief in the traditional ideals of the nuclear family as the primary contemporary measure of social respectability and value" but he hastens to add that "this enjoyment or rights" comes as a result of the perpetuated global marginalization of others left behind—"cosigned to outcast status" because of the inaccessibility of mobility (culture and/or class) (101). In other words, Eng ponders the motives behind the desire to access this version of queer kinship, and if transnational adoption becomes a tool for perpetuating an economics-based liberal ethos that re-energizes inequality and oppression as well as heteronormative ideals. In other words, transnational adoptions, in queer contexts, reiterate power inequalities of economics, race, and gender despite the progressive sentiments that surround these acts.

Again, it appears that the line is drawn between liberal and radical politics, as liberal thinkers seek solutions within these power systems and radicals aim to disrupt those systems altogether. It is also worth providing a note on the recent trend in some scholarship to frame transnational adoption as inherently queer. While the methodological frameworks afforded by queer studies are alluring, without nuance, these approaches run the risk of erasing and/or appropriating queer subjectivity and, moreover, often overlook the fact that, as Eng and others argue, transnational adoption is deployed as a heteronormatizing device regardless of the gender identities and sexual orientations of the adoptive parent(s).

CONCLUSION

I'd like to close with a return to the discussion on reproductive justice. Mostly, mainstream conversations about reproductive rights focus on the meaningful and necessary rights of people to access health care, contraception, and abortions as they affect their own bodies, despite the important work of organizations like SisterSong that draw on notions of reproductive justice to protest forced sterilization and other ways that (mostly Black, Indigenous, People of Color [BIPOC] and poor) people are prevented from parenting. White, Western liberal feminists are particularly keen to decry reproductive injustices in other parts of the world, as I have discussed earlier in this essay. But I think that it is also imperative that we consider parenting rights, and specifically here, the rights of non-Western, mostly women of color to parent their own children, as part of this discussion. For instance, how does adoption fit within our conversations about *choice* and *access*? And how do we square the liberal idealism of transnational and transracial adoption with the historic and ongoing ways that women of color have been deemed unfit mothers or have been alienated from their own children because they are compelled and historically, *forced* to be caretakers for children in white families— as enslaved women, as servants, and as migrant laborers? Furthermore, how can we reckon with the ways that transnational adoption all but erases first mothers, since as scholar Hosu Kim argues, "[t]he misrecognition of birth mothers and their sightlessness is useful for maintaining the status quo in the transnational adoption practice" (9)? What are we to make of the ways that, in some contexts, a young person's first mother need not give consent for adoption to occur (Kim, *Birth Mothers* 7–8)? And of course, how can Western liberals discuss reproductive justice for women whose states enforce sterilization and contraception while benefiting from a transnational adoption industry that seemingly supports that hegemonic context? In other words, is transnational adoption a quiet complicity with patriarchal, misogynistic, and oppressive social practices that shame unwed mothers,

coerce abortions and sterilization? These questions reveal how adoption broadly, and transnational and transracial adoption specifically, invite us to deepen our conversations about kinship, gendered and raced *labor*, and reproductive justice and hopefully encourage us to think with even greater nuance about how individual and collective rights as well as the good intentions of liberalism impact and play into power imbalances and oppressions.

REFERENCES

Adoptee Rights Campaign. http://adopteerightscampaign.org/. Accessed October 24, 2017.

Choy, Catherine Ceniza. *Global Families: A History of Asian International Adoption in America.* New York UP, 2013.

Dorow, Sara K. *Transnational Adoption: A Cultural Economy of Race, Gender, and Kinship.* New York UP, 2006.

Dubinsky, Karen. "The Fantasy of the Global Cabbage Patch: Making Sense of Transnational Adoption," *Feminist Theory*, vol. 9, no. 3 (2008): 339–45.

ElAwar, Daniel Drennan. "The New Abolition: Ending Adoption in Our Time." *Dissident Voice: a radical newsletter in the struggle for peace and social justice*, August 18, 2012, http://dissidentvoice. org/2012/08/the-new-abolition-ending-adoption-in-our-time/.

Eng, David. *The Feeling of Kinship: Queer Liberalism and the Racialization of Intimacy.* Duke UP, 2010.

Fronek, Patricia, Denise Cuthbert, and Indigo Willing. "Intercountry Adoption: Privilege, Rights and Social Justice." *The Intercountry Adoption Debate: Dialogues Across Disciplines*, eds. Robert L. Ballard, Naomi H. Goodno, Robert F. Cochran, and Jay A. Milbrandt. Cambridge Scholars, 2015, pp. 348–65.

Grice, Helena. "Transracial Adoption Narratives: Prospects and Perspectives." *Meridians*, vol. 5, no. 2 (2005): 124–48.

McKee, Kimberly. "The Transnational Adoption Industrial Complex: An Analysis of Nation, Citizenship, and the Korean Diaspora." PhD diss., Ohio State University, 2013.

Kim, Hosu. *Birth Mothers and Transnational Adoption Practice in South Korea: Virtual Mothering.* Palgrave, 2016.

Kim, Jodi. *Ends of Empire: Asian American Critique and the Cold War.* U of Minnesota P, 2010.

Roberts, Dorothy. "Feminism, Race, and Adoption Policy." *Adoption Matters: Philosophical and Feminist Essays*, eds. Sally Haslanger and Charlotte Witt. Cornell UP, 2005, pp. 234–46.

Selman, Peter. "The Rise and Fall of Countries of Origin." *Proceedings of the First International Korean Adoption Studies Research Symposium*, eds. Kim Park Nelson, Eleana Kim, and Lene Myong Petersen. IKAA, 2007, pp. 55–76.

Spivak, Gayatri Chakravorty. "Can the Subaltern Speak?" *Colonial Discourse and Post-Colonial Theory: A Reader*, eds. Patrick Williams and Laura Chrisman. Harvester Wheatsheaf, 1994, pp. 90–105.

Wills, Jenny Heijun. "The Gift of the Good Life: 'Anchor Babies' and Asian Adoptees." *The Good Life and the Greater Good in a Global Context*, ed. Laura Savu Walker. Lexington, 2015, pp. 159–72.

Wills, Jenny Heijun. "Transnational and Transracial Adoption: Multiculturalism and Selective Colour-Blindness." *American Multicultural Studies: Diversity of Race, Ethnicity, Gender, and Sexuality*, ed. Sherrow O. Pinder. Sage, 2013, pp. 101–14.

DEAN SPADE

49. WHAT'S WRONG WITH RIGHTS?

Rights discourse in liberal capitalist culture casts as private potentially political contests about distribution of resources and about relevant parties to decision making. It converts social problems into matters of individualized, dehistoricized injury and entitlement, into matters in which there is no harm if there is no agent and no tangibly violated subject.

—Wendy Brown, *States of Injury*

As the concept of trans rights has gained more currency in the last two decades, a seeming consensus has emerged about which law reforms should be sought to better the lives of trans people.[1] Advocates of trans equality have primarily pursued two law reform interventions: anti-discrimination laws that list gender identity and/or expression as a category of nondiscrimination, and hate crime laws that include crimes motivated by the gender identity and/or expression of the victim as triggering the application of a jurisdiction's hate crime statute. Organizations like the National Gay and Lesbian Task Force (NGLTF) have supported state and local organizations around the country in legislative campaigns to pass such laws. Thirteen states (California, Colorado, Hawaii, Illinois, Iowa, Maine, Minnesota, New Jersey, New Mexico, Oregon, Rhode Island, Vermont, Washington) and the District of Columbia currently have laws that include gender identity and/or expression as a category of anti-discrimination, and 108 counties and cities have such laws. NGLTF estimates that 39 percent of people in the United States live in a jurisdiction where such laws are on the books.[2] Seven states now have hate crime laws that include gender identity and/or expression.[3] In 2009, a federal law, the Matthew Shepard and James Byrd, Jr. Hate Crimes Prevention Act, added gender identity and/or expression to federal hate crime law. An ongoing battle regarding if and how gender identity and/or expression will be included in the Employment Non-Discrimination Act (ENDA), a federal law that would prohibit discrimination on the basis of sexual orientation, continues to be fought between the conservative national gay and lesbian organization, the Human Rights Campaign (HRC), legislators, and a variety of organizations and activists seeking to push an inclusive bill through Congress. These two legal reforms, anti-discrimination bills and hate crime laws, have come to define the idea of "trans rights" in the United States and are presently the most visible efforts made by nonprofit organizations and activists working under this rubric.

The logic behind this law reform strategy is not mysterious. Proponents argue that passing these laws does a number of important things. First, the passage of anti-discrimination laws can create a basis for legal claims against discriminating employers, housing providers, restaurants, hotels, stores, and the like. Trans people's legal claims when facing exclusion in such contexts have often failed in the past, with courts saying that the exclusion is a legitimate preference on the part of the employer, landlord, or business owner.[4] Laws that make gender identity/expression-based exclusion illegal have the potential to influence courts to punish discriminators and provide certain remedies (e.g., back pay or damages) to injured trans people. There is also a hope that such laws, and their enforcement by courts, would send a preventative message to potential discriminators, letting them know that such exclusions will not be tolerated; these laws would ultimately increase access to jobs, housing, and other necessities for trans people.

Hate crime laws are promoted under a related logic. Proponents point out that trans people have a very high murder rate and are subject to a great deal of violence.[5] In many instances, trans people's lives are so devalued by police and prosecutors that trans murders are not investigated or trans people's murderers are given less punishment than is typical in murder sentencing. Proponents believe that hate crime laws will intervene in these situations, making law enforcement take this violence seriously. There is also a symbolic element to the passage of these laws: a statement that trans lives are meaningful, often described by proponents as an assertion that trans people are human. Additionally, both proponents of anti-discrimination laws and hate crime laws argue that the processes of advocating the passage of such laws, including media advocacy representing the lives and concerns of trans people and meetings with legislators to tell them about trans people's experiences, increases positive trans visibility and advances the struggle for trans equality. The data-collection element of hate crime statutes, through which certain government agencies keep count of crimes that fall into this category, is touted by proponents as a chance to make the quantity and severity of trans people's struggles more visible.

The logic of visibility and inclusion surrounding anti-discrimination and hate crime laws campaigns is very popular, yet there are many troubling limitations to the idea that these two reforms comprise a proper approach to problems trans people face in both criminal and civil law contexts. One concern is whether these laws actually improve the life chances of those who are purportedly protected by them. An examination of categories of identity that have been included in these kinds of laws over the last several decades indicates that these kinds of reforms have not eliminated bias, exclusion, or marginalization. Discrimination and violence against people of color have persisted despite law changes that declared it illegal. The persistent and growing racial wealth divide in the United States suggests that these law changes have not had their promised effects, and that the structure of systemic racism is not addressed by the work of these laws.[6] Similarly, the . . . history of the Americans with Disabilities Act (ADA) demonstrates disappointing results. Courts have limited the enforcement potential

of this law with narrow interpretations of its impact, and people with disabilities remain economically and politically marginalized by systemic ableism. Similar arguments can be made about the persistence of national origin discrimination, sex discrimination, and other forms of pervasive discrimination despite decades of official prohibitions of such behavior. The persistence of wage gaps, illegal terminations, hostile work environments, hiring/firing disparities, and bias-motivated violence for groups whose struggles have supposedly been addressed by anti-discrimination and hate crime laws invites caution when assuming the effectiveness of these measures.

As I discussed, . . . hate crime laws do not have a deterrent effect. They focus on punishment and cannot be argued to actually prevent bias-motivated violence. In addition to their failure to prevent harm, they must be considered in the context of the failures of our legal systems and, specifically, the violence of our criminal punishment system. Anti-discrimination laws are not adequately enforced. Most people who experience discrimination cannot afford to access legal help, so their experiences never make it to court. Additionally, the Supreme Court has severely narrowed the enforceability of these laws, . . . making it extremely difficult to prove discrimination short of a signed letter from a boss or landlord stating, "I am taking this negative action against you because of your [insert characteristic]." Even in cases that seem as obvious as that, people experiencing discrimination often lose. Proving discriminatory intent has become central, making it almost impossible to win these cases when they are brought to court. These laws also have such narrow scopes that they often do not include action taken by some of the most common discriminators against marginalized people: prison guards, welfare workers, workfare supervisors, immigration officers, child welfare workers, and others who have significant control over the lives of marginalized people in the United States. In a neoliberal era characterized by abandonment (reduction of social safety net and infrastructure, especially in poor and people of color communities) and imprisonment (increased immigration and criminal law enforcement), anti-discrimination laws provide little relief to the most vulnerable people.

In addition to these general problems with law reforms that add gender identity/expression to the list of prohibited characteristics, trans litigants have run into specific challenges when seeking redress from discrimination under these laws. Even in jurisdictions where these laws have been put in place, trans litigants have lost discrimination cases about being denied access to a sex-segregated facility.[7] In the employment context, this often means that even when a worker lives in a jurisdiction where discriminating against trans people is supposedly illegal, denying a trans person access to a bathroom that comports with their gender identity at work is not interpreted as a violation of the law. Of course, given the staggering unemployment of trans populations emerging from conditions of homelessness, lack of family support,[8] violence-related trauma, discrimination by potential employers, effects of unmet health needs, and many other factors,[9] even if the legal interpretations of trans people's bathroom access demands were better it would not scratch the surface of trans poverty.[10] However, these interpretations in employment cases involving bathrooms are particularly dangerous because they can be applied by courts to other high-stakes settings where trans people struggle in systems that rely on sex-segregation. Because trans people frequently face violence and discrimination in the context of sex-segregated spaces like shelters, prisons, and group homes, and because bathroom access is often the most contentious issue between trans workers and their employers, these anti-trans legal interpretations take the teeth out of trans-inclusive laws and are an example of the limitations of seeking equality through courts and legislatures.

Critical race theorists have developed analyses about the limitations of anti-discrimination law that are useful in understanding the ways these law reforms have and will continue to fail to deliver meaningful change to trans people. Alan Freeman's critique of what he terms the "perpetrator perspective" in discrimination law is particularly helpful in conceptualizing the limits of the common trans rights strategies.[11] Freeman's work looks at laws that prohibit discrimination based on race. He exposes how and why anti-discrimination and hate crime statutes do not achieve their promises of equality and freedom for people targeted by discrimination and violence. Freeman argues that discrimination law

misunderstands how racism works, which makes it fail to effectively address it.

Discrimination law primarily conceptualizes the harm of racism through the perpetrator/victim dyad, imagining that the fundamental scene is that of a perpetrator who irrationally hates people on the basis of their race and fires or denies service to or beats or kills the victim based on that hatred. The law's adoption of this conception of racism does several things that make it ineffective at eradicating racism and help it contribute to obscuring the actual operations of racism. First, it individualizes racism. It says that racism is about bad individuals who intentionally make discriminatory choices and must be punished. In this (mis)understanding, structural or systemic racism is rendered invisible. Through this function, the law can only attend to disparities that come from the behavior of a perpetrator who intentionally considered the category that must not be considered (e.g., race, gender, disability) in the decision she [or he] was making (e.g., hiring, firing, admission, expulsion). Conditions like living in a district with underfunded schools that "happens to be" 96 percent students of color,[12] or having to take an admissions test that has been proven to predict race better than academic success,[13] or any of a number of disparities in life conditions (access to adequate food, health care, employment, housing, clean air and water) that we know stem from and reflect long-term patterns of exclusion and exploitation cannot be understood as "violations" under the discrimination principle, and thus remedies cannot be won. This narrow reading of what constitutes a violation and can be recognized as discrimination serves to naturalize and affirm the status quo of maldistribution. Anti-discrimination law seeks out aberrant individuals with overtly biased intentions.[14] Meanwhile, all the daily disparities in life chances that shape our world along lines of race, class, indigeneity, disability, national origin, sex, and gender remain untouchable and affirmed as non-discriminatory or even as fair.

The perpetrator perspective also obscures the historical context of racism. Discrimination is understood as the act of taking into account the identity that discrimination law forbids us to take into account (e.g., race, sex, disability) when making a decision, and it does not regard whether the decision-maker is favoring or harming a traditionally excluded group. In this way, the discrimination principle has been used to eviscerate affirmative action and desegregation programs.[15] This erroneously conceptualized "color-blindness" undermines the possibility of remedying the severe racial disparities in the United States that are rooted in slavery, genocide, land theft, internment, and immigration exclusion, as well as racially explicit policies that historically and presently exclude people of color from the benefits of wealth-building programs for US citizens like Social Security, land grants, and credit and other homeownership support.[16] The conditions that created and continue to reproduce such immense disparities are made invisible by the perpetrator perspective's insistence that any consideration of the prohibited category is equally damaging. This model pretends the playing field is equal, and thus any loss or gain in opportunity based on the category is harmful and creates inequality, again serving to declare the racial status quo neutral. This justification for systemic racism masquerading as a logic of equal opportunity gives rise to the myth of "reverse racism," a concept that misunderstands racism to suggest parallel meanings when white people lose opportunities or access through programs aiming to ameliorate impacts of racism and when people of color lose opportunities due to racism.

Discrimination law's reliance on the perpetrator perspective also creates the false impression that the previously excluded or marginalized group is now equal, that fairness has been imposed, and the legitimacy of the distribution of life chances restored. This declaration of equality and fairness papers over the inequalities and disparities that constitute business as usual and allows them to continue. Narrowing political resistance strategies to seeking inclusion in anti-discrimination law makes the mistaken assumption that gaining recognition and inclusion in this way will equalize our life chances and allow us to compete in the (assumed fair) system. This often constitutes a forfeiture of other critiques, as if the economic system is fair but for the fact that bad discriminators are sometimes allowed to fire trans people for being trans.[17] Defining the problem of oppression so narrowly that an anti-discrimination law could solve it erases the complexity and breadth of the systemic, life-threatening

harm that trans resistance seeks to end. Not surprisingly, the rhetoric accompanying these quests for inclusion often focuses on "deserving workers," otherwise known as people whose other characteristics (race, ability, education, class) would have entitled them to a good chance in the workforce were it not for the illegitimate exclusion that happened.[18] Using as examples the least marginalized of the marginalized, so to speak, becomes necessary when issues are framed so narrowly that a person who faces intersecting vectors of harm would be unlikely to benefit from anti-discrimination law. This framing permits—and even necessitates—that efforts for inclusion in the discrimination regime rely on rhetoric that affirms the legitimacy and fairness of the status quo. The inclusion focus of anti-discrimination law and hate crime law campaigns relies on a strategy of simile, essentially arguing "we are just like you; we do not deserve this different treatment because of this one characteristic." To make that argument, advocates cling to the imagined norms of the US social body and choose poster people who are symbolic of US standards of normalcy, whose lives are easily framed by sound bites that resound in shared notions of injustice. "Perfect plaintiffs" for these cases are white people with high-level jobs and lawful immigration status. The thorny issues facing undocumented immigrants, people experiencing simultaneous discrimination through, for example, race, disability, and gender identity, or people in low-wage jobs where it is particularly hard to prove discrimination, are not addressed by anti-discrimination law. Laws created from such strategies, not surprisingly, routinely fail to protect people with more complicated relationships to marginality. These people, who face the worst economic vulnerability, are not lifted up as the "deserving workers" that anti-discrimination law advocates rally to protect.

Hate crime laws are an even more direct example of the limitations of the perpetrator perspective's conception of oppression. Hate crime laws frame violence in terms of individual wrongdoers. These laws and their advocates portray violence through a lens that oversimplifies its operation and suggests that the criminal punishment system is the proper way to solve it. The violence targeted by hate crime laws is that of purportedly aberrant individuals who have committed acts of violence motivated by bias. Hate crime law advocacy advances the fallacy that such violence is especially reprehensible in the eyes of an equality-minded state, and thus must be punished with enhanced force. While it is no doubt true that violence of this kind is frequent and devastating, critics of hate crime legislation argue that hate crime laws are not the answer. First, as mentioned above, hate crime laws have no deterrent effect: people do not read law books before committing acts of violence and choose against bias-motivated violence because it carries a harsher sentence. Hate crime laws do not and cannot actually increase the life chances of the people they purportedly protect.

Second, hate crime laws strengthen and legitimize the criminal punishment system, a system that targets the very people these laws are supposedly passed to protect. The criminal punishment system was founded on and constantly reproduces the same biases (racism, sexism, homophobia, transphobia, ableism, xenophobia) that advocates of these laws want to eliminate. This is no small point, given the rapid growth of the US criminal punishment system in the last few decades, and the gender, race, and ability disparities in whom it targets. The United States now imprisons 25 percent of the world's prisoners although it has only 5 percent of the world's population.[19] Imprisonment in the United States has quadrupled since the 1980s and continues to increase despite the fact that violent crime and property crime have declined since the 1990s.[20] The United States has the highest documented rate of imprisonment per capita of any country.[21] A 2008 report declared that the United States now imprisons one in every 100 adults.[22] Significant racial, gender, ability, and national origin disparities exist in this imprisonment. One in nine black men between the ages of 20 and 34 are imprisoned. While men still vastly outnumber women in prisons, the rate of imprisonment for women is growing far faster, largely the result of sentencing changes created as part of the War on Drugs, including the advent of mandatory minimum sentences for drug convictions. An estimated 27 percent of federal prisoners are noncitizens.[23] While accurate estimates of rates of imprisonment for people with disabilities are difficult to obtain, it is clear that the combination of severe medical neglect

of prisoners, deinstitutionalization of people with psychiatric disabilities without the provision of adequate community services, and the role of drug use in self-medicating account for high rates.[24]

In a context of mass imprisonment and rapid prison growth targeting traditionally marginalized groups, what does it mean to use criminal punishment–enhancing laws to purportedly address violence against those groups? This point has been especially forcefully made by critics who note the origins of the contemporary lesbian and gay rights formation in anti-police activism of the 1960s and 70s, and who question how current lesbian and gay rights work has come to be aligned with a neoliberal "law and order" approach.[25] Could the veterans of the Stonewall and Compton's Cafeteria uprisings against police violence have guessed that a few decades later LGBT law reformers would be supporting passage of the Matthew Shepard and James Byrd, Jr. Hate Crimes Prevention Act, a law that provides millions of dollars to enhance police and prosecutorial resources? Could they have imagined that the police would be claimed as protectors of queer and trans people against violence, while imprisonment and police brutality were skyrocketing? The neoliberal reframing of discrimination and violence that have drastically shifted and undermined strategies of resistance to economic exploitation and state violence produce this narrow law reform agenda that ignores and colludes in the harm and violence faced every day by queer and trans people struggling against racism, ableism, xenophobia, transphobia, homophobia, and poverty.

These concerns are particularly relevant for trans people given our ongoing struggles with police profiling, harassment, violence, and high rates of both youth and adult imprisonment. Trans populations are disproportionately poor because of employment discrimination, family rejection, and difficulty accessing school, medical care, and social services.[26] These factors increase our rate of participation in criminalized work to survive, which, combined with police profiling, produces high levels of criminalization.[27] Trans people in prisons face severe harassment, medical neglect, and violence in both men's and women's facilities. Violence against trans women in men's prisons is consistently reported by prisoners as well as by researchers, and in court cases, testimony from advocates and formerly imprisoned people reveal trends of forced prostitution, sexual slavery, sexual assault, and other violence. Trans people, like all people locked up in women's prisons, are targets of gender-based violence, including sexual assault and rape, most frequently at the hands of correctional staff. Prisoners housed at women's facilities who are perceived as too masculine by prison staff are often at significantly increased risk of harassment and enhanced punishment, including psychologically damaging isolation, for alleged violations of rules against homosexual contact. These prisoners also face a greater risk of assault motivated by an adverse reaction to gender nonconformity.[28]

Since the criminal punishment system itself is a significant source of racialized-gendered violence, increasing its resources and punishment capacity will not reduce violence against trans people. When advocates of hate crime laws frame the criminal punishment systems as a solution to the violence trans people face, they participate in the false logic that criminal punishment produces safety, when it is clear that it is actually a site of enormous violence. Criminal punishment cannot be the method we use to stop transphobia when the criminal punishment system is the most significant perpetrator of violence against trans people. Many commentators have used this support of the expansion of punishment regimes through the advent of hate crime advocacy as an example of co-optation, where resistance struggles that have named certain conditions or violences come to be used to prop up the very arrangements that are harming the people who are resisting. A new mandate to punish transphobic people is added to the arsenal of justifications for a system that primarily locks up and destroys the lives of poor people, people of color, indigenous people, people with disabilities, and immigrants, and that uses gender-based sexual violence as one of its daily tools of discipline against people of all genders.[29]

Much of the thinking behind the need for hate crime and anti-discrimination legislation, including by advocates who recognize how limited these interventions are as avenues for increasing the life chances of trans people, is about the significance of having our experiences of discrimination and violence named in law. The belief that being named in this way has a benefit

for the well-being of trans people has to be reexamined with an understanding that the alleged benefits of such naming provides even greater opportunity for harmful systems to claim fairness and equality while continuing to kill us. Hate crime and anti-discrimination laws declare that punishment systems and economic arrangements are now nontransphobic, yet these laws not only fail to eradicate transphobia but also strengthen systems that perpetrate it.

This analysis illuminates how law reform work that merely tinkers with systems to make them look more inclusive while leaving their most violent operations intact must be a concern of many social movements today. For example, prison abolitionists in the United States argue that the project of prison reform, which is usually aimed at reducing certain kinds of violence or unfairness in the prison system, has always functioned to maintain and expand imprisonment.[30] Prison reform efforts aimed at reducing a variety of harms, such as gender and sexual violence, medical neglect and abuse, and overcrowding, to name but a few, have often been made by well-meaning people who wanted to address the horrors of prison life. But these reform efforts have been incorporated into the project of prison expansion, mobilized as rationales for building and filling more and more prisons. Abolitionists caution that a system designed from its inception as a technology of racialized control through exile and punishment will use any rationale necessary to achieve that purpose. . . . [An] example of particular interest to feminism and trans politics is the 2003 National Prison Rape Elimination Act (NPREA). While passed in the name of preventing sexual assault, the NPREA has been used to further enforce and increase penalties against prisoners for consensual sexual activity, including activities such as handholding. Abolitionist activists doing prisoner support work have pointed out that because some of the main tools the act uses are punishment tools, those tools have become just another part of the arsenal used by punishment systems to increase sentences, target prisoners of color and queer and trans prisoners, and expand imprisonment. It is unclear whether the new rules have reduced sexual violence, but it is clear that they have increased punishment.[31] Activists considering using law reform as a tool, then, have to be extraordinarily vigilant to determine if we are actually strengthening and expanding various systems' capacities to harm, or if our work is part of dismantling those capacities.

In both prison and immigration reform contexts, trans activists are raising concerns about the danger of dividing affected populations by mobilizing ideas about who constitutes a "deserving" or "undeserving" subject. Campaigns that focus on immigrants portrayed as "hard-working" (code for those who do not need support like public benefits or housing) and "law-abiding" (code for those not caught up in the criminal punishment system), or that frame immigration issues in terms of family unity relying on heteropatriarchal constructs, further stigmatize those who do not fit the "deserving" frame, and create policies that only benefit a narrow swath of affected people. Similarly, campaigns about imprisonment that only focus on people convicted of nonviolent crimes, "political" prisoners, or people exonerated by the introduction of new evidence, risk refining the system in ways that justify and legitimize the bulk of its continued operation by eliminating its most obvious contradictions. Three concerns about law reform projects permeate many sites of resistance. First, these projects change only what the law says about what a system is doing, but not its actual impact. Second, they refine a system in ways that help it continue to target the most vulnerable people, while only partially or temporarily removing a few of the less vulnerable from its path. And finally, law reform projects often provide rationales and justifications for the expansion of harmful systems.

Alan Freeman's critique of the perpetrator perspective helps us understand how a discrimination-focused law reform strategy that aims to prohibit the consideration of certain categories of identity in the context of certain decisions (who to hire, fire, evict, house, or assault) misconceives how the violences of racism, ableism, xenophobia, transphobia, sexism, and homophobia operate. Freeman's work shows how discrimination law fails to remedy the harms it claims to attend to, and actually can empower systems that maldistribute life chances. Reconceptualizing the theory of power and struggle that underlies such law reforms allows us to turn our attention to other systems in law that produce structured insecurity and shortened life spans for trans people, and consider alternative avenues of intervention.

As I argue, . . . examining the operation of legal systems that administer life changes at the population level, such as welfare systems, punishment systems, health care systems, and immigration systems, can expose how law operates to sort people into subpopulations facing different exposures to security and insecurity. Looking at sites of the legal administration of societal norms, we can see how certain populations come to have such pervasive experiences with both abandonment and imprisonment. From that vantage point we can strategize about how to use legal reform tools as part of a broader strategy to dismantle capitalism's murderous structures while we build alternative methods of meeting human needs and organizing political participation. Because of the obvious failures of the most popular contemporary law reform strategies to address harms trans people are facing, trans experience can offer a location from which to consider the broader questions of the neoliberal co-optation of social movements through law reform and the institutionalization of resistance, and from which to reframe the problems of violence and poverty that impact marginalized populations in ways that give us new inroads to intervention.

NOTES

1. I shared an earlier version of some of the text in this chapter in my keynote remarks at the Temple Political & Civil Rights Law Review's 2008 Symposium, Intersections of Transgender Lives and the Law. Those remarks were published as "Keynote Address: Trans Law and Politics on a Neoliberal Landscape," *Temple Political & Civil Rights Law Review* 18 (2009): 353–373.
2. National Gay and Lesbian Task Force, "Jurisdictions with Explicitly Transgender-Inclusive Non-Discrimination Laws" (2008), thetaskforce.org/downloads/reports/fact_sheets/all_jurisdictions_ w_ pop_8_08.pdf.

3. National Center for Transgender Equality, "Hate Crimes" (2008), www.nctequality.org/Hate_Crimes.asp.2008.

4. See *Ulane v. Eastern Airlines*, 742 E2d 1081 (7th Cir. 1984), where the Seventh Circuit Court of Appeals found that a transwoman who was dismissed from her job as an airline pilot was not protected under the sex discrimination clause of Title VII of the Civil Rights Act of 1964, holding that "Title VII does not protect transsexuals"; and *Oiler v. Winn Dixie, Louisiana Inc.*, No. Civ. A. 00–3114, 2002 WL 31098541 (E.D.La. Sept. 16, 2002), where the US District Court for the Eastern District of Louisiana found that a man who was fired from his job for occasionally cross-dressing outside of work was not protected under Title VII sex discrimination, even though his behavior had nothing to do with his job performance.

5. Rebecca L. Stotzer, "Gender Identity and Hate Crimes: Violence Against Transgender People in Los Angeles County," *Sexuality Research and Social Policy: Journal of NSRC* 5 (March, 2008), 43–52.

6. .Angela P. Harris, "From Stonewall to the Suburbs? Toward a Political Economy of Sexuality," *William and Mary Bill of Rights Journal* 14 (2006): 1539–1582.

7. See *Goins v. West Group*, 619 N.W.2d 424 (Minn. App. Ct. 2000), where the Minnesota Supreme Court held that employers may restrict bathroom and locker room access based on birth sex; and *Hispanic Aids Forum v. Estate of Bruno*, 16 Misc.3d 960, 839 N.Y.S.2d 691 (N.Y. Sup., 2007) where a New York Supreme Court judge ruled in favor of a nonprofit organization that was facing eviction based on its failure to comply with a landlord's demands that it disclose the birth-sex of its clients. In *Ettsity v. Utah Transit Authority*, 502 F.3d 1215 (10th Cir. 2007), the Tenth Circuit held that a trans woman bus driver who was fired because she used women's restrooms as needed at various stops on her bus route was not protected by Title VII's prohibition against sex discrimination and gender stereotyping.

8. A . . . survey of 6,450 transgender and gender-nonconforming people in the United States found that 57 percent had experienced significant family rejection. Jamie M. Grant, Lisa A. Mottet, and Justin Tanis, *Injustice at Every Turn: A Report of the National Transgender Discrimination Survey*, Executive Summary (Washington, DC: National Gay and Lesbian Task Force and National Center for Transgender Equality, 2011), www.thetaskforce.org/downloads/reports/reports/ntds_summary.pdf.

9. The same study found that 19 percent of transgender and gender non-conforming people had been refused medical treatment due to their gender, 28 percent had postponed medical care when they were sick or injured due to discrimination, and 48 percent had postponed care when they were sick or injured because they could not afford it. The study also found that respondents reported a rate of HIV infection over four times the national average, with rates higher among trans people of color. Grant, et al., *Injustice at Every Turn*.

10. The study also confirmed that trans people live in extreme poverty. Respondents were nearly four times more likely to have a household income of less than $10,000/year compared to the general population. National Gay and Lesbian Task Force and National Center for Transgender Equality, "Injustice at Every Turn."

11. Alan David Freeman, "Legitimizing Racial Discrimination Through Anti-Discrimination Law: A Critical Review of Supreme Court Doctrine," in *Critical Race Studies: The Key Writings That Formed the Movement*, ed. Kimberlé Crenshaw, Neil Gotanda, Garry Peller, and Kendall Thomas (New York: The New Press, 1996), 29–45.

12. See *San Antonio Independent School District v. Rodriguez*, 411 US 1 (1973), where the US Supreme Court held that the severe imbalance in a school district's funding of its primary and secondary

schools based on the income levels of the residents of each district is not an unconstitutional violation of equal protection rights under the Fourteenth Amendment.

13. David M. White, "The Requirement of Race-Conscious Evaluation of LSAT Scores for Equitable Law School Admission," *Berkeley La Raza Law Journal* 12 (2000-2001): 399; Susan Sturm and Lani Guinier, "The Future of Affirmative Action: Reclaiming the Innovative Ideal," *California Law Review* 84 (July 1996): 953.

14. Freeman, "Legitimizing Racial Discrimination Through Anti-Discrimination Law."

15. *Milliken v. Bradley*, 418 US 717 (1974); *Parents Involved in Community Schools v. Seattle School District No. 1*, 551 US 701 (2007).

16. Mazher Ali, Jeanette Huezo, Brian Miller, Wanjiku Mwangi, and Mike Prokosch, *State of the Dream 2011: Austerity for Whom?* (Boston: United for a Fair Economy, 2011), www.faireconomy.org/files/ State_of_the_Dream_2011.pdf.

17. Dan Irving, "Normalized Transgressions: Legitimizing the Transsexual Body as Productive," *Radical History Review 100* (2008) 38–59.

18. Irving, "Normalized Transgressions." Several significant famous trans discrimination cases follow this pattern, with both media and advocates portraying the assimilable characteristics of the trans person in order to emphasize their deserving nature. One example is the highly publicized case of Dian Schroer who won a lawsuit after she lost a job at the Library of Congress when she disclosed her trans identity. *Time* magazine described her as an ex-Special Forces colonel. . . . Schroer was a dream candidate, a guy out of a Tom Clancy novel: he had jumped from airplanes, undergone grueling combat training in extreme heat and cold, commanded hundreds of soldiers, helped run Haiti during the U.S. intervention in the '90s—and, since 9/11, he had been intimately involved in secret counterterrorism planning at the highest levels of the Pentagon. He had been selected to organize and run a new, classified antiterror organization, and in that position he had routinely briefed Defense Secretary Donald Rumsfeld. He had also briefed Vice President Cheney more than once. Schroer had been an action hero, but he also had the contacts and intellectual dexterity to make him an ideal congressional analyst. Schroer's public persona as a patriot and terrorist-fighter was used by advocates to promote the idea of her deservingness in ways that those concerned about the racist, anti-immigrant, imperialist War on Terror might take issue with. Critics have similarly pointed out dynamics of deservingness that determine which queer and trans murder victims become icons in the battle for hate crime legislation. White victims tend to be publicly remembered (e.g., Harvey Milk, Brandon Teena, Matthew Shepard), their lives memorialized in films and movies *(Milk, Boys Don't Cry, Larabee)*, and laws named after them (Matthew Shepard Local Law Enforcement Enhancement Act). The names of these white victims and the struggles for healing and justice on the part of their friends and family are in greater circulation than victims of color through media and nonprofit channels even though people of color lose their lives at higher rates. Sanesha Stewart, Amanda Milan, Marsha P. Johnson, Duanna Johnson, and Ruby Ordeñana are just a few of the trans women of color whose murders have been mourned by local communities but mostly ignored by media, large nonprofits, and lawmakers.

19. Roy Walmsley, "World Prison Population List," 7th ed. (London: International Centre for Prison Studies, 2005).

20. US Department of Justice, "Key Crime and Justice Facts at a Glance" (2009), www.ojp.usdoj.gov/ bjs/glance.htm.

21. Walmsley, "World Prison Population List."

22. The PEW Center on the States, *One in 100: Behind Bars in America 2008* (2008), www.pewcenteronthestates.org/uploadedFiles/8015PCTS_Prison08_FINAL_2-1-1_FORWEB.pdf.

23. Government Accounting Office, "Information on Criminal Aliens Incarcerated in Federal and State Prisons and Local Jails," congressional briefing, March 25, 2005, http://gao.gov/new.items/d05337r.pdf.

24. Lauraet Magnani and Harmon L. Wray, *Beyond Prisons: A New Interfaith Paradigm for Our Failed Prison System,* a report by the American Friends Service Committee, Criminal Justice Task Force (Minneapolis: Fortress Press, 2006).

25. Anna M. Agathangelou, D. Morgan Bassichis, and Tamara L. Spira, "Intimate Investments: Homonormativity, Global Lockdown, and the Seductions of Empire," *Radical History Review* no. 100 (Winter 2008): 120–143; Morgan Bassichis, Alex Lee, and Dean Spade, "Building an Abolitionist Trans Movement with Everything We've Got," in *Captive Genders,* ed. Nat Smith and Eric A. Stanley (Oakland, CA: AK Press, 2011); Magnani and Wray, *Beyond Prisons.*

26. Dean Spade, "Documenting Gender," *Hastings Law Journal* 59 (2008):731; Chris Daley and Shannon Minter, *Trans Realities: A Legal Needs Assessment of San Francisco's Transgender Communities* (San Francisco: Transgender Law Center, 2003).

27. Joey L. Mogul, Andrea J. Ritchie, and Kay Whitlock, *Queer (In) Justice* (Boston: Beacon Press, 2011).

28. D. Morgan Bassichis, *"It's War in Here": A Report on the Treatment of Transgender & Intersex People in New York State Men's Prisons* (New York: Sylvia Rivera Law Project, 2007), http://srlp.org/files/warinhere.pdf; Alexander L. Lee, *Gendered Crime & Punishment: Strategies to Protect Transgender, Gender Variant & Intersex People in America's Prisons* (pts 1 & 2), GIC TIP J. (Summer 2004), GIC TIP J. (Fall 2004); Christopher D. Man and John P. Cronan, "Forecasting Sexual Abuse in Prison: The Prison Subculture of Masculinity as a Backdrop for 'Deliberate Indifference,'" *Journal of Criminal Law and Criminology* 92 (2002):127; Alex Coolman, Lamar Glover, and Kara Gotsch, *Still in Danger: The Ongoing Threat of Sexual Violence Against Transgender Prisoners* (Los Angeles: Stop Prisoner Rape and the ACLU National Prison Project, 2005), www.justdetention.org/pdf/stillindanger.pdf; Janet Baus and Dan Hunt, *Cruel and Unusual* (New York: Reid Productions, 2006).

29. Morgan Bassichis, Alex Lee, and Dean Spade, "Building an Abolitionist Trans Movement with Everything We've Got," in *Captive Genders: Transembodiment and the Prison Industrial Complex,* ed. Nat Smith and Eric A. Stanley (Oakland, CA: AK Press, 2011); Agathangelou, Bassichis, and Spira, "Intimate Investments"; Dean Spade and Craig Willse, "Confronting the Limits of Gay Hate Crimes Activism: A Radical Critique," *Chicano-Latino Law Review* 21 (2000): 38; Sarah Lamble, "Retelling Racialized Violence, Remaking White Innocence: The Politics of Interlocking Oppressions in Transgender Day of Remembrance," *Sexuality Research and Social Policy* 5 (March 2008): 24–42.

30. Angela Y. Davis, *Are Prisons Obsolete?* (New York: Seven Stories Press, 2003).

31. Gabriel Arkles's work has exposed how rules that purport to protect prisoners from sexual violence are frequently used to punish consensual sexual or friendship relationships, prohibit masturbation, and target queer and gender non-conforming prisoners. The existence of such rules can also increase risks of sexual behavior and create opportunities for blackmail and abuse by corrections officers. See letter from Chase Strangio and Z Gabriel Arkles to Attorney General Eric Holder, May 10, 2010, page 9, http://srlp.org/files/SRLP%20PREA%20comment%20Docket%20no%20OAG-131.pdf; Gabriel Arkles, *Transgender Communities and the Prison Industrial Complex,* lecture, Northeastern University School of Law, February 2010. Arkles's lecture offers as an example of this type of problematic policy-making, Idaho's Prison Rape Elimination Provision (Control No. 325.02.01.001, 2004), www.idoc.idaho.gov/policy/int3250201001.

pdf, which includes a prohibition on "male" prisoners having a "feminine or effeminate hairstyle." Email from Gabriel Arkles, February 21, 2011 (on file with the author). Further controversy has emerged around the NPREA since the Department of Justice proposed national standards "for the detection, prevention, reduction, and punishment of prison rape, as mandated by" the NPREA, which exclude immigration facilities. See National Juvenile Defender Center & the Equity Project, Transgender Law Center, Lambda Legal Education and Defense Fund, National Center for Lesbian Rights, American Civil Liberties Union, Sylvia Rivera Law Project, National Center for Transgender Equality, "Protecting Lesbian, Gay, Bisexual, Transgender, Intersex, and Gender Nonconforming people from Sexual Abuse and Harassment in Correctional Settings," Comments Submitted in Response to Docket No. OAG-131; AG Order No. 3244-2011 National Standards to Prevent, Detect, and Respond to Prison Rape, April 4, 2011, 47–48 (on file with the author); Human Rights Watch, ACLU Washington Legislative Office, Immigration Equality, Just Detention International, National Immigrant Justice Center, National Immigration Forum, Physicians for Human Rights, Prison Fellowship, Southern Center for Human Rights, Texas Civil Rights Project, Women's Refugee Commission, "US: Immigration Facilities Should Apply Prison Rape Elimination Act Protections: Letter to US President Barack Obama" (February 15, 2011), http://www.hrw.org/es/news/2011/02/15/us-immigration-facilities-should-apply-prison-rape-elimination-act-protections.

ASHWINI TAMBE

50. INDIAN AMERICANS IN THE TRUMP ERA: A TRANSNATIONAL FEMINIST ANALYSIS

Transnational feminist theory is frequently understood to be only concerned with the cross-border circulation of people, capital, or ideas. My goal in this brief essay is to also illustrate its uses at a different scale: intensely local, nation-oriented political practices and identities. I focus on the context of the aftermath of the 2016 US election of Donald Trump and specifically how Indian Americans have responded to rising levels of xenophobia. I note how progressive organizing has given rise to flexible transnational solidarities. I also focus on a contradiction in mainstream Indian American political leanings: even as they oppose a rightward tilt in the United States, some support a right-wing government in India. I probe this contradiction by shifting focus to India and describe its history of education and religion to explain why the political identity of some Indian Americans varies depending on geography. In both locations—India and the United States—I analyze the role of state policy in shaping political and economic identities. While gender is not a central category in my exploration, transnational feminism's analytic angles and philosophical commitments inform my approach. I treat this case as an exercise in using a transnational feminist lens to better understand political contradictions and offer a potential expansion of how we understand transnational feminism.

Before describing the context, let me revisit the broad contours of transnational feminist theory. Unlike other uses of "transnational," transnational feminist theory does not just mark connections that cross borders; rather, it places networks under critical scrutiny to diagnose how power operates in asymmetric and multidirectional ways (Grewal and Kaplan; Modern Girl Around the World Group; Tambe). It holds that national frameworks can limit research and movement agendas; but even as it draws connections across

national locations, it is critical of universalizing narratives that purvey imperial or parochial interests (Sangtin Writers and Richa Nagar). Apart from decentering both national and universalizing orthodoxies, transnational feminist approaches also unsettle nationalisms. Drawing on a longstanding feminist critique of the patriarchal underpinnings of nationalism—including many anticolonial nationalisms—transnational feminists urge critical perspectives on ethnic, religious, and economic nationalisms. Transnational feminism is also attuned to the constitutive power of transnational forces such as capital and migration in shaping apparently local problems. Unpacking transnational elements of local phenomena allows for a more fluid understanding of how these phenomena emerge and avoids their reification. Indeed, a signature contribution of transnational feminist approaches has been to understand identity categories in historically specific, non-universalizing ways (Swarr and Nagar). In this essay, I illustrate several of these elements of transnational feminist analysis and their political relevance in the late 2010s.

INDIAN AMERICAN IDENTITY IN TRANSNATIONAL PERSPECTIVE

Let us start with how transnational feminism approaches identity. Every identity category conveys a constellation of associated meanings—racial, sexual, economic, gendered, and national. An important insight of transnational feminist theory is that these meanings are site-specific: they accrue in the context of geographic and historical location. Racial formations vary widely across location, and so the meaning of racial categories, and the political alignments these meanings spur, are also not stable. They are often shaped in unseen ways by state policy. The economic meanings associated with the term "Indian American" have long been shaped by US state practices, for instance. The 1965 Immigration and Naturalization Act, which sought to attract skilled labor to the country, dictated which immigrants from India would be allowed to enter. Its preferential quotas for those in technical and medical professions has led, over the last fifty years, to the association between Indian Americans and these professions. Effectively, this law has meant that a large component of this 4 million-strong ethnic group is wealthy; it has the highest median annual income of $88,000 (Pew Research Center). In the Britain, by contrast, Indians (or Asians, in common parlance) are associated with a broader range of jobs, such as those in restaurants and transportation; theirs is a much more strongly working-class identity. Although Indians migrated to both North America and the Britain long before the 1960s, the largest numbers of Indian immigrants in the United States arrived after the 1965 Act, thereby defining the class coordinates of Indian American identity (Bhatt and Iyer).

A second principle of transnational feminist approaches is to stay attuned to shifts in meanings of identities. Political changes, in particular, can sometimes generate rapid reconfigurations. The category "Indian American" has gained new meanings in the context of a rightward tilt in US electoral politics. In the first twelve months after the election of Donald Trump, there has been a discernible shift in how Indian Americans are viewed. For two decades, the relative prosperity of the majority of Indian Americans meant that they were primarily described as a wealthy immigrant group. But rising xenophobia and economic nationalism have now led to marking Indian Americans, like several other immigrant groups, as unwelcome outsiders. In February and March 2017, a string of hate crimes across the United States targeted Indians. The first hate crime casualty in the wake of Donald Trump's inauguration was an Indian man: in February 2017, Srinivas Kuchibotla was murdered by a white man, Adam Purinton, who yelled "get out of my country" as he shot him. (Chillingly, the first person killed in a hate crime following the 9/11 attacks was also of Indian origin—a Sikh man, Balbir Singh Sodhi, was murdered on September 15.) Six Indian-origin men have been killed by shooting or stabbing in Kansas, Washington, Idaho, California, and South Carolina in incidents being investigated as hate crimes or potential hate crimes (Press Trust of India; AB Wire; Fuchs; Burch; Indo-Asian News Service).

The category Indian American is, in this historical moment, becoming unmoored from its class-based referents. It is now a far more racially charged status. Long hailed in conservative discourses as a "model minority"—itself a dubious phrase that reinforces anti-black and anti-Latino racial hierarchies, as Vijay Prashad notes—Indian Americans no longer feel cushioned from incidents of random violence. To be clear, Indian Americans have been targeted in the past by sporadic hate crimes, such as in 1987 in New Jersey when gangs that called themselves "dot-busters" targeted Hindu women who wore *bindi*s on their foreheads. But a sudden spike in violence after Donald Trump's election is clear: the 150 recorded incidents of hate against Indian Americans in the first half of 2017 have already outstripped the total for the entirety of the previous year (Modi). The violence in 2017 also appears to be spread across the country, with 30 percent of incidents in California and 30 percent in New York state, and the rest distributed across the US South and Midwest (Modi). Groups recording incidents of hate against Indian Americans note that verbal and written assaults have risen starkly since the election—those harboring racist views feel more emboldened to express them verbally through casual forms of microaggression such as jokes about purported terrorist links, questions about citizenship, or just fewer smiles (Modi). Police officers question the immigration status of Indians in irrelevant situations (Bartolotta).

Islamophobia is undeniably a major motivation for much of the hostility. Middle Eastern and Muslim people have been the target of sustained animosity since 9/11. To uninformed US eyes, South Asian Sikhs, Hindus, and Muslims are indistinguishable from Middle Eastern people. In two of the attacks mentioned above, the murderers mistook their targets for Iranians or Arabs. Indian American vulnerability is, in one sense, of a piece with that faced by Middle Eastern Americans.

In addition, though, the current targeting of Indian Americans draws from a sense of white economic entitlement. Indian Americans are strongly associated with the information technology sector and targeted as agents of globalization who "take away opportunities" from purportedly deserving Americans. The murder of Gagandeep Singh on August 29, 2017, in Bonner, Idaho, is telling: he was a 22-year-old Sikh software engineering student who worked as a cab driver, and he was murdered by a 19-year-old white man, Jacob Coleman, who claimed to have been upset about being denied entry into Gonzaga University (Cockburn). It is also telling that hate crimes are concentrated in California and New York, where Indians can be found in large numbers and where they have an identity distinct from Arab Americans. The narrative that foreigners "steal" jobs and opportunities has a long precedent in US history: Mexican, Chinese, and Japanese immigrants have borne similar scapegoating for economic downturns at various successive times (Takaki; Balderamma and Rodriguez; Prashad). Indian Americans are dealing with a contemporary inflection of this scapegoating.

The current nativism does not simply privilege those born in the United States; it is also white supremacist. In media stories about the elections, the terms "poor," "working class," and "rural," used to refer to those most disenfranchised by economic globalization, are code words for a white underclass. This racially limited sense of the term "poor" and indeed of "working class" blurs from view the poverty that urban Black and immigrant workers have struggled with for decades. The needs of women workers for childcare, healthcare, and eldercare are also consistently overlooked when the prototypical working-class figures are unemployed white male factory workers. The media focus on this disenchanted subsection of the white population ignores the struggles of those who have neither enjoyed the security of racial privilege nor the benefits of full citizenship. Implicitly, this framing pits class against race, and the US-born white working class against those from elsewhere. Feminist theory's standard invocation to think about categories such as class, race, gender, and nation in interconnected ways has yet to make serious inroads into mass media discourses. Intersectional feminists such as Patricia Hill Collins reject the compulsion to accord primacy to single categories and instead analyze categories in connection with each other, reminding us to specify, which women? which workers? which people of color? Transnational feminist theory also presumes that identity categories are connected, but it offers an important nuance: it sees these categories as mutually constitutive—they come into being and into meaning through each other, with no prior stable meaning. They also emerge in historically specific ways. In US popular culture, for instance, the term "working class" has long held a negative valence (unlike countries with stronger social democratic leanings), but is now being reconfigured in sympathetic ways as a vulnerable white identity. Both intersectional and transnational feminist approaches push us to question such unstated racial/gendered/nationalist uses of the term "working class." The virulence of white supremacist discourse in this moment calls for a robust critical response.

SOUTH ASIAN ACTIVISM AGAINST XENOPHOBIA

The response of Indian Americans to xenophobia has been remarkably vocal and organized. Several progressive organizations are tracking the increase in hate crimes and specifically attending to those most vulnerable. One such group is SAALT (South Asian Americans Leading Together), a staffed organization that engages national policies affecting South Asians. The South Asian group Desis Rising Up and Moving (DRUM) was one of the first organizations in the country to respond to the Trump administration's January 2017 ban on travelers from Muslim-majority countries by mobilizing a rally at JFK airport in New York City (Rosenberg). The South Asian-led New York Taxi Workers Alliance called for a one-hour work stoppage at the airport to protest the ban (Rosenberg). DRUM has also spearheaded creating "Hate-Free Zones"—a neighborhood-based system for defending those who are vulnerable to hate crimes and deportation—in Jackson Heights, New York, in the wake of the November 2016 elections (Connelly).

Most progressive Indian American activism takes place under a "South Asian" banner that includes immigrants from Pakistan, Bangladesh, Sri Lanka, and Nepal. This transnational ethic overcomes animosities bred by nationalist discourses between Indians and Pakistanis, and Bangladeshis and Pakistanis. It stands for solidarity across multiple religions—Hindu, Muslim, Sikh, Jain, Christian, and Buddhist. Progressive South Asian organizations are also transnational in the connections forged with other US racial/ethnic groups, such as Latinx and Caribbean immigrant rights groups. They are focused on building solidarity with other threatened groups and meeting the needs of diverse working-class constituencies. They are responding to the increased crackdowns on undocumented immigrants who hail primarily from Central America and the Caribbean. Hindu temples such as Shanti Bhavan Mandir in Queens (New York), like churches and other places of worship, are proposing to shelter people who want to resist deportation efforts of Immigration and Customs Enforcement (ICE).

Another creative idea engaged by South Asian activists is asking those with the security of citizenship to behave like "less assimilated" immigrants—to not reveal their citizenship, speak languages other than English in public, wear non-assimilative clothing—as a means to confuse the clear divide drawn between insiders and outsiders. Such intra-ethic and interethnic solidarity practices imply that the best way to counter white nationalist targeting of specific minority groups is to refuse hierarchies between "good" and "bad" immigrants.

Many of these activist initiatives are women-led. SAALT'S executive director for its first decade was lawyer Deepa Iyer, and its current board consists mostly of women. The New York Taxi Workers Alliance was founded by Rutgers women's studies graduate Bhairavi Desai. Four of DRUM's board members are women. Perhaps it is not an accident that transnational politics comes easily to such activists: they embody and fight multiple oppressions simultaneously and recognize the value of coalitions. Their work is a reminder that the transnational can be found not just at junctions of national boundaries, but even within local sites that are oriented toward national politics. Countries such as the United States are constitutively transnational, as historians of the Americas frequently point out, and it is important to assert transnational connections and solidarities within its bounds as a corrective to assimilationist and racially homogenous visions of national identity (Bayly et al.; Briggs et al.).

ELECTORAL LEANINGS AND CONTRADICTIONS

The relatively vigorous mobilization by Indian Americans is not surprising when one considers their leanings in US electoral politics. Of all Asian American groups,

they are most likely to lean left of center, according to the Pew Research Center ("Five Facts"). The majority of Indian Americans—over 65 percent—have historically voted Democrat (Bhattacharya), notwithstanding a small but visible pocket of Trump supporters (Ali). Becoming a racial minority in the United States has frequently pushed Indian Americans to align against a Republican party hospitable to racist candidates.

And yet, although a majority of Indian Americans are critical of the Trump administration, some are uncritical supporters of a right-wing party running the government in India, the Bharatiya Janata Party (BJP). Under the BJP government, there has been an alarming rise in the persecution of Muslims and Christians for private practices such as embarking on romantic relationships with Hindus. In the last two years, mobs have lynched Muslim men for eating beef and Dalits for skinning cows (Nair). Ironically, and much to the frustration of progressive Indian American activists, some of those Indian Americans who feel fragile in the face of white nationalism in the United States seem oblivious to the threats posed by Hindu nationalism to religious minorities in India. Some diasporic Indians even financially support the BJP (Sabrang Communication). The Overseas Friends of the BJP is an organization with chapters in the United States, United Kingdom, and Canada (and with 4,000 members in the United States alone) that seeks to improve the public image of the BJP and whose volunteers campaigned for the BJP in India. When BJP leader Narendra Modi visited the United States in 2014, he received a "wildly enthusiastic reception" (Sengupta).

Unpacking this contradiction requires closer attention to Indian history. The Indian state has subsidized higher education in India almost since the country's independence. Many Indians who arrived in the United States after 1965 and especially in the 1990s were upper-caste Hindus who benefited from the highly affordable training in institutions subsidized by the Indian state. The Indian state funded such institutions for decades because upper-caste planners prioritized higher education over primary and secondary education. The principal beneficiaries of higher education subsidies have been upper-caste students who sailed into elite institutions by drawing on accumulated cross-generational investment in learning that did not require the boost of free public schooling. Yet very few Indians in the technology and medicine fields view themselves as beneficiaries of the Indian state's largesse. Instead, their orientation toward the Indian state is frequently cynical and contemptuous—they view the Indian state as an obstacle to their personal success. Rather than recognizing the state-funded scaffolding that facilitated their well-being, they frequently espouse anti-state free market fundamentalism.

There are notable similarities between right-wing tactics in India and the United States. Both the BJP and the US Republican party combine economic and religious conservatism. More specifically, they strive to make dominant groups feel threatened and vulnerable. Much of the BJP's success relies on the sedimenting of two ideas: that education and employment quotas for lower-caste and Dalit (formerly termed "untouchable") Indians in universities and government jobs threaten upper-caste Hindus, and that Muslims (both Indian and Pakistani) threaten Hindu survival. The idea that the Hindu majority in India is besieged might seem bizarre to outside observers, but there is nothing laughable about the violence that the militant right in India promotes. Vigilante gunmen have shot four journalists and activists critical of Hindu extremism over the period from 2013 to 2017 (Gopal and Joshi). So, it is frustrating when Indian Americans who rail against hate crimes in the United States remain unperturbed by hate crimes in their countries of origin. It is possible to speculate that their sense of being a besieged minority in the United States *fuels* their endorsement of the BJP's call to defend "besieged" upper-caste Hindus in India.

These contradictory political ideologies among some Indian Americans highlight the transnational feminist insight that geographic differences matter: political leanings vary depending on how identities are socially construed. As a racial minority in the United States, Indian Americans are broadly oriented against the xenophobic right; however, this does not imply, or lead to, an empathetic political position toward minorities in India. Many immigrant Indians continue to nurture their caste- and class-based identifications, incorporating the new injuries and affective states they experience in the United States. Indeed the problematic gender, caste, and class exclusions embedded in Hindu nationalism, recede from view as Indian Americans observe their old homeland from a distance. In this respect they are not unique; other diasporic groups, such as some US Jewish organizations, espouse hardline political positions on matters pertaining to the "homeland" but not in the countries where they actually live. They nurture a sense of injury that draws from their treatment in one locale without bearing its full political consequence in the other. Such diasporic groups support through remote means—blogging, funding, social media—the growth of right-wing forces in distant locations. Such practices remind us to not restrict the ambit of our analyses of local politics to national boundaries and to deeply engage with the history of all relevant locations, as Leela Fernandes urges.

I began this piece by arguing for the potential of transnational feminist analysis to illuminate local politics and to spur solidarities. In order to understand the complexities of political identities such as those of Indian Americans, it was necessary to not only examine the history of Indians in the United States but also to understand the context of Indian education policies. I have delved into both local histories in order to dissect the contradiction of how political ideologies vary across geography. In so doing, I have de-emphasized circulation, which is typically an important category in transnational analyses. Implicit in the notion of circulation is that entities—whether capital, bodies, ideas, or identities—travel across borders in an intact form. Instead, I suggest considering how political leanings and ideologies are geographically contingent: they are responsive to different histories, and they accrue new meanings and generate new solidarities all the time.

Transnational feminist theory is also especially valuable for its trenchant critiques of nationalism as we examine right-leaning trends in contemporary electoral politics around the globe. In the 2010s, several countries—India, Turkey, Philippines, Russia—have witnessed the rise of authoritarians such as Narenda Modi, Recep Erdogan, Rodrigo Duterte, and Vladimir Putin. There has been a worrisome rise in virulent nationalisms—white nationalism in the United States and Europe, economic nationalism in the Britain and United States, religious nationalism in India and Turkey, or militarist nationalism in Russia and the Philippines. A combination of economic nationalism and xenophobia has propelled dramatic policy shifts such as Britain's exit from the European Union. Trump appears on the scene in the United States in the wake of successful polarizing strategies by right-leaning politicians in several locations.

So what is the ideal political response to this moment? The transnational and interethnic solidarity demonstrated by groups such as DRUM and SAALT offers an important model. These groups implicitly refuse the right-wing narrative that working-class people support xenophobic cultural nationalism. Instead, they draw on a more expansive understanding of the term "working class," centering the people of color who comprise this group. They forge links with other movements, such as that of the Dreamers and Black Lives Matter. Indeed, they exemplify what we might see as a specifically working-class cosmopolitanism—a form of mutual understanding and respect borne out of actual contact between working people. Intercultural understanding is not, as US right-wing commentators narrate it, an elite luxury. It is exercised in everyday situations where working people need to get along: taxi drivers and convenience store owners who observe and serve hundreds of diverse customers per week, or salons shared by Indian and African American hairdressers, or Indian restaurant kitchens where non-Indian staff make Indian food. It is illustrated in the unique example of the Punjabi Mexican American community of Yuba City, California, which was formed, as Karen Leonard describes, by intermarriage between Punjabi and Mexican farmers in the early 1900s. These examples are a reminder of the value of forging connections and alliances across different identities around common issues, planks, and priorities. Transnational feminist theorists such as Grewal and Kaplan offered this suggestion in the 1990s as a corrective to a feminist politics built around sameness. It remains an urgent and even more widely useful strategy today.

REFERENCES

AB Wire. "Indian American Store Clerk Stabbed to Death in Modesto, Calif." *American Bazaar Online*. May 7, 2017. https://www.americanbazaaronline.com/2017/05/07/indian-american-sikh-man-stabbed-over-cigarette-dies-in-modesto-city425127/.

Ali, Rozina. "Hindus for Trump." *The New Yorker*, November 7, 2016. https://www.newyorker.com/magazine/2016/11/07/hindus-for-trump.

Balderamma, Francisco, and Raymond Rodriguez. *Decade of Betrayal: Mexican Repatriation in the 1930s*. University of New Mexico Press, 2006.

Bartolotta, Devin. "Bel Air Woman's Immigration Status Questioned in Own Neighborhood" *CBS Baltimore*. January 27, 2017. http://baltimore.cbslocal.com/2017/01/27/bel-air-womans-immigration-status-questioned-in-own-neighborhood/.

Bayly, Chris, Sven Beckert, Matthew Connelly, Isabel Hofmeyr, Wendy Kozol, and Patricia Seed. "AHR Conversation: On Transnational History." *American Historical Review*, vol. 111, no. 5, December 2006, pp. 1441–1464.

Bhatt, Amy, and Nalini Iyer. *Roots and Reflections*. University of Washington Press, 2013.

Bhattacharya, Suryatapa. "This Survey Shows How Indian-Americans Plan to Vote in the U.S. Election," *Wall Street Journal*, May 27, 2016. https://blogs.wsj.com/indiarealtime/2016/05/27/this-survey-shows-how-indian-americans-plan-to-vote-in-the-u-s-election/.

Briggs, Laura, Gladys McCormick, and J. T. Way. "Transnationalism: A Category of Analysis." *American Quarterly*, vol. 60, no 3, September 2008, pp. 625–648.

Burch, Audra D. S. "He Became A Hate Crime Victim; She Became a Widow." *New York Times*, July 8, 2017. https://www.nytimes.com/2017/07/08/us/he-became-a-hate-crime-victim-she-became-a-widow.html?mcubz=3.

Cockburn, Harry. "Asians 'Being Victimised' Because of Trump's Policies, Says Family of Murdered Sikh Man." *The Independent*, August 31, 2017. http://www.independent.co.uk/news/world/americas/murder-idaho-gagandeep-singh-taxi-driver-jacob-corban-coleman-racial-hatred-manmohan-singh-raju-a7922081.html.

Collins, Patricia Hill. *Black Feminist Thought: Knowledge, Consciousness, and the Politics of Empowerment*. Hyman, 1990.

Connelly, Joel. "Washington Is Declared a 'Hate Free Zone' by Inslee, Democratic Politicians." *San Francisco Chronicle*, December 19, 2016. http://www.sfchronicle.com/local/politics/article-Comments/Washington-declared-Hate-Free-State-by-Inslee-10806801.php.

Fernandes, Leela. *Transnational Feminism in the United States: Knowledge, Ethics, Power*. NYU Press, 2013.

Fuchs, Chris. "California Police Search for Suspects in Stabbing Death of Indian Man." *NBC News*, May 9, 2017. https://www.nbcnews.com/news/asian-america/california-police-search-suspects-stabbing-death-indian-man-n757116.

Gopal, Vikram, and Yogesh Joshi. "Gauri Lankesh's Death Brings Focus Back on Kalburgi, Pansare, Dabholkar Murders." *Hindustan Times*, September 7, 2017. http://www.hindustantimes.com/india-news/gauri-lankesh-s-killing-brings-focus-back-on-murders-of-right-wing-critics-kalburgi-pansare-dabholkar/story-XgzqWPjEJFyqhgIcVQUMaN.html.

Grewal, Inderpal, and Caren Kaplan. *Scattered Hegemonies*. University of Minnesota Press, 1994.

Indo-Asian News Service. "Sikh Driver Stabbed to Death in Taxi." *India Abroad*, August 31, 2017. https://www.indiaabroad.com/campus/sikh-american-cab-driver-stabbed-to-death-in-taxi/article_ec9b7c24-8e6e-11e7-ace5-a318b5393ef8.html.

Leonard, Karen. *Making Ethnic Choices: California's Punjabi Mexican Americans*. Temple University Press, 1994.

Modern Girl Around the World Group. *The Modern Girl Around the World*. Duke University Press, 2009.

Modi, Radha. "This Week in Hate." *SAALT*, August 25, 2017. http://saalt.org/category/blog/hate-crimes/.

Nair, Supriya. "The Meaning of India's 'Beef Lynchings.'" *The Atlantic*, July 24, 2017. https://www.theatlantic.com/international/archive/2017/07/india-modi-beef-lynching-muslim-partition/533739/.

Pew Research Center. "Five Facts about Indian Americans." *Fact Tank*, 2014. http://www.pewresearch.org/fact-tank/2014/09/30/5-facts-about-indian-americans/.

Prashad, Vijay. *Karma of Brown Folk*. University of Minnesota Press, 2000.

Press Trust of India. "Indian Origin Man Shot Dead in the United States." *Times of India*, March 4, 2017. http://timesofindia.indiatimes.com/nri/us-canada-news/indian-origin-businessman-shot-dead-in-the-us/articleshow/57462656.cms.

Rosenberg, Eli. "Protest Grows 'Out of Nowhere' at Kennedy Airport After Iraqis Are Detained." *New York Times*, January 28, 2017. https://www.nytimes.com/2017/01/28/nyregion/jfk-protests-trump-refugee-ban.html.

Sabrang Communication. *The Foreign Exchange of Hate: IDRF and the American Funding of Hindutva*. 2002. http://www.sacw.net/2002/FEHi/FEH/.

Sangtin Writers and Richa Nagar. *Playing With Fire*. Minneapolis: University of Minnesota Press, 2006.

Sengupta, Somini. "Narendra Modi Outlines Goals for India on Eve of a Visit With Obama." *New York Times*, September 28, 2014. https://www.nytimes.com/2014/09/29/world/asia/narendra-modi-madison-square-garden-obama.html?hp&action=click&pgtype=Homepage&version=HpSumSmallMedia&module=first-column-region&region=top-news&WT.nav=top-news&_r=0.

Swarr, Amanda, and Richa Nagar. "Dismantling Assumptions: Interrogating "Lesbian" Struggles for Identity and Survival in India and South Africa." *Signs: Journal of Women in Culture and Society*, vol. 9, no. 2, 2004, pp. 491–516.

Takaki, Ronald. *A Different Mirror: A History of Multicultural America*. Little Brown and Co., 1993.

Tambe, Ashwini. "Transnational Feminist Studies: A Brief Sketch" *New Global Studies*, vol. 4, no. 1, 2010, article 7.

BARBARA BOSWELL

51. AFRICAN WOMEN'S LITERATURE AS FEMINIST THEORY

At the heart of the teaching and theorizing enterprise of feminist studies, in the Global South and elsewhere, is a political engagement with epistemology—not only the processes and trajectories of knowledge production but also the very fabric of what counts as knowledge. The arena of knowledge production is contested terrain: not everyone has access to the tools, methods, and educational opportunities needed to construct what is considered knowledge in formal academic spaces; not all knowledges, once produced, are considered as carrying equivalent weight. Feminist theory originating in the Global North, most notably the United States, has been exhaustively critiqued during the second wave of US feminism for its eurocentrism and, in transnational contexts, its unreflexive, imperialist tendencies, which flatten out differences by making white, middle-class, American women the center of its analysis (hooks 1981; Crenshaw 1989; Baca Zinn and Dill 1996). This universalizing tendency leaves out those at the margins of its theory construction—women of color in the United States; lesbians, queer and trans women; and so-called third world women in the Global South.

Gayatri Spivak's well-cited question, "can the subaltern speak?" remains salient when one considers global feminist theory-making. The circuits of dissemination and the politics of citation of theory produced in Western locations often sees theory constructed in the Global South—Africa, Latin America, Asia—left unexamined and not cited in the ongoing production of global feminist knowledge. African feminist Amina Mama wryly sums up this tendency:

> The words and testimonies of rural women, township women, sex workers and slaves are elicited, organised into soundbites, to be replayed during prime time, authenticating someone else's argument at some other location, or otherwise appropriated as raw material in the global economy of knowledge production. What this comes down to is this: the more we speak, the more they write. (Mama 20)

Mama here points out the invisibilization of postcolonial, African women as reasoning subjects and knowledge producers in their own right.

For feminists working in the Global South it is imperative to strategize around this exclusion. This requires a critical engagement with epistemology, one that asks us in the field of gender and feminist studies to approach knowledge production through the lens of power, to note how asymmetrical power relations at the global and local levels inflect the outcomes of epistemic endeavors, and to deconstruct approaches to knowledge production that naturalize the West as the only source of legitimate knowledge. Those of us engaged in teaching, writing, and reading from the location of the interdiscipline of feminist studies are therefore tasked with pointing out the gaps in seamless constructions of Eurocentric, androcentric paradigms of knowledge production as complete.

Our investment in feminism requires us to think, read, and write critically about the absence of African and other postcolonial feminist theory in our work. We are additionally tasked with filling in those gaps with our scholarship; and enabling newer generations to produce decolonial, feminist knowledges that are ultimately liberatory and that decenter the West as the only site of feminist knowledge production. We have a responsibility to read widely, actively searching for texts and theories that decenter North America and Europe as the only sites where feminist knowledge is made.

This essay offers a reading of African feminist fiction as a site of knowledge production with potential to subvert dominant epistemological power relations. Following on African feminist literary critic Juliana Nfah-Abbenyi's formulation of literature as theory, it seeks to make a case for viewing African women's literature as theory. Such theory works to demonstrate how gender relations are embedded within both local and global sets of power relations, and specifically global economic relations. Nfah-Abbenyi argues that "reclaiming and recovering" African women's fiction writing is a form of indigenous theory-making "not common to feminist politics and praxis." (274) Writing fiction, especially for African women excluded from global circuits of knowledge production, becomes a crystallization of lived experience and a form of self-recovery that creates new worlds and ways in which readers can see themselves reflected, as well as new ways of interpreting the world. Recovering women's fiction, then, is a way of reframing the idea of theory as that which always, self-consciously names itself as such.

Departing from this standpoint articulated by Nfah-Abbenyi, I examine three short stories by African women as sites of theory production. The three works of fiction foregrounded are short stories by women located on different parts of the continent at different historical moments in relation to colonialism: they are South African writer Gcina Mhlophe's "The Toilet" (first published in 1987), Ghanaian writer Ama Ata Aidoo's short story "Lice" (first published in 1987), and Ugandan Doreen Baingana's "Tropical Fish" (first published in 2005). I aim to tease apart the ways in which these writers construct gender, and womanhood in particular, in the different political and social locations from which they write. I argue that these short stories can provide an entry point into the politics of decolonial gender, sexuality, and knowledge construction.

Poet, short story writer, and playwright Gcina Mhlophe's short story "The Toilet" was published during the height of apartheid, legislated racial segregation, in South Africa. In this semi-autobiographical narrative, the young African woman who is the first-person narrator, relates her journey from worker in a clothing factory in Johannesburg, South Africa cutting loose threads from garments to writer of poems and stories. The protagonist lives illegally in a white suburb of Johannesburg with her sister, who is a domestic worker for a white family. Black South Africans during apartheid were prohibited from white suburbs and urban spaces without the conditional access given by the dreaded pass book, a document that all black South Africans had to carry in order to be granted "legal" access to cities designated white by apartheid law. Without a passbook to legalize her presence in the city, the black protagonist's mere presence in her sister's servant's cottage is therefore illegal. The white family that employs her sister as a domestic worker does not know of the narrator's presence in her sister's tiny living space, and she consequently has to hide and remain out of sight for most of the daylight hours in Johannesburg. Part of the unnamed character's development as an artist is possible because she discovers a public toilet in a park in which she locks herself for hours to write her poems and stories.

The problem with this temporary writing haven, however, is that the toilet is reserved for whites, and the narrator's use of this space is a dangerous transgression, punishable by law. But in using the toilet as a "room of her own," Mhlophe's character not only flouts apartheid law but also transgresses apartheid's ideological code, which has set up an educational system that deliberately excludes women from the realm of cultural and literary production, with its aim of positioning African women as "drawers of water and hewers of wood" within the apartheid political economy. Yet the character uses the space of the toilet as an incubator for her dreams of being a performer and writer:

> The toilet was very small—the walls were wonderfully close to me—it felt like it was made to fit me alone. I enjoyed that kind of privacy. I did a lot of thinking while I sat there on that toilet seat. I did a lot of daydreaming too—many times imagining myself in some big hall doing a really popular play with some other young actors. (Mhlophe 13)

The image Mhlophe conjures is of a thinking African woman, with dreams, aspirations, and critical faculties—the antithesis of the characters encountered in the fiction of men like Alan Paton, Chinua Achebe, and JM Coetzee. She has a work and family life, and balances the two under the constraints of one of the most oppressive political systems ever imposed on human beings. She reflects on her life and produces strategies for creating a better life. She is creative, re-configuring space and her abject status, and is the creator of her own literary worlds.

This short story does the theoretical work of placing African women's experiences as imaginative agents at the center of discussions about the production of art and knowledge. It demonstrates what Caribbean feminist literary critic Carole Boyce Davies (2002) terms the "migratory subjectivity" of the character—the ability to imaginatively and physically cross borders and boundaries meant to exclude black women from literary production in order to narrate their own experiences and realities, whether in fiction or other forms of writing. Mhlophe shows readers that space is not a neutral commodity, equally accessible to all people; it is always racialized, always gendered. So is literary and knowledge production. Who gets to write, and under what circumstances they are allowed to be published, are deeply political issues, layered with power differentials based on race, gender, sexual orientation, and place in the world: with "place" meaning both location and the "place" society designates for a domestic worker, cultural worker, laborer, or thinker. Mhlophe's politicizing of writing and her theorization of imagination as a tool of resistance additionally helps readers think of themselves as imaginative, creative beings, a consciousness critical for beginning to think of themselves as producers of knowledge.

The second short story that foregrounds the political economy of living and producing knowledge in Africa is Ghanaian writer Ama Ata Aidoo's "Lice" In this story, readers encounter married mother of two, Sissie, whose battles straddle both the personal and public realms: her husband's infidelities exacerbate the tough economic cond.itions she faces in her low-paying job as a teacher. Additionally, as the story unfolds, Sissie battles sexual harassment from the school principal, scuppering her chances of being promoted at her workplace, has to care for an injured child with very little resources, and witnesses this child undergo a painful medical procedure without any anesthesia because the hospital has run out of medical supplies. The last straw comes for Sissie when she discovers her young daughter's head crawling with lice early one Saturday morning. She sets on a plan to douse her daughter's head with paraffin in order to kill the lice,

but when Sissie accidentally grabs a can of petrol instead of the paraffin, her thoughts and actions become more sinister, turning to suicide. Sissie douses not only her daughter's head, but also her own, their clothes, the bed and the floor. She strikes a match and is about to unleash tragedy on herself and her daughter when her other child's cough from a different room jolts her awake and back to life. She stamps out the match and narrowly avoids disaster.

One thread Aidoo deftly weaves through the story is the persistent drone of Sissie's radio by her bedside, tuned to a station that broadcasts only world news. The story starts:

> Life has its problems. Without further ruining
> one's already bad nerves listening to the World
> News first thing in the morning. And when
> you are
>
> just a woman
> an ordinary wife with a normal
> marriage
> ignored, double timed
> a harassed mother
> a low-paid teacher in a rotten
> Third World educational system
>
> what should you want with world news anyway?
> (Aidoo 66)

Sissie's rhetorical question to herself, about why someone as insignificant as her would need to listen to "World News" anyway, is filled with irony. Upon listening to the news, she immediately chastises herself: "Sissie knew she should know better" (66). Though she is geographically a million miles away from the West, the economic policies produced by Washington and London during the 1980s have everything to do with Sissie's life.

While Sissie contemplates her larger life problems and the immediate one of her daughter's head lice, the radio chimes in that Ronald Reagan has won a landslide victory, securing a second term as US President. And after Sissie resists suicide's seductive call, the story concludes with the following sentence: "To end the news, these were the main headlines: President Reagan . . ." (74). While the story thus deals with the day to day intimate and structural hardships of life for this particular African woman, it is framed at the beginning and end, and interrupted in the middle, by "world news," specifically the re-election of Ronald Reagan as US President.

The story's structure and framing of Sissie's life immediately positions her, and the challenges she faces, within the transnational movements of power and capital. The recurring message, via the transistor radio, of Reagan's re-election invokes "Reagonomics," a set of economic policies that were disastrous for Africa, often increasing poverty and worsening inequality. Through Aidoo's "Lice," readers are introduced to the concept of what became known as the Washington Consensus, policies implemented by Ronald Reagan and US financial and government institutions, alongside the World Bank and International Monetary Fund's Structural Adjustment Programs (SAPs) to secure repayment of debts owed to the so-called first world by third world countries. Readers whose curiosity is piqued by the story to do further research on Ghana will learn that it started participating in World Bank and International Monetary Fund SAPs in 1983 (Konadu-Agyemang), one year prior to Reagan's re-election. Feminist geographer Konadu-Agyemang notes that in Ghana and elsewhere in Africa, "the IMF and World Bank inspired structural adjustment programs often consisting of a package of actions that included currency devaluation, reducing inflation, downsizing the public service, drastic cutbacks on government expenditure on education, health and welfare, financial reforms, privatization of public enterprises, export promotion and other policies geared towards economic growth" (473). Implementing SAPs in Ghana meant the retrenchment of 300,000 public sector workers, as well as cuts in government allocations to health and education, which subsequently had to be subsidized by individual citizens' user fees, thus reducing access to education and health services for the poor. While these measures were aimed at reducing Ghana's debt burden to first world monetary institutions, its consequence was increased economic hardship and poverty, especially for women. Structural adjustment programs in Ghana and elsewhere in the developing world has led to what feminist scholars of political economy have termed the feminization of poverty in Africa (Mikell; Chant), meaning that

women suffer disproportionately from the effects of increased economic inequality. Aidoo's short story demonstrates with exquisite and economical language use the effects of these programs on one woman's life. It produces a theory of gender that locates its construction within a global world order. Flows of capital between the West and the postcolonial, and the resultant debts owed by developing nations, structure the lived experiences of one African woman. Her story is about much more than a philandering husband: it is also about how the material conditions of her life are directly produced by economic policies embraced by the United States.

What her story makes lucid is that Africa does not exist in an atemporal, ahistorical vacuum, outside of time. Moreover, interconnected global political and economic systems are embedded within power structures shaped by history: the country's history as former colony is alluded to when Sissie refers to Ghana as "Euro-Africa and Afro-Europe" (Aidoo 67). This designation foregrounds not only the colonial relationship, but also the shadow those historically uneven and exploitive relationships casts over present day Ghana. The story, through its subtext of Reagan's re-election and his economic politics, also makes visible the ongoing exploitation of neocolonial relations between the west and one postcolonial nation. It points to the ways in which Ghana exists within a globalized political economy, and how this political economy has material consequences on women's lives. The story thus immediately reframes how gendered identities and relations are shaped not just by patriarchy but by wider political, colonial, and economic systems. Gender is thus not only the roles or expectations this society places on men and women, but it is also produced by globalized power relations between nations (see Sparr; Afshar and Dennis).

The third story, "Tropical Fish" by Doreen Baingana, locates a young African women's sexual agency within a web of global, neocolonial, and local patriarchies. Set at Makerere University, which once styled itself as the "Harvard of Africa," the novel shows how Christine's choices of sexual partners and access to reproductive health care hinges on a transactional sexual relationship with a white British expatriate, Peter. "Sex was like school, something I just did," reflects the cynical Christine (80). Her relationship with Peter is not unlike the extractive relationship he has with the Ugandan nation and its resources. His business venture extracts and exports rare and endangered tropical fish from Uganda to sell them for a fortune in Europe.

Aware that Peter's lavish lifestyle in Uganda, complete with servants and a mansion in the diplomatic quarters, is afforded by his race, gender, and national privilege, Christine stifles the urge to reveal that she knows his class status back in Britain:

> Whenever he whined about the insects everywhere, the terrible ice cream, and only one Chinese restaurant, I wanted to tell him I knew he was lower class, Cockney, and doing much better here, practically stealing our fish, than he ever would in Britain. So he should just shut up. But of course I didn't. Our Lady of the Smiles and Open Body. (87)

Savvy and unsentimental, Christine's sexual coming-of-age is embedded within these exploitive economic relations, which complicates her exercise of sexual agency. She sees herself, when she is with Peter, as "the sweet, simpering self I reserve for men," a blank slate onto which Peter projects all his fantasies (81).

While she enjoys sex with Peter and the luxurious lifestyle he offers, their relationship is devoid of intimacy. They meet only to have sex, never conversing with each other. When Christine has an abortion after an unwanted pregnancy, she is disgusted to hear the only words Peter has to offer when she turns to him for comfort: "Do you want some money?" (92). She refuses his money, hurrying away and melting into a crowd of anonymous bodies on an overcrowded minibus taxi. She is disposable and easily replaceable for Peter, who has many young women to choose from as potential sexual partners given his wealth and unearned privilege derived from his British expatriate status in Uganda. The story shows how Christine's burgeoning sexuality, as well as her subjectivity as a young, middle class woman, is inflected by neocolonialism and a British man's plunder of rare African resources. Her gendered subjectivity as a postcolonial African woman is thus produced within global economic patterns that continue the economic disparities wrought by colonization.

According to Nfah-Abbenyi, whose recasting of African women's stories as African theory frames this discussion, fictional narrative has the potential to reconstitute and reconstruct "the multiple, shifting, and sometimes contradictory identities and subjectivities of African women in their writing. They (stories) show how these same contradictions are valuable and empowering tools necessary to subverting gender(ed) dichotomies and exigencies, contradictions that are paramount to describing African women's identity, subjectivity and agency" (275). "Tropical Fish," in demonstrating Christine's agency as well as her location within global neocolonialism, gives the reader a complex picture of female subjectivity. Here is a comfortably middle-class woman, who has access to one of Africa's most exclusive universities, whose imbrication in the neocolonial global world order nevertheless leaves her vulnerable to sexual exploitation by a British man. Moreover, in telling the story from her perspective, not relying on stultifying stereotypes of African women as objects and perpetual victims, it demonstrates her agency and an interiority not often afforded African women in men's fiction.

Language, and the imaginative possibilities offered by stories, is an integral part of the decolonizing project of African feminism. Through the stories African women tell, they produce cartographies of the worlds they inhabit, and also counterhegemonic maps; signposts toward more just economic and gender orders. The power of these stories demonstrate the importance of feminist theorizing the local and the global from particular African locations, critiquing power within these settings and showing how it operates to marginalize and oppress certain categories of women. They demonstrate Crenshaw's (1989) theory of intersectionality, pointing to the limitations of a single-axis approach to formulating and redressing gender oppression, which predates the formulation of the term, intersectionality. They point to the embeddedness of local cultures within world economic systems that invariably inflect them, and assist in reflecting an imperialist feminist gaze back to the United States, making the complicity of the global economic order clear in the conditions facing African women, who might otherwise be pitied as victims of regressive African masculinities. Most importantly, these works show the political importance of the imagination. Imagination allows a vision of a different, more just world; the spark often needed to move into the action required to make small and large changes to the world. African feminist imagination enables us to continue the process of decolonization by seeing structures of oppression, articulating a critique against them, and imagining what could exist beyond them.

REFERENCES

Afshar, Haleh, and Carolyne Dennis, eds. *Women and Adjustment Policies in the Third World*. Springer, 2016.

Aidoo, Ama Ata. "Lice." *The Picador Book of African Short Stories*, edited by Stephen Gray. Picador, 2000, pp. 66–74.

Baca Zinn, Maxine, and Bonnie Thornton Dill. "Theorizing Difference from Multiracial Feminism." *Feminist Studies*, vol. 22, no. 2, 1996, pp. 321–331.

Baingana, Doreen. *Tropical Fish: Stories Out of Entebbe*. University of Massachusetts Press, 2005.

Chant, Sylvia. *Gender and the Feminization of Poverty: Exploring the Feminization of Poverty in Africa, Asia and Latin America*. Edward Elgar Publishing, 2007.

Crenshaw, Kimberlé. "Demarginalizing the Intersection of Race and Sex: A Black Feminist Critique of Antidiscrimination Doctrine, Feminist Theory and Antiracist Politics." *University of Chicago Legal Forum*, vol. 1989, no. 1, 1989, pp. 139–167.

Davies, Carole Boyce. *Black Women, Writing and Identity: Migrations of the Subject*. Routledge, 2002.

hooks, bell. *Ain't I a Woman? Black Women and Feminism*. South End Press, 1981.

Konadu-Agyemang, Kwadwo. "The Best of Times and the Worst of Times: Structural Adjustment Programs and Uneven Development in Africa: The Case of Ghana." *The Professional Geographer*, vol. 52, no. 3, 2000, pp. 469–483.

Mama, Amina. "Why We Must Write: Personal Reflections on Linking the Alchemy of Science with the Relevance of Activism." *Agenda* vol. 16, no. 46, 2000, pp. 13–20.

Mhlophe, Gcina. "The Toilet." *Love Child*. UKZN Press, 2002, pp. 11–18.

Mikell, Gwendolyn, ed. *African Feminism: The Politics of Survival in Sub-Saharan Africa*. University of Pennsylvania Press, 1997.

Nfah-Abbenyi, Juliana Makuchi. "Gender, Feminist Theory, and Post-Colonial (Women's) Writing." *African Gender Studies: A Reader*, edited by Oyeronke Oyewumi. Palgrave Macmillan, 2005, pp. 259–278.

Sparr, Pamela, ed. *Mortgaging Women's Lives: Feminist Critiques of Structural Adjustment*. Palgrave Macmillan, 1994.

Spivak, Gayatri Chakravorty. "Can the Subaltern Speak?" *The Norton Anthology of Theory and Criticism*, edited by Vincent B. Leitch. W. W. Norton and Company, 2001, pp. 2197–2208.

CHERRÍE MORAGA

52. LA GÜERA

It requires something more than personal experience to gain a philosophy or point of view from any specific event. It is the quality of our response to the event and our capacity to enter into the lives of others that help us to make their lives and experiences our own.

—Emma Goldman[1]

I am the very well-educated daughter of a woman who, by the standards in this country, would be considered largely illiterate. My mother was born in Santa Paula, Southern California, at a time when much of the central valley there was still farm land. Nearly thirty-five years later, in 1948, she was the only daughter of six to marry an Anglo, my father.

I remember all of my mother's stories, probably much better than she realizes. She is a fine story-teller, recalling every event of her life with the vividness of the present, noting each detail right down to the cut and color of her dress. I remember stories of her being pulled out of school at the ages of five, seven, nine, and eleven to work in the fields, along with her brothers and sisters; stories of her father drinking away whatever small profit she was able to make for the family; of her going the long way home to avoid meeting him on the street, staggering toward the same destination. I remember stories of my mother lying about her age in order to get a job as a hat-check girl at Agua Caliente Racetrack in Tijuana. At fourteen, she was the main support of the family. I can still see her walking home alone at 3 a.m., only to turn all of her salary and tips over to her mother, who was pregnant again.

The stories continue through the war years and on: walnut-cracking factories, the Voit Rubber factory, and then the computer boom. I remember my mother doing piecework for the electronics plant in our neighborhood. In the late evening, she would sit in front of the TV set, wrapping copper wires into the backs of circuit boards, talking about "keeping up with the younger girls." By that time, she was already in her mid-fifties.

Meanwhile, I was college-prep in school. After classes, I would go with my mother to fill out job applications for her, or write checks for her at the supermarket. We would have the scenario all worked out ahead of time. My mother would sign the check before we'd get to the store. Then, as we'd approach the check-stand, she would say—within earshot of the cashier—"oh honey, you go 'head and make out the check," as if she couldn't be bothered with such an insignificant detail. No one asked any questions.

I was educated, and wore it with a keen sense of pride and satisfaction, my head propped up with the knowledge, from my mother, that my life would be easier than hers. I was educated; but more than this, I was "la guera": fair-skinned. Born with the features of my Chicana mother, but the skin of my Anglo father, I had it made.

No one ever quite told me this (that light was right), but I knew that being light was something valued in my family (who were all Chicano, with the exception of my father). In fact, everything about my upbringing (at least what occurred on a conscious level) attempted to bleach me of what color I did have. Although my mother was fluent in it, I was never taught much Spanish at home. I picked up what I did learn from school and from overheard snatches of conversation among my relatives and mother. She often called other lower-income Mexicans "braceros," or "wet-backs," referring to herself and her family as "a different class of people." And yet, the real story was that my family, too, had been poor (some still are) and farmworkers. My mother can remember this in her blood as if it were yesterday. But this is something she would like to forget (and rightfully), for to her, on a basic economic level, being Chicana meant being "less." It was through my mother's desire to protect her children from poverty and illiteracy that we became "anglocized"; the more effectively we could pass in the white world, the better guaranteed our future.

From all of this, I experience, daily, a huge disparity between what I was born into and what I was to grow up to become. Because, (as Goldman suggests) these stories my mother told me crept under my "guera" skin. I had no choice but to enter into the life of my mother. *I had no choice.* I took her life into my heart, but managed to keep a lid on it as long as I feigned being the happy, upwardly mobile heterosexual.

When I finally lifted the lid to my lesbianism, a profound connection with my mother reawakened in me. It wasn't until I acknowledged and confronted my own lesbianism in the flesh, that my heartfelt identification with and empathy for my mother's oppression—due to being poor, uneducated, and Chicana—was realized. My lesbianism is the avenue through which I have learned the most about silence and oppression, and it continues to be the most tactile reminder to me that we are not free human beings.

You see, one follows the other. I had known for years that I was a lesbian, had felt it in my bones, had ached with the knowledge, gone crazed with the knowledge, wallowed in the silence of it. Silence *is* like starvation. Don't be fooled. It's nothing short of that, and felt most sharply when one has had a full belly most of her life. When we are not physically starving, we have the luxury to realize psychic and emotional starvation. It is from this starvation that other starvations can be recognized—if one is willing to take the risk of making the connection—if one is willing to be responsible to the result of the connection. For me, the connection is an inevitable one.

What I am saying is that the joys of looking like a white girl ain't so great since I realized I could be beaten on the street for being a dyke. If my sister's being beaten because she's Black, it's pretty much the same principle. We're both getting beaten any way you look at it. The connection is blatant; and in the case of my own family, the difference in the privileges attached to looking white instead of brown are merely a generation apart.

In this country, lesbianism is a poverty—as is being brown, as is being a woman, as is being just plain poor. The danger lies in ranking the oppressions. *The danger lies in failing to acknowledge the specificity of the oppression.* The danger lies in attempting to deal with oppression purely from a theoretical base. Without an emotional, heartfelt grappling with the source of our own oppression, without naming the enemy within ourselves and outside of us, no authentic, non-hierarchical connection among oppressed groups can take place.

When the going gets rough, will we abandon our so-called comrades in a flurry of racist/heterosexist/what-have-you panic? To whose camp, then, should the lesbian of color retreat? Her very presence violates the ranking and abstraction of oppression. Do we merely live hand to mouth? Do we merely struggle with the "ism" that's sitting on top of our own heads?

The answer is: yes, I think first we do; and we must do so thoroughly and deeply. But to fail to move out from there will only isolate us in our own oppression—will only insulate, rather than radicalize us.

To illustrate: a gay male friend of mine once confided to me that he continued to feel that, on some level, I didn't trust him because he was male; that he felt, really, if it ever came down to a "battle of the sexes," I might kill him. I admitted that I might very well. He wanted to understand the source of my distrust. I responded, "You're not a woman. Be a woman for a day. Imagine being a woman." He confessed that the thought terrified him because, to him, being a woman meant being raped by men. He *had* felt raped by men; he wanted to forget what that meant. What grew from that discussion was the realization that in order for him to create an authentic alliance with me, he must deal with the primary source of his own sense of oppression. He must, first, emotionally come to terms with what it feels like to be a victim. If he—or anyone—were to truly do this, it would be impossible to discount the oppression of others, except by again forgetting how we have been hurt.

And yet, oppressed groups are forgetting all the time. There are instances of this in the rising Black middle class, and certainly an obvious trend of such "unconsciousness" among white gay men. Because to remember may mean giving up whatever privileges we have managed to squeeze out of this society by virtue of our gender, race, class, or sexuality.

Within the women's movement, the connections among women of different backgrounds and sexual orientations have been fragile, at best. I think this phenomenon is indicative of our failure to seriously address ourselves to some very frightening questions: How have I internalized my own oppression? How have I oppressed? Instead, we have let rhetoric do the job of poetry. Even the word "oppression" has lost its power. We need a new language, better words that can more closely describe women's fear of and resistance to one another; words that will not always come out sounding like dogma.

What prompted me in the first place to work on an anthology by radical women of color was a deep sense that I had a valuable insight to contribute, by virtue of my birthright and background. And yet, I don't really understand first-hand what it feels like being shitted on for being brown. I understand much more about the joys of it—being Chicana and having family are synonymous for me. What I know about loving, singing, crying, telling stories, speaking with my heart and hands, even having a sense of my own soul comes from the love of my mother, aunts, cousins. . . .

But at the age of twenty-seven, it is frightening to acknowledge that I have internalized a racism and classism, where the object of oppression is not only someone outside of my skin, but the someone inside my skin. In fact, to a large degree, the real battle with such oppression, for all of us, begins under the skin. I have had to confront the fact that much of what I value about being Chicana, about my family, has been subverted by anglo culture and my own cooperation with it. This realization did not occur to me overnight. For example, it wasn't until long after my graduation from the private college I'd attended in Los Angeles, that I realized the major reason for my total alienation from and fear of my classmates was rooted in class and culture. CLICK.

Three years after graduation, in an apple-orchard in Sonoma, a friend of mine (who comes from an Italian Irish working-class family) says to me, "Cherríe, no wonder you felt like such a nut in school. Most of the people there were white and rich." It was true. All along I had felt the difference, but not until I had put the words "class" and "color" to the experience, did my feelings make any sense. For years, I had berated myself for not being as "free" as my classmates. I completely bought that they simply had more guts than I did—to rebel against their parents and run around the country hitch-hiking, reading books and studying "art." They had enough privilege to be atheists, for chrissake. There was no one around filling in the disparity for me between their parents, who were Hollywood filmmakers, and my parents, who wouldn't know the name of a filmmaker if their lives depended on it (and precisely because their lives didn't depend on it, they couldn't be bothered). But I knew nothing about "privilege" then. White was right. Period. I could pass. If I got educated enough, there would never be any telling.

Three years after that, another CLICK. In a letter to Barbara Smith, I wrote:

> I went to a concert where Ntosake Shange was reading. There, everything exploded for me. She was speaking a language that I knew—in the deepest parts of me—existed, and that I had ignored in my own feminist studies and even in my own writing. What Ntosake caught in me is the realization that in my development as a poet, I have, in many ways, denied the voice of my brown mother—the brown in me. I have acclimated to the sound of a white language which, as my father represents it, does not speak to the emotions in my poems—emotions which stem from the love of my mother.
>
> The reading was agitating. Made me uncomfortable. Threw me into a week-long terror of how deeply I was affected. I felt that I had to start all over again. That I turned only to the perceptions of white middle-class women to speak for me and all women. I am shocked by my own ignorance.

Sitting in that auditorium chair was the first time I had realized to the core of me that for years I had disowned the language I knew best—ignored the words and rhythms that were the closest to me. The sounds of my mother and aunts gossiping—half in English, half in Spanish—while drinking cerveza in the kitchen. And the hands—I had cut off the hands in my poems. But not in conversation; still the hands could not be kept down. Still they insisted on moving.

The reading had forced me to remember that I knew things from my roots. But to remember puts me up against what I don't know. Shange's reading agitated me because she spoke with power about a world that is both alien and common to me: "the capacity to enter into the lives of others." But you can't just take the goods and run. I knew that then, sitting in the Oakland auditorium (as I know in my poetry), that the only thing worth *writing* about is what seems to be unknown and, therefore, fearful.

The "unknown" is often depicted in racist literature as the "darkness" within a person. Similarly, sexist writers will refer to fear in the form of the vagina, calling it "the orifice of death." In contrast, it is a pleasure to read works such as Maxine Hong Kingston's *Woman Warrior*, where fear and alienation are described as "the white ghosts." And yet, the bulk of literature in this country reinforces the myth that what is dark and female is evil. Consequently, each of us—whether dark, female, or both—has in some way *internalized* this oppressive imagery. What the oppressor often succeeds in doing is simply *externalizing* his fears, projecting them into the bodies of women, Asians, gays, disabled folks, whoever seems most "other."

> call me
> roach and presumptuous
> nightmare on your white pillow
> your itch to destroy
> the indestructible
> part of yourself
>
> *Audre Lorde[2]*

But it is not really difference the oppressor fears so much as similarity. He fears he will discover in himself the same aches, the same longings as those of the people he has shitted on. He fears the immobilization threatened by his own incipient guilt. He fears he will have to change his life once he has seen himself in the bodies of the people he has called different. He fears the hatred, anger, and vengeance of those he has hurt.

This is the oppressor's nightmare, but it is not exclusive to him. We women have a similar nightmare, for each of us in some way has been both oppressed and the oppressor. We are afraid to look at how we have failed each other. We are afraid to see how we have taken the values of our oppressor into our hearts and turned them against ourselves and one another. We are afraid to admit how deeply "the man's" words have been ingrained in us.

To assess the damage is a dangerous act. I think of how, even as a feminist lesbian, I have so wanted to ignore my own homophobia, my own hatred of myself for being queer. I have not wanted to admit that my deepest personal sense of myself has not quite "caught up" with my "woman-identified" politics. I have been afraid to criticize lesbian writers who choose to "skip over" these issues in the name of feminism. In 1979, we talk of "old gay" and "butch and femme" roles as if they were ancient history. We toss them aside as merely patriarchal notions. And yet, the truth of the matter is that I have sometimes taken society's fear and hatred of lesbians to bed with me. I have sometimes hated my lover for loving me. I have sometimes felt "not woman enough" for her. I have sometimes felt "not man enough." For a lesbian trying to survive in a heterosexist society, there is no easy way around these emotions. Similarly, in a white-dominated world, there is little getting around racism and our own internalization of it. It's always there, embodied in some one we least expect to rub up against.

When we do rub up against this person, *there* then is the challenge. *There* then is the opportunity to look at the nightmare within us. But we usually shrink from such a challenge.

Time and time again, I have observed that the usual response among white women's groups when the "racism issue" comes up is to deny the difference. I have heard comments like, "Well, we're open to *all* women; why don't they (women of color) come? You can only do so much. . . ." But there is seldom any analysis of how the very nature and structure of the group itself may be founded on racist or classist assumptions. More importantly, so often the women seem to feel no loss, no lack, no absence when women of color are not involved; therefore, there is little desire to change the situation. This has hurt me deeply. I have come to believe that the only reason women of a privileged class will dare to look at *how* it is that *they* oppress, is when they've come to know the meaning of their own oppression. And understand that the oppression of others hurts them personally.

The other side of the story is that women of color and working-class women often shrink from challenging white middle-class women. It is much easier to rank oppressions and set up a hierarchy, rather than take responsibility for changing our own lives. We have failed to demand that white women, particularly those who claim to be speaking for all women, be accountable for their racism.

The dialogue has simply not gone deep enough.

I have many times questioned my right to even work on an anthology which is to be written "exclusively by Third World women." I have had to look critically at my claim to color, at a time when, among white feminist ranks, it is a "politically correct" (and sometimes peripherally advantageous) assertion to make. I must acknowledge the fact that, physically, I have had a *choice* about making that claim, in contrast to women who have not had such a choice, and have been abused for their color. I must reckon with the fact that for most of my life, by virtue of the very fact that I am white-looking, I identified with and aspired toward white values, and that I rode the wave of that Southern Californian privilege as far as conscience would let me.

Well, now I feel both bleached and beached. I feel angry about this—the years when I refused to recognize privilege, both when it worked against me, and when I worked it, ignorantly, at the expense of others.

These are not settled issues. That is why this work feels so risky to me. It continues to be discovery. It has brought me into contact with women who invariably know a hell of a lot more than I do about racism, as experienced in the flesh, as revealed in the flesh of their writing.

I think: what is my responsibility to my roots-both white and brown, Spanish-speaking and English? I am a woman with a foot in both worlds; and I refuse the split. I feel the necessity for dialogue. Sometimes I feel it urgently.

But one voice is not enough, nor two, although this is where dialogue begins. It is essential that radical feminists confront their fear of and resistance to each other, because without this, there *will* be no bread on the table. Simply, we will not survive. If we could make this connection in our heart of hearts, that if we are serious about a revolution—better—if we seriously believe there should be joy in our lives (real joy, not just "good times"), then we need one another. We women need each other. Because my/your solitary, self-asserting "go-for-the-throat-of-fear" power is not enough. The real power, as you and I well know, is collective. I can't afford to be afraid of you, nor you of me. If it takes head-on collisions, let's do it: this polite timidity is killing us.

As Lorde suggests in the passage I cited earlier, it is in looking to the nightmare that the dream is found. There, the survivor emerges to insist on a future, a vision, yes, born out of what is dark and female. The feminist movement must be a movement of such survivors, a movement with a future.

September, 1979.

NOTES

1. Alix Kates Shulman, "Was My Life Worth Living?" *Red Emma Speaks.* (New York: Random House, 1972), p. 388.
2. From "The Brown Menace or Poem to the Survival of Roaches." *The New York Head Shop and Museum* (Detroit: Broadside, 1974), p. 48.

SARA AHMED

53. LESBIAN FEMINISM

I write this . . . out of a conviction: in order to survive what we come up against, in order to build worlds from the shattered pieces, we need a revival of lesbian feminism. This . . . is an explanation of my conviction.

Right now might seem an odd time to ask for such a revival. Lesbian feminism might seem to be passé precisely because lesbian feminism posed feminism as a life question. Many of the critiques of lesbian feminism, often as a form of cultural feminism, were precisely because of this attachment to life. Alice Echols, in her book *Daring to Be Bad*, which gives a history of radical feminism in the United States, describes: "With the rise of lesbian-feminism, the conflation of the personal with the political, long in the making, was complete and unassailable. More than ever, how one lived one's life, not commitment to political struggle, became the salient factor" (1989, 240). Note this *not*: the question of how we live our lives is separated from a commitment to political struggle; more than that, the focus on how we live our lives is implied to be a weak substitute for political struggle or a withdrawal of feminist energy from that struggle. We can hear a similar implication in Juliet Mitchell and Rosalind Delmar's argument: "The effects of liberation do not become the manifestations of liberation by changing values or for that matter by changing oneself, but only by challenging the social structure that gives rise to the values in the first place" (cited in Echols 1989, 244). The suggestion is not only that life change is not structural change but that focusing on how one lives one's life might be how structures are not transformed.

I want to offer an alternative argument by returning to the archives of lesbian feminism. When a life is what we have to struggle for, we struggle against structures. It is not necessarily the case that these struggles always lead to transformation (though neither does one's involvement in political movements). But to struggle against something is to chip away at something. Many of these structures are not visible or tangible unless you come up against them, which means that the work of chipping away, what I call diversity work, is a particular kind of work. The energy required to keep going when you keep coming up against these structures is how we build things, sometimes, often, from the shattered pieces.

Lesbian feminism can bring feminism back to life.

HETEROGENDER AS WALL

I write as a lesbian. I write as a feminist. This *as* is an individual claim but also a claim I make for others. To describe oneself as a lesbian is a way of reaching out to others who hear themselves in this *as*. But of course lesbian feminism means more than speaking as lesbian and speaking as a feminist; this *and* is too loose as a connecting device. Lesbian feminism also implies a stronger connection between these words. I think it is this stronger connection that makes lesbian feminism a site of so much anxiety, as explored by Victoria Hesford (2013) in her powerful analysis of the figure of the feminist as lesbian. This stronger connection is then heard as a charge against those feminists who are not lesbians as not being feminists. The charge of this connection could be heard not as a charge against something or somebody but as a charge with something. Perhaps we can recall the charge of willfulness: a charge that is electric. The connection between lesbian and feminist is not something that can be prescribed even if some of our histories include this prescription or even if lesbian feminism is heard as prescription (to be a lesbian you must identify as feminist; to be a feminist you must identify as lesbian). The connection is a connection to be lived: living as a lesbian is how I live a feminist life.

. . . I have been trying to bring feminist theory home by generating feminist theory out of ordinary experiences of being a feminist. The book [this was written for] could have been called *Everyday Feminism*.[1] Feminist theory is or can be what we might call, following Marilyn Frye, "lived theory," an approach that "does not separate politics from living" (1991, 13). We can think of life as data collection: we gather information. And being a lesbian, living one's life as a lesbian, gives us plenty of data. Lesbians collect information about the institutions that govern the reproduction of life: it is almost too much data; we don't have time to interpret all the material we collect. If living a lesbian life gives us data, lesbian feminism gives us the tools to interpret that data.

And by data I am once again referring to walls. . . . I [have] offered a rethinking of heterogender as a traffic system, a way of directing human traffic. When a flow is directed, it becomes a momentum. . . . I began to rethink the materiality of power in terms of walls, the hardenings of history. We can rethink heterogender as another brick wall, one that is encountered by those who are not going in the right direction. When you are not going the right way, a flow is an obstruction. Lesbians know a lot about obstruction.

But it might seem now for lesbians that we are going with the flow. Hey, we can go; hey, here in the United Kingdom we can even get married. And if you talk about what you come up against now, those around you may blink with disbelief: hey, what's up, stop complaining dear, smile. I am not willing to smile on command. I am willing to go on a smile embargo, if I can evoke Shulamith Firestone's (1970, 90) "dream action" for the women's movement. Talking about walls matters all the more when the mechanisms by which we are blocked are less visible.

The everyday is our data.
A wall can be an atmosphere. A wall can be a gesture.

A queer experience: You are seated with your girlfriend, two women at a table, waiting. A straight couple walks into the room and is attended to right away: sir, madam, over here, sir, madam. Sometimes if you do not appear as you are expected to appear, you do not appear. There are many who do not appear under this word *couple*: sir, madam. The gaze slides over you, as if you are not there. This is not so much about being seen, as about being seen to, having your needs attended to: after all when the *sir, madam* becomes a question—"Is that sir, or madam?"—you are being seen, your body turned into a spectacle.

This queer experience might be better articulated as a lesbian experience or something women in particular experience: as if without a man present at a table, or a body visible as man, you do not appear. I have experienced much solidarity among women around these sorts of experiences: say you are pressed up against a busy bar, two women who do not know each other, and over and over again, the men are served first. You look at each other both with frustration but sometimes affection, as you recognize the other woman recognizes that situation as one in which she is perpetually thrown, recognizes being in that situation; you too, me too, she too, we too. When women are seated together you might not register as being there at all. For some, you have to become insistent to be the recipient of a social action; you might have to announce your presence, wave your arm, saying, "Here I am!" For others, it is enough just to turn up because you have already been given a place at the table before you take up that place. I have used *willfulness* to describe the consequences of this differentiation.

Of course more than gender is at stake in the distribution of attention. But gender is at stake in the distribution of attention. Feminist philosophers have taught us for over a century how man becomes universal; woman particular. Women become relatives, only registered as existing when existing in relation to men. We can now deepen the formulation I [have] offered . . .: women as female relatives. To become woman is to become relative: not only in the sense of kin (connected by blood or marriage) but also in the fundamental sense of considered (only) in relation or proportion to something else. We encounter the universal as a wall when we refuse to become relative. And note how we come to understand these distinctions (such as universal and relative) not as abstractions, but in everyday social life, which is to say, through being in a world with others. No wonder that by starting here, by starting with what gets thrown up in a concrete exchange, we generate concepts: sweaty concepts. We muscle in on a world from trying to be in a world.

Lesbian feminism gives us the tools to make sense of the sexism that becomes all the more striking when women exit from the requirements of compulsory heterosexuality (which is, in effect, a citational relational, a requirement to live a life by citing men). For her to appear, she might have to fight. If this is true for women, it is even truer for lesbians. Women with women at a table are hard to see (and by *table* here I am referring to the mechanisms of social gathering, a table as what we are assembled around). For a gathering to be complete, a man is the head. A table of women: a body without a head.

Data as wall.

You turn up at a hotel with your girlfriend and you say you have booked a room. A hesitation can speak volumes. This reservation says your booking is for a double bed. Is that right, madam? Eyebrows are raised; a glance slides over the two of you, catching enough detail. Are you sure, madam? Yes, that's right; a double bed. You have to say it, again; you have to say it, again, firmly. . . . I introduced a formula: rolling eyes = feminist pedagogy. Another formula:

Raised eyebrows = lesbian feminist pedagogy.

Really, are you sure? This happens again and again; you almost come to expect it, the necessity of being firm just to receive what you have requested. Disbelief follows you wherever you go, still. One time after a querying—are you sure madam, are you sure, madam—you enter the room: twin beds. Do you go down; do you try again? It can be trying. Sometimes it is too trying; it is too much; and you pull your two little beds together; you find other ways of huddling.

A history can become concrete through the repetition of such encounters, encounters that require you to put the whole of your body, as well as your arms, behind an action.[2] Maybe these actions seem small. Maybe they are small. But they accumulate over time.

They can feel like a hammering, a chip, chip, chip against your being, so that eventually you begin to feel smaller, hammering as hammered down.

Actions that seem small can also become wall.

AN ORDINARY BATTLE

An ordinary is what we might be missing when we feel that chip, chip, chip. An ordinary can be what we need to survive that chip, chip, chip. Susan Griffin remembers a scene for us, a scene that has yet to happen:

> I remember a scene. . . . This from a film I want to see. It is a film made by a woman about two women who live together. This is a scene from their daily lives. It is a film about the small daily transformations which women experience, allow, tend to, and which have been invisible in this male culture. In this film, two women touch. In all ways possible they show knowledge of. What they have lived through and what they will yet do, and *one sees in their movements how they have survived*. I am certain that one day this film will exist. (cited in Becker et al. 1981, emphasis mine)

Lesbian feminism: to remember a scene that has yet to happen, a scene of the ordinary; of the movements, little movements, which tell the story of our survival. It is a touching scene. Sometimes you have to battle for an ordinary. When you have to battle for an ordinary, when battling becomes ordinary, the ordinary can be what you lose.

Even if we lose it, we have a glimpse of it.
A loss can be a glimpse.
Moments can become movements.

Think of this: how for many women, life has been understood as a sphere of immanence, as dwelling in, not rising above; she is there; there she is; not transcending things by creating things. A masculinist model of creativity is premised on withdrawal. She is there; there she is: engaged in the endless repetitive cycle of housework. We can follow Adrienne Rich, who makes this starting point into an instruction: "Begin with the material," she says, with "matter, mma, madre, mutter, moeder, modder" (1986, 213). Lesbian feminism is materialist right from the beginning. If women are expected to be here, in matter, in materiality, in work, at work, this is where lesbian feminism begins. We begin in the lodge where we are lodged. We begin with the lodge when we are dislodged.

A poignant lesbian scene of ordinary life is provided by the first of the three films that make up *If These Walls Could Talk* 2 (dir. Jane Anderson, 2000). We begin with that ordinary: we begin with its warmth. The quietness of intimacy: Edith and Abby, going to see a film together, coming home together. Yes maybe there are comments made by some kids on the street, but they are used to it: they have each other, a place to return to; home becomes shelter, a place to withdraw to.

Everything is shattered, when Abby slips and falls. Everything shatters.

We are in the hospital waiting room. Edith is waiting to hear how Abby is. Another woman arrives, visibly upset, and says, "They just took my husband in. He had a heart attack." Edith comforts her. When this woman asks about Edith's husband, Edith replies, "I never had a husband." And the woman says, "That's lucky, because you won't have the heartbreak of losing one." The history of heterosexuality is presented as a history of broken hearts, or even just a history of hearts. To be recognized as having a heart is to be recognized as having the potential to be broken. With such recognition comes care, comfort, support. Without recognition, even one's grief cannot be supported or held by the kindness of another.

And so Edith waits. The temporality of this wait feels like a shudder, as each moment passes, as we wait with her, the mood of the film becoming unbearably sad, as it lingers over her loss by lingering. When she asks the hospital staff to see Abby they say, "Only family are allowed." She is excluded from the sphere of intimates. She is a nonrelative, or not-family. The nurse asks, "Is she any relation of yours, madam?" She replies, "I'm a friend, a very good friend." They respond only with another question, "Does she have any family?" The friend disappears in the weight of the address. The recognition of family ties as the only ties that are binding means Abby dies alone; it means Edith waits all night, alone. Their relationship is hidden as friendship, while friendship itself becomes produced as a lesser tie, less binding, another land of fragile. The power of the distinction between friends and family is

legislative, as if only family counts, as if other relationships are not real, or simply are not.

When lesbian grief is not recognized, because lesbian relationships are not recognized, then you become nonrelatives. You become unrelated; you become not. You are alone in your grief. You are left waiting.

We know this history. It is a history of what we know.

Support is how much you have to fall back on when you fall. . . . I suggested that heterosexuality can be understood as an elaborate support system. . . . I considered how fragility is unevenly distributed. To leave a support system can mean to become more fragile, less protected from the bumps of ordinary life. Class of course can be understood in these terms. To be middle or upper class is to have more resources to fall back on when you fall. What is behind you can be what holds you up; what is behind you can stop you from going down.

To say that heterosexuality can do the work of holding you up when you fall shows how intersectionality is not only about stopping and starting, . . . but also a matter of ups and downs. Maybe if the life you live severs a family tie or snaps a bond, one that would otherwise have held you up when things break up, then you have left not only heterosexuality but the stability of a class position as a way of accessing resources.[3] To leave heterosexuality can be to leave those institutional forms of protecting, cherishing, holding. When things break, your whole life can then unravel. So much feminist and queer invention comes from the necessity of creating our own support systems.

When family is not there to prop you up, when you disappear from family life, you have to find other ways of being supported. When you disappear from family life: does this happen to you? You go home, you go back home. And it feels like you are watching yourself disappear: watching your own life unravel, thread by thread. No one has willed or intended your disappearance. Just slowly, just slowly, as talk of family, of heterosexuality as the future, of lives that you do not live, just slowly, just slowly, you disappear. They welcome you; they are kind, but it is harder and harder to breathe. And then when you leave, you might go and find a lesbian bar or queer space; it can be such a relief. You feel like a toe liberated from a cramped shoe: how you wiggle about! And we need to think about that: how the restriction of life when heterosexuality remains a presumption can be countered by creating spaces that are looser, freer, not only because you are not surrounded by what you are not but because you are reminded there are many ways to be. Lesbian bars, queer space: wiggle room.

The loss of possibility can be experienced as a physical restriction. The remainder of this short film depicts the arrival of Abby's family for the funeral. Before they arrive, Edith removes traces of their relationship from the house, including photographs from the wall, exposing the lighter spaces underneath. If relationships leave traces on the wall so too does the removal of those relationships. The house is figured as a zone of intimacy; their love literally occupies the walls, keeping them busy. The house is not represented as property, but as a space in which they have extended themselves; mementos, cards, photographs; their intimacy leaves an impression on the walls. A photo of them marching, traces of the lesbian and gay histories of activism that allow this zone to become theirs. The objects that Edith takes down are objects that embody their love, which create their own horizon. These objects betray their secret. The removal of signs of their intimacy empties the house, re-creating the house as a vacant space, as if the walls too must wait.

> **If the walls could talk, what would they say?**
> **We need the walls to talk.**
> **What a story.**

When Abby's family arrive, the house is transformed from a zone of intimacy into property. The house was in Abby's name. There is no will. The objects, the house itself; it belongs to Abby's family.

> **The walls, too; they belong too.**
> **They hold up the master's residence; the family home.**

When Abby's family arrive, they occupy the house. Edith becomes their guest. Abby's nephew says, "I have no problem with you staying here. Maybe we can work out some sort of rental situation." Staying becomes a question of receiving his hospitality: he has the power to lend the house, which is the same power as the power to take it away. Indeed, the objects that embody their lesbian intimacy are taken away, by being transformed into property, as something that can be taken: they keep asking, "What was Aunt Abby's?" as a way of asking, "What is ours?" When a lesbian feminist past is reassembled as a heterosexual present, the future, her future, is lost.

> **It is a situation.**
> **A sad, sad situation.**

The sadness of the situation unfolds through things: they embody Edith's life; her life with Abby. But for Abby's relatives, these things were Abby's; they become objects that are inheritable. In particular, Abby's china porcelain birds, her most loved and precious objects, become the site of contestation over family values and the value of family. The daughter of her nephew—Alice, let's give her a name—says to Edith, "They are beautiful." When Alice picks up one of the birds, Edith says, "I gave her that one. It's a lovely gift." In the following exchange between Edith and Alice, we have a partial recognition of loss—which in underdescribing that loss works to annul the force of recognition. "It must be very sad for you to lose such a good friend." To which Edith replies, inadequately, "Yes it is." At this moment, Edith's face is blank, her eyes glimmering; she withholds. The affirmative response, "Yes it is," becomes a disavowal of the loss, a way of keeping the loss a secret, a way of keeping what was lost a secret.

It is at this moment that Edith is undone. For having said yes to this, Alice says, "I think you should have something of hers to remember her by. I would really like for you to pick one of these birds to have as a keepsake." These objects that signify her love for Abby, and Abby's love, are taken away in the very gesture of being returned: of being turned into a gift, a keepsake, as if she must be grateful for this return. The objects that Abby loved most, which were part of her, become kinship objects for Ted's family; they become family relatives, maybe even female relatives (if hers then ours), what can be inherited, objects to be passed down the family line, objects that give family its form.

It is this loss, the loss of what her lover loved, that is too much.

> **Too much; it is too much.**
> **Things shatter.**

There are many ways to tell the story of recognition because there are many stories to tell. The desire for recognition is not necessarily about having access to a good life or being included in the institutions that have left you shattered. It is not even necessarily an aspiration for something: rather, it comes from the experience of what is unbearable, what cannot be endured. The desire for a bearable life is a desire for a life where suffering does not mean you lose your bearings when you become unhoused, when the walls come up, when they secure the rights of some to occupy space by the dispossession of others. The desire for a bearable life is a desire to have an ordinary life, an ordinary that is far more precious than property; indeed, an ordinary is what is negated when things become property, when things become alienable things, when things become family possessions.

I am not saying a desire for an ordinary does not take an institutional form, or that a zone of intimacy that covers the walls does not end up being an aspiration for a property, making things ours, so they cannot be taken away. There is more in an aspiration not to be unhoused than an aspiration for a house. To aspire is to breathe. With breath comes imagination. With breath comes possibility.

Perhaps a lesbian feminist struggle for recognition comes out of rage against the injustice of how some dwell by the dispossession of others. Perhaps the signs of this struggle are neutralized by being represented as a gift. As Sarah Schulman (1998, 102) has shown, when recognition is understood as a gift from the straight world, our collective labor and struggle are forgotten. It is like Edith being given the bird as a keepsake, as if that bird was theirs to give, rather than something that matters because it marks what was created by her and Abby being together; the effort to be together.

We have to keep trying. We want the walls to come down. Or, if they stay up, we want the walls to talk, to tell our story. A story too can shatter: a thousand tiny little pieces, strewn all over the place. Lesbian feminism: in making an ordinary out of the shattered pieces of a dwelling, we dwell.

> **We dwell, we tell.**
> **How telling.**

A WILLFULNESS ARCHIVE

I have noted how actions that are small can also become wall. Lesbian feminism might involve small actions. Maybe the chip, chip, chip of hammering can be transformed into a hammer: if he is a chip off the old block, we chip, chip, chip away at that block. Chip, chip, chip, who knows, eventually it might come right off. To persist in chipping at the blocks of heteropatriarchy, we have to become willful. I want to think of lesbian feminism as a willfulness archive, a living and a lively archive made up and made out of our own experiences of struggling against what we come up against, developing some of my arguments. . . .

We could begin with the very figure of the lesbian feminist; how willful she is, how striking. She is without question a killjoy figure; so often coming up as being anti, antisex, antifun; antilife. The investment in her misery needs to be understood as just that: an investment. To live out a lesbian life is to become willingly estranged from the causes of happiness. No wonder she causes unhappiness.

It is important to note here that the investment in the misery of lesbians can also be detected even within queer studies. In some queer literatures, lesbian feminism itself appears as a miserable scene that we had to get through, or pass through, before we could embrace the happier possibility of becoming queer. For instance, Beatriz Preciado (2012), in a lecture on queer bulldogs, refers to lesbians as ugly with specific reference to lesbian styles, fashions, and haircuts. The lesbian appears as an abject figure we were all surely happy to have left behind, even if she continues to stalk queer talks as a reminder of a failed project. I suspect this reference to the ugliness of lesbians is intended as ironic, even playful. But of course contemporary sexism and homophobia is often ironic and playful. I don't find it particularly amusing.

And indeed what is also noticeable is how this investment in miserable lesbians leads to an erasure of the inventiveness in lesbian histories . . . as a desire to be ordinary in a world in which your desires take you out of the ordinary. The bits and pieces from lesbian histories that are understood as more redeemable (for example, butch/femme as erotic styles or modes of being) become rewritten as a queer history, or a history of how queerness came to be. Of course there were moments in lesbian feminist history when butch and femme were critiqued as imitating the gender system, or when the butch lesbian was herself rendered a pale imitation of a man (moments that exposed the class as well as racial specificity of lesbian ideals); but that was not exhaustive either as a moment or as a critique. Lesbians are not a step on a path that leads in a queer direction.

> **A willful lesbian stone is not a stepping stone. Try stepping on a stone butch and see what happens.**

More is at stake in lesbian feminism as a politics of willfulness than how the figure of the lesbian feminist is menacing and miserable. Willfulness is also behind us. We can listen to who is behind us. Julia Penelope describes lesbianism as willfulness: "The lesbian *stands against* the world created by the male imagination. What *willfulness* we possess when we claim our lives!" (1992, 42, first emphasis mine). Marilyn Frye's radical feminism uses the adjective *willful*: "The willful creation of new meaning, new loci of meaning, and new ways of being, together, in the world, seems to me in these mortally dangerous times the best hope we have" (1992, 9). Together these statements are claims to willfulness as a lesbian and radical feminist politics, and I want us to think about the connections between them: willfulness as standing against; willfulness as creativity.

When a world does not give us standing, to stand is to stand against that world. And when a world does not give us standing, we have to create other ways of being in the world. You acquire the potential to make things, create things. Lesbian feminism: the actualization of a potential we have to make things. A movement is assembled by those who keep encountering in their everyday life what they stand against. Lesbian feminism is radical feminism (in the sense of feminist at its root) and thus lesbian feminism demands our full involvement; as Marilyn Frye describes, "Bodily energy, ardour, intelligence, vitality" all need "to be available and engaged in the creation of a world for women" (1991,14).

To be engaged in the creation of a world for women is to transform what it means to be women. Let me explain what I mean by this by going back to the words. The history of the word *woman* teaches us how the categories that secure personhood are bound up with a history of ownership: *woman* is derived from a compound of *wif* (wife) and *man* (human being); woman as wife-man also suggesting woman as female servant. The history of woman is impossible to disentangle from the history of wife: the female human not only as in relation to man but as for man (woman as there for, and therefore, being for). We can make sense of Monique Wittig's (1992) audacious statement, "Lesbians are not women." She argues that lesbians are not women because "women" is being in relation to men: for Wittig, "women" is a heterosexual category, or a heterosexual injunction. To become a lesbian is to queer woman by wrestling her away from him. To create a world for women is to cease to be women for. To be a woman with a woman or a woman with women (we do not need to assume a couple form) is to become what Wittig calls an "escapee" or a stray. To be a lesbian is to stray away from the path you are supposed to follow if you are to reach the right destination. To stray is to deviate from the path of happiness. We deviate from the category "women" when we move toward women. Or if a lesbian is a woman, if we wrestle her away from this history, she is a willful woman.

Willful woman: how striking! Willful woman: how queer! By holding on to the figure of the lesbian as full of potential, we are not giving up on queer; rather, we are refusing to assume being queer means giving up on lesbian feminism.[4] . . . I drew on Eve Kosofsky Sedgwick's discussion of how the potential of queer resides in how it is cleaved to everyday childhood scenes of shame. Queer arrives as an affective inheritance of an insult.[5] That queer became an insult directed to sexual minorities refers us back to earlier meanings of queer as odd or strange. The lesbian as a figure might even overinherit queerness: in a heteropatriarchal world there might be nothing odder, or more striking, than women who have as their primary sexual and life partners other women. Lesbians: queer before queer.

Lesbian feminism: how revolting! We are revolting against the requirement to be in relation to men; we are revolting against the demand to be female relatives. Lesbian feminism: how we revolt; how we become revolting. The classic piece "Woman Identified Woman" by Radicalesbians thus begins with an explosive speech act: "A lesbian is the rage of all women condensed to the point of explosion" (1970, n.p.). This speech act renders the lesbian herself into a tipping point, a breaking point, what I called in the previous chapter feminist snap. She comes to embody the collective rage of women against the requirement to live their lives in relation to men, to become female relatives to the male universal. Such a rage, however, is only part of the story being told; becoming lesbian is an energetic becoming, a redirecting of women's energies away from the labor of maintaining relationships with men as our primary relationships.

A lesbian withdraws from a system that requires that she make herself available to men. Many antifeminist as well as antilesbian arguments explain and pathologize her withdrawal. One of the primary ways is through the explanation that lesbianism begins with disappointment; that some women become lesbians because they are not desirable to men; she is understood as a weak substitute, she yet again as not he. She can't get him so she settles for her.[6]

The rendering of the lesbian into an abject figure is an orientation device, a way of signaling the danger of not orientating your life as a woman around men. She acquires utility as a reminder of the unhappy consequence of getting things wrong. This statement by Radicalesbians shows exactly how abjection is used as a warning:

> As long as the label "dyke" can be used to frighten women into a less militant stand, keep her separate from her sisters, keep her from giving primacy to anything other than men and family—then to that extent she is controlled by the male culture. Until women see in each other the possibility of a primal commitment which includes sexual love, they will be denying themselves the love and value they readily accord to men, thus affirming their second-class status. As long as male acceptability is primary— both to individual women and to the movement as a whole—the term lesbian will be used effectively against women. Insofar as women want only more privileges within the system, they do not want to antagonize male power. They instead seek acceptability

for women's liberation, and the most crucial aspect of the acceptability is to deny lesbianism—i.e., to deny any fundamental challenge to the basis of the female. But why is it that women have related to and through men? By virtue of having been brought up in a male society, we have internalized the male culture's definition of ourselves. That definition consigns us to sexual and family functions, and excludes us from defining and shaping the terms of our lives. (1970, n.p.)

The dyke is frightening. To become a dyke is not to be frightened off from militancy. To become a dyke is thus to become militant. She represents a cutoff point. For feminisms that are about becoming acceptable (code: more acceptable to men, or more acceptable to those who are being asked to give up some of their power), lesbians are still unacceptable; lesbianism stands for what is unacceptable; the woman who goes astray is the one who does make becoming acceptable to men her way. Or the work of being lesbian without losing face is the work of becoming as acceptable as one can be, the kind of diversity work . . . described . . . as institutional passing. Shiny happy lesbians: you can polish yourself by removing traces of dykes and other more frightening lesbian tendencies.

If in becoming woman we have already been directed a certain way, then to become woman in a different way requires a reorientation. To become woman can often mean, in this context, becoming unrelated. It requires work; the effort of redirection, turning away from men as turning the wrong way. At the end of the film *A Question of Silence*, . . . we witness this work. When Janine exits the courtroom her husband signals to her to come to him. He beeps the horn of his car, aggressively. I hear that beep as the sound of patriarchy: attend to me; turn to me; listen to me; come back to me. But Janine does not turn to him, return to him; she turns instead toward the other women who have left the room. It is a subtle movement. It is a small step. But it is the beginning of a reorientation. When eventually Janine can turn away from the man who demands her attention, toward other women, it is only because something has already snapped, a bond not only to an individual man as a sexual and life partner, but to the world that makes that bond that which demands the fullness of her attention. Snap is what allows her turning, what allows her to see the women who are already there: right by her side. To identify as lesbian is to turn toward women, which, given the system we live in, requires an active and perpetual turning away from men.

In the statement "Woman Identified Woman," this turning toward women is described in terms of energy. They note, "On one level, which is both personal and political, women may withdraw emotional and sexual energies from men, and work out various alternatives for those energies in their own lives" (Radicalesbians 1970). I think woman identification has been read too quickly as being about gender expression. Woman identification here is about refusing as women to identify with male culture. To refuse to identify is to withdraw your own energy from relationships to men. You often have to become willful to withdraw that energy because you are expected to allocate it that way. Even to withdraw your energy from relationships to men will then be pathologized as hatred of men. This is why the lesbian appears so regularly as a man hater. And this is why woman identification makes woman such a willful subject; she is willful when she is not willing to put her energies into her relationships with men; she is willful by how she redirects her attention. We could reclaim Adrienne Rich's (1993) somewhat maligned term "lesbian continuum" on similar grounds: not as taking the sex out of lesbianism (by putting friendships between women on the same continuum with sexual relationships) but as a call to redirect our attention.[7] To attend to women, we have to unlearn how we have learned to screen women out. We have to learn not to pass over her, just as we have been passed over.

It is something to aim for. When you aim not to reproduce a world that directs attention to men, you are threatening. When your being threatens life, you have to wrap life around being.

You have to wrap life around being. I would suggest that it is transfeminism today that most recalls the militant spirit of lesbian feminism in part because of the insistence that crafting a life is political work. Transfeminist manifestos carry the baton of radical lesbian manifestos such as "Woman Identified Woman": from Sandy Stone's (2006) "The Empire Strikes Back: A Posttranssexual Manifesto" to Julia Serano's (2007) "Trans Woman Manifesto" and Susan Stryker's (1994) "My Words to Victor Frankenstein." These texts assemble a politics from what they name: showing not only how the sex-gender system is coercive, how it restricts what and who can be, but how creativity comes from how we survive a system that we cannot dismantle by the force of our will alone (no matter how willful we are).

The monsters will lead the way. Susan Stryker describes how the transsexual appears as monster within some lesbian and gay writing. Rather than distancing herself from this figure, Stryker claims her, becomes her; a proximity initiated as a politics of transgender rage: "Through the operation of rage, the stigma itself becomes the source of transformative power" (1994, 261).

Remember, resonance.
Abject within feminism
Monstrosity

When lesbians insisted on speaking within feminist spaces, we were rendered monstrous: think back to Betty Friedan's description of a lesbian presence as a "lavender menace," a description that lesbian feminists such as Rita Mae Brown were willing to take up as their own. For Stryker, being willing to be the monster becomes a matter of how you live your life: "May your rage inform your actions and your actions transform you as you struggle to transform your world" (1994, 254). A political struggle can be the struggle to transform your world. It can take willfulness to bring politics back to life.

Willfulness might seem to be about an individual subject, as the one who has to become willful just to exist. She matters; to become a subject for some is to become a willful subject. But it is important not to reduce willfulness to individualism, as I have noted previously. We can think here of the character Molly Bolt from Rita Mae Brown's (1973) classic lesbian novel, *Rubyfruit Jungle*. It is interesting to note how this novel has been challenged by some critics for its individualism. Kim Emery in her reading of the novel strains hard (in the best way) to be sympathetic. But she notes, "I find it difficult to read *Rubyfruit Jungle* as being anything other than the simplistic, essentialist, and effectively anti-feminist aggrandizement of American individualism that critics like Bonnie Zimmerman hold it to be" (Emery 2002, 126). Emery in her reading also draws upon Rita Mae Brown's feisty lesbian feminist text *A Plain Brown Rapper*, in which Brown

(1976, 126) describes woman identification as an on-going activity, as a persistent practice of selfhood and solidarity. I think reading Molly Bolt through the lens of willfulness allows us to understand that actions that can be diagnosed as individualism provide the basis of lesbian feminist rebellion against social norms and conventions such as the family. When you fight against the family, you are often understood as fighting for yourself. Rebellion is dismissible as individualism. The word *willfulness* registers this dismissal.

I offered a reading *of Rubyfruit Jungle* in my book *The Promise of Happiness* (Ahmed 2010) as one instance of the genre of what I called female troublemaker fiction. Somewhat surprisingly (even to myself, looking back) Molly Bolt did not pop up in *Willful Subjects* (Ahmed 2014), though maybe she lent a hand to the many will-ful arms that haunted the pages. Molly is appealing. She captures something for us as lesbian readers precisely because of her willful energy: she is too much; she has to be too much, if she is not to be brought down by what she comes up against. It would be easy to dismiss this concern with character as individualism. For those who have to struggle to be, to become an individual is a profoundly communal achievement.

It is not surprising that girls who want girls are found to have wills that are wanting. A willful les-bian might be the one who makes bad object choices. A bad choice is when you willingly want the wrong things, the things you are supposed to give up, as well as willfully not wanting the right things, those that would or should secure your happiness. A willful les-bian archive is thus not only an unhappy archive, even though it includes unhappiness. As Elizabeth Freeman suggests, we might be able to glimpse in our archives "historically specific forms of pleasure" that have not been "subsumed into institutional forms" (2005, 66). Molly is not subsumed; her pleasures leak all over the place. She says in response to a question of how many women she has slept with: "Hundreds. I'm irresistible" (200). *Rubyfruit Jungle* offers us a story of a queer girl who refuses to give up her desires, even if they take her outside the horizon of happiness, even though they get her into trouble. When Molly is brought to the dean's office after rumors of lesbianism at film college, she is asked by the dean about her problem with girls, and replies:

"Dean Marne, I don't have any problems relating to girls and I'm in love with my roommate. She makes me happy." Her scraggly red eyebrows with the brown pencil glaring through shot up. "Is this relationship with Faye Raider of an, uh—intimate nature?" "We fuck, if that's what you're after." I think her womb collapsed on that one. Sputtering, she pressed forward. "Don't you find that somewhat of an aberration? Doesn't this disturb you, my dear? After all, it's not normal." "I know it's not normal for people in this world to be happy, and I'm happy." (127)

Rather than being disturbed by being found disturb-ing, Molly performs the ultimate act of defiance, by claiming her happiness as abnormal. It is as if queers, by doing what they want, expose the unhappiness of having to sacrifice personal desires, in the perversity of their twists and turns, for the happiness of others.

The lesbian who persists is misdirected.
She is willing to be misdirected.
She is willing to miss.
Willfulness: not missing what you miss.

Despite all her charm, and her rather infectious en-thusiasm for lesbian life worlds, it is not that Molly's experiences are happy ones, in the sense that she is able to make and get her way. Indeed, throughout, her experiences involve discrimination: violence and rejection from would-be lovers, who cannot bear the consequences of following queer desire out of the forms of recognition delivered by a straight world. She is just not defeated by these experiences. Of course, we need to take care to avoid turning characters such as Molly into good object lessons: as if we could create a moral imperative from the example of her fictional life. But we can still be infected by her enthusiasm that spills all over the pages, her refusal to be brought down. For me, as a lesbian feminist reader, characters like Molly Bolt with a spring in their step pick me up; feisty characters whose vitality is not at the expense of their lesbian desire, but how their desire roams across the pages.

If we think of lesbian feminism as a willfulness archive, we are not simply directing our attention to characters such as Molly Bolt, however appealing.

A willfulness archive would derive as much from our struggle to write ourselves into existence as from who appears in what we write. This intimacy of standing against and creativity can take the form of a book.

> **A willful girl in a book**
> **A willful girl as a book**
> **I am rather taken by you**

Gloria Anzaldúa describes her book *Borderlands/La Frontera: The New Mestiza* as follows: "The whole thing has had a mind of its own, escaping me and insisting on putting together the pieces of its own puzzle with minimal direction from my will. It is a rebellious, willful entity, a precocious girl-child forced to grow up too quickly" ([1987] 1999, 88). A book, a survival strategy, comes alive, acquires a life of its own, a will of its own, a willful will; history by the bone, own but not alone.

Lesbian feminism of color: the struggle to put ourselves back together because within lesbian shelters too our being was not always accommodated. I think of a brown history, a mixed history as a lesbian history, another way in which we can tell a history of women being in relation to women. I think of my own history, as a mixed lesbian, so many sides, all over the place. I think of all that lesbian potential as coming from somewhere. Brownness has a lesbian history, because there are brown lesbians in history; whether or not you could see us, whether or not you knew where to find us.

Intersectionality: let's make a point of how we come into existence. I am not a lesbian one moment and a person of color the next and a feminist at another. I am all of these at every moment. And lesbian feminism of color brings this all into existence, writing of all existence, with insistence, with persistence. There can be so much labor to bring ourselves about. When being is laboring, we are creating more than ourselves. Lesbian feminism of color is a lifeline made up out of willful books that had to insist on their own creation. Books are themselves material, paper, pen, ink, even blood. Words come out of us, like sweat, like blood; tears. Your texts are littered with love. Words can pulse with life; words as flesh, leaking; words as heart, beating.

A poem weeps

Audre Lorde spoke of herself as a writer when she was dying. For Lorde, writing was a survival strategy. She says, "1 am going to write fire until it comes out of my ears, my eyes, my noseholes—everywhere. Until it's every breath I breathe. I'm going to go out like a fucking meteor!" (1988, 76–77).

> **And so she did**
> **And so she did**

She goes out; she makes something. She calls this capacity to make things through heat "the erotic." Lorde describes, "There is a difference between painting a black fence and writing a poem, but only one of quantity. And there is, for me, no difference between writing a good poem and moving into sunlight against the body of a woman I love" (1984a, 58). Words flicker with life, like the sunlight on her body.

> **A love poem**
> **A lover as poem**

I am warmed by the thought; of how we create things; of how we break open a container to make things. We watch the words spill. They spill all over you. I think too of Cherríe Moraga's poem "The Welder." Moraga speaks of heating being used to shape new elements, to create new shapes, "the intimacy of steel melting, the fire that makes sculpture of your lives, builds buildings" (1981, 219). We build our own buildings when the world does not accommodate our desires. When you are blocked, when your very existence is prohibited or viewed with general suspicion or even just raised eyebrows (yes they are pedagogy), you have to come up with your own systems for getting things through. You might even have to come up with your own system for getting yourself through.

> **How inventive**
> **Quite something**
> **Not from nothing**
> **Something from something**
> **A kitchen table becomes a publishing house**

We assemble ourselves around our own tables, kitchen tables, doing the work of community as ordinary conversation. Lesbian feminist world making is nothing extraordinary; I have tried to show how lesbian feminist world making is quite ordinary. The ordinary can be what you are for. For: it comes from not. To stand against what is, we make room for what is not. Or even:

we are for what is not. We might think of the work of making room as wiggling, a corporeal willfulness; like that toe that wiggles about in a shoe. A lesbian does not toe the line. Lesbians (as lesbians well know) have quite a wiggle; you have to wiggle to make room in a cramped space. We can be warmed by the work required to be together even if we sometimes wish it was less work. To recall the vitality of lesbian feminism as a resource of the present is to remember that effort required for our shelters to be built. When we have to shelter from the harshness of a world, we build a shelter.

Lesbian feminism gives us the tools to build a world in which we become each other's building blocks. We love our cobuilders; they are our lovers, which is not to say that we might not struggle at times to agree about what we are making. We have to find spaces that are for women: and for women means, for those who are assigned or assign themselves as women, for those who willfully accept being women as their assignment. And women's spaces are gradually being eroded, often through the assumption that they are no longer necessary. I have addressed this problem in relation to women's studies. . . . The time for women's studies is not over until universities cease to be men's studies. We must be willful to will this cessation.

We are willful when we are not willing to cease. To recall the vitality of lesbian feminism as a resource of the present is to stay attuned to that effort required for those shelters to be built, brick by brick; she had a hand in it.

> **Helter-skelter**
> **What a shelter**

The roots; back to routes. *Skelter* from *skelt:* "to hasten, scatter hurriedly." Scattered; shattered; confusion. The helter?

> **Just there for the rhyme**
> **Poetry in motion**

To build from the ruin; our building might seem ruined; when we build, we ruin. It is a lesbian feminist hope: to become a ruin, to ruin by becoming.

How easily though without foundations, without a stable ground, the walls come down. We keep them up; we keep each other up. We might then think of fragility not so much as the potential to lose something, fragility as loss, but as a quality of relations we acquire, or a quality of what we build. A fragile shelter has looser walls, made out of lighter materials; see how they move. A movement is what is built to survive what has been built. When we loosen the requirements to be in a world, we create room for others to be.

CONCLUSION: INTERSECTIONALITY IS ARMY

We could think of lesbian feminism as willful carpentry: she builds with her own hands; she is handy. Maybe I am thinking too of your arms, your strong butch arms and what they can do, whom they can hold; of how they can hold me. If a feminist history is army, . . . that history is also a history of lesbian arms.

> **I think of being held by your arms**
> **Yes, I do**

I want to return one last time to the Grimm story. I keep coming back to the story because the arm keeps coming up. Is the willful child a lesbian? Is the arm a lesbian? The arm certainly seems queer: to come up is to be way ward.

We could tell a few lesbian stories about arms. When arms are not employed, they disobey; they wander away. Arms can be "matter out of place," to borrow an expression from the anthropologist Mary Douglas ([1966] 2002, 44), the sign of an improper residence. If you have the wrong arms, it means you are assumed to be in the wrong place. An example: A butch lesbian enters the female restroom. The attendant becomes flustered and says, "You are not supposed to be here." The butch lesbian is used to this: how many of her stories are restroom stories; to pass as male becomes a question mark of your right to pass into female space. "I am a woman," she says. We might have to assign ourselves with gender if we trouble the existing assignments. With a reassignment, she can go to the restroom. When she comes out, the attendant is embarrassed; the attendant points to her arm, saying, "So strong." The butch lesbian allows the moment to pass by joking, giving the attendant a show of her arms.

With arms we come out, with arm we come in. If the strong arms are called upon to answer a questioning of a right to be there, they are called upon to assert a right to be there. However, these moments do not always pass so easily. Many of these histories of passing or of not passing are traumatic.[8] Arms don't always help us get through. When arms are wayward, they can be beaten. If we told queer history as a history of arms, we would show the material consequences of being wayward. Arms after all can be gendering assignments. J. Halberstam in *Female Masculinity* notes with some surprise how Havelock Ellis uses the arm as a gender test in the case of Miss M.: "Miss M. he thinks, tries to cover over her masculinity but gives herself away to Ellis when he uses a rather idiosyncratic test of gender identification: 'with arms, palmed up, extended in front of her with inner sides touching, she cannot bring the inner sides of the forearms together as nearly every woman can, showing that the feminine angle of the arm is lost'" (Halberstam 1998, 80). If the arminess of the queer female arm is detected by a straightening rod, the arm is not straightened. The arm can be the fleshy site of a disagreement. The wayward arm is another call to arms.

You note the connection between the strong arms of the black woman (who has to insist on being woman) . . . and the strong arms of the butch lesbian (who has to insist on being woman) discussed here. These arms can, of course, belong to the same body. Throughout feminist history many women had to insist on being women before they became part of the feminist conversation. Trans women have to insist on being women; trans women often have to keep insisting, again and again, often in the face of violent and repeated acts

of misgendering; any feminists who do not stand up, who do not wave their arms to protest against this misgendering, have become the straightening rods. An antitrans stance is an antifeminist stance; it is against the feminist project of creating worlds to support those for whom gender fatalism (boys will be boys, girls will be girls) is fatal; a sentencing to death. We have to hear that fatalism as punishment and instruction: it is the story of the rod, of how those who have wayward wills or who will waywardly (boys who will not be boys, girls who will not be girls) are beaten. We need to drown these antitrans voices out, raising the sound of our own. Our voices need to become our arms: rise up; rise up.

We can make an army connection: if gender norms operate to create a narrow idea of how a female arm should appear, a white arm, a slight arm, an arm that has not labored, an arm that is delicately attuned to an assignment, then many who understand themselves as women, who sign up to being women, will be deemed not women because of their arms. It is the arms that lead us astray.

Arms not only have a history; they are shaped by history; arms make history flesh. No wonder arms keep coming up. It is the arms that can help us make the connection between histories that otherwise do not seem to meet. There are many arms; arms that are muscular, strong, laboring arms, arms that refuse to be employed, striking arms; arms that are lost in service to the industrial machine; broken arms.

Intersectionality is arm.
Intersectionality is army.

NOTES

1. I acknowledge here the feminist digital media site Everyday Feminism, launched in 2012, with its mission to "help people heal from and stand up to everyday violence, discrimination, and marginalization through applied intersectional feminism" (http://everydayfeminism.com/, last accessed September 18, 2015).

2. When writing this sentence about how women have to get their whole body behind an action, I was reminded of Iris Marion Young's description of "throwing like a girl." . . . A girl throws by not putting the whole of her body behind the action. Young gives us a phenomenological account of how the girl comes to experience her body as restriction. But one aspect of her account we could reflect upon is the extent to which it accepts that a girl, when throwing like a girl, throws in a way that is less good than a boy (in other words, the extent to which it accepts the association of femininity and failure). It might seem obvious that her way of throwing is deficient: that the boy throws faster and farther than the girl. But if we think of how the girl has

to put so much energy into accomplishing things, because of the obstacles that she encounters, things that are in her way, could we not see her way of throwing as wisdom: she is saving her energy for more important things? See also Dahl (2015) for an important queer femme critique of how feminists associate femininity with failure.

3. This would be true of course only for those who have lost connection to middle-class or resource-rich families. My argument here suggests that we need to rethink the distinction between a politics of recognition and a politics of redistribution (see Butler's [1997] critique of Nancy Fraser's use of this distinction). Sexuality, race, and gender as a series of norms are very much about access to resources that cannot be separated from the class system (indeed, which mess with that system at certain points). We can witness this messiness when we return to life, which is to say, to ups and downs, to the distribution of vulnerability across a life course as well as a social system (see also Butler 2004).

4. I was very struck, when I gave a lecture in February 2015 on living a lesbian life, based on material from this, . . . how my argument was translated as calling for a return to lesbian feminism by giving up on queer.

5. We could show how Sedgwick's argument can be applied to queer studies: that the potential for queer studies resides in how queer cleaves to those scenes of shame. In other words, queer is all the more queer because of what queer refers to. I add this because I have detected some anxiety within queer studies about the status of queer as a literal referent. We can queer the referent. We might even become rather literal about this; go back to the letter. We preserve histories by the words we use, which does not mean that the act of preservation should not be contested (which histories, which words, who, when, where?). Let's think about the word *reference*. It is itself a rather queer word. To refer is to relate or to carry back. Heather Love (2007) describes "feeling backward" as a way of doing queer history. Perhaps we can do feminist and queer theory by using backward terms, terms that point us back. To use terms that go back is not to make these terms into a ground: going back is another invitation to go back again; referral as deferral. We can refuse the injunction to move forward by assuming that going back is what would stop us from moving at all. Words can keep histories alive, or words remind us of how histories arc alive. To use queer as if it can simply be freed from this history would be to lose something; it would detach queer from the very histories that render queer affective or charged. When we lose that charge, queer can end up being reorganized around the same old bodies, doing the same old things. We need to retain that charge in how we use the word: pointedly. And, . . . we can then use queer to question how queer can be taken up as if it replaces other words (such as lesbian) that are assumed to be more containing, because they are assumed to be always and only about identity. . . . [I] also aim to show how some words become pointers of identity (identity words), attached to bodies who are deemed too attached to themselves, by how other words are freed or detached from bodies, becoming lighter, even universal. We need the heavier words to point us back, to teach us how lighter words that are assumed to be detached still point to some bodies more than others.

6. For a much longer discussion of the figure of the "contingent lesbian" (derived from a reading of psychoanalysis and inversion), see chapter 2 in my book *Queer Phenomenology* (Ahmed 2006).

7. We might return as well to Alice Walker's powerful womanist prose. As I noted . . . in her *In Search of Our Mothers' Gardens,* Walker defines a womanist as a "black feminist or feminist of color" and as "usually referring to outrageous, audacious, courageous or *willful* behavior" (2005, xi). Walker also describes a womanist as a "woman who loves women, sexually and nonsexually" (xi). A womanist is a queer as well as a willful black woman or woman of color.

8. For discussions of bathrooms as places of gender policing, see Cavanagh (2010) and Halberstam (1998, 20–29).

JOSÉ MUÑOZ

54. QUEERNESS AS HORIZON: UTOPIAN HERMENEUTICS IN THE FACE OF GAY PRAGMATISM

I begin this . . . on futurity and a desire that is utopian by turning to a text from the past—more specifically, to those words that emanate from the spatiotemporal coordinate Bloch referred to as the no-longer-conscious, a term that attempts to enact a more precise understanding of the work that the past does, what can be understood as the performative force of the past. A 1971 issue of the gay liberation journal *Gay Flames* included a manifesto by a group calling itself Third World Gay Revolution. The text, titled "What We Want, What We Believe," offered a detailed list of demands that included the abolition of capital punishment, the abolishment of institutional religion, and the end of the bourgeois family. The entire list of sixteen demands culminated with a request that was especially radical and poignant when compared to the anemic political agenda that dominates contemporary LGBT politics in North America today.

> 16.) We want a new society—a revolutionary socialist society. We want liberation of humanity, free food, free shelter, free clothing, free transportation, free health care, free utilities, free education, free art for all. We want a society where the needs of the people come first.
>
> We believe that all people should share the labor and products of society, according to each one's needs and abilities, regardless of race, sex, age or sexual preferences. We believe the land, technology and the means of production belong to the people, and must be shared by the people collectively for the liberation of all.[1]

When we consider the extremely pragmatic agenda that organizes LGBT activism in North America today, the demand "we want a new society" may seem naive by the present's standards. Many people would dismiss these demands as impractical or merely utopian. Yet I contend that there is great value in pulling these words from the no-longer-conscious to arm a critique of the present. The use of "we" in this manifesto can be mistakenly read as the "we" implicit in the identity politics that emerged after the Third World Gay Revolution group. Such a reading would miss the point. This "we" does not speak to a merely identitarian logic but instead to a logic of futurity. The "we" speaks to a "we" that is "not yet conscious" the future society that is being invoked and addressed at the same moment. The "we" is not content to describe who the collective is but more nearly describes what the collective and the larger social order could be, what it should be. The particularities that are listed—"race, sex, age or sexual preferences"—are not things in and of themselves that format this "we"; indeed the statement's "we" is "regardless" of these markers, which is not to say that it is beyond such distinctions or due to these differences but, instead, that it is *beside* them. This is to say that the field of utopian possibility is one in which multiple forms of belonging in difference adhere to a belonging in collectivity.

Such multiple forms of belonging-in-difference and expansive critiques of social asymmetries are absent in the dominant LGBT leadership community and in many aspects of queer critique. One manifesto from today s movement that seems especially representative of the anemic, shortsighted, and retrograde politics of the present is "All Together Now (A Blueprint for the Movement),"[2] a text written by pro-gay-marriage lawyer Evan Wolfson that appeared

---

on his website, freedomtomarry.org. Wolfson's single-minded text identifies the social recognition and financial advantages offered by traditional marriage pacts as the key to what he calls "freedom." Freedom for Wolfson is mere inclusion in a corrupt and bankrupt social order. Wolfson cannot critique the larger ideological regime that represents marriage as something desirable, natural, and good. His assimilationist gay politics posits an "all" that is in fact a few: queers with enough access to capital to imagine a life integrated within North American capitalist culture. It goes almost without saying that the "all" invoked by the gay lawyer and his followers are normative citizen-subjects with a host of rights only afforded to some (and not all) queer people. Arguments against gay marriage have been articulated with great acumen by Lisa Duggan and Richard Kim.[3] But it is Wolfson's invocation of the term *freedom* that is most unsettling.

Wolfson and his website's rhetoric degrade the concept of freedom. Homonormative cultural and political lobbyists such as Wolfson have degraded the political and conceptual force of concepts such as freedom in the same way that the current political regime of the United States has degraded the term *liberation* in the case of recent Middle Eastern foreign policy. I invoke Wolfson here not so much as [a] . . . problem or foil but merely as a recent symptom of the erosion of the gay and lesbian political imagination. Wolfson represents many homonormative interests leading the contemporary LGBT movement toward the goal of "naturalizing" the flawed and toxic ideological formation known as marriage. The aping of traditional straight relationality, especially marriage, for gays and lesbians announces itself as a pragmatic strategy when it is in fact a deeply ideological project that is hardly practical. In this way gay marriage's detractors are absolutely right: gay marriage is not natural—but then again, neither is marriage for any individual.

A similar but more nuanced form of what I am referring to as gay pragmatic thought can be seen in Biddy Martins work, especially her psycho-analytically inspired diagnosis that queer critique suffers from an androcentric bias in which queerness presents itself as the "extraordinary" while at the same time fleeing the charge of being "ordinary." Being ordinary and being married are both antiutopian wishes, desires that automatically rein themselves in, never daring to see or imagine the not-yet-conscious. This line of thought that I am identifying as pragmatic is taken from its vernacular register. I am not referring to the actual philosophical tradition of American pragmatism of Charles Peirce, William James, or John Dewey. But the current gay political strategy I am describing does share an interest in empiricism with that school. Gay pragmatic organizing is in direct opposition to the idealist thought that I associate as endemic to a forward-dawning queerness that calls on a no-longer-conscious in the service of imagining a futurity.

The not-quite-conscious is the realm of potentiality that must be called on, and insisted on, if we are ever to look beyond the pragmatic sphere of the here and now, the hollow nature of the present. Thus, I wish to argue that queerness is not quite here; it is, in the language of Italian philosopher Giorgio Agamben, a potentiality.[4] Alain Badiou refers to that which follows the event as the thing-that-is-not-yet-imagined,[5] and in my estimation queerness too should be understood to have a similar valence. But my turn to this notion of the not-quite-conscious is again indebted to Bloch and his massive three-volume text *The Principle of Hope.*[6] That treatise, both a continuation and an amplification of German idealist practices of thought, is a critical discourse—which is to say that it does not avert or turn away from the present. Rather; it critiques an autonaturalizing temporality that we might call *straight time*. Straight time tells us that there is no future but the here and now of our everyday life.[7] The only futurity promised is that of reproductive majoritarian heterosexuality, the spectacle of the state refurbishing its ranks through overt and subsidized acts of reproduction. In *No Future*, Lee Edelman advises queers that the future is "kid stuff."[8] Although I believe that there is a lot to like about Edelman's polemic—mostly its disdain for the culture of the child—I ultimately want to speak for a notion of queer futurity by turning to Bloch's critical notion of utopia.

It is equally polemical to argue that we are not quite queer yet, that queerness, what we will really know as queerness, does not yet exist. I suggest that holding queerness in a sort of ontologically humble state, under a conceptual grid in which we do not claim to always already know queerness in the world, potentially staves off the ossifying effects of neoliberal ideology and the degradation of politics brought about by representations of queerness in contemporary popular culture.

A posterior glance at different moments, objects, and spaces might offer us an anticipatory illumination of queerness. We cannot trust in the manifestations of what some people would call queerness in the present, especially as embodied in the pragmatic debates that dominate contemporary gay and lesbian politics. (Here, again, I most pointedly mean U.S. queers clamoring for their right to participate in the suspect institution of marriage and, maybe worse, to serve in the military.) None of this is to say that there are not avatars of a queer futurity, both in the past and the present, especially in sites of cultural production. What I am suggesting is that we gain a greater conceptual and theoretical leverage if we see queerness as something that is not yet here. In this sense it is useful to consider Edmund Husserl, phenomenology's founder, and his invitation to look to horizons of being.[9] Indeed to access queer visuality we may need to squint, to strain our vision and force it to see otherwise, beyond the limited vista of the here and now.

To critique an overarching "here and now" is not to turn ones face away from the everyday. Roland Barthes wrote that the mark of the utopian is the quotidian.[10] Such an argument would stress that the utopian is an impulse that we see in everyday life. This impulse is to be glimpsed as something that is extra to the everyday transaction of heteronormative capitalism. This quotidian example of the utopian can be glimpsed in utopian bonds, affiliations, designs, and gestures that exist within the present moment. Turning to the New York School of poetry, a moment that is one of the cultural touchstones for my research, we can consider a poem by James Schuyler that speaks of a hope and desire that is clearly utopian. The poem, like most of Schuyler's body of work, is clearly rooted in an observation of the affective realm of the present. Yet there is an excess that the poet also conveys, a type of affective excess that presents the enabling force of a forward-dawning futurity that is queerness. In the poem "A photograph," published in 1974 in the collection *Hymn to Life*, a picture that resides on the speaker's desk sparks a recollection of domestic bliss.

A PHOTOGRAPH

Shows you in a London
room; books, a painting,
your smile, a silky
tie, a suit. And more.
It looks so like you
and I see it every day
(here, on my desk)
which I don't you. Last Friday was grand.
We went out, we came
back, we went wild. You
slept. Me too. The pup
woke you and you dressed
and walked him. When
you left, I was sleeping.
When I woke there was
just time to make the
train to a country dinner
and talk about ecstasy.
Which I think comes in
two sorts: that which you
Know "Now I am ecstatic"
Like my strange scream
last Friday night. And
another kind, that you
know only in retrospect:
"Why, that joy I felt
and didn't think about
when his feet were in
my lap, or when I looked
down and saw his slanty
eyes shut, that too was
ecstasy. Nor is there
necessarily a downer from
it." Do I believe in
the perfectibility of
man? Strangely enough,
(I've known unhappiness enough) I do. I mean it.
I really do believe
future generations can
live without the intervals
of anxious
fear we know between our
bouts and strolls of
ecstasy. The struck ball

finds the pocket. You
smile some years back
in London, I have
known ecstasy and calm:
haven't you too? Let's
try to understand, my
handsome friend who
wears his nose awry.[11]

The speaker remembers the grandness of an unspec-
tacular Friday in which he and his addressee slept in
and then scrambled to catch a train to a dinner out
in the country. He attempts to explain the ecstasy he
felt that night, indicating that one moment of ecstasy,
a moment he identifies as being marked both by
self-consciousness and obliviousness, possesses a potentially transformative charge. He then considers another moment of ecstasy in retrospect, a looking back
at a no-longer-conscious that provides an affective enclave in the present that staves off the sense of "bad
feelings" that mark the affective disjuncture of being
queer in straight time.

The moment in the poem of deeper introspection—
beginning "Do I believe in / the perfectibility of /
man?"—is an example of a utopian desire inspired
by queer relationality. Moments of queer relational
bliss, what the poet names as ecstasies, are viewed as
having the ability to rewrite a larger map of everyday
life. When "future generations" are invoked, the poet
is signaling a queerness to come, a way of being in the
world that is glimpsed through reveries in a quotidian life that challenges the dominance of an affective
world, a present, full of anxiousness and fear. These
future generations are, like the "we" invoked in the
manifesto by the Third World Gay Revolution group,
not an identitarian formulation but, instead, the invocation of a future collectivity, a queerness that registers
as the illumination of a horizon of existence.

The poem speaks of multiple temporalities and the
affective mode known as ecstasy, which resonates alongside the work of Martin Heidegger. In *Being and Time*
Heidegger reflects on the activity of timeliness and its
relation to *ekstatisch* (ecstasy), signaling for Heidegger
the ecstatic unity of temporality—Past, Present, and
Future.[12] The ecstasy the speaker feels and remembers
in "A photograph" is not consigned to one moment. It
steps out from the past and remarks on the unity of an
expansive version of temporality; hence, future generations are invoked. To know ecstasy in the way in which
the poem's speaker does is to have a sense of timeliness's motion, to understand a temporal unity that is
important to what I attempt to describe as the time of
queerness. Queerness's time is a stepping out of the linearity of straight time. Straight time is a self-naturalizing
temporality. Straight time's "presentness" needs to be
phenomenologically questioned, and this is the fundamental value of a queer utopian hermeneutics. Queerness's ecstatic and horizonal temporality is a path and a
movement to a greater openness to the world.

It would be difficult to mistake Schuyler's poem
for one of Frank O'Hara's upbeat reveries. O'Hara's optimism is a contagious happiness within the quotidian
that I would also describe as having a utopian quality. Schuyler's poetry is not so much about optimism
but instead about a hope that is distinctly utopian and
distinctly queer. The poem imagines another collective belonging, an enclave in the future where readers
will not be beset with feelings of nervousness and fear.
These feelings are the affective results of being outside
of straight time. He writes from a depressive position,
"(I've known un- / happiness enough)," but reaches
beyond the affective force-field of the present.

Hope for Bloch is an essential characteristic of not
only the utopian but also the human condition. Thus,
I talk about the human as a relatively stable category.
But queerness in its utopian connotations promises a
human that is not yet here, thus disrupting any ossi-
fied understanding of the human. The point is to stave
off a gay and lesbian antiutopianism that is very much
tainted with a polemics of the pragmatic rights discourse that in and of itself hamstrings not only politics
but also desire. Queerness as utopian formation is a
formation based on an economy of desire and desiring.
This desire is always directed at that thing that is not
yet here, objects and moments that burn with anticipation and promise. The desire that propels Schuyler's "A
photograph" is born of the no-longer-conscious, the
rich resonance of remembrance, distinct pleasures felt
in the past. And thus past pleasures stave off the affective perils of the present while they enable a desire that
is queer futurity's core.

Queerness is utopian, and there is something queer about the utopian. Fredric Jameson described the utopian as the oddball or the maniac.[13] Indeed, to live inside straight time and ask for, desire, and imagine another time and place is to represent and perform a desire that is both utopian and queer. To participate in such an endeavor is not to imagine an isolated future for the individual but instead to participate in a hermeneutic that wishes to describe a collective futurity, a notion of futurity that functions as a historical materialist critique. In the two textual examples I have employed we see an overt utopianism that is explicit in the Third World Gay Revolution manifesto, and what I am identifying as a *utopian impulse* is perceivable in Schuyler's poetry. One requires a utopian hermeneutic to see an already operative principle of hope that hums in the poet's work. The other text, the manifesto, does another type of performative work; it *does* utopia.

To "read" the performative, along the lines of thought first inaugurated by J. L. Austin, is implicitly to critique the epistemological.[14] Performativity and utopia both call into question what is epistemologically there and signal a highly ephemeral ontological field that can be characterized as a *doing in futurity*. Thus, a manifesto is a call to a doing in and for the future. The utopian impulse to be gleaned from the poem is a call for "doing" that is a becoming: the becoming of and for "future generations." This rejection of the here and now, the ontologically static, is indeed, by the measure of homonormative codes, a maniacal and oddball endeavor. The queer utopian project addressed here turns to the fringe of political and cultural production to offset the tyranny of the homonormative. It is drawn to tastes, ideologies, and aesthetics that can only seem odd, strange, or indeed queer next to the muted striving of the practical and normalcy-desiring homosexual.

The turn to the call of the no-longer-conscious is not a turn to normative historical analysis. Indeed it is important to complicate queer history and understand it as doing more than the flawed process of merely evidencing. Evidencing protocols often fail to enact real hermeneutical inquiry and instead opt to reinstate that which is known in advance. Thus, practices of knowledge production that are content merely to cull selectively from the past, while striking a pose of positivist undertaking or empirical knowledge retrieval, often nullify the political imagination. Jameson's Marxian dictate "always historicize"[15] is not a methodological call for empirical data collection. Instead, it is a dialectical injunction, suggesting we animate our critical faculties by bringing the past to bear on the present and the future. Utopian hermeneutics offer us a refined lens to view queerness, insofar as queerness, if it is indeed not quite here, is nonetheless intensely relational with the past.

The present is not enough. It is impoverished and toxic for queers and other people who do not feel the privilege of majoritarian belonging, normative tastes, and "rational" expectations. (I address the question of rationalism shortly). Let me be clear that the idea is not simply to turn away from the present. One cannot afford such a maneuver, and if one thinks one can, one has resisted the present in favor of folly. The present must be known in relation to the alternative temporal and spatial maps provided by a perception of past and future affective worlds.

Utopian thinking gets maligned for being naively romantic. Of course, much of it has been naive. We know that any history of actualized utopian communities would be replete with failures. No one, other than perhaps Marx himself, has been more cognizant about this fact than Bloch. But it is through this Marxian tradition, not beside or against it, that the problem of the present is addressed. In the following quotation we begin to glimpse the importance of the Marxian tradition for the here and now.

> Marxism, above all, was first to bring a concept of knowledge into the world that essentially refers to Becomeness, but to the tendency of what is coming up; thus for the first time it brings future into our conceptual and theoretical grasp. Such recognition of tendency is necessary to remember, and to open up the No-Longer-Conscious.[16]

Thus we see Bloch's model for approaching the past. The idea is not to attempt merely to represent it with simplistic strokes. More nearly, it is important to call on the past, to animate it, understanding that the past has a performative nature, which is to say that rather than being static and fixed, the past does things. It is in this very way that the past is performative. Following a Blochian thread, it seems important to put the past into play with the present, calling into view the tautological nature of the present. The present, which is almost exclusively conceived through the parameters of straight time, is a self-naturalizing endeavor. Opening up a queer past is enabled by Marxian ideological tactics. Bloch explains that

> Marxism thus rescued the rational core of utopia and made it concrete as well as the core of the still idealistic tendency of dialectics. Romanticism does not understand utopia, not even its own, but utopia that has become concrete understands Romanticism and makes inroads into it, in so far as archaic material in its archetypes and work, contain a not yet voiced, undischarged element.[17]

Bloch invites us to look to this no-longer-conscious, a past that is akin to what Derrida described as the trace. These ephemeral traces, flickering illuminations from other times and places, are sites that may indeed appear merely romantic, even to themselves. Nonetheless they assist those of us who wish to follow queerness's promise, its still unrealized potential, to see something else, a component that the German aesthetician would call *cultural surplus*. I build on this idea to suggest that the surplus is both cultural and *affective*. More distinctly, I point to a queer feeling of hope in the face of hopeless heteronormative maps of the present where futurity is indeed the province of normative reproduction. This hope takes on the philosophical contours of idealism.

A queer utopian hermeneutic would thus be queer in its aim to look for queer relational formations within the social. It is also about this temporal project that I align with queerness, a work shaped by its idealist trajectory; indeed it is the work of not settling for the present, of asking and looking beyond the here and now. Such a hermeneutic would then be *epistemologically and ontologically humble* in that it would not claim the epistemological certitude of a queerness that we simply "know" but, instead, strain to activate the no-longer-conscious and to extend a glance toward that which is forward-dawning, anticipatory illuminations of the not-yet-conscious. The purpose of such temporal maneuvers is to wrest ourselves from the presents stultifying hold, to know our queerness

as a belonging in particularity that is not dictated or organized around the spirit of political impasse that characterizes the present.

Jameson has suggested that for Bloch the present is provincial.[18] This spatialization of time makes sense in relation to the history of utopian thought, most famously described as an island by Thomas More. To mark the present as provincial is not to ridicule or demean the spots on queerness's map that do not signify as metropolitan. The here and now has an opposite number, and that would be the then and there. I have argued that the *then* that disrupts the tyranny of the *now* is both past and future. Along those lines, the here that is unnamed yet always implicit in the metropolitan hub requires the challenge of a there that can be regional or global. The transregional or the global as modes of spatial organization potentially displace the hegemony of an unnamed here that is always dominated by the shadow of the nation-state and its mutable and multiple corporate interests. While *globalization* is a term that mostly defines a worldwide system of manufactured asymmetry and ravenous exploitation, it also signals the encroaching of the there on the here in ways that are worth considering.

The Third World Gay Revolution group was an organization that grew out of the larger Gay Liberation Front at roughly the same time that the Radicalesbians also spun off from the larger group in the spring/summer of 1970. Although they took the name Third World Gay Revolution, the group's members have been described by a recent historian as people of color.[19] Their own usage of the term "Third World" clearly connotes their deep identification with the global phenomenon that was decolonization. It is therefore imperative to remember this moment from the no-longer-conscious that transcended a gay and lesbian activist nationalist imaginary. For Heidegger "time and space are not co-ordinate. Time is prior to space."[20] If time is prior to space, then we can view both the force of the no-longer-conscious and the not-yet-here as potentially bearing on the *here* of naturalized space and time. Thus, at the center of cultural texts such as the manifesto "All Together Now (A Blueprint for the Movement)" we find an ideological document, and its claim to the pragmatic is the product of a short-sighted here that fails to include anything but an entitled and privileged world. The there of queer utopia cannot simply be that of the faltering yet still influential nation-state.

This is then to say that the distinctions between here and there, and the world that the here and now organizes, are not fixed—they are already becoming undone in relation to a forward-dawning futurity. It is important to understand that a critique of our homosexual present is not an attack on what many people routinely name as lesbian or gay but, instead, an appraisal of how queerness is still forming, or in many crucial ways formless. Queerness's form is utopian. Ultimately, we must insist on a queer futurity because the present is so poisonous and insolvent. A resource that cannot be discounted to know the future is indeed the no-longer-conscious, that thing or place that may be extinguished but not yet discharged in its utopian potentiality.

Bloch explains the Kantian nature of his project as the "saving" of a "rationalist core." It is worth remarking that Kant's rationalism is not merely held up in this instance; indeed *rationalism itself is refunctioned*. No longer is rationalism the ruler used by universalism to measure time and space. In Bloch's work rationalism is transformed via a political urgency. Rationalism is not dismissed but is instead unyoked from a politics of the pragmatic. Herbert Marcuse discussed the "irrational element in rationality" as an important component of industrial society's nature. Irrationality flourishes in "established institutions"—marriage is perhaps one of the very best examples of an institution that hampers rational advancement and the not-yet-imagined versions of freedom that heteronormative and homonormative culture proscribe.[21] In Marcuse's analysis the advancements in rationality made by technological innovations were counteracted by gay pragmatic political strategies that tell us not to dream of other spatial/temporal coordinates but instead to dwell in a broken-down present. This homosexual pragmatism takes on the practical contours of the homonormativity so powerfully described by Lisa Duggan in her treatise on neoliberalism, *The Twilight of Equality?*[22] Within the hermeneutical scope of a queer utopian inquiry rationalism is reignited with an affective spark of idealist thought.

Abstract utopias are indeed dead ends, too often vectoring into the escapist disavowal of our current moment. But a turn to what Bloch calls the no-longer-conscious is an essential route for the purpose of arriving at the not-yet-here. This maneuver, a turn to the past for the purpose of critiquing the present, is propelled by a desire for futurity. Queer futurity does not underplay desire. In fact it is all about desire, desire for both larger semiabstractions such as a better world or freedom but also, more immediately, better relations within the social that include better sex and more pleasure. Some theorists of postmodernity, such as David Harvey, have narrated sex radicalism as a turning away from a politics of the collectivity toward the individualistic and the petty.[23] In his *A Brief History of Neoliberalism* Harvey plots what he views as the condition of neoliberalism. In his account, "The narcissistic exploration of self, sexuality and identity became the leitmotif of bourgeois urban culture." In this account, the hard-fought struggles for sexual liberation are reduced to a "demand for lifestyle diversification." Harvey's critique pits the "working-class and ethnic immigrant New York" against elites who pursue "lifestyle diversification."[24] The experiences of working-class or ethnic-racial queers are beyond his notice or interest. Harvey's failing is a too-common error for some, but not all, members of a recalcitrant, unreconstructed North American left. The rejection of queer and feminist politics represented by Harvey and other reductive left thinkers is a deviation away from the Frankfurt School's interest in the transformative force of *eros* and its implicit relationship to political desire. The failings and limits of commentators such as Harvey have certainly made queer and utopian thinkers alike wary of left thought. Thus, I suggest a turn to previous modes of Marxian philosophy, such as the work of Marcuse or Bloch. The point is not to succumb to the phobic panic that muddles left thinking or to unimaginative invocations of the rationalism cited by neoliberal gays and lesbians. The point is once again to pull from the past, the no-longer-conscious, described and represented by Bloch today, to push beyond the impasse of the present.

I swerve away from my critique of the failures of imagination in the LGBT activist enterprises to Harvey for a very specific purpose. Harvey represented a fairly more expansive and nuanced critique in his previous work on postmodernity, writing that was thoughtfully critiqued by queer theorists such as Judith

Halberstam.[25] But Harvey's work has become, like that of many Marxist scholars, all too ready to dismiss or sacrifice questions of sexuality and gender. Furthermore, these mostly white writers have, as in the example I cited in the preceding paragraph, been quick to posit race and class as real antagonisms within a larger socioeconomic struggle and sexuality and gender as merely "lifestyle diversification." In many ways they are performing a function that is the direct opposite of white neoliberal queers who studiously avoid the question of ethnic, racial, class, ability, or gender difference. This correspondence is representative of a larger political impasse that I understand as being the toll of pragmatic politics and antiutopian thought.

Concrete utopias remake rationalism, unlinking it from the provincial and pragmatic politics of the present. Taking back a rationalist core, in the way in which Bloch suggests we do in relation to romanticism, is to insist on an ordering of life that is not dictated by the spatial/temporal coordinates of straight time, a time and space matrix in which, unfortunately, far too many gays, lesbians, and other purportedly "queer" people reside.

To see queerness as horizon is to perceive it as a modality of ecstatic time in which the temporal stranglehold that I describe as straight time is interrupted or stepped out of. Ecstatic time is signaled at the moment one feels ecstasy, announced perhaps in a scream or grunt of pleasure, and more importantly during moments of contemplation when one looks back at a scene from ones past, present, or future. Opening oneself up to such a perception of queerness as manifestation in and of ecstatic time offers queers much more than the meager offerings of pragmatic gay and lesbian politics. Seeing queerness as horizon rescues and emboldens concepts such as freedom that have been withered by the touch of neoliberal thought and gay assimilationist politics. Pragmatic gay politics present themselves as rational and ultimately more doable. Such politics and their proponents often attempt to describe themselves as not being ideological, yet they are extremely ideological and, more precisely, are representative of a decayed ideological institution known as marriage. Rationalism need not be given over to gay neoliberals who attempt to sell a cheapened and degraded version of freedom. The freedom that is offered by an LGBT position that does not bend to straight time's gravitational pull is akin to one of Heidegger s descriptions of freedom as unboundness. And more often than not the "rhetorical" deployment of the pragmatic leads to a *not-doing*, an antiperformativity. Doing, performing, engaging the performative as force of and for futurity is queerness's bent and ideally the way to queerness.

NOTES

1. Third World Gay Revolution, "Manifesto of the Third World Gay Revolution," in *Out of the Closets: Voices of Gay Liberation*, ed. Karla Jay and Allen Young (New York: New York University Press, 1992), 367.
2. Evan Wolfson, "All Together Now (A Blueprint for the Movement)," *Advocate*, September 11, 2001; available online at http://www.freedomtomarry.org/evan_wolfson/by/all_together_now. php (accessed February 6, 2009).
3. See Lisa Duggan, "Holy Matrimony!" *Nation*, March 15, 2004, available online at http://www. thenation.com/doc/20040315/duggan; and Lisa Duggan and Richard Kim, "Beyond Gay Marriage," *Nation*, July 18, 2005, available online at http://www.thenation.com/doc/20050718/kim.
4. Giorgio Agamben, *Potentialities: Collected Essays in Philosophy*, ed. and trans. Daniel Heller-Roazen (Stanford, CA: Stanford University Press, 1999).
5. Alain Badiou, *Being and Event* (London: Continuum, 2005).
6. Ernst Bloch, *The Principle of Hope*, trans. Neville Plaice, Stephen Plaice, and Paul Knight, 3 vols. (Cambridge, MA: MIT Press, 1995).
7. Here I draw from Judith Halberstam's notion of time and normativity that she mines from a critique of David Harvey. I see her alerting us to a normative straight temporality that underscores

heterosexual and heteronormative life and constructs straight space. My notion of time or critique of a certain modality of time is interested in the way in which a queer utopian hermeneutic wishes to interrupt the linear temporal ordering of past, present, and future. See Judith Halberstam, *In a Queer Time and Place: Transgender Bodies, Subcultural Lives* (New York: New York University Press, 2005).

8. Lee Edelman, *No Future: Queer Theory and the Death Drive* (Durham, NC: Duke University Press, 2004).

9. *Edmund Husserl, Ideas Pertaining to a Pure Phenomenology and to a Phenomenological Philosophy,* trans. K. Rojcewicz (New York: Springer, 1991).

10. Roland Barthes, *Sade, Fourier, Loyola* (New York: Hill and Wang, 1976), 23.

11. James Schuyler, *Collected Poems* (New York: Farrar, Straus and Giroux, 1993), 186–187.

12. Martin Heidegger, *Being and Time,* trans. Joan Stambaugh (Albany: State University of New York Press, 1996), 329.

13. *Fredric Jameson, Archaeologies of the Future: The Desire Called Utopia and Other Science Fictions* (New York: Verso, 2005), 10.

14. J. L. Austin, *How to Do Things with Words* (Cambridge, MA: Harvard University Press, 1962).

15. Fredric Jameson, *The Political Unconscious: Narrative as a Socially Symbolic Act* (Ithaca, NY: Cornell University Press, 1981).

16. Bloch, *Principle of Hope,* 1:141.

17. Ibid.

18. Fredric Jameson, *Marxism and Form: Twentieth-Century Dialectical Theories of Literature* (Princeton, NJ: Princeton University Press, 1972).

19. Terrence Kissack, "Freaking Fag Revolutionaries: New York's Gay Liberation Front, 1969–1971," *Radical History Review* 62 (1995): 104–135.

20. This economical summary is drawn from Michael Inwood's useful book: Michael Inwood, *Heidegger: A Very Short Introduction* (Oxford: Oxford University Press, 2000), 121.

21. Herbert Marcuse, *One-Dimensional Man: Studies in the Ideology of Advanced Industrial Society* (Boston: Beacon, 1964), 17.

22. Lisa Duggan, *The Twilight of Equality? Neoliberalism, Cultural Politics, and the Attack on Democracy* (Boston: Beacon, 2003).

23. David Harvey, *A Brief History of Neo-Liberalism* (Oxford: Oxford University Press, 2005).

24. Ibid, 46–47.

25. Halberstam, *In a Queer Time and Place.*

ANGELA WILLEY

55. BIOPOSSIBILITY: A QUEER FEMINIST MATERIALIST SCIENCE STUDIES MANIFESTO, WITH SPECIAL REFERENCE TO THE QUESTION OF MONOGAMOUS BEHAVIOR

What has made me laugh as a feminist scientist, and what has allowed me to bring humor to my political project, has been the realization that each and every biological experiment I conducted in the lab was in fact an experiment in uncertainty, an experiment in transforming uncertainty into materiality. There is much room for feminist philosophies of subjectivity and theories of embodiment to guide these transformations from uncertainty to materiality. To do this, however, we must turn to the actual molecular matters of biology with desires for social justice.

—Deboleena Roy (2007)

On August 6, 2013, the *New York Times* ran a feature titled "Monogamy and Human Evolution" (Zimmer 2013) that sought to explore controversies in research on the origins of human monogamy. The piece ends with a report on a study speculating that perhaps monogamy is more than a descriptive feature of humanity but in fact just what made us human in the first place. The argument, in a nutshell, goes that when dads started hanging around, they had time to hunt and bring food back to their young and that this bringing home of the not-so-metaphorical bacon introduced unprecedented high protein calories that caused brains to grow large and develop the attendant faculties that distinguish humans from other primates. In other news, legal historian John Witte Jr. declared monogamy a unique site of consensus for God and Darwin in his op-ed (2012), while others, like evolutionary biologist David Barash, have insisted that "homo sapiens [are actually] a mildly polygamous species" (2009). There is a lot for a queer feminist science studies scholar to say about monogamy's place in public discourse these days, especially given debate surrounding the shifting legal status of gay marriage, intensifying as it has anxieties and hopes about the institutionalization of nondyadic relationship structures.[1] The naturalization of the nuclear family form in which material resources and care are privatized, the scientization of Christian sexual mores and its flip side in the reification of compulsory sexuality, and the racially gendered nature of these discourses matter to my argument, but they are not my focus here. Rather, I aim to bracket my critiques of the politics of scientific discourse from my curiosity about the biopolitical conditions of possibility for becoming monogamous in order to focus attention on the latter. I therefore introduce these narratives not to unpack the historical and cultural baggage contained in their logics but rather to gesture to it while highlighting the stakes of how we understand our nature for queer feminist politics writ large. The implications of queer and feminist critiques of scientific epistemology, practice, and categories of analysis are too often reduced and consigned to some flattened category of "social constructionism" rather than read or elaborated for their potential to reorient our understandings of what "human nature" is. This manifesto aims to redress that very problematic.

So it is with desire for "social justice"—as feminist endocrinologist and science studies scholar Deboleena Roy (2007) writes in the epigraph above—that I turn to the molecular and to the materialization of monogamy. As a manifesto for a queer feminist critical materialist science studies, this essay is a speculative exploration of the uses of a materialism grounded in the epistemological interventions of feminist and postcolonial science studies and queer historicizations of sexuality. It seeks to offer a curious and creative approach to the materiality of embodiment, an approach that is critically alert to how certain disciplinary ways of knowing (Science with a capital S) have been constructed as less mediated than others (humanistic approaches to corporeality and embodiment). So rather than turning to a materialist genealogy that relies on Science to ground a materialist politics that might reshape our worlds, I turn to a genealogy grounded in a queer, feminist, and antiracist vision of the vital body as a source of knowledge and resistance. Specifically, I turn to a reading of Audre Lorde's "Uses of the Erotic" (1984; originally published as a pamphlet in 1978) to develop a theory of biopossibility, which I then deploy to offer a queer feminist critical-materialist account of monogamy.

It is my contention that a queer feminist critical-materialist approach should ask: How do we engage the molecular with queer feminist desires for new biocultural stories and forms? As we create new approaches to science's proper objects, how do we ground them in queer and feminist critiques of the stability of those very objects—hormones (Fausto-Sterling 2000), muscles (Giordano 2013), chromosomes (Richardson 2012), and brains (Jordan-Young 2010), for example? How do we passionately challenge a view of biology as flat and predictable (Davis 2009) without locating our salvation in a framing that romanticizes nature's agency (Herzig 2004), contingency (Blencowe 2011), self-organization (Cooper 2008), or plasticity (Pitts-Taylor 2010)? That is to say, such an approach should begin by querying the contexts that inform the intelligibility of our understandings of nature, deterministic or otherwise. I offer *biopossibility* as a conceptual resource in our collective toolbox, one that might aid in the project of holding the material-discursive conditions of scientific knowledge production and the materialization of bodies in the same frame.

I define *biopossibility* as a species- and context-specific capacity to embody socially meaningful traits or desires. I use *biopossibilities*, rather than *biological*

possibilities, in an express effort to problematize the presumed locus of the *logical*. The study of *bios* in the natural sciences—in biology, as it were—has certainly been no more successful than the body theory produced within the humanities at illuminating the nature of embodiment. *Biopossibility* seeks to capture conceptually the way our creaturely capacities depend on the constraints of both intelligibility and matter, concepts whose comediation has been described most capaciously by Donna Haraway's concept of "natureculture" (2008, 249).[2] I intend biopossibility as a tool for naturecultural thinking. A capacity to embody is always naturecultural such that new biopossibilities emerge through "entangled" processes of biopolitical becoming (Barad 2007). In this naturecultural world, nothing is "merely" textual, and everything matters. That is to say, the intelligibility of a biopossibility and our capacity to actually embody it are interconnected in nonlinear ways. A theory of biopossibility does not require that we map or otherwise simplify those processes in order to name them: indeed, it actively resists the division between the pretheoretical realms of nature/biology and culture/language (the proper objects of the sciences and humanities, respectively). In so doing, it queers knowledge by resisting service to evidentiary schemas that support fixed ideas of what we are and might become (Winnubst 2006, 199) . . . .

RETHINKING BIOLOGY: TOWARD A FEMINIST MATERIALISM

While feminist critiques of science have been more concerned with knowledge production than with processes of materialization and new materialist approaches more concerned with matter than with critical engagements with science, this essay integrates their approaches to articulate new conceptual and methodological tools for approaching bodies from what I call a critical queer feminist materialist science studies perspective. It is my contention that the articulation of new materialist engagements with matter as a project in tension with feminist critiques of science is an obstacle to bringing into being materialities with which we are willing to live, to paraphrase Roy (2007), and that biopossibility, in bringing the approaches together conceptually, might aid that project.

The tension between these fields might best be framed by rehearsing a debate that originated in the pages of the *European Journal of Women's Studies* with Sara Ahmed's impassioned critique of what she calls new materialism's "founding gestures" (Ahmed 2008). This ongoing conversation reveals the need for new conceptual resources that problematize biology as the locus of claims about the materiality of bodies. Ahmed argues that the new materialist move to recoup the biological for feminism is being framed as an intervention into the "anti-biologism" of feminism, which she assesses as an unfair caricature of feminism (23–24). In her response to Ahmed, Noela Davis argues that Ahmed's counterexamples actually illustrate the problem: the importing of an old materialism, a stable albeit misrepresented body, into feminist projects (Davis 2009). Davis insists on the importance of taking feminism to task for critiquing science in such a way that biology and culture are allowed to be or made to seem separate.

I am indebted to insights on each side of this debate and want to home in on a slippage that I believe happens on both sides, making it difficult to chart a path that takes the following insights seriously: first, that feminist interventions into representations of the material body in science are not sufficient and, second, that feminist resources for thinking about materiality exist. In feminist debates about materialism, *biology* is used to refer not only to the science of bodies but also to the body itself. This slippage is important because it makes it appear as though the science of biology were an unmediated representation of the body itself, a fallacy whose debunking is at the heart of critical feminist science studies. My hope is that critical attention to this slippage will help us not to avoid it altogether (I'm not entirely certain this is possible) but to make us alert to its effects so that we might find ways to orient ourselves to the invention of new conceptual resources.

In both Ahmed's (2008) assessment of new materialism and Davis's (2009) rebuttal, Elizabeth A. Wilson's work figures as an exemplary site of intervention into a feminist theory inhospitable to the integration of biology. In Ahmed's assessment, this supposed intervention names an "imaginary prohibition" against engaging biology in feminist thought.

In Davis's article, Wilson's work cogently articulates a difficult and necessary intervention that Ahmed's "deflationary logic" (Van der Tuin 2008) obscures. As Wilson's framing of the relationship between feminism and materialism has been such productive terrain for this debate, and because her work on the importance of receptors outside the brain has been so influential for my own work on neuroscience, I return to two oft-cited passages from her books and then back again to Ahmed's critique of new materialism in order to illustrate this slippage on both sides.

In her introduction, Wilson asserts that "feminist theories have usually been reluctant to engage with *biological data:* they retain, and encourage, the fierce *anti-biologism* that marked the emergence of second wave feminism" (2004, 13; emphasis added).[3] Here "anti-biologism" is the cause of feminist reluctance to engage with data. Feminist reluctance to engage with data is in fact well supported by feminist engagements with the processes by which data are produced, engagements that have occurred in feminist science studies. Yet, "anti-biologism" suggests a reluctance to think about embodiment, and this obscures a long history of lively feminist debate about how to talk about the leaky, bleeding, desiring body (Roy and Subramaniam). In another frequently referenced passage from the introduction to her earlier work, Wilson refers to feminism's "distaste for biological detail," "despite an avowed interest in the body" (1998, 14–15). Here, "biological detail" takes on a very narrow meaning, one confined to the kind of detail only accessible through very specific scientific approaches that privilege reductionist explanations over others. Bodies are reduced to this detail through the suggestion of an inconsistency between an avowed commitment to the body and a distaste for data. In this move, feminist theories of embodiment and corporeality are represented as disingenuous, not really theories of bodies but of something else, ostensibly the body's outside: culture. In this interchangeable use of "biological detail," "the body," and "biological data," there is no conceptual space for engaging feminist skepticism about science and its privileged epistemic status. All critiques of science are rhetorically subsumed into the category of "anti-biologism," where they serve as implicit evidence of the hypocrisy of feminist claims to care about bodies.

At the same time, Ahmed's reclamation of those feminisms does not resist this slippage but rather reiterates it. She points to examples of feminist health materials researched and disseminated in the 1970s and 1980s that drew directly on scientific research, as well as to feminist science studies scholars who helped to revise and improve scientific information, not to a rich and conflicted history of debate about bodies, sciences, and the feminist stories we tell. Both Wilson and Ahmed enact a slippage between biology as the study of the body—or the body produced within the context of scientific inquiry—and biology as the body itself. With this slippage in mind, I argue that we must insist on some distinction between feminist critiques of science and feminist refusals to engage bodies, refusals rightly critiqued by Wilson and others. This will necessitate drawing a distinction between engaging data and asking new questions about bodies and then carefully accounting for the interface between data and new modes of conceptualization. This in turn will require a certain kind of resistance to disciplinary divides, which, despite the widespread institutionalization of some forms of interdisciplinarity, remain quite fixed.

Let me be clear that my perspective is not that feminist uses of scientific concepts or data are to be avoided. It is rather that nuanced and careful narratives about relationships between feminism, science, and the body enable the work of producing new knowledges about bodies in a naturecultural world. As a critical methodology, biopossibility calls for the interruption of storytelling conventions in which data and the body are conflated. Projects that frame their materialist queries against feminist, social constructionist, or humanist approaches to making sense of things lend those queries an easy epistemic authority.[4] That authority is established by simultaneously distancing new materialism from approaches or perspectives already the object of derision and by associating it, implicitly or explicitly, with an objectivist agenda.[5] I switch the designating terms—opting for "feminist materialist" rather than "materialist feminist"—to denote a different sort of materialism, not a different sort of feminism. Rather than distancing myself from the cultural or textual approaches of feminism or the humanities, I seek to distinguish this materialist project from the epistemological agendas of a Science (with a capital S) that would demand that nature itself, however complex, speak. I do so by offering biopossibility as a conceptual alternative to biology in interdisciplinary feminist research on bodies.

LORDE'S MATERIALISM: TOWARD A THEORY OF EROTIC BIOPOSSIBILITY

Audre Lorde is an important figure for a feminist genealogy of materialist thought. Here I focus on a reading of her "Uses of the Erotic, the Erotic as Power" (1984), one of the most famous works by one of the most influential feminist thinkers of the twentieth century. Deeply committed to both embodiment and politics in her writing, Lorde is among those figures whose work has variously been characterized as both essentialist and antiessentialist. As such a border figure, she has allowed us to hold the agentive force of both the body and politics without placing them in hierarchical relation as causal elements in the making of experience. Lorde's erotic provides resources for holding our analyses of embodiment accountable to our critical engagements with "culture" and vice versa.

For Lorde, bodies are not simply oppressed by or drawn into the service of power, they are also a critical site of resistance. The political potential of connection between individuals is one of the defining features of Lorde's erotic, one that has inspired much thinking about the importance of relationships to social change. She writes: "The erotic functions for me in several ways, and the first is in providing the power which comes from sharing deeply any pursuit with another person. The sharing of joy, *whether physical, emotional, psychic, or intellectual*, forms a bridge between the sharers which can be the basis for understanding much of what is not shared between them, and lessens the threat of their difference" (Lorde 1984, 56; emphasis added). I would like to draw attention to Lorde's care in interrupting a reading that would reduce the "sharing" she speaks of to sexual or romantic exchanges. The "physical" is far broader than the sexual, and the "emotional" far more so than the romantic. The sexual and the romantic become both dislodged from each other and subsumed within two of four larger categories, shrinking them down to size in the schema of the potential for human connection. These other less celebrated forms of human connection become larger when they stand parallel to physical and emotional sharing. The range of sharing that might be imagined to cultivate this bridge of understanding opens up our vision of types of interactions that provide this power. In the lingo of popular neurometaphors, it helps us to think more creatively about what we are "wired" for.

The displacement of sexual, romantic love, which I discuss in more detail below, is not the only function of the erotic: "Another important way in which the erotic connection functions is the open and fearless underlining of my capacity for joy, in the way my body stretches to music and opens into response, harkening to its deepest rhythms so every level on which I sense also opens to the erotically satisfying experience whether it is dancing, building a bookcase, writing a poem, or examining an idea" (Lorde 1984, 56–57). For Lorde, the erotic openly and fearlessly underlines our capacity for joy. This "underlining" marks a kind of knowing. Body knowledge does not begin from activities categorized in advance but rather from a capacious aptitude for joy. It opens us, at every level, to what Lorde calls "the erotically satisfying experience," whatever it may be. Dancing, listening, building, writing, examining, and sharing are all potential avenues to erotic fulfilment here.

But why refer to her theory of the erotic as biopossibility? Surely, we must read Lorde's words as in part an act of resistance to the scientization of sexuality and desire, which has certainly tended toward what Lorde critiques as the pornographic. I use *biopossibility* to refer to Lorde's theory of the erotic in order to challenge the locus and authority of claims about the material body in the sciences and to mark an alternative conceptual terrain. *Matter* is too often conflated with scientific ways of knowing it. *Biology,* the study of the body in the sciences, leaves little space for interdisciplinary feminist innovation. Like other feminist scholars trying to rethink the corporeal—notably Stacy Alaimo in *Bodily Natures*—I have found resources in Lorde (Alaimo 2010, 85–87). Lorde's words often viscerally capture a body that exceeds scientific and social reductionism. It is at once material and palpably situated. Most important, bodies for Lorde are a source of power, agential in that they resist annihilation. In other words, for Lorde, there is something in

our embodiment that is oriented toward what new materialists like Elizabeth Grosz might call "life" (see also Huffer). Others have turned to aspects of Baruch Spinoza's monism or to Lucretius on that "something" in our breast that makes it possible to resist an outside force.[6] This Western philosophical tradition of trying to account for what is without God has been a powerfully authorizing resource for new materialisms, but alternate—and feminist—genealogies are full of generative potential. Lorde's joy—an embodied sense of fulfillment that stems from what she calls erotic experience—for example, offers not only another account of that vibrancy in our nature but an expressly and specifically grounded queer feminist theory of the similarity of seemingly disparate environmental and experiential stimuli. This account lends itself to an innovative theory of affective biopossibility.

Lorde's erotic is at once difficult to pin down and richly elaborated with examples. She postulates that there is no qualitative difference between the experiences of building a bookcase, thinking about an idea, making love to a woman, listening to music, and writing a poem. These are all potential experiential stimuli for the realization of a capacity that she refers to as both "joy" and "fulfillment." *Joy* here is unlike *happiness*. It is something immediate and visceral, something that can be motivational in terms of behavior—"rewarding," in neurochemical lingo—and can thus inform an orientation to certain practices, activities, and objects in everyday life. According to Lorde, if we do not fear the erotic, and it is thus able to open us internally to the joys different experiential stimuli can bring, we will become accustomed to the feeling, and we will desire its repeated effects. This logic is often explained in terms of stimulation of reward centers—as the neurochemical support for habitual behavior—in ways that often lend themselves to reductive stories about gene-brain-behavior connections.[7]

Lorde offers an account of how and why the vital capacity for joy gets written out of our stories of human nature: "In order to perpetuate itself, every oppression must corrupt or distort those various sources of power within the culture of the oppressed that can provide energy for change. For women, this has meant a suppression of the erotic as a considered source of power and information within our lives" (1984, 53). This is a powerful statement about the place of the erotic in the nexus of power/knowledge. Knowledge of the erotic is dangerous because its capacities are potentially transformative. Because all of this potential is innate, its suppression has required that we understand it not as power but as a liability. We have been taught to suspect this depth of feeling and to believe that our strength lies in overcoming it. While the erotic can be a "replenishing and provocative" force in our lives, orienting them toward joy and change, it is often distorted and misappropriated (54).

Lorde makes the distinctly materialist claim that the rich concept of human need is a key principle in bringing into being a world in which we would like to live. That need, importantly, is neither prescriptive nor confining: it does not codify sex, bonding, or even sociality as its driving force. Rather, it is a need for the freedom to realize this diffuse capacity for an embodied sense of fulfillment. And naming that capacity, for Lorde, paves the way for a decidedly naturecultural ethics. She writes: "That deep and irreplaceable knowledge of my capacity for joy comes to demand from all of my life that it be lived within the knowledge that such satisfaction is possible" (Lorde 1984, 57). Lorde's biopossibility of the erotic offers an expressly politicized ontology of becoming that depends on an epistemic renegotiation. We must be willing to critique sexuality as we know it in order to understand this reontologization of the erotic body. If we understand ourselves as erotic rather than (self-evidently or universally) sexual, our creatureliness has a different valence, with implications for how we imagine success, adulthood, wellness, and so on. Possibility is at the heart of this conception of humanness. If "the erotic is a measure between our sense of self and the chaos of our strongest feelings . . . an internal sense of satisfaction to which, once we have experienced it, we know we can aspire" (57), the idea that we are creatures motivated by an instinct that is sexual or reproductive or that we are motivated by social pressures to conform to such a script seems inadequate. We are rather, in this formulation, always becoming, where bodily capacity for what we might call reward, fulfillment, or joy constitutes a condition of possibility for those becomings. [8]

We can read Lorde's biopossibility as a critique of the reduction of the vast potential of the erotic to the narrow concept of sexuality, a reduction[9] enabled by misogynist and racist fears of women's power. Read as an analysis of the biopolitical perpetuation of sexuality, the project is indeed powerful. Still, Lorde's primary task is not to critique sexuality but rather to attend to the biological resources rendered unintelligible by its imposition as an explanatory frame. The erotic comes from the root *eros*, which Lorde defines as a broad and diffuse conception of something we might call love. This love is something rather akin to Gayatri Chakravorty Spivak's "risky love" (2011, 56). Spivak argues that while love is always haunted by reproductive heteronormativity, it can still inform an orientation toward the world and its inhabitants that might in turn inform political praxis.[10] Lynne Huffer, too, embraces the possibility of such reappropriation, suggesting that we might yet evoke and reclaim love in ways that challenge its "schmaltzified, narcissistic, possessive structures" (2013, 130). I read Lorde's eros as springing from such a feminist conception of love—both claimed and queered. As Cynthia Willet explains, "while Freudian and post-Freudian writers portray love as the threat of immersion, black writers like Lorde and Walker present love as a force for the expansion of the human personality in relationship with others. [Lorde's] eros is most decidedly a primary source for, and not a primitive threat to, subjectivity" (2001, 180). Eros here is not the primordial sexual, romantic love of Freudian discourse. Lorde's account of eros emerges in the struggle to articulate an account of embodied capacities that does not center sexuality while still accounting for its embodied existence as a biopossibility we have realized and named. A biopossibility of the erotic, then, is an approach to embodied desire and behavior attuned to relationships between knowledge politics and materialization. Lorde's eros can help us to approach calcified forms of embodiment as biopossibilities, neither reducible to text nor essential to human nature.

REVISITING THE MATTER OF MONOGAMY

In particular, Lorde's biopossibility of the erotic has opened up conceptual space for me to reengage the material of monogamy gene research, research that underlies vast neuroscientific data not only on pair-bonding and promiscuity but on attachment, social processing disorders, and affiliative behavior in general (Donaldson and Young 2008). Lorde provides resources for undoing the categories that structure this research without dismissing its findings or simply appropriating its data. I have studied Larry Young's laboratory at Yerkes Primate Research Center, which uses a "monogamous" vole species as a neural model for healthy attachment in humans, because its multi-million-dollar funding situates it at the cutting edge of neuroscientific research on affiliative behavior.[11] My ongoing interest in the contexts that make the laboratory's frames, models, and conclusions intelligible has been haunted—at moments enchanted, to call up Jane Bennett (2009)—by the materialist turn in the humanities in general and within feminist theory in particular. This haunting enchantment is nurtured by the specter of the extratextual realness of the objects of my analysis.

Over the years, many people have been curious about my research in Young's laboratory, and several have asked me some version of the question, "so . . . *is* there a monogamy gene?" As they say in the lab, there is always a "quick and dirty" answer. Mine is that it depends on how you define both *gene* and *monogamy*. I have been apt to argue that "the monogamy gene" is a misleading or useless formulation; simply put, it's the wrong question. By this, do I mean to say that bodies do not matter in any way to our understanding of the reproduction of monogamy-centric culture, that *biology* is but another discourse drawn into the maintenance of the status quo, and nothing more? Not exactly. Embodied desire is doubtless part of the naturecultural world in which we navigate the ethics of belonging. Rather than asking whether the human (or the prairie or meadow vole for that matter) is a monogamous or pair-bonding species (or conversely a promiscuous one), however, it may be fruitful to think about the capacity to form attachments as a biopossibility that can inform our understandings of certain becomings without foreclosing as-yet-unrealized or unintelligible biopossibilities.

My fieldwork in the laboratory suggests that the monogamy that apparently characterizes human biology is not necessarily sexual, nor is it necessarily exclusive. These findings call into question the will to

distinguish monogamy not only from promiscuity or polygamy but also from friendship. If we agree to define monogamy as a behavioral responsiveness to a familiar individual in a scenario that is not necessarily sexual or exclusive (as this is what is actually measured), and if we understand that the expression of a gene depends on multiple, complexly mediated, and often ill-understood processes of transcription that allow for the articulation of correlative relationships between variations in DNA and complex social behaviors, it is possible to talk about monogamy's molecular substrates. That is to say, one condition of possibility for the behaviors associated with what we call pair-bonding is molecular. Attachment to other animals is thus a biopossibility among humans and prairie voles in a way that it is not for members of all species.

Yet when we name species (or other biological types) monogamous or nonmonogamous, social or asocial, we obscure the contingency of those biopossibilities. Even as the categories themselves remain stable, the molecular complexity of the processes has become the object of increasing attention. In 1999 the Young Laboratory discovered a genetic variation between two species of voles: the prairie vole (*Microtus ochrogaster*) and the meadow vole (*Microtus pennsylvanicus*), considered behaviorally monogamous and promiscuous, respectively. Not all of the monogamous voles had the genetic variation, and not all who did have it showed a partner preference, but for both the lab and the press, the integrity of the categories themselves stayed intact and remains the primary descriptor of the two types, which serve as models for healthy and unhealthy social variation in humans. In 2004 the laboratory succeeded in genetically modifying a promiscuous vole to make it monogamous according to measures of partner preference, the test used to measure monogamy by scoring an individual vole's preference for proximity to a familiar ("partner") over an unfamiliar ("stranger") vole (Lim et al. 2004; Hammock and Young 2005). With this gene story, the laboratory became famous. By 2008, however, the Young Laboratory had explicitly acknowledged that this genetic variation did not fully account for the behavioral differences between species considered monogamous and promiscuous (Donaldson and Young 2008). In 2009, researchers there succeeded in attaining the resources (approval for vole genome mapping) to better understand the complex regulatory processes that produce behavioral differences among vole species. And this world of complexity, with its attention to epigenetic and other factors in making voles (and humans) monogamous, offers us a rich language surrounding regulatory elements and transcription factors that mediate what we call monogamy (McGraw, Thomas, and Young 2008). While the scope of their referents remains conceptually narrow, the naming of a category of important but unknown variables is ripe with potential for naturecultural thinking.

In light of Lorde's insights about the embodied likeness of experiences considered sexual and not, I turn to the known and unknown factors that mediate gene expression and that in so doing bring into being certain biopossibilities. Social neuroscience seeks to understand what Thomas R. Insel, director of the National Institute of Mental Health and forefather of monogamy gene research, calls "dark matter," those processes that link "receptive" input to "expressive" behavioral output (Insel 2010). The dark matter metaphor directly analogizes the biosciences and physics, suggesting a system that is complicated but ultimately mappable (Willey and Subramaniam). Simple models that have treated genes as an on/off switch for behaviors or treated single hormones as key to human characteristics are indeed widely outmoded and regarded as too reductive to be of any use at all, despite their startling persistence in popular scientific and medical discourse (Moss 2013). Complex systems modeling, which is reshaping the biosciences, offers possibilities that Mendelian genetics discourse never could, including the provision of evidence to support the undoing of the very categories it seeks to model.

EROTICIZING MONOGAMY'S DARK MATTER

I aim to eroticize representations of the dark matter of monogamous and nonmonogamous pathways, both drawing on and problematizing the story that Insel's review of the neuroscience of affiliative behavior tells in order to question the integrity of the categories themselves. In brief, the two species of vole I mentioned—prairie voles and meadow voles,

respectively—are used to represent monogamous and promiscuous affiliative pathways in this research. The former models "healthy" affiliative behavior, and the latter, social processing disorders, such as autism. The idea is that some genetic variation in the two species leads to different outcomes or expressions of the receptive experiential input of copulation (Insel 2010). The research attempts to map and compare the processes that produce these pathways from copulation to pair-bonding in monogamous prairie voles and from copulation to not pair-bonding in promiscuous meadow voles. Researchers increasingly understand the factors that facilitate the transcription from gene to behavior as complex but continue to treat them as ultimately stable and measurable.

The genetic marker associated with monogamous species of voles is a microsatellite of the Vla receptor gene, which affects the distribution of arginine vasopressin receptors in the forebrain (Hammock and Young 2005). The story goes that a concentration of arginine vasopressin receptors in the reward centers of the brain is a precondition for as-yet-unmapped transcription factors to effect monogamous behavior in males. A concentration of oxytocin receptors in the same regions is associated with monogamous behaviors in females. Drug therapies and gene manipulations, in this account, have turned "promiscuous mammals into stay-at-home dads" (Zarembo 2004). The ability to turn the promiscuous pathway monogamous is precisely the point of this research. In clinical applications, the neurochemical capacity to form pair-bonds in voles is the model for healthy affiliative behavior in humans, and, conversely, the inability to form pair-bonds is the model for disordered affiliative behavior, like autism. The ability to turn a promiscuous vole monogamous (or more accurately, to make a vole who is largely independent by measures of partner preference more responsive to other animals) suggests the possibility of making an adult or child diagnosed with autism more responsive to familiars (e.g., parents or a partner; Hammock and Young 2006).

Understanding a bit about the workings of these hormones and how they are administered in experimental and clinical settings can help to illuminate what is meant by monogamous and promiscuous pathways in ways that the data obscure. The gendered nature of the story of monogamy hormones contains within it the idea that what we call monogamy is not monolithic. It domesticates this insight within a familiar gendered schema but still, I think, is instructive as a model of variance. The gendered story is undermined by the research itself, but the different processes by which the same receptive input (copulation) and expressive output (pair-bonding behavior) are represented as linked by wholly disparate processes in females and males opens the black box of monogamy's dark matter to readings that complicate its meanings. Oxytocin is the maternal hormone associated with nurturance and gendered feminine: thus, scientists understand pair-bonding behavior in females as both like a mother's bond with an infant and adaptive in the service of that bond. In other words, in this schema female monogamy is mediated by functional mechanisms that support the reproduction of the nuclear family through nurturance. In mating research, vasopressin is studied for its role in species-specific behaviors like territoriality and aggression and supports a different monogamy story. In this tale of complementary heterosexual mating strategies, male monogamy is mediated by functional mechanisms that support the reproduction of the nuclear family through mate guarding—jealousy and protection.[12] Feminist science studies scholars have had a lot to say about the imposition of these types of gendered narratives onto biology and the ways in which they misrepresent or actually materialize the effects they purport to describe. These insights guide me here in my reading of monogamy's dark matter.

While genetic markers for the distribution of oxytocin and vasopressin receptors in the reward centers of the brain are usually represented as sexually dimorphic explanations for mammalian monogamy, oxytocin has been used to effect behavioral changes in both males and females. Oxytocin and vasopressin have a more fluid relationship than the frame of the monogamy gene suggests. In nonmammalian vertebrates, oxytocin and vasopressin are considered one thing—a hormone known as vasotocin. In mammals, a certain amount of cross-receptivity among their receptors accounts for at least some of the apparent discrepancy between laboratory and clinical effects, gendered and

not (Chini and Manning 2007). That is to say, oxytocin seems to be binding with vasopressin receptors, which suggests that in spite of a great deal of hetero-intuitive theorizing, we do not know what monogamy is, or, in another manner of speaking, what mechanisms enable pair-bonding behavior.

In addition to their high-affinity binding with each other, oxytocin and vasopressin systems are highly mediated by cortisol systems (Bartz and Hollander 2006; Moss 2013) and testosterone.[13] They share some high-affinity binding sites with other hormones, like dopamine (Kodavanti and Curras-Collazo 2010). In controlled experiments, oxytocin was injected directly into vole forebrains in order to induce behavioral changes. But in human trials, oxytocin is not injected into the brain but rather administered intranasally. This means that subjects taking oxytocin to modify behavioral outputs will have high circulating levels of the hormone in their bloodstream, but it may or may not cross the blood-brain barrier to allow binding with those receptors (Donaldson and Young 2008). This in turn points to the importance of binding sites outside the brain.[14] Sites of concentration of oxytocin and arginine vasopressin receptors in other parts of the human body tend to be higher-affinity binding sites both between oxytocin and vasopressin (Lolait, O'Carroll, and Brownstein 1995) and with other hormones (Chini and Manning 2007). The cross-receptivity of various hormones with oxytocin and vasopressin receptors throughout human bodies suggests not only the fragility of the ideological commitment to understanding monogamy in gendered ways (Willey and Giordano 2011) but also that dark matter is best understood not as a pathway shrouded in shadow but rather as a collision of indiscrete systems.

When we start to think natureculturally about the reality of the vast array of factors that contribute to variation in circulating levels of various hormones (diet, movement, interaction, etc.) at different stages of evolutionary time—hours, days, years, and generations (Dumit 2014; Jablonka and Lamb 2014)— the biology of monogamy starts to look very messy indeed. In a white paper bid to get the prairie vole genome sequenced (McGraw, Thomas, and Young 2008), Young's laboratory references this complexity time and again. While the significance of the prairie voles' monogamous nature and its exemplary status as a model for human sociality are the main point of this white paper, the promise of unmasking what is unknown is at the heart of the case for genome mapping: "It should be noted that the simple presence or absence of this microsatellite is not associated with social organization in other Microtus species . . . suggesting that variation in other genes or regulatory elements also contribute to natural variation in social behavior. . . . Taking advantage of the genetic diversity in laboratory populations of prairie voles can lead to exciting insights into how variation in gene regulation affects behavior in rodents as well as in humans"(5). Here, the behavioral diversity that has been noted by critics but largely ignored in the laboratory's research is explicitly named, so too is the complexity of that diversity (Fink, Excoffier, and Heckel 2006; Willey and Giordano 2011). Other genes and regulatory elements are acknowledged as important in the production of behaviors we call monogamous and promiscuous, social and asocial. The phrase "regulatory elements" seems to refer to a broad range of potential factors that are usually understood—in the conception of nature as fairly stable that operates within the rubric of slow evolutionary time—as external to the animal. Those factors, belonging thus to the realm of the social yet necessary for the expression of genetic traits, pose a problem for the boundaries of the biological: "The prairie vole brain is exquisitely sensitive to the influence of social experience which shapes the expression of behaviorally relevant genes. *The molecular mechanisms by which social experience alters brain gene expression and thereby behavior is unknown*" (McGraw, Thomas, and Young 2008, 4; emphasis added). Importantly, those mechanisms by which "rates of molecular and chromosomal evolution in mammals" (6) conspire to produce monogamous and nonmonogamous effects are unknown. I depart from the ambitions of the white paper in my skepticism about their ultimate knowability. This suspension of knowledge opens up space for thinking critically about the intertwined processes of naming and becoming and makes space for raising ethical questions about pharmacology, storytelling, and other regulatory elements within our control. That is to say, it opens space for thinking about the complex field of ethical relations between epistemology and ontology, between what we know and what we are. Lorde's erotic suggests that part of this relationship is the exercise of power inherent in the naming of these possibilities, which itself forecloses potential materializations. Biopossibility provides a linguistic and conceptual resource for holding this onto-epistemological production of types in our view as we choose how to map matter.

CONCLUSION

Lorde's biopossibility of the erotic is a theory of a capacious aptitude for joy that can be realized in many possible ways: touching, listening, thinking, talking, moving, building. In the verbs Lorde uses to characterize the experiences that reveal our erotic capacity, a world of biopossibility emerges. This biopossibility opens up space for thinking natureculturally not only about friendship, community, and our coevolution with nonhuman animals but also about human relationships to things—both abstract and material. To what, apart from (or perhaps above or alongside) coupling and child rearing, might our deepest desires be oriented? What might we become? If the factors that coconspire to make some behaviors more rewarding than others vary for individual animals, whose social contexts are a vitally important regulatory element on a variety of temporal evolutionary scales, we might begin to think of pairing off as an overdetermined biopossibility.

Biopossibility allows us to apprehend behaviors intelligible as monogamous and nonmonogamous, and the processes we understand as their molecular substrates, as one set of culturally and historically mediated expressions of our creaturely capacities in a naturecultural world. Demonstrating as it does the biopolitical intelligibility of this story, biopossibility serves as a tool for holding discourse and materialization within the same frame. As such, it can serve as a resource for fleshing out the insight that material variation among bodies is delimited (and enabled) by discourse (Sieben 2011, 277). In challenging the a priori biological distinction between the sexual and the nonsexual, Lorde's biopossibility of the erotic upsets the idea that human nature is monogamous or nonmonogamous (or pluralistic with regard to monogamous or nonmonogamous difference) and in so doing lends itself to a rethinking of the privileged status of science in the turn to materiality. This is not because the sciences are without resources for feminisms but because engagement with data cannot generate the resources to "disorganize" (Roy 2007) the categories that organize our lives: here, monogamous and promiscuous, social and asocial. Data neither reveal nor engender possibilities for materialities with which we can live. That requires the critical-creative work of queer feminist imagining.

NOTES

1. See, e.g., Burgett (2005), Aviram (2008), Tweedy (2010), Brake (2012), Sheff (2013), and Nair (2015).
2. Attempts to further pin these two realms down tend to keep them separate, slipping us right back into a nature/nurture debate by positing a causal relationship: biology creates culture or culture creates biology.
3. See Hemmings (2005) for a discussion of the political ramifications of the stories we tell about feminist waves in general and of a reactionary 1970s in particular.
4. See the *differences* special issue "Feminist Theory Out of Science" (Roosth and Schraeder 2012a) for an example of an approach that deliberately eschews this framing; see especially Grosz (2010) and Roosth and Schraeder (2012b) for explicit articulations of the import of feminist theory to reimagining materiality.
5. See Coole (2013) for a discussion and refutation of new materialism as neopositivist.
6. On Spinoza, see Van der Tuin and Dolphijn (2010). On Lucretius, see Bennett (2009).
7. See the classic Hubbard and Wald (1999) and the more recent Keller (2010) for in-depth discussions of the reductive stories about gene-brain-behavior connections.
8. See Ginzberg (1992) for a counterreading of Lorde's *eros* as antiessentialist.
9. See Huffer (2013) for a refreshing queer feminist approach to sexual ethics that elegantly complicates a frame that dismisses feminism as moralistic.
10. Kristina Gupta (2013) picks up on this riskiness in Lorde's use of *eros*, arguing that that frame in fact reifies sexuality.
11. See Insel (2010), Willey and Giordano (2011), and Willey (2014).
12. See feminist neuroscientist Sari van Anders and colleagues' discussion of the "aggression paradox" in research on bonding and hormones (Van Anders, Goldey, and Kuo 2011).
13. See Van Anders and Goldey (2010) for an explication of the undertheorized importance of testosterone to pair-bonding. The authors discuss testosterone's effects on both male and female pairing and on both territorial and nurturant bonding in ways that complicate and challenge the gendered bonding stories of approaches that look at different hormones in male and female bodies.
14. See Wilson (2012) for a brilliant discussion of the importance of receptors outside the brain.

REFERENCES

Ahern, Todd H., and Larry J. Young. 2009. "The Impact of Early Life Family Structure on Adult Social Attachment, Alloparental Behavior, and the Neuropeptide Systems Regulating Affiliative Behaviors in the Monogamous Prairie Vole *(Microtus Ochrogaster)*." *Frontiers in Behavioral Neuroscience* 3 (August):1–19.

Ahmed, Sara. 2008. "Open Forum: Imaginary Prohibitions; Some Preliminary Remarks on the Founding Gestures of the 'New Materialism.'" *European Journal of Women's Studies* 15(1):23–39.

Alaimo, Stacy. 2010. *Bodily Natures: Science, Environment, and the Material Self*. Bloomington: Indiana University Press.

Aviram, Hadar. 2008. "Make Love, Now Law: Perceptions of the Marriage Equality Struggle among Polyamorous Activists." *Journal of Bisexuality* 7(3–4):261–86.

Barad, Karen. 2007. *Meeting the Universe Halfway: Quantum Physics and the Entanglement of Matter and Meaning*. Durham, NC: Duke University Press.

Barash, David P. 2009. "Monogamy Isn't Easy, Naturally." *Los Angeles Times*, November 22. http://articles.latimes.com/2009/nov/22/opinion/la-oe-barash.

Bartz, Jennifer, and Eric Hollander. 2006. "The Neuroscience of Affiliation: Forging Links between Basic and Clinical Research on Neuropeptides and Social Behavior." *Hormones and Behavior* 50(4):518–28.

Bennett, Jane. 2009. *Vibrant Matter: A Political Ecology of Things*. Durham, NC: Duke University Press.

Blencowe, Claire Peta. 2011. "Biology, Contingency and the Problem of Racism in Feminist Discourse." *Theory, Culture and Society* 28(3):3–27.

Brake, Elizabeth. 2012. *Minimizing Marriage: Marriage, Morality, and the Law*. Oxford: Oxford University Press.

Burgett, Bruce. 2005. "On the Mormon Question: Race, Sex, and Polygamy in the 1850s and the 1990s." *American Quarterly* 57(1):75–102.

Chapkis, Wendy. 1997. Live Sex Acts: Women Performing Erotic Labor. New York: Routledge.

Chini, Bice, and Maurice Manning. 2007. "Agonist Selectivity in the Oxytocin/Vasopressin Receptor Family: New Insights and Challenges." *Biochemical Society Transactions* 35(4):737–41.

Coole, Diana. 2013. "Agentic Capacities and Capacious Historical Materialism: Thinking with New Materialisms in the Political Sciences." *Millennium* 41(3):451–69.

Cooper, Melinda. 2008. *Life as Surplus: Biotechnology and Capitalism in the Neoliberal Era*. Seattle: University of Washington Press.

Davis, Noela. 2009. "New Materialism and Feminism's Anti-biologism: A Response to Sara Ahmed." *European Journal of Women's Studies* 16(1):67–80.

Donaldson, Zoe R., and Larry J. Young. 2008. "Oxytocin, Vasopressin, and the Neurogenetics of Sociality." *Science* 322(5903):900–904.

Dumit, Joseph. 2014. "Plastic Neuroscience: Studying What the Brain Cares About." *Frontiers in Human Neuroscience* 8 (April):1–4.

Fausto-Sterling, Anne. 2000. *Sexing the Body: Gender Politics and the Construction of Sexuality*. New York: Basic.

Fink, Sabine, Laurent Excoffier, and Gerald Heckel. 2006. "Mammalian Monogamy Is Not Controlled by a Single Gene." *Proceedings of the National Academy of Sciences* 109(23):10956–60.

Foucault, Michel. 1990. *The History of Sexuality*. Vol. 1, *An Introduction*. Translated by Robert Hurley. London: Penguin.

Ginzberg, Ruth. 1992. "Audre Lorde's (Nonessentialist) Lesbian Eros." *Hypatia* 7(4):73–90.

Giordano, Sara. 2013. "What's Political about Plantarflexion Muscles? A Feminist Investigation into the Boundaries of Muscles." Paper presented at the thirty-fourth annual conference of the National Women's Studies Association, Cincinnati, November 9.

Grosz, Elizabeth. 2010. "The Practice of Feminist Theory." *differences* 21(1):94–108.

Gupta, Kristina. 2013. "Compulsory Sexuality and Its Discontents: The Challenge of Asexualities." PhD dissertation, Emory University.

Hammock, Elizabeth A. D., and Larry J. Young. 2005. "Microsatellite Instability Generates Diversity in Brain and Sociobehavioral Traits." *Science* 308(5728):1630–34.

Hammock, Elizabeth A. D., and Larry J. Young. 2006. "Oxytocin, Vasopressin and Pair Bonding: Implications for Autism." *Philosophical Transactions of the Royal Society* B 361(1476):2187–98.

Haraway, Donna. 2008. *When Species Meet*. Minneapolis: University of Minnesota Press.

Hemmings, Clare. 2005. "Telling Feminist Stories." *Feminist Theory* 6(2):115–39.

Herzig, Rebecca. 2004. "On Performance, Productivity, and Vocabularies of Motive in Recent Studies of Science." *Feminist Theory* 5(2):127–47.

Holland, Sharon Patricia. 2012. *The Erotic Life of Racism*. Durham, NC: Duke University Press.

Hubbard, Ruth, and Elijah Wald. 1999. *Exploding the Gene Myth: How Genetic Information Is Produced and Manipulated by Scientists, Physicians, Employers, Insurance Companies, Educators, and Law Enforcers*. Boston: Beacon.

Huffer, Lynne. 2013. *Are the Lips a Grave? A Queer Feminist on the Ethics of Sex*. New York: Columbia University Press.

Huffer, Lynne. 2017 "Foucault's Fossils: Life Itself and the Return to Nature in Feminist Philosophy." In Anthropocene Feminism, ed. Richard Grusin. Minneapolis: University of Minnesota Press.

Insel, Thomas R. 2010. "The Challenge of Translation in Social Neuroscience: A Review of Oxytocin, Vasopressin, and Affiliative Behavior." *Neuron* 65(6):768–79.

Jablonka, Eva, and Marion J. Lamb. 2014. *Evolution in Four Dimensions: Genetic, Epigenetic, Behavioral, and Symbolic Variation in the History of Life*. Rev. ed. Cambridge, MA: MIT Press.

Jordan-Young, Rebecca M. 2010. *Brain Storm: The Flaws in the Science of Sex Differences*. Cambridge, MA: Harvard University Press.

Keller, Evelyn Fox. 2010. *The Mirage of a Space between Nature and Nurture*. Durham, NC: Duke University Press.

Kodavanti, Prasada Rao S., and Margarita C. Curras-Collazo. 2010. "Neuroendocrine Actions of Organohalogens: Thyroid Hormones, Arginine Vasopressin, and Neuroplasticity." *Frontiers in Neuroendocrinology* 31(4):479–96.

Lim, Miranda M., Zuoxin Wang, Daniel E. Olazábal, Xianghui Ren, Ernest F. Terwilliger, and Larry J. Young. 2004. "Enhanced Partner Preference in a Promiscuous Species by Manipulating the Expression of a Single Gene." *Nature* 429(6993):754–57.

Lolait, Stephen J., Anne-Marie O'Carroll, and Michael J. Brownstein. 1995. "Molecular Biology of Vasopressin Receptors." *Annals of the New York Academy of Sciences* 771(1):273–92.

Lorde, Audre. 1984. "Uses of the Erotic, the Erotic as Power." In *Sister Outsider: Essays and Speeches*, 53–59. Trumansburg, NY: Crossing.

McGraw, Lisa A., James W. Thomas, and Larry J. Young. 2008. "White Paper Proposal for Sequencing the Genome of the Prairie Vole *(Microtus orchragaster)*." White paper, National Human Genome Research Institute. http://www.genome.gov/Pages/Research/Sequencing/SeqProposals/VoleWhitePaper_and_LOS.pdf.

Moss, Lenny. 2013. "Moral Molecules, Modern Selves, and Our 'Inner Tribe.'" *Hedgehog Review* 15(1). http://www.iasc-culture.org/THR/THR_article_2013_Spring_Moss.php.

Nair, Yasmin. 2015. "The Secret History of Gay Marriage." *Yasmin Nair blog*, June 25. http://yasminnair.net/content/secret-history-gay-marriage.

Pitts-Taylor, Victoria. 2010. "The Plastic Brain: Neoliberalism and the Neuronal Self." *Health* 14(6):635–52.

Richardson, Sarah S. 2012. "Sexing the X: How the X Became the 'Female Chromosome.'" *Signs: Journal of Women in Culture and Society* 37(4):909–33.

Roosth, Sophia, and Astrid Schraeder, eds. 2012a. "Feminist Theory Out of Science." Special issue, *differences* 23, no. 3.

Roosth, Sophia, and Astrid Schraeder. 2012b. "Feminist Theory Out of Science: Introduction." *differences* 23(3):1–8.

Roy, Deboleena. 2007. "Somatic Matters: Becoming Molecular in Molecular Biology." *Rhizome* 14 (Summer). http://www.rhizomes.net/issue14/roy/roy.html.

Roy, Deboleena, and Banu Subramaniam. "Matter in the Shadows: Feminist New Materialism and the Practices of Colonialism." In *Mattering: Feminism, Science and Materialism*, ed. Victoria Pitts-Taylor. New York: New York University Press, 2016.

Sheff, Elisabeth. 2013. *The Polyamorists Next Door: Inside Multiple-Partner Relationships and Families*. Lanham, MD: Rowman & Littlefield.

Sieben, Anna. 2011. "Heteronormative Pheromones? A Feminist Approach to Human Chemical Communication." *Feminist Theory* 12(3):263–80.

Spivak, Gayatri Chakravorty. 2011. "'Love: A Conversation.' Conversation with Serene Jones, Catherine Keller, Kwok Pui-Lan, and Stephen D. Moore." In *Planetary Loves: Spivak, Postcoloniality, and Theology*, ed. Stephen D. Moore and Mayra Rivera, 55–78. New York: Fordham University Press.

Tweedy, Ann E. 2010. "Polyamory as a Sexual Orientation." *University of Cincinnati Law Review* 79(4):1461–1515.

Van Anders, Sari M., and Katherine L. Goldey. 2010. "Testosterone and Partnering Are Linked via Relationship Status for Women and 'Relationship Orientation' for Men." *Hormones and Behavior* 58(5):820–26.

Van Anders, Sari M., Katherine L. Goldey, and Patty X. Kuo. 2011. "The Steroid/Peptide Theory of Social Bonds: Integrating Testosterone and Peptide Responses for Classifying Social Behavioral Contexts." *Psychoneuroendocrinology* 36(9):1265–75.

Van der Tuin, Iris. 2008. "Deflationary Logic." *European Journal of Women's Studies* 15(4):411–16.

Van der Tuin, Iris, and Rick Dolphijn. 2010. "The Transversality of New Materialism." *Women: A Cultural Review* 21(2):153–71.

Willett, Cynthia. 2001. *The Soul of Justice: Social Bonds and Racial Hubris*. Ithaca, NY: Cornell University Press.

Willey, Angela. 2014. "Why Do Voles Fall in Love? Interview with Feminist Science Studies Scholar Angela Willey." Interview conducted by Kristina Gupta. Kristina Gupta blog, June 28. http://www.kristinagupta.com/2012/06/28/why-do-voles-fall-in-love-interview-with-feminist-science-studies-scholar-angela-willey/.

Willey, Angela, and Sara Giordano. 2011. "'Why Do Voles Fall in Love?' Sexual Dimorphism in Monogamy Gene Research." In *Gender and the Science of Difference: Cultural Politics of Contemporary Science and Medicine*, ed. Jill A. Fisher, 108–25. New Brunswick, NJ: Rutgers University Press.

Willey, Angela, and Banu Subramaniam. 2017. "Inside the Social World of Asocials: White Nerd Masculinity, Science, and the Politics of Reverent Disdain." *Feminist Studies*.

Wilson, Elizabeth A. 1998. *Neural Geographies: Feminism and the Microstructure of Cognition*. New York: Routledge.

Wilson, Elizabeth A. 2004. *Psychosomatic: Feminism and the Neurological Body*. Durham, NC: Duke University Press.

Wilson, Elizabeth A. 2012. "Gut Feminism." *differences* 15(3):66–94.

Winnubst, Shannon. 2006. *Queering Freedom*. Bloomington: Indiana University Press.

Withers, Deborah M. 2010. "What Is Your Essentialism Is My Immanent Flesh! The Ontological Politics of Feminist Epistemology." *European Journal of Women's Studies* 17(3):231–47.

Witte, John, Jr. 2012. "Why Monogamy Is Natural." *Faith Street*, October 2. http://www.faithstreet.com/onfaith/2012/01/02/why-monogamy-is-natural/12105.

Zarembo, Alan. 2004. "DNA Tweak Turns Vole Mates into Soul Mates." *Los Angeles Times*, June 17. http://articles.latimes.com/2004/jun/17/science/scimonogamy17.

Zimmer, Carl. 2013. "Monogamy and Human Evolution." *New York Times*, August 2. http://www.nytimes.com/2013/08/02/science/monogamys-boost-to-human-evolution.html.

ANALOUISE KEATING AND KAKALI BHATTACHARYA

56. DECOLONIZING RELIGION, TRANSFORMING SPIRIT: THE IMAGINAL IN GLORIA ANZALDÚA'S AUTOHISTORIA-TEORÍA

Typically, mainstream feminist theory and the academic field of Women's and Gender Studies (WGS) enact an unspoken, often unrecognized binary between the secular and the religious, prioritizing the former while almost entirely ignoring the latter. As Niamh Reilly explains, while feminist religious studies scholars investigate the sexism in patriarchal religions, feminist scholars in other disciplines adopt secular approaches that avoid religion entirely or reduce it to identity issues. Karlyn Crowley makes a related point, arguing that North American WGS has been shaped by "a Western progress narrative" (256) that embraces secularity while rejecting its presumed opposite, religion/spirituality, as oppressive, "atavistic, and uninformed" (245). Given the conservative, heteronormative teachings found in many organized religions as well as the "spirit-phobia" (Keating 55) that compels most academics to avoid mentioning spirit, souls, the sacred, or other apparently incorporeal things, this hyper-secularity is not surprising.

However, when scholars conflate religion with spirituality and then downplay or avoid them, they limit their scholarship and WGS by shutting out those for whom religion and/or spirituality are more complex than this knee-jerk rejection presumes. Because so many of those ignored are women of color and women of the Global South, this dismissal inadvertently reinforces exclusionary divisions and white-supremacist thinking. Moreover, because the division between secularity and religion relies on binary (either/or) thinking and unwarranted faith in a (pseudo-)universal reason and other Enlightenment-based principles, this unquestioned hyper-secularity reinforces the status quo and prevents us from developing ontologies and epistemologies that move partially outside the Cartesian framework separating reality into binary opposites:

mind/body, subject/object, spirit/matter, male/female, and reason/intuition.

Rather than engage directly in this debate, we focus on Gloria Anzaldúa's innovative but seldom-explored theory of autohistoria-teoría to demonstrate that spirituality—when defined broadly and not conflated with organized religion—offers knowledge creation and metaphysical alternatives to dichotomous body/spirit paradigms. We argue that autohistoria-teoría provides a de/colonial approach to conventional Enlightenment-based frameworks (Bhattacharya). A de/colonial approach enacts complex both/and negotiations acknowledging colonial forms of oppression while, simultaneously, enacting anti-colonial resistances like reclaiming language, land, and spiritual practices. Incorporating spirituality and imaginal journeys, autohistoria-teoría bridges personal narratives, theory-building, and creative inquiry into self and self-in-relation-to others. It facilitates transdisciplinary methodological moves that open additional, expansive engagements in transformational cross-disciplinary inquiry in the humanities, social sciences, and related fields, enabling us to generate new types of questions and unexpected insights.

We center spirituality rather than religion because the former is more ubiquitous; less constrained by external authorities; and less frequently associated with colonization, conquest, environmental destruction, and other forms of oppression. Unlike most religions, which typically have sacred texts, specific ethical/moral codes, specially trained leaders, and hierarchical structures, spirituality is grounded in the individual's relationship with self, community, nature, spirit, and/or cosmos. For example, Akasha (Gloria) Hull describes spirituality as a "conscious relationship with the realm of spirit, with the invisibly permeating, ultimately positive, divine, and evolutionary energies that give rise to and sustain all that exists" (2); similarly, Elisa Facio and Irene Lara define spirituality as "a conscious, self-reflective way of life and a way of relating to others, to ourselves, and to 's/Spirit' . . . in a manner that honors all of life as an interconnected web" (4). In de/colonial praxis, spirituality goes beyond epistemological, ethical dimensions to include social critique, metaphysical exploration, and personal/collective transformation.

AUTOHISTORIA-TEORÍA

Anzaldúa coined the term "autohistoria-teoría" to distinguish her work from mainstream autobiography and cultural narratives. When she reflected on her writing and that of some women of color, she realized that this work—whether "autobiography, memoir, fictitious narratives, [or] personal and theoretical essays"—included dreams, visions, prayers, and other elusive, nontangible experiences in unique ways not found in the conventional forms. Rather than redefine existing genres more expansively, Anzaldúa decided that this work merits its own genre and method ("autohistorias-teorías"). Autohistoria-teoría exceeds the status quo and takes risks: it combines self-writing with theorizing, fact with fiction, embodiment with knowledge production, and the personal with the social. Key traits include strategic use of fictional, poetic elements; creation of individual/collective selfhoods; use of nonlinear narrative; and acceptance of multiplicity–multiple realities, truths, perspectives, epistemologies, and worlds.

While incorporating historical, biographical, and/or memoir-like details, autohistoria-teoría reaches beyond physical-material reality to document memories, spectral visits, shamanic journeys, and other forms of spirituality. By so doing, it moves beyond the dichotomous Cartesian framework described above. Anzaldúa's final book, *Light in the Dark/Luz en lo oscuro: Rewriting Identity, Spirituality, Reality*, illustrates this movement. While she includes memories of verifiable incidents that occurred in physical reality, Anzaldúa also shares reflections on spirit worlds; interactions with her creative muse, la naguala; and interconnections with animals, reptiles, trees, plants, and imaginal worlds in which she is constantly crossing boundaries, forever in the in-between spaces. She cultivates a writing practice unrestricted by formal, academic, or popular genre conventions—an alchemical method legitimizing additional epistemologies, ontologies, and metaphysics for our (real, imaginal, and/or dream) worlds. She gives us examples, guidelines, and (most importantly) permission to remember and create spiritual connections.

By definition, autohistoria-teoría investigates self-identity-related issues, especially experiences and oppressive societal forces that fragment us. These fragmentations provoke emotional, geographic, economic, spiritual, philosophical, familial, professional, and other forms of exile as we are separated and labeled—for example, as too feminist/not feminist enough, too queer/not queer enough, and too radical/not radical enough. When we internalize these labels, we reinforce this process. Carrying these fragmentations in our bodies, spirits, and beings, we imprint their narratives in our consciousness. At times we refuse to acknowledge them; at other times we simply forget their presence; and at still other times we overidentify with one or two fragments while entirely ignoring the rest.

Employing autohistoria-teoría enables us to retrieve these fragments, enacting the *Coyolxauhqui imperative*–the term Anzaldúa coined to describe knowledge production as "an ongoing, healing process of making and unmaking" (*Light* 20) in which there is no final resolution. When we heed Coyolxauhqui's imperative, we strive to integrate internal fragmentations, reconstructing and reframing self-identity and insights. The Coyolxauhqui imperative invites us to confront our shadow-beasts, aspects of ourselves that we "don't want to own" (132). Leaning on Jungian archetype and precolonial myth, Anzaldúa coined the term *shadow-beast* to investigate self-fragmentation's impact. Psychologist Carl Jung posited that we share inherited potentials, or archetypes, that variously manifest in consciousness, emerging as motifs like mother, child, trickster, and shadow.

Drawing on her own experiences, Anzaldúa explains that "[t]he shadow-beast and attendant desconocimientos (the ignorance we cultivate to keep ourselves from knowledge so that we can remain unaccountable) have a tenacious hold on us." Rather than run from her shadow-beasts, she confronts them. By thus excavating her experiences, she (sometimes) achieves new insights: "Grappling with (des)conocimientos, with what I don't want to know, opening and shutting my eyes and ears to cultural realities, expanding my awareness and consciousness, or refusing to do so, sometimes results in discovering the positive shadow: hidden aspects of myself and the world" (*Light* 2).

Anzaldúa uses autohistoria-teoría to enact this self-excavation. As she exposes (both to herself and to readers) personal and cultural traumas, struggles for visibility, and identity development, she explores creativity, spirituality, and writing itself. Through writing, she creates a coherence that works toward healing her fragmented parts while generating new knowledge. A process of self-reflection and identity development, autohistoria-teoría demands that we honestly scrutinize our wounds. We journey into the hidden parts of consciousness, where perhaps disintegration and reintegration occur, propelling us to places and ways of knowledge production, with a renewed sense of self. Autohistoria-teoría as method uses self-reflective writing to conduct shadow work and spiritual healing. Shadow work is the work one must do to journey inward and engage with the darker parts of one's memories, consciousness, painful events, or stuck places to understand how such journey could be insight-provoking in ways that were previously unknown. This method is always in flux, never fixed, just as our fragmentations are not essentialized, frozen into one meaning or another, but exist dynamically, in relation to each other and the world (Bhattacharya and Payne).

Autohistoria-teoría (both as method and text) takes a wide variety of forms, depending on writer and context (the event, environment, writer's current state, and countless other influences). Keeping the fragmentations in play resists duality-based discourses and makes space for contradictions rising from various parts of ourselves. A deeply embodied method, autohistoria-teoría displays the material effects of those discourses with which we identify, those we accommodate, and those we resist. Writing autohistoria-teoría expands our angle of vision, enabling us to sort through competing discourses; as we reflect on our cognitive dissonance (provoked by these competing discourses), we detect those that are oppressive and our relationship with them.

Autohistoria-teoría enables us to move beyond Cartesian binary frameworks into what Anzaldúa calls an *alchemical synthesis* of numerous self-fragmentations. In this synthesis the writer is researcher of self, self in relation to other, and self in relation to sociocultural discourses. This multiplicity can liberate us from dualistic writing that separates mind from body, conscious from unconscious, and real from imaginal. Autohistoria-teoría invites us to imagine de/colonial possibilities. No longer writing *about* the Other in ways that further commodify and exoticize, we write from *within* our own experiences *as* Other, enacting border crossings and building bridges among multiple parts of our narratives and our self.

But this potentially transformative autohistoria-teoría occurs only when we're willing to meet and work with our shadow-beasts. Anzaldúa asks her readers the critical question: "Are you sure you're ready to face the shadow-beast guarding the threshold—that part of you holding your failures and inadequacies, the negativities you've internalized, and those aspects of gender and class you want to disown? Recognizing and coming to terms with the manipulative, vindictive, secretive shadow-beast within will take the heaviest toll" (*Light* 137). Fully acknowledging this heaviest of tolls, we present exemplars of autohistoria-teoría that engage in this shadow work. Although shadow work is not autohistoria-teoría's sole purpose, when we write from spaces of alchemical synthesis with vulnerability and honesty, there's a good chance we'll run into the dark, shadowy parts of self and society.

ENACTING AUTOHISTORIA-TEORÍA: ANALOUISE'S NARRATIVE

I was overweight until early adolescence, when I went on a radical diet (*500 calories per day: hard-boiled eggs, saltine crackers, cottage cheese, diet soda*) and lost about thirty pounds very quickly. When I stopped dieting my stomach had shrunk so much that I'd automatically vomit up most of the food I'd just eaten. I had no idea why; nor did the doctors my parents took me to see. (*But of course no one knew: it wasn't until about a year later that my condition was given a name: "bulimia nervosa."*) I soon realized that I could easily purge whatever I ate, with no apparent pain or negative consequence. Because it seemed like a magical way to eat whatever I wanted (*and I wanted to eat a lot!*) while also maintaining an acceptable body weight and size (*but–acceptable to who? why didn't I ask this question years ago?*), I embraced this unexpected gift. No more dieting! How lucky was *I*, I thought to myself. Even when introduced to the term "bulimia," I denied that it applied to me. (*I was deeply immersed in my desconocimientos, my culturally inscribed willed ignorance.*)

By my mid-twenties this "gift" had taken over my life. I'd gone from binging once a week (*on "special" occasions*) to binging multiple times each day. Whenever I was happy, sad, depressed, lonely, demoralized—really, no matter what I was feeling—I used food to process (*or, rather, to smother*) emotions, stress, loneliness, alienation, and despair. I'd eat copious amounts of sweets (*doughnuts, cake, cookies, candy bars . . . you name it, I ate it*), drink a large diet soda, and easily vomit up everything I'd devoured. Every time I tried to quit (*and I tried often!*), I'd be fine for a week or two, but whenever I slid into depression I'd immediately return to this binge-purge cycle. My personal hell. Trapped in what Anzaldúa would call a "Coatlicue State," I was paralyzed—unable to move forward, unable to find my way out.

An ancient Mesoamerican earth goddess, Coatlicue is typically portrayed as a headless figure, with a skirt made of writhing serpents, a necklace of human skulls, hands, and hearts; and two blood-serpents spurting out of her neck. However, this horrific depiction is ancient propaganda suppressing previous egalitarian cosmologies that revered female deities. As Anzaldúa explains, "The male-dominated Azteca-Mexica culture drove the powerful female deities underground by giving them monstrous attributes . . . They divided [Coatlicue,] who had been complete, who possessed both upper (light) and underworld (dark) aspects" (*Borderlands* 49). Like Anzaldúa's shadow-beast, Coatlicue represents the repressed, disavowed parts of ourselves—those aspects we fear, deny, or in other ways try to ignore—often because we've been taught that they're insignificant, shameful, or worse.

Upon first encountering Anzaldúa's discussion of Coatlicue, I experienced a full-body jolt, an electrical connection. Recognizing that Coatlicue's division mirrored my own, I acquired new insight: The bulimia tore me asunder, dividing me from my self, numbing

me into temporary satisfaction with my place, as defined by US racialized gender roles. I reread Coatlicue's fierce visage as masking incredible power and goodness, her serpents as promising transformation and rebirth. Instead of running *away from* Coatlicue, I ran *toward* her. Through meditation, imaginal journeys, altar-making, tattoos, and other spiritual practices, I tried to enter her presence, to face and embrace her. Although I often stumbled and fell, I learned to appreciate the complexity behind her fierce gaze, acknowledge my dissatisfaction with conventional race-gender roles, and embrace my own power.

ENACTING AUTOHISTORIA-TEORÍA: KAKALI'S NARRATIVE

The mangalsutra was the black necklace with a gold, heart-shaped pendant that went around my neck when I married for the first and only time. *Mangal* means well-being, or a wish for someone's well-being, and *sutra* means thread, or the source, as I recall from my early childhood Sanskrit classes in Kolkata, India. Wikipedia tells me some other meaning and I ignore it. I remember how older, Bengali Indian women would say, "Tomar mangal hok," as I bowed and touched their feet in reverence when meeting after a long time. Their response usually meant, "Let all that is well and good happen to you in your life." I viewed this necklace as a reminder that my marriage would be the source and thread of my well-being, wrapped around my neck, a daily reminder of cultural heritage, and an imagined aspiration. Anzaldúa describes a similar awareness that attends to embodied knowledge from ancestors and cultural rituals, informing our values and subsequent actions.

I fell in love with a man from India during my doctoral studies at the University of Georgia. We met online in a Kolkata chat room. Nostalgia took hold of me; feeling isolated at a predominantly White university, I desperately wanted connection with *my people.* After chatting online for a year or so, I traveled to India to meet him, who would become my future husband. We had a fairytale summer romance, traveling all over India, wanting to learn every detail of each other's lives, meeting one another's friends and relatives. On the last day of my visit he proposed to me after knowing me online for a year and in person for a month.

I accepted. How could I not, when someone loved me enough to make such a grand gesture?

That winter my entire family traveled to Kolkata for my wedding. Sitting across the room from my fiancé's father, aunt, and grandmother, my parents and I were informed that the amount of gifts we offer in dowry directly reflected our class and character. My fiancé stayed silent—a silence I interpreted as respectful disagreement. My parents offered to cancel the wedding, but people were arriving in Kolkata from the United States, Canada, and elsewhere for the celebration. Loans had been taken out for wedding expenses. What would I say to people? That I'd made the wrong choice? That they'd taken on unnecessary debt because of my poor judgment? I felt paralyzed and longed for the wholeness of the happy married life I'd imagined. Yet I felt fragmented into shards, fearing to call back these fragments into wholeness. Not yet ready to heed the Coyolxauhqui imperative, I was soon married. My fragmented parts remained in flux and in contest with each other. In later years I would heed Coyolxauhqui's imperative, move toward healing and wholeness, excavate into wounds, and remain aware of the (im)possibility of achieving wholeness. At the moment, though, I dropped into the Coatlicue state, paralyzed by the chaos of living in an oppressive story and desiring a liberatory narrative. In this third space, Anzaldúa explains, one sinks into the depths of despair, loneliness, and self-resentment, which made calling back the fragmented parts of me to a wholeness even more challenging.

The marriage lasted six years. Six years of holes punched in walls, abuse, and screaming matches that required police intervention; the discovery of several extramarital affairs; and my resentment, heightened anxiety, depression, panic attacks, and two suicide attempts. All because I had not walked away when I had the chance, for which I paid the highest price with my life and well-being. I continued sinking into the Coatlicue state. My anti-anxiety, antidepressant, and sleep-aid medications were at their maximum allowable dosage, numbing me so thoroughly that I walked through life a zombie. Only when my psychiatrist warned that I would be drug-dependent for the rest of my life did I decide to end the marriage, become drug-independent, and look squarely at the darkness enveloping me. I acknowledged that I'd have to completely fall apart before I could make sense of my life, become healthy, and undertake the healing journey. Now ready to heed the Coyolxauhqui imperative and integrate my fragments, I removed my mangalsutra.

OUR COYOLXAUHQUI IMPERATIVE: PULLING IT TOGETHER

This essay explores autohistoria-teoría, Anzaldúa's multi-theory method of holistic knowledge production, and uses this exploration to de/colonize Western academic spirit-phobia. Although Anzaldúa's theories of mestiza consciousness and borderlands have impacted decolonial feminist scholarship (Facio and Lara; Mody; Pérez), scholars have yet to examine autohistoria-teoría's de/colonial potential. To honor autohistoria-teoría's boundary-crossing while enacting our own de/colonial maneuvers, we transgressed academic conventions: After presenting Anzaldúa's theory, we illustrated it with two highly-personal autohistorias-teorías. Despite potential risks, we delved into fragmented, suppressed parts of ourselves, exploring how these parts played out in our lives. The act of writing within, from, and about painful fragmentations while reintegrating them compelled us to journey into hidden aspects of consciousness, challenge Western academic writing conventions, and work with metaphysical spirit-driven understandings of self-in-relation-to world.

Prior to this, AnaLouise had never written about her bulimic years or her confrontation with Coatlicue. By enacting autohistoria-teoría, her writing self connected with other parts of self, parts that mirror others, and sociocultural discourses about body image and body-shaming. Engaging with meditation and imaginal journeys allowed AnaLouise to dissolve dichotomous mind/body, religion/secularity boundaries and connect her spiritual identity with Coatlicue. As Anzaldúa notes, this shadow work can take the heaviest toll as we unload the weight of decades of spirit-draining programming.

Kakali's narrative concludes by recognizing the need to unpack social scripts about being a wife, a daughter, and a culturally respectful woman and to begin a healing process informed by the Coyolxauhqui imperative. Like AnaLouise, Kakali made herself vulnerable, sharing a personal narrative that risks misinterpretation—the possibility that Western readers will impose an exotic sensibility on her autohistoria-teoría and thus reinforce stigmatized, colonial understandings of patriarchy and women in India. However, like all autohistoria-teoría, Kakali's narrative goes beyond the personal; it exceeds cultural borders and resonates with those who have experienced similar paralyzing Coatlicue states–the inability to take an action that perhaps was more difficult, highlighting our failures, inadequacies, and effects of internalized oppressive narratives that provoke us to be self-destructive to escape (*enhance?*) our pain. Not discussing such events empowers the shadow-beast to create fragmentations, leading Kakali to continuously disown those parts of herself.

Academic spirit-phobia has its source in Western ethnocentric, Cartesian frameworks separating body from mind and relegating spirit to the immaterial. Autohistoria-teoría offers a de/colonial praxis enabling us to challenge this framework by redefining spirit to include embodied experiences and complex journeys into consciousness and other realms. While colonial sensibilities urge us to mark such experiences as backward and unworthy of legitimization, autohistoria-teoría invites us to embrace them. Our sample autohistoria-teorías focused on episodes in our lives when mind/body dualities paralyzed us (throwing us into Coatlicue states). As we explored how these oppressive dualities negatively impacted us physically, mentally, and spiritually, we confronted our personal shadow-beasts and moved toward reintegrating repressed fragments. We performed spirituality-driven understandings of our gendered/racialized identities, thus challenging how knowledge-making is privileged in western academia. Doing so required critical awareness of self, identification of repressed personal/cultural truths, and acceptance of alternative ontological frameworks.

REFERENCES

Anzaldúa, Gloria. "Autohistorias-teorías—*Mujeres que cuentan vidas:* Personal & Collective Narratives that Challenge Genre Conventions." Box 94, Folder 2, Gloria Evangelina Anzaldúa Papers. Nettie Lee Benson Latin American Collection, University of Texas, Austin.

Anzaldúa, Gloria. *Borderlands/La Frontera: The New Mestiza.* Spinsters/Aunt Lute, 1999; 1987.

Anzaldúa, Gloria. *Light in the Dark/Luz en lo oscuro: Rewriting Identity, Spirituality, Reality.* Edited by AnaLouise Keating. Duke UP, 2015.

Bhattacharya, Kakali. "Performing Gender as 'Third-World-Other" in Higher Education: De/colonizing Transnational Feminist Possibilities." *Creative Approaches to Research*, vol. 6, no. 3, 2013, pp. 30–47.

Bhattacharya, Kakali, and Payne, Rachél. "Mixing Mediums, Mixing Selves: Arts-based Contemplative Approaches to Border Crossings." *International Journal of Qualitative Studies in Education*, vol. 29, 2016, pp. 1–18. doi:10.1080/09518398.2016.1201163.

Crowley, Karlyn. "Secularity." *Rethinking Women's and Gender Studies.* Edited by Catherine M. Orr, Ann Braithwaite, and Diane Lichentstein. Routledge, 2012.

Facio, Elisa, and Irene Lara, "Introduction." *Fleshing the Spirit: Spirituality and Activism in Chicana, Latina, and Indigenous Women's Lives.* Edited by Elisa Facio and Irene Lara. U of Arizona P, 2014.

Hull, Akasha Gloria. *Soul Talk: The New Spirituality of African American Women.* Inner Traditions, 2001.

Jung, Carl. "Phenomenology of the Self." *The Portable Jung*, Trans. R.F.C. Hull, Penguin Classics, 1976, pp. 139–62.

Keating, AnaLouise. "'I'm a Citizen of the Universe': Gloria Anzaldúa's Spiritual Activism as Catalyst for Social Change." *Feminist Studies*, vol. 34, no. 1–2, 2008, pp. 53–69.

Mody, Monica. "The Borderlands Feminine: A Feminist, Decolonial Framework for Re-membering Motherlines in South Asia/Transnational Culture." *The Integral Review*, vol. 37, no. 1, July 2017, pp. 87–98.

Pérez, Emma. *The Decolonial Imaginary: Writing Chicanas into History.* Indiana UP, 1999.

Reilly, Niamh. "Rethinking the Interplay of Feminism and Secularism in a Neo-Secular Age." *Feminist Review*, no. 97, 2011, pp. 5–31.

ELI CLARE

57. MOVING THROUGH CURE

CHOOSING DISABILITY

Collectively in the white Western world, we go to such lengths to un-choose disability. We wear seat belts. We don't dive into shallow water. We vaccinate against polio and measles. Certainly these actions are about avoiding death, but our avoidance quickly mashes into the un-choosing of disability. Consider for instance public service announcements and advertisements that warn against unsafe and drunk driving. Many of them use disability as the cautionary tale, showing photos of tragic-appearing teenage boys in wheelchairs. One ad from Utah's "Zero Fatalities" campaign in 2009 reads: "Nothing kills more Utah teens than auto crashes. Not fazed? Okay, how does the thought of spending the rest of your life in a wheelchair grab you? Look, every year far too many Utah teens go from cool to crippled in a blink of an eye."[1] Disability and death are paired together, the first considered a more powerful argument against unsafe driving than the second.

We un-choose disability in hundreds of ways. We condone genetic testing for pregnant people and rarely question the ethics of disability-selective abortion. Some pro-choice activists justify late-term abortions with talk about fetal abnormalities—or in plainer language, disability. We accept as a matter of course that sperm banks screen out donors with a whole host of body-mind conditions considered undesirable, including deafness, alcoholism, cystic fibrosis, depression, and schizophrenia. We walk to end breast cancer, run to end diabetes, bike to end multiple sclerosis, dump ice water on our heads to end ALS. We want to control how, when, and if disability and death appear in our lives.

In 1963 my mother was twenty-six, a newly married working-class student struggling through graduate school. Every day she answered to professors who believed women belonged not in the classroom but at home, tending children. In the spring of that year, she discovered she was pregnant with me. That pregnancy was unplanned. It completely changed the course of her life.

I grew up knowing she desperately didn't want a disabled child. She made that clear in a thousand ways. She was an intensely unhappy mother. Maybe she didn't want *any* children. Yet her grief, guilt, bitterness about my cerebral palsy was so distinct, so personal; at ages ten, eleven, twelve, I believed she didn't want *me*. I may have been right. But for sure, if she could have un-chosen disability, she would have.

There are also moments when disability is actively chosen. Prospective foster or adoptive parents fill out agency paperwork requesting a disabled child—or more likely in the language of those bureaucracies, a "special needs" child. Pregnant people decide to keep their fetuses predicted to have Down syndrome. Or they decide against genetic testing altogether, letting the crapshoot of disability run its course unimpeded. Deaf people using alternative insemination to become pregnant seek out deaf sperm donors, wanting to increase their likelihood of having deaf children. Transabled people, sometimes called disability wannabes or amputee wannabes, feel a need to be disabled.[2] Many have sought out surgeons, planned self-amputations, or staged disabling events, manifesting their desire in actual disability. Or, unable to acquire a disability, they use crutches, braces, wheelchairs anyway.

How the world treats people who, in some fashion, choose disability reveals so much. When transabled people come out, putting words to their desire, they most often encounter revulsion, anger, disbelief. The medical-industrial complex pathologizes them, labeling their so-called troubled body-minds with the recently invented Body Identity Integrity Disorder. People who choose to increase the likelihood of having a disabled or deaf child are deemed categorically selfish and immoral. They're accused of burdening their children and sometimes publicly shamed by the media. People who forego genetic testing, deciding not to intervene in the possibility of disability, are seen as vaguely foolish. People who choose against selective abortion after a positive test for a variety of genetic conditions are frequently perceived as downright irresponsible. And people who adopt or foster disabled children—the world treats them as martyrs engaged in charity work. The act of choosing disability in the white Western world is never neutral, simply one choice among many, but rather pathologized, shamed, or sensationalized. In contrast, un-choosing disability is celebrated and framed as a collective imperative.

Beyond this binary of choosing and un-choosing lives the many ways we claim disability and chronic illness. We make peace. We accept. We celebrate. We let go. We find pride. We live with ambiguity. We face mortality. We reject pity and overcoming. We build community and grow accustomed to isolation. We seek interdependence. We turn away from expectations of hyperproductivity. We insist on what we know about our own body-minds. We learn to balance loss and pride. We deal with frustration and pain. *I'm* loath to define claiming. Sometimes it lives near an active choosing of disability; other times it shares much in common with un-choosing; often it is laced with contradiction.

I know hard-of-hearing people who have thrown their hearing aids away and stopped struggling to be part of the non-deaf world. People who might have been able to walk again after their disabling accidents and chose to become wheelchair users. People who much prefer hearing voices or experiencing emotional highs and lows than managing the impacts and side effects of psychotropic drugs. To many non-deaf people, nondisabled walkies, and people without psych disabilities or psych labels, these choices seem unimaginable. But from the inside, they make all the sense in the world. They pave the way for finding community

and connection. They allow for greater and easier mobility. They allow us to be ourselves

On my forty-fifth birthday a friend writes me, "I'm so glad you were born crippled." She's a queer, disabled, white, working-class activist. We've organized together, sat together, struggled together. The word *crippled* makes me smile. In disability communities, many of us call each other *crip*, practicing the art of refashioning and reclaiming language full of hurt, but typically we veer away from *crippled*; it's too much. My friend uses that riskier word with affection. It contains a whirl of pain and centuries of history. The word *born* settles into me as inconvertible truth: I was indeed born forty-five years ago crippled. But *glad* is her gift to me, both surprise and revelation. *Glad* leans against un-choosing, my mother's dismay, a whole world of devaluing and eradication. *Glad* is more than uppity pride and stubborn resistance. *Glad* is matter-of-fact, unmovable in its conviction that the world needs disabled body-minds. *Glad* is a powerful claiming.

AIRPORTS AND CORNFIELDS

I.

It's late spring in the San Francisco airport. I walk down a long concourse toward the plane that will take me home, I've been in the Bay Area for a long weekend with three hundred LGBTQ disabled people—queer crips as many of us like to call ourselves. I walk slowly, unable to keep up with the frenzied pace. People stream around me. A white businessman with a rainbow flag sticker on his briefcase hurries past an African American woman and her grandson; a Latino man speaking quiet Spanish into his cell phone stands next to a white teen joking in twangy English with her friends; an Asian American woman pushes her cleaning cart by, stopping to empty the trash can. I know something is missing, but I don't know what. I let my exhaustion and images from the weekend roll over me. Suddenly I realize everyone around me has two arms and two legs. They're walking rather than rolling; speaking with their lips, not their hands, speaking in even, smooth syllables, no stutters or slurs. They have no canes, no crutches, no braces, no ventilators, no face masks, no oxygen tanks, no service dogs. Their faces don't twitch nor their hands flop; they don't rock back and forth. They hold their backs straight, and their smiles aren't lopsided. They move as if their body-minds are separate and independent from the others around them. For a split second, they all look the same.

That fleeting experience of sameness reminds me of monocultures—ecosystems that have been stripped, through human intervention, of a multitude of interdependent beings and replaced by a single species. I think of a wheat field with its orderly rows of one variety of grass, a clearcut forest replanted with one variety of tree.

I know there were many kinds of humans in the San Francisco airport. I was surrounded by differences created through race, language, citizenship, age, class, gender, sexuality, geography, spirituality, nationality, body-mind shape and size, and disability and chronic illness I didn't perceive. Yet, even with my recognition of human diversity, that moment at the airport when everyone looked the same has stayed with me.

II.

It's early autumn, and I step into an agribusiness cornfield. Rows envelop me, the whole world a forest of corn beginning to turn brown. Leaves and husks rattle overhead. I walk along the furrows between rows, step onto the mounds upon which the stalks grow. A repetition of the same plant fills the space. Nothing chirps or rasps, squawks or buzzes; the cicadas and grasshoppers have gone dormant for the season. I see no traces of grouse, pheasant, fox. If it were a rainy day, I'd see brown water running down the slight slope I'm standing on, washing the dirt away before my very eyes.

In a monoculture, a world of damage lies beneath the obvious sameness. During that autumn walk, I couldn't smell the pesticide residue, but it hung in the air I was breathing. I couldn't see the petroleum-based fertilizers in the dirt, but they were present in large quantities. I didn't know how depleted the earth was, each corn stalk sucking nutrients from the soil and giving nothing in return. Nor did I notice the six or seven inches of topsoil that had already been washed away in the last hundred and fifty years. I had no visceral awareness of all the invasive pests—the true armyworm, the European corn borer, the corn rootworm, among many others—that breed and eat with abandon in monoculture cornfields, which in turn force agribusiness farmers to spray endless rounds of pesticides.

Simply put, monocultures do an immense amount of damage. So much labor and violence goes into creating and maintaining them. Their existence requires hundreds of eradications and removals.[3]

The history of agribusiness corn, soybeans, wheat, and beef haunts me. I return to an old black-and-white photo, scratched and faded at the edges, taken in the 1870s.[4] It starkly portrays the violence on which these monocultures were created. At the center looms a mountain of bison skulls—thousands upon thousands heaped on top of each other, maybe as many as 180,000. No single skull is distinct; instead they blur together, becoming a geometric pattern of bone. Soon they will be ground into fertilizer. Amidst these bones are two men. Both wear dark suits, and each stands with a foot resting on a skull that's been pulled out of the jumble. One is posed at the base of the pile; the other, twenty-five feet above him on top of the mountain. They make me shiver. They are braggarts—maybe bison hunters or government officials or land speculators. Their body-mind language proclaims, "Look, look at what I own."

My heart breaks and breaks again. Starting in the early 1800s, white hunters killed these big shaggy creatures indiscriminately, thirty million in less than a century. They left the carcasses to rot, took only tongues and skins with them to sell. Later white homesteaders collected the bones for fertilizer. The U.S. government encouraged this slaughter as one strategy among many to conquer the Indigenous peoples of the Great Plains. The Lakota medicine man John (Fire) Lame

Deer (Lakota) described the connection between his nation and bison: "The buffalo was part of us, his flesh and blood being absorbed by us until it became our flesh and blood. Our clothing, our tipis, everything we needed for life came from the buffalo's body. It was hard to say where the animal ended and the man began."[5] So when, in 1867, Colonel Richard Irving Dodge commanded, "Kill every buffalo you can! Every buffalo dead is an Indian gone," he was calling for genocide.[6] Native peoples were starved, brutalized, killed, driven onto reservations.

White colonial settlers claimed the land as their own, dividing it into neat rectangles, fencing it, and establishing herds of cattle. The near eradication of the prairies started here. The grazing and migration patterns of bison had been integral parts of these ecosystems, whereas cows destroyed the grasses, giving nothing back. And then white farmers literally tore up the prairie with their plows. They planted monocultures of wheat, corn, and soybean. One hundred seventy million acres of tallgrass prairie used to exist in North America; seven million are left now. Today when we eat corn or steak produced on agribusiness farms in the Great Plains, we are connected all the way back to that mountain of skulls. Monocultures start with violence, removal, and eradication.

III.

The shadows, legacies, and ongoing realities of environmental destruction and genocide, incarceration and involuntary sterilization rise up. They haunt me. The desire for eradication runs so deep. It is revealed in specific moments, places, and histories—in a fleeting experience of sameness at the San Francisco airport, in an agribusiness cornfield before it's mowed for the winter, in a hundred-and-forty-year-old photo of a mountain of bison skulls. But the desire for eradication is also a pattern reaching across time and space. The un-choosing of disability fits into this pattern, one force among many, threatening to create a human monoculture.

INTERDEPENDENCE

Leaves to stones, earthworms to grizzly bears, prairie grasses to bison—life is connected to life.

I'm at a crip dance. We lean into each other—hands on waists, hands on hips, hands on metal and wood and wheels, canes waving in the air, crutches stomping out the beat. We slide in and through pain, shimmy and strut. We dance with our tongues, our eyes, our sip-and-puff wheelchairs. We dance lying on the floor. We dance into tremors and spasms, through anxiety, inside hallucinations. We take breaks, stretch our backs, our legs, our shoulders. We dance all night.

No single part of an ecosystem can be changed without changing every other part.

I'm at a crip gathering. A woman smoking pot as pain management and a woman with environmental illness made sick by marijuana smoke end up rooming next door to each other, an arrangement that doesn't work at all. We reorganize who is sleeping where to create more access for both of them. We sit with people having seizures, monitor their breathing, keep the space around them as safe as possible. We don't call 9-1-1. We figure out food together. Fragrance-free shampoo and shower chairs in gender-neutral restrooms are the norm.

If we spray DDT to eradicate mosquitos, bald eagle and condor eggs become too fragile to hatch.

I remember all the times I've talked friends and lovers through panic attacks and flashbacks; sat with them during nighttime terrors; brought them tea, Rescue Remedy, or Klonopin, depending on their preferences. All the times they've done the same for me.

If we burn coal to light our homes and power our computers, the air we breathe becomes toxic.

I stay overnight with a friend. She lives in a big, collective house. In the morning I putter around the kitchen. I can tell crips live here. There are straws in the silverware drawer, a sign on the refrigerator reminding people to keep the pantry peanut-free, and ice packs galore in the freezer. From the next room, I hear my friend L., a white, power-chair-using, self-described femmegimp, talking with her care shifter (the person helping her with her morning routine). They're exchanging first-date stories, L. buoying the confidence of the care shifter with tips, jokes, and appreciation. Their stories are interrupted by logistics—which scarf L. wants to wear, what eye shadow will match, when paratransit is coming.

The interdependent relationships between disabled people and the people who provide care for us are often messy and fraught with power imbalances rooted in racism, sexism, homophobia, transphobia, ableism, and capitalism. These imbalances frequently cause abuse and neglect for the person receiving care, low wages and exploited labor for the person providing care, and harassment flying in multiple directions. And yet interdependence exists whether it's laced with easy banter and mutuality or with struggle, hierarchy, and exploitation.

White Western culture goes to extraordinary lengths to deny the vital relationships between water and stone, plant and animal, human and nonhuman, as well as the utter reliance of human upon human. Within this culture of denial, when those of us who don't currently need help dressing ourselves or going to the bathroom try to imagine interdependence, we fail. In conjuring a world where we need care to get up in the morning and go to bed at night, we picture an overwhelming dependency, a terrifying loss of privacy and dignity. We don't pause to notice that our fears reflect not the truth but the limits of our imagination.

Part of claiming disability is choosing this messy, imperfect work-in-progress called interdependence.

WANTING A FLAT CHEST

I thought I understood self-acceptance and love—definitely not a simple practice but nonetheless guided by a certain set of principles—until my gendered and sexed self started speaking. When I listened, I discovered an unshakable desire to reshape my body-mind using medical technology—first with chest reconstruction surgery and later with hormone replacement therapy.

All of our body-minds are in motion from the moment of birth to the moment of death. Ask anyone in the throes of puberty or old age. Ask the U.S. soldier back from Afghanistan, dealing with a recent traumatic brain injury; the Afghan civilian whose leg has been shattered in a bomb attack. Ask the person who has lost or gained a hundred pounds; the woman leaving her fifteen-year heterosexual marriage because she's fallen head over heels in love with another woman. Ask the family who over three or four generations climbs out of poverty, maybe through luck or white privilege, education or marrying up.

I remember the last time I went flat chested and bare skinned, age nine camping with my family in Idaho. Dusk licked my ribs, sternum, collar-bone. My mother ordered me to put a T-shirt on, right then and there. I protested, "But why, Dad gets to go without a shirt?" Of course, there was no real answer, only a "because."

Our body-minds tumble, shift, ease their way through space and time, never static. Gender transition in its many forms is simply another kind of motion. I lived in a body-mind assigned female at birth and made peace with it as a girl, a tomboy, a dyke, a queer woman, a butch. But uncovering my desire to transition—to live as a genderqueer, a female-to-male transgender person, a white guy—challenged everything I thought I knew about self-acceptance and love.

I am the girl whose breasts develop slowly—fourteen and still not needing the training bra my mother bought me for Christmas. I feel impatient, embarrassed, disconnected from the girls in my school who whisper about their boyfriends and show off in the locker room. But when my breasts do grow, changing the shape of my body-mind in a matter of months, I'm utterly dismayed. I hate the attention my mother pays me.

During this time and place in history, doctors have the authority to name and classify sex and gender, just as they do disability. At the very moment we take our first full-bodied breath, wailing into the world, they declare "boy" or "girl." When that decision doesn't come easily, when a baby emerges with genitals that don't match what they typically associate with male or female body-minds, they make the birth a medical emergency. They diagnose the newborn with one of the many conditions that falls under the umbrella of disorders of sex differentiation. And then they often perform infant genital surgery to create a penis or vulva that more closely matches their vision of boy or girl. Most of these surgeries are not medically necessary, but rather cosmetic, blatantly enforcing what is normal and cutting away that which is declared abnormal.[7]

After my birth, a nurse laid me in an incubator and gave me antibiotics through a tiny IV drip, no one touching me except to turn me under the heat lamp. But before that, the doctors declared me a girl, just as they would name me mentally retarded two and a half years later, confident in their authority to categorize body-minds.

I am the tomboy who spends the summer between my sophomore and junior years of high school working in the woods with twenty other teenagers. We wear blue chambray work shirts with the Youth Conservation Corps logo embroidered on them. I often layer a T-shirt underneath but forgo a bra. My choice of undergarments is obvious and worries the other girls on my crew. They bully and lecture me all summer. I shrug them off, but one of the crew leaders, a twenty-three-year-old hippie guy, starts asking me pointedly why I don't wear a bra. His eyes rake my body-mind.

Decades later, I discovered that I wanted a flat chest. Arriving at that desire, and then accepting it, took a long time. My body-mind politics told me that plastic surgery, particularly for cosmetic reasons, was bad, a tool of the patriarchy, enforcing sexist and racist standards of beauty, encouraging body-mind mutilation and hatred. I thought about rich, white, cisgender women and nose jobs, tummy tucks, and breast enlargements. I thought about upper-middle-class families spending thousands of dollars on synthetic growth hormones in hopes that their short sons might grow up to be tall men. I thought about poor people who can't get the most basic of health care. During her pregnancy with me, my mother had no health insurance, received almost no prenatal care, and so the ovarian cyst that grew alongside me wasn't detected until the crisis of my birth.

I am the dyke whose breasts hang loose under one layer of cloth. I live at a women's peace camp and rage against sexism and men. Many of us go topless, relishing the feel of sun, wind, water on our skin.

Plastic surgeons make so much profit from people who want to change the appearance of their body-minds. Certainly the doctors specializing in double-incision mastectomies and phalloplasties, facial feminization and tracheal shave surgeries, oophorectomies and vaginoplasties become millionaires off of transsexuality and trans people who want and can afford surgery to change our sexed and gendered selves. My politics argued that I needed to change the world and claim my body-mind as it was.

I am the stone butch who traces my lovers' breasts. I lavish them with my fingertips, tongue, tremoring touch. Learn how to bite, pinch, suck, drawing our heat to the surface. Yet when my lovers reach toward my breasts, I can't feel their hands on me.

GENDER IDENTITY DISORDER

My relationships with mental retardation, cerebral palsy, schizophrenia, and gender identity disorder (GID) range widely. The first of these diagnoses has fallen by the wayside, even as it still stalks me in the form of hate speech. The second found me during my parents' search for a cure and is convenient shorthand when I request disability access, navigate the medical-industrial complex, or deal with random curiosity, but it has never orchestrated a life-changing revelation. The third I narrowly escaped, grateful not because seeing visions and hearing voices are inherently bad or wrong, even when they create havoc, but because the medical treatment and social conditions accompanying that diagnosis are often dreadful. But the fourth, I actively sought out.

I started my search not because I needed a diagnosis for my gender-queer self, nor because I thought of my desire to reshape my gendered and sexed body-mind as a disorder. Instead I wanted chest reconstruction surgery, and in turn my surgeon wanted a letter of recommendation from a therapist confirming that I had GID and was a good candidate for surgery. In the scheme of providing medical technology for gender transition in 2002, this surgeon was neither conservative nor liberal. According to the 2001 Standards of Care created by the Harry Benjamin International Gender Dysphoria Association, he could have asked for much more or much less.[8] He might have operated without a letter, but he clearly wanted one.

Like diagnoses in general, GID can be thought of as a static category that describes a specific body-mind condition and directs a course of treatment. Or it can be thought of as a tool embedded in time, space, culture, and science. In 2002 GID lived in the *Diagnostic and Statistical Manual of Mental Disorders, Fourth Edition, Text Revision* (*DSM-IV-TR*) and is traceable over the decades.

One strand of this history starts with the first edition of the *DSM* in 1952. The body-mind experiences of trans and gender-nonconforming people were placed in the overarching *category* "Sexual Deviations," which included homosexuality, transvestism, pedophilia, fetishism, and sexual sadism. From there, the diagnosis that became known in 1994 as GID twisted and turned through four editions of the *DSM*. In 1980, as lesbian, gay, and bisexual identities and experiences were being removed from the *DSM-III*, "Sexual Deviations" became "Paraphilias," and "Transvestism" became "Transvestic Fetishism." Transness also appeared in two other diagnoses: "Transsexualism," used for adults and adolescents, and "Gender Identity Disorder of Childhood." The 1987 revision of the *DSM-III* added "Gender Identity Disorder of Adolescence and Adulthood, non-transsexual type" to this convoluted heap of diagnoses. The 1994 *DSM-IV* combined most of these diagnoses into "Gender Identity Disorder," with one symptom list for adults and another for youth. "Transvestic Fetishism" remained the same.[9]

At this point, my head is spinning. The criteria for each diagnosis keep shifting; the lines between categories blur. The words *disorder, paraphilia, fetish* echo through the maze; shame, violence, and hatred follow close behind. There is nothing neutral about the *DSM*.

My search for a GID diagnosis started with the *DSM-IV-TR*. In 2002 the most conventional treatment, laid out in the Standards of Care, began with three months of psychotherapy, which led to hormone replacement therapy and then to any one of a number of surgeries, including chest reconstruction.[10] After finding a surgeon

who didn't require hormones before surgery, I started looking for a therapist who had the same philosophy and didn't require three months of therapy, partly because none of this health care was covered by insurance. I found a social worker through word of mouth in the local trans community. She wanted five sessions.

She posed a lot of questions—a few of them insightful, many of them irrelevant, and several of them directly offensive. I vividly remember the moment when she asked, "Was your father a cross-dresser; did he have any sexual fetishes or perversions?" She didn't inquire about my mother; evidently her behavior was inconsequential. I paused. The ironies overwhelmed me. To my knowledge, my father wasn't a cross-dresser, but I certainly was, wearing his work clothes throughout my teenage years. I adored the faded blue denim jeans and flannel shirts he handed down to me, even as my mother hated seeing me, her eldest crippled daughter, dressed in his clothes. But he was also a child molester, a pedophile in the language of the *DSM*. That reality shaped my entire childhood. I would have far preferred a cross-dressing father.

These inappropriate questions about my father were made appropriate by the *DSM-IV*. The diagnosis GID lived next to "Transvestic Fetishism," which was placed next to "Pedophilia," the latter two lumped together as "Paraphilias" and all three listed in the same chapter. Within this scheme, my therapist's questions made clinical sense. In other words, the taxonomic structure of the *DSM* shaped her understanding of GID, my father, and me.

At the end of our five sessions, I received the letter and diagnosis I needed. I was able to navigate the whole process with my sense of self intact, because I had a community network, I was familiar with the routine of therapy, and I knew just how honest to be.

But wait, the maze isn't finished. The *DSM-IV* has become the *DSM-5*, and GID is now gender dysphoria (GD), focused not on trans people's gender identities per se but rather on the distress those identities may cause us. This new diagnosis now has its own chapter rather than being grouped with "Sexual and Gender Identity Disorders." At the same time, "Transvestic Fetishism" has become "Transvestic Disorder," complete with an expanded criteria list, remaining grouped with "Sexual Dysfunctions." The move from GID to GD didn't simply happen but resulted from trans activists putting significant pressure on the working groups that created the *DSM-5.*[11]

In exploring this maze, I'm struck by how much the *DSM* has changed over time. These transformations underline how intensely diagnoses are made up. There is nothing inevitable, natural, or inherent about GID or GD. They are fabricated categories that reflect current white Western cultural and scientific beliefs and practices. Academics call this idea social construction, but I believe the blunter phrase *made up* reveals more about the relationship between diagnoses and the body-minds they categorize. Simply put, the *DSM* is a highly constructed projection placed on top of particular body-mind experiences in order to label, organize, and make meaning of them from within a specific worldview.

Many trans activists pose fundamental challenges to GID and GD. We want to know why these diagnoses live in the *DSM*. We object to the ways in which the medical-industrial complex defines our genders as disordered. We resist the pathology foisted on us.

And yet I want us to reach farther: to imagine dismantling the *DSM* itself, discarding the concepts of *disorder* and *defect*, and developing other means of accessing medical technology beyond white Western diagnosis. Yes, I am suggesting a rebellion.

CLAIMING OURSELVES

Gloria, every time I see the Foundation for a Better Life billboard of Whoopi Goldberg overcoming dyslexia, I think of you in 1959, a six-year-old girl called stupid by her teachers and held back in the first grade.[12] You taught yourself to write by turning over a sheet of big block alphabet letters and tracing them backward, the lines and curves finally coming into focus. You strained your way through public school, nourished and embattled long before Individualized Education Plans and the Americans with Disabilities Act. You narrowly escaped special ed. I imagine you in the mid-1970s at college on a rich white campus not so far from the poor Black neighborhood where you grew up.

In the years we knew each other, you never stopped wondering how you escaped the gut-aching poverty of your childhood, landing in college, the first and only one in your family to graduate. You watched your brothers and sisters struggle with drugs and alcohol, unplanned pregnancies, senseless arrests. Your escape haunted you.

I remember us watching *Whoopi Goldberg: Live on Broadway* on VHS, shortly after it was released, sitting in your apartment, a bowl of popcorn between us, the VCR whirring away.[13] Whoopi Goldberg was brilliant, shape-shifting from Black man junkie visiting Anne Franks house to white surfer teen getting an illegal abortion, from a young Black girl wishing for long, straight, blonde hair to a physically disabled Black woman planning her wedding. We laughed, fell silent, talked about those stories of survival and violence for days. But you never connected your dyslexia to Whoopi Goldberg's.

You worked hard not to overcome dyslexia but to get an education and a steady job after you graduated, to keep it in spite of a doubting, hostile boss, to stay safe and strong amidst daily harassment. You wrote and studied for years, becoming a poet and public health nurse. You proved yourself over and over again, never asking for disability access even as reading and writing remained slow, deliberate acts, never naming your dyslexia a disability. There are so many reasons why people don't identify themselves as disabled. Might you have adopted that word if you had known some disabled women of color? If the disability rights movement had been less white?[14]

You and I built our relationship on stories. We sat in movie theaters and pizza joints, poetry readings and creative writing workshops, sat for hour upon hour talking about our lives, listening hard, laughing harder. Our relationship hovered between first date and articulated passion, both of us newly out as lesbians. I was full of fear, longing, an inability to open my body-mind to another human being, and you were struggling to reconcile your queerness with your Baptist family and church, the God who had sustained you through so much.

You wrote me in half a love poem:

> We've taken each other
> to the attic of ourselves
> one continuous speaking
> vision . . .

When we first met, I had recently arrived in the city that was your home, a young disabled queer fleeing the backwoods of Oregon, gulping down new ways of thinking, new ways of being. We told stories as if we believed words alone could bridge the chasm between your thirty and my twenty, your Black and my white, your urban and my rural. I remember you, me, our one continuous speaking vision with so much gratitude and tenderness.

You told me about your dyslexia—about teaching yourself to write, the misery of school, your frequent struggles to read maps. You named your shame and hurt but never connected those experiences to disability. In our relationship, I was the disabled one.

I told you stories that now thirty years later I've repeated dozens of times: being called *retard* and *monkey*, struggling to keep up in school, my slow, slurred speech not being understood, strangers gawking unabashedly. But back then, saying those words out loud was brand new. I could reveal those moments for the first time precisely because you listened through your own lived experiences of dyslexia and ableism.

But there are other disability stories I didn't tell then, can barely tell now: stories about hearing voices and seeing visions, about psych hospitalizations and being housebound for weeks in order to stay alive. I'm loath to talk about the times I've had to flee queer public space, triggered by some expression of kinky sex or description of violence, a performance or conversation, slipping out of my body-mind into the past. I don't tell these stories because they're mired in shame; because I don't want them to be true; because unlike my tremoring hands, I can hide these experiences most of the time; because I'd rather not claim that kind of disability.

Writer and performer Leah Lakshmi Piepzna-Samarasinha reflects on the twine of gender, race, sexuality, and disability: "Queer women of color . . . do not want any more identities than we already have to wrestle with. Our bodies are already seen as tough, monster, angry, seductive, incompetent. How can we admit [the] weakness, vulnerability, interdependence [of disability] and still keep our jobs, our perch on the 'thin edge of barbwire' we live on?"[15] What did you claim and hide? What did I?

Gloria, my questions make me want to return to our one continuous speaking vision. I remember the few times we danced together—body-minds awkward, unable to find our rhythm. But our stories knew exactly how to waver and flex, slur and limp, burst in jagged letters across the dance floor. This time, through the cracks and across the chasms, we might claim disability together as strength and vulnerability, interdependence and hard work, risk and fear. Claim, as white, disabled, lesbian poet Laura Hershey writes, "our beautiful crip bodies, broken or bent, and whole."[16] Claim ourselves as common as morning coffee.

NOTES

1. "Drive Stupid and Score Some Kickin' New Wheels," Don't Drive Stupid advertisement, accessed April 4, 2016. http://2.bp.blogspot.com/_iw4mpIACIU4/S3axcnaXowI/AAAAAAAAACk/BjJhuz4DSmA/s1600-h/dontdrivestupid-001.jpg.

2. For more about transabled people, see Stevens, "Interrogating Transability"; *Whole* (dir. Melody Gilbert, 2003).

3. For more about environmental injustice and long-term processes that harm both the human and the nonhuman world, see, for example, *Nixon, Slow Violence and the Environmentalism of the Poor.*

4. "Bison Skull Pile," photograph, circa 1870 (Burton Historical Collection, Detroit Public Library), Wikimedia Commons, accessed April 4, 2016, https://commons.wikimedia.org/wiki/File:Bison_skull_pile-restored.jpg.

5. Erdoes and Lame Deer, *Lame Deer, Seeker of Visions,* 269.

6. Smits, "The Frontier Army and the Destruction of the Buffalo," 328. For more about bison and Native peoples, see Jawort, "Genocide by Other Means."

7. For more about intersex politics and the medical treatment of intersex people, see the website Intersex Initiative, accessed December 22, 2015, http://www.intersexinitiative.org; Emi Koyama, "'Zines by Intersex Initiative," Eminism.org, accessed December 22, 2015, http://eminism.org/store/zine-intersex.html.

8. For details, see WPATH, "The Standards of Care—Historical Compilation of Versions 1–6."

9. For more detail, see Lev, "Gender Dysphoria."

10. For more detail, see WPATH, "The Standards of Care—Historical Compilation of Versions 1–6."

11. Lev, "Gender Dysphoria."

12. Gloria Thomas (not her real name) was a writer and close friend when I was twenty and twenty-one. See the billboard Foundation for a Better Life, "Overcaem Dyslexia," Values.com, accessed July 8, 2009, http://www.values.com/inspirational-sayings-billboards/20-hard-work.

13. *Whoopi Goldberg: Live on Broadway* (dir. Thomas Schlamme, 1985).

14. For more about whiteness in the disability rights movement and people of color identifying as disabled, see Morales et al., "Sweet Dark Places"; Morales, *Kindling*; Schalk, "Coming to Claim Crip"; Thompson, "#DisabilityTooWhite."

15. Morales et al., "Sweet Dark Places," 94–95.

16. Morales et al., "Sweet Dark Places," 94–95.

JAYNA BROWN

58. A WORLD ON FIRE: RADICAL BLACK FEMINISM IN A DYSTOPIAN AGE

The term *black feminism* has been reinvigorated over the past few years.[1] It proliferates through social media with a renewed audibility, as activists, artists, and writers use it to evoke a plurality of meanings, stakes, and commitments. This reinvigorated movement has led to a powerful spread of political energies. Many people, like those organizing in Black Lives Matter and Millennial Activists United, both activist collectives founded by black queer women, have taken it as foundational, as a condition to being "woke" in their fight to dismantle a variety of interlocking systems of oppression, including police violence, the prison industrial complex, and economic and environmental exploitation.[2] The term *intersectionality*, coined by law theorist Kimberlé Crenshaw (1989), has become commonplace and now enjoys an institutional life. Rooted in black feminist activism, the term is inviting to all disenfranchised peoples, as it refers to the ways sexism, racism, and classicism, as well as ableism, ageism, and trans- and homophobia, are intersecting systems of oppression. In the academy, forceful work is being done where black feminism meets queer theory. Radical black feminisms, my subject in this essay, are already queer, as they critique normativity and normativizing processes and challenge a "politics of respectability," the long-engrained anxieties about hypersexualization that have kept more moderate black feminist discourse from exploring sexualities. But from this new conjuncture of black feminism and queer theory come more complex models for understanding subjectivity, identity, and community and deep theoretical explorations of sexuality, desire, and pleasure. The application and circulation of black feminism, then, is shaping its meanings and possibility. This burgeoning of academic and activist energies is recalibrating the work of earlier black and women of color feminists for a new political moment.

But the process of black feminism's incorporation has had troubling consequences. Visibility comes at the expense of black feminism's more radical and unruly instantiations. Visibility means marketability, and neoliberal market feminism makes a profit branding selected language and iconography taken from these more radical versions. In this climate, freedom is equated with personal wealth. Branded personas and celebrity culture have become surrogates for a collective struggle of liberation. The much-touted concepts of empowerment and autonomy have been bled of their political resonance, subsumed under the ethos of possessive individualism. Where there has been an embrace of desire in black queer theory, the politicization of pleasure has fallen short of a full critique of the sociopolitical formations that shape these pleasures. In the context of high capitalism, desire becomes equated with privatized consumption and is drained of collective meaning. Intersectionality continues to be useful as a way for women of color to be legible in a political and judicial framework, as Crenshaw intended. But in many cases it has lost its force as a tool to nuance situatedness in relation to systems of oppression and has become a term signaling an argument for political and social inclusion, that is, coverage by social contract under the banner of "diversity."[3] These appeals for inclusion under the social contract can become substitutes for substantive critiques of the state. The idea of revolution, so crucial to a radical black / women of color feminism, becomes a product rather than a practice, a hollow posture rather than a situated provocation for the kinds of intense dialogue and contingent rapprochement we need around the very concept.

My interest is in tracing an anarchistic impulse in black radical feminist art and activism that refuses to be subsumed within neoliberal market feminism. Although I could begin much earlier, I look to the late 1970s and early 1980s and focus specifically on the film *Born in Flames* (1983), directed by the "anarcha-feminist" filmmaker Lizzie Borden. The film is part of a crucial era that saw the radical politicization of black women and women of color and a burgeoning of intellectual and artistic work and activism. Women were articulating a rage and refusal to compromise their needs and priorities in accordance with white feminisms—in their liberal, socialist, or separatist varieties—or in compliance with masculinist and heterosexist black and brown struggle, with its militarism and hierarchical structure. Along with other poor women and women of color, lesbian and straight, they saw themselves as linked to revolutions across the global South, but not as a subordinated class. They argued that black women, who suffered at the nexus of racism, sexism, heterosexism, and economic oppression in the United States, were in the position to lead a revolutionary movement for *all* peoples.

Born in Flames is an important text to revisit today as it invites us to rejuvenate a version of noncompliance that dances and screams and blows things up, that refuses and disrupts rather than appeals. The film imagines the galvanizing of a radical ethos among working-class and poor black women, women of color, and white women, with lesbians as its central organic intellectuals. I explore the ways that the film envisions the formation of a counterpublic and its commons, formed through pirating the airwaves and by meeting women where they are in their daily lives. This is a counterpublic not herded into a single square and a commons not necessarily under anything, but held on a different bandwidth.

The creation of a basis for the public happens in the unofficial, unsanctioned spaces of black, brown, and poor women's lives. There is no town hall, no Rancièrean dissensus, only the power of the disenfranchised to recognize and hear each other. Women organize and debate in kitchens and bedrooms, on fire escapes, and in the streets, where girls jump rope and dance. Women consider the many different political tactics at hand, not with dramatic scenes of suffering, but with a stolid pragmatism. Do we close down the child care center while we strike or try to keep it open independently? Do we take up arms? Women disagree with each other in this film as they contemplate various approaches to revolution. But the starting point in their discussions is that it will be a decentralized and collective process of change. There will be no leaders, no authority, no dictates, mandates, or directives; all rules and rule makers are there to be questioned.

The film is anarchistic in its politics. It insists on a nonhierarchical organizing principle. It is not interested in recognition, validation, or redress from the state or any existing institution. It does not search for protection under the social contract or for universal consensus. As the film's character DJ Honey says, revolutionary change demands that we "deconstruct, and reconstruct, all the laws that suppress, and oppress, all of us."[4] But the aim is not a revolution designed to create another nation-state or another centralized form of governance. What the film ultimately asks us to understand is that revolutionary change is not a destination but a practice. This practice is based in a continual questioning and requires that we defy and destabilize dominant paradigms and then that we sit in the ambiguity of not knowing what might be.

Formal anarchism was famously and pejoratively referred to as "utopian socialism" by Friedrich Engels (1970), who called it reformist, as its vision of change was not based in the properly scientific process of historical materialism. What makes the film anarchist is that it refuses to offer any formula or solution. It provokes, stirs things up, unsettles us. *Born in Flames* ends with an explosion, the results of which we can only guess. But the film holds within it a utopian urge, a pulse, a rhythm that will not sync with any system or structure of dominance. Its utopian impulse gestures not to a then and there but to a here and now we must all tune into.

Contemporary black feminisms have been inspired by a few texts published in the late 1970s and early 1980s, though they are perhaps less aware of the climate of activism out of which these texts came. Women published short and easily accessible forms of literature—broadsheets, open letters, poetry, essays—which reflected the activist ethos of collectivity and coalition then shaping intellectual work. Women set up small periodicals and presses, but much of this literature was initially typed up and mimeographed at low cost to be handed out at meetings and demonstrations and read in the streets, living rooms, and basements.

Black women were establishing organizations, like the National Black Feminist Organization (NBFO) and the Third World Women's Alliance (TWWA). Seeking a more radical politics, a group of black women activists split with the NBFO in 1974 and formed the Combahee River Collective. Borden began making *Born in Flames* in 1978, just after the Combahee River Collective (1981) had issued "A Black Feminist Statement." Borden finished making the film in 1983, not long after the publication of the anthology *This Bridge Called My Back: Writings by Radical Women of Color* (1981) by Kitchen Table: Women of Color Press, a press started by the black lesbian feminist Barbara Smith, one of the Combahee River Collective founders, at the urging of her friend Audre Lorde. Both manifesto and anthology were to become the establishing texts of a Third World / Women of Color feminist curriculum. While these texts did not function as instruction or doctrine in the making of *Born in Flames,* the film reflects the political positions expressed in them.

Predating the term *intersectionality,* the Combahee River Collective's statement articulated succinctly for us the intertwined structures of oppression—patriarchy, racism, sexism, heterosexism, and capitalism—shaping our lives. It emphasizes, as the film does, an antihierarchical ethos. And, importantly, the statement puts emphasis on economic oppression, critiquing capitalism in a way that many contemporary iterations of black feminism do not. Yet official, organized socialism was insufficient, as its analysis did not include the specific positionalities of women of color.

This ambivalent relationship to socialism, and socialist feminism, is key to the film's narrative. Like the Combahee River Collective statement, *Born in Flames* criticizes the notion of the universal subject of any organized economic system. It centers on the prosaic, the daily lives of working-class women of color. A montage central to the film features scenes of women's hands—wrapping chicken, taking care of children, cutting hair, washing dishes, serving food, putting condoms on penises, working on building sites—engaged in everything from office work to sex work. Toward the beginning of the film, working women—in grocery stores, offices, and construction sites—welcome us. As the camera pans by, they turn their heads and smile at us, in direct address and with recognition.

Set in New York City, the film opens on the ten-year anniversary of a socialist revolution in the United States. But this revolution has not addressed the needs of poor women and women of color, whose lives and well-being remain precarious. In response, a number of women organize a revolutionary association called the Women's Army. Central to the army's formation is a radical black lesbian named Adelaide Norris, who is mentored by an older black woman activist named Zella Wiley, played by the inimitable activist Florynce Kennedy. All of the members of the army who can be identified are under government surveillance, whose intelligence we are privy to. The spies have a hard time of it, for the army is not organized according to any military hierarchy. Instead, it is a system of affiliated cells, each working independently, but in coordination with one another. Norris loses her job when the government changes workfare programs to prioritize male heads of families, and she decides that it is time to revolutionize and take up arms. She goes to North Africa, where she trains with women engaged in their own struggles for liberation. After she returns to the United States, she is captured at the airport and taken to prison, where she dies of a supposed suicide. Many women have been reluctant to work with the army, including those involved in the media: a group of white women journalists and two pirate DJs, Honey and Isabel, each with her own station, who feature prominently in the film. But after Norris is killed, women across the political and racial spectrum join forces. After their studios are bombed, DJs Honey and Isabel band together, steal rental trucks, and set up their radio stations on the go. The army's first action is to seize the means of media production, and it takes over the major radio and television stations at gunpoint. In the film's final scene, the Women's Army blows up a radio transmission tower atop one of the World Trade Center buildings.

The film celebrates a punk sensibility, and the process of making the film reflects its radical and collective politics. Borden (1987) made the film for less than $40,000, and its "aesthetics of cheapness," as she calls it, gives the film permission to run the streets. Borden filmed the footage of people in the streets by holding a camera out the window of her beat-up car, for which she forged a fake filming permit. Other sites include a Grand Union grocery store, where she filmed while rolling through the aisles in a wheelchair. She then interlaced this footage with staged scenes, all filmed either in her downtown loft or in people's apartments. Borden shot most of the footage of protests at actual demonstrations around New York City. To shoot the final scene, a single cameraperson followed the actor, played by a friend of Borden's, the lesbian filmmaker Sheila McLaughlin, up to the roof of the World Trade Center building, where McLaughlin planted a fake bomb at the foot of the radio tower. The explosion was created in postproduction; Borden and the effects person, Hisao Taya, blew glitter through straws onto the film. There is a powerful porousness between the film's fiction, the concreteness of the city, and the realness of the participants' lives.

Borden was part of the downtown art scene, where she worked editing films. She drew some actors, including McLaughlin, Hillary Hurst, and Marty Pottenger, from lesbian theater groups, and several of the male characters were from other theater ensembles, like the Wooster Group. She knew others from the punk scene, and those who acted and performed in *Born in Flames* include Bush Tetras' guitarist Pat Place and keyboardist Adele Bertei, Borden's then girlfriend, who plays DJ Isabel in the film.

But Borden did not just look for actors to appear in the film. Instead, she sought out people to participate in its conception, beginning only with the idea of a film that featured a women's army and pirate DJs. Borden held meetings in her loft, but was not satisfied, as the people who came were mostly other white women from the downtown art scene. A few of these women, including filmmaker Kathryn Bigelow and screenwriter Becky Johnston, contributed initially, while others, including Irish filmmaker Pat Murphy, stayed on.

Borden made the film in response to the stark divisions she saw among women. "*Born in Flames* came out of a lot of the inequalities I saw when I came to New York. Also, the alternative movements—the gay movement, the women's movement—were very divided and reproduced the divisions of the dominant culture," Borden (1987) says. "Black women were still very isolated from white women, who were very isolated from Latin and Asian women, who were invisible. . . . I began to be involved with Black women for the purpose of making the film. I wanted to construct a paradigm that I didn't see happening in the culture." She concluded that the film needed to be from black women's perspectives, and she felt strongly that this could not be a film made by a white team. "Then, as now, [it was] time for white women to just listen," she said to me (Borden 2017).

Borden went first to community centers in Harlem. Many of the women she met there who agreed to be in the film would not commit to it, as they were suspicious of her intentions. "They didn't trust me and suspected I was appropriating," Borden (2017) told me. Borden was also going to women's bars, where she met Alexa Evans in 1979, the first woman outside the downtown scene to commit to making the film. Through Evans, Borden met Honey, who plays DJ Honey in the film, then living with Evans. "Meeting Honey was the first turning point. She gave me the heart of the film," Borden (2017) said. Borden held a deep and loving relationship with Honey until she died in 2010. Borden then approached Jeanne Satterfield, who plays Norris and whom Borden used to watch playing basketball at the Twenty-Third Street YMCA. She was then introduced to Kennedy, the seasoned activist and radical civil rights lawyer, who signed on immediately. "I was thrilled, as she was so well known and busy, I couldn't believe she agreed," said Borden (2017). The film emerged out of the input and commitment of these women, who either volunteered their time or accepted the $25 a day Borden could afford to pay them. "The film was shaped by the women who agreed to participate," she said (Borden 2017). The plot developed as each joined, and, besides Norris's lines, the women improvised all of the dialogue or wrote their own monologues.

Borden told me that she wanted more than anything for the film to have a pulse, a pulse that coursed below and around language, a pulse that people, outside of the art world or academia, could tune into. For the film's theme song, Borden approached Mayo Thompson from the art collective Art and Language, and in 1981 he recorded "Born in Flames" with his band Red Krayola. She immediately took the song's title for the film (which was originally called *Les Guérrillères,* in reference to the novel by Monique Wittig). Bertei's all-women punk band, the Bloods, wrote the other signature song, "Undercover Nation," which the band performs in the film. The music, combined with Honey's and Isabel's broadcasts, is about the rejection of ladylike melodies and is an embrace of rhythm and dissonance that invites the unexpected. Music and poetic manifesto signal the porousness between this world and a world that is possible.

Media—television and especially radio—are a crucial means by which women come together in the film, and in their ultimate act of revolutionary struggle they seize the means of media production. The film was made in an era when media were centralized, and as such the film's version of revolutionary action may seem dated in our era where media have dispersed and now stream through our lives in a way that destroys any binary between an official public sphere and a counterpublic alternative. But the film is prescient of the kinds of dispersed, networked media of its future, both their powers of surveillance and their fugitive uses. Dissenting currents form in the film as women take over the airwaves and redirect them. A counterpublic coheres and disperses, sonically, through music, poetic manifesto, and polemic address. Wherever they are— on the subway, in the streets, in the kitchen—women turn their dials and tune in. The commons is a shared vibration, which builds, gathering energy.

The revolution begins with the hijacking of the airwaves. The film is framed by the broadcasts of the two pirate radio DJs. We listen to the soft, contemplative address of DJ Honey at Phoenix Radio, where we are invited to engage politically by 1970s R & B and reggae. Tuning to another frequency, we hear the defiant provocations of DJ Isabel at Radio Ragazza and listen to the dissonant thrash of punk rock. The aim is not to speak truth to power but to call out other disenfranchised subjects. As DJ Isabel says: "Wake up! Get it together! It's time to fight!"

Music is the film's *mise en scène*. The first visual moment of the film coincides with the first note of "Born in Flames," and the song continues to play under the film's introductory scenes. After establishing shots of New York City, the first scene takes place on a grainy

TV screen, as a white male news broadcaster announces a "week of celebration" for the tenth anniversary of the peaceful socialist revolution. Then, in contrast, we are brought into the clandestine darkness of a radio booth where we are introduced to DJ Isabel. "Hi there. This is Isabel from Radio Ragazza, bringing you a little tune that you'll be hearing an awful lot of these days, from the makers of our revolution. You may not be hearing it here, but you'll be hearing it everywhere else you go. Happy anniversary!" "Born in Flames" is established as the chorus of the film, its refrain. These are the lyrics, which are hard to follow in the film:

> At a new life we took aim
> We set the vast conglomerates aflame
> The working class avowed its name
> Of America's mysteries, none remain
> We broke the hidden tyrannies
> Of the reptilian joint-stock companies
> Nor did their armed brutality
> Ever bring us to our knees
> We are born in flames
> Into the darkness of the past
> We've thrown the shamans of the ruling class
> The struggle of the exploited mass
> Has broken the oppressors' lash
> We are born in flames
> The war of great heroic deeds
> Confirmed the death of inhuman creeds
> The people now can fill their needs
> On truth and reason now we feed
> We are born in flames
> Against external perturbation
> The party-hearth of culture education
> Achiever of all history's confirmation
> Our social democrat consolidation
> In brotherhood and sisterhood
> We are prepared to give our blood
> Defend new life—crush those who would
> Deny the right for which we stood
> We are born in flames
>
> (Thompson 1979)[5]

The film alternates between official voices—TV broadcasts and the conversations between Federal Bureau of Investigation (FBI) agents in briefings on surveillance of the Women's Army—and the unofficial voices and rhythms generated in the Phoenix Radio and Radio Ragazza studios. These accompany quotidian scenes of women in the public spaces of the city: encountering sexual harassment in the streets and on the subway, going to and from work, demonstrating and protesting. All the while, we are listening to music.

After we meet Isabel, "Born in Flames" segues into a song by the Staple Singers, as DJ Honey begins her broadcast. "Good evening. This is Honey coming directly to you from Phoenix Radio. A free radio station. A station not only for the liberation of women but for the liberation of all through the freedom of life which is found in music." Honey gives us the first of the film's manifestos; she speaks, and the music plays, as men and women inhabit the city streets, listening to the radio on their boom boxes. In a city park, girls dance to the music, playing from their boom box:

> We are all here because we have fought in the wars of liberation. And we all bear witness to what has happened since the war. We still see the depression from the oppression that still exists both day and night. For we are the children of the light. And we will continue to fight. Not against the flesh and blood, but against the system that has named itself falsely. For we have stood on the promises far too long now, that we can all be equal under the cover of a social democracy. Where the richer get richer, and the poor just wait on their dreams.

On these free radio stations, the voice of the people can be heard and music is transformed from a commodity to a frequency on which we can sense what "freedom of life" might feel like.

In the next scene, following another television report of an official demonstration of the Labor party, we join two unsmiling white women on the subway, listening to Radio Ragazza on their boom box. "Undercover Nation" comes on, and as they tune in, turn it up, and nod their heads to the music, we find ourselves in the Ragazza studio, where the Bloods are performing the song live. "Wake up, wake up, could this be you?" sings Isabel/Bertei. Sonically and visually, the film shows how media technologies can be creatively used and claims itself as part of this process. Since the lyrics have been publicly unavailable, I include them in full:

> Headlines screaming while she's watching the race
> Reading back the constitution
> Leather-legged or a dancer in space
> Talkin' 'bout evolution
> She's got a black suit and a red dress
> She's got a chest full of the poet's mess
> She's got a hangover and her mother's on the phone
> Wake up, wake up, she isn't alone
> A manifesto scrawled in a tenement room
> Talkin' 'bout a declaration
> Warpaint and feathers, another young brave
> In the undercover nation
> She's got a black cat and the wings of a dove
> She's got an iron fist in a velvet glove
> She just got evicted 'cause her rent was due
> Wake up, wake up, could this be you?
> I know a girl who used to think:
> Lonely hearted hunter don't say nothing
> The hungry and the hurt got only one law left
> Unsung, undone, only one place left to run
> But it's changing, it's all changing, watch it change
> Will you stand by while you watch your brother die?
> Will you close your eyes when you hear the
>   mothers cry?
> Wake up! wake up!

(Bertei et al. 1983?)[6]

While it calls for us to see and feel and hear the discontent and dissent of people living under an oppressive social and economic system, part of the power of the film is that it does not emotionally ask us to agree with any one person's or party's solution. While the formation of a collective involves the recognition of shared conditions, the film refuses a white liberal feminist model of personal discovery or catharsis through an awakening to the experience of personal injury, a therapeutics of shared trauma, or salvific wish. The way the film sees the formation of counterpublics is through the gathered force of shared outrage and a focus on realpolitik. Brechtian in its approach, the terms by which we identify are based in revolutionary action, rather than self-centered emotional appeal.

The film creates a radical dialogic space of many voices. Its model of organization is a dispersed and mobile web of often-tenuous affiliations and leaves us with no surety as to the future, only a temporary vision of unity. While it calls us to a shared resolve and a shared ethics, it reminds us that collectivity is often full of conflict and ambivalence. The film is aimed at breaking us away from dominating paradigms. But it is explicitly not interested in creating consensus. What the film tells us is that the fight for a new kind of worlding does not require that all agree or are assimilated into one body.

While radio broadcasts tend to the declarative, scenes of the Women's Army "induction meetings," as the FBI agent calls them, reveal the kinds of questions and differences that exist between women. These meetings are led primarily by another activist in the army, Hurst; the FBI agents puzzle over what title to give her, as they can't comprehend the nonhierarchical nature of the relationships between the army's members. "We don't know how to find out at any given time who is in charge," they complain.

Not all women agree to join the Women's Army. Isabel thinks they are too soft to have any real effect. Honey is working with some other women and doesn't want to break ranks. The white women intelligentsia does not take the army seriously as a movement and considers it sectarian and reactionary. The white women assess the army as "restless" and potentially "counterrevolutionary" and the situation as "a kind of gratuitous desire for excitement and romanticism." Their political position reflects an investment in an existing governmental system and the idea of progress.

In one scene, Norris challenges their lack of perspective. "I don't understand how you as women can say that women's grievances are separatist. You can't even see how it's affecting you. You know you're pressed too, and it's pathetic that you can't even see it." Norris tries to get them to connect politics to the immediate experiences of women of color. She begins by describing the hardships of her mother's life. "There are plenty of women nowadays living in that same manner, black women, Latin women, young women, living in that same lifestyle," she argues. A white woman replies: "Everyone had a hard time during the revolution. But if we remove the only structure that exits for progress, we dissipate everything. It will be worse than it was before." Norris ends the conversation: "I knew you wouldn't understand. . . . Look, if you're not going to write about it, at least come out of class guilt." The film critiques white

women's universalism, as well as recognizes the work that must be done utilizing their privilege.

In a pivotal scene, Norris meets with her mentor, Wiley, played by Kennedy. The meeting follows a women's demonstration, filmed during an actual demonstration in Washington Square Park. The scene was shot in Kennedy's bedroom. Kennedy is lying down on her bed, as she was having health problems and had undergone major surgery during the years the film was made. Her back was still bothering her, after an action she took at the age of nineteen, for which she was picked up and thrown from a seat at a lunch counter.

Norris expresses dismay at the lack of unity. "These three thousand women were so separated. It wasn't even unified. If we were all together, it would be a lot different," Norris says in frustration. Wiley/Kennedy gives her some words of wisdom:

> You've heard my story about the division. They always talk about unity, we need unity, unity, but I always say, if you were the army, and the school and the head of the health institutions, and the head of the government, and all of you had guns, which would you rather see come through the door, one lion, unified, or five hundred mice? My answer is five hundred mice can do a lot of damage and disruption. If you having a meeting and everybody's all, you know, gussied up . . .

This scene between two activists, one experienced and the other young, shows the crucial importance of intergenerational organizing. Wiley/Kennedy's experienced perspective gives us a nuanced model of power and stresses the importance that women of color don't subordinate their specific concerns within a women's movement, based in the idea of a false universal subject.

There is a profound intimacy to this scene as Wiley/Kennedy and Norris engage in a quiet conversation. It conveys a quality of mutual care, but it is not based in an intimacy that requires a private space divorced from the political sphere. Seeing Wiley/Kennedy, her body directly affected by the violence of an oppressive state, demonstrates the absurdity of a retreatist definition of intimacy.

Born in Flames is based in an expansive kind of love. As DJ Isabel says, "The scope and capabilities of human love are as wide and encompassing as this vast universe we all swirl in." But *love* is a complicated and freighted word. The film calls us to think of organizing along affective registers other than injury, but also to complicate our notions of affect beyond a simple language of emotion. It calls us to feel in our bodies, through the sonic pulse of the music, as much rage and defiance as we do the soft, sweet caress of affection. Revolution, it seems to say, requires a fierce love, made of sweat, blood, and struggle.

The army's initial actions are locally focused, self-organized acts of unarmed resistance. In one of the film's most noted scenes, a group of women on bicycles, blowing whistles, surround a group of men physically assaulting a woman in the street. In another scene Norris intervenes as a man hassles a woman on the subway. "We wouldn't exactly call them terrorists," says an FBI agent. "The problem is the vigilante sensibility." But as Norris continues to develop politically, the film begins to ask, what if we launch a women's revolution? Should it be a velvet one or one with spikes or both? What is to be said on the issue of the use of force? In the quiet bedroom scene, Norris conveys to Wiley/Kennedy her ambivalence and tells her of her newly made decision to turn to armed struggle. Norris contemplates what direction to go politically. "At this point . . . I've been seriously questioning myself and questioning my abilities and what I have and don't have and where I can go, and I think it's that time, that we really pick up arms and really be prepared." Wiley/Kennedy replies: "What took you so long?"

Women in the film defend the right of the oppressed to use violence. There will be no compromises. Unlike in the masculinist revolutionary movements in the United States and across the global South (the Third World, as it was called), this violence was not conceptualized as cathartic retribution, as it is for Frantz Fanon in *The Wretched of the Earth* (2004). The model for liberation is not a "Manichean" battle to the death between men, by which the (male) colonized subject could restore his manhood (Fanon 2004: 43). As DJ Honey states, the fight is "not against the flesh and blood, but against the system that names itself falsely." The system in the film is a fictional socialist government, but the film gestures to any organized and centralized system claiming to represent all peoples.

Some women in the film approach the use of violence with caution. But there is a current in the film that considers uncompromised revolutionary violence, here

explicitly in conversation with Fanon, as the right of the oppressed. Wiley/Kennedy, wearing not a hijab but a kaffiyeh, voices this. "We have a right to violence," she says. "All oppressed people have a right to violence. I wanna tell you something, it's like the right to pee. Gotta have the right place, gotta have the right time, gotta have the appropriate situation, and I am absolutely convinced that this is it." Yet the ways that violence is considered, and taken up in the film, are not therapeutic in the same way that Fanon writes it as so for the colonized.

The film keeps alive the way the black power movement in the United States was inspired by independence movements and successful revolutions in Africa and Asia. As Norris develops politically, she begins to see the struggle of black women and women of color in this global context. Through Wiley's associations, she connects with revolutionaries from the Western Sahara and travels there to train with them.

The concept of an army is reconceived in the film, and pointedly missing from the film are the romanticized cadres of a male lumpenproletariat, military hierarchies, or a call for the foundation of any nation-state. *Born in Flames* speaks in important ways to the film *The Battle of Algiers* (1966) and to Fanon's works, with their centralization of disaffected angry young men as the leaders of the revolution. In a widely celebrated scene from *The Battle of Algiers*, three Algerian women are recruited for a mission to smuggle bombs through a checkpoint. To the rousing sound of war drums, they don Western dress and use their beauty to disarm the guards. The scene argues for the participation of Arab women in the war against colonial oppression. But their sole act in the film is to follow instructions and seduce the colonizers. We do not hear their voices or see their perspectives. Once they complete their mission, they disappear from the film. Freedom from male domination is not part of the vision of a nationalist liberation.

In *Born in Flames* the words of an Algerian woman revolutionary, with whom Norris trains, speak back to the silence of the women in *The Battle of Algiers*. "These women were fighting, with the men at first, with the men for territories, for things that seemed right at the time," she says.

> And then after the fight was over, they were pushed back in the kitchens, back in the homes, NO, and there's more and more women now that want a

change, they want to go for their own, that understand that this fight is not the right fight and that the world is round and big and it's our world and the women can move free in the world and there's no need for territory and there's no need to sit in the home and be protected by the men. . . . It is very good that you are here. Because you are telling us about your world, about the women in your world, but you must be very careful, because the violence is dangerous and there's not that many of you.

The film powerfully juxtaposes black women in the United States on a union strike with footage of Algerian women training in their own army.[7] The woman revolutionary asserts that there is no need for territories, for nation-states, and, in concordance, Norris states explicitly: "The only armed activity we see is against the media, the television and radio stations."

Norris's alleged suicide in prison galvanizes the different factions; Honey, Isabel, and the white women intelligentsia join the army. "Is there anything I can do?" Honey asks Wiley. "The most important thing of all is media, our media . . . communications," Wiley replies. "Your, our job, but mainly your job, is to see that it can't be quieted. That it can't be bullshitted out." As the women hijack the radio and television stations, they force the DJs and television operators to replace the official news with a broadcast of Wiley. Once Honey and Isabel are on the road, they make powerful statements on their pirate stations. Even the white women retract their earlier cynicism and declare themselves, though not without a hint of hope for reform.

Broadcasting from the newly joined Phoenix and Ragazza Radio studio, housed in the back of a rental truck, Isabel gives the film's final and most powerful manifesto:

I'd like to open up by making a statement on behalf of Adelaide Norris and the Women's Army. Her murder serves as a warning for women everywhere of the struggle we face, and the truth will be heard and the story must and shall be told. It is not only the story of women's oppression; it is the story of oppression, but of sexism, racism, bigotry, nationalism, false religion, and the blasphemy of the state-controlled church, the story of environmental poisoning and nuclear warfare, of the powerful over the powerless for the sake of sick and depraved manipulations that abuse and corner the human soul like a rat in a cage. It is all of our responsibilities, as individuals and together, to examine, and reexamine everything, leaving no stones unturned. Every word that we utter, every action, and every thought, we are all, women and men, the prophets of this new age and for those of us [who] would be safer in the sensibilities of racism, separatism, and martyrdom, if you can't help us in building this living church, then step out of the way. The scope and capabilities of human love are as wide and encompassing as this vast universe that we all swirl in, one for all, and all for oneness. This fight will not end in terrorism and violence. It will not end in nuclear holocaust. It begins in a celebration of the rights of alchemy. The transformation of shit into gold. The illumination of dark, chaotic night into light. This is the time of sweet, sweet change for us all.

With the familiar jump to official broadcast, we then hear the beginnings of the end of the socialist experiment. "The management of this station fears that oversocialization has transformed our democracy into a welfare state. If we are to survive our ideals, we must carefully consider their implications. This, in the midst of our celebration, is the opinion—" But the official opinion is interrupted, as the radio tower explodes in a cloud of smoke.

We are left with the surety that the battle will continue. And it must, for we live in a world of terror, where the police and vigilantes continue to gun down black people in cold blood and white supremacists march the streets, sanctioned by their elected leader, who occupies the White House. That is the dystopia of our present, our world on fire. Watching *Born in Flames* now, while it gives us no answers or blueprints, does incite us to make revolution real, to make it our daily practice, to struggle over what we want the world to look and feel like. "Revolution: it's not neat or pretty or quick," says Pat Parker (1981: 238). It is urgent that we take up the problems the film poses—how to participate in the formation of counterpublics and what radical change means. The film demands that we wake up from neoliberal dreams of meritocracy and the idea that the government and its contracts will, or ever did, protect us. Our actions, it suggests, should not be based in recognition from a nation-state, or in amassed wealth, but in remaining joyfully ungovernable.

NOTES

1. This essay's title draws on Cherríe Moraga, "Refugees of a World on Fire" (1983), the foreword to the second edition of *This Bridge Called My Back: Writings by Radical Women of Color*.
2. Black Lives Matter's "Guiding Principles" (2017) also challenge heteronormativity, committing to the rights of trans and queer people of color.
3. Jennifer C. Nash (2017) has written a balanced and thoughtful critique of intersectionality and contestations over its uses in a review of several recently published titles.
4. All quotations from the film are from *Born in Flames* (1983).
5. Lyrics courtesy of Borden.
6. Lyrics courtesy of Borden.
7. The footage of Algerian women training in the 1980s was brought back by a friend of Ed Bowes, who worked on the film and gave it to Borden to use.

REFERENCES

The Battle of Algiers. 1966. Directed by Gillo Pontecorvo. Rizzoli, Rialto Pictures.

Black Lives Matter. 2017. "Guiding Principles." http://blacklivesmatter.com/guiding-principles. (accessed August 18, 2017).

The Bloods. 1983. "Undercover Nation." In *Born in Flames* sound track.

Borden, Lizzie. 1987. "Anarcha-Filmmaker: An Interview with Lizzie Borden." By Alexandra Davon and Catherine Tammaro. *Kick It Over*, no. 18. www.kersplebedeb.com/mystufif/video/review/lizzie_borden.html.

Borden, Lizzie. 2017. Author interview, August 16. London and Los Angeles.

Born in Flames. 1983. *Directed by Lizzie Borden. 90 min*. New York: First Run Features.

Combahee River Collective. 1981. "A Black Feminist Statement." In *This Bridge Called My Back: Writings by Radical Women of Color*, edited by Cherríe Moraga and Gloria Anzaldúa, 210–18. New York: Kitchen Table: Women of Color Press.

Crenshaw, Kimberlé. 1989. "Demarginalizing the Intersection of Race and Sex: A Black Feminist Critique of Antidiscrimination Doctrine, Feminist Theory and Antiracist Politics." *University of Chicago Legal Forum* 140: 139–67.

Engels, Friedrich. 1970. "Socialism: Utopian and Scientific." In *Marx/Engels Selected Works*, 3: 95–151. Moscow: Progress Publishers.

Fanon, Frantz. 2004. *The Wretched of the Earth*. Translated by Richard Philcox. New York: Grove.

Moraga, Cherríe. 1983. "Refugees of a World on Fire." Foreword to *This Bridge Called My Back: Writings by Radical Women of Color*, edited by Cherríe Moraga and Gloria Anzaldúa, 2nd ed., i–iv. New York: Kitchen Table: Women of Color Press.

Moraga, Cherríe, and Gloria Anzaldúa. 1981. *This Bridge Called My Back: Writings by Radical Women of Color*. New York: Kitchen Table: Women of Color Press.

Nash, Jennifer C. 2017. "Intersectionality and Its Discontents." Review of *Intersectionality: Origins, Contestations, Horizons*, by Anna Carastathis; *Intersectionality*, by Patricia Hill Collins and Sirma Bilge; and *Pursuing Intersectionality, Unsettling Dominant Imaginaries*, by Vivian May. *American Quarterly* 69, no. 1: 117–29.

Parker, Pat. 1981. "Revolution: It's Not Neat or Pretty or Quick." In Moraga and Anzaldúa, *This Bridge Called My Back: Writings by Radical Women of Color*, 238–42. New York: Kitchen Table: Women of Color Press.

Thompson, Mayo. 1979. "Born in Flames." In *Born in Flames* sound track.

ANGELA Y. DAVIS

59. TRANSNATIONAL SOLIDARITIES

Hrant Dink remains a potent symbol of the struggle against colonialism, genocide, and racism. Those who assume that it was possible to eradicate his dream of justice, peace, and equality must now know that by striking him down countless Hrant Dinks were created, as people all over the world exclaim, "I am Hrant Dink." We know that his struggle for justice and equality lives on. Ongoing efforts to create a popular intellectual environment within which to explore the contemporary impact of the Armenian genocide are central, I think, to global resistance to racism, genocide, and settler colonialism. The spirit of Hrant Dink lives on and grows stronger and stronger.

I am very pleased that I'm been accorded the opportunity to join a very long list of distinguished speakers who have paid tribute to Hrant Dink. I can say I'm a little intimidated by that prospect as well. I know that those of you who have made it a regular practice to attend these lectures have had the opportunity to hear Arundhati Roy and Naomi Klein, Noam Chomsky, and Loïc Wacquant. So I hope I live up to your expectations.

Let me also say that I am very pleased that the commemoration of the life and work of Hrant Dink has provided me with an occasion for my very first visit to Turkey. It's hard to believe that it has taken so many decades for me to actually visit this country, since I have dreamed of Istanbul since I was very young, and especially since I learned about the formative influence of Turkish geographies, politics, and intellectual life, and this very university, on a formative influence and close friend, James Baldwin. I can also share with you that as a very young activist—and as I grow older it seems I grow younger as well in my memories and thoughts—I remember reading and feeling inspired by the words of Nâzim Hikmet,

as in those days every good communist did. And I can say that when I myself was imprisoned, I was encouraged and emboldened by messages of solidarity and by various descriptions of events organized on my behalf here in Turkey. As I said, I can't believe this is my first trip to Turkey. When I was in graduate school in Frankfurt, my sister made an amazing trip to Turkey, so I'll have to tell her that I finally caught up with her fifty years later.

And since this is my first trip to Turkey, I would like to thank all of those who personally joined the campaign for my freedom in those days, or whose parents were involved, or perhaps whose grandparents were involved in the international movement for my defense. I think far more important than the fact that I was on the FBI's Ten Most Wanted list—which draws applause these days; it tells you what happens if you live long enough, the transformative power of history—is that vast international campaign that achieved what was imagined to be unachievable. That is to say, against all odds we won in our confrontation with the most powerful figures in the US at that time. Let's not forget that Ronald Reagan was the governor of California, Richard Nixon was the president of the US, and J. Edgar Hoover was the head of the FBI.

Often people ask me how I would like to be remembered. My response is that I really am not that concerned about ways in which people might remember me personally. What I do want people to remember is the fact that the movement around the demand for my freedom was victorious. It was a victory against insurmountable odds, even though I was innocent; the assumption was that the power of those forces in the US was so strong that I would either end up in the gas chamber or that I would spend the rest of my life behind bars. Thanks to the movement, I am here with you today.

Angela Davis, "Transnational Solidarities," (Chapter 10) in *Freedom is a Constant Struggle* (Chicago: Haymarket Books: 2016): pp. 129–145. Reprinted with permission.

My relationship with Turkey has been shaped by other movements of solidarity. More recently, I attempted to contribute to the solidarity efforts supporting those who challenged the F-type prisons here in Turkey, including prisoners who joined death fasts. And I've also been active in efforts to generate solidarity around Abdullah Ocalan and other political prisoners, such as Pinar Selek.

Given that my historical relationships with this country have been shaped by circumstances of international solidarity, I have entitled my talk "Transnational Solidarities: Resisting Racism, Genocide, and Settler Colonialism," for the purpose of evoking possible futures, potential circuits connecting movements in various parts of the world, and specifically, in the US, Turkey, and occupied Palestine.

The term "genocide" has usually been reserved for particular conditions defined in accordance with the United Nations Convention on the Prevention and Punishment of the Crime of Genocide, which was adopted on December 9, 1948, in the aftermath of the fascist scourge during World War II. Some of you are probably familiar with the wording of that convention, but let me share it with you: "Any of the following acts committed with intent to destroy, in whole or in part, a national, ethnic, racial, or religious group as such, killing members of the group, causing serious bodily or mental harm to members of the group, deliberately inflicting on the group conditions of life calculated to bring about its physical destruction in whole or in part, imposing measures intended to prevent births within the group, and forcibly transferring children of the group to another group."

This convention was passed in 1948, but it was not ratified by the US until 1987, almost forty years later. However, just three years after the passage of the convention, a petition was submitted to the United Nations by the Civil Rights Congress of the US, charging genocide with respect to Black people in the US. This petition was signed by luminaries such as W. E. B. Du Bois, who at that time was under attack by the government. It was submitted to the UN in New York by Paul Robeson and it was submitted in Paris by the civil rights attorney William L. Patterson. Patterson was at that time the head of the Civil Rights Congress. He was a Black member of the Communist Party, a prominent attorney

who had defended the Scottsboro Nine. His passport was taken away when he returned. This was during the era in which communists and those who were accused of being communists were seriously under attack.

In the introduction to this petition, one can read the following words: "Out of the inhuman Black ghettos of American cities, out of the cotton plantations of the South, comes this record of mass slayings on the basis of race, of lives deliberately warped and distorted by the willful creation of conditions making for premature death, poverty, and disease. It is a record that calls aloud for condemnation, for an end to these terrible injustices that constitute a daily and ever-increasing violation of the United Nations Convention on the Prevention and Punishment of the Crime of Genocide." The introduction continues, "We maintain, therefore, that the oppressed Negro citizens of the United States, segregated, discriminated against, and long the target of violence, suffer from genocide as the result of the consistent, conscious, unified policies of every branch of government."

Then they go on to point out that they will submit evidence proving, in accordance with the convention, the killing of members of the group. They point to police killings—this is 1951—killings by gangs, by the Ku Klux Klan, and other racist groups. They point out that the evidence concerns thousands of people who have been "beaten to death on chain gangs and in the back rooms of sheriffs' offices and in the cells of county jails and precinct police stations and on city streets, who have been framed and murdered by sham legal forms and by a legal bureaucracy. They also point out that a significant number of Black people were killed allegedly for failure to say "sir" to a white person, or to tip their hats, or to move aside.

I mention this historic petition against genocide first because such a charge could have also been launched at the time based on the mass slaughters of Armenians, the death marches, the theft of children and the attempt to assimilate them into dominant culture. I had the opportunity to read the very moving memoir *My Grandmother*, an Armenian Turkish memoir by Fethiye Çetin. I'm certain everyone in this room has read the book. I also learned that as many as two million Turks might have at least one grandparent of Armenian heritage, and that because of prevailing racism, so many people have been prevented from exploring their own family histories.

Reading *My Grandmother,* I thought about the work of a French Marxist anthropologist whose name is Claude Meillassoux. This imposed silence with respect to ancestry reminded me that his definition of slavery has the concept of social death at its core. He defined the slave as subject to a kind of social death—the slave as a person who was not born, *non née.* Of course, there's grave collective psychic damage that is a consequence of not being acknowledged within the context of one's ancestry. Those of us of African descent in the US of my age are familiar with that sense of not being able to trace our ancestry beyond, as in my case, one grandmother. Deprivation of ancestry affects the present and the future. Of course, *My Grandmother* details the process of ethnic cleansing, the death march, the killings by the gendarmes, the fact that when they were crossing a bridge, the grandmother's own grandmother threw two of her grandchildren in the water and made sure they had drowned before she threw herself into the water. And for me the scene so resonated with historical descriptions of slave mothers in the US who killed their children in order to spare them the violence of slavery. Toni Morrison's novel *Beloved,* for which she received the Nobel Prize, is based on one such narrative, the narrative of Margaret Garner.

I also evoke the genocide petition of 1951 because so many of the conditions outlined in that petition continue to exist in the US today. This analysis helps us to understand the extent to which contemporary racist state violence in the US is deeply rooted in genocidal histories, including, of course, the genocidal colonization of indigenous inhabitants of the Americas. A recent book by historian Craig Wilder addresses the extent to which the Ivy League universities, the universities everyone knows all over the world—you mention the name Harvard and that is recognizable virtually everywhere in the world—Harvard, Yale, Princeton, et cetera, were founded on and are deeply implicated in the institution of slavery. But—and in my mind this may be the most important aspect of his research—he discovers that he cannot tell the story of slavery and US higher education without also simultaneously telling the story of the genocidal colonization of Native Americans.

I think it's important to pay attention to the larger methodological implications of such an approach. Our histories never unfold in isolation. We cannot truly tell what we consider to be our own histories without knowing the other stories. And often we discover that those other stories are actually our own stories. This is the admonition "Learn your sisters' stories" by Black feminist sociologist Jacqui Alexander. This is a dialectical process that requires us to constantly retell our stories, to revise them and retell them and relaunch them. We can thus not pretend that we do not know about the conjunctures of race and class and ethnicity and nationality and sexuality and ability.

I cannot prescribe how Turkish people—I've learned in the days since I've been here (actually, this is only my second and a half day here) that it might be better to refer to "people who live in Turkey." I cannot prescribe how you come to grips with the imperial past of this country. But I do know, because I have learned this from Hrant Dink, from Fethiye Çetin, and others, that it has to be possible to speak freely, it has to be possible to engage in free speech. The ethnic-cleansing processes, including the so-called population exchanges at the end of the Ottoman Empire that inflicted incalculable forms of violence on so many populations—Greeks and Syrians, and, of course, Armenians—have to be acknowledged in the historical record. But popular conversations about these events and about the histories of the Kurdish people in this space have to occur before any real social transformation can be imagined, much less rendered possible.

I tell you that in the United States we are at such a disadvantage because we do not know how to talk about the genocide inflicted on indigenous people. We do not know how to talk about slavery. Otherwise it would not have been assumed that simply because of the election of one Black man to the presidency we would leap forward into a postracial era. We do not acknowledge that we all live on colonized land. And in the meantime, Native Americans live in impoverished conditions on reservations. They have an extremely high incarceration rate—as a matter of fact, per capita the highest incarceration rate—and they suffer disproportionately from such diseases as alcoholism and diabetes. In the meantime, sports teams still mock indigenous people with racially derogatory names, like the Washington Redskins. We do not know how to talk about slavery, except, perhaps, within a framework of victim and victimizer, one that continues to polarize and implicate.

But I can say that, increasingly, young activists are learning how to acknowledge the intersections of these stories, the ways in which these stories are crosshatched and overlaid. Therefore, when we attempt to develop an analysis of the persistence of racist violence, largely directed at young Black men, of which we have been hearing a great deal over this last period, we cannot forget to contextualize this racist violence.

Here in Turkey you are all aware that this past fall and last summer in Ferguson, Missouri, all over the country—in New York, in Washington, in Chicago, on the West Coast—and, indeed, in other parts of the world, people took to the streets collectively announcing that they absolutely refuse to assent to racist state violence. People took to the streets saying, "No justice, no peace, no racist police." And people have been saying that, contrary to routine police actions and regardless of the collusion of district attorneys with the police, that Black lives do matter. Black lives matter. And we will take to the streets and raise our voices until we can be certain that a change is on the agenda. Social media have been flooded with messages of solidarity from people all over the world in the fall, not only with respect to the failure to indict the police officer who killed Michael Brown in Ferguson, Missouri, but also as a response to the decision of the grand jury in the case of Eric Garner [in New York City]. These demonstrations literally all over the world made it very clear that there is vast potential with respect to the forging of transnational solidarities.

What this means in one sense is that we may be given the opportunity to emerge from the individualism within which we are ensconced in this neoliberal era. Neoliberal ideology drives us to focus on individuals, ourselves, individual victims, individual perpetrators. But how is it possible to solve the massive problem of racist state violence by calling upon individual police officers to bear the burden of that history and to assume that by prosecuting them, by exacting our revenge on them, we would have somehow made progress in eradicating racism? If one imagines these vast expressions of solidarity all over the world

as being focused only on the fact that individual police officers were not prosecuted, it makes very little sense. I'm not suggesting that individuals should not be held accountable. Every individual who engages in such a violent act of racism, of terror, should be held accountable. But what I am saying is that we have to embrace projects that address the sociohistorical conditions that enable these acts.

For some time now I have been involved in efforts to abolish the death penalty and imprisonment as the main modes of punishment. I should say that it is not simply out of empathy with the victims of capital punishment and the victims of prison punishment, who are overwhelmingly people of color. It is because these modes of punishment don't work. These forms of punishment do not work when you consider that the majority of people who are in prison are there because society has failed them, because they've had no access to education or jobs or housing or health care. But let me say that criminalization and imprisonment could not solve other problems.

They do not solve the problem of sexual violence either. "Carceral feminism," which is a term that has begun to circulate recently—carceral feminisms, that is to say, feminisms that call for the criminalization and incarceration of those who engage in gender violence—do the work of the state. Carceral feminisms do the work of the state as surely as they focus on state violence and repression as the solution to heteropatriarchy and as the solution, more specifically, to sexual assault. But it does not work for those who are directly involved in the repressive work of the state either. As influenced as many police officers may be by the racism that criminalizes communities of color—and this influence is not limited to white police officers; Black police officers and police officers of color are subject to the same way in which racism structurally defines police work—but even as they may be influenced by this racism, it was not their individual idea to do this. So simply by focusing on the individual as if the individual were an aberration, we inadvertently engage in the process of reproducing the very violence that we assume we are contesting.

How do we move beyond this framework of primarily focusing on individual perpetrators? In the case of Michael Brown in Ferguson, Missouri, we quickly learned about the militarization of the police because of the visual images of their military garb, military vehicles, and military weapons. The militarization of the police in the US, of police forces all over the country has been accomplished in part with the aid of the Israeli government, which has been sharing its training with police forces all over the country since the period in the immediate aftermath of 9/11. As a matter of fact, the St. Louis County Police chief, whose name is Timothy Fitch—and St. Louis, of course, is the setting in which the Ferguson violence took place; Ferguson is a small town in St. Louis County—this chief received "counterterrorism" training in Israel. County sheriffs and police chiefs from all over the country, agents of the FBI, and bomb technicians have been traveling to Israel to get lessons in how to combat terrorism.

The point that I'm making is that while racist police violence, particularly against Black people, has a very long history, going back to the era of slavery, the current context is absolutely decisive. And when one examines the ways in which racism has been further reproduced and complicated by the theories and practices of terrorism and counterterrorism, one begins to perhaps envision the possibility of political alliances that will move us in the direction of transnational solidarities. What was interesting during the protests in Ferguson last summer was that Palestinian activists noticed from the images they saw on social media and on television that tear-gas canisters that were being used in Ferguson were exactly the same tear-gas canisters that were used against them in occupied Palestine. As a matter of fact, a US company, which is called Combined Systems, Incorporated, stamps "CTS" (Combined Tactical Systems) on their tear-gas canisters. When Palestinian activists noticed these canisters in Ferguson, what they did was to tweet advice to Ferguson protesters on how to deal with the tear gas. They suggested, among other things: "Don't keep much distance from the police. If you're close to them, they can't tear gas," because they would be tear-gassing themselves. There was a whole series of really interesting comments for the young activists in Ferguson, who were probably confronting tear gas for the first time in their lives. They didn't necessarily have the experience that some of us older activists have with tear gas.

I'm trying to suggest that there are connections between the militarization of the police in the US, which provides a different context for us to analyze the continuing, ongoing proliferation of racist police violence, and the continuous assault on people in occupied Palestine, the West Bank, and especially in Gaza, given the military violence inflicted on people in Gaza this past summer.

I also want to bring into the conversation one of the most well-known political prisoners in the history of the US. Her name is Assata Shakur. Assata now lives in Cuba, and has lived in Cuba since the 1980s. Not very long ago she was designated as one of the ten most dangerous terrorists in the world. And since it was mentioned that I was on the FBI's Ten Most Wanted list, I would like you to think about what would motivate the decision to place this woman, Assata Shakur, on that list. You can read her history. Her autobiography is absolutely fascinating. She was falsely, fraudulently charged with a whole range of crimes. I won't even mention them. You can read about it in her biography. She was found not guilty on every single charge except the very last one. I wrote a preface to the second edition of her autobiography. Assata, who is actually younger than I am by a few years, is in her late sixties now. She has been leading a productive life in Cuba, studying and teaching and engaging in art. So why would Homeland Security suddenly decide that she is one of the Ten Most Wanted terrorists in the world?

This retroactive criminalization of the late-twentieth-century Black liberation movements through targeting one of the women leaders at that time, who was so systematically pursued, is, I think, an attempt to deter people from engaging in radical political struggle today. This is why I am always so cautious about the use of the term "terrorist." I am cautious, knowing that we have endured a history of unacknowledged terror. As someone who grew up in the most segregated city of the South, my very first memories were of bombs exploding across the street from my family's house simply because a Black person had purchased a house. We actually knew the identities of the Ku Klux Klan people were who were bombing houses and bombing churches. You may be familiar with the bombing of the Sixteenth Street Baptist Church that happened in 1963, when the four young girls, who were all very close to my family, died. But you should know that that was not an unusual occasion. Those bombings happened all the time. Why has that not been acknowledged as an era of terror? So I'm really cautious about the use of that term, because there is almost always a political motivation.

Let me say, as I move toward my conclusion, that I want to be little bit more specific about the importance of feminist theory and analysis. I'm not simply speaking to the women in the audience, because I think feminism provides methodological guidance for all of us who are engaged in serious research and organized activist work. Feminist approaches urge us to develop understandings of social relations, whose connections are often initially only intuited. Everyone is familiar with the slogan "The personal is political"—not only that what we experience on a personal level has profound political implications, but that our interior lives, our emotional lives are very much informed by ideology. We ourselves often do the work of the state in and through our interior lives. What we often assume belongs most intimately to ourselves and to our emotional life has been produced elsewhere and has been recruited to do the work of racism and repression.

Some of us have always insisted on making connections, in terms of prison work, between assaults on women in prison and the larger project of abolishing imprisonment. And this larger project requires us to understand where we figure into transnational solidarity efforts. This means that we have to examine various dimensions of our lives—from social relations, political contexts—but also our interior lives. It's interesting that in this era of global capitalism the corporations have learned how to do that: the corporations have learned how to access aspects of our lives that cause us to often express our innermost dreams in terms of capitalist commodities. So we have internalized exchange value in ways that would have been entirely unimaginable to the authors of *Capital*. But this is the topic of another lecture.

What I want to point out is that the megacorporations have clearly grasped the ways in which what we often consider to be disparate issues are connected. One such corporation, G4S, which is the largest security corporation in the world—and, I evoke G4S because I am certain that they will attempt to take advantage in France of the current situation in a way that evokes Naomi Klein's analysis of disaster capitalism—G4S, as some of you probably know, has played such an important role in the Israeli occupation of Palestine: running prisons, being involved in checkpoint technology. It's also been involved in the deaths of undocumented immigrants. The case of Jimmy Mubenga is important. He was killed by G4S guards in Britain in the process of being deported to Angola. G4S operates private prisons in South Africa. G4S is the largest corporate employer on the entire continent of Africa. G4S, this megacorporation that is involved in the ownership and operation of prisons, that provides armies with weapons, that provides security for rock stars, also operates centers for abused women and for "young girls at risk." I mention this because it seems that they have grasped the connection in ways that we should have long ago.

Speaking of megacorporations, I heard that students have successfully protested Starbucks. Is today the last day Starbucks will be available on this campus? Hallelujah. Especially since Turkish coffee far exceeds what Starbucks could ever hope for.

My last example is also an example from the US, but it reflects a global pandemic from which no country is exempt. I'm referring to sexual violence, sexual harassment, sexual assault. Intimate violence is not unconnected to state violence. Where do perpetrators of intimate violence learn how to engage in the practices of violence? Who teaches them that violence is okay? But this is, of course, another question. I do want to evoke the case of a young woman by the name of Marissa Alexander. You know the names of Michael Brown and Eric Garner. Add the name of Marissa Alexander to that list, a young Black woman who felt compelled to go to extremes to prevent her abusive husband from attacking her. She fired a weapon in the air. No one was hit. But in the very same judicial district where Trayvon Martin—you remember his name—was killed, and where George Zimmerman, his killer, was acquitted, Marissa Alexander was sentenced to twenty years for trying to defend herself against sexual assault. Recently she faced a possible resentencing to sixty years, and therefore she engaged in a plea bargain, which means that she will be wearing an electronic bracelet for the next period.

Racist and sexual violence are practices that are not only tolerated but explicitly—or if not explicitly, then implicitly—encouraged. When these modes of violence are recognized—and they are often hidden and rendered invisible—they are most often the most dramatic examples of structural exclusion and discrimination. I think it would be important to go further developing that analysis, but I am going to conclude by saying that the greatest challenge facing us as we attempt to forge international solidarities and connections across national borders is an understanding of what feminists often call "intersectionality." Not so much intersectionality of identities, but intersectionality of struggles.

Let us not forget the impact of Tahrir Square and the Occupy movement all over the world. And since we are gathered here in Istanbul, let us not forget the Taksim Gezi Park protesters. Oftentimes people argue that in these more recent movements there were no leaders, there was no manifesto, no agenda, no demands, so therefore the movements failed. But I'd like to point out that Stuart Hall, who died just a little over a year ago, urged us to distinguish between outcome and impact. There is a difference between outcome and impact. Many people assume that because the encampments are gone and nothing tangible was produced, that there was no outcome. But when we think about the impact of these imaginative and innovative actions and these moments where people learned how to be together without the scaffolding of the state, when they learned to solve problems without succumbing to the impulse of calling the police, that should serve as a true inspiration for the work that we will do in the future to build these transnational solidarities. Don't we want to be able to imagine the expansion of freedom and justice in the world, as Hrant Dink urged us to do—in Turkey, in Palestine, in South Africa, in Germany, in Colombia, in Brazil, in the Philippines, in the US?

If this is the case, we will have to do something quite extraordinary: We will have to go to great lengths. We cannot go on as usual. We cannot pivot the center. We cannot be moderate. We will have to be willing to stand up and say no with our combined spirits, our collective intellects, and our many bodies.